CLAYTN-FOR REF

310120036901374

R 292.1303 ROMAN, LUKE

Roman, Luke

Encyclopedia of Greek and Roman Mytho

Georgia Law requires Library materials
to be returned or replacement costs paid.
Failure to comply with this law
is a misdemeanor. (O.C.G.A. 20-5-53)

D0706809

CLAYTON COUNTY LIBRARY SYSTEM
FOREST PARK BRANCH
4812 WEST STREET
FOREST PARK, GEORGIA 30297-1824

ENCYCLOPEDIA OF

GREEK AND ROMAN MYTHOLOGY

LUKE ROMAN
AND MONICA ROMAN

CLAYTON COUNTY LIBRARY SYSTEM
FOREST PARK BRANCH
4812 WEST STREET
FOREST PARK, GA 30297-1824

Facts On File
An imprint of Infobase Publishing

Encyclopedia of Greek and Roman Mythology

Copyright © 2010 by Luke Roman and Monica Roman

All rights reserved. No part of this book may be reproduced or utilized in any form or by any means, electronic or mechanical, including photocopying, recording, or by any information storage or retrieval systems, without permission in writing from the publisher. For information contact:

Facts On File, Inc.
An imprint of Infobase Publishing
132 West 31st Street
New York NY 10001

Library of Congress Cataloging-in-Publication Data

Roman, Luke.
  Encyclopedia of Greek and Roman mythology / Luke Roman and Monica Roman.
      p. cm.
  Includes bibliographical references and index.
  ISBN 978-0-8160-7242-2 (hc : alk. paper) 1. Mythology, Classical—Encyclopedias. I. Roman, Monica. II. Title. III. Title: Greek and Roman mythology.
  BL715.R65 2009
  292.1'303—dc22
                              2009001235

Facts On File books are available at special discounts when purchased in bulk quantities for businesses, associations, institutions, or sales promotions. Please call our Special Sales Department in New York at (212) 967-8800 or (800) 322-8755.

You can find Facts On File on the World Wide Web at http://www.factsonfile.com

Excerpts included herewith have been reprinted by permission of the copyright holders; the author has made every effort to contact copyright holders. The publishers will be glad to rectify, in future editions, any errors or omissions brought to their notice.

Text design by Erika K. Arroyo
Composition by Hermitage Publishing Services
Cover printed by Art Print, Taylor, Pa.
Book printed and bound by Maple-Vail Book Manufacturing Group, York, Pa.
Date printed: January, 2011
Printed in the United States of America

10 9 8 7 6 5 4 3

This book is printed on acid-free paper and contains 30 percent postconsumer recycled content.

CONTENTS

INTRODUCTION

This reference work is designed to provide concise summaries of the major figures of classical mythology, and, at the same time, synopses and discussions of major works of Greek and Roman literature from the eighth century B.C.E. through the second century C.E. While there are many reference works on classical mythology, the distinctive feature of this encyclopedia is the inclusion of extensive discussion of classical authors and literary works to enable the study of ancient mythology in the light of ancient literature. In addition, we have selectively documented the representation of the classical myths in visual art, ranging from ancient statues to famous paintings of the Renaissance and later eras. Myths were not narrated solely in verbal form, and the artistic representations often surprise us by emphasizing scenes or dimensions of a story less prominent or even omitted in textual versions. The underlying aim of this book is to enable the student to appreciate ancient myth in the light of ancient literature and fine art, rather than presenting myth as a fossilized set of stories abstracted from the multiple contexts of their telling.

MYTHOLOGY AND LITERATURE IN THE GREEK AND ROMAN WORLD

At the most basic level, myths are simply stories. The Greek word *mythos*, from which our word *myth* comes, had various meanings, including "speech," "story," and, later, "myth" or "fable." In modern English, the term *myth* often implies a belief that is demonstrably false yet has nonetheless achieved widespread credence. Magazines and newspapers contrast myths with the true facts gleaned from scientific study. In the ancient world, by contrast, there was no strict, consistently applied division between mythic knowledge and rationally discovered truth. Ancient philosophers and historians in some instances challenge the authority of myth as a fundamental source of knowledge, but they do not wholly reject it.

For the archaic Greek poets Homer and Hesiod (ca. eighth/seventh century B.C.E.), the traditional stories constitute divinely inspired knowledge. The historian Herodotus (fifth century B.C.E.) never suggests that there is anything inherently false in traditional stories or myths; nor does he imply that there is any better basis for understanding history. The Athenian historian Thucydides (fifth century B.C.E.) does claim that he has methods for bringing greater accuracy to the study of history yet refers to Homer's *Iliad* in measuring the scale of past wars as a basis of comparison for the Peloponnesian War. There was no clear dividing line between history and myth; indeed, it is not clear that the ancients had a clearly defined category corresponding to our "myth." Rather, there were inherited stories, above all the stories of the poets, and these stories were sometimes questionable and sometimes contained an element of truth.

It was never the case that the ancients simply believed their myths with dogmatic insistence. The divinely inspired Hesiod knew that the Muses mixed truth with falsehood. Yet the classical writers frequently refer to myths as a source of knowledge of the past, and they almost never *categorically* equate myth with falsehood. Ovid's *Metamorphoses* (ca. 8 C.E.), arguably the most sophisticated treatment of myth surviving from the ancient world, traces a series of transformations from the dawn of creation down to the apotheosis of Julius Caesar. Mythical figures such as Heracles, Midas, and Orpheus, Roman founder-figures such as Aeneas and Romulus, and the emerging mythology of the Roman imperial family all form part of a continuous narrative fabric. In Ovid's poem, the new myths of imperial power are not obviously or fundamentally different from the age-old stories of gods and heroes.

Philosophers mounted the most radical opposition to the authority of the traditional stories. In classical Greece, the poets, and above all Homer, were still considered the prime sources of knowledge. Homer offered not only precious insight into the past but also knowledge of the gods, religion, warfare, and proper conduct in all areas of life. It is therefore not surprising that Plato, as he strove to define a new kind of knowledge called philosophy, challenged the authority of poetry and the poets' stories. Even so, Plato does not forgo mythic modes of exposition altogether. Some of the more famous passages in Plato, such as the story of Er in the *Republic*, assume a mythic format. Plato is not so much banishing myth from the realm of rational discourse as inventing a new style of philosophical mythmaking. The Roman poet Lucretius (first century B.C.E.), a follower of the Greek philosopher Epicurus, continues the philosophical tradition of reworking inherited myths and fashioning new philosophically informed myths in the name of an antitraditionalist form of knowledge.

The uses of myth inevitably change across different periods and contexts, but characterizing the nature of such change is not a straightforward undertaking. It is potentially misleading, for example, to suppose that classical authors' attitude toward and use of mythology became more sophisticated over time. There never was a phase of natural, unselfconscious mythmaking, despite the romantic tendency to posit one. Homeric epic itself represents an immensely sophisticated narrative undertaking based on the skilled manipulation of mythological traditions.

Yet while mythographical self-consciousness, narrative sophistication, and awareness of multiple, diverging mythic traditions appear to have been present in the earliest extant poetry, later centuries did contribute at least one crucial factor to the dissemination and reworking of myth: the institution of the library. The most famous library of the ancient world was the great library at Alexandria, Egypt, built and developed under the Ptolemies in the third and second centuries B.C.E. The Ptolemies patronized eminent writer/scholars, some of whom served as head librarians and worked on creating canonical texts of Greek literature (see *Voyage of the Argonauts* and Callimachus). This immense focus on literature forms part of a complex awareness of Greek culture in the wake of the conquests of Alexander the Great and subsequent division of the conquered territories among Greek ruling elites. Some scholars have employed the term "diaspora" to describe this sustained engagement with Greek culture in locations geographically removed from the original Greek city-states. The project of sustaining Greekness amid non-Greek native populations thus becomes inextricably related to the poet/scholar's erudition and the production of canonical texts, which in turn furnish material for further erudite poetic creations enriched with a dense fabric of literary allusions.

Mythology in this period thus became an object of study and literary display, as well as a key repository of Greekness. Mythography emerges as an area of study in its own right: Scholars, gifted with a vast library, are able to sift and compare different versions of myths and record them in texts of their own. One key arena of mythographical knowledge is the writing of scholia, or commentaries on classic works, which require, among other forms of attention, mythological elucidation. The post-classical period also saw the rise of new rationalizing interpretations of mythology such as the work of Euhemerus (fourth century B.C.E.), who saw the stories of the gods as being originally developed out of the deeds of great men. It was not modern scholars, then, who first developed methodologies for the interpretation of myth but the ancients themselves. Rationalizing approaches, however, did not constitute a rejection of myth per se, so much as a new mode of engagement with the inherited stories.

The increasingly cosmopolitan literary exploitation and perpetuation of myths deriving from the Greek city-states continued throughout the Roman period, above all in the period of the Second Sophistic. Lucian (second century C.E.) drew on mythic figures and situations with erudite humor in his dialogues and satirical sketches. Athenaeus (second/third century C.E.), in his *Deipnosophistae* (Philosophers at dinner), describes a series of banquets at which learned topics were discussed, including literature and mythology. Lucian was from Samosata in Syria, while Athenaeus hailed from Naucratis in Egypt. Greek culture by this period was a thoroughly cosmopolitan and diasporic phenomenon. Throughout the Roman period, mythology formed part of the body of knowledge that conferred the status of an educated person in the broader Mediterranean world.

One of the locations where Greek mythology flourished was, of course, Rome. The emperor Tiberius, while in retreat on the island of Rhodes, enjoyed discussing abstruse mythological questions, such as the name assumed by Achilles on the island of Scyros while disguised as a girl, or the identity of Hecuba's mother. Yet as the example of Tiberius also illustrates, too much Greekness could be seen in Rome as a bad thing, despite the fact that Romans assimilated Greek culture throughout their history in voracious and sometimes brilliant fashion. A further layer of complexity arises in the question of *Roman* myths and gods. The Romans had their own gods, rites, and, to a certain extent, their own traditional stories. The Roman gods are popularly viewed as simply the "equivalent" of Greek gods. Yet Roman gods such as Jupiter and Juno enjoyed their own independent existence and cult as Italic deities. Over time, they were aligned with the Greek gods and merged on the mythological plane. This book does not offer separate entries on Zeus and Jupiter, since in mythology they are best viewed together, yet it is important to remember the process of syncretization, not simply the outcome of their (apparent) common origin.

Whether or not there can be said to be a distinctly Roman mythology is a matter of contention. There is little evidence for a narrative fabric of myths comparable to and autonomous of Greek mythology. The Roman myths that do exist—or, as they are often called, legends—concern quasi-historical figures, beginning with Romulus and including the great figures that people Livy's history, such as Camillus and Coriolanus. Yet this series of legends concerning the deeds of great men is clearly not quite the same thing as Greek mythology, with its stress on the supernatural and the interactions of men, gods, heroes, and monsters. Ultimately, the Romans come to integrate their own legendary history with the myths of the Greek city-states. Bridging figures, such as Aeneas, Heracles, Diomedes, Hippolytus, Evander, and Orestes, who, in some myths, travel from the Greek or Trojan world to Italy, and in some cases found cities, are particularly salient examples of such integration. The resultant fusion is called "classical mythology" by modern textbooks.

Greek culture was the prestige culture for the Romans, and in assimilating it, the Romans were deliberately adding cultural prestige to their already established military and political supremacy. Greek culture was present at Rome from the beginning not least because there were significant Greek communities in Italy, especially southern Italy. Rome's first writers, such as Ennius, came from a bi- or even trilingual background and were fluent in Greek language and culture. The incorporation of Greek culture in Roman society began in earnest, however, in the late third and second centuries B.C.E., when Rome was reaching the definitive stage of military supremacy with the defeat of its major rival, Carthage. The first known works of Roman literature adapt the major Greek genres: tragedy, comedy, and epic. Yet even in this early period, adaptation of Greek literature served distinctively Roman ends, such as the commemoration of military victory and the deeds of eminent men.

The processes of Hellenization accelerate in the first century B.C.E., as Rome continues to absorb the cultural riches of the cities it conquered, and as the stakes of intra-elite competition intensify in the dangerous political environment of the late republic. The generation of poets that flourished around the middle of the first century B.C.E. marks a major watershed: Catullus and his contemporaries espouse the erudite poetics of the Alexandrians, explicitly following in the path of Callimachus and Apollonius. This pattern equally defines the early works of Virgil and becomes the dominant paradigm among the Augustan poets. Mythology is key in these developments: one need only cite Virgil's *Aeneid*, Ovid's *Metamorphoses*, Horace's odes, and the love elegies of Propertius. The Augustans, like Catullus, work on the Alexandrian model: They treat mythology with a sophisticated erudition fueled by an emerging book trade and Rome's first public libraries. The intensified Greekness of Roman poetry of the first century B.C.E. does not mean,

of course, that Roman interests were not being served. Catullus's mythological poetry confronts questions of social disintegration and compromised virility in late republican Rome, while Virgil's *Aeneid* traces the hero Aeneas to Italy and, through this legendary narrative, ponders the immense contemporary task of repairing a damaged society.

Aeneas was a figure of special significance in the Augustan period, since Julius Caesar traced his ancestry back to Aeneas via the hero's son Ascanius/Iulus, and thus ultimately to the goddess Venus. Greek mythology, as Ovid elegantly demonstrates in the closing books of his *Metamorphoses*, is adapted to serve Rome's conversion of men into gods during the emergence of imperial government. Other social uses of mythology were less tied to the prestige of a single family. Greek mythology formed part of the idiom of educated speech (as demonstrated magnificently by Trimalchio's bungling of mythology in Petronius's *Satyricon*) and supplied rhetoricians and schoolboys with stock examples (exempla) with which to adorn their arguments. Such developments might seem to provide support for the old view that the Romans were artificial and political, whereas the Greeks displayed a richly imaginative, almost childlike genius. The notion of the originality of the Greeks versus the artificial imitations of the Romans still persists despite being an evident relic of romantic thought. The Romans were deliberate, calculating, consciously imitative, and at times politically pragmatic in their adaptation of Greek mythology and literature, but this does not mean that they lacked genius and originality in their adaptation; nor is it true that the Greeks were free of deliberation, self-consciousness, artifice, and social and political motives in creating, adapting, and disseminating their own myths. The Greeks deserve full credit for creating their myths, yet it is undeniable that some of the best versions of Greek mythology are Roman.

STUDYING MYTHOLOGY TODAY

In studying classical mythology, we need to consider not only the Greeks and Romans who made the myths but also our own role as readers and interpreters. How do we determine the meaning of a given myth? This question is as old as the myths themselves: As we have already mentioned, the ancients derived various meanings from their myths and applied different schemes of interpretation. The last two centuries, however, have seen an unusually fertile range of approaches to the interpretation of mythology. The main ones are enumerated in university-level courses and textbooks: ritualist, structuralist, psychoanalytic, sociological. In each instance, the interpreter attempts to understand the deeper meaning of the myth for those who tell it. In the sociological approach, for example, mythology is read as a "charter" for a society's beliefs, a blueprint of social attitudes and codes. While all these approaches have served to stimulate inquiry into classical mythology and have enabled important insights, they are all equally hampered by a questionable premise. Modern methodologies of mythological interpretation have in common the notion that there is an underlying narrative that encodes a deeper meaning—a distillation of that society's psychic impulses, social beliefs, systems of meaning, or ritual practices. In short, modern interpretations of mythology tend to assume the existence of a stable set of stories that affirm social concepts. Modern approaches for the most part—there are some exceptions—posit a stable entity designated as *the* myth, which exists independently of its individual manifestations and whose fundamental meaning can be elicited through the correct mode of interpretation.

Myths, however, undergo constant metamorphosis from telling to telling, as Ovid's great poem demonstrates. There is no such thing as *the* myth, since each author or visual artist tells the story in a different way and emphasizes different aspects of it. Accordingly, there is no single, fundamental meaning; rather, the story's meaning changes depending on the interests and emphases of its teller. A major tendency of the modern discipline of mythology is to extract an independent set of myths from the literary texts and visual images that narrate them. On this conception, an original, true story, or ur-story, underlies the numerous (imperfect, biased, partial) tellings. The search for an ur-narrative is irresistible, not least because it suggests the promise of a fundamental set of stories that a society tells to itself as a collectivity. Myths are sometimes described as the shared dreams of a culture that reveal a society's underlying desires, anxieties, and contradictions. Mythology, in this reading, furnishes a key for unlocking the secrets of the collective unconscious. Sigmund Freud's use of the Oedipus myth is a remarkable instance of such an ambition. Yet this type of reading cannot do justice to the diversity and richness of the ancient literary texts and the mutability of the myths themselves.

ABOUT THIS BOOK

If one accepts, as we do, the Ovidian view of myth as a body of stories in constant flux, it is necessary to abandon the hope for a stable, transparent set of communal stories that produce a unified meaning. Abandoning such hope, however, is far from dispiriting. One is left with the rich diversity of texts and images that re-create the myths in their constantly shifting forms. We have accordingly designed our reference book so as best to do justice to the diversity of mythic narrative in literary and visual media. Encyclopedias, dictionaries, and textbooks on mythology are, in fact, especially prone to editing out the diversity of classical myth and thereby effacing the importance of the *different* tellings. There is an understandable tendency in any reference work to create the impression of factual consistency—in this instance, the impression that the classical myths are stable narratives easily susceptible to informational summary. Indeed, there are many advantages to factual clarity and simplicity, since a summary of the basic outlines of the most common versions of the story of Heracles, for example, will be more useful to a beginning student of mythology than a treatment weighed down with every variant version extant in ancient literature. This leaves the danger, however, that the student will be left with the notion that there is essentially one Heracles consistent across all ancient texts. Informational reference works tend to have a homogenizing effect on their subject.

We have attempted to deal with both potential problems by offering, on the one hand, concise entries on mythological figures that contain the most important versions of the myths and the ones that are the most prominent in the major works of ancient literature and, on the other hand, longer entries on ancient authors and their individual works. The entries on mythological figures are based on a close reading of the primary sources. In creating these entries, we have striven to bring to light important differences in the Greek and Roman versions of the myth, rather than producing a streamlined narrative. We have also included references to the major classical sources; these references are necessarily selective but allow the reader to consult the ancient works themselves. Mythological figures are listed under their Greek names, with cross-references indicated under the Roman names. The index can assist in finding entries.

Entries on the more important literary works include an introduction to the work, a synopsis, and critical commentary. Users of this reference book, then, can begin by consulting the entry on Heracles and become acquainted with his story. They can then go on to read about the different representations of Heracles in Apollonius of Rhodes's *Voyage of the Argonauts*, the eighth book of Virgil's *Aeneid*, Sophocles' *Trachiniae*, Ovid's *Metamorphoses*, and so forth. Conversely, a reader of Statius's *Thebaid* who is interested in the character of Hypsipyle can read the mythological

entry detailing her basic story and, in addition, consult the entry on Apollonius's *Voyage of the Argonauts*, where she plays an important role. Cross-references to other entries are designed to facilitate this movement between entries on mythological figures and entries on ancient authors and works. As we said above, the underlying aim is to enable the student to appreciate ancient myth in the light of ancient literature, rather than presenting myth as a fossilized set of stories abstracted from the multiple contexts of their telling. In the same spirit, we have included information on the visual representation of classical myths in various media. Myths were not narrated solely in verbal form, and the artistic representations often surprise us by emphasizing scenes or dimensions of a story less prominent or even omitted in textual versions.

We have based our selection of entries on their relevance to and prominence in the central works of classical literature and art. This reference work is not meant to be an exhaustive repository of mythological figures. More unusual mythological figures and, in general, recondite detail may be sought in Pierre Grimal's richly erudite *Dictionary of Classical Mythology*. The distinguishing feature of our book, by contrast, is the inclusion of substantial entries on literary works, particularly those that are significant in mythological terms. This latter criterion guided our selection of literary entries. There is an individual entry, for example, on each of Euripides' plays, because the subject matter of Euripidean tragedy is mythological. By contrast, there is only one synthetic entry on Aristophanes, and no entries on his individual works, because Aristophanes' comedies, while they do sometimes include mythological elements, are not predominantly focused on myth but rather on a comic vision of contemporary Athenian society. At the same time, some works and authors, while important in mythographical terms, are less likely to appear on an undergraduate reading list, and, in general, are more obscure. Thus, while we have included a brief informational entry on Diodorus Siculus, there is no extensive discussion of his work. In effect, two criteria are at work in determining the inclusion and extent of literary entries: the importance of the work in literary terms and its relevance to our understanding of mythology.

The myths of the classical world may be classed among the richest legacies of Western civilization. We hope that our reference work contributes to the understanding and enjoyment of these astonishing stories.

Achelous A river god who engaged in a legendary combat with HERACLES. Classical sources are Apollodorus's *LIBRARY* (1.8.1, 2.7.5), Diodorus Siculus's *LIBRARY OF HISTORY* (4.34.3, 4.35.3), Hyginus's *Fabulae* (31), Ovid's *META-MORPHOSES* (9.1–100), Philostratus's *IMAGINES* (4.16), and Sophocles' *TRACHINIAE* (9–21). During the 11th of his Twelve Labors, Heracles descended to HADES, where he met the ghost of MELEAGER. There, Meleager extracted from Heracles the promise that on the hero's return from the underworld he would find and marry his sister DEIANIRA. Heracles successfully battled Achelous in a wrestling match for the hand of Deianira. The battle was hard fought because the river god was capable of changing form. Achelous became a snake, then a bull. Heracles pulled off one horn and defeated him. This horn was associated with a cornucopia, or horn of plenty. The combat of Achelous and Heracles was frequently represented in antiquity; Philostratus's *Imagines* includes a description of a painting showing various scenes from the myth.

Achilleid STATIUS (ca. 92–96 C.E.) The *Achilleid*, an unfinished epic poem on which STATIUS worked between the publication of his *THEBAID* (91/92 C.E.) and his death (ca. 96 C.E.), tells the beginnings of the story of the hero ACHILLES.

Only one book and a portion of the following book exist. Statius's epic is notable for following the entire life story of a single hero, rather than relating a more concentrated series of connected events forming part of a single phase of action. As elsewhere, Statius displays a playful yet rigorous self-consciousness as he simultaneously enacts well-established epic conventions, examines their mechanisms and internal tensions, and sometimes pushes them to their breaking point. In the surviving fragment, Statius pays special attention to the category of gender and its complex interaction with the inherited codes of the epic genre.

SYNOPSIS

Book 1

The poet addresses the muse (see MUSES) and bids her tell of Achilles. Homer has made him famous, but there is more to be told about the hero. Statius, already author of the *Thebaid*, will tell the hero's entire life. He asks the emperor Domitian to grant pardon that he does not yet write an epic on his deeds; Achilles will furnish the prelude.

PARIS is leaving Sparta with HELEN and making for Troy. THETIS, observing his ship, is alarmed and delivers a speech: She recognizes the fulfillment of a prophecy made by PRO-TEUS—war is coming, and her son Achilles will wish to join it. She wishes she had done more to prevent this unhappy outcome but will ask Neptune (see POSEIDON) for a storm to oppose Paris's ship. In pitiable tones, she approaches Neptune and asks him to oppose the ship carrying Paris, robber and profaner of hospitality. Neptune replies that the war between Greece and Troy has been ordained by Jupiter (see ZEUS) and cannot be prevented: He consoles her with a prophecy of Achilles' heroic career. She conceives of another plan and seeks out the dwelling of CHIRON, who has charge of Achilles. Chiron eagerly runs to meet her and leads her into the cave. She tells of her presages of doom and demands that he hand over Achilles to her immediately: Concealing her true aim, she claims that she is going to take him to the edge of Ocean (OCEANUS) and purify him. Chiron assents and comments that Achilles seems to be growing more aggressive and violent, less liable to listen to his tutor.

Achilles at that moment returns, holding lion cubs he has just captured, and embraces his mother. PATROCLUS follows closely behind. They have a banquet together, and Achilles sings songs of heroes. Thetis stays awake afterward, trying to think of a good hiding place for Achilles: After ruling out various possibilities, she chooses the island of Scyros. She calls forth her two-dolphin chariot, picks up the slumbering Achilles in her arms, and carries him down to the sea. As she departs with her son, Chiron and the local deities lament. Waking up the next day, a disoriented Achilles asks where he is. Thetis explains to him her concern about his mortality and the coming danger, and, drawing on mythical exempla, encourages him to wear women's clothing. Achilles resists until he sees Deidamia, daughter of Lycomedes, king of Scyros, participating in festivities of Pallas and becomes immediately infatuated. His mother perceives this and encourages him to join their dancing in woman's guise. He allows the woman's clothing to be placed on him. She fashions him into a woman and coaches him on feminine demeanor. Thetis then presents him to the king as Achilles' sister, asking him

to keep her safely secluded. The group of girls accepts him happily. Thetis addresses the island and bids it keep Greek ships far away.

AGAMEMNON, in the meanwhile, stirs up war, inciting indignation at Paris's deed. The poet lists the numerous communities joining the expedition—all except Thessaly, since Achilles is too young and Peleus too old. The Greek fleet gathers at Aulis, including well-known heroes, but all yearn for the absent Achilles. He is hailed already as the greatest of the Greeks and most likely to defeat HECTOR. Protesilaus presses TIRESIAS to reveal to them the location of Achilles. Tiresias goes into a prophetic trance and sees that Achilles is on the island of Lycomedes, shamefully wearing women's clothing. TYDEUS and Ulysses (see ODYSSEUS) decide to seek him out and bring him back. They depart. In the meanwhile, Deidamia alone suspects that Achilles is a man, for he has been courting her, teaching her to play the lyre, while she teaches him to weave. She half-knows that he is a man and desires her but will not allow him to confess. In a grove sacred to BACCHUS, the women are celebrating a triennial rite at which no men are allowed to be present. Achilles, however, begins to regret his lost male pursuits and complains that he cannot even play the man's part in love. He rapes Deidamia, then reveals himself to her as Achilles. He consoles her with the greatness of his lineage and commits to protecting her from her father's anger. Feeling love for Achilles herself, and also fearing for his safety, she keeps his secret, conceals her pregnancy, and eventually gives birth.

In the meantime, Ulysses and DIOMEDES navigate the Cyclades and approach Scyros. The two heroes disembark and begin walking toward the palace. Diomedes wonders why Ulysses purchased Bacchic wands, cymbals, and other objects, and Ulysses does not yet say why but bids him bring all these along with a shield, a spear, and the trumpeter Agyrtes. Ulysses introduces himself and Tydeus and claims to be spying out approaches to Troy. Lycomedes invites them to be his guests.

Rumor spreads of the Greek leaders' arrival. Achilles is eager to see them and their arms. The women are invited to join the banquet along with the guests. Deidamia strives to conceal Achilles, but he begins to give himself away by his unmaidenlike demeanor. In order to draw Achilles out Ulysses craftily speaks of war and the ignoble choice of those who remain behind.

The next day Tydeus brings forth the gifts. The maidens, including Achilles, perform Bacchic rites and dances, but Achilles stands out as unfeminine. Afterward, the women flock to the Bacchic gifts and adornment, while Achilles rushes to the weapons. Ulysses whispers to him that he knows who he is and encourages him to join the war; the trumpeter blows a blast on the trumpet, and Achilles is revealed as a man. Deidamia cries out, and Achilles addresses Lycomedes, revealing his identity and his relation with Deidamia, asking for her in marriage and placing his grandson at his feet. Lycomedes is won over. That night, Deidamia laments that their marriage is so soon to be over, that Achilles departs for war and will soon forget about her or take other women as his companions. He promises her that he will stay true to her and bring her back gifts from Troy. The poet observes that Achilles' words are destined to remain unfulfilled.

Book 2 (fragmentary)

Achilles, splendid now in his arms, makes sacrifice and addresses his mother, informing her that he is joining the expedition against Troy. Deidamia, holding her child Pyrrhus (see NEO-PTOLEMUS), follows his departure with her eyes. Achilles is momentarily regretful as he gazes toward her but is drawn back to his warlike spirit by Ulysses, and he asks to hear the causes of the war. Ulysses tells of the rape of Helen and whips up Achilles into a bellicose rage by imagining how it would be if someone similarly seized Deidamia. Diomedes then asks Achilles to recount his own upbringing. Achilles tells them how Chiron raised him to be very tough and strong.

He was trained in running, hunting, warfare, and other manly pursuits. He recalls all that he can, then remarks that his mother knows the rest.

COMMENTARY

With the *Achilleid*, Statius continues his daring and highly original adaptation of the epic tradition to unconventionally framed mythological themes. In the *Thebaid*, Statius took a mythological sequence—the Seven against Thebes—with strong tragic associations and, in adapting them to epic narrative, went out of his way to intensify the presence of tragedy and tragic paradigms within the space of epic. Statius is a writer at once intensely and self-consciously traditional, and at the same time audaciously original. In the present instance, Statius writes the story of the hero Achilles— a figure so famously and indelibly represented by Homer in his *Iliad* that there would seem to be no plausible area for improvement or emulation. Statius points out, however, that there is *more* to Achilles' story than Homer wrote about, and this "more" constitutes an important justification for his epic. Statius will fill in the interstices with episodes Homer does not include, yet in such a way as to transform our perception of the properly heroic episodes that Homer does include and that Statius now commits to rewriting (although, in the event, the poem remained incomplete, and Statius did not arrive at the Iliadic portion of Achilles' narrative). Provocatively, Statius will write "the entire hero," i.e., the whole story of his life, instead of a mere distillation of his heroic career. In making this choice, Statius violates the epic convention, spanning the period from Homer's practice to Horace's precepts, of commencing epic narration in medias res, i.e., starting in the midst of an ongoing development rather than from the very beginning.

Statius was exceptionally alert to questions of beginning and ending, as, for example, the beginning of his *Thebaid* demonstrates, and he was thus equally aware of the consequences that choices of beginning and ending point have for narrative structure. Aristotle, in writing about tragedy, was dubious that a person's life afforded the basis for poetic unity, i.e., unity of action. The collection of incidents that happen to fall into an individual life are potentially quite arbitrary and do not meet the requirements of literary coherence. Statius, in endowing his epic poem with a biographical structure, thus constantly undergoes the risk of arbitrariness and unstructured flow of incidents, and yet, if he had completed the poem, it nonetheless seems likely that he would have made this tension between structure and deviation into a matter of masterful play and manipulation. Certainly the surviving episodes betray an acute awareness of plot and deviation, narrative momentum and delay, the essential and the arbitrary. Statius, then, takes epic structure itself as one of his main objects of attention.

Where should he start, then? Playing, again, with his own premise, Statius begins, not with Achilles, but with Paris in the act of abducting Helen, thus bringing on Troy the Greek expedition. The abduction is a reasonable beginning point, given that the war will determine Achilles' destiny, yet the hero is as yet notably absent. He is still absent in the following sequence, because it is his mother, Thetis, who takes center stage. Moreover, when we do finally see Achilles, he is a fairly mature young man and is in the process of being transferred from Chiron's care to Scyros. Thus, we might ask if Statius has truly written the "entire hero." Later, however, Achilles will imitate AENEAS by rehearsing his own embedded narration (Book 2 in the *Aeneid*), in which he tells Ulysses and Diomedes of his childhood feats and education under Chiron; for everything that he does not remember, he refers to his mother, who would no doubt recall even his infant years with maternal affection. In a sense, then, the poet effectively completes the circle and covers the territory of Achilles' youthful years insofar as is possible. Statius seems aware of the subtle game he is playing:

We are reading an epic in which, at the beginning, there is no hero, and where the opening sequence of events is determined by a woman, and later there is a feminized hero. Epic is traditionally gendered male in its broad outline, although, of course, women sometimes play crucial roles. Here Statius seems determined to bring to the fore the paradox of female determination of male heroism, as Achilles' mother masterfully takes control of the plot. We see her manipulating and deceiving Chiron, pressuring Neptune, and, in a magnificent scene, cradling the (presumably large and muscular) sleeping Achilles in her arms as if he were an infant and sweeping him off to Scyros on her two-dolphin sea chariot.

Thetis thus tries to take control of the plot, but there are also limits to her intervention. The epic mythology of Achilles cannot be deflected endlessly, since it is destined, as well as established beyond doubt in the literary tradition, that he will go to Troy, fight, and ultimately die on the battlefield. Thetis, in some sense, opposes the epic identity that her son must inevitably assume. Statius thus once again engages in subtle play on the underlying identity of genre. In his epic's opening scenario, a masculine warrior Achilles is constantly trying to burst out of the feminine identity his mother has foisted on him for his own protection—a struggle between two gender positions that is at the same time a self-conscious dialogue of genres. One sign of Achilles' thus far unfulfilled epic potential is the density of references in these opening books to lyric, and especially songs played on the lyre. These songs are typically songs of heroes, such as Homer himself represented Achilles as singing when, sequestered in his tent, he received the embassy of Greek heroes. Since Homer, singing songs of heroism is a nonactive alternative to heroic deeds for Achilles, and thus Statius takes full advantage of this glancing mention in the *Iliad* to make Achilles into a young lyric poet. Other lyric references suggest nonheroic generic identifications; for example, when Achilles suffers from the symptoms of intense, overpowering desire for Deidamia, the language used recalls the famous symptomology of desire in Sappho fragment 31, later adapted into Latin by Catullus. Achilles' desire, then, rehearses a lyric literary history, from Greek to Latin, from Catullus to Statius. Achilles is supposed to be an epic hero, yet, for the time being, he has been assimilated to a feminine gender identity and to lyric and erotic literary associations. Despite his yearning to be a warrior, Achilles must first define his manhood within the erotic, feminine frame of the Scyros episode. Becoming impatient with his shameful, female disguise, he announces that he will prove his manhood at least in the love arena, and then proceeds to rape Deidamia. The token of his manhood—Deidamia's pregnancy—remains concealed for the present.

The entire Scyros episode plays on the ambiguity of gender and genre. There is a male hero hiding, latent, beneath the disguise, just as there is an epic trajectory of action that is still latent with the present scenario of delay, feminine wiles, and desire. Statius evokes an Achilles who sometimes presents a "tomboy" version of feminine beauty—not entirely surprisingly or anomalously, since ancient Greeks and Romans viewed the period of boyhood that immediately precedes manhood as one during which the boy remains "smooth" and effeminate in appearance and thus potentially attractive to older men. Statius is particularly interested, as in the *Thebaid*, in looking, gazing—the provocative game of trying to see through the ruse of gender ambiguity. Not surprisingly, Ulysses turns out to be an expert at uncovering such ruses, as he is a notoriously deft hand at creating them. At other times, however, Achilles cuts a less ambiguous figure, and we can see his ungraceful, hard masculinity despite the feminine costume. For example, right before he is revealed by Ulysses' trick of the gifts, Achilles participates in the dance with the other maidens, but he has become clumsy

and masculine in his movements, despite all his training in feminine comportment, first under the tutelage of his mother, then under Deidamia. Statius depicts with great subtlety the emergence of a truly masculine Achilles out of his feminine persona, a process that, while exaggerated by the circumstances of hiding and disguise in Achilles' story, is not totally out of keeping with the all-important passage to manhood as enacted generally in Roman culture. In general, Statius devotes much insightful attention to the construction of gender through habits of body, dress, speech, gait, and gaze, although, as Achilles' sometimes unfeminine behavior suggests, there is a limit to such construction and artificial formation. Gender is shown to be at once natural and a cultural construct.

When Achilles' masculine identity is finally unambiguously revealed, all aspects of his manhood—sexual, martial, political—are brought to the fore at once in a quasi-theatrical scene, all the more so since it involves a dramatic surprise, props, and a change of costume. Ulysses lays out the gifts for men and women, and Achilles predictably cannot stay away from the weapons. After laying his hands on them, he needs little in the way of further encouragement, and a clarion blast almost comically announces the theatrical entrance of "Achilles the Warrior" onto the stage of the epic. Then he reveals the other outcome of his manhood—his relationship with Deidamia, the pregnancy, and, in a further dramatic touch, the child himself. There is probably play here on the word *arma* in Latin, which means primarily "arms" (as in the famous Virgilian incipit, "arms and the man") but can also refer to male genitalia. Achilles' weaponry is now fully on display in every possible sense. Finally, he makes his maiden speech as a warrior/leader/negotiator by persuading Lycomedes not to punish him and Deidamia for their transgression, to accept their union, and even to contribute to the war effort. The nice rhetorical flourishes of this brief but lively speech are reminiscent of

Roman declamation, the rhetorical practice speeches that became especially popular as both educational tool and form of literary display in the early imperial period. Statius observes that Achilles "wins" his point, using the same term that is normally used for military conquest.

Achilles' first major public victory, then, is as a declaimer or orator. He is assuming his manhood, though not yet fully as a warrior, and manhood turns out to include a broader variety of traits than simply martial might and valor. Indeed, the diversity of Achilles' pursuits and acquisitions might be interpreted not so much as shameful but as reflective of shifting definitions of virility in Roman culture. In Statius's period, literary and rhetorical activity was increasingly set alongside political activity as a prime criterion of virile accomplishment and prestige, and since at least the second century B.C.E. Romans assimilated what might be termed aesthetic practices into the arena of masculine identity: dancing, composing and reciting poetry, wearing fine clothing, speaking in a sophisticated style influenced by Greek rhetoric, and so on. Achilles' feminine phase might be seen as an aberration in epic terms, but viewed from another perspective, it might be seen as offering the finishing touches to his education, which, already under Chiron, included a wide array of cultural competencies and not simply warfare and use of weapons. There were highly prestigious models for this broadened range of ability. The emperor Domitian prided himself, as the opening passage recalls, on both his military and his literary accomplishments.

Statius is careful to recall his own *Thebaid*, to which he proudly refers in the present epic's opening lines, but not to cover the same ground again too closely. For example, the present epic, like the *Thebaid*, is replete with Bacchic references and especially with references to Bacchic rites and objects as signifiers of the feminine and/or effeminate. The concern with masculinity and its inversion is thus an important element of continuity from one epic to the next, but whereas the Bacchic references in the *Thebaid* largely concern the paradox of an unwarlike, Bacchic city at war, the Bacchic rites at Scyros concern the paradox of a male hero concealed amid maidens—a mild yet significant variation. To take another example, Statius describes Thetis's process of deliberation as she rules out possibilities for a hiding place for her son. She considers Lemnos briefly, but then eliminates it as being dangerous because of the women's famous assault on their men. Statius thus subtly alludes to the extended HYPSIPYLE episode in the *Thebaid* while announcing his intention not to repeat his previous performance.

Scyros fits nicely into the well-established epic nexus of woman/island/delay; we might compare CALYPSO, CIRCE, DIDO, and Hypsipyle, where some or all of these elements are in play. Statius is therefore deciding, as self-conscious epic poet, where to set the woman/island/delay sequence of the *Achilleid*. As in other cases, the hero eventually must leave a comfortable setting and erotic relationship to achieve his destiny—whether that means returning to Ithaca, going to Italy, or joining the Greek expedition in Troy. Notable in this case is that the delay occurs immediately at the outset of the narrative and near the beginning of the hero's life, before he has accomplished anything of note. Moreover, it is not merely the hero's return to the path of destiny that is delayed by his stay on Scyros but the very emergence of his identity as male warrior. Statius, as usual, at once displays a keen attentiveness to his poem's traditional features and refashions epic conventions to suit his distinctive project.

Another element in the *Achilleid* that promises to respond to the *Thebaid* is the poet's interest in the pathos of departure and parental grief and anxiety. Statius as epic poet tends to focus at least as much attention, if not sometimes considerably more attention, on the emotions of sadness and worry that epic destinies inflict on parents and wives of the warriors. We might recall Argia, wife of POLYNICES, in the *Thebaid*, and that poem's many scenarios of parental grief and bereavement. The *Achilleid* opens with a representation of Thetis's all-consuming worry about her son that is highly reminiscent of both Atalanta and Argia in the *Thebaid* and suggests that this epic, too, will be devoted to evoking the poignant dimension of war. Even the hardened centaur Chiron cannot help shedding a tear as Achilles is removed from his care—a scene of departure echoed by the scene of Achilles' departure from Scyros. Deidamia's speech is highly affecting, and even the great warrior Achilles has to be distracted and made to forget Scyros by Ulysses and Diomedes. He is still, after all, a young man very much in love. Statius's attention to such psychological states is more acute than that of some of his predecessors, for whom the delaying woman figure seems simply to fade from view the minute the hero departs. Statius shows us the process and the techniques whereby memory is made to fade and is replaced with other things. In this as in other areas, Statius examines the conventions and plot machinery of the epic genre even as he enacts them.

The political dimension of the *Achilleid* is hard to characterize, both because the poem is a fragment and because of Statius's typically complex and elusive stance—perhaps necessarily so, given the dangers of speaking openly under an emperor, and especially an emperor such as Domitian. It is worth noting, however, that Statius, in suggesting that he will one day write an epic on Domitian's deeds, remarks that his *Achilleid* will serve as a "prelude" to this putative epic. If Achilles plays the opening act to Domitian, what is the relation between the two? It is possible to sketch only a few possible directions of thought on this topic. It is notable, as mentioned above, that Achilles, like Domitian, is accomplished both in war and in literature. It is also striking that he is compared with, and sometimes associatively assimilated to, Jupiter, to whom Domitian himself was often assimilated in contemporary panegyric. The opening lines of the poem recall how

Achilles, had he been born of Jupiter, would have replaced him on the throne; specifically, he states that Achilles would have succeeded him as ruler. In other words, the strong concern with inheritance under the Flavians—for whom imperial rule was inherited from father by son—seems to be reflected in the epic's opening theme. Achilles is a son greater than his father—so also, perhaps, is Domitian, the successor to both his brother Titus and his father, Vespasian. These ideas, however, must remain tentative and relatively undeveloped due to the unfinished state of Statius's epic.

Achilles   A Greek hero. Son of Peleus, king of Phthia of Thessaly, and Thetis, a sea nymph and daughter of Neseus. Achilles is the central character of Homer's Iliad and Statius's Achilleid. Other sources include Apollodorus's Library (3.13.6), Homer's Odyssey (11.470ff), Hyginus's *Fabulae* (96, 106, 107), and Ovid's Metamorphoses (12, 13). Achilles' childhood and early career, including his education by the centaur Chiron on Mt. Pelion and his battle with the Amazons during which he kills their queen, Penthesileia, are described in the *Epic Cycle*. Because of a prophecy that he would die an early death in battle, Thetis tried to make him invulnerable by dipping him into the river Styx. The heel by which she held him was, however, unprotected: Achilles was to die from an arrow shot into that heel by Paris. Another of Thetis's attempts to protect her son is most fully treated in Statius's unfinished *Achilleid*. She sends him, dressed as a girl, to the court of Lycomedes, king of Scyros, where he spends nine years, during which time he begets a son, Neoptolemus, with one of Lycomedes' daughters. Eventually, Odysseus finds him and persuades him to join the Greeks in the war against the Trojans.

The main poem in which Achilles is represented, and the work with which he is inextricably associated, is Homer's *Iliad*, in which he is characterized by his prowess in battle and his ungovernable temper. Homer either is not

Achilles and Ajax playing a board game. *Detail from a black-figure amphora, ca. 500 B.C.E. (Staatliche Antikensammlungen, Munich)*

aware of, or more likely, designedly omits, most of the legends mentioned above as being sub-heroic. Certainly he does not bring up Achilles' transvestitism, for example. For Homer, Achilles is the hero par excellence, and yet a hero who also turns away from his own army and violates aspects of the heroic code. At the opening of the *Iliad*, he quarrels with AGAMEMNON because the leader of the Greek expedition has taken away the young woman BRISEIS, the prize awarded him by the Greeks. He resists killing Agamemnon through ATHENA's intervention but swears an impressive oath that he will withdraw from the fighting and that the Greeks will appeal to him in vain in their hour of need. His motivation is not sentimental or "romantic";

rather, he is driven by the threat of damage to his honor. The "prize" *(geras)* awarded to him is a concrete embodiment of how much his community values and honors him, and thus to have it taken away is an insult to his heroic dignity. His deepest interest in life is to maximize his glory *(kleos)*, a priority reflected in his well-known choice to live a brief but glorious existence rather than a long, ordinary one. He is even willing to harm his own side to enhance his *kleos* as warrior. The Greek concept of the hero was not based on a calculation of the warrior's social utility and helpfulness in straightforward terms; rather, a hero's greatness is defined by how extraordinary he is, how far he transcends the lives of ordinary mortals.

Achilles, in withdrawing from battle, makes an extraordinary choice and intensifies expectations about his return. His mother, Thetis, in the meanwhile, obtains from ZEUS an assurance that he will turn the tide of battle against the Greeks precisely to make them understand how much they need Achilles and how much his loss means to them.

The Greeks send an embassy to Achilles to persuade him to return to battle, offering to return Briseis to him and to give him other magnificent gifts in addition, yet he still refuses. Only when his dear friend PATROCLUS, who donned Achilles' armor, has perished in battle at the hands of HECTOR, is he willing to return to the war. Most of the epic is taken up in expectation of Achilles' return, and so, when at last he does, the effect is spectacular. He fills the Trojans with terror, chokes the rivers with blood, and even battles a river god. At length, he meets Hector face to face and defeats him in one-to-one combat. At this point, the extremity of Achilles' character once again manifests itself. He will not return Hector's body but instead abuses it, dragging it around the walls of Troy behind his chariot. It is only when PRIAM goes to Achilles' tent under cover of darkness, with HERMES as a guide, that Achilles relents and agrees to return the body. In this much-discussed episode, Achilles weeps in grief, recalling his own father, Peleus, at home. The hero's terrible, unrelenting anger, which the *Iliad* declared in its opening line to be its subject matter, now does finally relent as the two warriors from opposing camps are brought together, at least temporarily, in a shared experience of pity for the mortal condition.

Achilles' death occurs outside the scope of the *Iliad*, when he is shot by an arrow from the skilled archer Paris, helped by the hand of APOLLO. Upon his death, the impetus of the Trojan War is logically inherited by his son Neoptolemus, whose name means "New War." When, in the *Odyssey*, ODYSSEUS meets Achilles in HADES, Achilles famously proclaims that he would rather be a serf in the world above than a king among the dead, yet he rejoices upon hearing of his son Neoptolemus's deeds and fame.

A very different perspective on Achilles is provided by Catullus ca. 64. In the latter part of this poem, the FATES, who are attending the wedding of Peleus and Thetis, sing a dark prophecy as a somber version of a marriage song. They predict the birth of Achilles and outline his grim career: slaughter on the plains of Troy, the choking of the rivers with blood, and, after his death, the sacrifice of the Trojan Polyxena to Achilles' shade. Catullus's poem, written during the discord of the late Roman Republic, scrutinizes the dark side of heroism, the violent and destructive elements in masculinity. Achilles' story is accordingly viewed through a deeply pessimistic lens.

In visual representations of the classical period, Achilles frequently appears fully armed. For example, in an Attic black-figure calyx krater from ca. 520 B.C.E. (Toledo Museum of Art, Ohio), Achilles carries a shield and spear and wears a Corinthian helmet. In some images, he is shown playing a board game with his companion-at-arms AJAX. The motif of the board game appears also on an Attic black-figure amphora of the sixth century B.C.E. (Staatliche Antikensammlungen, Munich). In the postclassical period, Peter Paul Rubens prepared a series of designs entitled *The History of Achilles* in ca. 1630–35 (copy in the Detroit Institute of Arts). Another postclassical image is Luca Giordano's *The Story of Achilles* of 1705 (Alte Pinakothek, Munich).

Acis (Akis)   See GALATEA; POLYPHEMUS.

Acontius and Cydippe   A young man from Chios. Classical sources are Callimachus's *Aetia* (3.1.26) and Ovid's *HEROIDES* (20, 21). Acontius fell in love with Cydippe and followed her to the temple of ARTEMIS. He wrote on an apple the words "I swear by Artemis that I will marry

Acontius." Cydippe picked up the apple and read the inscription aloud, inadvertently swearing an oath by Artemis to marry Acontius. Cydippe's parents, however, arranged for her to be engaged to another man, and she became ill as the time for the marriage neared. Cydippe's father discovered from the Delphic oracle that Cydippe's illness was caused by the potential betrayal of the oath she had sworn to Artemis. Acontius was then accepted as a husband for Cydippe.

Actaeon A Boeotian hunter. Son of Aristaeus and AUTONOE. Grandson of CADMUS. Classical sources are Apollodorus's *LIBRARY* (3.4.4), Diodorus Siculus's *LIBRARY OF HISTORY* (4.81.4), Hyginus's *Fabulae* (180, 181), Ovid's *METAMORPHOSES* (3.131–252), and Pausanias's *Description of Greece* (9.2.3). Actaeon was raised by the centaur CHIRON, who was tutor

also to the heroes ACHILLES and JASON and the gods APOLLO and ASCLEPIUS. In Ovid's *Metamorphoses*, Actaeon surprised ARTEMIS and her nymphs bathing on Mount Cithaeron in Boeotia. Outraged that she had been seen nude, Artemis transformed Actaeon into a stag. His own pack of dogs failed to recognize him, gave chase, and, after capturing him, tore him apart. In other accounts, Actaeon offended Artemis either by attempting to seduce her or by boasting of his superior hunting skills. Apollodorus's *Library* provides a coda to the myth in which Actaeon's howling dogs afterward searched fruitlessly for their master until Chiron created a sculptural likeness of Actaeon to console them. In yet another version of the myth, ZEUS punished Actaeon with death for his amorous pursuit of SEMELE, one of Zeus's consorts. The myth of Actaeon was a popular theme in art, literature, and dance.

Diana and Actaeon. *Lucas Cranach, ca. 1540 (Wadsworth Atheneum, Hartford, Connecticut)*

In antiquity, visual representations of the myth of Actaeon commonly depicted his death. An example is a black-figure krater attributed to the Pan Painter from ca. 470 B.C.E. (Museum of Fine Arts, Boston). Here Artemis stands with drawn bow before the falling figure of Actaeon while his hounds tear at his throat and torso. There is a magnificent relief of Actaeon attacked by his dogs from a temple frieze in Selinunte, Italy, from ca. 465 B.C.E. (Museo Archeologico, Palermo). After the fifth century B.C.E., artists take more interest in Actaeon's physical transformation into a stag, for example, Titian, *Diana and Actaeon*, 1556–59 (National Gallery of Scotland, Edinburgh), or in Actaeon's discovery of the bathing Artemis and her company. This theme was particularly well explored by a variety of artists from the 15th century onward. Some examples are Lucas Cranach's *Diana and Actaeon* from ca. 1540 (Wadsworth Atheneum, Hartford). Here, Actaeon's spying on Artemis and his metamorphoses occur simultaneously. Another example of this theme is Jean-Baptiste Camille Corot's *Diana Surprised at the Bath* from ca. 1836 (Metropolitan Museum of Art, New York). Later literary interpretations of the myth of Actaeon appeared in verse by Giovanni Boccaccio, *The Hunt of Diana*, ca. 1334, and Petrarch in ca. 1336. William Shakespeare's *A Midsummer Night's Dream*, ca. 1595–96, evoked Actaeon and Diana in the characters Titania and Bottom. The myth of Actaeon is also the subject of several ballets choreographed by Bronisława Nijinska and Rudolph Nureyev.

Admetus   See *ALCESTIS*; TIBULLUS.

Adonis   A lover of APHRODITE. Son of King Cinyras of Paphos and Myrrha (Smyrna). Classical sources are Apollodorus's *LIBRARY* (3.14.3–4), Hyginus's *Fabulae* (58, 248, 251) Ovid's *METAMORPHOSES* (10.476, 519–559, 708–739), and Theocritus's *Idylls* (15, 30). Adonis is one of a group of mortal youths whose beauty attracted the amorous attention of the gods and goddesses; others include ENDYMION, GANYMEDE, and HYACINTHUS. Both APHRODITE and PERSEPHONE loved Adonis.

Because Myrrha neglected to worship Aphrodite, the goddess punished her by making her fall in love with her own father, Cinyras. With her nurse's help, Myrrha tricked her father into beginning an incestuous relationship with her. When Cinyras discovered the truth, he tried to kill her, but before he could do so, the gods mercifully transformed her into a myrrh tree. Adonis was born of the myrrh tree (he is associated with vegetation and fertility) and given by Aphrodite into the protection of Persephone. Both goddesses fell in love with the youth, and eventually Adonis divided his time between them. Despite Aphrodite's protective care, Adonis was killed by a boar while hunting. An anemone grew on the spot where he died, and a red rose where Aphrodite's tears fell.

Representations of Adonis hunting and the moment of his death appear in early antique reliefs and pottery, where the emphasis is usually placed on the youth's beauty and tragic death. Depictions of Adonis in the company of one or both the goddesses with whom he was associated appear from about the fifth century B.C.E. A Pompeian fresco from the first century B.C.E. shows Adonis with Aphrodite. Aphrodite's love for Adonis is a subject that appears frequently among Renaissance and baroque painters. Examples include Titian's *Venus and Adonis* from 1553–54 (Prado, Madrid). This theme was also explored by Paolo Veronese, Peter Paul Rubens, Nicholas Poussin, and the sculptor Antonio Canova. William Shakespeare wrote a poem based on the myth, *Venus and Adonis* (1592–93).

Adrastus   The leader of the expedition of the Seven against Thebes. King of Argos, and for a certain period, of Sicyon. Classical sources are Aeschylus's *SEVEN AGAINST THEBES*, Euripides' *SUPPLIANT WOMEN*, and Statius's

THEBAID. Adrastus quarreled with his cousin, the seer AMPHIARAUS. Later they made peace, and Amphiaraus married Adrastus's sister Eriphyle on the understanding that she would resolve any disputes between them. One night, POLYNICES, exiled from Thebes, where his brother Eteocles maintained his rule, and TYDEUS, exiled from Calydon, took shelter at Adrastus's palace on a stormy night, where they quarreled and fought. Adrastus broke up the fight and offered to help reinstate both, giving to Polynices his daughter Argia in marriage, and to Tydeus his other daughter, Deipyla. Polynices's alliance with Adrastus is the origin of the first Argive expedition against Thebes. Polynices secured Amphiaraus's participation by bribing his wife, Eriphyle, with the fatally cursed necklace of HARMONIA (see discussion of Statius's *Thebaid*). The expedition failed, and Adrastus alone survived by escaping on his divine horse Arion. In Euripides' *Suppliant Women*, Adrastus seeks help from Athens and THESEUS in recovering the bodies of the slain Argive heroes, which CREON of Thebes refuses to hand over for burial. The sons of the slain heroes, called the Epigoni, mounted a second, successful expedition against Thebes. The story of Adrastus and the Seven against Thebes is well represented in ancient literature: Aeschylus and Statius are major sources.

Aeacus Ruler of the Myrmidons. Son of Aegina (a river nymph) and ZEUS. Sources are Apollodorus's *LIBRARY* (3.12.6), Hesiod's *THEOGONY* (1,003), Hyginus's *Fabulae* (52), and Ovid's *METAMORPHOSES* (7.469). Aeacus had a reputation for sound judgment and piety. Zeus transformed ants on the island of Aegina into the Myrmidons, and Aeacus reigned over them. According to Ovid, the population of the island had been destroyed by a plague brought upon them by the jealousy of HERA. Aeacus married Endeis, and their sons were PELEUS and TELAMON. With Psamathe (a NEREID), Aeacus had a son,

Phocus. Peleus and Telamon were jealous of Phocus and killed him. When Aeacus discovered the murder, he exiled his sons. Aeacus was an honored figure in HADES in addition to MINOS and Rhadamanthys.

Aeetes A ruler of Colchis. Son of HELIOS and Perseis (a sea nymph). Classical sources are Apollodorus's *LIBRARY* (1.9.1, 1.9.23), Apollonius of Rhodes's *VOYAGE OF THE ARGONAUTS* (2.1,140–4.240), Diodorus Siculus's *LIBRARY OF HISTORY* (4.45.1–49), Hesiod's *THEOGONY* (956), Homer's *ODYSSEY* (10.135), and Hyginus's *Fabulae* (3, 12, 22, 23). Aeetes was the brother of CIRCE and PASIPHAE and the father of Chalciope, MEDEA, and Apsyrtus. He received PHRIXUS and the Golden Ram at Colchis and married him to his daughter Chalciope. The ram was sacrificed, and the Golden Fleece was dedicated to ARES by Aeetes. Later Aeetes refused to allow JASON to take away the fleece, but the hero was aided by Aeetes' daughter Medea. In Medea's attempt to escape with Jason, she killed Apsyrtus and dispersed the pieces of his body in the sea. Aeetes was forced to stop to pick them up, giving Jason and Medea the chance to escape.

Aegeus A king of Athens and father of the hero THESEUS. Classical sources are Apollodorus's *LIBRARY* (3.15.5), Euripides' *MEDEA* (663–758), Hyginus's *Fabulae* (37, 43), Ovid's *METAMORPHOSES* (7.403, 420), Pausanias's *Description of Greece* (1.22.5, 1.27.8), and Plutarch's *Life of Theseus* (3.12–17.22). While Aegeus was still childless, he traveled to Delphi to consult the Oracle about his future heirs. The prophecy warned him not to beget a child before he should return to Athens but in opaque terms that Aegeus did not understand. He consulted Pittheus, King of Troezen, and while there fathered Theseus by Aethra, the daughter of Pittheus. Suspecting that Aethra was pregnant with his child, Aegeus left behind, hidden under a stone, a sword and shoes for the child. He asked Aethra to send his son to him once he was capable of lifting the stone. When Theseus reached young manhood, he found the tokens left by his father and went to Athens to claim his birthright. Aegeus recognized him as his son by the sword that he bore. Aegeus had by then married MEDEA, and she, perceiving Theseus to be a threat to the position of her own children with Aegeus, tried at first to discredit and then to poison Theseus. When Aegeus discovered her schemes, he drove her out of Athens.

After his adventures in Crete, Theseus returned by ship to Athens. Aegeus had asked Theseus to hang a white sail as a sign that Theseus had survived his adventures, but Theseus neglected to hang the correct sail. When Theseus's ships were sighted without the sail in question, Aegeus assumed the worst and, in his grief, threw himself into the sea, thus giving his name to the Aegean Sea. In literature, Aegeus often plays an important but subsidiary role. In Euripides' *Medea*, Medea finds it convenient to marry Aegeus because he offers her escape and shelter. A particularly affecting representation of the tragedy of Aegeus's death occurs in Catullus c.64: Theseus's "forgetful/inconsiderate" abandonment of the Cretan princess Ariadne is symmetrically punished by his later "forgetful" omission to raise the white sail and the resulting death of his father.

Aegeus appears at the Delphic Oracle in a red-figure kylix from ca. 430 B.C.E. (Antikensammlung, Berlin). The theme of Aegeus's recognition of Theseus by his sword was also represented by artists. A postclassical example is Hippolyte Flandrin's *Theseus Recognized by His Father* of 1832 (École des Beaux-Arts, Paris).

Aegisthus   Son of THYESTES. Classical sources are Aeschylus's *AGAMEMNON* and *LIBATION BEARERS*, Apollodorus's *LIBRARY* (Epitome 2.14), Euripides' *ELECTRA*, Homer's *ODYSSEY* (1.29–43, 3.248–312, 4.512–537), Hyginus's *Fabulae* (88), and Sophocles' *ELECTRA*, Aegisthus was the sole surviving son of Thyestes after ATREUS killed his brother's children and served them

to Thyestes in a meal. In another version, Thyestes committed incest with his daughter Pelopia in order to have a son to avenge him, and Aegisthus was born of their union. When he grew up, Aegisthus became CLYTAEMNESTRA's lover and helped her to kill AGAMEMNON, son of Atreus. Agamemnon's son ORESTES later killed Aegisthus.

Aeneas   Trojan hero and founder of the Roman race. Son of Venus (APHRODITE) and ANCHISES. Father of Ascanius (also Iulus). Aeneas is the hero of Virgil's *AENEID* and one of the heroes of Homer's *ILIAD*. An additional classical source is Ovid's *METAMORPHOSES* (13.623–14.608). The *Homeric Hymn to Aphrodite* (see *HOMERIC HYMNS*) tells how Aphrodite fell in love with the mortal Anchises, and the product of their union was the hero Aeneas. In Homer's *Iliad*, Aeneas is among the more impressive Trojan warriors. He is also unusually favored and protected by the gods. When Aeneas faces DIOMEDES in battle, Aphrodite attempts to rescue him, and after Diomedes wounds Venus, Apollo completes the rescue. Later, in Book 20, POSEIDON saves Aeneas from ACHILLES. Poseidon then predicts that Aeneas's line will survive the war to rule over the Trojans in later years. Accounts of Aeneas's escape from Troy vary. Either he departed for Mount Ida before the fall of Troy with his family, or as in Virgil's version, he departed in the midst of Troy's sack.

Stories of Aeneas's escape and subsequent wanderings go back to the sixth century B.C.E. Various versions exist in the Greek poets and mythographers. The story takes on a new significance when the Romans begin to adapt it in the third century B.C.E. to explain the origins of their civilization. As Rome emerged as a major force in the Mediterranean world, it was necessary to find a sufficiently prestigious foundation myth and founder figure. Troy has the advantage of being a glorious civilization, favored by the gods, and endowed with heroic, mythological, and literary pedigree, yet distinct from, and even opposed to, Greece. The Romans came into conflict with the great Hellenistic kingdoms in the third and second centuries B.C.E., and, in general, would have found it unacceptable to be derived from a civilization to which they already owed a considerable portion of their culture.

As Roman founder figure, Aeneas departs from Troy and, in his subsequent wanderings, sojourns in various places—e.g., Crete, Epirus, Carthage, Sicily—until finally landing in Italy at Cumae. This basic narrative framework exists in early Roman poets such as ENNIUS and Naevius starting in the third century B.C.E. The canonical account, inevitably, is the version contained in Virgil's fully extant *Aeneid* (ca.19 B.C.E.). According to Virgil, Aeneas leaves Troy in the midst of the Greek sack with his son, called both Ascanius and Iulus; his father, ANCHISES; his wife, Creusa; and his household gods, the Penates. He loses track of his wife during their flight, and her spirit appears to him, urging him to continue pursuing his destiny. Aeneas leaves Troy along with a substantial group of Trojan fugitives in several ships. They do not know what their final destination is to be. There are several failed attempts, in which dire omens and other disastrous events indicate that they must depart from a given place. At length, Aeneas learns that Italy is their goal. On their way to Italy, Juno (see HERA), who still angrily opposes the Trojans, wrecks the fleet and causes it to wash ashore in Carthage. There Aeneas becomes involved in a serious love affair with DIDO, queen of Carthage. Admonished by Mercury (HERMES), he departs, and Dido commits suicide. Eventually, after stopping in Sicily and celebrating the funeral games of his father, who died during the journey, Aeneas comes to Cumae, where the SIBYL offers prophecies and instructions for visiting the underworld. In the underworld, Anchises shows him the souls of future Romans waiting to take on bodily form in the world above. After departing from the underworld, Aeneas sails up the Tiber and lands in Latium, where king Latinus offers him his daughter in marriage in accordance with a prophecy that his daughter Lavinia is destined to marry a foreigner. Juno causes TURNUS, Lavinia's favored suitor hitherto, to take up arms against Aeneas. EVANDER, a Greek from Arcadia established on the Palatine, offers Aeneas support and gives him a tour of the future site of Rome. After several books of warfare, Aeneas kills Turnus in one-on-one combat.

Virgil ends his epic with the death of Turnus. Aeneas later founds Lavinium. He dies, in some versions by mysterious disappearance, and is deified as Jupiter Indiges (see the account in Ovid's *Metamorphoses* 14). Aeneas is the founder of the Roman race and the Roman civilization, not the founder of the city. This latter honor goes to the eponymous ROMULUS, a descendant of Aeneas. Aeneas's Trojans intermarry with the native Latins, and their descendants become the Romans. Aeneas was of special interest in the Augustan period because Julius Caesar and his adoptive son the emperor Augustus claimed descent from Aeneas; the name of Aeneas's son Iulus resembles the name of the Julian clan. Aeneas enjoyed a prominent place amid the statuary of Augustus's Forum and on the reliefs of the Ara Pacis, a major monument of Augustan Rome. The Virgilian Aeneas is competent at wandering adventures, like ODYSSEUS, and dominant in battle, like Achilles, but he also adds qualities of his own: He is dutiful (*pius*), patient, self-sacrificing, pragmatic, enduring of many labors. Homer's Trojan warrior has become the quintessential Roman hero.

Aeneid VIRGIL (ca. 19 B.C.E.)

INTRODUCTION

Virgil's poetic career proceeded from humble to grand. He began by composing a collection of 10 elegant pastoral poems, the *Eclogues* (ca. 39 B.C.E.), went on to complete his didactic poem on farming in four books, the *Georgics* (ca. 29 B.C.E.), and finally, as the culmination of his career, produced his epic on the founding of Roman civilization by the Trojan hero AENEAS. The *Aeneid* was published unfinished after Virgil's death in 19 B.C.E., and some incomplete half-lines attest to the fact that the work had not yet received the poet's "final hand." The poem, despite these minor flaws, is a masterpiece and constitutes Virgil's most ambitious treatment of his central themes: violence and civilization, the immense labor of creating and sustaining human society, and the land of Italy itself as the site of violent struggle, idyllic habitation, exilic nostalgia, and agricultural toil.

At the opening of the third book of the *Georgics*, Virgil appears to advertise his as yet unpublished epic. He proclaims he will build a great temple that will honor Octavian (the future emperor Augustus). To what extent the *Aeneid* stands as a proud monument to Augustan society and Augustus as *princeps* ("first citizen," "leader") remains a matter of intense and complicated debate. The epic treats the story of Aeneas's exile from conquered Troy and his subsequent wanderings. It was prophesied by Homer that Aeneas's line would survive Troy's fall, and Virgil's epic traces his story from the terrible moment when the Greeks enter and sack the city, to his perplexed wanderings by sea, through his eventual arrival in Italy, where, according to destiny, he is to found a new community that will become the basis for the Roman race. Before he founds this community, however, he must contend with the local inhabitants, the Latins, with whom, against his will, he becomes engaged in a bloody conflict. At the close of the epic, in order to marry King Latinus's daughter Lavinia and found Lavinium, he must slay his implacable rival, TURNUS, in one-to-one combat, in a duel that replays, on Italian soil, the final combat of ACHILLES and HECTOR as narrated in Homer's *ILIAD*.

Virgil's ambitions in the *Aeneid* are immense. He aims, first of all, to encapsulate in epic form the labor of founding Roman civilization and its moral, political, and religious dimensions. Second, in adapting Roman historical legend to the epic form, he incorporates and assimilates within his poetic vision Homer's *Iliad* and *ODYSSEY*, Apollonius of Rhodes's *VOYAGE OF THE ARGONAUTS*, and the *Annales* of the Roman epic poet ENNIUS, to name only his most important models. The task of writing the classic epic of Roman civilization near the end of the first century B.C.E. was not an easy one. The epic genre was not exactly out of fashion but had been rendered problematic for poets whose practice was informed by the sophisticated poetics of craft and erudition inherited from Hellenistic Alexandria. Virgil does not produce an outright panegyric or narration of Augustus's deeds yet manages to incorporate reference to and awareness of Augustus and the moral concepts and civilizing ideology with which he was associated into his richly erudite and sophisticated mythological narrative.

SYNOPSIS

Book 1

The poet introduces his subject matter: the founding of Roman civilization. Juno (see HERA) is then identified as the goddess who caused all of Aeneas's labors and wanderings: She is still bitter about the judgment of PARIS and GANYMEDE and has heard a prophecy that the race deriving from Aeneas would one day overthrow her beloved Carthage. Profoundly indignant that she cannot act on her hatreds with the freedom granted to other gods and goddesses, Juno bribes AEOLUS to release the winds under his control with the promise of a nymph in marriage. The winds are released, and Aeneas, who is sailing with his fleet, is introduced in a moment of terror as the storm descends. The ships are in great danger, and that of Orontes is overwhelmed before Aeneas's eyes, but Neptune (see POSEIDON) observes the seas in turmoil, chastises the unruly winds, and calms the seas. The remainder of the fleet makes for the nearby shore of Libya. Aeneas climbs a peak to look for signs of the other ships, and shoots seven deer, one for each of his ships. Aeneas and his fleet hold a feast and mourn for the comrades whom they believe they have lost. Among the gods, Venus (see APHRODITE) turns to Jupiter (see ZEUS) and complains of her son Aeneas's fate. Jupiter consoles her by revealing the destiny of the future Romans. They will have empire without limit, and one day Augustus Caesar will bring a new golden age. The gods dispatch Mercury (see HERMES) to ensure a hospitable welcome for the Trojans in Carthage. The next morning, Aeneas goes to explore the nearby area and meets his mother, Venus, disguised as a maiden huntress. She informs Aeneas and his comrade Achates about Carthage and its ruler, DIDO, and encourages him to approach her; he rebukes her for mocking him with disguises and images. Aeneas and Achates arrive in the city, which is in the process of being built and is bustling with activity. When Aeneas perceives that events of the Trojan War are depicted on the walls of the temple of Juno, he realizes that the inhabitants know about the Trojans and sympathize with them; he is much heartened. He then sees Dido, and suddenly, his comrades from all the other ships except Orontes' appear on the scene. While Aeneas and Achates remain hidden, Ilioneus steps forward and beseeches Dido for hospitality, and she graciously offers to receive them and even to accept them as fellow settlers. Aeneas and Achates are then revealed; Aeneas addresses Dido and she leads him into the palace. Venus, in the meanwhile, comes up with a scheme to control Dido and ensure her loyalty to Aeneas: She instructs her son Cupid (see EROS) to take on the appearance of Aeneas's son, Ascanius, and, when Ascanius is sent for, to take his place (the real Ascanius has been plunged into magically induced slumber). At the palace, Cupid sits on Dido's lap and breathes a profound love into her, gradually erasing the memory of her attachment to her dead husband, Sychaeus. As

the evening proceeds, Dido asks Aeneas to tell the story of his adventures.

Book 2

Although the memory is painful to him, Aeneas agrees to tell the story of the fall of Troy. He relates how the Greeks hid themselves on the nearby island of Tenedos, and the Trojans, thinking they had departed for good, came out of the gates of their city to discover the wooden horse. During the debate as to what to do with it, LAOCOON suggests that the Greek gift is a trick and makes the hollow horse resound with his spear. At that moment, the captive Greek spy Sinon is dragged onto the scene: He gains the Trojans' sympathy by a brilliant speech in which he pretends to be a deserter victimized by Ulysses (see ODYSSEUS) and whom Ulysses threatened to sacrifice; he persuades them that the horse was made as an act of atonement to appease Minerva (see ATHENA) for the theft of the Palladium. The Trojans are convinced by his story and convinced, furthermore, that it is right to accept the horse when two serpents appear from Tenedos and strangle Laocoon and his sons before settling at the feet of Minerva's statue on the citadel. That night, the Greeks descend from the horse, open the gates for their comrades, and commence sacking the city. Aeneas, waking from a terrifying dream in which HECTOR appeared to him and admonished him to flee the city, throws himself furiously into the midst of the fighting. He eventually makes his way to the palace, sees the headless corpse of PRIAM, slain by NEOPTOLEMUS, and remembers his own father and family. He turns around and sees HELEN. For a moment, he considers killing her, but he is stopped by the appearance of his mother, Venus. She shows him the terrible revelation that it is the gods, not Helen, who are responsible for the destruction of Troy. He goes home, consults with his family, and on a sign from Jupiter, they decide to flee. Aeneas carries his father on his shoulders and leads his son, Iulus/Ascanius, by the hand, but in the confusion, he loses sight of his wife, Creusa.

Desperately, he retraces his steps to find her, but in vain. Finally, her shade appears to him and bids him go on without her to achieve his destiny. He returns to the group of companions preparing to follow him into exile.

Book 3

Aeneas's narration continues. He tells how they built a fleet and he departed with his son, father, companions, and household gods (Penates). They attempt a landing at various places, but in each case omens prevent a long-term stay: In Thrace, Aeneas pulls up some green boughs to deck the altar in preparation for offering a sacrifice; they bleed and eventually the groaning voice of Polydorus arises from the ground. He was a Trojan prince whom PRIAM had sent to the Thracian king along with a large amount of gold; after the fall of Troy, the king had Polydorus killed and kept the gold. The Trojans depart and next go to Delos, where Aeneas receives a prophetic admonition that they must seek out their "ancient mother" from which their stock derives. Anchises interprets this on various grounds to mean Crete. They begin to establish a new Pergamum in Crete, when a pestilence falls on them. In a dream, the Penates tell Aeneas that he must seek out Italy/Hesperia, the land of origin of the Trojan founder figure Dardanus. They sail for several days and take shelter from bad weather on the island of Strophades, where the HARPIES dwell. They engage the Harpies in battle, and the chief harpy, Calaeno, delivers a worrisome prophecy: "They must sail for Italy but, because of their mistreatment of the Harpies, they will be condemned to violence and hunger until, in their desperation, they will be driven to eat their own tables." They go on to Actium, where they celebrate the Trojan athletic games, which Aeneas commemorates with an inscription. From there, they go to Buthrotum at Epirus, where Priam's son HELENUS rules alongside ANDROMACHE. She had been Neoptolemus's slave and bore his children, but when Neoptolemus was killed by ORESTES, Helenus ruled a

portion of his kingdom and took Andromache as his wife. They have constructed a duplicate Troy in miniature, and Andromache does honor to Hector's cenotaph. Helenus offers Aeneas advice and various prophecies that will guide him on his journey: the portent of the white sow, the dangers of SCYLLA and CHARYBDIS, the importance of offering prayers to Juno, the necessity of consulting the Sibyl of CUMAE. They then sail off, avoiding Charybdis and passing by Aetna; as they pass the island of the Cyclopes, they stop to rescue Achaemenides, a Greek who was stranded there when Ulysses's crew left hastily. They depart just in time as the Cyclopes begin to approach. They sail past other cities of Sicily until Aeneas's father, Anchises, dies at Drepanum. On this sad note, Aeneas ends his story. .

Book 4

Dido by now is hopelessly and painfully in love with Aeneas. She struggles with her guilt over betraying her dead husband, Sychaeus, to whom she had pledged lifelong loyalty, and debates with her sister Anna what to do. Dido is so obsessed with her love that she ignores all else; even the construction of her town comes to a halt. Venus and Juno discuss the development and propose to promote the relationship between the two, but each with her own, very different motivation—Juno to keep Aeneas from Italy, Venus to keep him safe for the time being. The next day, Dido, Aeneas, and their companions go on a hunt; there is a storm (summoned by Juno); they seek shelter in the same cave, where, with Juno's connivance, they consummate a questionable "marriage." Rumor, personified as a terrifying birdlike monster with an eye, mouth, and ear for every feather, brings the news to Iarbas, a neighboring king whom Dido rejected as suitor. He complains to Jupiter, who gives him a favorable hearing and dispatches Mercury to remind Aeneas of his destiny. Aeneas is terrified by the god's apparition. He makes plans to depart and prepares to explain his departure to Dido.

When she learns of his plans, she becomes furious and reproaches Aeneas bitterly. He protests that he departs to seek Italy against his will. She vows that she will, as a shade, continue to pursue him in vengeance even after death. After their conversation, she sends Anna to beg him to stay, but Aeneas refuses to be swayed. Dido is assailed by visions and portents. On the pretence that she is seeking a magical cure for her love, she begins preparations for his funeral pyre. Mercury urges Aeneas to flee immediately. Dido observes his departure, pronounces a terrible curse on Aeneas and his descendants, and commits suicide with the sword that had been Aeneas's gift to her. Juno in pity sends down IRIS to release Dido's soul by cutting a lock of her hair.

Book 5

The sight of Dido's funeral flames fill the departing Trojans with grim forebodings. Prevented from seeking Italy directly by bad weather, they make for the land of Aeneas's brother Eryx in Sicily. When they land, Aeneas announces that they will celebrate his father's funeral games on the first anniversary of his death. He presides as the Trojans and Sicilians compete in a boat race, a foot race, a boxing match, and an archery contest. Ascanius and other Trojan boys then put on an equestrian display that prefigures Rome's *lusus Troiae*. Juno, in the meanwhile, dispatches Iris to stir up the Trojan women. In the guise of Beroe, she rouses their indignation at their wandering life, suggests that they settle down in the land of Eryx, and incites them to burn the ships. Ascanius, Aeneas, and others hear of the fire, rush to the scene, and the women scatter. In response to Aeneas's prayer, Jupiter quenches the flames with a thunderstorm. Aeneas then decides that those who wish to stay will found their own community under the leadership of Acestes. Venus, in the meanwhile, seeks assurance from Neptune that Aeneas and his remaining companions will make it safely to Italy. He assures

her that they will arrive safely at the cost of a single life, "one for many." The god Sleep then overpowers the helmsman Palinurus, who is thrown into the ocean. Aeneas himself sadly steers the ship the rest of the way.

Book 6

The fleet anchors at Cumae. On his way to consult the Sibyl, Aeneas pauses to view the temple of Apollo on the acropolis. DAEDALUS dedicated this temple after his flight from Crete. Its doors depict the episodes in Cretan mythology in which Daedalus himself was involved except for his own son's death. Aeneas then offers a sacrifice as bidden by the priestess of Apollo and hears the voice of the Sibyl emanating from the cave. She predicts a second "Trojan War" on Italian soil. He then asks how he may descend to the underworld to meet his father, and she instructs him to seek the golden bough. In the meantime, Misenus, one of Aeneas's comrades, is drowned after challenging TRITON to a music contest. Aeneas obtains the golden bough, and the Trojans bury Misenus. Aeneas proceeds to a deep cave by Lake Avernus, where he offers a sacrifice, before descending to the underworld with the Sibyl as his guide. On the near side of the river STYX, where the unburied are detained, he meets Palinurus, who tells his story; Aeneas promises to bury him and name a place after him. They present the bough to CHARON, and he ferries them across. On the other side, Aeneas sees and addresses Dido, who refuses to speak with him. He then meets Deiphobus, Helen's lover after Paris's death, whose visage still exhibits the mutilations that the Greeks inflicted on him before they killed him. Aeneas then goes on to visit TARTARUS and its fabled punishments and, finally, the abode of the blessed, ELYSIUM, where he meets Anchises. Anchises explains the process of transmigration, whereby souls are purged of their flaws in preparation for taking on new bodily form, and then points out the souls whose future selves will constitute Rome's notable men and heroes. The procession reaches its climax in the figure of Augustus, but ends, somewhat mournfully, with the figure of his heir designate, Marcellus, who died young. They leave the underworld through the ivory gate of false dreams.

Book 7

Aeneas performs funeral rites for his nurse Caieta, who died during his absence, and sails forth from Cumae, past CIRCE, where they hear the roaring of Circe's victims in their animal forms. Aeneas's fleet enters the Tiber; the poet addresses his muse, Erato, and announces the commencement of the battle narrative. The king of the local people, Latinus, has a daughter, Lavinia, who, according to a prophecy, is to marry a non-Latin stranger. Aeneas and Iulus, in the meanwhile, spread a feast out on the grass, placing food on top of wheat cakes; when they eat the cakes too, Iulus remarks that they have eaten their tables, and Aeneas perceives that they have fulfilled the prophecy and arrived at the land destined for them. Aeneas then sends envoys to Latinus's palace. The king realizes that Aeneas must be the stranger fated to marry his daughter and responds favorably. Juno is furious at the Trojans' success and decides that if she cannot halt their progress, she will at least make it bloody, resolving to employ the powers of the underworld to wreak havoc. Accordingly, she calls upon the fury Allecto, who afflicts Latinus's wife, Amata, with madness and drives her to despair that her daughter is to be given in marriage to a foreigner. Amata takes Lavinia up into the mountains and initiates a Bacchic frenzy. Allecto then appears in the dreams of the Rutulian Turnus, to whom Lavinia is currently betrothed, and infects him with a frenzied rage for battle. Finally, she brings it about that Iulus, while hunting, shoots a pet stag of the royal household. The people of Latium are roused to anger; fighting breaks out between the Trojans and local peoples. Allecto reports back to Juno, who dismisses the Fury abruptly. All of Latium cries out for war, and Latinus, besieged, withdraws into the palace and gives up his rule. Since Latinus refused to open the gates of war according to Roman custom, Juno herself smashes them open. For the remainder of the book, the poet rehearses a catalog of Italian peoples and their leaders in war, ending with an evocative description of the Volscian Camilla.

Book 8

As the opposing hosts gather, Tiberinus appears to Aeneas in his sleep to elaborate on the portent of the white sow with a litter of 30 and suggests an alliance with EVANDER, the Arcadian who occupies the future site of Rome. The next day, as predicted, Aeneas sees the white sow. He then goes with his companions to see Evander. Evander agrees to the alliance and extends his hospitality to Aeneas. As they are performing the rites of HERACLES, Evander takes the occasion of the feast to give a colorful explanation of the origins of these rites. They were in memory of Heracles' killing of CACUS for having stolen his cattle. Evander then offers a history of Latium from the earliest period and a tour of key sites of proto-Roman topography: the Asylum, the Lupercal, the Argiletum, the Capitol, and, finally, his own simple dwelling. In the meantime, Venus seduces her husband, Vulcan (see HEPHAESTUS), and persuades him to make armor for Aeneas. In the middle of the night, Vulcan rises and visits his CYCLOPES to instruct them to put aside their other work to make armor and, especially, a mighty shield fit for a hero. The next morning, Evander addresses Aeneas and offers him the leadership of the Etruscans: They have risen against their tyrant, Mezentius, and driven him out; Mezentius has now taken refuge with Turnus. Evander also offers to send his own son Pallas with Aeneas so that he may learn the art of war under his tutelage. Evander sends his son off with a farewell speech full of pathos and foreboding. As Aeneas is on his way to the Etruscan camp, he is met by Venus, who presents him with the shield and armor. He is struck with admiration, particularly of the shield, although he does not fully understand its message—it represents the future deeds and history of the Roman people, with special emphasis on Augustus's victory over Antony and Cleopatra at Actium, and his consequent triumph.

Book 9

Iris comes down to speak to Turnus and informs him that Aeneas is away from the Trojan camp. It is a good time to attack. As Turnus and his army advance on the camp, the Trojans withdraw behind defensive works. Turnus and his followers then begin to set the fleet on fire to draw them out. These ships were said to be made of trees from the grove of CYBELE, the Phrygian mother goddess; Jupiter promised her that they would one day assume the form of immortal sea goddesses. Cybele warns off the Rutulians, and to their horror, they see the ships, now taking the form of goddesses, sail off into the sea. Turnus, however, is not intimidated but taunts the Trojans and rallies his followers with promise of victory. Two Trojans, Nisus and Euryalus, joined by an idealized homoerotic bond, decide to attempt to break through the Rutulian lines at night and bear a message to Aeneas in Pallanteum. They fall upon the camp of their sleeping, drunken enemies and wreak havoc. However, the gleam of Euryalus's newly acquired helmet gives them away. The older man, Nisus, escapes, but when he realizes that the youth Euryalus has been left behind, he turns back. Nisus cannot save Euryalus but rushes to his death to slay the man who killed him. The Rutulians put their heads on spears and display them before the Trojan camp, where Euryalus's mother sees them. Turnus and his allies besiege the Trojans. Ascanius slays the Rutulian warrior Numanus Remulus. APOLLO, in human form, praises Ascanius but warns him to withdraw from further battle. Two Trojans open the gates to lure the enemy in to join battle. The enemy accept the challenge and rush in. Fighting starts and now Turnus himself enters. The Trojans shut the gates, but Turnus remains inside and wreaks havoc among them. Finally, the Trojans regroup in massed ranks to attack him. Realizing that he has done as much damage as he could, Turnus leaps into the Tiber, and the current carries him back to his comrades.

Book 10

On Olympus, the gods hold a council. Jupiter reminds the company that war is not supposed to take place now, and not between Latins and Trojans, but later, between Rome and Carthage. Venus and then Juno speak, supporting the Trojans and Latins, respectively. Jupiter announces that discord still rules the day, and that each side must make its own fortune or misfortune. In the meanwhile, battle continues among the mortals. Aeneas has made an alliance with Tarchon and the Etruscans. As he is returning by ship to the camp, he meets the sea goddesses, who, before their transformation, had been his fleet. One of them, Cymodocea, addresses Aeneas to warn him of a threat to his camp and propels him on his way. When he arrives and disembarks, he goes on a violent rampage. At the same time, Pallas puts on his own display of martial excellence, slaying a series of foes until he, in turn, is slain by Turnus. Turnus despoils the corpse of his distinctive sword-belt, which represents the murder of the sons of Aegyptus by the DANAIDS. Aeneas, driven by grief and rage, renews his onslaught with pitiless violence. On Olympus, Juno persuades Jupiter to allow her to save Turnus for the time being, even if she cannot change the final outcome of the conflict. She takes on the appearance of Aeneas and lures Turnus onto a ship, which takes him, in a state of shame and frustration, to Ardea. Mezentius now goes on a violent rampage, killing Trojans and their allies until Aeneas wounds him in the groin, and Mezentius's son Lausus provides cover for his father's retreat. Aeneas ends up slaying Lausus with considerable remorse. He makes a point of returning his body without stripping it of its armor. When Mezentius hears of his son's death, he accepts his fate and turns back to face Aeneas despite his own wounds. Before he dies at Aeneas's hands, Mezentius pleads to be buried in the same tomb as his son.

Book 11

Aeneas fulfills his vow to Mars (see ARES) by attaching Mezentius's bloody spoils to a tree as a trophy *(tropaeum)* representing the defeated enemy. He then sends Pallas's body back to Evander. Envoys from the Latins arrive to ask for a truce while the dead are buried. Aeneas graciously grants it, and both sides bury their dead. Aeneas suggests, moreover, that he is open to a peace agreement, to which the Latin Drances, an enemy of Turnus, responds positively. But Evander calls on Aeneas for vengeance when he learns of Pallas's death. The Latins are in doubt as to the course to pursue. Eventually, the envoys whom they sent to make an alliance with Diomedes return with the news that they have failed. Diomedes does not wish to engage in further warfare and provoke the anger of the gods, as had so many of the Greek heroes, to their great cost. He respects Aeneas as a brilliant warrior and urges the Latins to make peace with him. In the council, King Latinus gives initial support to the path of peace; Drances opposes Turnus's drive to war more vigorously and angrily. Turnus responds with disdain for Drances and his proposals and declares that if need be he will face Aeneas in one-to-one combat as an alternative for all-out war. Word comes suddenly that the Trojans are renewing their attack. Diana (see ARTEMIS) commands Opis, one of her companions, to go down to the battlefield and punish anyone who wounds her devotee, the warrior Camilla, with the goddess's own arrow. The Trojan and Rutulian forces clash. Camilla distinguishes herself in the battle, slaying many opponents. Arruns looks for his chance to kill her, and while she is intently pursuing the Trojan Chloreus for his brilliant golden garb and armor, he deals her a

death blow with his spear. Opis kills him with an arrow she shoots from the top of a tumulus. The Trojans gain the momentum from different directions, and Aeneas and Turnus head for the walls of the city. Night falls before any further fighting ensues.

Book 12

Turnus's spirits are now high, and he calls for the duel with Aeneas. Latinus suggests that Turnus should retire from the dispute and save his own life. Amata also begs him not to fight the Trojans. Turnus refuses both. He then dispatches his herald Idmon to issue the challenge to Aeneas. Turnus arms himself while both Trojans and Rutulians prepare to view the duel. Juno now bids Juturna—a river deity, Turnus's sister and one-time paramour of Jupiter—to go offer what help she can to Turnus on this fatal day. Aeneas and Latinus announce the terms of an agreement: If Aeneas loses, his people will withdraw into Evander's community and offer no further challenge; if Aeneas wins, the two peoples will be joined on equal terms, and he will found Lavinium. Turnus now looks pale and weak. Juturna assumes the form of Camertus, one of the leaders, and argues for a general battle, in which they will outnumber the Trojans, rather than a duel in which Turnus is doomed to die. The augur Tolumnius is encouraged by a propitious omen: An eagle dropped a swan that it held in its talons, and the swan flew away safely; he predicts the departure of the predator Aeneas and casts a spear at the enemy. The truce is broken, and battle begins afresh. Aeneas is wounded by an arrow from an unknown source, and he withdraws, leaving the field open to Turnus, who goes on a rampage. Iapyx the healer works unsuccessfully on Aeneas's wound until, unbeknown to him, Venus puts magic herbs into the water. Aeneas returns to the battle and searches for Turnus. Encouraged by Venus, Aeneas decides to attack the city itself. In despair, Amata hangs herself. Turnus is fighting at the edge of the plain when he hears the uproar coming from the city. He wants to rush back to its defense. Juturna, who has disguised herself as his charioteer Metiscus but whom he now recognizes, tries to persuade him to follow a safer course. But when he hears of the events in the city, he can be restrained no longer, and he returns immediately to take up the duel with Aeneas. As they fight, Turnus's sword, actually Metiscus's, which he picked up by mistake, shatters. Juturna eventually returns his own sword to him, while Aeneas struggles to retrieve his spear from a tree. Jupiter now forbids Juno, whom he has sequestered in a cloud, to interfere any further. Juno yields; she admits that she can protect Turnus no longer but demands that the race resulting from the merging of the two peoples keep the Latin name, tongue, attire, and manners. Jupiter agrees. Then he sends down one of two terrifying hell-creatures called Dirae, which changes into an ill-omened screech owl and appears before Turnus as a chilling portent: A numbness comes over him; his sister Juturna recognizes the sign of doom and withdraws into the river. As the fight resumes, Turnus picks up an immense stone and hurls it at Aeneas, but he senses that he has lost his own strength and capacity, and the stone falls short of the mark. Aeneas hurls a spear and pierces Turnus's thigh. Turnus falls before Aeneas and begs that his body be returned to his kin; implicitly, he begs for his life. Aeneas hesitates but then sees the sword-belt stripped from Pallas. Full of anger, Aeneas offers up Turnus as a sacrifice to Pallas's shade and drives his sword into him. Turnus's shade passes to the underworld.

COMMENTARY

Virgil's epic tells the story of the origins of Roman civilization. He could have chosen a broader narrative span for his epic if he had wanted. Previous epic poets, notably Ennius, narrated Rome's history from the beginning up to recent times. Virgil elected to focus, like Homer and Apollonius in the Greek tradition, on a single hero and his story, moreover, a hero who could not have been better chosen as a link between Greek and Roman traditions of epic: He literally travels from one into the other. It was prophesied in Homer that Aeneas's line would survive the destruction of Troy. This survival provides a basis for the mythology of his voyage from Troy to Italy, where he eventually merges his people with the indigenous Latins to form the Roman race. Both Greek and Roman writers, for generations before Virgil, had been generating mythological origins-stories to put Rome on the cultural map in a way that was in keeping with its emerging status in the world. A major power needs a significant origin and a founder of importance, whereas Rome seemed to leap out of relative insignificance onto the world stage in the third and second centuries B.C.E. The story of Aeneas, providing a link between Rome and an important center endowed with mythological prestige, makes sense of its apparently sudden and arbitrary greatness.

It is significant that what becomes the Roman origin myth is a story of cultural transfer, assimilation, and ethnic fusion. Virgil's epic participates in a broader process of investing Rome with its own mythology, a mythology intertwined with diverse places and traditions of the Italian mainland and Sicily, where Greek meets Roman, and Rome emerges out of a diversity of Italic peoples. Such origins-stories, or etiologies, are not uncommon in Greco-Roman antiquity. Typically ancient cities had stories of their founders and foundation narratives that they preserved and embroidered with great civic pride. There is a difference in scale, however, in the case of Rome. This is not the etiology of a city but of a civilization and, ultimately, of an empire. For Virgil, then, the story of Aeneas's flight to Italy takes on cosmic dimensions that put it into a different category than other tales of migration and colonization; whereas Homer's Zeus upholds the destiny that will bring down a rich and powerful city, Virgil's Jupiter promises the future Romans "empire without end."

The immense scope of cosmic and imperial time, however, conceals the more immediate interests of the Augustan principate. Augustus is tracing not only the origins of Roman civilization in general but the origins of Augustus and his adoptive family (the Julian *gens*). Aeneas's son is called both Ascanius and Iulus. The latter name was already connected with the Julian clan by Julius Caesar, who claimed to have been descended from the goddess Venus via Anchises-Aeneas-Iulus. Augustus, who was adopted as Julius Caesar's son by the terms of the latter's will, therefore could claim the same divine and heroic lineage. It would be too simple to state that Aeneas simply represents or symbolizes Augustus and his virtues, but it is also impossible to extricate Virgil's representation of Aeneas from Augustus. Romans of aristocratic families aspired to reembody the virtue (*virtus* = manly excellence) and character (*mores*) of their ancestors (*maiores*). At an aristocratic Roman funeral, according to the historian Polybius, actors would wear masks (*imagines*) representing the illustrious ancestors of the deceased. The *Aeneid* accomplishes such a procession of lineage in reverse: Aeneas, when he carries the shield made by Vulcan at the end of Book 8, is bearing the image of his future descendants, those who will inherit and strive to reanimate a portion of his virtues and mores. Augustus is the most significant of those descendants: He carries within him the *virtus* of the founder of Roman civilization. Virgil thus succeeds in making the origins and destiny of Rome converge with the origins and destiny of the ruler and the imperial family. This focus on origins and founding is in keeping with contemporary concerns. The Augustan historian Livy likewise focuses special attention on foundation in his vast work, *From the Foundation of the City (Ab urbe condita)*, and confesses, in the prologue, that he prefers to focus on this earlier period rather than the more disturbing developments of recent history. Both Virgil and Livy, of course, are diverting our gaze (at least temporarily and partially) from the conflicts

of the late republican period and, in particular, from the civil wars that culminated in the conflict between Octavian (later Augustus) and Mark Antony. Augustan monuments and works of literature have a tendency to bypass recent history in order to associate the princeps ("first citizen" = Augustus) with the ancient past and, in particular, with the founder figures ROMULUS and Aeneas. Suetonius records that Augustus considered adding the honorific "Romulus" at the end of his name but finally decided on Augustus. The name "Augustus" ("Revered One," "Grand One") itself has associations with primordial sanctity and, in particular, with the "august augury" whereby Romulus founded Rome. King Latinus's palace is described in the *Aeneid* as an "august building" (*tectum augustum*). Indeed, one strategy of Augustan writers such as Livy and Virgil is to "discover" the qualities that define "Augustus" already present and immanent in Rome's ancient past.

As founder of a civilization, Aeneas is an especially important ancestor of Augustus, who viewed himself as one who founded Rome anew. For Livy, as for Romans generally, there is not just one single founder of Rome but, rather, multiple founders who either contributed important aspects to Roman civilization (e.g., Numa) or reestablished Rome on a more secure footing after a disastrous reversal or setback (Camillus, Augustus). Virgil comments that it was an "immense labor" to found the Roman race, and we, as readers, are meant to feel the immensity and complexity of Aeneas's task, as he attempts to deal with his people's frustrations, his own doubts, the sometimes enigmatic signs sent by the gods, and the resistance of enemies, including the goddess Juno herself. Roman readers of Virgil's time would have understood the implications of this grim view of history. They had lived through terrible times, but with the help of Virgil's narrative, they could begin to appreciate—and perhaps view Augustus through the lens of—a new kind of heroism, the dutiful (*pius*) heroism of Aeneas, who wins out in the end through patience, endurance, and piety. Aeneas, significantly, is a reluctant warrior, albeit a fierce and merciless one when the moment requires. He is not gratuitously aggressive, not a violent, hubristic character like Mezentius, but is rather a humane hero. Having witnessed the catastrophic havoc of the sack of Troy, he is sensitive to the sufferings of others and is deeply cognizant of the value of peace. Above all, he is bound, by duty to the gods, to carry out his sometimes violent mission of wandering and eventual settlement. It is hard not to see a parallel with the way that Augustus might have liked to be understood: a hero of divine blood who, despite his disinclination to violence and love of peace, was bound to avenge the death of his father, Julius Caesar, and to free Rome from the oppression of his hubristic adversary.

The key aspect of Aeneas's struggle, his labor of foundation, is that it is ultimately *for* something. The effect of this sense of purpose behind immense struggle, chaos, and discord can be understood when we perceive the similarity between Aeneas's war with the Latins and civil war. Technically, of course, it is not a civil war, but Romans of Virgil's time could not help viewing the conflict between these two strands of the Roman race as a battle of Romans against Romans. The war might also be seen to resemble the Social War of the earlier half of the first century B.C.E., in which Rome fought against communities of Italy that sought citizen rights. In the *Aeneid*, too, different communities of Italy are pitted against each other, and the question of potential Roman unity is posed against the background of Italian strife. But the civil wars of the closing decades of the republic are perhaps especially pertinent, since Virgil's readers had just lived through these conflicts and were currently living through Augustus's attempt to refound Roman society on a new, more secure footing. Like the comrades of Aeneas, Romans of the Augustan age may have been tempted to despair, to think that all the struggle had been for nothing. Yet Virgilian

narrative frames the possibility that the destiny envisaged by the gods requires a period of suffering and struggle before a great civilization can be founded—an age of darkness before a renewed Golden Age. Virgil offers paradigms of redemption and justification that *could* potentially be applied to Augustus and the society that he is attempting to found after a period of great violence in which he was himself very controversially involved.

Teleological drive and elements of resistance to that drive define the narrative of the *Aeneid*. In the opening lines, Virgil frames Aeneas's wanderings in terms of the drive to found Roman civilization. The constant stream of prophecies, portents, dreams, and signs forms a key feature of the very syntax of the Trojans' journey. On a larger scale, the procession of heroes in the underworld in Book 6 and on the shield of Aeneas in Book 8 famously endows the immediate narrative with a more profound sense of historical purpose. Jupiter's prophecies are especially authoritative from a Roman perspective and make an important early appearance in Book 1, precisely at a moment when Aeneas seems impotent and helpless, and his expedition thrown into disarray. The mechanism of the plot of the epic, however, depends on forces that oppose, complicate, even call into question in moral terms the otherwise relentless teleological drive toward Italy, the foundation of Roman civilization, and, ultimately, the Augustan principate. One such force is represented by the goddess Juno and the hell forces that she musters and throws into Aeneas's way. Forces of order (typically male, celestial, rational) are opposed to the forces of chaos (typically female, chthonic/Tartarean, irrational). Neptune in Book 1, when he calms the chaos of the water after Juno instigates the release of the winds, appears as a paradigm of the authoritative statesman—perhaps even as a princeps—who calms civic turmoil. Obstructions and hell raisings, however, are so crucial to the plot and to Aeneas's heroism that we may wonder, as Blake claimed of Milton, if Virgil was at least partly of the devil's party. Certainly his description, for example, of Allecto and the havoc she wreaks on human minds and hearts is poetically thrilling.

A similar poetic power resides in Virgil's famous tendency to linger on the victims of Aeneas's forward narrative momentum. These victim narratives come in both micro- and macro-units of narrative. A small example is the mention of the death of one of Aeneas's companions—such as his nurse Caieta at the opening of Book 7. Palinurus and Creusa offer examples of more expansive narratives about those left behind. Their deaths evoke pity and are especially designed to do so, but they are explicitly framed as sacrifices necessary for the narrative to continue on its forward path. We as readers, like Aeneas, feel these losses, but must also accept them to continue voyaging/reading.

On the grandest scale, narratives of sacrifice dominate entire books and portions of the epic. The first, Odyssean half of the epic is dominated by the Dido episode, beginning with the Trojans' arrival in Carthage in Book 1 and ending in Dido's refusal to speak with Aeneas in the underworld in Book 6. Dido is one of the most prominent victims in the poem. Her death is brought about directly by Aeneas's need to continue on his destined course to Italy. In terms of the Homeric tradition, Dido corresponds with delaying temptresses such as Circe and CALYPSO. In terms of Roman history, her curse on Aeneas constitutes an origins story for Rome's terrible and nearly catastrophic conflict with Carthage in the Punic Wars of the third century B.C.E. Dido represents an enemy of Roman progress and civilization on many levels. And yet Virgil evokes a great degree of pity for her, exploring her emotions in exquisite detail in some of his most unforgettable poetry. She is perhaps the most complex character in the poem. OVID would later claim that of the entire *Aeneid*, people really read only the Dido episode, and St. Augustine would confess that he wept over Dido. Modern readers have tended to concur with these estimates of Dido's centrality. And yet we must give up Dido if we want the narrative to continue and Roman civilization to come into being.

The second half of the *Aeneid* focuses in a broadly comparable fashion on the figure of Turnus. It is his previous engagement with Lavinia that causes the war, and he is the chief figure who continues to motivate the conflict with the Trojans that dominates this half of the epic. His death marks the end of the war narrative and of the poem. He is hardly a wholly unsympathetic character. He is not disposed to be recklessly violent and adversarial until Allecto overpowers his mind. He is brave and lives according to the hero's code of honor. Virgil is careful, of course, to create a strong justification for his death. He killed Pallas without remorse and arrogantly stripped him of his sword-belt; these actions are in contrast with Aeneas's honorable treatment of the slain Lausus. But then again at certain moments the fury of battle has challenged the limits of even Aeneas's sense of restraint.

The question throughout is not simply whether or not to engage in violence but how violence and morality interact. The more disturbing dilemma arises at the end of Virgil's text, which has furnished a topic of vigorous debate among scholars. Aeneas kills Turnus in anger, driven by "fury"—often a negative thing in the moral scheme of the *Aeneid*. Even more disturbingly, there is no ameliorative or rationalizing frame concluding the poem. The epic simply ends as Turnus's soul descends to the underworld. We do not see even the hints of the emergence of a peaceful social order, rituals of social unity, the beginnings of less divisive relations between Trojans and Latins, or the like. Readers are free to fill in such elements by implication, yet they must make the decision to do so. Whereas throughout the rest of the epic, the sheer fact of forward narrative drive as justified by the necessity of destiny tended to prevent us from lingering too long on any particular sacrifice or victimization, the ending provides no such mechanism: We are left with the raw fact of Aeneas's violence as foundational act. Not accidentally, the killing resembles and prefigures the prefoundational slaying of Remus by Romulus. By the end of the poem, we have had occasion to contemplate, and perhaps accept, the indissoluble link between violence and civilization, warfare and the emergence of the Roman state. We can choose to refuse or resist the justifying, teleological drive that makes of Turnus a necessary martyr for the foundation of Lavinium and the fusion of the two races; but the cost of such resistance is the negation of Roman civilization.

In creating his epic of civilization, Virgil draws on the two epic poems of Homer that enjoy the status of master texts of Greek civilization. They represent and exemplify Greekness, Greek paradigms of behavior, character, and excellence. It was Virgil's immense ambition to combine the scope and subject matter of the two Homeric epics into his single 12-book poem. Broadly speaking, Books 1–6 engage in a sustained dialogue with Homer's *Odyssey*. Aeneas is a hero wandering from place to place in search of his elusive destination; he stays in one location with a woman who is not his wife for a long period of time until warned to leave by Mercury; he encounters dangers at sea and continual harassment at the hands of an opposing deity; and, like Odysseus, he departs on his wanderings with the city of Troy as starting point. At the end of this half of the epic, Aeneas, like Odysseus in *Odyssey* 11, descends to the underworld to hear a prophecy: He also meets a dead parent, and in a pointed evocation of the Ajax episode in the *Odyssey*, the shade of Dido refuses to enter into a dialogue with him. (Dido also resembles the Sophoclean Ajax in that she kills herself, significantly, with her "enemy's" sword.) Finally, a series of smaller episodes are unabashedly Odyssean: the Cyclops; Circe; Scylla. In the case of Circe, Virgil knowingly alludes to the *Odyssey* even when he chooses *not* to engage in an extensive imitation: Aeneas does not land on the shore of Circe; as they sail

by, he merely hears the sounds of her captive beasts.

The division, of course, is not perfect and is not meant to be. For example, the funeral games of Book 5 have the funeral games of Patroclus in the *Iliad* as their chief model. The Iliadic model, however, largely dominates throughout Books 7–12, at the opening of which Virgil announces the commencement of his "greater task." Here Virgil adapts the conventions of Homeric battle narrative to Italy and a Homeric hero to a conflict among peoples on the Italian peninsula. Of course, imitation and reminiscence are not simply duplication. Virgil's hero is very different from a properly Homeric hero: Aeneas is a hero of duty, endurance, and pained remembrance, a hero who carries for so long the burden and trauma of catastrophic failure. Yet he is also not quite Homeric in his success. Aeneas, as some scholars have noted, goes from being another Hector—dutiful, protective of his family, a defender of Troy, one of history's noble losers—to an ACHILLES: terrifying, merciless, formidable in battle, the slayer of Turnus in one-to-one combat outside the walls of his adversary's city. This Trojan/Roman version of Achilles does not have as deepest impulse, however, the maximization of personal *kleos* and glory as, arguably, the Homeric Achilles does. Achilles is intensely aware of the limitations of his mortality and the need to shine all the more brightly while he is alive. Aeneas, by contrast, even in the heat of battle, carries the burden of the civilization that he is endeavoring to establish. He is a hero defined by his social responsibilities rather than by his breathtaking refusal of them.

A final epic model to be considered is Apollonius' of Rhodes's *Voyage of the Argonauts*. Virgil, like Apollonius, has created an epic of astonishing geographical and ethnographic erudition: In the Alexandrian manner, his poem displays a rich knowledge of local rites and traditions. Indeed, scholars have noted how Virgil's imitation of Homer is often mediated by and/or intertwined with his allusions to

Apollonius, who himself was a keen student of Homer. Apollonius created his own un-Homeric hero in the figure of Jason. He is often "resourceless" and weak and requires an immense amount of help along the way. The same cannot quite be said of Aeneas, but it is probably true that Apollonius's antihero opened up a new set of possibilities, including the interesting constellation of strength and weakness, confidence and self-doubt, that constitutes Virgil's Aeneas.

Throughout the *Aeneid*, the labor of cultural transfer undergone by the hero is paralleled by the comparable labor of the epic poet. Just as Aeneas must carry his Trojan Penates to Italy—an immense task, as it turns out—so must Virgil transfer a Greek epic hero and Greek epic traditions into a Latin framework and the Italian landscape. Virgil must laboriously trace Aeneas's path from Troy—the location of the *Iliad*—to Italy and Rome. In establishing his own originality as epic poet, moreover, Virgil must be careful not simply to repeat Homer. This literary requirement finds its echo within the poem's narrative in the recurrent theme of the dangers of mere replication and (attempted) restoration of the past. The weary and frustrated Trojan women who attempt to burn the boats in Sicily demand to know why they cannot re-create their own Troy and give familiar Trojan names to local rivers. Similarly, Andromache and Helenus make their own miniature, replica-Troy, complete with a paltry Simois and Scamander. Here repetition becomes a failure to progress, to make a new and satisfying social order of one's own. Andromache is first seen offering rites at Hector's cenotaph: She is still caught in a shadow image of her old life, tending to an empty tomb. The Trojans themselves, in Book 3, engage in a series of abortive foundations. They fail, in part, because they have not adequately understood how profound is the transformation their community must undergo: how far they must travel from the familiar, and how hard the struggle must be to establish themselves in their new land.

The poet must learn the same lesson of laborious adaptation. The path of progress toward Roman civilization and the path toward poetic originality are at some level the same.

On these fronts, Virgil engages with his Greek epic models quite explicitly and contrastively. In particular, the Odyssean and Argonautic paradigm of return, or *nostos* ("return journey"), is found to be incapable of expressing the Roman concept of civilization and is accordingly revised. The Odyssean Aeneas is indeed wandering in search of his true home, and he is even going back, as the prophecy demands, to the land of Troy's origins: the land of Dardanus. This "return journey," however, is not *nostos* in the Odyssean sense of a return to one's own original land, household, and wife; nor is it a circular return to civilization with an emblematic object in tow according to the Argonautic pattern. Jason goes to the edges of the known world and brings an originally Greek object back to Greece from the barbarian realm of Colchis. The poem ends at the moment of that all-important return. Aeneas, by contrast, is transferring his Trojan Penates to a new place where they will attain a new meaning, where he will find a new Latin wife in place of his lost Trojan one, and where the distinction between civilized and barbarian becomes problematic. (Are not Aeneas's Trojans, as the Latins tauntingly insist, effeminate Easterners, who wear perfume and strange clothing?) There is no clear end point, moreover, included within the poem's central narrative frame, unless, perhaps, we construct one ourselves by leaping ahead to Augustus's Golden Age. The actual ending of the poem represents only one stage on a very long journey. Aeneas, like Moses, will not live to see the promised land of Rome, much less imperial Rome. The satisfyingly closed circle of the Greek *nostos* no longer suffices. The *Aeneid* points toward a more difficult but also more fruitful paradigm of transfer, ethnic fusion, and assimilation. This pattern is in keeping, after all, with the assimilative pattern of Roman history and Roman historical legend.

The mythological theme with which Virgil's epic ends provides a focus for such concerns with intermarriage and ethnic synthesis. Aeneas slays Turnus when he sees the sword-belt of Pallas displayed by his adversary. This sword-belt, we recall, depicted the story of the Danaids, who, when forced to marry the sons of Aegyptus, are instructed by their father, DANAUS, to kill their husbands on their marriage night. The myth is grimly appropriate to the current situation. The Trojans are in effect seeking to join the Latin race through intermarriage (primarily, Aeneas with Lavinia), while Turnus and his allies are resisting this attempt at synthesis. The story is also appropriate to the Augustan context, when the emperor was laying stress on the importance of marriage. Aeneas, by killing Turnus, is opening up the path to his own otherwise obstructed marriage to Lavinia. Despite this implication, the myth is not wholly grim. One of the Danaids, Hypermnestra, chooses not to kill her husband. Racial fusion may be feasible after all. For the Trojans and Latins, it was ultimately possible to live together as one community, and together they formed the Roman people. Virgil has shown us, however, the immense cost in suffering and human life incurred by this founding synthesis.

Aeolus (1) (Aiolos) Either a minor god or a mortal with sovereignty over the winds. Classical sources are Homer's ODYSSEY (10.1–77), Ovid's METAMORPHOSES (1.268, 14.223ff), and Virgil's AENEID (1.50–86). In the *Odyssey* and Ovid's *Heroides*, Aeolus is a mortal who lives on the floating island of Aeolia, and has been given control over the winds by the Olympian gods. His six daughters, the Aioliades, married his six sons, and the clan lived in isolation from the rest of the world. When ODYSSEUS arrived in Aeolia with his shipmates, Aeolus received him hospitably and provided him with a wind-filled ox skin to use on their homeward journey. Aboard ship, Odysseus's men opened the ox

skin, believing it to contain wine, and unwittingly loosed a storm that returned the ship to its point of departure in Aeolia.

In the *Aeneid*, Aeolus is a minor god. The winds under his command were so destructive that Aeolus kept them captive in a cavernous dungeon. HERA bribed Aeolus (with the offer of a nymph in marriage) to free the winds so that they might blow AENEAS's ship off course. The release of the winds represents cosmic and political disorder that NEPTUNE, in his role of celestial statesman, brings under control.

According to some authors, it is the same Aeolus whose children, Canace and Macareus, committed incest. The incestuous unions of Aeolus's children are the tragic subject matter of Euripides' *Aeolus* and of Ovid's *Heroides* (11), an epistolary first-person narrative by Canace, one of the daughters of Aeolus. In this version of the story, Canace carried on a romantic relationship with her brother Macareus in secret. Aeolus was furious when he discovered their affair. He took the infant born to the couple and exposed it, and forced Canace to kill herself.

Aeolus (2) Son of Hellen and the nymph Orseis. Ancestor of the Aeolians. Father of, among others, SISYPHUS, ATHAMAS, Salmoneus, Canace, and ALCYONE. This Aeolus may be the one whose children committed incest. There is some confusion in the sources (see AEOLUS [1]).

Aeolus (3) Son of POSEIDON and Melanippe. The story of Aeolus and his brother Boetus is the subject of two dramas by EURIPIDES.

Aeschylus (ca. 525 B.C.E.–ca. 456 B.C.E.) Aeschylus was an Athenian tragic playwright who was born in the 520s B.C.E. and died in 456 or 455 B.C.E. Aeschylus fought in the battle of Marathon and won the first prize at the tragic competition 13 times. He produced his first play in 499 B.C.E. Out of an oeuvre of approximately 90 plays, only six tragedies securely attributable to Aeschylus have survived. The *Prometheus Bound*, traditionally ascribed to him, is probably not by Aeschylus. Aeschylus was a great formal innovator and is said to have introduced the second actor to the tragic stage. Aeschylus's major themes are human suffering and its causes, the justice of the gods, and the roles of violence, persuasion, justice, sex, sacrifice, and hubris in human society. Many of his plays fall within a continuous tragic tetralogy consisting in three tragedies and a satyr play. This format allows Aeschylus to explore the human, theological, and cosmic dimensions of a given mythic sequence in all its depth through its development in successive phases. The individual story (such as the myth of Orestes or the Danaids) often takes place against the background of a broader concern with the emergence of human civilization and its central institutions (law courts, marriage). Aeschylean tragedy does not tend to focus on intricate character portraiture or on nuances and surprises of plot but on the terrible unfolding of destined actions and their consequences for mortals' comprehension of their own condition. A dynamic and even dominant chorus is a prominent feature of his plays. Aeschylus's most ambitious extant work, and the only tragic trilogy to survive from the ancient world, is the *Oresteia*, comprising *Agamemnon*, *Libation Bearers*, and *Eumenides*. Aeschylus, an Athenian, also betrays throughout his works a concern with the polis (*Seven against Thebes*, *Suppliants*) and Athens in particular (*Persians*, *Eumenides*).

Aeson Son of Cretheus; king of Iolcus. See Jason.

Aethra See Demophon.

Agamemnon Leader of the Greek forces in the Trojan War. King of Argos or Mycenae. Son of Atreus and Merope. Brother of Menelaus and husband of Clytaemnestra. Agamemnon's children by Clytaemnestra were Orestes, Electra, and Iphigenia, although in earlier sources his daughters are named Chrysomethis, Laodice, and Iphianassa. Agamemnon appears throughout Homer's *Iliad* and in the following tragedies: Aeschylus's *Agamemnon* and *Eumenides* and Euripides' *Iphigenia at Aulis* and *Hecuba*. Additional classical sources are Homer's *Odyssey* (11.404), Hyginus's *Fabulae* (98, 117), and Ovid's *Metamorphoses* (12.25). In one legend, Agamemnon killed Clytaemnestra's first husband, Tantalus, and their children. The Dioscuri, her brothers, subsequently forced Agamemnon to marry her. After Paris abducted Helen, wife of Menelaus, Agamemnon assembled the Greek heroes for the expedition against Troy. The Greek fleet was held up at Aulis by unfavorable winds, and the prophet Calchas declared that Artemis was offended by Agamemnon (the reasons depend on the version; see Iphigenia). According to Calchas, Agamemnon would obtain favorable winds if he sacrificed his own daughter Iphigenia. The story of Iphigenia's sacrifice is not in Homer and first appears in the *Cypria*, a poem of the Epic Cycle. According to Euripides' *Iphigenia at Aulis*, Agamemnon sends for Iphigenia on the pretext of marriage to Achilles. Agamemnon struggled miserably with his choice: undermine an expedition morally required by the support of Zeus, and politically required because of the immense commitment of the Greek army, or defile himself by killing his own kin. He decided to go through with the sacrifice, although in most versions, Iphigenia was replaced by an animal, often a deer, at the last moment by Artemis. (For very different versions, see Aeschylus's *Agamemnon*, and Euripides' *Iphigenia at Aulis*.)

Homer's *Iliad*, set in the ninth year of the Trojan War, begins with and is premised on the quarrel between Agamemnon and Achilles. Calchas reveals that the cause of the plague afflicting the Greeks is the captive Chryseis, daughter of Chryses, priest of Apollo. Agamemnon must accordingly give up Chryseis, allotted

The Sacrifice of Iphigenia. *Fresco from the House of the Tragic Poet, Pompeii, first century* C.E. *(Museo Archeologico Nazionale, Naples)*

to him as a prize of war, and demands that Achilles give him his own concubine BRISEIS in compensation. Achilles allows Agamemnon to take Briseis but is deeply aggrieved at the loss of his prize. Agamemnon's ruinous quarrel with Achilles leads to the death of many Greeks.

Later, Agamemnon realizes his error and claims that delusion or folly led him into the quarrel. Other episodes are similarly discrediting and reveal Agamemnon as weak and easily discouraged. For example, in Book 14, when the Trojans are routing the Greeks, he suggests flight by sea and is rebuked by ODYSSEUS. Agamemnon has his moment of excellence in battle in Book 11, but other heroes—DIOMEDES, AJAX, Achilles—are more impressive overall. Agamemnon is protective of his brother and his brother's interests. In the *Iliad*, he talks Menelaus out of facing HECTOR in a duel. In Athenian tragedy, Agamemnon is often accused of sacrificing his own family, and Iphigenia in particular, for the sake of his brother.

When Agamemnon returned from Troy, his wife, Clytaemnestra, killed him along with his captive concubine CASSANDRA. Homer gives a greater role to AEGISTHUS, Clytaemnestra's lover, in the murder of Agamemnon, while Aeschylus awards the dominant part in the action to Clytaemnestra. Agamemnon's son Orestes and daughter Electra later avenge his death by killing Aegisthus and Clytaemnestra—a popular subject in Greek tragedy. (See Aeschylus's *LIBATION BEARERS*, Euripides' *ELECTRA* and *ORESTES*, and Sophocles' *ELECTRA*.) There are few if any wholly positive representations of Agamemnon, although he is honored by his children after his death, as they seek to avenge his murder. In tragedy, Agamemnon is primarily a victim or a catalyzing memory. In Euripides' *Hecuba*, Agamemnon is an anxious figure controlled by his public image and political expediency.

The sacrifice of Iphigenia was represented in a Pompeian fresco from the first century C.E., which represents many of the main points of the myth. In this image, Iphigenia is being brought to be sacrificed, while Agamemnon, his head covered, appears distraught. Next to Iphigenia is Calchas, who declared that Iphigenia had to die for the Greek fleet to sail. Overhead, Artemis is shown arriving with the hind that will take Iphigenia's place in the sacrificial rites.

Agamemnon AESCHYLUS (458 B.C.E.)

INTRODUCTION

Aeschylus's *Agamemnon* is the first tragedy in a tetralogy that includes the *LIBATION BEAR-* *ERS*, the *EUMENIDES*, and the lost satyr play *Proteus*. The plays won first prize at the tragic competition at Athens in 458 B.C.E. The three plays comprising the tragic trilogy, known as the *Oresteia* after the character Orestes, are the only such trilogy still extant. This late work by Aeschylus is thematically complex, densely layered in its figurative language and interconnected imagery, and dramatically powerful. The subject is the troubled "house of Atreus," i.e., the household of the ruling family of Argos that includes ATREUS, father of AGAMEMNON and MENELAUS. This family has a dark mythological history. TANTALUS, the grandfather of Agamemnon, reportedly attempted to serve up his own son PELOPS to the gods as a stew; Atreus, his father, served his brother Thyestes the flesh of his own children. Agamemnon himself sacrificed his daughter IPHIGENIA to enable the Greek expedition to make its way to Troy. At the opening of the present play, Agamemnon is about to return from war, yet the household is full of anxiety. CLYTAEMNESTRA, Agamemnon's wife, has taken AEGISTHUS, son of Thyestes, as a lover, and plans to kill her husband. Aeschylus's play represents the ineluctable curse on a royal household and the cycle of vengeance that afflicts it for generations.

SYNOPSIS

The scene opens in front of the royal palace at Argos. The watchman is lying on the roof of the palace. He begs the gods to release him from his toils; he lies awake night after night, ordered by Clytaemnestra to watch out for a beacon fire signaling the capture of Troy. He laments the misfortune of the house and its present degradation. He sees the beacon, cries out in joy, and dances, but the speech ends on a more sinister note, as he suggests that he knows more about the house than he is willing to say openly. The watchman exits.

The Chorus of Argive elders enters. They observe that it is now the 10th year of war since Agamemnon and Menelaus went to Troy. The two brothers are compared to vultures shrieking and circling around a nest from which their chicks have been taken. ZEUS, guardian of guest-host relations, has sent the FURIES (Erinyes) as punisher, ordaining the death of Trojans and Danaans. They, the members of the Chorus, are old and thus have remained behind. They then turn to face the palace and address Clytaemnestra, asking her what news she has received that she sends messengers and sacrifices. They are anxious, but wonder if there might be cause for joy. The Chorus further sings how a sign appeared and was interpreted by the prophet CALCHAS: Two eagles (the Atreidae) attacked and fed upon a pregnant hare (Troy). Calchas also declared that ARTEMIS was angry at the eagles' feasting and feared that Artemis might bring about a delay that would lead to a sacrifice and a source of avenging anger in the house of Agamemnon. The Chorus then praises Zeus who defeated CRONUS and instituted the law of learning through suffering. It then tells how Calchas prophesied that only Iphigenia's sacrifice would free the Greeks of the opposing winds that kept them in Aulis, and that Agamemnon, constrained to carry out an expedition demanded by Zeus, found himself with an impossible choice and was compelled to commit the evil act of sacrificing his own daughter. It describes the scene in which, Iphigenia, gagged, is carried to the altar and attempts to elicit pity from those around her, but it claims that they did not see what happens next.

Clytaemnestra enters. The Chorus questions her respectfully regarding the recent news. She relates that Troy has been captured; the beacon-fire signal has passed from Mount Ida near Troy to Argos. Then she imagines the different fates of conquerors and conquered in Troy. If the conquerors restrain themselves from violating the city's gods and ravaging what they should not, they will return home safely. The Chorus praises her speech, and she exits.

The Chorus then sings of the destruction of Troy and PARIS through the agency of Zeus. Paris, as guest of Menelaus, stole his wife, and brought inevitable destruction down on himself and his city. The Chorus describes the desolation of Menelaus and then the consequent desolation of the households from which Greek soldiers departed, only to return as ash in urns. Finally, the chorus wonders whether or not the beacon is a reliable sign and questions the tendency of a woman to be quickly persuaded.

Clytaemnestra enters. She observes that a herald is arriving; he will confirm through more certain knowledge the message of the beacons. The herald expresses relief that he has come back to Argos after 10 years and hails Zeus, APOLLO, and HERMES, and the royal palace itself. He confirms the destruction of Troy and Agamemnon's imminent arrival. Troy has suffered profoundly. In dialogue with the herald, the Chorus declares that it has been longing for the return of the army, just as the army longed to return, and hints that all has not been well in the house. The herald then goes on to describe the experience of the army at Troy. They lived in deplorable conditions and lost many comrades, and yet he claims at the end that the city and her generals are to be praised, and that the Greeks have achieved glory. Clytaemnestra, who has been apparently (though debatably) present throughout this exchange, then breaks in. She sneers now at those who criticized her feminine credulity, anticipates the return of her husband, and bids that a message be brought to him to the effect that she has been a faithful watchdog of the house and has known no other man.

The Chorus ostensibly approves her speech, then questions the messenger about Menelaus. He does not know exactly what happened to Menelaus, but then, very reluctant to mar his good news with an unpleasant story, tells how a storm devastated the Greek fleet. The herald's own ship managed to escape the damage. He does not know about the rest of his companions but harbors a hope that Menelaus lives and will one day return.

The Chorus then sings of Helen and relates her name etymologically to the Greek word meaning "destroy." She was a true destroyer of men, ships, and cities. Her marriage was ruinous to Troy; she is like a lion cub reared in a house—at first charming, later violent and the cause of ruin. The Furies brought about her marriage. The Chorus then contrasts the just household and its happy outcomes with the wealthy yet immoral household that ends in ruin.

Agamemnon enters in his chariot with CASSANDRA. The Chorus addresses him with respect and makes a sharp distinction between flattery that is only seemingly sincere and an authentic expression of support and gratitude. The Chorus's previous criticism of the expedition should be sufficient proof of their honesty. Agamemnon expresses gratitude to the gods for the fall of Troy, displays his awareness of false praise and hidden malice, praises ODYSSEUS's loyalty to him, and suggests that if there is any "disease" in the city, it will be treated by knife and cautery. Clytaemnestra then tells of her own grief and suicide attempts as she heard dark rumors of her husband's demise, and attempts to explain Orestes' absence as a maneuver to protect him from harm. She praises Agamemnon as protector of the household and bids the handmaids spread purple tapestries before his path. Agamemnon is reluctant to be exposed to envy and charges of hubris by trampling fine tapestries worthy of the gods. Clytaemnestra presses him with diverse arguments and pleas, and at last he reluctantly agrees to walk across them, expressing misgivings even as he does. Clytaemnestra hails the return of the king to the house as a sign of renewal and prays that Zeus accomplish her prayer.

The Chorus expresses a persistent sense of foreboding, an inward dirge that is quickly sung. The Chorus, however, cannot fully and publicly announce its fears. Clytaemnestra enters. She calls on Cassandra to come in and accept her lot as slave of an ancient, noble house. Cassandra does not respond despite the Chorus's encouragement, and Clytaemnestra dismisses her as crazed. Clytaemnestra exits.

Cassandra proclaims that the house to which she has been brought is a place of slaughter the Chorus comments, sometimes with admiration and sometimes with perplexity, as she continues to speak in a prophetic frenzy dense with metaphor and riddling speech. She alludes to ancient crimes of the house but moves quickly to the imminent murder of Agamemnon, then to her own murder. She then refers to her upbringing in Troy and the fate of the city. Next, she shifts to a clearer mode of speech and describes the grim history of the house of Atreus. Then she tells how she denied Apollo full intercourse with her and he cursed her with prophetic knowledge that no one will believe. The Chorus claims to believe her. Cassandra first refers to Thyestes' children's fate, then to Clytaemnestra as a deceitful murderess and monster. The Chorus accepts her account of Thyestes' children but is confused by the rest. It cannot comprehend that Agamemnon is being killed. Cassandra curses her art. She foresees her own brutal death but also prophesies the coming of Orestes as avenger. Cassandra prays that her killer will pay for their act and exits into the house.

The Chorus hears the offstage cries of Agamemnon as he is being stabbed. The Chorus debates as to what action should be taken. In rapid-fire dialogue, the Chorus comes to the conclusion that it should wait to see whether Agamemnon is truly dead. Clytaemnestra appears on stage, standing over the bodies of Agamemnon and Cassandra. Putting aside pretense, Clytaemnestra now admits to slaughtering Agamemnon. She threw a net over him and stabbed him three times. She compares herself, splashed with her dying husband's blood, to the crop rejoicing in rain sent by Zeus. The Chorus is shocked. Clytaemnestra is not easily cowed. The Chorus states that because she has committed this murder, she must go into exile. Clytaemnestra reminds it that Agamemnon sacrificed his own child and was not sent into exile. The Chorus predicts doom as her punishment, but Clytaemnestra swears she has no fear with Aegisthus as her protector. Agamemnon, moreover, has paid for his promiscuity. The Chorus prays for death and refers again to Helen as origin of the war. Clytaemnestra chides it for these sentiments. Singing in response, Clytaemnestra and the Chorus debate her act of murder. For her, the death was merited; for the Chorus, it is a tragedy brought about by the daimon (spirit/fate) and the "spider" Clytaemnestra. The Chorus laments the fate of the house and wishes that death had come to them before it had to see Agamemnon murdered.

Aegisthus enters. He recalls the murder of Thyestes' children by Atreus and the ghastly banquet. Aegisthus was the one surviving child of Thyestes, and Atreus was Agamemnon's father. Thus by bringing this scheme to fruition, Aegisthus has achieved vengeance, or, as he says, "Justice." The Chorus rebukes him, but he threatens it with physical punishment and deprivation. The Chorus asks why he did not do the deed himself; Aegisthus responds that he was more suspect in Agamemnon's eyes. The conflict between the Chorus of Elders and Aegisthus threatens to become violent, when Clytaemnestra intervenes and urges calm. The two sides exchange a few more insults, before Clytaemnestra, in the play's final words, announces her aim to rule the house and order all things.

COMMENTARY

The *Agamemnon* begins Aeschylus's great trilogy on the house of Atreus and the cycle of violence that besets the ruling family of Argos. As in other instances, Aeschylus has created a trilogy of interconnected mythic subject matter that represents a chronological progression from one play to the next (cf. his Theban and Danaid trilogies). In this case, all three tragedies are extant. The *Oresteia* is the only such trilogy to survive out of the corpus of Athenian

tragedy. The *Oresteia* would appear to resemble the other Aeschylean trilogies in its overall thematic orientation. In each case, the mythology treated in dramatic form concerns violence between members of the same family, the repercussions and cycles of violence that result from earlier violent acts, and after much suffering, a peaceful outcome, achieved in the context of the polis. (The ending of the Danaid trilogy, while the subject of much learned speculation, is not known, and thus cannot be confirmed as conforming to the pattern. However, it seems possible, if not probable, that a resolution of the violence between the Danaids and the sons of Aegyptus was achieved in the final play.) In the case of the present trilogy, Aeschylus is concerned not only with the cessation of a cycle of violence but with the emergence of polis institutions and of civilization itself out of a more primitive system of retributive justice.

To appreciate the complexity and sustained exploration of myth made possible by the trilogy form, it is helpful to compare the present play with a play that does not form part of a trilogy, the *Persians*. The elements of similarity and difference are instructive. In both plays, a Chorus of elders and the Queen have assumed a prominent role while the King is involved in a war across the sea; the King has a grim homecoming from war, and the master of an abundantly wealthy house is brought low by the gods. We see vividly the consequences of an ambitious and destructive foreign war, for the army, the populace, and above all the ruling household. In the *Agamemnon*, however, the King's return from war is only the first in a series of violent events within the royal household that will supply the subject for subsequent plays. Perhaps more important, the final play in the trilogy will also begin to salvage the hopes of the household within the context of the institutions of the Athenian polis. The Persian King's exemplary fate is self-contained and encompassed within a single play. He affords a powerful yet one-dimensional paradigm of hubris. The present trilogy is more complex:

The aristocratic household comes into contact with the polis, male opposes female, gods are set against gods, and a new order is seen emerging out of the old. Aeschylus enriches the complexity of these interactions as they unfold over the course of three plays.

The trilogy form, then, is well suited to the content of the *Oresteia* and its various stages of conflict and ultimate resolution on the human and cosmic level. Across the different phases of action, there is one continuous and consistent presence that pervades the drama: the house itself. In the *Agamemnon*, the house is often personified by the speakers: e.g., the house, if it could speak, would tell terrible tales. We are aware of the house as physical space and social entity from the very outset of the play: The watchman lies on top of the palace roof in the opening scene and refers obliquely to the misfortunes of the house. His words and emotions, suspended between hope and fear, seem to encapsulate the situation of the house as a whole, as the time approaches for Agamemnon's fateful return. Later, when Cassandra arrives on the scene, her first impression is of the evil nature of the house to which she has been brought as captive, a sense of wrongness inhering in the very place. Subsequently, in her prophetic raving, she will allude to key episodes in the house's history, and particularly Thyestes' feasting on his own murdered children. And yet the violence goes back even further: Tantalus, the grandfather of Atreus and Thyestes, is said to have committed various crimes against Zeus and the gods and, in particular, to have served up his own son Pelops in a stew to the gods. The mythology of this particular household presents an unusually consistent and relentless example of a family curse. In Aeschylus's trilogy, the house itself seems to drive the pattern of violence bridging the family's successive generations, as if it were itself an autonomous agent bent on carrying out its dark designs.

At other moments, Zeus is awarded the central role as divine cause of the story's inevitable unfolding: his telos (end/goal) will be fulfilled, though it may not be understood at present. The trilogy form, with its successive stages of conflict and movement toward its final resolution, is thus coherent with the teleological dimension of Aeschylean tragedy. In the first play, a violent act, premised on previous violence, is committed by Clytaemnestra and Aegisthus; in the second play, that violent act is avenged; in the third play, it is atoned for and expiated as the trilogy's title character, Orestes, moves out of the royal household of Atreus and into the institutional fabric of the city-state. The movement from one play to the next, with one act of violence answering another and perpetuating the pattern, poses, in a lucid and powerful form, the central question: How does the cycle of revenge killing stop? How can violence provide the conditions for an emerging civilization?

The chain reaction of violence is already a major theme in the *Agamemnon* and is symbolized in a famous speech by Clytaemnestra. She tells the Chorus how the system of beacon fires relayed the message of Troy's fall from Mount Ida to Argos, bringing her the news before the arrival of the army. One fire leads to the kindling of another in a sublime yet sinister succession of signs, a trail of fire that is first ignited with the burning of the city of Troy itself. It is no accident that the entire trilogy begins with the stirring scene of the watchman sitting on the roof, waiting for a sign of his master's return, and then rejoicing (inappropriately, as it turns out) when the beacon signal appears. Clytaemnestra, for her part, is proud of her communication system and even arrogant. The Chorus dismisses her supposed knowledge as a woman's delusion, and now she demonstrates to it her command of knowledge and mastery of modes of communication. Yet the playwright's irony goes deeper and undercuts her triumphant tone. Clytaemnestra fails to control fully the chain reaction of fire; she, too, will fall victim to the path of violence that goes from Troy to Argos, engulfed in flames of her own making. The message is clear. It is impossible to create such a chain or cycle without becoming part of the pattern oneself.

The framing of mythic narrative in terms of an inevitable chain of consequences and an eventual telos goes back to Homer's ILIAD itself, the most important poetic predecessor for Aeschylus's *Oresteia*. In the *Iliad*, Zeus is the major figure on the divine level who drives the narrative toward its final goal of the destruction of Troy, although this episode is not itself narrated within the scope of the epic. Zeus effectively presides over the entire expedition in his capacity as protector of guest-host relations (Zeus *xenios*), since it was Paris's transgression as Menelaus's guest that spurred the war. Aeschylus is even more insistent and explicit about the chain of causation, on both human and divine levels, that determined the war and continues to determine the destiny of those who participated in it. In choral passages, he emphasizes Paris's violation of the guest-host relation and the consequent necessity of the expedition. Yet, when Agamemnon and his army were trapped at Aulis by contrary winds, Artemis demanded the sacrifice of his own daughter Iphigenia for the expedition to go forward.

Aeschylus's concept of sacrifice and Artemis's role is complex. Artemis, as a goddess, is both huntress and a figure associated with care of young animals. Artemis feels both anger and pity at the omen of the two eagles (representing Agamemnon and Menelaus) feasting on the pregnant hare (representing Troy) and, in her anger, demands of them this sacrifice of their own young as a kind of prospective compensation for the killing of the "hare" and her young. Agamemnon must sacrifice his own daughter, in other words, to compensate for the destruction of Troy and its many offspring. Indeed, Aeschylus's language specifically refers to the sacking of Troy as a sacrifice, to which the battles of the Trojan War itself are "preliminary rites." Finally, in Clytaemnestra's words, Agamemnon is a sacrifice to the Furies. He

paid in advance for the destruction of Troy with the sacrifice of his daughter, and finally, on returning home, he pays for this latter sacrifice with his own life. Iphigenia's death created an avenging fury in the house, and thus when Agamemnon reenters his own home, his doom is sealed.

Agamemnon is not only paying for his daughter's death when he is slaughtered in his bath, however; he is also paying for the killing of Priam and the sacking of his city. It is significant that the destruction of Troy is figured by Aeschylus as the drawing of a net over its inhabitants, a net with a particularly dense mesh so that no one can escape it. The language of sacrifice here is intertwined with the language of the hunt. When Agamemnon comes home to Argos, he is no longer the hunter but the prey, and Clytaemnestra draws over him a similarly tight and ineluctable net—this time an actual, physical mesh—to immobilize him before stabbing him to death. The king of Argos and leader of the Trojan expedition must be slain like the king of Troy.

Another link between Priam and Agamemnon relates to the great riches of their households and the attitude toward wealth. The question of the preservation and squandering of wealth comes up when Agamemnon first arrives home and is greeted by his wife after a long absence. In a sinister scene, Clytaemnestra welcomes her husband home, while literally laying the path for his killing. The queen has vastly expensive, purple-dyed tapestries rolled out before him and encourages the king to tread on them as he enters the palace. Agamemnon is hesitant because it is wrong, he feels, to tread hubristically on tapestries that are appropriate as gifts for the gods, and it is wrong to waste household wealth in a display of conspicuous consumption. An Eastern king such as Priam might act this way, but Agamemnon feels he would be tempting fate. Yet Clytaemnestra's powers of persuasion are in the end too much for him, and, in a fatal act of submission, he enters his own house on the path made by the purple tapestries. This symbolic gesture of pride, however unwillingly made, might be seen as the tipping point that enables his fall—an act that, in the eyes of the gods, justifies in advance his punishment. Wasting wealth wantonly, moreover, symbolizes and in fact contributes to the destruction of the household, which, as we have seen, is being ruined on multiple levels. The Chorus throughout the play expresses its preference for a modest yet safe existence as opposed to the dangers that the mighty and wealthy undergo. Agamemnon now assumes the role of arrogant rich man primed for his fall. Finally, we might note that he is made parallel yet again with Priam, who is represented as being capable of treading on tapestries himself and who has already fallen in a sacrificial killing, just as Agamemnon is about to fall.

Of course, none of these killings would be seen as proper sacrifices in the eyes of ancient Greeks. Human sacrifice was seen as the extreme instance of an alien rite, a mark of the barbaric, and in variant myths, represented, for example, in Euripides, Artemis saves Iphigenia at the last moment by replacing her with a hind. The use of sacrificial language to describe what are properly seen as murders—for example, in the disturbing idea of a human sacrifice to the Furies—intensifies the perversion of ordinary ritual and the sense of cosmic wrong that inheres in the house of Atreus. Sacrifice to the gods is not happening in the normal, healthy manner; therefore the royal household is in profound moral disorder. Even in Iphigenia's case, where there might be said to be a true human sacrifice demanded by a god, the Chorus only describes the scene of her sacrifice up to the last moment before the killing. It claims not to have seen what happened and refuse to speak of it, only grimly noting that Calchas's art is not fallible. This conspicuous omission leaves some room for ambiguity, and while we may assume that the killing was carried out, this most persuasive instance of human sacrifice—as opposed to murder figured

as sacrifice—remains shrouded in silence and mystery.

It may be that Aeschylus does not wish to confirm explicitly a human sacrifice demanded by Artemis and wishes to leave some room for vagueness and ambiguity, yet neither does he wish to diminish any of the burden of Agamemnon's choice and ultimate guilt as killer of kin. To represent the animal substitute for Iphigenia would be to undermine the full horror of the cycle of violence afflicting the house and to soften the edges of Agamemnon's insoluble dilemma. To abandon the expedition would make him a deserter, the betrayer of his own army, and, worst of all, violator of the command of Zeus *xenios*, yet to sacrifice his own daughter makes him evil and subject to the Furies; and, of course, it also causes his own death. The Chorus makes it clear that Agamemnon is constrained by necessity, impelled by the conflicting impulses of two gods, and thus faces an impossible choice, and that, in sacrificing his daughter, he is committing a sacrilegious act and has a mind warped by the evil drive for war. Modern readers may be struck by the apparent illogic of this situation—he cannot make *any* good or acceptable choice yet is blamed when he does make a choice—but for the Greeks, he is an intensely tragic figure precisely at this moment. He is caught somewhere between morally informed free will and the inescapable, controlling power of the gods. He must make a choice that is judged in ethical terms while remaining utterly subject to the force of divine destiny.

This kind of situation is typical of tragedy as opposed to epic. In Homer, Zeus presides over the fate of human actors, and gods constantly intervene in the action, yet there is considerable focus on the ability of the epic hero to create his own fame (*kleos*) through deeds. Despite great suffering (ODYSSEUS), and/or early death (ACHILLES), the Homeric hero wins a good name through his own unique abilities and the gods' unusual favor. We are constantly surprised, in the case of Odysseus, how the hero, through the combination of divine help and his own unconquerable wits, is able against the odds to get out of the most unpromising situations. Tragedy takes a very different perspective on its heroes, and it is significant that Aeschylus chooses Agamemnon and his household as the opening focus of his trilogy. Agamemnon's fatal homecoming is cited in the *Odyssey* as a negative example of what Homer's hero must avoid, just as Clytaemnestra's example counters that of the virtuous Penelope. In the *Iliad*, Agamemnon is, despite some properly heroic exploits, a lesser hero than Achilles, and comes off as blustering and hubristic in the epic's opening scene of confrontation. Aeschylus, then, has carefully chosen a figure who can be effectively associated with the dark side of war, a man who does not win an unambiguously good *kleos,* and who utterly fails, in the end, to be the master of his destiny. Agamemnon is controlled by his own violent acts and the curse of his household, and we are shown not heroism in a positive sense but the heroism of a figure singled out for unusual suffering and doom. In representing the dark side of the Trojan War, Aeschylus also understandably focuses on the phase of the *nostoi* (return journeys) of the Greek heroes. Some return journeys were successful, like that of Odysseus, and yet even he spent 10 years getting home and was allowed to return only after much suffering and the total loss of his companions. Other Greek heroes were punished for impious acts committed during the sacking of the city, and, in an episode alluded to in the present play, Menelaus was driven off course to Egypt and was able to return to Sparta only after delays and trials of his own. (This allusion to Menelaus's fate anticipates the subject of the tetralogy's lost satyr play, *Proteus,* which, in telling the story of Menelaus's sojourn in Egypt, would have treated the same mythological nexus in a somewhat lighter manner.) The immense cost of war is a persistent theme, and Aeschylus is especially insistent that the price of violence must be paid for with further suffering and death. Aeschylus's post-

Homeric vision of war and the aristocratic warlord aggressively and brilliantly rewrites Homer's version of the undertaking. Homer never flinched from representing the cost of war—the loss of the warrior to his parents, his wife and children, and his homeland—but he did so without detracting from the ennobling vision of the warrior's courage in facing death and without fundamentally questioning the aristocratic value system built around excellence in battle and the glorious fame of the warrior. Achilles in some ways goes against the heroic code by withdrawing from battle, but only ultimately to maximize his own *kleos* and make himself the most famous and admired of the Greek warriors.

The Aeschylean depiction of the Trojan War is very different, and the perspective on war is not the Olympian perspective of the epic poet describing signal deeds on the battlefield but of more marginal figures who suffered because of the war. The herald, who has returned from the war, is satisfied that the war has ended with the capture of Troy but lingers, in his speeches, on the tedium, weariness, and physical toils and torments of the battlefield. Many of the details of his description are a far cry from the brilliant flashes of valor transmitted by Homeric epic: They lived in cramped, filthy quarters aboard the ships, and on land, the dew soaked their clothes and filled their hair with lice.

A different but related perspective emerges from those who remained at home in Greece. The Chorus of Argive elders powerfully evokes the tragic loss of men from the homeland. Warriors went to Troy and came back as ash in urns. This negative assessment goes hand in hand with a judgment of Helen that is much harsher than Homer's. In Homer, Helen is hardly morally absolved, but there is a great deal of nuance and subtlety in his character sketches of the heroine in both epics. Her immense beauty is a curse also to her, and she is very much subject to the power of the goddess Aphrodite. The Aeschylean Chorus, however, links her name, through a false but rhetorically effective etymology, with the Greek word for "destroy" and makes her into the destroyer of Greece. There is a savage grief and anger in its odes that cannot be assuaged even by the eventual victory. The epic narrative of war has been assimilated and transformed to fit Aeschylus's tragic vision. The mythology of the imploding royal household and the mythology of ruinous war merge in the figure of Agamemnon, who headed the war effort and whose house is in the course of being destroyed by events relating to the war. Both the war and the revenge killings at Argos are framed by a broader causal sequence initiated by earlier originating events: the theft of Helen, the crimes of Atreus and Tantalus. War is no longer the arena of heroic, glory-conferring exploits but functions both as consequence and cause in an inevitable chain of violent acts.

A masterpiece of Aeschylus's mature style, the *Agamemnon* weaves an intertwining fabric of diverse mythological themes and shifting temporal frames. The play is a notably long one and is enriched by a complex orchestration of metaphors that are activated and reactivated in changing contexts. Aeschylus's poetic style sometimes seems stilted, grandiose, and overly complex to modern readers, yet it is integrally related to the manner in which he builds up a dense interrelation of themes and images across multiple characters and narrative frames. It will be helpful to consider a few examples briefly. A legal metaphor is employed, to take one notable instance, when Priam is described as the great adversary at law of the Atreidae. Later in the trilogy, of course, a forensic setting will be crucial to Orestes' absolution, and we might already begin to contemplate the shift from the "legal dispute" of two royal households engaged in a violent conflict over a stolen woman and the legal institutions of the Athenian polis. To take another strand of imagery, the Atreidae are first described as vultures deprived of their chicks (i.e., their initial reaction of outrage to the theft of Helen), and later

as two eagles, one black and one white, devouring a pregnant hare (their sacking of Troy). Animal metaphors are rife: Cassandra is first like a swallow singing incomprehensible notes (in Clytaemnestra's description), then like a nightingale singing out her grief. Clytaemnestra (in Cassandra's metaphor) is a lioness who lies with the wolf while the lion is away.

Many metaphors in the play concern sound and expressive speech (e.g., the shrieking of birds), but some are also about silence. The watchman, in the play's opening scene, declares that he has an "ox standing on his tongue." One reason for the special difficulty and at times near opacity of Aeschylean language in this play is the practical need for silence, circumspect speech, and coded expression in a palace where an assassination plot is in progress. The watchman and the Chorus cannot always give full expression to their anxieties and their criticisms of Clytaemnestra's behavior. Clytaemnestra, at least until near the end of the play, employs a kind of doublespeak, whereby her words, ostensibly acceptable and welcoming, have a sinister second meaning when considered in the light of her murderous intentions. When, upon Agamemnon's return, Clytaemnestra delivers an enigmatic speech that culminates with a prayer to Zeus to "bring these things to pass," it is not clear what these things are; and in retrospect, it seems likely that she prays for the death of her husband, which she herself is about to accomplish.

The most dramatic instance of blocked, tortured speech that both reveals and conceals the truth is the scene in which the Trojan prophetess Cassandra has a dialogue with the Chorus. Cassandra's words come in thick, frantic waves of semiopaque prophecy, and the Chorus sometimes confesses itself baffled and other times recognizes the glint of truth in what she says. The scene comes at the climax of the play. We know that while she is speaking, Clytaemnestra is preparing the imminent murder of Agamemnon, and toward the end of the exchange we hear the king's death cries from within the palace. The dramatic power of the scene is considerable. The audience is driven to an extreme of suspense as they await the outcome of Clytaemnestra's murderous design, and as Cassandra's prophetic frenzy grows more and more intense with the approach of the moment of death. Cassandra is a perfect distillation of the play's obstructed and stifled modes of speech. For the act of breaking off intercourse with Apollo, she has been punished with the fate of always offering true prophecy that no one believes. Her prophetic communication, like her union with the god, is pointedly unfulfilled. Now she struggles to make her prophetic vision understood, but whenever she nears the crucial point—that Agamemnon is in the course of being murdered—the Chorus seems to have a fog come over its mind, and it fails to comprehend. She reveals her prophet's knowledge of the whole dark history of the house—indeed, she seems to sense the evil in the place viscerally—but cannot make clear to her listener the episode in its history that is taking shape that very moment. At one point she declares that she will speak clearly and not cryptically, but even then she is able to communicate clearly only her insights about the past. Not just in this play, but in Athenian tragedy generally, the Chorus is typically unable to intervene to prevent tragic outcomes. In this instance, Aeschylus provides an ingeniously appropriate reason for their inaction.

Cassandra's scene is the culmination of the play on many different levels: With her knowledge of the past and foreboding of the future, she alone seems able to perceive fully the mythic pattern of the house and heroically attempts to break through the heavy veil of secrecy and silence as the murderous act is being put in motion. As prophet, narrator of myth, singer, and weaver of dense, difficult language, Cassandra is in a certain sense a surrogate poet or tragic playwright. Her tortured, twisted words, however, offer only the most dramatic example of the theme of the perversion of song and distortion of language throughout the play. We hear, variously, of a paean to the Fury, a wedding song that turns to a dirge, the Furies's dirge sung without a lyre in the singer's mind, and, finally, the ghastly cacophony of the choir of Furies. The song and revelry of the Furies—drunk not on wine but on blood—represent a kind of antisymposium, and their song is a perverted version of the traditional poetry of the Greek drinking party. Tragic poetry, in the *Agamemnon*, is inspired by these anti-Muses, the Furies, and reflects the perversion of the social and cosmic order in its grim, troubled cadences.

Perhaps the most crucial disturbance that arises both in the play's network of human relations and in the cosmic fabric itself is the unbalancing of male-female relations and roles as understood in ancient Greek terms. Clytaemnestra is characterized by a strikingly masculine role that is implicitly or openly criticized throughout the play. She dominates discourse to an extent considered inappropriate for a woman; she has cunning, bold, violent designs like a man, and she appears to covet power over Argos. By entrapping Agamemnon, rendering him weak and passive with the net, and then stabbing him, she reverses the "natural" relation between man and woman, husband and wife. She appears to be similarly in control of Aegisthus and to have taken the man's role from him. In Homer, Aegisthus is represented as Agamemnon's murderer, and it is precisely this scenario that is feared in the case of Odysseus. A male suitor will claim his wife and throne and murder him in the event of his return. Clytaemnestra defies this expected narrative pattern and the constraints of her gender role. Many of her comments about the injustice and condescension that women must suffer are sharply eloquent, and in this and other respects, she is an important predecessor of the Euripidean Medea. She is the most brilliant and disturbing character in the play and perhaps in the entire extant Aeschylean oeuvre.

The conflict between male and female, as the trilogy goes on, will become a driving force in the action and one of its central themes. We glimpse already the outlines of this conflict. The watchman in the opening scene is in the service of his mistress yet remains loyal to the master of the household, Agamemnon. The male Chorus of Argive elders expresses disgust at Clytaemnestra's act when it is revealed, an act that, however, she justifies in the name of her murdered daughter, Iphigenia. The Chorus likewise expresses its hatred of Helen, the cause of the Greeks' and Trojans' suffering in war. Certain aspects of Clytaemnestra's language, however, hint at an even deeper divide than the one between mortal men and women, and a deeper unbalance. In her speech upon Agamemnon's entrance into the house, she likens him to a godlike figure whose return brings warmth and life to the house, yet the metaphoric language she employs is deeply ambiguous and almost opaque. Later, after killing him, she is more direct. As Agamemnon died, he splattered her with blood, and the blood for her was like the rain of Zeus that fertilizes the earth. Clytaemnestra thus employs the primal paradigm of the fertilization of Earth by the sky god in the context of her murder of her husband and the "rain" of his blood. She thus signals her action's place in a broader cosmic disturbance in the relations between the sexes. Later in the trilogy, the gods themselves will take sides in the family's conflict, and the question of male/female relations will remain crucial to the resolution on human and divine levels.

The last speaker in the play is appropriately Clytaemnestra, who signals her intention to rule Argos alongside Aegisthus. But the last important character to make an appearance in the play is Aegisthus, near the end. He reveals his own story and motivations. Atreus, father of Agamemnon and Menelaus, fed to Thyestes, father of Aegisthus, two of his own children; Aegisthus, the third, survived and has now finally obtained vengeance by designing this plot against Agamemnon. Aegisthus is a much weaker character than Clytaemnestra, yet his late, surprise appearance comes as a revelation. He is the embodiment of the house's dark history of crime and vengeance, and, as his own words seem to suggest, he will fall victim to it in turn. The scene is set for the next phase in the cycle of violence.

Agave   Daughter of CADMUS and HARMONIA. Wife of Echion; their son was Pentheus. Agave appears in Euripides' BACCHAE. Additional classical sources are Apollodorus's LIBRARY (3.5.2–3), Hyginus's *Fabulae* (184), and Ovid's *METAMORPHOSES* (3.511–7.33).

Pentheus, king of Thebes, refused to accept the worship of DIONYSUS in Thebes. He was torn limb from limb by his own mother, Agave, and his aunt, AUTONOE, in a Bacchic frenzy. Their unwitting murder of Pentheus was brought about by Dionysus in revenge for Pentheus's lack of piety toward him. Agave was exiled from Thebes for the murder of Pentheus.

Aglaurus and Herse   Daughters of Aglaurus and Cecrops, king of Athens. Textual sources are Apollodorus's LIBRARY (3.14.2–3), Euripides' ION (23ff, 270ff), Hyginus's *Fabulae* (166), Ovid's *METAMORPHOSES* (2.708–832), and Pausanias's *Description of Greece* (1.18.2). Cecrops had three daughters, Aglaurus, Herse, and Pandrosus. ATHENA had consigned for safekeeping a casket or box in which ERICHTHONIUS had been hidden with the instruction to the daughters of Cecrops not to open it. Either all three sisters disobeyed or only Pandrosus obeyed the goddess's command and was saved. They opened the casket and became alarmed when they saw Ericthonius, serpentlike, and protected by two snakes. An attendant of Athena's temple revealed the disobedience of the daughters of Cecrops, and for her trouble the attendant was transformed into a crow. Athena afflicted the sisters with a madness that caused them to throw themselves from the Acropolis (or into the sea).

In another version, Herse and Pandrosus were able to resist the temptation but not Aglaurus, who incurred the goddess's wrath and was punished by being inflicted with a passionate envy of Herse, with whom HERMES had fallen in love. At first Aglaurus demanded gold of Hermes to help him woo Herse, but then she sent him away. On another occasion, when Hermes attempted to enter Herse's room, Aglaurus blocked his entry by sitting on the threshold. With his wand, Hermes opened the door and transformed Aglaurus into a black stone. In Apollodorus's *Library*, Herse bore a son, Cephalus, to Hermes, and Aglaurus had a daughter, Alcippe, by ARES. The myth was depicted in a 16th-century painting by Paolo Veronese, *Hermes, Herse and Aglauros* (Fitzwilliam Museum, Cambridge, United Kingdom).

Ajax (Aias)   The Greater Ajax, a Greek hero of the Trojan War. Son of Telamon, king of Salamis and Periboea. Ajax is one of the heroes of Homer's ILIAD and the central character in Sophocles's *AJAX*. Additional classical sources are Apollodorus's LIBRARY (Epitome 5.6–7), Homer's ODYSSEY (11.541–567), Hyginus's *Fabulae* (107), Ovid's METAMORPHOSES (12.624–13.398), and Pindar's *Isthmian Odes* (6.41–54). According to Apollodorus and Pindar, HERACLES prayed to Zeus that Telamon might have a male son. An eagle appeared to Heracles soon afterward, and thus Ajax was named after *aietos*, or "eagle." Ajax, like ACHILLES, has an invulnerability story: Heracles wrapped the infant Ajax in his own lion skin, thus making him invulnerable except in the part of his body that touched Heracles' quiver; this was where he would later receive his mortal wound.

According to Homeric tradition, Ajax was of great size and second only to Achilles in military prowess. His weaponry included a seven-layered oxhide shield. Book 7 of the *Iliad* centers on the duel between Ajax and the Trojan warrior HECTOR, who had challenged the warriors of the Greek army to a single combat to the death. The winner would receive the weaponry of the vanquished as his prize, and the body of the vanquished would be returned to his friends for proper burial. The Argives drew lots and Ajax was selected as their champion. Zeus stopped the duel at a climactic moment in the combat. Afterward, the heroes peaceably exchanged gifts; Hector received Ajax's purple war belt, and Ajax gave Hector a silver-studded sword.

Ajax was part of the embassy of Greek warriors who attempted to persuade Achilles to reenter the battle; his speech appealed to Achilles' friendship and came closest to persuading Achilles to rejoin the fight—Achilles was more moved by Ajax's directness, honesty, and adherence to the heroic code than by ODYSSEUS's skilled oratory. After Achilles' death, it was Ajax who brought his body back to the Greek army.

During Patroclus's funeral games, Ajax wrestled with Odysseus and, after Achilles' death, engaged in rhetorical battle with Odysseus over the distribution of Achilles' arms. Ajax reacted with fury when the arms were eventually given to Odysseus. He ran himself through with a sword in the very place where he was vulnerable, and died.

Sophocles treated the hero's death differently; in his version, after the distribution of Achilles' arms to Odysseus, Ajax went mad and slaughtered a herd of sheep, believing them to be Greeks. When he came to his senses and discovered what he had done, he committed suicide but was nonetheless given an honorable burial. Ajax's resentment of Odysseus continued in death: when, in the *Odyssey*, Odysseus descended to HADES, he met the ghost of Ajax, who glared darkly at him and refused to speak to him.

In visual representations, Ajax is depicted as a bearded, sometimes nude warrior. He appears frequently with Achilles or in the context of the events of the Trojan War. The two warriors, Ajax and Achilles, were sometimes depicted on vase paintings playing at dice together. An example is a black-figure amphora vase painted by Exekias dating from ca. 540 B.C.E. (Vatican Museums, Rome). His combat with Hector was also a popular theme; an example is an Attic red-figure cup from ca. 485 B.C.E. (Louvre, Paris). Other themes appearing on vase paintings and coins include Ajax's combat with Odysseus over the arms of Achilles and his suicide.

Ajax SOPHOCLES (ca. 440 B.C.E.) Sophocles' *Ajax* was probably produced in the late 440s B.C.E. around the time of the *ANTIGONE*. As in the *Antigone*, Sophocles presents an isolated hero who turns against his own community and ends up embracing a radically solitary death. According to the post-Iliadic mythological tradition, after ACHILLES' death, the Greeks voted to decide who of the Greek heroes was most worthy of inheriting his armor. The armor went to ODYSSEUS. Ajax, feeling dishonored and deeply resentful of Odysseus' tricks and skill in speaking, committed suicide. In the version that Sophocles here adapts (or possibly, invents), Ajax decides to kill the Greek chieftains but is driven mad by ATHENA and slays and tortures herd animals instead. His suicide thus derives from the immense shame he experiences on coming to his senses and realizing what he has done. Sophocles' play is a profound exploration of the dark side of heroism. For all that Ajax is diminished and rendered ignominious by his shameful deeds, he remains an object of power and awe. Sophocles himself, according to the biographical tradition, was conspicuously involved in hero cults in Attica and was revered as a hero after his death. This play goes to the heart of the tensions of the heroic code and the paradoxes of the hero's greatness.

SYNOPSIS

When the scene opens, Athena and Odysseus are in front of the tent of Ajax. Odysseus is pacing about, scanning the ground for tracks.

Athena addresses him, asking what he is looking for. Odysseus states that he has heard that Ajax butchered a flock and its guard dogs the night before. Athena replies that the report is true, that Ajax wanted to kill the sons of Atreus, Odysseus, and other Greek chieftains because the armor of Achilles was awarded to Odysseus rather than to him, but that she made him go insane and slaughter livestock even as he thought he was killing his enemies. Athena proposes to summon Ajax. Odysseus is afraid, but Athena summons him anyway. Ajax, still demented, comes out of the tent. he claims that he holds "Odysseus" prisoner and that he plans to flog and kill him.

Enter the Chorus of sailors from Salamis who sailed to Troy with Ajax. It stresses its dependence on Ajax and its reluctance to believe Odysseus's story.

Tecmessa enters. She reveals to the Chorus that Ajax has gone mad and has indeed slain livestock. His mind is now clear but he is suffering immense shame and horror at his deed. The Chorus fears that it will become the object of the Greeks' hatred and a target for reprisal. In a long speech, Tecmessa describes how Ajax departed the night before with the aim of killing his enemies, and now that his sanity is restored, he is completely shattered. Ajax groans from within, then calls for his son Eurysaces. Tecmessa opens the door and reveals Ajax inside, dejected, in the midst of slaughtered bulls and sheep. The Chorus attempts in vain to calm and console him. Ajax speaks of his own death, then, in a long speech, complains of the Atreidae and Odysseus and recalls how Athena destroyed his sanity. Finally, he begins to contemplate how he can recoup some of his honor and come to a suitably noble end. In a long speech of her own, Tecmessa reminds Ajax of her own hard fortune in life as a freeborn woman who became a captive, of his duty to protect her and her son. She states that being "noble" means remaining loyal to those who have been kind to one.

Ajax asks to see his child. Tecmessa confesses that she removed the child because she was afraid that Ajax might kill him in his dementia. She now calls the servants to bring in Eurysaces. He is brought before Ajax, who delivers another long speech in which he entrusts him to his half-brother TEUCER to bring up after his own death, bequeaths him his famous sevenfold oxhide shield, and requests that the rest of his armor be buried with him. Tecmessa begs him to abandon his dark mood and dark intentions, but he responds harshly and has the doors to his tent shut.

The Chorus laments Ajax's shameful madness and its own fate. Ajax comes from the tent carrying a sword. Again he speaks at length, claiming that his mood, which was once as hard as a sword, has lost its "edge," that he is affected by pity for his wife and child; that he is going to cleanse himself and bury his sword, which was given to him by his enemy HECTOR, and that like all things, he, too, must learn to yield, and humble himself before the sons of Atreus. Ajax exits to the side; Tecmessa and Eurysaces go inside the tent. The Chorus exults, filled with joy at Ajax's decision and newfound wisdom.

A messenger enters. He reports that Teucer has just come back from Mysia, that he was treated abusively by the Greeks, and that Teucer declared that Ajax must be made to stay indoors until his arrival. CALCHAS the prophet had told him that if Teucer wanted to see his brother alive again, Ajax must remain in his tent that entire day. The reason, explained Calchas, is that the goddess Athena is angry with Ajax because he had, on one occasion, declared that he had no need of the help of the gods and, on another, of the help of Athena specifically. Athena means to have her revenge on this very day.

Tecmessa enters with Eurysaces. The Chorus asks her to listen to the messenger's news. She is desperate and fearful, knowing that Ajax has already gone out, and commands the Chorus to split up into search parties to find Ajax. All exit.

Ajax enters. He stands alone on the stage with his sword. He fixes his sword in the ground, blade pointing upward. Ajax recalls that the sword was a gift from his enemy Hector, and then, in his farewell speech to life, invokes ZEUS, HERMES, the FURIES, HELIOS, Death, Salamis, and the springs and streams of Troy. In particular, he asks Zeus to guarantee that Teucer will take care of his body and protect it from his enemies, the Furies to punish the Greeks, and Helios to bring news of his fate to his father and mother. He then falls on his sword.

The members of the Chorus enter in two groups, still searching for Ajax. Tecmessa follows them. She goes to where Ajax has fallen, sees him, and cries out. The Chorus and Tecmessa lament. She insists that he should not be seen and covers him with a garment. The Chorus and Tecmessa continue their lamentations, blaming Odysseus and the sons of Atreus. Teucer is heard shouting offstage. He enters and hears from the Chorus that his half-brother is dead, and he immediately sends Tecmessa to fetch Eurysaces to ensure his safety.

As soon as she has left, Teucer uncovers Ajax's face, and he, too, begins to lament bitterly. He imagines that Telamon will not welcome him home when he returns without Ajax and will reproach him for being illegitimate. He predicts that he will be forced to go into exile and observes that the hospitality gifts exchanged between Hector and Ajax have become the instrument of death for each.

MENELAUS enters with two heralds. He forbids Teucer to bury Ajax's body. He explains himself at length: Ajax was a scofflaw and tried to kill the Greek leaders; laws must be respected in a polis as in an army. He threatens Teucer himself at the close. Teucer refuses to obey and insists that Ajax was his own master, not subordinate to Menelaus. The Chorus does not fully approve of either speech. The two men trade insults and continue to threaten and contradict each other over the question of Ajax's burial until Menelaus leaves.

A moment later, Tecmessa enters with Eurysaces. Teucer places three locks of hair, his own, Tecmessa's, and Eurysaces', into Eurysaces' hands as a suppliant's offering and instructs him to stay near Ajax while he prepares a grave. He exits.

The Chorus now complain of war and reminisces about Ajax. Teucer enters expecting AGAMEMNON's arrival. Agamemnon enters with his retinue and immediately begins to bluster at Teucer, insulting him, dwelling particularly on his low birth. Teucer rebukes him in an answering speech. He reminds him how Ajax defended Agamemnon and stood up to Hector, then points out Agamemnon's own dubious origins and the notorious events in his family's past, and defends the nobility of his own parents. He insists that he will not be moved from Ajax's corpse.

Odysseus enters and declares that he was Ajax's enemy yet admires him as a brave hero. He insists that enmity ought not to extend beyond the grave. Agamemnon reluctantly agrees not to prevent the burial, then exits.

The Chorus praises Odysseus's wisdom. Odysseus proclaims his willingness to be Teucer's friend rather than his enemy, offering even to participate in the burial of Ajax's body. Teucer praises his attitude and calls on the Furies to destroy Agamemnon and Menelaus for their lack of respect for the dead. He suggests, however, that Odysseus not touch Ajax's body for fear of offending the dead. Odysseus respects his wish and exits. Teucer and the others begin to bury Ajax. All exit.

COMMENTARY

Like Aeschylus's *Oresteia* and many other Greek tragedies, the *Ajax* takes as its subject post-Iliadic mythology: episodes that Homer does not mention or narrate directly, often related to heroes' *nostoi* ("return journeys"), episodes that in many cases bring out the darker side of heroism. In Book 11 of the *ODYSSEY*, Homer alludes to the dispute between Achilles and Odysseus. When Odysseus travels to the underworld,

Ajax, still resentful, refuses to speak with him. Homer, however, is relatively reticent on the topic and is not nearly as interested as the tragedians in the darker aspects of heroism and the dementia of heroes. Tragedy is interested in precisely such aspects of human behavior and action and also needs to occupy areas of the mythological tradition not already authoritatively narrated by Homer. Yet Sophocles also develops themes already present in Homer. The *ILIAD* is very much concerned with tensions within the Panhellenic expedition to Troy. The relative weakness of Menelaus and even Agamemnon in comparison with some other Greek heroes, as well as the loss of life and the years spent away from home to retrieve Menelaus's wife, all come up in the dispute between Agamemnon and Achilles. In the *Ajax*, there are once again questions of honor, the unity of the Greek chieftains, and the distribution of prized objects. And once again a dominant but alienated warrior is set against the two nominal leaders of the expedition.

Ajax fits the paradigm of the Sophoclean hero type. He is intensely self-isolating, in tension with and even dangerous to his community and those closest to him, and he relentlessly follows his own path and adheres to his own principles. He resembles Antigone in many respects, who also carries her principles to the extreme and opposes the leader of her polis, and values her sense of honor and what is right over her own life. We might also compare the obsessive concern with the burial of dead heroes with the same theme in the *Antigone*. Antigone insists on performing burial rites for her dead brother, Polynices, and, as her reward, ends up being immured alive in a tomblike cave instead of achieving her normal role in life as a wife. Ajax buries his sword in the ground and kills himself, praying before he does so that his brother Teucer will be able to protect his body and oversee his burial. The closing sequence of the play concerns precisely this, the burial of Ajax. This latter part of the play, in which a sibling fights against the polis leader to ensure the proper burial of someone who made himself an enemy of his own community, affords a very precise correspondence with the situation in the *Antigone* (hence the hypothetical dating of the play).

Proper burial signifies acceptance of the hero's special status, his place in the community, even if he harmed or tried to harm members of the community. The community must make the decision that the importance both of the hero and of burial customs transcends the sum of the mundane interests of its members. Sophocles is at pains to demonstrate how many people Ajax harms by his decisions and how profoundly. Tecmessa's speeches drive home that she may face slavery again and will have to bear the taunts of the rest of the Greeks: Their son, Eurysaces, will have no father, and thus he, too, will be humiliated and mistreated. Ajax's parents will not have him to care for them in their old age, and his father, Telamon, who is alluded to many times throughout the play, will suffer shame on hearing of his son's actions. The Chorus of Salaminian sailors constantly draws attention to the ways in which Ajax's dishonor implicates it and makes it subject to the angry reprisals of the rest of the Greek army. Teucer expands on the fact that he will now have to go home to their father, Telamon, without Ajax, he will face his father's harsh rebukes, and he will, ultimately, have to go into exile. Essentially, everyone in contact with Ajax is grievously harmed by his action. The only person who appears to benefit is his enemy Odysseus. And yet it was Ajax's intention to kill him and the other Greek chieftains too. The difficult insight that lies at the heart of Sophocles' play, and that the Athenian audience could be expected to contemplate, is that although Ajax's intentions and his effect on all those around him are overwhelmingly negative, he still deserves a degree of honor and even reverence after his death. This seeming paradox relates to the Greek concept of the hero as a figure who is at once extraordinary, isolated, destructive, and awe-inspiring, a figure who surpasses ordinary mortal bounds and whose value transcends, to a certain degree, the moral scruples that constrain us in our everyday lives.

One path of approach to the question of the harm caused by the hero, on the one hand, and his value, on the other, is the theme of intertwining friendship and enmity that runs through the play. Ajax, like Achilles, is a character who breaks with the ordinary version of the heroic code by doing harm to those who should be his friends. He attempted to harm his enemies, as would be normal, but instead destroyed livestock. Hector was his enemy, but he nonetheless exchanged gifts with Ajax as a guest-friend; in a further twist, however, this act of friendship carried the seed of destruction, since Ajax ultimately killed himself with his friend/enemy's sword—a deadly gift—and even Ajax's gift to Hector is construed by Sophocles as having done him harm. The very parallelism of these two figures, however, links them and makes them something more than mere enemies. They are both great bulwarks of their respective armies who meet an early death in part through the gifts they gave each other. Even if they are not, properly speaking, friends, heroes of the stature of Ajax and Hector have more in common with each other than with some of their ostensible allies. Finally, Teucer finds in Odysseus an unexpected ally and friend at the end of the play. Odysseus supports Teucer's insistence on proper burial of Ajax, and though enemies previously, they accept each other as friends.

Many of these concerns with what it means to be a friend (*philos*) come to a head in the speeches of Ajax and Tecmessa on nobility. Ajax stresses that being noble means not fearing death and not living in dishonor merely for the sake of survival in a minimal sense. Tecmessa seeks to remind him that men have obligations to their friends and those who have shown them kindness. She stresses his links with others, whereas he isolates himself by his own heroism and the hard principles by which he lives and by which he wishes to be remembered. Neither viewpoint is necessarily meant to be undermined or defeated by the other: Both stand in eloquent and rich tension as a comment on the potential contradictions of the heroic code.

Sophoclean heroes are typically isolated: Antigone, OEDIPUS, PHILOCTETES. In some cases, they are afflicted by intense shame and are made, for physical and/or moral reasons, to appear repulsive to others. Philoctetes lives like an desperate animal and is tormented by a reeking wound. Oedipus is marked by the shame of having killed his father and married his mother. In the case of Ajax, the intensification of his shame, brought about by his very unheroic, vindictive slaying of herd animals, isolates him further from his fellow human beings. His place in society was predicated on his sense of honor and excellence; once he has lost that, he can no longer find a way to go on living with others. He could continue existing physically, but without the sense of self that previously defined and sustained him. The theme of hunting highlights Ajax's distance from those around him. At the opening of the play, Odysseus is like a hound searching for Ajax's tracks and hunting him down. Later, when Ajax is suspected of having committed suicide, a desperate hunt is on for the hero: Tecmessa and the Chorus, divided into different groups, go on a frantic manhunt. One important outcome of the hunting metaphor is to create a distinction between the pack, on the one hand, and the tragically individuated quarry, on the other.

The staging of the play contributes a further element to the dynamic of isolation and shame. Instead of the entrance to a royal palace, the central door of the stage of the *Ajax* opens onto Ajax's tent, where, at the outset, he is inside by himself amid the horrific carnage of his slaughter of the herd. He occupies a sequestered domain of horror and madness. In the central action of the play—Ajax's suicide—he stands alone on the stage in a deserted area, where he delivers his final soliloquy. For the rest of the play, Ajax is a corpse, hidden beneath a mantle that Tecmessa puts over him. The massive, silent hulk of his body remains present in the closing scenes as Teucer and the Atreidae trade insults back and forth. His very silence and death are eloquent in this instance. Ajax does not take part in the dialogue that will determine the fate of his body, and while his status in the community is being negotiated in a wordy debate, he remains a silent, inert presence. He is even careful to prevent his possessions from being circulated communally after his death. He leaves the object that is the most closely identified with him—his massive shield—to his son, Eurysaces, and proclaims that the rest of his armor will be buried with him. His suicidal act is all about bringing things to an end. He ends himself, ends the competition for honor through the distribution of armor. In broader terms, he represents the end of a form of heroism.

Ajax's tragedy is that he finds himself in an unthinkable situation. He is himself the author of deeds that have no place in his code of action, and he is at risk of losing his heroic status. It is true that he aimed to kill the Greek chieftains—a questionable act to begin with—but this outcome would at least have been in accordance with his own conception of forthright action against enemies. What actually happens resembles the extremity of Euripides' *BACCHAE*, where a god taunts a hubristic mortal then destroys him by undermining the integrity and rigidity of his own moral position to an extreme degree. Here Ajax is punished by being made the author of the undoing of his own ideal of manly excellence and the warrior's nobility of action. The repeated mention of Telamon underscores Ajax's loss of a sense of connection with the heroic example of his father. The heroic chain of inheritance has been broken with Ajax; he even goes so as far as to lament that his father was allowed to maintain his glory as a hero untainted, whereas he must accept dishonor.

The chief instrument of Ajax's undoing is the madness that Athena inflicts on him. Madness, as in the *Bacchae*, signifies the god's destruction of a mortal's identity and basic dignity. He loses not simply his position in life but his sense of self and the purpose behind his existence. As in Agave's terrible moment of realization in Euripides' play, it is the return of clarity that is the most destructive and painful. Ajax realizes that it is too late, and that he cannot go back to being who he was.

Particularly notable in this version of the Sophoclean hero estranged from his community is the emphasis on the hero's culpability. Antigone and Philoctetes are not clearly culpable to the same degree. Even Oedipus seems less obviously culpable than Ajax. Oedipus may be intellectually arrogant, and given to violent outbursts, but it is also clear that an intricate web of destiny has victimized him. Ajax, by contrast, seems to invite his own doom. On two occasions, he hubristically proclaimed his lack of need for divine support, and he specifically refused Athena's help. It is thus all the more ironic when, in his demented state, he calls Athena his ally. She stood by the warrior in battle—but drove him to slaughter livestock, not human enemies. It is also clear that he aimed to carry out a slaughter of his fellow Greeks—a slaughter that does not seem morally justifiable. Other versions of the story were available. For Pindar, Ajax's suicide simply followed from the disgrace of not receiving Achilles' armor. Sophocles has maximized the horror and shame by elaborating a version in which Ajax slays and tortures herd animals as part of an abortive plan to slay the Greek chieftains.

It is thus perhaps all the more dramatic in this instance that Sophocles maintains the keen sense of pity for Ajax—above all through the powerful characterization of Tecmessa—and maintains the sense of his greatness even as he falls on his own sword. Like Oedipus, he will be revered as a hero after his death—as an example and an object of awe. And like Oedipus in Sophocles' *OEDIPUS AT COLONUS*, the hero Ajax has a connection with Athens. The Chorus of Salaminian sailors stresses its place of origin—an important site of Athenian patriotism—and apostrophizes Athens conspicuously. Ajax does the same shortly before his death. The Athenians themselves honored Ajax's memory in their own way by sitting as spectators before this dark and fascinating play.

Alcestis EURIPIDES (438 B.C.E.) Euripides' *Alcestis* was produced in 438 B.C.E. and won second prize in the tragedy competition. The story concerns ADMETUS, king of Thessaly: He has learned that he must die unless he can find someone to die in his stead. His parents refuse, and the one person who agrees to do so is his own wife, ALCESTIS. At the opening of the action, Alcestis is near death. The play was presented fourth in order, the place usually occupied by a satyr play—a humorous type of play where heroic mythology is typically treated in a less serious manner. Indeed, we hear that an earlier tragedian, Phrynicus, had produced a satyr play on Alcestis and Admetus. The present play alludes to aspects of the satyr play but is best described as an unconventional tragedy. Euripides often challenges the conventions and high seriousness of the tragic genre and presents his audience with sub-heroic or otherwise perplexing characters and situations. Admetus hardly seems to fit the profile of the hard, unyielding tragic hero, yet his experience of grief and loss nonetheless achieves a profound resonance. The *Alcestis* is a play above all about the necessity of death and its implications for the human condition.

SYNOPSIS

APOLLO enters and stands before the house of Admetus at Pherae in Thessaly. He explains that he has been in the service of Admetus, king of Thessaly, as a lowly shepherd, because, angry that ZEUS had killed his son ASCLEPIUS with a lightning bolt, he killed Zeus's smiths, the CYCLOPES. He was therefore condemned to become a mortal's servant. Yet because Admetus revered and honored Apollo, Apollo became his friend and has protected him from death until this day. Admetus must now perish, unless he can find someone willing to die in his place. He tried his relatives and those near him, but only his wife, Alcestis, would agree to die for him. She is, at this moment, in her husband's arms, on the point of dying. The god Death is just now arriving. Death enters.

He complains that Apollo contrived to save Admetus and now appears still to defend Alcestis. Apollo wants to know why Alcestis cannot live to an old age. Death replies that he is inflexible, as always. Apollo warns that a man (HERACLES) is coming to Admetus's house and will take Alcestis away from Death. Death insists that he will take Alcestis. Death exits by the central door leading to Admetus's house. Apollo also exits.

The Chorus of citizens of Pherae enters. It wonders whether or not Alcestis is still alive, scans for signs of her death, and debates among itself about the matter. It laments that nothing can be done to save her from death, and that there is no one who can save mortals from death, now that Asclepius himself has been struck down by Zeus.

A serving maid enters. The Chorus asks about Alcestis. She replies that the queen will die soon. The Chorus laments. In a long speech, the maid describes Alcestis's final day. She bathed and prayed to the Spirit of the Hearth for her children's happiness in life, then went to the marriage bed and wept, and predicted that her husband would soon have another wife. She kissed her children farewell, and the household began to lament. The maid repeats that Alcestis is now dying and that Admetus is inconsolable. She also reports that Alcestis is asking to see the sun once more. She goes in to announce the presence of the Chorus to the king.

The Chorus prays to the gods, and to Apollo in particular, for some means of escape from death. The Chorus then addresses Admetus, remarks on his grief, and imagines that life will no longer be worth living for him. While it is thus lamenting, Alcestis is carried out on a litter accompanied by Admetus, her children, and servants of the house. Alcestis and Admetus converse: She addresses once more the sun, her land, and her marriage chamber. Then she observes that Death has come for her, and CHARON is summoning her. Admetus begs the gods not to let her die and implores her to fight against death. In a long speech, Alcestis describes the sacrifice she is making for him at that very moment and her reasons for making it; she notes that his parents, who are near death, did not wish to make this sacrifice and thus save their children from orphanhood and him from being a widower. In recompense, she asks him to promise her not to marry again, and thus make his children subject to an unsympathetic stepmother. Admetus promises: He will spend his life in mourning her and hating his parents; he will not enjoy any of the usual pleasures in life; he will continue to be devoted to her, will be buried alongside her, and will seek her in the underworld. On hearing this promise, she commends the children to his care. She now begins to sink into death and bids her children and husband farewell. She dies. Admetus laments, and their son expresses his grief and shock. The Chorus consoles Admetus with the observation that all must die. Admetus proclaims public mourning for his wife throughout Thessaly.

The Chorus sings in praise of Alcestis, proclaiming her to be a subject of future poetry. Heracles enters. He asks after Admetus and reveals that he is stopping at Pherae on the way to Thrace, where his next labor requires him to procure the chariot of Diomedes. Admetus enters. Heracles notes signs of mourning and asks who has died. Admetus gives a somewhat obscure reply; he acknowledges that someone has died, but not that it is his own wife; he even hints that it was some woman outside the family. Heracles suggests that perhaps it is not a good time for guests, but Admetus insists on extending him hospitality. The Chorus is astounded by the decision to entertain a guest during the period of mourning. Admetus stresses the importance of hospitality *(xenia)*, and reveals that he did not tell Heracles openly about Alcestis's death because, in that case, Heracles would not have agreed to stay. Admetus goes into the palace.

The Chorus praises Admetus's liberality and hospitality. Apollo himself was happy to live with him. Admetus reenters, followed by a covered litter. He announces that the deceased (he does not name Alcestis) is being carried to the place of cremation and burial. Pheres, Admetus's father, enters. He comes to offer his last respects and praises Alcestis as a paragon of womanhood. Admetus, in a long speech, scathingly criticizes his father, calling him a coward who is ungrateful for the good treatment he has received; he renounces filial relation to him and claims to be the "child" of Alcestis rather than of his parents. Admetus declares that he will not bury his father. Pheres responds with equally harsh words: He does not owe his son his life, having given him everything else; it is not a Greek custom for fathers to die for their sons; it is Admetus who is a coward, who kills his wife to stay alive himself; perhaps Admetus will live forever by persuading a succession of wives to die for him. Admetus and Pheres exchange a series of brief, bitter remarks: Pheres warns that Alcestis's brother Acastus has vowed vengeance; Admetus disowns his father. The body of Alcestis is borne off as the Chorus laments; all exit.

A servant enters from the house. In a soliloquy, he complains that the guest currently staying in the house is the worst they have ever had: He is insensitive to the mourning of a household, he drinks a huge amount of wine, and he sings drunken songs—off key. Heracles enters. He chastises the servant for his gloomy demeanor, observes that all must die, but that in the meanwhile we should enjoy life, love, and wine. The servant insists that the current troubles of the household preclude revelry.

Heracles cannot understand the seriousness of this, since he is still under the impression given him by Admetus that a woman "outside the family" has died. When, during the ensuing dialogue, it becomes clear that Alcestis died, Heracles is appalled that he allowed himself to be misled into accepting Admetus's hospitality. The servant exits after giving Heracles directions to the funeral. Heracles, moved by Admetus's nobility of spirit in extending hospitality even at such a time, resolves to bring Alcestis back from the clutches of Death. He exits.

Admetus and the Chorus enter. Admetus laments his widowhood and expresses envy for the dead. The Chorus responds to and consoles him as he gives voice to his desolation. Admetus now regrets his condition. Everything in his household and life reminds him of his dead wife, and many see him as an unmanly coward. The Chorus sings of the terrible goddess Necessity and stresses the finality of Alcestis's death; it predicts that she will be worshipped as a god or hero. Heracles enters, leading a veiled woman by the hand. He first chides Admetus for misleading him as to the object of the household's mourning, then asks him to keep the woman safe for him in his house, claiming to have won her as a prize at an athletic event. Admetus regrets misleading Heracles but points out that to have driven Heracles to another host would have been worse. He begs Heracles to take the woman to someone else: He does not wish to invite criticism or impropriety, and it upsets him to look at her, since she resembles Alcestis. In the following exchange, Heracles still does not reveal who the woman is but attempts to persuade Admetus to remarry. He refuses, but at Heracles' insistence allows him to lead the woman into the house. Admetus is persuaded to take her hand against his instincts and then to look upon her. He is amazed to see Alcestis. Heracles reveals that he wrestled with Death to obtain her back, and that Alcestis is silent because she cannot speak until she has fulfilled her obligations to the gods of the underworld. Heracles must depart for his next labor, though urged to stay on as a guest. Admetus orders celebrations with dancing and sacrifices to the gods, and proclaims his own happiness.

COMMENTARY

The *Alcestis* lacks the element of horror central to some of the better-known Euripidean tragedies such as the *Medea* and the *Bacchae*. Yet other features of this early play are typical of Euripidean tragedy. A god introduces the play in a divine prologue speech (Apollo, in this instance), and three gods appear on stage: besides Apollo, we also see Heracles and Death. Heracles, of course, is only partially or debatably a divine figure, but in this case, he plays, very effectively, the role of deus ex machina. As in the *Medea*, a character who just happens to be passing through, and who receives a favor from the central character, plays a major role in the plot. Most significantly, we might note the unconventional role of a woman in relation to motherhood, death, and heroism. Euripides' Medea character kills her own children and her husband's new bride and father-in-law, humbles and destroys Jason, and magnificently controls the plot of the play throughout. In the *Alcestis*, too, a woman makes a highly unusual choice that makes her famous, and that astonishes her husband and reduces him to a wretched existence of deprivation. In particular, we might compare the scene in which Medea flies away at the end of the play and abandons Jason to his empty existence, and the scene here when Alcestis departs for the other world: She, too, leaves her husband prostrate and defeated. As in the *Medea*, so here we note a woman's powerful concern for her "bed" and her husband's fidelity—in this case posthumous. Alcestis might be read as a kind of inverse Medea, and whereas she is represented consistently as a paragon of womanhood, it remains intriguing that the effect on her husband of her magnificent departure is highly reminiscent of the final exit of Euripides' greatest villainess.

Another way of viewing this relation is to observe that Euripides displays an interest in weak or displaced virility. The obvious flaw at the heart of Admetus's behavior is that he has allowed his wife to die in his stead and is thus a coward. His wife is better able to face the simple fact of death than he is and is clearheaded about her reasons for doing so. The flaw affects not only Admetus but his father as well, from whom we might presume Admetus to have inherited some aspects of his character. Admetus is deeply bitter that his parents, who had not long to live anyway, would not agree to die in his stead, and thus condemned his wife to death and himself to widowhood. When his father comes onstage to offer his last respects to Alcestis, the father and son bicker unpleasantly. Euripides, as elsewhere, involves his characters in sometimes shockingly petty motives and quarrels: They stoop to low insults and even sarcasm, as when Pheres suggests that Admetus will resort to a succession of dead wives to prolong his own life. The effect of grotesque unmanliness is intensified if we recall that the two men, father and son, are arguing as to who is the greater coward in front of Alcestis's covered corpse. The silent body refutes and diminishes both of them.

Admetus has a tragic flaw but it is not a normal or expected one for a hero: Tragic heroes are more often foolhardy and reckless of their lives. The sadness he experiences at losing Alcestis and his own fear of death, moreover, are very ordinary qualities. Admetus perhaps brings them into high relief by his unusual story, and, like other tragic heroes, he does aspire to extraordinary status, yet he does so for all too ordinary motives. His wife is the extraordinary character who will be treated like a god, not Admetus. Still, the destruction of Admetus's virile integrity is not total, as in, for example, the *Bacchae*, when Pentheus is made to dress up as a woman to spy grotesquely on the Bacchantes, and then is slain by women, chief among them his own mother. Admetus is not fully and irredeemably ignoble: He does not even seem to have fully realized what he was doing until he had done it. Euripides is also careful to endow him with at least one highly significant virtue: He is a good host, a worthy friend of Apollo and Heracles. Apollo protected him from death in the first place because he was such a pleasant master and kindly host; Heracles chose to save Alcestis because, despite his immense bereavement, he insisted on extending hospitality to the wandering hero. Hospitality *(xenia)* was, since the time of Homer, the litmus test of Greekness and civilization, whereas the archetypal monster or villain was someone who violated the bonds of the guest-host relation (e.g., POLYPHEMUS, who eats his would-be guests). In its broad structure, the story of Admetus's hospitality to Heracles correlates with other mythological narratives in which a god, disguised and wandering among mortals, is offered hospitality only by a truly good person, who is subsequently rewarded (e.g., BAUCIS AND PHILEMON). Thus we know that, on some level, however questionably he has acted in the present instance, Admetus is good, precisely because he is a superlative host.

While Admetus is not a typical tragic character but merely a good, if flawed, man, the play nonetheless achieves real tragic intensity by evoking directly and unostentatiously the simple facts of death and loss. Absent from this scenario are the sublime tragic ironies of a mighty hero whose actions have contributed to his own magnificent but fearsome downfall. The *Alcestis* presents instead, with touching simplicity, a scene of death such as occurs often in human life: A beloved family member dies as her family stands by in grief and dismay. Compared with other tragic deaths, Alcestis's occurs in painstaking slow motion. When the action of the play opens, she is dying but not yet dead, and she remains in this transitional state of semidarkness for several hundred lines. First we see the grim figure of Death approaching the house. Then we hear the maid's speech, in which she recalls the poignancy of Alcestis's final day of life. Finally, in a highly unusual scene of onstage death,

Admetus and Alcestis engage in a prolonged conversation as gradually, line by line, she fades from the world of the living. Euripides lingers on the simple, unbearable fact of loss, the minute changes in Alcestis whereby she goes from being able to speak and see to an increasingly inert figure who cannot lift her head and eyes to look upon her children. After she is gone, her son's naive yet powerful speeches of lament are also remarkable in a genre that rarely awards speech of any length to children. He is dismayed by the stillness of his mother's eyes and hands, her inability to hear him crying out to her.

Euripides, as elsewhere, displays a rich interest in pathos itself—intense emotions of pain, shock, and loss. We might compare the death scene described above with Medea's murder of her children and the sounds of their terrified, uncomprehending cries offstage. Pity, fear, grief—such emotions are the stuff of tragedy, yet it is worth considering how the present version of the ruin of a royal household has a different structure and focus from other tragedies. When the house of Atreus collapses before our eyes in Aeschylus's *Oresteia*, we have a sense of cosmic ruin on multiple levels and the essential derangement of right and wrong: the killing of the king, the violent triumph of a woman over her husband, the derailing of royal succession and political stability, the murder of family members by family members according to a terrible curse that goes back generations. Here the ruin, although royal, is more homely, local, and, for all that, more touching. When Alcestis's son laments that without her "the whole house is ruined," he is picturing primarily a house without a comforting maternal presence in it, no one to care for him and his sister. Later, when Admetus's true desolation is beginning to dawn on him more forcefully, the details that haunt him are his wife's empty bed, the chairs that she would sit in, the unwashed floors, and crying children. He cannot bear to see his wife's childhood friends. Admetus's grief is the grief of an ordinary man who cannot endure the absence of a specific person, who, though perhaps he did not fully realize it at the time, created the basis for his happiness and his very enjoyment of life.

Euripides does not mind contraposing the intensely poignant with the absurd. The play does not descend into farce but is pervasively tinted with mildly humorous and colloquial elements: Charon is characterized as a peevishly impatient ship's captain who does not want to wait for a tardy passenger; Heracles, in the speech of Admetus's servant, is represented according to his more humorous character type as a big drinker and maladroit symposiast. In conversation with the Chorus, he grumbles wearily and endearingly about his labors, the now all too predicable dangers to which he is exposed. Besides the low, sarcastic wrangling of Pheres and Admetus, we might also consider the confusing and oafishly clumsy version of a sophists' debate between Heracles and Admetus on the questions of death and life, being and nonbeing. Despite the evident incoherence and evasiveness of Admetus's responses, an untroubled Heracles goes off to enjoy wine and revelry without a worry. But later, when he learns of Alcestis's death, he is genuinely stupefied by the revelation. Even the strange story of a shepherd Apollo that introduces the play sets a different tone for the tragedy. Instead of a merciless, punitive, and terrifying tragic god, we have role-playing and an amusing fish-out-of-water scenario: The hyper-refined Apollo must play his lyre while tending a flock of sheep. Instead of announcing his intent to punish a hubristic mortal, he declares his sympathy and inclination to save him.

The play's pervasive theme is simply death. The occasionally gruff, colloquial manner of the Death character does not make him the less relentless and less fearsome. The characters' conversations and the Chorus's songs are full of references to Charon, Acheron, HADES, Death, and ORPHEUS. Orpheus, is a hero particularly relevant in the present context, as a figure who attempted (without success) to retrieve his dead wife from the underworld. The necessity of death and of accepting one's death even while appreciating life and the sunlight of the world above frequently affords the subject of aphorisms and choral interjections. This emphasis might seem strange or pointless, given that the central feature of the present myth is a miraculous instance of return from death—Heracles' retrieval of Alcestis. The deeper lesson for Admetus, however, is the acceptance of mortality. He gradually realizes the extent of his desolation, that his own life was not worth preserving at the expense of his wife's. The experience of having his wife taken away demonstrates this to Admetus: He has lost friends, enjoyment of life, and reputation—why does he remain alive? Previously, he was willing to sacrifice anyone or anything to remain alive, but now, in a telling reversal, he envies the dead and sees no purpose in his life. Admetus did not come to this realization immediately. Right after his wife's death, his son was the one who expressed his grief most directly and poignantly. Admetus was more guarded; later, as Alcestis's body is being carried out, he does not use her name but only calls her "the deceased," just as he would not tell Heracles honestly of her death but only of the death of a woman "outside the family." Tellingly, it is only just before Heracles restores Alcestis to him that Admetus achieves full, tragic awareness of his loss and his error in sacrificing her. He realizes that in condemning her to death, he has ended his own life for all intents and purposes, and thus has gained nothing.

Admetus must learn the importance of living a worthwhile life rather than merely living. This is an insight that other tragic heroes, such as Ajax, possess from the outset. Heroes, from Achilles onward, typically value a glorious and noble life over the mere preservation of life. Admetus is not such a hero but an ordinary man who must be driven by an extreme circumstance to glean this insight. Nor has he or Alcestis been saved from death: Rather,

Admetus now has another chance to face his death in a more satisfactory way. The miraculous return of Alcestis in the closing scene may seem like a gaudy theatrical effect, the surprise reappearance of a character thought dead with ample use of suspense and dramatic irony—a recognition scene of the familiar type. This crowd-pleasing theatricality, however, is a conscious effect knowingly employed by Euripides. Admetus has been made into the spectator of a drama in which his wife disappears and is then miraculously returned to him in a dramatic reversal of expectations. This mock bereavement gives him an opportunity to understand what the loss of his wife would really mean: He undergoes an experiment in death that leaves him wiser at its close. The members of Euripides' audience are perhaps similarly encouraged to contemplate the significance of mortality in their own case and to discern the serious message behind the play's apparently frivolous cheating of death.

Alcestis and Admetus   Daughter of Pelias. Wife of Admetus, king of Pherae in Thessaly. Alcestis is a central character of Euripides' *ALCESTIS*. Additional classical sources are Apollodorus's *LIBRARY* (1.9.14–15) and Hyginus's *Fabulae* (50, 51). Pelias decreed that only someone who could yoke together a lion and a boar would be an eligible suitor for Alcestis. At this time APOLLO was indentured to Admetus (in expiation of his killing of the CYCLOPES), and he helped Admetus to yoke together the lion and the boar and win the hand of Alcestis. Admetus neglected to offer a sacrifice to ARTEMIS for the marriage, and this oversight incurred her wrath. Admetus found his marriage chamber filled with serpents, which he interpreted as a portent of an early death. Apollo counseled Admetus to appease Artemis with a sacrifice and encouraged him to ask the FATES if someone else could die in his stead, but no one would agree to die in his place except Alcestis. After her death Alcestis was brought back from

HADES and reunited with Admetus. Alcestis was resurrected either by the grace of PERSEPHONE or by the virtue of HERACLES, who was said to have wrestled Hades (or Thanatos) for her.

Alcmaeon   See AMPHIARAUS.

Alcmene (Alcmena)   Mother of the famous Greek hero HERACLES. Daughter of King Electryon of Mycenae and wife of AMPHITRYON. Granddaughter of PERSEUS. Classical sources are Apollodorus's *LIBRARY* (2.4.8, 2.8.1ff), Hyginus's *Fabulae* (29), and Pausanias's *Description of Greece* (5.18.3). While Electryon was king of Mycenae, his sons became embroiled in a battle with the sons of Pterelaus and were slain. Electryon left Mycenae in the charge of Amphitryon while he pursued the sons of Pterelaus to avenge the deaths of his sons. Electryon also married Alcmene to Amphitryon. Before Electryon left on his quest, an errant club thrown by Amphitryon accidentally killed Electryon. Amphitryon fled with Alcmene to Thebes and then departed to avenge the death of Electryon's sons at the instigation of Alcmene, who refused to sleep with him until he did so. While Amphitryon was away avenging the murder of her brothers, Zeus, disguised as Amphitryon, visited Alcmene and persuaded her that he was her husband. According to Apollodorus and Hyginus, Zeus prolonged his time with her for several days. It was then that Alcmene became pregnant with Heracles. In some versions, on the following night, Amphitryon returned to Alcmene, and she conceived Iphicles, Heracles' twin brother, with him.

Zeus decreed that the child about to be born, a descendant of Perseus, would reign in Argos. Zeus was outwitted by HERA, however, who arranged to delay the birth of Heracles by seven days. Heracles' cousin EURYSTHEUS, son of Sthenelus, also a descendant of Perseus, was born first, and thus was entitled to the throne of Argos.

Following the death of Amphitryon, Alcmene married Rhadamanthys in Boeotia and, according to Pausanias's *Description of Greece*, she was buried and worshipped at Thebes.

Alcmene appears on an Attic red-figure stamnos vase painted by the Berlin Painter and dating from ca. 480 B.C.E. (Louvre, Paris). Here, Alcmene is flanked by Amphitryon and Athena. She draws Iphicles into the protection of her arms while the infant Heracles wrestles with the serpents sent by Hera to harm him.

Alcyone and Ceyx   Alcyone, daughter of AEOLUS and Enarete, was married to King Ceyx of Trachis. Classical sources are Apollodorus's *LIBRARY* (1.7.4), Hyginus's *Fabulae* (65), and Ovid's *METAMORPHOSES* (11.410–748). According to the *LIBRARY*, Alcyone and Ceyx were transformed into birds, the halcyon (kingfisher) and gannet (ceyx), respectively, for their impiety in comparing themselves to HERA and ZEUS. Ovid and Hyginus suggest a different version of the myth; here the gods were kindly disposed toward the married couple, and when Alcyone threw herself into the sea after Ceyx drowned in a shipwreck, they were both transformed into halcyons. In Ovid's *Metamorphoses*, Alcyone had a premonition of Ceyx's death in the shipwreck, and the text lingers on the couple's final farewells before Ceyx goes on his sea voyage and describes the storm and shipwreck in detail. Unaware of Ceyx's death at sea, Alcyone continued to pray at the altar of HERA for his safe return. Hera then persuaded Morpheus to appear to Alcyone in her sleep in the guise of Ceyx and reveal his death to her. A grief-stricken Alcyone found Ceyx's body floating on the sea at the place where she had last seen him. She then flung herself into the water and was transformed into the seabird. When she touched the body of her dead husband, he, too, was metamorphosed into a halcyon. According to Ovid, during the winter season halcyons build their nests on the sea for seven days, during which time the sea is peaceful, as Aeolus keeps the winds in check, and the

bird couple are able to nurture their young. This is the basis for the modern term *halcyon days*, meaning a time without storm or strife, a time of calm and peace.

Allecto   See FURIES.

Aloadae (Ephialtes and Otus)   The Aloadae were Ephialtes and Otus, giant twin sons of ALOEUS or of Iphimedia and POSEIDON. Classical sources are Apollodorus's *LIBRARY* (1.7.4), Homer's *ILIAD* (5.385), and Hyginus's *Fabulae* (28). Iphimedia loved Poseidon, and she bore him the handsome giant twins Ephialtes and Otus (according to Hyginus's *Fabulae* and Virgil's *Aeneid*, their father is ALOEUS). At the age of nine years the Aloadae were nine cubits broad and nine cubits high. In adulthood, Ephialtes and Otus resolved to overthrow the Olympian gods. They piled Mount Pelion on Mount Ossa upon Mount Olympus in an attempt to reach the heavens. Ephialtes and Otus succeeded in imprisoning ARES for 13 months in a brazen pot until, alerted by Eeriboea, stepmother of the Aloadae, HERMES rescued Ares. Ephialtes attempted to seduce HERA and Otus, ARTEMIS. According to Apollodorus's *Library*, Artemis transformed herself into a deer and placed herself between them so that Ephialtes and Otus accidentally killed each other while trying to hunt her. Hyginus's *Fabulae* gives an alternate version of the story; either APOLLO surprised the Aloadae in their attempt to scale the mountains to the heavens and killed them, or Artemis was raped by Otus and Apollo sent the deer in their midst, which provoked their deaths. Hyginus writes that the Aloadae were punished by the Olympian gods by being consigned to HADES, where they were bound together back-to-back by serpents to a column.

Alpheus and Arethusa   A river god, and son of OCEANUS and TETHYS, Alpheus loved Arethusa, a follower of ARTEMIS. Classical sources are Hesiod's THEOGONY (338), Lucian's *Dialogues of the Sea-Gods* (3), Ovid's METAMORPHOSES (5.572–642), Pausanias's *Description of Greece* (5.7.2), and Virgil's AENEID (3.694). The Alpheus is a large river in Elis, flowing from Arcadia and running through the Peloponnesus. According to Ovid, who provides the most detailed treatment, Arethusa was a nymph and disciple of Artemis. Returning from the hunt one day, Arethusa disrobed and bathed in the waters of the Alpheus. The river god Alpheus fell in love with her and began to speak to her, whereupon Arethusa fled in fright. Alpheus, taking human form, chased after her. Arethusa called to Artemis for help. The goddess created a cloud of mist around her, and Arethusa was transformed into a stream of water. Alpheus, taking on water form, leapt into the stream, but the earth opened and the stream progressed underground to emerge in a bay near Syracuse, Sicily, near the island of Ortygia, a location sacred to Artemis. Here, the waters of the Alpheus mingle with the spring of Arethusa. In another version of the myth, in Pausanias's *Description of Greece*, Alpheus began life as a mortal hunter who fell in love with Arethusa and chased her to Ortygia, where she turned into the spring; Alpheus, for love of Arethusa, was transformed into a river. The spring of Arethusa was, and still is, a symbol of Syracuse. It was believed that the spring maintained a connection, via a passage under the ocean, with the Apheus River in Greece. Strabo reports stories that a cup, thrown into the river at Olympia, leapt out of the fount of Arethusa, and that when oxen were sacrificed at Olympia, the waters of the fountain were discolored.

Amazons A race of female warriors. Classical sources are Apollodorus's LIBRARY (2.3.2, 2.5.9), Diodorus Siculus's LIBRARY OF HISTORY (2.45, 4.28.2), Herodotus's *Histories* (4.110ff), HOMER'S ILIAD (3.185–189, 6.186), and Pausanias's

Description of Greece (1.2.1, 1.41.7). The Amazons were said to have descended from ARES, god of war, and Harmonia. Their name *Amazon* was interpreted by the ancients to mean "breastless" and to refer to the practice of cutting off the right breast to facilitate use of a javelin. Cults and shrines dedicated to the Amazons appear in Greece and Asia Minor. Depending on the source, the Amazons established a colony in Thrace, or Scythia. Apollodorus places them in Themiscyra, on the Thermodon River in Boeotia.

The Amazons lived in isolation from men, mingling with foreign men only to reproduce, and raising only female offspring. In epic, they fight various heroes in several Amazonomachies. HERACLES' Ninth Labor, which required him to bring back the girdle of the Amazonian queen Hippolyte (given to her by Ares) provoked an Amazonomachy. According to Apollodorus, Hippolyte had been inclined to present the girdle to Heracles, but HERA, taking the form of Hippolyte, roused the Amazons to war. Hippolyte was killed in the ensuing chaos. THESEUS joined Heracles in the Amazonomachy and abducted the Amazon Antiope (or Melanippe), who later gave him a son, HIPPOLYTUS. The Amazons retaliated by attempting to storm Athens and were defeated by Theseus and the Athenians. In another Amazonomachy, the Amazons were defeated by the hero BELLEROPHON.

During the Trojan War, the Amazons fought on the side of Troy against the Athenians and Greeks. The Amazonian army joined forces with King PRIAM in return for his offer to purify the Amazonian queen PENTHESILEA of blood-guilt for her accidental killing of her sister Hippolyte (or Glauce or Melanippe). Penthesilea, a daughter of Ares, was killed in the Trojan War by ACHILLES.

The Amazonomachy was a popular theme in art of the classical period, particularly in the Amazons' combat against Heracles and Theseus. An Attic black-figure amphora excavated at Tarquinia from ca. 525 B.C.E. (University

Museum, University of Pennsylvania) shows two Amazons struggling against Heracles. Achilles' killing of Penthesilea is represented on an Attic black-figure amphora painted by Exekias and dating from ca. 530 B.C.E. (British Museum, London).

Amores OVID (ca. 16 B.C.E.) The dating of Ovid's *Amores* is highly uncertain. Work on the *Amores* probably commenced around 25 B.C.E., but the extant edition of three books was not published until 16 B.C.E. or later. In a verse preface to the entire work, Ovid presents his three books as a second edition, reduced in length from the original five-book collection. The *Amores* represent Ovid's foray into love elegy, a genre fashionable in the Augustan period. The basic premise of love elegy is the poet's obsessive pursuit of his mistress *(domina);* love is an incurable illness that undermines the poet's virility. Traditionally, the poet designates his elegiac mistress by a pseudonym. Ovid names Corinna as his mistress in the fifth poem of his first collection, although he already appears to be in love and suffering from love's symptoms. It is not always clear whether Ovid is writing about Corinna, or simply a generic *puella* ("girl-friend"). He does not assume the persona of a lover chronically obsessed with a single woman.

While Ovid's predecessors largely maintain the fiction of an emotionally demanding love affair, Ovid unapologetically presents elegiac love as a set of generic conventions. In *Amores* 1.1., Ovid claims to have been beginning the composition of an epic poem, when Cupid (EROS) stole a metrical foot, converting hexameter poetry (the meter of epic) into the elegiac couplet (one hexameter line followed by a pentameter line, the meter of love elegy). For Ovid, literary conventions shape the lover's behavior and personality, not the other way around. Like other elegists, Ovid employs mythological exempla (examples, comparisons), yet his examples sometimes subvert the nominal message. In

Amores 1.3, for example, the Ovidian lover addresses an unnamed woman and insists that he is faithful and monogamous, not a "circus-rider" of love who jumps from horse to horse. Yet the mythological exempla employed near the elegy's end to prove poetry's capacity to immortalize women include LEDA, Io, and EUROPA—all women seduced by the notoriously philandering Jupiter (see ZEUS). Here as elsewhere, Ovidian love is a game premised on multiple layers of deception. Ovid's manipulation of genre, convention, and literary persona in this early work lays the foundations for his later, more ambitious engagement with elegiac subject matter in the ARS AMATORIA.

Amphiaraus A seer at Argos, Amphiaraus participated in the expedition of the Seven against Thebes. Classical sources are Aeschylus's SEVEN AGAINST THEBES (568ff), Apollodorus's LIBRARY (3.6.3), Hyginus's *Fabulae* (73), Pausanias's *Description of Greece* (5.17.7, 9.41.2), and Statius's THEBAID. The famous seer Melampus was Amphiaraus's ancestor. Amphiaraus fought with his cousin ADRASTUS but was later reconciled with him and married Adrastus's sister Eriphyle, who was empowered to resolve any disputes between them. Adrastus and POLYNICES wanted Amphiaraus to join the expedition against Thebes, but Amphiaraus, who had foreseen its failure, refused. Polynices bribed Eriphyle with the necklace of HARMONIA to induce Amphiaraus to join them. The war ended in failure, and Amphiaraus was killed, but not before asking his son Alcmaeon to avenge him by killing Eriphyle. Alcmaeon's murder of his mother aroused the vengeful FURIES. In other stories, Amphiaraus was swallowed by a cleft in the earth and descended to the underworld, still living in his chariot: Statius's *Thebaid* presents a vivid and dramatic version of this latter story. Aeschylus's *Seven against Thebes* characterizes Amphiaraus as a good and honorable man, unlike his hubristic fellow warriors.

Amphion and Zethus Twin sons of ANTIOPE and ZEUS. Classical sources include Apollodorus's *LIBRARY* (3.5.5–6), Homer's *ODYSSEY* (11.260–265), Hyginus's *Fabulae* (7, 8, 9), and Philostratus's *IMAGINES* (1.10).

The origins of Amphion and Zethus are as follows. According to Ovid, Zeus transformed himself into a satyr to seduce Antiope. Pregnant with his child and fearing the wrath of her father, Nycteus, Antiope fled to Sicyon, where she married Epopeus. Antiope's disgrace caused Nycteus to commit suicide, but his brother Lycus pursued and captured Antiope, killing Epopeus as well. Lycus brought Antiope back from Sicyon, and during that journey she gave birth to Amphion and Zethus in a cave. He forced her to abandon the children, but a herdsman found and raised them. Antiope was imprisoned by Lycus and maltreated by his wife, Dirce, a nymph of a spring sacred to DIONYSUS. After many years, she was reunited with her sons, either because she managed to escape or because Amphion and Zethus rescued her. The brothers punished Lycus and Dirce for their treatment of their mother—Dirce, memorably, by yoking her to a bull that killed her, and Lycus, either by killing him or by forcing him to give up his throne to Amphion.

Homer recounts that Amphion and Zethus built the fortifications of Thebes, Zethus using his great strength and Amphion the magical music of his lyre to move the foundation stones. Philostratus's *Imagines* (1.10) evokes a scene in which Amphion sings and plays his lyre, a gift from HERMES, while the stones, moved by his music, assemble themselves into the foundation walls of Thebes. Amphion married NIOBE, whose overweening pride in her children offended APOLLO and ARTEMIS and brought about their deaths.

Amphion was associated with music and Zethus with agriculture and the hunt; their attributes were, respectively, the lyre and the hunting dog. In visual representation, they appear together as young male nudes. An imperial Roman copy of a Greek original sculptural group from ca. first century B.C.E. shows Amphion and Zethus in the act of yoking Dirce to a bull (National Archeological Museum, Naples). The same theme appears in a ca. first-century B.C.E. wall painting from the House of the Vettii, Pompeii.

Amphitrite A NEREID (sea nymph). Daughter of Doris and NEREUS (or OCEANUS and TETHYS). The wife of POSEIDON, Olympian god of the sea. Classical sources are Apollodorus's *LIBRARY* (1.2.7, 1.4.5), Hesiod's *THEOGONY* (243, 254, 930), Homer's *ODYSSEY* (5.422, 12.60), and Pausanias's *Description of Greece* (1.17.3). Amphitrite is mentioned only briefly in texts and has no myths specific to her. In Apollodorus's *Library*, Amphitrite is not a Nereid but an OCEANID, born of the TITANS Oceanus and Tethys. Hesiod's *Theogony* describes Amphitrite as fair-ankled and gives her the ability to calm the waves of the sea. By Poseidon, Amphitrite conceived Rhodos and TRITON. In Pausanias's *Description of Greece*, THESEUS dived to the bottom of the sea and was given a golden crown by Amphitrite. In Homer's *Odyssey*, Amphitrite represents the sea's more threatening capacity; she breeds sea monsters, and her great waves crash against the rocks, imperiling sailors.

In visual representations of the classical period, Amphitrite often appears with Poseidon and other maritime creatures. She and Poseidon mount a chariot drawn by horses in the Attic black-figure François Vase from ca. 570 B.C.E. (Museo Archeologico Nazionale, Florence). Amphitrite appears with Theseus in the Attic red-figure *Euphronios* cup from ca. 500 B.C.E. (Louvre, Paris), offering the hero a wreath. In the postclassical period, Amphitrite often appears in the retinue of Poseidon. Amphitrite's identity is sometimes confused with the sea nymph GALATEA and the goddess APHRODITE and associated with similar iconographic elements—shells, dolphins, mermen, sea nymphs, and other creatures of the sea.

Amphitryon Stepfather (sometimes father) of the Greek hero HERACLES. Son of King Alcaeus of Tiryns. Husband of ALCMENE (a descendant of PERSEUS). Classical sources are Apollodorus's LIBRARY (2.4.5–11), Diodorus Siculus's LIBRARY OF HISTORY (3.67.2), and Hyginus's *Fabulae* (29). King Electryon of Mycenae, father of Alcmene, left Amphitryon in charge of Mycenae so that he could pursue the Teleboans and avenge the deaths of his sons. But Electryon was killed accidentally by a club thrown by Amphitryon. Amphitryon accepted responsibility for avenging the death of Electryon's sons, but Sthenelus, Electryon's brother, banished him and Alcmene from Mycenae. He fled with Alcmene to Thebes, where he was purified by CREON.

To persuade Creon of Thebes to accompany him on his pursuit of the Teleboans, Amphitryon promised to kill a fox that was ravaging Cadmea. He borrowed a magical hound from Cephalus. This hound never failed to catch its prey and had been given to Cephalus by his wife PROCRIS, who had originally received it as a present from ARTEMIS. ZEUS intervened by turning both fox and hound to stone. In company with Cephalus and Creon, Amphitryon then continued on his quest for vengeance. At Taphos, Amphitryon discovered that King Pterelaus of the Teleboans had golden hair that made him invulnerable. Pterelaus's daughter Comaetho fell in love with Amphitryon and for his sake pulled out her father's hair, thus enabling Amphitryon to kill him and to conquer the city. Amphitryon later killed Comaetho. Her betrayal of father and city recalls those of ARIADNE on behalf of THESEUS, SCYLLA for MINOS, and MEDEA for JASON: In each instance, the man on whose behalf the heroine commits her betrayal proves ungrateful.

While Amphitryon was carrying out his revenge, his wife, Alcmene, was visited by Zeus. Zeus took on Amphitryon's appearance and described the victory over Pterelaus's sons in such convincing detail to Alcmene that she accepted him as her husband. That night she conceived Heracles by Zeus, but the next evening Amphitryon returned and, in some versions, became pregnant by him too. As a result, Alcmene bore twin sons: Heracles, whose father was Zeus, and Iphicles, whose father was Amphitryon.

Amphitryon and Heracles fought on the same side in a war against the Minyans, during which Amphitryon died in battle. Pausanias's *Description of Greece* places his grave at Thebes.

Amphitryon appears on an Attic red-figure stamnos vase painted by the Berlin Painter and dating from ca. 480 B.C.E. (Louvre, Paris). Here, he stands next to Alcmene as she draws Iphicles into the protection of her arms, while the infant Heracles wrestles with the serpents sent by Hera to harm him.

Anaxarete See IPHIS.

Anchises Son of Capys and Themiste. A consort of APHRODITE, on whom he fathered AENEAS. Classical sources are the *Homeric Hymn to Aphrodite*, Homer's ILIAD (5.260–272, 20.230–240), Pausanias's *Description of Greece* (8.12.8–9), and Virgil's AENEID (2.634–804; 3.707–715; 6.106–117, 679–899). In the *Homeric Hymn to Aphrodite*, ZEUS, annoyed that she had led him into so many intrigues, persuaded EROS to shoot Aphrodite with an arrow to cause her to fall in love with Anchises, whom she saw herding sheep on Mount Ida. She seduced him without at first revealing her identity. Afterward she revealed her divinity to him, predicted the birth of his son, Aeneas, and made him promise never to reveal their relations. He, however, became indiscreet after drinking too much wine. Zeus struck him with a thunderbolt as punishment, and he was left lame. He was rescued from the burning of Troy by his son and accompanied him on the first part of his travels, giving advice and interpreting omens (on one occasion, erroneously). He never reached Rome, but died in Sicily. Aeneas buries him with great honor in the Homeric funeral episode in Book 5 of the *Aeneid*, and, in Book 6, Anchises guides his son through HADES. It is fitting that Aeneas's father should present to him the parade of great men and heroes, who, for Romans of Virgil's time, represented the revered ancestors of the Roman people.

Anchises's myth became very important in the Roman period. As forebear of the Roman race through his son Aeneas, he gave the Romans the right to claim descent from Venus, just as Romulus, the son of Mars (see ARES) and founder of Rome, gave them the right to claim descent from Mars. The Romans could thus claim descent from two divine founders, the goddess of love and the god of war. Julius Caesar further enriched the connection by claiming descent from the line of Aeneas and his son, Iulus. This made the Julian family descendants both of the founder of Rome and of a goddess. Finally, with Augustus, the adopted son of the deified Julius Caesar, as first emperor, the origins-story became enshrined among the central patriotic myths of the Roman state. Of particular importance is the *pietas* ("dutifulness") demonstrated by Aeneas toward his father: The Romans of the Augustan era frequently depicted the pious Aeneas carrying his aged father on his shoulders away from the burning ruins of Troy while leading Ascanius by the hand.

Andromache   A Trojan princess. Daughter of Etion and wife of HECTOR. Classical sources are Euripides' ANDROMACHE and TROJAN WOMEN, Homer's ILIAD (6.390–502, 24.723–745), and Virgil's AENEID (3.294–348). Andromache's father and brothers were killed during the Trojan War. Her farewell to Hector as he departs for battle against the Greeks is the subject of Book 6 of Homer's *Iliad*. ASTYANAX, son of Andromache and Hector, is murdered during the fall of Troy, and Andromache her-

self is taken as a spoil of war by NEOPTOLEMUS (the son of ACHILLES), who later marries her and fathers children on her. After his death, she marries PRIAM's son Helenus and with him constructs a miniature Troy in Epirus, where she continues faithfully to make offerings to Hector at his cenotaph. Andromache was famous for her virtue and fidelity, and her character was often used to represent the sufferings of Trojan women during war. Early visual representations of Andromache center on her farewell to Hector and her grief over the deaths of Astyanax and Hector. A postclassical example is Jean-Louis David's *Andromache Mourning Hector* of 1783 (Louvre, Paris).

Andromache   EURIPIDES (ca. 430 B.C.E.)   Euripides' *Andromache* was produced between 430 and 424 B.C.E., most likely in 426. His play, often criticized for fragmentation and lack of lucid structure, might equally be appreciated for the subtle interconnections among its different plot segments and characters. ANDROMACHE, the title character, unwillingly bore a son to her captor, NEOPTOLEMUS, son of ACHILLES, who apparently prefers her to his own wife, HERMIONE, with whom he has no offspring. ORESTES, in the meanwhile, seeks to abduct Hermione for himself and plots to have Neoptolemus killed. PELEUS, the father of Achilles and grandfather of Neoptolemus, mourns his dead grandson and calls on his wife, the goddess THETIS, for aid. Thematic concerns that potentially unify these diverse strands of plot include marriage and the potentially destructive outcome of marriages, the devastating effects of war and military subjugation on human relations, and the ignoble character of Spartans (MENELAUS, HELEN, Hermione) by contrast with the good character of Phthians (Achilles, Peleus, Neoptolemus) and Trojans (Andromache). The closing epiphany of Thetis offers a measure of consolation for the weak victims and survivors, such as Peleus and Andromache, who have seen their world destroyed by the ambitions of the powerful and unscrupulous.

SYNOPSIS

The scene is set in Thessaly at Phthia, before the shrine of Thetis. Andromache, Hector's widow, was given to Achilles' son Neoptolemus after the fall of Troy, and she bore him a son. Neoptolemus then married Hermione, daughter of Menelaus and Helen. Hermione began to persecute and threaten Andromache, claiming that Andromache used drugs on Neoptolemus to render them unable to conceive a child. Now Andromache has taken refuge at Thetis's shrine, in fear for her own life and that of her son, whom she has hidden in a secret place. Neoptolemus is not there to protect her and his son—he had insulted APOLLO after the god caused his father's death, and now he is at Delphi, trying to make amends. Hermione enters and rebukes Andromache harshly for ruining her marriage. Andromache replies that it is Hermione's unpleasant character, not drugs, that makes Neoptolemus despise her. After a bitter exchange, Hermione exits. The Chorus of Phthian women sings of the Judgment of PARIS and the destruction it caused. Menelaus enters with Andromache's son, announcing that he has found him. He threatens to kill the boy if Andromache does not leave the safety of the shrine; she thus will have to sacrifice her life to save her son. At length, after exchanging insults, Andromache agrees to be led away and comes forth, only to discover that Menelaus intends to let his daughter decide whether or not the boy dies. Andromache excoriates his treacherous Spartan character before leaving with Menelaus and her child.

After the choral ode, Andromache and her son, their hands bound, return onstage with Menelaus. They are being led to their doom, when Peleus, Achilles' father, enters. Peleus and Menelaus exchange long, insulting speeches, until, at length, Menelaus gives way and withdraws but promises that he will return. Andromache thanks Peleus and exits with her son. Hermione's nurse enters and reports that Hermione is desperate and suicidal: Her father has abandoned her, and she fears her husband's anger when he returns. The nurse attempts to console her. Orestes enters, as if by chance, on his way to the oracle at Dodona. After inquiring about Hermione's situation, he reveals that he long resented that Menelaus gave Hermione to Neoptolemus after he had first promised her to him. Orestes had then asked Neoptolemus to relinquish his rights, but Neoptolemus referred insultingly to Orestes' murder of his mother, CLYTAEMNESTRA. He now takes advantage of the present crisis by offering to restore her to her father, presumably with the intention of marrying her himself. She defers the question of marriage to her father but agrees to leave with him. Orestes darkly hints that Neoptolemus's insulting comment will be punished at Delphi. They exit.

After the choral ode, Peleus enters and learns that Hermione has left with Orestes, and that Orestes intends to have Neoptolemus murdered. Before he has time to take steps to save his grandson, a messenger enters and reports that, with the god's support, a gang of Delphians killed Neoptolemus. The body is brought in, and Peleus laments his grandson's death. Thetis appears: She bids them take Neoptolemus's body back to Delphi for burial. She predicts that Andromache will marry HELENUS in Molossia, and that thus the descendants of Troy and Phthia will rule Molossia. She promises that Peleus will, in time, become a god and that they will live together once again. All exit.

COMMENTARY

Andromache has frequently been criticized as an incoherent, rambling play without a dramatic or thematic core. The opening section deals with the love triangle involving Neoptolemus, Hermione, and Andromache. Neoptolemus is absent; the drama is played out first between Hermione and Andromache, then between Menelaus and Andromache, and, finally, between Peleus and Menelaus. At that point, not quite 800 lines into the play, Andromache makes her final exit, after thanking

Peleus for protecting her from Menelaus. The title character has simply left the stage. The second significant sequence, and second "love triangle," involve Orestes, Hermione, and the still absent Neoptolemus. At the end of their conversation, at about line 1,000, Orestes and Hermione make their final exit. The third and final part of the play belongs to Peleus, who first learns of the tragic death of his grandson Neoptolemus, then is consoled by the epiphany of his wife, Thetis. The three phases of action are subtly and intricately interconnected yet retain a degree of independence. There is no unbroken arc of tragic downfall, as in some tragedies, whereby a single protagonist moves inexorably toward his or her doom. The central, heroic death of the tragedy is that of Neoptolemus, who never appears on stage.

More recent interpretations have attempted to discern threads of thematic unity pervading the play, and/or have revived the play's reputation by positing, on Euripides' part, a masterful manipulation of tragic structure and conventions. On this reading, Euripides plays with his audience's expectations of dramatic coherence, interweaving a complex plot that always threatens to lapse, but never quite lapses, into incoherence: He creates a subtle tension between fragmentation and unity, challenging us to ponder the connections and the larger significance. There is more potential and probably more justification in this line of interpretation than in the older view that Euripides simply lost control of his plot, or was unable to create a more integrated plot. It still remains to be decided, however, what theme or themes in particular unify the playwright's bold experiment in plot structure and to what extent the play succeeds.

As in so many of Euripides' tragedies, the action of *Andromache* takes place in the post–Trojan War period. The heroes of this period inhabit a world morally devastated and gutted by the war nearly to the same extent that Troy itself was physically devastated. Many of the truly great and admirable heroes, such as

Achilles, are dead; Achilles' son remains significantly absent and will himself be dead by the end of the play. Peleus represents a more old-fashioned style of virtue and integrity, but he is old and weak: He manages to scare off the blustering, cowardly Menelaus, but just barely, and the Chorus sings of his deeds of old in battle with CENTAURS on the *Argo* and with HERACLES at Troy. Other choral odes are concerned with the Judgment of Paris and its catastrophic outcomes. The war looms large in the background, and the present situation is almost entirely determined by it. Menelaus gave Hermione to Neoptolemus instead of Orestes to recruit him as a warrior at Troy; Orestes' hands have been stained with blood in the aftermath of AGAMEMNON's return from Troy; Andromache's entire situation is determined by her status as a prisoner of war. Peleus's case is perhaps the most poignant: He is the father of the Greeks' greatest warrior, Achilles, who perished through Apollo's agency; now his grandson, Neoptolemus, dies at the hands of the same god at Delphi.

The present play allows us to see how relations of power and hegemony play out in the domestic and sexual spheres. Hermione takes her place alongside Clytaemnestra as a Greek wife who becomes homicidally jealous of a Trojan captive. In Euripides' consciously subheroic and ignoble milieu, she fails in her project—indeed, fails miserably. Aeschylus's Clytaemnestra displayed a disdainful hauteur in the face of CASSANDRA and had her pitilessly murdered. Hermione does not hesitate to lower herself to exchanging low, degrading insults with her slave rival. Like other Euripidean heroines, she is obsessed with sex and, specifically, with exclusive sexual possession of her husband. She accuses Andromache of using drugs to make her unattractive to her husband, which makes her vulnerable to Andromache's triumphant sneer: It is not drugs, but Hermione's unattractive personality, that drives Neoptolemus from her bed. This motif allows Andromache to dwell in detail on a savage portrayal of Hermione's Spartan snobbery and her misplaced idolization of her father, Menelaus; nor does she miss the opportunity to allude to Helen's questionable virtue. The most provocative point scored by Andromache, however, is her frank reference to HECTOR's extramarital affairs, and how she served as wet nurse to his bastard children: Is Hermione too self-centered to do the same for Neoptolemus? Andromache's ferocious, and ferociously competitive, criticism of Hermione's wifely comportment has the added outcome of portraying Homer's morally flawless hero Hector in a markedly subheroic light.

Ironies abound: Andromache is a slave, but the slave clearly is victorious over the legitimate Greek wife when it comes to Neoptolemus's bed. The slave, moreover, has no scruples about picking apart her mistress's character. Neoptolemus himself married into the family of Menelaus, victorious coleader of the Greek expedition against Troy, yet appears to have fallen in love with one of the defeated Trojan captives. Relations of military/political domination do not align with domestic/sexual desire and are notably subverted by the crosscurrents of sexual rivalry. Heroic valor of an Homeric cast, moreover, does not make the transition to the post–Trojan War world of intrigue, secret resentment, and deceit. Orestes, instead of facing Neoptolemus in a heroic duel, arranges to have him ambushed at Delphi, while running off with his wife. Neoptolemus for a moment looks as if he will be able to defend himself against the pack of treacherous Delphians who surround him, as if his heroic virtue will result in a display of traditional, Homeric excellence in battle; yet in the end, the subheroic mob overcomes him and mangles his body grotesquely after he has fallen.

Orestes himself is hardly the morally tortured and ultimately vindicated figure of Aeschylus's *Oresteia*: He is "Clytaemnestra's son," murderous, treacherous, an adulterer motivated to crime by petty resentment and lust. He waylays Hermione as if meeting her by chance; it turns out, however, that he has carefully calculated the moment of his arrival: Neoptolemus is away, and his wife is vulnerable and in need of a protector. Orestes is somewhere between a rescuer and an abductor: Women could not easily or safely travel alone in the ancient world, and Menelaus ignobly abandoned his daughter. Hermione has little choice but to go with the opportunist Orestes. Nor does he present himself even nominally as a devoted suitor: He is openly motivated by hatred of Neoptolemus and, in any case, cannot find anyone to marry him, given his well-known status as matricide. Hermione, for her part, is now fulfilling her mother's role as abducted wife of a Greek hero. Menelaus, never the bravest of the Greek heroes, is here utterly weak and unimpressive. He exchanges bitter taunts with Peleus, only to crumble completely and depart, leaving his own daughter unprotected and vulnerable to retribution. Neoptolemus's reputation is relatively untarnished but, significantly, he is absent: The inheritor of the honest warrior ethos of his father, Achilles, he is constantly expected, and his arrival is constantly deferred, until, finally, he is brought onstage as a corpse. It would be difficult to make a stronger statement of the demise of the Greek heroic spirit of the Trojan War: Its last, great representative—heir of Achilles, sacker of Troy, a hero whose name means "New War"—has been killed by ambush and the deceit of a conniving matricide who did not fight in the war.

Marriage and the destructiveness it causes constitute a major theme of the play: Neoptolemus's marriage to Hermione dooms him; Helen's marriage and subsequent abduction, as Euripides frequently reminds us, was the cause of the war; and, before either of these, the marriage of Peleus and Thetis was the beginning of the strife *(eris)* among the three goddesses. Euripides often connects desire, sexual possession, and violence, and this play is no exception, although the outcomes are notably oblique. The murder takes place some distance away, at Delphi, and Menelaus and Hermione fail in their self-assigned task as Euripidean domestic murderers. We might expect the sexual rival and her offspring to be killed. Yet Hermione cannot rise to the level of a MEDEA, HECUBA, or even a PHAEDRA, and, rather than taking on a masculine role in a masterful act of vengeance, she continually takes shelter behind a man. As in her mother's case, however, the question of Hermione's marriage results in violence between men. Contracting a bad marriage is the ultimate cause of Neoptolemus's end, as Peleus querulously observes.

The play's resolution through the intervention of Thetis as dea ex machina thus logically involves a realignment of marriages in a more positive way. Andromache will be married to the Trojan seer Helenus in Molossia, and Neoptolemus and Andromache's son, Molossus, will be the founder of the race: Thus Peleus's Phthian race, and the Trojan race, will live on in Molossia. Marriage expands in significance to encompass the founding of communities: Whereas up to this point, the noble lines of the Greek and Trojan heroes appeared on the verge of extinction in a subheroic world, in part because of the destructive consequences of marriages, the ending suggests new hope for continuation. On the divine level, Peleus will be made immortal and will return to his divine consort, from whom he appears to have been separated for some time. Peleus and Thetis are at the origin of the Trojan War in many ways, as the Roman poet Catullus will later perceive. Their wedding saw the introduction of Strife, and they were the parents of the great hero of the war, Achilles. Now Peleus and Thetis, according to Thetis's speech, will see their son Achilles again on an island that his ghost was supposed to haunt; Neoptolemus will be properly buried at Delphi, the shrine of his own and his father's divine nemesis; and Peleus will return to his wife's embrace. The Trojan War is being put to rights, buried, and its dead heroes assigned their proper *kleos* ("fame"); a cycle in history is ending. Peleus, in his closing

words, cannot help observing the value of good matches in marriage and the destructiveness of bad matches, no matter the dowry. This comment carries a not too oblique criticism of Neoptolemus's match with Hermione and confirms the excellence of his own with Thetis.

The dating of the play—usually set between 430 and 424 B.C.E.—falls within the broader period of the Peloponnesian War, but if the date of *Andromache* is specifically 426 B.C.E., as some scholars think, the massacre of Plataean prisoners in 427 B.C.E. would explain the play's fiercely anti-Spartan sentiments. In any case, it seems reasonable to assume that the play belongs roughly to the mid-420's B.C.E. (By the time the *Helen* was produced in 412 B.C.E., after the failure of the Sicilian expedition, the bias tilts in Sparta's favor and away from the illusory gains of a large-scale war of conquest: Helen of Sparta is herself significantly reevaluated in a kind of tragic palinode, or recantation.) Spartan characters in the play are consistently presented as dissemblers, cowards, hypocrites, and shallow materialists: Hermione comes onstage boasting of her father's wealth, while Menelaus, who accuses Peleus of being "all talk," is in fact himself capable of little more than empty vaunting. The divide between Phthia, Achilles' homeland, and Sparta, is significant: Achilles and Neoptolemus were the hard-fighting soldiers who won the war, and Achilles died on the fields of Troy; the Spartan Menelaus, by contrast, both survives and profits. The war was waged to retrieve his wife, and though as warrior he was far inferior to Achilles, he benefited from its success through the acquisition of plunder and the recovery of his wife. The splintering of a Panhellenic expedition into resentment, recrimination, and conflict in the postvictory period not accidentally recalls the intensifying conflict between Athens and Sparta after the Persian Wars in which they fought as allies.

What does all this amount to? In the end, Euripides' challengingly fragmented play is difficult to characterize by any one theme or statement. Yet it is still possible to discern broader patterns that are coherent with his other plays and suggestive of the playwright's deeper preoccupations. As elsewhere, Euripides represents a subheroic world of petty, twisted motivations and ignoble actions, where hypocritical villains vaunt their power over characters of greater integrity and inferior strength. He removes revered heroes of mythology from their pedestal and represents a world in crisis. The play culminates with the disturbing description of a treacherous killing supported by the god Apollo in his very shrine. Yet even as Euripides undermines our sense of the gods' justice, he (at least partially) recovers it with a divine epiphany, as in so many other instances. We are left stranded between the all too realistic presentation of a degraded world presided over by unjust, or possibly nonexistent, gods and an extraordinary intrusion of divine presence at the end that averts a total sense of purposelessness. Which do we believe more, the epiphany or the moral chaos that preceded it? Finally, the *Andromache* resembles Euripides' other plays in its persistent concern with speech (Logos), and the manifold, often dishonest, and malevolent uses of the spoken word. His characters talk each other alternately into rage and submission. Gods, like Thetis, speak in a very different way, without pettiness or subterfuge, with directness, placidity, and clarity—yet another way in which the gods so clearly do not belong to our world.

Andromeda Daughter of King Cepheus and Queen Cassiopeia of Ethiopia. Wife of the hero Perseus and ancestor of Heracles. Classical sources are Apollodorus's Library (2.4.3), Hyginus's *Fabulae* (64), Lucian's *Dialogues of the Sea-Gods* (14), Ovid's Metamorphoses (4.663–5.249), and Philostratus's Imagines (1.29). Andromeda's mother, Cassiopeia, insulted the Nereids, daughters of Poseidon, by claiming that she (or her daughter) were superior to

Perseus and Andromeda. *Piero di Cosimo (attrib.), ca. 1510 (Galleria degli Uffizi, Florence)*

them in beauty. In punishment, Poseidon sent a sea monster to destroy the land. Cepheus was informed by an oracle that only the sacrifice of his daughter would appease the monster. Perseus, who had recently procured the head of the Gorgon MEDUSA, saw Andromeda bound to a rock awaiting death. He fell in love with her and, having gained the consent of her father to marry her, rescued her, slaying the sea monster either by sword or using the Gorgon's head. Cepheus's brother Phineus, who had been promised Andromeda's hand in marriage, attacked Perseus to recover Andromeda, but Perseus defeated Phineus and his allies using the severed head of Medusa to turn them to stone.

Eventually, Perseus and Andromeda traveled from Argos to Tiryns, where they remained and Perseus became king. Their children were Alcaeus, Electryon, Heleius, Mestor, Sthenelus, Gorgophone, and Perses, an ancestor of the Persian kings.

The rescue of Andromeda by Perseus from Poseidon's sea monster was a popular theme in classical art. An example is an Apulian red-figure krater attributed to the Sisyphus Group from ca. 430 B.C.E. (J. Paul Getty Museum, Malibu). It shows Perseus asking for Andromeda's hand in marriage while Andromeda is chained nearby. A Roman fresco from Pompeii of the first century C.E. also depicts the myth. Andromeda is sometimes shown still bound with chains to the rock or at the moment in which Perseus takes her arm to deliver her from her fate. A sea creature representing the monster is also often present. A postclassical painting of the myth is Piero di Cosimo's *Perseus and Andromeda* of ca. 1510 (Galleria degli Uffizi, Florence).

Anemoi (Venti) The winds. The progeny of Eos (Aurora) and Astraeus or, according to some accounts, TYPHOEUS. Classical sources are Hesiod's *THEOGONY* (378, 869) Homer's *ODYSSEY* (5.291), and Ovid's *METAMORPHOSES* (1.56–67). The Anemoi are storm winds associated with the four cardinal points: BOREAS, the North Wind; NOTUS, the South Wind; ZEPHYRUS, the West Wind; and EURUS, the East Wind. Hesiod and Homer also mention four lesser winds. At times, the winds were represented as men, sometimes winged. For Homer, Ovid, and Virgil, the winds were subject to AEOLUS's control.

Antigone Daughter of OEDIPUS and Jocasta, sister of POLYNICES, ETEOCLES, and Ismene. Antigone appears as a character in Sophocles' *ANTIGONE* and *OEDIPUS AT COLONUS* and Euripides' *PHOENICIAN WOMEN*. Other classical sources include Apollodorus's *LIBRARY* (3.5.9, 3.7.1), Hyginus's *Fabulae* (72), and Pausanias's *Description of Greece* (9.25.2). In Sophocles' well-known version of Antigone's story, Oedipus has already gone into exile and met his death, and Oedipus's sons Polynices and Eteocles have killed each other in a civil war over control of Thebes. Creon, ruler of Thebes, decrees that no one may offer burial to Polynices, whom he defines as a traitor, whereas Eteocles defended the city and deserves full honors. Antigone, however, considers it sacrilegious not to offer burial rites to dead kin, a violation of the laws of the "gods below." In defiance of the decree, Antigone casts some dirt on her brother's corpse as a rite of burial. Creon condemns her to be entombed alive in a cave. Creon's son Haemon, to whom she was betrothed, finds that Antigone has hanged herself in the cave; he then kills himself with his sword. Creon's wife, Eurydice, commits suicide. Antigone, by her death, ends up destroying her adversary Creon's household. In the *Oedipus at Colonus*, Antigone accompanies her aged blind father into exile. In her extreme stubbornness and doomed existence, she resembles her father. The extant ending of Aeschylus's *SEVEN AGAINST THEBES* shows Antigone in defiance of the edict forbidding Polynices's burial, but this ending is probably a later addition to the play's script, influenced by the popularity of Sophocles' *Antigone*. Euripides also wrote a (lost) *Antigone*, and in his *Phoenician Women* has Antigone attempt unsuccessfully to persuade Eteocles and Polynices not to fight each other. Hyginus presents a variant version in which Polynices's wife, Argia, helps Antigone carry Polynices's body onto Eteocles' pyre, and in which Haemon, to whom Creon entrusts Antigone's execution, instead deposits her with shepherds. Antigone then becomes pregnant with Haemon's son. Creon later recognizes the son by a special birthmark as a Theban when the young man comes to Thebes for a competition. Haemon, despite an attempt by Heracles to intercede on his behalf, is condemned to death by Creon and kills himself and Antigone. In Apollodorus (3.5.8), however, Haemon is killed by the sphinx and thus is already dead by the time Antigone defies Creon's decree.

Antigone Sophocles (441 B.C.E.) An ancient introduction to the *Antigone* states that Sophocles owed to the popularity of his play his election as one of the generals for the campaign against Samos of 441 B.C.E. This statement has been conventionally accepted as a basis for dating the *Antigone* to ca. 441 B.C.E., although the evidence is far from secure. The *Antigone* is one of three extant plays by Sophocles devoted to the misfortunes of the Theban royal house. These plays—*Oedipus the King*, *Antigone*, and *Oedipus at Colonus*—make up what is often termed Sophocles' Theban cycle, but it is important to recall that they did not form part of a connected trilogy and were written and produced separately on different occasions. In the present play, Oedipus's sons Polynices and Eteocles, doomed by their father's curse, have both perished in mutual slaughter on the field of battle. Creon, ruler of Thebes, has decreed that no one may offer burial to Polynices on pain of death, since he was the one who led his army against the city, whereas Eteocles was defending the polis (city-state). Oedipus's daughter Antigone, however, refuses to ignore her obligations both to her dead brother and to the "gods below," i.e., the chthonic (subterranean) deities who preside over rites offered to the dead. The confrontation between the ruler of Thebes and a young unmarried woman, who would have been seen as a mere "girl" in the ancient Greek perspective, is striking and unexpected. The female Antigone is certainly not a hero in the conventional sense, yet she displays many of the character traits of the Sophoclean tragic hero: She is stubborn and unrelenting in her adherence to her principles.

SYNOPSIS

The opening scene of Sophocles' *Antigone* takes place at nighttime, in front of the royal palace of Thebes. The armies of Argos have just been defeated and are retreating from Thebes. Among the casualties are the sons of Oedipus, Eteocles and Polynices, who fought on opposite sides, Eteocles defending the city and Polynices with the attacking forces. The brothers are dead, having killed each other in battle. Their uncle, Creon, has assumed the kingship. Antigone and Ismene, sisters of Eteocles and Polynices, enter the scene. As Antigone emerges from the royal palace, she motions to Ismene that she wishes to speak with her. She reveals that yet another sorrow, in addition to the death of their mother, father, and two brothers, awaits them: Polynices is to be denied burial. While Eteocles has been given a hero's burial, Polynices will not receive that honor because he fought on the side of the invading army. Creon has decreed that Polynices's body shall not be mourned over, nor given any traditional burial rites. Anyone who disobeys this stricture shall be stoned to death inside the city walls. Antigone is in despair over this sacrilege. Antigone then asks Ismene whether she will go with her to bury their slain brother with the proper rites. Ismene, fearful of violating Creon's orders, attempts to convince Antigone of the madness of such a course. Angered by her sister's caution, Antigone defends her right to give Polynices proper burial and thus to honor the gods. Ismene sympathizes but refuses to defy Creon's will. She urges Antigone not to reveal her plans to anyone, but Antigone rejects this idea and exits.

As day breaks, a Chorus composed of Theban elders and their leader enters, chanting about the victory of Thebes over Argos and the defeat of Polynices. Creon and his attendants come out from the palace, and the Chorus reveals that Creon has gathered his subjects for an announcement. He recounts to his subjects the recent history of Thebes up to his accession to the throne. He explains that his first command as king concerns the treatment of Polynices's body—no one, on pain of death, is to give him a burial. Creon declares that Polynices, though a member of the royal family, was a traitor to Thebes. He argues that the integrity of the city depends on the conviction that ties of kinship are secondary to good citizenry. On behalf of the Chorus, the leader accepts Creon's injunctions regarding Polynices's body.

A sentry, breathless from running, enters the scene, and from his speech it is clear he has some news he is afraid to give Creon. The sentry reveals that Polynices's body has indeed been buried with the proper rites, but the sentries were not able to see who had done this. The leader of the Chorus suggests that perhaps it was the work of the gods. This comment angers Creon, who rages at the sentry, claiming that it is more likely that the guards were bribed to allow the burial of Polynices. Turning on the sentry with threats of dire punishment, Creon orders him and his fellow guards to produce the perpetrator of this act. The sentry tries to say that he has not been corrupted, but Creon refuses to acknowledge any judgment other than his own and quickly exits, returning to the palace. The sentry decides to run off rather than try to find the culprit and exits.

The Chorus now meditates on man's resourcefulness in mastering his environment but despairs over the impulsive and reckless aspects of his nature. During the ode, Antigone, accompanied by the sentry who had earlier rushed away, enters the scene, and the Chorus wonders aloud whether she is brought in as a prisoner and whether she has not committed an act of "mad defiance" against the king's laws.

Creon enters the scene, where he is informed by a relieved sentry that they have indeed captured the culprit. The sentry relates that after the guards uncovered Polynices's corpse, they were keeping close watch on it, when a windstorm obscured their view of the body. When the storm died down, they saw Antigone in the act of performing the burial rites. Creon turns to Antigone for confirmation, and she admits the charge and also that she knew that what she did was illegal. She defends her actions by claiming a higher moral directive: She had chosen to honor the laws of the gods and in so doing to break the laws of mere mortals. Furious, Creon declares that Antigone will die for her defiance, and accuses Ismene of the same crime. He orders his attendants to produce her and condemns her to die. Antigone accuses Creon of tyranny; he rejoins that she showed utter disloyalty to Thebes in burying Polynices. Antigone argues that ties of blood have stronger claims than the state, and, furthermore, that all deaths equally deserve burial rites. The attendants now bring Ismene, weeping, from the palace. Creon accuses her of sharing in Antigone's crime and demands that she confess. Ismene confesses that she did indeed participate in the crime, but Antigone contradicts her: Her sister shall share neither in the credit for the deed nor in the punishment. Ismene pleads with Creon for Antigone, asking if he can possibly condemn to death his son Haemon's betrothed. Creon answers resolutely that he has no qualms on that score. He insists that Antigone will not be spared and orders the guards to remove Ismene and Antigone to the palace. While the women and guards enter the palace, the Chorus gathers and decries the ruin of the house of Oedipus. Haemon enters and the Chorus wonders about his reaction to the fate of his betrothed. Initially, Haemon calmly affirms his loyalty to his family, and his father responds by explaining the circumstances of his decision. Haemon quietly suggests that public sympathy for Antigone's principles is strong and that Creon might reconsider and not be so intransigent. The Chorus echoes Haemon's thoughts, but Creon is annoyed by the advice. In the ensuing dialogue between father and son, Haemon argues ever more passionately in Antigone's defense, while Creon becomes increasingly bitter. Convinced of his father's poor judgment and intractability, Haemon storms off, hinting that Antigone's death will be followed by the death of another and that he will never see his father again.

The leader of the Chorus turns to Creon and warns him of the possibility of future violence, but Creon dismisses his anxiety. The leader asks if Creon means to kill both girls, and Creon states that Ismene will be spared but that Antigone will be killed immediately. He describes how she will die—he intends to wall her up alive. When he leaves, the Chorus reflects on the invincibility of love. Antigone is led out from the palace by the guards.

Antigone laments to the Chorus about the wedding that she will be denied. Contemplating her fate, the Chorus wonders whether Antigone is still another casualty of Oedipus's history and she agrees. As Creon enters, the Chorus reminds Antigone that her passionate defense of her principles has brought her into conflict with royal authority and that this cannot be accepted. Creon demands Antigone be taken away to her death, but Antigone continues to lament her lost nuptials and her cursed family. She remains convinced that her actions were right. Creon demands again that she be removed. Antigone accepts that her fate has been determined by her reverence for the gods and is taken away by the guards. Creon is unmoved.

The Chorus sings about several mythological figures that have suffered similarly at the hands of fate. Tiresias is then led in. He comes to proffer Creon advice, and Creon is willing to listen. Tiresias says that he has studied the omens and sees that the gods are outraged by Creon's treatment of Polynices's body: As a consequence of his actions, Thebes is threatened by plagues and other misfortunes. He advises Creon to relent. Creon reacts angrily to Tiresias's words, insulting his prophesies and insinuating that Tiresias is corrupt. Enraged, Tiresias prophesies that the Furies will destroy Creon both for having desecrated a dead body and for the murder of an innocent. Tiresias exits.

Frightened by Tiresias's prophecies, the leader of the Chorus urges Creon to reverse his judgment and finally succeeds in convincing him. He asks Creon to set Antigone free, and Creon rushes off to do this. The Chorus pleads with the gods to defend Thebes, but it is too late. A messenger enters to announce that Haemon is dead. Eurydice, mother of Haemon and wife of Creon, enters and demands that the messenger explain himself. The messenger had accompanied Creon to the body of Polynices; they had already performed the burial rites when they heard Haemon cry out. Creon rushed to the vault in which Antigone had been walled up and found Haemon holding Antigone's dead body in his arms: She had hanged herself by the time Haemon reached her. While his horrified father watched, Haemon fell on his sword and died. When the messenger finishes his recitation, Eurydice turns wordlessly and goes into the palace.

Creon enters with Haemon's body, borne on a bier by attendants. He is in despair over the consequences of his actions when the messenger comes out from the palace to announce even more woe—Eurydice is also dead. Creon cries out as the body of Eurydice is brought forth on a bier. The messenger tells him that Eurydice blamed him for the deaths, then stabbed herself. Creon acknowledges his guilt and kneels in prayer, begging to die, but his prayers are unanswered. A distraught Creon is led by the messenger and his attendants into the palace. The Chorus remarks that fate will, in the end, teach us about wisdom, good judgment, pride, and the reverence due to the gods.

COMMENTARY

The major theme of Sophocles' *Antigone* is the limits of the polis (city-state). Antigone's uncle Creon (whose name means, generically, "ruler") decrees that the dead Eteocles represented Thebes, and that Polynices was the enemy of Thebes; therefore, no one may offer Polynices burial rites. His decree, as Antigone insists, cuts heedlessly across family ties and dishonors the laws of the gods of the underworld. Here then is the conflict between the family as an integral unit and the polis that, in its extreme form, recognizes only citizens and laws that apply to citizens.

Antigone's perspective suggests that the laws of the polis can go only so far in ignoring the ancient ties of kin. By offering burial rites to her brother, she insists that the city cannot deny her the right to honor her dead kin—something more primal and essential than the polis's decrees, just as the laws of the gods of the underworld represent a primal power that must not be disregarded by the polis. It is important here that Antigone is female, especially connected with the family and less so with the polis, that is, the public sphere of government. Not only Antigone but Tiresias also is connected with those more primal powers, and he understands the need to honor them. Sophocles thus recasts the old conflict between the ruler's and the prophet's authority (a motif as old as Homer) to fit the present conflict between polis and kinship ties, a ruler's decree and the laws of the dead. The central irony of the play is that when his own son dies, Creon will learn the value of kin, but by then it is too late.

As Antigone comes into conflict with her community's ruler, she affords yet another example of the Sophoclean hero, whose chief characteristic is refusal to concede or give in: an unconquerable stubbornness that typically leads to his or her (magnificent) destruction. The suitable character for comparison is Oedipus, who persists in learning his own origins, relentlessly seeking this object until it destroys him. Likewise, Antigone is so uncompromising that she will not renounce the actions demanded by her convictions, even when threatened with death. This refusal to compromise is the quintessential heroic, but also antisocial, trait. The hero, as also in the case of Sophocles' Ajax, refuses to accept the *communis opinio*, the reasonable viewpoint of consoling, moderating influences around him or her, but presses on unbendingly to his or her self-chosen doom. This is the hero's autonomy: to control the conditions of his or her own death. Antigone's sister Ismene serves as an effective foil to her sister's unbending nature: She does not wish to stray into madness and continually urges compromise.

What goes counter to the heroic paradigm in Sophocles' tragedy is the simple fact that Antigone is a woman: Heroes tend to be men. In a certain sense, Creon should be the tragic hero: He is the one left at the end utterly shattered, destroyed by his own perversely stubborn actions, his royal household imploded. It is a tragedy with two closely related tragic figures, and, despite the strong romantic prejudice in favor of Antigone, it is not clear that either one of them is fully in the right. Antigone goes obstinately against her own community, not listening to reason, ultimately destroying herself and the man she expects to marry. Ruthless as he is, Creon is attempting to establish policies that defend the integrity of the polis.

Given Antigone's focus on death, her own death is therefore appropriate: She will be entombed alive, enclosed in a space of death. This is in some sense the logical outcome of her actions. She was always devoted to the rites of the dead, perhaps even perversely focused on death and the dead body of her brother, and so finally ends up being enshrouded in a living death. Her story falls under the rubric of myths of "failed transitions." As a young woman of marriageable age, engaged but not yet a married women, she is at a liminal stage between girlhood and womanhood. Many Greek myths represent instances of failed transition, where the central figure dies before moving from one condition to another. Antigone's end is at the same time a version of the "perverted ritual" motif in tragedy, e.g., not a normal sacrifice, but a human sacrifice. Here her entombment is a ghastly travesty of the rite of marriage: Her tomb is a marriage chamber.

Antilochus Son of Nestor. See MEMNON; NESTOR.

Antiope (1) Consort of ZEUS and by him mother of AMPHION and ZETHUS. Daughter of either Nycteus, king of Beotia, or of the river god Asopus. The subject of a lost play by EURIPIDES. Classical sources include Apollodorus's *LIBRARY* (3.5.5), Hyginus's *Fabulae* (7, 8), Ovid's *METAMORPHOSES* (6.110–111), and Pausanias's *Description of Greece* (1.38.9, 9.25.3). In Ovid's *Metamorphoses*, Zeus transformed himself into a satyr to seduce Antiope. Pregnant with his child and fearing the wrath of her father, Nycteus, Antiope fled to Sicyon, where she married Epopeus. Antiope's disgrace caused Nycteus to commit suicide, but his brother Lycus pursued and captured Antiope, killing Epopeus as well. Lycus brought Antiope back from Sicyon, and during that journey she gave birth to Amphion and Zethus in a cave. Antiope was forced by Lycus to abandon her twins, but they were discovered and raised by a cattle herder. Antiope was imprisoned by Lycus and maltreated by Lycus's wife, Dirce, a nymph of a spring sacred to DIONYSUS. After many years, either Amphion and Zethus rescued Antiope or she escaped her imprisonment and was reunited with her sons. Lycus and Dirce were punished for their treatment of Antiope; Dirce, memorably, by being yoked to a bull causing her death. Lycus was either killed as well or forced to give up his throne to Amphion. According to Homer's *Odyssey*, Amphion and Zethus afterward established the fortifications of Thebes.

Dionysus inflicted Antiope with madness in retribution for Dirce's death. According to Pausanias's *Description of Greece*, she wandered about in this condition until SISYPHUS's grandson, Phocus, found and cured her. Antiope married Phocus and was buried in Tithorea.

In the postclassical period, painters represented the subject of Antiope within the larger theme of Zeus's loves and transformations. Anthony van Dyck's *Jupiter and Antiope* of ca. 1616 (Museum Voor Shone Kunsten, Ghent) is good example of this treatment. It shows the god in the form of a satyr, with his attribute, the eagle, observing the sleeping Antiope. This is a variation on another related theme: a lone satyr observing a reclining nymph or APHRODITE herself, sometimes in the presence of EROS.

Antiope (2) (or Hippolyte or Melanippe) An Amazon. Consort of the hero THESEUS. Antiope was abducted by Theseus during the Amazonomachy that took place in the course of HERACLES' Ninth Labor, the quest for the girdle of Hippolyte, the Amazon queen. The Amazons attempted to storm Athens but were defeated by the Athenian forces under Theseus's leadership. Antiope bore Theseus a son, HIPPOLYTUS.

Aphrodite (Venus) Olympian goddess of love. Daughter of URANUS or ZEUS. Aphrodite appears throughout Homer's *ILIAD* and Virgil's *AENEID*. Additional classical sources are the *Homeric Hymn to Aphrodite*, Apollodorus's *LIBRARY* (1.3.1, 3.9.2, 3.12.2, 3.14.3), Euripides' *HIPPOLYTUS* (1–57), Hesiod's *THEOGONY* (188–206), Homer's *ODYSSEY* (8.266–366), and Ovid's *METAMORPHOSES* (10.534ff). Aphrodite was aligned with the Roman goddess of love, Venus. In some versions of the story of her birth, Aphrodite is the daughter of DIONE and Zeus. In

Venus and Cupid. *Lucas Cranach, ca. 1509*
(Hermitage Museum, St. Petersburg)

another account, she descends parthenogeneti-cally from Uranus (Heaven). CRONUS castrated his father, Uranus, and cast the genitals away. When they touched Earth, they produced the FURIES and the GIANTS. Cast into the sea, the genitals produced Aphrodite. Aphrodite's rising from the sea is perhaps one of the most iconic mythological images.

Aphrodite was married to HEPHAESTUS but deceived him with ARES, god of war.

In Ovid's *Metamorphoses*, Ares' affair with Aphrodite was discovered by APOLLO, who betrayed their affair to Aphrodite's husband, Hephaestus. Enraged, Hephaestus created a fine bronze net in which the lovers were captured, then displayed for the entertainment of the Olympian gods. Her children with Ares were Anteros, EROS, Deimos, HARMONIA, and Phobos. Eros was worshipped at Thespiae and Athens, both singly and with Aphrodite. Anteros was also a love deity; he represented either Reciprocal Love or Love Avenged. Aphrodite and Hephaestus had no offspring.

Aphrodite also had affairs with several mortal men, notably ADONIS and ANCHISES. Adonis was the son of MYRRHA (Symrna). Myrrha had neglected to worship Aphrodite, and so Aphrodite punished her by making her fall in love with her own father. With her nurse's help Myrrha tricked her father into beginning an incestuous relationship with her. When he discovered the truth, he tried to kill her, but before he could do so, the gods mercifully transformed her into a myrrh tree. Adonis was born of the myrrh tree and given by Aphrodite into the protection of PERSEPHONE. Both goddesses fell in love with him, and eventually Adonis divided his time between them. Despite Aphrodite's protective care, Adonis was killed by a boar while hunting.

According to the *Homeric Hymn to Aphrodite*, Aphrodite annoyed Zeus because she continually caused him to fall in love with mortal women and humiliate himself in their pursuit. In retribution, he caused her to become enamored of the mortal Anchises. By Anchises, Aphrodite became pregnant with AENEAS, hero of Virgil's *Aeneid*, which is the story of Aeneas's exile from conquered Troy and his subsequent wanderings. Aphrodite protects Aeneas as he travels to Italy, where he will found the Roman race. Aphrodite/Venus therefore enjoys a special status within the Roman pantheon of gods as the divine parent of a founder figure. Julius Caesar, who claimed descent from Aeneas and so also from Venus, built a temple to Venus Genetrix ("Venus the Begetter") in his forum.

Another important myth for Aphrodite is the Judgment of PARIS. At the wedding of PELEUS and THETIS, Eris (Discord or Strife) threw a golden apple into the midst of the revelers that was to be given to the most beautiful of ATHENA, Aphrodite, or HERA. Since none wished to be the arbiter of the competition, Zeus asked HERMES to bring the three goddesses to Mount Ida to be judged by Paris. The goddesses attempted to sway Paris's judgment. Paris accepted Aphrodite's proposal, the love of the most beautiful mortal woman, HELEN, and presented her with the golden apple. Paris sought Helen in Sparta and returned with her to Troy, thereby setting off the Trojan War.

Aphrodites' anger and desire for retribution are displayed in several of her myths. The mortal PSYCHE possessed a beauty that aroused Aphrodite's envy. Aphrodite asked Eros to make Psyche fall in love with a monster, but on seeing her, Eros fell in love with her himself. Psyche betrayed the trust of Eros but succeeded in winning him back after performing a variety of tasks imposed on her by Aphrodite. In Homer's *Iliad*, DIOMEDES succeeded in wounding Aphrodite. As retribution for Diomedes' injury to her, Aphrodite incited Diomedes' wife, Aegiale, to infidelity. Diomedes was forced to flee the threat to his life posed by her lovers. Aphrodite was also responsible for Eos's infatuation with ORION as punishment for Eos's affair with Ares.

Throughout ancient literature, Aphrodite/Venus represents the power of love and sexual desire, which, in the ancient conception, can be pleasurable and good but equally can be bitter, humiliating, and enslaving. In her own way, Aphrodite is as destructive as her lover Ares, and she was feared as well as adored. Yet avoiding Aphrodite could be dangerous too, as the example of HIPPOLYTUS shows. Hippolytus, the son of THESEUS, refused to show piety

to Aphrodite, and so the goddess inflicted a destructive passion upon PHAEDRA, stepmother to Hippolytus. Aphrodite's revenge resulted in the deaths of Hippolytus and Phaedra and the ruin of Theseus.

Aphrodite was one of the most frequently represented of the gods in classical and postclassical art. Aphrodite—in sculpture, relief, fresco, and painting—symbolized the feminine ideal of beauty, and her physical charms were central to her depictions. The earliest Hellenistic sculptures of Aphrodite emphasized the symmetry and proportion of the classical female nude. The influence of these representations on postclassical artists was lasting. Lucas Cranach's painting *Venus and Cupid* from ca. 1509 (Hermitage Museum, St. Petersburg) owes much to its classical forbearers. Here, the nude Aphrodite with long flowing hair is accompanied by Cupid. Cranach's image echoes perhaps the most famous image of Aphrodite, that of Botticelli. His *The Birth of Venus* of ca. 1485 (Galleria degli Uffizi, Florence) remains the most famous image of the goddess of love, one whose iconography has remained almost unchanged from the classical period. Aphrodite was often shown with her son Eros or in the context of the myth of Adonis. Other themes are her affair with Ares and love for Adonis.

Apollo Olympian god of the sun. Son of LETO (daughter of the TITANS COEUS and PHOEBE) and ZEUS. Brother of ARTEMIS, goddess of the moon and the hunt. Apollo appears throughout Homer's *ILIAD*. Additional classical sources are the *Homeric Hymn to Apollo*, Apollodorus's *LIBRARY* (1.3.2, 1.4.1, 3.10.2), Euripides' *ION*, Hesiod's *THEOGONY* (94–95, 346), Homer's *ODYSSEY* (8.226ff), Horace's *Odes* (1.31), Hyginus's *Fabulae* (49–51, 53), Ovid's *METAMORPHOSES* (1.439–568, 6.382–400, 11.153–171), and Pindar's *Pythian Odes* (I, 3.1–47, 4.176ff, 8.12ff, 9.1–70).

Apollo's domains are the arts, music, medicine, and prophecy. Apollo is "Phoebus," meaning "bright," which recalls the name of his maternal grandmother, Phoebe. The bow is his particular weapon; thus he is often called by the epithet Far-Shooter. Apollo is termed "Pythian" for his defeat of the Python on the site where the oracle of Delphi was later established. Apollo's attributes are the bow and the lyre, and his tree is the laurel.

The *Homeric Hymn to Apollo* establishes the god's birth on the island of Delos after a long search by Leto to find a site that would accept his birth. Fearing HERA's wrath, none would accept her except Delos. On Delos, Leto leaned against a palm tree in her labor pains. In some texts Apollo is born at the same time as Artemis, but the *Homeric Hymn to Apollo* and the *Orphic Hymn to Leto* put Artemis's birth later. Yet others sources suggest that Artemis was first born and helped deliver Apollo. In the *Homeric Hymn to Delian Apollo*, the goddesses assisting Leto during her labor persuaded IRIS, with the promise of a necklace of golden thread, to summon EILEITHYIA, goddess of childbirth, whom Hera had kept away for nine days and nights to prevent the births of Apollo and Artemis.

The sanctuary on Delos was the site of worship of Apollo, Artemis, Zeus, and Leto. Apollo's most important site, however, was located at Delphi, the site of the most famous oracle of antiquity. Apollo killed the monstrous Python (a serpent or dragon) that had been ravaging

Apollo and the Muses on Parnassus. *Engraving after Anton Raphael Mengs, 1784 (Metropolitan Museum of Art, New York)*

the countryside and established both the oracle and the Pythian Games in Delphi. Later Apollo would fight HERACLES over the tripod of the Delphic Oracle, a battle that Zeus stopped by separating them with a thunderbolt.

Apollo attempts, in several myths, to seduce women who have committed themselves to chastity. Two examples are the wood nymph DAPHNE, a follower of Artemis, and the Cumean sibyl. In the *Homeric Hymns to Artemis*, the closeness of the relationship between the siblings is emphasized. Artemis is said to have led the Muses in dance at the home of her brother in Delphi. In defense of any injury committed against their mother, Leto, Artemis and Apollo were ferocious and quick with retribution.

Both Apollo and Artemis fought on the side of the Olympian gods against the GIANTS in the GIGANTOMACHY. During the Trojan War, both Artemis and Apollo sided with the Athenians, but, at a certain point in the conflict, Apollo (in Homer's *Iliad*) argued that the Olympians should not fight each other for the sake of mere mortals. Artemis scolded her brother for his lack of valor, but since she opposed Hera in her defense of the Trojans, Hera attacked her and forced her to flee.

Apollo also helped repulse another challenge to Olympian authority, this time by the ALOADAE, the twin giants Ephialtes and Otus. According to Hyginus's version of the myth, either Apollo surprised them in the midst of their attempt to reach Olympus and killed them, or Artemis was raped by Otus and Apollo killed the Aloadae by sending a deer into their midst. The Aloadae, trying to hunt the deer, accidentally killed each other.

In his role as god of music and poetry, Apollo has a close association with the MUSES, with whom he shares a domain on Mount Parnassus. HERMES' association with Apollo is based on a shared interest in music; several myths and functions link the two gods. Hermes is credited with the creation of the lyre, which he later presented to Apollo, shortly after having stolen cattle from Apollo's herd. Accord-

ing to Apollodorus's *Library*, Hermes gave his pipe to Apollo in exchange for his trademark *cadaceus* ("golden wand") and was also said to have been taught the art of divination by the elder god. Hermes competed with Apollo for the affections of CHIONE. In Ovid's *Metamorphoses*, Chione was impregnated on the same day by Apollo and Hermes and she conceived twins: Autolycus, a trickster figure, took after his father, Hermes, while Apollo bestowed musical skills on his son Philammon. Artemis shot Chione with an arrow when she claimed superiority over the goddess of the hunt.

Apollo defended his musical skill in two separate contests with MARSYAS and PAN. The double flute (sometimes called "Pallas's reed") was said to have been invented by either ATHENA or Marsyas. Marsyas's skill on the double flute led to a musical contest with Apollo. The competition, judged by the Muses, was won by Apollo. For his hubris, Marsyas was hung by Apollo from a pine tree and flayed alive. In Book 11 of Ovid's *Metamorphoses*, Pan entered into a musical contest with Apollo, which was judged in favor of Apollo and his lyre. King MIDAS, who was in the audience, expressed a preference for Pan's double flute, and for this remark, Apollo gave Midas asses' ears.

The *Homeric Hymn to Apollo* highlights the frightening aspect of Apollo. Apollo and Artemis are both partial to meting out violent punishment for impiety or challenges to their functions (chastity, musical skill) and domains, or in defense of Leto. Their joint punishments of NIOBE and TITYUS were motivated by a desire to avenge their mother's honor. Niobe, wife of AMPHION, King of Thebes, had a number of children—between five and 10 of each sex, depending on the source—called Niobids. She was very proud of her children and boasted that she was a superior mother to Leto, who had only two children. Apollo and Artemis sought revenge on her behalf; Apollo's arrows killed the male children and Artemis's the female. Tityus attempted to rape Leto and was either killed by the arrows of Apollo and Artemis or the thunderbolt of Zeus.

Many of Apollo's myths feature unsuccessful love affairs in which the god is thwarted, deceived, or refused by the object of his affections. In Ovid's *Metamorphoses* the Cumean sibyl tells AENEAS that she refused Apollo and rejected his offer of eternal youth in return for her favors.

In Ovid's *Metamorphoses*, Apollo, having defeating the Python, saw EROS and told him to leave bows and arrows to those more capable of using them. Eros decided to have his revenge for this insulting comment, specifically by demonstrating his deadly skill with the bow and arrow: He shot Apollo with a gold-tipped arrow that incited desire, and Daphne, a wood nymph, with a lead-tipped arrow that repelled it. Daphne, in any case, already appears to have been averse to marriage, as she was a follower of chaste Artemis. Apollo pursued her until, despairing of escape, Daphne prayed to her father, the river god Peneus, for her beautiful form to be changed. She metamorphosed into a laurel tree (Daphne means "laurel" in Greek). Since he could not possess her as his wife, Apollo made her his tree and the laurel became his attribute.

HYACINTHUS was a mortal youth from Sparta also loved by Apollo. Hyacinthus was unwittingly killed when a discus thrown by Apollo was blown off course by ZEPHYRUS, the west wind, who, in some versions of the myth, was also enamored of the youth. A distraught Apollo attempted to revive Hyacinthus but could not. A flower arose from the drops of blood shed by Hyacinthus—the hyacinth.

Apollo also attempted to win over CASSANDRA, daughter of King PRIAM of Troy. He endowed Cassandra with prophetic abilities, but she would not give in to his amorous advances, so Apollo deprived her of the ability to convince others of the truth of her prophecies. HECUBA, mother of Cassandra and wife of Priam, was said to be Apollo's lover and bore him a son, TROILUS.

Another unsuccessful love was Marpessa, daughter of Evenus, who chose her mortal suitor Idas over Apollo, because of her fear that Apollo would one day abandon her.

In the myth of Coronis, Apollo was again supplanted by a mortal in the affections of a loved one. Apollo loved Coronis and discovered from a raven that Coronis was betraying him. In a rage, he drew his bow and killed her, but not before she revealed that she was pregnant with his child. Apollo turned the raven from white to black for its part in the affair. He repented of his actions and tried to save Coronis, but his skill in medicine failed him. Apollo then took the unborn child, ASCLEPIUS, and had him raised by CHIRON. Asclepius was famed for his skills in medicine, which he either came by naturally as the son of Apollo or learned from Chiron. Asclepius's skill was so great that he managed not only to save many lives but also to resurrect some who had died. When he saved HIPPOLYTUS in this manner, Zeus became angry with him and struck him down with a thunderbolt. Apollo was angered by the death of his son, and, in Apollodorus's *Library*, was said to have killed in revenge the CYCLOPES, who made Zeus's thunderbolts. Apollo was forgiven for this crime but was made to place himself in the service of Admetus, king of Thessaly, in expiation. Admetus asked for Apollo's help in winning the hand of ALCESTIS, daughter of Pelias. In gratitude for Admetus's good treatment of him, Apollo helped Admetus accomplish the task of yoking together a lion and a boar so that Admetus could marry Alcestis. Apollo also helped Admetus to avoid dying on his fated day: the consequences of this avoidance form the subject of Euripides' *Alcestis*.

Euripides' tragedy *Ion* tells the story of Ion, son of Apollo by CREUSA, daughter of King ERECTHEUS of Athens (in Hesiod, Ion is not given divine parentage but is instead the son of Xuthus). Creusa exposed Ion after his birth, but the child was raised by Apollo and became an attendant at the god's temple in Delphi.

Other children of Apollo include ARISTAEUS, by the nymph Cyrene; Dorus, Laodocus, and Polypoetes, by Phthia; Miletus and Mopsus, who had the gift of prophecy.

Apollo is one of the most frequently represented gods in classical and postclassical art. In visual representation, Apollo typifies the perfectly formed classical male nude; he is often crowned with laurel and known by his attributes, the bow and arrow. Apollo is sometimes pictured with the Muses on Parnassus. An example of this presentation is Raphael Morghen's neoclassical engraving after Anton Raphael Mengs, *Apollo and the Muses on Parnassus* from 1784 (Metropolitan Museum of Art, New York). Here, the arrangement of the Muses recalls Raphael's *Apollo and the Muses* in the Stanza della Segnatura from 1510–11 (Vatican Museums, Rome). The Muses, holding their attributes, surround Apollo in a half-circle. Apollo wears a laurel crown and carries a lyre. Apollo appears with Artemis on an Attic red-figure amphora from ca. 520 B.C.E. (Louvre, Paris). Here, Artemis gestures in shock at the scene before her in which Tityus attempts to abduct Leto, and Apollo reaches forward to grasp his mother. Artemis prepares to come to the assistance of Apollo with her quiver and arrows as Apollo wrestles with HERACLES for the Delphic tripod on an Attic red-figure belly amphora from ca. 500 B.C.E. (British Museum, London). The most famous classical sculpture of Apollo is the *Apollo Belvedere*. A well-known later representation of the myth of Apollo and Daphne is Gianlorenzo Bernini's famous *Apollo and Daphne* sculpture from 1622–25 (Galleria Borghese, Rome). The Marsyas myth inspired many classical and postclassical artists despite the gruesomeness of Marsyas's death. Apollo stands over the body of Marsyas, holding aloft his flayed skin, in Melchior Meier's engraving *Apollo, Marsyas, and the Judgment of Midas* of 1582 (Metropolitan Museum of Art, New York).

Apollodorus (fl. second century B.C.E.) A scholar and writer from Athens who flourished in the second century B.C.E. and participated in the intellectual culture of Alexandria. Apollodorus wrote the *Chronica*, a work of chronology and intellectual history, a treatise entitled *On the Gods*, and a commentary on Homer's catalogue of ships. Apollodorus was probably not the author of the *LIBRARY*, a comprehensive study of mythology and an important source for versions of the Greeks myths, but the work is still traditionally known as "Apollodorus's *Library*."

Apollonius of Rhodes (ca. 295 B.C.E.–ca. 247 B.C.E.) A major Greek poet of the third century B.C.E., author of the *VOYAGE OF THE ARGONAUTS* (the *Argonautica*). Apollonius may have come from Rhodes or merely lived there for a certain period. His literary career, however, was centered in Alexandria, where Ptolemy I Soter (367–282 B.C.E.) and Ptolemy II Philadelphus (308–246) provided substantial support to literary culture. Apollonius was among the scholars and poets who benefited from the patronage of the Ptolemies: He was head librarian of the Alexandrian library and served as tutor to Ptolemy III Euergetes, son and heir of Ptolemy II Philadelphus. Apollonius's only extant work is the *Voyage of the Argonauts*, an epic poem on the hero JASON's retrieval of the golden fleece. Apollonius's poetry is deeply and conspicuously learned in the Alexandrian style: His epic poem includes a dense fabric of allusions to local rites, ethnography, etiologies, mythological variants, and geography. Apollonius takes Homer as his constant point of reference, yet his poem's hero, Jason, is markedly un-Homeric in certain aspects: He has neither the warlike ferocity of Achilles, nor the resourcefulness of Odysseus. At the same time, Apollonius awards a central role to the power and resourcefulness of a woman (MEDEA) and the force of erotic attraction. Apollonius's learned epic of travel and adventure was a major model for Virgil's *AENEID*.

Apuleius Apuleius was born in 125 c.e. at Medaurus in Africa Proconsularis. The exact date of his death is unknown but was sometime after 170. In 158–159, Apuleius wrote the *Apologia*, a speech delivered at Sabathra defending himself against charges of using magic to cause a woman to marry him. Apuleius's major work is his *Metamorphoses*, a novel in Latin prose sometimes called *The Golden Ass*. The *Metamorphoses* is 11 books in length. In this novel, the first-person narrator, Lucius, a young man from Corinth, is transformed into an ass through an experiment in magic and goes through various adventures before being turned back into a human being by the goddess Isis. The *Metamorphoses*, underappreciated until recent decades, is an immensely sophisticated narrative that opens up multiple perspectives onto a rich cultural and social world. Apuleius's novel is truly cosmopolitan in its dense interweaving of Greek and Roman cultural elements within the broader fabric of the empire. Apuleius's most significant contribution to mythology is the detailed telling of the story of Cupid (Eros) and Psyche in Books 4–6. The story is an internal narrative told by a housekeeper of some robbers who have captured Lucius and a young woman named Charite. Scholars have observed parallels between Lucius's story and Psyche's. She too, undergoes trials because of her inappropriate curiosity and is saved in the end through divine intervention. The story of Cupid and Psyche is a rare instance of a fairy tale preserved in an ancient literary text.

Arachne Daughter of Idmon of Colophon. The classical source is Ovid's *Metamorphoses* (6.1–145). Arachne was a young Lydian woman renowned for her skill in weaving. She boasted that her skills surpassed those of Athena, the goddess of weaving. The goddess visited Arachne in the form of an old woman and warned her to behave more modestly. When Arachne gave an insolent reply, the goddess revealed herself, and the two engaged in a contest. In Ovid's account (which is nearly the sole source for the myth), Athena's tapestry depicted the 12 Olympian gods and the punishment and defeat of mythological figures who challenged their authority. Arachne's tapestry, by contrast, represented the unjust, exploitative, or otherwise discreditable behavior of the gods toward mortals. Although Arachne's tapestry was flawless, Athena angrily ripped it up and struck Arachne with her shuttle. Arachne tried to hang herself, but Athena wished to make an enduring example of her. She transformed Arachne into a spider and made her spin webs ceaselessly (and, it is implied, ignominiously and artlessly).

The story does not appear to have been a major or well-known myth before Ovid, who incorporates it as a magnificent set piece in Book 6 of his *Metamorphoses*. The story is both a prime example of the origins story *(aetion)* that is the poem's defining narrative type and a suggestive encapsulation of the broader themes and patterns of Ovid's mythological epic. Ovid, who wrote under, and was eventually exiled by, the emperor Augustus, may also have been commenting on the relation between art and tyrannical power. In the ancient world, weaving was a common metaphor for poetry: Arachne's rebellious artistry and Athena's brutally censorious reply have seemed to many to offer a provocative allegory of the writer's role under an autocratic regime.

Arcas (Arkas) Son of Zeus and the nymph Callisto. Classical sources are Ovid's *Fasti* (2.155–192) and *Metamorphoses* (2.469, 496–507) and Pausanias's *Description of Greece* (8.4.1, 10.9.5). According to Pausanias, Arcas was the king of Arcadia, the region to which he gave his name. He was said to have introduced agriculture (through the instruction of Triptolemus) to Arcadia. He also encouraged the production of bread, clothing, and the arts of weaving. Arcas was married to the Dryad Erato and with her had three sons.

The story of Arcas's origins is as follows. His mother, Callisto, was an Arcadian nymph and favorite of ARTEMIS who became pregnant by Zeus.

When Callisto gave birth to Arcas, HERA became enraged with what she perceived was the flagrant display of her husband's infidelity, and she transformed the nymph into a bear. (In another version, it was Zeus who changed Callisto to protect her from Hera.)

Zeus gave Arcas into the care of MAIA (one of the PLEIADES). As a young man, Arcas came upon Callisto as a bear while hunting. Zeus stayed Arcas's hand before he killed Callisto and placed mother and son in the heavens as the constellations Ursa Major and Arcturus. Under the directions of the Delphic Oracle, Arcas's bones were brought back to Arcadia and buried near an altar dedicated to Hera.

The infant Arcas appears on an Apulian red-figure chous vase dating from ca. 350 B.C.E. (J. Paul Getty Museum, Malibu). On one side of the vase Callisto is changing into a bear and HERMES, an appropriate intermediary as the son of Maia, takes the young Arcas protectively into his arms.

Ares (Mars) Olympian god of war. Son of HERA and ZEUS. Ares appears throughout Homer's *ILIAD*. Additional classical sources are the *Homeric Hymn to Ares*, Apollodorus's *LIBRARY* (1.4.4, 1.7.4, 2.5.9, 3.4.1), Hesiod's *THEOGONY* (921, 934), Homer's *ODYSSEY* (8.266ff), Ovid's *METAMORPHOSES* (4.172–187), and Pausanias's *Description of Greece* (1.21.4, 1.28.5). Ares was identified with the Roman god of war, Mars. For Romans, Mars was an important god, second only to Zeus in the Olympic pantheon. In Hesiod's *Theogony*, Ares is the only son of Hera and Zeus and brother to HEBE (goddess of youth) and EILEITHYIA (goddess of childbirth). In an alternate account, according to Ovid's *Fasti*, CHLORIS gave Hera a magic flower that helped her conceive Ares spontaneously because Hera wished to match Zeus's feat in producing ATHENA. Ares is accompanied by Deimos (Fear) and Phobos (Panic) and drives a chariot with four horses. His animals are the dog and the vulture, scavengers of war. His attributes are a helmet, shield, and sword or spear. Ares represents the more violent, destructive capacity of war in contrast to the controlled and wisely waged war associated with Athena. In Homer's *Iliad*, Ares is the "bane of mortals," and in the *Orphic Hymn to Ares*, the bloodthirsty god desires war for its own sake. By contrast, in the *Homeric Hymn to Ares* he advocates war in defense of the city and in other righteous causes.

Ares at times finds himself in opposition to Athena. He is not an invulnerable warrior: During the Trojan War, he first assured Athena that he would not interfere in the battle, but he was persuaded by APOLLO to fight on the side of the Trojans and while doing so was injured by DIOMEDES, who was guided by Athena. When he received the wound, Ares gave a tremendous cry, heard by all in the battlefield, and hastened to Olympus, where his wound was healed and where Zeus decried Ares' love of violence. Later on during the Trojan War, Athena injured him by throwing a stone against his neck, which knocked him out. Athena stood over him laughing and boasting of her superiority as a warrior, and Ares was led away by APHRODITE. In another instance, HERACLES got the better of Ares, and the god was forced to return to Olympus to be healed of his wound.

The ALOADAE, giant twin sons of Iphimedeia and POSEIDON, managed to imprison Ares for 13 months in a brazen pot until he was rescued by HERMES.

Ares favored the AMAZONS, who were said to be his descendants. PENTHESILEIA, an Amazon and the daughter of Ares, was killed during the Trojan War by ACHILLES, and Ares was prevented by Zeus from entering the conflict to avenge her death. Ares' sons by Astyiche, Ascalaphus and Ialmenus, fought during the Trojan War on the Greek side. Ascalaphus was killed during the conflict, and Ares was

Venus and Mars. *Sandro Botticelli, ca. 1485 (National Gallery, London)*

restrained by Athena from avenging his death. Ares stood trial on the Hill of Ares for his murder of Halirrhothius, who had raped Ares' daughter Alcippe.

Ares' most famous amorous alliance was with Aphrodite. Their offspring were Anteros, Eros, Deimos, Harmonia, and Phobos. In Ovid's *Metamorphoses*, Ares' affair with Aphrodite was discovered by Helios, who betrayed them to Aphrodite's husband, Hephaestus. Hephaestus created a fine bronze net in which the lovers were captured and then displayed to the ridicule of the Olympian gods.

Ares' domains were Thrace and Thebes, where he was associated with its founder, Cadmus. Directed by an oracle to establish a city at Thebes, Cadmus looked for a spring before offering a sacrifice and found one guarded by the dragon of Ares. Cadmus killed the dragon and, advised by Athena, planted its teeth in the ground. These sprang up from the ground as fully grown warriors. Cadmus atoned for the crime of killing Ares' dragon by placing himself in the god's service for eight years. Cadmus was afterward rewarded by ascending to the throne of Thebes and was given Harmonia, daughter of Ares, in marriage.

Ares was represented in depictions of the Olympian pantheon with his attributes, helmet,

shield, and spear. In the *Ares Borghese*, a freestanding sculpture of ca. 125 C.E. (Louvre, Paris), Ares stands nude, wearing a helmet. In classical and postclassical paintings, Ares/Mars appears frequently with Aphrodite, as in a Pompeian wall painting from the first century C.E. A postclassical example is Sandro Botticelli's *Venus and Mars* from ca. 1485 (National Gallery, London). Here, the sleeping god of war is surrounded by satyrs playing with his helmet and spear while Aphrodite looks on. Hephaestus's entrapment of Ares and Aphrodite was also a commonly depicted theme in postclassical painting.

Arethusa   See Alpheus.

Argonautica   See *Voyage   of   the Argonauts*.

Argonauts   See Jason *Voyage   of   the Argonauts*.

Argus (Argos) Argus *Panoptes*, or "All-Seeing," a hundred-eyed herdsman. Son of Gaia. Classical sources are Aeschylus's *Prometheus Bound* (561–575), Apollodorus's *Library* (2.1.3), and Ovid's *Metamorphoses* (1.568–746). Argus is sometimes said to be a giant. Traditionally, Argus has a hundred eyes that cover his body, but sources vary as to the precise number. In some sources, Argus is the son of Gaia (Earth), but in Apollodorus's *Library*, he is made to be the son of King Agenor of Argos. In this human, heroic form, he performed many deeds, including the killing of a certain bull that ravaged Arcadia (he took its skin as a cape) and of a satyr that had stolen Arcadian cattle. He also killed the monstrous ECHIDNA. In myth, Argus is the servant of HERA and appears in the story of Io. Io was the consort of ZEUS and, to avoid Hera's wrath, was transformed into a white heifer that Hera set Argus to guard over. He tethered Io to an olive tree in a sacred grove. This made it impossible for Io to escape or for Zeus to rescue her until Zeus commanded HERMES to intervene. Disguised as a shepherd, Hermes lulled Argus to close all his eyes in sleep with the aid of his reed pipe and the story of its invention by PAN. After Argus fell asleep, Hermes beheaded him and thereafter assumed the epithet Argeiphontes or "Argus-slayer." In honor of his service to her, Hera plucked out Argus's many sightless eyes and placed them on the tail of her bird, the peacock. Afterward, Hera sent a gadfly to drive Io mad. Chased by the gadfly, Io fled to Egypt, where the ghost of Argus still haunted her.

In antiquity, visual representations of Argus occur in the context of the myth of Io. He is usually depicted as a large, bearded, male nude whose body is covered with eyes and frequently shown protecting the tethered heifer Io and/or in combat with Hermes, as on an Attic red-figure hydria from ca. 460 B.C.E. (Museum of Fine Arts, Boston). Here, Argus stands beside the bovine Io, with his chest, arms, and legs covered in eyes, and defends himself against Hermes, who unsheathes his sword. Zeus and Hera are also present. Hermes deals Argus the death blow in an Attic red-figure stamnos from ca. 430 B.C.E. (Kunsthistorisches Museum, Vienna). Argus's body is here painted with white eyes.

Ariadne   Daughter of MINOS, king of Crete, and Pasiphae. Classical sources are Apollodorus's *LIBRARY* (Epitome 1.7–10), Diodorus Siculus's *LIBRARY OF HISTORY* (4.61.5), Hyginus's *Fabulae* (42, 43), Ovid's *METAMORPHOSES* (8.170–182), and Plutarch's *Life of Theseus*. Ariadne belonged to a line of fascinating and unusual women. Her mother, Pasiphae, mated with a bull and gave birth to the MINOTAUR. She was related on her mother's side to the witch CIRCE and to MEDEA. Her sister PHAEDRA married THESEUS.

Ariadne fell in love with Theseus when he came as one of seven young men and seven young women to be offered to the Minotaur in his labyrinth, as the tribute that Minos exacted from Athens every nine years for the murder of his son, Androgeos.

Theseus, the son of King Aegeus of Athens, had insisted on volunteering to be one of the victims. He slew the Minotaur and, by unrolling and rerolling a spool of thread that Ariadne gave him, was able to escape from the labyrinth. Having betrayed her father and her country for her lover, Ariadne fled with Theseus, but he abandoned her on the island of Naxos. The god DIONYSUS and his followers came upon her as she was wandering, desolate and despairing, on the island. He fell in love with her and carried her away to be his bride, giving her a golden diadem that was afterward transformed into a constellation.

Among the many treatments of the myth, CATULLUS's poem 64 is outstanding for its extended description of Ariadne on the beach, its examination of her emotions, and its complex reinterpretation of the myth in the light of Roman ethics and late republican society. In general, Ariadne was a favorite theme in the Hellenistic and Roman period: Her story is a prime example of the myths of suffering in love and the emotional plight of heroines that poets of this period enjoyed exploring. Apollonius of Rhodes, in his *VOYAGE OF THE ARGONAUTS*, makes much of her structural similarity to Medea. Like Medea, she is a foreign women who falls in love with a Greek, helps him accomplish his heroic

Bacchus and Ariadne. *Titian, 1520–23 (National Gallery, London)*

quest, leaves behind her father and fatherland for him, then is abandoned by him.

Ariadne and Theseus, in particular her abandonment and subsequent rescue by Dionysus, have been frequently represented in the visual arts and in opera. This theme occurs in vase painting from the fifth century B.C.E. onward. Ariadne appears on the François Vase from ca. 570 B.C.E. (Museo Archeologico, Florence). Perhaps the most famous painting of Dionysus's rescue of Ariadne is Titian's *Bacchus and Ariadne* 1520–23 (National Gallery, London).

Aristaeus   See *GEORGICS*.

Aristophanes (ca. 450 B.C.E.–ca. 386 B.C.E.) Greek poet of the Old Attic Comedy. Aristophanes was born between 460 and 450 B.C.E. and died ca. 386 B.C.E. Eleven plays by Aristophanes are extant: *Acharnians* (425), *Knights* (424), *Clouds* (423), *Wasps* (422), *Peace* (421), *Birds* (414), *Lysistrata* (411), *Thesmophoriazusae* (411) *Frogs* (405), *Ecclesiazusae* ("Assembly-Women," 392 or 391),

Plutus (388). Surviving titles of lost plays include *Banqueters* (427), *Babylonians* (426), *Amphiaraus* (414), an earlier version of *Plutus* (408), *Aiolosikon* (after 388), and *Cocalus* (after 388). Central features of Aristophanic comedy are boisterous action and deliberately fantastic and preposterous premises, sexually explicit and obscene language, constant puns and wordplay, and personal attacks and satire on politicians and other culturally prominent figures (e.g., EURIPIDES, Socrates). Old Comedy is a form of drama that makes sense in a face-to-face democratic society. Aristophanes comments on issues of the day, deeply familiar to his Athenian audience, although without excessive dogmatism. The Chorus is an integral part of the action, and local references are crucial. Aristophanes' later plays suggest the beginnings of the transition to New Comedy. The Chorus plays a less integral role, and there is more attention to the mechanism of plot and story line. New Comedy, with its stock characters and repetitive plots, is designed to be comprehensible to a broad audience not necessarily rooted in a single city-state. There is relatively little myth in comedy by comparison with tragedy, because comedy by definition represents ordinary life, not the exalted world of heroes. Yet Aristophanes creates his own outrageous "myths" that turn reality upside down in revealing and thought-provoking ways: e.g., a city-state of birds. Aristophanes does sometimes write about mythological characters, usually in a spirit of comic deflation. The title of the lost *Amphiaraus* suggests something along these lines. A notable instance in the extant plays is the character of DIONYSUS in *Frogs*. Dionysus goes down to Hades to bring back Euripides from the dead in order to save Athens, but he ends up judging a contest between Euripides and AESCHYLUS and choosing to bring back Aeschylus instead. Aristophanes presents a comic portrait both of the god Dionysus—so dear to the Athenian theater—and of two of Athens's most revered tragedians.

Ars Amatoria OVID (ca. 1 B.C.E.) The *Ars Amatoria* ("The Art/Technique of Love"), published around 1 B.C.E., is a didactic poem in three books on the techniques of seduction. Books 1 and 2 are written for men; Book 3 is notionally meant to aid women. "Didactic" is a term for the genre of poetry that teaches. Some known topics include astronomy, farming, philosophy, and snakebites. Ovid's combination of the didactic genre with erotic subject matter and meter (elegiac couplets) produces provocative and witty effects. Love is conventionally an emotion not susceptible to manipulation or systematic, rational control, yet Ovid insists that he will subject Love precisely to such rational control. In making these claims, and setting himself up as an urbane, calculating *praeceptor amoris* ("teacher of love"), Ovid is playing with the conventions and underlying assumptions of elegiac love poetry, including his own *Amores*. Ovid's manual for carrying out love affairs is often conspicuously "by the book," i.e., it repeats, as didactic advice and conscious strategy, the well-known literary motifs of elegiac poetry, which, however, stress the lover's *inability* to control his behavior and utter lack of a rational strategy. Ovid picks apart the elegiac fiction and discovers a level of self-serving calculation beneath previous elegists' protestations of powerlessness. If the *domina* ("mistress") of previous elegy was an appropriately dominating figure, now she becomes the target of a series of cynical strategies of control and exploitation.

Love has become a complicated, absorbing game, the expanded playing field of which encompasses the entire city, its vast, colonnaded structures and large, diverse population. Ovid has taken the fiction of elegiac exclusivity—the *una puella* ("one and only girl") of Propertius—and converted it into a large-scale mode of urban behavior. His lover is an eroticized version of the flaneur. Ovid at the same time expands the scope of elegiac mythological narration. The opening of Book 2, for example, offers a version of the story of DAEDALUS and ICARUS that doubles as an extended meditation on *ars* ("technique," "art"), both poetic and otherwise. Ovid's exile poetry singles out the *Ars* as one of the two causes of his exile: a poem *(carmen)* and a mistake *(error)*. The ostensible content of Ovid's *Ars Amatoria*—love affairs conducted outside of marriage—went against the grain of the emperor Augustus's marriage and adultery legislation, although Ovid was careful to build plausible denials of adulterous intent into his poem. Scholarly opinion, however, is divided on the extent to which Augustus was truly motivated by Ovid's poem in ordering his relegation. The *Ars Amatoria* is both an intriguing intervention in the ideological climate of the later Augustan principate and an example of Ovid's interest in combining genres and modes of poetic exposition in innovative ways.

Artemis (Diana) Olympian goddess of the hunt and the moon. Daughter of LETO (daughter of the TITANS COEUS and PHOEBE) and ZEUS. Twin sister of APOLLO. Artemis appears in Euripides' *HIPPOLYTUS* and *IPHIGENIA IN TAURIS*. Additional classical sources are the *Homeric Hymn to Artemis*, Apollodorus's *LIBRARY* (1.4.1, 1.7.3, 1.9.15, 2.5.3, 3.8.2), Hesiod's *THEOGONY* (918–920), Homer's *ILIAD* (21.468) and *ODYSSEY* (5.121), Hyginus's *Fabulae* (9, 98, 189), and Ovid's *METAMORPHOSES* (2.415–465, 3.156–252, 6.205, 6.416, 7.745, 12.28). The Romans syncretized Diana, also a moon goddess, with Artemis, and worship of Diana was practiced on the Aventine Hill, at her sanctuary near Lake Nemi, and in Campania.

Like Apollo, Artemis is also "Phoebe," or "bright," like her maternal grandmother. Among Artemis's epithets are "torch-bringer," because as goddess of the moon she brings light to darkness. Artemis carries a quiver and arrows, and she lets loose a "rain of arrows" and is "arrow-pouring," while Apollo is the "far-shooter" because of his association with archery. Artemis's domain is the woods, particularly those of Arcadia, where she is both protector and huntress of animals. In the *Orphic Hymn to Artemis*, she is associated with female chastity but also with childbirth. In cult practice, this aspect of Artemis was important.

The circumstances of Artemis's birth vary according to the source. In some, she is born at the same time as Apollo, in others, earlier or later. The *Homeric Hymn to Apollo* and the *Orphic Hymn to Leto* describe the long search by Leto to find a site where she could give birth. Fearing HERA's wrath, none would accept her, except for Delos. In the *Homeric Hymn to Delian Apollo*, the goddesses assisting Leto during her labor persuaded IRIS (the messenger of the gods) to summon EILEITHYIA, goddess of childbirth, whom Hera had kept away for nine days and nights, to prevent the births of Apollo and Artemis. Apollodorus's *Library* maintains that Artemis helped deliver her brother shortly after her own birth. Artemis is sometime called "Cynthia," after Mount Cynthus on Delos. The sanctuary on Delos was the site of worship of Apollo, Artemis, Zeus, and Leto.

Apollo and Artemis are both partial to meting out violent punishment for impiety or challenges to their functions (chastity, musical skill) and domains, or in defense of Leto. Their joint punishments of NIOBE and TITYUS were motivated by a desire to avenge their mother's honor. Niobe, wife of king Amphion of Thebes, had a number of children—between five and 10 of each sex, depending on the source—called Niobids. She was very proud of her children and boasted that she was a superior mother to Leto, who had only two children. Apollo and Artemis sought revenge on her behalf; Apollo's arrows killed the male children and Artemis's the female. Tityus attempted to rape Leto and was killed by either the arrows of Apollo and Artemis or the thunderbolt of Zeus.

Both Apollo and Artemis fought on the side of the Olympian gods against the GIANTS and the Titans. During the Trojan War, both Artemis and Apollo sided with the Athenians, but at a certain point in the conflict, Apollo, according to Homer's *Iliad*, argued that the Olympians should not fight each other over mere mortals. Artemis scolded her brother for his lack of valor, but since she opposed Hera in her defense of the Trojans, Hera attacked her and forced her to flee. Leto later retrieved the quiver and arrows that Artemis had hastily left behind on Olympus.

Artemis and Apollo also jointly helped repulse the challenge to the Olympians posed by the ALOADAE, the twin giants Ephialtes and Otus. In Apollodorus's *Library*, Artemis trans-

formed herself into a deer, and while trying to hunt it, Ephialtes and Otus accidentally killed each other. According to Hyginus's version of the myth, either Apollo surprised the Aloadae in the midst of their attempt to reach Olympus and killed them or Artemis was raped by Otus and Apollo killed the Aloadae by sending a deer into their midst, whereupon the Aloadae accidentally killed each other.

Artemis and Apollo. *Detail from an Attic cup, Briseis Painter, ca. 470* B.C.E. *(Louvre, Paris)*

In several texts, Artemis is characterized as an aloof figure, and though she is associated with positive aspects, such as the protection of the young and chaste or women during childbirth, she has, like Apollo, a dark and terrifying aspect as well. She is wrathful if proper piety is not shown to her or if her companions, domain, or animals are threatened. Artemis permitted Heracles to capture the Ceryneian hind only when the hero persuaded her that it was a Labor laid on him by EURYSTHEUS.

In retribution for King Oeneus of Calydon's failure to worship her, Artemis sent a wild boar to ravage the countryside. This boar was hunted in the famous Calydonian Boar hunt led by MELEAGER. Another who neglected to sacrifice to Artemis was Admetus, husband of ALCESTIS. In punishment Artemis filled his marriage chamber with serpents, a portent of an early death. In another myth, Artemis first demanded, then prevented AGAMEMNON's sacrifice of his daughter IPHIGENIA (the subject of Euripides' tragedy *Iphigenia among the Taurians*), substituting a deer in place of the young girl. Artemis made Iphigenia guardian of her temple, or made her immortal.

In the *Homeric Hymn to Aphrodite*, Artemis is singled out as one of three goddesses—along with ATHENA and HESTIA—over whom love has no sway. Defense of purity is the central theme of Artemis's best known myths, those of CALLISTO and HIPPOLYTUS and the hunters ACTAEON and ORION. In Ovid's *Metamorphoses*, Actaeon surprised Artemis and her nymphs bathing on Mount Cithaeron in Boeotia. Enraged that she had been seen nude, Artemis transformed Actaeon into a stag. His own pack of dogs failed to recognize him, gave chase, and devoured him. Another hunter, Orion, attempted to seduce either Artemis or one of her followers and was punished: The goddess sent a scorpion to sting him to death.

Callisto was an Arcadian wood nymph and follower of Artemis. Seeing the nymph in the woods of Arcadia, Zeus became enamored of her, and, disguising himself as Artemis, sur-

prised her. The nymph recognized Zeus when he embraced her, but, defenseless, she was unable to resist him. Despite her innocence, she was banished by Artemis from her company.

Artemis hears the prayers of those who wish to remain chaste and guard their virtue. In Ovid's *Metamorphoses*, she transformed Nyctimene into a crow because she did not wish to be seduced by Poseidon.

Another favorite of Artemis was the virtuous and chaste youth Hippolytus, son of THESEUS. Theseus's wife, PHAEDRA, became enamored of Hippolytus and attempted to seduce him, but he chastely refused, being a devotee of Artemis. Phaedra, scorned, accused Hippolytus of attempting to rape her. Theseus then called on the help of Poseidon to kill Hippolytus. In Euripides' tragedy *Hippolytus*, Artemis revealed to Theseus that in his blindness he brought about the death of his blameless son. According to some sources, at the request of Artemis, Hippolytus was revived by the famed healer ASCLEPIUS and lived on in his new incarnation as Virbius at the sanctuary of Diana at Aricia.

Artemis also showed favor to PROCRIS, wife of the hunter CEPHALUS. Tricked by Eos (Dawn) into believing her husband had been unfaithful, Procris joined the company of Artemis on Crete. However, the goddess refused to accept her presence because she kept company only with unmarried young women. Artemis was moved, however, by Procris's devotion to Cephalus and presented her with a javelin that never missed its mark and a dog that always captured its prey. On the same theme of marital affection and loyalty, Artemis took pity on the nymph Egeria, who, in Ovid's *Metamorphoses*, was lamenting her dead husband, Numa, in Artemis's grove. Artemis transformed her into a spring.

In visual representations, Artemis is depicted as a young, clothed huntress holding a bow, arrows, and quiver, and accompanied by animals (especially hunting dogs). Her central attribute is the crescent or full moon. At times the crescent moon appears at her forehead, giving her the appearance of being horned.

Artemis, carrying a bow and accompanied by a hind, is shown with Apollo on the tondo of an Attic red-figure cup by the Briseis Painter dating to ca. 470 B.C.E. (Louvre, Paris). Here, she carries a quiver and gestures in shock at the scene before her in which Tityus attempts to abduct Leto. Artemis prepares to assist Apollo with her quiver and arrows as Apollo wrestles with HERACLES for the Delphic tripod on an Attic red-figure belly amphora from ca. 500 B.C.E. (British Museum, London).

Ascanius (Iulus) See AENEAS; AENEID.

Asclepius (Asklepios) Greek god of medicine. Son of APOLLO and CORONIS (Arsinoe). Classical sources are the *Homeric Hymn to Asclepius*, Apollodorus's *LIBRARY* (3.10.3), Hyginus's *Fabulae* (49) and *Poetica Astronomica* (2.23), Lucian's *DIALOGUES OF THE GODS* (15), Ovid's *FASTI* (6.746–754) and *METAMORPHOSES* (2.600–634), Pindar's *Pythian Odes* (3.1–45), and Virgil's *AENEID* (7.760–783). Sources disagree as to Asclepius's mother: The *Homeric Hymn to Asclepius* and Ovid's *Metamorphoses* say that she is Coronis, daughter of King Phlegyas of Thessaly, while Apollodorus's *Library* maintains that she is Arsinoe, daughter of Leucippus (the question is debated in Pausanias's *Description of Greece*, which favors Coronis as his mother). Nor do the sources agree as to whether Asclepius was divine or whether he was accorded that status after he was struck down by ZEUS.

In the *Homeric Hymn*, Asclepius skillfully cures disease, and in the *ORPHIC HYMN*, Asclepius charms misery away and wards off evil. His attribute is a caduceus (a staff entwined by two serpents), and he deals with fevers, sores, wounds, and illnesses of all kinds. He provides potions, treatment, and even surgery to all who require it. In Virgil's *Aeneid*, Asclepius is "Phoebus-born," and in Ovid's *Metamorphoses*, he is the most skilled of healers, killed by Zeus because he dared to restore the dead to life. Diodorus Siculus's *LIBRARY OF HISTORY* ratio-

nalizes Asclepius's resurrection of the dead by maintaining that Asclepius was so skilled that he could effect cures in cases that had been despaired of. According to Pindar's *Pythian Odes*, Asclepius was bribed to resurrect the dead, but in most other accounts, he was simply making use of all his skills as physician.

The story of Asclepius's origins, interestingly, involves a failed medical intervention. Apollo loved his mother, Coronis, and discovered from a raven that Coronis, already pregnant with Asclepius by Apollo, was betraying him with the mortal Ischys. In a rage, Apollo drew his bow and killed Coronis, but not before she revealed that she was pregnant with his child. Apollo repented his actions and tried to save her, but even with all his skills as a healer, he was unsuccessful and she died. (On another occasion, Apollo attempted to save another lover, Leucothoe, and again failed.) In Pindar's *Pythian Odes*, ARTEMIS killed Coronis for her betrayal of Apollo. Apollo rescued the unborn child from the pyre burning the body of Coronis and brought it to the centaur CHIRON. Chiron raised Asclepius and taught him the arts of healing. Chiron's daughter Ocyrhoe prophesied that Asclepius would possess incredible healing skills and be able to return the dead to life, but that his gift of resurrecting the dead would imperil his own life and he would be struck down by his grandfather's (Zeus's) thunderbolt.

Among the mortals whom Asclepius is said to have restored to life are Capaneus, Glaucus (the young son of MINOS, who had died by falling into a pot of honey), HIPPOLYTUS, Hymenaeus, Lycurgus, and Tyndareus (father of the DIOSCURI). Diodorus Siculus mentions that Asclepius was struck down by Zeus because he prevented so many souls from entering HADES that the lord of the dead complained about the lack. In Virgil's *Aeneid*, Asclepius resurrected Hippolytus at the request of Artemis after her young follower had been killed in a chariot accident. In Ovid's *Fasti*, Asclepius touched Hippolytus three times with healing herbs and three times spoke healing words to him in order to revive him. Asclepius's skills challenged the omnipotence of Zeus, who then killed Asclepius with a thunderbolt. In some sources, Apollo, angered by Zeus's killing of Asclepius, revenged himself by killing the CYCLOPES who fashioned Zeus's thunderbolts.

There was a temple of Asclepius on Tiber Island in Rome. The temple's origins were attributed to a moment of crisis in Roman history. In the third century B.C.E., Rome was suffering from a plague, and the senators were directed by the Delphic Oracle to seek the aid of Asclepius. The Romans sailed to Epidaurus in Greece in search of the god; he entered the ship in the form of a snake. On the ship's return to Rome, Asclepius descended at Tiber Island, which he chose to make his new home.

Asclepius married Epione, and their daughter was HYGEIA (Health). She shared her father's abilities. In the *Orphic Hymn to Asclepius*, Hygeia is Asclepius's mate, but in other sources, she is his daughter, a skilled healer in her own right, and goddess of Health. Asclepius and Hygeia were sometimes worshipped jointly. Asclepius passed on his skills to his sons, Machaon and Podaleirius, who accompanied AGAMEMNON during the Trojan War.

Asteria Daughter of the TITANS COEUS and PHOEBE. Sister to LETO. Classical sources are Apollodorus's LIBRARY (1.2.2, 1.2.4), Hesiod's THEOGONY (414), Hyginus's *Fabulae* (53), and Ovid's METAMORPHOSES (6.108). Asteria escaped the amorous pursuit of ZEUS by being transformed into a quail. In this form, she threw herself into the sea and gave her name to the island of Ortygia ("quail"). Ortygia is sometimes known as or conflated with the island of Delos, the location in which Leto gave birth to her children, APOLLO and ARTEMIS. Asteria married PERSES and their child was HECATE.

Astyanax Young son of HECTOR and ANDROMACHE. The classical sources are Euripides' ANDROMACHE (10) and TROJAN WOMEN (118), Homer's ILIAD (6.400, 24.734), and Ovid's METAMORPHOSES (13.415). Astyanax, whose name means "lord of the town," ought to have inherited his father Hector's role as protector of the city of Troy. Precisely to head off any possibility of later vengeance, ODYSSEUS or NEOPTOLEMUS killed Astyanax after the defeat of Troy by throwing him from the walls of Troy. In the *Iliad*, Andromache laments the fate of the fatherless boy. In Euripides' *Trojan Women* Astyanax was HECUBA's (Hector's mother's) one remaining hope and consolation, and the announcement of his death is the terrible climax of a long series of catastrophes.

Atalanta (Atalante) Mythological Greek heroine. Wife to Hippomenes and mother of Parthenopaeus by either her husband or ARES. Classical sources are Apollodorus's LIBRARY (1.8.2, 3.9.2), Hyginus's *Fabulae* (185), Ovid's METAMORPHOSES (10.560–704), and Propertius's *Elegies* (1.1.9). Atalanta's parentage is uncertain; Apollodorus gives her father as Iasus, Ovid as Schoeneus, and Euripides as Maenalus.

Atalanta was exposed at birth on Mount Parthenion and raised by a bear. When she came of age, Atalanta chose to become a huntress and follower of ARTEMIS. She took part in the famous Calydonian Boar hunt. King Oeneus of Calydon (Aetolia) had neglected to perform a harvest sacrifice to Artemis; as a consequence, the goddess sent a wild boar to ravage the country. Oeneus's son MELEAGER gathered a group of hunters including Atalanta, the DIOSCURI, JASON, PHOENIX, THESEUS, and TELAMON to hunt the boar. Atalanta struck the first successful blow, but Meleager managed to finish it off. He then gave the prized hide to Atalanta, with whom he was in love. This act of generosity on his part set in motion a series of events leading to his death.

Atalanta's most famous myth is her race with Hippomenes (a grandson of POSEIDON). According to Ovid, an oracle counseled Atalanta not to marry but predicted that she would, nonethe-

Atalanta and Hippomenes. *Guido Reni, ca. 1620–25 (Galleria Nazionale di Capodimonte, Naples)*

less, marry and that the marriage would alter her. Atalanta's father insisted on her marrying, and she agreed to accept the suitor who would beat her in a foot race. Those suitors she defeated would be killed. She won all her races until Hippomenes saw her win a race and fell in love with her. He appealed to APHRODITE for her help, and the goddess gave him three golden apples to use in the race. Accordingly, Hippomenes threw the apples down during the race, and while Atalanta paused to pick them up, he pulled ahead and won both the race and the bride. In some versions, Atalanta loved Hippomenes and hoped that he would win. Hippomenes neglected to thank Aphrodite, and the couple, made heedless by passion, desecrated one of CYBELE's sanctuaries by making love within it. As punish-

ment for their offence, Aphrodite turned them into lions, and thus the prophecy of Atlanta's marriage was realized.

Representations of Atalanta as a huntress and participant in the Calydonian Boar hunt occur on pediments, vases, and in engravings from the sixth century B.C.E. onward, for example, on the François Vase from ca. 570 B.C.E. (Museo Archeologico Nazionale, Florence). Here, the enormous boar tramples hunters and is surrounded by the heroes. Representation of Atalanta's race with Hippomenes and the episode of the golden apples occurs in a number of postclassical paintings, such as Guido Reni's *Atalanta and Hippomenes* from ca. 1620–25 (Galleria Nazionale di Capodimonte, Naples).

Athamas A king of Boeotia. Son of AEOLUS. Husband of INO (daughter of CADMUS and HARMONIA). The children of Athamas and Ino were Learchus and Melicertes (or Melicerta). Classical sources are Apollodorus's *LIBRARY* (1.9.1–3), Diodorus Siculus's *LIBRARY OF HISTORY* (4.47), Hyginus's *Fabulae* (1–5), Ovid's *METAMORPHOSES* (4.416–542, and Pausanias's *Description of Greece* (1.44.7–8). Euripides' *Ino* and Sophocles' *Athamas* survive in fragmentary form. There are several, sometimes contradictory, versions of the story of Athamas, Ino, and their children. Athamas had two children, PHRIXUS and Helle, by Nephele (a cloud goddess), before his marriage to Ino. Ino bore her stepchildren malice and plotted against them. First, she arranged to have the crops fail, in response to which Athamas sent a messenger to consult the Delphic Oracle. Ino persuaded the messenger to say on behalf of the Oracle that the sacrifice of Phrixus would renew the fertility of the crops. Athamas prepared to sacrifice his son, but before the child was killed, he and his sister Helle were carried off by their mother, Nephele. Nephele placed them on a Golden Ram that had been given to her by HERMES to journey through the sky. Helle fell off the ram into the sea and drowned and gave her name to the waters, the Hellesponte. Phrixus survived and was received by king AEETES in Colchis, where he married one of the royal daughters. Phrixus sacrificed the Golden Ram to ZEUS, and its fleece was placed in a grove sacred to ARES. This fleece would later be sought by JASON and the Argonauts.

HERA was infuriated by Ino's pride in her nephew, DIONYSUS, and she persuaded one of the FURIES, Tisiphone, to incite madness in Athamas and Ino. In Ovid's *Metamorphoses*, Tisiphone, whose head writhed with snakes, threw two snakes and a venomous potion at the couple, which caused their insanity. Athamas dashed his son against the wall, killing him, and in grief and madness Ino with Melicertes in her arms threw herself from a nearby cliff into the sea. APHRODITE, the mother of Harmonia and grandmother of Ino, took pity on them and asked POSEIDON to transform the two into marine deities: Ino became known as Leucothea, and Melicertes as Palaemon.

Athamas was said to have been exiled from Boeotia, founded his own settlement in Thessaly, and married Themisto, who bore him Erythrius, Leucon, Schoenus, and Ptous. In another version of the death of Ino, that of Hyginus's *Fabulae* (based on Euripides' *Ino*), the time line of events is reversed: Athamas, believing Ino to be dead, married Themisto, who bore him Erythrius, Leucon, Schoenus, and Ptous. Themisto, wishing to do away with the children of her predecessor, unwittingly killed her own children instead of those of Ino. Following this, Athamas was driven to the madness that provoked his killing of Learchus and Ino's attempted suicide.

Athena (Minerva) Olympian goddess of wisdom and war. Athena appears throughout Homer's *ILIAD* and *ODYSSEY*. Additional classical sources are the *Homeric Hymns to Athena*, Aeschylus's *EUMENIDES* (397–1,047), Apollodorus's *LIBRARY* (1.3.6, 2.4.3, 3.14.1, 3.14.6), Diodorus Siculus's *LIBRARY OF HISTORY* (3.70.1–6), Hesiod's *THEOGONY* (886ff), Hyginus's *Fabulae* (164–166), Ovid's *METAMORPHOSES* (4.790–803, 6.1–145), and Sophocles' *AJAX* (1–133). The Greek goddess Athena was later syncretized with the Roman Minerva, who was similarly associated with intelligence and war. In some accounts, Athena was the daughter of METIS (a personification of intelligence) one of the TITANS, and first wife of ZEUS. In Hesiod's *Theogony*, Metis was swallowed by Zeus because of the threat of succession her second child would represent. Zeus learned from GAIA and URANUS that Metis would bear Athena and that Metis's second child would overthrow him, so Zeus swallowed Metis, who was already pregnant with Athena. Zeus had terrible pains in his head, HEPHAESTUS struck him with an ax, and Athena emerged, fully grown, wearing a helmet and carrying her armor. Athena carries a shield, aegis, and spear. Her shield is decorated with the head of MEDUSA given to her by PERSEUS and can turn her enemies to stone. She is associated with the owl and the olive tree.

Athena's warlike capacity is sometimes distinguished from that of ARES, who is associated with the more violent, bloodthirsty aspects of war. In some myths, Athena and Ares come into conflict. During the Trojan War, Ares was injured by DIOMEDES, who had been guided by Athena. Athena also injured Ares by throwing a stone against his neck that knocked him down. Athena stood over Ares, laughing and boasting of her superiority as a warrior.

Athena argued with POSEIDON for patronage of the city of Athens. Zeus adjudicated in favor of Athena as she had planted the first olive tree on Attic soil.

Athena is a patron of the arts and music and as such has associations with APOLLO and the MUSES. In Ovid's *Fasti*, MARSYAS discovered the double flute after it had been invented by Athena (the double flute is sometimes called "Pallas's reed"). Ovid mentions a March festival celebrating Athena's invention, which involved a procession of the guild of flute players. Seeing that in the playing of the instrument her cheeks puffed up unattractively, Athena threw it away on a riverbank, where Marsyas found it and became adept at playing it. In some sources, Marsyas was punished by the goddess for his temerity in having acquired the instrument, and in others, Marsyas's skill on the double flute led to his ill-fated musical contest with Apollo.

Athena is a chaste goddess and has no lovers. In the *Homeric Hymn to Aphrodite* Athena is singled out as one of three goddesses—the others are ARTEMIS and HESTIA—over whom love has no sway. Despite her chastity, she is sometimes identified as the mother of ERICHTHONIUS, an early king of Athens. Details of Erichthonius's parentage and birth vary. In Homer's *Iliad*, Erichthonius, whose lower half was serpent-

shaped, was born of Earth (Gaia) but nurtured by Athena. In other sources, Hephaestus tried to violate Athena, but she fought him off. As he released her, his sperm fell to the ground and impregnated Gaia, from whom Erichthonius was born. Athena consigned a casket or box, in which Erichthonius was hidden, to the daughters of King Cecrops of Athens, AGLAURUS, Herse, and Pandrosus, and instructed them not to open it. Herse and Pandrosus resisted the temptation but not Aglaurus, who incurred the goddess's wrath (versions vary according to the source). As punishment, Athena afflicted Aglaurus with a terrible jealousy of HERMES' love for Herse.

Athena Parthenos. *Antiochos, first-century* B.C.E. *copy of a Greek fifth-century* B.C.E. *original (Palazzo Altemps, Rome)*

In addition to her responsibility for the infant Erichthonius, Athena nurtured the newborn HERACLES. Heracles' mother, ALCMENE, fearing HERA, exposed Heracles in a field where he was found by Athena. The goddess was struck by the infant's vigor and cared for him. Athena was thereafter his protector and appears in many of the hero's myths. She helped Heracles succeed in driving the birds from Lake Stymphalos, and he brought the golden apples of the HESPERIDES to her. ODYSSEUS was another favorite. She provides aid to Odysseus at several critical moments in Homer's *Odyssey*.

Athena's most famous myth is the story of ARACHNE. Arachne was a skilled weaver who claimed her efforts surpassed those of Athena, the patron goddess of weaving. The goddess visited Arachne in the form of an old woman and warned her to behave more modestly. When Arachne gave an insolent reply, the goddess revealed herself, and the two engaged in a contest. In Ovid's account (which is nearly the sole source for the myth), Athena's tapestry depicted the 12 Olympian gods and the punishment and defeat of mythological figures who challenged their authority. Arachne's tapestry, by contrast, represented the unjust, victimizing, or otherwise discrediting behavior of the gods toward mortals. Although Arachne's tapestry was flawless, Athena, in her anger, ripped it up and struck Arachne with her shuttle. Arachne tried to hang herself, but Athena wished to make an enduring example of her: She transformed Arachne into a spider and made her spin webs ceaselessly (and, it is implied, ignominiously and artlessly).

Athena was frequently represented in the visual arts of antiquity. In a marble freestanding sculpture of the first century B.C.E. (a Greek copy of a statue from the fifth century B.C.E.), Athena wears a peplos and helmet; she possibly carried a shield and spear in the original sculpture. An Athena Parthenos colossal statue from ca. 430 B.C.E. used for cult purposes at the Acropolis in Athens shows the goddess holding a spear and wearing an aegis and helmet.

A serpent on her shield refers to Erichthonius. Reliefs carved on the statue represented the Amazonomachy, the Centauromachy, and the GIGANTOMACHY.

Atlas   A TITAN. Son of the Titan IAPETUS and of the sea nymph Clymene (or the OCEANID Asia). Brother of EPIMETHEUS and PROMETHEUS. Classical sources are Apollodorus's LIBRARY (1.2.3, 2.5.11), Hesiod's THEOGONY (507–517), Homer's ODYSSEY (1.51), Hyginus's *Fabulae* (150, 192), Ovid's METAMORPHOSES (4.630–662), Philostratus's IMAGINES (20), and Virgil's AENEID (4.246–250, 481). By Pleione, Atlas had seven daughters, the PLEIADES (Alcyone, Asterope, Electra, Celaeno, MAIA, MEROPE, and Taygete), and one son, Hyas. His children were immortalized in the heavens: Hyas was killed by a lion and became the constellation Aquarius, and the lion became the constellation Leo. His grieving sisters were transformed into the Pleiades constellation. Homer identifies the nymph CALYPSO as another of Atlas's daughters. HERMES is the son of the Pleiad Maia and thus a grandson of Atlas. Atlas is also said to be the father of the HESPERIDES by Hesperis. Depending on the source, Atlas either holds the heavens on his shoulders, which prevents them from meeting Earth, or he safeguards the pillars that hold the heavens. He also protects his daughters, the Hesperides, and the golden apples in their keeping.

After the Olympian gods defeated the Titans in the Titanomachy, ZEUS punished Atlas by making him carry the bronze dome of the heavens on his shoulders or back. During his Twelfth Labor, HERACLES sought Atlas's help in obtaining the golden apples of the Hesperides. Atlas obligingly offered to fetch the apples if Heracles would temporarily hold the heavens up in his stead. Atlas returned with the fruit but refused to change places again with Heracles, but he was tricked by Heracles into resuming his burden. According to some versions, Atlas was released from his punishment, either by Zeus or by Heracles, and was

Perseus and Atlas. *Engraving, Johann Wilhelm Bauer, illustration for Ovid's* Metamorphoses, *1703 (University of Vermont)*

required merely to guard the two tall pillars that henceforward bore the weight of the sky.

Ovid's *Metamorphoses* describes an encounter between PERSEUS and Atlas, during which the former used the Gorgon's head to turn Atlas into stone, in revenge for having been denied hospitality. Atlas became the mountain range in North Africa known by his name.

Because of his physical connections to the heavens, Atlas was said to have superior knowledge of the stars and constellations and is closely associated with astronomy. The fate of his children also attests to this connection.

In the visual arts, Atlas is shown as a large, mature, bearded man bearing a weight representing the heavens on his bent shoulders. A common visual theme is Atlas's encounter with Heracles. Pausanias describes two items at the Temple of Zeus depicting this theme: the chest of Kypselos and a painted screen showing Atlas, Heracles, and Prometheus. This theme is

depicted on an Attic black-figure lekythos attributed to the Athena Painter from ca. 475 B.C.E. (National Archaeological Museum, Athens) and in relief on a metope from the Temple of Zeus at Olympia from ca. 470–457 B.C.E. On a black-figure vase by the Athenian Painter, Atlas stands before Heracles holding the golden apples of the Hesperides. Heracles holds the heavens and can be identified by his club and lion skin. Perseus, holding the head of Medusa, confronts Atlas in an engraving by J. W. Bauer from 1703. Here, Atlas is outlined against the mountain range with which he is associated. A second-century Roman copy of a Greek original sculpture shows Atlas straining under the weight of a globe (Museo Archeologico Nazionale, Naples), which provided the inspiration for John Singer Sargent's *Atlas and the Hesperides* of 1922–24 (Museum of Fine Arts, Boston). On both the Roman sculpture and Sargent's painting, the constellations are outlined on the sphere carried by Atlas.

Atreus Son of Pelops and Hippodamia. Father of AGAMEMNON and MENELAUS. Classical sources are Aeschylus's AGAMEMNON (1583–1602), Apollodorus's LIBRARY (Epitome 2.10), Homer's ILIAD (2.105ff), Hyginus's *Fabulae* (86, 88), and Seneca's *Thyestes*. Atreus and his younger brother Thyestes disputed the kingship of Mycenae. Thyestes committed adultery with his brother's wife, Aerope, and obtained from her the golden lamb, which, the brothers had agreed, symbolized the right to the throne. Zeus, appalled, reversed the course of the sun, and Atreus banished Thyestes.

Later, Atreus pretended reconciliation with his brother, lured him back to Mycenae, and, in revenge for his brother's adultery, served up his own children to him as a stew. Then Atreus showed Thyestes his sons' heads and hands, so that he would know that he had eaten his own children.

AEGISTHUS, Thyestes' son by an incestuous relationship, later killed Atreus; he completed his revenge on his uncle's line by seducing Agamemnon's wife, CLYTAEMNESTRA, and helping her kill her husband, afterward marrying her and taking over the throne. In Homer, the myth appears to have taken a different form: Atreus and Thyestes are not at odds with each other. In later versions, and especially in tragedy, the mythology of Atreus and his sons represents the curse of a household that destroys itself over successive generations. Aeschylus's trilogy *Oresteia*, especially the first play, *Agamemnon*, traces the path of violence through previous generations and the avenging spirits that inhabit the house of Atreus. Seneca's play *Thyestes* dwells with particular horror on the murder of Thyestes' children and his unknowing consumption of them.

Attis (Atys) A young shepherd from Phrygia, a disciple of CYBELE. Classical sources are Catullus's Poem 63, Diodorus Siculus's LIBRARY OF HISTORY (3.58.4ff), Ovid's FASTI (4.183) and METAMORPHOSES (10.104), and Pausanias's

Description of Greece (7.17.9–12). In one version of the story of Attis, the young follower of Cybele demonstrated his dedication to the goddess with self-emasculation. Following his example, later disciples of Cybele, called the *Galli*, also made themselves eunuchs.

In another version, that of Ovid's *Fasti*, Attis fell in love with Sagaritis, a NAIAD, breaking his vow of chastity to Cybele. Cybele revenged herself on the nymph by wounding Sagaritis's tree and thereby killing her. Filled with grief and madness, Attis castrated himself. According to Ovid's *Metamorphoses*, Attis was himself transformed into a pine tree.

In another myth, according to Diodorus Siculus's *Library of History*, Cybele was exposed as an infant by her father, Maeon, but survived and was raised by leopards and other wild beasts. While still young, she was recognized and received into her father's household, but he became furious when he discovered that she had become pregnant by Attis. Maeon put Attis to death, and Cybele wandered in grief, accompanied by MARSYAS and, for some time, by APOLLO. In response to plague and crop failure, the people of Phrygia provided a proper burial for Attis and established rites for Cybele.

Pausanias's *Description of Greece* puts forward yet another version of the story of Attis Attis was born a eunuch, offended ZEUS and, was killed by a boar sent by the god. Still in Pausanias, another story has Attis born from a hermaphrodite deity Agdistis, who originated from Zeus's sperm falling to earth. The gods castrated Agdistis and from her sexual organs grew an almond tree; the river nymph Nana plucked a nut from it, and, placing it on her body, became pregnant with Attis. Later, Agdistis fell in love with Attis and to prevent him from marrying someone else drove Attis into madness. In the grip of insanity, Attis castrated himself.

In representations, the pine tree or almond tree and the Phrygian cap are attributes of Attis, who is depicted as a beautiful youth. In the postclassical period, Attis is rarely represented in the visual arts; however, the myth has inspired literary works and operas, for example, Jean-Baptiste Lully's *Atys* of 1676.

Autonoe Daughter of CADMUS and HARMONIA. Autonoe married ARISTAEUS and their son was ACTAEON. Classical sources are Apollodorus's *LIBRARY* (3.4.2–4), Euripides' *BACCHAE*, and Hesiod's *THEOGONY* (975–978).

In Euripides' tragedy *Bacchae*, Pentheus, king of Thebes and grandson of Cadmus and Harmonia, was slaughtered by his own mother, Agave, and his aunt Autonoe in a Dionysiac frenzy. Their unwitting murder of Pentheus was brought about by DIONYSUS as retribution for Pentheus's lack of piety for the god. Autonoe later left Thebes for Megara, where she died. Autonoe and Aristaeus's son, the hunter Actaeon, was killed by ARTEMIS.

Bacchae Euripides (ca. 408–406 B.C.E.) Euripides' *Bacchae* was produced posthumously in 405 B.C.E. as part of a tragic tetralogy that included the *Iphigenia at Aulis*. The play is set in Thebes, a city of special importance to Athenian tragedy. Oedipus's tragic downfall occurred at Thebes, as did the conflict between his sons Polynices and Eteocles. Finally, in Sophocles' *Antigone*, Thebes provides the setting for the death of Oedipus's daughter and destruction of Creon's family. Euripides' *Bacchae* traces the dark mythological inheritance of Thebes back to an earlier phase, when Pentheus rules Thebes and attempts to repress the worship of Dionysus. The god punishes Pentheus by deranging his mind: He dresses up as a woman in order to spy on the women of Thebes as they carry out Dionysiac rites on the mountain, and his own mother, Agave, participates in his murder. The key role played by the god Dionysus underpins the intensely metatheatrical aspect of the play. This late tragedy by Euripides honors the terrible power of the god in whose honor Athenian tragedies were performed.

SYNOPSIS

The action takes place in front of the royal palace of Thebes. On the left, the path leads to Cithaeron, and on the right, to the city of Thebes. In the center of the stage lies Semele's tomb, covered in vines. Dionysus, son of Semele, enters wearing a fawn skin and smiling mask and carrying a thyrsus. Dionysus voices his pleasure at observing Semele's tomb covered in vines by Cadmus, former king of Thebes. He has made his way, he says, from Lydia, Phrygia, and cities throughout Asia Minor, establishing his rites among the people there. Here in Thebes, Dionysus continues, Semele's sisters have slandered him, claiming that he is not immortal and not the son of Zeus. To punish them, Dionysus has driven the women of Thebes mad, possessed by his worship. Among the women are Autonoe, Ino, and Agave, mother of the current king of Thebes, Pentheus. Cloaked in fawn skins and carrying thyrsi, the women of Thebes are attending to the Dionysian rites on Mount Cithaeron. Dionysus is here in Thebes to confront the impiety of Pentheus, but he has disguised himself as a mortal. Dionysus summons his followers, women gathered from distant Asian lands, the Bacchae, and they enter, also costumed in fawn skins and ivy crowns, while carrying thyrsi, timbrels, and flutes.

The Bacchae sing the praises of Dionysus, exhorting others to follow him. They describe his mythical birth (see Semele) and his triumphant ascendancy as a god.

The Bacchae form two semicircles as the blind seer Tiresias enters. He is an unlikely sight, clothed in Dionysian costume, using his thyrsus as a guiding stick. He calls out to Cadmus, who emerges, bent over with age, wearing a similar costume. In a semicomic dialogue, the two men exchange remarks about the irony of two such old men participating in this new cult, which requires so much physicality and strength. Though they alone of Theban men take part in the rites, they do so because they believe in the traditional respect and honor due to the gods. Cadmus observes his grandson, Pentheus, entering from the city in agitated conversation with his attendants. He is discussing the Dionysian rites taking place and hopes to prevent more of the same by imprisoning the worshippers. Moreover, a foreigner has been observed among the revelers, and Pentheus hopes to capture him too.

Pentheus comes on the two older men and, remarking on their clothing, is disgusted at the sight. The Chorus leader objects to Pentheus's obvious disrespect for the god. Tiresias responds that he, Pentheus, is mad and foolish not to apprehend the greatness of Dionysus, who has given men the gift of wine, commands prophetic powers, and is able to infect an army with panic. Further, Tiresias says, Dionysus does not, as Pentheus contends, encourage obscene behavior in women. Chaste women continue to be so even if they should take part in Dionysiac rites. For his part, Cadmus attempts to persuade Pentheus to join them in the worship of the new god. He asks why Pentheus should withhold his respect if all of Thebes is participating. Cadmus also asks Pentheus to bear in mind the example of his cousin Actaeon, torn limb from limb by his hounds because he did not respect Artemis.

Furious, Pentheus rejects their entreaties and arguments. He commands his attendants to imprison the male foreigner attending the rites, and they leave to do his bidding. Tiresias decries Pentheus's folly, and he and Cadmus exit, while Pentheus enters the palace. The Bacchae respond to Pentheus's impiety by observing that ill befalls the man who does not recognize the limitations of his understanding and accept the traditional and natural respect due to the gods. True wisdom for men, according to the Bacchae, lies in recognizing a superior authority.

Pentheus emerges from the palace as his attendants arrive bearing Dionysus, captive, between them. The attendants inform Pentheus that the stranger came cooperatively and that the women Pentheus had previously imprisoned for participating in the rites have been mysteriously liberated.

Pentheus examines Dionysus, questioning him about his origins and relationship to Dionysus, never suspecting that he is speaking to the god himself. Dionysus is careful not to reveal his identity, and in the ensuing dialogue Pentheus is frustrated by Dionysus's obfuscations. Annoyed, Pentheus cuts away the god's long blond curls, takes his thyrsus, and orders his imprisonment in the stables. The Bacchae become agitated and beat at their drums. Once Pentheus exits and Dionysus has been led away, the Bacchae repeat their recital of Dionysus's birth, express their anger at Pentheus's impiety, and call on Dionysus to avenge this behavior with justice.

Thunder and lightning are heard, Dionysus calls out to the Bacchae from within and calls on thunder, lightning, and earthquake to raze the palace of Thebes. An earthquake shatters the palace and flames leap up from the tomb of Semele to engulf it.

The Bacchae, amazed, prostrate themselves before Dionysus, who emerges unharmed, calmly stepping through the ruins of the royal palace of Thebes. The Chorus leader expresses anxiety for Dionysus, and he reassures them that his safety was never in question and his escape from Pentheus's captivity never in doubt.

An agitated Pentheus comes out from the ruins and demands of Dionysus how he managed to escape. Dionysus calmly responds that Dionysus has made possible his escape.

A messenger arrives from Cithaeron, a herdsman who has spied on the female revelers in the mountain and has come to report what he has seen. He tells Pentheus that Autonoe, Ino, and Pentheus's own mother Agave are leading groups of dancing women through the forests and that he has witnessed many of their miracles. The Maenads, or Dionysiac revelers, have produced water from rock and milk and wine from the ground. The herdsman helped lay an ambush for Agave, but the women beat them off and fled. The women then came upon a herd of cattle, which they tore apart with their bare hands. Afterward, the women pillaged and destroyed an entire village, and despite attack by the men of the village, who fought them with spears, they were unharmed and the men forced to flee. These acts of physical strength and the miracles that accompanied them awed the herdsman, who now can only acknowledge the greatness of divinity these acts represent. The messenger exits.

Pentheus turns to his attendants, preparing to call his army to march on the women. Dionysus gives him a clear warning not to prepare to do violence against the worshippers of a god and suggests that even now Pentheus can still repent.

Because Pentheus does not heed the warning, Dionysus suggests a plan in which Pentheus can first observe the revelers in disguise, before he marches on them. Despite some misgivings, Pentheus is tempted by the plan and enters the palace to reflect on it. When he is gone, Dionysus reveals that he has already bewildered Pentheus, otherwise he would never have even considered this plan. Further, Dionysus reveals that this plan, which Pentheus will accept, will lead him to his death, a just fate for his impiety.

Dionysus enters the palace after Pentheus to aid him in his disguise and exits later in triumph. Pentheus also exits; he is dressed in a linen dress over a fawn skin, carries a thyrsus, and wears a blond wig. He is completely under the thrall of the god. Dionysus arranges Pentheus's costume and leads him to Cithaeron, meaning to offer the young man as a sacrifice to the women who will kill him. The young man and the god exit as the Bacchae call on justice to visit Pentheus's impiety.

A messenger arrives bearing the news that Pentheus has been killed. He describes the scene thus: Dionysus placed Pentheus on a tree in full view of his followers and commanded them to take revenge on the man who mocked and disdained their faith. Led by a maddened Agave, who did not recognize her son or acknowledge his cry of repentance, the women tore Pentheus limb from limb. Agave impaled Pentheus's head on her thyrsus and is now coming toward the royal palace. The messenger exits while the Bacchae sing triumphantly at Pentheus's humiliation and death.

Agave enters bearing her grisly staff and the Bacchae praise her. Cadmus, father of Agave, enters, accompanied by attendants bearing the dismembered corpse of his grandson Pentheus. He calls Agave out of her madness, and she gradually becomes aware of the death of her son and her own actions bringing it about. Agave is grief-stricken, and Cadmus observes that Dionysus has shattered the entire family. No male heir remains; his daughters are murderers and the palace in ruins because of Pentheus's lack of piety. The Chorus leader remarks that the scene before them should be a lesson for those who deny the immortality of Dionysus.

Dionysus appears above the palace and in his speech explains that the sufferings of the royal house of Thebes are a consequence of the questioning of his immortality and the violence threatened against him by Pentheus. Because of their murder of Pentheus, Agave and her sisters will be exiled from Thebes, while Cadmus and his wife, Harmonia, will be transformed into serpents and also go into exile. Cadmus pleads with the god, but to no avail. Agave and Cadmus bid each other a tearful farewell and move off to their appointed destinies in exile.

The Bacchae's final words concern the unexpected events brought about by the superior authority and power of the gods.

COMMENTARY

Euripides' *Bacchae* is remarkable for focusing on a myth whose central figure is of thematic significance for the genre of tragedy: Dionysus himself. Greek tragedies were performed during festivals of Dionysus. These performances took place in the precinct of the god, and a representation of the god in statue form was located near the stage so as to watch as spectator the plays that were performed in his honor. Dionysus was a god associated with transformation, disguise, inebriation, and ecstatic states; he was also a terrifying god with destructive tendencies. He was an appropriate patron god for ancient theater, but the Greeks themselves, by a common saying, often observed that the plays' content had "nothing to do with Dionysus." Some recent scholarship has challenged this idea, attempting to link the cultic, religious, and civic background of the Dionysian festivals to the content and performance of the plays. To whatever extent these recent arguments persuade, it is striking that Euripides, in his late play the *Bacchae*, demonstrates a keen awareness of Dionysus's role as tragic god and powerfully plays on the interrelation among Dionysiac cult, myth, and tragedy.

The myth of Pentheus is an especially appropriate episode in Dionysus's mythology for introducing the question of tragedy's origins. Thebes, by this point in the history of the genre, has been established as the location par excellence of tragic plots: One need only recall the SEVEN AGAINST THEBES (Aeschylus), ANTIGONE (Sophocles), and OEDIPUS THE KING (Aeschylus), among others. Thebes is an eminently tragic city-state from the Athenian viewpoint. Dionysus, the son of Semele and Zeus, is related to the Theban royal family. Pentheus is his cousin. When Cadmus realizes the full horror of Pentheus's demise at the hands of his own mother near the play's end, he laments the destruction of their household and family—a familiar tragic motif here modified by the inclusion of a divine figure within the family matrix. Dionysus brings about the death of his cousin at the hands of his aunt to punish both his cousin's resistance to his rites and his aunts' denial of his divinity—a family tragedy in which the god proves his divinity by destroying his mortal relations.

Just as Dionysus both belongs to a mortal family and brutally demonstrates his distance from it, he appears simultaneously as a foreign and a Greek god. The Greeks conceptualized Dionysus as a god who came from elsewhere, presumably because of his connection with questionable qualities such as violence, wildness, and drunkenness. In fact, he is among the oldest Greek gods: His name has been discovered on Linear B tablets. The essential tension in Dionysus's identity recurs here in an intensified form: Dionysus returns from Asia as an invading barbarian to his native Thebes. The Chorus of Asian Bacchae further embodies the duality. We cannot tell to what extent they are meant to give voice to Greek values. As in Euripides' MEDEA, concepts of foreign and barbarian are at the heart of the play. The opposition is highly marked but by no means uncomplicated. Greekness itself threatens to dissolve or implode if an inadequate respect for the irrational and the exotic is manifested. The old men Cadmus and Tiresias break with tradition and consciously violate norms of virility and old age in dressing up to dance for Dionysus, but it is Pentheus's overzealous Greek maleness that is presented as the true madness, the true derangement of tradition. The Chorus compares him to a wild beast and a monster.

Pentheus resembles the character of CREON in Sophocles' *Antigone*: Stubborn, devoted to the primacy of the polis over irrational religious beliefs, a misguided rationalist, he, too, ends up destroying his own family by resisting the traditional claims of the gods and overriding the feminine with an overly rigid version of the masculine ethos. But whereas in the *Antigone*, the laws of the polis are set in opposition to the laws of the dead, Euripides sets up an explicitly topographical opposition between city and wilderness. The polis and its laws are challenged by the numinous powers associated with the wilderness outside the city, the Bacchic hunting grounds of Mount Cithaeron. Pentheus's aggressive masculine approach, moreover, is contrasted with the female Bacchae and Dionysus's languid, effeminate manner. Women, as in Sophocles, manifest a deeper connection with cults and rites not sanctioned by the polis.

Too strict and puritanical an opposition, however, is precisely the cause of the crisis instigated by Pentheus. The polis, according to the tragedians, can survive only if it incorporates a healthy awareness of its own limitations and the importance of deeper obligations and greater powers. The male-female divide is key to the Euripidean (and, to some extent, the Sophoclean) articulation of this awareness. The god's appearance is effeminate and Asian, and he is dynamically represented by the Chorus of Bacchae, who offer him songs of praise throughout the play and whose ecstatic singing and dancing drive the play forward with powerful surges of rhythm. The men of Thebes, and above all Pentheus, resist the god in large part because his worship seems too much like a morally dubious emancipation of women. But in Euripides, it rarely pays to overestimate the male/polis–centered/rationalistic dimension. Even Medea was praiseworthy in her way—barbarian, female, irrational, and destructive, a good figure to compare with the god Dionysus. Medea may not be admirable, but she presents essentially the same challenge for men—a divine force of irrational destructiveness that it would be wiser to fear and revere than to challenge directly.

Dionysus represents a crucial wild element in civilization itself: What is more essential to Mediterranean civilization than wine, and yet what potentially brings people closer to savagery? And yet if we were to tame Dionysus fully, he would not be Dionysus—he

would not be wild. This paradox is at the core of Dionysus's identity and the play's meditations, yet it is not one that Pentheus is able to accept: The failure to accept this paradox is catastrophic. We can trace his attempts, and ultimate failure, to control and defeat the wild, dangerous energies of Dionysiac cult through the highly conspicuous metaphor of the hunt. Near the play's opening, an arrogant Pentheus proclaims that he will "hunt" and capture the stranger who has corrupted his city's women. The women themselves, of course, are involved in hunting of their own: They hunt wild animals and, in a trademark Dionysiac rite, rip them apart limb from limb. Hunting is a key point of contact with civilization and the wild: Dionysiac rites represent an extreme version of this confrontation, where the hunters take on characteristics of wild animals themselves. Pentheus's hypercivilized model ultimately fails, however. In a grim irony, he is ripped apart by the hunting Bacchae, and his head is brought back from the wilds into the city of Thebes by the deranged Agave as a glorious "trophy." Euripides does not fail to uncover a deeper mythological layer within this Theban pattern: Pentheus's cousin Actaeon failed to respect sufficiently the wild divinity of Artemis and ended up being ripped apart by his own hounds, the hunter converted into quarry. Finally, we might recall the hunting enthusiast Hippolytus in another Euripidean play: He, too, ended up being mangled to the point of unrecognizability by his own horses for the crime of disdaining another powerful god representing an irrational destructive force: Aphrodite. The Chorus, in the present play, explicitly links the pleasures of wine and Aphrodite, and so, even if Euripides insists that the Bacchae are sexually chaste, he does draw a link between these essential yet potentially destructive elements of human life.

Just as Pentheus's excessive resistance to wild, uncontrolled Dionysiac hunting ultimately makes him a victim of the hunt, his arrogant virility becomes an object lesson in hubris by collapsing into its opposite by play's end. He poses himself the option of either advancing on the women with his army—the virile, polis-sanctioned mode of attack—or of disguising himself in women's clothes and spying on the women amid their supposed orgies. The choice is an impossible one—he will be defeated either way—but it is significant that Dionysus destroys and makes an example of Pentheus by exploiting the ruler's desire to *see* while remaining concealed himself. Dionysus is a god specifically associated with disguise and deception, and he has demonstrated those powers in this very play. Pentheus, however, is unable to handle such transitions, and his transvestitism is grotesque and bathetic, not sleek and beguiling like the god's. He has invested the Bacchic rites, moreover, with his own puritanical notions. Since the women are uncontrolled and outside the polis, they must be engaging in multifarious sexual acts. This possibility revolts, fascinates, and, ultimately, deranges Pentheus. He wants to see, to be a spectator, but to remain untouched himself, apart. This kind of spying on sacred rites, however, is strictly wrong, and for his punishment he is absorbed brutally into them: He is pulled down from his isolationist perch, and in a symbolic erasure of his identity, he is pulled limb from limb and mangled until unrecognizable.

Pentheus, then, fails to become a successful spectator, and fails to participate safely in the Dionysiac acts of deception, disguise, doubling, and mimesis. This metatheatrical dimension of the play would have been intensified by the physical environment of the Theater of Dionysus when the play was being performed before an Athenian audience. The god himself—as represented by his statue—looked on as Pentheus's tragedy unfolded. Dionysus's many ironic references to himself in the third person would have been further enriched by the god's presence in statue form. Athenians in the theater were themselves successfully, safely, and (presumably) chastely participating in the worship of Dionysus, even as they watched Pentheus's failure to incorporate Dionysiac cult into the Theban polis. They were spectators at a drama that did *not* engulf and destroy them. They could feel themselves reasonably (if never wholly) in control of their responses to the god's dangerous duality. The young male Athenian chorus members, moreover, were aware of being able to dress up as women and Asians without losing their identity as Athenian males. The young Pentheus, in the liminal state of young adulthood, does not become a fully mature Theban male. Instead, his identity is erased before it can be properly established. The aged Cadmus and Tiresias, on the other hand, are able to assume Bacchic outfits with the proper humility. Dionysus teaches us, among other things, that an ability to dress up, try on new and unfamiliar identities through acting and disguise, is an important component of our ordinary identity as citizens.

The story of Pentheus, however, does not represent a successful transition into maturity; nor does it offer a resolution of the conflicts between civilization and savagery, male and female, identity and disguise. Cadmus and Tiresias might seem like successful models of integration and flexibility, yet they still cut slightly ridiculous figures in their Bacchic garb, and the justifications they offer for dressing up in Bacchus's honor come off as sophistic and self-interested. The closure of the play, moreover, punishes Pentheus and his family with stark extremity that goes beyond ordinary notions of justice: The god has demonstrated his power and above all his power to destroy, derange, and transform in terrible ways. The Chorus—who in most ancient tragedies represents a kind of *communis opinio*—exults ecstatically at the gruesome death of Pentheus. The messenger, by contrast, demurs. Finally, Cadmus laments his son's death with a pathos that begins to make the death seem not only cruel but also even pointless. Cadmus himself, as Euripides is careful to emphasize, undergoes a long, drawn-out punishment and banishment in the form of a serpent that he hardly merits. The singing and dancing of the Bacchic Chorus—whose effect must have been electrifying from their first appearance on stage—by the end is infused with a sense of cruelty and crazed violence.

Euripides' tragedy, as in other instances, provides a pitiless demonstration of a god's brutality and inexorable will. Our value systems are ultimately powerless to suture the rifts created by divine violence. Euripidean gods belong to another order of morality and of necessity. The best human beings can do is to be aware of, and to treat with the proper humility and reverence, the terrible power of the gods, rather than attract their violence and punishment through disregard.

Bacchus   See DIONYSUS.

Baucis and Philemon   An elderly Phrygian couple who gave hospitality to HERMES (Mercury) and ZEUS (Jupiter). The main textual source for this myth is Ovid's *METAMORPHOSES* (8.616–724). The story of Baucis and Philemon is told by Lelex at a banquet held by the river god ACHELOUS in honor of THESEUS. The stories told by the banquet guests concern Zeus's ability to metamorphose and dispense justice to pious mortals. PIRITHOUS objected to Achelous's story, which, he felt, attributed too much power to the gods. Lelex answered the criticism with the story of Baucis and Philemon. Zeus and Hermes were

Jupiter *[Zeus]* and Mercury *[Hermes]* in the House of Philemon and Baucis. *Adam Elsheimer, ca. 1608 (Gemäldegalerie, Dresden)*

wandering, disguised, in Phrygia in search of hospitality. Household after household refused to host the travelers. Only Baucis and Philemon, an older, humble and pious couple living in a straw-thatched cottage, received them. This couple bore their poverty with dignity and did not let their humble surroundings prevent them from providing food and shelter to the disguised gods. During the simple meal, Baucis and Philemon were surprised to find the food and wine magically replenishing themselves. Zeus and Hermes revealed their true identities and led them into the nearby mountain. The area in which they had lived was inundated by the gods, destroying the inhospitable population. The house of Baucis and Philemon, meanwhile, was turned into a temple, and the gods fulfilled the couple's wish to be together in eternity by transforming them, upon their deaths, into an entwined oak and linden tree guarding the temple.

In the 18th century, Jean de la Fontaine's fables included a story based on that of Baucis and Philemon. Early-modern northern painters produced many versions of the theme, including Adam Elsheimer's *Jupiter and Mercury in the House of Philemon and Baucis* from ca. 1608 (Gemäldegalerie, Dresden), Peter Paul Rubens's 1620 *Landscape with Philemon and Baucis* (Kunsthistoriches Museum, Vienna), and Rembrandt van Rijn's *Philemon and Baucis* from 1658 (National Gallery of Art, Washington). Elsheimer's painting shows the humble interior of Baucis and Philemon's cottage as they offer Zeus and Hermes hospitality. The seated gods, dressed in rustic garb, have yet to reveal their true identities.

Bellerophon A Corinthian hero. Son of Glaucus (or POSEIDON) and Eurymede. Grandson of SISYPHUS. Classical sources are Apollodorus's LIBRARY (1.9.3, 2.3.2), Hesiod's THEOGONY (319–325), Homer's ILIAD (6.186f), Horace's ODES (4.11), Hyginus's *Fabulae* (57), and Pindar's *Isthmian Odes* (7.45) and *Olympian Odes* (13.60). Euripides wrote two plays, *Bellerophon*

and *Stheneboea* (now lost), based on the story of Bellerophon. In Homer, Bellerophon is a great warrior who, in a reversal of fortune, eventually earned the disfavor of the gods. According to Pindar's *Olympian Ode* 13, ATHENA gave him a charmed bridle to capture the winged horse PEGASUS as he drank from a spring. Astride this marvelous horse, Bellerophon fought and defeated the AMAZONS and killed the CHIMAERA. According to Pindar, when Bellerophon attempted to ride to Mount Olympus to join the gods, Pegasus threw him off his back.

At the beginning of his adventures, Bellerophon found himself in exile at the court of Proteus as a consequence of a (possibly unwitting) murder that he had committed. Depending on the source, the victim was either his own brother or Belarus, a tyrant of Corinth. Proteus's wife Stheneboea (sometimes called Anteia) attempted to seduce Bellerophon. He resisted her advances, so she accused him of attempting to rape her and asked her husband to kill Bellerophon. (The myth is similar to that of HIPPOLYTUS, who also rejected an adulterous liaison and was made the target of false accusations.) Proteus was unwilling to violate the laws of hospitality by personally killing his guest. Instead, he sent the young man to Stheneboea's father, king Iobates of Lycia, with a letter detailing the accusations and asking him to kill Bellerophon. Equally unwilling to kill the young man himself, Iobates set him several tasks, the first of which was to slay the fire-breathing Chimaera. Bellerophon used a spear to insert a piece of lead into her throat, which her fiery breath melted and caused her to choke to death. Afterward Bellerophon battled with the Solymi and the Amazons, defeating them both. Finally, Iobates engineered an ambush by Lycian warriors, but, here again, Bellerophon triumphed. His success in overcoming these trials convinced Iobates that Bellerophon enjoyed the favor of the gods. He accepted him into his household, made him his successor, and gave him his daughter, Anticlea, in marriage. Anticlea and Bellerophon produced three children: Isander, Hippolochus, and Laodamia. According to Homer, Bellerophon angered the gods (possibly because he had attempted to ride Pegasus to Mount Olympus), and he ended his days miserably.

In the visual arts, Bellerophon is often represented riding Pegasus in the act of slaying the Chimaera. A Laconian black-figure kylix attributed to the Boread Painter from ca. 570 B.C.E. (J. Paul Getty Museum, Malibu) is one example. A similar image is depicted in a Palmyrian floor mosaic of the imperial period. Images of Bellerophon are thought to be the iconographic model for later representations of St. George slaying the dragon.

Bibliotheca   See LIBRARY.

Boreadae (Calais and Zetes)   The Boreadae, twin sons of BOREAS, the North Wind, and OREITHYIA (daughter of ERECTHEUS). Textual sources are Apollodorus's LIBRARY (1.9.21), Apollonius of Rhodes's VOYAGE OF THE ARGONAUTS (2.211–223, 2.164–434), Hyginus's *Fabulae* (14, 19), and Ovid's METAMORPHOSES (6.675–722). In Ovid's *Metamorphoses*, Calais and Zetes showed no signs of having inherited their father's divine status until manhood, when they sprouted wings on their backs. In Hyginus's *Fabulae*, they have wings at their heads and feet. Calais and Zetes joined the expedition of the Argonauts in the company of JASON and HERACLES. Their central myth is the rescue of King PHINEUS of Thrace. Phineus had been granted prophetic gifts by APOLLO, but either his misuse of them or his maltreatment of his sons brought the HARPIES' wrath down upon him. They tormented him by snatching food away from his mouth but allowed him just enough, a reeking morsel of food, to allow him to linger in a weakened, aged, and blind state. When the crew of the *Argo* came upon him in this condition, Calais and Zetes resolved to liberate him. Being sons of Boreas, they were endowed with wings and chased the Harpies to the Strophades. The Harpies were protected

by their sister IRIS (goddess of rainbows and herald of the Olympian gods), who pledged that the Harpies would cease to torment Phineus. Diodorus Siculus's *Library of History* has an alternate version of the story in which Phineus's sons were imprisoned by him, freed by the Boreadae and by the crew of the *Argo*, and Phineus was killed by Heracles. Sources vary as to the ending of the myth: either Calais and Zetes freed Phineus or were themselves killed by the Harpies. According to Apollonius of Rhodes and Hyginus, Calais and Zetes were later killed by Heracles. Heracles blamed them for having convinced the crew of the *Argo* to abandon him in Propontis while he searched for his companion HYLAS, and he revenged himself on them by killing them both. Heracles built a barrow at the graves of Zetes and Calais that shook with winds blown by their father, Boreas. The winged Boreadae are shown rescuing Phineus in an Attic red-figure column-amphora attributed to the Leningrad Painter from ca. 460 B.C.E. (Louvre, Paris), while in a Chalcidian black-figure cup (Wagner Museum, University of Würzburg) from ca. 530 B.C.E. the Boreadae give chase to the Harpies.

Boreas   The personification of the North Wind. According to Hesiod, the progeny of Eos (Aurora) and ASTRAEUS; elsewhere, the son of TYPHOEUS. Classical sources are Apollodorus's LIBRARY (3.15.1), Apollonius of Rhodes's *Voyage of the Argonauts* (2.211–223), Hesiod's THEOGONY (378) and *Works and Days* (504f), Homer's ILIAD (20.221), Ovid's METAMORPHOSES (6.675–722), and Pausanias's *Description of Greece* (1.19.5, 8.27.14). The Anemoi were four storms winds associated with the four cardinal points: Boreas the North Wind, NOTUS the South Wind, ZEPHYRUS the West Wind, and EURUS the East Wind. Boreas brings the bitter coldness of the winter winds from the north. In his *Works and Days*, Hesiod recommends avoiding the bitter cold and moist wind blown from Thrace by "swift-pathed" Boreas in January and February.

A cult was established in Athens in gratitude to the North Wind after a storm destroyed the approaching Persian fleet in 480 B.C.E. In Homer's *Odyssey*, Boreas sent a wind to blow ODYSSEUS's ship off course in obedience to Zeus. Boreas loved OREITHYIA, daughter of King ERECTHEUS of Athens, and carried her off by force after he failed to win her by persuasion. Their offspring were Calais and Zetes, twins who seemed human until they came of age and sprouted wings. The BOREADAE, as the youths were known, later joined the expedition of the Argonauts. Two daughters were also born to the couple, Chione and Cleopatra; the latter married the Thracian king PHINEUS. In Homer's *Iliad*, Boreas, in the form of a stallion, mated with the mares of Erectheus, producing 12 swift mares. In the *Orphic Hymn to Boreas*, the North Wind is called on to bring good, rather than cold, weather.

In visual representations, Boreas is shown as an older, bearded male figure with hair stiffened by cold. His abduction of Oreithyia was a popular theme in classical painting. An example of this typical representation is an Attic red-figure pelike attributed to the Niobid Painter from ca. 460 B.C.E. (Wagner Museum, University of Würzburg). A postclassical example is a lunette fresco from the Galatea stanza of the Villa Farnesina (Rome) painted by Sebastiano del Piombo in ca. 1511.

Briareus   See HUNDRED-HANDED ONES.

Briseis   Concubine of ACHILLES. Daughter of Brisis. Classical sources are Homer's *ILIAD* (1.181–187, 318–348; 2.688–694; 9.328–945; 19.245–302; 24.675–676) and Ovid's *HEROIDES* (3). Briseis was married to Mynes. During the Trojan War, ACHILLES killed Mynes and captured Briseis as his slave but was forced to give her to AGAMEMNON, who had himself given up his captive, Chryseis, to her father, Chryses, when it was revealed that her capture was the cause of a plague afflicting the Greeks. After being obliged to release Briseis, Achilles refused to reenter the battle.

Cacus A fire-breathing creature Hercules (see HERACLES) encountered during his Tenth Labor. Classical sources are Livy's *History* (1.7.4–15), Ovid's *FASTI* (1.543–582, 5.643–652), and Virgil's *AENEID* (8.190ff). The story of Caucus is a Roman addition to the myths of the Twelve Labors of Hercules. In Hercules' Tenth Labor, he was sent to fetch the cattle of GERYON, a triple-bodied warrior whom he defeated. The herd of beautiful cattle were driven by Hercules from Erythia (modern Spain) through (in the Latin addition to the story) Rome. According to Livy, Ovid, and Virgil, Heracles encountered the cattle thief Cacus in Rome. In Livy, Cacus is simply a covetous shepherd, but Virgil's Cacus is a part-human, fire-breathing monster fathered by Vulcan (see HEPHAESTUS). Cacus is equally grotesque in Ovid, who notes that he lives in caves on the Aventine Hill; in other versions, he inhabits the Palatine. While Hercules was being entertained by EVANDER, Cacus stole several cattle from him and devised a plan for confusing him about their location; he pulled the cows backward into a cave, making it seem as if the cattle had walked away from the cave (a trick similar to the one perpetrated by HERMES on APOLLO). When Hercules came to drive his herd away, some of these bellowed for the lost cattle. The hidden cattle answered, revealing their hiding place. Hercules recovered his cattle and killed Cacus with his club. Hercules afterward instituted the rite of Greek-style sacrifice at Rome's Ara Maxima (Greatest Altar).

Cadmus Founder of Thebes. Son of King Agenor of Tyre, in Phoenicia. Husband to HARMONIA (daughter of APHRODITE and ARES) and brother to EUROPA. The children of Cadmus and Harmonia are AUTONOE, AGAVE, INO, and SEMELE, and a son, Polydorus. Cadmus appears in Aeschylus's *SEVEN AGAINST THEBES* and *EURIPIDES' BACCHAE*. Additional classical sources are Apollodorus's *LIBRARY* (3.4.1–2), Diodorus Siculus's *LIBRARY OF HISTORY* (5.49.1–6, 58.2), Herodotus's *Histories* (1.166ff), Hesiod's *THEOGONY* (937), Hyginus's *Fabulae* (6), Ovid's *METAMORPHOSES* (3.1–136, 4.561–603), Pausanias's *Description of Greece* (9.5.1–3) and Strabo's *Geography* (9.2.3). Sources are not agreed on the parentage of Cadmus, neither do they agree about the number and name of his siblings. Cadmus's brothers are, variously, Cilix, PHINEUS, Phoenix, and Thasus, and it is usually agreed that his sister is Europa. Following the abduction of Europa by ZEUS in the form of a bull to Crete, Cadmus and his brothers were sent by their father, King Agenor, to return with her or face exile themselves. The brothers did not find Europa but did move onto the European continent and there established several settlements. Cadmus, in particular, was renowned as the founder of the city of Thebes. He was also believed to have brought the Phoenician alphabet—the basis of the Greek alphabet—to Greece. The Cadmea, the citadel of Thebes, is named after the founder of the city.

Accompanied by his mother, Telephassa, in his search for Europa, Cadmus first arrived in Thrace, where they were warmly received. Cadmus consulted the Delphic Oracle, which advised him to abandon the search for Europa. Instead, he was advised to follow a certain cow and establish a city on the spot where the cow would fall down exhausted. This was Thebes. According to Pausanias's *Description of Greece*, the cow Cadmus followed had the markings of the full moon on her flanks. Before Cadmus could sacrifice the cow, he searched for a spring. He found one protected by a dragon, Ares' off-spring, who proceeded to slaughter Cadmus's companions. Cadmus killed the dragon, and, following ATHENA's advice, planted the dragon's teeth in the soil. These sprang up to become fully armed Spartan warriors. Alarmed, Cadmus threw a rock among the warriors to provoke a fight among them. Only five Spartoi ("sown men") survived the battle: Echion, Oudaeus, Chthonius, Hyperenor, and Pelorus. Cadmus atoned for his killing of Ares' dragon by giving himself into the god's servitude for eight years. He was finally rewarded for his toils by ascending to the throne of Thebes and was given Harmonia, daughter of Aphrodite and Ares, in marriage. According to Diodorus Siculus's *Library of History*, their wedding was hosted by the Olympian gods, and the couple were presented with extraordinary gifts. Cadmus gave Harmonia a golden necklace. In some accounts, it was given to her directly by its maker, HEPHAESTUS, or even given to Cadmus by his sister, Europa, who had received it from Zeus. This necklace was later associated with the ill fortune suffered by the descendants of Cadmus and Harmonia. Eventually Cadmus ceded the throne of Thebes to his grandson, PENTHEUS, and settled in Illyria with Harmonia, where, after death, they were transformed into snakes and brought to Elysium. According to Hyginus's *Fabulae*, they metamorphosed into serpents because Cadmus had killed the dragon of Ares.

Though Cadmus and Harmonia appear to have been favored by the gods, their descendants suffered misfortunes. Semele, mother of DIONYSUS, was tricked into bringing about her own death by HERA. Ino's care of her nephew Dionysus attracted Hera's wrath, and she afflicted Ino with a madness that caused Ino to throw herself into the sea with her son Melicertes. In Euripides' tragedy *Bacchae*, Cadmus was humiliatingly forced to submit to the authority of Dionysus. In the same play, Pentheus was slaughtered by his own mother, Agave, and his aunt Autonoe in a Dionysiac frenzy. Their unwitting murder of Pentheus was brought about by Dionysus in revenge for Pentheus's lack of piety toward him.

In visual representation Cadmus is sometimes shown battling the dragon guarding the Spring of Ares, as in a red-figure calyx krater from ca. 360 B.C.E. (Louvre, Paris). Here Cadmus, shown with Harmonia, is preparing to kill the dragon coiled against rocks near the site of the spring.

Calaeno   See HARPIES.

Calais   See BOREADAE.

Calchas   A Greek seer. Son of Thestor. Classical sources are Homer's *ILIAD* (1.68–100, 2.303–330) and Euripides' *IPHIGENIA AT AULIS*. Calchas joined the Greek expedition against Troy and was the chief seer of the Greek army. He exposed the reason for the plague afflicting the army in Homer's *Iliad*, which led to the quarrel between ACHILLES and AGAMEMNON. He also made prophecies motivating other major decisions during the Trojan War (e.g., the construction of the wooden horse). According to Euripides, Calchas delivered the prophecy demanding Iphigenia's sacrifice.

Callimachus (fl. third century B.C.E.) Callimachus was a poet and scholar from Cyrene who lived and worked in Alexandria and flourished under Ptolemy II and III in the third century B.C.E. He produced a rich and varied body of work, which survives largely in fragments: *Aetia* ("Origins") in four books, *Iambi* (13 poems), and the *Hecale*. Callimachus also wrote hymns to ZEUS, APOLLO, ARTEMIS, DELOS, ATHENA, and DEMETER; these survive in full and loosely imitate the manner of the *HOMERIC HYMNS*. Finally, he wrote epigrams and other erudite works. Callimachus's approach to mythology reflects his interest in the recherché and the uncommon. Callimachus participates in a broader Alexandrian tendency to carve out subheroic episodes within heroic mythology. In the *Hecale*, for example, Callimachus relates how THESEUS receives hospitality from the aged Hecale on the way to the bull of Marathon. Callimachus avoids the unbroken sweep of epic narrative, preferring shorter, carefully crafted segments of narration. In the prologue to his *Aetia*, he famously enunciates some of his key poetic principles: He values the narrow, the slender, and the finely crafted over the loud, the large, and the bombastic. He expresses this preference through a series of concrete metaphors, e.g., the superiority of the pure, narrow stream to the vast, muddy river. Callimachus's aesthetic preferences and water metaphors enjoyed an extended afterlife among the Roman poets, by whom he was revered as a master of literary craft and the sophisticated, erudite style: CATULLUS, HORACE, VIRGIL, Propertius, and Ovid all write in an avowedly Callimachean tradition, albeit laying claim to different aspects of that tradition. The Augustan poets defend their Callimachean cult of poetic craft against the demand for an epic on Augustus's or Agrippa's deeds. This type of strategy has been classified as the Callimachean "refusal"

(recusatio). The Augustans are not so much reproducing Callimachus's programmatic statements as adapting Callimachean metaphors and terminology to their own situation.

Callirhoe (1) An OCEANID (sea nymph), daughter of OCEANUS and TETHYS. Classical sources are Apollodorus's *LIBRARY* (2.5.10) and Hesiod's *THEOGONY* (288ff). Callirhoe was married to the warrior CHRYSAOR (son of MEDUSA and POSEIDON), and their son was the warrior GERYON.

Callirhoe (2) A river nymph, daughter of ACHELOUS (a river god). The main classical source is Apollodorus's *LIBRARY* (3.7.5). Callirhoe was married to ALCMAEON and by him she had two sons, Amphoterus and Acarnan. She sent Alcmaeon to acquire the golden necklace of HARMONIA, and Alcmaeon was killed during the attempt. Callirhoe became the consort of Zeus and asked him to grant her the favor of magically aging her sons so that they could avenge the death of their father.

Callirhoe (3) A young Calydonian woman. The classical source is Pausanias's *Description of Greece* (7.21.1–5). Callirhoe rejected the advances of Coresus, a priest of DIONYSUS. Coresus informed Dionysus, who inflicted the population with madness. Callirhoe was to be sacrificed to appease the god but at the last moment Coresus spared her and killed himself. Callirhoe took her own life out of remorse and the spring where she died was given her name.

Callisto (Kallisto) An Arcadian wood nymph and follower of ARTEMIS. Daughter of King Lycaon. Classical sources are Apollodorus's *LIBRARY* (3.8.2), Hyginus's *Fabulae* (177), Ovid's *FASTI* (2.155–192) and *METAMORPHOSES* (2.409–531), and Pausanias's *Description of Greece* (1.25.1, 8.3.6), ZEUS disguised as Artemis, appeared to Callisto when she had fallen asleep alone in the forest. She recognized Zeus when he embraced her, but she had lain her bow aside and, defenseless, was unable to resist his advances. Callisto became pregnant by Zeus with a son, ARCAS. She was too ashamed to reveal to Artemis what had taken place. However, nine months later, a distraught Callisto's pregnancy was revealed by the other nymphs (they had disrobed her before bathing). Despite her innocence, Artemis banished her from her company. When Callisto gave birth to Arcas, HERA became enraged with what she perceived was the flagrant display of her husband's infidelity, and she transformed Callisto into a bear. In some versions of the myth, it was Zeus who transformed Callisto into a bear to protect her from Hera's wrath.

Arcas was given by Zeus into the care of MAIA (one of the PLEIADES). As a young man, Arcas came upon Callisto as a bear while hunting. Zeus stayed Arcas's hand before he killed her and placed mother and son in the heavens as the constellations Ursa Major and Minor. A furious Hera persuaded TETHYS and OCEANUS to circumscribe the path of the constellations so that they never descended below the horizon into the sea.

The infant Arcas appears on an Apulian red-figure chous vase dating from ca. 350 B.C.E. (J. Paul Getty Museum, Malibu). On one side of the vase, Callisto is changing into a bear and Hermes, an appropriate intermediary as the son of Maia, takes the young Arcas protectively into his arms. Postclassical artists painted several versions of the story of Callisto, focusing on the seduction of Callisto by Zeus as in Peter Paul Rubens's painting *Jupiter and Callisto* of 1613 (Staatliche Kunstsammlungen, Kassel, Germany).

Calydonian Boar hunt See MELEAGER.

Calypso A nymph or PLEIAD. Daughter of ATLAS and Pleione or of HELIOS and Perseis. Classical sources are Apollodorus's *LIBRARY*

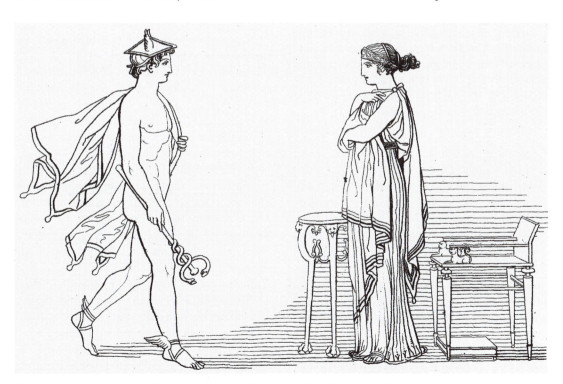

Mercury Orders Calypso to Release Odysseus. *Engraving, John Flaxman, 1810*

(Epitome 7.24), Hesiod's *Theogony* (1,017), Homer's ODYSSEY (1.13–15, 48–59; 5.13–281; 7.244–269). Ovid's *Ars Amatoria* (2.125), and Hyginus's *Fabulae* (125), Propertius's *Elegies* (1.15.9). Calypso lived on the island Ogygia, where ODYSSEUS came to be shipwrecked. She fell in love with him and kept him there for either one, three, or seven years (depending on the source) until HERMES, commanded by ZEUS, requested that she release Odysseus. Calypso reluctantly and sadly allowed Odysseus to depart for Ithaca. This scene is the subject of the neoclassical engraving by John Flaxman, *Mercury Orders Calypso to Release Odysseus*, illustrating Homer's *Odyssey*. During their affair one or more sons were born to Calypso.

Canace   See AEOLUS (1).

Capaneus   Son of Hipponous. Capaneus was one of the Seven against Thebes. Classical sources are Aeschylus's SEVEN AGAINST THEBES (422–451), Homer's ILIAD (2.564), and Statius's THEBAID (3.598, 4.165, 6.731, 10.827). As Capaneus scaled the walls of Thebes, he declared that not even ZEUS could stop him with his thunderbolts; yet Zeus killed him with a thunderbolt. Capaneus is a prime example of hubris.

Cassandra   A Trojan prophetess. Daughter of HECUBA and PRIAM. Cassandra appears in Aeschylus's AGAMEMNON and Euripides' TROJAN WOMEN. Additional classical sources are Apollodorus's LIBRARY (3.12.5), Homer's ILIAD (24.699), Hyginus's *Fabulae* (93, 108, 117), and Virgil's AENEID (2.245ff, 3.183). In Aeschylus's *Agamemnon*, Cassandra tells how APOLLO gave her the power of prophecy in return for the promise of sex, but she went back on her word and refused him. Apollo left her gift of prophecy intact but condemned her never to be believed. Cassandra predicts many important events—such as the disastrous outcome of PARIS's abduction of HELEN and the murder of AGAMEMNON

and herself—but fails to affect the outcome, since no one believes her. The tragedians exploit to powerful effect the maddening inability of her audience to understand her. Cassandra often appears to be mad or raving, unable to express herself clearly, which makes it somewhat more plausible when her interlocutors cannot understand her. Homer does not mention her prophetic powers but gives her a prominent place as Priam's most beautiful daughter and one of the mourners of the dead HECTOR. During the sack of Troy, the lesser AJAX, son of Oileus, dragged Cassandra away from the statue of ATHENA where she had taken refuge, thereby loosening the statue from its plinth, and raped her. Athena subsequently caused him to die by drowning at sea. Cassandra was awarded to Agamemnon as his concubine after the sack of Troy and was killed along with him by CLYTAEMNESTRA on their return.

Catullus   (ca. 84 B.C.E.–ca. 54 B.C.E.)   Catullus was a young man of wealth and good connections from Verona in Cisalpine Gaul. He probably lived until the age of 30 (84 to 54 B.C.E.), although the details of his life are highly uncertain. Catullus is notable as the first in a line of Roman poets of provincial origin who devoted themselves full-time to the composition of erudite, first-person poetry, often on convivial or erotic topics. Roman poetry of the previous century belonged for the most part to one of the public genres: tragedy, comedy, or epic. Poets in Catullus's time continued to write epic poetry, but they also turned increasingly to smaller genres, such as epigrams and lyric poetry, and nonheroic subject matter. While Greek influence on Roman poetry had always been strong, Catullus and his contemporaries brought these Hellenizing tendencies to a new degree of intensity: Metrical, syntactic, and dictional features of the "new poets" gave their poetry a refined, esoteric style that flaunted its Greekness and sophistication. Cicero, with no small disdain, referred to them in a letter as *neoteroi* ("the more recent ones," or "new poets"), from which we get the term "neoteric." While we do not have the poetry of Catullus's fellow "new poets" except in fragments, they appear to have participated in an elegant cultural milieu centered in Rome. Catullus, we know, especially prized the qualities of urbanity, wit, charm, and elegance—qualities that were explicitly opposed to a severe traditionalist ethos, and that were as important in poetry as they were in life.

Catullus valued erudite poems of high quality as opposed to weighty, bombastic ones and, in general, was highly influenced by the Alexandrian aesthetic associated with CALLIMACHUS, THEOCRITUS, Philetas, APOLLONIUS OF RHODES, and the epigrams of the Greek Anthology. Specific Alexandrian features that can be found in Catullus include an interest in framed mythological narratives and a complex layering of myths, focus on subheroic mythology and/or the darker side of heroism, an emphasis on female figures, irrational emotions and unsuccessful eros, and a rich display of geographical, cultic, and mythological erudition. Some of the erudition may have been encouraged and enriched by the presence of the Greek scholar and poet Parthenius of Nicaea, who was brought to Rome by Catullus's fellow neoteric poet C. Helvius Cinna and who influenced both him and C. Cornelius Gallus—another poet of broadly neoteric affinities who wrote love poetry and mythological/aetiological poetry. Parthenius's extant *Erotika Pathemata* ("Sufferings in Love"), dedicated to Gallus, is a collection of recherché love stories of the kind that neoteric poets would have found useful for their poetry.

The Catullan collection consists of 116 poems divided into three sections: short poems in various meters, often called the "polymetrics" (1–60); a series of longer poems in various meters, called the *carmina maiora* (61–68); and epigrams in elegiac couplets (69–116). To complicate matters, however, poems 65–116 are all in the elegiac meter and thus form their own subcategory, as do poems 1–64 (poems in various meters, short and long). Scholars debate

to this day to what degree the extant collection represents Catullus's ordering and intentions. In poem 1, he dedicates a "little book" of "trifling compositions" to his friend Cornelius Nepos—a book that many have supposed to be a collection of polymetric poems, possibly 1–60. On balance, it is impossible to say (although hard to abstain from attempting to guess) whether or not the extant collection represents a collection designed and published as such by its author.

The polymetrics and epigrams concern largely scenes and figures from contemporary Roman life. These shorter poems, written often in a satirical, facetious, or invective manner, contain only the rare mythic reference. In the fragmentary poem 2b, for example, Catullus appears to compare himself to ATALANTA loosening her girdle and thus losing her virginity in marriage. It is in the longer poems, or *carmina maiora*, that Catullus engages in more extensive treatment of myths. Significantly, he does not write in the traditional genres of epic and tragedy but prefers the exquisitely crafted mini-epic (sometimes called "epyllion") in the sophisticated modern style. Just as the epyllion eschews traditional epic form and narrative structure, so it opposes itself to the heroic values of epic. Catullus's friend Cinna labored nine years over his learned epyllion on Smyrna (see MYRRHA), the mythic figure who conceived ADONIS through incestuous union with her father. Catullus similarly displays an interest in feminine (or feminized) mythic figures, often involved in unhappy or otherwise doomed love, and in the darker aspects of male heroism.

To a certain degree, in subverting the epic hero, Catullus is following in the tradition of Alexandrian poets such as Apollonius of Rhodes. But he is also viewing Alexandrian mythology through a distinctly Roman lens. Catullus, who lived and wrote in the age of Caesar and Pompey, when the institutions and traditions of Roman public life were beginning to fall apart and the traditional political career became problematic, was profoundly skeptical of the heroic ideal of *virtus* ("manly excellence"). The great dynasts were monopolizing power and offices in an unconstitutional manner and ripping apart the republic through their rival ambitions: "manliness" becomes a problematic quality. All but the most powerful are deprived of their traditional virile role of political participation. Catullus himself, as a poet and aesthete, presents a novel style of virile identity, and in some cases flaunts a quasi-effeminate sophistication. His exploration of myth is thus related to his own poetic autobiography and his interest in the degradation of *virtus* in his turbulent times.

In poem 63, the mythic figure ATTIS wakes to the terrible realization that he castrated himself in a moment of ecstatic worship of CYBELE, the Anatolian goddess sometimes referred to as the Great Mother. The Phrygian cult of the Great Mother was traditionally supposed to have been brought to Rome in 204 B.C.E.: An annual festival, the Megalesia, was celebrated in her honor. Romans continued to view the cult as foreign, however; her castrated priests, the Galli, were foreign, and Romans were not allowed to take part in her rites. In most legends, Attis is Cybele's Phrygian lover. Catullus, however, presents a less familiar version in which Attis is a Greek youth who sails to Phrygia out of devotion to the goddess. Catullus's version allows Attis's self-destructive, unmanly, "Eastern," ecstatic frenzy to be contrasted with his previous male identity as defined and fostered by the civic institutions of the Greek city-state: the forum, the palaestra, the gymnasium. He has lost that identity now and regrets the excessive frenzy that drove him to destroy his own masculinity.

Catullus, who represents himself as subject to deranging passions and compromised in his masculinity, might be suspected of exploring myths of personal significance to himself. Whether or not this is true of Attis, poem 68 undeniably interweaves personal biography and mythic narrative. This highly experimental poem connects the story of Laodomia, who enjoyed only a single day of marriage with her husband, Protesilaus, before he died immediately on landing on the shore of Troy, with Catullus's loss of his brother, and his love affair with Lesbia. The themes of grief, loss, marriage, and death are inextricably combined as Catullus shuttles between autobiography and myth. Myth is merged with first-person narration in a manner that perhaps prefigures the elegiac love poetry of Propertius and Ovid. And once again, as in the Atalanta simile, Catullus associates himself closely with a female figure.

Catullus's most ambitious and important mythological work is poem 64. Here he focuses his most intensive poetic labors on a richly erudite mythic narrative, layered and interwoven to a remarkable degree. In the outermost frame of the story, PELEUS, voyaging among the heroes of the ship *Argo*, sees THETIS rise out of the ocean, is inflamed with desire, and ends up marrying her. Catullus then describes the wedding and the guests, which include both mortals and gods. On the wedding couch is an amazing tapestry, woven with the stories of heroic mythology. Specifically, the tapestry tells the story of ARIADNE, THESEUS, and Bacchus. The framing story of Peleus and Thetis thus frames the story of another union of god and mortal. As depicted in the tapestry, Ariadne is abandoned on the island of Dia by Theseus, who has just slain the MINOTAUR and is returning to the Greek mainland. In a long soliloquy (which, incidentally, the visual medium of textile could not represent), she laments her sad fate and Theseus's faithlessness. At the end of her speech, however, the god Bacchus and his train of followers arrive amid cacophonous music and revelry. The god will make Ariadne his bride, while her prayers to the gods will doom the forgetful Theseus: He neglects to change the black sail on his ship to a white one, and his father, Aegeus, understanding the black sail to mean that his son has been killed by the Minotaur, throws himself into the sea. In the final section of the poem, we move back to the framing narrative of the wedding. The Parcae (Fates) arrive and sing a ghastly wedding song about the future deeds of the couple's famous son-to-be, ACHILLES. The song of the Parcae emphasizes the darker side of Achilles' accomplishments, such as the glutting of the rivers of Troy with dead bodies and the sacrifice of the virgin Polyxena to his shade.

The central connection between the framed story and framing story is the marriage of a mortal and a god: Peleus and Thetis, Ariadne and Bacchus. In both stories, moreover, male heroism is set in a questionable light. Theseus is a faithless deserter, rather than a brave monster-slaying hero, and Achilles' deeds, represented as glorious in Homer, come off as ghastly and excessively violent in the speech of the Parcae. The most attractive figure in the poem, in whom commentators have seen glimmers of Catullan autobiography, is not accidentally the female Ariadne: She was abandoned by her unscrupulous lover, just as Catullus was abandoned by the callous and faithless Lesbia, and now weaves a rich web of lamenting words. It is hard to imagine a more carefully designed subversion of the traditional values of heroic epic than Catullus's central focus on the emotionally fraught, helpless, and hyperarticulate Ariadne. The very use of the tapestry is an epic motif turned against itself. As an extended description of an artwork, or ecphrasis, the passage recalls Homer's Shield of Achilles. But rather than describing the scenes represented in metal on an epic hero's mighty weapon forged by the god Hephaestus, Catullus makes the emotional complaint of a female figure the centerpiece of a finely wrought tapestry.

Catullus's use of mythology coheres with his counterclassical aesthetic and countertraditional sensibility. He integrates mythic narrative with the themes of his own literary autobiography and his interpretation of present social conditions. The world of gods and heroes, however, ultimately belongs to the past. In a coda to poem 64, the poet laments the hopelessly vitiated morals of contemporary Rome: The gods abhor our behavior and no longer mingle with mortals as they did at the weddings of Peleus and Theseus; they no longer deign to be seen in the clear light of day. The profoundly *different* world of the inherited myths has become a measure of the corruption of contemporary Roman society.

Cecrops   See AGLAURUS AND HERSE; ATHENA.

centaur   Hybrid creature whose upper half is human and lower half is horse-shaped. The progeny of IXION and a cloud. Classical sources are Apollodorus's LIBRARY (1.2.3, 2.5.4, 3.4.4, 3.10.3, Epitome 1.20), Hyginus's *Fabulae* (33, 62), and Ovid's METAMORPHOSES (9.123, 12.210–536). Ixion attempted to seduce HERA, he thought with some success, but Zeus had created a cloud in her shape to deceive him. The offspring of Ixion's union with the Hera-shaped cloud was Centaurus, from whom centaurs descend. An alternate version sees CRONUS, in the form of a horse, seducing Philyra, daughter of OCEANUS and producing CHIRON as the ancestor of the centaurs.

Hybrid creatures such as centaurs represented the potential savagery of the human being, but they were sometimes capable of civilized behavior. By contrast, SATYRS, who were considered a more benign, if lascivious species, were, from the point of view of civilization, unredeemable creatures.

Several heroes of classical literature participated in wars against the centaurs, or centauromachies, including HERACLES and THESEUS. The battle of Lapiths and centaurs is a famous instance of a centauromachy. PIRITHOUS, king of the Lapiths in Thessaly and son of Ixion, invited the centaurs to his wedding with Hippodame. During the wedding feast the centaurs, led by Eurytus, drank wine and became unruly. Eurytus attempted to carry off the bride but was prevented by Theseus, who killed him. In Ovid's *Metamorphoses*, the battle is a gruesome, violent struggle in which the combatants made use of whatever weapon lay at hand in the wedding hall: votives, antlers, cups and candelabrum, a fire brand, an altar and nearby trees. The myth emphasized the centaurs' violation of the rules of hospitality.

On another occasion, the centaur Nessus attempted to abduct Heracles' bride DEIANIRA, and Heracles killed him with an arrow. Nessus tricked Deianira, however, into preserving some of his blood as a love potion, and years later she unwittingly poisoned Heracles with it.

Chiron and Pholus are exceptions to the view of the centaurs as essentially uncivilized. Chiron was a centaur skilled in medicine and trusted by the Olympian gods; he was the tutor of ACHILLES, ASCLEPIUS, JASON, and DIONYSUS. Pholus was a centaur who offered Heracles hospitality while he was on his way to perform his Third Labor, the capture of the Erymanthian Boar. He offered Heracles wine and thereby attracted the attention of other, less civilized centaurs. Pholus was killed and, according to some accounts, Chiron himself was fatally wounded in the ensuing fray.

The Battle of the Lapiths and centaurs appears as a theme many times in ancient art. It is the subject of a metope of the Temple of Zeus at Olympia dating from the fifth century B.C.E. and a wall painting from Pompeii of the first century B.C.E. It was treated by Michelangelo in his *Battle of the Lapiths and Centaurs*, a relief that depicts not the violent struggle as much as the twisting, intertwined form of hybrid centaurs and their human enemies, blurring the distinction between the species. A more generalized notion of centauromachy also appeared on the François Vase from 570 B.C.E. (Museo Archeologico Nazionale, Florence). In the postclassical period, versions of the centauromachy were painted by Piero di Cosimo and Peter Paul Rubens. An episode of some interest is Heracles' struggle with Nessus, as in the Nessus amphora from ca. 600 B.C.E. (National Museum, Athens) and in sculptural form in Jean Boulogne's bronze *Heracles and Nessus* of 1600 (Rijksmuseum, Amsterdam).

Cephalus (Kephalus) An Athenian hunter. Son of AEOLUS. Classical sources are Apollodorus's *LIBRARY* (1.9.4, 2.4.7, 3.15.1), Hyginus's *Fabulae* (189), and Ovid's *Ars Amatoria* (3.687–746) and *METAMORPHOSES* (7.668–862). Cephalus was married to PROCRIS, daughter of ERECHTHEUS and sister of ORITHYIA. Ovid tells the story of the tragic death of Procris by the hand of her unwitting husband. One morning Eos, goddess of dawn, fell in love with him when she saw him out hunting and carried him off. Cephalus protested his love for his wife and a scorned Eos sent him back to Procris, although, according to some sources, not before he fathered on her a son, Phaethon. In one version of the myth, Eos caused Cephalus to be suspicious of Procris's fidelity or tricked him into believing that she had been unfaithful. Cephalus therefore set about testing Procris to put his mind at ease. He changed his appearance (with the help of Eos) and attempted to seduce his wife. The faithful Procris resisted his advances for a long time, but Cephalus finally observed her hesitating and revealed his true identity to her. A distraught Procris sought refuge in the woods of ARTEMIS (in some sources, on the island of Crete), but Artemis refused to accept her into her company because she was married. She was, however, moved by Procris's story and did not send her away empty-handed but presented her with a javelin that never missed its mark and a dog that always tracked its prey. Cephalus eventually won Procris back by begging forgiveness. The couple lived together happily for some time, and Procris presented her husband with the javelin and hound. But later Procris heard rumors that he was unfaithful to her. Following him one day into the woods, she surprised him and he, thinking that she was a wild animal, killed her with his javelin.

In visual representations, Cephalus is depicted as a hunter, sometimes carrying the javelin given to him by Procris. Another visual theme is Cephalus as the object of Eos's affection, as in a red-figure cup from ca. 440 B.C.E. (Antikenmuseen, Berlin). Here Eos is carrying

Cephalus away with her. A postclassical example of this theme is Nicholas Poussin's *Cephalus and Eos* of 1624 (National Gallery, London), in which the hunter tries to free himself from her amorous embrace. The marital love between Cephalus and Procris is treated in Pierre Narcisse Guérin's *Cephalus and Procris* of 1810 (Louvre, Paris) and Claude Lorraine's *Landscape with Cephalus and Procris Reunited by Diana* of ca. 1630 (National Gallery, London). Here, the reconciliation of Cephalus and Procris, orchestrated by Artemis, is the focus of the image. The goddess's gifts of the javelin and hound are also depicted.

Cerberus   A three-headed dog that guards the entrance to HADES. Offspring of ECHIDNA and TYPHOEUS. Classical sources are Apollodorus's *LIBRARY* (2.5.12), Hesiod's *THEOGONY* (311, 769), Homer's *ILIAD* (8.368) and *ODYSSEY* (11.623), Pausanias's *Description of Greece* (3.25.6), and Virgil's *AENEID* (6.417–425). HERACLES' Eleventh Labor was to retrieve Cerberus for king EURYSTHEUS of Mycenae. Heracles was given permission by Hades, lord of the underworld, to take Cerberus on the condition that Heracles subdue the dog without weapons. Heracles grasped it around the neck until Cerberus conceded defeat. Later, Heracles returned Cerberus to Hades. A Caeretan black-figure hydria from ca. 530 B.C.E. (Louvre, Paris) shows the three-headed hound being mastered by Heracles. A postclassical representation of Cerberus by William Blake, *Cerberus*, a watercolor from 1824–27 (Tate Gallery, London), shows a similarly fearsome three-headed creature gnashing its teeth.

Cerberus. *Illustration for* The Divine Comedy, *William Blake, 1824–27 (Tate Gallery, London)*

Ceres See Demeter.

Ceyx See Alcyone.

Charon A guardian of Hades. Son of Erebus and Nyx. Classical sources are Aristophanes's *The Frogs* (180–270), Diodorus Siculus's Library of History (1.92), Pausanias's *Description of Greece* (10.28.1–2), and Virgil's Aeneid (6.298–301). Charon ferried the dead, brought to him by Hermes, across the river Styx (Acheron) to the underworld. Every soul he transported paid for the passage, and if the soul had not received the proper burial rites, Charon was forbidden to deliver her or him to Hades. During Heracles' Eleventh Labor, to retrieve Cerberus, the hound guarding Hades, Heracles physically attacked Charon until the ferryman agreed to bring him across to the underworld. In some myths, a ruthless Charon forces the

Charon Crossing the Acheron. *Illustration for Dante's* Inferno, *Gustave Doré, ca. 1857*

dead to row themselves to the underworld while he steers. In visual representations, Charon is shown as an old man ferrying his boat, as in a white-ground red-figure lekythos vase attributed to the Reed Painter, dating from ca. 425 B.C.E. (British Museum, London). A postclassical image of Charon is the 19th-century engraving *Charon Crossing the Acheron* by Gustave Doré.

Charybdis A female creature living in a cave above a narrow sea passage across from another monster, Scylla. The offspring of Gaia and Poseidon. Classical sources are Apollodorus's Library (1.9.25), Apollonius of Rhodes's Voyage of the Argonauts (4.789ff), Homer's Odyssey (12.73–126, 222–59, 426–427), Ovid's Metamorphoses (13.730–734), and Virgil's Aeneid (3.420–432). In the *Library* and the *Odyssey*, Charybdis sends up a spray of water that she has sucked from the sea, and these thrice-daily occurrences formed deadly whirlpools. Jason and the Argonauts were successfully guided past Charybdis with the protection of Hera. Odysseus survived Charybdis's whirlpool by clinging to a fig tree beside it until it spat up the wreckage of his ship. He then leapt onto a plank and paddled himself to safety.

Chimaera A fire-breathing creature. Offspring of Echidna and Typhoeus. Sister of Orthus (a dog), Cerberus, who guards the gates of Hades, and the Hydra of Lerna. The Chimaera mated with Orthus, and their progeny was the Sphinx and the Nemean Lion. Classical sources are Apollodorus's Library (1.9.3, 2.3.1), Hesiod's Theogony (319–325), Homer's Iliad (6.179), Hyginus's *Fabulae* (57), and Ovid's Metamorphoses (9.647). Like the Sphinx and the Griffon, Chimaera, or "she-goat," is composed of different animal parts. Hesiod describes her as having three monstrous heads: a lion's, a goat's, and a dragon's. In Homer, she has the head of a lion, the body of a goat, and a serpent's tail. The main associative animal is the goat. The Chimaera ravaged the countryside but was ultimately defeated by the hero BELLEROPHON. Riding on the PEGASUS, Bellerophon used a spear to thrust a piece of lead into the Chimaera's throat. It was melted by her fiery breath and choked her to death.

Visual representations of the Chimaera are usually based on Homer's description of the tripartite beast. Bellerophon riding on the winged horse Pegasus is often shown with the Chimaera. A Laconian black-figure kylix attributed to the Boread Painter from ca. 570 B.C.E. (J. Paul Getty Museum, Malibu) is one example. Here the leonine head tops a goat's torso completed with a serpent's head for a tail. A similar image is depicted in a floor mosaic of the imperial period in Palmyra, Syria, dating from ca. 260 C.E. The Chimaera is rare in the art of later periods. It appears in the work of the French symbolist poets Gustave Flaubert and Stéphane Mallarmé and their contemporary, the painter Odilon Redon, who provided illustrations of the Chimaera for Flaubert's prose poem *The Temptation of St. Anthony* (1874).

Chione   Daughter of King Daedalion (son of Lucifer, the Morning Star). Textual sources are Hyginus's *Fabulae* (200) and Ovid's *METAMORPHOSES* (11.291–345). Chione was impregnated on the same day by APOLLO and HERMES and conceived twins: Autolycus, a trickster figure, took after his father, Hermes, while Apollo bestowed musical skills on his son Philammon. ARTEMIS shot Chione with an arrow when she claimed superiority over the goddess of the hunt. Her grieving father, Daedalion, was transformed into a hawk.

Chiron   A CENTAUR, friendly to the Olympian gods and tutor to several heroes. Son of Philyra and CRONUS. Classical sources are Apollodorus's *LIBRARY* (1.2.3, 2.5.4, 3.4.4, 3.10.3), Apollonius of Rhodes's *VOYAGE OF THE ARGONAUTS* (1.554–8, 2.510, 2.1229–42), Diodorus Siculus's *LIBRARY OF HISTORY* (4.12.3–13), Homer's *ILIAD* (4.218,

11.830–832), Ovid's *METAMORPHOSES* (2.630–649), Pausanias's *Description of Greece* (5.19.8), and Pindar's *Pythian Odes* (3.1–45). Chiron is the prime example of the "civilized centaur." He was skilled in medicine and, as such, linked to APOLLO. He was trusted by the Olympian gods and was the tutor of ACHILLES, ASCLEPIUS, JASON, and DIONYSUS.

The following story of Chiron's death appears in Apollodorus and Diodorus Siculus. A centauromachy broke out when HERACLES visited the civilized centaur Pholus. Chiron was fatally wounded in the fight of Pholus and Heracles against a group of savage centaurs. Being immortal, Chiron could not die but lay in excruciating pain until PROMETHEUS offered to exchange his mortality for Chiron's immortality.

After his death, Zeus set Chiron in the sky as the constellation Centaurus. In the classical period, Chiron was frequently depicted alongside the heroes he mentored, as in an Attic red-figure stamnos vase from ca. 500 B.C.E. (Louvre, Paris). Here, the young Achilles is given into the care of Chiron by his father, PELEUS. In a similar scene, painted on an Attic red-figure amphora vase from ca. 520 B.C.E. (Louvre, Paris), Chiron carries the infant Achilles in his hand. In both vase paintings, Chiron wears human garb and stands on human legs while the torso and rear legs of a horse emerge from his back. Chiron's role as tutor of the young hero Achilles is also represented in postclassical painting, for example, Gustav Moreau's *The Education of Achilles (The Centaur)* of 1884.

Chloris   See FLORA.

Chrysaor   Son of MEDUSA and POSEIDON. Classical sources are Apollodorus's *LIBRARY* (2.4.2, 2.5.10), Diodorus Siculus's *LIBRARY OF HISTORY* (4.17), Hesiod's *THEOGONY* (278, 979), Hyginus's *Fabulae* (151), and Ovid's *METAMORPHOSES* (4.782–786). The hero PERSEUS beheaded Medusa, and at the moment of her death, the warrior Chrysaor and the winged horse Pegasus sprang from her neck. Pegasus was later acquired by the hero Bellerophon. Chrysaor, so named because of his attribute—a golden sword—married an Oceanid named Callirhoe. Their offspring was Geryon, a three-headed, or three-bodied, warrior. Chrysaor was killed by Heracles when Chrysaor attempted to prevent him from acquiring a herd of cattle belonging to Geryon in Heracles' Tenth Labor. A black-figure (white-ground) pyxis from ca. 525 B.C.E. (Louvre, Paris) depicts the death of Medusa and the birth of Chrysaor and Pegasus.

Circe Daughter of Helios and Perseis. Classical sources are Apollodorus's *Library* (1.9.24), Apollonius of Rhodes's *Voyage of the Argonauts* (4.559–591, 659–752), Hesiod's *Theogony* (956f, 1,011–1,014), Homer's *Odyssey* (10.133–574), Hyginus's *Fabulae* (125), Ovid's *Metamorphoses* (13.966–14.71, 14.247–440), and Virgil's *Aeneid* (7.10–20). Circe belongs to a family of formidable and sometimes magical figures: Aeetes is her brother; Medea, her niece; and Pasiphae, her sister. A goddess known for her skill in magic and drugs, Circe plays a notable role in the two major Greek epics of adventure and sea travel. In Homer's *Odyssey*, Odysseus and his companions arrive on the island of Aeaea after departing from the land of the Lastrygonians. Eurylochus and others of Odysseus's crew come upon Circe's palace and are invited inside to a feast. At the end of the feast, Circe waves her wand, turning the men into various animals and herding them into a stable. Eurylochus, who is standing on guard outside, reports the news to Odysseus, who is waiting at the ship. As Odysseus makes his way toward Circe's palace, Hermes appears to him and instructs him to place a magic herb in the drink Circe will give him. The herb will prevent her enchantment from working, and Odysseus should then draw his sword and make her swear an oath. All this occurs as Hermes predicted: Circe fails to transform Odysseus, she swears that she will not harm Odysseus and

his companions, and she turns the others back into men. Odysseus and his companions spend a month with Circe, while the hero himself shares the goddess's bed. Their union is said to have produced the hero Telegonus and other children. Circe later gives Odysseus instructions for traveling to Hades, the land of the dead. As in the case of Calypso, Odysseus significantly prefers to return to his mortal wife, Penelope, rather than remain as the consort of a goddess. Circe, however, is a more menacing version of the female figure obstructing the hero's journey, or *nostos* (homeward voyage): She resembles the Sirens and the lotus eaters in her capacity to seduce the unwary into thoughtlessness and loss of identity.

In Apollonius of Rhodes's *Voyage of the Argonauts*, Circe plays a cameo role as Medea's aunt: She purifies Jason and Medea after the murder of Apsyrtos but refuses to offer hospitality to Jason. The fact that Circe, a notorious witch, morally recoils from the epic's hero is a disturbing revelation and demonstrates one way in which Apollonius differentiates his antihero from Odysseus. Virgil does not fail to allude to Circe in the Odyssean adventure portion of his *Aeneid* but pointedly refuses to include a fully developed episode: Her role is reduced to a glancing mention.

The transformation of Odysseus's men is vividly portrayed on an Attic black-figure cup from ca. 550 B.C.E. (Museum of Fine Arts, Boston). Here, Odysseus, sword in hand, stands before Circe, who holds a cup of potion, and his men, some of whom have been partially changed into animals.

Clytaemnestra Daughter of Tyndareus and Leda. Sister of Helen and the Dioscuri (Castor and Pollux). Clytaemnestra married Agamemnon and their children are Electra, Iphigenia, and Orestes. Clytaemnestra appears in Aeschylus's *Agamemnon*, *Libation Bearers*, and *Eumenides*; Euripides' *Electra* and *Iphigenia at Aulis*; and Sophocles'

ELECTRA. Additional classical sources are Homer's *ILIAD* (1.113–115) and *ODYSSEY* (11.409–453, 24.199–202). In earlier sources, Clytaemnestra and Agamemnon's daughters are named Chrysomethis, Laodice, and Iphianassa. In one legend, Agamemnon killed Clytaemnestra's first husband, TANTALUS, and their children, and was subsequently forced to marry her by her brothers, the Dioscuri. This beginning of their marriage boded ill for the remainder. After Agamemnon went to war, Clytaemnestra took AEGISTHUS, the surviving son of THYESTES, as a lover. Aegisthus, whose father had been the deadly enemy of Agamemnon's father, ATREUS, may have had reasons of his own to seduce Clytaemnestra (as revealed at the end of Aeschylus's *Agamemnon*). On Agamemnon's return, Aegisthus and Clytaemnestra murdered him and his captive concubine CASSANDRA. In Aeschylus, Clytaemnestra takes an active role and murders Agamemnon by trapping him in a net in his bath. Homer, in the *Odyssey*, mainly focuses on Aegisthus's actions as usurper. Years later, Orestes avenges his father's murder by killing Aegisthus and Clytaemnestra. In the tragedians, he has the help of Pylades and his sister Electra. Homer represents him as the sole avenger. In Aeschylus's and Euripides' *Electra*, but not in Sophocles' *Electra* or in Homer, the FURIES afterward hound Orestes.

The most important development in the tradition occurs in Aeschylus, where Aegisthus is no longer the main actor, and Clytaemnestra dominates. The Aeschylean Clytaemnestra is a character of astonishing power, a woman who usurps a masculine role and, in the process, disrupts the natural order of the Greek cosmos. In Sophocles and Euripides, Clytaemnestra is still a central character, but she never quite recovers her Aeschylean grandeur and dominance. Her motives for killing her husband are debatable. One possible interpretation is that she simply desired power for herself. Less convincing is the idea that Agamemnon's choice to bring home Cassandra as his concubine was experienced by Clytaemnestra as an insult. She appears to have planned his murder long before Cassandra's arrival. In the tragedians, Clytaemnestra often stresses Agamemnon's sacrifice of Iphigenia as a motivating factor. Aeschylus's *Agamemnon* vividly describes the scene of sacrifice, and Euripides' *Iphigenia at Aulis* subtly sketches the origins of Clytaemnestra's alienation from her husband and the beginning of long years of resentment of his betrayal of their trust.

Clytie (Clytia) An OCEANID (Ocean nymph). Daughter of the TITANS OCEANUS and TETHYS. The main classical source is Ovid's *METAMORPHOSES* (4.169–270). Clytie loved HELIOS, but he was inflamed by APHRODITE (he had betrayed her tryst with ARES to her husband, HEPHAESTUS) to love LEUCOTHOE. Filled with envy, Clytie betrayed the secret affair between Helios and Leucothoe to Leucothoe's father, Orchamus. Orchamus was ashamed of Leucothoe's conduct and buried her alive. Helios attempted to save Leucothoe, but even his warms rays could not revive her dead body. The god poured nectar over her corpse, and her body was transformed into a frankincense bush. Despite her rival's defeat, Helios would not love Clytie, and the nymph was driven mad with despair. She sat on the ground and was, over the course of nine days, slowly transformed into a sunflower (or heliotrope), a flower whose face follows the sun around the sky.

Coeus (Koios) A Titan offspring of GAIA (Earth) and URANUS (Heaven). Brother of HYPERION, IAPETUS, CRIUS, CRONUS, MNEMOSYNE, OCEANUS, PHOEBE, RHEA, TETHYS, THEIA, and THEMIS. Classical sources are Apollodorus's *LIBRARY* (1.2.2) and Hesiod's *THEOGONY* (132–136, 404–410). Cronus, encouraged by Gaia, castrated his father with a flint (or adamant) sickle, liberated his siblings, and succeeded Uranus. Following a 10-year battle for supremacy against the Olympian gods, the Titans were in turn defeated and imprisoned in

TARTARUS. Coeus married his sister Phoebe, and their daughters were Asteria and LETO (mother of APOLLO and ARTEMIS). Coeus appears in the genealogies of Hesiod, Apollodorus and Ovid but has no specific myths.

Coronis Consort of APOLLO and mother of ASCLEPIUS. Daughter of King Phlegyas of Thessaly. Textual sources are the *Homeric Hymn to Asclepius*, Apollodorus's *LIBRARY* (3.10.3), Hyginus's *Fabulae* (202), Ovid's *METAMORPHOSES* (2.542–636), Pausanias's *Description of Greece* (4.3.2), and Pindar's *Pythian Odes* (3). In the *Homeric Hymn to Asclepius* and Ovid's *Metamorphoses*, Coronis is said to be the mother of the famous healer, Asclepius, while Apollodorus and Pausanias maintain that his mother is Arsinoe, daughter of Leucippus. Apollo loved Coronis and discovered from a raven that Coronis was betraying him with an Arcadian youth named Ischys. In Hyginus's *Fabulae*, the raven had been set by Apollo to guard over Coronis and so was simply fulfilling his duty. In Ovid's *Metamorphoses*, however, the raven was simply passing by, observed the lovers, and, despite encountering a crow that tried to dissuade it from bearing bad news to the god, reported what he had seen to Apollo. For his pains, he was turned from white to black. A furious Apollo drew his bow and killed Coronis, but not before she revealed that she was pregnant with his child. Apollo repented his actions and tried to save her with his skill in medicine but failed. Apollo then took the unborn child, Asclepius, to the centaur CHIRON, who raised him. In Pindar's *Pythian Odes*, Coronis was killed by ARTEMIS, in revenge for her betrayal of Apollo. Either Artemis shot her with arrows or sent a plague that killed her.

Cottus (Kottos) See HUNDRED-HANDED ONES.

Creon (1) Regent or king of Thebes on various occasions. Son of Menoeceus and brother of JOCASTA. Creon appears in Sophocles' *OEDIPUS THE KING*, *ANTIGONE*, and *OEDIPUS AT COLONUS*; Euripides' *SUPPLIANT WOMEN*; and Statius's *THEBAID*. Additional classical sources are Apollodorus's *LIBRARY* (2.4.6, 2.4.11, 3.5.8, 3.6.7, 3.7.1), Hyginus's *Fabulae* (67, 72), and Pausanias's *Description of Greece* (1.39.2). Creon's name simply means "ruler." After OEDIPUS killed LAIUS, Creon took control of the city, but the SPHINX began to terrorize the Thebans. Oedipus solved the Sphinx's riddle, the Sphinx threw herself from her rock in despair, and Creon gave Oedipus both the kingship of Thebes and Jocasta in marriage. In Sophocles' *Oedipus the King*, Oedipus sends Creon to consult the oracle at Delphi to discover the cause of the plague afflicting the city. Creon becomes ruler or regent after Oedipus's self-blinding and retirement, and also after the death of ETEOCLES and POLYNICES. In Sophocles' *Antigone*, Creon forbids Polynices's burial and condemns ANTIGONE to death when she defies his decree. Creon's son Haemon, who was Antigone's fiancé, kills himself by her corpse, and Creon's wife, Eurydice, then hangs herself. In another version, the Sphinx killed Haemon. In Sophocles' *Oedipus at Colonus*, Creon attempts to persuade Oedipus to return to Thebes because of a prophecy stating that Oedipus's tomb will guarantee Thebes's power, but Oedipus refuses. During the assault of the Seven against Thebes, Creon's son Menoeceus sacrifices himself to guarantee Thebes's safety. (Statius has Creon cynically manipulate Menoeceus's death for political purposes in his *Thebaid*.) After the war with Argos, Creon refuses to hand over the bodies of the slain Argive heroes, according to Euripides' *Suppliant Women* and Statius's *Thebaid*. In Statius's epic, THESEUS slays Creon in battle.

Creon (2) A king of Corinth. MEDEA killed Creon, along with his daughter, by means of a poisoned robe. See JASON.

Creusa See AENEAS; *AENEID*.

Crius (Krius) A TITAN, the offspring of GAIA (Earth) and URANUS (Heaven). Brother of HYPERION, IAPETUS, COEUS, CRONUS,

MNEMOSYNE, OCEANUS, PHOEBE, RHEA, TETHYS, THEIA, and THEMIS. Classical sources are Apollodorus's *LIBRARY* (1.1.3) and Hesiod's *THEOGONY* (132–136, 375–377). Crius married Eurybia, daughter of Pontus, and their children were Astreus, Pallas, and Perses. Crius appears in the genealogies of Hesiod and Apollodorus but has no specific myths.

Cronus (Kronos) A TITAN, ruler of the gods before Zeus. Son of URANUS and GAIA. Husband and brother of RHEA. Father of HESTIA, DEMETER, HERA, HADES, POSEIDON, and ZEUS. Classical sources include Apollodorus's *LIBRARY* (1.1–2.4), Hesiod's *THEOGONY* (137–138, 154–187, 453–506) and *WORKS AND DAYS* (109–126), Homer's *ILIAD* (14.200–204, 271–279), Ovid's *FASTI* (1.235–238, 3.795–808, 4.197–210) and *METAMORPHOSES* (1.113–115, 6.126, 9.498, 14.320), and Virgil's *AENEID* (7.45–49, 8.319–329, 357A). In the Roman period, Cronus was syncretized with the Italic god Saturn (Saturnus). According to the succession myth retailed in Hesiod's *Theogony*, Uranus (Heaven), anxious to avoid being deposed by one of his children, kept all his offspring imprisoned in their mother Gaia (Earth). Gaia, in pain, devised a plan: She fashioned a sickle of adamant and encouraged her sons to take vengeance on their father. Cronus accepted the challenge, and when Uranus came to have intercourse with Gaia at night, Cronus lay in wait, hiding, and castrated his father with the sickle. Drops of blood from the severed genitals, when they fell on Gaia, impregnated her with the Erinyes (see FURIES), and GIANTS, and the Melian nymphs. When Cronus cast the genitals into the sea, foam rose up around them, and from the foam arose APHRODITE.

Cronus, having thus defeated his father and taken his place as ruler, raped his sister Rhea, and she gave birth to Hestia, Demeter, Hera, Hades, Poseidon, and Zeus. Cronus, in order to avoid succumbing to the same fate as his father, swallowed his children; Gaia and Uranus had predicted that he was destined to be overpowered by his son. Rhea, grieving for her children, sought the advice of her parents, Gaia and Uranus, who told her to hide Zeus in a cave in Crete. She did so, and, in Zeus's place, gave Cronus a stone wrapped in swaddling clothes, which he swallowed. At length, Cronus vomited up the stone along with his other children, and Zeus drove out his father and became king in his place. Cronus ended up being confined to TARTARUS, along with the other defeated Titans, as Homer attests in the *Iliad*. Apollodorus offers an account with minor differences: Gaia summoned all the Titans to attack Uranus and gave the sickle to Cronus; they attacked as a group, and Cronus castrated Uranus. There is no mention in Apollodorus of the Titans' imprisonment within Gaia. Apollodorus, moreover, records that Rhea gave birth to Zeus in Crete and put him in the care of the Curetes and the nymphs Adrasteia and Ida: The Curetes stood guard over the cave where Zeus was kept and banged their shields with their spears to conceal the sounds of the baby from Cronus. Finally, Metis, as Zeus's accomplice, gave Cronus a drug that caused him to vomit the stone and Rhea's other children. The war with the Titans ensued. According to Apollodorus and Ovid's *Metamorphoses*, the centaur CHIRON was Cronus's son by Philyra.

Homer and Hesiod agree in designating Cronus as "crooked-counselled," and their picture of him is generally negative. Yet another strand within Cronus's mythology identifies him as the ruler of the world in humanity's Golden Age. According to Hesiod's *Works and Days*, human beings in the time of Cronus's rule lived a carefree life untroubled by toils, and the earth produced crops for them of its own accord. A similar mythology becomes associated with the Italic Saturn in the Roman tradition. According to Ovid's *Fasti* and Virgil's *Aeneid*, Saturn, driven from the throne by Jupiter, went into hiding in Latium (modern Lazio, the region of Italy that includes Rome), and from his "hiding" (Latin, *latens*), Latium received its name. Saturnus's rule was Italy's Golden Age. In Virgil's *Aeneid*, Latinus, king of the Latins at the time of the Trojan hero AENEAS's arrival, derived his ancestry from Saturn: Saturn was the father of Picus, who sired Faunus (see PAN), who was, in turn, the father of Latinus. This makes Saturn the founder of the race of Latin kings and, thus, one of the ancestors of the Romans. According to Ovid's *Metamorphoses*, Saturn's wife was his sister Ops (Abundance). A Temple of Saturn, first built in the early fifth century B.C.E., was one of the major monuments of the Roman Forum. The Roman festival in Saturn's honor, the Saturnalia, was celebrated in December: During the Saturnalia, Romans exchanged gifts, feasted, drank, wore leisure suits instead of the toga, and gambled. Slaves were allowed freedom of speech and dined before their masters; everyone wore the *pilleus*, a cap normally worn by freed slaves.

Cupid   See EROS.

Cybele   Anatolian mother goddess. In mythology, the daughter of King Maeon of Phrygia and Dindyme. Classical sources are the *Homeric Hymns to the Mother of Gods*, Apollonius of Rhodes's *VOYAGE OF THE ARGONAUTS* (1.1,092–1,152), Catullus' Poem 63, Diodorus Siculus's *LIBRARY OF HISTORY* (3.58.1–3.59.8), Livy's *History of Rome* (29.5ff), Lucretius's *De Rerum Natura* (2.594–643), Ovid's *FASTI* (4.179–244) and *METAMORPHOSES* (10.102–105, 686–704; 14.530–561), Pausanias's *Description of History* (7.17.9–12), and Virgil's *AENEID* (10.252–255). Cybele was a mother goddess worshipped throughout Asia Minor. She was associated with wild nature, mountains, and fertility. Her cult was introduced into the Greek world starting in the fifth century B.C.E., and was Hellenized over time. In 204–205 B.C.E., during the Second Punic War, the Romans transferred the black, aniconic stone representing Cybele from her cult center at Pessinus in Phrygia to her new temple on the Palatine Hill in Rome. The Romans called Cybele the "Great Mother" (Latin *Magna Mater*), and her festival, the Megalesia, was incorporated into the Roman religious calendar. Cybele's cult was asso-

ciated with orgiastic frenzy, and her priests, the Galli, were self-castrated. The Romans distanced themselves from some aspects of Cybele's cult by allowing only Easterners to serve as priests at her temple in Rome.

In Diodorus Siculus's *Library of History*, Cybele was exposed as an infant by her father, Maeon, but survived and was raised by leopards and other wild beasts. In youth, she was beautiful and virtuous and was said to have invented the multi-reed pipe, the kettledrum, and cymbals. MARSYAS, also associated with the playing of the reed pipe, was a follower. While still young, she was recognized and received into her father's household, but he became furious when he discovered that she had become pregnant by the Phrygian youth ATTIS. Maeon put Attis to death, and Cybele wandered in grief, accompanied by Marsyas, and, for some time, by APOLLO. After being punished by plague and crop failure, the people of Phrygia provided a proper burial for Attis and established rites for Cybele.

There are several versions of the myth of Attis; the central one is Attis's self-emasculation as an act of dedication to Cybele.

In Apollonius of Rhodes's *Voyage of the Argonauts* and Lucian's *Dialogues of the Gods*, Cybele is merged with Rhea, mother of the Olympian gods. Cybele's attendants were called Corbyantes, in some sources identified with the Curetes, who made a great din to hide the cries of the infant ZEUS (hidden by Rhea so that CRONUS would not swallow him). These calls and music were seen as originating aspects of her later worship. Following the example of Attis, the disciples of Cybele, called the Galli, were self-made eunuchs. The musical instruments played by her devotees and her association with lions and wolves are mentioned in the *Homeric Hymn to the Mother of the Gods*. In Catullus's poem 63, the procession resembles a Dionysiac frenzy. The Dionysiac connection is reinforced in Apollodorus's *LIBRARY*, who maintains that DIONYSUS had been initiated into her worship before he established his own cult.

Cybele was represented in reliefs, coins, painting, and sculpture. Her attributes are a turret crown and wild beasts, often a lion. She rides a lion and wears a turret crown in a silver sculptural group from 200 C.E. (Museum of Fine Arts, Boston).

Cyclopes One-eyed creatures. Classical sources are Apollodorus's *LIBRARY* (1.1.2, 1.1.4–5, 1.2.1), Hesiod's *THEOGONY* (139–146), Homer's *ODYSSEY* (9.104–115), Hyginus's *Fabulae* (49), Pausanias's *Description of Greece* (2.2.1, 2.25.8, 7.25.6), Theocritus's *Idylls* (2), and Virgil's *AENEID* (3.616–681, 8.424–454) and *GEORGICS* (4.170ff). The Cyclopes were enormously strong beings with a single eye set in the middle of their foreheads. The Cyclopes born of GAIA (Earth) and URANUS (HEAVEN) were named Brontes, Steropes, and Arges, names associated with thunder, lightning, and thunderbolts. The Cyclopes were hidden away by Uranus in the earth until they were released by CRONUS. The TITANS confined them to TARTARUS until they were released, this time by ZEUS. In gratitude, the Cyclopes forged thunderbolts for Zeus, an invisibility helmet for HADES, and POSEIDON's trident. The Cyclopes were also critical in assuring the defeat of the Titans by the Olympian gods. The Cyclopes are sometimes found in the forge of HEPHAESTUS. A thunderbolt killed ASCLEPIUS, son of APOLLO, and the god was said to have slain the Cyclopes in revenge. In Homer's *Odyssey*, Odysseus's encounter with the Cyclops POLYPHEMUS is recounted in Book 9.

Cyclops EURIPIDES (ca. 450 B.C.E.) Euripides' *Cyclops* is the only surviving example of a satyr play from antiquity. Otherwise, only fragments survive, including a large number of lines from Sophocles' play *Trackers*. The satyr play presented a more boisterous, drunken, and rowdy version of heroic mythology than the tragedies it typically followed. A satyr play was typically performed in the fourth place following a playwright's trilogy of tragedies. It is called a "satyr" play because the chorus was composed of SATYRS—mythical wild male creatures with ani-

mal features, often interchangeable with "Sileni," and forming part of the sacred troupe *(thiasos)* of DIONYSUS. Satyrs and Sileni are only partly civilized and often embody untamed energies and desires normally restrained by civilization, especially sexual impulses and drunkenness. SILENUS, prime companion and teacher of Dionysus, is also known as the father of the satyrs. A "satyr play" with its chorus of Dionysiac revelers, thus forms an appropriate part of the festival of Dionysus—more appropriate in some ways than tragedy proper—and, as Aristotle suggests, may represent an earlier component of the festivities than the tragedies themselves. As tragedy developed into its known form, the satyr play appears to have been preserved, if only in the fourth place, as an honored relic of the earlier form of dramatic performance in Dionysus's honor.

The *Cyclops* presents in dramatic form the story of ODYSSEUS and POLYPHEMUS familiar from Homer's *ODYSSEY*, and while the often bawdy jokes and pranks of the satyrs are evidently meant to contrast with the higher tone of epic, Euripides remains surprisingly faithful to the underlying plot of Homer. The play recapitulates and comments on the central themes of the Homeric episode, while weaving in a Dionysiac subplot: Silenus and the satyrs, attempting to rescue Dionysus from the band of Lydian pirates, end up as captives of the Cyclops, who makes them his slaves. As Odysseus completes his epic feat of blinding the Cyclops, the Dionysiac troupe remains present as a constant source of comic relief and facetious commentary. At the end, they will have the opportunity to escape the oppressive Cyclops, and win their freedom.

SYNOPSIS

The scene is set in front of the cave of the Cyclops in Sicily near Aetna. Silenus enters. He complains of the many tasks he has to perform in the service of Dionysus, including the present one: Having heard that Lydian pirates captured Dionysus and intended to sell him as a slave, he took his sons, the satyrs, on a sea voyage to find him. They were driven by the East Wind to the shores of Sicily and the land of the CYCLOPES. One of the Cyclopes, Polyphemus, made them his slaves. The Chorus of satyrs enters. As they have been put to work as shepherds, their entry song concerns the herd and their pastoral labors. Silenus calls for silence and announces the arrival of a Greek ship. The sailors and their captain are coming toward the cave. Odysseus and his crew enter. Odysseus asks for food and water and introduces himself. Silenus reveals that they have come to the uncivilized land of the Cyclopes. They have no cities, laws, government, or agriculture. Moreover, they eat their visitors rather than treating them hospitably. Odysseus offers to trade some wine for food. Silenus happily agrees and drinks some of Odysseus's excellent wine.

A satyr asks Odysseus whether or not the Greeks raped Helen after sacking Troy. Odysseus is given his food. They hear the Cyclops coming, but Odysseus refuses to flee. The Cyclops Polyphemus enters and asks who the strangers are and why they have his lambs and cheese. Silenus comes out of the cave, having made himself appear to have been bruised in a fight, and claims that the strangers beat him for attempting to obstruct their robbery. Polyphemus decides that he will eat the strangers. Odysseus insists that he purchased the food by giving wine to Silenus. Polyphemus asks where they are from, and Odysseus tells him that they have come from Troy. Then Odysseus beseeches Polyphemus as the son of POSEIDON not to eat them. He refers to the gods, to the fact that he and his companions fought on behalf of Greece, and to the laws of hospitality. But as long as there is food in his cave, the Cyclops cares for nothing and no one, not ZEUS himself. He worships his own stomach and still intends to eat Odysseus's crew. Polyphemus herds Odysseus and his crew into the cave; they exit. The Chorus expresses disgust at the Cyclops's cannibalism.

Odysseus enters with members of his crew. In conversation with the Chorus leader, he describes the horrors of the Cyclops's cave, and how he made a stew out of two of Odysseus's men. Odysseus, however, gave Polyphemus some of his wine, and he has begun to be tipsy. He offers the satyrs hope of liberation and enlists their help in his plan. He intends to convince Polyphemus to drink all the wine by himself and then, when he is drunk and sleepy, destroy the monster's one eye with a sharpened, heated wooden spike. The Chorus members are eager to take an active role.

Polyphemus enters drunk. The Chorus sings enthusiastically with him about drinking, eros, and marriage. Odysseus persuades him that it is best to drink alone, in his own cave. When asked his name, Odysseus replies that it is "Nobody." Polyphemus (and, when he gets the chance, Silenus) continues to drink until he is quite drunk. Polyphemus and Silenus go into the cave. Odysseus summons the satyrs to help him with his plan, and they respond with unabated enthusiasm. Odysseus enters the cave. The Chorus sings of the coming blinding of Polyphemus. Odysseus returns. The satyrs are now trying to get out of helping with the task, and Odysseus calls them cowards. He enters the cave with his crew. The Chorus chants an incantation to help Odysseus. The Cyclops is heard bellowing in the cave as Odysseus and his crew drive the stake into his eye. Polyphemus comes out to the entrance of the cave. The satyrs taunt him as he complains that "Nobody blinded me." They all escape from the cave toward Odysseus's ships as Polyphemus gropes in vain for them. Odysseus reveals his identity, and Polyphemus declares that Odysseus will be cursed to wandering because of his actions. Odysseus announces his departure as Polyphemus rages impotently. The satyrs proclaim their intention to go with Odysseus's crew and then seek Dionysus. Odysseus, Silenus, and the Chorus exit.

COMMENTARY

Dionysus is the absent hero of the play. The play begins with a reference to him and his capture by pirates and ends with the proclamation of the Chorus's intention to seek him out. Throughout the play, the audience sees Dionysus's *thiasos* (sacred troupe) singing and dancing before them. In a few notable instances, praises of Dionysus have been conspicuously inserted amid the dialogue. Greek plays, we recall, were performed at festivals of Dionysus, above all at the City Dionysia that took place in Athens and included the tragic competition at the Theater of Dionysus—a theater located within the god's sacred precinct. Dionysus was in some sense present to oversee the tragic competition in his honor, not only as the festival's honored god, but also in more physical terms: His statue was placed in the theater, and thus "viewed" the action of the plays. It was often observed by Athenian theatergoers that the tragedies had "nothing to do with Dionysus." Whatever the truth of this commonplace saying, it certainly cannot be said with any plausibility of satyr plays, and certainly not of this one.

As protagonist, the god may be physically absent throughout the play, but in another sense, he is not absent at all: He is the spirit of wine; he is wine itself personified and manifested in divine form; and wine *is* present in the play. Euripides no doubt chooses Book 9 of the *Odyssey* as the play's basic mythological framework because of the striking prominence of wine in this episode—both as the hero's unusual weapon against his monstrous foe and as a symbol of Greek civilization and its superiority over barbarians. Wine turns out to be the play's true hero: It tames Polyphemus, makes him vulnerable to Odysseus and his men, and acts as liberator of the satyrs and Silenus in more than one sense. Dionysus, from this perspective, may be considered the hero of the play—absent from its action yet powerfully present as the inebriating force inherent in wine.

One underlying premise both of the present play and of its Odyssean model is that barbarians do not understand how to drink wine properly and cannot enjoy its effects moderately and nonself-destructively. Wine, after all, is one of the central tokens of Greek and Mediterranean civilization as opposed to barbaric lands. Silenus, at one point, offers the Cyclopes a semifacetious lesson on wine drinking: how to recline properly while drinking, how to savor the wine, how to mix the wine first with water. Silenus, of course, is an expert wine drinker and symposiast. Polyphemus, however, is eager to gulp down the wine indiscriminately and does not bother to mix it with water first—a necessary precaution for a civilized symposium. Odysseus, moreover, succeeds in persuading Polyphemus to drink alone, in his cave, without company. This solitary gulping of wine is the antithesis of the Greek symposium, and Polyphemus comes off as the very opposite of the members of the Dionysiac *thiasos*. The Chorus members are joined together in drinking and in worship of the god, whereas Polyphemus is a solitary, godless drunkard.

The fact that Polyphemus cannot handle his wine is just one, albeit important and highly emphasized, facet of his broader lack of civilization as a Cyclops. This theme is taken over directly from the *Odyssey*. As in Homer's epic, so in this play, it is made clear that the Cyclopes do not have laws, government, agriculture (including viticulture), or any of the other elements of civilized society. The Cyclops also lacks proper religion and respect for the gods. Though born from the god Poseidon, he proclaims his indifference to his father's temples and to Zeus himself. He is uncivilized because radically self-isolating and self-sufficient, i.e., he has no need for or interest in society and its religion. He enjoys himself in his cave without any care of Zeus or the rest of the world. This means, of course, that he has no respect for the laws of hospitality upheld by Zeus *xenios*. Here, too, a theme is taken deliberately from the *Odyssey*: Instead of feeding and hosting guests and strangers, Polyphemus eats them. He is thus the worst host imaginable and an outrageous violator of *xenia*. Guest-host relations constitute another of the central litmus tests for Greekness and civilized behavior.

He who treats a guest or host badly is barbaric and will be punished. The foreign prince PARIS violated his host MENELAUS's hospitality, and the Trojan War ensued under Zeus's guidance. Polyphemus here horribly mistreats the strangers who should be treated as guests, and, as in the *Odyssey*, is duly punished.

In general, Euripides follows quite closely the actual events and central themes of the Odyssean narrative: the eating of Odysseus's men, Odysseus's use of wine to overpower the Cyclops, his assumption of the name "Nobody" as a clever ruse, and the exchange of "hospitality" gifts. The last of these items is especially closely reproduced: Odysseus gives Polyphemus a "gift" (the wine that will enable his blinding), while Polyphemus, as his "*xenia*-gift," offers Odysseus the privilege of being eaten last. Odysseus himself is not quite his usual heroic self, yet he remains relatively true to his epic character in broad outlines: He does not lower himself to the level of the Chorus's bawdy discourse and remains brave in comparison with the cowardly and entertainingly base Silenus and satyrs. On the one hand, Euripides has carefully chosen an Odyssean episode, which, in its extravagance (a one-eyed cannibal) and elements of wit and humor (the Cyclops's drunkenness, Odysseus's pseudonym) is already adaptable to the format of the satyr play and, in hindsight, can be construed as having its own protosatiric elements. On the other hand, Odysseus, who, in the epic, is a clever, witty foil to Polyphemus's unmannered brutishness and naïveté, now plays the role of "straight man" to the Chorus. Dionysus's *thiasos* has been inserted into the basic narrative of the Odyssey, on which it provides a continual, rowdy commentary. The Chorus of satyrs uses Odysseus's heroic feat as material for its gleefully low humor and as background for its scene-stealing antics.

The nature of the satyrs' lively, disruptive humor generally concerns their strong interest in drinking and sex. The satyrs' comments have intermittent phallic references, and they make

it clear that they see sex as the perfect accompaniment to drinking. In their present situation of enslavement and hard work, they are perhaps particularly liable to fantasize about such things and linger on them. When a hero from the Trojan War arrives somewhere and meets another hero or character, it is traditional according to epic conventions for him to be asked questions about the progress or outcome of the war and how various well-known figures have fared—whether they are dead, on their way home, or have successfully returned. The only thing the satyrs ask Odysseus is whether the Greeks, after capturing Troy, gang-raped Helen as an apt punishment for her "marriage" to more than one man. As the trap is being laid for Polyphemus, the Chorus sings a wedding song that alludes grimly to his coming fate: The bridegroom's eye gleams in anticipation of the bride, the torches are lit, and so on. These remarks are perhaps especially ironic, given the phallic image of the giant stake plunging into the Cyclops's eye cavity: He will be penetrated and made weak and impotent—not exactly the bridegroom he might hope to be. Immediately before the blinding, the drunken Cyclops admits that he prefers boys and expresses a desire to make Silenus his GANYMEDE—once again, an inappropriate choice, since Silenus is too old to be the object of pederastic affection (the Cyclops can do nothing right as a symposiast—not even choose an appropriate object of pederasty). The declaration of this desire, too, is grimly ironic, since it is Polyphemus who is about to be violated by the wooden spike.

The satyr play is basically a tragedy in a different key. The subject matter is similarly mythological, and the themes are often similar as well. For example, in tragedy mortals typically dwell on the opaque designs and attitudes of the gods: Do they truly exist, and if so, do they pity mortals and attempt to help them, or not? In the *Cyclops*, Odysseus asks the same questions. Here also are themes of chance, hubris, and a tyrant toppled and brought low. In seeing Polyphemus blinded, we view the intense sufferings of one who, because he violated the laws of the gods, has been severely punished. There is also the extravagance of horror and carnage we see in many tragedies (e.g., *AJAX*, the story of Atreus and Thyestes, etc.). Odysseus describes the horrors of the Cyclops's cave in a satyric version of the tragic "messenger speech." Cannibalism itself is a well-known tragic theme. We might also note the theme of the absent god who nonetheless seems to be constantly behind the action, in this instance, Dionysus. Finally, the form of the play corresponds, albeit more briefly, with the main elements of a tragedy: prologue, parados, episodes punctuated by choral song, and exodos. Silenus, as in other Euripidean prologue speeches, outlines the basic situation. The play employs *stichomythia* (single-line retorts exchanged back and forth), and there are contests in speech between two protagonists where one persuades the other to take a path of action decisive for his fate. Particularly notable is the Chorus's inability to intervene directly in the action: When it comes to it, they are too cowardly to help Odysseus blind Polyphemus and sing a supportive song instead. Euripides here appears to comment knowingly and even sardonically on the well-known limitations of the tragic Chorus: It can help only with words.

The Chorus's dialogue with a main protagonist, in which the actor's response forms part of the choral song, is also a feature of many tragedies. In the *Cyclops*, the Chorus of satyrs at one point absorbs Polyphemus into their drunken song: The Chorus speaks the strophe, the Cyclopes the antistrophe, and the Chorus closes with the epode (the three formal units of the choral ode). This song occurs near the blinding episode in the latter part of the play and strikes a very different note from their song at the beginning. The Dionysiac Chorus of satyrs first entered singing about pastoral matters and addressing

the goats that were in their care. In other words, as slaves of Polyphemus, they had to sing his pastoral tune. By the end of the play, he has to sing to their drunken Dionysiac tune—i.e., he has, effectively, been assimilated to their mode of song. Of course, as a tuneless, clumsy, one-eyed monster, Polyphemus performs this kind of song and movement with laughable awkwardness, and his performance becomes part of the humor—the brutish Polyphemus attempting to become fluid and Dionysiac. A humorous version of a tragic tyrant, Polyphemus finds himself humiliated by the god (in this case, Dionysus, god of wine) by being transformed into his own opposite. As the play goes on, the Chorus marks this shift in mood. At first cowed, long-suffering, and absorbed into its pastoral occupation, it builds up enthusiasm and Dionysiac rowdiness, until at last, it exits, alongside Odysseus, in triumph.

Liberation is a major theme and dynamic of the play, as of other satyr plays, insofar as scholars have been able to reconstruct them. The Chorus and Silenus were on a mission to save Dionysus, but they have been thus far completely ineffective (only succeeding in getting themselves enslaved), and in any case, Dionysus, as we know, does not need saving. He is able to free himself at any time, as Euripides' *BACCHAE* demonstrates. Dionysus, moreover, is the one who saves them, without even being present: The force inherent in wine defeats the Cyclops and ensures their liberation with Odysseus. Freedom is perhaps not surprisingly the theme of this most Dionysiac play performed at Dionysus's festival. Wine/Dionysus was seen as having liberating, loosening, and freeing effects: liberation from pain and sorrow, for example. Even more concretely, the City Dionysia were in honor of Dionysus Eleuthereus ("Dionysus the Liberator").

D

Daedalion See CHIONE.

Daedalus An Athenian inventor and crafts-man of great skill. Classical sources are Apollodorus's LIBRARY (3.15.8ff, Epitome 1.8–15), Diodorus Siculus's LIBRARY OF HISTORY (4.76.1–79.2), Homer's ILIAD (18.590), Hyginus's *Fabulae* (39, 40), Pliny's *Natural History* (7.56.168), Ovid's METAMORPHOSES (8.152–262), and Virgil's AENEID (6.14–33). Daedalus's parentage is uncertain; his father was either Palaemon, a sculptor, or Eupalamus, an architect. Daedalus himself was an architect, sculptor, and inventor. He built three-dimensional wooden works, machines, and sculptures (for example, of HERACLES). What is generally agreed on is that Daedalus fled or was forced into exile from Athens to Crete for the murder of his nephew, Talos. The story goes that Daedalus killed Talos by throwing him off the Acropolis because he was jealous that Talos had invented the saw.

In Crete, Daedalus was accepted at the court of King MINOS, where he proved himself useful to the royal family. Ovid relates that when Minos's wife, Pasiphae, was enflamed with passion for a bull and desired to mate with it, Daedalus helpfully built her a wooden cow in which she could mate with the animal. He constructed an intricate labyrinth to house the MINOTAUR, the monstrous half-man, half-bull offspring of this union. But it was also Daedalus who revealed to ARIADNE how to help THESEUS escape from the labyrinth after killing the Minotaur, by giving him a ball of thread to unroll as he entered the monster's lair and then to rewind as he left the labyrinth.

Minos imprisoned Daedalus in the labyrinth, possibly because of the aid he gave Ariadne. Daedalus constructed wings that attached to the shoulder with wax in order to escape from the island of Crete with his son ICARUS. Daedalus warned Icarus not to fly too high, but Icarus ignored his father's warnings, and the heat of the sun melted the wax. Icarus lost his wings and plunged to his death. His distraught father landed in Sicily, either at Cumae or Camicus, and took shelter with King Cocalus. Minos pursued him to Sicily but died there, possibly through Daedalus's agency.

Danae Consort of ZEUS and by him, mother of PERSEUS. Daughter of Eurydice and King Acrisius of Argos. Classical sources are Apollodorus's LIBRARY (2.4.1–5) Homer's ILIAD (14.319ff), Horace's *Odes* (3.16), Ovid's METAMORPHOSES (4.605–611), Pindar's *Pythian Odes* (12), and Virgil's AENEID (7.371–372, 408–413). Euripides and Sophocles both wrote tragedies, now lost, based on the myth of Danae. An oracle foretold

Danae and the Shower of Gold. *Titian, 1553–54 (Hermitage Museum, St. Petersburg)*

that Acrisius would die at the hand of Danae's son, so Acrisius imprisoned her in an underground chamber of bronze. Zeus, in the form of a shower of gold, was nonetheless able to visit her, and she gave birth to the hero Perseus. In a second attempt to forestall the oracle, Acrisius cast Danae and the infant Perseus adrift in a wooden chest, but they survived the ordeal. According to Apollodorus, Danae and Perseus drifted to the island of Seriphos, where they were rescued and offered shelter by King Polydectes. He became enamored of Danae and sent Perseus on a quest to capture the head of the Gorgon MEDUSA. Eventually, through a complicated series of incidents, Perseus unwittingly killed Acrisius and fulfilled the oracle. In a later, Roman version of the story, Danae and Perseus drift to Latium, where Danae marries Pilumnus, with whom she founds the city of Ardea, near Nemi.

Depictions of Danae occur on vase painting from the fifth century B.C.E. onward. Such rep-

resentations are often thematically related to the loves of Zeus. There is a particular interest in Zeus's transformation into a golden shower. In some paintings, Zeus is depicted as a shower of golden rain and in others as a shower of golden coins. An example of the latter is the red-figure krater from ca. 490 B.C.E. (Hermitage Museum, St. Petersburg). Scenes in which Danae and Perseus are cast adrift by Acrisius are common, as in an Attic red-figure lekythos attributed to the Providence Painter from ca. 480 B.C.E. (Toledo Museum of Art, Toledo, Ohio). In postclassical representations of the theme, Zeus's seduction of Danae is central. Many such images relied on formal conceptions already established in Attic vase painting: a nude or seminude Danae set on a low couch close to the picture plane with the shower of gold falling over her torso. She is often in the company of attendant or hovering cupids. Versions of this visual theme include Correggio's *Danae* of ca. 1531 (Galleria Borghese, Rome), Titian's *Danae and the Shower of Gold* of 1553–54 (Hermitage Museum, St. Petersburg), Rembrandt's *Danae* of 1636–37 (Hermitage, St. Petersburg), and Gustav Klimt's *Danae* of 1907–08 (private collection).

Danaus and Danaids Danaus was the son of Belus, the brother of Aegyptus, and father of 50 daughters, the Danaids. The Danaids appear in Aeschylus's SUPPLIANTS. Additional classical sources are Aeschylus's PROMETHEUS BOUND (850ff), Apollodorus's LIBRARY (2.1.4), Horace's *Odes* (3.11), Hyginus's *Fabulae* (168, 170), Ovid's HEROIDES (14), and Pindar's *Pythian Odes* (9.111–116). The 50 sons of Aegyptus wished to marry their cousins, the Danaids, who were unwilling. Aeschylus's *Suppliants* tells how the Danaids flee to Argos, where their father, Danaus, persuades King Pelasgus to receive them as suppliants. Aeschylus's play was part of a tetralogy, the subsequent plays of which do not survive except in fragments. Other sources, including the *Prometheus Bound*, relate how the Egyptians followed them and continued to demand marriage. Danaus assented but commanded his daughters to kill their husbands on their wedding night. Only one daughter, Hypermnestra, defied her father and spared her husband, Lynceus, either because of love or because he spared her virginity. On this story, see the letter from Hypermnestra to Lynceus in Ovid's *Heroides* and Horace's *Odes*. At this point, the mythological tradition becomes uncertain. In some versions, Danaus attempts to marry off his daughters by offering them as prizes in a race. In others, Lynceus avenges his brothers' deaths by freeing the imprisoned Hypermnestra and killing Danaus and the other Danaids. Lynceus and Hypermnestra, according to the *Prometheus Bound*, subsequently rule and originate a race of kings. The Danaans, a term used to designate the Greeks, are supposed to arise from the line of Danaus and his daughters. In Roman versions,

the Danaids are punished in the underworld by having constantly to refill leaky vessels. One of the Danaids, Amymone, was rescued by POSEIDON from a satyr attempting to rape her while she went to fetch water; she was then seduced by Poseidon. Amymone was the subject of the satyr play completing Aeschylus's tetralogy on the Danaid myth. The Danaids were of special interest in Augustan Rome: Statues of Danaus and the Danaids adorned the portico of Augustus's Palatine Apollo complex (described by PROPERTIUS and Ovid), while Virgil represented this myth on the crucial baldric of Pallas in his AENEID. It is possible that the destruction of aggressive Egyptians was meant to recall Augustus's defeat of the Egyptian Cleopatra at Actium. Hypermnestra's act of defiance, however, is viewed in a positive light by the Augustan poets.

Daphne A nymph, daughter of the river god Peneus. Classical sources are Hyginus's *Fabulae* (203), Ovid's METAMORPHOSES (1.452–567), and Pausanias's *Description of Greece* (10.7.8).

In Ovid's *Metamorphoses*, Apollo, proud and haughty after defeating the Python, told EROS to leave bows and arrows to those more capable of using them. Eros decided to have his revenge for this insulting comment by demonstrating his deadly skill with the bow and arrow: He shot Apollo with a gold-tipped arrow that incited desire, and Daphne, a wood nymph, with a lead-tipped arrow that repelled it. Daphne already appears to have been averse to marriage, as she was a follower of chaste ARTEMIS. Apollo pursued her, until, despairing of escape, Daphne prayed to her father, the river god Peneus, for her beautiful form to be changed. She metamorphosed into a laurel tree (Daphne means "laurel" in Greek). Since he could not possess her as his wife, Apollo made her his tree and the laurel became his attribute. Victorious Roman generals wore laurels. The door of the emperor Augustus's house is framed by laurel trees, and although Ovid does not mention it, laurels are associated with poets, as in the case with Apollo himself, patron god of poetry. The story of Daphne is singled out for extended treatment by Ovid and is among his mythological epic's first stories of metamorphosis. It may be no accident that it tells the origins-story of a tree associated with poetry and with a god who was especially favored under Augustus.

The myth of Apollo and Daphne is the subject of a mosaic in the House of Dionysus, Paphos. For postclassical artists, the myth of Daphne has been a rich source of inspiration: A famous example is Gianlorenzo Bernini's *Apollo and Daphne* of 1622–25 (Galleria Borghese, Rome). A mid-16th-century engraving after Baldassare Peruzzi (Metropolitan Museum of Art, New York), *Apollo's Pursuit of Daphne* exemplifies the most common representation of the myth: The god pursues the fleeing nymph in the foreground, and in the background, Daphne has begun her transformation into the laurel tree. An addition here is the fig-

Apollo's Pursuit of Daphne. *Engraving Master of the Die (after Baldassare Peruzzi), mid-16th century (Metropolitan Museum of Art, New York)*

ure of Peneus, who reclines in the background. Peneus has answered the desperate plea of his daughter to evade Apollo's grasp and caused her transformation.

Deianira Daughter of Althaea and King Oeneus of Calydon. Sister of MELEAGER. Wife of the greatest of Greek heroes, HERACLES. The fullest treatment of Deianira and Heracles' story is Sophocles' *TRACHINIAE*. Other classical sources include Apollodorus's *LIBRARY* (1.8.1, 2.7.5), Diodorus Siculus's *LIBRARY OF HISTORY* (4.34.1, 4.38.1), Hyginus's *Fabulae* (33, 34, 36), Ovid's *METAMORPHOSES* (9.5–133), and Pausanias's *Description of Greece* (6.19.12). During one of his Twelve Labors, Heracles descended to HADES, where he met the ghost of Meleager. Heracles promised Meleager that upon his return from the underworld that he would find and marry Meleager's sister Deianira. First, Heracles successfully defeated the river god ACHELOUS in a wrestling match for her hand in marriage. Then the centaur NESSUS, who was carrying Deianira across a river, attempted to violate her. Heracles killed him with an arrow dipped in the poisonous blood of the HYDRA. The dying Nessus tricked Deianira into collecting some of his blood, telling her it could be used as a love potion. Many years afterward, when Heracles fell in love with Iole, Deianira gave him a robe with the potion, unwittingly causing his death. In grief and horror at what she had done, Deianira committed suicide.

In visual representations, Deianira is frequently shown being rescued from Nessus by Heracles. An example is an Attic black-figure hydria from ca. 560 B.C.E. (Louvre, Paris). Here, a bearded Heracles pursues Nessus, who is escaping with Deianira astride his back. The scene also occurs on a wall painting at the House of the Centaur in Pompeii. An Attic red-figure pelike from ca. 440 B.C.E. (British Museum, London) focuses on the tragic death of the hero brought about by the wife who loved him. Here, Heracles, identified by his

The Abduction of Deianira by the Centaur Nessus.
Guido Reni, 1621 (Louvre, Paris)

lion skin and club, holds out his hand for the (poisoned) tunic Deianira is presenting to him.

In a 17th-century image of the myth, *The Abduction of Deianira by the Centaur Nessus* (Louvre, Paris) by Guido Reni, Deianira is being spirited away by Nessus as Heracles reacts in the background of the image.

Demeter (Ceres) The goddess of agriculture. Daughter of the Titans Cronus and RHEA. Demeter's Olympian siblings are HADES, HERA, HESTIA, POSEIDON, and ZEUS. Classical sources include the *Homeric Hymns to Demeter,* Apollodorus's LIBRARY (1.1.5, 1.5.1, 2.1.3, 2.5.12, 3.6.8, 3.12.1, 3.14.7), Hesiod's THEOGONY (453–506, 969–974), Homer's ODYSSEY (5.125–8), Hyginus's *Fabulae* (146, 147), and Ovid's *METAMORPHOSES* (5.346–571). Demeter is associated with the fertility of crops, especially of

grain. Later, the Romans syncretized her with the goddess Ceres. In the *Theogony*, the *Homeric Hymn*, and the *Odyssey*, Demeter loved the hero Iasion, and their son Ploutos (meaning "wealth") was conceived, appropriately considering her sphere of activity, on a thrice-plowed field. In some accounts, when Zeus became aware of their affair, he struck Iasion dead with a thunderbolt, on the grounds that a mortal was not to have such relations with a god. In other accounts, Iasion survived.

Demeter's brother Poseidon forced himself upon her, and she became pregnant with two children; Despoine, a goddess worshipped in the Eleusian Mysteries, and Aerion, a dark-colored horse, because when Poseidon came upon her, Demeter had transformed herself into a mare in an unsuccessful attempt to avoid his advances. Demeter is the fourth wife of her brother Zeus, and their daughter is PERSE-PHONE, with whom Demeter is closely associated in mythology and cult practice.

In a myth recounted by Ovid, she punished ERYSICHTHON for having violently and insolently cut down a grove of trees sacred to her. She cursed him with perpetual hunger, and eventually Erysichthon, driven to madness by his hunger, consumed himself.

Central to the Demeter myth is the abduction of her daughter Persephone by Hades, and her imprisonment in the underworld. Demeter, disguised as an old woman, searched the world in vain for her daughter. Though no one had seen Persephone, many offered the disguised goddess comfort or food. In return for their kindness, Demeter taught them agriculture and initiated them into her rites.

In the course of her wanderings, Demeter arrived in Eleusis and became the nurse of DEMOPHON, the son of King Celeus. Because of her attachment to the child, Demeter hoped to make him immortal by dipping him in ambrosia and burning his mortality away in the fire, but she was discovered in the act and prevented from doing so by Celeus's wife, Metaneira, and the child remained mortal. Demeter shed her disguise and asked the Eleusinians to build her an altar so that by their worship they would secure the boy honors after his death. This myth is evidently intended to explain the origins of Demeter's cult at Eleusis and the Eleusinian mysteries. According to some sources, Demeter, after failing to immortalize Demophon, gave Demophon's brother TRIPTOLEMUS a chariot with dragon wings and seeds of wheat so that he could spread the practice of agriculture throughout the world.

When both altar and temple were finished, the goddess took shelter there, keeping away from the other gods and, in her grief at the loss of her daughter, neglected to assure the fertility of the crops causing famine. Finally, Zeus persuaded Hades to return Persephone to the upper world and her mother, but since Persephone had eaten a pomegranate seed while in the underworld, she was fated to remain there for part of every year. Her time in the underworld coincides with winter and her reappearance above with spring and summer, the seasons of fertility and growth.

Demeter and Persephone, also known as Kore ("girl"), are the central cult figures in the practice of the Eleusinian Mysteries. The sanctuary to Demeter and Kore in Eleusis, west of Athens, was originally housed in a temple dating to the Geometric period, but as the cult grew in importance and popularity, it was replaced and enlarged. The festival spanned seven days in autumn, during which initiates presented themselves at the shrine to offer sacrifices and perform rituals, the precise nature of which is not fully known. Another major festival of Demeter is the Thesmophoria. This festival took place in autumn, lasted for three days, and excluded men.

In the classical period, visual representations of Demeter and Persephone were put on vases, reliefs, coins, and mosaics. Demeter is usually depicted as a fully clothed matron-type figure. She may be standing, seated, or riding in a chariot, and she carries such attributes as a scepter, sheaf of wheat, ears of corn, and, occa-

sionally, a crown of flowers. It is common to find the goddess and her daughter together, where both are clothed in long gowns, as on an Attic red-figure, white-ground lekythos from ca. 450 B.C.E. (National Museum, Athens). Here, Persephone pours libations on the ground before Demeter. A colossal statue of Demeter (Vatican Museums, Rome) shows the goddess carrying a sheaf of wheat and holding a scepter. In a few instances, Demeter and Persephone are joined by Triptolemus in a wheeled or winged chariot (Demeter's gift to him), as in a bas-relief from Eleusis dating to ca. 440 B.C.E.

Demophon (1) Son of Metaneira and Celeus of Eleusis. See DEMETER.

Demophon (2) and Acamas Demophon, a king of Athens, and Acamas were sons of PHAEDRA and THESEUS. Classical sources are Apollodorus's LIBRARY (Epitome 1.18, 1.23, 5.22, 6.16), Hyginus's *Fabulae* (59), Ovid's *HEROIDES* (2), and Pausanias's *Description of Greece* (10.25.8). Demophon and Acamas are, with some variations in the sources, linked with the bringing of the Palladium to Athens. Their father, Theseus, abducted HELEN, but she was rescued by her brothers, the DIOSCURI. In revenge, the Dioscuri kidnapped Theseus's mother, Aethra. Aethra became either a servant or a handmaiden to Helen and accompanied her to Troy. Acamas and Demophon undertook the rescue of their grandmother Aethra in Troy. Pausanias's *Description of Greece* mentions that Demophon was given permission by Helen and AGAMEMNON to return with Aethra, but other sources maintain that Aethra was liberated only after the fall of Troy. While on their way to rescue Aethra, Demophon and Acamas came to Thrace, where Demophon fell in love with Phyllis, daughter of the king. After a time, Demophon wished to return home but promised Phyllis that he would return to her in a year's time. Phyllis presented Demophon with a casket and instructed him to open it only if he should decide not to return to her. After a year passed without Demophon's return, Phyllis killed herself (either by throwing herself into the sea or hanging herself). Demophon opened the casket and was driven mad by the sight of its contents. Diodorus Siculus writes that trees growing on Phyllis's grave had leaves (*phylla*, in Greek) that fell every autumn in grief over her death. In another version of the myth, Phyllis was transformed upon her death into an almond tree that blossomed when Demophon embraced it. In some sources, Acamas, rather than Demophon, is the hero of these adventures.

Demophon and Acamas are pictured on an Attic black-figure amphora from ca. 545 B.C.E. (Antikenmuseen, Berlin). Here, the brothers are accompanied by horses and carry spears.

Deucalion and Pyrrha   The son of Clymene and PROMETHEUS. Deucalion's wife is Pyrrha, daughter of EPIMETHEUS and PANDORA. Classical sources are Apollodorus's LIBRARY (1.7.2–3), Hyginus's *Fabulae* (153), Ovid's METAMORPHOSES (1.125–415), and Pindar's *Olympian Odes* (9.42–53). When Zeus sent a flood to destroy human civilization, he elected to save only the worthy Deucalion and Pyrrha. They built a chest and took refuge in it for nine days and nights, until the flood brought them to Parnassus. They repopulated the earth by throwing rocks over their shoulders. The rocks thrown by Deucalion became men and those thrown by Pyrrha, women.

Dialogues of the Gods   LUCIAN (ca. 150)   The *Dialogues of the Gods* were written by Lucian, a Greek author from Samosata in Syria, who lived in the second century C.E. (ca. 115–80). Lucian traveled throughout the Mediterranean world as a lecturer or sophist, i.e., a typically itinerant practitioner of public, rhetorical display and instruction. The cultural milieu in which Lucian wrote has been called the "Second Sophistic" (ca. later first and second centuries C.E.) because of its (debatable) revival of the practices of the sophists of the fifth cen-

tury B.C.E. Eighty-two works in prose surviving from the ancient world are ascribed to Lucian, but not all have an equal claim to authenticity. His best-known works are his satirical dialogues, a form that Lucian developed by combining features of the Platonic dialogue, comedy, and mime. Among his satirical dialogues, the *Dialogues of the Gods* are among the most admired. In these brief, humorous sketches, Lucian normally presents two gods in dialogue to flesh out a familiar episode in their mythology. The tone is refreshingly direct and humorously quotidian. HERMES, for example, complains to his mother, MAIA, of being exploited as the gods' errand boy; he is especially exhausted with attending to the details of his father ZEUS's love affairs. In another brief exchange, PROMETHEUS offers Zeus the crucial prophecy regarding THETIS's offspring and thereby wins his freedom. Lucian wears his erudition lightly, and the effect is one of exquisitely maintained levity and wit.

Diana   See ARTEMIS.

Dido   Queen of Carthage. Also called Elissa, daughter of Mutto, king of Tyre. The principal classical source for the story of Dido is Virgil's AENEID (1.335–756, 4.1–705, 5.1–7, 6.450–476). There may be a precursor in Naevius's *Punic War*, although his fragmentary preservation makes this uncertain. An additional classical source is Ovid's HEROIDES (7). Dido, according to Virgil's narrative, was deceived by her treacherous brother Pygmalion, then king of Tyre, who murdered her husband, Sychaeus (elsewhere called Sicharbas), for his treasure. She fled her native Tyre and set up a new colony in Carthage, where she reigned as queen of the emerging city-state. In *Aeneid* Book 1, the Trojan hero AENEAS took refuge on her shores after enduring a terrible storm at sea. He was encouraged to see relief sculptures of scenes from the Trojan War depicted in Carthage, and even more so when Dido offered him and his men hospitality in her

Dido Performing a Sacrifice. *Manuscript illustration, fifth century* C.E. *(Vatican Library, Rome)*

land. He, like Dido, was an exile, and she both pitied and admired his astonishing sufferings. To make her son Aeneas secure in Carthage, Venus (see APHRODITE) determined to make Dido fall in love with him. She replaced Aeneas's son, Ascanius/Iulus, with her own son, Cupid (see EROS), and in a strange and sinister scene, Dido unwittingly drew the poison of love into herself as she held Ascanius in her arms. During a hunting expedition, Aeneas and Dido took shelter in a cave from a storm. They there consummated what the love-struck Dido mistakenly considered a "marriage." Eventually, Jupiter (see ZEUS), swayed both by the angry prayers of a rival suitor of Dido (the neighboring King Iarbas) and by his concern that Aeneas was failing to fulfill his destiny to found Rome, dispatched Mercury (see HERMES) to send Aeneas on his way to Italy. Reluctantly, Aeneas announced his departure to the incredulous and irate queen. He remained unshaken by her pleas and feared for his men's safety as they made hasty preparations for departure. Dido killed herself in despair. Later, when Aeneas descended to the HADES, Dido refused to speak to him, just as AJAX refuses to speak to ODYSSEUS in Book 11 of Homer's *ODYSSEY*.

Virgil's etiological myth offers Dido's enduring rage as an explanation of the calamitous enmity of Carthage and Rome during the Carthaginian wars. At the same time, Virgil assimilates the Dido myth to epic paradigms of female obstruction of the hero's journey and purpose: She resembles the Homeric CALYPSO and CIRCE. Finally, she comes to resemble a tragic heroine, driven by madness and the FURIES and, ultimately, bringing about her own destruction. Virgil, however, profoundly transforms the myth for his own purposes. Dido's story was likely, in its origins, a colonization and foundation myth in its broader emphasis. Virgil subordinated

Dido's foundation story to his own myth of cultural transfer: the foundation of Rome.

A crucial stage in the transmission of Virgil's epic was the copying of manuscripts in the late antique and medieval periods. An illustration from an illuminated manuscript of the fifth century C.E., *Dido Performing a Sacrifice* (Vatican Library, Rome) shows Dido and her court engaged in a sacrificial rite.

Diodorus Siculus (fl. first century B.C.E.) A Greek historian from Agyrium, Sicily, often referred to as Diodorus Siculus (Diodorus of Sicily). Diodorus lived and wrote in the first century B.C.E. but very little is known of his life. He is the author of the *LIBRARY OF HISTORY (Bibliotheke)*, a history of the world from its legendary beginnings to 60 B.C.E. in 40 books. Fifteen Books are extant: 1–5 and 11–20. He focuses on the history of Greece, Sicily, and, starting in the period of the Punic Wars (third century B.C.E.), Rome. Diodorus's project is thus truly world historical in scope. He also provides extensive treatment of what we would categorize as myth, treating mythology prior to the Trojan War. Diodorus, like most ancient writers, includes mythology within his broader view of world history.

Diomedes A major hero of the Trojan War. Son of Tydeus and Deipyle, husband of Aegiale. Diomedes appears throughout Homer's *ILIAD*. Additional classical sources include Apollodorus's *LIBRARY* (1.8.5–6, 3.7.2–3, Epitome 5.8, 5.13, 6.1), Homer's *ODYSSEY* (3.141–182), Hyginus's *Fabulae* (102, 108, 175), Ovid's *METAMORPHOSES* (14.457–511), and Virgil's *AENEID* (8.9–17, 11.222–295). Diomedes fought on the side of the Greeks during the Trojan War. Before the war, he took part in the expedition against Thebes as one of the Epigoni, the sons of the Seven against Thebes. He also was known for avenging his grandfather Oeneus. The sons of Agrius, Oeneus's brother, drove him from the throne of Calydon. Diomedes killed most of the sons of Agrius and restored his family to the throne. Two of the sons

of Agrius who managed to survive, however, later ambushed and killed Oeneus.

Diomedes was one of the greatest Greek heroes of the Trojan War—possibly the greatest after Achilles. In Book 5 of the *Iliad*, Diomedes goes on an unstoppable onslaught. In particular, he wounds the goddess APHRODITE while she attempts to protect AENEAS; subsequently, he has to be warned away from Aeneas four times by APOLLO before he desists; and, with Athena's encouragement, he wounds the god Ares in the belly. Diomedes, in this extraordinary sequence, appears invincible and a rival to the gods in warfare. In *Iliad* 6, Diomedes encounters the Trojan Glaucus. In conversation, the two discover that there was a relation of hospitality and friendship between the families dating to an exchange of gifts between their grandfathers, Oeneus and BELLEROPHON; instead of fighting, they exchange armor. In other episodes, Diomedes is often associated with Odysseus in feats that involve cunning, deception, and/or transgression. In the night raid scene in *Iliad* 10, Diomedes and Odysseus kill the Trojan spy Dolon and massacre a larger number of sleeping Thracians and their leader, Rhesus. Diomedes is also said to have aided Odysseus in the murder of PALAMEDES, the expedition to obtain the hero PHILOCTETES (in Apollodorus and Hyginus), and the theft of the Palladium, Athena's sacred statue, from Troy (Apollodorus). Diomedes is also listed among the soldiers hiding in the Trojan Horse. At the funeral games in honor of PATROCLUS, Diomedes wins the chariot race.

Diomedes, like other Greek heroes of the Trojan War, encounters serious difficulties returning home, in part because of the sacrilegious behavior of the Greeks generally during the sack of Troy and in part because Aphrodite still harbors a grudge against him for wounding her in battle. In Ovid's *Metamorphoses*, Diomedes' comrades despair of wandering and complain of Aphrodite's ill treatment of them, and they are transformed into birds. According to various, mostly late, sources, including Servius's commentary on the *Aeneid*, Aphrodite punishes Diomedes by making his wife commit adultery while he is away at Troy. On returning home, he either leaves of his own accord after discovering her infidelity or is driven out by her adulterer. (Ovid's *Ibis* lists Diomedes' wife Aegiale among examples of immoral women.) Finally, in some accounts, Diomedes ends up arriving in Italy, where he helps king Daunus in warfare, receives a tract of land from him, marries his daughter, and founds Italian communities. In Virgil's *Aeneid*, Turnus and his Latin allies seek Diomedes' support against Aeneas, but he refuses, not wishing to incite Venus (Aphrodite) to further anger against him.

Dione   An early Greek goddess and consort of ZEUS. Classical sources are the *Homeric Hymn to Apollo*, Apollodorus's LIBRARY (1.1.3, 1.2.7, 1.3.1), Hesiod's THEOGONY (353), Homer's ILIAD (5.370–417), and Hyginus's *Fabulae* (82, 83). There was a cult of Dione, alongside that of Zeus, at Dodona, and her name is the feminine version of *Zeus*. There are few myths relating to Dione; instead, she is variously conceived by ancient authors as a NEREID, an OCEANID, or a TITAN. In Hesiod's *Theogony*, Dione is the daughter of OCEANUS and TETHYS. In Apollodorus's *Library*, Dione is both the name of a Titan and a Nereid (daughter of NEREUS and Doris) whose union with Zeus produces Aphrodite. However, according to Hyginus's *Fabulae*, Dione is the daughter of the Titan ATLAS; she married TANTALUS, by whom she had a son, PELOPS. In Homer's *Iliad*, which provides the fullest treatment of her, Dione is the mother of APHRODITE. In the *Iliad*, Aphrodite sought the comfort and aid of her mother on Mount Olympus, after having been injured by DIOMEDES during the Trojan War. Dione healed her injured arm with herbs and consoled her by listing the various injuries that the gods had suffered at the hands of mortals.

Dionysus (Bacchus)   Greek god of wine in the Olympic pantheon of gods. Son of SEMELE (daughter of CADMUS, king of Thebes) and ZEUS. Dionysus appears in Euripides' BACCHAE. Additional classical sources are the *Homeric Hymns to Dionysus*, Apollodorus's LIBRARY, (3.4.2–3.5.3), Diodorus Siculus's LIBRARY OF HISTORY (3.67–74, 4.2–5, 5.75.4–5), Homer's ILIAD (6.130–143), Hesiod's THEOGONY (940–942, 947–949), Lucian's DIALOGUES OF THE GODS (3, 12, 22), and Ovid's METAMORPHOSES (3.253–315, 511–733; 11.85–145). Dionysus is the god of wine and of the harvest. Dionysus used to be considered a foreign god who only later joined the Olympians, but the discovery of his name on Linear B tablets (ca. 1250 B.C.E.) confirms his status as one of the older Greek gods. The Roman called him Bacchus after one of his cult titles and associated him with the Italic Liber Pater. Dionysus was said to be effeminately beautiful. He appeared mild but could be dangerous, as he is presented in Euripides' *Bacchae*. In the *Homeric Hymns* dedicated to Dionysus, of which there are three, Dionysus is "ivy-crowned" and terrible when roused. Dionysus wears a panther skin, his cortege is pulled by panthers, and his attributes are vegetal: grapes, ivy, and myrtle. His entourage includes SILENI, maenads, and SATYRS. Dionysus carries a thyrsus, or ivy-covered staff, with which he is able to induce frenzy.

Dionysus is also able to change form at will. In the *Orphic Hymn to Dionysus*, the god is "two-horned" and "bull-faced." During his rites, goats and bulls were sacrificed, and, unusually, his rites appear to have involved offerings of raw meat: In the *Orphic Hymn* Dionysus is the "eater of raw flesh." Because of Dionysus's association with wine and the freedom from ordinary restraint its consumption induces, the Dionysiac rites, at least in myth, were wild revelries that included dancing, shrieking, and orgiastic and more violent elements, such as ripping apart animals and consuming raw flesh. In reality, behavior in cult practice may not have been so uncontrolled. His followers—Bacchantes or maenads—were female, though men could participate in a lim-

Bacchus. *Michelangelo Caravaggio, ca. 1595 (Galleria degli Uffizi, Florence)*

ited role. In alternate years, Dionysus's female worshippers would "go to the mountain" to celebrate his rites. The departure from the civilized space of the polis for the wilds is a key theme of Dionysiac worship.

Dionysus is called the twice-born god because of the curious story of his birth. According to Apollodorus's *Library* and Ovid's *Metamorphoses*, HERA became aware of Zeus's love for Semele. Disguised as Semele's nurse, she persuaded Semele to ask him to show himself to her in his full divinity as proof that he was, indeed, Olympic Zeus. Zeus had already promised to grant Semele a request, and he was obliged to fulfill his promise. Zeus manifested himself in the form of a lightning bolt, and Semele perished in the blaze. Zeus plucked the unborn Dionysus from her womb and sewed him into his thigh until the child was ready to be born. After his birth, Dionysus was given into the care of King ATHAMAS and his wife, INO, sister of Semele. Ino's care of her nephew Dionysus attracted the wrath of Hera, who

inflicted a madness on her that caused Ino and her son Melicertes to throw themselves into the sea. Afterward, Zeus transformed Dionysus into a goat to prevent Hera from finding him, and he was brought by HERMES to Nysa. In the *Homeric Hymns*, his birthplace is Nysa, where the nymphs raised him and became his first adherents. In youth, Dionysus discovered wine, which was his gift to humanity. At this time, Hera afflicted him with madness. In its grip he wandered to Egypt, Syria, and India. When he had recovered, he established Dionysiac rites in Syria, India, and Greece.

Dionysus could be ruthless to those who resisted his authority. Lycurgus refused to accept Dionysus's worship in Thrace, and, in retribution, Dionysus afflicted him with madness. In another version of the story, according to Homer's *Iliad*, Lycurgus killed Dionysus's nurses, and Dionysus was forced to shelter with THETIS beneath the sea. Zeus punished Lycurgus by blinding him.

In Euripides' tragedy *Bacchae*, PENTHEUS, grandson of Cadmus and now king of Thebes, was slaughtered by his mother, AGAVE, and his aunt AUTONOE in a Dionysiac frenzy. Their unwitting murder of Pentheus was brought about by Dionysus as retribution for Pentheus's lack of piety toward him. Agave was punished because she slandered Dionysus's mother, Semele. Later, Dionysus would descend into HADES by way of the bottomless Alcyonian Lake and return with Semele, whom he made immortal.

In the *Homeric Hymns*, Dionysus encountered Tyrrhenian pirates who kidnapped him for ransom. They tried unsuccessfully to bind him. The helmsman recognized him as a god and attempted to persuade the crew to release him, but they refused. Suddenly vines grew aboard ship, wine ran throughout, and Dionysus terrified the pirates by taking the shape of a lion. The pirates were transformed into dolphins as they leapt overboard, but Dionysus promised good fortune to the helmsman who had recognized his divinity.

King MIDAS also encountered Dionysus. Dionysus granted Midas the ability to turn everything he touched to gold either because Midas recognized Dionysus's divinity or because he was responsible for rescuing SILENUS, one of the god's companions.

Having established his cult in Greece, Dionysus came to the island of Naxos, where he fell in love with ARIADNE, who had been abandoned there by THESEUS. Dionysus carried her off to become his bride, and they had a son named Oenopion. A wreath that he gave Ariadne was placed as a constellation in the sky, the Corona Borealis. By APHRODITE, Dionysus was said to have sired the god Priapus.

In visual representations of the classical period, Dionysus is often shown on vase paintings accompanied by satyrs and his attributes: grapes, vines, and ivy. An Attic black-figure amphora from ca. 560–525 B.C.E. by the Amasis Painter (Antikenmuseum Kä, Basel) shows Dionysus, satyrs, and maenads at a vintage. In postclassical art, the character of the god, mild yet threatening, was captured in Michelangelo Caravaggio's *Bacchus* of ca. 1595 (Galleria degli Uffizi, Florence). In this image, Dionysus, crowned with grape leaves, is shown with his customary attributes: vegetal motifs and wine.

Ariadne's rescue by Dionysus has been a richly employed theme in the visual arts. The theme occurs in vase painting from the fifth century B.C.E. onward. One example is the François Vase from ca. 570 B.C.E. (Museo Archeologico Nazionale, Florence). The most famous postclassical painting of this theme is Titian's *Ariadne in Naxos* of ca. 1520 (National Gallery, London).

Dioscuri (Castor and Polydeuces or Pollux) Twin sons of LEDA and ZEUS (or Tyndareus, king of Sparta). The Dioscuri appear as the dei-ex-machina in Euripides' *ELECTRA* and *HELEN*. Additional classical sources are the *Homeric Hymns to the Discuri*, Apollodorus's *LIBRARY* (3.10.7, 3.11.2, Epitome 1.23), Homer's *ILIAD* (3.236–244) and *ODYSSEY* (11.298–304), Ovid's *FASTI* (5.699–720) and *METAMORPHOSES* (8.301–302, 372–377), Pindar's *Pythian Odes* (11.61–4) and *Nemean Odes* (10.49–90), and Theocritus's *Idylls* (22.137–213). Spartan heroes with problematic parentage and claims to immortality, Castor and Pollux are known as the Dioscuri, "sons of Zeus," but also as the "Tyndaridae," the "sons of Tyndareus." They were skilled horsemen and are associated with hunting, boxing, wrestling, and sailing. Leda, Tyndareus's wife, was impregnated by Zeus in the form of a swan. The brothers were born from one egg, and from another were born their sisters, HELEN and CLYTAEMNESTRA. Some sources claim that only Polydeuces was fathered by Zeus, and therefore only he inherited his immortality, whereas Castor was the son of Tyndareus, and as such was born a mortal like him. When he died, Zeus granted him immortality at the request of his brother. In still other sources, both men were mortal. In the *Iliad*, the twins share their mortality, taking turns living in the underworld.

The Dioscuri took part in the Calydonian Boar hunt alongside MELEAGER and were part of the crew of the *Argo*. In one episode of the voyage, Polydeuces defeated Amycus in a boxing match. The Dioscuri pursued THESEUS when he abducted their sister Helen and rescued her. In revenge they abducted Theseus's mother, Aethra. Their central myth is the abduction and rape of the daughters of Leucippus, which led to Castor's death. After their deaths, they took their place in heaven as the constellation Gemini (the Twins).

In visual representations, the Dioscuri usually appear together, young males of athletic build, often as horsemen, sometimes wearing caps decorated with stars. A metope of the Sicyonian building at Dephi, dating from the sixth century B.C.E., shows the abduction of the daughters of Leucippus. The Prado Group dating from the first century C.E. represents the Dioscuri and behind them a female figure holding what seems to be an egg. In this Roman sculptural group, Castor and Pollux are shown nude and wear laurel crowns. The remains of the temple of Castor and Pollux can be seen in the Roman Forum. According to Roman tradition, it was built and dedicated to the gods following the defeat of the Latin League at the battle of Lake Regillus in the fifth century B.C.E., a victory the Romans attributed to the aid of the Dioscuri. Images of Castor and Pollux also appear throughout the imperial period on coins. Colossal statues of the Dioscuri frame the entrance to the Campidoglio in Rome, designed by Michelangelo in 1536–1546. Here, Castor and Pollux, wearing caps, stand with horses.

Also in Rome, another colossal pair of Dioscuri, copies of ancient bronzes, are displayed in front of the Palazzo Quirinale. In postclassical painting, Peter Paul Rubens's *Rape of the Daughters of Leucippus* of ca. 1616 (Alte Pinakothek, Munich) shows the muscular horsemen carrying off Leucippus's barely clad daughters as a cupid hangs onto the bridle of their horse.

Jean-Philippe Rameau's opera *Castor et Pollux* of 1737 focuses on the question of their immortality.

Dryads See NYMPHS.

E

Echidna A female serpentine monster, offspring of Phorycs and Ceto. Sister of the GRAEAE and the GORGONS. Textual sources are Apollodorus's LIBRARY (2.1.2, 2.3.1, 2.5.11, 3.5.8, Epitome 1.1) and Hesiod's THEOGONY (295–332). Alternately, her parents are given as GAIA and TARTARUS. In Hesiod's THEOGONY, Echidna is part beguiling, beautiful woman and part monstrous snake, immortal and ageless. She eats raw flesh and lives in a cave deep in the earth in Arima. The offspring of Echidna and TYPHOEUS are CERBERUS, the three-headed dog who guards the entrance to HADES; the CHIMAERA; the HYDRA OF LERNA; and Orthus, the dog that guards the cattle of Geryon (see HERACLES). The Lernian Hydra and Orthus were slain by HERACLES, and he successfully carried Cerberus from Hades as part of his Twelve Labors. The Chimaera was slain by BELLEROPHON. Echidna, possibly by mating with her offspring Orthus, is also said to be the mother of the NEMEAN LION and the SPHINX. Echidna was killed by ARGUS Panoptes, the "All-Seeing."

Echo A nymph from Mount Helicon in Boeotia. Classical sources are Ovid's META-MORPHOSES (3.356–510), Pausanias's *Description of Greece* (9.31.6–9), and Philostratus's IMAGINES (1.23). Echo distracted HERA with conversation while ZEUS pursued his love interests. Eventually, Hera became aware of Echo's motives and cursed her with the inability to speak, except in repetition of the words of others. She was pursued by the amorous PAN but fled from his advances. Echo's most famous myth is her hopeless love for the youth NARCISSUS. With her limited speech she was unable to make him understand her. Narcissus rejected her, and in her grief, the nymph withered away, her bones became stones, and she was left with nothing but a voice.

Echo and Narcissus were represented on several wall paintings in Pompeii. One example, now in the National Archaeological Museum in Naples, shows Narcissus sitting beside the stream showing his reflection while a cupid points at him. Narcissus faces away from the seated Echo who gazes sadly at him. The theme was popular with artists in the postclassical period as well. Examples include Nicholas Poussin's *Echo and Narcissus* of 1628–30 (Louvre, Paris), Benjamin West's *Narcissus* of 1805 (Alexander Gallery, New York), and J. W. Waterhouse's *Echo and Narcissus* of 1903 (Walker Art Gallery, Liverpool).

Eclogues VIRGIL (CA. 38 B.C.E.) Virgil's *Eclogues* was his first major poetic work, a slender, elegantly arranged collection of 10 poems in the erudite Alexandrian style. Virgil deliberately imitates Theocritean bucolic and initiates the Augustan pattern of writing Roman versions of Greek poetic masterpieces. The *Eclogues*, probably published around 38 B.C.E., revises THEOCRITUS's pastoral model at an unexpected moment in Roman history. If we assume the publication date is correct, Virgil's idyllic pastoral world made its appearance in the midst of bitter partisan conflict, in the wake of the murder of Julius Caesar (44 B.C.E.), and, most strikingly, the land confiscations carried out by Octavian (later the emperor Augustus) in 42–41 B.C.E. Due to the efforts of Octavian to settle his veterans on arable land, the Italian countryside was in tumult: Old owners were driven out, and revolts were put down with force. Eclogues 1 and 9 refer directly to the confiscations; it even appears that Virgil himself lost some of his land. (Scholars argue about the details of Virgil's situation and the extent to which autobiography informs the poetry: His patrons, Varus, Pollio, and, if the "young man" and "god" praised in Eclogue 1 can be thus identified, Octavian, are supposed to have helped to recover some of his land, although this, too, is far from certain.) Virgil's pastoral collection thus presents a paradox: He offers an oasis of tranquility amid chaos and violence that infects the pastoral world itself. The pastoral refuge offers shelter to the pastoral singer and his audience, yet there can be no truly secure place of safety, given the current conditions.

Virgil imitates Theocritus's bucolic poetry, yet he goes further than Theocritus in defining and distilling the essence of the pastoral genre. Theocritus did not clearly demarcate his rural poems from his urban ones: Both types of Theocritean poem represent in hexameter verse ordinary persons of low status going about their everyday lives; the rural does not clearly correspond to a separate set of ethical associations. Virgil creates a more coherent and exclusive pastoral milieu but, at the same time, incorporates a greater sense of menace through reference to non- or antipastoral elements: war, arms, violence, eviction, exile. This simultaneous narrowing of generic identity and intensification of the threat to that

identity are at some level quite logical: The pastoral gains definition and clarity through the recurrence of antipastoral motifs, and vice versa. Virgil creates a pastoral world, or a pastoral "myth": He evokes a literary landscape, neither fully Italian nor totally Greek, peopled with NYMPHS, Dryads, herdsmen, shepherd-singers, and the god PAN. Departure from that world, as in the case of Meliboeus at the beginning and Gallus at the end of the collection, intensifies the pathos and fragility pervading Virgil's bucolic fiction.

In other cases, Virgil incorporates mythology proper into his pastoral landscape of notionally illiterate shepherd-singers. Eclogue 2 reworks Theocritus's story of POLYPHEMUS and GALATEA, while Gallus in Eclogue 10 recalls the Theocritean Daphnis. Eclogue 4 proclaims that the order of time is running backward: We will see first a new heroic age, and then a new golden age heralded by the birth of a mysterious boy. (Scholars have offered various answers to the boy's identity: The leading candidate has traditionally been the putative future son of Antony and Octavia. For Christian interpreters of the late antique period, Virgil's poem prefigured the birth of Christ.) Eclogue 6 constitutes the most ambitious engagement with mythology in the *Eclogues*: two boys and a NAIAD bind SILENUS, the companion of Bacchus (see DIONYSUS), and demand that he sing them a song. His song includes the story of the flood, the golden age, PROMETHEUS, HYLAS, Pasiphae, ATALANTA, PHAETHON's sisters, SCYLLA, and Tereus and Philomela—a veritable catalog of myths of interest to erudite poets of the immediately preceding and present generation. Much of the *Eclogues* is about song itself—a society built around song, mythic singers such as ORPHEUS and Linus, traditions of song passed from gods to mortals, and from great poets of the past to poets of the present. It is only appropriate that Virgil should begin his distinguished career as poet by building up the impression of poetry's numinous power, legendary associations, and deep traditions.

Eileithyia (Ilithyia)   The Greek goddess of childbirth. Daughter of Hera and Zeus. Sister of Ares and Hebe. Classical sources are the *Homeric Hymn to Apollo* (97–119), Apollodorus's *Library* (1.3.1.), Hesiod's *Theogony* (921–923), Homer's *Iliad* (11.269–272, 16.187–188, 19.95–133), Ovid's *Metamorphoses* (9.280–323), Pausanias's *Description of Greece* (1.18.5, 6.20.2–6), and Pindar's *Nemean Odes* (7.1–4). Hera and Artemis also share an association with childbirth. Eileithyia keeps company with Hera and on occasion prevents the birth of Zeus's illegitimate children at Hera's behest. The birth of Apollo was delayed by nine days and nights because Hera, jealous of her rival Leto, kept Eileithyia from attending the birth. Finally, the other goddesses in attendance, Amphitrite, Dione, Rhea, and Themis, persuaded her to arrive and allow for Apollo's birth by offering her a golden necklace. Hera also arranged to delay Heracles' birth by seven days so that Eurystheus, son of Sthenelus and cousin to Heracles, should be born first and rule over Mycenae instead of Heracles. Eileithyia prevented the birth of Heracles by sitting with crossed legs on the threshold of the door of the room where Heracles was to be born, until Alcmene sent a false report of Heracles' birth. Eileithyia relaxed her limbs and finally allowed Heracles to be born.

In classical art, Eileithyia appears in childbirth scenes, even unconventional ones such as the birth of Athena. While Eileithyia observes, an adult Athena emerges from the head of Zeus in a scene on a black-figure amphora from ca. 550 B.C.E. (Louvre, Paris).

Electra (1)   Daughter of Agamemnon and Clytaemnestra. Sister of Orestes and Iphigenia. Electra appears in Aeschylus's *Libation Bearers*, Euripides' *Electra* and *Orestes*, and Sophocles' *Electra*. An additional classical source is Hyginus's *Fabulae* (117–122). Though not mentioned in Homer,

Electra emerges as a major figure in Athenian tragedy. After Clytaemnestra and Aegisthus murder Agamemnon and Cassandra, Electra is deeply angry with her mother. According to Sophocles' *Electra*, she saved Orestes by sending him away from the palace at the time of the murders. According to Euripides' *Electra*, she lives a life of humble drudgery, married to a peasant, who, however, has chosen to spare her virginity. In both cases, she resents her mother's high lifestyle and exchanges harsh words with her. Orestes, who has been staying with his uncle Strophius, returns with his companion Pylades. Orestes and Electra are reunited, and their reunion is brought about in artfully arranged recognition scenes by each of the three tragedians. (See the discussions of Aeschylus's *Libation Bearers*, Sophocles' *Electra*, and Euripides' *Electra*). Together Electra and Orestes plot the murder of Clytaemnestra and Aegisthus. Orestes and Pylades murder Agamemnon. In Aeschylus, Electra plays no direct role in the murder. In Sophocles, she is fiercer in her hatred of Clytaemnestra and more grimly fixated on her death—an intransigent Sophoclean heroine. In Euripides, she plays an active role, holding the sword along with Orestes at the moment of the murder. At the end of Euripides' *Electra*, Orestes is exiled and Electra is to marry Pylades. In Euripides' *Orestes*, the citizens of Argus vote to execute Electra and Orestes for their crimes, but Apollo intervenes to avert the crisis: Electra once again is to marry Pylades, while Orestes will marry his cousin Hermione.

Electra (2)   Daughter of Atlas and Pleione. See Pleiades.

Electra (3)   Daughter of Oceanus and Tethys.

Electra Euripides (ca. 413 B.C.E.)   The precise date of performance of Euripides' *Electra* is not known: An apparent reference to the Sicilian Expedition has often suggested a date of 413 B.C.E., although not all scholars agree that this reference is decisive in dating the play. The question is an important one, not least because Sophocles's *Electra* is often conventionally dated to the same approximate period (ca. 418–410 B.C.E.). Since both dates are hypothetical, we do not know which play came first and which playwright is responding to his predecessor in his handling of the theme. In Euripides' play, Electra, daughter of the treacherously slain AGAMEMNON, is married to a peasant. Electra's mother CLYTAEMNESTRA, who was responsible for the murder of her father, arranged the marriage in an attempt to humiliate Electra and neutralize any threat to her own power. Electra's brother ORESTES has returned from exile, accompanied by his friend Pylades, and after a complicated recognition sequence, the brother and sister together plan the murder of Clytaemnestra and her accomplice and lover, AEGISTHUS. Euripides, who is treating the same mythic subject matter as Aeschylus's *LIBATION BEARERS*, stresses the shaky moral underpinnings of the murder, the pettiness of the murderers' motives, and the subsequent sense of horror and remorse. Electra herself plays a strikingly active role in planning and carrying out the killings.

SYNOPSIS

The scene is the Argive hills overlooking to the left the road to Argus and to the right the passes to Sparta. A farmer stands before a cottage at center stage and speaks about the recent history of Argos: Agamemnon's war in Troy, his triumphant return, then his murder at the hands of his wife's lover, Aegisthus. In addition, Agamemnon's son, Orestes, was forced to flee to save himself from Aegisthus, and Agamemnon's daughter Electra was for many years kept from a suitable marriage until, finally, she was forced to marry him, a low-born farmer. Aegisthus had feared that Electra might have children of noble birth, strong enough to avenge their grandfather's death. The farmer has not forced Electra to consummate their marriage.

Electra enters, her head is shaved in mourning, and she bears a water jug. Usually, the task of collecting water is left to a slave, but Electra performs it, she says, to remind herself of the lowly status her marriage has imposed on her. The farmer asks her why she persists in such tasks, but Electra insists that she wishes to contribute to the household. They exit together.

Orestes and Pylades enter, after first making sure that they are alone. Orestes thanks Pylades for his loyalty. It is revealed that they have come to Argos in secret and that he intends to avenge his father. Orestes declares that he has performed rites at his father's grave on his arrival and is now looking for his sister, who he hopes will be his partner in vengeance.

Both men notice Electra returning with a full water jug and mistake her for a slave. Electra is singing about her life, her mother's betrayal of her husband, her brother's exile, and her father's death. She is met by a Chorus of Argive peasant women who invite her to perform rites with it. Electra replies that she is too distraught to do so, and, moreover, has no finery for such an occasion. The Chorus attempts to persuade her to honor the gods nonetheless, but she resists and at this point observes Orestes and Pylades. She does not recognize her brother and takes the strangers for criminals, but Orestes, having heard her song, knows who she is and approaches her. He does not wish to reveal himself and so pretends that he is Orestes' friend and sympathetic to his plight and to hers. Encouraged, Electra reveals her present condition: her removal from Aegisthus's house and her marriage to a farmer, the unusual state of her marriage, and the reason why Aegisthus wished to prevent a noble marriage. Still without revealing himself, Orestes probes her desire to revenge her father's death. He is satisfied with her resolve for vengeance when Electra bitterly describes the funeral rites denied her father and the prosperity in which Clytaemnestra and Aegisthus now live compared to her poverty and loss of status and her brother's life in exile.

Electra's husband enters and demands to know who the strangers are. Assured by Electra that they are friends of Orestes and sympathetic to his wife, he insists on inviting them into his home. Orestes is struck by the noble character of the farmer despite his lack of status or wealth. Orestes and Pylades enter the cottage. Outside, the Chorus delights that Electra has such sympathetic visitors, but Electra chides her husband, replying that she has nothing to offer guests. She bids him find one of her father's former servants to bring some fare for the guests. This man, now an old shepherd, saved Orestes as a child and helped him flee. Electra follows Orestes and Pylades into the cottage while the farmer sets out toward the Argive hills. The Chorus sings of the Trojan War and warns Clytaemnestra that she may pay with her life for her murder of Agamemnon.

The Old Man appears with the gift of a newborn lamb. He greets Electra and startles her by asking if Orestes has somehow secretly come into Argus; rites have apparently been performed at Agamemnon's tomb. He holds a lock of hair that was left at the grave up to Electra's own head. Electra dismisses the idea, saying that if Orestes were to enter Argus, he would do so boldly. The Old Man asks if there are any signs by which she would recognize her brother were he to come; she replies in the negative, as she has not seen her brother since they were both children.

Orestes and Pylades emerge from the cottage and greet the Old Man. Electra explains who he is. The Old Man is arrested by the sight of Orestes and, after looking at him searchingly, recognizes Orestes by a scar above his eye. Electra is stunned and delighted by the revelation. The brother and sister embrace. The Old Man and Electra are overjoyed by his appearance in Argus. Quickly they begin to discuss plans for revenge. The Old Man warns them that they have no allies remaining in

Argos; thus, any plan will have to be put into action by Orestes alone.

On his way to Electra's cottage, the Old Man had observed Aegisthus preparing to sacrifice a bull to the nymphs. Orestes decides to seek him out, contrive to be invited to the sacrifice, and find an opportunity to kill him. Electra proposes that in the meanwhile the Old Man bring a message to Clytaemnestra saying that Electra has recently had a baby. Electra is convinced her mother will come to her immediately on hearing this news, and Electra will take that opportunity to murder her. Electra, Orestes, and the Old Man call on the gods to favor their plans, Electra and Orestes calling in particular on Agamemnon for protection. The Old Man leads Orestes and Pylades off to find Aegisthus, and Electra enters the cottage.

The Chorus sings of ATREUS and THYESTES. They call out to Electra to emerge when they hear shouting in the distance. Electra comes outside and impatiently awaits news of the success of their plan. A messenger arrives with the report of Orestes' victory and Aegisthus's death: As Orestes had hoped, when Aegisthus noticed him and Pylades, he invited both to share in the sacrifice to the nymphs. Aegisthus gave Orestes the honor of butchering the bull, but he was alarmed by an ill omen: The bull was missing a part of his liver. While Aegisthus reached down to continue examining the entrails, Orestes smashed his ax down on him, breaking his back and killing him. When the messenger finishes his narration, the Chorus bursts out in joyful song. Electra is triumphant.

Orestes, Pylades, and servants enter bearing the corpse of Aegisthus. Electra's next speech, charged with bitterness and venom, is addressed to the dead Aegisthus. She condemns his adultery with her mother and hints at his other adulteries. She calls his marriage into her family social climbing. She describes Aegisthus as in every way a lesser man than her father, whose place he usurped, and as a man unable even to recognize his own inferiority. Thus, she finishes, his death is well deserved.

The corpse is carried indoors, and Clytaemnestra is seen approaching. Orestes and Electra quickly debate their plans. Orestes hesitates to kill his mother, but Electra is adamant. Orestes is unwilling to believe that the oracle of Phoebus would urge matricide. Electra is insistent. She sends Orestes inside the house and tells him that Clytaemnestra should be killed when she enters the house.

When Clytaemnestra arrives, she and Electra exchange accusations. Clytaemnestra defends her participation in the murder of Agamemnon by pointing to his sacrifice of their daughter Iphigenia. Electra retorts that if this justifies Agamemnon's death, then she herself would be justified in killing Clytaemnestra to avenge her father's death. She adds that her mother was always self-interested, even before the death of Iphigenia, and cites her treatment of Electra and Orestes following Agamemnon's death. If Clytaemnestra had been motivated primarily by care for her children, Electra claims, Clytaemnestra would not have deprived them of their home, their comforts, and their status. Electra at length persuades Clytaemnestra to enter the cottage with her on the pretext that she needs Clytaemnestra's help in carrying out the customary sacrifice on the 10th day after a child's birth.

After a moment, Clytaemnestra's cries are heard from inside the house; she asks her children for mercy. Outside the Chorus announces that justice has been meted out to Clytaemnestra and that terrible deed has met terrible deed.

Electra and Orestes emerge from the cottage. Behind them, the doors of the house are opened to reveal the bodies of Aegisthus and Clytaemnestra lying together. The brother and sister are stunned by what they have done and are overcome by horror and remorse. Only now, when it is too late, do they seem to realize the brutality and impiety of their actions. They are inconsolable. They describe their mother's piteous cries and their violence to her—Electra, too, placed her hand on the sword to deal the death blow. The Chorus joins in their lament.

The DIOSCURI, Castor and Polydeuces, twin brothers to Clytaemnestra, appear hovering over the roof of the house. Looking down on the siblings, the Dioscuri tell them that justice was not wrought the right way by Electra and Orestes, and they even cast doubt on Apollo's wisdom. The matricide will call the Furies on Orestes, and he must make his way to Athens to face trial for this murder, but he will be acquitted: He must then found a city bearing his name in Arcadia. Electra will be given to Pylades as his wife. Electra and Orestes accept their fates: They will never be together, and they will never return home to Argos. Electra and Orestes tearfully take leave of each other. The Chorus bids them farewell and comments on the good fortune of mortals who do not lead lives filled with grief.

COMMENTARY

In focusing on the figure of Electra, Euripides inevitably invites comparison with the treatments of other tragedians (Sophocles' *Electra*, Aeschylus's *Libation Bearers*) and thereby all the more effectively showcases his own unique style and approach. Unlike Aeschylus, Euripides focuses a great deal of attention on the character of Electra, but unlike Sophocles, he does not present her tragic situation in a noble or heroic light. Electra comes off as a sulky, envious, resentful, self-absorbed figure, who is too young and too inexperienced to comprehend truly the horror of the events that she instigates. In fact, almost none of the play's characters is particularly admirable. It is true that they do not have very good options: Euripides carefully reproduces the Aeschylean scenario of the impossible decision—the choice to kill kin or leave the death of kin shamefully unavenged. But in Euripides' play, mixed among the lofty, if terrible, motives that drove Aeschylus's characters are more sordid, banal interests: envy, sexual desire, personal vanity, resentment of others' material wealth.

Electra consistently displays a melodramatic sense of her own suffering, albeit in an inconsistent manner that sometimes comes off as simple moral confusion. In the opening scene, she appears as a servant, with shorn hair and carrying a water vessel on her head—a pointedly unheroic figure. Euripides was famous for lowering his heroes and heroines, dressing them in rags; yet here, Electra has made some effort to dramatize her own abasement. She praises the self-restraint of her husband (who has abstained from intercourse with her), but in other moments, she reveals her disdain for his social position and humble material resources: He is not worthy of marriage to a princess such as herself, and no amount of noble sentiments can conceal her underlying revulsion. Electra introduces him to the visiting stranger (Orestes) as a man of good character in humble circumstances, but when it comes to hospitality, she harshly indicates that his house and food are inappropriate for noble guests. Conversely, bitter comments about her mother's materially rich and sexually promiscuous life seem more like a display of envy than of moral integrity.

Even in the midst of action, Electra is not particularly appealing: She is vicious and petty toward her mother, Clytaemnestra. One moment she glories in their plan of bloody revenge, then the next, she weakly anticipates defeat. When Orestes has killed Aegisthus and rumors are beginning to circulate, Electra assumes the worst, prepares for suicide, and has to be talked patiently out of her despair. It takes some time to persuade her that Orestes has prevailed, and in her aristocratic snobbery, she fails even to recognize the bringer of the good news as Orestes' servant. One of the most disturbing and yet brilliant scenes has an only momentarily embarrassed Electra finally speaking her mind and "bravely" rehearsing all her resentments to the corpse of Aegisthus. Euripides could not demonstrate more lucidly that the motives of the tragic agents in his play are messier and more ignoble than the morally required vengeance for the killing of kin. Many of her comments revolve around Aegisthus's lack of manliness—a

shrewd commentary on his mythological tradition, but hardly a justification that meets the standards for heroic homicide. Electra unlooses a whole bundle of complaints—some serious and some petty—at a moment when words have become superfluous.

The characters are often shown moving from high-sounding sentiments—the kinds of utterances they *think* they should mouth as exalted figures on a tragic stage—to the peevish snobbery that more accurately represents their attitude. Orestes utters a long, sententious speech on the mismatch between external attributes and true merit, praising the poor but virtuous man by contrast with the aristocratic coward. Elsewhere, however, he reveals his own aristocratic bias and snobbish instincts, as when he first observes Electra's dwelling and describes it as being worthy of a cowherd or ditchdigger. Orestes and Electra inhabit a world of ethical confusion where it is impossible to know where (if anywhere) truly noble qualities dwell: They are affected by a profound sense of inconsistency and moral panic as they try to live up to the tragic destinies they fail even remotely to comprehend.

This sense of moral confusion pervades the killing sequences. Specifically, Euripides allows the "bad" characters, Aegisthus and Clytaemnestra, to appear reasonably (although not totally) sympathetic, and, in Clytaemnestra's case, to display moments of appealing honesty. We begin to perceive just how immature the killers are, and how circumscribed their viewpoints. Clytaemnestra's speech and the moral complexity it evinces are not truly answered but simply silenced by violence. Clytaemnestra's speech brilliantly picks apart the gendered logic driving the entire Trojan War. She pointedly asks: If Menelaus (instead of Helen) had been abducted, would she herself have been required to sacrifice Orestes (instead of Iphigenia) so that the Greek forces could set out to rescue Menelaus? In Aeschylus's *EUMENIDES*, Athena finally resolved the vengeance-cycle by insisting on her preference for the male (Agamemnon, Orestes, polis institutions) over the female (Clytaemnestra, Iphigenia, the Furies), whereas the Euripidean Chorus merely responds: "You should defer to your husband." We might recall Medea. She, too, is a murderess driven by sexual betrayal, and she too offers a provocative critique of ancient gender systems. The scene of murder is itself reminiscent of the other play: Here we hear offstage the cries of the mother begging her children's mercy as they kill her, whereas in the *Medea*, we hear the pitiful cries of the children.

It is significant that neither Clytaemnestra nor Aegisthus conveniently delivers a hubristic speech that might serve to justify and catalyze their murder: Aegisthus is genial and hospitable; Clytaemnestra is darker, but she is at times regretful and penitent and invites Electra to articulate her feelings. Neither comes off as excessively overbearing or tyrannical. Both figures, moreover, are shown piously sacrificing at the moment of their deaths: They are engaged in an act of devotion to the gods and thus incriminate their murderers at the moment of their demise. This coincidence of killing with animal sacrifice also frames the murders as a perversion of ritual—a well-worn tragic motif, here intensified to the point of baroque ingenuity. Just as Agamemnon perversely sacrificed Iphigenia like an animal, now Aegisthus and Clytaemnestra fall in the same manner. In comparison with the Aeschylean trilogy, however, Euripides' play devotes little space to resolving the cycle of violence. The speech of the Dioscuri at the end suggests a path to expiation, but we do not see Orestes suffering and struggling through a trial of atonement—and that makes a very important difference.

Euripides often seems to play at the edges of the tragic genre and to wreak havoc on tragic seriousness and tragic conventions. It is worth considering a signal example of Euripides' travesty of high tragic seriousness and his flirtation with the bathetic and the parodic. A key element in the Electra story since Aeschylus, and

a common motif in Greek tragedy generally, is the recognition sequence in which one character (here Electra) comes to recognize another character (here Orestes) by some irrefutable token or object. In this play, the Old Man notes first the signs of sacrifice at Agamemnon's tomb, and then a lock of hair that he swears is the twin of Electra's. Electra is immediately rude and dismissive: How can the Old Man be so foolish? He then goes on to suggest other possible tokens, running through a veritable repertoire of familiar devices: footprints, an unforgettable style of clothing. Electra continues to be contemptuous. Finally, Orestes arrives, and after some time, the Old Man finally persuades her on the basis of the oldest and most trite recognition token of all, dating back to Homer's *Odyssey*—the scar—that the stranger is indeed Orestes. The entire episode might even be labeled a recognition comedy: It takes an immense amount of time to be resolved after many false starts, it brings out the main character's worst qualities rather than her virtues, it parodies Aeschylus mercilessly, and the necessity for drawing it out at such length is never made wholly clear.

The recognition scene seems to deconstruct tragic conventions and even hints at their futility. There is a darker side to such futility, however. In the speech of the Dioscuri at the end of the play, the twin gods reveal that their sister Helen, in accordance with an alternate version of the myth, never went to Troy: Instead, Zeus sent a mere image *(eidolon)* of Helen to Troy "so men might die in hate and blood" (tr. Vermeule). This is a terrible revelation. Throughout the play, Helen features strongly as the catalyst of the war and thus as the origin of the intrafamilial violence in the house of Atreus. If Helen had not gone off with Paris, Agamemnon would not have had to sacrifice Iphigenia to initiate the expedition, and he would not have returned with CASSANDRA. None of the killings would have taken place—and yet this originating factor turns out to be a phantasm created by a sadistic Zeus. Euripides leaves his audience with a devastating sense of the futility of everything.

In this context, it may or may not be relevant that in the closing lines of the play, the Dioscuri announce their eagerness to fly to the help of the Athenian fleet on its way to Sicily (and thereby allow us to hypothesize the date of the play). These eminently Euripidean dei ex machina have (at least nominally) sorted out the ending of the Electra story, but now they must go off to sort out another impossibly muddled exchange of violence for violence. Are the origins for this massive expedition of warriors as illusory and phantasmic as that of the Trojan expedition? Euripides' meditations on violence, the banality of evil, and the moral confusion these cause may well have a historical resonance that goes well beyond the mythic frame of the house of Atreus.

Electra Sophocles (fifth century b.c.e.) The date of composition and production of Sophocles' *Electra* are unknown. In this play, Sophocles engages persistently with Aeschylus's Libation Bearers, at once paying homage to, and ringing the changes on, his predecessor's play. Sophocles treats the subject of Aeschylus's middle play: Electra's oppressive existence in her slain father's palace, followed by Orestes' return and slaying of Aegisthus and Clytaemnestra. Two major differences are the self-containedness of Sophocles' play, which does not form part of a broader trilogy of interconnected subject matter, and its focus on Electra as protagonist. Orestes' role remains significant, yet his story is simplified: There is no mention of his hounding by the Furies, and the matricide itself comes off as less morally disturbing than in Aeschylus and Euripides. Stress is laid, rather, on the liberation of the palace through the slaying of the usurper Aegisthus. Electra's character, by contrast, is more closely rendered than in Aeschylus and receives more attention. As an outspoken, strong-willed woman, she resembles her mother, yet profoundly hates her; she appreciates the virtue of feminine modesty, yet feels obliged to cast it aside to denounce Clytaemnestra's and Aegisthus's misdeeds. Like Antigone, she refuses to yield to tyrannical power. Sophocles writes his own version of the mythology of the house of Atreus while maintaining his signature trait: the tight focus on the unyielding temper of a hero or heroine in the face of difficult if not overpowering circumstances.

SYNOPSIS

The scene is set before the palace of Agamemnon at Mycenae. Orestes, Pylades, and Orestes' servant, his aged tutor, enter. The servant points out Mycenae and its landmarks to Orestes and urges the two young men to form a plan. Orestes recalls that Apollo's oracles commanded him to carry out his vengeance by stealth. The servant is to go to the palace, pretending to be a Phocian stranger, and report that Orestes is dead; meanwhile, Orestes and Pylades will make offerings at Agamemnon's tomb. Electra is heard from within, crying out in distress, but they decide to carry out their tasks instead of waiting to listen to her. All three exit. Electra enters from the palace. She laments the murder of her father and her solitude. The Chorus enters and begins an exchange with Electra: It sympathizes with her sorrow and attempts to console her. Together they lament Agamemnon's death, but Electra cries out for vengeance, whereas the Chorus recommends prudence. Electra claims that she cannot restrain her rage. She describes her humiliating position in the palace ruled by Aegisthus and her mother's shamelessness. She relates that although Orestes has repeatedly sent to say that he is coming, he has not yet appeared.

Chrysomethis, Electra's sister, enters. She differentiates herself from Electra: She admits that Electra is right to rage, but she feels that she is powerless to do anything and, therefore, must restrain herself. Electra sharply rebukes her cowardice and her taking their mother's side. The Chorus advises them to be reconciled to each other. Chrysomethis warns Electra of a new source of danger: Clytaemnestra and Aegisthus plan to imprison Electra if she does not stop complaining. Electra is not intimidated; she welcomes this fate. Chrysomethis announces that she is departing to make offerings to Agamemnon's tomb, as commanded by Clytaemnestra. According to Chrysomethis, her mother had dreamed that she saw Agamemnon take Aegisthus's scepter and plant it at the household altar, from which it grew into a tree that overshadowed all of Mycenae. Electra pleads with her sister not to make a false offering from Clytaemnestra but a true one, locks of hair from Electra and herself. Chrysomethis agrees but enjoins silence from the Chorus. She exits.

The Chorus takes courage from the dream. It believes that Clytaemnestra will be punished. Nonetheless, it laments the woes of the household, going back to the chariot race of Pelops and Oenomaus. Clytaemnestra enters and rebukes Electra for her continual complaints, claiming that justice was on her side when she killed Agamemnon because he had killed Iphigenia for his brother Menelaus's sake. Electra replies that Agamemnon sacrificed his daughter not for Menelaus's sake, but because he had once displeased Artemis by killing her hind. But even if Menelaus had been the cause, her mother would not have been justified in killing Agamemnon; moreover, there is certainly no justification for remaining with Aegisthus. The dialogue ends in bitter recriminations, and Clytaemnestra prays to Apollo to fulfill her prayers regarding the ambiguous dream.

The servant of Orestes enters and asks whether it is King Aegisthus's house. He greets Clytaemnestra and, as planned, reports that Orestes is dead. Electra cries out in distress. Clytaemnestra is eager to get the news. The servant tells how Orestes competed splendidly at the Delphian Games but was killed when he crashed his chariot: His body, dragged along by it, was mangled beyond recognition. Envoys

are now bringing his remains in an urn. Clytaemnestra expresses ambivalence: His death relieves her anxiety, yet he was her child; on the whole, however, she is not deeply saddened. Clytaemnestra and Electra exchange bitter remarks. Clytaemnestra and the servant exit, leaving the despairing Electra behind to long for death and, together with the Chorus, to lament Orestes' demise and the extinction of their hopes. Chrysomethis enters. She reports happily that Orestes is alive and present. Electra is incredulous; Chrysomethis tells how she found offerings and a lock of hair at the tomb and realized the hair must be that of Orestes. Electra contradicts her story with the story of the servant, and Chrysomethis is persuaded. Electra tries to enlist Chrysomethis's help in a plot to murder Aegisthus, but Chrysomethis is overawed by Aegisthus's strength in comparison with their weakness. Electra endeavors to do the work alone. The two sisters have an adversarial exchange, and Chrysomethis exits.

The Chorus ponders the discord in the house of Atreus and praises Electra's generosity of spirit. Orestes enters. He introduces himself as a Phocian visitor and presents Orestes' "remains" in an urn. Electra laments bitterly. Orestes confirms that he is speaking with Electra and is dismayed to see her brought so low. He learns of her situation and, once he is sure that the Chorus is trustworthy, gradually reveals that Orestes is alive, and that he is actually Orestes. They embrace joyfully. Orestes counsels restraint and silence, but Electra cannot restrain herself. They begin to plan the murder. The servant enters and chides them for speaking out unguardedly. He reports that his deception has worked: They think Orestes is dead. Orestes tells Electra that this is the man to whom she entrusted him as a child. The servant announces that the time is ripe: Clytaemnestra is alone. Orestes and Pylades enter the palace. Electra prays to Apollo for success; the Chorus anticipates the act of vengeance that is under way. Clytaemnestra is heard crying out from within. Orestes and Pylades emerge to report that the deed was successfully carried out. Aegisthus is now seen approaching. Electra sends Orestes and Pylades back to the palace. Aegisthus asks after the Phocian strangers; she replies that they are inside and confirms the report of Orestes' death: Aegisthus may view his mangled corpse inside Aegisthus is triumphant. The palace doors open to show a shrouded corpse beside Orestes and Pylades. Aegisthus lifts the cloth to see the dead Clytaemnestra. Orestes and Electra refuse to let Aegisthus speak for himself, and Orestes drives him inside the palace to kill him where his father died. The Chorus proclaims the liberation of the house of Atreus.

COMMENTARY

Sophocles' *Electra* covers the same mythological ground as Aeschylus's *Libation Bearers*. The most obvious difference between the two is that, whereas Aeschylus's play is part of a trilogy of tragedies—the *Oresteia*—Sophocles' play is a self-contained drama focusing on Electra. This focus on the female sibling is itself notable. In the *Libation Bearers*, Electra's sense of victimization is both amplified and diluted by the presence of the Chorus of captive women, who are similarly enslaved, cut off from loved ones, and enveloped in despair. She is not radically alone. Orestes' role, moreover, is arguably the more crucial one: His unbearable dilemma—to leave his father unavenged or kill his mother—is at the center of the play. When the play ends, the advancing Furies, visible only to Orestes, single him out as the key figure of the following play, the *Eumenides*.

The title of Sophocles' *Electra* thus already conveys important information about his approach to the subject. It soon emerges that Electra is an isolated, quasi-heroic female figure on the model of Antigone; although much uncertainty surrounds the dating of Sophocles' plays, the *Electra* and *Antigone* are often thought to have been composed in the same period of the playwright's career. In both cases,

a female member of the royal family defiantly opposes those in power by openly supporting a brother who is either dead or believed to be dead. To underline further the central figure's isolation and extremity of defiance, Sophocles in both instances creates a more conventional, timid sister, who serves as foil: Ismene in *Antigone*, Chrysomethis in *Electra*. The substitution is marked; Chrysomethis, as bearer of Clytaemnestra's hypocritical offering to Agamemnon's tomb, replaces Aeschylus's Chorus of captive servants, who were highly sympathetic to Electra and showed some courage in supporting the siblings' plans. Sophocles' Electra is much more radically isolated, and her dialogues with Chrysomethis set up a series of oppositions reminiscent of the *Antigone*: concern with personal safety and comfort versus a brave devotion to principles; respect for the powerful versus defiance; a more modest female role versus a more daring, masculine character; hypocrisy versus relentless, dangerous honesty; a diplomatic style versus a harsh, at times sarcastic manner of engaging with others. In the case of both female protagonists, their status as women, and thus nominally weak and vulnerable, highlights all the more sharply their indomitable temper.

Sophocles in general tends to focus on individual character and the uniquely inflexible temperament of the hero. The choice to maintain such a focus in his *Electra*, where the subject matter extends significantly beyond the title character backward and forward in time, is all the more intriguing. Not accidentally did Aeschylus find the house of Atreus apt for treatment in trilogy form: The consequences of violent acts extend from generation to generation, from divine to human levels of causation, in a manner that enmeshes multiple characters in the same "net" of doom. Aeschylus's point is that none of the characters can simply take fate into his or her own hands; their decisions come already overburdened with the weight of the past. It will take the intervention of the gods and the institution of a new court in Athens to resolve the knotty impasse of the royal house of Argos.

For Electra, the key issue is one of individual choice, whether to give in to those in power or to continue voicing her complaints and exhibiting resistance to a state of affairs that she must, on principle, abhor. This choice, as she herself tell us, was already made long ago, and thus in some sense the play affords the spectacle of her spirited maintenance of that choice. At a key point in the plot, when Aegisthus comes on stage shortly before his ambush and murder, Electra affects to have made peace with those in power, to have finally given in and subordinated herself. Of course, this pose is mere pretense, a part of the deceit that leads Aegisthus to his doom. Here Electra recalls not Antigone, but AJAX, who similarly affects to have decided to reconcile with the Greek leaders and yield; in fact, he has finally decided to kill himself. The preoccupation with death is another trait of Sophoclean heroes: Several of them pursue a course of action that leads to their death (Ajax, Antigone, OEDIPUS), and others are obdurate to the point of wishing for death (PHILOCTETES, Electra). Death is the ultimate means of not compromising, of solidifying personal self-determination in the face of superior forces beyond one's control. More than once, Electra appears to accept or welcome death as the outcome of her inflexible choice.

One peculiar consequence of the focus on Electra's character and determination is that there is correspondingly little interest in the ethics of Orestes' action. Orestes does not require Pylades' support to steel his resolve to kill his mother; Pylades, who is present as a companion to Orestes, as indicated by the servant's opening speech, does not speak at all throughout the play. One inference is that Sophocles has no interest in creating dialogue around Orestes' choice and has, therefore, devoted a character (Chrysomethis) to bringing out aspects of *Electra*'s character. Electra's role is systematically foregrounded in the Sophoclean

version of the myth. For Sophocles, Clytaemnestra did not send Orestes into exile to get him out of Aegisthus's way; Electra sent him off with his tutor to save his life. In Aeschylus, the nurse describes the sweet labor of taking care of Orestes as a child, thereby undermining Clytaemnestra's claims to motherhood and nursing of the baby Orestes. In Sophocles' play, it is Electra who plays this role: She declares that Orestes was her child, that she cared for him and was steadfastly devoted to his welfare. In general, she is more active in the plot, and while men still do the actual killing, her role in tricking Aegisthus is crucial.

Orestes' particular fate as matricide and subsequent object of the Furies' hounding is correspondingly much diminished. The order in which the murders take place is itself significant. In both Aeschylus's and Euripides' versions, Aegisthus is killed first, then Clytaemnestra. The reasoning behind this ordering should be clear: Clytaemnestra's murder is the more morally problematic of the two killings. As Orestes himself proclaims in *Libation Bearers*, the killing of Aegisthus is legally allowed; there is no crime in slaying an adulterous lover and usurper. The morally problematic slaying is thus logically the final, culminating action of the play. Nor should we be surprised that the appearance of the Furies follows shortly after Orestes' murder of his parent. Sophocles chooses the reverse order, however: Clytaemnestra is killed first, offstage, in an almost casual manner. Then, in a sequence significantly reminiscent of the Aeschylean slaying of Clytaemnestra, Aegisthus is driven into the palace in the final scene with much greater dramatic focus. The effect of this choice is that the pollution and hounding incurred by kin killing are de-emphasized, while the just ridding of the palace of a usurper is emphasized. Sophocles comes close to reproducing the emphasis and perspective of Homer's *ODYSSEY*, where Aegisthus, as usurper of Agamemnon's role, is singled out as the object of Orestes' vengeance. Elsewhere, Sophocles refers to the myth of AMPHIARAUS: The prophet was swallowed alive by the earth on the expedition against Thebes; his wife, bribed by the offer of HARMONIA's necklace, had persuaded him to go despite his own premonitions, and their son in turn killed her in vengeance. It is significant that Sophocles applies this relatively straightforward mythic paradigm of wifely perfidy (she was bribed to send her husband to his doom) and justified vengeance.

Agamemnon's murder and Clytaemnestra's perfidy, by contrast, have some moderately plausible justification. In a long speech, Sophocles' Clytaemnestra justifies herself: She killed Agamemnon in revenge for having sacrificed their daughter Iphigenia; there was no good reason for him to kill her, if it was only to gratify his brother; since Menelaus' interests were being served, why did he not offer up one of his own for sacrifice? One key motivation for giving Clytaemnestra this long speech of self-justification is to give Electra a chance to refute her, which she does at length. Whereas Clytaemnestra protests that Agamemnon displayed a perverse preference for Menelaus and his family over his own kin, Electra demonstrates, by telling the story of Agamemnon's slaying of the hind of Artemis, that he was not motivated by the desire to gratify his brother but compelled by the anger of the goddess to sacrifice Iphigenia. This argument may seem a bit oblique, but divine anger will probably have struck the Greek audience as a more compelling reason than deference toward one's brother. On the other hand, it is significant that the tragic tradition must constantly invent reasons for downplaying the culpability of Agamemnon and making Clytaemnestra the truly guilty and evil one. If we believe that Agamemnon was driven to his terrible choice by the gods, whereas Clytaemnestra used Iphigenia as a pretext to clear the way for her lover Aegisthus, then we will be persuaded that Orestes' act is (barely) just. The argument is not entirely convincing, and we can see Sophocles adding further refinements with the story of Artemis's hind.

Clytaemnestra and Aegisthus, who were not sympathetic characters in Aeschylus, are now even less so. According to Electra, her mother celebrates the day of her husband's murder with a festival. Whereas in the *Libation Bearers*, Clytaemnestra and Aegisthus at least feigned dismay at the report of Orestes' death, in Sophocles their response to the story of his death is nearly unconcealed delight. Aegisthus is a simple usurper, and he is never allowed to defend his actions, as he did in a certain sense at the end of Aeschylus's *Agamemnon*. Orestes drives him into the palace before he can speak, even though he, as the surviving son of THYESTES, had some plausible justification for killing the son of Atreus, at least within the logic of Greek vengeance killing (a logic within which Orestes himself still acts). The Sophoclean Clytaemnestra and Aegisthus are more straightforwardly cold, manipulative characters. We might also compare Sophocles' play to Euripides' *Electra*, though we cannot be certain of its relative dating. Euripides seems to go out of his way to generate sympathy for Orestes' and Electra's victims: The murderous couple have settled into an anxious, quasi-repentant middle age and appear to wish to live out their lives in peace. Aegisthus is shown as genial, hospitable, and pious; he is actually offering a sacrifice at the moment that he is murdered. Orestes is at once a murderer and a violator of Aegisthus's hospitality. The Euripidean Clytaemnestra is also killed during an act of piety, and in Aeschylus, Clytaemnestra pitiably begs her son for her life.

Sophocles generally plays down moral Orestes' dilemma. There is no allusion to his later hounding and punishment, and the Chorus wholeheartedly endorses his act. Allusions to Furies are relatively sparse, and one instance, significantly, identifies Aegisthus and Clytaemnestra as a "double Fury" of which Orestes rids the palace. Clytaemnestra's dream is also notably altered: Whereas in the *Libation Bearers*, the dream identified Orestes as a viper biting his own mother's breast, in

Sophocles' *Electra*, it refers to the wresting of power from the usurper Aegisthus. The sinister resonance of the poisonous snake imagery of the Aeschylean dream is replaced by a dream signifying the restoration of proper succession and rule. The underlying themes of the play stress, not matricide, but the removal of an illegitimate ruler and the restoration of the house. The last words of the play, spoken by the Chorus, proclaim that the race of Atreus, after having suffered much, has at last completed its passage to liberation; the play's very last word stresses completion *(telos)*. This is surprising, and perhaps even consciously provocative, on the part of Sophocles. The whole point of Aeschylus's ending of the *Libation Bearers* is that the story is *not* yet finished: What end, the Chorus asks, can there be to fury? The ending has not yet been found, and the closural scene of Orestes being hounded off the stage by the Furies is only a paradoxical closure, for it signals the beginning of a new struggle. The fortunes of the house of Atreus cannot truly be repaired until Orestes has undergone purification and been absolved by a court in Athens. Sophocles' play, by contrast, is emphatically self-contained. The crucial act of liberation has been completed.

Sophocles has sharpened the characterization of Electra at the expense of simplifying Orestes' moral dilemma. It may be argued that the most complex and absorbing scene in the play is Electra's exchange with Clytaemnestra, where they debate their differing views of the justification, or lack of justification, for Agamemnon's murder. Electra is at first subtly manipulative. She affects to be placidly accommodating to be allowed to speak her mind; the next moment, she launches into a savage, at times sarcastic, condemnation of her mother's life and actions. Her relationship with her mother is complex. She, like Clytaemnestra, displays what may seem to many a deficit of feminine "shame," i.e., the sense of modesty and restraint appropriate to women in Greek moral thought. Electra displays a comparably

indomitable spirit, a harsh temper, skill in adversarial speech, and a vindictive streak. Electra points to this tension in her own character at the end of her long speech: Her mother should not be surprised if she, Electra, is skilled in the arts of bitter speech, for she has inherited her nature/temperament *(physis)* from Clytaemnestra. In Aeschylus's play, stress is placed on Orestes' difficult role as inheritor of the tradition of male kin slaying in the house of Atreus (Atreus-Agamemnon-Orestes); like his father, he is driven by the gods to kill his own female kin. In Sophocles' version, by contrast, it is Electra's difficult legacy as her mother's daughter that comes to the fore.

There is a valid question as to how successful Sophocles' play is in integrating the focus on Electra's character into the broader mythological fabric of the house of Atreus. *Antigone* is unquestionably compelling in its dramatization of a young woman's simple act of casting dust on her brother's body. Sophocles achieves a relentless focus and drive as he moves from this act to her entombment at the end—an embodiment of her isolation and detachment from society and, ultimately, from life itself. The plot strands of Sophocles' *Electra*, by contrast, are multiple: Orestes is a major actor alongside his sister, and their opponents, Clytaemnestra and Aegisthus, are likewise dual. The ending, however self-contained Sophocles strives to make it, only makes us think ahead to the question of Orestes' absolution. In some sense, Sophocles has attempted to set an Antigone-like protagonist in the midst of a complicated, multiphase myth that does not easily permit such focus. To maintain focus and to produce a self-contained play, Sophocles has arguably simplified Orestes' act of matricide to a problematic degree.

On the other hand, Sophocles' handling of this complex plot is highly skilled, and he elegantly unfolds its various scenes of recognition, suspense, and surprise. Like Euripides, Sophocles was evidently unimpressed by Aeschylus's recognition scene, in which Orestes, whom

Electra does not even know by appearance, is somehow identified on the basis of a lock of hair. This scene is at once subtly incorporated in the form of a prerecognition scene assigned to Chrysomethis, who discovers Orestes' lock of hair, and displaced by the later recognition proper between Orestes and Electra. The ruse of Orestes' supposed death is also brilliantly handled. His death is narrated by the servant in a false-messenger scene, which is all the more effective and believable for its employment of the rich descriptive detail conventional in tragic messenger scenes. Sophocles thus plays on the conventions of the genre in such a way that the exigencies of the plot (deception) converge with the inversion of traditional features (a messenger's lengthy, veristic description of something that did *not* happen). The final twist comes with the revelation of "Orestes'" body, which turns out to be Clytaemnestra's. Aegisthus, at the very moment that he has begun to triumph in his own good luck and security, looks on his adulterous lover's body and realizes his own fate: a fitting ending for a well-crafted play.

Elpenor   See *ODYSSEY*.

Elysium (Elysian Fields)   See HADES.

Endymion   A mortal youth loved by SELENE (Greek goddess of the Moon). Son of Calyce and Aethlius or perhaps even of ZEUS. Classical sources are Apollodorus's *LIBRARY* (1.7.5–6), Apollonius of Rhodes's *VOYAGE OF THE ARGONAUTS* (4.57–58), Lucian's *DIALOGUES OF THE GODS* (19), and Pausanias's *Description of Greece* (5.1.3–5). Endymion is one of a group of mortal youths whose beauty attracts the amorous attention of the gods; others include ADONIS, GANYMEDE, and HYACINTHUS. Selene fell in love with the beautiful Endymion, to whom Zeus granted perpetual sleep in which he would neither grow old nor die. Selene

would visit Endymion in a cave on Mount Latmus during the dark phase of the Moon. There are variations in the story, mainly one in which Endymion figures as the first king of Elis in the Peloponnesus. Another tradition makes him the ancestor of the Aetolians.

In classical art, Endymion is represented variously as a hunter or shepherd, as in an imperial-era Roman mosaic (Bardo Museum, Tunis). Here, the goddess, holding a crescent moon, observes the sleeping Endymion. The associations between Endymion's endless sleep and death are made by sarcophagi reliefs, as in the *Endymion Sarcophagus* from the early third century C.E. (Metropolitan Museum of Art, New York). There are several postclassical versions of Endymion, including Titian's *Landscape with Endymion* from ca. 1520, Parmigianino's *Diana and Endymion* of ca. 1540 (Frick Art Museum, Pittsburgh), François Boucher's *Endymion* of ca. 1729 (National Gallery, Washington), and Anne-Louis Girodet's *The Sleep of Endymion* from 1791 (Louvre, Paris).

Ennius   (239 B.C.E.–169 B.C.E)   Quintus Ennius was a Roman poet of Messapian origin who lived from 239 to 169 B.C.E. He is supposed to have been brought to Rome by M. Porcius Cato in 204 B.C.E. and given citizenship by Q. Fulvius Nobilior, Ennius's noble patron, in 184 B.C.E. In addition to teaching Latin and Greek grammar to the sons of aristocratic households, Ennius wrote a number of literary works that largely survive in fragments. He wrote over 20 tragedies, the *Epicharmus* (a poem on the gods and the universe), the *Euhemerus* (a prose treatise on theology), the *Hedyphagetica* (a poem on gastronomy), the *Sota* (humorous, abusive poetry in the style and meter of Sotades of Maroneia), and informal verse in diverse meters that comes down to us under the title of *Satires*. His most famous and influential work is the *Annales*, an epic poem in 15 books on Roman history from the fall of Troy to recent events. Ennius, like Virgil and LIVY, does not draw a clear line between legend and history. He represents an important early example of a Roman writer tracing the origins of Rome through such legendary figures as Aeneas and Romulus. Ennius brought about changes in the nature of Roman epic that were decisive for the later tradition: He replaced Saturnian meter—an early Italic verse form—with dactylic hexameters along the lines of the Greek tradition, and the Latin Camenae with the Greek Muses.

Enyo   See Gorgons.

Eos (Aurora)   A Greek personification of dawn. Daughter of the Titans Hyperion and Theia. Sister of Helios (god of the Sun) and Selene (goddess of the Moon). Classical sources are Apollodorus's Library (1.2.2–4, 1.4.4–5, 1.9.4, 3.12.4–5), Hesiod's Theogony (371–382), Homer's Odyssey (15.249–251, 23.241–246), Hyginus's Fabulae (189), and Ovid's Metamorphoses (7.661–865, 13.576–624). In the Theogony, Eos "shines for all those on the earth and for the immortal gods that possess the broad sky" (translation G. Most), and in Homer, Eos is "rosy-fingered" dawn. Eos drives a horse-drawn carriage across the sky, bringing Dawn in her wake. According to Hesiod, Zeus prevented Eos, Selene, and Helios from shining during the Gigantomachy to enable the Olympian gods to defeat the giants. At the end of the Odyssey, during the nighttime reunion of Odysseus and Penelope, Eos was persuaded by Athena to hold back the dawn. Eos reined in her colts, until Odysseus and his wife had sufficiently rejoiced in each other's presence. In the Homeric Hymn to Aphrodite, Eos is said to have became so enamored of Tithonus (son of King Laomedon of Troy) that she carried him away to be her husband. At her request, Zeus bestowed immortality on Tithonus, but since she had neglected to ask for eternal youth as well, he grew ever older until he literally shrank away. Finally, he disappeared, leaving behind only his voice.

Eos and Tithonus had two sons, Emathion and Memnon. Emathion died as he was trying to protect the Golden Apples of the Hesperides, which Heracles was seeking during his Twelve Labors. Memnon, an Ethiopian warrior, was killed by Achilles during the Trojan War. Ovid writes that following her son's death, Dawn's glow was dulled and the tears she wept became the dew. She begged Zeus to honor Memnon's death, and he did so by transforming the ashes that rose from his funeral pyre into birds called Memnonides.

Eos fell in love with several mortals. According to Homer, she was in love with Orion and carried him off to be her consort. According to Apollodorus, Aphrodite caused Eos to fall in love with Orion as punishment for having once been the lover of Ares. Eos also abducted the hunter Cephalus, who rejected the goddess in favor of his wife, Procris.

Eos is iconographically linked with Helios, the sun god. He is represented driving a chariot across the sky, and Eos is also often depicted in a chariot, though a less grand one. In antiquity, she is shown winged and fully clothed, sometimes in the company of her brother and sister, as on an Attic red-figure cylix krater from ca. 430 B.C.E. (British Museum, London). Here, Helios drives a four-horse chariot while Eos pursues the hunter Cephalus (shown with his hunting dog) on foot and Selene rides on horseback. Eos is sometimes shown wearing a cap under which her hair is gathered, for example, in an Attic red-figure cup from ca. 485 B.C.E. (Louvre, Paris), where a grieving Eos clasps the motionless body of her son Memnon, his eyes closed in death. In visual representations of the classical period, a common thematic treatment is Eos's loves, as in an Attic red-figure cup from Vulci dating to ca. 470 B.C.E. (Museum of Fine Arts, Boston). Here Eos holds Tithonus around the neck and wrist as the young man tries to flee from her, but she has him firmly in her grip, and her glance is already directed heavenward. In the postclassical period, Nicholas Poussin painted Eos's abduction of Cephalus in his *Cephalus and Eos* of 1624 (National Gallery, London). Here, again, the hunter struggles to free himself from the goddess's grasp. During the Renaissance and baroque periods, the figure of Eos/Aurora continued to provide a rich source of inspiration for artists emphasizing the metaphorical potential of "light-bringing" or "illuminating" Eos.

Epaphus   Son of Io and ZEUS. Ancestor of the DANAIDS. Textual sources are Aeschylus's *SUPPLIANTS* (40–48, 312–315) and *PROMETHEUS BOUND* (846–854), Apollodorus's *LIBRARY* (2.1.3–4), Herodotus's *Histories* (2.153, 3.27, 3.28), and Ovid's *METAMORPHOSES* (1.748f). Epaphus's name resembles the Greek word for "touch," which refers to the story that Zeus fathered Epaphus on Io simply by touching her. Io, the consort of Zeus, was transformed into a white heifer. In some version of the myth, she was transformed by Zeus to protect her from HERA's jealousy, and in others she was changed by Hera herself. Hera sent a gadfly to madden the bovine Io. Chased by the gadfly, Io left Greece and in her wanderings met PROMETHEUS, who advised her to found a colony in Egypt, the city of Memphis. Hera ordered the Curetes to abduct Epaphus, but Io found him in Syria and returned with him to Egypt. Epaphus was commanded by Zeus to reign over Egypt and, in some sources, founded the city of Memphis. According to Aeschylus, Epaphus married Libya (who gave her name to the country), and their son was Agenor. In another source, Epaphus married Cassipoea, with whom he conceived Libya, and in yet another version of the story, Epaphus married Memphis, daughter of the Nile, named the city after her, and their daughter was Libya. Epaphus is the ancestor of Belus and Danaus and the Danaids, who eventually return to Greece from Egypt. In Ovid's *Metamorphoses* (Book 1), Epaphus is the companion of PHAETHON. Epaphus's skepticism provoked Phaethon to seek his father, HELIOS, which ultimately led to Phaethon's death.

Epimetheus   Son of IAPETUS (a TITAN) and the sea nymph Clymene. Brother of ATLAS and PROMETHEUS. Classical sources are Aeschylus's *PROMETHEUS BOUND*, Apollodorus's *LIBRARY* (1.2.3, 1.7.2), Hesiod's *THEOGONY* (507–616) and *WORKS AND DAYS* (47–105), Hyginus's *Fabulae* (142), and Plato's *Protagoras* (320ff). Epimetheus, whose name means "afterthought," is the diametrical opposite of his brother Prometheus, whose name in ancient etymology was thought to mean "forethought." Epimetheus is muddleheaded where Prometheus is clever and wily. They earned the enmity of the Olympian gods by defending humanity and advancing its interests, although sources vary as to the specific offence that aroused the gods' ire. According to Plato, the gods had charged Epimetheus and Prometheus with the responsibility of distributing positive qualities among men and animals. Epimetheus began by giving out a number of virtues to the animals and, too late, realized that he had very little left to give humans. Prometheus, therefore, tried to steal gifts (fire, the practical arts) for men from the gods to make up for what they lacked because of his brother's thoughtlessness. According to Hesiod, Prometheus tried to trick Zeus into accepting the inferior portion of the sacrificial animal at Mekone. Zeus allowed Prometheus to carry out his trick but, then, as a punishment, took fire away from humankind. Prometheus then stole fire back. In retribution, Zeus ordered HEPHAESTUS to create a woman, PANDORA. The gods provided her with every gift and charm to make her attractive to men, and Epimetheus, despite having been warned by Prometheus against taking gifts from Zeus, accepted Zeus's offering of Pandora for a wife. And so, unintentionally, Epimetheus introduced suffering into the world of men. The gods had given Pandora a storage jar containing all the evils of the world, which she set loose on humanity when she opened the jar.

Epimetheus and Pandora had a daughter Pyrrha, who married DEUCALION, the son of Prometheus. They alone of humanity survived the deluge sent by Zeus and afterward repopulated the earth.

In classical art, Epimetheus appears in representations of the myth of Pandora. An example is an Attic red-figure krater from ca. 475–425 B.C.E. (Ashmolean Museum, Oxford). Here, the first mortal woman is seen rising from the ground while Epimetheus waits to receive her in the company of Zeus and Hermes.

Erato   See MUSES.

Erichthonius (Erecthonius)   An early king of Athens. Son of ATHENA (or GAIA) and HEPHAESTUS. Classical sources are Apollodorus's *LIBRARY* (3.14.6), Euripides' *ION* (20–24, 260–274), Homer's *ILIAD* (2.546f), Ovid's *METAMORPHOSES* (2.552–565), Pausanias's *Description of Greece* (1.2.6, 1.18.2), and Virgil's *Georgics* (3.113–114). Erichthonius is sometimes confused with his descendant Erechtheus, both of whom are associated with early Attic history and cult practices on the Acropolis. Details of Erichthonius's parentage and birth vary. In Homer's *Iliad*, Erichthonius, whose lower half was serpent-shaped, was born of Earth (Gaia) and nurtured by Athena. In Ovid's *Metamorphoses*, Erichthonius has no mother. In other sources, Hephaestus tried to rape Athena but she fought him off. As he released her, his sperm fell to the ground and impregnated Gaia, giving rise to Erichthonius. Athena consigned a box, in which Erichthonius was hidden, to the daughters of King Cecrops of Athens, AGLAURUS, Herse, and Pandrosus, and instructed them not to open it. Herse and Pandrosus resisted the temptation, but not Algaurus, who incurred the goddess's wrath (versions vary according to the source). As punishment, Athena afflicted Aglaurus with a terrible jealousy of HERMES' love for Herse. In Apollodorus's *Library*, Erichthonius became king of Athens after driving out Amphictyon, and he married Praxithea (a NAIAD), on whom he fathered a son, Pandion.

Erinyes   See FURIES.

Eriphyle   See AMPHIARAUS.

Eris (Strife)   See PARIS.

Eros (Cupid)   God of love and desire. Classical sources are Apollonius of Rhodes's *VOYAGE OF THE ARGONAUTS* (3.119–166, 275–298; 4.445–451); APULEIUS's *METAMORPHOSES*; Euripides' *IPHIGENIA IN AULIS* (543–551), *MEDEA* (627–634), and *HIPPOLYTUS* (1,268–1,282); Hesiod's *THEOGONY* (120–123, 201); Horace's *Odes* (2.8.13–16); Lucian's *DIALOGUES OF THE GODS* (6, 20, 23); Ovid's *METAMORPHOSES* (1.452–476, 5.362–384); Sophocles' *ANTIGONE* (781–800) and *TRACHINIAE* (441–444); and Virgil's *AENEID* (1.657–722). Eros is the god of love and lust whose name signifies physical or sexual love and from which the word "erotic" is derived. In Greece, Eros was worshipped in Thespiae and Athens among other cult centers, both alone and with APHRODITE. The Roman Cupid, personifying love, was later merged with the Greek Eros. There are multiple versions of Eros's parentage. Hesiod's *Theogony* holds that Eros is one of the primordial beings, the child of Chaos and brother of GAIA, Erebus, NYX (Night), and TARTARUS. According to Hesiod, Eros overpowers the rational thought of mortals and immortals alike and is the companion of Aphrodite, goddess of love. In other sources ARES and Aphrodite are said to be the parents of Eros, HARMONIA and Anteros, also a love deity (Reciprocal Love or Love Avenged). In another tradition, Eros is the son of IRIS, messenger of the gods, and ZEPHYRUS, the West Wind. In Aristophanes' *Birds*, Eros is born from an egg of Erebus and Nyx and emerges with wings of gold.

In literature, Eros is represented variously as a playful, beautiful youth or a mischievous little boy. His attributes are bows and arrows and his flower is the rose. Eros can also appear as multiple figures, called "erotes." Eros's power, like

Aphrodite's, is universal; there is no realm or boundary that he cannot breach. Eros's arrows can cause a frenzy of passion, such as the painful, unnatural love of PHAEDRA for her stepson HIPPOLYTUS, and it can bewitch and confuse its victim. In Sophocles' *Trachiniae*, HERACLES' love for Iole is viewed as a sickness by Heracles' wife DEIANIERA. In Ovid's *Metamorphoses*, Eros, instructed by Aphrodite, directed his arrow at the heart of HADES, who fell in love with PERSEPHONE and carried her off to be his bride.

In Apollonius of Rhodes's *Voyage of the Argonauts*, Eros, at the bidding of Aphrodite (who has promised him a beautiful toy once belonging to ZEUS), pierces the heart of MEDEA with his arrow, causing her to full in love with the hero JASON. The force of Medea's passion, according to Virgil's *Eclogues*, would later cause her to murder her own children. In the *Aeneid*, Virgil attributes DIDO's love for AENEAS to the work of Eros, again acting on behalf of his mother, Aphrodite, to ensure the safety of her other son, Aeneas. In Lucian's *Dialogues of the Gods*, Eros's youthful mischievousness is rebuked by Aphrodite, who scolds him for causing so much trouble among the Olympian gods with his indiscriminate use of the arrows of love.

In Ovid's *Metamorphoses*, APOLLO, having defeated the Python, haughtily told Eros to leave bows and arrows to those more capable of using them. Eros had his revenge for this insult, specifically by demonstrating his deadly skill with the bow and arrow: He shot Apollo with a gold-tipped arrow that incited desire, and DAPHNE, a wood nymph, with a lead-tipped arrow that repelled it.

In Apuleius's second-century C.E. *Metamorphoses* (also known as the *The Golden Ass*), Eros (Cupid) succumbed to his own weapons when he fell in love with PSYCHE. Psyche, a mortal whose beauty was universally admired, drew the envious attention of Aphrodite. The goddess of love asked Eros to make Psyche fall in love with the most wretched creature alive, but seeing her, Eros pricked himself accidentally with his arrow and fell in love with

Eros and Psyche. *Fresco from the House of Terenzio Neo, in Pompeii, first century* C.E. *(Museo Archeologico Nazionale, Naples)*

Psyche himself. She was brought by Zephyrus to an isolated place where Eros would visit her by night, never showing Psyche his true form. Driven by the envy and curiosity of her sisters, Psyche one night examined the sleeping god by the light of a candle. Eros awoke, became enraged, and fled. Psyche, however, loved Eros and to win him back agreed to perform a variety of tasks imposed on her by Aphrodite, in which she was ultimately successful. The myth inspired several later retellings of which the best known is the fairy tale *Beauty and the Beast*.

Eros is one of the most frequently depicted of all Greek and Roman mythological characters. He is variously represented as a beautiful young man or a small boy, usually nude. He can be winged, as in an Attic red-figure amphoriskos from ca. 425 B.C.E. (Museum of Fine Arts, Boston) or not, and usually carries bows and arrows or is garlanded with flowers, in particular, roses. Eros appears during wedding scenes or in the company of Aphrodite. Erotes appear on an Attic red-figure pyxis from ca.

350 B.C.E. (University Museum, University of Pennsylvania) depicting the marriage of HEBE and Heracles on its lid. The Renaissance tradition of the putto draws on the classical example of Eros as a cherubic little boy. In postclassical painting, Eros appears in scenes of romantic love, whether reciprocated, as in the case of Aphrodite and ADONIS, or unrequited love, as in the case of ECHO and NARCISSUS. The various themes is which Eros is shown include his education, chastisement, or the myth of Psyche. This last theme is the subject of a charming Pompeian fresco from the House of Terenzio Neo dating to the first century C.E.

Erysichthon An impious mortal from Thessaly. Classical sources are Callimachus's *Hymns* (6.24–115) and Ovid's *METAMORPHOSES* (8.738–778). Erysichthon violated a grove sacred to DEMETER (Ceres) and as punishment was afflicted with unending, inexhaustible hunger. His daughter, Mnestra, who had the capacity to change shape, acquired food for her desperate father by undergoing a series of transformations. Yet she could not save him, and in the end, he devoured himself.

Eteocles Elder son of JOCASTA and OEDIPUS. Brother of POLYNICES. Eteocles appears in Aeschylus's *SEVEN AGAINST THEBES*, Sophocles' *OEDIPUS AT COLONUS*, and Statius's *THEBAID*. Additional classical sources are Apollodorus's *LIBRARY* (3.6.1) and Hyginus's *Fabulae* (68). Eteocles and Polynices agreed to share the Throne of Thebes in turn. After Eteocles' first reign he refused to honor his agreement with Polynices, and Polynices responded by laying siege to Thebes. (For the story of the two brothers' conflict, see POLYNICES.) Aeschylus's *SEVEN AGAINST THEBES* takes the perspective of the Theban leader Eteocles attempting to rally defense of his city, while the invaders are represented as violent and hubristic. The Eteocles of Statius's *Thebaid*, by comparison, is a more sinister and tyrannical figure.

Eumenides   See FURIES *EUMENIDES*.

Eumenides AESCHYLUS (458 B.C.E.) Aeschylus's *Eumenides*, written in 458 B.C.E., is the third play in his *Oresteia*, on the subject of the house of Atreus, which also included a fourth, satyr play. "Eumenides" is a positive, euphemistic term for the terrifying Erinyes, or FURIES, who punish the shedding of kindred blood in Greek mythology. At the end of the previous play in the trilogy, *Libation Bearers*, the Furies appeared and began to hound ORESTES for killing his mother, CLYTAEMNESTRA, in vengeance for her murder of her husband and Orestes' father, AGAMEMNON. APOLLO, however, had commanded Orestes' crimes and was accordingly committed to helping him. At the beginning of the present play, Orestes is at Apollo's shrine of Delphi, where he has undergone purification. The Furies have been put to sleep by the god. Apollo instructed Orestes to go to Athens, where, to be free of the Furies, he will have to be acquitted in a trial presided over by ATHENA. This final play in the trilogy will be concerned with finding a resolution to the cycle of revenge and violence afflicting the house of Atreus. Such a resolution, however, will not be found within the house itself but in the emerging institutions of the Athenian polis. The solution will also involve renegotiating, on both the divine and the human level, the conflict between male and female that has pervaded the trilogy.

SYNOPSIS

The play opens at Delphi in front of the sanctuary of Apollo. The Pythia enters. The Pythia offers a genealogy of prophets and prophecy going back to Earth herself, and a history of Phoebus Apollo's association with the site of his oracle at Delphi. She also honors Pallas Athena, DIONYSUS, and ZEUS. She enters the temple to see who is there and comes out aghast. She has seen a man (Orestes) with blood dripping from his hands in the suppliant's seat. In front of him, sleeping, are gorgonlike women of horrible appearance. She calls on Apollo's help and exits. The doors open to show Orestes, the Furies, Apollo, and HERMES. Apollo asserts his commitment to aid Orestes and shows how he has put the Furies to sleep. He commands Orestes to continue fleeing from their relentless pursuit until he reaches Athens. There his case will be judged, and he will be freed of his affliction. He asks Hermes to look after Orestes. Apollo, Orestes, and Hermes exit. The ghost of Clytaemnestra enters. She berates the Furies for sleeping and complains of her treatment at the hands of her matricidal son. They moan in their sleep as Clytaemnestra continues to taunt them until they wake up. Clytaemnestra encourages them to pursue and torment Orestes. The Chorus of Furies expresses rage at the fact that its "prey" has been allowed to get away and complains that the youthful upstart Apollo is aiding a matricide.

Apollo enters. He threatens it with his bow, proclaiming that it is vile and violent and does not belong in his shrine. It blames Apollo for encouraging Orestes' act and giving him harbor. It does not put the killing of Agamemnon in the same category as the murder of Clytaemnestra, because it was not an instance of the shedding of kindred blood, i.e., they were married, not kin. Apollo criticizes their lack of interest in upholding marriage vows. The Chorus of Furies will continue to pursue Orestes, and Apollo to aid Orestes. The Furies and Apollo exit separately.

The scene is now the Athenian Acropolis, in front of the temple of Athena. Orestes enters. He prays to be received by Athena, for he comes at the behest of Apollo. The Chorus of Furies enters. It is still hunting Orestes, following his trail like hounds and demanding his punishment. Orestes insists that, guided by Apollo, he has gone through a long process of purification and is no longer an unclean presence; he calls on Athena to aid him. The Chorus continues to claim him as its own for punishment: It will drain away his life. It sings a fearsome song

proclaiming its rights and powers of vengeance for the shedding of blood. It claims to operate independently of the Olympians and vaunts its power to overthrow men and entire households. Athena enters. She has come from Troy, is amazed to see Orestes and the Furies, and asks who they are. Athena learns that Orestes is a matricide, and the Furies agree to allow her to adjudicate his case. He explains that he has been purified by sacrifices and running waters and thus is allowed to speak. He presents his case: He avenged the death of Agamemnon by killing his mother and was driven to do so by Apollo. Athena, facing the dilemma of either leaving Orestes to his fate or provoking the Furies to afflict the land with plague, decides to set up a court and select judges. Athena exits.

The Chorus complains of the overthrow of laws and justice; it will no longer oversee the doing of justice. It speaks of the vengeance and doom that will fall on the transgressor. Athena enters guiding 12 chosen jurors and a herald. She bids the herald to announce the trial. Apollo enters and is challenged by the Chorus. He defends his presence at the trial. Athena commands the Furies to present their case. They interrogate Orestes and confirm that he killed his mother on Apollo's orders. The Furies insist on the primacy of blood ties. Apollo claims the authority of Zeus and recounts vividly the manner of Agamemnon's murder. The Chorus points out that Zeus shackled his own father, Cronus. Apollo replies angrily that shackling is less permanent than death. Apollo goes on to argue that the mother is only the nurse of the male seed; the male is the true parent, as proven by the case of Pallas Athena, brought forth without need of a womb. The time comes for the casting of votes. Athena proclaims that henceforth the judges will deliberate on the present ground, called the Hill of Ares. She calls on the jurors to consider their votes. The Chorus and Apollo in the meanwhile quarrel over the outcome and their respective rights. Athena proclaims that she will vote on Orestes' side, since she, having no mother, supports the male side, that of the father; her vote will break a tie. Athena proclaims that the ballots are equal, and thus Orestes is acquitted. Orestes thanks Athena for saving his household. He will go home but first swears that his city (Argos) will never oppose Athens. He promises to be a friend to Athens and exits.

The Chorus of Furies complains of being dispossessed and angrily threatens to poison and bring pollution on the land. Athena encourages it: It should not feel that it is beaten—it was a fair ballot, supported by the gods. She exhorts it not to take its anger out on Athens and promises its own place underground where it will accept offerings. In a long exchange, the Chorus reiterates its angry chant and threats, and Athena answers them each time with diplomatic words that are by turns threatening and mollifying. Athena urges it to accept an honored place in a city-state that will grow greater over time. She continues to insist on her point, and at length, the Chorus begins to ask about the place of honor offered it and to be persuaded. The Chorus of Furies accepts its new place in the city and blesses the land instead of cursing it. It further banishes civil discord from the city. Now, as kindly deities (Eumenides), it is led by Athena and the citizens of Athens in a procession to its new abode.

COMMENTARY

In the third play of the *Oresteia* trilogy, Aeschylus begins to work toward resolving the dilemmas that have thus far kept his characters trapped within the horizon of painfully destructive alternatives. The interest in resolution, however difficult that may be, appears to be an Aeschylean trait. Not only here, but probably also in the Danaid trilogy, patterns of reciprocal violence are resolved or ameliorated by the end of the third play. At the start of the present play, Orestes has killed his mother in vengeance for the killing of his father and is being hounded by the Furies, who first made their appearance at the end of the last play, *Libation Bearers*. So far no clear principle of resolution

has emerged: Each death must be punished by another answering death. Even Orestes, for whom there is no obvious human avenger, is in danger of falling victim to the same pattern. The Furies have been literally sucking the life out of him, wasting him away with torment and sapping his life force to send him down to the underworld for further punishment. The Furies, the deities embodying his mother's rage, are taking vengeance for the spilling of her blood.

At the beginning of the *Eumenides*, the dark pattern of the previous plays is still in operation. One notable element of continuity is the use of hunting as a metaphor. Previously, Agamemnon was caught in a fatal net by the hunter Clytaemnestra, and Orestes, in turn, hunted down and killed his mother and her lover. The brutal treatment of humans as animal quarry underscores the moral disorder of the house and its descent into anarchy and violence. Now, the Furies are a group of hunters, or rather hunting dogs, who sniff out the guilty Orestes and track him relentlessly as he flees. The pattern is thus confirmed: The victorious hunter becomes the hunted. The pattern of gender alternation likewise continues unflagging: Woman (Clytaemnestra) hunts man (Agamemnon); man (Orestes) hunts woman (Clytaemnestra); female divinities (Furies) hunt man (Orestes). We can trace the pattern back even further, if we wish: Agamemnon previously killed Iphigenia like a sacrificial animal. Even further back, the male eagles, symbol of Zeus and kingly power, slaughtered the pregnant hare and her young, i.e., MENELAUS and Agamemnon destroyed Troy, figured in the metaphor not only as female (pregnant) but also as a *hunted* animal.

Another element of continuity is Clytaemnestra herself and her presence on stage as ghost or ghostly dream figure. She appears to the sleeping Furies at Delphi and goads them awake with her sharp, taunting words. This scene counterbalances the looming presence of Agamemnon's tomb at the opening of *Libation Bearers* and the implicit presence of his angry spirit whom his children address and who is the notional object of appeasement for Clytaemnestra and her servants. The dead continue to exert their force over the living in vivid ways. Clytaemnestra, in particular, has emerged as a crucial element of continuity in the trilogy. She was a magnificent force of malevolence and ruin in the *Agamemnon*, the target of Orestes' vengeance and object of his painful doubts and equivocations in *Libation Bearers*, and now, with stunning confidence and arrogance, she commands the Furies as her personal cadre of avengers, castigating them for their delay and motivating them with shame. She is the one continuous presence throughout the three plays and still drives the mechanism of violence and retribution by lashing the Furies back into action.

It could be said that the Furies are equally an element of continuity from beginning to end. While the Furies did not make an appearance as characters or chorus in the two earlier plays, they were often alluded to as dark presences in the house. For example, they were imagined singing in a sinister chorus. Now, indeed, the Furies constitute the Chorus. Aeschylus has been building up to their terrible appearance on stage throughout the trilogy, and now we actually see them in corporeal form on the stage, singing their grim songs.

The Furies, in Greek mythology, are concerned with retribution for killing, especially of kin. They are also generally associated with upholding proper behavior and the cosmic order and are linked with night, darkness, death, and the underworld. In the Aeschylean conception, they are tightly focused on punishment for kin killing and have a ghastly physical appearance that reflects their domain of concern and their methods of punishment. Their eyes ooze; they are compared to Gorgons; their robes are black; their breath reeks; and they are generally repulsive. We can imagine that an entire Chorus of Furies in elaborate costume chanting grimly and advancing on their "quarry" Orestes would have had a terrifying and thrilling effect on the audience.

From such a perspective, this third play really is the culmination of the trilogy: The dark deities who have been lurking in the background of the house of Atreus have now appeared fully embodied on stage.

The Furies, as they insist, have a place ordained, fixed, primeval. They do not seem to belong to the same order of being as the other gods and the Olympians, in particular. They describe themselves as outcasts and divided from the Olympian peers by their appearance, their chthonic associations, and their garments: They wear black, whereas the Olympians are described as white-robed. Athena, when she first sees them, does not recognize them and has to ask their identity; it turns out she did know about them but apparently had not met them before. Apollo is especially disdainful of them and treats them as repulsive beings unworthy of appearing within the precincts of his sanctuary. They are associated with the most horrible things—violence, pain, torture, death. The word clusters associated with them often involve the mixing or pouring out or spewing forth of liquid—blood, venom, vomit. They are represented as chewing, grinding, and sucking the life blood out of their victims. By contrast with the clean, perfect outlines of the Olympians, there is an emphatically nasty corporeality about these creatures; they are "unclean."

The Furies, however, have certain valid claims to make even in the face of Olympians such as Apollo. They do have an important role appointed to them, as they insist: Without fear of punishment, mortals would not obey laws and would live in anarchy. The prohibition against killing kin is an especially important moral rule to uphold. Orestes, moreover, indisputably did kill his mother, and thus their role should be clear: to punish him relentlessly. While Apollo's stance is highly adversarial, Athena recognizes early on that these deities must be treated diplomatically, that they cannot simply be pushed aside, and that their function remains important in human society and thus must be maintained, even while undergoing transformation.

The separate status of the Furies has given them a certain degree of autonomy, and thus, early in the play, they claim the right to ignore the demands of the Olympians and denounce Apollo's interference within their realm of authority. They also seem to belong to an older order of being, just as they represent an older, increasingly outmoded vision of justice. The relative youth of the Olympians, Apollo especially, is frequently referred to, and in general, the Furies speak as the outraged protectors of traditional values: The young gods are ruining everything and promoting anarchy. Aeschylus is thus setting up a series of interlocking oppositions: new and old; Olympian and chthonian; gods associated with immortality and deities associated with death; light and dark. Aeschylus sets the stage for a conflict of cosmic dimensions that will require a confrontation of and negotiation among divine powers for resolution.

We witness on stage a divine power struggle in process. The youthful Apollo, son of Zeus and an Olympian himself, opposes the ancient Furies and, in opposing them, claims Zeus's authority for his acts. Zeus is at the center of the play's action and resolutions, although we do not see him on stage. In the end Athena, likewise, sides with her father, Zeus, and with Apollo. When Apollo defends the rights of fathers, the Furies sharply point out that Zeus shackled his own father, Cronus. Apollo is furious, since they have not only undermined his argument to some degree; they also dared to challenge his father's legitimacy and rule. The stakes are thus high in Orestes' trial. The legitimacy of the Olympian order is also on trial. If Orestes is not acquitted, then Phoebus's prophetic authority risks being impugned, and the killing of Agamemnon, the mortal representative of Zeus's kingly authority, is insufficiently condemned. Zeus supported Agamemnon's expedition to Troy. A failure to support the

son's right to avenge his father's murder ultimately undermines Zeus.

The trial brings these issues to a head. The Furies are in effect the prosecution, while Apollo provides the defense. Two issues emerge as key in arriving at a decision. First, there is the question of blood. The Furies insist that their special mission is retribution for spilling the blood of kin. Since Agamemnon and Clytaemnestra were married but not kin, the killing of Clytaemnestra by Orestes falls within their concern, not the earlier killing of husband by wife that motivated Orestes. Apollo, in answering this argument, points to the sacred status of marriage vows, to the marriage of Zeus and HERA, and to the divinity of APHRODITE—hence the holy status of all that belongs within her realm of concern. Here, the Furies do not seem to be on very strong ground. Yet even if we accept Apollo's point and value the relation of marriage as much as relations of blood, the crucial issue remains unresolved: Orestes has still killed his mother, and if, on Apollo's argument, he has not done something more evil than his mother did in killing his father, we as yet have no grounds for arguing that he is in any way less culpable or more excusable.

The resolution of this dilemma ultimately coincides with the resolution of the gender dynamic that runs throughout the trilogy. The male Orestes killed his mother for killing her husband, and now Orestes is pursued by the female deities who are driven by his mother's ghost. The male god Apollo supports him, and, it appears, Zeus supports his son in turn. It is in this context that Apollo presents an argument of pivotal importance: The woman's womb, he suggests, is only the container of the seed that derives from the male; and thus the male, and not the female, is the true parent of the child. The priority of the male parent therefore justifies Orestes' killing: His father was the more important of his two parents; hence it was his moral responsibility to avenge his father's death, even if it meant killing the mother (the less crucial parent). Apollo supports his argument by pointing to Pallas Athena herself: She was born without the participation of a mother, directly brought into being by Zeus.

For Aeschylus, Zeus is the central figure of the divine order, and thus also the most important figure for human beings as they strive to act and understand their fate. This was not always so. The opening speech of the Pythia alludes to an earlier time, when Earth (GAIA) was the first god to offer prophecy. After her came THEMIS, another goddess, and finally PHOEBE. It was only when Phoebe ceded the seat of prophecy to Phoebus that it fell into the hands of a male god. In the theogonic vision of the Greeks, Earth produced a series of challenges to male sky gods, and it was only with the reign of Zeus that a stable, patriarchal power structure came into being. Orestes' murder of his mother in his father's name is thus set within the context of a broad cosmic vision that includes the ascension of Zeus as king of the gods. The references to Zeus's bird, the eagle, in connection with Agamemnon, and Clytaemnestra's perverse, murderous references to the fertilization of Earth by the sky god in the trilogy's first play are thus brought full circle in the third play. The rent in the cosmic fabric caused by Clytaemnestra's audacious slaying of the king is being repaired as the Olympian gods reassert the divine and human order based on the priority of the male.

Key to this restoration is the mediating role played by Athena in her city, Athens. Athena, as Apollo shrewdly pointed out in making his argument, playing to the most important judge in the case, was born from Zeus without a mother. When Athena herself announces her crucial vote, she reiterates this fact and further states that she supports her father and supports the male in general. She, after all, is female, but, as a warrior, is male in appearance, and, as a virgin, distances herself from the traditional female roles of wife and mother. When she arrives on the stage, she is fresh from the scene of the Trojan War, an expedition supported by her father, Zeus. She is in general associated

closely with male Greek heroes, such as ODYS-SEUS, and here gives her support to Orestes. Yet she remains female as well, and this dual status makes her the ideal negotiator to bring about a resolution of the conflict.

In a long interchange, Athena mixes threats with promises to persuade the Furies to accept their new role within the city rather than to poison it and set themselves against the Olympians. Unlike Apollo, she is respectful of them and respectful of their rights. She is thus not purely adversarial and male in this regard. Along with such mollifying remarks, however, she includes a reference to force, the thunderbolt of Zeus. She is still a warrior and still supports, and is supported by, her father, even as she adopts a diplomatic stance. In the end, the Furies are persuaded to accept their new role as beneficent deities that protect the city and uphold its order in a positive sense. Athena, then, resolves the crisis of the house of Atreus and, at the same time, resolves the gendered opposition that has driven the sequence of violent acts from the start of the trilogy.

It is no accident that Athena accomplishes this in the city that shares her name, Athens, in a play that was performed by an Athenian playwright before an Athenian audience. Aeschylus connects his ancient mythological theme with pride in the institutions of his own city-state. The larger pattern of the trilogy and its resolution in the third play suggests, in broad terms, a movement from the irresolvable violence and implosion of the royal household to the beneficial institutions of the polis. Such a theme would in itself have pleased Aeschylus's audience in democratic Athens and coheres with a broader tendency in Athenian tragedy to connect the ancient myths with contemporary cults, communities, and institutions (compare, for example, Sophocles' *OEDIPUS AT COLONUS* or the cult of Medea's children in Euripides' *MEDEA*). Ultimately, Aeschylus suggests, the aristocratic household cannot regulate itself, since it has no institution outside itself to impose a procedural resolution on its cycle of revenge violence, i.e., kin kill kin without any outside body to intervene or regulate. Athena's/Athens's court provides an institution capable of imposing such resolution.

The Areopagus is the specific court to which Aeschylus refers. Its name means "Hill of Ares," and the playwright means to suggest that Orestes' case, tried, as Athena declares, on the Hill of Ares, is the first homicide case brought before that court. Until the middle of the fifth century B.C.E., this court had special powers that put the state itself within its purview. In 461 B.C.E., however, Ephialtes brought about a radical reform of the court, newly circumscribing the scope of its power. This reform was highly controversial, and Ephialtes himself ended up being murdered. Aeschylus's play, produced only a few years later in 458 B.C.E., surely reflects and in some way comments on these developments in Athenian politics. It is not wholly clear, however, whether Aeschylus, in focusing on the court's function in adjudicating homicide, approves the limitation of scope, or whether he is lauding its ancient status and foundation by the goddess Athena herself so as to promote its importance and oppose its reform. On balance, the former seems more likely, since the entire theme of the play is (in the case of the Furies) about the value of *accepting* a valued if circumscribed role within the polis, a lesson that might easily be transferred to Aeschylus's own day. Athena's remarks about the value of external wars as opposed to internal discord cohere both with the broader themes of the trilogy and with the internal unrest in Athens surrounding Ephialtes' reforms. Possibly Aeschylus means to demonstrate the value of compromise, diplomacy, and civic cohesion over polarization and violence. It is clear that Aeschylus's representation of Orestes' story and the court's foundation is highly relevant to developments at the time of the play's composition.

The Areopagus is not the only topic of present relevance. The city of Argos is also of recent concern to the playwright and his audience. Aeschylus intriguingly set his trilogy on the house of Atreus in Argos, not in Mycenae, where Agamemnon is more usually supposed to have ruled. One possible motive for this shift comes to our attention in the *Eumenides:* After Orestes is acquitted and announces his attention to return to Argos, he says, with semiprophetic overtones, that his city will always maintain good relations with Athens in the future. Argos, starting in the late 460s and repeatedly throughout the century, offered support to the Athenians in the conflict with Sparta. While their contribution was not decisive, the Argives were noteworthy allies. Here, too, the chronology fits with the composition of the *Oresteia* and suggests that Aeschylus is celebrating a contemporary development.

Orestes' final speech announces his intention to return to Argos and to repair his house's fortunes. Thus, while the polis proves itself capable of resolving the aristocratic household's apparently irresolvable violence, the restoration of that household remains a significant concern for Aeschylus. The house, from the beginning of the trilogy, has been a major focus of the drama and has at times taken on the appearance of a character in its own right. The house observes, in silence, the succession of murders that culminates in the departure of the surviving male heir, Orestes, into exile. The prime function of the Furies, in their own words, is to drive matricides out of their houses. They did so in the case of Orestes. Now, however, the Furies, who lived off the blood of the house throughout the three plays, have been placated and have accepted a new, positive position within the Athenian polis. Orestes is free to return home.

Euripides (ca. 485 B.C.E.–ca. 407 B.C.E.) Euripides was an Athenian tragic playwright who was born in the 480s B.C.E. and died in 407–406 B.C.E. He wrote approximately

90 plays, of which 17 securely Euripidean tragedies and one satyr play, the CYCLOPS, survive. The *Rhesus*, transmitted to us as part of his oeuvre, is probably not genuinely Euripidean. Euripides first produced plays for the tragic competition in Athens in 455 B.C.E., while his last plays, which included the IPHIGENIA AT AULIS and BACCHAE, were produced posthumously. Euripides won first prize in the Athenian dramatic competition only four times in his life. In 408, Euripides left Athens for the court of King Archelaus of Macedon and died there. Euripides' extant plays are characterized by a great variety of subject, themes, and moods, yet certain pre-occupations are recurrent: the Trojan War and its resonance with the contemporary Peloponnesian War; the formidable and often destructive passions of female characters; the cynical maneuvers of those in power; the moral chaos of a fragmented world; the experience of immense suffering and the effects of such experiences on the victim. Euripides was seen as having a propensity for innovation, a virtuoso's facility with morally dubious turns of argument and verbal tricks, and a preoccupation with dark subject matter and ignoble characters. Sophocles is reported by Aristotle as having declared that Euripides represented people not "as they ought to be" but "as they were." Certainly many of Euripides' central characters are represented in a subheroic light: Jason, in the MEDEA, is a weak, self-serving, and, in the end, broken man. Orestes and Electra, in the ELECTRA, are by turns self-pitying, bloodthirsty, confused, and repentant: They lack clarity of moral purpose. Euripides' later plays often feature a deus ex machina at the close and a complicated plot involving recognition and escape. In many cases, e.g., the ION and ALCESTIS, Euripides presses at the boundaries of tragic conventions. His apparent lack of consistent success with Athenian audiences is more than compensated by the fascination he holds for modern readers. See also ANDROMACHE, HECUBA, HELEN, HERACLEIDAE, HERACLES, HIPPOLYTUS, IPHIGENIA AMONG THE TAURIANS, ORESTES, PHOENICIAN WOMEN, SUPPLIANT WOMEN, and TROJAN WOMEN.

Europa A consort of ZEUS. Daughter of Telephassa and King Agenor of Tyre, in Phoenicia. Sister of CADMUS. Classical sources are Apollodorus's LIBRARY (3.1.1–2), Diodorus Siculus's LIBRARY OF HISTORY (40.6.2, 5.78.1), Herodotus's *Histories* (4.147.5), Homer's ILIAD (14.321–322), Horace's *Odes* (3.27), Lucian's *Dialogues of the Sea-Gods* (15), and Ovid's FASTI (5.605–616) and METAMORPHOSES (2.833–875).

Sources vary as to Europa's parentage. Some give her mother as Argiope or Perimede and her father as Phoenix, while others disagree on the names of her brothers, variously, Cadmus, Cilix, Phoenix, and Thasus. They were said to have founded several ancient settlements during their search for their sister.

Zeus is said to have seen Europa playing near the sea with other maidens and to have become enamored of her. He transformed himself into a bull to carry her off. Ovid's *Metamorphoses* provides details of the abduction. Zeus asked his son HERMES to drive a herd of cattle near the playing maidens, while he metamorphosed into a beautiful white bull, mingled with the herd, and attracted Europa's attention. Charmed by the beauty and gentleness of the white bull, Europa garlanded his horns with flowers and finally sat on the bull's back. Slowly Zeus made for the sea, and, once immersed, with a fearful Europa holding on to his horns, he swam with her to Crete. When Zeus arrived with Europa on the island of Crete, he resumed his own shape, and according to Ovid's *Fasti*, the bull went into the heavens and became the constellation Taurus. Europa's father, Agenor, sent his sons to search for her but without success. Europa's brother Cadmus, on the advice of the Delphic Oracle, followed a bull to the location where he would found the city of Thebes.

Three sons were born from the union of Zeus and Europa: MINOS, Rhadamanthys, and

The Rape of Europa. *Titian, 1559–62 (Isabella Stewart Gardner Museum, Boston)*

Sarpedon (though Homer cites only the first two as their issue). Zeus gave Europa three presents: the bronze man of Talos, which protected the island of Crete; a javelin that never missed its mark; and a hound that always found its prey. The hunting dog and javelin were later given to Procris. Afterward, Europa married King Asterius of Crete, and her children by Zeus were adopted by him and brought up in his household; they eventually inherited his kingdom. Minos, or possibly a descendant of the same name, was the king of Crete involved in another myth in which a bull features promi-

nently, that of the Minotaur. Rhadamanthys was said to have introduced a legal system to Crete and married Alcmene, mother of Heracles. Minos and Rhadamanthys became judges in Hades after their deaths.

In classical art Europa's abduction by Zeus in the shape of a bull was a popular theme. Ovid's *Fasti* describes the young yellow-haired Europa being carried on the bull's back; gradually becoming aware of her predicament, she holds the bull's mane in one hand and her garments are blown in the wind as they travel across the sea to Crete. The Ovidian passage is quite similar to many classical and postclassical artists' representation of the scene. Europa is shown thus on an Archaic temple metope from 600 B.C.E. A Roman wall painting from the House of Fatal Love, Pompeii, dating to the first century B.C.E., fills in the scene with a group of Europa's friends watching her astride the bull's back. Postclassical examples of the myth of Europa include Titian's *The Rape of Europa* from 1559–62 (Gardner Museum, Boston) and Rembrandt's *The Abduction of Europa* from 1632 (J. Paul Getty Museum, Los Angeles).

Eurus   One of the ANEMOI, or Four Winds, offspring of Eos (Aurora) and Astraeus, according to Hesiod's THEOGONY. Some accounts claim that their father was TYPHOEUS. The Anemoi are storm winds associated with the four cardinal points: BOREAS, the North Wind; NOTUS, the South Wind; ZEPHYRUS, the West Wind; and Eurus, the East Wind, which brings the Dawn with it.

Eurydice   See ORPHEUS.

Eurystheus   A king of Mycenae. A descendant of PERSEUS, son of Sthenelus and cousin to HERACLES. Classical sources are Apollodorus's *LIBRARY* (2.4.12–2.5.12, 2.8.1), Euripides' *HERACLEIDAE* (928–1,052), and Pindar's *Pythian Odes* (9.79–81). Perseus had several children of whom two were Electryon, father of ALCMENE, and Sthenelus. ZEUS had decreed that a child about to be born, a descendant of Perseus, would reign over the Argolid. He intended Heracles to be this child, but HERA arranged to delay the birth of Heracles by seven days so that Eurystheus, son of Sthenelus, would be born first and should rule instead of Electryon's grandson Heracles.

Heracles was commanded by the Olympian gods through the Delphic Oracle to perform labors that would purify him of slaying his kin and also win him immortality. Heracles was initially reluctant to undertake the Twelve Labors,

because they entailed subjugation to his cousin Eurystheus. In many sources, Eurystheus is described as a lesser man than Heracles, an ungracious and cowardly master. Throughout his trials, Eurystheus made Heracles feel the indignity of his servitude, particularly in the task that called on him to clean out the Augean Stables. Though some sources acknowledge only 10 tasks, the commonly accepted number of tasks set for Heracles by Eursytheus is 12. These are **1.** The Nemean Lion **2.** The Hydra of Lerna **3.** The Erymanthian Boar **4.** The Ceryneian Hind **5.** The Stymphalian Birds **6.** The Augean Stables **7.** The Cretan Bull **8.** The Mares of Diomedes **9.** The Girdle of Hippolyte **10.** The Cattle of Geryon **11.** Cerberus in Hades **12.** The Apples of Hesperides

Euripides' the *Heracleidae* concerns the fate of Heracles' children after his death. In this tragedy, Eurystheus's hatred of Heracles extended to his children, the Heracleidae, after Heracles' death. Eurystheus exiled them from Trachis, and they found refuge in Athens. Once they had grown to adulthood, Eurystheus went to war against them. The Heracleidae, in the company of Iolaus and under the leadership of the Athenian king Demophon (son of THESEUS), prepared for war against Eurystheus. The Athenians were counseled to sacrifice a maiden to ensure military success, and Heracles' daughter Macaria volunteered. The sacrifice was performed, and Hyllus, Iolaus, and Demophon led the Athenians to victory. The tragedy ends as the captive Eurystheus is brought before Heracles' mother, ALCMENE, who orders his death.

Evander   An Arcadian hero. Classical sources are Livy's *From the Foundation of the City* (1.5.1–2), Ovid's *FASTI* (1.461–586, 5.91–100), Pausanias's *Description of Greece* (8.43.2, 8.44.5), and Virgil's *AENEID* (8.51–369, 455–607). Evander is sometimes identified as the son of HERMES and a nymph. In Rome, his mother is called Carmenta/Carmentis, a prophetess associated with song *(carmen)*.

Evander came to Rome from Arcadia and was allowed by Faunus to settle on the left bank of the Tiber on the Palatine Hill. He was said to have introduced the art of writing to the local population. In LIVY's history of Rome, Evander welcomes Hercules (HERACLES), defends him, and proclaims his divinity after killing CACUS, and establishes the cult of the Ara Maxima in Heracles' honor. In Virgil's *Aeneid*, Evander, a Greek, welcomes the Trojan AENEAS in Italy and becomes his ally. He tells Aeneas the story of Heracles and Cacus, gives him a tour of the future site of Rome, and sends his son Pallas with Aeneas to war. When TURNUS kills Pallas, he strips Pallas's distinctive baldric (see DANAUS AND DANAIDS). At the end of the epic, Aeneas recognizes the baldric on Turnus and kills him. The name of the Palatine was believed to derive from "Pallas" by some ancient authors.

Fasti OVID (ca. 8 C.E.) *Fasti* means "calendar" in Latin. Ovid's calendar poem is incomplete, covering only January to June. Each of its six books is devoted to a single month. Ovid wrote the *Fasti* in the years leading up to his exile in 8 C.E., and he appears to have continued revising it while in exile. He discusses the rites celebrated on the various days of the Roman calendar, their nature, their settings, and their origins. This format produces a literary work at once provocatively fragmented and diverse in its subject matter. Ovid discusses inter alia religion, history, mythology, and city monuments. Recent scholarship has appreciated how Ovid's poem on the calendar explores the ways in which the emperor Augustus appropriated and influenced aspects of Roman religion, space, and time. By adding new festivals to the Roman calendar connected with himself and his rule, by reviving and transforming existing rites and cults, and by building and restoring numerous temples, Augustus effectively made himself part of the densely bundled set of practices modern scholars term "Roman religion." Ovid's erudite, Alexandrian poem displays the poet's etiological knowledge while making forays into sensitive political and cultural territory. On one level, Ovid's poem coheres with the movement toward more overtly "Roman" and patriotic subject matter in the later works of Augustan poets; e.g., Propertius's fourth book of elegies and HORACE's fourth book of odes. And yet, precisely by showing how deeply Augustus pervades the social and religious fabric, Ovid's poem betrays its critical edge. Some scholars have suspected that Ovid stopped with June to avoid writing about July and August, named after Julius Caesar and Augustus, respectively. The poem contains notable mythological narratives, including the story of the rape of Proserpina (see PERSEPHONE), which merits comparison with Ovid's versions of the myth in the roughly contemporary *METAMORPHOSES*.

Fates (Moirai, Parcae) Greek personifications of fate. Classical sources are Aeschylus's *PROMETHEUS BOUND* (515–517) and *EUMENIDES* (723–728, 956–967f), Apollodorus's *LIBRARY* (1.3.1, 1.6.2–3, 1.8.2, 1.9.15), Aristophanes' *Frogs* (448–453), Euripides' *ALCESTIS* (10–14), Hesiod's *THEOGONY* (217–223) and *Shield of Heracles* (258–263), Homer's *ILIAD* (13.602; 18.119; 20.127–128; 24.49, 209–210) and *ODYSSEY* (7.197–198), and Pindar's *Pythian Odes* (4.145–146). The Fates, or Moirai (from the Greek word for "share" or "portion"), represent the Greek conception of destiny as fixed at birth and unknown to mortals. The Romans would later blend their own version of the Moirai, the Parcae, with the Greek notion of fate. The Fates, who are personified in Homer's *Odyssey* as spinners weaving together the threads of mortal lives at birth, are usually three sisters. In Hesiod's *Theogony*, their mother is Nyx (Night). She gave birth parthenogenetically to Atropos, Clotho, and Lachesis, but later in the poem, their parentage is attributed to Zeus and Themis (Titan goddess of Law). In this context, the Fates embody concepts of Rightness and are made to be the sisters of Dike (Justice), Eirene (Peace), Eunomia (Lawfulness), and the Horae (Seasons). In the *Theogony*, the Fates shape destinies both good and evil, but in the *Shield of Heracles*, they are bloodthirsty creatures whose fangs drip with the blood of the dying. In the *Prometheus Bound* and *Eumenides*, the Fates shape destiny in ways that even Zeus cannot.

According to one conception of his powers, only Zeus is aware of what is in store for humans, but even he is limited in what he can do to change specific destiny. In a dialogue written by Lucian, between Minos, judge of Hades, and Sostratus, a dead soul, the tension between personal responsibility and destiny shows an awareness of the limits of concepts of predestination. In Homer's *Iliad*, Zeus contemplates saving his son Sarpedon, whose destiny is to die at the hands of Patroclus. Hera persuades Zeus to accept his death because to do otherwise would upset the natural order. When the natural order is transgressed, for example, in a killing of a family member, the related figures of the Furies appear. The Fates were pictured as female figures weaving or binding thread together. They appear on the sixth-century François Vase (Museo Archeologico Nazionale, Florence), where they accompany Hermes and Maia.

fauns Hybrid creatures, part human male and part animal. Classical sources are Ovid's *Metamorphoses* (193–196) and Virgil's *Eclogues* (6). Fauns have human torsos and goats' legs. They have in common with satyrs and Sileni (followers of Silenus) their sylvan domain and their association with revelry and music. In Ovid's *Metamorphoses*, fauns are classed with other sylvan creatures and bucolic divinities and have been granted by Zeus the right to live in peace in the woods and forests. Fauns are to be distinguished from centaurs, who have human torsos and horses's legs and are more violent in nature, and satyrs, who resemble fauns physically but are more lascivious. Satyrs, fauns, and Sileni as well as their female counterparts, nymphs and maenads, participate in the Bacchic processions of Dionysus. Fauns were followers of Pan, a bucolic god of Arcadia. Romans merged the figure of Pan with that of Faunus, who, likewise, was a bucolic god. In the *Orphic Hymn to Silenus*, Silenus leads the Bacchanalia and is followed by satyrs, Naiads, and Bacchantes.

Fauns were frequently depicted by classical vase painters in one of two themes: the satyrs' amorous pursuit of a woodland nymph or a Bacchanalia. An Attic black-figure amphora from ca. 560–525 by the Amasis Painter (Antikenmusem Kä, Basel) shows Dionysus, satyrs, and maenads at a vintage.

Flora (Chloris) A nymph who represents springtime. The main classical source is Ovid's *Fasti* (5.183ff). The Romans aligned Chloris with Flora, who is also associated with vegetation, especially grains. In the *Fasti*, Flora is carried off by Zephyrus, one of the *Anemoi*, or winds associated with the cardinal points. (He was following the courtship example of his brother, Boreas, who had also abducted his bride.) Flora and Zephyrus were married, and Flora carried Spring perpetually with her. Zephyrus granted her the privilege of reigning over flowers. Flora claimed that she gave Hera a flower from the field of Olenus, which caused Hera to conceive Ares parthenogenetically.

The most famous instance of the representation of Flora is Sandro Botticelli's *Primavera* from ca. 1478 (Galleria degli Uffizi, Florence). Zephyrus, depicted as a forceful youth blowing wind through his mouth arriving on the right-hand side of the image, is preceded by his bride, Flora, under whose feet flowers spring and out of whose mouth tumble more blossoms.

Furies (Erinyes) Female personifications of curses and vengeance. Offspring of GAIA (Earth) and URANUS (Heaven). Sisters of the GIANTS and the TITANS. The Roman Furies absorbed the characteristics of the Greek Furies. Classical sources are Apollodorus's *LIBRARY* (1.1.4), Hesiod's *THEOGONY* (182–187), Homer's *ILIAD* (9.453–456, 566–572; 19.259–260; 418; 21.412–414) and *ODYSSEY* (2.135, 15.234, 20.77–78), Ovid's *METAMORPHOSES* (4.451–511), Pindar's *Olympian Odes* (2.38–42) and Virgil's *AENEID* (6.570–572, 7.324–571, 12.845–886). Aeschylus, Ovid, and Virgil refer to the Furies as the Daughters of Night, but in the *Theogony*, the Furies were born of Gaia, fertilized by the blood of Uranus's genitals after he was castrated by his son CRONUS. Apollodorus and the *Orphic Hymn* give their names as Tisiphone, Megaera, and Alecto. They are sometimes designated euphemistically as Eumenides ("kindly ones") or Semnai ("revered ones"). The Furies are the Eumenides of Aeschylus's tragedy *EUMENIDES*. Their appearance is ghastly. Aeschylus describes them as being dressed in black, with Gorgon-like snakes for hair. In other sources, we are told that blood drips from their eyes. The Furies' most important function is to avenge intrafamilial homicide. But they also punish other crimes, such as perjury, disrespect for elders, and violations of the laws of hospitality. The Furies are pitiless in their pursuit of justice, and as chthonic deities, they oversee punishments in HADES. In Aeschylus's *Oresteia*, they pursue ORESTES relentlessly for having murdered his mother CLYTAEMNESTRA until finally, in the last play of the trilogy, *Eumenides*, ATHENA persuades the Furies to accept a new role as protectors of Athens, under the name *Eumenides*. A sanctuary dedicated to the Furies was located in Athens.

In visual representations, the Furies were sometimes represented as winged creatures. A Fury appears, whip in hand, with SISYPHUS on an Apulian red-figure krater from ca. 330 B.C.E. (Antikensammlungen, Munich) and in an Attic black-figure lekythos from 470 B.C.E. (National Museum, Athens).

G

Gaia (Ge) A Greek goddess personifying Earth. Classical sources are the *Homeric Hymn to Earth*, Aeschylus's *Eumenides* (1–11), Apollodorus's *Library* (1.1.1–5, 1.2.1. 1.2.6, 1.3.6, 1.6.1–1.7, Hesiod's *Theogony* (116–200, 233–239, 453–506, 617–735, 820–900), and Pausanias's *Description of Greece* (1.2.6, 5.14.10, 7.25.13, 8.29.4, 10.5.5–7).

Gaia's cult was practiced throughout Greece, particularly at Delphi. According to Hesiod, Gaia was one of the four spontaneously generated primeval deities. Chaos ("gaping void") came into being at the beginning of time, followed first by Gaia and then by Eros and Tartarus. Gaia gave birth to Ourea (Mountains) and Pontus (Sea). She produced the sea gods Eurybia, Keto, Nereus, Phorkys, and Thaumas. With Tartarus, she produced the monster Typhoeus and the Giants. She gave birth to Uranus (Heaven), and she later conceived with him the Titans: Coeus, Crius, Cronus, Iapetus, Hyperion, Mnemosyne, Oceanus, Phoebe, Rhea, Tethys, Theia, and Themis. Uranus and Gaia also produced the Hundred-Handed Ones and the Cyclopes. Uranus consigned the Hundred-Handed Ones and the Cyclopes to Tartarus and prevented the birth of his many children by keeping them inside Gaia, in the earth. Cronus, encouraged by Gaia, castrated him. Gaia was then able to give birth to the other children. Cronus succeeded his father, but Uranus foretold the eventual downfall of the Titans. During the Titanomachy (the battle between the Olympian gods and the Titans), Gaia favored the Olympians and suggested to Zeus that he free the giants, Hundred-Handed Ones, and Cyclopes from Tartarus and to enlist them on his side against the Titans. With these reinforcements, the Olympians were victorious, the Titans defeated and imprisoned in Tartarus.

In visual representations of the classical period, Gaia was depicted as a buxom, mature woman, in keeping with her association with fertility and maternity. She appears together with Atlas in an Apulian red-figure krater from ca. fourth century B.C.E. (Dallas Museum of Art, Texas), where she is holding the tree that will bear the golden apples of the Hesperides (her gift to Hera at her marriage to Zeus). Gaia is shown coming to the aid of one of the giants in a relief of the Great Altar of Zeus at Pergamon dating from the second century B.C.E. (Pergamonmuseum, Berlin).

Galatea A Nereid (sea nymph). One of the 50 daughters of Nereus and Doris. Classical sources are Apollodorus's *Library* (1.2.7), Hesiod's *Theogony* (250), Homer's *Iliad* (18.45), Lucian's *Dialogues of the Sea-Gods* (1), Ovid's *Metamorphoses* (13.738–897), Philostratus's *Imagines* (2.18), and Theocritus's *Idylls* (11).

According to Theocritus, the Cyclops POLY-PHEMUS fell in love with Galatea. He attempted to woo her with love songs, but Galatea was in love with Acis, son of Faynus (see PAN), and did not respond to his overtures. Philostratus's *Imagines* describes a painting of the myth. In a landscape of harvesting Cyclopes, a lovelorn Polyphemus, pan pipes under his arm, a single bushy eyebrow crowning his single eye atop a broad nose, watches Galatea astride a team of four dolphins. Polyphemus offered Galatea his wealth of flocks of sheep and orchards, but Galatea would not be tempted. Surprising Acis and Galatea in an embrace one day, Polyphemus was overcome with jealous rage and crushed the fleeing Acis with a boulder. Ovid informs us that after his death, Acis was transformed into a river god.

In the classical period, visual representations of the myth of Galatea and Polyphemus

Triumph of Galatea. *Fresco Raphael, 1511 (Villa Farnesina, Rome)*

were popular and occurred in a variety of media. Polyphemus is often shown in a pastoral setting playing or carrying a pan pipe, as in a first-century B.C.E. fresco from the Imperial Villa at Boscotrecase (Metropolitan Museum of Art, New York). Here, Galatea and Polyphemus are shown in a rocky landscape surrounded by a flock of goats. Galatea shares iconographic similarities with APHRODITE; her attributes are also dolphins and other sea animals. She holds a windblown cloth above her head and is often accompanied by Nereids and TRITONS. These iconographic elements greatly influenced postclassical images of Galatea, such as Raphael's *Triumph of Galatea* of 1511 in the Villa Farnesina (Rome), which is placed beside its thematic pair, Sebastiano del Piombo's *Polyphemus.* Another famous example is Annibale Carracci's paired frescoes, *Polyphemus Wooing Galatea* and *Polyphemus Slaying Acis* in the Palazzo Farnese from ca. 1597 (Rome). A postclassical example of the theme is Gustave Moreau's *The Cyclops (Observing a Sleeping Nymph)* from ca. 1898 (Rijksmuseum, Amsterdam).

Ganymede   A mortal youth from Troy. Son of Tros and Callirrhoe. Classical sources are the *Homeric Hymn to Aphrodite* (202–217), Apollodorus's LIBRARY (2.5.9, 3.12.2), Euripides' TROJAN WOMEN (821–840), Homer's ILIAD (5.265–267, 20.231–235), Lucian's DIALOGUES OF THE GODS (8.10), Ovid's METAMORPHOSES (10.152–161), Pindar's *Olympian Odes* (1.40–145), and Virgil's AENEID (1.28, 5.253). Ganymede is one of a group of mortal youths who attract the amorous attention of the gods; others include ADONIS, ENDYMION, and HYACINTHUS. Virgil and Pindar relate that Zeus became enamored of Ganymede because of his beauty. In Diodorus Siculus's LIBRARY OF HISTORY, the *Homeric Hymn to Aphrodite*, and the *Iliad*, Ganymede was carried off by an eagle (either Zeus's eagle or the god himself in the form of the bird) to become Zeus's cupbearer on Olympus. Zeus was said to have compensated Ganymede's family with a gift of beautiful horses.

The story of Ganymede's abduction was a popular theme in classical imagery in sculpture, relief, and pottery. Some images focused on the compelling visual moment in which Ganymede is physically carried away by the eagle, while others emphasized his function as cupbearer to the Olympian gods. A late Roman mosaic (Sousse, Tunisia) shows the boy wearing a Phrygian cap in the presence of Zeus's eagle, while a red-figure bell krater from ca. 525–475 B.C.E. (Louvre, Paris) depicts Ganymede holding a hoop, as a symbol of his youthfulness, and a rooster, a typical gift that suitors presented to young boys. Ganymede as cupbearer is represented on an Archaic red-figure kylix (National Museum, Tarquinia). The more overtly erotic aspects of the myth were popular with post-classical painters, a prime example of which is Antonio Correggio's *Ganymede* from ca. 1530 (Kunsthistoriches Museum, Vienna).

Ganymede. *Antonio Correggio, ca. 1530 (Kunsthistorisches Museum, Vienna)*

Georgics VIRGIL (29 B.C.E.) Virgil published his *Georgics*, a didactic poem in four books on farming, in 29 B.C.E., the same year as Octavian's celebration of a triple triumph in Rome, and shortly following Octavian's victory over Antony and Cleopatra at Actium (31 B.C.E.) and Alexandria (30 B.C.E.). Virgil's first work, the *ECLOGUES*, was published ca. 38 B.C.E. in the midst of the turbulent crises of the waning years of the Roman republic. By 29 B.C.E., Octavian, the future emperor Augustus, was decisively triumphant over his enemies, while Virgil became associated with the great patron of the Augustan age, Maecenas, and with Octavian himself. At the opening of the *Georgics*, Virgil makes Maecenas his primary addressee but also addresses Caesar (i.e., Octavian), and, in a striking instance of early Augustan panegyric, hesitates among the various divine roles that Octavian may choose to assume. The topic of his poem is not Octavian or his deeds but the ostensibly humble and practical topic of farming. Farming and the land are traditional Roman concerns, and the farmer *(agricola)* is a Roman figure endowed with symbolic importance. The sturdy small-holder of the Italian countryside represents the archetypal citizen/soldier and exemplar of old-fashioned, rustic values and behavior. In recent years, farming and land had become contentious issues. Octavian, in an effort to settle his veterans in the late 40s B.C.E., had to expropriate land from Italian landowners, causing discontent in the countryside. Virgil appears to have initially suffered from the confiscations (see discussion of his *Eclogues*). After this shaky beginning, however, Augustus and his poets and architects would stress the benefits of peace, the bounty and fertility of the land, and the "golden age" tranquility of the Italian countryside.

Virgil's *Georgics* contributes to the Augustan focus on the land of Italy and farming; indeed, a uniting theme of all three of his major works is Italy and the potentially destructive conflict over Italian land. (The civil wars were fresh in Italian memories, nor had the Social Wars of the early decades of the first century B.C.E. between Rome and its Italian allies been forgotten.) Virgil's didactic poem on farming is written in the tradition of Hesiod's *WORKS AND DAYS*, but also imitates Homer and Hellenistic didactic poetry. A more recent model for Virgil is the didactic poem of Lucretius, *On the Nature of Things*, written around the middle of the first century B.C.E. Virgil's view of things, however, is markedly different from the Epicurean Lucretius's rationalizing vision of the universe. For Virgil, nature and the cosmos are difficult to read, at times opaque, although traditional lore and religious practices can help; above all, relentless hard work (Latin, *labor*) is required to prevent slippage into disorder. While Virgil focuses on farming, he builds several famous digressions into his poem, e.g., the myth of the golden age and the portents preceding Julius Caesar's murder in Book 1; the praises of Italy in Book 2; the description of the "temple" the poet plans to build in honor of Octavian in Mantua at the opening of Book 3; the cattle plague at Noricum at the end of the same book; and the description of the old man of Tarentum in Book 4. The most famous digression is mythological: At the end of Book 4,

Virgil tells the story of Aristaeus, ORPHEUS AND EURYDICE. Aristaeus, the son of APOLLO and the nymph Cyrene, is said to have played a part in causing Eurydice's death. He desired her, and while he was chasing her, a poisonous snake bit her foot. In punishment for this, Aristaeus lost all the bees he was keeping. He then learned from PROTEUS how to appease Eurydice by making sacrifice: From the decaying flesh of the slain oxen there came forth swarms of bees. This closing epyllion ("mini-epic") of Virgil's didactic poem combines the productive, social image of the regenerated bees with the intense pathos of Orpheus's personal loss. The Orphic passage recalls the neoteric style of CATULLUS's generation, while the regenerated bees may express the hopes of the present generation for expiation of the violence of the recent past. Taken together, Orpheus and Aristaeus encapsulate the distinctive vision and power of Virgilian poetry.

Geryon   See CHRYSAOR; HERACLES.

giants   The offspring of GAIA (Earth) and URANUS (Heaven). Classical sources are Apollonius of Rhodes's *VOYAGE OF THE ARGONAUTS* (1.940–1010), Diodorus Siculus's *LIBRARY OF HISTORY* (5.71.2–6), Euripides' *HERACLES* (177–178), Hesiod's *THEOGONY* (185), Homer's *ODYSSEY* (7.58–60), and Pausanias's *Description of Greece* (1.25.2, 8.29.1–4). The giants were conceived when the blood of Uranus, after his castration by Cronus, fell on Earth. Gaia sent the giants to destroy the Olympians in retribution for their imprisonment of her offspring the TITANS, in HADES. The subsequent battle was called the GIGANTOMACHY. Enormously large and strong, the giants had dragon's scales for feet. In Ovid's *METAMORPHOSES* the giants had serpents' feet and 100 hands. According to Ovid, the giants were slain by the thunderbolts of ZEUS. The giants included Alcyoneus, Clytius, Enceladus, Ephialtes, Eurytus, Gration, Hippolytus, Mimas, Pallas, Polybotes, and Porphyrion.

Poseidon Battles the Giant Polybotes. *Detail from an Attic kylix, ca. 475 B.C.E. (Bibliothèque nationale de France, Paris)*

The Gigantomachy was a popular theme and frequently depicted on vases, architectural relief, and sarcophagi. According to Euripides, one such relief decorated the outside of the temple of Apollo at Delphi. In ancient art, the giants were large, sometimes nude figures. They were often bearded and sometimes represented as serpent-footed, as, for example, in a late imperial mosaic from the triclinium at Piazza Armerina (Sicily) and the second-century B.C.E. Gigantomachy frieze of the Pergamon Altar. On the relief of the Siphnian Treasury at Delphi from ca. 525 B.C.E., the giants are shown fighting Olympians. The giant Polybotes has human form in an image on the tondo of an Attic red-figure kylix of ca. 475 B.C.E. (Bibliothèque nationale de France, Paris) as he fights POSEIDON.

Gigantomachy The battle between the GIANTS (offspring of GAIA) and the Olympian gods. Classical sources are Apollodorus's *LIBRARY* (1.6.1) and Diodorus Siculus's *LIBRARY OF HISTORY* (5.71.2–6). The defeat of the TITANS by the Olympians was followed by the war with

a race of giants descended from Gaia (Earth). Gaia sent the giants to destroy the Olympians in retribution for their imprisonment of her offspring the Titans. The giants challenged the Olympian gods, hurling rocks and flaming trees at the heavens. According to Ovid, the giants were slain by the thunderbolts of ZEUS, but other sources suggest more protracted engagement with giants. An oracle prophesied that the giants were undefeatable without the aid of a mortal. The mortal was HERACLES, who went on to slay the giant Alcyoneus. According to Apollodorus's *Library*, who cataloged the deaths of the giants, Heracles shot an arrow into Alcyoneus, but without killing him, because the giant was able to revive and regain his strength while he touched his native earth. On the advice of ATHENA, Heracles dragged Alcyoneus away from the land where he had been born and there killed him. Either Zeus or APOLLO killed Porphyrion, who tried to violate HERA, while Gration was slain by ARTEMIS. Ephialtes was killed by an arrow in each eye aimed by Apollo and Heracles, while DIONYSUS used his thyrsus to kill Eurytus. HECATE set Clytius afire with torches, and HEPHAESTUS used heated metal to kill Mimas. ATHENA also participated in the war; she skinned Pallas and used his skin as a shield for her body, and she killed Enceladus, who, according to Virgil's *AENEID*, lies under Sicily's Mount Etna. POSEIDON crushed Polybotes with a piece of the island of Cos, and HERMES, invisible while wearing the helmet of Hades, killed Hippolytus.

The Gigantomachy was a popular theme and frequently depicted on vases, architectural relief, and sarcophagi. According to Euripides, one such relief decorated the outside of the temple of Apollo at Delphi. In ancient art, the giants were large, sometimes nude figures, often bearded, and sometimes, though not always, represented as serpent-footed. Examples in which they were depicted as snake-footed include the late imperial mosaic from the triclinium at Piazza Armerina (Sicily) and the second-century B.C.E. Gigantomachy frieze of the Pergamon Altar. On the relief of the Siphnian Treasury at Delphi from ca. 525 B.C.E., the giants are shown fighting the Olympians.

Glaucus (1) (Glaukos)   A sea god. Glaucus had the torso of a man and lower half of a fish. Classical sources are Apollonius of Rhodes's *VOYAGE OF THE ARGONAUTS* (1.1,310–1,328), Euripides' *ORESTES* (362–369), Hyginus's *Fabulae* (199), Ovid's *METAMORPHOSES* (13.898–14.69), Pausanias's *Description of Greece* (9.22.6–7), and Philostratus's *IMAGINES* (215). According to Ovid's *Metamorphoses*, Glaucus began life as a mortal fisherman living in Boeotia. Spreading his catch on a field one day, Glaucus was amazed to find the fish move about and escape back into the sea. Speculating that the grass on which they had been laid had magical power, Glaucus ate some and was transformed into a merman. He fell in love with the nymph SCYLLA, but she fled from his advances. He sought CIRCE's aid, but she loved Glaucus herself. When she was scorned by him, she revenged herself upon Scylla. Circe poisoned the waters in which Scylla was accustomed to bathe, and the nymph was transformed into a monstrous canine creature. She appears in the maritime adventures of Apollonius of Rhodes's *Voyage of the Argonauts* and Homer's *ODYSSEY*.

Glaucus had prophetic abilities, which he displayed in Euripides' *Orestes* by revealing the death of AGAMEMNON to his brother MENELAUS and again in Apollonius of Rhodes's *Voyage of the Argonauts*, where he emerged from the sea to insist that HERACLES abandon his search for the youth HYLAS and return to the Twelve Labors. In Diodorus Siculus's *Library of History*, he also reveals the future destinies of the members of the Argonautic expedition.

In appearance, Glaucus is usually mature, long-haired, and bearded, and is recognizable for his merman shape. According to Philostratus's *Imagines*, Glaucus is accompanied by singing kingfishers.

Glaucus (2)   A Lycian hero of the Trojan War. Son of Hippolochus. Cousin of SARPEDON. The principal classical source is Homer's *ILIAD* (2.876, 6.119–235, 12.310–470, 16.493ff). Glaucus and Sarpedon fought on the side of the Trojans during the Trojan War. During the fighting, Glaucus came upon DIOMEDES, fighting on the side of the Greeks. The two remembered the friendship between their families—dating to an exchange of gifts between their grandfathers, Oeneus and BELLEROPHON—and they peaceably exchanged armor. When Sarpedon was badly injured during battle, Glaucus attempted to rescue him but was prevented because he sustained a wound himself. He prayed to APOLLO to be quickly cured, a prayer that the god granted. Glaucus was not able to save Sarpedon but brought back his body. Sarpedon's armor, in the meantime, had been stripped by the Greeks.

Glaucus fought HECTOR for the possession of PATROCLUS's body, but while doing so, he was killed by AJAX. Under the direction of Apollo, Glaucus's body was borne back to Lycia by the winds.

Golden Fleece   See JASON; *VOYAGE OF THE ARGONAUTS*.

Gorgons   Daughters of the sea gods Phorcys and Ceto. Sisters of the GRAEAE. Classical sources are Apollodorus's *LIBRARY* (3.10.3), Euripides' *ION* (989–1,017), Hesiod's *THEOGONY* (270–283), Homer's *ILIAD* (5.738–742), Hyginus's *Fabulae* (64, 151), Ovid's *METAMORPHOSES* (4.614–620, 770–803), Pausanias's *Description of Greece* (1.24.7, 5.18.5, 9.34.2) and Pindar's *Pythian Odes* (12.6–27). The Gorgons are the monstrous sisters Sthenno, Euryale, and, most famous of all, Medusa. Described by Apollodorus as having serpentine hair, a fierce gaze, a fierce glance, and vicious teeth, the Gorgons were so frightening in appearance that they turned to stone anyone who looked on them. In one version of the myth, unlike her sisters Medusa was originally mortal and beautiful, but ATHENA discovered that Medusa and POSEIDON had sex in her sanctuary, and she destroyed Medusa's beauty and turned her into a monster.

The Gorgons appear in the myth of the hero PERSEUS. The hero was sent by King Polydectes to retrieve the head of Medusa. Perseus was fortunate enough to have the help of Athena and HERMES, who gave him a sickle of adamant, the cap of Hades (which gave him invisibility), and winged shoes. He compelled the Gorgons' almost equally unlovely sisters, the Graeae, to reveal Medusa's whereabouts. He found Medusa asleep, and while Athena held her shield as a mirror to guide him so that he would not have to look at her directly, he cut off Medusa's head with his sickle. The winged horse PEGASUS and the warrior CHRYSAOR sprang from her neck. Perseus was afterward pursued by the remaining Gorgons, whom he avoided by wearing the cap of Hades. In some versions of the myth, Perseus killed all three Gorgons. After further adventures, Perseus returned the magical objects to Hermes and Athena, and gave Medusa's head to Athena, who placed it on her shield.

In the classical period, Medusa appears frequently in images depicting Perseus's adventures. The Gorgons, like the Graeae, are depicted as winged creatures, as in a red-figure hydria attributed to the Pan Painter from ca. 500 B.C.E. (British Museum, London). Here, the Gorgon's winged and headless body falls to the ground as Perseus strides away with Medusa's head peeking out of his bag. Medusa's horrifying appearance is the focus of an Attic red-figure amphora attributed to the Berlin Painter from ca. 490 B.C.E. (Antikensammlungen, Munich). Here, Medusa runs from Perseus; she has wings and serpents for hair, and her tongue hangs between her fanged teeth. Caravaggio's *Medusa* from ca. 1592 (Galleria degli Uffizi, Florence) shows the gruesome severed head of Medusa with its still writhing snakes. The birth of Pegasus from Medusa's headless corpse is another theme. A white-ground lekythos attributed to the Diospos Painter from ca. 500 (Metropolitan Museum of Art, New York) shows the wing-sandaled hero Perseus fleeing from the decapitated body of Medusa while from her neck springs the fully formed Pegasus.

Medusa. *Michelangelo Caravaggio, ca. 1592 (Galleria degli Uffizi, Florence)*

Graces (Charites, Gratiae) Greek goddesses representing grace, charm, and beauty. Classical sources are Apollodorus's LIBRARY (1.3.1), Hesiod's THEOGONY (64–65, 907–911, 945–946), Homer's ILIAD (5.338, 14.263–276, 18.382–387) and ODYSSEY (8.362–366, 18.192–194), Pausanias's *Description of Greece* (3.18.9–10, 6.24.6–7, 9.35.1–7), and Pindar's *Olympian Odes* (14.3–17). The Graces live in Olympus with the MUSES, with whom they share similar characteristics. Cults dedicated to them appear in Athens and elsewhere in Greece. The Charites were later identified with the Roman Gratiae. There is some variation in the names and functions of the Graces. Homer mentions them in association with APHRODITE but gives neither their names nor their number. In his *Theogony*, Hesiod described the Graces as three daughters of Zeus and Eurynome, named Aglaea, Euphroysne,

The Three Graces. *Raphael, ca. 1504 (Musée Condé, Chantilly, France)*

and Thalia. Here, they represent poetry, dance, singing, and festivity. Aglaea, also sometimes called Charis (Beauty), in Homer, is the wife of HEPHAESTUS. Because of their associations with beauty, both aesthetic and moral, the Graces are often attendants to the Olympian deities with similar associations: Aphrodite, HERA, APOLLO, DIONYSUS, HERMES, and EROS.

In the classical period, the Graces appear in vase paintings, bas-reliefs, and sculptural works. On a wall painting from Pompeii dating to the first century B.C.E., the Graces appear unclothed with their arms around each other's shoulders. This type of representation would come to influence postclassical artists, as in Botticelli's depiction of the three Graces in his *Primavera* of 1478 (Galleria degli Uffizi, Florence). In this image, the Graces appear with figures symbolizing Spring. Raphael's *The Three Graces* from ca. 1504 (Musée Condé, Chantilly) shows the nude, graceful trio in their characteristic pose.

Graeae (Graiai)   Daughters of the sea gods Phorcys and Ceto, sisters of the GORGONS. Classical sources are Apollodorus's *LIBRARY* (2.4.2) and Hesiod's *THEOGONY* (270–273). The Graeae, also known as the Crones, are winged, gray-haired hags that share between them a single tooth and a single eye. In Hesiod's *Theogony*, two of the Graeae are named Pemphedro and Enyo, while in Aeschylus, a third is mentioned that Apollodorus calls Deino. PERSEUS captured the eye of the Graeae, forcing them to reveal the location of the Gorgons. He afterward defeated the Gorgon Medusa. The haplessness of the Graeae stands in contrast to the murderous strength of the Gorgons.

The Graeae are the model for the witches that appear in Shakespeare's *Macbeth*. In classical art, the Graeae appear within the context of the myth of Perseus, as in an Attic red-figure krater of ca. fifth century B.C.E. (Archaeological Museum, Delos). Here, Perseus, in winged sandals and the cap of Hades, furtively steals the eye from the seated Graeae.

Gyges, Gyes   See HUNDRED-HANDED ONES.

H

Hades (Pluto, Dis) Olympian god of the underworld. Son of the TITANS Cronus and RHEA. The brother of DEMETER, HERA, HESTIA, POSEIDON, and ZEUS. Classical sources are the *Homeric Hymn to Demeter* (1–87, 334–433), Apollodorus's LIBRARY (1.1.5–1.2.1), Hesiod's THEOGONY (453–506, 765–778, 850), Homer's ILIAD (5.394–402, 15.187–193, 20.61–66), Hyginus's *Fabulae* (146), Lucian's *Dialogue of the Dead* (passim), Ovid's METAMORPHOSES (5.346–424), Pausanias's *Description of Greece* (6.25.2–3), and Strabo's *Geography* (3.2.9). Hades' eponymous realm is the underworld, the kingdom of all dead souls. Together with his wife, PERSEPHONE, who joins him in ruling the underworld, they are the prime deities of the underworld. The name *Hades*, according to ancient etymology, means "invisible"; thus, Hades is sometimes called the ruler of the invisible world, or underworld. His helmet, the cap of Hades, causes its wearers to become invisible. It was used by the hero PERSEUS when he killed MEDUSA, and ATHENA wore it in the *Iliad*. Hades was sometimes conceived of as the "other Zeus," but unlike Zeus, no cults were dedicated to him. He was also referred to as Pluto, meaning "wealth," and this aspect of his characterization was more favorably viewed. In the Roman period, Hades/Pluto was merged with a similar god, Dis.

The story of Hades' origins is as follows. Cronus married his sister Rhea, who gave birth to Olympian gods, including Hades, but Cronus swallowed each child whole shortly after its birth. When Zeus, the youngest child, was born, Rhea wrapped up a stone in swaddling clothes and gave it to Cronus in lieu of the infant. Zeus forced Cronus to disgorge his other children into the world. Hades joined Zeus and Poseidon in the TITANOMACHY, the protracted battle of the Olympian gods against the Titans. Zeus eventually fulfilled the prophecy that he would unseat his father, and the Olympians triumphed over the Titans. Poseidon was given the sea as his domain, Zeus ruled over the heavens, and Hades' reign extended over the underworld. According to Homer, the gods determined this division of the world by casting lots.

The myths concerning Hades are few. In Homer's *Iliad*, Hades is wounded by HERACLES during an encounter in Pylos. The most important myth of Hades is the abduction of Persephone. The abduction of Demeter's daughter Persephone is vividly described in Ovid's *Metamorphoses*: Hades seized the girl from among her maiden companions in a Sicilian meadow. Demeter refused to return to Olympus but wandered over the earth, seeking her daughter. In her grief, she neglected the harvest, and a famine ensued. Finally, Zeus persuaded Hades to return Persephone, but she had eaten one or more pomegranate seeds (sources vary as to the number) while in the underworld, and she was fated to remain there for part of every year. Persephone's time in the underworld coincides with winter, and her reappearance above with spring and summer.

Like Hades, Persephone occupies a dual role. As Demeter's daughter, she is connected with youthful vitality, but as goddess of the underworld, she is also connected with death. Persephone is the "Hera of the Dead," according to Virgil, in the same way that Hades is the "other Zeus." It is thus appropriate that Hades' union with Persephone does not result in any offspring.

Hades' kingdom is seldom visited by the living, and, of the dead, only ALCESTIS and EURYDICE were permitted to return to the world above, although in Eurydice's case, the return to life was ultimately unsuccessful. On the rare occasion when a hero such as ODYSSEUS or AENEAS travels to Hades, they must

pay their respects to Hades and Persephone. Others who, through guile or courage, trespass in Hades include HERACLES and THESEUS. Theseus's friend PIRITHOUS decided to kidnap and marry Persephone. Theseus joined him in the unsuccessful attempt, and they were both imprisoned in Hades. Heracles' visit to the underworld while he was performing his Twelfth Labor had better results; Persephone welcomed him and allowed him to take CERBERUS, the three-headed hound guarding the entrance of Hades. Heracles was also given permission to rescue Theseus, and, in some versions Pirithous, from their underworld prison.

In classical art Hades was commonly depicted as a bearded, solemn figure. Hades' abduction of Persephone was a popular visual theme. An example is a red-figure hydria from the fourth century B.C.E. (Metropolitan Museum of Art, New York) that shows a flee-

Pluto Abducting Persephone. *Fresco, Luca Giordano, 1682–83 (Palazzo Medici Riccardi, Florence)*

ing Hades with Persephone in his grasp. The myth of Persephone as an allegory of the afterlife was used by artists on sarcophagi. A wall painting from a royal tomb at Vergina, dating from the fourth century B.C.E., shows the main iconographic elements of this theme: a bearded Hades carrying off the struggling Persephone in his chariot. Postclassical representations include Luca Giordano's fresco *Pluto Abducting Persephone* of 1682–83 (Palazzo Medici Riccardi, Florence) and Gianlorenzo Bernini's *The Abduction of Persephone* of 1622 (Villa Borghese, Rome), which forms a thematic pair with the *Apollo and Daphne* sculptural group. In their associations with the fertility of the earth, Hades and Persephone are sometimes shown with attributes of a cornucopia or vegetation, as in an Attic red-figure kylix from ca. 450 B.C.E. (British Museum, London). A similar scene is carved in marble relief dating to ca. 480 B.C.E. (Museo Nazionale, Reggio Calabria). Here the chthonic deities are enthroned, and Hades holds a cornucopia, while Persephone holds a sheaf of wheat.

Hades (Underworld) The eponymous realm of HADES, ruler of the kingdom of all dead souls. Classical sources are Hesiod's THEOGONY (227, 310–312, 361, 383–403, 769–776, 777–805) and WORKS AND DAYS (167–173), Homer's *Odyssey* (11, passim), Ovid's METAMORPHOSES (4.434–464, 10.15–77), Pausanias's *Description of Greece* (8.17.5–18.6, 9.39.8, 10.28.1–8), and Virgil's AENEID (6, passim). Much of the geography of Hades is drawn from Homer's *Odyssey* and Virgil's *Aeneid*. Dead souls whose bodies have received proper burial are brought to Hades by CHARON, who ferries them across the river STYX. The river Acheron flows through Hades, and the river Lethe brings oblivion to those who drink its waters. CERBERUS, the three-headed dog, guards the entrance to Hades, providing a gruesome welcome to new arrivals and preventing any exit. Hades' kingdom is seldom visited by the living. On the

rare occasion when a hero such as ODYSSEUS or AENEAS travel to Hades, they must pay their respects to Hades and Persephone. Others that through guile or courage trespass in Hades include HERACLES, THESEUS, and ORPHEUS. Of the dead, only ALCESTIS and EURYDICE were permitted to leave Hades.

MINOS, Rhadamanthys, and AEACUS are the three judges of the underworld. In Virgil's *Aeneid*, Minos has the task of deciding whether a soul will proceed to Elysium or TARTARUS, and in Dante's *Divine Comedy*, Minos directs the soul to the appropriate circle of hell.

In Book 11 of the *Odyssey*, CIRCE sends Odysseus to consult the seer TIRESIAS in Hades. Following her directions, Odysseus and his crew sail to the end of the world to find Hades. Odysseus offers sacrifices to the dead, promises to bury the body of his companion Elpenor with the proper rites, and calls on Persephone. Tiresias's ghost appears before Odysseus and, after drinking the blood of the sacrificed animals, prophesies a treacherous journey home for Odysseus and his crew. Odysseus also speaks to his mother's ghost, whom he cannot embrace, but who recognizes and speaks to him after she also has drunk sacrificial blood. Following the appearance of his mother, a host of female ghosts sent by Persephone, the mothers of heroes—ALCMENE, ARIADNE, ANTIOPE, LEDA, and Megara—speak to Odysseus. The ghost of AGAMEMNON comes before Odysseus. He is enraged at his murderers, his wife, CLYTAEMNESTRA, and her lover, AEGISTHUS. Odysseus also speaks with other heroes of the Trojan campaign: ACHILLES, Antilochus, and PATROCLUS. He attempts to make amends to AJAX, whom he defeated in the contest over Achilles' arms, but Ajax cannot forgive him and refuses to speak with him.

Odysseus sees ORION hunting in Hades and finds MINOS holding court as a judge in the underworld. He also sees the less fortunate inmates of Hades: TITYUS tormented by vultures eating his liver, TANTALUS with food and water continually receding from his grasp, and Sɪsʏᴘʜᴜs eternally pushing his enormous boulder. Odysseus comes upon Hᴇʀᴀᴄʟᴇs, who is still powerful in death. Though he had hoped to speak with more heroes, Odysseus is overcome by the crowd of ghosts around him; he turns back to his ship and speeds away from Hades. The next morning, having reached safety, Odysseus and his crew fulfill their promise to the ghost of Elpenor and perform the proper burial rites for his corpse.

In Book 6 of the *Aeneid*, Aeneas descends to Hades to communicate with his father, Aɴᴄʜɪsᴇs. Aeneas was instructed by the Cumaean Sibyl on how to accomplish this: perform the burial rites for his dead shipmate and obtain the golden bough for Persephone. When he had fulfilled her prescriptions and offered animal sacrifices to both Hades and Persephone, the Sibyl led him into Hades, through gloomy halls where he encountered Grief, Conscience, Disease and Old Age, Dread, Hunger, and Poverty. Further on, Aeneas recognizes War, Strife, Death, and his twin Sleep. The inhabitants of Hades include centaurs, beasts, ghosts, and famous monsters such as Briareus, the Cʜɪᴍᴀᴇʀᴀ, the Gᴏʀɢᴏɴs, the Hᴀʀᴘɪᴇs, and Sᴄʏʟʟᴀ. The Sibyl guided Aeneas past the crowd of dead souls awaiting Charon's transport to Hades. His gift for Persephone, the golden bough, assured him passage in Charon's boat. The Sibyl gave Cerberus drugged food to enable Aeneas to enter Hades. In the Fields of Mourning, an area for those who suffered cruelly in their love, Aeneas encountered Dɪᴅᴏ, the lover he abandoned, but she refuses to speak to him. Further on, Hades divides into Elysium and Tartarus. Tartarus, guarded by the Hʏᴅʀᴀ, is reserved for the worst transgressors, mortal or immortal. The Tɪᴛᴀɴs were consigned to Tartarus by Zeus, and they were joined by others who earned the enmity of the gods, including Ixɪᴏɴ, Sisyphus, Tantalus, and Tityus. Aeneas found Anchises in the fields of Elysium, where reside the virtuous dead, and, after learning from him about the future destiny of Rome, emerged from Hades through the Ivory Gate (the gate of false dreams).

The Christian conception of hell shares similarities with Hades as a place for the dead, many of whom exist in torment. Hades, however, includes its own paradise in Elysium. In the Christian geography of the afterlife, the heavens occupy a physically separate space above the human world, which for the Greeks and Romans had been the domain of the Olympian gods. Following the tradition of Homer and Virgil, Dante's early 14th-century *Divine Comedy* describes his own exploration of the levels of hell under Virgil's guidance.

Harmonia Daughter of Aᴘʜʀᴏᴅɪᴛᴇ and Aʀᴇs. Wife of Cᴀᴅᴍᴜs. The daughters of Harmonia and Cadmus are Aᴜᴛᴏɴᴏᴇ, Aɢᴀᴠᴇ, Iɴᴏ, and Sᴇᴍᴇʟᴇ. Their son is Polydorus. Classical sources are Apollodorus's *Lɪʙʀᴀʀʏ* (3.4.2), Hesiod's *Tʜᴇᴏɢᴏɴʏ* (933–937, 975–978), Pausanias's *Description of Greece* (9.12.3), and Pindar's *Pythian Odess* (3.86–103). In establishing the city of Thebes, Cadmus killed the dragon of Ares, then made atonement by serving the god for eight years. Cadmus was afterward rewarded by the Olympians with his marriage to Harmonia. At their wedding, Cadmus gave Harmonia a golden necklace (in some accounts its maker, Hᴇᴘʜᴀᴇsᴛᴜs, gave it to her). Harmonia's necklace brought its future owners, descendants of Cadmus, ill fortune. Eventually, Cadmus ceded the throne of Thebes to his grandson Pᴇɴᴛʜᴇᴜs and settled in Illyria with Harmonia where, after death, they were transformed into snakes and brought to Elysium. According to Hyginus's *Fabulae*, the transformation occurred because Cadmus had killed Ares' dragon. Though Cadmus and Harmonia appear to have been favored by the gods, their descendants suffered misfortunes. In Euripides' tragedy *Bacchae*, Pentheus, grandson of Cadmus and Harmonia and now king of Thebes, was slaughtered by his own mother, Agave, and his aunt Autonoe in a Dionysiac frenzy. Autonoe later fled Thebes, and her son ACTAEON offended ARTEMIS and was killed. Semele, mother of Dionysus, was tricked by HERA into provoking her own death, and Ino's care of her nephew Dionysus attracted the ire of Hera, who incited the madness that caused Ino and her son Melicertes to throw themselves into the sea.

In visual representation, Harmonia is often shown with Cadmus and the dragon at the Spring of Ares. An example is a red-figure calyx krater from ca. 360 B.C.E. (Louvre, Paris). An Attic red-figure (white-ground) epinetron from ca. 430 B.C.E. (National Archaeological Museum, Athens) depicts the wedding of Harmonia and Cadmus attended by the gods.

Harpies   Daughters of Electra (an OCEANID) and Thaumas (son of GAIA and Pontus). Sisters to IRIS, herald to the Olympian gods. Classical sources are Apollodorus's *LIBRARY* (1.9.21), Apollonius of Rhodes's *VOYAGE OF THE ARGONAUTS* (2.164–499), Hesiod's *THEOGONY* (265–269), Homer's *ILIAD* (16.148–151) and *ODYSSEY* (20.61ff), and Virgil's *AENEID* (3.209–267). Sources disagree as to their parentage and number. Their names are usually Aello, Celaeno, Ocypete, and Podarge. The Harpies ("snatchers" in Greek) are winged creatures and travel through the air. They personify the storm winds and are often associated in their myths with other air or wind deities such as the sons of BOREAS and the winds.

In Virgil's *Aeneid*, they are monstrous bird-creatures with female faces and clawed hands. They are accompanied by a horrible stench and befoul food. In the *Aeneid*, the Harpy Celaeno prophesies to AENEAS and his company that they will arrive in Italy but not before becoming so racked with hunger that they eat their own tables. Aeneas also sees the Harpies in his descent to HADES, among other monsters and dark creatures.

The Harpies figure in the story of PHINEUS, king of Thrace and son of Agenor. Phineus had been granted prophetic gifts by APOLLO and either his misuse of them or his maltreatment of his sons caused him to be tormented by the Harpies. The Harpies snatched food from his mouth but allowed him just enough, a reeking morsel of food, to allow him to linger in a weakened, aged, and blind state. When the crew of the *Argo* came upon him in this condition, Zetes and Calais (the BOREADAE) resolved to liberate him. Being sons of Boreas, they were endowed with wings and were thus able to chase the Harpies to the Strophades. There, the Harpies were defended by IRIS, who made a pledge to the Boreadae that they would cease their torment of Phineus.

In another myth, the Harpies carried off the daughters of Pandareus, who had stolen from the gods and thus incurred the wrath of ZEUS. The gods killed Pandareus and his wife but, according to Homer (*Odyssey* 20), took pity on the daughters: Aphrodite, Artemis, and Athena cared for them and bestowed skills and attributes on them. Nevertheless, just as Aphrodite was arranging their marriage, they were snatched away by Harpies and handed over to the Erinyes (see FURIES). As in the myth of Phineus, the Harpies represent a ruthless form of justice or fate acting independently of conventional sources of authority.

In classical art, the Harpies were depicted as winged females or as monstrous, clawed females. The winged Boreadae are shown rescuing Phineus on an Attic red-figure column-amphora attributed to the Leningrad Painter from ca. 460 B.C.E. (Louvre, Paris), while in a Chalcidian black-figure cup (Wagner Museum, University of Würzburg) from ca. 530 B.C.E. the Boreadae are shown chasing the Harpies.

Hebe   Olympian goddess of youth and cup-bearer of the gods. Daughter of HERA and ZEUS. Sister of ARES (god of war) and EILEITHYIA (goddess of childbirth). Wife of HERACLES, following the hero's apotheosis. Textual sources are Apollodorus's *LIBRARY* (1.3.1, 2.7.7), Euripides' *HERACEIDAE* (915ff), Hesiod's *THEOGONY* (921–

922, 950–955), Homer's *ILIAD* (4.2–3, 5.719–723) and *ODYSSEY* (11.601–604), and Ovid's *METAMORPHOSES* (9.397–403). Hebe shared the function of cupbearer of the Olympian gods with GANYMEDE (Pausanias's *Description of Greece* gives Ganymede as an alternate name for Hebe). Hebe, who personifies youth, is commonly found in the company of the Olympian gods but has few myths of her own. She was worshiped in connection with her mother, Hera, or with Heracles. Homer's *Iliad* and *Odyssey* provide only a few details, such as Hebe's pouring of nectar into golden goblets for her fellow gods.

Hebe's parentage is established in Hesiod's *Theogony*, which also notes her marriage to the deified Heracles. Heracles' marriage to Hebe reconciled him with his enemy, Hera, and he received immortality and eternal youth. Hebe also restores Heracles' nephew IOLAUS, king of Thessaly, to youthfulness in Euripides' *Heracleidae*. Hebe's marriage to Heracles, according to Apollodorus's *Library*, produced two sons, Alexiares and Anicetus.

The lid of an Attic red-figure pyxis from ca. 350 B.C.E. (University Museum, University of Pennsylvania) shows the marriage of Hebe and Heracles. In this image, Hebe is represented as a white-painted figure in a long robe whom a nude Heracles, holding his club, takes by the hand as flying erotes (see EROS) hold back Hebe's veil.

Hecate Goddess of magic and prosperity, associated with ARTEMIS, DEMETER, and PERSEPHONE. Daughter of the TITANS ASTERIA (sister of LETO) and Perses. Classical sources are the *Homeric Hymn to Demeter* (22–63, 438–440), Apollodorus's *LIBRARY* (1.2.4), Apollonius of Rhodes's *VOYAGE OF THE ARGONAUTS* (3.477–478, 528–530, 1,035–1,041, 1,207–1,224), Euripides' *MEDEA* (395–397), Hesiod's *THEOGONY* (411–452), Pausanias's *Description of Greece* (1.43.1, 2.30.2), and Virgil's *AENEID* (4.511, 609; 6.247, 564–565). Hecate was a goddess with highly varied associations, forms, and appearances. Her cult also varied greatly, depending on period and context. She is most consistently associated with witchcraft, crossroads, the underworld, graves, the night, and barking dogs. Hecate is also linked with the number three: She is often described as triple-formed or triple-faced. In mythology and cult, Hecate is linked with Artemis, Demeter, and Persephone. She accompanied Demeter in her search for Persephone, bearing flaming torches in her hands. Hesiod's *Theogony* devotes a surprisingly long and fervent passage to the praise of Hecate and her manifold powers: She offers protection to many as well as various gifts but does not appear in her more familiar guise of goddess of witchcraft, the nocturnal, and the sinister. There is little in the way of an independent mythological tradition of Hecate, but she is typically invoked by mythological figures—MEDEA, for example—who practice witchcraft.

In classical art Hecate is represented in triple form or in association with figures from Hades. She is holds twin torches on a red-figure volute krater from ca. 330 B.C.E. (Antikensammlungen, Munich) in a scene showing HERACLES subduing CERBERUS in Hades.

Hector (Hektor) Son of PRIAM, King of Troy, and HECUBA. Husband of ANDROMACHE and father of ASTYANAX. Brother of PARIS. Classical sources are Apollodorus's *LIBRARY* (Epitome 4.2–8), Homer's *ILIAD* (passim), Hyginus's *Fabulae* (106), and Pausanias's *Description of Greece* (9.18.5). Hector is a central figure in the *Iliad*, the chief Trojan warrior and opponent of ACHILLES. Homer makes much of the contrast between the characters of Hector and Paris: On the one hand, the mild-mannered lover Paris, who must be goaded into action, and on the other, the duty-driven Hector, who in the end dies in the struggle to protect his city. Hector is frequently described by Homer as a formidable fighter, but his most important function in the Homeric narrative is to die. He is a prime example of Homer's ability to sympathize with dying warriors on both sides of the war, and the epic poet's ability to evoke the immense pathos

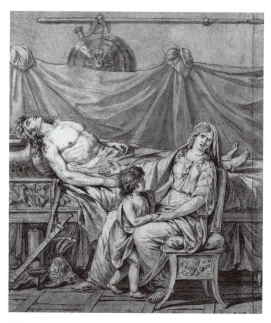

The Grief of Andromache. *Jacques-Louis David, 1782 (Musée du Petit Palais, Paris)*

and cost of war even as he insists on the glory of martial achievement. Hector slays Achilles' comrade PATROCLUS when Patroclus, wearing Achilles, armor in an attempt to turn the tide of war back in the Greeks' favor, approaches the walls of Troy. The death of Patroclus causes Achilles to reenter battle after his famous withdrawal. Book 7 of Homer's *Iliad* centers on the duel of Hector and AJAX. Hector challenged the warriors of the Greek army to a single combat to the death, where the victor was to receive the weaponry of the vanquished and the body of the dead hero would be given back into the care of his allies for proper burial. The Argives drew lots, and Ajax was selected as their champion, but Zeus stopped the duel before either was killed. Afterward, the heroes exchanged gifts; Hector received Ajax's purple war belt, and Ajax gave Hector a silver-studded sword.

Achilles eventually met Hector in a duel. Hector fled around the walls of Troy; Achilles was aided by the deceit of Athena, who appeared in the guise of one of Hector's com-

rades and encouraged him to stop and face Achilles. Achilles killed Hector in the ensuing confrontation. In his dying words, Hector begged that his dead body be treated well and returned to his father. Achilles instead dragged Hector's body around the walls of Troy and then kept it in his tent. The gods, appalled by Achilles' treatment of the corpse, preserved the body. Priam finally made his way to Achilles' tent and successfully negotiated the return of his son's body. Homer emphasizes the pathos of the future fate of Andromache, who will be taken off into slavery and another man's bed, and of young Astyanax, who will be killed by the Greeks.

In classical art, Hector's duel with Ajax and combat with Achilles were common themes. An example of the former is an Attic red-figure cup from ca. 485 B.C.E. (Louvre, Paris), and of the latter, an Attic black-figure hydria from ca. 520 B.C.E. (Museum of Fine Arts, Boston). A fine postclassical depiction of the Hector myth is Jacques-Louis David's *The Grief of Andromache.*

Hecuba   Daughter of Dymas or of Cisseus. Wife of PRIAM, and mother of 19 of his 50 sons, including HECTOR and PARIS. Hecuba appears in Euripides' TROJAN WOMEN and HECUBA. Additional classical sources are Apollodorus's LIBRARY (3.12.5, Epitome 5.23), Ovid's METAMORPHOSES (13.422–575), Homer's ILIAD (6.251–311; 22.79–92, 405–409, 430–436; 24.193–227, 283–301, 747–60), Pausanias's *Description of Greece* (10.27.2), and Virgil's AENEID (2.506–558, 7.319–320). When Paris was born, Hecuba dreamed that she was giving birth to a torch that would destroy Troy and had him exposed. In Homer's *Iliad*, Hecuba plays a limited but dignified role. In Euripidean tragedy, she becomes a more complex character. In Euripides' *Trojan Women*, Hecuba's seemingly endless suffering frames the play; she emerges as an impressive and majestic figure even in her downfall. Hecuba must endure the sacrifice of her daughter POLYXENA, the murder of her grandson ASTYANAX, and the enslavement of the Trojan women, including herself; she was awarded to ODYSSEUS as captive slave. In the same play, she attempts to persuade MENELAUS to kill HELEN. In Euripides' *Hecuba*, a darker story emerges. The first part of the play concerns the sacrifice of Polyxena; in the latter part, Hecuba learns that the Thracian king Polymestor, to whom her son, Polydorus, had been entrusted, murdered Polydorus and took his gold. Going from passive victim to violent avenger, Hecuba blinds Polymestor and kills his sons. At this point the tradition diverges: Hecuba is transformed into a dog either while being transported by ship to Greece, or while being stoned by the Greeks as punishment for her violent crime, or while being pursued by Polymestor's companions. Ovid's *Metamorphoses* (Book 13) offers a version of the story of Hecuba and Polymestor.

Hecuba EURIPIDES (ca. 425 B.C.E.) The date of the *Hecuba* is not definitely known, but it is usually considered to have been produced in 425–424 B.C.E. Euripides writes about an episode that occurs after the fall of Troy, when HECUBA and other Trojan women are beginning their lives as captive slaves, and the Greeks are preparing to depart for their homes. Hecuba, who has already lost so many of her children, now suffers a twofold misfortune. First, her daughter POLYXENA is sacrificed to appease ACHILLES' spirit; then, her son Polydorus is discovered to have been treacherously murdered by his guardian, King Polymestor of Thrace. This latter discovery motivates Hecuba to change from an attitude of passive suffering to active revenge. Her revenge is terrible: She blinds Polymestor and kills his children. Hecuba not only forces Polymestor to experience the wrenching pain of losing his children; she simultaneously renders him incapable of obtaining revenge in turn. Hecuba provokes in Polymestor the feelings of fury she herself experienced while denying him the satisfying outlet she had. *Hecuba* is a study in human evil and the relation among suffering, degradation, and violence.

SYNOPSIS

The scene is set in the Thracian Chersonese before the tent of Hecuba. The ghost of Polydorus, the son of Hecuba and PRIAM, explains how he was sent to King Polymestor of Thrace for safekeeping, but after the fall of Troy, Polymestor killed him, threw his body into the sea, and took the gold that Priam had sent with him. Polymestor's ghost exits. Hecuba enters. She has dreamed of the death of her son Polydorus and daughter Polyxena. The Chorus of captive Trojan women enters. It reports that the ghost of Achilles demanded the sacrifice of a young maiden, and ODYSSEUS persuaded the Greeks to sacrifice Polyxena. Hecuba summons Polyxena and tells her of the Greeks' plans. Odysseus enters, and although Hecuba reminds him how she once saved his life, he insists on taking Polyxena. Polyxena herself nobly declares her willingness to die. Hecuba begs to die in her place, but Odysseus refuses and leads Polyxena away. After the choral ode, the Greek herald Talthybius enters with news of Polyxena's death: She freely offered herself up to NEOPTOLEMUS's sword. Hecuba laments. Hecuba's handmaid, followed by other women carrying a shrouded corpse, brings to Hecuba the news of the death of her son Polydorus, whose body washed up onto the shore. Hecuba is now overwhelmed with grief. AGAMEMNON enters to ask about the burial of Polyxena. Hecuba seeks his help in punishing Polymestor; he refuses to help openly but agrees to turn a blind eye. Hecuba sends a handmaid to summon Polymestor and his sons. When Agamemnon leaves, the Chorus sing of the destruction of Troy and HELEN's culpability for the war. Polymestor enters with his sons. On the pretext of revealing to him the location of Priam's gold and her own jewels, Hecuba leads him and his sons into the tent. Polymestor is heard screaming within. Hecuba emerges, then Polymestor. Hecuba and her attendants have blinded him and murdered his sons. Agamemnon enters and presides over an impromptu trial. Polymestor and Hecuba explain their motives, and Agamemnon concludes that Polymestor is guilty of murdering his ward out of greed for gold. In the closing dialogue, the blind Polymestor predicts that Hecuba will drown at sea after being transformed into a dog, and that Cassandra and Agamemnon will be killed by Clytaemnestra. Agamemnon sends Polymestor away and prepares for the return journey to Argos.

COMMENTARY

The main character of the play, Hecuba, is a slave. She was the wife of Priam, king of Troy, and has now been captured by the victorious Greeks. Her family and kingdom are largely destroyed, and she now must live out the dismal aftermath of the fall of Troy. The Chorus, whose singing and dancing set the broader tone for the play, is composed of captive Trojan women. The stage setting speaks to the condition of the protagonist: It is not set before the doors of the royal palace, but before the tent that the female Trojan prisoners occupy in the Greek army's camp. The catastrophic situation of the Trojan women was a recurrent one in the ancient world: It was normal practice to enslave and sell defeated enemies. Yet Hecuba's situation is especially appropriate for tragedy. She was once the queen of a great city and is now a miserable slave. As the play continues, her sufferings intensify, and we come to realize how far even the greatest mortals can fall.

The theme of slavery forms part of the play's broader reflections on compulsion, freedom, necessity, and the nature of evil. Polyxena is a case in point. Like her mother, she is a slave, yet, when faced with death, she insists on freely choosing it. Before she is led off, she explicitly reflects on the life she would have had to lead as a slave: compulsion, humiliation, forced service as the bedmate of the highest

bidder. In the description of her death given by the herald Talthybius, we learn that she specifically demanded to be freed, so that she could freely present her neck to the sword, and so die nobly. She makes a final, spectacular display of her beauty, tearing her robe and revealing her breasts, yet, as Talthybius comments, even in falling onto the ground dead, she manages to do so in such a way as to preserve her modesty. She is singled out for doom in the way that others were not, yet, as we are reminded throughout the play by the enslaved female Chorus, she also manages to avoid the grinding misery of a slave's life that awaits the others.

Slavery, then, is not simply a matter of domination and social position. Certainly, raw compulsion plays a role in a person's range of choices, as, for example, when Odysseus brusquely reminds Hecuba that she cannot insist on her own preferences, even self-destructive ones (i.e., when she demands to be allowed to die in place of, or at least alongside, her daughter). Yet freedom and slavery depend also on ethical orientation and force of will. The free action of political figures such as Agamemnon are hedged round with cautious considerations of public opinion and expedience. Agamemnon sympathizes with Hecuba's need for Polymestor to be punished, yet, as he himself admits, his hands are tied. The army would mutter that he is motivated by his connection with Cassandra. He is enslaved by his own public image and the constraints it imposes on his actions. Hecuba is quick to point up the irony. She, although a slave, pursues her aims freely; he, the leader of the Greek army, cannot.

Agamemnon is skillfully inserted by Euripides amid this complex of themes. Already in the mythic and tragic tradition, he is a figure marked by compulsion and the grim necessities foisted on him by his own role as leader of the expedition. In Aeschylus's *Oresteia*, he was caught between the horror of killing his own daughter and the impossibility of abandoning an expedition supported by Zeus: Necessity drove him to kin killing. Now, by a certain narrative symmetry, the return voyage requires the sacrifice of another maiden, not his own daughter, but the daughter of his enemy and counterpart Priam. The sacrifice scene is reminiscent of Aeschylus's description of the sacrifice of IPHIGENIA: Both are virgins of royal blood sacrificed before a sympathetic Greek army.

We are also not allowed to forget the later consequences of Agamemnon's act: He will be killed by his own wife on his return to Argos. Besides the killing of Iphigenia, the main justification of Clytaemnestra's murderous plan is her husband's relations with the enslaved Cassandra, to which the present play refers several times. Agamemnon, who now, as leader of the Greek army, sententiously passes judgment on others' sorrows, will soon be engulfed in his own misfortune. In the play's closing dialogue, Polymestor predicts the death of Cassandra and Agamemnon. Agamemnon silences Polymestor, and, in his final words, expresses with ignorant optimism his hope for a successful return to Argos. The ominous implications are clear: Agamemnon thinks he is free to depart, but the dark necessity that determines his fate is even now drawing him into its net. His own tragedy is about to begin.

It is possible to read in Hecuba's violence a demonstration of the potential, motivating principles behind Clytaemnestra's subsequent actions. With immensely cruel irony, Euripides even has Agamemnon express utter disbelief at the idea that women could successfully plan and commit violence against men. What Agamemnon does not seem to realize is that in tragic mythology women, when motivated by powerful emotions such as bereavement, are perfectly capable of violent acts (above all, in Euripides). His incredulousness is the basis of his future vulnerability, and, finally, his death. Polymestor clearly also underestimates Hecuba. Perhaps the audience does too. Throughout the earlier portion of the play, the focus has fallen on Hecuba as grieving woman and enslaved victim. Her sudden conversion into murderess comes as a shock and inspires

a sobering realization: Passive suffering can be converted into violent rage, a slave can become a purposeful agent of vengeance, a woman can maim and kill. Hecuba is almost by definition a long-suffering victim. After Priam's death, she represents fallen Troy in all its wretchedness, and, unlike Priam, she continues to drag out her existence after Troy's fall. Her capacity for violence reminds us of the potential effect of degrading treatment on the conquered.

How do we evaluate this change in Hecuba? On one level, what she accomplishes is simply a harsh form of justice. Polymestor killed her son, his guest and ward; she kills his sons. According to Hecuba's grim metaphor, Polymestor, who both killed her son and stole his money, has "paid his debt." Hecuba further observes that there are deep, unchanging laws overseen by the gods, and these laws cannot be broken. The maintenance of such primal justice transcends the expediencies and institutions of human society. In the trial that follows Hecuba's revenge, her arguments demolish Polymestor's self-serving claims of loyalty to the Greeks and political necessity. If he was such a good friend to the Greeks—and his status as barbarian undermines any such claim from the outset—he ought to have rendered up Polydorus to them before, not after the fall of Troy. No, Polymestor's motivation was greed; he pretends to be the "friend" of whoever will best serve his purposes. Agamemnon judges, therefore, that the punishment exacted was just.

Agamemnon, however, is not really a reliable judge. He has shown himself to be utterly controlled by political expediency and has already committed himself to supporting Hecuba's cause tacitly. Euripides, moreover, encourages us to view Hecuba's act within the broader mythic context of revenge killing and female violence: Her plan is compared to the DANAIDS' murder of the sons of Aegyptus, and the Lemnian women's slaying of their male family members—both highly questionable actions on moral grounds, especially the latter one. Finally, the explicit anticipation of Clytaemnestra's murder of Cassandra and Agamemnon at Argos poses the question of revenge more sharply. Agamemnon, who here judges revenge killing an acceptable form of justice, will soon himself fall victim to the cycle of revenge killing dramatized in Aeschylus's *Oresteia*. The three central figures of the present play's final scene—Hecuba, Polymestor, and Agamemnon—are tainted by violent acts, and in particular, the killing of children. Each figure lives out his or her own tragedy, and none is capable of truly assuming moral authority. The blinded Polymestor appears to assume the prophetic "inner sight" of other similar figures in Greek mythology—TIRESIAS, OEDIPUS—yet in the present degraded context, he can only be viewed as a grotesque travesty of the blind seer. He is a seer who only recently ran around on all fours in vain pursuit of his tormentors, and whose main motivation in life has been greed. Polymestor's prophecy is the last resort of exasperated fury.

It is tempting to speak of the "dehumanization" of Hecuba, how the suffering to which she is subjected by the victorious Greeks robs her of her humanity. Yet it is not clear whether she becomes less "human" throughout the course of the play, or more so. The savage need to make Polymestor feel the same pain she feels, to match child killing with child killing, and, by blinding him, render him as powerless and impotent as herself, might be seen as an unpleasant but all too accurately depicted aspect of human nature. The animal metaphors are indeed striking: Polymestor, emerging from the tent, rushes around like an animal on all fours and later compares himself to a wounded animal hunting a pack of hounds. Later, as predicted by Polymestor, Hecuba herself will be transformed into a dog. One could argue that it all began earlier when Polyxena, a human being, was sacrificed instead of the usual type of victim, an animal. This metaphorical nexus, and the way in which the roles of hunter and hunted are confounded, recall Aeschylus's

Oresteia, in which revenge killing is equally the focus, and in which the first act of violence is a human sacrifice. These animal metaphors suggest, not a loss of humanity per se, but an uncivilized state of humanity.

The violence of feminine emotions is a special theme of Euripides, and the present play is reminiscent of the *MEDEA*. In a certain sense, Euripides combines two plot types, two tragic scenarios. On the one hand, there is the sequence of unbearable sufferings to which the protagonist is subjected, as in the *TROJAN WOMEN*; on the other hand, there is a chilling sequence of female revenge, as in the *Medea*. The pivotal moment of the play is the revelation of Polydorus's death. Polyxena's death is a terrible blow for Hecuba, but Polydorus's corpse provokes a further, different reaction: fury and an insatiable desire for revenge. The long-suffering Hecuba becomes a Medea-type character, who commits daring, ingenious acts and survives to taunt her male victim at play's end with the destruction of his family. Women, on the Euripidean reading, are devoted to their family and their "bed," i.e., exclusive sexual relations with their husband, but, when pushed beyond a certain point, become capable of destroying everything they previously devoted themselves to maintaining.

Hecuba does not destroy her own family, yet the killing scene is carefully designed as a grim perversion of the domestic: The women draw Polymestor indoors, enfolding him in feminine talk and touch; they examine the "Thracian" weave of his clothing, remove his weapons, and dandle his children in an affectionate manner, passing them from hand to hand until they are out of sight. The seamless merging of domestic kindliness and murder is especially chilling here and recalls Medea's capacity to mollify Creusa with a poisoned gift, or to kill her own children in their home. Medea's violent, unfeminine revenge nonetheless occurs in the domestic sphere. She deprives Jason of his children, and the capacity to make more children (i.e., with Creusa). When Polymestor first enters, Hecuba for a long time will not answer or look at him. She offers feminine modesty as a pretext, although her real reason must be her intense loathing for the man who killed her son and whom she is about to kill. The effect is brilliantly disturbing: Polymestor's long string of nervous pleasantries only intensifies the impression of Hecuba's malign presence and his impending doom.

Euripides' play about Hecuba presents a different figure than the stately, long-suffering queen we might expect. Her Euripidean rage destroys this venerable image of Priam's wife but also makes her into a memorable and significant literary character, later treated by Ovid and Dante. Euripides reminds us of the violent rage that potentially lies concealed within suffering and subjugation—an insight that may have been particularly relevant during the Peloponnesian War. Aeschylus's Clytaemnestra appears as an evil woman, capable of violence and of justifying her violence in subtle ways, but the same cannot be said of the Hecuba represented in the earlier half of the play. Hecuba still appears as the noble victim, a queen fallen from greatness. The problem of evil is not explicable by inherently bad character. By the play's end, Hecuba has recovered some of her grandeur at the expense of her moral integrity; she has achieved revenge and will be memorialized by the site of Cynossema ("dog's tomb"). The Chorus of captive women, however, will not achieve any such distinction. It is bleak words end the play. For it, there is only a long life of unremitting servitude.

Helen Daughter of Zeus and Leda. Helen appears in Euripides' HELEN, ORESTES, and TROJAN WOMEN. Addition classical sources are Apollodorus's LIBRARY (3.10.7–3.11.1, Epitome 3.1–6, 3.28, 5.8–22, 6.29), Herodotus's *Histories* (2,112–2,120), Homer's ILIAD (3.121–447, 6.313–369, 24.761–776) and ODYSSEY (4.81–85, 120–305, 15.56–181), Pausanias's *Description of Greece* (1.35.1, 2.22.6), Theocritus's *Idylls* (18), and Virgil's AENEID (2.567–603). Zeus seduced Leda in the form of a swan, and Helen was subsequently born from an egg. Helen's mortal father was TYNDAREUS, the husband of Leda. Her brothers were the DIOSCURI, and her sister was CLYTAEMNESTRA.

While PARIS is the most famous abductor of Helen, there is a story of an earlier abduction by THESEUS. Theseus, with the help of PIRITHOUS, kidnapped Helen with the intention of marrying her, but Helen's brothers the Dioscuri rescued her. Helen was said to be the most beautiful woman in the world and had many suitors. Her father, Tyndareus, made all her suitors swear an oath that they would uphold the rights of whichever one of them should marry her. MENELAUS was chosen as her husband and after the death of Tyndareus he became king of Sparta.

Paris's abduction of Helen sparked the Trojan War. The story begins with the famous Judgment of Paris. At the wedding of PELEUS and THETIS, Eris (Discord or Strife) threw a golden apple into the midst of the revelers, which was to be given to the most beautiful of ATHENA, APHRODITE, or HERA. Since none wished to be the arbiter of the competition, ZEUS asked HERMES to bring the three goddesses to Mount Ida and there be judged by Paris. The goddesses attempted to sway Paris's judgment. By Athena, Paris was offered wisdom and unparalleled military victory; Aphrodite offered him the love of the most beautiful mortal woman—Helen; and Hera promised him the rule of Asia. Paris accepted Aphrodite's proposal and presented her with the golden apple. He stayed as a guest at Menelaus's palace, while Menelaus himself was away in Crete at a funeral, and carried Helen off with him to Troy. In some accounts, Helen went with Paris willingly. In other accounts, he forcibly abducted her. Because her former suitors had sworn the oath to defend the rights of Helen's husband, her removal from Menelaus triggered the war against Troy.

The Love of Helen and Paris (detail). *Jacques-Louis David, 1788 (Louvre, Paris)*

A radically variant tradition, best represented by Herodotus's *Histories* and Euripides' *Helen*, insists that Helen never went to Troy but remained in Egypt throughout the war. In this version, the gods, for reasons that vary depending on the author relating them, fashioned a phantom image of Helen, and this phantom image went to Troy, causing the war and the loss of so many lives. In Euripides' *Helen*, Menelaus began to take the phantom image home with him after the war, when suddenly she disappeared. He then came to Egypt, where he met the real Helen, and he escaped with her from the barbarian ruler Theoclymenus.

Helen's reputation and character in literature vary widely. Homer's *Iliad* represents Helen in a relatively positive light, given that she is the cause of the war. Aphrodite bullies her ruthlessly, and it seems clear that Helen deeply regrets the destruction she has caused and does not fully admire her second husband, Paris. Helen's terrible beauty, in the Homeric viewpoint, comes from the gods, and this divine aspect of Helen makes her an object of admiration and wonder, aside from any questions of blame. In Athenian tragedy, Helen's name is normally evoked as the cause of immense destruction, although Euripides' *Helen* is more sympathetic. She appears vain in Euripides' *Orestes*, but at the end she is saved from harm by being made immortal. The hero Aeneas, in a disputed passage in Virgil's *Aeneid*, briefly considers killing Helen for all the havoc she caused. There is a story that the Greek poet Stesichorus, writing in the sixth century B.C.E., was at first critical of Helen but then was struck blind. He subsequently composed a recantation, or palinode. The rhetorician Gorgias wrote a speech in praise of Helen. Helen was a figure who clearly inspired strong, and often opposing, viewpoints throughout classical antiquity.

Helen EURIPIDES (ca. 412 B.C.E.) Euripides' *Helen* was produced in 412 B.C.E. In this play, Euripides develops an alternative trajectory of the HELEN story: Rather than actually going to Troy, she spends the duration of the war in Egypt. In the Euripidean version, HERA was angry at PARIS for awarding APHRODITE the golden apple as the most beautiful of the goddesses, and decided to punish him by creating a phantom image of Helen out of ether. Thus, Paris did not possess Helen, and yet Troy, because of the mistaken impression created by the phantom Helen, still had to suffer the consequences of the Greek expedition. As a result, countless heroes perished and lives were destroyed for a mere illusion. Euripides brilliantly explores themes of doubling, mimesis, deception, and theatricality, while at the same time reflecting on the destructiveness of war in the context of the failed Sicilian Expedition. *Helen*, like the approximately contemporary *IPHIGENIA AMONG THE TAURIANS*, ends "happily" with a successful escape, yet the implications of Euripides' tragedy remain troubling and provocative.

SYNOPSIS

The scene is set in front of the palace of Theoclymenus, king of Egypt; the tomb of Proteus, Theoclymenus's father, is in the foreground. Helen, alone on stage, tells of the Egyptian royal family and her own lineage. She goes on to relate how she was granted to Paris as a result of the contest of the three goddesses, and how, subsequently, Hera, angry at Paris for choosing Aphrodite, substituted a phantom image of Helen, not Helen herself. The war over the false Helen was waged between Trojans and Greeks. ZEUS, in the meantime, had HERMES take her to Egypt, since the king of Egypt at that time, Proteus, was considered to have considerable self-restraint. When he died, however, his son Theoclymenus came to the throne, and, lacking his father's self-restraint, began pursuing Helen. Now she is a suppliant at Proteus's tomb, seeking to maintain her honor and chastity in the expectation that, as prophesied by Hermes, she will one day return to Sparta and live with her husband, MENELAUS. The Greek hero TEUCER enters. He is astonished by the woman's "similarity" to the hated Helen, declares that he would like to kill her, but then controls his anger and apologizes. He identifies himself as Teucer, son of TELAMON. He was exiled by his father, when his half-brother AJAX killed himself at Troy because he had not been awarded Achilles' armor. He also reports that Troy fell seven years ago, and that Menelaus took back Helen, but has not yet arrived home, and is rumored to be dead; Helen's mother, LEDA, is said to have killed herself in shame. The DIOSCURI are said to be dead and yet not dead, and to have killed themselves out of shame for their sister. Teucer has come to consult the prophetess Theonoe, daughter of Proteus, regarding the foundation of his new Salamis. Helen warns him of the murderous Theoclymenus. After thanking her and praising

her for having a character "very different" from Helen's, Teucer exits.

Helen laments her fate. The Chorus of captive Greek women enters. She continues to rehearse woefully what she learned from Teucer: the death of Leda and the Dioscuri, her husband lost at sea. She laments that Hera and Aphrodite have brought about strife between Greece and Troy. Then, in a long speech, she describes her unfortunate condition: She has done nothing wrong, yet suffers from a bad reputation, and now that her husband is dead, there is no one who will know her true identity by sure signs. She considers suicide. The Chorus consoles her, casting doubt on some of Teucer's information. The Chorus persuades her to consult Theonoe as to whether or not her husband is still alive. Helen continues to lament her own fate and that of Troy, and then enters the palace with the Chorus.

Menelaus enters. He expresses the wish that PELOPS had never lived to beget his line. He has been wandering since the fall of Troy, and now, shipwrecked, wasted with hunger, and clad in rags, he seeks help from the palace; he has left "Helen" in a cave, guarded by his surviving comrades. He knocks at the palace gate. An old woman, the porter, opens the door. She tells him to go away, informing him that he is in Egypt, that the ruler, Proteus's son, hates Greeks, and that Helen, daughter of Tyndareus of Lacedaemon, is within: She came to Egypt before the Greek expedition to Troy. She, too, warns Menelaus of the king's hostility toward Greeks before she departs, closing the door behind her. Menelaus is momentarily confounded. Can there be two Helens, two Tyndareuses, and two Lacedaemons? He concludes that there is simply a duplication of names, resolves to await the king, and withdraws to the background.

The Chorus enters and reports that Theonoe has revealed that Menalaus is not dead but still wandering from land to land. Helen enters and gladly reports the same news. At this point, Menelaus comes forward, and Helen, not recognizing him in his current state, is afraid that he is a thug sent by Theoclymenus. After some time she recognizes him, but he remains confused by her resemblance to Helen. She insists she is Helen, and tells him how Hera fashioned the phantom Helen from ether. Menelaus is still unconvinced. A messenger enters. The messengers reports that the "Helen" in the cave vanished after revealing Hera's trick and proclaiming the true Helen's innocence. Menelaus is now convinced and joyfully embraces his wife. Helen tells him that Leda committed suicide from shame and that their daughter HERMIONE has neither child nor husband. The messenger expresses wonder at the present turn of events. Menelaus orders him to bring the news to their friends, who are waiting for them by the shore. The messenger, commenting on the ignorance of prophets, exits.

Helen warns Menelaus that he is in danger from Theoclymenus. Menelaus wishes to face him in combat, but Helen demurs. She suggests that they persuade Theonoe not to reveal Menelaus's presence to her brother Theoclymenus. They swear an oath to each other that they will die if they cannot escape together. Theonoe enters. She must either obey Hera, who now favors Menelaus and Helen, and conceal his presence, or obey Aphrodite and her brother's command by warning him of Menelaus's arrival. She is about to inform her brother, when Helen supplicates her. She beseeches her to adhere to her father Proteus's commitments rather than bending to her brother's will to buy his gratitude. Menelaus, stating that womanly tears are not appropriate for him, insists that she be worthy of her father and that he and Helen will die rather than give in to Theoclymenus. Theonoe is persuaded to support Menelaus and Helen and vows not to tell her brother, although they must devise their own escape. She exits. Helen proposes that Menelaus pretend to bring the news of his own death and that she demand a cenotaph burial at sea in a ship. They can then meet with his crew and use the ship to escape. She exits.

The Chorus sings of Helen and her strange destiny: She is the daughter of Leda and Zeus and is yet deemed faithless and godless by Greece. Theoclymenus enters with attendants. He is dismayed that Helen seems to have disappeared, but then Helen enters in mourning clothes. She reports that her husband has died at sea, as testified by Theonoe and the man (actually Menelaus) by the tomb. For his part, Menelaus provides a detailed account of the Greek funeral ceremony customary for a man perished at sea. The ceremony requires, among other things, a ship; the wife's presence on the ship, moreover, is essential. Menelaus, Helen, and Theoclymenus exit.

The Chorus sings of the abduction of PERSEPHONE, and how Aphrodite was the first to succeed in distracting DEMETER from her grief and making her laugh. It hopes that Helen may find a way to appease the goddess and make atonement for whatever act caused Aphrodite to hate her. Helen enters. She reports that everything is going smoothly and asks the Chorus to keep their secret. Menelaus and Theoclymenus enter. Theoclymenus somewhat grudgingly gives Helen permission to go on the ship and happily anticipates their marriage. He exits. Menelaus calls on Zeus and the gods for aid, and then he and Helen leave also.

The Chorus wishes Helen a speedy and successful return to Greece. The king enters from the palace. A messenger arrives with the news that Menelaus, who falsely reported his own death, has succeeded in departing on the ship with Helen. Theoclymenus is enraged, not least by his sister's betrayal. In rapid-fire dialogue, he announces his murderous designs on his sister, while the Chorus attempts to dissuade him. The Dioscuri appear from above. They command Theoclymenus to check his anger; it is Helen's destiny to return now with her husband; they address Helen herself and guarantee her a safe return journey; they promise her that she will be worshipped as a goddess and receive rites along with her brothers, and that an island on the Attic coast where she stayed on her travels will be named after her, and that Menelaus, after his death, will dwell on the Island of the Blessed. Theoclymenus agrees to desist and hails Helen's noble spirit. All exit.

COMMENTARY

The similarity between *Helen* (412 B.C.E.) and *Iphigenia among the Taurians* (ca. 414 B.C.E.) is quite close. A Greek woman vitally connected with the Trojan War, stranded in a barbarian land and under the control of a barbarian tyrant who displays a propensity for killing Greeks, meets, in a dramatic recognition scene, her beloved kinsman or husband, and subsequently escapes with him by fooling the tyrant with a sham ceremony. Like Iphigenia, Helen is closely associated with a leader of the expedition (in her case, Menelaus), and because of a mysterious divine intervention, her true fate and location are unknown. Iphigenia is supposed to have died in the sacrifice, but really resides among the Taurians, while Helen is supposed to have been taken to Troy, but really remains in Egypt. Finally, in each case, the play ends with the intervention of a deus ex machina (ATHENA, Dioscuri), who prevents the barbarian king from pursuing the Greeks as they escape by sea.

Both plays were written during the Peloponnesian War, close to the time of the Sicilian Expedition. The positive representation of the Spartan Helen may suggest an inclination for peace on the playwright's part, while the elements of romance and escape in a foreign land would have provided the Athenian audience with a much-needed distraction. Both plays are suspenseful and broadly (but hardly uniformly) optimistic in tone, and both emphasize the cultural solidarity of Greeks as opposed to intra-Hellenic strife; yet in the background of both plays there looms an immensely destructive war waged for questionable purposes.

The myth represented in Euripides' *Helen* is a particularly interesting one. Homer's *ILIAD* and *ODYSSEY* tell the traditional story: Helen, abducted by Paris, resides in Troy during the war that the Greeks wage to obtain her. Helen is not represented in a totally negative light by Homer, since it is clear that her destructive role is forced on her by Aphrodite, and yet in the broader picture she is not wholly innocent and is perceived to be the cause of many deaths and great destruction. The lyric poet Stesichorus (sixth century B.C.E.) is said to have first written of her in the traditional fashion as the cause of destruction and, later, when he was blinded as a punishment for what he wrote, to have written a palinode, recanting his earlier criticism of Helen and claiming that she never went to Troy. The historian Herodotus records a comparable version. Helen, on the way to Troy with Paris, was detained in Egypt by Proteus. In Euripides' play, Helen did not even board a ship with Paris but was deposited for safekeeping with Proteus in Egypt by Hermes: Only her phantom image (Greek *eidolon*) was sent to Troy.

How seriously should we take this myth? Helen is traditionally the cause of the Trojan War, and thus the justification for the most important sequence of events in Greek mythology. Aeschylus, in *AGAMEMNON*, linked her name with the Greek word for "destroy," and elsewhere poets, including Euripides, play on the similarity of Helen and Hellas (Greece): She stands for Greece, the most beautiful Greek woman, but also the cause of Troy's destruction and many Greek deaths. Yet the version of the myth that Euripides presents reduces Helen's centrality as cause of the Trojan War to mere report, a falsity foisted on the Greeks by the gods. It is merely her name that resides in Troy, a name that has become a byword for disgrace and faithlessness, and that has caused such mayhem; her body is innocent of wrongdoing and has remained in Egypt throughout the war. Helen is forced to adopt two identities at once, a virtuous one and an evil one: She experiences a split reality.

Euripides is engaging in subtle play with the categories of illusion, reality, and story. The "real" Helen is not the one the world knows, and when Teucer meets her, he mistakes the real Helen for a copy or likeness. In the same speech, Teucer compares the palace of Theoclymenus to the palace of Pluto (see HADES), king of the underworld, a place associated with insubstantial wraiths (*eidola*) and dreams. Egypt, for the Greeks, is likewise a land of mysterious inversions of reality, of phantoms and likenesses. While Euripides' play, in large part, insists on Helen's innocence as substantiated by the alternative myth of her residence in Egypt, we cannot help recalling that the play itself offers a representation or mimetic likeness that has no inherent priority over other versions of the myth. The playwright has sculpted his "Helen" out of words, just as the gods in the myth shape the phantom Helen out of ether.

Throughout the play there is a thematic concern with doubling and mimesis, naming, truth, and illusion. The origins of Helen, born from Leda's egg and the swan-formed Zeus, are a fantastic story, not easy to believe. Teucer arrives with the stories of Leda's suicide and the death of her brothers, the Dioscuri: Helen is then in the difficult position of mourning deaths that she has experienced only by rumor. The Dioscuri are an appropriate duo for the play, since, as twins, they reflect the play's theme of doubling and likeness: Helen, in being split into two identical selves, has come to resemble her twin brothers. Their reality is also dual; they are dead, yet immortal, and their story about them, as Teucer reports, is double. Menelaus, when he arrives in Egypt, is confounded by the doubling of reality: Can there be two Spartas, two men named Tyndareus?

The choice of Teucer as representative of the Greek expedition in Egypt is intriguing and potentially relates to the same complex of themes. In an immediate sense, Teucer has experienced catastrophic loss due to the war notionally caused by Helen. He has lost his brother Ajax and now has been exiled by his father, Telamon. His misfortune contin-

ues and even intensifies after the war itself. Helen can thus assess from his example how much suffering her "name" has caused among the Greek heroes. In addition, the scene with Teucer, who comes from Salamis, an island closely associated with Athens, may implicitly suggest rapprochement with Sparta. When he first sees the Spartan Helen, he wishes to kill her because of her physical similarity to "Helen," but by the end of their dialogue, they are friendly to and sympathetic with each other. Finally, we might include Teucer among examples of doubling. According to Telamon, he should have died at Troy like his brother, yet the duality of these two brothers is imperfect: One is legitimate, the other a bastard son; one perished by his own hand at Troy, one survived. Teucer, moreover, since he has been exiled, is destined to found a new homeland for himself, a second Salamis. This doubling produces further ironies: The beloved, legitimate son dies shamefully, while the rejected, illegitimate son reproduces his father's city. The figure of Teucer, in other words, recapitulates many of the themes associated with Helen herself: exile, doubling, a bad reputation unjustly assigned, the death of brothers.

Life and death are part of the play of illusion. The same word often used of Helen's phantom image (*eidolon*) is also used of the empty images or wraiths of the dead in the underworld. The Dioscuri are perfect as presiding deities of the play—twins, half-dead, half-immortal, dead and living by alternation. A key shift in the play comes when the central characters, Helen and Menelaus, begin to employ the strategies of doubling, illusion, and false death on their behalf, i.e., they take control of tendencies that have hitherto victimized them. Menelaus will "die," but only by report (Logos), just as, previously, Helen (to her grief) went to Troy only in name. The trick is old and trite, as Menelaus himself concedes, and goes back to Aeschylus's *LIBATION BEARERS*, but it nonetheless succeeds. In reclaiming their own reality, Menelaus and Helen produce a triumphant, metatheatrical ruse—a strategic play within a play that facilitates their escape.

With complex irony, Euripides has his characters assume theatrical roles morally antithetical to the moral integrity that they have been attempting to reclaim. The false burial ceremony, with its counterfeit rites designed to fool the barbarian Theoclymenus, simulates a false Greekness. The barbarian Theoclymenus, moreover, becomes a model host to Menelaus, who in turn betrays his hospitality, stealing Helen by deceit. Menelaus, in other words, must play the part of guest turned robber, i.e., the part of Paris. Helen, to prove she is not "Helen," i.e., the faithless traitor and destroyer of Greek lives, must assume the very character of "Helen," an ingenious trickster and escape artist by ship. The two characters live out an inverted reality in a foreign land, a place of exotic unreality, to recover their proper existence in Sparta. Whereas previously the false report/name of Helen in Troy overshadowed the true Helen residing in Egypt, now the false report of the dead Menelaus allows the real Menelaus to escape from Egypt by the device of a false cenotaphic burial. Menelaus is reported dead but absent in body; in reality, he is alive and present. The themes of life and death, insubstantial phantom and solid bodily reality, report and reality thus end up applying to Menelaus just as much as they apply to Helen.

If there was no true Helen in Troy, this simple alteration wreaks havoc with vast stretches of Greek mythology: the *Iliad*, the *Odyssey*, the story of the return voyages, and so on. All the stories of Greek heroes associated with Troy are thereby infused with a bitter sense of futility. It may not be accidental that this motif arises in a play performed after the spectacular failure of Athens' Sicilian Expedition, an expedition that was immensely destructive for the Athenians, based on a hope that turned out to be delusive. The gods in particular are revealed in a sinister light by Euripides' play: They fashioned a phantom Helen so that human beings

would destroy themselves for no reason. The messenger, before exiting, reflects on the emptiness of prophecy and mendacity of prophets, for neither the Greek prophet Calchas nor the Trojan HELENUS revealed the nullity and pointlessness at the heart of the war.

The question of divine justice and truth as revealed through prophets pervades the play. As in *Iphigenia among the Taurians*, the gods are at least in part revalidated by the play's ending. Theonoe, whose name refers to divine knowledge, turns out to be a true prophet of Menelaus's survival and, after some hesitation, sides with her pious father, Proteus, rather than her impious, violent brother. She does need to be persuaded, however, to follow the path of moral integrity and courage: Her initial instinct is to tell her brother immediately of Menelaus's presence in Egypt. The appearance of the Dioscuri at the end, moreover, prevents Theoclymenus from carrying out further violent designs. The two gods then reveal Helen's and Menelaus's future destinies, which seems to make good their previous suffering to some extent: An island will be named after Helen, while the gods will grant Menelaus a dwelling on the Island of the Blessed. Even Hera, Helen's victimizer, who created her phantom image and caused the Trojan War out of pique, has come around by the end and supports the couple's escape from Egypt. Only Aphrodite remains hostile and destructive.

The appearance of gods ex machina, however, is an exceptional circumstance and goes to show how brittle and fragile the sense of justice and meaningful resolution is in Euripidean tragedy; divine intervention, as in *Iphigenia among the Taurians*, is required to salvage something from a hopeless muddle, a world in which arbitrary destruction, loss of identity, and confused wandering appear to be the norm. Euripides, as elsewhere, radically polarizes the options, so that we are asked to choose between belief in the gods' capacity to order our lives and a violent chaos. As elsewhere, radical division that threatens to fracture our sense of the wholeness of reality and of our lives is a central Euripidean theme. *Helen* ends "happily" yet remains tragic in many of its core aspects: The audience has had occasion to appreciate the arbitrary power of the gods over human lives, the constant possibility of radical reversals of fortune, and the evanescence and fragility of human perceptions and knowledge.

Helenus A Trojan seer. Son of HECUBA and PRIAM. Classical sources are Homer's *ILIAD* (6.76, 12.94, 13.576, 24.249) and Virgil's *AENEID* (3.333). In the *Iliad*, Helenus is wounded by MENELAUS. He is later captured by ODYSSEUS and reveals that PHILOCTETES' bow is required for the capture of Troy. After the war, Helenus and ANDROMACHE were given to NEOPTOLEMUS as captive slaves. When ORESTES killed Neoptolemus, Helenus and Andromache married and ruled in Epirus, where they recreated a "little Troy," according to Virgil's *AENEID*. Helenus and Andromache host the wandering hero, AENEAS, and Helenus offers prophecies of the remainder of his voyage to Italy.

Heliades Daughters of Clymene and HELIOS. Classical sources are Hyginus's *Fabulae* (154) and Ovid's *METAMORPHOSES* (2.340–365). Sisters, whose names are alternately given as Aegiale, Aegle, and Aetheria or Helia, Merope, Phoebe, Aetheria, and Dioxippe. Their brother was the ill-fated PHAETHON, who drove his father's chariot recklessly across the sky to his death. In their grief, his sisters were transformed into poplar trees and their tears into amber.

Helios (Sol) Greek god of the sun. Son of the TITANS HYPERION, the sun god, and THEIA. Brother of Eos and SELENE, who, respectively, represent the Dawn and the Moon. In some cases, Helios is conflated with the god APOLLO. Classical sources are the *Homeric Hymn to*

Demeter (22–27, 62–89), Apollodorus's *LIBRARY* (1.2.2, 1.4.3, 1.4.6, 1.9.28, 2.5.10–11, Epitome 2.12, 7.22), Apollonius of Rhodes's *VOYAGE OF THE ARGONAUTS* (4.964–969), Hesiod's *THEOGONY* (371–374, 956–962), Homer's *ILIAD* (3.277, 19.259) and *ODYSSEY* (8.270–271, 12.127–241), Ovid's *METAMORPHOSES* (1.750–2.380, 4.169–270), Pausanias's *Description of Greece* (2.1.6), and Pindar's *Olympian Odes* (7.54–76). Helios drives a blazing chariot across the sky from east to west bringing daylight hours. He is preceded by Eos, who drives her own, lesser chariot, followed by Selene, after Helios's disappearance on the western horizon. According to Apollodorus, Helios cured the hunter ORION of blindness. PHAETHON, Helios's son by Clymene, recklessly drove his father's chariot across the sky to his death. Also by Clymene, Helios's daughters were Leucothoe (see CLYTIE) and Eurynome. Helios was also the father, by Perseis, of the sorceress CIRCE, AEETES (king of Colchis), and PASIPHAE (wife of MINOS). MEDEA was his granddaughter, and Helios provided her with his chariot as means of escape after she murdered her children. The HELIADES are also daughters of Helios. The Heliades guarded the herds of Helios on the island of Thrinacia. In Homer's *Odyssey*, the crew was warned not to eat the cattle of Helios, but driven by hunger, they neglected the warning and were later punished by death at sea.

In visual representations, Helios is often shown in his chariot, sometimes in the company of his sisters, as in an Attic red-figure cyclix krater from ca. 430 B.C.E. (British Museum, London).

Helle See ATHAMAS; PHRIXUS.

Hephaestus (Vulcan) Olympian god of the forge and of fire. Son of ZEUS and HERA. Hephaestus appears in Euripides' *ALCESTIS* and *HERACLES* and Sophocles' *TRACHINIAE*. Additional classical sources are the *Homeric Hymn to Hephaestus* and the *Homeric Hymn* to *Apollo* (316–320), Apollodorus's *LIBRARY* (1.3.5–6, 1.4.3, 1.7.1, 1.9.26, 2.4.11, 2.5.6, 3.4.2, 3.14.6), Apollonius of Rhodes's *VOYAGE OF THE ARGONAUTS* (1.202–206, 850–860), Hesiod's *THEOGONY* (570–584, 927–929, 945–946) and *WORKS AND DAYS* (60–71), Homer's *ILIAD* (1.571–608, 5.9–24, 18.368–617, 21.328–382) and *ODYSSEY* (7.91–94, 8.266–366), Hyginus's *Fabulae* (148, 166), Lucian's *DIALOGUES OF THE GODS* (11, 13, 17, 21), Pausanias's *Description of Greece* (1.20.3, 2.31.3), Pindar's *Olympian Odes* (7.35–38), and Virgil's *AENEID* (8.416–454). Hephaestus was later identified by the Romans with Vulcan, their own god of fire. Hephaestus's domain is the forge, and he represents blacksmiths, artisans, and sculptors. He is sometimes paired with ATHENA. It was from these two Olympians that PROMETHEUS stole the crafts that would enable humanity to survive and prosper. Hephaestus is a remarkable figure among the pantheon of Olympian gods; he does not possess physical perfection nor does he elicit the fearful respect of the other gods. Within the realm of his forge, however, Hephaestus's creations are masterpieces, described in some detail in the *Iliad* and *The Aeneid* and on this account his praises are sung in the *Homeric Hymns*. Hephaestus built incredible mansions on Mount Olympus for himself and the Olympian gods, the bronze man of Talos, and fantastic armor for the gods and mortal heroes.

There are different versions of the origins of Hephaestus. According to Apollodorus and Homer, he was the son of Zeus and Hera, but in Hesiod, the *Homeric Hymn*, and Hyginus, he was born of Hera parthenogenetically. Hephaestus was known as the "Lame One," either because he was born with a deformity or because of an incident in his childhood in which either Zeus or his mother threw him down from Olympus. In Homer's version of the myth, Hephaestus was crippled from birth, and in disgust, his mother, Hera, threw him down to earth, where he was rescued and raised by EURYNOME and THETIS. To take revenge on his mother, Hephaestus created a golden throne

for Hera, which, once she sat on it, held her down and prevented her from rising. DIONYSUS persuaded Hephaestus (in some accounts, by making him drunk) to return to Olympus and free his mother.

In some sources, Hephaestus was married to one of the three GRACES, but, more commonly, his wife was said to be APHRODITE. Notoriously she deceived him with ARES, god of war. Hephaestus was informed of their affair by HELIOS, and he devised an incredibly fine chain-link net to ensnare the entwined lovers, whom he then exhibited to the mockery of the other gods. The union of Aphrodite and Ares produced HARMONIA, wife of CADMUS and ancestor of OEDIPUS. Hephaestus presented Harmonia with a finely worked, yet cursed, necklace that brought suffering to her descendants.

In the *Iliad*, Hephaestus was married to Charis, one of the Graces. It was Charis who received Thetis warmly into their home when she came to ask Hephaestus to make arms for her son ACHILLES. Hephaestus obliged her unhesitatingly in gratitude for Thetis's care of him in infancy. The shield Hephaestus created for Achilles, with its five layers of bronze, is famously described in Book 18 of the *Iliad*.

Virgil tells a comparable story in the *Aeneid*. Here Hephaestus's wife is Venus (Aphrodite), who requested arms for her son AENEAS. Hephaestus descended to his forge in an underground cavern on a volcanic island off the coast of Sicily, where, amid the roar of an enormous furnace and scorching heat, he created spectacular arms for Aeneas: a crested helmet, a breastplate of bronze, sword, spear, and shield. Again, the shield was exquisite; Hephaestus carved onto its surface the very history of Rome.

In another myth, Hephaestus attempted to rape Athena. She broke away from his amorous grasp, but as she did so, his seed fell on the earth and from it was born ERICHTHONIUS, an early ruler of Athens.

Hephaestus appears as a minor character in other myths. He broke open Zeus's aching head

Vulcan *[Hephaestus]* at His Forge with Mars and Venus. *Engraving, after Parmigianino, 1543 (Metropolitan Museum of Art, New York)*

from which ATHENA emerged fully formed. According to Hesiod, Hephaestus created PAN-DORA, the first mortal woman, out of clay. Hephaestus also gave aid to the giant ORION, helping to lead the blind hunter toward the west to regain his vision. At the command of Zeus, Hephaestus chained PROMETHEUS to the boulder that would be the site of his torments. During the Trojan War, Hephaestus was on the side of the Greeks, and in *Iliad* 21, at Hera's urging, subdues the river Scamander with flame in order protect Achilles.

In visual representations, Hephaestus is often bearded, stocky, and muscled. He is sometimes depicted wearing the round cap associated with artisans and shown riding a donkey on his return to Olympus, as in an Attic red-figure skyphos

from ca. 430 B.C.E. (Toledo Museum of Art, Toledo). His attributes are blacksmith's tools, which he is shown carrying in the François Vase of ca. 570 B.C.E. (Museo Archeologico Nazionale, Florence). Here, Hephaestus carries a large hammer on his return to Mount Olympus. Other themes include the creation of Pandora and his attendance at the birth of Athena. An example of the latter is an Attic red-figure kylix from ca. 560 B.C.E. (British Museum, London), on which Hephaestus holds the mallet with which he struck Zeus's head to allow the birth of Athena. Pausanias's *Description of Greece* refers to a similar scene carved in relief around the base of the pedestal of the statue of Athena on the Acropolis. In a wall painting from Pompeii from the ca. first century B.C.E., Hephaestus, surrounded by the Cyclopes, presents Thetis with the arms that he made for Achilles (Museo Archeologico Nazionale, Naples). A visual theme popular in the postclassical period was Hephaestus's capture of Aphrodite and Mars in the golden net, as in Martin Van Heemskerk's painting *Mars and Venus* of 1536. In Enea Vico's engraving, *Vulcan at His Forge with Mars and Venus*, after a work by Parmigianino, from 1543 (Metropolitan Museum, New York), Hephaestus works at his forge in the foreground of the image while in the background Aphrodite embraces Ares in her bed. On the same theme, Hephaestus (identified as Vulcan) appears in Andrea Mantegna's *Parnassus* from 1497 (Louvre, Paris). Among the frescoes of the Villa Farnesina (Rome), painted in 1508–13 by Baldassare Peruzzi, a grand fresco over the fireplace in the Room of Perspectives shows Hephaestus working in his forge. Other postclassical images include Peter Paul Rubens's *Vulcan Forging the Thunderbolts of Jove* from ca. 1616 (Museum of Ancient Art, Brussels) and François Boucher's *The Forge of Vulcan* of 1747 (Louvre, Paris).

Hera (Juno) Olympian goddess of marriage. Wife of ZEUS. Daughter of the TITANS CRONUS and RHEA. Classical sources are the *Homeric Hymn to Hera*, Aeschlyus's *PROMETHEUS BOUND* (1.81, 365–369), Apollodorus's *LIBRARY* (1.1.6, 2.1.3–4, 2.4.8, 3.6.7, 3.8.2, Epitome 3.2), Apollonius of Rhodes's *VOYAGE OF THE ARGONAUTS* (passim), Hesiod's *THEOGONY* (326–332, 453–506, 921–929), Homer's *ILIAD* (passim), Hyginus's *Fabulae* (5.13, 22, 102, 150), Lucian's *DIALOGUES OF THE GODS* (9, 18, 22), Ovid's *METAMORPHOSES* (1.568–746), Pausanias's *Description of Greece* (2.13.3, 2.17.1–7, 8.22.1–2, 9.2.7–3.8), Pindar's *Nemean Odes* (1.33–72), and Virgil's *AENEID* (passim). Juno, Roman goddess of marriage and childbirth, was syncretized with the Greek goddess Hera. Juno gave her name to the month of June, which was seen as a propitious time for weddings. Hera married her brother Zeus and had four

children by him: ARES (god of war), EILEITHYIA (goddess of childbirth), HEBE (goddess of eternal youth), and HEPHAESTUS (god of fire and the forge). In some sources, Hera is said to have conceived Hephaestus parthenogenetically. Hera is said to have thrown Hephaestus from Mount Olympus because he was lame; in some versions, the fall caused his lameness. Hephaestus revenged himself on Hera by creating for her a throne that bound her to it went she sat on it. Hephaestus was eventually persuaded by DIONYSUS to return to Mount Olympus and liberate Hera.

The majority of Hera's myths represent the goddess as a jealous and vindictive wife. Zeus's extramarital loves were numerous, and his infidelities attracted Hera's wrath. She sometimes directed her anger at Zeus but was more commonly angry toward Zeus's consort and the offspring of the affair. The myth of Io is a good example. Io was an attendant of the Temple of Hera at Argos when she came to Zeus's attention. According to Ovid's

Juno. *Rembrandt van Rijn, ca. 1660–65 (Metropolitan Museum of Art, New York)*

Metamorphoses, Zeus set a cloud cover over the place in which he was seducing Io. Hera descended from Mount Olympus in the hope of catching Zeus in his deceit, but he heard her coming and quickly transformed Io into a cow (in some sources, Hera turned Io into a cow herself). Hera suspiciously asked for the heifer as a gift, and Zeus was obliged to acquiesce. Hera then set ARGUS, the All-Seeing, to watch over Io, whom he tethered to an olive tree in Hera's sacred precinct. HERMES, commanded by Zeus, freed Io and beheaded Argus. In honor of his service to her, Hera plucked out Argus's many sightless eyes and placed them on the tail of her bird, the peacock. Io was liberated from Argus's surveillance, but while she was still in bovine form, Hera sent a gadfly to drive her mad. Chased by the gadfly, Io fled to Egypt. According to Aeschlyus's *Prometheus Bound*, it was the ghost of Argus, in the form of a gadfly, that pursued and tormented her.

When CALLISTO gave birth to her son, ARCAS, by Zeus, Hera was furious with the flagrant display of her husband's infidelity and transformed her rival into a bear. Many years later, Arcas, hunting in the woods, came upon Callisto in bear form. Zeus stayed Arcas's hand before he killed her and placed mother and son in the heavens as the constellations Ursa Major and Ursa Minor. An angry Hera persuaded OCEANUS and TETHYS to circumscribe the path of the constellations.

Hera tricked Zeus's consort SEMELE into bringing about her own death. Semele's son by Zeus, DIONYSUS, was given into the care of Semele's sister INO, but Ino's care of her nephew attracted Hera's fury, and she inflicted a madness upon her that caused her to throw herself into the sea. In order to protect Dionysus, Zeus transformed him into a kid goat.

The birth of APOLLO was delayed by nine days and nights because Hera, jealous of her rival LETO, kept Eileithyia from attending the birth. Finally, the other goddesses in attendance persuaded Eileithyia (with the bribe of a golden necklace) to arrive and allow for Apollo's birth.

The most famous instance of Hera's enmity was that of HERACLES. Zeus had impregnated ALCMENE and decreed that the child about to be born would reign over the Argolid. Hera, aided by Eileithyia, delayed Heracle's birth by seven days and nights so that EURYSTHEUS, son of Sthenelus and cousin to Heracles, should be born first and rule instead of Heracles. According to Diodorus Siculus, Alcmene, fearing for the infant Heracles, exposed him in a field, where he was found by ATHENA. The goddess was struck by the child's vigor and persuaded Hera to nurse him. Hera agreed but, alarmed by the strength of the baby, gave him back to Athena, who took Heracles back to Alcmene to be nursed. Hera sent two serpents to kill him in his cradle, but Heracles strangled them. Hera's resentment continued during Heracles' later adventures, but eventually Hera was reconciled with him, and he was married to her daughter Hebe.

In the Judgment of PARIS, Hera offered Paris the rule of the world in exchange for his decision in her favor, but he rejected her offer for APHRODITE's. As a result, Hera sided with the Greeks in the Trojan War and was especially protective of ACHILLES.

IXION attempted to rape Hera, but Zeus tricked him into mating with a cloud, and the offspring of this union was Centaurus, father of the CENTAURS. Hera was also attacked by the giant Porphyrion during the GIGANTOMACHY, and he was killed by Zeus.

In Apollonius of Rhodes's *Voyage of the Argonauts*, Hera was sympathetic to the crew of the *Argo* and helped them navigate safely past SCYLLA and CHARYBDIS.

In classical art, Hera has a matronly appearance and is shown fully clothed. She often wears a crown and is depicted alongside Zeus. An example of this presentation occurs on a red-figure calyx krater from ca. 420 B.C.E. (Museo Arqueológico Nacional de España, Madrid). Hera appears in representations of the myths of Heracles or in the Judgment of Paris. A postclassical example of the regal Hera is Rembrandt's 17th-century *Juno* (Metropolitan Museum of Art, New York).

Heracleidae (The Children of Heracles)
EURIPIDES (ca. 430 B.C.E.) The dating of Euripides' *Heracleidae* is uncertain, but it is believed to have been produced around 430–429 B.C.E. Euripides here enacts the classic tragic scenario of supplication, in which a victimized group, driven from their home, seeks protection from another city-state. Euripides' play examines the relations between city-states and foregrounds the role of his own Athens as pious defender of divine laws. The play's action has implications for later legendary history, since the descendants of HERACLES' children (called the Heracleidae) were believed to have invaded and occupied the Peloponnese. The play's ending, in which the condemned EURYSTHEUS prophesies his own protective power as buried hero, anticipates the contemporary conflict between Sparta and Athens.

SYNOPSIS

The scene is set before the Temple of ZEUS at Marathon. After Heracles' death, Eurystheus, king of Argos and Mycenae, fearing that Heracles' sons would grow up to avenge their father, sent his herald to each city where the children sought sanctuary, using intimidation to have them expelled. After wandering throughout Greece, accompanied by their grandmother ALCMENE and Iolaus, their old kinsman and their father's comrade at arms, the children have at last come to Athenian territory at Marathon. Iolaus, standing as a suppliant before the temple, summarizes the situation: Two small boys are with him, the girls are inside the temple with Alcmene, while HYLLUS and the older boys have gone to find a refuge elsewhere in case a quick escape is needed. Copreus, Eurystheus's herald, enters. In an adversarial exchange, Copreus

assaults Iolaus, and Iolaus calls on the men of the town to protect him. The Chorus of old men of Marathon comes to his defense, insisting on the sanctity of the altar and Iolaus's status as suppliant. The two kings of Athens, Demophon and Acamas, enter. They learn of the situation, then listen to the respective arguments of Copreus and Iolaus. Demophon announces his intention to protect the suppliants for three reasons: They have taken refuge at the altar of the god; they are bound to each other through kinship; and Heracles performed a service for Demophon and Acamas's father, THESEUS, by rescuing him from the underworld. Before leaving, Copreus announces that an army headed by Eurystheus awaits him and will attack Athens. Iolaus expresses his gratitude to Demophon. Demophon exits. When he reenters after the choral ode, he brings dire news: The oracles insist that a well-born young woman must be sacrificed to PERSEPHONE. It would be madness for him to sacrifice his own child or to demand that one of his own citizens do so. Iolaus is in despair. Heracles' daughter Macaria enters and, on learning the situation, offers herself as a sacrifice. Iolaus expresses his admiration, and, after bidding them farewell, Macaria exits to meet her end. After the choral ode, an attendant enters to announce that Heracles' sons, including Hyllus, have arrived with a troop of soldiers. He summons Alcmene, and she rejoices at the news. Iolaus resolves to join the battle despite his age, and despite the protests of Alcmene and the attendant, he leaves prepared for battle. After the choral ode, another attendant enters with news of victory: All the children are alive; Hyllus and Demophon have distinguished themselves by their bravery; Iolaus was transformed, apparently by Heracles and his wife HEBE (Youth), into his youthful self and captured Eurystheus. They then bring in Eurystheus in chains; Alcmene taunts him and orders that he be killed. The Chorus is affronted at the idea of putting to death a prisoner of war without trial. Alcmene suggests that she take responsibility for having him killed so that the city of Athens will not be polluted by his death. The Chorus agrees. Eurystheus reveals an oracle of Apollo stating that if Eurystheus's body is buried at Athena's shrine, his spirit will defend Athens in the future. In particular, he will oppose the descendants of the children of Heracles when they come as invaders. He is led away, and all exit.

COMMENTARY

Euripides' *Heracleidae* begins with the familiar tragic scenario of supplication. In Aeschylus's SUPPLIANTS, Euripides' SUPPLIANT WOMEN, and Sophocles' OEDIPUS AT COLONUS, a group (or an individual), driven from their home, seek refuge in another city-state by means of the rite of supplication. By assuming suppliant status, the refuge seekers ensure that they cannot be killed, assaulted, or expelled without serious consequences for those who do so. They are protected by the god at whose altar they seek refuge, and thus have the power to bring pollution to the land. Politics both within the city-state and among city-states at this point can become complicated, however; offering refuge to asylum seekers typically will offend, and may trigger an aggressive response from the city-state that has expelled them or seeks them for its own purposes. The citizens of the supplicated city-state may worry that the consequences of protecting suppliants may be damaging to themselves; the suppliants, for their part, are by definition weak and cannot offer substantial benefits in return. In Euripides' *Suppliant Women*, Sophocles' *Oedipus at Colonus*, and the present play, the supplicated city-state is Athens. Athenian playwrights, perhaps not surprisingly, tend to represent Athens as a place of democracy, justice, and piety. They do not impiously send away suppliants or allow them to be assaulted; nor do they ignore the justice of their claims. In Euripides' *Suppliant Women*, for example, the Athenian Theseus condemns, and forcibly corrects, Creon's impious refusal to allow burial of the Argive dead. Here, the Athenians

at Marathon stand up for Heracles' persecuted children.

The set of oppositions that emerges is familiar and falls along the same lines as similar scenarios in Sophocles and Aeschylus: The foreign tyrant figure, here Eurystheus as represented by the herald Copreus (cf. Creon in *Oedipus at Colonus*), hubristically threatens both the suppliants and the supplicated leader, in this case, Demophon (cf. Theseus in *Oedipus at Colonus*). Moreover, as in Aeschylus's *Suppliants* and Euripides' *Suppliant Women*, an older male figure acts of protector and representative of a larger group, either of women or of children. There follows a military conflict or confrontation, in which the supplicated city-state usually defeats the army of the foreign tyrant. Euripides, then, is working within a fairly conventional framework.

The dominant tone of the play is political, and the focus is the relations among city-states. Elements of contemporary relevance are thus inevitable. The play, usually dated to around 430–429 B.C.E., must be read in the context of the Peloponnesian War and Euripides' earlier, more enthusiastically pro-Athenian stance. Here Athens represents piety, respect for kinship, and hospitality; Demophon, although occupying a leader's role, appears to rule jointly with his brother Acamas without conflict and to be dutifully democratic in respecting the citizens' wishes. Notably, when the sacrifice of a well-born maiden is demanded, he declares that he will not consider the possibility of sacrificing an Athenian. The Chorus of old men of Marathon stands up for the rights of suppliants and prisoners of war. The play ends with an Athenian victory in battle.

The closing scene between Alcmene and Eurystheus, however, presents a somewhat more complicated picture. Alcmene, who has played only a small role in the drama up to this point, brutally orders Eurystheus's death. The Chorus objects that he is a prisoner of war, and that killing him would pollute the city. Alcmene undertakes to have the killing carried out herself, thus avoiding the pollution of Athens. Athens, for its part, will benefit from the hero's grave; like Oedipus in *Oedipus at Colonus*, the dead Eurystheus will constitute a force of resistance against future invaders. Specifically, Eurystheus will repel the advance of the descendants of Heracles' children. The prophecy has contemporary relevance: The Heracleidae were believed to have invaded and subsequently ruled over the Peloponnese, and thus the Spartans would have been considered their descendants. Athens, as in the case of the Sophoclean Oedipus, neatly avoids being polluted by the hero's death while benefiting from the protective power of his tomb. The Spartans are doubly undermined: Their ancestors, the Heracleidae, are shown to be in the Athenians' debt; the victim of their ancestors will ward off their attack.

The closing focus on hero cult, Athens, and etiology are typical of Euripides. The violent turn of Alcmene is more surprising, given that her character has not been built up in any significant way throughout the play, and we have had little or no opportunity to appreciate her motives for revenge until she is actually carrying it out. The questionable ethics of the act are made clear by the Chorus's response, significantly balancing its earlier expression of horror at Copreus's violent treatment of the suppliant Iolaus. The ending in some ways resembles the ending of HECUBA. A female character, previously a victim, takes violent revenge on her victimizer. On one possible interpretation, she has been brutalized by her suffering, and cannot refrain from offering a response in kind to the cruelty to which she has been subjected for so long. In both the *Hecuba* and the *Heracleidae*, moreover, the victim himself gives voice to a prophecy of a future punishment: Hecuba will die at sea after being transformed into a dog; the descendants of the Heracleidae will be defeated by Eurystheus's ghost. In the *Hecuba*, however, Euripides has drawn a much more detailed portrait of the female avenger and presented the ethi-

cal derangement of her act more vividly. In the *Heracleidae*, Alcmene sentences Eurystheus to death after briefly rebuking him and easily persuades the Chorus to be complicit in her act. The ethical problem never fully emerges or presents itself for examination.

The other important death in the play is the self-sacrifice of Macaria, who volunteers to die as the victim required by the oracle. Here, too, we might feel that the importance of the act has been glossed over: She appears onstage only at the moment of her choice, and the only person to mourn her is Iolaus himself, who does express his grief, but only momentarily. Later he becomes more focused on personal participation in battle; Macaria's act is largely self-contained. Her speeches are vivid and forceful. She is fiercely disgusted by the idea that they would seek refuge and support from the Athenians but refuse to undergo any dangers or make any sacrifices themselves. She displays, as Iolaus appreciatively notes, the character of her father, Heracles, and a proud nobility. She disdains the idea of deciding on a sacrificial victim by lot, proclaiming "I won't be butchered as a gambling debt" (translated by Ralph Gladstone). Still, the episode in itself offers a dutiful display of virtue without much in the way of accompanying pathos.

There is little sustained focus in the play, and the only candidate for a main protagonist is Iolaus, Heracles' aged comrade in arms. Euripides sometimes offers vivid touches of characterization verging on the humorous, but the overall impression is that of a quintessentially minor character placed in a central role. The emphasis falls on his old age—strangely, since a nephew of Heracles should not necessarily be decrepit at this point. His age, moreover, is emphasized almost to the point of absurdity. The sequence in which he makes himself ready for battle, and shrugs off the warnings of Alcmene, is ridiculously long, and at times comic. Alcmene has to act as Iolaus's "nursemaid" as he goes into battle. We are surely in the presence of Euripides' interest in the subheroic—a tendency here taken to the extreme. Not only is Heracles dead at the outset of the play, there is no decidedly heroic presence to take his place. Demophon is no Theseus, and Eurystheus is a weak and morally repugnant figure. As reported in the messenger speech, Iolaus miraculously recovers his youth in battle and captures Eurystheus. The point of all this focus on Iolaus's age, however, is difficult to comprehend. There may be some contemporary reference, or a reference to a lost work of another tragedian.

Heracleidae, while not one of Euripides' best works, affords interesting points of comparison with broader themes and structures in his oeuvre.

Heracles (Hercules) The most famous of all Greek and Roman heroes. Son of ALCMENE and AMPHITRYON (or ZEUS). Heracles appears in Euripides' *ALCESTIS* and *HERACLES* and Sophocles' *TRACHINIAE*. Heracles also appears in Apollonius of Rhodes's *VOYAGE OF THE ARGONAUTS* and many other sources. A selection of classical sources are the *Homeric Hymn to Heracles*, Apollodorus's *LIBRARY* (2.4.8–2.7.8), Diodorus Siculus's *LIBRARY OF HISTORY* (4.9–39), and Hyginus's *Fabulae* (29–36). Some stories of Heracles were Greek and Roman in origin, but others were adaptations of legends from the wider ancient world. It is likely that intermingling and overlapping traditions of local heroes from different regions have been amalgamated into the figure of Heracles. Under the circumstances, it is not surprising that the image that emerges of the hero is complex and at times contradictory, and that a chronological narrative of his adventures is difficult.

Like many heroes, Heracles sprang from the union of a god (Zeus) and a mortal woman. Although mortal by birth, he became the greatest hero of Greek myth and finally achieved divine status. Cult practice throughout Greece offers testimony of his status as both god and as hero. In his *Histories*, Herodotus made a distinction between the cults of Heracles the deity and Heracles the hero. In legend, Heracles occupies a place between mortal and divine. His hero/god status forms of part of his image in the *Odyssey*. Heracles' courage and physical strength are divine, but he also displays all-too-human flaws.

In some sources, he is called Alcides after his mortal grandfather, but generally he is known by his more familiar name. Heracles's name means "Glory of Hera" or "glorious through Hera." His life was marked by Hera's hatred of him—the cause of many of the hardships that the hero endured—and not their mutual devotion. Nevertheless, the name is appropriate enough since, according to Diodorus Siculus, Heracles owed his fame to the heroism with which he overcame these hardships. The goddess thus unwittingly and unwillingly contributed to the creation of his glorious reputation.

With the important exception of Hera, the Olympian gods were kindly disposed toward him as the favored son of Zeus, and he enjoyed the powerful protection of ATHENA. He participated in many wars and adventures (some of which date from well after his putative lifetime), including an Amazonomachy, several Centauromachies, and the GIGANTOMACHY. His help was critical in the gods' victory over the GIANTS. He featured in the adventures of THESEUS, joined the expedition of JASON and the Argonauts, and freed Prometheus from the punishment inflicted on him by Zeus. He was absent from some notable events, such as the Calydonian Boar hunt led by MELEAGER, although he later came to marry Meleager's sister DEIANIRA.

ORIGINS

Heracles was descended from PERSEUS, king of Mycenae. Electryon and Sthenelus were both sons of Perseus. Electryon, king of Mycenae, and father of Alcmene, left Amphitryon in charge of Mycenae while he pursued the Teleboans to avenge the deaths of his sons. But Electryon was killed accidentally by a club thrown by Amphitryon. Amphitryon vowed to pursue the Teleboans on Electryon's behalf. While

Heracles and Three Other Figures in a Landscape.
Albrecht Dürer, 1496–97 (British Museum, London)

be born first and become ruler. The sources name various places as the site of Heracles' birth, but it is often placed at either Thebes or Argos.

Fearing the wrath of Hera, Alcmene exposed the infant Heracles in a field as soon as he was born, where he was found by Athena. She was struck by the infant's vigor and persuaded Hera to suckle the child, but he nursed so vigorously that he hurt the goddess, and she cast him from her. Athena then took Heracles away to be reared by his own mother. From then on, Athena was his protector. In another episode of his infancy, Heracles killed two serpents that Hera had sent to kill him and his twin brother in their cradle.

Raised by Amphitryon and taught by him to drive a chariot, Heracles was also instructed in archery, wrestling, and singing. While Heracles was still a child, he killed his lyre instructor Linus, in a fit of indignant fury. As punishment, Amphitryon sent him to mind cattle on Mount Cithaeron. There Heracles stayed until his 18th year, when he killed the lion of Cithaeron. In the same period of his life, a famous incident occurred that would later inspire many classical and post-classical artists, writers, and composers: the "choice of Heracles," or, later, "Heracles at the crossroads." The young hero was met at the crossroads by two women, the female personifications of Virtue and Vice. The more sensual female, Vice, represented the path of ease and pleasure in contrast to Virtue and a life of labor and heroism. Heracles chose Virtue.

While still young, Heracles organized the young men of Thebes to liberate their city from the Minyans, whose leader Heracles himself killed in battle. In gratitude CREON, king of Thebes, gave his daughter Megara to him in marriage. Hera now caused a madness to descend upon Heracles. While in its grip, he killed Megara and his children by her. According to some sources, Heracles killed only his sons and abandoned Megara. (For a very different version of Heracles murderous frenzy,

he was away, Zeus took on his appearance and described his victory over the Teleboans in such convincing detail to Alcmene that she accepted him as her husband. By him she conceived Heracles, but the next evening Amphitryon returned, and as a result, Alcmene bore twin sons: Heracles, whose father was Zeus, and Iphicles, whose father was Amphitryon. Several sources insist on Alcmene's innocence in this betrayal of Amphitryon. According to Diodorus Siculus, her natural chastity would have made it impossible to seduce her.

When Alcmene was about to give birth, Zeus decreed that the child about to be born, a descendant of PERSEUS, would reign over the Argolid. Hera thwarted him by delaying Heracles' birth for seven days, so that EURYSTHEUS, son of Sthenelus and cousin to Heracles, would see Euripides' *Heracles*.) In penance for this crime, Heracles went into exile and was forced to serve Eurystheus, now king of Mycenae, for whom he performed the famous Twelve Labors.

THE LABORS OF HERACLES

Though some sources acknowledge only 10 tasks, the conventionally accepted number is 12. Different texts have arranged them in different orders. One common ordering is:

1. The Nemean Lion
2. The Hydra of Lerna
3. The Erymanthian Boar
4. The Ceryneian Hind
5. The Stymphalian Birds
6. The Augean Stables
7. The Cretan Bull
8. The Mares of Diomedes
9. The Girdle of Hippolyte
10. The Cattle of Geryon
11. Cerberus in Hades
12. The Apples of Hesperides

The Olympians commanded Heracles through the Delphic Oracle to perform a series of tasks. These would not only purify him of the killing of his wife and children but would also win him immortality. At first, Heracles was reluctant to undertake the Labors, because they entailed subjugation to his cousin Eurystheus, a subjugation he felt bitterly because, had it not been for the enmity of Hera, he would now have been king of Argos and Mycenae. In many of the texts, Eurystheus is described as a lesser man than Heracles, an ungracious and cowardly master. From the beginning and throughout the trials, he endeavors to make Heracles feel the indignity of his position.

Heracles' First Labor was a combat against the Nemean Lion, an enormous lion impervious to all weapons. Heracles defeated it by cornering it in a rocky impasse and strangling it. He then skinned it and wore its hide. It provided him with protection in his further adven-

tures. In his very first labor, Heracles acquired the attribute, the lion skin, by which he would become universally known.

His Second Labor was the defeat of the Hydra of Lerna, a nine-headed serpent born of the union of Echidna and Typhoeus. To help the Hydra, Hera sent a crab that bit Heracles' foot. The crab was afterward placed in the heavens as the constellation Cancer. Heracles cut off each of the serpent's heads and asked Iolaus, his nephew and companion, to sear each wound shut to prevent more heads from growing; he was thus able finally to kill the monster. Heracles then dipped his arrows in the Hydra's poisonous blood. The Hydra became a constellation located south of Cancer. In his second task, Heracles provided himself with a formidable weapon—poison-tipped arrows—these, however, would later come to figure in his own death.

In his Third Labor, that of the Erymanthian Boar, Heracles was required to bring the boar back alive from Arcadia to Eurystheus. This was difficult because it required not only great strength but judgment and good timing. Heracles captured the creature and brought it back to Eurystheus on his shoulders.

The Fourth Labor was similar: He had to bring the Ceryneian Hind back alive. The hind was sacred to Artemis. Heracles pursued it and, at length, captured it in a net.

Heracles then went on to his Fifth Labor: to drive the birds out of the region of the Stymphalian Lake in Arcadia, where they had become a nuisance. This he achieved by shaking a bronze rattle (or bronze castanets) given to him by Athena, until the birds took flight. Once they were in the air, he shot them down with his bow and arrows.

The Sixth Labor that Eurystheus imposed was cleaning the stables of King Augeas, which had become polluted by many years of accumulation of dung. Heracles accomplished this by breaching the wall of the stable and diverting the river Alpheus to flow through it, cleansing the stable of its squalor.

In his Seventh Labor, Heracles captured the Cretan Bull, brought it before Eurystheus, then released it. Later, this bull ravaged Marathon until it was slain by Theseus.

Heracles subdued the man-eating mares of Diomedes of Thrace as his Eighth Labor. According to some sources, he tamed them by feeding them the body of their master, Diomedes.

As his Ninth Labor, Heracles fought the Amazons, and captured the belt, or girdle, of Ares from Hippolyte. In one version of the myth, Hippolyte at first willingly offered the belt, but Hera incited the battle by spreading false rumors.

Heracles' Tenth Labor was to fetch the cattle of Geryon, a triple-bodied warrior born of Chrysaor (offspring of Medusa and Poseidon). This adventure took Heracles to the island of Erythia, near the boundaries of Europe and Libya. The fantastic herd was guarded by Orthus, a dog (offspring of Echidna and Typhoeus), which Heracles dispatched with a blow from his club. He then defeated Geryon in battle and herded the cattle toward Greece. A later addition to the story appears in Livy's *From the Foundation of the City*, Ovid's *Fasti*, and Virgil's *Aeneid* in which Heracles encountered Cacus. In Livy, Cacus is simply a covetous shepherd, but in Virgil, he is a part-human fire-breathing monster fathered by Vulcan (see Hephaestus). He is equally grotesque in Ovid, who notes that he lives in caves on the Aventine Hill in Rome. While Heracles was being entertained by Evander, Cacus stole several of the cattle and devised a plan to hide them by confusing Heracles. He pulled the cows backward into a cave, making it seem that the cattle had walked away from the cave rather than gone in (a trick similar to the one perpetrated upon Apollo by Hermes). When Heracles came to drive his herd away, some of these bellowed for the stolen animals. The hidden cows responded, thereby revealing their hiding place. Heracles recovered his cattle and killed Cacus with his club. Hera sent gadflies to madden and disperse the herd, but Heracles managed to bring a sufficient number back to Eurystheus.

Heracles' Eleventh Labor was to fetch Cerberus, the three-headed dog (offspring, like the Hydra and Orthus, of Echidna and Typhoeus) that guarded Hades. Athena and Hermes guided him in his descent to the underworld. Hades (Pluto) agreed to allow Heracles to take Cerberus on condition that he subdue the dog without using his weapons. Heracles managed this by grasping the dog around the neck until Cerberus conceded defeat. While still in the underworld, Heracles released Theseus from his imprisonment there and spoke with the ghost of Meleager, whose sister, Deianira, he promised to marry on his return from Hades. Later, Heracles returned Cerberus to Hades.

Heracles' Twelfth Labor sent him to the Garden of the Hesperides, at the extremity of the known world, to fetch the apples of the Hesperides. Atlas, whose task was to hold the heavens on his shoulders, agreed to bring the apples to Heracles if the hero would temporarily bear his burden. But when Atlas returned with the apples, he refused to take back the weight of the heavens. Heracles tricked Atlas into reassuming his burden and brought the apples to Eurystheus. In Diodorus Siculus's *Library of History*, the Hesperides, Atlas's daughters, had been abducted by pirates. Heracles rescued them, and Atlas helped the hero in gratitude. Another version relates that Heracles killed Ladon, the dragon that protected the tree of the Hesperides, and acquired the apples without the aid of Atlas. Heracles presented the apples to Athena, and she later returned them to the Garden of Hesperides.

FURTHER ADVENTURES

Some of Heracles' adventures occurred during the period when he was performing the Twelve Labors but do not form part of them. He wrestled and killed the giant Antaeus. Since

Antaeus remained invincible as long as he remained in contact with the earth (his mother, GAIA), Heracles lifted him off the ground and crushed him. He also killed Busiris of Egypt, who put all strangers in the land to death. He cleared Crete and Libya of wild beasts. One of his exploits echoed the most famous episode in the life of his ancestor Perseus: the rescue of ANDROMEDA from a sea monster sent by Poseidon. In Troy, he saved Hesione, daughter of King Laomedon and sister of PRIAM, from a similar fate. Heracles saved her in exchange for the mares that Zeus had given as recompense for having abducted GANYMEDE, but Laomedon refused to make good on his promise of payment. In revenge, Heracles returned to lay siege to Troy. He captured the city, killed the king, and gave Hesione in marriage to his follower, Telamon.

Heracles displayed enormous strength and capacity for battle. During the Gigantomachy, Heracles' arrow struck the giant Alcyoneus but failed to kill him, since the giant could revive and regain his strength as long as he touched his native soil. On Athena's advice, Heracles dragged Alcyoneus away from the land where he had been born, and there he was able to kill him.

Heracles had repeated conflicts with CENTAURS. He inadvertently caused one Centauromachy (battle with centaurs) during a friendly visit to the centaur Pholus. Pholus was entertaining him hospitably, but the opening of a flask of wine unleashed a savage attack by centaurs of the surrounding area. Heracles subdued the majority of them, but Pholus was injured by a poisoned arrow and died. Heracles gave him burial. In another episode, the centaur NESSUS tried to assault Deianira, the hero's second wife. Nessus offered to carry her across a river, but once she was on his back, he attempted to abduct her. Heracles shot and killed him with his poisoned arrow. The dying Nessus had his revenge, however. The blood that he convinced Deianira to collect, to use as a love potion should her husband turn his attentions elsewhere, was a deadly poison and eventually killed Heracles. In yet another adventure, Heracles is also said to have killed the centaur Eurytion, either because he was on the point of marrying Heracles' own fiancée or because he was carrying away the daughter of Heracles' friend Dexamenus by force. According to Diodorus Siculus, Heracles was purified of the centaurs' blood by the institution of the Lesser Mysteries, which DEMETER established for his sake.

Heracles underwent a second period of servitude, this time in expiation for the murder of Iphitus, son of King Eurytus of Oechalia. Sources disagree as to the method and motivation for the murder. In Apollodorus's *Library*, Heracles is said to have fallen in love with Iole, sister of Iphitus, and competed in an archery match to win her. Though he won the competition, Eurytus refused Heracles the prize, and in a rage Heracles killed him and his sons. To purify himself of this murder, Heracles became the slave of Queen OMPHALE of Libya. First, however, he sought guidance from the Delphic Oracle, and when he received no response from it, he angrily grasped the tripod of the Oracle and was obliged to fight with APOLLO over its possession. Zeus intervened between his sons, sending a thunderbolt to separate them, and eventually reconciled them. The sources do not agree on Heracles' relationship to Omphale. In some, she became his mistress and bore him a son, Agelaus; in others, he was simply her servant. According to Ovid, while Heracles was in Omphale's employ, he was made to dress in feminine clothes while she wore his lion skin.

Heracles also participated in military campaigns against the Iberians and Celts and put down lawlessness and savagery along the roads of Europe. In Sicily, Heracles defeated Eryx in a wrestling match, acquired his land, then passed it on to its native inhabitants. Heracles and his army sacked Sparta and restored the exiled Tyndareus (father of the DIOSCURI) to the throne.

LOVES AND OFFSPRING

Heracles' first wife was Megara, with whom he had several children. In Euripides' *Heracles (Heracles Furens)*, Heracles murdered her and their children in a fit of madness induced by Hera. In other sources, Heracles spared Megara but passed her on as a wife to his nephew and companion, Iolaus. To purify himself of these murders, Heracles was indentured to King Eurystheus and was forced to perform the Twelve Labors. Deianira was Heracles' second wife. Heracles won her hand in marriage by defeating the river god ACHELOUS in a wrestling match.

Heracles had numerous offspring, some from his wives, some from the many extramarital liaisons for which he was famous. The Thespiades (the daughters of king Thespius) alone bore him 50 children. These went on to settle the island of Sardinia. The most famous of Heracles' progeny are HYLLUS and three other sons by Deianira. Euripides' *Heracleidae* concerns the fate of these children after their father died. In this tragedy, Eurystheus, who bore Heracles great enmity throughout his life, continued to persecute his children after his death. With the aid of Demophon, son of Theseus and now king of Athens, and accompanied by Iolaus, the Heracleidae began to mobilize for war against Eurystheus. The Athenians were advised to ensure military success by sacrificing a maiden. Heracles' daughter Macaria offered herself. The sacrifice was performed, and Hyllus, Iolaus, and Demophon led the Athenians to victory. In his account of Heracles' life, Apollodorus lists many more children born of his amorous encounters. After his death and apotheosis, Heracles married HEBE, the daughter of Zeus and Hera; with her, he had two more sons, Alexiares and Anicetus.

According to Theocritus's *Idylls*, Heracles also loved the Argive youth HYLAS. Hylas accompanied Heracles when he joined the expedition of the Argonauts. During the voyage, the crew put in at Propontis and made camp while Hylas was sent to fetch water. He found a spring but the nymphs there fell in love with him, drew him into the water, and held him fast. Heracles searched for him frantically, even allowing the Argonauts to sail on without him, but he was unable to discover what had became of Hylas. Eventually, grief-stricken, he was forced to concede defeat and to continue on his journey to Colchis, on foot and alone.

DEATH

Sophocles' *Trachiniae* describes the death of Heracles by the unwitting agency of his wife Deianira. Many years before, Heracles had shot an arrow dipped in the poisonous blood of the Hydra and used it to kill the centaur Nessus as he attempted to abduct Deianira. Before he died, Nessus encouraged Deianira to collect the blood around his wound and keep it as a love potion for Heracles should his attentions stray elsewhere. When Heracles brought his mistress Iole into their home, Deinaria accordingly presented him with a robe that she had anointed with this "love potion." Heracles put on the robe and was immediately seized by agonizing pain. Maddened by his torment, he killed Lichas, the servant who had brought him the poisoned tunic. Realizing too late that she had unknowingly poisoned her husband, Deianira killed herself. In the midst of dreadful suffering, Heracles asked his son Hyllus to build a funeral pyre on Mount Oeta, and there he ended his own life.

Apollodorus's *Library* is the main source for the story of Heracles' apotheosis. A cloud appeared beneath the hero as he mounted his funeral pyre and carried him off to the heavens, where he became immortal. In Diodorus Siculus's *Library of History*, Heracles died in the conflagration of the funeral pyre, but his bones were never found, possibly a sign of his transformation into a god. In yet other sources, Athena brought Heracles up to Mount Olympus at Zeus's behest. Hera was finally persuaded, after his apotheosis, to be reconciled with the hero.

REPRESENTATION

Classical artists depicted Heracles frequently and in a variety of media: coins, reliefs, sculpture, mosaics, wall paintings, and vase paintings. Like many other heroes, such as Theseus and Perseus, Heracles is depicted as a large male, often nude, with strongly defined musculature. Unlike many others, however, Heracles is often represented bearded, and thus not a youthful hero so much as one in the prime of life. He is easily identified by his attributes: a club and a cape made from the hide of the Nemean Lion. The Twelve Labors of Heracles were often represented in antiquity. Some were individual scenes. A black-figure oinochoe from ca. 500 B.C.E. (Harvard Art Museum, Cambridge) shows Heracles subduing the Cretan Bull; on a black-figure (white-ground) oinochoe from ca. 520 B.C.E. (British Museum, London), a victorious Heracles grasps the standing Nemean Lion in its final throes; a Caeretan black-figure hydria from ca. 530 B.C.E. (Louvre, Paris) shows Heracles, carrying his club and clothed in his lion skin, in front of Eurystheus with the three-headed hound Cerberus; a Caeretan black-figure hydria from ca. 525 B.C.E. (J. Paul Getty Museum, Malibu) depicts the nine-headed Hydra grasped by Heracles as he raises his club over it. The Labors were also treated serially, as in the carved reliefs of the Twelve Labors of Heracles on the Metopes of the Temple of Zeus at Olympia from ca. 470 B.C.E. (Olympia Archaeological Museum, Athens). Heracles frequently appears with Athena, with whom he had a special relationship. Of 12 metopes, she is present in four. Heracles' death was also depicted, for example, in an Attic red-figure pelike from ca. 440 B.C.E. (British Museum, London), where Heracles is reaching out his hand for the poisoned tunic that Deianira is presenting to him; he still holds one of his attributes, the lion skin, but he has deposited the other, his club, on the ground. An Attic red-figure pelike from ca. 410 B.C.E. (Antikensammlungen, Munich) depicts not just his death but also his apotheosis. In a section of the image, the hero is about to throw himself on the funeral pyre; and in another, he is shown in a chariot driven by Athena rising toward Mount Olympus.

Artists in the postclassical period continued to find Heraclean myths a rich source of inspiration, primarily in painting and sculpture. The influence on postclassical artists of the *Farnese Heracles* sculpture from the first century C.E. was immense. Antonio del Pollaiuolo's *Heracles Slaying the Hydra of Lerna* from ca. 1460 (Galleria degli Uffizi, Florence) shows Heracles wearing his lion's skin and dispatching the Hydra with his club; his Heracles is a strong, virile, dominant presence. Albrecht Dürer's *Heracles and Three Other Figures in a Landscape* of 1496–97 (British Museum, London) shows the muscular strength of the hero. Many postclassical artists recognized the moralizing potential of "Heracles at the crossroads," the scene of his choice between Virtue and Vice. It was a theme that lent itself well to the religious environment in which Renaissance and baroque artists lived and worked, and was therefore frequently represented in these periods. Examples of the theme are Albrecht Dürer's engraving *Heracles (at the Crossroads)* from 1498 and Annibale Carracci's *Heracles at the Crossroads* from 1595–97 (Galleria Nazionale di Capodimonte, Naples). Carracci's work formed part of a series of frescoes dedicated to the life of Heracles from the Camerina of the Palazzo Farnese, Rome, which also included a series on the loves of the gods.

Heracles Euripides (ca. 416 B.C.E.) Euripides' *Heracles* was produced around 416 B.C.E. As in Sophocles' TRACHINIAE, the final phase of the hero's life is catastrophic, despite his heroic achievements. Euripides has rearranged the usual ordering of events, however, and placed HERACLES' killing of his family chronologically after his Twelve Labors, not before them, thereby providing a tragic culmination to his career. The idea that ZEUS's son, the greatest hero of Greece, could be brought to so pitiful and shameful an end not by any misdeed of his own but by the jealousy roused in HERA by Zeus's adulterous intrigues is disturbing, and affords one of the play's central preoccupations. Is the divine ordering of human lives guided in any way by justice?

SYNOPSIS

The scene is set in Thebes before the house of Heracles, near an altar of Zeus the Savior. AMPHITRYON, Megara, and Heracles' three children sit before the altar as suppliants. Amphitryon recalls the origins of Thebes, and how Megara, son of Creon, was married to Heracles. Heracles, however, desired to reestablish himself and his family in Argos, from which Amphitryon had been banished for killing his father-in-law, Electryon. To secure his return, Heracles offered to give EURYSTHEUS the price of his labors, which he has been accomplishing; he has descended to the underworld to perform his last labor, which is to retrieve CERBERUS, but has not returned. In the meanwhile, Lycus, who usurped the throne of Thebes after killing Creon, intends to slay Megara and her entire family to destroy potential rivals. They are now taking refuge at the altar of Zeus. Megara is in despair and wonders if there is any point in drawing out life. Amphitryon attempts to encourage her.

The Chorus of old men of Thebes enters and expresses sympathy for the plight of the family. Lycus enters with his retinue. He taunts them, sarcastically belittling Heracles' reputation, calling him cowardly, and openly declaring his motives for wishing to destroy Megara's children. Amphitryon indignantly defends Heracles' reputation, calls Lycus himself a coward, and laments that no one has stepped forward to help the children of Heracles. Lycus announces his intention to set a fire around the altar and burn them, and threatens the Chorus for expressing sympathy for Megara's family. The Chorus reviles Lycus, calling him non-Theban and an immigrant. Megara and Amphitryon

consider how best to face their fate. Megara asks Lycus to allow the house to be opened up so that they might place funeral adornments on the children. Lycus consents, and exits. Megara and her children enter the house. Amphitryon criticizes Zeus bitterly, accusing him of sneaking into other men's beds without later showing any concern for his offspring. Amphitryon exits.

The Chorus sings in praise of Heracles' Twelve Labors but ends on a pessimistic note: Heracles has failed to return from the land of the dead, where his children will soon go. Megara, Amphitryon, and the children, dressed for burial, enter from the house. She mourns her children's dashed hopes and calls on Heracles to rescue them. Amphitryon calls on Zeus and prepares for the end. Heracles enters. He learns that Lycus has usurped the throne violently and is now preparing to kill his family. Heracles declares his intention of killing Lycus and defending his family. In consultation with Amphitryon, he decides to wait at the house until Lycus returns. In the interval, he relates how he captured Cerberus and freed THESEUS from the underworld. As he goes into the house with his family clinging to him, Heracles expresses his love for his children.

The Chorus sings of the unpleasantness of old age and the lack of a reward in life for good actions. It ends with a new commitment to song and the MUSES, praising Heracles' deeds. Lycus enters, and Amphitryon comes forth from the house. Lycus calls for his victims, and Amphitryon affects to be reconciled to his fate. Tricked by Amphitryon into believing that Megara and her children are still fruitlessly praying for Heracles' return, Lycus enters the house with his retinue to retrieve her. Amphitryon follows him into the house so that he can enjoy the sight of Lycus being killed.

The Chorus sings in triumph, praising Heracles as the offspring of Zeus and proclaiming that good conduct is rewarded by the gods; Lycus's death cries are heard from within. IRIS, the messenger goddess, and Lyssa, goddess of madness, descend onto the roof of the house from above. The Chorus cries out in fright. Iris declares that the anger of Hera is being directed at Heracles and his house: Zeus preserved his life until his labors were accomplished, but now he must incur the pollution of killing his own kin; otherwise Hera's authority as goddess will be undermined. Lyssa announces her lineage from Night and Heaven (URANUS) and expresses reluctance to harm so renowned a hero. Iris rebukes her. Lyssa is still reluctant but states that, since she is obliged, she will invade Heracles' breast and fill him with madness; he will kill his children and not realize what he is doing. Lyssa descends into the house while Iris rises into the sky.

The Chorus laments the reversal of Heracles' fortune. Amphitryon is heard crying out within. A servant comes forth in the role of messenger. He reports the children's death to the Chorus, then tells how it happened: Heracles was carrying out a purification ceremony with his family, since he had just killed Lycus; in the middle of the ceremony, he stopped and declared that he might as well kill Eurystheus first and purify himself afterward; he then moved about the house under the illusion that he was traveling to Mycenae, stopping on his way to participate in the Isthmian games; upon "arriving," he proceeded to kill his children and wife in the belief that he was killing Eurystheus's children. At length Pallas ATHENA appeared and stunned him with a stone before he could kill his father. The servants helped Amphitryon tie Heracles to a pillar to prevent him from doing more damage on returning to consciousness.

The Chorus laments the immensity of Heracles' misfortune, as the hero, tied to the pillar and surrounded by his slaughtered family, is wheeled out on a rolling stage device (the *eccyclema*) from the doors of the house. Amphitryon enters. He begs them to allow Heracles to sleep longer and fears that he will add further to his own defilement by killing his father. Heracles awakens. In dialogue

with Amphitryon, he gradually learns that he has killed his wife and children in a fit of madness. He considers suicide, but then sees his friend Theseus enter. He veils his head because he fears that the sight of him will pollute Theseus. Theseus, who has come because he heard of Lycus's threats against Heracles' family, learns from Amphitryon what Heracles has done. He bids Heracles unveil himself and proclaims his intention to join Heracles in misfortune as a sign of true friendship. Heracles removes the veil. He is defiant toward the gods, and Theseus advises him to restrain himself. Heracles argues that his life is not worth living, and as proof recounts his life, starting with Amphitryon's killing of his father-in-law and continuing through his last "labor," the killing of his children; he has nowhere to go: Hera has triumphed over a guiltless man. Theseus argues that all beings, gods included, suffer misfortune and commit bad actions; Heracles should not wish to have a better fate than the gods. Theseus offers to host Heracles in Athens, where he will be welcomed as a great hero. Heracles declares that he does not believe the stories about the misdeeds of the gods, for true gods need nothing. He agrees, however, to follow Theseus to Athens. He addresses his father and dead wife and children one last time. Theseus encourages Heracles to depart with manly fortitude, yet Heracles finds it hard to do so. Heracles asks Amphitryon to bury his family and promises to bury him after his death. He departs for Athens with Theseus. The Chorus laments the loss of its friend and then also exits.

COMMENTARY

Euripides' *Heracles* is founded on a deviation from the usual Heraclean mythology. In most accounts, he kills his family in a fit of madness early on, and in expiation for this he must carry out the labors assigned to him by Eurystheus. In the present version, he carries out the labors to win the right for himself and his father to return to Argos, from which Amphitryon was banished for killing his father-in-law, and it is only after finishing the Twelve Labors that he is driven mad by Hera and kills his family.

This reordering of events has important outcomes for the framing of Heracles' life in Euripides' play. First, and most important, it makes the murder of his family the terrible culmination of his career as a hero, not its beginning. As Heracles himself states in dialogue with Theseus, his last "labor," and most difficult, was reserved for the end, the killing of his family. Euripides thus maximizes the effect of reversal of fortune—from famous hero to tainted pariah—and leaves Heracles polluted by a murder that he cannot easily expiate by subsequent labors (they have already been completed). Euripidean tragedy brings into focus the difficult question of what is the purpose of the hero's life, given that it concludes with seemingly pointless slaughter. For all that he may receive the honors of a hero in Athens, he has been brought low and tainted; he has shelter only by Theseus's mercy and is now the recipient of aid from a hero whom he previously saved.

For Sophocles, also, Heracles' final "end" (*telos*) coincides with the return to his household. In the *Trachiniae*, the hero has been brought low, first by desire, then by his wife's (DEAINIRA) unknowing act of poisoning. Heracles' heroic itinerary reaches its final phase, not in the far-off lands where his labors were gloriously completed, or on the field of battle, but in his home. For both tragedians, in other words, making Heracles into a properly tragic hero involves detaching him from the serialized catalog of exploits, bringing him to a stop with the implosion of his house in classic tragic fashion. He is converted from a hero that conquers monsters and makes lands safe for civilization to a hero who tragically destroys his own kin and reputation. Along these lines, we might also compare him with Sophocles' AJAX—a similarly isolated figure, who undermines the basis of his previous reputation by slaughtering

a herd of sheep in a state of madness. There, too, a goddess causes the madness as a means of punishing the hero, and the scene of violence occurs inside the hero's tent/home. Returning home, ever since Aeschylus's *AGAMEMNON*, is a problematic proposition for heroes. The home is an extension or symbol of the hero's self, and thus the inevitable site of self-destruction.

Another consequence of Euripides' innovative version of Heraclean mythology is that emphasis is placed on the kin slaying committed by Heracles' father, Amphitryon. Certainly, Euripides gives Amphitryon a very strong paternal role, in view of the usual identification of Zeus as his true father. Amphitryon boasts that he shared his wife and the act of begetting Heracles with Zeus, and identifies himself with his son to a great extent: His entire happiness and sense of self evidently depend on Heracles. When Heracles is away, he assumes his son's role as protector of the family, albeit ineffectually. Heracles, as killer of his kin, becomes truly his father's son. In his speech to Theseus late in the play, he begins his life story with his father's act of kin slaying and states that a life begun in this crooked fashion cannot be straightened out again. In Euripides' version, then, Heracles is not only the tragic murderer of his own family and destroyer of his household; he is also subject, like so many other tragic protagonists, to an ancestral curse.

The theme of the household is physically embodied in aspects of the staging of the play. The play is set in front of Heracles' house, which affords a visual focus throughout the action. The house comes under siege by Lycus and his attendants. Later, when Heracles returns, his family clings to him as his massive form enters the house. Lycus is lured into the house to be killed, but subsequently, when Iris and Lyssa arrive, the goddess of madness initiates her attack on Heracles by physically invading the household from above, a destructive dea ex machina. Heracles' madness takes the form of an attack on the household, resulting in the slaughter of his family but also in the ravaging of the house's structure. At the end of his frenzy, Heracles is tied to a significantly broken pillar. In symbolic terms, Heracles is the pillar of the household, its main force and support. The shattered pillar to which he is tied provides all too accurate an image of the hero as failed support-structure of his house. Comparably, after he regains consciousness, Heracles declares that he has "put the topmost layers of stones on the wall" of his house's catastrophe. The hero's connection with his household, however, is severed once he has destroyed his family. At the play's end, he is led away from his home by Theseus to Athens, where he will lead the life of an honored exile.

Heracles' madness and violence against his own kin can be interpreted as a failed transition. Heracles is a hero associated with wandering, banishment, and labors of expiation. Heracles has not led a normal life as citizen and master of his household, since he has spent much of his life devoted to his famous labors *(ponoi)*. He has no stable domestic space or civic identity. It is no accident, then, that in this play, as well as in Sophocles' *Trachiniae*, the hero who frees the world of monsters comes to grief on returning to his own household and family. The Twelve Labors are respectfully praised by the Chorus as a quasi-canonical unit, and when Heracles returns home, he proclaims "farewell to my labors." His labors, however, have not been completed. After Heracles kills his family, his father calls him "man of much toil" *(polyponos)*, which now has a somewhat different meaning. Heracles confirms the idea, when he states that his final labor was the killing of his own children, the "coping stone" of the destruction of his house.

Heracles has failed to make the transition from violent labors to stable home life. His murderous frenzy perfectly mimics this failure. Even though he remains within the walls of his house, he is under the deluded impression that he is traveling from place to place in his usual manner and carrying out violent, heroic deeds. Heracles crucially mistakes his own

house for the broader world in which he normally wanders and wreaks heroic havoc. Nor is it accidental that the moment the madness comes on him as he is carrying out a rite of purification for his slaying of Lycus, a rite that, if completed, should have ensured his successful transition from violent warrior to protective father and husband. The border between the realm of "labors" and home is never fully established. Another emblem of this fatal intermingling of the two realms is that he kills his family with arrows steeped in the HYDRA's blood. He never manages to put aside his warrior identity. Indeed, at the play's close, Heracles comes to the terrible realization that he must keep with him the weapons with which he both carried out his labors and murdered his family—an apt symbol of his divided mythic legacy.

The catastrophic outcome of Heracles' return to his own house enacts a reversal of fortune, and this theme dominates the play: Heracles goes from being the most famous of Greek heroes to the "most unfortunate man in the world." Ship imagery traces the change. He first offers a tow line to his children; then he is moored like a ship to the shattered pillar; finally, in the play's closing lines, he is "towed" by Theseus toward Athens. The theme is a persistent one in Greek tragedy generally, and is also recurrent among Euripidean tragedies of the penultimate decade of the fifth century B.C.E. In *IPHIGENIA AMONG THE TAURIANS* (414), *ION* (414), and *HELEN* (412), a grim fate is averted by a surprise revelation or exciting escape from danger. In the *TROJAN WOMEN* (415), however, we see a reversal of fortune of another type: The royal family of Troy falls from its high station and its members are slaughtered or enslaved by the Greeks. *Heracles* (416) combines both types of plot in an interesting way. The opening portion of the tragedy, in which Lycus threatens Heracles' family, conforms with the former type, where members of a family escape a terrible fate at the last moment. Euripides has ingeniously set up his audience to be lulled into a false sense of relief.

The scene unfolds before the altar of Zeus the savior, and it seems only logical, as Amphitryon pointedly insists, that Zeus should come to his descendants' aid when they are in distress. The family's impending doom threatens to render pointless Heracles' labors on behalf of humanity and his divine ancestry. Later, when Heracles returns to punish Lycus, he is hailed as savior in place of Zeus. Finally, when Lycus is slain, the Chorus crows that the outcome proves the gods' support of just conduct.

The story, at this point, might be completed. Lycus, the hubristic tyrant, is brought low by the anger of the gods and the timely return of Heracles, just as, in *Helen* and *Iphigenia among the Taurians*, the protagonists escape from a barbaric tyrant at the last moment. The benevolence and justice of the gods has seemingly been established. It is at this point—some 800 lines into the play—with Heracles and his family within the house and Lycus slain, that Iris and Lyssa descend, throwing the apparently secure situation into turmoil again. Whereas in other plays, the descent of dei ex machina signifies a positive divine intervention on behalf of the protagonists, here the intervention is wholly destructive. Now the true reversal of fortune—from good to bad—takes place, and Heracles' story reaches its true ending.

Whereas the outcome of *Iphigenia among the Taurians* vindicates the justice of the gods in the protagonists' eyes, the present play comes close to demolishing the sense of divine justice. The sight of the altar of Zeus "the savior" on the stage is increasingly tinged with a dark irony, and Amphitryon's speeches against Zeus become bolder and more fiercely embittered. Even Lyssa, the hellish, snake-haired goddess of madness, displays moral scruples about following Hera's directives. She is reluctant to incite Heracles' insanity and has to be forced to do so. Ironically, she is the only one to show "good sense," to appreciate the wrongness of destroying the son of Zeus, who has accomplished so much for humanity. The Chorus, as it woefully observes the house being battered

under Heracles' murderous assault, compares his violence to the violence of Athena against Enceladus in the GIGANTOMACHY. There is an unpleasant grain of truth in the comparison. Heracles, son of Zeus, is carrying out a violent act endorsed by the Olympian regime. Athena herself will descend later, to stun Heracles and prevent him from doing further damage, but the slaughter itself has evidently been condoned. Zeus the savior has chosen not to intervene on his son's behalf. Heracles himself, in the face of these shattering events, echoes the thinker Xenophanes in declaring that true divinities are not motivated by petty reasons of pride or a desire to master others: They are self-sufficient. This dogma would appear to be contradicted by the action of the play, yet aptly represents Heracles' attempt to come to grips with the disturbing theological implications of his own life.

We should not forget that these terrible events occur at Thebes, a prime setting of tragedy. The action takes place in the margins of central Theban tragic myths. Lycus, the usurper, takes the place of Creon, son of Menoeceus, who took the throne after OEDIPUS's banishment. Mythic emblems of Thebes recur at intervals throughout the play, e.g., the motif of the Sown Men. Finally, when Heracles kills his family, the Chorus characterizes it as a Bacchic frenzy that ends in death, not the making of wine. DIONYSUS, after all, is associated with madness and delusion, and Heracles' awakening to the realization of his own kin slaying resembles that of Agave. Like the kin killer Oedipus, he will not end his days in Thebes. Sophocles' Oedipus is received in the Attic town of Colonus; Medea similarly speeds off from Corinth to Athens as a guest of Aegeus at the end of Euripides' play. Euripides thus conforms to the tragic pattern whereby a hero who can no longer dwell in his own community is received with honor by Athens. Theseus wins the reputation for loyal friendship and acquires the honor of being Heracles' host, even though, as he himself states, he is not subject to pollution for helping a friend. Athens thus appropriates the heroes of other communities, remaining largely untainted by the hero's violent deeds, yet adding to its own prestige by furnishing his final resting place. The theme of the hero's appropriation was enacted before Euripides' audience: Heracles was honored at Athens as the subject of Euripides' play.

Hercules See HERACLES.

Hermaphroditus A mythic figure with both female and male physical characteristics. Son of APHRODITE and HERMES. Classical sources are Diodorus Siculus's LIBRARY OF HISTORY (4.6.5), Ovid's METAMORPHORES (4.285–388), and Strabo's *Geography* (14.2.16). In Ovid's *Metamorphoses*, the youth Hermaphroditus bathed in a fountain at Salmacis. A nymph fell in love with him, but Hermaphroditus rejected her. The nymph (sometimes called Salmacis) wrapped herself around him, praying that she might never be parted from him. Her prayers were answered as their two bodies became one. The waters in which he bathed were afterward said to deprive men of virility.

In classical art, Hermaphroditus was represented with both female and male physical attributes. In a red-figure lekythos from the fourth century B.C.E. (Museum of Art, Rhode Island School of Design), Hermaphroditus has a female head and breasts and male genitalia and is winged. The *Borghese Hermaphrodite*, a Roman copy from the second century C.E. of a Greek sculpture from the second century B.C.E., shows the sleeping figure of Hermaphroditus. A postclassical painting by Bartholomeus Spranger, *Salamacis and Hermaphroditus*, from ca. 1585 (Kunsthistorisches Museum, Vienna) depicts the myth as recounted in Ovid.

Hermes (Mercury) A messenger and herald of the Olympian gods. Son of MAIA (a PLEIAD)

and ZEUS. Hermes is the Olympian god of travelers, prosperity (commerce), thieves, and fertility; he is also a psychopomp ("guide of souls"). Classical sources are the *Homeric Hymn to Demeter* (334–384) and the *Homeric Hymn to Hermes*, Apollodorus's LIBRARY (1.6.2–3, 1.9.16, 2.1.3, 2.4.2–3, 3.2.1, 3.10.2, 3.14.3), Diodorus Siculus's LIBRARY OF HISTORY (5.75.1–3), Homer's ILIAD (24.334–469, 679–694) and ODYSSEY (5.28–148, 10.275–308, 24.1–10), Lucian's DIALOGUES OF THE GODS (1, 2, 4, 11, 12, 14, 16, 17, 21, 25), Ovid's METAMORPHOSES (1.671, 2.686, 8.627ff), Pausanias's *Description of Greece* (2.3.4, 9.22.1–2), and Philostratus's *Imagines* (1.26). Hermes was aligned with the Roman god Mercury, and, according to Roman tradition, a temple in his name was erected in the fifth century B.C.E. in Rome.

Hermes is a youthful, trickster figure in the Olympian pantheon. Hermes' attributes are a wand (*caduceus*), a wide-brimmed hat (*petasus*), a purse, and winged sandals (*talaria*). His wand is magical. It can either bring on sleep or rouse from sleep. Hermes is both messenger and guide to Hades; in this role, he brings the dead to CHARON, to be transported across the river STYX. In general, Hermes is associated with mediation and crossing of boundaries.

As messenger of the gods, Hermes is sometimes credited with having invented speech. Diodorus Siculus maintained that Hermes perfected clear and concise speech and such verbal skills as a messenger requires. In the *Orphic Hymn to Hermes*, Hermes is a judge of contests, a friend of mortals, a trickster, and skilled in speech. Among his epithets are *Cyllenius* in reference to his birthplace, Mount Cyllene in Arcadia. *Hermes Koinos* is another epithet, which Diodorus Siculus interprets in light of Hermes' ability to negotiate for the common good.

Hermes is said to have invented the lyre, which he later presented to APOLLO, with whom he shares interests in music and prophecy. In Ovid's *Fasti*, Hermes attached seven strings to a tortoise shell, one for each of the seven Pleiades, in honor of his mother, Maia. In the

Parnassus. *Andrea Mantegna, 1497 (Louvre, Paris)*

Homeric Hymn to Hermes, the first song Hermes sang, accompanying himself on the newly created lyre, celebrated his own birth. In Apollodorus's *Library*, Hermes exchanged his pipe with Apollo for his trademark golden wand and was taught by the elder god the art of divination. Hermes is also credited with inventing the reed pipe (in some sources this is attributed to PAN, whose parentage is sometimes attributed to Hermes and a nymph).

Hermes, on the day he was born, both created the lyre and stole 50 cows from the flock of his older brother Apollo. He obscured the tracks of the stolen cattle in an attempt to mislead their owner. In Ovid's version, Hermes hid the cattle but was witnessed by one old man named Battus. He bought Battus's silence with a cow, and Battus insisted he would be as silent as a stone. Later, Hermes returned in disguise and successfully bribed Battus to reveal the cattle's location. For this disservice, Battus was transformed by Hermes into flint.

Hermes' motivation for the cattle theft is not clear, in Apollodorus's *Library* and the *Homeric Hymn to Hermes*, he claimed hunger. In Apollodorus, he afterward roasted two of the cattle and ate a portion, but in the *Homeric Hymn* he did not eat the cattle at all.

Philostratus's *Imagines* describes a painting that features the main outlines of Hermes' birth and theft of the cattle. Hermes is shown hiding the cattle in a crevice of the earth and slipping back into swaddling clothes while Apollo confronts a confused Maia with Hermes' misdeeds. In the same painting, Hermes also attempts to steal Apollo's weapons, but when he is caught, Apollo is more charmed than aggrieved (a scene also described in Horace's *Odes* [1.10]).

Hermes and Apollo shared the same love interest; they competed for the affections of CHIONE. In Ovid's *Metamorphoses*, Hermes and Apollo impregnated her with twins on the same day. Autolycus, a trickster figure, took after his father, Hermes, while Apollo bestowed musical skills on his son Philammon.

Many myths feature Hermes in his role as guide: He brought the newborn ION, son of Apollo, to Apollo's temple at Delphi in Euripides' *Ion*, returned PERSEPHONE to her mother, DEMETER, following her abduction, and escorted PANDORA to her earthly husband, EPIMETHEUS. He also led ATHENA, APHRODITE, and HERA to Mount Ida for the Judgment of PARIS. He guided PERSEUS to the GRAEAE in his quest to slay MEDUSA. In Homer's *Iliad*, Hermes guided PRIAM to ACHILLES' tent so that the king could offer a ransom for his son HECTOR's body.

Hermes has a close relationship to Zeus, whom he sometimes aided in the subterfuge necessary for his extramarital seductions, as in Zeus's affairs with EUROPA, GANYMEDE, and Io. Hermes was commanded by Zeus to free his beloved Io, who had been transformed into a white heifer and was watched over by ARGUS, servant of HERA. Disguised as a shepherd, Hermes lulled the herdsman into closing his many eyes in sleep with the aid of his reed pipe. Hermes then beheaded Argus (in other versions, he killed the Argus with a stone) and thereafter assumed the epithet *Argeiphontes*, or "slayer of Argus." Hermes also accompanies Zeus in the myth of BAUCIS AND PHILEMON. In

Apollodorus, Hermes killed the giant Hippolytus in the GIGANTOMACHY.

Hermes is associated with fertility and prosperity. A *herm*, a phallic pillar surmounted by a head, was placed in towns and on thresholds as a good omen. Despite this link to fertility, Hermes' offspring were few—when they can be said with authority to be his—and his loves were few. Some authors, but not all, identify Autolycus, Cephalus, Eurytus, Eudorus, and Pan as sons of Hermes. Another offspring attributed to him is HERMAPHRODITUS, whose mother was APHRODITE. In Ovid's *Metamorphoses*, Hermes fell in love with Herse (see AGLAURUS AND HERSE), daughter of King Cecrops of Athens, and when Herse's sister Aglaurus became inflamed by Envy (at the instigation of Athena), Hermes turned her to stone. In Apollodorus's *Library*, Hermes loved Apemosyne, descendant of King MINOS of Crete.

In addition to his more prominent functions as messenger and guide, Hermes was associated with prosperity in commerce—he is said to have invented weights and measures—and created the first wrestling schools. Hermes' broad domain of responsibility is the basis for a comic complaint, in Lucian's *Dialogues of the Gods* (4), about the incredible quantity of work for which the young god is responsible.

Visual representations of Hermes in antiquity depict a youthful god, sometimes bearded and sometimes not, wearing easily identifiable attributes: winged sandals, helmet, and *caduceus*. Postclassical images such as Andrea Mantegna's *Parnassus* of 1497 (Louvre, Paris) follow similar iconographic conventions. He is shown stealing the cattle of Apollo on an Attic black-figure hydria from the sixth century B.C.E. (Louvre, Paris). Hermes appears in images that represent the underworld as on an Apulian red-figure volute krater from ca. 330 B.C.E. (Antikensammlungen, Munich). Here HADES and Persephone are shown with other figures associated with the world of the dead, including ORPHEUS, SISYPHUS, and Hermes.

Another popular theme for Hermes is his combat with Argus, often in the presence of the bovine Io, as on an Attic red-figure hydria from ca. 460 B.C.E. (Museum of Fine Arts, Boston). Here the Hundred-Eyed Argus defends himself from Hermes, who unsheathes his sword. Hermes deals Argus the death blow in an Attic red-figure stamnos from ca. 430 B.C.E. (Kunsthistoriches Museum, Vienna), which draws on the same myth.

Hermione Daughter of MENELAUS and HELEN. Hermione appears in Euripides' *ANDROMACHE* and *ORESTES*. Additional classical sources are Apollodorus's *LIBRARY* (Epitome 3.3, 6.14, 6.28), Homer's *ODYSSEY* (4.1–14), Ovid's *HEROIDES* (8), Pausanias's *Description of Greece* (1.33.8), and Virgil's *AENEID* (3.327–332). Menelaus, while away at Troy, promised Hermione to NEOPTOLEMUS to secure his support of the war. She had previously been promised to ORESTES, either by Menelaus or TYNDAREUS. In Euripides' *Andromache*, Hermione is deeply jealous of Neoptolemus's concubine ANDROMACHE, with whom he has had a child, Molossus. Neoptolemus departs for Delphi to discover the reason for Hermione's childlessness, and Orestes arranges to have him murdered there in a riot. (In other versions, Orestes himself kills him.) In the same play, Orestes carries Hermione away with him and makes her his wife. Their child is Tisamenus. In Euripides' *Orestes*, APOLLO commands Orestes to marry Hermione, at whose throat Orestes has been holding a sword in a bid to force Menelaus to defend him against the hostile citizens of Argos.

Hero and Leander Mythological lovers from Asia Minor. Classical sources are Musaeus's *Hero and Leander*, Ovid's *HEROIDES* (18, 19), and Virgil's *GEORGICS* (3.258–260). The fullest treatment of this story is given in a poem by the fifth century C.E. poet Musaeus. Hero, a priestess of APHRODITE, lived in Sestos, across the Hellespont strait (now the Dardanelles) from Abydos, where her lover Leander lived. With Hero's torch to guide him, Leander swam across the strait to meet her nightly. In Ovid's *Heroides*, the young lovers send letters back and forth. Leander laments that the rough sea sometimes prevents him from going to her. She begs him to swim only when the seas are calm. The wind extinguished her torch one night during a storm, and Leander drowned in the rough seas. In her sorrow, Hero threw herself from her tower and died. The story has inspired many postclassical poetic works, such as Christopher Marlowe's *Hero and Leander* (1593) and Byron's *Written after Swimming from Sestos to Abydos* (1810).

Herodotus (fl. fifth century B.C.E.) Herodotus of Halicarnassus, the first historian of the classical world and sometimes called the "father of history," flourished in the fifth century B.C.E. Herodotus's history, or his "inquiries" to adopt a more precise translation of his work's title, is nine books in length. In broad terms, Herodotus treats the conflict between Greeks and barbarians, East and West. Specifically, he examines the origins and history and the conflict between Greece and Persia. The Persian Wars took place in the early decades of the fifth century B.C.E. Decisive Greek victories took place at Marathon (490 B.C.E.) and Salamis (479 B.C.E.); the Athenians played a central role in both cases. Herodotus narrates the history of the wars, but also explores their background. He first discusses the Lydian king Croesus, then the Persian kings Cyrus, Cambyses, Darius, and Xerxes. He includes in his discussion the internal politics of their realms, their contact with neighboring kingdoms, and their encounters with Greece.

Herodotean history does not follow a straight line. It is full of detours and anecdotal episodes. Herodotus openly relies on oral tradition, the information he has collected in his various conversations and travels, and the traditions retailed by particular peoples and ethnic groups. In many cases, Herodotus must negotiate among differing versions; there is no clearly objective truth but a web of sometimes conflicting opinions among which the historian must strive (when possible) to choose the most likely or persuasive. Herodotus, like Thucydides, does not draw a hard, clear line between history, myth, and legend. For Herodotus, the series of abductions of mythological heroines such as MEDEA and HELEN form part of the history of conflicts between Greeks and barbarians culminating in the Persian Wars. In Book 2, Herodotus considers different versions of the Helen myth and chooses the version in which she never goes to Troy, but instead remains in Egypt. His basis for choosing this version is a rationalist evaluation of likelihood, suggesting perhaps a historian's perspective as opposed to a poet's. Herodotus for a long time was denigrated in favor of the more "scientific" approach to history of Thucydides, but now, given the postmodernist enthusiasm for subjective involvement in the construction of history, Herodotus has become the object of renewed appreciation.

Heroides OVID (ca. 16 B.C.E.) The precise date of publication of Ovid's *Heroides* (Heroines) is not known, but it is believed that Heroides 1–15 are among his earlier works, possibly published around the same time as the second edition of his *Amores* (sometime after 16 B.C.E.). Heroides 1–14 are all single, unanswered letters addressed by mythological heroines to male heroes, who, in most cases, abandoned or otherwise betrayed them. Some scholars suspect that letter 15, from the poet SAPPHO to her lover Phaon, is not authentically Ovidian, on the grounds that Sappho is a historical and not a mythological figure. The objection in itself is not decisive, since ancient writers did not always draw a strict distinction between the two. Sappho's biography, in any case, is a

species of myth, and Phaon is a mythic figure. Heroides 16–21 are distinct: They are paired letters exchanged, in each case, between a hero and a heroine. Scholars, on stylistic grounds, date these paired letters later, roughly to the period of composition of Ovid's *FASTI* in the early years C.E.

SYNOPSIS

The following is a summary of the 21 letters of the *Heroides*. 1: PENELOPE writes to her husband Ulysses (see ODYSSEUS) to tell him of her longing for his return. 2: Phyllis, a Thracian princess, writes to DEMOPHON, son of THESEUS; she was seduced and then abandoned by Demophon, and now laments his behavior. 3: BRISEIS, a captive slave, writes to her former master and lover ACHILLES. Achilles was obliged to give her up to AGAMEMNON; she reproves him for giving her up so easily and wishes to return to him. 4: PHAEDRA, wife of Theseus, writes to HIPPOLYTUS, his son by the Amazon Hippolyte, and attempts to seduce him. 5: OENONE, a nymph whom PARIS married in his youth, pleads with him to give HELEN back to the Greeks and return to her. 6: Hypsipyle, with whom JASON sojourned on Lemnos, writes to her former lover (she claims they were married), rebukes him for taking up with MEDEA, and warns him of Medea's dangerous nature. She ends her letter with a curse. 7: DIDO, queen of Carthage, writes to her lover AENEAS, who is on the point of departing for Italy. She begs him to stay and threatens to kill herself with the knife he gave her if he does not. 8: Hermione, daughter of MENELAUS and HELEN, writes to ORESTES, to whom she was first promised by her maternal grandfather, Tyndareus. Menelaus, however, offered her to Pyrrhus (also called NEOPTOLEMUS), Achilles' son, in return for his help in the Trojan War. She is unhappy as Pyrrhus's wife and exhorts Orestes to claim her as his bride. 9: DEIANIRA writes to her husband, HERACLES, who has fallen under the spell of Iole, daughter of King Eurytus, whose city, Oechalia, he has just sacked. She compares Heracles' great deeds of the past with his ignoble position now, contemplates her own suicide, and desperately regrets sending Heracles the robe she now realizes was poisoned. 10: ARIADNE, daughter of King MINOS, writes to Theseus, whom she aided in his plans to slay the MINOTAUR. He has abandoned her and is now sailing to Athens. She begs him to sail back to her and anticipates her own death. 11: Canace, daughter of AEOLUS, writes to her brother Maraceus, with whom she has committed incest. She became pregnant, attempted abortion, failed, and gave birth. The nurse tried to remove the baby from the palace but was discovered. Aeolus has ordered Canace to commit suicide and the baby to be exposed. 12: Medea writes to Jason, who has now taken a new wife, Creusa, daughter of the king of Corinth. She reminds Jason of all that he owes her and asks him to come back to her bed. She threatens unspecified revenge if he does not. 13: LAODAMIA writes to her husband, Protesilaus, who has departed for the Trojan War. She begs him to be careful to stay alive so that he may return to her. (Protesilaus is said to have been the first to land on Trojan soil, and the first to die. In some versions, Laodamia, because she grieves so deeply, is allowed to be with Protesilaus for three hours after his death at Troy. She then commits suicide to remain with him.) 14: Hypermnestra, one of the 50 daughters of Danaus, writes to Lynceus, the only surviving son of the 50 sons of Aegyptus. Danaus instructed all his daughters to kill, on their wedding night, their 50 cousins, who had pursued them aggressively and forced them to consent to the marriage. Hypermnestra alone spared her husband. Her father, Danaus, imprisoned her, and she now asks Lynceus to come and save her. 15: The poet Sappho writes to her lover Phaon, who has left her and gone to Sicily. She implores him to return and threatens to commit suicide by leaping from the Leucadian cliffs. 16: Paris writes to Helen. Menelaus has departed for Crete, and he sees this to be the perfect opportunity to commence their love affair. Moreover, he urges her to return to

Troy with him. He advances many arguments: APHRODITE gave Helen to him, therefore she is rightfully his; he is very handsome; he is driven by love; her beauty is so great she cannot expect to remain chaste; Troy has great wealth and will afford her great luxury. 17: Helen responds to Paris. She is pleased by his love but does not feel Troy offers any great advantages; nor is she willing to give up her position as Menelaus's wife and her good name. She fears war and destruction. For the time being, however, she expresses cautious interest in his adulterous propositions. 18: LEANDER from Abydos writes to HERO of Sestos. Leander has already crossed the Hellespont by swimming to visit his lover, Hero. Now the rough seas obstruct him, and he hopes they will soon relent; he imagines his dead body washed up on shore and discovered by Hero. 19: Hero responds to Leander. She is eager to see him, and encourages him to brave the waters. But she is also anxious for his safety and relates how she dreamed that a dead dolphin was washed up on shore. 20: Acontius writes to Cydippe. He tricked her by rolling an apple before her with an inscription stating "I will swear I will marry Acontius" on it; she read it aloud and thus unwittingly made an oath to marry him. He admits the deception, but urges her to accept him nonetheless. He observes that she is engaged to be married to another man, and that she has become ill; the goddess Diana (see ARTEMIS), in whose temple she made her "oath," is punishing her for not keeping her word. 21: Cydippe responds to Acontius. She deplores his trickery and argues that an oath made unwittingly and without active intention is not a true oath. Nonetheless, she appears to be indifferent to her promised husband and to harbor feelings of love for Acontius despite herself. In the letter's closing words, she bids him come to her.

COMMENTARY

Ovid's *Heroides* are a series of letters notionally composed by mythological heroines and heroes in elegiac couplets, the meter characteristic of

Latin love elegy. The salient feature of originality in this Ovidian collection is the combination of the epistolary mode with elegiac genre and mythological subject matter. Most Roman love elegy is spoken by a first-person lover identified, in broad terms, with the poet himself. The love elegist speaks as a lover defined generically and conventionally within a literary fiction of *amor* (love/passion), and thus only in a complicated way can the lover/speaker represent the biographical author. Still, the terms of the fiction work to merge the identities of lover and poet. In Ovid's *Heroides*, the meter, style, subject, and many of the individual flourishes and motifs are those of love elegy, yet the writers are diverse mythological figures, mostly women, rather than the male poet-lover. There are limited precedents both for sustained mythological focus and for ventriloquism of female figures in previous elegy. Yet Ovid, in combining these different strands, has created a literary work of a new and different kind.

Previous elegists, including Ovid himself, inserted mythological comparisons into their first-person discourse as a way of expanding, complicating, and illustrating some aspect of their love affair. The new form of the *Heroides* allows Ovid to rewrite major myths and mythic sequences from an elegiac perspective. Among Ovid's enduring interests is the juxtaposition of different genres and the sometimes sharply dissonant and ironic effects of their differing perspectives on the same event or situation. The myths that make up the *Heroides* have been treated, in many cases famously and definitively, in other genres, above all in tragedy and epic. Ovid inserts his letters in the interstices of epic and tragic narratives, challenging the reader to relate the subjective utterances of the heroines to the traditional elements of their story. For example, Briseis writes to Achilles, and in so doing, shifts the emphases of the Homeric narrative. Achilles, in her view, ought to have made a greater effort to keep her, and could still claim her if he wished to do so. In the *Iliad*, the key factor is

Achilles' sense of honor, and Briseis is a token or trophy exchanged between two men in a struggle for authority. In the *Heroides*, Briseis has a viewpoint and a will of her own, which she does not hesitate to express.

The epistolary mode adds its own distinctive set of concerns and perspectives. The epistle is, at times, almost provocatively partial and limited in its vision. The letter writer is distanced from the person he or she is addressing; the writer does not even enjoy the expanded scope of knowledge achieved by direct dialogue. Is Ulysses dead or alive? How would Hippolytus view Phaedra's passion for him? The letter writer must produce his or her side of the entire communication in ignorance of these crucial pieces of the puzzle. The epistle provides a form of mythological narrative, if it can even be termed narrative, that is emphatically *not* omniscient, *not* synoptic, *not* objective, and thus thrives on the already rich ambiguities of mythological traditions. At the same time, the epistolary form returns the reader to the material act of writing itself, whereas most previous elegiac poetry privileges fictions of voice and song. We are reminded that much of what we call myth depends on written traditions and written modes of preservation and circulation. The letter writer's perspective, however partial and slanted, is in this sense truer to the sometimes crooked paths of mythography than synoptic narrative. As we read the letter writers of the *Heroides* deliberately and even artfully construing their situation from their own inevitably biased viewpoints, we may have occasion to observe that the writing of myth by mythographers and poets is not fundamentally more objective or less calculating.

A further element in this mix of genres, styles, and modes is the presence of rhetoric and, in particular, the contemporary phenomenon of declamation. Declamation was the delivery of rhetorical practice speeches on set themes. In the Augustan period, declamation ceased to be exclusively a pedagogical practice and became an arena of adult display and competition as well. According to Seneca the Elder, who wrote on declamation and famous declaimers, Ovid himself practiced declamation. One form of declamation is the *suasoria*, a speech persuading a historical or mythological figure to follow a certain course of action. Many of Ovid's *Heroides* broadly fit the profile of a verse *suasoria*. These letter writers are not shy about their underlying aim of persuading others to do what they want them to do, and at times assume the manner of a lawyer fluidly and authoritatively summoning arguments to support his case.

The declamatory speakers of the *Heroides* inhabit scenarios strongly reminiscent of other, nonelegiac poetic genres. Tragedy and especially Euripidean tragedy is a constant presence. Euripides was a playwright unusually interested in female characters, their emotions, and their sometimes violent or otherwise destructive actions. Ovid intentionally adopts several Euripidean heroines as elegiac letter writers: Helen, Phaedra, Hermione, and Medea are obvious examples. The action of the *Medea* lies behind both Medea's and Hypsipyle's letters. Hermione's letter to Orestes covers the same tangled web of gossip as Euripides' *Andromache* and the ending of his *Orestes.* Tyndareus, Hermione's grandfather, promised her to Orestes, but later, when Menelaus needed the help of Achilles' son Pyrrhus (Neoptolemus) in the war, he promised her to Pyrrhus. She now urges Orestes to assert his claim. Ovid's Hermione is an active figure who plays an important role in influencing her own fate. Orestes appears at an opportune moment to abduct her in Euripides' *Andromache* and arranges to have Neoptolemus killed at Delphi for an insult that the latter once dealt him. In Ovid's letter, Hermione emerges as the principal mover of the plot. She urges Orestes to fight battles on her behalf, just as Menelaus waged war for Helen. The metaphoric "battles of love" so common in elegiac poetry in this context imply real violence. The terms in which Hermione frames their story, moreover,

carry strongly tragic undertones. The letter is packed with references to their shared family members and ancestors (ATREUS, Pelops, TANTALUS) and, in the closing lines, refers to their common descent from Tantalus. The result is a letter of seduction pervaded by a sense of sinister menace and barely contained violence.

In letter 14, which Hypermnestra addresses to Lynceus, tragic subtexts are similarly discernible. Hypermnestra, alone among the daughters of Danaus, chose not to kill her husband on the night of their marriage, although she had been ordered to do so by her father. Her father accordingly imprisoned her. She now writes to Lynceus to rescue her. The story of the Danaids is the subject of an Aeschylean trilogy, of which the only surviving play is the *SUPPLIANTS*. We do not know what form the story took in the lost plays of Aeschylus's trilogy, but in other versions, Lynceus and Hypermnestra end up ruling together and become the progenitors of the dynastic line of Argive kings. Sometimes Hypermnestra is said to have been tried for disobedience and acquitted; in other accounts, Lynceus slays Danaus and the other Danaids to avenge his brothers' deaths.

Hints of future violence and royal succession lie behind Hypermnestra's elegiac plea to Lynceus. Indeed, Hypermnestra speaks very little, if at all, of love. She does relate the myth of Io in some detail, which establishes a further connection with Aeschylus, where Io is frequently mentioned as an ancestor of the Danaids. Letter 14, then, assimilates tragic subject matter to elegiac form and, at the same time, converts elegy into a medium for exploration of markedly tragic themes. The tragedy of the Danaids displaces love in a poem written in elegiac couplets, the metrical form most closely associated with erotic poetry in Ovid's times. Finally, it is worth considering some contemporary ideological associations of Hypermnestra's letter: One of the most prominent monuments built by the emperor Augustus, the portico of the temple of Apollo on the Palatine, features a statue group representing the story of the Danaids. The myth apparently celebrates Augustus's victory over the Egyptian Cleopatra in the battle of Actium (31 B.C.E.), just as the Danaids triumphed over the sons of Aegyptus; and yet in doing so, the Danaids would seem to oppose the great value Augustus placed on marriage. Certainly, the mythological tradition did not represent the Danaids in a wholly positive light. Ovid, in depicting Hypermnestra's difficult choice between a lack of *pietas* (dutifulness) toward her father and an impious violation of the marriage bond, reworks in textual form the ambiguities of Augustus's monument.

Ovid's *Heroides* do not simply tell stories in epistolary form; rather, his poetic letters explore how and why we tell ourselves stories, how we use those stories to persuade others and ourselves. A letter presents discourse in action, the workings of rhetoric and persuasion, which necessarily includes self-persuasion. Medea's letter to Jason, like her monologues in Euripides' play, forms part of the process of deliberation that finally culminates in the terrible choice to kill her children. Hypermnestra's account of her choice to spare Lynceus's life at once works on Lynceus, persuading him that he owes her his life and, at the same time, justifies her own action to herself. By reliving the moment of her decision that night, Hypermnestra is able to articulate her reasons for rejecting the planned murder: She was simply not suited, morally or temperamentally, to commit the violent crime, however deserving of their fate the sons of Aegyptus may have been.

Ovid thus exploits the tension between two simultaneously operative tendencies of the letter. On one reading, the letter represents the letter writer's exploration of her own emotions and thoughts. We may doubt whether the abandoned Ariadne's words will ever reach the heedless Theseus; they come close to pure monologue, although we may imagine that she *hoped* the letter might somehow come into his hands. On another reading, the letter is the medium of rhetorical speech, communication

designed to influence another's behavior and have an outcome on events in the world. By contrast with the letters of abandoned heroines (Oenone, Ariadne, Phyllis, Deianira, Sappho), the letters exchanged between Paris and Helen clearly reach their addressees and form part of a delicate series of negotiations leading directly to an adulterous affair. Far from writing to her faithless lover from some remote location, Helen exchanges letters with Paris in a milieu that closely resembles the classic scenario of Ovidian love elegy, in which notes are shuttled back and forth between lovers by household servants. The written word is a prelude to action. We might equally note Hypsipyle's highly effective curse of Jason, or Phaedra's ultimately catastrophic overture to Hippolytus. In most of the letters in Ovid's collection, however, both dimensions—the soliloquizing and the rhetorical—are inextricably combined. Writing to someone else is a means of forming one's own thoughts, and vice versa.

In an extreme version of epistolary isolation, Deianira writes to Heracles, who has left her in favor of Iole. She displays throughout the letter her intense concern for him and for his reputation. Deianira attempts to remind Heracles of his past deeds and reputation for manly accomplishment; at the same time, she brings out the dissonance between this reputation and his current humiliating role as subservient lover of Iole. We realize only later in the letter that she does not really hope now to gain him back, and that Heracles is doomed by the poisoned robes she has already sent him. Deianira herself will die by suicide. In a tragic scenario recalling Sophocles' TRACHINIAE, Deianira, soon to be dead, writes to her already doomed husband; effectively, one corpse writes to another. It is hard to imagine a letter that offers *less* hope of any positive outcome in the world. Deianira's letter is a text that confirms and distills in verbal form the now irreversible tragedy of its writer.

Some of the myths appear to be chosen for their meta-epistolary dimension. Phaedra, for example, ended up destroying Hippolytus in Euripides' *Hippolytus* by means of a letter she left for Theseus, which accused Hippolytus of rape. The theme of the destruction, through use of the written word, of an innocent man accused of violating another's wife goes back to the story of BELLEROPHON in Homer's *Iliad*. Ovid's letter to Hippolytus begins with Phaedra's questions: How can a letter hurt you? This remark naturally makes the reader think of ways in which letters really can harm a person. Phaedra has begun her dangerous career as letter writer, and if we have read Euripides, we know where it all ends.

Oenone's letter begins with a similarly explicit reference to the epistolary medium: She wonders whether Paris really will read her letter, or if Helen will not permit him. One might equally wonder whether so heedless and distraction-prone a character as Paris, who is in the midst of kindling an immense war through his theft of another man's wife, will take the time to read his former wife's missive. Oenone's apparently earnest desire to return to the way things were, to have Paris again as her husband in their primitive, sylvan setting, even after he has been recognized as Priam's son and started the Trojan War, is appealingly naive. Equally naive and appealing is her desperate declaration that, if necessary, she could embrace the life of a great man's wife and lie in a purple marriage bed. Throughout the letter, Oenone contrasts the more sophisticated and luxurious milieu in which Paris now lives and the pastoral haunts of their early, innocent love. The contrast, of course, is both a contrast of values (urban/rustic, simple living/luxury) and of genres (epic/pastoral). Evoking a distinctively pastoral mode of writing, Oenone recalls to Paris the vows he wrote on the bark of trees. Oenone belongs to an earlier period in the Paris narrative, and thus falls out of the picture when he takes Helen as his wife. Ovid's inspiration is to show us that Oenone continues to exist, remember, and desire even after she has disappeared from her lover's view. In some versions of the myth, however, Paris later seeks Oenone's healing powers, when he has been wounded by Philoctetes. She at first refuses, but then repents; by that time, however, Paris is already dead, and Oenone commits suicide. Ovid, in referring to Oenone's healing powers, shows his awareness of these later outcomes.

The aesthetic subtlety of the *Heroides* resides to a great degree in the play between two perspectives of reading: on the one hand, the fictional perspective that the letter writer notionally inhabits; and on the other hand, the tacit yet pervasive perspective of the mythographer/poet, who builds in hints of later outcomes, allusions to diverging options within the mythological tradition, and analogical references to other myths. Ovid is at his best when he delicately maintains the fiction of the letter writer's limited perspective even while incorporating an allusive and mythographically sophisticated level of meaning. Hypsipyle, for example, is on one level an angry, jealous former lover of Jason; on another level, she has evidently read Apollonius's *Voyage of the Argonauts* and comments on the plot developments. Despite her knowledge of Jason's busy life, she is irritated that he has not found time to write her a letter. Like other heroines in the collection, moreover, she insists that their relationship was a marriage, and not only that, a very public one that included Juno (see HERA) and HYMEN. Ovid strands his readers in interpretive aporia: Is Hypsipyle, like Dido (the writer of the letter immediately following in the collection), dressing up a fleeting liaison as marriage to exert control over Jason, or has the existing mythological tradition merely fossilized a version that is, conveniently, advantageous for the male hero?

Hypsipyle, again like Dido, pronounces a terrible curse against Medea, which closes the letter. Whereas her complaints about Jason's behavior represent Hypsipyle's reading of the *Voyage of the Argonauts*, the curse constitutes a prospective narration of Euripides' *Medea*. In Ovid's innovative version, the abandoned

Hypsipyle becomes the motivating force behind the grim events at Corinth, just as the abandoned Dido, in Virgil's *Aeneid*, furnishes an origins story for the conflict between Rome and Carthage. The mythological commentary goes yet deeper, however. Hypsipyle's condemnation of Medea contains strong indications that she is, in fact, the equivalent of Medea. She, too, has been involved in the murder of family members, and has used violence to avenge male sexual betrayal. She alludes to her status as leader of a violent troop of women. Hypsipyle later states that she would, if possible, have splashed her face with Medea's blood and would have been Medea for Medea. Jason's two most important lovers, on this reading, are at some level doubles, or at least broadly comparable figures. The story does not end there, however. Later in the collection, in letter 12, Ovid will provide us an opportunity to test this hypothesis and to reconsider the situation from Medea's perspective.

The following letter, in which Dido addresses the departing Aeneas, represents another case of differing perspectives within the mythological tradition. Ovid, in particular, has his eye on Virgil's recently completed *Aeneid*, where the Dido episode receives intensive treatment. Dido is by no means complacent with Aeneas's decision to depart for Italy in Virgil's epic. Yet in Ovid's version, she arguably goes further: She sneers, for example, at the idea of Aeneas's signal act of *pietas* ("dutifulness") in Augustan ideology, his rescue of Anchises and Iulus from the burning city of Troy. She states, moreover, that Aeneas is morally unworthy of worshipping the Penates (household gods); they were better off not being rescued from the flames, if the impious Aeneas must be the one who rescues them. Dido's critique directly confronts the most ideologically laden myths of Romanness in the Augustan period. Most shockingly of all, she declares that Aeneas is abandoning not only her but his unborn child as well. Virgil makes it clear, for readers who might be worried, that Dido did *not* become pregnant with

Aeneas's child. Virgil needs to make this clear, since otherwise Aeneas's departure effectively kills (through Dido's suicide) a member of the Julian *gens* ("clan")—a deeply unacceptable outcome for many reasons. Do we believe Dido's claim of pregnancy in her current letter? Again, Ovid makes it difficult to know for certain whether he is correcting Virgil's whitewashed version, or whether Dido is to be understood as bending the truth in her desperate attempt to persuade Aeneas.

Near the end, we learn that as she is writing her letter, Dido has lying on her lap the dagger that Aeneas gave her. The opening of *Aeneid* Book 4 compares Dido to a deer fatally "wounded" by a hunter; at the end of the book, she kills herself with Aeneas's gift. Ovid encourages us to reread his letter with the knowledge of the dagger's fatal presence. We see here one of many instances in which Ovid evokes the image of the writer—the writer's tears, imprisonment (Hypermnestra), lingering illness (Cydippe). In letter 11, Canace, writing to her brother and incestuous lover Macareus, similarly holds the stilus in one hand and a sword in the other. When she has finished writing, she will obey her father's command and kill herself. At the opening of the letter, she explains to Macareus that if some letters are blotted out, it is because her blood has spilled on them. The presumably clean, spruce papyrus of Ovid's *Heroides* evokes a proto-text marked both with ink and with the tears and/or blood of the writer.

Throughout these letters, it is possible to discern an interesting set of links connecting writing, the writer's body (physical body or body of work, *corpus*), sharp tools that leave marks on paper or flesh (stilus, blade), and the writer's death. At the end of the *Metamorphoses*, Ovid proclaims that he will not wholly die and that he will live on through the eternity of his poem. This interest in poetic immortality recurs implicitly within the fiction of epistolary writing in the *Heroides*: The heroines, like Ovid, are leaving a text that will endure after their death, providing a record of their thoughts and experiences. We are reading, as it were, the first draft of an emerging mythological tradition. Ovid is, on the one hand, writing *after* many of the canonical texts that established the narrative profile of these myths (Homer, Virgil, the tragedians), and yet, in another sense, he locates the act of writing *before* the canonization of myth, at the moment when the mythological figure herself is first writing down her story. After her death, the document she leaves will furnish the raw materials for an enduring tradition. It is no accident that so many of Ovid's heroines commit suicide at some point after they complete their letter: The *Heroides* shows us the process whereby a living person becomes a text.

The idea of writing and temporal endurance often arises in yet another form in the closing lines of Ovid's letters. Many of the letters of the *Heroides* end with a prospective epitaph, e.g., Dido requests an inscription memorializing not her marriage to Sychaeus but Aeneas as the cause of her death. The motif of the prospective epitaph derives from the genre of love elegy. In these cases, it is the male poet/lover who imagines his death and future commemoration. Ovid now incorporates this motif into the letters of his heroines, layering yet another imagined scene of writing within his epistolary fiction. Ovid offers a further instance of writing that endures and preserves the memory of the writer. Ovid's epistolary writing thus tacitly explores the dynamics of literary immortality and canonization.

Another aspect of the *Heroides* that implicitly examines the nature of the literary work is the persistent interest in absence, copies, and imitation. Laodamia, separated from her husband, Protesilaus, who had departed for the Trojan War, desperately yearns for him to survive and return, to the extent that she has a waxen copy of Protesilaus made and develops a somewhat disturbing relationship with it: She speaks words of love to it and embraces it. She states that if only a voice were added

to it, it would become Protesilaus. Underlying this story is a deeper Ovidian concern with erotic attraction, the desire to create images of the desired object, and the power of art as mimesis. We might compare the myth of PYG-MALION in Ovid's *Metamorphoses*. Laodomia's is a particularly poignant case of absence and loss. She never truly possessed Protesilaus, who departs for war immediately after they are married, and dies, first of all the Greeks, on landing in Troy. In some versions, her loss even inspires sympathy among the gods, who allow her to spend three hours with Protesilaus before he returns to Hades. She then commits suicide to remain with him. In another version, Laodamia's father, finding out about his daughter's unusual relationship with a statue, has the statue burned. She then throws herself into the fire with it and perishes. This latter version presents an even more radical conception of Laodamia's infatuation with the copied or surrogate Protesilaus. Is it possible that she loves the image of Protesilaus she has created as intensely as she loves the man?

These reflections on copies, absence, and doubling play into the broader epistolary fiction, wherein the written word functions as a representative or surrogate of the living, speaking person. Rhetorical devices of vividness—e.g., evocations of the writer's tears and physical presence—only underline further the irremediable fact of separation. The effect of distance is fairly obvious in the unanswered letters of abandoned women throughout the collection. Their words are addressed all too often to a man who has already ceased to listen. Perhaps paradoxically, however, the paired letters placed at the end of the collection, in which one mythological letter writer responds to another, rather than alleviating the sense of isolation, in some ways actually intensify it. The correspondents are islands unto themselves, and communication occurs across a vast gulf. In one instance, the gulf is a literal one: Leander and Hero correspond across the fatal waters of the Hellespont. Their misunderstandings create yet another gulf, however. Hero, while worrying about Leander's safety, cannot help eagerly encouraging him to swim across to her—with tragic results. Paris and Helen will become lovers, and thus physical separation is hardly their problem. Yet, in his masterful depiction of the lovers' mismatched sentiments, Ovid emphasizes the vast gulf between their differing perspectives. Helen is inclined to pursue the affair while her husband is away but is opposed to giving up her position as Menelaus's wife; Paris is eager both to seduce and to possess, enumerating all the attractions of his Trojan wealth. The gulf between their two perspectives contributes to the catastrophe of their physical union.

The collection ends with a pair of letters that, arguably perhaps to an even greater extent than Phaedra's letter to Hippolytus, explore the dangers and capacities of the written word. Acontius fell in love with Cydippe and, in order to possess her, caused her to pick up an apple with the words "I swear to marry Acontius" written on it. She unwittingly read the inscribed words aloud in Diana's sanctuary. Subsequently, her parents arranged her engagement to another man, and Cydippe became sick. Acontius interprets her sickness to mean that Diana is punishing Cydippe for violating her oath. Cydippe, who deplores Acontius's tactics, offers a cogent critique of his idea of the binding power of an oath: She insists that intention determines the meaning and force of words, and that there can be no binding oath without intention behind the speech. The paired letters, then, revolve around a very literary debate—specifically, an argument over writing, reading, intention, and meaning. Her own feelings, however, run contrary to her logic, as it emerges in the course of her letter that she does not feel any love for the man she is supposed to marry, but does appear to be inclined to accept Acontius.

"Sickness," in elegiac love poetry, is one of the prime metaphors for the condition of love. The symptoms are especially intense when the desiring lover must endure absence from the beloved. Cydippe's flagging energy and mounting fatigue as the letter goes on create a brilliant closural effect in the collection's final letter. The *Heroides* are coming to an end, just as the letter writer's capacity to go on writing is dwindling: Cydippe's hand, by the end, can barely support the stilus. The only means of curing the sickness draining her spirit is reunion with her lover Acontius. The collection's closing words—in which Cydippe expresses the wish that she will soon be with Acontius—are also its most hopeful. As Cydippe comes to the end of letter writing, she also comes nearer to the end of absence and separation, and closer to a cure.

Herse   See ALGAURUS AND HERSE.

Hesiod (ca. eighth century B.C.E.)   Major Greek poet of the eighth or possibly seventh century B.C.E., around the time of Homer. Hesiod was a native of the town of Askra. Unlike Homer, Hesiod reveals aspects of his life and personality in the first person; for example, he has a brother, Perses, with whom he had a dispute over inheritance, and he won a prize at a poetry contest at a festival. Hesiod's two major extant works are THEOGONY and WORKS AND DAYS. Hesiod's *Theogony* and *Works and Days* exemplify two distinct poetic modes: *Works and Days* largely concerns the labors and rhythms of human life, while the *Theogony* is concerned with the creation of the world and generation of the gods. In the *Works and Days,* Hesiod speaks in a somewhat irritable didactic voice, taking his brother Perses to task for his failings, whereas in the *Theogony*, he speaks as an inspired poet who enjoys a special relation with the Muses and thus special access to knowledge about the gods and the world's origins. These differences sometimes provoke questions regarding the identity of Hesiod, e.g., whether or not the same poet wrote the two poems. The differences, however, can equally be explained by differences in theme, genre, and perspective.

Hesione Daughter of King LAOMEDON of Troy. Classical sources are Apollodorus's *LIBRARY* (2.5.9, 2.64) and Ovid's *METAMORPHOSES* (11.211–217). Hesione was saved from a sea monster by HERACLES.

Hesperides Guardian nymphs of the tree bearing the golden apples. The Hesperides were associated with evening and song. Classical sources are Apollodorus's *LIBRARY* (2.5.11), Diodorus Siculus's *LIBRARY OF HISTORY* (4.26.2–4), Hesiod's *THEOGONY* (215–216, 274–275, 335–336, 517–520), and Sophocles' *TRACHINIAE* (1,089–1,100). According to Hesiod, the Hesperides were the daughters of NYX (Night) and Erebus (Darkness), but later sources attributed their parentage to ATLAS and Hesperis.

GAIA had given a tree bearing golden apples as a gift to HERA at her wedding to ZEUS. Hera placed the tree in the Garden of the Hesperides, thought to be located near the Atlas Mountains, at the westernmost extremity of the known world—to be guarded by the Hesperides. Their number varies in the sources, ranging from three to seven. The names of four are known: Aegle, Arethusa, Erythia, and Hesperethusa. According to some sources, the tree was also guarded by the dragon Ladon, (offspring of ECHIDNA and TYPHOES).

The golden apples featured in the myths of ATALANTA and Hippomenes and in the Twelve Labors of HERACLES. Heracles' Twelfth Labor sent him to the Garden of Hesperides to fetch the golden apples. Atlas, whose task was to hold the heavens on his shoulders, agreed to bring the apples to Heracles if the hero would temporarily take his burden but, when he returned with the apples, Atlas refused to take it back. Heracles, however, tricked Atlas into assuming his burden once more, and brought the apples to King EURYSTHEUS of Mycenae. In Diodorus Siculus's version of the story, Atlas aided Heracles in gratitude to the hero for having rescued the Hesperides, his daughters, who had been abducted by pirates. Another version relates that Heracles killed Ladon and acquired the apples without Atlas's help. Athena later returned them to the Garden of Hesperides, but the Hesperides, in grief at their loss, had been transformed into trees: elm, poplar, and willow.

In classical art, on vases and coins, and in paintings, the Hesperides are often shown in the company of Heracles. An example is an Attic red-figure hydria from ca. 420 B.C.E. attributed to the Meidias Painter (British Museum, London). In this image, Heracles is seated facing the Hesperides, who flank the tree of golden apples, around which Ladon is coiled. Renaissance and baroque artists seldom represented the Hesperides; not until the 19th century did painters and poets turn to these myths for inspiration. Alfred Tennyson's poem *The Hesperides*, of 1830, is based on the myth. Postclassical images include Edward Burne-Jones's *The Garden of the Hesperides* from ca. 1869–73 (Kunsthalle, Hamburg) and Frederick Leighton's *The Garden of the Hesperides* from ca. 1892 (Lady Lever Art Gallery, Cheshire, England). In this last, the Hesperides drowse under the tree of golden apples, abundant with fruit, while Ladon is entwined sinuously around the tree and one of the Hesperides.

Hestia Goddess of the hearth. Daughter of the TITANS CRONUS and RHEA. Classical sources are the *Homeric Hymn to Aphrodite* (21–32) and the *Homeric Hymns to Hestia*, Hesiod's *THEOGONY* (453–506), Pausanias's *Description of Greece* (5.11.8, 5.14.4), Pindar's *Nemean Odes* (11.1–7), and Virgil's *AENEID* (1.292, 2.296). Hestia was associated with domesticity. She was a virgin goddess and, like ARTEMIS and ATHENA, immune to love. Hestia personified the hearth and was associated generally with the home and the family, but she has no myths of her own. The Roman goddess Vesta was syncretized with the Greek Hestia. A temple dedicated to Vesta was built in the Roman forum where the sacred flame was tended by the Vestal Virgins. Vesta was a goddess a great importance for the Romans: Her flame was thought to guarantee the security of Rome.

Hippolyte See AMAZONS, HIPPOLYTUS, THESEUS.

Hippolytus Son of THESEUS and the Amazon ANTIOPE (or Hippolyte). Hippolytus is one of the central characters of Euripides' HIPPOLYTUS. Additional classical sources are Apollodorus's *LIBRARY* (3.19.3, Epitome 1.18–19), Diodorus Siculus's *LIBRARY OF HISTORY* (4.62), Hyginus's *Fabulae* (47), Ovid's *METAMORPHOSES* (15.497–545), Pausanias's *Description of Greece* (1.22.1–3, 2.27.4, 2.32.3–4, 2.32.10), and Virgil's *AENEID* (7.765–780). After the death of Hippolytus's mother, Theseus married PHAEDRA, with whom he had two sons, Acamas and Demophon. Theseus was at one time exiled from Athens and came to live in Troezen, near Athens. It was at this time, when Hippolytus was a young man, that Phaedra became enamored of him. Hippolytus was a follower of ARTEMIS and chastely refused Phaedra's advances (the advances and, later, false accusations made against the hero are similar to those in the myth of BELLEROPHON and Stheneboea, and in the biblical story of Joseph and Potiphar's wife). Sources differ on the

The Death of Hippolytus. *Jean-Baptiste Lemoyne, 1715 (Louvre, Paris)*

events that followed. In some, a scorned Phaedra told Theseus that Hippolytus had attempted to seduce her. Theseus was unsure whom to believe and sent for Hippolytus, who succumbed to an accident while driving his chariot. Theseus called on one of three curses that his father, Poseidon, had given him, to wish for Hippolytus's death. As Hippolytus was driving his chariot away from Troezen to exile, a bull sent up from the sea panicked the horses and Hippolytus was dragged to his death while tangled in the reins.

In Euripides' *Hippolytus*, Phaedra's passion for the young man was incited by APHRODITE in anger for Hippolytus's lack of piety toward her. The goddess's plan, to cause Phaedra's love for her son-in-law to result in his death, absolves Phaedra from some measure of responsibility, and this play treats Phaedra with more sympathy than other accounts.

According to the *Aeneid*, after Hippolytus's death, Artemis interceded on his behalf, and he was revived by ASCLEPIUS, then hidden by the goddess Trivia in Italy, in a grove sacred to her. A son, Virbius, is attributed to Hippolytus, though in some sources Hippolytus takes on the identity of Virbius following his resurrection.

In classical art, Hippolytus appears with Theseus and Phaedra or at the moment of his death. An example of the latter is an Apulian krater from 350 B.C.E. (British Museum, London). An 18th-century baroque sculpture, *The Death of Hippolytus* (Louvre, Paris) by Jean-Baptiste Lemoyne, shows Hippolytus cast headfirst, legs askew, against the wreckage of the chariot, reins still clutched in his hands. The complex story of the attraction of Phaedra to her stepson and his chaste resistance is the subject of a wall painting from Herculaneum dating to 75 B.C.E.

Hippolytus EURIPIDES (428 B.C.E.) Euripides' *Hippolytus* was produced in 428 B.C.E. and won first prize in the competition for tragedy. HIPPOLYTUS, the son of THESEUS by an Amazon, is a devotee of the goddess ARTEMIS but disdains love and the goddess ᴀᴘʜʀᴏᴅɪᴛᴇ. Aphrodite, at the opening of the play, announces her intention to punish Hippolytus by making ᴘʜᴀᴇᴅʀᴀ, wife of ᴛʜᴇsᴇᴜs and stepmother to Hippolytus, fall in love with him. Phaedra's unchaste desire for her stepson was possibly incestuous and certainly shocking in the eyes of the Greek audience, yet Euripides seems to go out of his way to represent Phaedra as struggling with her desire and unwilling to undermine her modesty. The indiscreet nurse, however, overcomes Phaedra's reticence and is instrumental in bringing about the catastrophic outcome. This version of the play was preceded by an earlier version that apparently presented Phaedra as more shameless and overt in her declaration of love for Hippolytus. Yet even if Euripides has softened the moral impact of Phaedra's infatuation, his representation of the gods' power to shatter human lives remains stark and unmitigated.

SYNOPSIS

The action takes place before the house of Theseus in Troezen. At the beginning of the play, Theseus is away in foreign lands. The prologue consists of a soliloquy by Aphrodite. She remarks on Hippolytus's chastity, his dedication to Artemis, and his constant companionship with the immortal huntress. Aphrodite's power is universal, but Hippolytus has not yielded to the temptations of love and continues to refuse to do so. Thus, he has drawn on himself the ire of the goddess of love. Aphrodite resolves to punish his lack of piety with suffering and death. She has already begun to punish this proud young man by causing his stepmother, Phaedra, to become infatuated with him. Aphrodite now reveals how he will die: Theseus will invoke one of three curses, which his father, ᴘᴏsᴇɪᴅᴏɴ, conferred on him, to bring about Hippolytus's death. Aphrodite exits.

Hippolytus sings the praises of Artemis and lays a wreath at her altar on his return with his companions from a hunting trip. In a dialogue with one of the servants he reveals the depth of his devotion to the goddess of the hunt. The old servant attempts to alert Hippolytus to the danger of neglecting the worship of Aphrodite, but Hippolytus argues that he has chosen to worship one goddess, Artemis, above all others, and then exits. The old servant is left behind to pray to Aphrodite on Hippolytus's behalf.

The Chorus, composed of women of Troezen, servants of the household, enters and discusses the state of its mistress, Phaedra. For some days now, she has refused to eat, is feverish, and appears to be dying. The Chorus proposes various reasons for Phaedra's obvious spiritual anguish and physical decline; it speculates that perhaps she has been punished by Artemis for neglecting to sacrifice to her, or that perhaps her husband has betrayed her with another, or that a messenger has brought her some other distressing news. Its speculations continue as Phaedra is led outdoors, supported by her nurse.

Phaedra is restless and agitated, and the nurse worries aloud about the source of her distress. Phaedra speaks of longing to join a hunt like Artemis. The nurse is alarmed that Phaedra may have gone mad. Phaedra admits that she feels as if she has lost her sanity, but she cannot understand how she could deserve this fate. The Chorus asks the nurse whether she knows why Phaedra is unwell, and the nurse responds that she has attempted many times to learn the cause, but Phaedra has been silent on this point. Since Theseus is currently away, however, and no one but the nurse can help their mistress, the Chorus again presses her to find out why Phaedra is suffering. The nurse begins her inquiries again but is met with Phaedra's silence. The nurse urges her to consider that if she dies and can no longer protect the interests of her children at Theseus's court, then Hippolytus, her stepson, will surely displace them. Phaedra reacts to the mention of Hippolytus's name, and the nurse begins to question her relentlessly. Phaedra maintains that her honor lies in her silence, but the nurse entreats and supplicates her until she begins to guess that love is the source of Phaedra's unhappiness. Phaedra relents and, under further questioning, provides enough clues to have the nurse put into words what she refuses to say herself, that Phaedra is in love with her stepson Hippolytus.

The nurse's first reaction is panic, and she calls curses down on them all. She laments the destructive power of Aphrodite, and exits.

The Chorus expresses horror at Phaedra's love for Hippolytus and sorrow for her and for the ruin that will surely follow the revelation of that love. In Phaedra's response, she laments that virtue alone is not enough to guarantee an untroubled life. She explains that when she first became aware of her unhealthy passion for Hippolytus, she tried to conceal it by silence and then to conquer it; when neither method gave her peace, she resolved to die. But although prepared to die, Phaedra cannot accept that her reputation for virtue should be compromised.

The nurse returns and begs forgiveness for her abrupt departure. She has come, on reflection, to provide some solace. She argues that since love is not a force that can be withstood, there is no point in dying because one is in love. Even the gods themselves are subject to it. In her opinion, therefore, Phaedra must surrender to it and endure it. The Chorus agrees with the nurse's arguments, but Phaedra does not. In her view, the nurse's interpretation ignores the fact that her love is still not virtuous, even if she is has no control of it.

The nurse retorts that, in the balance, Phaedra's life is worth more than her virtue, that if the cure to her affliction is Hippolytus, surely that is not a great price to pay to save her own life. Phaedra is shocked at the suggestion, but the nurse presses her to consider the importance of her own life. Phaedra is adamant that she will not consider this option of giving in to her passion. The nurse then says that she will fetch some magic charms that may help. Suspicious, Phaedra asks for details, but the nurse is evasive. When Phaedra asks her directly

whether she will tell Hippolytus her secret, the nurse tells her only that Aphrodite will help her in her endeavors. She exits. The Chorus sings of the destructive force of love.

Hippolytus and the nurse enter in the midst of a dialogue, while Phaedra, unobserved, listens. Phaedra's secret has evidently been revealed by the nurse. Hippolytus is disgusted, but the nurse begs him not to expose Phaedra. He responds with a long speech condemning the wickedness of women and the burden they represent to their fathers, families, and husbands. He castigates the nurse for suggesting that he defile the sanctity of his own father's marriage. Before he leaves, he promises to remain silent but again expresses his hatred of women and their lack of chastity.

Phaedra emerges and, when the nurse returns, rages at her for her betrayal. She suspected what the nurse meant to do and had hoped to prevent it by insisting that the nurse keep silent. The nurse responds that Phaedra would have felt differently if she had succeeded with Hippolytus instead of failing, and that Phaedra should not lose all hope. Phaedra abruptly dismisses her. Turning to the Chorus, Phaedra asks that it remain silent about all it has already witnessed and is yet to witness. The promise is given. In the ensuing dialogue with the Chorus, Phaedra reveals that she has now made the decision to die, and that in death her name will remain honorable, although she does not specify how. In her last speech, Phaedra acknowledges the bitter victory that Aphrodite has achieved, and she predicts that her death will punish Hippolytus for his arrogance and excessive chastity. She enters the palace.

The Chorus sings of the farthest reaches of the world, where it would rather be, and of the voyage that Phaedra made from Crete to Athens when she came to marry Theseus. It anticipates that Phaedra will hang herself. The nurse emerges from the palace and calls out for help, but it is too late—Phaedra is dead.

Theseus enters and immediately perceives that something is wrong. He questions the

Chorus, asking whether his father has died, or perhaps one of his children. The Chorus tells him that Phaedra has killed herself but can offer no explanation why. Theseus sees his wife's corpse inside the palace doors. He enters, laments, and asks why she killed herself. He finds a letter in her hand, reads it, and discovers that Phaedra has accused Hippolytus of having raped her; his sorrow gives way to fury. Turning toward the sea, Theseus uses one of three curses bestowed on him by his father, Poseidon, to kill Hippolytus. The Chorus pleads with him to take the curse back, but Theseus, now beyond reason, refuses to listen and orders that Hippolytus be banished. He foresees that Hippolytus will either die in exile or be struck down by Poseidon. The Chorus again urges restraint as Hippolytus and his companions enter.

Hippolytus heard Theseus shouting and has come to investigate. At the sight of Phaedra's corpse, he, too, is shocked and asks how she died. Theseus tells Hippolytus that he knows all and angrily denounces Hippolytus as a hypocrite who has trumpeted his piety and chastity so as to hide his real character. Theseus banishes Hippolytus. Hippolytus insists on his virtue and swears by Zeus that he did not dishonor his father's marriage.

Theseus does not believe him and rejects the suggestion that they wait for a trial or an oracle. Hippolytus wonders out loud whether he should betray his oath to keep silent about Phaedra's love for him but, in the end, decides to keep silent. Theseus again commands Hippolytus to go into exile, then exits. Hippolytus bemoans the oath that prevents him from defending himself and bids farewell to Athens and Troezen and the company of Artemis. He leaves the stage together with his companions. The Chorus sings of the uncertainty of human life and laments Hippolytus's exile.

One of Hippolytus's servants enters with a message for Theseus, who now enters: Hippolytus has had an accident in his chariot and is on the point of death. As Hippolytus was leaving Troezen, a bull evoked by Theseus's curse rose out of the sea and attacked Hippolytus's chariot. The terrified horses panicked; Hippolytus was thrown from the chariot and dragged along the ground as he cried out that he was innocent. As Theseus waits for the dying Hippolytus to be brought before him, the Chorus sings of the power of Aphrodite and Eros over all mortals and immortals.

The goddess Artemis appears above the palace. She proclaims Hippolytus's virtue and explains that the goddess of love instigated his death. Artemis tells Theseus that Phaedra's false accusations stemmed from the madness of love inflicted on her by Aphrodite. She accuses Theseus of having caused his son's tragic death by drawing hasty conclusions and by refusing to heed Hippolytus's oath or to wait for the oracle's pronouncement. Theseus is overcome with sorrow as Hippolytus is brought in. He is in great pain and is dying. Artemis identifies Aphrodite as the cause of all their misfortunes. In revenge, she promises to punish with death a mortal devoted to Aphrodite and promises also that Hippolytus will receive great honor in Troezen. In the future, young women about to be married will cut their hair and dedicate it to Hippolytus. Artemis reconciles Theseus and Hippolytus and departs. As his last act, Hippolytus forgives his father and dies. Theseus laments the loss of his son, who displayed such great virtue, and he resolves to remember the sufferings brought on him by Aphrodite.

COMMENTARY

When the play *Hippolytus Stephanephorus* (Hippolytus Garland-Bearer) was presented in Athens in 428–429 B.C.E., it won first prize. Euripides' *Hippolytus* had been preceded by another version of the play, entitled *Hippolytus Calyptomenus* (Hippolytus with Head Covered), by the same author. The earlier version caused something of a scandal: The representation of Phaedra was apparently far less sympathetic than in this second play. The topic was clearly potentially disturbing, as Euripides had chosen a story that depicts the unchaste desires of a married woman directed toward her own husband's son.

One central concern is the havoc that Phaedra's desire wreaks on the integrity of the Greek *oikos* ("household"). Behind the more colorful aspects of the myth, there are prosaic worries about inheritance and legitimate and illegitimate children. Hippolytus is the illegitimate son of Theseus by ANTIOPE, an Amazon. Theseus has his own legitimate children by Phaedra. The legitimate children must inherit his estate and position. Pausanias tells us that Hippolytus was sent to Pittheus's house in Troezen in the first place to avoid a conflict over inheritance and succession. His natural enemy in such a struggle would be Phaedra herself, his stepmother and the mother of his rivals. Her love for him thus appears all the more strange and unnatural. Yet, in a sense, she is true to her role as stepmother. It is her love and the letter that she leaves that cause Hippolytus's death. Thus, it is she, in effect, who kills him, thereby leaving the field free for her own children.

Euripides, as we know from other plays, is interested in family dynamics, and like other tragedians, he often depicts the destruction or implosion of a household. Here, the family dynamic seems especially tense. All of its most important members seem to operate separately in their own sphere, with little communication among them. Phaedra nurses her "illness" on her own; Hippolytus, before he hears of Phaedra's infatuation, contentedly pursues his life of hunting in the wilds; and Theseus, until late in the play, is absent altogether. The members of the household follow parallel yet separate paths, until they merge with tragic results. This separateness relates to a major Euripidean theme, here pursued with particular lucidity: the irreconcilability of divided viewpoints, modes of living, spheres of concern. Strikingly, the three main figures—Hippolytus, Phaedra, Theseus—do not meet until Theseus confronts Hippolytus with his supposed crime, and by then, Phaedra is already dead. The first damage

is done by surrogate: The nurse informs Hippolytus of Phaedra's desire. This act apparently occurred without Phaedra's consent. The second damage is also done by surrogate, specifically by the medium of writing: Phaedra leaves a letter for her husband, Theseus, to find, accusing Hippolytus of rape. The two pivotal acts of communication that bring about the doom of all three characters are performed by surrogate, without direct dialogue between the persons involved. The setting itself is the final factor contributing to a sense of isolation. The tragedy does not unfold in Theseus's Athens, or Phaedra's Crete, but in Troezen, a kind of neutral zone that Phaedra describes as "this extremity of land, this anteroom of Argos" (tr. David Grene).

Euripidean characters often inhabit a divided world of extremes. In this play, the two main characters are closely associated with opposing goddesses: Artemis and Aphrodite. Each is tragically isolated from moderating influences that might make them more nuanced, less extreme characters. Phaedra is consumed by desire that makes her so sick that she is in danger of dying. Hippolytus, for his part, pursues a life so exclusively devoted to Artemis and her typical pursuits that he courts his own kind of extremity. This extremism is brought out in each instance in the characters' dialogue with humbler, more sensible characters. For example, Hippolytus, in dialogue with the servant, insists on the validity of his exclusive devotion, while the servant more reasonably recommends moderation, and, above all, some degree of respect for the power and greatness of Aphrodite. The deities who represent the diverse extremes, moreover, are kept separate from each other and do not interfere in each other's domains or engage with each other diplomatically (as elsewhere often occurs in Greek mythology). At the beginning, Aphrodite appears alone on stage, announcing in cruelly lucid terms that this is the day appointed for Hippolytus's punishment. At the end of the play, Artemis appears and announces that she will in turn take vengeance by punishing one of Aphrodite's followers. The two deities do not enter into dialogue with each other but merely take out their anger on separate human victims. The strict autonomy of the goddesses corresponds to the radical isolation of the two extremes of character represented in the human domain by the chaste Hippolytus and the eros-consumed Phaedra.

Both figures have complementary faults and virtues, although it may be that Hippolytus is the more virtuous of the two. Phaedra understands the wrongness of her desire but cannot control it, and because of this, she has resolved to die. She is no hypocrite, even if she wishes to continue to be known for her virtue after her death. In fact, the good virtuous intention of preserving her honor is what leads her to the destructive action of writing the letter falsely accusing Hippolytus. Hippolytus, by contrast, has no unchaste desires; and though Theseus accuses him of maintaining a false pretense of virtue, he is not a hypocrite either. His fault, in contrast to Phaedra's self-denigration, is arrogance and a belief that his purity is the only quality that needs cultivating. It is Hippolytus, in the end, who is honored by being incorporated into the cultic fabric of Troezen, and who, in the closing lines of the play, displays a nobly forgiving attitude toward his father. Yet both characters are compelling, complex, and by turns, repellent and sympathetic. Euripides has created a subtle study in complementary opposites.

As in his *Medea*, the female character displays destructive erotic passion, while the male character is emotionally colder. Men and women appear to inhabit separate worlds, and as if to stress this point, the virginal Hippolytus, on learning of Phaedra's desire, embarks on a long, misogynistic diatribe. In his critique of women, he stresses a financial metaphor, designating them as counterfeit coin and lamenting their drain on household resources. There is less in the way of a critique of men in the *Hippolytus*, since Phaedra is a less outrageous and

empowered character than Medea, yet there are hints of an alienated perspective. Phaedra refers to herself as a woman and, thus, as an object of hatred to all. She is acutely aware of the sense of "shame" (in the positive sense of modesty) that she should display and, at the same time, of the "shame" (in a negative sense) that she now brings on herself by her unchaste desire. For Phaedra, being a woman is a hard fate. As in the *Medea*, the terrible power of Aphrodite, especially over women in the Euripidean representation, is key to woman's difficult condition.

Identity is determined not only by gender in the *Hippolytus* but also by mythic genealogy. Hippolytus, who devotes himself to the wilds rather than to love, has an Amazon mother, which perhaps in part explains his unusual and extreme character. His place is more uncertain than Phaedra's—a son of Theseus, yet illegitimate, a devotee of Artemis, who, however, can only avenge, not save, him. He is destroyed in his youth by the power of Aphrodite. He never properly comes of age nor initiates his own heroic career like his father; in that sense, his identity is incomplete. The erasure, or partial erasure, of his identity is signified by the mangling of his body at the play's close. Counterbalancing this destruction of identity, however, is the grim recognition scene, in which Theseus finally perceives the true character and worth of his son, and in which Artemis guarantees him a place in the cultic life of Troezen and confirms his status as hero. Phaedra, for her part, is a Cretan woman, a descendant of Europa (who was seduced by a bull), daughter of Pasiphae (who fell in love with a bull), and sister of Ariadne (who was abandoned by Theseus and was later married to Dionysus). Love for the women of her family is generally a painful, tragic, and transgressive affair. She herself recognizes this painful inheritance and, in the course of the story, assumes her place in the mythic pattern. The story of Hippolytus and Phaedra was sufficiently absorbing that later writers were inspired to rewrite it to suit their own interests and themes. Ovid includes a self-narrative on the part of Hippolytus in his *Metamorphoses*. In the Neronian period (first century C.E.), the story was taken up by Seneca in his tragedy *Phaedra*, which, as announced by the title, focuses on Phaedra rather than Hippolytus. Finally, it is necessary to mention Racine's magnificent *Phèdre* (1677), which draws on the entire rich tradition of the myth going back to Euripides.

Hippomedon   See SEVEN AGAINST THEBES.

Hippomenes   See ATALANTA.

Homer (eighth–seventh century B.C.E.) Epic poet and, according to ancient tradition, author of the ILIAD and ODYSSEY. Scholars usually date the Homeric epics to the eighth or seventh century B.C.E. Several cities claimed to be the birthplace of Homer; the most reliable clue to his origins is the Ionian dialect of his poetry.

While the ancients consistently name Homer as the author of the *Iliad* and *Odyssey*, a great deal of uncertainty surrounds the identity of the author(s) of the two Homeric epics, the circumstances of their composition and performance, and the mechanics of their creation and transmission as literary texts. The most we can reliably state is that the *Iliad* and *Odyssey* have come down to us as the works of "Homer," a figure of legend overlaid with diverse, sometimes contradictory biographical tradition who at some level provides a name to which these two great works can be attached. The idea of an author is a familiar one in the Western tradition, and for a long time Homer was presumed to be an early example of a literary creator, one of a long line of such creators, who brought into being unitary, original texts to which they could claim ownership. Scholarship in the last few decades, however, has increasingly focused on the Homeric poems as the products of oral culture and oral compositional techniques.

Close study of metrical and lexical features of the poems, and in particular the repeated use of stock phrases that can be used, in varying combinations, in recurrent metrical positions, has led some scholars to conclude that Homeric epic derives from an oral tradition based on a highly trained memory and an improvisational repertoire of themes, phrases, and type scenes.

The study of the orality of the Homeric poems has revolutionized our understanding of their composition and the question of authorship. To simplify a complex debate, an oral compositional milieu undermines the notion of a single, unitary author who could claim ownership of the poem and who created it in its present form in a more or less integral act of composition. A further issue within this set of investigations concerns the unity of Homeric epic. Since the 18th century, some scholars have doubted whether the Homeric epics were unified compositions; there are discrepancies and instances of discontinuity in their plot, which might suggest that originally separate song traditions were later merged into a larger epic. Certain episodes—e.g., the deeds of DIOMEDES in *Iliad* 5—hint of independent song traditions attached to local heroes that were later integrated within the Panhellenic scheme of Homeric epic. Neither minor inconsistency of plot, however, nor the existence of independent, oral song traditions constitutes a decisive argument against the composition of the Homeric epics by a single individual. A single author could have composed one or both of the Homeric epics, drawing on a rich oral tradition, synthesizing and transforming its elements. The carefully structured plots of both epics weigh heavily against the idea that the poems as we have them are the outcome of patchwork composition.

Yet difficult questions remain. In particular, if we accept that the epics derive from oral tradition, how did they get into their current written form? On some theories, writing played an essential part in the very composition of the poems. Many scholars have difficulty imagining how an epic poem 24 books in length could be performed, unless it was stretched out over successive nights of entertainment. It is possible, then, that a poet steeped in oral traditions, but also acquainted with the new technology of writing, at once drew on traditional material and at the same time used writing to create a new kind of work on a new, monumental scale.

Homeric Hymns ANONYMOUS (ca. eighth century B.C.E.) The *Homeric Hymns* are not written by Homer but are so called because their meter (dactylic hexameter) and style resemble Homer's. There are 33 hymns extant by different authors from different periods. They range in date from the eighth century B.C.E. to the Hellenistic period. Some of the hymns are quite short; they invoke the god or goddess and enumerate the god's genealogy, qualities, and areas of expertise. The four better-known hymns, by contrast, are long and contain substantial narratives about the god or goddess. These are the hymn to DEMETER, the hymn to HERMES, the hymn to APOLLO, and the hymn to APHRODITE. The hymn to Demeter tells of the abduction of PERSEPHONE, Demeter's search for her, Demeter's disguise as a mortal and employment at the house of Celeus, king of Eleusis, her thwarted attempt to confer immortality on Celeus's son DEMOPHON, and the origins of the Eleusinian mysteries. The hymn to Apollo tells of LETO's difficulties in finding a place to give birth to him, Apollo's slaying of the serpent, the foundation of his cult at Pytho, and the foundation of his cult at Delphi. The hymn to Hermes tells of the god's theft of Apollo's cattle and his invention of the lyre. The hymn to Aphrodite tells how ZEUS, irritated at the humiliation he has undergone in being made to desire mortal women, arranges to have Aphrodite fall in love with the Trojan ANCHISES, who will become the father of AENEAS. Especially notable in the hymns is the interest in relating the origins of cult (Apollo's cult at Delphi, the Eleusinian mysteries) and of other aspects of human society (the lyre, agriculture, sacrifice).

Horace (65 B.C.E.–8 B.C.E.) Quintus Horatius Flaccus came from Venusia (modern Venosa, Italy) and, according to his *Satires*, was the son of a freedman. Horace was educated, however, at an expensive school in Rome and afterward completed his education in the usual manner of the Roman upper classes by going to Athens. He held the position of military tribune under Brutus, one of the chief assassins of Julius Caesar, and fought on the side of the tyrannicides at the battle of Philippi in 42 B.C.E. After Brutus and Cassius were defeated, Horace returned to Italy, albeit with his patrimony reduced. He took a scribal position in Rome, began writing poetry, and eventually was admitted into the circle of friends of Maecenas, a close associate of Octavian. By 30 B.C.E., when Octavian had eliminated his rival Mark Antony and achieved undisputed dominance, Horace had published his two books of *Satires* (ca. 35 B.C.E. and 30 B.C.E., respectively) and a book of *Epodes* (30 B.C.E.). His most ambitious work, the *Odes*, came in two installments: Books 1–3 were published as a unit in 23 B.C.E.; a fourth book was added later, apparently at Augustus's request, in 13 B.C.E. After completing *Odes* 1–3, Horace returned to the more conversational style and hexameter line of his *Satires*, and published *Epistles* Book 1 (ca. 20–19 B.C.E.) and Book 2, composed of three longer epistles, one of which is the so-called *Ars Poetica*. The epistles of this second book were written at different points between 19 B.C.E. and 10 B.C.E. Horace also received the commission to write the *Saecular Hymn*, performed by choruses of girls and boys for Augustus's Saecular Games of 17 B.C.E.

Horace's *Odes* represent his most self-consciously poetic work and his most serious bid for literary immortality. In the last ode of the third book (3.30), he declares that he has "erected a monument more lasting than bronze." The *Satires* and *Epistles* simulate conversation (*sermo*)—the poet's musings, personal letters, and ethical discussions in hexameter verse. The *Epodes* imitate the iambic invective of the Greek poets Archilochus and Hipponax, yet without the dangers of truly vitriolic personal attack. Satire, too, ought to be a dangerous genre of personal attack, yet, in Horace's hands, it becomes a carefully tended discourse of ethical self-regulation and self-sufficiency. The common feature of Horace's works in diverse genres is authorial self-representation. In broad terms, Horace's literary self prefers the simple, tranquil lifestyle of the countryside and seeks out the autonomy afforded by seclusion. This picture is complicated, however, by the poet's many points of connection with the city—his powerful friends, the importance of the city as focus of literary society, and above all his association with Maecenas and Augustus.

Horace's most significant use of myth can be found in his *Odes*. Following the tradition of Greek lyric, he employs myth as an illustration and expansion of the sentiments he expresses as a first-person speaker. Figures from heroic mythology, such as PARIS or TEUCER, appear in his lyric poems, but they are adapted to the scale and distinctive focus of lyric. Horace does not present sweeping narratives in his odes, but carefully selected speech occasions that distill or compress the meaning of the myth to suit the needs of his lyric treatment. Epic is nominally the opposite of lyric, the genre against which the lyric poet defines his less exalted and more personal focus, and yet Horace constantly adapts and assimilates the heroic mythology of epic for his own purposes. Horace's apparently narrow definition of lyric's literary domain is thus misleading: He manages to incorporate a broad range of subject matter, including mythological material proper to tragedy and epic.

Horae (Horai, Seasons) Goddesses of the seasons. Classical sources are the *Homeric Hymn to Apollo* (194–195), Hesiod's THEOGONY (901–906), Homer's ILIAD (5.749–751, 8.393–395, 433–435), Ovid's METAMORPHOSES (2.116–118), Pausanias's *Description of Greece* (1.40.4, 2.17.4, 5.11.7, 9.35.2), and Pindar's *Olympian Odes* (13.6–10) and *Pythian Odes* (9.59–65). In Hesiod, the Horae are the daughters of THEMIS (goddess of Justice or Law) and ZEUS. In the *Theogony*, there are three Horae; they were named Dike (Justice), Eirene (Peace), and Eunomia (Lawfulness) and are thus connected to concepts of rightful natural order. In other sources, the Horae (named Auxo, Carpo, and Thallo) are more closely related to the growing seasons. The Horae are also associated with the GRACES (Charites). In Homer's *Iliad*, the Horae stand at the entrance gates to Olympus, admitting those who have the right to enter, while in Pindar's *Pythian Odes* 9, the Horae together with GAIA, make ARISTAEUS immortal by giving him nectar and ambrosia. In Homer and Ovid, the Horae prepare the horses of the gods.

Hundred-Handed Ones (Hekatonkheires) Briareus, Gyges (Gyes), and Cottus (Kottos), the three giants with 100 hands and 50 heads each. Offspring of the TITANS URANUS and GAIA. Brothers of the Cyclopes. Classical sources are Apollodorus's LIBRARY (1.1.1–1.2.1), Hesiod's THEOGONY (617–735, 807–819), Homer's ILIAD (1.396–406), and Virgil's AENEID (10.565–568). Hesiod describes the Hundred-Handed Ones as possessing immense strength. Cronus viewed them as a threat and imprisoned them in TARTARUS. During the Titanomachy, in which the Olympian gods battled the Titans, ZEUS released the GIANTS, Cyclopes, and Hundred-Handed Ones from Tartarus and defeated the Titans with their help. During the battle, the Hundred-Handed Ones gathered rocks in their 300 hands and flung them at the Titans, burying them under their weight. The Olympian gods then imprisoned the Titans in Tartarus behind bronze walls and a bronze gate, and set the Hundred-Handed Ones as guards over them.

Hyacinthus (Hyakinthos) A mortal youth from Sparta loved by APOLLO. Classical sources are Apollodorus's LIBRARY (1.3.3, 3.10.3), Euripides' HELEN (1,465–1,475),

Lucian's DIALOGUES OF THE GODS (16), Ovid's METAMORPHOSES (10.162–219, 13.394–398), Pausanias's *Description of Greece* (3.1.3, 3.19.3–5), and Philostratus's IMAGINES (1.24). Like ADONIS, ENDYMION, and GANYMEDE, Hyacinthus was a beautiful mortal youth who attracted the amorous attention of a god. Hyacinthus was killed accidentally when a discus thrown by Apollo was blown off course by ZEPHYRUS, the West Wind, who, in some versions of the myth, was also enamored of Hyacinthus. Apollo attempted to revive him but in vain. A flower arose from the drops of blood shed by Hyacinthus—the hyacinth—giving the flower its bright red color; on its leaves were marked the letters "ai, ai," meaning "alas, alas." An Attic red-figure cup from ca. 480 B.C.E. shows a winged Zephyrus pulling the youth toward him in an embrace (Museum of Fine Arts, Boston). Postclassical paintings emphasized his relationship with Apollo instead. One such example are the frescoes in Palazzo Farnese, Rome, where the myth of Hyacinthus was represented twice, by Annibale Carracci and Domenichino. Many artists focused on the moment of Hyacinthus's death, for example, G. B. Tiepolo's *The Death of Hyacinth* of ca. 1752 (Thyssen-Bornemisza, Lugano).

Hydra of Lerna A nine-headed serpent born of the union of TYPHOEUS and ECHIDNA. Classical sources are Apollodorus's LIBRARY (2.5.2), Diodorus Siculus's LIBRARY OF HISTORY (4.11.5–6), Euripides' HERACLES (419–421) and ION (194–200), Hesiod's THEOGONY (313–319), Ovid's METAMORPHOSES (9.69–74) and Sophocles' TRACHINIAE (573–574, 714–718). Heracles' Second Labor was to kill the Hydra of Lerna. HERA, according to some sources, had raised the hydra and now sent a crab to help it. The crab bit Heracles' foot and was afterward placed in the heavens as a constellation. Heracles cut off each of the hydra's heads and asked Iolaus, his nephew and companion, to sear shut the wounds so that no new heads could regrow, a tactic that finally killed the

Hercules Battles the Hydra. *Antonio Pollaiuolo, 15th century (Galleria degli Uffizi, Florence)*

hydra. The hydra also became a constellation. Afterward, Heracles dipped his arrows in the hydra's poisonous blood (or venom), thus arming himself with a formidable weapon, which came to play a role in Heracles' death. A Caeretan black-figure hydria from ca. 525 B.C.E. (J. Paul Getty Museum, Malibu) shows the nine-headed serpent grasped by Heracles as he raises his club over it. A similar representation characterizes the 15th-century oil on panel by Antonio Pollaiuolo, *Heracles Battles the Hydra* (Galleria degli Uffizi, Florence). In this image, the artist has set the struggle between Heracles and the hydra against a vast landscape.

Hygeia Greek goddess of Health. Daughter of ASCLEPIUS, god of medicine. Classical sources are the *Orphic Hymn to Hygeia* and Pausanias's

Description of Greece (1.23.4, 5.20.3). There is no mythology proper to Hygeia, but she was worshipped in cult together with Asclepius. Asclepius married Epione, and from this union was born Hygeia, who shared her father's healing skills. Asclepius was also said to have passed on his skills to his sons, Machaon and Podaleirius, who accompanied AGAMEMNON during the Trojan War. In the *Orphic Hymn to Asclepius*, Hygeia is Asclepius's wife, but in other sources, she is his daughter, a skilled healer in her own right, and goddess of health. In the *Orphic Hymn to Hygeia*, Hygeia, hated only by HADES, whom she deprives of victims, is eternally youthful. She brings joy, wards off disease, and without her goodwill a large fortune is useless. Hygeia was represented in antiquity on various media-reliefs, ceramics, coins, and sculpture. She often appears, sometimes alone and sometimes in the company of Asclepius, with a snake. An example is an imperial period freestanding sculpture (Vatican Museums, Rome). Here, Asclepius is seated and Hygeia stands beside him. A snake wrapping itself around the leg of the chair on which Asclepius is seated meets Hygeia's outstretched hand.

Hyginus (ca. first century) Very little is known about the author of the mythological handbook that now is known by the title *Fabulae* (Fables, or Stories) but in antiquity probably had the title *Genealogiae* (Genealogies). There is one well-known Hyginus who might have written such a handbook: Gaius Julius Hyginus, a Spaniard who lived in the first centuries B.C.E. and C.E., and, as freedman of the Roman emperor Augustus, served as librarian of the prestigious Palatine Library. Most scholars, however, doubt that Gaius Julius Hyginus was the author of the *Fabulae*. It is evident, in any case, that the text underwent multiple redactions by different authors over time, and thus it is not truly the work of a single writer. The work begins with a theogony and then proceeds through various sections devoted to mythic cycles, specific heroes, mythological figures, and categories. Modern scholars of myth tend to cite the *Fabulae* with caution, owing to the various errors and misunderstandings that were incorporated into the text over time by authors of less than perfect erudition.

Hylas An Argive youth, "golden-haired" Hylas was loved by HERACLES. Son of Theodamas. Classical sources are Apollodorus's LIBRARY (1.9.19, 2.7.7), Apollonius of Rhodes's *VOYAGE OF THE ARGONAUTS* (1.1,207–1,357), Propertius's *Elegies* (1.20.5–32), Strabo's *Geography* (12.4.3), and Theocritus's *Idylls* (13.36–75). Hylas and Heracles joined the expedition of JASON and the Argonauts. During the voyage, the crew arrived at Propontis, made camp, and Hylas was sent to fetch water. He found a spring and the nymphs residing in it fell in love with him. They drew him into the water and held him fast. In Propertius's *Elegies,* the nymphs are Hamadryads, tree nymphs from the tree shadowing the spring. Heracles engaged in a frenzied search for Hylas but was not able to find him. Heracles called out Hylas's name three times but was not able to hear Hylas's replies from within the spring. The Argonauts left Heracles behind in Propontis, but eventually the grief-stricken hero conceded defeat and journeyed to Colchis on foot. Heracles' companion Cius remained and founded a city that bore his name. Together with Heracles, Cius established rites for the lost Hylas that involved ritually calling out the name of Hylas. In Apollonius of Rhodes's *Voyage of the Argonauts* the prophetic sea god GLAUCUS emerged from the sea to tell the crew of the *Argo* that Hylas had wed a nymph and to insist that Heracles abandon his search and return to his destiny of accomplishing the Twelve Labors.

In classical art Hylas is represented with Heracles and the Argonauts or with the nymphs who abduct him. In paintings and mosaics Hylas is shown holding a water jug while the nymphs attempt to restrain him. A postclassical image in this iconographic tradition is J. W. Waterhouse's *Hylas and the Nymphs* of 1896 (Manchester Art Gallery, Manchester, England).

Hyllus Son of Heracles, one of the Heracleidae. Hyllus appears in Euripides' *HERACLEIDAE* and Sophocles' *TRACHINIAE*. Additional classical sources are Apollodorus's *LIBRARY* (2.7.7–2.8.2), Diodorus Siculus's *LIBRARY OF HISTORY* (4.57), Herodotus's *Histories* (8.131), Pausanias's *Description of History* (1.41.2–3, 8.5.1), and Strabo's *Geography* (19.4.10). Some sources name Omphale or a nymph as Hyllus's mother, but the generally accepted version is that Hyllus was the son of Heracles' second wife, DEIANIRA.

In the *Trachiniae*, Sophocles describes Hyllus as a loyal and obedient son. When Heracles brought his mistress, Iole, into the house, Deianira gave him a robe that, unknown to her, was covered with a deadly poison. In despair at what she had inadvertently done, she took her own life. Hyllus promised the dying Heracles that he would marry Iole himself after his father's death. Then, on his father's orders, he built the funeral pyre on Mount Oeta, where Heracles ended his life. Hyllus grieved for his father's fate but at the same time demonstrated sympathy for his anguished mother. Hyllus was one of the leaders of the Heracleidae in Euripides' play of the same name. In the company of Iolaus and DEMOPHON, the king of Athens, Hyllus waged a successful war against King EURYSTHEUS, his father's lifelong enemy. Hyllus and the other Heracleidae were also said to have conquered the Peloponnesus after Eurystheus's death. But they were not allowed to hold it in peace. Eurystheus's successor, ATREUS, in league with the Tegeatans led by Echemus, again made war against Hyllus and the Heracleidae. Echemus finally killed Hyllus in single combat.

Hymen (Hymenaeus) Greek god of marriage. Son either of APHRODITE and DIONYSUS or of APOLLO and a MUSE. Classical sources are Euripides' *TROJAN WOMEN* (310–340) and Ovid's *METAMORPHOSES* (4.758–764, 9.762–797, 10.1–7). Hymen appears frequently together with either or both of two goddesses whose presence at marriages is particularly appropriate: Aphrodite, the personification of love, and HERA, goddess of marriage as an institution. In the *Metamorphoses*, both Aphrodite and Hera accompany Hymen, clad in his saffron-colored mantle at the wedding of PERSEUS and ANDROMEDA and the marriage of IPHIS and Ianthe.

It was traditional to chant *hymen o hymenaie* in Greek wedding songs. Over time, Hymen was understood to be a god of marriage invoked in the songs. Hymen/Hymenaeus then becomes a figure in myth and a conventional figure in mythic marriage scenes. In Ovid's *Metamorphoses*, at the wedding of Perseus and Andromeda, the marriage fires were lit, incense was burned, wedding hymns were sung to the accompaniment of the lyre and flute, while Eros and Hymen shook the bridal torches.

Hymen's presence, however, was not enough to guarantee good fortune if the wedding was marred by unfavorable portents. The marriage of ORPHEUS AND EURYDICE is an example of an ill-starred ceremony, despite Hymen's presence. According to Ovid, the torches that Hymen held sputtered and refused to burn, an evil presage fulfilled in the bride's untimely death.

References to Hymen and the marriage rites associated with him are evoked by a half-mad CASSANDRA in Euripides' *Trojan Women*. The tragic irony of her invocation of Hymen is all the more bitter because she is one of the defeated Trojan women parceled out among the victors.

In art, Hymen is depicted as a youth and is sometimes confused with Eros. His attribute is the burning torch, and he often wears a crown of flowers in his hair. Representations of Hymen were popular in early-modern paintings, where he is frequently shown with either Aphrodite or Eros, or both. An example is Peter Paul Rubens's *The Marriage of Marie de'Medici to Henri IV by Proxy* from 1622–25 (Louvre, Paris), where he is shown as a very young, fair-haired boy carrying a burning torch.

Hyperion A Titan, the offspring of Gaia (Earth) and Uranus (Heaven). Brother of Iapetus, Coeus, Crius, Cronus, Mnemosyne, Oceanus, Phoebe, Rhea, Tethys, Theia, and Themis. Classical sources are the *Homeric Hymn to Helios*, Hesiod's Theogony (132–136, 371–374), and Homer's Odyssey (1.24). Hyperion was associated with light, and brightness, and, like Helios, often represents the sun. Hyperion married his sister Theia. Their offspring are Eos (Dawn), Helios (Sun), and Selene (Moon). In the *Homeric Hymn to Helios*, Hyperion's wife is named Euryphaessa; like Theia, she is said to be his sister. According to Diodorus Siculus, Hyperion is also associated with astronomy. While Hyperion appears in the genealogies, beginning with Hesiod, he does not otherwise appear in myth.

Hypermnestra See Danaids.

Hypnos (Hypnus) A personification of sleep. Son of Erebus and Nyx (Night). Twin brother of Thanatos (Death). Classical sources are Homer's Iliad (14.225–362, 16.666–683), Ovid's Metamorphoses (11.592–649), and Pausanias's *Description of Greece* (2.31.3, 5.18.1). Hypnos is winged, can fly through the air, and, in Homer's *Iliad*, lives on the island of Lemnos. According to Homer, Hera descends from Mount Olympus to request that Hypnos lull Zeus to asleep. He refuses, pointing out that when he had previously put Zeus to sleep at her request, Zeus had awakened furious, and Hypnos had escaped his wrath only by the protection of Nyx. Hera finally persuades Hypnos by offering one of the Graces, Pasithea, as his wife. Also in the *Iliad*, after the death of Sarpedon during the Trojan War, Hypnos and Thanatos are charged by Apollo to convey

Sarpedon's body to his native Lycia for burial. In Ovid's *Metamorphoses*, Hera sends the messenger goddess Iris to the cave of Hypnos in the myth of Alcyone.

Hypsipyle Queen of Lemnos, daughter of Thoas, lover of Jason. Classical sources are Apollodorus's Library (1.9.14, 1.9.17, 3.6.4, Epitome 1.9), Apollonius of Rhodes's Voyage of the Argonauts (1.609–909), Homer's Iliad (7.467–475, 14.230, 21.40–41, 23.740–749), Hyginus's *Fabulae* (74), Ovid's Heroides (6), and Statius's Thebaid (4.715–6.192). In Apollonius of Rhodes's *Voyage of the Argonauts*, Jason and his companions arrive at the island of Lemnos. The women of the island neglected the rites of Aphrodite, and as punishment, the goddess made the men of the island passionately desire the Thracian slave girls they captured in war, but not their own wives. (In Apollodorus's version, the Lemnian women were no longer attractive to their husbands because Aphrodite afflicted the women with a horrible smell.) The Lemnian women therefore killed, not only the slave girls and their husbands, but all the males of the island to avoid later reprisals. Hypsipyle saved her father, Thoas, son of Dionysus and Ariadne, by setting him to drift in a hollow chest on the sea. According to Apollonius, Thoas was still the king of Lemnos, despite the fact that Hypsipyle appeared to rule the island in his absence.

At first, when the Argonauts arrived, the Lemnians thought their enemies the Thracians were arriving. On realizing their error, they decided to receive the Argonauts into their homes in the hope of producing children who could later defend them from invading enemies and sustain them in old age. The Lemnians became the lovers of the Argonauts, and Jason became Hypsipyle's lover; in Apollonius, she is quite willing, but according to her first-person narrative in Statius, she was taken by Jason against her will. At length, Heracles grew impatient and demanded that they depart to complete their quest. The Argonauts left the Lemnians on amicable terms. In Ovid's *Heroides*, however, Hypsipyle is a violently jealous lover, who views herself as Jason's wife and bitterly resents the fact that he has taken up with MEDEA. In Apollonius, Hypsipyle alludes to the possibility of children by Jason, and elsewhere we hear that she had two children by him, Euneus and Thoas or Nephrophonus; Euneus is mentioned more than once in Homer's *Iliad*.

Hyginus, Apollodorus, and Statius relate a further development of Hypsipyle's story. Hypsipyle, according to Statius, received the help of Dionysus in securing her father Thoas's safety. Afterward, however, the other Lemnian women discovered what she had done and were resentful of her deception, or (in Statius) of her innocence. They killed her father and sold her into slavery (Apollodorus), or Hypsipyle herself departed for the shore, where she was captured by pirates and sold into slavery (Statius). She ended up as the slave of king Lycurgus of Nemea: She was assigned as the nurse of Opheltes, the son of Lycurgus and his wife Eurydice. When the Argive heroes in the expedition of the Seven against Thebes reached Nemea, there was a drought, and they could not find any water. Hypsipyle led them to the one spring that still had water. She either left behind Opheltes in order to do so (Apollodorus), or left him asleep in the grass as she told the Argives her story (Statius); the child was killed by a serpent sacred to Jupiter. The Argives killed the serpent (in Statius, CAPANEUS killed it, declaring his indifference to its protector god), and the child was buried. Opheltes was also called Archemorus ("beginning of doom"), because his death was the first death of the war. In Statius, Lycurgus called for Hypsipyle's death as punishment for her neglect, but AMPHIARAUS and ADRASTUS persuaded the Nemeans to pardon her, though Eurydice remained savagely angry. Unexpectedly, her two sons Thoas and Euneus appeared and were reunited with their mother. Finally, it was decided that Archemorus would be honored as a hero. The Nemean segment of Hypsipyle's mythology has evidently been merged with the Lemnian segment; originally, there appears to have been two distinct traditions.

Ianthe   See Iphis.

Iapetus (Iapetos)   A Titan. The offspring of Gaia (Earth) and Uranus (Heaven). Brother of Hyperion, Coeus, Crius, Cronus, Mnemosyne, Oceanus, Phoebe, Rhea, Tethys, Theia, and Themis. Classical sources are Apollodorus's Library (1.2.3), Hesiod's Theogony (132–136, 507–511), and Homer's Iliad (8.478–481). Following a 10-year battle for supremacy against the Olympian gods, the Titans were defeated and Iapetus was imprisoned in Tartarus with Cronus and the other Titans. Iapetus married Cymene, daughter of Oceanus (though in Apollodorus, Iapetus's wife is another Oceanid named Asia). The children of Clymene and Iapetus are Atlas, Epimetheus, Menoitius, and Prometheus. Menoitius was slain by Zeus during the Titanomachy, but Atlas, Epimetheus, and Prometheus feature in important myths that establish the relationship between the world of the Olympian gods and that of mortals. The descendants of Iapetus are Deucalion and Pyrrha, who were the sole human survivors of the great flood and were responsible for repopulating the earth. While Iapetus appears in the genealogies of Apollodorus and Hesiod, he does not otherwise appear in myth.

Icarus   Son of Daedalus. Classical sources are Apollodorus's Library (Epitome 1.12–13), Diodorus Siculus's Library of History (4.77.5–9, Hyginus's Fabulae (40), Ovid's Metamorphoses (8.183–235), and Virgil's Aeneid (6.14–33). Icarus's father, Daedalus, was the master artisan and inventor of King Minos's court in Crete. Daedalus created the famed labyrinth that contained the Minotaurs, and then, for having helped Theseus, was himself imprisoned by Minos. Daedalus constructed wings on which he and Icarus could escape and warned Icarus to fly neither so high that the sun would melt the wax attaching the wings to the shoulders, nor so low that the spray from the sea would weigh them down. Icarus could not prevent himself from flying too high, however, and fell to his death into the sea. The body of water into which he fell, or, in Ovid's account, a nearby island, Icaria, was named after him. In Apollodorus's Library, Icarus's body was found by Heracles, who gave it a proper burial. In gratitude Daedalus created a statue of Heracles at Pisa. Virgil claims that Daedalus built a temple on his arrival in Italy and three times attempted to represent in relief sculpture his son's death, and three times failed to do so. Ovid was even more interested in Daedalus as a paradigm of the artisan, and Icarus as a representation of the dangers and limits of art. He tells the story at length both in his

The Fall of Icarus. *Woodcut, Albrecht Dürer (attrib.), 1493*

Metamorphoses and at the beginning of the second book of his *Ars Amatoria.*

In classical art, Icarus is depicted as a young man with wings attached to his back accompanied by Daedalus or alone. He is shown thus in a first-century C.E. fresco from the Villa Imperiale at Pompeii. Here, Icarus has fallen into the sea as Daedalus soars above him. A postclassical example of the same theme is a 15th-century woodcut by Albrecht Dürer, *The Fall of Icarus* (1493), which shows a dismayed Daedalus watching Icarus tumble through the sky scattering feathers in his wake. Pieter Brueghel (Bruegel) the Elder integrated Icarus's fall into a landscape in *The Fall of Icarus* of 1569 (Musée Royaux des Beaux-Arts, Brussels). The myth of Icarus has inspired poetic tribute by W. H. Auden and William Carlos Williams.

Iliad HOMER (ca. eighth–seventh century B.C.E.) While we know little to nothing about the poet called Homer, the epic poems ascribed to him were probably composed in the eighth or seventh centuries B.C.E. Sometimes scholars have argued that the *Iliad* was composed earlier than the *Odyssey*, but there is no secure basis for this argument. The style of the poems strongly suggests that they come out of an oral tradition of improvisatory song, but their transmission as texts demands the intervention of writing at some stage. To what extent writing is integral to the composition of Homeric epic is debated. In short, a great deal of uncertainty surrounds the identity of the author(s) of the Homeric epics, the date of their composition, and the circumstances in which they came to be written. For further discussion, see HOMER.

Homer's *Iliad* narrates the consequences of the Greek hero ACHILLES' quarrel with AGAMEMNON, the leader of the expedition against Troy. Deprived of BRISEIS, the captive woman allotted to him as his share of the plunder, and thereby deprived, as he sees it, of the honor due to him, Achilles withdraws from battle, causing the tide of war to go against the Greeks. Achilles finally returns to battle late in the epic, after his comrade PATROCLUS dies at the hands of HECTOR. The central themes of the epic are human mortality and the anger that drives Achilles' action in complex ways.

SYNOPSIS

Book 1

The poet asks the MUSE to sing of the anger of Achilles and its destructive outcome. Chryses, a priest of Apollo, whose daughter Chryseis has been given to Agamemnon, leader of the Greek expedition, as a prize of war, prays to APOLLO, who sends a plague on the Greeks. The seer CALCHAS informs the Greeks that Chryseis must be returned to her father. Agamemnon consents angrily but demands that one of the other Greek chieftains give him their prize in compensation. Achilles and Agamemnon quarrel over this demand; ATHENA prevents Achilles from killing Agamemnon on the spot, and Agamemnon claims and takes Briseis, Achilles' prize. Achilles withdraws to his tent and appeals to his mother, the goddess THETIS, for help; she, in turn, successfully supplicates ZEUS, who agrees to turn the tide of war against the Greeks to make them appreciate the loss of Achilles from the battlefield. HERA, who supports the Greek side, learns about Zeus's agreement with Thetis and quarrels with him. HEPHAESTUS succeeds in dissolving the tension, and the gods turn to feasting.

Book 2

Zeus decides to undermine the Greeks by sending a false dream to Agamemnon to make him think the Greeks are on the verge of victory. Agamemnon, on waking, is filled with confidence but decides to test his men by suggesting that they sail home. The men begin to rush toward the ships; only the quick reaction of ODYSSEUS prevents a mass exodus. Thersites then starts to complain about Agamemnon, but Odysseus rebukes him and strikes him down. Odysseus and NESTOR deliver encouraging speeches and offer sacrifice, but Zeus does not grant Agamemnon's prayer. The Greek army gathers, and the poet asks the Muse to tell him of the Greek ships and their commanders: A catalog follows. The messenger goddess IRIS bids Hector gather together the Trojan contingents: A catalog of these also follows.

Book 3

The armies advance toward each other, and PARIS, seeing MENELAUS, retreats. Rebuked for cowardice by his brother Hector, Paris proposes that he meet Menelaus in a duel. The winner will take HELEN and her property, and the war will be resolved. The two sides agree to the duel. Helen, informed by Iris of the upcoming duel, comes down to the walls of Troy, where she points out the Greek heroes to PRIAM and describes their qualities. The duel begins, and Menelaus is on the point of victory, when APHRODITE carries Paris away in a cloud of mist to Helen's bedroom; Aphrodite forces a reluctant Helen to return to Paris and make love to him. Menelaus, in the meanwhile, searches in vain for the vanished Paris, and Agamemnon declares victory for the Greeks.

Book 4

Zeus teases Athena and Hera by suggesting that the war be ended and Menelaus be allowed to take Helen home. Hera is outraged, since she wants Troy destroyed. Athena descends to make the Trojans break the truce, which she achieves by taking human form and persuading the Trojan Pandarus to shoot an arrow at Menelaus. Athena ensures that the arrow only grazes him. Agamemnon then surveys the troops and makes speeches to the Greek heroes, some full of praise and some taunting, to raise their spirits for battle. Battle commences, with Apollo supporting the Trojans, while Athena supports the Greeks.

Book 5

Athena now inspires the Greek Diomedes with valor. He begins a furious onslaught on the Trojans. He is wounded by Pandarus, but Athena heals him and enables him to distinguish between men and gods. She warns him not to attack any god except for Aphrodite. Thus, when Aphrodite, Aeneas's mother, intervenes to save her son from Diomedes, who is about to kill him, Diomedes turns on her, gives pursuit, and manages to wound her below the palm of her hand. She retreats to Olympus, where her mother, Dione, consoles her. Diomedes still pursues Aeneas, but Apollo warns him off and removes Aeneas from the field. ARES, at Apollo's bidding, encourages the Trojans. The fighting continues, and deaths mount up on both sides. Athena goes to Diomedes, who has retreated from Ares in accordance with Athena's previous instructions, and bids him to join her now in attacking Ares. He wounds Ares, who returns complaining to Olympus. Zeus is unsympathetic but has Paeon heal him.

Book 6

The Greeks gain the advantage in battle. The Trojan prophet HELENUS advises Aeneas and Hector to rally the troops and Hector to go into the city of Troy and tell the women to offer a sacrifice to Athena. With the help of Hector and Aeneas, the Trojans rally, and Hector departs for the city. The Trojan GLAUCUS and Diomedes meet in battle. When Glaucus tells of his ancestry, including the story of his grandfather BELLEROPHON, Diomedes realizes that they are guest-friends, because his grandfather Oeneus hosted Bellerophon once and they exchanged gifts. The two warriors agree

to avoid each other in battle, and they exchange armor—Glaucus's gold armor for Diomedes' bronze. Hector arrives in Troy and gives his mother, HECUBA, instructions for the sacrifice to Athena; they perform the sacrifice, but it is in vain. Hector then visits with Paris and Helen and at last goes to seek his own family. He meets his wife, ANDROMACHE, and his son, ASTYANAX, with the knowledge that he may be seeing them for the last time. Hector and Paris return to battle together.

Book 7

Apollo and Athena agree to have Hector challenge the Greeks to a duel. Helenus divines the gods' will and tells Hector, who issues his challenge to the Greeks. Menelaus wishes to take up the challenge, but Agamemnon dissuades him. At length, Ajax is chosen by lot. They fight with spears and rocks, and are about to engage in close combat with swords, when heralds intervene and the duel is called off. The two heroes exchange gifts. Nestor proposes to the Greeks that they negotiate a truce to allow for cremation of the dead and also that they build walls to protect their ships. The Greeks accept his suggestions. For their part, the Trojans promise that if the Greeks depart, they will return all the property Paris took from Menelaus, except his wife, whom Paris refuses to give up. The Greeks refuse this offer, but both sides agree to a truce for cremation. The Trojans and Greeks cremate their dead, and the Greeks build a wall and fortifications. The Trojans and Greeks feast as Zeus thunders ominously.

Book 8

Zeus warns the gods not to support either side, then goes to Mount Ida. The Greeks are in retreat. Diomedes saves Nestor with Odysseus's help and goes on an onslaught, which is stopped at last by a thunderbolt from Zeus. Hector taunts Diomedes as Zeus continues to thunder in support of the Trojans. Hera tries to get POSEIDON to help. When he refuses, she inspires Agamemnon to rally the Greeks. It is TEUCER'S turn to go on an onslaught, until Hector stops him by smashing his bow with a rock. Hector now drives the Greeks back to the ships, at which point Athena and Hera prepare to join battle on the Greek side. Zeus, enraged, sends Iris to warn them off. Then, on Olympus, he informs the disgruntled goddesses that he will not relent until Achilles returns to battle after Patroclus's death, as it is fated. A confident Hector instructs the Trojans to encamp around the Greeks and hem them in.

Book 9

Agamemnon expresses his despair and frustration with the failing expedition. Nestor suggests offering an apology and compensation to Achilles. Agamemnon agrees to offer back Briseis in addition to many other lavish gifts. Nestor chooses Phoenix, Ajax, and Odysseus for the embassy. Achilles welcomes them hospitably. Odysseus appeals to him to save the Greeks from catastrophe and presents Agamemnon's offer of compensation. Achilles replies that he does not care for Agamemnon or his offer, and intends to return home. Phoenix, Achilles' childhood tutor and guardian, appeals to him in the name of their friendship and tells the story of MELEAGER, who from anger had once refused to fight for his city when it was under siege; he relented later and drove back the enemies, but by then he had forfeited the reward that he had been promised originally. Achilles is still not persuaded; instead, he invites Phoenix to stay with him. Finally, Ajax argues that it is normal to accept compensation even for murder, whereas Achilles refuses compensation for the mere loss of a captive girl. Achilles admits the force of Ajax's argument but remains deeply angry at Agamemnon. Odysseus and Ajax return to report the failure of the embassy, while Phoenix stays with Achilles.

Book 10

Agamemnon and Menelaus cannot sleep. They rouse Nestor, and then Odysseus and Diomedes. The Greek leaders hold a council, and Nestor recommends a surprise attack on the Trojan camp. Diomedes volunteers and selects Odysseus as his comrade. As they depart, they observe a lucky omen from Athena. Hector, in the meanwhile, seeks a volunteer to spy on the Greeks; Dolon offers himself. Odysseus and Diomedes intercept him as he is on his way to the Greek camp and find out from him how the camps and sentries of the Trojans and their allies are disposed; Diomedes kills Dolon, and they decide to attack the nearby camp of the Thracian leader Rhesus, who has a splendid chariot and horses. They slaughter the sleeping Rhesus and his men and take the horses. The Trojans wake up to discover the carnage, while Odysseus and Diomedes return in triumph.

Book 11

Zeus sends down the goddess Strife to the Greeks, whom she fills with warlike spirit. Agamemnon arms himself and goes on an onslaught; the Trojans fall back. Zeus sends Iris to tell Hector to stay back until Agamemnon is wounded. At length, Agamemnon is wounded and quits the field. Hector enters the fray and kills many Greeks, until Diomedes strikes him with a stunning blow and forces him to retreat. Then Paris wounds Diomedes in the foot with an arrow, and Diomedes also has to withdraw. Odysseus is left alone to face the Trojans, but Ajax and Menelaus come to help him. Paris then shoots the healer Machaon, whom Nestor rescues. As a harried Ajax retreats, Achilles observes the disarray of the Greeks and perceives Nestor taking Machaon back to the camp; knowing Machaon's importance to the Greeks, he sends Patroclus to ask after him. Patroclus arrives at Nestor's hut, and Nestor recounts to him the glorious deeds of his own youth. At length he suggests that Patroclus take the field in Achilles' place, leading the Myrmidons and wearing Achilles' armor. Patroclus, as he is helping the wounded Eurypylus, learns the extent of the Greeks' woes.

Book 12

The poet observes that one day, after the fall of Troy, Poseidon and Apollo will destroy the wall the Greeks have made. The Trojans decide to leave behind their chariots and assault the wall on foot. The two Lapiths, Polypoetes and Leonteus, courageously repel the Trojan advance. The Trojan Polydamas interprets the omen of an eagle that holds a snake in its talons and then drops it after it is bitten to mean that the Trojans should hold back; Hector rejects his advice and leads the Trojans forward. The two Ajaxes encourage the Greeks. The Trojans SARPEDON and Glaucus attack the wall. Ajax and Teucer hold them off, and Glaucus is wounded. Sarpedon leads his Lycians onward, and Hector smashes open the gate with a huge rock. The Trojans swarm inside, and the Greeks flee toward the ships.

Book 13

Zeus, satisfied with the Trojan position, and sure that the other Olympians would not dare intervene, turns his gaze to other lands. But Poseidon, taking the form of Calchas, inspires the two Ajaxes and the Greeks generally, and the Greeks stop Hector's advance. The two sides engage in fierce battle; among the warriors killed on both sides is Poseidon's grandson Amphimachus. Poseidon then encourages Idomeneus, who enters battle with Meriones. Greeks and Trojans, supported by Zeus and Poseidon, respectively, now engage in a prolonged, bloody hand-to-hand combat. At length the Greeks begin to gain the advantage, and the Trojans are in disarray. Hector gathers the Trojan troops and surveys their losses. Ajax challenges Hector, and an eagle appears; Hector responds fiercely, and fighting resumes.

Book 14

Nestor goes among the troops and discovers that Agamemnon, Diomedes, and Odysseus are wounded. Agamemnon suggests that they flee in their ships and is rebuked by Odysseus. Diomedes suggests that they return to the battlefield and encourage others to fight. Agamemnon takes his advice and is met on his way back to battle by Poseidon, who further inspires him. Meanwhile, Hera resolves to distract Zeus's attention from the battlefield. She seduces him with the help of Aphrodite; afterward, he is overpowered by Sleep, whose help Hera has also enlisted. Sleep then relays the news to Poseidon, who is now free to support the Greeks without restraint. The Greeks begin to gain momentum.

Book 15

Zeus wakes to observe the Trojans in flight and Hector lying wounded on the ground. He realizes Hera's deception and threatens her. Hera lays the blame on Poseidon. Zeus sends Iris to recall Poseidon. Poseidon reluctantly agrees to withdraw. Zeus sends Apollo to restore Hector to health. Apollo fills Hector with renewed energy and courage, and the Greeks gather to resist him. With Apollo's support, Hector routs the Greeks and leads the Trojans toward the Greek ships. Patroclus observes the fighting around the ships and, resolving to join the battle, goes to see Achilles. The fighting continues, with Hector and Ajax rallying their respective sides. Hector, filled with strength by Zeus, overpowers the Greeks. He reaches the ships and attempts to set them on fire as Ajax struggles to hold off the Trojans.

Book 16

Patroclus goes to Achilles' tent in tears and laments the predicament of the Greeks; he asks to fight in Achilles' armor. Achilles assents, but warns Patroclus not to go beyond saving the ships and attack Troy itself; that would diminish Achilles' own glory. In the meantime, Hector drives Ajax back and sets fire to the ships. Achilles gathers his Myrmidons to encourage them and prays to Zeus that Patroclus will drive back the Trojans and return alive. Zeus grants the first request but not the second. Patroclus and the Myrmidons join battle with the Trojans. Led by Patroclus, the Greeks go on the offensive, driving back the Trojans. Zeus is aware that his son the Trojan Sarpedon will soon die; he is reluctant to allow it, but Hera reminds him of the ineluctable fate of mortals. Zeus sends down a rain of blood in tribute. Patroclus kills Sarpedon and continues his onslaught. Zeus inspires Hector to flee and instructs Apollo to rescue Sarpedon's body and arrange his burial. Apollo warns off Patroclus, who retreats, but then presses forward again. Phoebus strikes Patroclus on the back with his hand, stunning him, shattering his spear, and knocking off his helmet, shield, and armor. The Trojan Euphorbus then wounds Patroclus, and Hector kills him. Hector taunts Patroclus, but before dying, Patroclus declares that Zeus and Apollo killed him, not Hector, and that Achilles will soon kill Hector.

Book 17

A fight arises over Patroclus's body, and Menelaus kills Euphorbus but is forced to retreat in front of Hector, who advances and strips Patroclus's armor (the armor that Achilles had lent him). Ajax advances in his turn and drives Hector back. The Lycian Glaucus accuses Hector of cowardice; Hector puts on Achilles' armor. Zeus pities Hector's imminent doom and so grants him supremacy in battle in the meantime. The Greeks and Trojans meet in the battle over Patroclus's body, rallied by Menelaus and Hector, respectively. A mist descends over this part of the battlefield. Achilles does not yet know the fate of his friend Patroclus. Zeus pities the horses of Achilles and arranges for them to escape back to the ships. The Greeks, supported by Athena, and the Trojans, supported by Apollo, continue to fight. Ajax despairs of sending the news of Patroclus's death to Achilles because of the mist, but Zeus dispels the mist. Menelaus sends Antilochus to tell Achilles. The Greeks realize that Achilles' help will not come immediately and so resolve to work together to carry Patroclus's body back to the ships. They retreat with the body, pursued by the Trojans.

Book 18

Antilochus reports to Achilles the news of Patroclus's death and Hector's possession of his armor. Achilles grieves deeply. Thetis hears him cry out and goes to him. She reminds him that he is doomed to die shortly after Hector, but Achilles is bent on revenge. Seeing that he is determined, Thetis departs to seek new armor for him. Hector makes constant attacks on the Greeks as they are bearing Patroclus's body to their own camp. He is on the verge of recapturing the body when Iris, sent by Hera, warns Achilles, who makes an appearance on the battlefield without his armor and terrifies the Trojans with his fierce shouting. The Trojans flee in panic, and the Greeks bring the body to safety. The Trojan Polydamas recommends that they retreat into the city, while Hector insists that they continue fighting. Athena undermines the Trojans' judgment, and they allow themselves to be persuaded by Hector. Achilles and the Greeks mourn Patroclus. Thetis goes to Hephaestus and asks him to make new armor for Achilles. Grateful to Thetis for sheltering him after he was thrown down from Olympus, Hephaestus makes the armor. Its designs are described in detail.

Book 19

Thetis brings the armor to the grieving Achilles and promises that Patroclus's body will be preserved from decomposition. He calls an assembly of the Greeks and renounces his destructive anger. Agamemnon claims that he had been led astray by Delusion, just as Zeus was when Hera tricked him into giving EURYSTHEUS supremacy instead of HERACLES. Moreover, he offers Achilles all the compensation that the embassy previously offered. Achilles is eager to fight. Odysseus recommends that they first eat, but Achilles refuses. The Greeks bring forth gifts for Achilles and also bring back Briseis. He still refuses to eat in his grief, but Zeus encourages Athena to infuse nectar and ambrosia into his chest. The Greeks, including Achilles, arm and take to the battlefield. Achilles' horse Xanthus, endowed with human speech by Hera, predicts his death.

Book 20

Zeus calls an assembly of the gods and gives them permission to help either side to prevent Achilles from completely routing the Trojans. When the Olympians take to the battlefield, there is a cosmic uproar that frightens HADES.

Apollo encourages Aeneas to face Achilles. The two warriors exchange words, compare lineages, and engage in battle. Achilles is on the verge of killing Aeneas. Poseidon, observing that Aeneas's line is destined to survive the destruction of Troy, saves him by removing him to the edge of the battlefield. Achilles, deprived of Aeneas, continues on his rampage. Apollo warns Hector not to approach Achilles, but when Achilles kills Hector's brother Polydorus, Hector challenges Achilles; Apollo, however, removes him before Achilles can kill him. Achilles continues his onslaught.

Book 21

Achilles slaughters the Trojans who have been driven into the river but sets aside 12 to be sacrificed in compensation for Patroclus's death. He kills the Trojan Lycaon mercilessly despite his supplication. As he continues to slaughter Trojans, the river god Scamander protests that Achilles is choking his waters with bodies. Achilles continues killing, and the river god attempts to drown him. Achilles is afraid, but Poseidon and Athena encourage him. At length, Hera orders Hephaestus to tame the river with fire. The parching flames subdue the river, who agrees not to make any further efforts to save the Trojans. Ares then challenges Athena, who strikes him with a boulder and lays him low. Aphrodite draws him from the battlefield, and encouraged by Hera, Athena strikes Aphrodite on the breast and knocks her down. Poseidon challenges Apollo, but Apollo disdains to fight another god for mere mortals. Hera humiliates Artemis by boxing her ears. HERMES refuses to fight LETO. Achilles drives the Trojans into flight. Priam opens the gates to let them in. Apollo takes on the appearance of the Trojan Agenor and lures Achilles away from Troy to help the Trojans escape.

Book 22

Apollo reveals his deception (that he took on the appearance of Agenor) to Achilles, who is furious. Hecuba and Priam plead with Hector not to face Achilles, but Hector decides that he must fight. Achilles rushes at Hector, and in a moment of panic, Hector flees around the walls of Troy. Zeus holds the two men's fate in the scales, and the balance sinks on Hector's side as a sign of his doom. Athena tricks Hector by assuming the appearance of Deiphobus and suggesting that they face Achilles together. Hector stops, challenges Achilles, and asks that they agree to return the body of the loser. Achilles refuses, hurls a spear, and misses; Athena returns his spear to him. Hector's spear is deflected by Achilles' spear, and as he seeks another discovers that he was tricked by Athena. Hector draws his sword, and Achilles pierces Hector's throat above the collarbone. Achilles again refuses to return his body, and Hector, in his dying words, predicts Achilles' death. Achilles drags Hector's body behind his chariot, and at the sight of their son's mistreated corpse, Priam and Hecuba begin to lament. Andromache then learns of his death and mourns her own fate and that of their son, Astyanax.

Book 23

The Greeks return to their ships, and the Myrmidons, led by Achilles, hold a funeral feast for Patroclus. Patroclus's spirit appears to Achilles in his sleep and requests that he be buried quickly, and that Achilles be buried alongside him when he should die. The next day, they build Patroclus's funeral pyre; Achilles slays the 12 captive Trojans, and they are burned together with Patroclus's body on the pyre. Achilles asks that Patroclus's bones be set aside and saved for his own burial, and the Greeks build a burial mound. Then Achilles brings out prizes for Patroclus's funeral games. Diomedes wins the chariot race; Epeius defeats Euryalus in boxing; Ajax, son of Telamon, and Odysseus wrestle to a draw; Odysseus defeats Ajax, son of Oileus, in the foot race; Ajax, son of Telamon, and Diomedes duel to a draw in armed combat. Polypoetes wins the shot put competition, and Meriones wins at archery. Achilles proclaims

Agamemnon winner of the spear-throwing contest without actually holding the competition.

Book 24

Achilles continues to grieve and mistreat Hector's body, which Apollo protects from disfigurement. The gods argue over whose side they should take. Zeus resolves on a plan and summons Thetis to warn Achilles of the gods' anger and to bid him accept a ransom. Achilles agrees. Zeus sends Iris to tell Priam to make his way to the Greek camp escorted by Hermes in order to ransom his son's body. Hecuba tries to restrain him, but Priam is determined, and the gods have assured him of success. Priam makes for the Greek camps in his chariot, accompanied by Idaeus, who drives the wagon of treasures to be offered as ransom. Hermes, pretending to be an attendant of Achilles, hails them and offers to escort them to Achilles' tent. Hermes reveals his identity before departing. Priam enters Achilles' tent, kisses his hands, and supplicates him in the name of his own father, Peleus. They both weep. Achilles announces that he will release Hector's body in accord with the gods' bidding. At Achilles' suggestion, they eat together. Achilles agrees to hold off fighting for 11 days to allow for Hector's funeral. They go to bed. Hermes rouses Priam and warns him to make his way home. Cassandra is the first to see them as they return with the body. Andromache and Helen lament Hector's death, and the Trojans perform his funeral rites.

COMMENTARY

Homer does not narrate events of his own times, or even events that occurred within recent memory. He tells of the aristocratic culture of palaces and warrior-heroes of the Mycenaean age, several centuries before his own time. While Homer is clearly not a "historian" in anything like the modern sense of the term, his stories contain elements of historical truth as filtered through generations of oral tradition. Significant places in Homer not infrequently coincide with major centers of Mycenaean culture (Pylos, Mycenae). His picture of heroic society—palace strongholds ruled by warrior-lords who control much of the production of the surrounding countryside—is broadly compatible with what archaeologists and historians know about Mycenaean culture, although inevitably Homer reproduces the society of his own times in greater detail. Excavations of Troy have revealed a destruction level that could be consistent with the sacking of the city in the late Mycenaean period. Material culture as represented in Homer, moreover, in some cases matches Mycenean technology rather than the material culture of Homer's own day. The correspondences, however, are not consistent, and most scholars now tend to see Homer's "world" as a complex mixing of elements from his own times with imperfectly remembered features of a vanished society.

The fascination exercised by the heroic age on Homer and his audience is inextricable from the fascination with the past itself. Mycenaean civilization, for reasons that remain mysterious, was largely destroyed around 1200 B.C.E. Greece in the eighth century B.C.E. was coming out of the subsequent Dark Age characterized by sparse population, ephemeral structures, and an unimpressive material culture compared with the rich finds of the Mycenaean period. The Homeric poems were produced in a society that preserved memories and some physical ruins of a glorious past age, when men inhabited mighty palaces. Homer's general view of human history suggests that men were greater and stronger in the past. He lavishes rich description on the magnificent trappings of warriors and their vast palaces. These heroes of the past, moreover, lived in constant contact with the gods: The gods took part in their battles, and the Homeric warrior has frequent occasion to realize that a god has been speaking with him in disguise, or has sent a message via the flight of birds or other omen.

Access to this past world is provided by the Muses, who play a major role both in Homer's poetry and in the poetry of Homer's approximate contemporary Hesiod. In the opening lines of both Homeric epics, the singer appeals to the Muse for inspiration for his song and the detailed knowledge of his subject. As Homer observes, we hear only the distant rumor of past deeds and heroes; for this reason, the Muses's divine knowledge is indispensable. The clearest demonstration of this principle is the "catalog of ships" in *Iliad* 2: It would be impossible for a poet, unaided, to recall the various contingents that made up the Greek expeditionary force and the names of their leaders and notable warriors, since the expedition occurred in the distant past. Recalling all the names of the heroes and details of their lives and genealogy not only provides an important background to the narrative that follows; it is a demonstration of the poet's divine connection with the Muse, his capacity to re-create a past world. Poetry is uniquely able to do this because of its connection with the past and the memorialization of past deeds. Memory, as Hesiod reminds us, is the mother of the Muses.

Arguably the defining feature of epic in its Homeric form is its universality of vision and Panhellenic scope. Heroism in Homer attains its significance against the background of the broader Hellenic world and the comparison of heroic figures and stories from different locations. It is worth recalling that the modern concept of the nation-state does not apply to ancient Greece, where individual strongholds and poleis ("city-states") shared a common language and culture but did not fall under the umbrella of a unified state structure. The idea of a Panhellenic identity, i.e., a larger idea of Greekness that distinguished Greeks from barbarian peoples, nonetheless began to emerge at around the same time as the Homeric poems. A notable example is the Olympic Games, at which Greeks from different communities came to together to participate in athletic competition. In the *Iliad*, the campaign against Troy is itself inherently Panhellenic, insofar as the expeditionary force consists of contingents from different Greek cities and communities. Herodotus would later view this war in

the context of a broader pattern of conflict between Hellenes and Easterners, culminating in the Persian Wars.

The tension between local community and Panhellenic expedition informs the entire epic and, at the same time, imbues it with a sense of grandeur and universality. The origins of the idea of immensity of scope that still inheres in the modern term "epic" can be traced back to the maximizing effect produced by Panhellenism in Homer. All the great heroes of the time go on the expedition to Troy. The Trojan War is thus a correspondingly vast demonstration of human courage in the face of death and of the potential for heroic valor in battle. The significance of individual achievement is magnified by our impression of the maximal scale of the conflict itself, which comprises East and West, Barbarian and Greek, and, on a cosmic level, the Olympian gods.

The epic's opening conflict between Achilles and Agamemnon plays out precisely such concerns. The expedition is in the ultimate interest of the sons of Atreus and, in particular, Menelaus. Achilles is resentful that he and his Myrmidons must face peril in battle and do the lion's share of the fighting, while the largest benefits go to the two brothers. Achilles' case is an emblematic intensification of tensions that arise inevitably when diverse groups are made to coalesce under the single banner of the Greek expedition, even though the interests of the various groups, and the degree to which they profit from the war, are not the same. The quarrel between Achilles and Agamemnon at the same time raises the larger question of the relative claims of different forms of virtue. Achilles is by far the superior warrior, but Agamemnon is the more kingly. We might think of the narrative as being one that pits Achilles' warlike brilliance against Agamemnon's kingly position, and ultimately finds Agamemnon wanting. Agamemnon has his moments of glory, but more often Homer views him negatively. Homer shows Agamemnon realizing his error (in alienating Achilles) and Achilles achieving the demonstration of his indispensable status that he sought.

Conflict, in ancient Greece, is never clearly distinguished from competition: They are part of the same thing. While Achilles' quarrel with Agamemnon and withdrawal from battle represent an extraordinary instance of dissension within the Greek ranks, this type of conflict is not necessarily different in kind from the ordinary modus operandi of Homeric warriors. They urge each other on to brave deeds by taunting and mocking each other; they are motivated to excellence in battle by the desire to surpass others. The showpiece event in Homeric epic—the one-on-one duel—exemplifies the competitive ethos at its most intense. Competition is not limited to the battlefield, however; decisions are made through competitive speech making in the assemblies of the Greeks and Trojans. Heroes vie with each other for authority and the reputation of sound strategic thinking. It is no accident that Patroclus's funeral games occupy a culminating position in the epic. Tensions among the Greek warriors are at once displayed and mitigated through friendly/competitive interaction. A Panhellenic field of action, on which warriors from different localities converge to demonstrate their prowess, whether in oratory, warfare, or athletics, provides an ideal staging for competition among Greek heroes.

Conflict and competition pervade the Greek universe. On the divine level, division among the Olympian gods propels and shapes the plot of the *Iliad*. Some gods favor the Greeks—Hera and Athena are the prime candidates—while others—Aphrodite, Ares, Apollo—favor the Trojans. Zeus is a special case, since he understands and accepts the inevitability of destiny, which includes the ultimate destruction of Troy; yet he both favors the Trojans personally and has agreed, at Thetis's behest, to support the Trojans for a certain period of time. For most of the epic, Zeus largely supports the Trojans to demonstrate the full significance of the loss of Achilles to the Greeks and thereby magnify his honor. Within this general scheme,

Hera and Athena inject tension and suspense by working against Zeus, bypassing him, and even deceiving him. In the end, Zeus always imposes his will through his kingly authority and the threat of force. In the meanwhile, however, developments on the field of battle undergo exciting twists and turns as the gods intervene on one side and then the other. Homer maintains an enlivening tension between destiny (on a narrative plane, the fixed, known outline of mythological events) and the element of surprise (in narrative terms, the uneven, twisting path of events created by resistance to and deferral of destined outcomes). As in many instances, Homer has established a pattern in epic narrative that will define central features of the later tradition. In Virgil's *AENEID*, for example, the opposition of Juno creates all the interesting wrinkles in the inevitable trajectory of destiny drawing Aeneas to Italy.

The presence of the gods is everywhere in Homer's world. Nearly every major event—and many of the minor ones—in the epic betrays the signs of divine causation, or occurs at the instigation of a god taking human form, or receives the affirmation of a sign sent by a god. Later thinkers, revealingly, mitigate and naturalize the gods' pervasive efficacy in Homer by ascribing their actions to allegory. For example, in *Iliad* 1, when Athena intervenes to stop Achilles from killing Agamemnon on the spot amid their quarrel, an allegorical reading might state that Homer's Athena does not literally intervene to restrain Achilles; rather, the poet is demonstrating how wisdom can temper anger and thereby prevent destructive violence. In such extraordinary scenes as the battle between Achilles and the river Scamander, it is especially tempting to mitigate or explain away the departure from naturalism as allegory. This line of reading, however, is potentially misleading, insofar as it underestimates the presence and continual efficacy of the gods in the heroic world as perceived by Homer and his audience. The gods are finely drawn characters in their own right, and it is their particular flaws and weaknesses as much as anything else that drive the plot. An overriding concern for naturalism is anachronistic in the context of the world of heroes—figures who come close to superhuman status themselves and who live their lives in contact with and under the supervision of the gods, their parents, and ancestors.

Without the very real presence of the gods, central and poignant aspects of heroes' existence would be incomprehensible. Heroes are, by definition, closer to godlike status than ordinary mortals, yet they remain mortal. Their particular interest lies in the poignancy of their not quite godlike status, of being so close to the gods, while remaining tragically subject to death. Brilliance and doom are inextricable in the battle sequences of the *Iliad*, where heroes alternately enjoy a period of apparently godlike invulnerability and irresistible power, and then succumb to wounds or death. The extended display of excellence in battle—called by Homeric scholars the hero's *aristeia*—derives its fascination from our awareness of its limitations. No mortal can hope for more than a brief flash of glory. Ultimately, death will conclude the hero's martial display.

The gods, as Homer shows us, can suffer humiliation and pain. Diomedes wounds Aphrodite and Ares. Their pain is real and all the more shocking for the fact that their flawless bodies, fed on ambrosia, are not used to being violated by weapons. Diomedes' display of martial excellence is thrilling, since he manages to challenge the gods and nearly achieves godlike status himself. He cannot, of course, truly hope to become the equal of a god, although for a brief, unforgettable span, he may seem godlike in his ability to dispense destruction while remaining unharmed himself. Patroclus represents another, more sternly phrased example of a challenge to a god. He is warned first by Achilles and then by the god Apollo not to press his attack on Troy too far. His progress is halted finally by a crushing blow from Apollo, which leaves him unarmed, disoriented, and vulnerable to his enemies.

Patroclus assumes the armor and appearance of a greater man, one who is himself closer to being a god than Patroclus, yet still mortal. A fortiori, Patroclus must die. This lesson pervades the *Iliad* and is uttered by Achilles himself: If the greatest heroes—including Achilles—are doomed to die, lesser men clearly cannot hope to escape mortality. On yet another level of meaning, Patroclus, as Achilles' surrogate, foreshadows his comrade's death, which is not represented within the compass of the epic's explicit narration. Achilles, too, will die at the hands of a mortal through the agency of his divine adversary, Apollo. Patroclus's nearly superhuman drive and attempt to take Troy prefigure Achilles' own failure to take Troy. Patroclus's fate keenly poses the questions of the limitations of mortal endeavor and of death—both his own and Achilles'.

These themes continue to resonate in the subsequent episode in which Achilles pursues and finally kills Hector. Hector makes the mistake of putting on Achilles' armor, which he stripped from Patroclus. The armor, both in its evident excellence and in its ultimate inability to ward off doom, has become an emblem of mortality, underscoring a meaningful sequence of deaths: Patroclus—Hector—Achilles. We never see the final link in the sequence but know that it is coming, and we prospectively mourn Achilles even as the poem concludes pointedly with the burial rites of Hector. Achilles himself wears immortal armor made by a god, yet he must die in it. Achilles' immortal horses employ human speech to predict his death. The immortal surrounds and sets off Achilles' mortal self.

The fact that the gods care about human death is at once natural and inexplicable. Should not the gods worry about their mortal favorites? And yet there are obvious limits to the gods' involvement in mortal affairs; the generations of men are almost risibly ephemeral from a divine perspective. It would be fruitless to take men's deaths too seriously when they are both frequent and inevitable. It is perhaps precisely because the Greek gods are highly anthropomorphic that the difference that death makes emerges so starkly. The gods are similar to us; they grieve and experience pain like us; they are petty, cruel, lustful, and angry like us; and yet, crucially, they do not die.

This dynamic of difference and similarity, indifference and sympathy, is well illustrated by the diverging paradigms represented by the gods' diverse reactions to mortal conflict and death. Zeus grieves for his son Sarpedon's death and even considers intervening to prevent it, yet Hera reminds him that he does not have a right to interfere with a mortal's destined time of death, and that allowing the gods to prevent the death of their favorites as a general practice would be unacceptable. The subsequent focus on Sarpedon's corpse and burial rites lays stress poignantly on the unavoidable fact of death, which cannot be warded off, even from the son of Zeus.

In other instances, however, the affairs of mortals fail to engage the full sympathy of the gods. In the battle leading up to Hector's death, the gods are permitted to take the field and, in a few instances, engage with each other in battle. Apollo, however, disdains to fight Poseidon over mere mortals, as Hermes refuses to fight Leto. A comparable scenario arises toward the beginning of the epic. At the end of Book 1, Zeus and Hera at first quarrel over his meeting with Thetis and plan to support the Trojans. Soon, however, Hephaestus's humorously maladroit manner dissolves the tension in laughter, and the gods enjoy their ambrosial repast. This easy, bloodless solution to quarreling contrasts pointedly with the quarrel we have just seen play out in the mortal world: The differences between Achilles and Agamemnon will not be painlessly resolved but will cause horrific losses for the Greeks on the battlefield. Agamemnon—an imperfect and at times blustering leader—cannot project the kingly authority of his divine counterpart Zeus, and fails to impose his will on a challenger. Hephaestus's humor effortlessly succeeds where the eloquence of Nestor failed.

The contrast is telling, since the entire epic is about the defining feature of the mortal, as opposed to immortal, condition—death. The *Iliad* is a record of deaths. Minor figures make up the majority of deaths, and sometimes Homer provides only a name. Even a relatively insignificant figure, however, often receives a brief, sympathetic description that memorializes his father, land of origin, and, in some cases, a further poignant detail (e.g., a new bride who will never see her husband again). The main line of narrative concerns a hero destined to die young yet to achieve great renown. Achilles' father, Peleus, will never see him again or have him as a comfort in his old age. Achilles' situation is an intensification of the situation of Homeric warriors generally.

By going to Troy, Achilles achieves great *kleos* ("renown"), yet is fated to die young, shortly after killing Hector. He chooses to maximize his *kleos* within his life's brief span, even at the cost of damaging his own side in the war. Achilles is relentlessly devoted to *kleos*. He withdraws from the war to intensify the effect of his return later on, and to make apparent the extent that he maintains the entire Greek war effort. Homer is attentive to this effect of intensification in his portrayal of Achilles. The hero's actions are extreme and conducted at a high degree of emotional intensity. He is condensing a lifetime's passionate devotion to *kleos* into a brief span. Homer's epic narrative embodies this principle of condensation in its temporal confinement. The entirety of the action occurs within a few weeks. By the end of 24 books, Homer's audience may feel that they have heard the story of an entire war. The *Iliad*, of course, represents only a small portion of the Trojan War, and yet Homer's narration presents each day of battle as critical and momentous. Length of time stands in inverse proportion to greatness of action, both in Achilles' life and in the narrative as a whole.

A heightened sense of the terrible cost of war *and* of the hero's glory are simultaneous and mutually irreducible in Homeric epic. It is misleading to argue either that Homer is anti-war or that he purely idealizes war. His mini-biographies of warriors at the moment of their death are constant reminders of the lives that they will not lead and of the pain their deaths will cause others. The physical description of death is fairly unsparing. Homer begins a long tradition of the graphic description of death in epic narrative that culminates with the horrific dismemberments of Lucan and STATIUS. In the larger picture, Homer is equally unsparing in reminding us of the ultimate outcome of the war: The destruction of Troy, the killing of the men, and the enslavement of the women and children. Women such as Andromache are aware that they will be forced to serve as concubines in other men's beds. Carnage, mass rape, the annihilation of a great civilization—this is the true ending of the story, and though Homer does not tell it, he shows us that he knows it. This destined ending supplies the present story with a key dimension of its meaning: Hector's defeat is the beginning of the end—for Andromache, Astyanax, and the rest of the Trojans.

Yet despite this awareness of destruction that tinges his narration, Homer is not "opposed to war" in the modern sense. War, in the Homeric view, is an inevitable feature of human society and its greatest arena of glory and accomplishment. The epic poet's verses embody the immortality of the warrior's fame. Hector, who imagines his future tomb, will have the consolation of enduring glory after his death. The deeds of past warriors are already part of the oral tradition, and thus inherent in the contemporary hero's outlook. Achilles, when he retires to his tent, sings the deeds of heroes. Nestor recalls the great battles and men of the past generation. Similarly, Homer's epic is a monument to the great men of the Trojan War. They lost their lives, but they have done deeds worth remembering, which, given the ephemerality and forgettable smallness of human life, is a difficult thing to do. Courage in the face of death is one of the few truly extraordinary and brilliant actions that mortals (and *not* the gods) are capable of performing.

Achilles, whose early death has been prophesied, is an especially clear example of such courage. In going to Troy, Achilles has already chosen a short, glorious life, i.e., he has chosen to die at Troy. Yet, although the choice has been effectively made, in another, equally important sense, we are able to watch him making this choice throughout the epic. Achilles withdraws from battle and does not return until near the end. So long as he remains in his tent, he puts off his doom. By returning to battle, then, Achilles accepts the inevitability of his life's end; for he is destined to die shortly after the death of Hector, and his chief purpose in returning to battle is to kill Hector. Part of Achilles' greatness is thus the courage that lies behind his decision to face his own death.

This decision, however, unfolds slowly throughout the narrative. We are able to appreciate, first, his reasons for withdrawal, and then watch as his resistance is broken down by the loss of Patroclus. Although the actual time taken up by these events is relatively short, the narrative time is vast: Achilles remains withdrawn from battle for most of the poem, and his return is (for the Greeks) painfully delayed. The narrative power of this delay is considerable, and may be counted as a central feature of Homeric epic.

In the *Odyssey*, Homer keeps his hero hidden through much of the poem—a mystery to his son and wife, a vagabond exiled from his home island. Even after returning to Ithaca, Odysseus remains in disguise as a beggar until very near the end. Homer builds up, with tremendous patience, the triumphant, violent return of his main character. The opening portion of the epic does not focus on Odysseus himself but on the story of his son, TELEMACHUS. Telemachus's promising yet ultimately minor feats in the realm of guest-host relations and foreign travel build up our anticipation of the masterful Odysseus.

Similarly, in the *Iliad*, Homer builds up intense anticipation of the return of Achilles. Patroclus serves a narrative function comparable to that of Telemachus in the *Odyssey*: Wearing Achilles' armor, he resembles his more powerful comrade. Yet, he must not go so far as to steal the spotlight from Achilles. Just as Odysseus warns Telemachus not to steal his glory in the archery contest, so Achilles explicitly admonishes Patroclus that he must not go so far as to capture Troy and thereby diminish his own prestige. In a certain sense, the entire preceding narration is a buildup to Achilles' final blaze of glory. We have heard of impressive deeds thus far, yet can only imagine how much greater will be the battle fury of the "best of the Achaeans." When Achilles does return, we are not disappointed. He chokes the waters of the Scamander with bodies and fights the river god himself. As in the *Odyssey*, the greatness of the hero can be measured by how much others miss him and suffer from his absence, and by the splendor of his eventual return.

Another example of Homer's interest in exquisitely drawing out the anticipation of Achilles' return through narrative delay is the lengthy description of the shield of Achilles in Book 18. This passage is apparently the first major example in Western literature of the ecphrasis, or extended description of a work of art. (In Greek, *ecphrasis* simply means "speaking out," or extended description of any significant object, person, building, or animal. Within this broader rhetorical category, however, a subcategory of ecphrastic description of works of art is distinguishable, especially within the epic tradition deriving from Homer.) Interpretation of the significance of the scenes depicted on the shield, however, is difficult. Hephaestus appears to represent the cosmos, and within this larger frame, human society, as embodied in two generic cities, the city at peace and the city at war. The single most striking feature of the description is the generic nature of the activities and human actors. The actors are not named, and many of their activities are recur-

rent and cyclical (activities associated with the harvest, procedures of law courts, typical strategies of war, etc.). Perhaps we are to understand that in the remote Olympian perspective of the divine artisan, human activity appears anonymous and generalized. No extraordinary figure distinguishes himself.

In the *Iliad*, as we know, quite the opposite is true. The central emphasis of the *Iliad* lies in the stress on individual names, identities, genealogies, and lands of origin. The drive of the narrative is to make heroes such as Ajax, Odysseus, Paris, Hector, and Achilles memorable, even unforgettable, for the audience. The scene in Book 3 in which Helen points out and describes the Greek heroes to Priam effectively introduces these personalities and establishes the importance of their particular traits for the epic. We might also think of the catalog of ships, in which Homer demonstrates how seriously he takes the task of recalling individual names of warriors. Achilles, above all, emerges as a highly distinctive and complex personality who imposes his will on an entire army and contravenes the heroic code with arresting boldness. Both in withdrawing from his own army, and later in sympathizing with Priam's grief, Achilles puts himself in tension with the basic rule of harming one's enemies and helping one's friends. With some justice, Achilles has been characterized as a kind of philosopher-warrior: He challenges the system of values in accordance with which he and his comrades are expected to live.

The designs of the immortal artisan, by contrast, afford little place for Achilles' distinctive personality and pattern of achievement. The immortal armor will protect Achilles (for a while anyway), and yet the armor embodies the rift between divine and human perspectives on life. Another, more immediate effect of the extended description of the armor is to effect further narrative delay and to build up even more anticipation of Achilles' return to battle. Homer awards several of his more important warriors "arming scenes," in which he describes how the warrior dons the various items of his equipment. In Achilles' case, he expands the "arming scene" to include an unparalleled scene of divine manufacture and artisanship, in which one feature of the armor—the designs incised on the shield—takes up a large portion of a book. Achilles is the central hero of Homer's epic. While other heroes may claim to be "the best," Homer makes it clear that Achilles performs at an altogether different level: His *aristeia* far surpasses that of any other warriors; his anger is more terrible; the destruction he personally wreaks is equivalent to that of an entire army. In one perspective, a central function of the battle narrative prior to Book 20 is simply to provide a background against which to appreciate Achilles' exceptional status. Other warriors challenge gods, seek revenge for slain comrades, go on an onslaught, and appear invulnerable, yet none combines all these feats with the relentless spirit and force of Achilles.

Throughout most of the epic, anger is Achilles' defining emotion. Anger is the first word of the epic ("The anger of Achilles, sing, O Muse") and is the cause of his withdrawal from the Greek army. He shows himself still to be angry in Book 9 when the embassy of Greek heroes seeks to persuade him to return to the fighting. In an intensely emotional response to Odysseus's carefully balanced and reasoned speech, he refuses Agamemnon's offer of immense wealth. Achilles displays a breathtaking and strangely admirable extremity not only on the battlefield but in verbal argument as well—the *other* great arena of competition and achievement in the *Iliad*. After Patroclus's death, when Achilles decides to return to battle, he calls an assembly of the Greeks and renounces his destructive anger, while Agamemnon blames his own deluded madness. In another sense, however, Achilles has not put anger behind him, but changed the object and nature of his anger. Whereas previously anger at Agamemnon drew him away from battle, now desire to avenge Patroclus's death and kill Hector motivates him to return to battle. After Achilles slays Hector,

in Book 23, he shows himself capable of a completely transformed mode of engagement with the rest of the Greeks and Agamemnon in particular. He serves as arbiter of the competition and, at the end, awards Agamemnon the prize in spear throwing without contest. It pays to recall at this point that the original quarrel between Agamemnon and Achilles concerned a question of honor, superiority, and Agamemnon's unlawful seizure of Achilles' "prize." Now Achilles generously concedes Agamemnon's kingly status and shows him honor by allowing him to forgo competition. As moderator of the competition, Achilles helps resolve tensions within the Greek army over issues of honor, status, supremacy, and the distribution of prizes.

Achilles, however, remains angry, and will not relinquish the body of Hector, which he continues to abuse. It eventually takes the intervention of the gods and Priam's personal visit to his tent to persuade Achilles to give up Hector's body and his own anger. Anger, for Achilles, is closely related in all its phases to death and the knowledge of his own mortality. A central dimension of Achilles' anger in the quarrel is his exasperated awareness that he has very little time to live and is now being deprived of one of the few things of any meaning or value to him any more—his honor. He will not live to enjoy vast estates, wealth, a wife, and children—all that really matters now is his renown and his honor as a warrior, the respect awarded to him by his comrades. This logic explains why Achilles furiously rejects the offer of the embassy in Book 9: Agamemnon cannot restore the honor owed him simply by restoring objects. Phoenix's story about Meleager for this reason misses the mark. Meleager, he points out, waited too long to return to the defense of his people and, therefore, failed to take advantage of the material reward offered him earlier. Achilles, however, fundamentally does not care for such rewards.

Achilles' later angry abuse of Hector's body reveals yet again the connection between his anger and the fact of death. He cannot accept

Patroclus's death and so continues to abuse the dead Hector. Patroclus's death, as discussed above, is a prefiguration and shadow image of his own imminent death at the hands of Apollo. There is, in Achilles, a raw element of rage at his own mortality, a fury at death. As he kills Trojans in Book 21, he refers to his own mortality. Achilles must die. How can they, much inferior men, presume to hope to live? He mercilessly inflicts on others the fate he soon must meet himself and abuses Hector's body to an irrational degree that suggests a brooding interest in, and ferocious dissatisfaction with, death. Ironically, the gods preserve the integrity of Hector's body even as Achilles attempts to disfigure it. He cannot make Hector's body reveal to him its actual death and disintegration. In the final book of the epic, Priam sets out, with the gods' help, to ransom his son's body. As many scholars have noted, his journey, undertaken at night and under the guidance of the god Hermes—known as the god who guides souls to the underworld—implicitly resembles a journey to the land of the dead. (Interestingly, in the *Odyssey*, Achilles turns out to be the king of the dead, although, as he tells Odysseus, he would rather live as the lowliest serf than rule as king in the underworld.) Achilles, reminded of the grief of his father, Peleus, sympathizes with Priam's desperate grief for his dead son. In aligning Priam with Peleus, Achilles sees himself in Hector and looks ahead to the great loss and desolation Peleus will feel when he is dead. When Achilles weeps, he is naturally weeping both for Peleus and for himself. Achilles approaches, in this closural scene, greater understanding and acceptance of his mortality, and perhaps for that reason is able to relinquish his terrible anger.

Imagines Philostratus (ca. 200)   There are two collections of "Images" or *Imagines* (both are translations of the Greek title *Eikones*). In one collection, there are 64 descriptions of paintings on largely mythological subjects,

and in another collection, there are 17 such descriptions. The question of authorship is tangled. There are four writers with the name Philostratus who belonged to the same family and lived in the second and third centuries C.E., and to whom various works in prose have been ascribed. Under one currently favored theory, the Elder Philostratus wrote the longer, and generally superior, collection of 64 descriptions of images, and his grandson, also named Philostratus, composed the second, imitating his grandfather's achievement. The descriptions consist in vivid commentary on notional paintings, i.e., examples of the kinds of painting one is likely to encounter. The paintings for the most part represent scenes in mythology, e.g., the battle of Hephaestus and the river Scamander as represented in the *Iliad*, or the dead Memnon. The preface to the longer collection specifies that the work's purpose is instructional: Young readers can learn how to appreciate and comment on paintings by studying Philostratus's example. In addition to providing versions of many classical myths, the *Imagines* demonstrate the importance of myth as subject matter of ancient painting.

Ino   Daughter of Cadmus and Harmonia. Wife of King Athamas of Boeotia. The children of Ino and Athamas were Learchus and Melicertes. Classical sources are Apollodorus's *Library* (1.9.1–3), Euripides' *Bacchae* (1,129–1,230) and *Medea* (1,282–1,289), Hyginus's *Fabulae* (1–5), Ovid's *Fasti* (6.489–550) and *Metamorphoses* (4.416–542), Pausanias's *Description of Greece* (1.42.7, 1.44.7–8, 3.24.4), and Pindar's *Olympian Odes* (2.28–30). Euripides' *Ino* and Sophocles' *Athamas* survive in fragmentary form. There are several, sometimes contradictory, versions of the story of Athamas, Ino, and their children.

The myth of Ino must be placed in the context of the tragedies that befall the house of Cadmus. The children of Cadmus and Harmonia were Autonoe, Agave, Ino, Semele, and a son, Polydorus. Though Cadmus and Harmonia appear to have been favored by the gods, their descendants suffered misfortunes. In Euripides' tragedy the *Bacchae*, Cadmus's grandson PENTHEUS was slaughtered by his own mother, Agave, and his aunts Autonoe and Ino in a Dionysiac frenzy. Their unwitting murder of Pentheus was brought about by DIONYSUS in revenge for Pentheus's lack of piety toward him.

Hera was angered by Ino's care of her nephew, Dionysus, and she persuaded one of the Furies, Tisiphone, to incite madness in Athamas and Ino. In Ovid's *Metamorphoses*, Tisiphone, whose head writhed with snakes, threw two snakes and a venomous potion at the couple that caused their insanity. Athamas dashed his son against the wall, killing him, and in grief and madness Ino with Melicertes in her arms threw herself from a nearby cliff into the sea. APHRODITE, the mother of Harmonia and grandmother of Ino, took pity on them and asked POSEIDON to transform the two into sea creatures. These were renamed Leucothoe (Ino) and Palaemon (Melicertes). The *Orphic Hymn to Leucothoe* describes Leucothoe as protective of sailors and ships in peril at sea. The Theban women who grieved for Ino were transformed by Hera into birds or stones.

Another version of the myth, by Apollodorus, expands on Ino's myth. Athamas had two children, PHRIXUS and Helle, before his marriage to Ino, by Nephele, a cloud goddess. Ino bore her stepchildren malice and plotted against them. First, she arranged to have the crops fail, in response to which Athamas sent a messenger to consult the Delphic Oracle. Ino persuaded the messenger to say, on behalf of the oracle, that the sacrifice of Phrixus would renew the fertility of the crops. Athamas prepared to sacrifice his son, but before the child was killed, he and his sister Helle were carried off by their mother, Nephele. Nephele placed them on a magical flying golden ram that had been given to her by HERMES. As they jour-

neyed through the sky. Helle fell off the ram into the sea and drowned, thereby giving her name to those waters—the Hellespont. Phrixus survived and was received by King AEETES in Colchis, where he married one of the royal daughters. He sacrificed the golden ram to ZEUS, and its fleece was placed in a grove sacred to ARES. It was the same fleece later sought by JASON and the Argonauts.

Athamas was said to have been exiled from Boeotia, founded his own settlement in Thessaly, and married Themisto, who bore him Erythrius, Leucon, Schoenus, and Ptous. In still another version of the death of Ino, that of Hyginus's *Fabulae* (based on Euripides' *Ino*) the time line of events is reversed. Athamas, believing Ino to be dead, married Themisto, who bore him Erythrius, Leucon, Schoenus, and Ptous. Themisto, wishing to do away with the children of her predecessor, unwittingly killed her own children instead of those of Ino. Athamas was then driven to the madness that provoked his killing of Learchus and Ino's throwing herself into the sea.

Io   Daughter of King Inachus of Argus (or the river god Inachus, or Iasus). Depending on her parentage, Io was either a nymph or a princess. Consort of ZEUS and by him, mother of EPAPHUS. Ancestor of the DANAIDS. Classical sources are Aeschylus's *SUPPLIANTS* (40–57, 291–324, 531–589) and *PROMETHEUS BOUND* (561–886), Apollodorus's *LIBRARY* (2.1.3), Herodotus's *Histories* (1.1, 2.41), Lucian's *DIALOGUES OF THE GODS* (7), Ovid's *METAMORPHOSES* (1.583–750), and Pausanias's *Description of Greece* (1.25.1, 2.16.1). Io is associated with the Egyptian deity Isis. In Lucian's *Dialogues of the Gods* ("Zeus and Hermes"), Zeus commanded HERMES to bring Io to Egypt, where she would become their goddess and have authority over the winds and the river Nile.

Io was an attendant of the temple of HERA at Heraion when she came to Zeus's attention. It was not unusual for Zeus to change shape while attempting seduction, but in this case it was Io who was transformed, by Zeus, into a white heifer of great beauty. Another instance of such a transformation occurs in the myth of CALLISTO, who is changed into a bear. In some versions of the myth, Io was transformed by Zeus to protect her from Hera's jealousy, and in others she was changed by Hera herself.

In Ovid's *Metamorphoses*, Zeus set a cloud cover over the place in which he was seducing Io. Hera descended from Mount Olympus with the hope of surprising the lovers, and Zeus quickly transformed Io into a cow. But Hera was suspicious and asked for the heifer as a gift. Zeus was obliged to acquiesce.

Hera set ARGUS, the "all-seeing," to guard over Io. He tethered Io to an olive tree in the grove of Heraion, sacred to Hera. This made it impossible for Io to escape or for Zeus to rescue her. She was unable even to communicate with her sisters and father, but only hover around them, until it occurred to her to write her name in the dirt with her hoof. Her father recognized her and commiserated with her but could not help her. Finally Zeus commanded HERMES to free Io. Disguised as a shepherd, Hermes lulled Argus into closing all his eyes in sleep with the aid of his reed pipe and the story of its invention by PAN. After Argus fell asleep, Hermes beheaded him and thereafter assumed the epithet Argeiphontes, or "Argus-slayer."

Io was liberated from Argus's surveillance, but Hera sent a gadfly to drive Io mad. Relentlessly chased by the gadfly and pursued by the ghost of Argus, Io fled to Egypt, crossing a body of water that afterward bore her name, the Ionian Sea. According to Ovid, Zeus eventually persuaded Hera to relent.

In Aeschylus's *Prometheus Bound*, Io, in her wanderings, met PROMETHEUS and was advised by him to journey away from Europe and to found a colony in Egypt. Along the way, she crossed the Thracian Strait, thereafter named the Bosphorus, which ancient etymology derived from the word for "cow." Prometheus also foretold that one of Io's descendants (HERACLES)

would eventually free him from his punishment by Zeus. After arriving in Egypt and meeting with Zeus, Io regained her human form.

Simply by touching her, Zeus fathered EPAPHUS on Io (Epaphus's name resembles the Greek word for "touch"), the ancestor of the Danaids. Hera commanded the Curetes to abduct Epaphus, but Io found him in Syria and returned with him to rule over Memphis, Egypt.

Herodotus's *Histories* makes the connection between Io's cow shape and the sacredness of the cow for the Egyptians, the country where she eventually settled.

In classical art, Io is depicted as a white heifer, often accompanied by the many-eyed Argus and Hermes. An example is a black-figure amphora from ca. 540 B.C.E. (Staatliche Antikensammlungen, Munich). In some images, Io is shown in human form, wearing horns to refer to her transformation—Io refers to herself, in Aeschylus's *Prometheus Bound*, as the "horned virgin." Postclassical artists found the story of Io and Zeus equally inspiring. Antonio Correggio's *Jupiter and Io* (Kunsthistorisches Museum, Vienna) from ca. 1530 is representative of this theme. Here Zeus takes the form of the cloud while seducing Io, rather than simply using the cloud to hide his indiscretion.

Iolaus   See HERACLES.

Iole   See HERACLES; *TRACHINIAE*.

Ion EURIPIDES (ca. 410 B.C.E.)   On the basis of its style and themes, the *Ion* is hypothetically dated late in Euripides' career, around 410 B.C.E. The play is set in Delphi, where Ion, the central character, is a temple servant. His mother, Creusa, an Athenian princess, was raped and impregnated by APOLLO, and he was exposed as a child. Apollo subsequently arranged to have the boy brought up at Delphi. When the play opens, Creusa and her foreign husband, Xuthus, are coming to Delphi to inquire about the reasons for their childlessness. In making a play about Ion, an early, legendary ruler of Athens and founder of the Ionian communities, Euripides brings his own city of Athens more closely into focus than in other plays. Like other late plays by this playwright, *Ion* has a more or less happy ending and incorporates other elements—such as an exciting escape scene and the miraculous reappearance and recognition of a child exposed and long thought dead—that might be associated with romance or comedy. The resemblance, however, can be misleading. Euripides here devotes himself to exploring the tragic resonance and heritage of Athens and its own distinctive mythological tradition. As in other tragedies, he explores themes of the justice and/or cruelty of the gods, children, and childlessness; the Greek and the foreign; and the sometimes dark politics of the household.

SYNOPSIS

The scene is set in front of the temple of Apollo at Delphi. HERMES enters and delivers the prologue speech. He gives his own genealogy, then tells the story of how Creusa, daughter of ERECHTHEUS, king of Athens, was raped by Apollo near the Long Cliffs at Athens and was impregnated. After giving birth, she exposed the child in the same cave where the rape took place, adorning him only with the typically Athenian gold serpents as protective tokens. Apollo then commanded Hermes to rescue the child and deposit him at his sanctuary at Delphi. He transported the baby in the wicker cradle in which he had been left exposed, and the child was found by a priestess, who pitied the boy and brought him up. He became a temple servant. Creusa, in the meanwhile, married a foreigner, Xuthus, son of Aeolus. They are childless, however, and have now come to Apollo's shrine at Delphi to inquire about children. Apollo has directed this outcome and wishes to tell Xuthus that the boy is his son. Apollo intends him to be called Ion, founder of the cities of Asia. Hermes exits.

Ion enters, accompanied by temple servants. He sends the temple servants off to cleanse themselves in the springs of Castalia. He then turns to his tasks: purifying and sweeping clean the temple, and keeping out birds with his bow. In a lyrical passage, he takes joy in his tasks and praises the god Apollo as his benefactor and "father." He refrains from driving off some unknown birds that are arriving. Ion exits into the temple.

The Chorus of Creusa's maidservants enters. It views the temple of Delphi with admiration, comparing it with Athenian temples; in particular, it admires its representation of mythological scenes: HERACLES slaying of the HYDRA with the help of IOLAUS, BELLEROPHON slaying the CHIMAERA, and the GIGANTOMACHY. Ion enters. It asks if it may enter the sanctuary. Ion replies that, as foreign, it may not. It asks if Phoebus's temple at Delphi is truly the "navel" of the world. He replies that it is and tells it how to ask a question of the god. It indicates that it comes from the house of Erechtheus at Athens. Creusa enters. Ion is impressed by her nobility but also observes that she is distressed. She alludes darkly to a past event and the injustice of the gods. She tells her name, father, and city, and answers his questions about Athenian legend: ERICHTHONIUS, ATHENA, the daughters of Cecrops, the daughters of Erechtheus, Erechtheus's death and burial, and the Long Rocks. She further reveals that she has come with her husband, Xuthus, a foreigner—who was able to marry her because he helped Athens defeat Euboea—to inquire about their childlessness. Ion reveals that he does not know who his parents are, but he is only Apollo's servant. They pity each other. She then claims that she has come to consult Apollo on behalf of a friend who claims to have been impregnated by Apollo and to have exposed the child. The story makes Ion think of himself. He warns that it would be improper to ask the god an awkward question he does not wish to answer. Creusa accuses the god of injustice.

Xuthus enters with his retinue. He has just come from the nearby oracle of Trophonius, who indicated only that they would not leave

Delphi without children. Xuthus announces his intention to seek Apollo's oracle and exits; Creusa expresses hope that Apollo will make good his past wrongdoing, and exits. Ion wonders aloud why the foreign woman criticizes the gods, but then before leaving, he rebukes Apollo and the other male gods for raping and impregnating mortal women: They set a bad example.

The Chorus addresses Athena and ARTEMIS and asks them to come to Delphi to plead with Apollo to provide the house of Erechtheus with children. It praises the blessings that children bring and then allude to the place where Creusa was raped. Ion enters and asks after Xuthus. The Chorus replies that he is arriving. Xuthus enters; he greets Ion happily and proclaims that Ion is his son. Ion thinks that he is deranged and is annoyed at Xuthus's attempted embraces. It emerges that the Oracle told Xuthus that the first person he would meet on coming to the sanctuary would be his son: This is Ion. Ion is persuaded only when he learns that once, at about the right time, Xuthus had come to Delphi, got drunk, and approached some of the young women of Delphi; one of them might have been impregnated by him and then exposed the child. Ion somewhat grudgingly accepts Xuthus as his father but then wonders who his mother is. Xuthus invites Ion to join him at the palace in Athens, where he will be high-born and rich. Ion, however, seems worried. He points out that he will be seen as both illegitimate and foreign by the autochthonous Athenians; furthermore, Creusa will now be isolated and resentful in her childlessness; finally, he enjoys his humble, yet respected, position at Delphi, where he leads a pure life. Xuthus responds that he must learn to accept his new position. He will take him to Athens as a foreign friend and visitor, not as his son, to avoid antagonizing his wife, but will gradually groom him for the kingship. Xuthus invites Ion to a special sacrificial feast to which his wife will not be invited. Xuthus exits. Ion expresses the hope that his mother will turn out to be

Athenian, for then, as a true citizen, he will have freedom of speech. He exits.

The Chorus, which has been forbidden to tell Creusa what has transpired, now laments their mistress's fate: She has been dishonored by her husband. It wishes that the boy may never come to their city.

Creusa and an old man, a servant of the household, enter. He accompanies Creusa to the shrine to learn the prophecy. They ask the Chorus about Apollo's response. Though Xuthus has forbidden it to tell on pain of death, it reveals that Xuthus alone has been given a child, and that the child was Ion. It does not know who the mother is. Creusa and the old man lament and express their outrage. The old man interprets the situation: Xuthus, plotting to exclude her from the royal house, conceived a child in secret by a slave woman, raised him at Delphi, then arranged to have the god declare that the child was his. Creusa expresses her indignation and, then, no longer willing to keep silent about her rape, sings a song in condemnation of Apollo. She recalls the circumstances and details of her rape, then complains bitterly that he allowed the child of their union to die and to be devoured by birds, while rewarding Xuthus with a child of his own to her dishonor. She now tells the old man the story of the rape and exposure; he expresses his horror. Presented with the options of burning down the god's temple, killing her husband, or murdering her husband's child, Creusa responds to the old man that she very much wishes to kill the child. Creusa has inherited from Erichthonius two drops of GORGON's blood, one of which is poison. They plot to have the old man place poison in Ion's cup at the sacrificial feast that her husband is holding secretly.

The Chorus addresses Enodia, goddess of the crossroads, and asks her to aid in the assassination, thus preventing a foreigner from taking over the royal house of Erechtheus. It complains that a foreigner will take part in the mystical rites of DIONYSUS, and that, whereas women are commonly blamed in song and legend, men commonly sire illegitimate children. A servant enters in search of Creusa. He reports that they are all in trouble with the authorities: Phoebus has exposed and prevented the plot. The servant then tells how Xuthus went off to make offerings to Dionysus on the peaks of Parnassus, but before going asked his son Ion to build a tent for the sacrificial feast. The servant describes at length how Ion did so, and how he covered the space with fine tapestries—one, acquired by Heracles from the AMAZONS, representing the sky, sun, moon, and constellations; one, a work of barbarians, representing Greek and barbarian ships, and scenes of hunting; and one, an Athenian tapestry representing Cecrops and his daughters. He then tells how the old man infiltrated the feast as a waiter, attempted to poison Ion but was prevented when another servant spoke a word of ill omen while they were holding their cups. The pious Ion ordered them all to throw their wine to the ground. Doves, allowed to live unharmed in Apollo's temple, came to drink the discarded wine, and the one that drank the wine from Ion's cup died in a fit of agony. The old man was made to reveal the plot, and the authorities at Delphi voted that Creusa should be put to death by stoning.

The Chorus laments. Creusa enters. She is desperate to escape. Ion and a group of armed Delphians enter. Ion expresses horror at her viperlike nature, and she takes refuge at the altar. They argue intensely over their respective justifications and rights. The priestess who raised Ion enters carrying a wicker cradle. She counsels him not to be violent. Bidden to do so by the god, she has retrieved the cradle in which he was brought to the temple, and the infant's clothes that he was wearing, as clues to help find his mother. The priestess exits. Ion speaks of his fate as an orphan, considers dedicating the objects to Phoebus, but then changes his mind and decides to uncover them. They have been miraculously preserved by the god. Creusa recognizes the cradle, realizes that Ion is her son, and runs to him from the altar.

Ion orders the Delphians to seize her. He does not believe her. She is able to describe from memory the objects inside, however: garments she wove herself embroidered with a Gorgon and serpents, a golden snake necklace, and a garland of olive leaves. Ion embraces Creusa as his mother. Creusa proclaims the rejuvenation of the house of Erechtheus and the earthborn race. She then reveals that his father is Apollo. Ion rejoices but is still confused by her account of Apollo's motives. At this point, Athena appears. She confirms Ion's parentage as authentic and bids them go to Athens to install Ion on the throne as a legitimate king. His four sons will give their names to the lands and tribes. Their descendants, in turn, will establish communities in both Europe and Asia, and their people will be called Ionians after him. Xuthus and Creusa will also have children: Dorus (giving his name to the Dorians) and Achaeus. She also reveals how carefully Apollo had arranged to keep the child safe. Finally, she orders Creusa to cherish in secret the knowledge that Ion is her son. Ion is convinced by Athena, and Creusa praises Phoebus and retracts her complaints. Creusa and Ion begin to make their way to Athens. All exit.

COMMENTARY

The play's probable date (ca. 410 B.C.E.) late in Euripides' career and its persistent display of interest in Athens and the etiology of Athenian cult and tradition link it on some key points with the *Iphigenia among the Taurians* (ca. 413 B.C.E.). In the *Ion*, Hermes makes the prologue speech, first giving his genealogy, while IPHIGENIA begins the prologue speech in *Iphigenia among the Taurians* by giving her own genealogy. In both plays, one family member, through the design of a god, goes to the foreign sanctuary where another family member, unbeknown to either, serves in the temple. They are eventually reunited through a complex recognition sequence, but only after one (or each of the two) nearly brings about the death of the other. Each had thought the other to be dead, and each experiences pity for the other's lot. In both cases, moreover, key characters (Iphigenia, ORESTES, Creusa) experience severe doubt regarding the designs and basic decency of the gods. Finally, at the close of both plays, the goddess Athena makes an appearance ex machina to bring about a satisfactory plot resolution and, at the same time, to reassure the main characters of the rationality of the gods' designs. In both instances, she sends the two family members to Athens, where they will lay some of the foundations of Athenian civilization. We are seeing here the conjunction of a set of concerns specific to Euripides' later work, in particular, an interest in etiology, Athenian and non-Athenian cults, and the self-consciousness of Athens in relation both to other Greek cities and to the broader world.

Yet whereas the mythological content of *Iphigenia among the Taurians*, as of most Euripidean tragedies, belongs to the broader mythological fabric of the Trojan War, and turns emphatically toward Athens only at the close, the *Ion* concerns a specifically Athenian set of myths. Euripides demonstrates that Athens, like other states with tragic myths, can boast of its own doomed royal house with a cross-generational history of violence. This tragic vision of Athenian legend is significant, given that the *Ion*, like other late Euripidean dramas, has been occasionally characterized as more comic than tragic, or somehow occupying a transitional point between the two genres. As always, such characterizations are misleading. Whether or not a play has a broadly unhappy ending does not necessarily constitute the chief criterion of tragedy, and here we might note in particular the guiding framework of the inherited familial taint or curse so central to tragic mythology.

The sense of a dark, ineluctable past that defines the characters' present horizons of action is a distinctly tragic feature, whereas comedy tends to focus on the present, the everyday, and the immediate: The past rarely extends beyond an earlier phase in a character's own lifetime. The Athenian royal house

into which Creusa is born as a princess has an appropriately dark history. HEPHAESTUS, attempting to rape Athena, spilled his semen on the ground, and the Earth was impregnated with Erichthonius (whose name refers to his status as earthborn). Athena hid him in a chest and forbade the three daughters of Cecrops to look at him; two looked, and all three were driven to madness and leapt to their deaths from the Acropolis. In the next generation, King Erechtheus, Creusa's father, to satisfy an oracle that demanded the sacrifice of virgins to repel an invader and thus save Athens, sacrificed his own daughters. Creusa was the only one not to be sacrificed, as she was a newborn child. When she arrives at Delphi and meets Ion, he questions her about the details of precisely these myths—the defining myths of Athens, from his viewpoint as a Delphian.

Creusa, then, belongs to a series of Athenian princesses who come to a bad end: Her own sisters were sacrificed by her father. Still, the house of Erechtheus cannot quite compete with the house of Atreus, with its long list of ghastly crimes extending back to Tantalus and Pelops, nor with the horrors of the Theban royal family. Presumably, this is a good thing. The misfortunes of Creusa's kin are alluded to in the play but do not weigh as heavily on her as the family histories of ANTIGONE and ELECTRA weigh on those characters. The play's broadly optimistic ending confirms that Athens's tragic legacy is not as intractable and deadly as that of other city-states. Athens is able to emerge from its dark tragic past whereas Mycenae needs the help of Athens and its institutions to lay to rest its demons.

Euripides thus wishes Athens to be taken seriously in tragic terms, even if the destructiveness of his city's tragic mythology remains within relatively moderate limits. Like other doomed royal households, the house of Erechtheus is identified with its own set of recurrent images and themes: snakes, gorgons, gigantomachy, earthborn creatures, and monsters. Autochthony—meaning originating from the earth and being indigenous to the land rather than coming from elsewhere—is the defining concept in this imagery set. The Athenian founder figure Erichthonius, we recall, came from the earth: the Gorgon and GIANTS are also children of Earth, and snakes, which are often seen as coming from of a hole in the ground, are animals that have a close association with the earth. In broader mythic terms, monsters of various kinds tend to be born of Earth and meet their end at the hands of heroes and gods associated with the sky. When the Chorus sees the temple at Delphi, it marvels at its relief sculptures and, in particular, the representation of the slaying of the hydra by Heracles, the Chimaera by Bellerophon, and the defeat of the giants by the Olympians. Apollo himself, the temple's god, was famous for slaying the monster Python before establishing his oracle. The combat between the Olympian gods and the giants presents an especially clear division between sky and earth, rational authority and brute nature. The Athenians had a somewhat more ambiguous relationship with earthborn creatures, since they included instances of such among their founders and legendary kings. The moment when the Chorus perceives the strongly Olympian artistic program on the temple of Apollo at Delphi is thus just as significant in its way as the moment when Ion asks Creusa about the peculiar mythology of her city.

The Athenians saw themselves as an especially privileged and pure race because of their autochthony, and yet being earthborn also has some dark and problematic mythic associations. It will be helpful to trace some aspects of this ambivalence through the play. Creusa, when she presents the idea of poisoning to the old man, begins by recalling the Gigantomachy, which she calls the "earthborn battle" at Phlegra; it was there, she goes on to say, that Gorgon was born of Earth. Athena killed the Gorgon and incorporated her image into her armor in the form of the aegis, a breastplate decorated with coils of snakes. Moreover, she

gave two drops of the Gorgon's blood to Erichthonius, the "earthy" one, and they were then passed to Erechtheus and thence to Creusa. The venom of the earthborn Gorgon, who was born at the battlefield of the gigantomachy, was thus passed on from Creusa's "earthman" ancestor to her. The drops of venom trace the genealogy of Athenian autochthony and now threaten to bring to an end the life of Ion, Athenian by birth, but brought up as the son of the Olympian Apollo. His double ancestry—by Creusa and Apollo—positions him precisely between the sky-and-earth lineage. Perhaps it was not by accident that he was conceived and exposed in a cave, from which he would later emerge, as if born within the earth. Following this scene, the Chorus exults that the blood from the "earthborn Gorgon" will kill Ion and prevent the invasion of the Erechtheid royal house by a foreigner. The deadly force of the earthborn Gorgon's blood, however, will be countered by the doves from Apollo's temple.

Another important passage illustrates some of the same mythological tensions. In his speech describing the thwarted assassination attempt, the servant describes in an ecphrasis—an extended description of a work of art—the images depicted on the tapestries that Ion uses to make the tent for the sacrificial feast. They include a tapestry acquired by Heracles as spoils from the Amazons that represents the heavens, evening star, night, constellations, and moon; a barbarian tapestry representing Greek and barbarian ships and hunt scenes; and an Athenian tapestry representing a half-serpentine Cecrops next to his daughters. Thus, we have representations of Athens, the cosmos, Hellas, and the barbarians—at once a woven map of Athens's place in relation to the world and a set of images that set up a contrast between the heavens and the earth. The Olympian-derived hero Heracles' tapestry representing the sky and heavens presents an especially sharp contrast with the Athenian tapestry, representing the snaky, earthborn Cecrops. These clashing images will surround Ion as he celebrates the sacrificial feast.

Another work of weaving is crucial to the pivotal recognition scene. Here, Creusa's own weaving of Ion's swaddling cloths included a Gorgon and serpents reminiscent of those depicted on Athena's aegis. The crib's other objects include the golden snakes placed on Athenian children in imitation of Erichthonius and a garland of olive leaves. The objects and woven garment placed by Creusa in Ion's crib, in other words, constitute a set of tokens of Athenian identity and autochthony. Athena herself plays no small role in this image set. She killed the Gorgon, and her aegis bears the image of the Gorgon and snakes. As a sky god who killed earthborn giants, she nonetheless appropriates the deadly power and formidable images of earthborn creatures. Athena is therefore appropriate as protector goddess of Athens, a city-state defined by its dual mythic heritage. In Euripides' tragedy, this dual heritage is embodied in the displaced figure of Ion. Ion is the site of a conflict between Olympian gods and the deadly, chthonic forces of earthborn monsters such as the Gorgon. Thanks to Apollo, he survives that conflict to become king of Athens. Creusa herself is impregnated by the sky god Apollo and manages to escape along with her son from the violence that has overtaken other female offspring of her line.

At some level, the play is a complicated household drama. Creusa has married outside her kin group and wants to preserve her line in the royal house of Erechtheus: A central struggle in the play is over which of the two members of the couple will bring back to Athens their own, singular child, begotten without the help of the other. Athena herself, as Euripides' reminds us, was conceived when Zeus swallowed METIS, without the help of HERA; Hera, in response, conceived Hephaestus all on her own. The conflict between Creusa and Xuthus represents a similar struggle on the mortal plane; whoever can be the one to bring back a child of his or her own to place

on the throne will be the winner. Children and childlessness are a central Euripidean theme. We might compare, for example, the terrible struggle over the children of Medea and JASON, precipitated by Medea's desire to destroy Jason by making him childless and to save her children from the fate of being mistreated and disrespected when Jason should have other children by the new wife. Children, as the Chorus of the present play reminds, are a great joy, and the life of the childless is much inferior to that of others, but that does not mean children do not also cause considerable pain and intense emotion for their parents. Creusa has been suffering her entire life under the misconception that her exposed child was not saved by Apollo but left to die.

Apollo's putative cruelty forms another major theme. Like other male gods, such as Zeus, he behaves ruthlessly toward mortal women whom he impregnates and then abandons. Ultimately, the outcome of the play and Athena's speech justify Apollo in his broader designs, but the pain of Creusa at her rape and mistreatment are real. This pain inspires one of the bolder passages in the play, Creusa's "anti-paean," in which, instead of offering a traditional song in praise of Apollo (a paean), she bitterly and sarcastically excoriates the god for behaving deplorably while continuing to be the subject of mortals' songs of praise. Even Apollo's son and servant, Ion, has a serious moment of doubt and pleads with the gods to provide a better example. Elsewhere, like the Chorus of the *Medea*, the Chorus of this play attempts to turn around the course of song and affix blame and bad reputation for sexual misdeed on men instead of women. It may well be that Euripides mitigates the force of these challenging statements with the characters' later self-corrections and recantations, yet it is hard not to wonder if he did not also relish the opportunity first to shock and thrill his audience with these sentiments all the more effectively for the fact that they have at least a grain of truth in them.

Ion's great accomplishments as king and founder of Ionia are not represented in the play; they are yet to come, prophesied by Athena but not enacted on stage. The playwright understandably is not as interested in this later career of his hero. He focuses on the moment of conflict and doubt, when Ion is not yet Ion, or has only just received his true name through the agency of the god Apollo. Becoming Ion means coming into a complicated legacy of rape and exposure, mortal and immortal, sky-and-earth ancestry. He is a good founder figure for the Athenians because of the revelation of his simultaneously divine and autochthonous origins, his moral purity and racial authenticity. The Athenian polis was notoriously exclusive in its definition of citizenship and increasingly strict as time went on. Euripides makes Xuthus the son of Aeolus and explicitly foreign. Ion's ancestry, by contrast, is carefully traced back to Athens's earliest autochthonous figures of legend. Ion's later history, however, expresses a somewhat different idea. He goes well beyond the boundaries of Attica to found communities that straddle Europe and Asia, while the shared sons of Creusa and Xuthus—Dorus and Achaeus—will go on to found communities of their own outside Attica. (Daughters are not mentioned—and given the terrible history of Athenian princesses, perhaps this omission is for the best.) The myth of Ion is thus well calibrated to give expression both to Athenian pride in autochthonous origins and to Athenian ambitions of expansion, colonization, and empire.

Iphicles   See Heracles.

Iphigenia   Daughter of Agamemnon and Clytaemnestra. Iphigenia appears in Euripides' *Iphigenia at Aulis* and *Iphigenia among the Taurians*. Additional classical sources are Apollodorus's *Library* (Epitome 2.10, 3.21–22), Homer's *Iliad* (9.145), Hyginus's *Fabulae* (98, 120, 122), Ovid's *Metamorphoses* (12.23–

38, 13.182–195), and Pausanias's *Description of Greece* (1.33.1, 2.22.6–7, 9.19.6–7). When Agamemnon and the Greek fleet were trapped by unfavorable winds at Aulis, Calchas prophesied that he must sacrifice his own daughter to gain fair winds for sailing. Artemis, angry at Agamemnon for killing a deer or a sacred goat, or for failing to fulfill a vow, or for boasting of his superiority in hunting, demanded the sacrifice. In Euripides' *Iphigenia at Aulis*, Agamemnon sends for Iphigenia on the pretext of marriage to Achilles, but in this play, as in other versions, Artemis replaces her with a deer in the moment before she is killed. Aeschylus's *Agamemnon* seems to imply that she was actually killed, although Aeschylus may have been aware of the story of her replacement. Agamemnon, both in the *Agamemnon* and the *Iphigenia at Aulis*, struggles with the choice between murdering his daughter and undermining the expedition of which he is leader. The tragic Clytaemnestra typically offers up Iphigenia's murder as justification for her murder of Agamemnon. In some versions, Artemis, after rescuing her, takes Iphigenia to Tauris and immortalizes her. In Euripides' *Iphigenia among the Taurians*, Iphigenia is a priestess forced to participate in human sacrifice. Orestes and Pylades arrive and, according to the custom of stranger sacrifice, are going to be killed. Orestes, Pylades, and Iphigenia manage to escape by an elaborate plan, and the barbarian king Thoas is about to pursue them, when Athena appears and orders him to let them go. She also predicts the establishment of the cult of Artemis at Brauron in Attica, which was closely associated with the figure of Iphigenia. For the Roman poet Lucretius, Iphigenia's sacrifice is a grim example of the destructive nature of superstition.

Iphigenia among the Taurians   Euripides (413 b.c.e.)   The title of Euripides' play is best rendered as *Iphigenia among the Taurians* rather than *Iphigenia at Tauris* on analogy with *Iphigenia at Aulis*. There is no place called

Tauris, but only a people called Taurians, who inhabited the modern Crimean peninsula. The play is not firmly but hypothetically dated to 414–413 B.C.E. on the basis of style and plot type. Euripides here develops the version of IPHIGENIA's sacrifice in which she is replaced by a deer at the last moment and placed by ARTEMIS among the Taurians. There she becomes a high priestess at Artemis's sanctuary, where a rite of stranger sacrifice is performed. As it happens, her brother, ORESTES, unbeknown to her, has just arrived at the opening of the play, and he and his companion and brother-in-law Pylades have been chosen to be the next victims of Artemis. The resolution is a happy one (she and her brother escape the barbarian land and its barbaric rites), but the tragic elements remain strong. Iphigenia and Orestes are the victims of powerful forces of the gods and fate; they belong to the cursed household of ATREUS; and they are both the objects of profound pity. Euripides' play at once interacts with Aeschylus's *Oresteia* and engages with broader themes of Greek and barbarian, male and female, in the context of the Trojan War and its consequence. Both Orestes and Iphigenia are involved in a desperate struggle to escape from cycles of violence and human sacrifice.

SYNOPSIS

The scene is set in the land of the Taurians. Iphigenia enters from the doors of a temple, where a bloodstained altar is seen inside; near the roof are objects taken from sacrificial victims. She gives her genealogy, starting with TANTALUS. Then she tells the commonly believed story of how her father, AGAMEMNON, on advice from the prophet CALCHAS, decided to sacrifice Iphigenia to Artemis to receive favorable weather to set sail for the expedition to Troy. ODYSSEUS was sent to lure her to the site of the sacrifice with a false story of marriage to ACHILLES; the sacrificial ritual was almost completed, but, just as the officiant was about to strike the death blow, Artemis replaced her with a deer

and took her away to Tauris, where the ruler, Thoas, made her high priestess of a rite of stranger sacrifice, in which her function is to prepare the victims. Iphigenia then relates her dream of the previous night. She dreamed that she was in her father's palace in Argos when the whole palace crashed to the ground. One pillar remained standing, and it had the form of a young man. She touched his forehead with the same water with which she anoints victims of human sacrifice in Tauris. She interprets the remaining pillar of the house to be Orestes, and the anointing with water as a sign of his death. Iphigenia exits into the temple.

Orestes and Pylades enter cautiously because they do not wish to be seen. They see the temple and note the signs of human sacrifice. Orestes relates that, while he was being hounded by the Furies, he turned to APOLLO for help, and the god bid him go to Tauris, find the statue of Artemis that fell from the sky, and bring it back to Hellas. This accomplishment would end his suffering. At the thought of being caught, however, he begins to panic, and Pylades must persuade him not to run back to the boat. He suggests instead that they enter the temple through the space between two beams and hoist the statue out. They exit.

The Chorus of temple maidens enters. They pray to Artemis and hear the voice of their high priestess Iphigenia calling them to worship. The Chorus asks why they have been called, and why Iphigenia looks worried. She tells her dream and her belief that Orestes, her brother, is dead; she then makes an offering to him. The Chorus laments and comments on the misfortunes of the house of Atreus across the generations. Iphigenia expresses her grief: given over as sacrifice by her father, forced to witness human sacrifice, exiled, she now must give up hope of seeing her brother grown up and installed as king. A herdsman runs in suddenly and reports that two young men from Hellas, one named Pylades, were captured—ideal victims for the goddess. He was ordered to tell them to make ready. Iphigenia asks him for the story of the capture. He relates how he and the other herds-man saw the two young Greeks and, from their appearance, had first thought that they were gods, but one of their number persuaded them that they were just shipwrecked sailors. Then they saw Orestes in a fit of madness, hounded by the Furies. He attacked their cattle with a sword. They called others to help them and surrounded the two, subdued them after a long fight, and brought them to the king. Iphigenia then sends the herdsman away to fetch the two victims.

Iphigenia declares that, after the dream portending her brother's death, she no longer pities the sacrificial victims; she relives in her mind her own near sacrifice at her father's hands, and she expresses her belief that Arte-mis cannot truly demand human sacrifice. The Chorus then sings of seafaring and the questionable motives that drive men to navi-gate the seas, of their wish that HELEN might be brought to Tauris as a victim, and of their longing to return to Hellas. They observe the victims' arrival. Iphigenia indicates that she now believes again that Artemis demands human sacrifice. The two young men are led in, and she engages them in conversation. Orestes, however, does not see the point of talking or evoking pity; so he refuses to tell who he is or where he is from. He will not tell his name but reveals he is from Mycenae and self-exiled. In response to her questions, he gives her news about other Greeks—Helen, MENELAUS, Cal-chas, Odysseus, Achilles. Finally, she asks about Agamemnon, and he reports that the king died by a woman's hand. He also tells her that Orestes survived but is not in Argos. Iphigenia then makes a proposal to him: He will be spared on condition that he take a letter to Argos for her, a letter that a previous, sympathetic victim wrote for her; Pylades, however, will have to die. Orestes replies that life would not be worth living for him if he betrayed his friend and so suggests Pylades for the task instead. Iphigenia praises him as worthy of being her brother, and agrees. Orestes asks how he will die, and

Iphigenia tells him; then when he says that he wishes that his sister could take care of his dead body, she replies that she will take care of it as if she were his sister in Argos. Iphigenia exits.

The Chorus expresses its pity for Orestes. Orestes and Pylades engage in a conversation initially at cross purposes. Orestes is puzzled why the priestess seems to know and care so much about Argos, while Pylades cannot understand why Orestes thinks him capable of letting his friend die in his place. He would be shamed forever if he did so. Orestes insists that Pylades go back to Argos and to his wife, ELECTRA, and rebuild the house of Agamem-non. He himself is angry that Phoebus has deceived and betrayed him by leading him to his death in a foreign land. Pylades reluctantly agrees to go back to Argos and build a tomb for Orestes.

Iphigenia reenters. She tells the two young men that Pylades must swear a vow that he will actually deliver the letter; Orestes demands that she in turn swear a vow that Pylades will be delivered from danger. They begin to swear their respective vows, but of a sudden it occurs to Pylades that if he is shipwrecked and loses the letter, he will be unable to fulfill his vow. Iphigenia answers that she will tell him what is in the letter so that, if necessary, he can deliver the message orally. She recites the contents of the letter: She greets Orestes, son of Agamem-non, informs him that she is still alive, and asks him to come to Tauris and save her from taking part in human sacrifice. She then explains how she was replaced by a deer at the last moment. Orestes is overcome by astonishment and won-ders if he is seeing a god. Pylades presents brother to sister, and they gradually become convinced of each other's identity as they recall details that only they would know, specifically, details of mythology of the house of Atreus that Iphigenia had woven into tapestries and certain gifts and keepsakes. They rejoice in their reunion and discuss their common fate. They have both escaped being sacrificed by their own kin.

Iphigenia begins to ask how Orestes can escape and finally suggests that he try to get away by sea. She wonders whether she, too, might escape. Pylades recommends that they leave immediately, but Iphigenia has still more questions. She learns of Pylades and Electra's marriage, CLYTAEMNESTRA's death, the Furies that hound Orestes, and Phoebus's oracle. The verdict of the Areopagus in Athens did not free him from all the Furies: The dissenters continued to hound him, forcing him to turn yet again to the oracle of Phoebus, which instructed him to retrieve the cult statue of Artemis from Tauris.

They then resolve to steal the wooden statue and attempt to escape together. Iphigenia determines upon a plan: They will claim that Orestes is a matricide and thus unworthy to be sacrificed—Pylades, too, because he aided in the killing—and thus in need of cleansing in seawater; further, that the cult statue must also be cleansed. Iphigenia then confirms the loyalty and silence of the other temple maidens from Hellas. Pylades and Orestes then go into the temple, but Iphigenia beseeches the goddess for help before she, too, leaves.

The Chorus recalls Hellas and laments its condition of exile in a strange land where it must attend barbaric rites. King Thoas enters with soldiers. He asks where the priestess is and whether the victims have been sacrificed yet. Iphigenia enters with the statue and explains that one of the strangers is a matricide, that they, along with the statue, need to be purified in the sea, and that Thoas must remain and purify the temple. He agrees. Iphigenia exits with the prisoners toward the sea; Thoas goes into the temple. The Chorus then sings of Apollo's oracular power and relates how he defeated the contradictory prophecies of dreams, making his daytime oracles the only valid ones.

A soldier enters. He asks for Thoas, explaining that the two prisoners escaped and are taking the priestess and Artemis's statue with them on a ship. The Chorus will not help him.

The soldier summons Thoas from the temple. Quickly, he explains the trick and reveals that one of the prisoners was Orestes. Secure in the conviction that his boats will prevent their escape, Thoas demands the whole story. The soldier details how they escaped under the pretext of a secret ritual, how a battle ensued, and how Orestes, Pylades, and Iphigenia were able to get on the boat with the statue but, subsequently, had trouble putting out to sea and how, when he left, they were struggling to keep it from running into the rocks. Thoas orders the Taurians to pursue the foreigners relentlessly and promises terrible punishments for all those involved. At this moment, the goddess Athena appears. She reveals to Thoas that Orestes and his ship have escaped with POSEIDON's help, and that it was Apollo who had instructed Orestes to take the statue. She then commands Orestes to continue to Greece; he is to stop at Athens and set up a temple at Halae, where the rites will recall the rites at Tauris, not as a duplication, but a warning; he is also to establish a cult in honor of Iphigenia in Brauron in Attica, where she will be buried. Thoas must swallow his wrath. He stands down in the face of the goddess and even releases the temple maidens from Hellas. The Chorus praises Athena.

COMMENTARY

Iphigenia among the Taurians falls into a category of Euripidean plays that are often described as incorporating aspects of comedy and romance at the expense of true tragic content. Athenian tragedy, however, is a much more diverse practice than is sometimes conceded, and its only firm criteria are derived from the occasions and conditions of its performance (in the tragic competition, at a festival of Dionysus), its basic formal features (a chorus, prologue, choral odes, episodes, exodus, etc.), and its mythological content. That said, we need to be aware how Euripides innovates within the tragic mode, and how he differentiates himself from his competitors and predecessors.

It is also worth attempting to characterize different phases in his career. The production of the play under discussion, for example, is usually dated to around 414–413 B.C.E. because of its close resemblance to the *Helen* (412 B.C.E.). Here, too, we have a Greek heroine stranded in a faraway land, unknown to her compatriots because of an illusion created by a god, rescued by a close relative (husband or brother) who is made known to her in a recognition scene, and who escapes with her by eluding the pursuit of a barbarian ruler. In this type of Euripidean tragedy, there is no central act of violence or horror that defines the tragedy and in which it culminates, but a complex plot involving recognition, deception, and escape with a more or less happy ending. In both instances, however, the action is located in the shadow of the Trojan expedition, which has destroyed the lives of many Greeks and continues to affect the protagonists of the plays. The Trojan War, on Euripides' reading, has created a great diaspora of heroes and heroines, who now must struggle to regain Greek soil and the society of other Greeks.

If indeed Euripides was to put on the *Helen* a year or two after the present tragedy, it is remarkable and intriguing that throughout *Iphigenia among the Taurians*, Helen is reviled as a "bad woman" and chief cause of the war. She emerges as a kind of anti-Iphigenia throughout the play. She was removed from Hellas with her own complicity to live with Paris in Troy, whereas Iphigenia was removed from Hellas against her will to serve in a foreign cult. The former is the cause of the war, the latter one of its signal victims. Helen's baneful effect on the land of her origin and her transfer from Greece to Troy is pointedly brought out through the verbal juxtaposition of Helen/Hellas by the Chorus, just as Aeschylus had played on the verbal similarity between "Helen" and the word for "destroy." It is interesting to contemplate, however, that Euripides may have already had in mind the counter-myth of Helen's stay in Egypt, while her mere image

went to Troy. In this version, both Iphigenia and Helen are Greek women displaced, misrepresented, and made to suffer because of the Trojan expedition. They are both presented by Euripides as false originating figures for the conflict—Iphigenia as sacrificial victim, Helen as nominal cause.

Euripides, in both plays, exploits alternative versions of the myth. A version in which Iphigenia is saved, transported to the land of the Taurians, and made immortal by Artemis already existed in the lost *Cypria*, a poem of the Epic Cycle (seventh–sixth century B.C.E.). Euripides, however, develops this story in new and interesting ways. In Euripides' play, Artemis makes Iphigenia a priestess in the land of the Taurians, not a goddess, and Euripides also appears to be responsible for the convergence of Iphigenia's story and the story of Orestes' wandering. This dimension of the plot in effect reopens the apparent closure of Aeschylus' *Oresteia*: Euripides imposes his own resolution, which interacts in complex ways with Aeschylus's *Eumenides*. For Aeschylus, the Athenian polis and the Areopagus offer a solution to the endless cycle of revenge killing that afflicts the house of Atreus. Polis institutions resolve a problem that the aristocratic *oikos* (household) shows itself incapable of resolving. But whereas Aeschylus converted the Furies into "Kindly Ones" and gave them a new home and set of duties to confine them, Euripides creates a dissenting party of Furies who refuse to accept the verdict and continue hounding the exasperated Orestes. The polis-based solution offered by Aeschylus does not suffice in Euripides' version. The hero is now required to leave not only the Athenian polis but Hellas itself, and go beyond the edges of the civilized Greek world to retrieve Artemis's cult statue from the Taurians. Against all expectation, however, he finds a member of his own family in this faraway place—his sister Iphigenia. The true resolution, in Euripides' version, thus includes a familial element and requires the discovery and complicity of Orestes' sister.

This aspect of the play has future implications as well. Whereas the house of Atreus was, in a certain sense, abandoned as irretrievably damaged by Aeschylus, who refocused his trilogy on the polis in his closing play, Euripides continues to focus on the royal household of Mycenae in a potentially positive sense. At different points throughout the play, the main characters look forward to the rebuilding and regeneration of the house of Atreus through either Orestes or Pylades (who turns out to be kin of Orestes). In Iphigenia's dream at the beginning, Orestes was figured as the last remaining pillar of his household. Both sister and brother hope to reestablish their father's kingdom. This shared adherence to the family is a highly prominent theme throughout the play. In the opening lines, Iphigenia introduces herself by tracing her ancestry from Tantalus through Pelops to Agamemnon. Later, during the recognition scene, brother and sister verify each other's identity by recalling key incidents in the mythology of the family and the tapestries that Iphigenia made of them. Pylades' importance is magnified to the extent that he is kin in the first place and now has married Electra.

The question of family, however, is complicated for Orestes and Iphigenia, especially as it concerns the central figure of Agamemnon. Orestes killed Clytaemnestra to avenge the slaying of Agamemnon, whereas Iphigenia went through the disturbing experience of having her father resolve to slay her as a sacrificial offering to Artemis. In Aeschylus's *Oresteia*, Clytaemnestra justified her slaying of Agamemnon, in large part, as retribution for his choice to sacrifice Iphigenia. Athena, however, resolves the impasse by awarding priority to the male: Agamemnon's death is the more important one and justifies the killing of Clytaemnestra. The resolution of the *Oresteia* thus depends on a very specific choice to privilege the male gender over the female.

Euripides, in attempting to work out the dynamics of a reintegrated royal household, strives to achieve a new gender equilibrium. According to the gendered logic of Aeschylus, Orestes should favor his father's cause, and Iphigenia should hate her father and take her mother's side. Iphigenia, however, while clearly still very bitter about the experience, broadly supports Orestes' path of action and sympathizes with him. Orestes, for his part, understands Iphigenia's equivocal feelings about her father. Even more important, Orestes, by saving his sister Iphigenia from a life in which she assists at human sacrifices, reverses the wrong done by his father, Agamemnon, who chose to make a human sacrifice of Iphigenia. As Iphigenia indicates in her letter to Orestes, serving as a priestess among the Taurians is a living death for her, and she reaches out to him from an open grave. In bringing her back to Hellas, Orestes, on a symbolic plane, brings back to life the sister his father condemned to death. At the same time, Iphigenia saves Orestes from the human sacrifice demanded by the Taurians. The traumatic event at Aulis, that originated the terrible split between male and female in Agamemnon's family, has thus been therapeutically addressed in Euripides' carefully symmetrical scenario: A male member and female member of the family are each given an opportunity to make the decision to *save* rather than sacrifice the other. The important regenerative dimension of this decision can be understood even more fully when we recall the sacrificial imagery applied to Agamemnon's slaying in the *Oresteia*: Putting a stop to human sacrifice effectively means putting a stop to the cycle of revenge killing that afflicts the house of Atreus.

For Euripides, the Aeschylean resolution was incomplete because it did not take into account the family; the family dynamic was merely overridden by the procedures of the state as instituted by Athena. Euripides, by contrast, is careful to bring the male and female representatives of the house of Atreus back into a harmonious, or in any case reasonably harmonious, relation. Euripides, however, does not ignore Athens and the polis in promoting the importance of familial integration in his play. Athens plays a small but prominent part. Athena, the divine protector of Athens and its eponymous goddess, plays the role of dea ex machina at the end, determining the final outcome of the play. If the divine brother and sister, Apollo and Artemis, who oversee the fates of Orestes and Iphigenia, respectively, each play a role in bringing the two together in the land of the Taurians to achieve their familial integration, Athena adds a civic dimension to their quest.

She instructs Orestes to go first to Athens, then to two sanctuaries of Artemis in Attica: Halae and Brauron. This etiological feature of her speech recalls a broader interest in Euripides' plays, in the origins of cult practices. At Halae, a kind of mock human sacrifice will be practiced, whereby a human "victim" has his throat grazed so as to draw a little blood. This rite will serve as a reminder of the necessity of never truly performing human sacrifice. At Brauron, Iphigenia will be revered alongside Artemis, especially by women giving birth. The divine version of Iphigenia envisaged here correlates with the story in the *Cypria*. Indeed, it seems plausible that her status as goddess is even dimly reflected in her position as prologue speaker for the play, a position often occupied in Euripides by a god. We might also recall the association of Brauron and Artemis with the initiation of young girls passing into womanhood. Both Iphigenia and Orestes are youthful figures, associated with the youthful brother and sister deities, Artemis and Apollo, and must succeed in a complicated ruse involving trickery, cunning, and role-playing—common elements in initiatory rites. Finally, Athena indicates that Orestes' case in Athens will set the precedent for future cases where the vote is tied.

Athena's instructions also relate to another major theme of the play: Greekness. The Chorus of Greek captive slaves of Thoas forced to attend to rites of human sacrifice frequently laments its condition of exile and expresses

its longing for its homeland. Iphigenia seems alienated from her very self as priestess of the foreign rite, and expresses disbelief that Artemis truly supports and demands the barbaric act. Thoas, for his part, exemplifies perhaps even excessively and cartoonishly the uncivilized barbarian. He openly recommends "barbaric" behavior and seems satisfied with his role as barbarian king. He does remark, however, on the irony of the Greek Orestes' matricide. He has committed an act more barbaric than the barbarians. The uncivilized land of the Taurians, where human sacrifice is a regular feature of religious life, functions as a symbolic place for members of the house of Atreus to come to terms with, and attempt to escape from, the violence of their family. The Taurian land is "good to think with" for the haunted Orestes and Iphigenia, as they attempt to reclaim both their Greek homeland and the peaceful, civilized mode of existence that Hellas should symbolize but that their own family and the Trojan War have recently perverted. At one point, when Orestes is in the depths of despair, he feels compelled to claim that the gods are simply out to deceive human beings and that everything is a lie: The chaos of his life has led him to believe that the world is simply moral chaos. Iphigenia herself appears confused about the true nature of Artemis. The play's resolution, however, makes clear the deeper designs and care of the Greek gods, as they help a family achieve reintegration, help Orestes and Iphigenia repatriate Artemis's cult statue, and help define with greater clarity the distinction between proper Greek cults and sanctuaries, on the one hand, and the barbaric, bloodstained altars of Thoas, on the other.

It is worth asking where Athens stands in all this. The Chorus seems highly critical of ambitious seafaring and the motivations of human beings as they sail to faraway lands. The Trojan War, moreover, is viewed with great bitterness as a bad war carried out by bad men for a bad reason. Perhaps the characters in the present instance have reasons to be bitter and are unable to appreciate the deeper necessity that motivated the war, but we are not afforded such an ameliorative perspective. We see only the suffering of the characters and their disillusionment and despair. Athens, too, was in the midst of a devastating, ambitious war and, in the years 415–413, was engaged in the misguided Sicilian Expedition. If this play was produced in 414 or 413, it is interesting to try to discern a political mood. Certainly the *Helen*, produced in 412 after the Sicilian Expedition came to grief, has been read in a political light. The playwright, however, provides no unequivocal statement, but only a searching inquiry into the struggles of individuals to reassemble their lives in war's devastating wake.

Iphigenia at Aulis Euripides (ca. 405 B.C.E.) Euripides' *Iphigenia at Aulis* was produced posthumously, probably in 405 B.C.E., the year after the playwright's death, and won first prize, along with the similarly posthumous the *BACCHAE*, at the tragic competition. Whereas Aeschylus, Sophocles, and Euripides himself devoted many plays to the aftermath of the Trojan War (*Oresteia*, *PHILOCTETES*, *ELECTRA*, *HELEN*), Euripides here focuses on the war's preliminaries. Agamemnon and Menelaus have assembled the Greek army and fleet at Aulis in preparation for the expedition against Troy. The winds are adverse, the fleet cannot sail, and the army is becoming restless. Calchas delivers a prophecy that Agamemnon must sacrifice his own daughter to win favorable winds. This prophecy puts Agamemnon in the impossible position previously explored in Aeschylus's *AGAMEMNON*: He cannot kill his own daughter, yet he cannot abandon an expedition that he has sworn an oath to carry out and that Zeus himself supports. Euripides now devotes an entire play to the story of his vacillation and its consequences. In the end, Agamemnon decides in favor of the sacrifice, yet an indignant Achilles still potentially stands as an obstruction to his plans. It is here that the play's title character becomes involved, and a true Euripidean heroine takes matters into her own hands. Iphigenia chooses to embrace death for the sake of Greek liberty. Artemis, however, intervenes at the last moment by replacing her with a deer. Both departures from the more usual myth are striking. Iphigenia comes into her own as a significant character: She plays an active role in shaping her own destiny and consciously assumes her role as an instrument of the destruction of Troy. At the same time, the goddess ensures that she is saved from death—the consequences of which Euripides had previously explored in *IPHIGENIA AMONG THE TAURIANS*. Orestes, who will play an important role along with his sister in this later phase of the myth, is still an infant, and Clytaemnestra has yet to become the murderer of her husband. The present play affords an opportunity to contemplate the beginnings of the tragedy of the house of Atreus.

SYNOPSIS

The scene is set in Aulis outside Agamemnon's tent. Agamemnon cannot sleep, and an old man, a slave belonging to Agamemnon and Clytaemnestra who came as part of Clytaemnestra's dowry, asks him to reveal his troubles. Agamemnon tells the story of Helen's marriage, the oath sworn to Tyndareus by all the suitors, the seduction of Helen by Paris, and the current expedition. He relates how Calchas prophesied that they would enjoy favorable winds for departing from Aulis only if Agamemnon's own daughter Iphigenia were sacrificed. Agamemnon has sent for Iphigenia on the pretext that she is being offered to Achilles in marriage. Agamemnon entrusts to the old man a letter canceling his previous communication and ordering Iphigenia to remain at home. The old man, and then Agamemnon, exit. The Chorus of young women of Chalcas enters. The Chorus sings of the Greek expedition to retrieve Helen, of the Greek heroes, and, above all, of Achilles. Menelaus and the old man enter. Menelaus has seized and read the letter. Agamemnon now returns and exchanges insults with his brother. A soldier enters and announces, to Agamemnon's horror, that Iphigenia, Clytaemnestra, and Orestes have arrived. Menelaus, apparently moved by Agamemnon's despair, recants his previous commitment to the sacrifice of Iphigenia. Agamemnon, however, has concluded that it is too late to change course. The army, urged on by Calchas, will demand her death, and if they should flee, the army will follow them to Argos and kill them all. Agamemnon and Menelaus exit. The Chorus sings of the destructive power of APHRODITE and the abduction of Helen. Clytaemnestra, Iphigenia, and Orestes enter, followed by Agamemnon. Iphigenia expresses her love for her father, who is devastated, but hides his intentions. Agamemnon and Clytaemnestra discuss the wedding, and Agamemnon tries to persuade Clytaemnestra not to attend. Clytaemnestra and Agamemnon exit. The Chorus sings of the coming destruction of Troy. Achilles enters, seeking to speak with Agamemnon about the delay of the expedition. Clytaemnestra comes in; when she speaks of the marriage, Achilles is confused. The old man enters and reveals Agamemnon's murderous plans to them both. Clytaemnestra asks Achilles to protect her child, and Achilles, angry that his name has been used in an ignoble ruse, agrees to do so if Agamemnon cannot be dissuaded from his purpose. They exit, leaving behind the Chorus to sing of the marriage of PELEUS and THETIS, the greatness of Achilles, and the proposed sacrifice of Iphigenia. Clytaemnestra enters and calls for Agamemnon to come. Then Iphigenia and Orestes are summoned. Clytaemnestra rebukes Agamemnon for intending to sacrifice their daughter, and Iphigenia begs her father for her life. Agamemnon responds that though he loathes sacrificing his own daughter, Greece demands the expedition to punish the barbarians for the theft of Helen. He exits. Iphigenia and Clytaemnestra lament. Achilles and his attendants enter, and Achilles reaffirms his commitment to protect Iphige-

nia. Iphigenia, however, has changed her mind and now resolves to die for the sake of Greece. Achilles praises her but insists that his promise of protection still holds. He exits. Slave attendants enter and lead Iphigenia away, who sings in praise of Artemis as she is led off stage. A slave attendant enters and reports to Clytaemnestra that a miracle occurred: The goddess Artemis replaced Iphigenia with a deer at the last moment. Clytaemnestra is skeptical, but Agamemnon returns and confirms the story. All exit.

COMMENTARY

The latter years of Euripides' life represent one of the darker phases of Athenian history. The disastrous Sicilian Expedition of 415–413 B.C.E. exhausted Athens's resources and capacity to carry on the war. In 404, two years after Euripides' death, Athens surrendered to Sparta. Euripides' attitude toward Athens, and more broadly, Greece, is informed by these developments, as can be seen especially in his later plays. The *Iphigenia at Aulis*, performed at some point after the playwright's death, displays many of the features and concerns of his later work. Heroism appears irremediably tainted by self-interest, cowardice, lust, and political ambition. The uncontrolled desires of the mob undermine the capacity of leaders to carry out rational plans and decision making. Vast military projects arise from risibly sordid, base, and possibly altogether phantasmal motivations. There is a sense that the great endeavors of the human world are so much "sound and fury" without any redeeming purpose or meaning. Frequently, as in the present case, Euripides rescues the hopeless situations of his later plays through the last-minute intervention of the deus ex machina. Such "happy" endings arguably suggest a more optimistic perspective concealed beneath the pervading mood of exasperation, yet it might equally be argued that the recurrent requirement of divine intervention speaks to the irretrievable, moral chaos of the human world. The gods must intervene to save the innocent and virtuous, because assuredly no one else will.

The character of Iphigenia, as in Euripides' *Iphigenia among the Taurians*, brings into play themes of sacrifice, the horror of war, the pointlessness of human suffering, and the relation between Greek and barbarian. Iphigenia may be particularly interesting to Euripides because she is the archetypal innocent victim—a young, unmarried girl who has done nothing wrong, who is to be sacrificed by her own father to enable the launching of a massively destructive war. Euripides is in general interested in the pathos of children's suffering and death (e.g., *MEDEA*). Among other things, this theme enables Euripides to display the ruthlessness of the world at large, which takes the few relatively untainted and still virtuous individuals and draws them into its violent, corrupt nexus. The contrast between the girl's tender expectation of marriage and genuine joy at seeing her father after long absence and the reality of what is being done to her in the name of political expediency is truly disturbing, and Euripides makes a point of intensifying the effect. The conversation between Agamemnon and Iphigenia plays pointedly on his dreadful knowledge of what he intends to do and her trusting affection for her father.

As in other tragedies such as Sophocles' *ANTIGONE*, Euripides at the same time develops a parallelism between marriage and death, showing how one can be made to sound like the other. The fact that there is some basic homology between the two intensifies the grim irony: Iphigenia will play the leading role in a ceremony; normally one would expect all her family members to be present at it. The ceremony will constitute a major transition for her. She will have to leave her former life behind and embrace the unknown. Iphigenia must leave her mother's care, never to return to the house of her upbringing; she must go on a long, lonely journey. Her mother will grieve for the loss of her daughter, and so on. The pathos is so great because Iphigenia does not merely die; she dies unmarried, and thus never truly commences her adult life and role.

Euripides seems to take a perverse interest in arranging matters as awkwardly and painfully as possible for his protagonist Agamemnon. The character himself periodically comments on his unbelievable bad luck and the systematic dismantling of all his plans. He can trace the path of misfortune back to the oath of the suitors and to Helen's fateful choice to marry his brother Menelaus. Now adverse winds have trapped him at Aulis with an increasingly restless and resentful army. The prophecy delivered by Calchas, that he must sacrifice his own daughter, is disastrous. When he has a temporary change of heart and tries to prevent his daughter from coming to Aulis, he fails; as luck would have it, Menelaus intercepts his communication. Then Iphigenia arrives, but not alone; Clytaemnestra and the infant Orestes are with her. Clytaemnestra insists on attending the "wedding." Everything is conspiring to place Agamemnon in the worst possible position. Finally, Clytaemnestra learns that the proposed marriage is a sham, and that Agamemnon intends to sacrifice Iphigenia. Euripides' tragedy at times threatens to become a grim comedy of errors. Euripides appears to be playing on Agamemnon's reputation, as established in the *ILIAD*, for example, as a blustering, weak, inconsistent leader. Here Agamemnon changes his mind frequently, while Menelaus on one occasion is allowed to deliver a blistering critique of his character. Menelaus himself is no better; he himself is inconsistent—happy to profit from the expedition and Iphigenia's death, but also temporarily swayed to pity by his brother's tears.

The ending would appear to repair Agamemnon's fortunes. Agamemnon gets credit both for his willingness to sacrifice his own family for the sake of the army and for the happy outcome of the sacrifice and intervention of the goddess. He now proceeds toward Troy as the admired leader of the expedition. We know, however, the true ending of his story (see *AGAMEMNON* by Aeschylus). Euripides leaves off where the epic battle proper begins, but his "prequel" has already brought out disturbing tensions within the expedition and cast an unflattering light on its central heroes. Agamemnon and Menelaus are unlikely leaders—at times cowardly, at other times cruel and self-interested. Perhaps the expedition would be better abandoned? The gathered mass of the army will not allow it. One cannot help thinking that the Sicilian Expedition is on the playwright's mind. The self-interest of elites and the bullying power of the mob to punish nonconforming elites combine to bring about questionable decisions. The patriotic bluster and pride motivating the prime actors—Greeks must not suffer barbarians to take their wives!—take on a distinctly Athenian resonance. While it is true that Greece wins the Trojan War, the victory, in Euripidean drama—as in tragedy generally—is viewed as a Pyrrhic one. We might recall Euripides' *Helen*, in which the play's title character is reviled by Greeks and Trojans alike as the cause of their mutual destruction.

The closing sequence of the play focuses ominously on Agamemnon's departure from his wife, Clytaemnestra, his anticipated absence, and eventual return. Clytaemnestra, having lost all faith in her husband, asks herself whether she can believe the news of Iphigenia's replacement with the deer: Is this simply another story fabricated to manipulate her? Agamemnon reassures her by stating that Iphigenia is now "with the gods"—a declaration that, in practical terms, reassures her of nothing; in the meanwhile, he leaves the infant Orestes in her charge. Euripides has carefully guided us to the threshold of Aeschylus's *Oresteia*. The Chorus, to help us appreciate the manifold ironies at work, offers a timely cue in the closing lines. They pray that Agamemnon will have a safe and successful voyage and return laden with plunder from Troy. For an audience steeped in Athenian tragedy, Clytaemnestra's already suspicious and resentful presence calls to mind the dire outcome of his return from Troy, while

the wordless Orestes speaks eloquently of yet another phase of violent retribution.

In general, the *Oresteia*, and subsequent treatments of the mythology of the house of Atreus in both Euripides' and Sophocles' *Electra*, afford a rich background for the present play. Consider, for example, the pivotal figure of the old servant who came to the house as part of Clytaemnestra's dowry. He proves his underlying loyalty to his mistress by informing her of Agamemnon's murderous plan. Not only does the servant's decision underline an already existing line of division within the house of Atreus that will only widen as time goes on; he prefigures the opening scene of Aeschylus's *Agamemnon*, when the watchman on the roof, loyal to his master, Agamemnon, waits for the beacon fire signaling his imminent return. In his parting words to Clytaemnestra, Agamemnon observes that it takes a long time to send a letter from Troy. Euripides may be slyly reminding us that Clytaemnestra will devise a method of communication (the beacon fires) that is very fast indeed.

Even as Euripides encourages us to look forward to later events, he also provides us with the opportunity to evaluate statements and justifications made at a later phase of the mythological story as represented in *earlier* plays. For example, Clytaemnestra in Sophocles' *Electra* justifies her actions by referring to Agamemnon's slaughter of Iphigenia, complaining that he carried out the murder to gratify his brother. Why did his brother not furnish the victim from his own family? Euripides responds by supplying a complex picture of the relation between the two brothers. His Agamemnon, far from simply wishing to gratify his brother, engages him in a heated argument and attempts to save his daughter. Menelaus, for his part, is persuaded and attempts to spare his brother the pain of killing his daughter. At some level, fear of the army and the irresistible momentum they have created overpowers both and takes away their ability to choose. Neither character comes off as laudable or noble, yet neither perfectly coheres with Clytaemnestra's characterization of them in Sophocles' *Electra* and Aeschylus' *Oresteia*.

In his later years, Euripides explored in depth the set of myths surrounding Agamemnon and his children (*Orestes, Iphigenia among the Taurians, Iphigenia at Aulis*) and the Trojan War and its aftermath (*Trojan Women, Helen,* the lost *Philoctetes*). A unifying strand—besides the obvious fact that Agamemnon is the leader of the Trojan expedition—is a persistent concern with interconnections between belief and reality. In the present play, a human sacrifice that, in Euripides' version, appears to have been a false story, a charade whose real violence is averted at the last moment, nonetheless produces lasting, and deadly, outcomes. Agamemnon's initial deception of his wife erodes her trust in him, and even if, in the end, his actions do not lead to the death of Iphigenia, the rift between Clytaemnestra and her husband is already irreparable. Euripides is particularly subtle in his exploration of how beliefs, even unfounded ones, motivate actions and ultimately shape reality. He brilliantly reframes the question of the reality of Iphigenia's sacrifice. It did not really happen (assuming we accept the report of the last-minute replacement), and yet, in term of its effects, it might as well have happened. Agamemnon is still guilty of the intention to have his child murdered; his wife has been turned prospectively into a murderer. The miraculous salvation of Iphigenia has not changed the tragic fate of the family in the longer term.

The prime instance of reality/unreality, both in Euripides' plays concerned with Agamemnon and in those concerned with the aftermath of the Trojan War, is Helen. She is a frequent focal point of late Euripidean choruses as the cause of war and the destruction of Greeks and Trojans alike. Yet Euripides' play on the topic converts the destructive Helen transported by Paris to Troy into a phantom maliciously fabricated by the gods. "Helen" of Euripides' play thus finds herself inhabiting two simulta-neous yet mutually exclusive realities—one in which she is to blame for everything; another in which she is to blame for nothing. This phantasmal view of the Trojan War takes on a disturbing contemporary resonance if applied to the Peloponnesian War and the Sicilian Expedition—a hugely destructive conflict over nothing, an all-consuming illusion.

The *Iphigenia at Aulis* also looks forward to the Trojan War itself and especially the events narrated in Homer's *Iliad*. In Euripides' tragic perspective, the division within the Greek army that led to Achilles' withdrawal from battle did not arise in Troy but was present from the outset at Aulis. He represents an army close to mutiny; the soldiers are suspicious of their leaders and impatient either to commence or to abandon an expedition that does not obviously further their own interests. Achilles already feels used and dishonored by Agamemnon. He is horrified at the employment of his name in the deception of Iphigenia and Clytaemnestra, and even now subverts the command of the sons of Atreus in the name of his honor and personal moral code. Specifically, Achilles' sense of honor is activated by Agamemnon's wrongful appropriation of a woman, as will recur in the case of the Homeric BRISEIS. The seeds of the Trojan War's discontents and the hazards of the heroes' return have been sown already in this preliminary stage. Odysseus is a ruthless operator; Agamemnon and Menelaus vacillate between ruthlessness and accommodation; Clytaemnestra is alienated from her husband; Achilles insists on following his own path. On some points, Euripides goes out of his way to surpass the divisions of the *Iliad*: Achilles' own Myrmidons refuse to support him in his plan to defend Iphigenia. Abandoned by his comrades, Achilles experiences a nearly total isolation.

Euripides approaches from a tragic angle the Iliadic question of Greek unity in war against a common enemy: Can the diverse Greek communities find enough common cause to work together? Greekness itself is at stake, as in other, later Euripidean plays. In Euripides' *Helen*, the heroine, stranded in Egypt while her phantom operates at Troy, must fend off a barbarian marriage to the local ruler. In *Iphigenia among the Taurians*, Iphigenia, who has miraculously escaped being a human sacrifice herself, now lives among barbarians as a priestess and must prepare victims for a rite of human sacrifice. Greeks are the preferred victims. In the present play, Agamemnon bases his final decision to go ahead with the sacrifice on the collective honor of Greece. Barbarians must not be allowed to abduct Greek wives with impunity. Iphigenia, after hearing her father's speech, appears to absorb the same lesson and resolves to forgo Achilles' protection. She must sacrifice herself for Greece and Greek freedom; she will be the cause of Troy's destruction. Yet if, as *Iphigenia among the Taurians* demonstrates, human sacrifice is a key signifier of barbarism, how can it be possible to vindicate Hellas through a distinctly barbaric rite? Why is everything staked on, and sacrificed for, Hellas, if, in doing so, we lose the moral integrity that defines core Greek values? The Trojan War that follows is another case in point: The Greek heroes, in destroying Troy, violate religious and moral imperatives and so bring down on themselves the anger of the gods, which prevents their successful return.

Euripides' tragedy hinges, as in other instances, around a female figure. Iphigenia is the title character, and she is the one who finally takes the outcome of the action into her own hands by resolving to go through with the sacrifice. Iphigenia at first appears to be a more innocent and less violent figure than Medea or the vengeful Hecuba of Euripides' play. Yet if we consider closely her words, this initial impression is in some respects misleading. Justifying her decision to die, Iphigenia in effect states that, instead of marrying a man, she is "wedding" herself to Greece, sacrificing herself for the sake of Greek honor and self-determination. She loses her life, marriage, the

production of children, for the sake of Greece and glory. Achilles, who should appreciate her decision to sacrifice long life in favor of enduring glory, admires her courage, and envies Greece its possession of her. Paradoxically, Achilles is so impressed with her decision that he wishes to take her home and make her his bride, thereby contradicting his own personal resolution to die young while achieving great renown. Carrying out this desire would equally deprive Iphigenia of the glorious sacrifice that causes Achilles to admire her. On Euripides' reading, a young woman is the author of the martial glory of Achilles, who otherwise might have returned home instead of going to Troy; at the same time, she becomes the author of Troy's downfall. As she is led offstage, Iphigenia hails herself in song as the conqueror of Troy. From one point of view, then, Iphigenia is a more violent figure than Medea or Hecuba; each of whom destroys a family—she consciously and deliberately consigns an entire city to destruction.

It does not pay to underestimate the power of female characters in Euripides. Medea famously stated that she would prefer to fight in battle many times rather than give birth once. Female strength, as the outcome of the *Medea* suggests, can be formidably destructive. The Trojan War, in Euripides' vision, is effectively framed by female causation: Helen inspires the expedition; Iphigenia enables it. After the war, Clytaemnestra will slay the triumphant commander on his return. The male figures are less impressive. Agamemnon, the play's central character, is vacillating and ineffectual. Menelaus is no more impressive. Achilles seems promising and receives a great outpouring of praise from the Chorus. Yet even Achilles by his own admission pales before Iphigenia: She turns out to be more ruthless, determined, and devoted to death than Achilles, whose thoughts turn toward marriage as his esteem for her increases. Achilles has a godlike status and expects to be able to face down an entire army with his handful of attendants. Euripides builds up the expectation of a deus ex machina intervention: Achilles will save Iphigenia at the last moment. As it turns out, it is the goddess Artemis who saves her, while the great Achilles fades from view. The immense buildup of Achilles followed by this wan anticlimax effects an even more powerful deflation of male heroism than the sordidly realist focus on Menelaus's and Agamemnon's personal flaws. In the *Iliad*, Achilles displays a magnificent disdain for death. In order for him to achieve such glory, Euripides insinuates, a brave young woman had to offer herself as preliminary sacrifice.

Iphis (1) Son of King Alector of Argus. Father of ETEOCLUS, one of the Seven against Thebes. Classical sources are Apollodorus' *LIBRARY* (3.6.3) and Pausanias's *Description of Greece* (2.18.5, 10.10.3). Iphis told POLYNICES how to bribe AMPHIARAUS to accompany him to war.

Iphis (2) and Anaxarete A humble youth from Cyprus. The classical source is Ovid's *METAMORPHOSES* (14.698–765). Iphis fell in love with the aristocratic Anaxarete, who spurned his affections. Despite his declarations of love and constant attentions, Anaxarete hard-heartedly mocked him. Iphis hung himself in grief on her threshold. When his funeral bier passed her window, Anaxarete coldly looked on and was transformed into stone. In Ovid, VERTUMNUS recounts this story to woo the nymph POMONA.

Iphis (3) and Ianthe Iphis (child of Ligdus and Telethusa) and Ianthe (daughter of Telestes). The classical source is Ovid's *METAMORPHOSES* (9.666–797). The story takes place in Crete, where Ligdus has decreed that if the child that his expectant wife is carrying is female, it is to be exposed. To save her newborn daughter, Telethusa endeavored, with the help of the

nurse, to convince Ligdus that she bore a son. The child was given a gender-neutral name, Iphis, and brought up as a boy. Later, a marriage was arranged between Iphis and Ianthe. The two young women fell in love, though Ianthe was completely unaware that she loved another woman. Iphis was ashamed of her love for another female but loved her anyway, and as the wedding day drew near, she and Telethusa prayed at the altar of Isis for help. The goddess was moved by the petition and transformed Iphis into a boy. The marriage of Iphis and Ianthe was attended by APHRODITE, HERA, and HYMEN.

Iris Greek goddess of the rainbow and winged messenger goddess of the Olympian gods. Daughter of Electra (daughter of OCEANUS) and Thaumas (son of GAIA and Pontus). Sister to the HARPIES, who are also winged. Classical sources are the *Homeric Hymn to Apollo* (102–114), Apollonius of Rhodes's *VOYAGE OF THE ARGONAUTS* (2.283–300, 4.753–779), Callimachus's *Hymns* (4.228–239), Hesiod's *THEOGONY* (265–269, 780–787), Homer's *ILIAD* (3.121–140, 8.397–425, 15.143–217, 18.165–202), and Virgil's *AENEID* (4.693–705, 5.605–615, 9.1–25). Next to Hermes, Iris is the most important herald of the Olympian gods. Hesiod, Homer, and the *Homeric Hymns* give her the epithet "swift" or "swift-footed." Iris flies across the sky delivering messages or providing summons to immortals and mortals (she will at times assume mortal shape for this purpose). In Ovid's *Metamorphoses*, she conveys the wishes of both ZEUS and HERA, but in the *Aeneid*, she is the particular envoy of Hera. In the *Theogony*, Iris has a specific ceremonial function, in a ritual oath of truth telling. She travels to the river STYX and brings its waters back to Olympus in a golden jug. The waters are used as a libation by which the gods swear an oath of truth.

In the *Homeric Hymn to Delian Apollo*, the goddesses assisting LETO during her labor persuaded Iris, with the promise of a necklace of golden thread, to summon EILEITHYIA, goddess of childbirth, whom Hera had kept away until then to prevent the births of APOLLO and ARTEMIS. But in the same episode recounted in Apollonius of Rhodes's *Voyage of the Argonauts* and in Callimachus's *Hymns*, Iris is shown to be loyal to Hera; in the latter, Iris does not leave Hera's side except at her command. Her loyalty to Hera is again shown in Euripides' *Heracles*, where, on Hera's behalf, Iris commands Lyssa, daughter of Nyx and goddess of madness, to afflict Zeus's son HERACLES with a fit of madness during which he murders his sons. In the *Iliad*, by contrast, Iris represents Zeus's interests against Hera and Athena, who support the Trojans. Also in the *Iliad*, Iris answers Achilles' prayers to summon BOREAS, the North Wind, and ZEPHYRUS, the West Wind, to ignite the funeral pyre of PATROCLUS. Given that her domain is the sky, Iris is associated with the ANEMOI, or winds. One source attributes the parentage of EROS to Iris and Zephyrus, but in other texts, she has no love interests.

In Apollonius's *Voyage of the Argonauts*, Iris defends her sisters the Harpies from the BOREADAE Calais and Zetes. She is treated satirically in Aristophanes' *The Birds* and comically in Lucian's *Dialogues of the Sea-Gods*.

In visual representations of antiquity, Iris can be identified either by a pair of winged sandals or by wings sprouting from her back. She sometimes carries a messenger's staff, or *kerykeion*, and is fully clothed, as in an Attic red-figure stamnos from ca. 480 B.C.E. (Louvre, Paris) in which Zeus is flanked by Iris and HERMES. She appears on the François Vase from ca. 570 B.C.E. (Museo Archeologico Nazionale, Florence) carrying a staff and accompanying CHIRON. In postclassical periods she is shown with her attribute the rainbow, as in François Le Moyne's *Juno, Iris, and Flora* from ca. 1737 (Louvre, Paris).

Ismene See *ANTIGONE; OEDIPUS AT COLONUS; SEVEN AGAINST THEBES*. See also ANTIGONE; OEDIPUS.

Ixion King of the Lapiths in Thessaly. Son of ARES. Classical sources are Aeschylus's *EUMENIDES* (717–718), Apollodorus's *LIBRARY* (Epitome 1.20), Diodorus Siculus's *LIBRARY OF HISTORY* (4.69.3–5), Homer's *ILIAD* (14.317–318), Hyginus's *Fabulae* (14, 62), Ovid's *METAMORPHOSES* (4.461, 9.123–124, 10.42), Pindar's *Pythian Odes* (2.21–48), and Virgil's *AENEID* and *GEORGICS* (3.37–39, 4.484). Ixion is one of a group—which includes SISYPHUS, TANTALUS, and TITYUS—of primordial violators of the social order and of divine authority. Ixion committed parricide, Tantalus was accused of cannibalism, Tityus tried to rape ZEUS's consort LETO, and the wily Sisyphus attempted to steal fire from the gods and defeat death. Their crimes varied, but all deeply offended morality and/or challenged the authority of the Olympian gods, especially that of Zeus, and their punishments were ingeniously devised to provide gruesome spectacle and admonition. In his descent to HADES in the *Odyssey*, Odysseus witnessed the torments of Sisyphus, Tantalus, and Tityus, and in the *Aeneid*, Aeneas encountered Tityus and Ixion. In Ovid's *Metamorphoses*, their punishments were momentarily stilled when ORPHEUS sang his lament for EURYDICE, his dead bride.

Ixion committed the first kinship murder. Ixion killed his father-in-law by throwing him into a fire pit to avoid paying him a dowry. Few were willing to purify Ixion of this crime, but Zeus agreed to do so. Then Ixion attempted to seduce HERA, but Zeus had created a cloud in her shape to deceive him. The offspring of Ixion's union with the Hera-shaped cloud was Centaurus, from whom CENTAURS descend. In punishment, Zeus commanded HERMES to affix Ixion to a burning wheel that would be placed in TARTARUS. The wedding of Ixion's son PIRITHOUS to Hippodame was the occasion of the Battle of the Lapiths and Centaurs, a centauromachy.

In visual representations, Ixion is depicted as a bearded male in the throes of his torment, and his attribute is a burning wheel, as in a fresco from the Ixion Room in the House of Vettii in Pompeii dating to the first century C.E. In an Attic red-figure kantharos vase from ca. 450 B.C.E. (British Museum, London), Ixion is held in the grip of Hermes and Ares before a seated Hera as ATHENA brings in the wheel that will be the instrument of his punishment. Postclassical images include Peter Paul Ruben's *Ixion, King of Lapiths, Tricked by Juno* from ca. 1615 (Louvre, Paris) and José Ribera's *Ixion* of 1632 (Prado, Madrid). Titian's cycle of paintings *The Four Condemned* included paintings of Ixion, Sisyphus, Tantalus, and Tityus.

Janus Roman god of doorways, gates, and entrances. Classical sources include Livy's *From the Foundation of the City* (1.19.1–4), Ovid's *FASTI* (1.63–288, 6.101–130), and Virgil's *Aeneid* (7.601–615, 7.180, 8.357, 12.198). Janus is a rare instance of a god who has no Greek counterpart; he was an Italic deity of great antiquity and enduring importance. In Latin, *ianua* is a door or entrance, and *ianus* is the term for a passageway or arch. The god, who is typically represented as having a double head, looking in two directions at once, is simultaneously the embodiment of the doorway and a symbol of transitions, both spatial and temporal. The month of January takes its name from Janus, who is associated with beginnings, in this case, the beginning of the Roman year. Janus thus presides over transitions from one space to another and from one segment of time to another. According to an old Roman tradition revived by Emperor Augustus, the doors of the Temple of Janus Geminus (Twin Janus) in the Roman Forum were closed when there was peace throughout the empire—putatively a rare event, but increasingly common throughout the imperial period as the closing of the gates became a propagandistic symbol of peace and security. The arch or *ianus* was a symbolic space through which an army and general passed at the beginning and end of a military campaign, and, thus, the closed gate symbolized the lack of

a need for armies to depart for war. The emperor Domitian, in the late first century C.E., appears to have replaced the Temple of Janus Geminus with a new shrine in his Forum Transitorium. Janus in some respects resembles Jupiter in his association with Rome's military security and power and, like Jupiter, is a divine father figure (sometimes called Janus pater, "father Janus"). As a primordial god of beginnings, he is associated with the creation of the world itself. Myths about Janus are sparse. He founded a settlement on the hill called the Janiculum and, like Saturn (see CRONUS), ruled over Italy in the Golden Age. He also hosted Saturn when Jupiter (see ZEUS) drove him into exile. Ovid, in the *Fasti*, tells how Janus raped the nymph Crane, later called Carna, and, in return for her lost virginity, gave her power over hinges of doors. Janus was the father of Canens (*Metamorphoses* 14.332–334) and of the river god and Alban king Tiberius, by the nymph Camasene.

Jason Son of AESON and Alcimede. Husband of MEDEA. Leader of the Argonauts. Jason appears in Apollonius of Rhodes's *VOYAGE OF THE ARGONAUTS*, Euripides's *MEDEA*, and Seneca's *MEDEA*. Additional classical sources are Apollodorus's *LIBRARY* (1.8.2, 1.9.16–28), Diodorus Siculus's *LIBRARY OF HISTORY* (4.40–53), Hesiod's *THEOGONY* (992–1,002), Hyginus's

Fabulae (12–14, 24, 25), Ovid's *METAMORPHOSES* (7.1–397) and *HEROIDES* (6, 12), and Pausanias's *Description of Greece* (2.3.6–11, 5.17.9–10). Jason's father, Aeson, was driven from the throne of Iolcus by his half brother Pelias, and Jason was sent to be brought up by the centaur CHIRON. In the meantime, an oracle warned Pelias to beware the man who could come wearing only one sandal. Later, Jason returned to claim the throne as his inheritance, wearing only one sandal. Pelias, aiming to get rid of Jason, stated that he would give Jason his kingdom in return for the golden fleece of the ram that carried PHRIXUS to COLCHIS on the Black Sea. The fleece, dedicated to ARES and guarded by a dragon, was now under the control of King AEETES of Colchis.

Jason, with ATHENA's help, had a boat built, the *Argo*, which according to some sources was the first ship ever built. HERA, who wished to punish Pelias for neglecting to honor her, gave her support to the voyage. Jason assembled the greatest heroes of the time, including

Jason and Medea. *Marble sarcophagus, second century C.E. (Palazzo Altemps, Rome)*

HERACLES, ORPHEUS, the DIOSCURI, TELAMON, PELEUS, the BOREADAE, and THESEUS. There are many versions of the voyage to Colchis, but the best known is Apollonius of Rhodes's *Voyage of the Argonauts*. Apollonius's account of their adventures includes the Argonauts' sojourn on the island of Lemnos, during which they help repopulate the island and Jason becomes the lover of Queen HYPSIPYLE (see Ovid's *HEROIDES* and Statius's *THEBAID*); the episode in which Jason and the Argonauts are hosted by King Cyzicus in the Propontis, and then later unwittingly engage in a battle at night that leads to Cyzicus's death; Heracles' search for the abducted HYLAS, which leads to his being left behind and excluded from the remainder of the expedition; the boxing match in which Polydeuces (Pollux, see DIOSCURI) defeats Amycus, king of the Bebrycians; the prophecy delivered by PHINEUS in return for being rescued from the HARPIES; the passage through the Symplegades, or clashing rocks, at the mouth of the Black Sea. When, at last, Jason arrives in Colchis, King Aeetes demands that he complete a series of deadly tasks in order to obtain the fleece: He must yoke fire-breathing bulls and sow dragon's teeth, from which armed men will spring up. With the help of Aeetes' daughter Medea, who has fallen in love with the Greek hero and is skilled in magic and drugs, Jason completes the tasks successfully. Medea gives him a balm to protect him from the fire-breathing bulls and instructs him to throw a rock in the midst of the armed men so that they fight and kill one another. She then uses a charm to lull the dragon to sleep, allowing Jason to steal the fleece. On their way back to Greece, in Apollonius's version, they tour the known world in a geographically expansive voyage. Their adventures include the treacherous murder of Medea's younger brother Apsyrtus, who has been sent after her (for another version of his death, see MEDEA); a visit to CIRCE, who purifies Jason for Apsyrtus's murder, but will not offer him hospitality; a visit to the land of the Phaeacians, where Medea and Jason must consummate their marriage in order not to be handed over to Aeetes' men by King Alcinous; and Medea's defeat of the great bronze giant Talos in Crete.

Apollonius's narrative ends upon the Argonauts return to Greece. Jason and Medea visited AESON, whom Medea rejuvenated by means of her magic skill. She promised the same to Pelias's daughters, who, on Medea's instructions, cut up their father into pieces and placed him into a cauldron, only to discover to their horror that he would never reemerge. Pelias's neglect of Hera was thus finally punished. Jason and Medea then fled to Corinth, where they lived without incident until Jason decided to marry Creusa, the daughter of King Creon of Corinth. Euripides' *Medea* tells how Medea, enraged, murders Creusa, Creon, and her own children before flying off to Athens on the chariot of HELIOS (Sun). Jason is left behind, a destroyed man. In some versions, he then killed himself, or was killed by a plank that fell from the hull of the rotting *Argo*, or by the ship's stern dedicated in Hera's temple.

In Apollonius's narrative Jason is not a conventional hero. He is typically "at a loss" and succeeds in the end because of the impressive heroes accompanying him, the support of the goddesses Hera and APHRODITE, and Medea's cunning and skill. His story conforms with the rite-of-passage pattern common in fairy tales: A young man must complete a series of seemingly impossible tasks to receive his reward. His tragic career, however, follows an entirely different trajectory. In Euripides' *Medea*, Jason is colorless, weak, and emotionally pallid. In the end, he is simply overpowered by the ferocity of his wife's character and, in the closing scene, gives the impression of a shattered mortal left in the wake of an angry divinity.

Jason and Medea appear on a marble sarcophagus of the second century C.E. (Palazzo Altemps, Rome). Here, nude and carrying a shield over his shoulder, Jason clasps hands with Medea, a gesture symbolizing their union. The initial complicity of the hero and the enchantress continues to be represented in postclassical works, in paintings by Gustave Moreau, *Jason and Medea* of 1865 (Musée d'Orsay, Paris), and J. W. Waterhouse, *Jason and Medea* of 1907 (private collection).

Jocasta Daughter of Menoeceus. Wife of LAIUS. Wife and mother of OEDIPUS. Jocasta appears in Sophocles' *OEDIPUS THE KING* and Euripides' *PHOENICIAN WOMEN*.

Jove See ZEUS.

Juno See HERA.

Jupiter See ZEUS.

Ladon See HESPERIDES.

Laius Son of Labdacus, great-grandson of CADMUS, and father of OEDIPUS. Classical sources are Apollodorus's *LIBRARY* (3.5.5–8) and Sophocles' *OEDIPUS THE KING*.

Laocoon A priest of APOLLO at Troy. Married to ANTIOPE. Their sons were Ethron and Melanthus. Classical sources are Apollodorus's *LIBRARY* (Epitome 5.17–18), Hyginus's *Fabulae* (135), Pliny's *Natural History* (36, 37), and Virgil's *AENEID* (2.40–233). The main story of Laocoon occurs at the close of the Trojan War. The Greek army built a wooden horse and left it for the Trojans, pretending to depart from the field of battle. Laocoon warned against accepting the Trojan gift, and this angered Apollo. Laocoon was commanded to prepare sacrifices to POSEIDON in the hope that the maritime god would send storms to destroy the departing Greek fleet. Before he could sacrifice the bull to Poseidon, two enormous snakes sent by Apollo came out of the water and, wrapping themselves around Laocoon and his sons, crushed them to death.

Laocoon and his sons are depicted in one of the most famous sculptural groups of the ancient period. In this early imperial Roman copy of a Greek original (Vatican Museums, Rome), Lao-

Laocoon and His Sons. *Marble, Roman copy of Greek original from the third century B.C.E. (Vatican Museums, Rome)*

coon struggles painfully, in a tour de force of marble musculature, against the serpents.

Laodamia (1) Daughter of BELLEROPHON. By ZEUS, the mother of SARPEDON. Classical sources are Diodorus Siculus's *LIBRARY OF HISTORY* (5.79) and Homer's *ILIAD* (6.196–206). She is mainly known as the mother of Sarpedon and, according to Diodorus Siculus, was killed by ARTEMIS, whom she had angered.

Laodamia (2) Daughter of Acastus and Astydamia. Wife of PROTESILAUS. Classical sources are Homer's *ILIAD* (2.695–710), Hyginus's *Fabulae* (103, 104), and Ovid's *Ars Amatoria* (3.17), *HEROIDES* (13), and *Tristis* (1.6.20). Euripides' tragedy *Protesilaus*, now lost, treated this subject. Laodamia was married to Protesilaus, the first Greek to die during the Trojan War. They had been married only a short time, and Laodamia begged HADES to have Protesilaus returned to her for a few hours. Her request was granted, her husband was restored to life, and, at the appointed hour, he returned to the land of the dead. In her grief, Laodamia committed suicide. In an alternate version of the story mentioned by Apollodorus, Laodamia created a wax image of Protesilaus, and when her father discovered it, he threw it into the fire and destroyed it. Laodamia threw herself into the fire after the melted image.

Laomedon A king of Troy. Son of Eurydice and Ilus. His children were Hesione and PRIAM. Classical sources are Apollodorus's *LIBRARY* (2.59, 2.6.4, 3.12.3–5, Epitome 3.24), Homer's *ILIAD* (5.638–651, 6.23–24, 7.452–453, 20.144–148, 237–238), Hyginus's *Fabulae* (89), Ovid's *METAMORPHOSES* (11.194–217), Pindar's *Olympian Odes* (8.30–46), and Strabo's *Geography* (13.1.32). Laomedon was famous for breaking his word, first to APOLLO and POSEIDON, then to HERACLES. Laomedon refused payment—in the *Metamorphoses*, a sum of gold, but in the *Fabulae*, sacrifices to the gods—for the walls or fortifications of Troy, which Apollo and Poseidon had built. As punishment, Apollo sent plagues, and Poseidon a sea monster. In a story that recalls ANDROMEDA and PERSEUS, an oracle advised that the king's daughter, Hesione, be sacrificed to the sea monster in appeasement. Heracles delivered Hesione from this fate and killed the sea monster in exchange for the mares that

Zeus had given Laomedon as recompense for his abduction of GANYMEDE. Although he had agreed to the bargain, Laomedon later failed to make good his promise of payment. Years later, in revenge, Heracles returned to lay siege to Troy. He captured the city, killed Laomedon, and married Hesione to his follower TELAMON. Priam succeeded his father as king of Troy.

Leda Wife of King Tyndareus of Sparta. Consort of ZEUS. Classical sources are the *Homeric Hymns to the Dioscuri*, Apollodorus's *LIBRARY* (1.7.10, 3.10.5–7), Euripides' *HELEN* (16–21, 213–216, 256–259), and Homer's *ODYSSEY* (11.298–300). Zeus appeared to Leda in the form of a swan, and their union produced the DIOSCURI, HELEN, and CLYTAEMNESTRA. In some accounts, the twin brothers were born of one egg and the twin sisters from another.

In classical art Leda is shown with Zeus in the form of a swan. The theme appeared in reliefs, ivories, paintings, and sculpture. Leda appears, embracing a swan, on an Apulian red-

Leda and the Swan. *Leonardo da Vinci, ca. 1505 (Copy of a lost drawing, private collection)*

figure loutrophoros vase from ca. 350 B.C.E. (J. Paul Getty Museum, Malibu). Leda was also a popular theme for postclassical artists. A famous example is Leonardo da Vinci's drawing *Leda and the Swan* of ca. 1505. Set against a landscape, Leda drapes her arms around Zeus, transformed into a swan, while putti gather flowers at her feet.

Lethe   See HADES.

Leto (Latona) Daughter of the TITANS Coeus and PHOEBE. Sixth wife of ZEUS, to whom she bore the Olympian gods APOLLO and ARTEMIS. Classical sources are the *Homeric Hymn to Apollo* (12–139), Apollodorus's LIBRARY (1.4.1), Hesiod's THEOGONY (404–410, 918–920), Hyginus's *Fabulae* (9, 53, 55), and Ovid's *METAMORPHOSES* (6.148–381). Hesiod remarked on Leto's exceptionally sweet, gentle disposition, and both the *Theogony* and the *Orphic Hymn to Leto* (34) single out Leto's somber clothes for mention—she is "dark-robed" in the former, "dark-veiled" in the latter—which may refer to cultic practices in which she was associated with Apollo and Artemis. Apart from the stories of NIOBE and TITYUS, Leto does not appear in many myths.

Leto had to search long before she could find a place to give birth to Apollo. Her labor pains with Apollo were prolonged for nine days and nights because HERA had kept EILEITHYIA, her daughter, the goddess of childbirth, from attending the birth. Finally, the other goddesses and nymphs in attendance, AMPHITRITE, DIONE, RHEA, and THEMIS, persuaded Eileithyia to arrive, and thus precipitated Apollo's birth.

While Leto was married to Zeus, Tityus attempted to seduce her. He was killed either by the arrows of Apollo and Artemis or the thunderbolt of Zeus. As punishment for his temerity, Zeus consigned Tityus to TARTARUS, where he was bound across nine acres for all time, while two vultures or serpents tore at his liver.

Leto's honor was also impugned by Niobe, who boasted that she was a superior mother to Leto, since she had a greater number of children, the Niobids (between five and 10 of each sex, depending on the source), whereas Leto had only two. To avenge her, Apollo and Artemis killed Niobe's children—Apollo the males with his arrows, Artemis the females with hers.

In visual representations, Leto appears with her children, Apollo and Artemis. She is shown in her function as religious figure and also in depictions of the myth of Tityus. An example of the latter theme is an Attic red-figure amphora from Vulci dating from ca. 520 B.C.E. (Louvre, Paris).

Leucothoe   See CLYTIE; HELIOS.

Libation Bearers AESCHYLUS (458 B.C.E.) Aeschylus's *Libation Bearers* is the second play in his tragic trilogy, the *Oresteia*, which also included the *Agamemnon*, the *Eumenides*, and a fourth satyr play, the *Proteus*. The four plays were produced in 458 B.C.E. and won first prize in the competition at Athens. While the *Libation Bearers* attracts less attention among modern scholars than the powerful, brooding *Agamemnon*, Greek tragedians found it a fertile terrain for creative exploration. Both Euripides and Sophocles produced their own, highly independent versions of the story of ORESTES and ELECTRA in their plays, which were both titled *Electra*. The potential for complicated plot twists involving recognition, deception, and surprise makes the subject attractive, while the characters of Orestes and Electra offer various possibilities for interpretation. But while later tragedians' versions do not form part of connected trilogies, Aeschylus's *Libation Bearers* plays a pivotal role in the broader development of his concerns across the three plays. The middle play of the trilogy at once represents the continuation of the pattern of revenge killing into the next generation of the house of ATREUS and begins to suggests the possibility of liberation from the relentless cycle of violence.

SYNOPSIS

The scene is set in Argos, before the tomb of AGAMEMNON. Ten years have passed since the last play. Orestes, son of Agamemnon, brought up and living hitherto in exile, enters with his companion Pylades. Orestes stands before the tomb, addresses HERMES as lord of the dead, leaves a lock of hair on the mound, and laments that he was not present to mourn his father's death. His sister Electra, daughter of CLYTAEMNESTRA and Agamemnon, and the Chorus of foreign slave women enters. They are wearing black and bearing urns to pour libations. The women complain of having been ill-treated by their mistress and of having been sent forth by Clytaemnestra to make libations. They lament their own fate. They were captured in war and enslaved and now lead a life of sorrow. Electra consults the serving women, asking how she can possibly address her father, and bids them to speak freely. Thereupon, she prays to Hermes, the underground deities, Earth (GAIA), and her father that Orestes return and that vengeance be visited on their enemies. Electra then discovers the strand of hair, observes that it matches her own, and concludes that it must be from Orestes. She weeps and notices two sets of footprints, one set very similar to her own.

Orestes now steps forward into view. After some moments of disbelief, Electra is persuaded that it is truly her brother. They greet each other and pray to ZEUS that he may direct them. They hope to win back and rebuild their father's house. Orestes reveals that APOLLO's oracle commanded him to avenge his father's death on pain of disease, exile, and madness; but he is also determined to recover the property he has lost; he is, moreover, distressed by the illegitimacy of the rule at Argos. In a long exchange, Electra, Orestes, and the Chorus chant in alternation, lamenting Agamemnon's death, calling on the gods of the dead, excoriating Clytaemnestra's cruelty and hypocrisy, complaining of their own dishonor, and calling finally on their own father as supporter of their

enterprise, and in general building themselves up to the act of vengeance they promise. After their chant finishes, Orestes asks why Clytaemnestra had them bring libations. The Chorus reveals that Clytaemnestra dreamed she gave birth to a snake, which drew blood when it nursed at her breast. Orestes interprets it to mean that the snake represents himself and that he will kill her. He then reveals his plan. Accompanied by his companion Pylades, and disguised as a foreigner, speaking the Parnassian dialectic of Phocis, he will gain entrance to the palace and slay AEGISTHUS, his mother's lover. Electra is to keep an eye on the palace, and the Chorus is to maintain silence. Orestes and Pylades exit, followed by Electra.

In the ode that follows, the Chorus recalls three myths relevant to the present situation: Althaea, angry that her son MELEAGER had slain her two brothers during a hunt, killed him by burning a log that represented his life; SCYLLA betrayed her father, Nisus, to MINOS for the bribe of a golden necklace; the women of Lemnos killed all their husbands for seeking other bedmates. The Chorus foresees the coming of vengeance through the agency of Orestes, who has returned at last. Orestes and Pylades reenter. They knock at the palace gate and request to be let in as visiting strangers. Orestes asks for Aegisthus in particular. Clytaemnestra comes out. She greets them and offers hospitality. Orestes introduces himself as a Daulian from Phocis, and then states that a stranger told him that Orestes was dead and that the news should be conveyed to his parents at Argos. Clytaemnestra laments that Orestes, who had been kept out of the way of the deadly reach of the house, has nonetheless been shot down from afar, as if by an archer. She directs them to the men's quarters. Orestes, Pylades, and Clytaemnestra exit.

The Chorus expresses its hopes for a successful outcome to the plot. Cilice, Orestes' old nurse, comes forth. She sorrows at the news of Orestes' death; she nursed and cared for him as a baby. Clytaemnestra, in the nurse's opinion, is concealing her joy at her news, and Aegisthus, who has been summoned by Clytaemnestra along with his men, will be openly delighted. The Chorus, intimating that there may be good news hidden behind the bad, persuades Cilice not to tell Aegisthus to bring his bodyguards but to come alone. Cilice leaves to carry out her message. The Chorus supplicates Zeus, Hermes, and Apollo for help in carrying out the scheme of vengeance and wiping out the old stain of blood. It will be an innocent murder; Orestes must remember his father's murder when his mother calls out to him as her son.

Aegisthus enters. He has heard the rumor of Orestes' death and wishes to question the messenger. The Chorus directs him to Orestes, and Aegisthus leaves to seek him out. The Chorus anticipates the outcome of the approaching confrontation. A cry is heard from within. One of Aegisthus's followers comes out. He declares that his lord has been killed and that he fears for Clytaemnestra's life. Clytaemnestra enters. She learns what is happening and asks for an ax to defend herself. Orestes and Pylades return. Clytaemnestra begs Orestes not to kill his own mother, and hesitating, he appeals to Pylades, who encourages him to respect the command of Apollo at any cost. Clytaemnestra and Orestes exchange bitter remarks, and she threatens him with punishment by the Furies, but Orestes has now made up his mind and is not to be shaken in his purpose. He announces the fulfillment of her dream about the snake, and he and Pylades drive her inside the palace.

The Chorus expresses pity for Aegisthus and Clytaemnestra but approves their slaying as an act of justice, just as justice also demanded the death of Priam and his sons. It expresses the hope that the house, now free from the murderous couple, will be restored and that Orestes will be absolved and freed from the Furies. The doors of the palace open to show Orestes standing over the bodies of Aegisthus and Clytaemnestra and the net that previously entangled Agamemnon. Orestes presents the two dead bodies and remarks, ironically, that they lie together as lovers still. He describes Clytaemnestra as a viper and the net as the device of a highway robber, and wishes that he may die without children before having such a wife. He then asserts that he takes no pride in this polluted victory. He defends his act as necessary but declares that he must go to Apollo's shrine at Delphi to be purified. The Chorus confirms that his act was well done. Orestes, however, sees the approach of his mother's Furies. They are horrible, but only he can see them. He exits. The Chorus observes that this was the third storm to afflict the royal house: first, the killing of Thyestes' children, then the murder of Agamemnon, and now the violence perpetrated by Orestes. The Chorus asks where the rage of ruin will come to an end.

COMMENTARY

The present play begins after a long period of waiting and expectation. The parallel with the previous play in the trilogy is striking. At the opening of *Agamemnon*, the watchman and the rest of the household were awaiting the return to Argos of the long-absent master. In this play, too, the male heir of Agamemnon, and thus rightful lord of the palace, has been absent 10 years and is almost despaired of by those who wish to see him again. In both instances, the absence of the male who is the rightful master of the house leaves Clytaemnestra effectively in control. Such parallelism is a major feature of *Libation Bearers* and bespeaks the playwright's awareness of the structures of recurrence that characterize the actions of those involved in a cycle of vengeance killings. The first two plays of the trilogy demonstrate, on the level of explicitly articulated theme and on the level of dramatic structure, the self-reproducing patterns of justice as revenge. The principle of "an eye for an eye" still essentially guides the actors and demands that Clytaemnestra's and Aegisthus's lives be given in return for Agamemnon's and Cassandra's. The parallelism extends even to role and gender: One man and one woman, one royal spouse and one lover/rival are found in each pairing.

A major question is this: How are Orestes and Electra different from Clytaemnestra and Aegisthus as revenge killers, or are they, in fact, no different? We should also consider the case of Agamemnon himself. As Electra concedes, IPHIGENIA was ruthlessly slain, but she does not mention that Agamemnon was the killer, and his culpability seems somehow reduced—perhaps because we know that he was not a willing killer and that he was driven by necessity. This fact of compulsion could form the basis for a parallel with Orestes, who must also kill a female family member and who is also driven to do so by the command of a god. In Orestes' case, however, the victim whom he must kill is herself guilty, unlike Iphigenia, and thus it can be argued that his culpability is even less. It may seem like splitting hairs to decide which kin killers are less culpable and which more, and yet these are precisely the decisions and distinctions that Aeschylus's trilogy is attempting to make. Clytaemnestra and Aegisthus carried out their violent plans gleefully and, afterward, gloried in their success. Orestes and Electra, by contrast, appear more somber in mood and must work themselves up to the act through a long buildup with the Chorus. There is never any question in the *Agamemnon* that Clytaemnestra will be emotionally capable of carrying out the murder of her husband. By contrast, in the *Libation Bearers*, the Chorus is concerned that Orestes might not be able to withstand his mother's pleas, and as it turns out, he requires Pylades' support to carry out the deed. Electra, for her part, wishes that she may be more temperate and of purer intentions than her mother in her own actions.

A dialectic of similarity and difference drives the play. Elements of continuity from the previous tragedy are marked by striking continuity of imagery and metaphor. A dense, luxuriant use of metaphor is a major means whereby Aeschylus knits together the com-

plex web of themes that spans the trilogy. The *Agamemnon* employed metaphors from sport and from wrestling in particular. In the present play, the murderous plot of Orestes and Electra is described in terms of "throwing" an opponent. Wrestling is perhaps especially appropriate as a metaphor, since it suggests a fierce contest in which the adversaries gain mastery over each other by turn: First, one has the upper hand, and then, with a quick move of reversal, the other; one wrestler "throws" his or her opponent and is thrown in turn. The alternating phases of domination and defeat in a close wrestling match correspond nicely to Clytaemnestra's and Aegisthus's careers. Net imagery is also carried over from the previous play. Whereas, previously, Agamemnon was caught in an actual net or mesh, now his murderers will be metaphorically netted by Orestes. In a more positive development, Orestes and Electra are described by the Chorus as the cork that keeps the whole fishing net, i.e., the household, afloat. While much of the continuity of imagery and metaphor stresses the relentlessly continuing pattern of revenge killing from one play and one generation to the next, some new twists on previous metaphors hint at the possibility of hope and a new direction for the household.

The complex set of animal images and associations also continues into the present play, with some new implications. The slain Agamemnon is the siblings' eagle-father, and they are the orphaned fledglings—a new twist on the metaphor of the robbed nest (i.e., the theft of HELEN) and shrieking eagles (Agamemnon and MENELAUS) from the previous play in the trilogy. Now Orestes prays to Zeus that he not allow the eagle's children to be destroyed, so that they may maintain the household and its sacrifices. Clytaemnestra and her murderous net is now figured as a viper with entangling coils. Later, however, we hear of Clytaemnestra's dream: She has given birth to a snake, which bites her when she brings it to her breast. The snake, in this case, is Orestes, the killer of his own mother. Near the end of the play, however, Orestes, standing over the slain bodies, describes her again as a poisonous viper, justly punished. The similarity of imagery for son and mother is disturbing, and that is part of the point: Both are kin-killers; in avenging his father and punishing his mother, he has manifested a fatal resemblance to both parents.

The Chorus gives the play its title: *Libation Bearers*. The choice of focus is significant. The Chorus consists of women captured in war and, subsequently, enslaved by the household: It is required to do Clytaemnestra's bidding. The fact that it evidently dislikes her, and consistently opposes her interests throughout the play, taking the side of Orestes and Electra instead, speaks to Clytaemnestra's character as an unkind mistress. More subtly, the focus on the Chorus of libation-bearing women brings to the fore Clytaemnestra's fundamental hypocrisy and moral confusion. After her dream of the snake, she sends these slaves to the tomb of Agamemnon to make libations in an attempt to appease the dead. Yet, there can be no appeasing the angry spirit of the murdered husband. Electra, sent on the same mission as the women, is keenly aware of the obscenity of making such an offering to her dead father on behalf of her living, unfaithful mother. For her, there is a serious problem: She cannot carry out an insincere rite, and yet the prayer she has been asked to make is itself inherently impious. The solution, which she works out with her fellow libation bearers, the Chorus, is to make her own, authentic prayer for the defeat of the ruling couple and the restoration of the fortunes of her house. As in other instances in tragedy, an attempt to ward off destiny by preventive action actually confirms the destined outcome. As a result of being sent to the tomb of Agamemnon, Electra succeeds in meeting Orestes, forming a conspiratorial bond with the Chorus, and offering a prayer to the gods for her mother's destruction. Clytaemnestra, appropriately enough, has sealed her own fate. The Chorus of libation bearers, then, is key to the central

arc of the play's action: It is the instrument of Clytaemnestra, an instrument that, like her own actions, turns against her.

Other aspects of the Chorus have significance in light of the play's broader concerns. The Chorus is composed of female slaves of the household, and they live in constant sorrow as they contemplate their condition and the fate of their husbands and family members in the war that made them slaves. Their sorrowful demeanor, despairing existence, memory of dead kin, and experience of loss of liberty are all features shared by Electra herself. Electra sees herself as living a slave's existence, deprived of honor and household. In her own words, she has been sold by her mother, who in turn bought Aegisthus for herself. The economic metaphors are more than just idle figures of speech. Not least among the brother and sister's concerns is Orestes' loss of property and inheritance, and the evident financial gain of Aegisthus at their expense. This set of concerns is also carried over from the *Agamemnon*. In that play, Clytaemnestra displayed a hubristic lack of concern for preserving the household wealth when she persuaded Agamemnon to trample on tapestries, undermining his own *oikos* (household), both symbolically and concretely. Thus, both the Chorus and Electra are effectively enslaved, and, as the Chorus states in its opening song, must suppress its true feelings and curb its tongues. The central drive of the play is toward liberation from this condition—although the liberation is necessarily violent and brings new constraints in its wake.

Finally, we might consider the importance of the dead and the cult offered to the dead as focalized through the Chorus. The action begins before Agamemnon's tomb, which serves as a constant visual reminder of the king's murder and his still angry spirit. The rites that the Chorus offers to the dead at first appear constrained and false, but later become true and sincere. This shift is crucial. The imagery of pouring libations, moreover, has significance insofar as it forms part of the sinister liquid imagery inherited from the previous play. The Furies of the *Agamemnon* were thirsty for human blood, and now the very ground, according to the Chorus, is glutted and caked with gore, which will not drain away; nor can the blood be washed away by their rites. It might justly be asked how the pouring of liquids into such ground could be effective in appeasing the dead Agamemnon. Yet the act of libation pouring that the Chorus and Electra perform will not be totally futile. Electra, as she attempts to articulate her prayer of vengeance, puts the emphasis on the act of pouring libations to her dead father, a rite that she has wrested from Clytaemnestra's control and at last made her own. She rejects her mother's hypocritical reasoning and prays for greater purity of action and for justice. The nexus of concerns surrounding the Chorus and its actions—freedom and slavery, hypocrisy and openness, false and true piety and cult, relations with the dead—are congruent with the central concerns of the play itself.

Recognition, surprise, and deception play important roles in this play, and in subsequent treatments of the subject by Sophocles and Euripides. Orestes and Electra, kept apart nearly their entire lives, are reunited in a famous recognition scene—a typical feature of tragedy and later the new comedy—where Electra recognizes first the lock of hair left by Orestes on his father's tomb and, later, his footprints. Euripides will parody and pick apart the logic of this scene hilariously in his version: The Euripidean Electra, with some justification, is scornful of the idea that you could recognize your kin on the basis of the similarity of a single lock of hair, or that the footprints of male and female kin would be unmistakably similar, not to mention the same size. What Aeschylus lacks in naturalism, however, he gains in efficiency and speed. Electra and Orestes are quickly joined and are working together nearly from the beginning of the play. Later, it is Clytaemnestra who will be forced to recognize her own son as her killer—a much grimmer recognition scene, and one, moreover, that is preceded by a deception. Orestes and Pylades adopt foreign dress and speech and affect to seek the hospitality of Aegisthus's house. This device may seem something less than heroic, yet in Aeschylus's tragic scheme, it is appropriate that Clytaemnestra and Aegisthus be killed by surprise and trickery, just as they had cunningly killed Agamemnon when he was not expecting an attack. For Aegisthus to plot to kill a man in his bath in his own house, after seducing his wife, is a potent violation of the laws of guest-host relations. Pylades' and Orestes' ruthless manipulation of the customs of hospitality to entrap Aegisthus is morally questionable, yet parallels and symmetrically punishes Aegisthus's own actions. That Orestes gains admittance by pretending to bear the news of his own death only heightens the irony: At the very moment Clytaemnestra and Aegisthus are secretly glorying in the perfection of their triumph through the removal of Agamemnon's surviving heir and sole rival to Aegisthus's position, the putatively dead Orestes kills *them*.

Orestes, like his father, must bear the burden of his own impossible choice. In his case, he must kill kin or leave kin unavenged; slay his own mother or ignore the dire command of a god. His father was driven by ARTEMIS to slay his own daughter; the son is driven by Artemis's brother Apollo to kill his mother. Already Aeschylus is setting up the explicit confrontation of the male and female principles that emerges in the final play of the trilogy: Orestes must choose between mother and father, father and sister, Apollo and his mother's Furies. Yet, as for his father, Orestes' impossible choice never really was a proper choice. The god's command is ineluctable, perhaps even more so in Orestes' case. Whereas his father was driven by Artemis, the son is driven by the male god Apollo, who speaks through his oracle and comes to occupy an increasingly commanding position in the trilogy. The trilogy's thematic privileging of the male is beginning to take form: Agamemnon's tomb dominates the scene; Apollo drives the action; Orestes is the central hero.

If male violence is downplayed and justified, female transgression is brought vividly to the fore as the object of condemnation. Shortly before Clytaemnestra's first appearance on stage, the Chorus recites myths that feature the excessive daring of women and the destruction of the men of their own families. The stories bring out different aspects of Clytaemenstra's treachery. Althaea's killing of Meleager illustrates the violence of female vengeance, the killing of one male family member to avenge the killing of other family members. Scylla betrayed her father, Nisus, by removing his protective purple hair for the sake of Minos. She thus fatally undermined father and king by giving way to the enticement of an enemy, as in the case of Clytaemnestra and Aegisthus. Finally, as the culmination of its catalog of female sin, the Chorus tells how the Lemnian women killed their husbands. Because they had neglected the rites due to Aphrodite, the women of Lemnos were afflicted with a terrible smell; their husbands took other consorts; and the women killed them in revenge. The murder of husbands evidently resembles the present situation, but so does the motivation of jealousy (cf. Agamemnon and Cassandra) and the outcome of female rule. Notionally, Aegisthus is king and Clytaemnestra queen only; yet Clytaemnestra's general character, and some specific indications in the present play, suggest that the queen is the one truly in control. She orders Aegisthus to come with his bodyguards, and even more tellingly, when Orestes comes and specifically asks for the man of the house to convey him some important news, it is Clytaemenstra who comes out the palace doors onto the stage.

Clytaemnestra is thus in charge of the palace, yet in other ways she is hardly the dominating figure that she was in the *Agamemnon*. She makes an appearance only after the play's halfway point and now seems more focused on preserving her position and safety than committing any further sublimely evil acts. She is clinging onto her life. There are limits to the audience's pity, however. One consequence of Orestes' ruse in pretending to be a man bearing the news of "Orestes'" death is that he can assess his mother's reaction to news of his supposed demise from close up. She puts on a show of sorrow, of course, but her actual words, when scrutinized, are a somewhat impersonal complaint about the antagonism of the house rather than the agonized cry of a bereft mother. Aegisthus, almost as if on cue, later repeats the party line about the malevolence of the house, as if this established pattern absolved them of personal guilt; by generalizing, they depersonalize their involvement. The nurse, who knows her master and mistress well, is skeptical of the claims of both Clytaemnestra and Aegisthus to sadness on hearing of Orestes' death, and on hearing of intruders in the house, Clytaemnestra is immediately prepared to defend herself with an ax. She is still a violent, self-interested person.

Even more telling is the nurse Cilice's description of her care for the baby Orestes. The playwright gives her a long speech to show her reaction to Orestes' death, in which she demonstrates how authentic grief for the loss of a loved one really sounds. We might compare her richly detailed, personal reminiscences with the barely mouthed pieties of her masters. For Clytaemnestra, Orestes' death is yet another addition to the house's horrors; for the nurse, it is the culmination of the house's misfortunes and the one that hurts her the most. In this speech, as in the speech of the herald in the *Agamemnon*, Aeschylus nears the limits of tragic decorum by including homely and quasi-comic details: the baby Orestes' crying at night, the difficulty of predicting when the baby would need to urinate, and the laundry that would have to be done as a consequence. The multitude of seemingly irrelevant details are, of course, very much to the point. The nurse took Orestes from his mother and brought him up and was, in a sense, his true mother. She knows and recalls, in a very physical, concrete, and thus believable manner, Orestes' babyhood. Clytaemnestra's appeal to her breast as a sign of her maternity as Orestes and Pylades advance on her has thus already been revealed by Cilice's speech as specious and self-serving. Clytaemnestra's status as Orestes' mother, while hardly obliterated, is at least crucially modified in a way that may work to mitigate the horror of his act, and at least partially explain its psychological plausibility.

The ending presents another major scene in which the playwright strives to establish parallels with the action of the first play of the trilogy. Just as, at the end of the *Agamemnon*, the palace doors opened to reveal Clytaemnestra standing over the bodies of Agamemnon and Cassandra, so now the palace doors open to reveal Orestes standing over the slain Clytaemnestra and Aegisthus. He, too, delivers a long speech for the occasion. The ending is worrisome, since we appear to have arrived back at the same point at which the first play ended. The cyclic nature of violence in the house of Atreus confirms itself in this powerful repetition of staging. The house opens its doors once again to reveal the double horror inside.

In other ways, however, the ending points toward the possibility of escape from the pattern. The Chorus expresses its hope for a better future for the house, and there are some signs that Orestes and Electra will not simply repeat the doomed pattern of their parents. Orestes justifies his act as basically right and lays considerable stress in his speech on the net used to kill Agamemnon, which has been laid alongside the bodies of Clytaemnestra and Aegisthus. Their slain corpses thus significantly share space with the inculpating object that justifies their slaying.

Orestes, however, also admits the horror of his act, and, as a consequence of this realization, rather than staying in Argos to rule tyrannically, as Clytaemnestra and Aegisthus had done, he goes into exile. At the end of the play, his destination is clear. He must seek out Apollo's shrine at Delphi, where the god has commanded him to seek purification. At the play's close, the Chorus approves Orestes' act despite his own deep misgivings. This combination of self-blame and external approval precisely inverts the ending of the *Agamemnon:* Clytaemnestra and Aegisthus unapologetically gloried in their murderous acts, while the Chorus reviled them. The moment the Chorus congratulates Orestes on his liberation of Argos by cutting off the heads of the two "snakes," the hero cries out in horror; for the Furies have appeared with snakes in their hair. The liberation is not complete; slaying the viper Clytaemnestra has only caused the snaked-wreathed Furies to appear. In the closing lines, the Chorus asks where the rage of ruin will come to an end. This question will define the action of the closing phase of the tragic trilogy in the *Eumenides*.

Library (*Bibliotheca*) (ca. first century C.E.) The *Library*, or *Bibliotheca*, ascribed to Apollodorus is a handbook of mythography. The author calls his work a "library" to stress its comprehensive scope. We have most of three books of the *Library*, as well as an epitome of the lost remainder of the work; thus, the work is often cited as "*Library* and Epitome." The work provides relatively unadorned, concise accounts of Greek mythology from its beginnings to the Trojan War and the death of Odysseus. A particular preoccupation of the author is genealogy. Unfortunately, we know little about the author of the *Library*. Presumably, the author, or someone else, chose to attach the name "Apollodorus" to the work because of the prestige of Apollodorus of Athens, a scholar of the second century B.C.E. The *Library*, however, cannot be the work of Apollodorus of Athens, and was more likely produced in the first century C.E. or even later. Throughout this reference, we have referred to this work as "Apollodorus's *Library*" for convenience, and to distinguish it from other works called the *Library*. The author of this *Library* is also sometimes designated "Pseudo-Apollodorus."

Library of History DIODORUS SICULUS (first century B.C.E.)   The *Library of History* was written by Diodorus Siculus ("Diodorus of Sicily"), a Greek writer of the first century B.C.E., who may have moved to Rome at some point in his life. We know very little about Diodorus himself. His *Library of History* originally comprised 40 books. Of these, books 1–5 and 11–20 survive. Diodorus covers an immense range, from the mythic beginnings down to 60 B.C.E. He thus includes mythic history up to and including the Trojan War, and subsequent history and historical legend through the Roman period. Diodorus's focus in the mythic portions is strongly ethnographic, and he includes not only the stories and traditions of the Hellenes but also of other cultures such as Egypt.

Livy (59 B.C.E.–17 C.E.)   Titus Livius, the Roman historian, came from the Italian town of Patavium, known for its stern morality. He lived from 59 B.C.E. to 17 C.E. and was on familiar terms with the emperor Augustus, who apparently affectionately chided him for being "Pompeian" in his sympathies. Livy's historical work, *From the Foundation of the City* (*Ab urbe condita*), comprised 142 books. Books 1–10 and 21–45 are extant, while summaries written later report the basic content and events of most of the other books. Livy covers the history of Rome from the wanderings of AENEAS to the Augustan age, in which he lived and wrote. Livy's history is written in a fluid Ciceronian style, with long, periodic sentences; he embellishes his stories at will and in impressive detail. Should we believe his stories? Livy suggests, in his preface, that there is a poetic quality to the early legends and that we are right to suspend our sense of disbelief. After all, Rome's greatness has earned it the respect of other nations; if any people have the right to claim "gods as

founders," *deos auctores*, i.e., MARS (see ARES), father of ROMULUS, and Venus (see APHRODITE), mother of Aeneas, it is Rome, ruler of the world.

Livy's focus on the city coincides with a period of intense urban renewal under Augustus, and his interest in early legendary history resembles at some level both Virgil's AENEID and Augustus's efforts to connect himself with founder figures such as Romulus and Aeneas, both claimed by the emperor as ancestors. Foundation, in the Roman view, is a continual, difficult process, not a one-time event. Aeneas founded the Roman race; Romulus founded and named the city of Rome. Later figures, such as Camillus, were considered founders of the city for the signal act of restoring it after a crisis. Augustus assumed the role of new founder of the city after the horrors of the civil war and many years of neglect of urban infrastructure and religion. Livy, then, in going back to the city's foundation (*ab urbe condita*), is investigating a process of contemporary relevance. Livy's stories of great men echo the procession of famous men in Virgil's underworld and the statues lined up along the sides of Augustus's new forum. Livy presents his history as a kind of "monument," on which examples of good and bad behavior are visible. In the atmosphere of the renewed moral integrity of Augustan Rome, Livy's history afforded a richly detailed account of the *mos maiorum* ("way of the ancestors"), as represented in picturesque tableaux of Rome's past.

Lotus-Eaters   See *ODYSSEY*.

Lucretius (mid-first century B.C.E.)   Titus Lucretius Carus, an Epicurean poet working at Rome. The life of Lucretius, the author of the *De rerum natura* (*On the Nature of Things*), is almost completely mysterious. Lucretius was praised by Cicero in a letter to Atticus of 54 B.C.E.—nearly the only hard piece of evidence about the poet in addition to the existence of his poem. Lucretius made the interesting decision to put the doctrines of the Greek philosopher Epicurus into Latin verse. The genre of his poem is didactic, a "teaching" poem; it is written in dactylic hexameter, the same meter as epic poetry, and it is six books in length. The poem's main addressee is Gaius Memmius, a prominent political figure of the 50s B.C.E. Lucretius praises him yet rejects political life. The aggressively rationalizing stance of the poem attacks our irrational fears of death and the illusions of romantic love and offers rational explanations for phenomena thought to be caused by the gods, such as thunder and lightning. Lucretius may be seen as involved in an effort to demythologize our experience of life. Lucretius does away with the traditional mythology of the underworld and insists that death is, precisely, nothing. Yet, like other philosophers on principle opposed to myth, Lucretius does not hesitate sometimes to use it to make his point. The poem's opening famously describes Venus's (see APHRODITE) infusion of nature in the springtime and addresses Venus as the "originator of the people of Aeneas." Later, Lucretius refers to the myth of IPHIGENIA in order to denounce superstition. Lucretius uses myth to draw us in, and then he dismantles myth.

Macaria See *HERACLEIDAE*; HERACLES.

Maenads See DIONYSUS.

Maia One of the seven PLEIADES, daughters of ATLAS and Pleione (an OCEANID). Classical sources are the *Homeric Hymn to Hermes* (1–19), Apollodorus's *LIBRARY* (3.10.1–3), and Hesiod's *THEOGONY* (938–939). Maia and her sisters were set in the sky as a constellation. ZEUS's relationship with Maia produced the Olympian god HERMES, messenger and herald of the Olympian gods. In the *Homeric Hymn to Hermes*, a timid Maia avoids the company of the other gods. Her domain is a cave in which she is visited by Zeus during the night, when HERA sleeps. There is no mythology attached to Maia, except for her role as one of the Pleiades and the mother of Hermes.

Marathonian bull See THESEUS.

Marpessa See APOLLO.

Mars See ARES.

Marsyas A SILENUS or SATYR. Son of Olympus and Hyagnis. Classical sources are Apollodorus's *LIBRARY* (1.4.2), Diodorus Siculus's *LIBRARY OF HISTORY* (3.59.2–5), Hyginus's *Fabulae* (165), Ovid's *FASTI* (6.695–710) and *METAMORPHOSES* (6.382–400), and Pausanias's *Description of Greece* (1.24.1, 2.22.8–9, 10.30.9). The double flute (sometimes called "Pallas's reed") was said to have been invented by either ATHENA or Marsyas. In Ovid's *Fasti*, Marsyas simply popularized the double flute after he found the instrument when Athena discarded it. Noticing that while playing the instrument, her cheeks puffed up unattractively, Athena threw it away on a riverbank, where Marsyas found it and became adept at playing it. In some sources Marsyas was punished by the goddess for his temerity in having acquired the instrument; in others, Marsyas's skill on the double flute led to a musical contest with APOLLO. The competition, judged by the MUSES, was won by Apollo. For his hubris, Marsyas was hung by Apollo from a pine tree and flayed alive. His fellow satyrs, fauns, and wood nymphs cried tears of sympathy that flowed into a stream henceforth called the Marsyas, located in Phrygia. The myth of Marsyas is sometimes confused with the musical contest between Apollo and the satyr PAN.

The musical contest between Apollo and Marsyas was popular with artists of the classical period and appeared in sculpture, painting, and relief, and on coins. The fifth-century sculptor Myron produced the sculptural Athena and

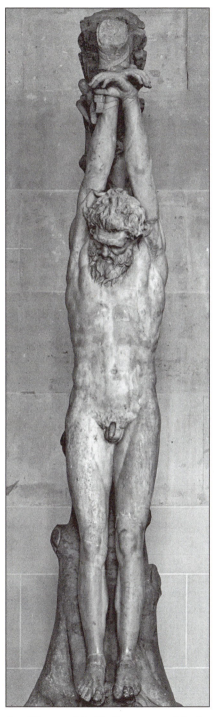

Marsyas Group, of which only copies (Frankfurt, Paris) remain. Here, Athena stands with a nude Marsyas, who beholds the double flute for the first time. Sculpted in marble, Marsyas stands with his hands bound above him in a Roman copy of a Greek original now in the Capitoline Museums, Rome. Another Roman copy of a Greek original, a marble sculpture of the first or second century B.C.E. (Louvre, Paris), shows a naturalistically represented Marsyas. Here, he is nude, bearded, and his hands bound above him. The contest is illustrated on an Attic red-figure pelike from ca. 340 B.C.E. (State Hermitage Museum, St. Petersburg) and Paestan red-figure lekanis lid from ca. 360 B.C.E. (Louvre, Paris), where Marsyas and Apollo are joined by the Muses. Postclassical images include Pietro Perugino's *Apollo and Marsyas* from 1523 (Louvre, Paris) and Titian's terrifying *The Flaying of Marsyas* from ca. 1570–75 (Archiepiscopal Palace, Kremsier, Czech Republic).

Mecisteus   See SEVEN AGAINST THEBES.

Medea   Princess of Colchis. Daughter of King AEETES and granddaughter of HELIOS. Wife of JASON. Medea appears in Euripides' *MEDEA*. Additional classical sources are Apollodorus's *LIBRARY* (1.9.16–28, Epitome 5.5), Apollonius of Rhodes's *VOYAGE OF THE ARGONAUTS* (3, 4 passim), Diodorus Siculus's *LIBRARY OF HISTORY* (4.48–52, 4.54–55), Hesiod's *THEOGONY* (956–962), Ovid's *HEROIDES* (6, 12) and *METAMORPHOSES* (7.1–400), and Pindar's *Pythian Odes* (4). In earlier accounts, such as Hesiod's *Theogony*, Medea appears as a divine or semidivine being, but not yet a witch. In Apollonius's *Voyage of the Argonauts* (3, 4 passim) and PINDAR's *Pythian Odes* (4), she helps the hero Jason obtain the golden fleece. According to Apollonius, she falls in love with him, gives him ointment to protect him from the fire-breathing bulls, and tells him how to defeat the sown men by throwing a stone in their midst. Then she puts to sleep the dragon guarding the

Hanging Marsyas. *Marble, Roman copy of the first or second century B.C.E. Greek original (Louvre, Paris)*

golden fleece, allowing Jason to steal it. Jason and Medea then escape, while Aeetes' fleet pursues them. In some versions, Medea kills her infant brother, Apsyrtus, and scatters his limbs on the sea to slow down her pursuers. In Apollonius's version, Apsyrtus is a young man treacherously murdered by Jason and Medea.

Medea has by this point in the story assumed the mythological role of foreign woman who betrays her father and homeland to help a Greek hero, who will later betray her. Apollonius aptly compares her to ARIADNE. She also represents the dangers and cunning of a barbarian woman: Jason successfully brings back the object of his quest to Greece, but he also brings back a foreign woman who will wreak havoc in Greece. It is not coincidental that Medea's aunt is CIRCE, the famous witch, whom

Medea about to Kill Her Children. *Eugène Delacroix, 1838 (Musée des Beaux-Arts, Lille)*

Jason and Medea, in Apollonius's account, visit on their voyage back to Greece.

On their return, Medea and Jason visit Jason's father, AESON, whom Medea rejuvenates using her magic skill. She offers the same boon to PELIAS, who maliciously sent Jason on the quest for the fleece in the first place. She persuades his daughters to cut him up into pieces and put him in a cauldron. Instead of emerging rejuvenated, he does not emerge at all. (The true and false rejuvenation of Aeson and Pelias, along with other episodes in Medea's story, are described in Ovid's *Metamorphoses* Book 7). The couple then flee to Corinth. Jason, however, decides to marry Creusa, daughter of the king of Corinth. At this point the events represented in Euripides' *Medea* commence. Creon, king of Corinth, fearing what she may do, allows Medea to remain one day in Corinth before leaving. She kills both Creusa and the king himself by sending her a poisoned robe. Creusa dies when she puts it on; Creon dies when he throws himself on her dead body. Then, after painful hesitation in Euripides' version, Medea kills her children to maximize Jason's pain and to prevent her enemies from triumphing over her by mistreating or harming her children. (At Corinth, there was a cult of the children of Medea.) She taunts the destroyed Jason as she departs magnificently on the magical flying chariot of Helios. She goes to Athens, where she has been promised refuge by AEGEUS, whom she promised to help with his problem of childlessness. She marries him and attempts unsuccessfully to poison THESEUS when he comes to Athens. In one legend, Medea becomes the bride of ACHILLES in Elysium.

Jason and Medea appear on a marble sarcophagus of the second century C.E. (Palazzo Altemps, Rome). Here, nude and carrying a shield over his shoulder, Jason clasps hands with Medea, a gesture symbolizing their union. The initial complicity of the hero and the enchantress continues to be represented in postclassical works, in paintings by Gustave Moreau, *Jason and Medea* of 1865 (Musée d'Orsay, Paris), and J. W. Waterhouse *Jason and Medea* of 1907 (private collection).

Medea's murder of her children has not been as frequently represented. In the postclassical period, Eugène Delacroix's *Medea about to Kill Her Children* of 1838 (Musée des Beaux-Arts, Lille) shows a partially clad Medea clutching her young children to her, a dagger in one hand.

Medea EURIPIDES (ca. 431 B.C.E.) Euripides' *Medea*, produced in 431 B.C.E., only won third prize in the dramatic competition. Euripides, if we judge from contemporary responses, was a controversial and notorious playwright, but hardly universally esteemed. Several of his tragedies, including the *Medea*, are nonetheless now ranked among the classics of Western literature. Many features of Euripidean drama that the playwright's fellow Athenians may have found disturbing or unsatisfying are the very ones that intrigue modern readers: An interest in the dark and irrational dimension of the human mind; a focus on female characters, children, and other marginal figures at the expense of traditionally male hero figures; highly formalized debates reminiscent of the Athenian law courts; and the ingenious modes of argumentation employed by contemporary teachers of rhetoric. Euripides' world offers little that is comforting or straightforwardly comprehensible to his tragic audience; instead, he represents a world fragmented by radically opposing ideas, arguments, and principles of behavior.

The *Medea* tells the story of a dangerously powerful woman from the distant land of Colchis, who, after helping the Greek hero JASON capture the golden fleece, fled with him back to Greece. At the beginning of the play, Jason has taken a new wife, the daughter of the king of Corinth, and *Medea* is filled with rage and thoughts of revenge. The form of revenge she ultimately chooses, however, has tragic consequences not only for Jason, whom she wishes to punish with the utmost severity, but also for herself. In addition to killing the new bride and the bride's father, she murders her own children. The horror of this act reverberates throughout the play and divides Medea against herself: She must either renounce her tenderness as mother or renounce her intention to be ruthless toward her enemies. In the end, she chooses to carry out her terrible plan, becoming a quasi-divine figure of vengeance. Jason is correspondingly humbled and will end his days in inglorious inertia beneath the prow of his ship, *Argo*. In pitting Medea against her faithless husband, Jason, Euripides sets woman again man, emotion against calculation, devotion and loyalty against expediency and profit. Ultimately, there is no resolution to this struggle: All that remains is the sense of awe and horror at the enormity of Medea's rage and its consequences.

SYNOPSIS

The opening scene takes place in Corinth in front of Medea's house. The nurse emerges from the house. She expresses the wish that Jason had never sailed to Colchis and had never brought Medea back to Greece, thereby setting into motion the series of events leading up to his present abandonment of Medea and marriage to the daughter of Creon, king of Corinth. According to the nurse, Medea suffers because, having betrayed her own father and country for the sake of Jason, she has now been betrayed by Jason. The nurse suspects Medea's sufferings will be channeled into revenge and that she is capable of violence toward Jason, his new bride, the bride's father, and even her own children. The children's tutor enters with the children and, turning to the nurse, begins a dialogue in which the nurse repeats her foreboding, and the tutor reveals a rumor that Creon will exile Medea and her children from Corinth.

Medea's voice is heard from inside the house, lamenting her fate. The nurse urges the children to stay out of their mother's sight, and the tutor takes them into the house. As the children enter the house, Medea is heard to curse them and their father.

A Chorus of Corinthian women enters the scene; it has come to inquire about Medea's agonized cries. After the nurse explains the cause of Medea's grief, it asks the nurse to bring Medea outside to it so that it may persuade her to be more temperate. Though the nurse is certain the Chorus's soothing words will have no effect on Medea, she does its bidding and enters the house. Medea emerges a few moments later and gives a speech to the Chorus in which she explains that she has come to speak with it only because, as a foreigner in its country, she does not want to offend it. She goes on to describe the difficulties of marriage for women. She succeeds in convincing the Chorus of the injustice of her situation and earns its sympathy. Medea extracts from it the promise that if she avenges herself, the Chorus will remain silent on her behalf.

Creon, the king of Corinth, enters and orders the immediate banishment of Medea and her children from Corinth. In the ensuing dialogue, Medea attempts to persuade Creon that he has nothing to fear from her, but Creon, fearful of Medea's desire for revenge on Jason, his daughter, and himself, continues to demand her exile. Medea finally accepts her banishment, but begs Creon to allow her to stay one day longer in Corinth. Against his better instincts, Creon relents and exits.

Turning to the Chorus, Medea crows that Creon's foolishness will be his folly. She declares that, in the one day Creon has granted her, she will avenge herself and bring about her enemies' deaths by poison. However, she hopes to find safe passage for herself before setting her plan in motion.

Jason and his attendants enter. He has heard about the order of banishment to which Medea and their children are now subject. Medea reproaches Jason furiously for his betrayal, pointing to the many adventures in which he owed his survival and success to her. Jason's no less bitter defense of himself depends on his argument that he helped Medea by bringing her to live in Greek society. Furthermore, he argues, his marriage to the princess is to

Medea's and their children's benefit: It assures them all a place within a noble Greek family and is an advantageous match both materially and socially. During this exchange, Jason argues that Medea should stop behaving irrationally and view the situation pragmatically, while Medea adamantly refuses to overlook or forgive Jason's betrayal of their marriage bed. She bitterly refuses Jason's offer of financial support in their exile. Jason and his attendants leave.

Following Jason's departure, the Chorus bemoans Medea's excess of passion, which had resulted in her exile from her native land and is now causing her banishment from Corinth, but at the same time it condemns Jason's betrayal of Medea.

AEGEUS, king of Athens and friend of Medea, enters. He had not been aware of the state of Medea and Jason's relationship and of her exile. She convinces him that she has been wronged by Jason and, moreover, that she can help him overcome his childlessness, but she does not tell him of her plans for revenge. Aegeus offers Medea sanctuary in Athens and swears by the gods that he will provide sanctuary no matter the circumstances of Medea's escape from Corinth. Aegeus departs.

Having secured asylum in Athens, Medea lays out her plan of vengeance to the Chorus and the nurse. First, Medea will speak with Jason and convince him that she has thought better of her anger and will ask him to allow their children to remain in Corinth. As a token of goodwill, she will send their children to the princess with gifts: a gown and a diadem. The children carry gifts that, unbeknown to them, are poisoned and will cause the death of the princess if she touches them, and the death of anyone who then touches the princess. Following this, Medea reveals her intention to kill the children. Their murder is necessary because, though it may grieve her, it will hurt Jason more, and Medea wishes to avenge herself on Jason as thoroughly as possible. She does not wish to be scorned by her enemies. The murder of her children, in its very ruthlessness, will prevent her from being viewed as weak, or as having the vulnerabilities of an ordinary woman. Medea dispatches the nurse to call Jason, and the Chorus attempts, unsuccessfully, to persuade her to abandon her plan.

When Jason arrives, Medea retracts her previous angry words, agrees with the pragmatic view of his marriage, and calls out their children to witness the end of their quarrel. Jason, flattered by Medea's acceptance of his view of the situation, agrees to try to convince the princess to intercede on behalf of the children so that they may remain in Corinth. Medea claims to accept her own exile and gives a dress and a golden diadem to the children to present to the princess. Jason, the children, and their tutor exit. The tutor returns to inform Medea that the princess has accepted the gifts and that the children will likely be granted a reprieve from exile. Medea is upset because the news means that her plan has been set in motion and that she cannot now turn back. The tutor mistakes her anxiety for sadness at being separated from her children, and Medea orders him indoors.

In the presence of her children, Medea then expresses torment at the thought of completing her plan. Hesitating momentarily, she contemplates escaping with her children. Medea reminds herself that this weakness is typical of a woman and commits herself once more to her original plan. Calling the children to her, Medea embraces them and has them go inside. The Chorus laments the anxieties that afflict those who have children, and Medea watches for some word from the palace. A messenger arrives. He reveals that the princess is indeed dead, poisoned by the gown and diadem, and that her father, Creon, is dead as well. The messenger describes in detail the princess's reception of Jason and the children and her delight in the gifts. Her horrific death is then described. Fire from the crown blazed around her head, the poisoned gown fastened to her skin, and she writhed on the ground and foamed at the mouth, until finally her flesh

melted away. Creon threw himself on her and, after struggling to free himself, finally succumbed to the poison of the gown.

Medea unhappily girds herself for the next part of her plan, the murder of her children, and rushes into the house. From within the house, the children are heard crying for help and attempting to escape their mother. The members of the Chorus wonder whether they should defend the children, but do not.

Jason enters and approaches the Chorus, asking after Medea and hoping to save the children from the certain vengeance of Creon's supporters. The Chorus reveals that Medea has murdered the children. Before Jason can enter the house, Medea is seen hovering above the house in a chariot drawn by dragons; it is the chariot of her grandfather, the sun god HELIOS. The bodies of the murdered children are with her. Jason is devastated. He expresses horror at her deed. He furiously regrets bringing a foreign wife to Greece, someone who would betray her father and her own land, and commit such acts for the sake of a scorned marriage bed. She is a monster, not a woman, he decides. Medea replies that she could not endure the thought that he should scorn her and continue to live peacefully while laughing at her. In the following exchange, Jason describes Medea as a wicked mother, while Medea counters that Jason bears the responsibility for their deaths. Jason asks for the bodies of the children so that he may bury them, but Medea refuses. Jason asks to touch the flesh of his children, and again, Medea refuses.

The Chorus offers the closing observation that it is impossible to know what the gods will bring to pass for mortals, as has been the case in this play.

COMMENTARY

The *Medea* begins and ends with domestic discord. It is not unusual for a Greek tragedy to result in the destruction of a household and, in particular, the killing of family members by family members. But this play is unusual in deriving tragedy from the core elements of domesticity itself. Medea and Jason's is not a royal household, and in many ways, they come off as a typically warring husband and wife. Medea complains in her first speech of the travails of marriage for the wife: She has no choice about marrying, since the alternative is worse; she must accept her husband as the master of her body and purchase this dubious privilege with a dowry; she must adapt to another family and learn the ways of strangers; she does not have the same outlets outside the house as the husband if the marriage turns out to be unsatisfactory; her happiness depends on him alone. In many ways, of course, Medea is not a typical wife with typical child-rearing problems: She is a powerful witch, expert in the use of poison, a daughter of a royal household descended from the god Helios who has been brought by Jason to Corinth from the Black Sea. But while Medea cannot simply be likened to an ordinary wife and mother, it is possible to see aspects of her situation as an intensification of the ordinary challenges faced by many Greek wives; she is isolated, cut off from her own family, and completely dependent on her husband for her happiness.

Medea's central complaints about her husband, Jason, concern their marriage. In marrying the king's daughter, he has violated the oaths of marriage and insulted Medea's bed. At the end of the play, when Medea has revealed the bodies of their murdered children to Jason, he complains bitterly that she killed her own children for the sake of her bed and sexual pleasure. Yet Medea herself, while she does complain of her violated marriage bed, is also driven by another motivation that is less domestic and less traditionally feminine: She declares repeatedly throughout the play that she is afraid of becoming the laughingstock of her enemies and suffering their mockery. It is for this reason that she cannot simply go into exile, as Creon demands, but must first kill the king, his daughter, and then her own children. If she were simply to depart as ordered, she would be passively doing the bidding of her enemies; and if she were to leave her children behind in her enemies' hands, she would feel similarly defeated and humiliated. Medea's concern with her standing and honor suggests a conception of self that is traditionally male. While she complains of the injustice of husbands and marriage as an institution from a distinctly female perspective, and gains the sympathy of the Chorus as a woman, in other respects Medea carries out her vengeance in a masculine manner. She surpasses men in daring and the ability to endure pain. Medea does not accept the traditional subordination of women to men in marriage, and even challenges key aspects of male heroism. Famously, she declares that she would rather go into battle three times than give birth once. Medea is simultaneously at war with her husband, and at war with her own role as mother and wife.

Euripides often chooses to adapt to the tragic stage myths that put male heroes in a bad light. Jason is the very type of the weak hero: He is physically attractive, like Homer's PARIS, but his main accomplishments as a hero required the constant aid of a woman—Medea. Medea, in turn, absorbs the heroic characteristics he lacks. She is able to overcome, in some cases kill, her enemies. She is also heroic in her single-mindedness and destructiveness. Though it may seem strange to modern readers, heroes in ancient Greece were difficult, dangerous figures, revered but also feared; they were honored like gods, and like gods could be terrifying, deadly, and inhuman. In Greek tragedy, heroes are especially liable to become cut off from the rest of society and to awe their audience with the terrible catastrophe that engulfed them. Medea is in many ways a typical tragic hero, stubborn, uninterested in banal motives of profit, expediency, and ordinary well-being, but devoted to rigorous principles of honor that ultimately lead to destruction. Medea's heroic stubbornness drives her to a perverse and disturbing extreme that is difficult to parallel in the mythology of self-destructive heroism. Her decision to murder her own children, however, is consistent with her grim focus on marriage and offspring. Jason violated her bed and their marriage oaths; she, therefore, with a terrible logic, destroys the offspring of their marriage and at the same time (by killing his virgin bride) cuts him off from all possibility of producing further offspring within another marriage. Aegeus, in conversation with Medea, complained that childlessness was the worst condition a man could suffer: Medea appears to have absorbed that lesson and applied it in taking revenge on Jason. This act of vengeance is indeed terrible, but it is specifically the act of an enraged wife. Even in achieving a very masculine vengeance, and in bringing low her enemies so that they cannot mock her, Medea locates her actions within the domestic (and notionally feminine) realm.

Euripides' originality resides in the fact that it is difficult, if not impossible, to map Medea's character and actions onto existing patterns of tragic heroism. Medea is difficult to accommodate to a known type, not least because her own internal contradictions are so profound. She acts as outraged wife and mother but pursues her violent ends like a man seeking revenge; one moment she speaks like a resentful housewife, another like an angry goddess. The themes of love and hate, friendship and enmity that run throughout the play are confounded by the contradictory nature of her actions. She claims to wish to do harm to her enemies, and to benefit those who are dear (Greek *philos*) to her. But in the end, to harm her enemy (Jason), Medea harms those who are dearest of all to her, her own children, and through them, herself. In this terrible act, the division within Medea between her role as loving mother and her role as honor-conscious avenger arrives at its culmination. Before the murder, Medea debates in a long soliloquy whether or not to kill them, and as she follows the twists and turns of her different options, changing her entire attitude from one line to the next, we are able to trace the fault lines in her conflicted mind. First, she concedes that, in killing her children, she will hurt herself twice as much as she will hurt Jason; but then she chides herself for such "soft," womanish arguments and recalls her aversion to being mocked by her enemies. Even as she goes in to kill her children, and steels herself to accomplish the "necessary" act, Medea cannot help expressing how "dear" they are to her, how "sweet." Euripides refuses to mitigate the fierce discord that divides the loving mother in Medea from the proud killer. He could have represented her as cold, unfeeling, and simply evil; instead, he establishes the psychological necessity for the children's murder but, at the same time, makes Medea's love for them as real, as tender, and as visceral as any mother's. It may even be tempting to see Medea as a radically fragmented figure, in whom multiple identities are combined. She is at the very least a figure in whom differing roles and motivations clash with terrible consequences.

Tragedies traditionally involve the implosion of a household, especially a royal one. We might recall the house of Atreus in Aeschylus's *Oresteia*. What is notable here is the highly independent, destructive agency of a single woman. Medea has already left her own household in ruins by murdering her own brother when fleeing from Colchis and tricked the daughters of Pelias into butchering their own father. We know that Euripides previously had written the play the *Daughters of Pelias*. Thus, in putting Medea back on the stage, Euripides is bringing back his own heroine with an awareness both of her mythic background and of his own previous work as playwright. But while Medea's previous history in the *Daughters of Pelias* prepares us for her household-destroying capacities, the Athenian audience was not necessarily prepared for the killing of her own children. This final act of violence is not mentioned in any earlier representation of the myth, and modern scholars sometimes hypothesize that Euripides invented this episode. If this is correct, the audience who first saw Euripides' *Medea* would have been as shocked as Jason to learn that she killed her own children; it would give point, moreover, to the Chorus's comment at the play's end that some things happened that were not expected. Certainly, Euripides expertly builds up suspense by putting expressions of fear and foreboding in the mouths of characters such as the nurse. Will she kill the king, the bridegroom? The killing of the children exceeds even the most pessimistic expectations and takes vengeance to a higher, almost sublime level.

It is no accident that the play revolves around children: They are the concrete product of intermarriage, the offspring of a dangerous foreign women. Colchis, Medea's land of origin, was seen by the Greeks as an exotic, dangerous place from which Jason and the other Greek heroes were lucky to escape with their lives. Medea herself is perceived as dangerous for several related reasons: She is foreign, and she is a women who has a formidable degree of knowledge—clever, capable, skilled in black magic, and poison. Being both female and foreign aligns Medea with the quality of cunning (Greek *metis*): magic and poison—perceived by the Greeks as dangerous weapons of cunning—are coherent with her foreign origin. She is often described by the Greek adjective *deinos*, which simultaneously means "formidable," "clever," "skilled," and "terrible." Medea's name is generally believed to derive from the Greek verb *medesthai*, "to devise." Medea thus represents a dangerous foreign influence in Greece and, perhaps, not surprisingly, destroys Greek families. She is an unusually strong, clever female who does not accept her subordination to her husband and does not even bow before the authority of a king. Given Medea's association with a dangerous foreignness, it makes sense that the play's long opening speech, delivered by the nurse, expresses regret that Medea ever left the land of Colchis to come to Corinth. There is a certain parallelism between this unrealizable wish and Jason's wish at the play's close: He wishes he had never begotten his children, i.e., that he had

never mingled foreign with Greek. His wish, essentially the same as the nurse's, represents a constant theme throughout the play.

But in the Euripidean perspective, figures associated with dark, irrational passions are not necessarily supposed to be driven out; it may even be appropriate to revere and respect them. The danger lies in the attempt to suppress the powerful, irrational force, to attempt to exclude it on the basis of a superficial conception of a rational social order. In this respect at least, Medea resembles the god DIONYSUS in Euripides' *Bacchae*. Dionysus was perceived by the Greeks as an invading foreign god. PENTHEUS, in attempting to exclude him from Thebes and suppress his worship, fails to show adequate respect to the god. Dionysus may not be fully Greek, but the Greeks need to show him honor so that he will not destroy them. Pentheus is accordingly punished: He ends up being driven mad and murdered by his own mother. Dionysus, of course, is both male and a god, neither of which applies to Medea. She does come close, however, to godlike status: In Greek mythology, Medea was traditionally seen as a divine being, and in the closing scene of the play, she appears as a semidivine figure of vengeance. She punishes Jason's failure to respect the power of eros and the sanctity of marriage oaths. Like Pentheus, he, too, must learn the limits of his rationalist perspective. Medea is the granddaughter of Helios, the sun god, and when she appears in the final scene, she is raised above the stage in Helios's chariot. It is possible that Medea herself, whose elevated position at the play's close recalls the Euripidean device of the deus ex machina, implicitly occupies the role of the play's presiding tragic deity.

Like the angry god of the *Bacchae*, Medea destroys the families of the men who attempt to oppose her and who reject the irrational forces she represents. She destroys both Jason and Creon, who, as the ruler the city of Corinth, banishes her from the land. In this light, the fact that the next stop on Medea's Greek itinerary is Athens becomes significant.

It is not accidental that the Chorus in *Medea*, as in other Greek tragedies, sings the praises of Athens. The Athenian audience and judges would appreciate such poetic honors. The question posed by the Chorus here, however, is crucial: How can a woman who killed her own children find a home in so civilized a city-state? From one perspective, she can never find a true home in any Greek city; she is too foreign and baneful a presence to be truly assimilated. The mythic tradition tells us that once in Athens, she will attempt to poison Aegeus's son THE-SEUS or otherwise get ride of him. This would be in keeping with her pattern of undermining royal households. But in another sense, the city of Athens is receiving Medea and doing her honor in the performance of Euripides' *Medea* at the city's festival of Dionysus: The city is showing her reverence, destructive and diffi-cult to assimilate as she is. In the play's closing scene, the heroine herself announces that she intends to establish a cult in Corinth in honor of her children. The Greek city-state is thus able to accommodate Medea at least to some degree, atoning for her murderous act with annual rites of sacrifice.

This suggestion of cultic resolution of the crisis of the *Medea*, however, is fairly modest and does not significantly mitigate the severity of the play's outlook. Medea's refusal to allow Jason even to touch the bodies of his dead children as she taunts him from her chariot at the play's close demonstrates the finality of their break and the absoluteness of the divide between the two perspectives—male and female, specious rationalizing argument and irrational rage. Within the span of the play, nei-ther character is able to affect the outlook of the other to any significant degree. The splintering of worldviews is radical and cannot be healed. When the play begins, dialogue between the two central protagonists, Jason and Medea, is already futile. They occupy different worlds: Dialogue only intensifies this sense of alien-ation. In their first encounter on stage, Medea and Jason trade hostile speeches in which, in typical Euripidean style, they trade point for point, each answering the other's arguments in highly formalized speeches. Jason stresses the expediency and rationality of his plan. He employs the language of profit and interest, denigrating what he portrays as Medea's obses-sive focus on her bed and sexual relations. But by his own admission, he is making a speech, presenting a series of carefully marshaled argu-ments as if in a law court. Medea dismisses him as a villain who lends plausibility to his vile deeds through eloquence. The Chorus, in more diplomatic language, says essentially the same thing. The debate between Jason and Medea proceeds from lengthy, formal speeches to the more heated exchange of one-line remarks back and forth. But the absoluteness of their enmity is only made more evident in this rapid-fire dialogue. Euripides, as in other plays, stages hypersubtle word battles that remind us of the contemporary figures of the demagogue and the rhetorical expert. He was infamous for the sophisticated rhetoric employed by his protago-nists, yet in this case, the flood of words only demonstrates the distance between the two main characters; it does not alter their tragedy, or put off the violence to come.

Jason really is wrong; he really did break his vows; yet Medea's response is wildly immoder-ate. Both characters are fatally flawed, but in different ways. Between Jason's spinelessness and Medea's ruthlessness, there is only a gulf of divided sensibilities. Medea is driven by her "spirit" (Greek *thumos*) to violent action, whereas Jason coldly weaves a fabric of mitigat-ing words around his betrayal. Medea engages in crafty, misleading speech of her own, when, later, she pretends to yield to Jason's arguments to be able to proceed unhindered with her deadly design; similarly, she pretends to speak in a reasonable, submissive manner to Creon to get what she wants from him. But for Medea, such speeches are useful only strategically in bringing about her plan: She does not really wish to justify herself, to put past actions in a good light as Jason attempts to do. Her words are inseparable from her actions. She does not care in the end to mitigate the purity of her hatred. The terse, brutal exchange between Jason and Medea in the final scene makes it clear that she has acted in such a way as to cause Jason as much pain as possible: She is not interested in covering this up with ameliorative language. Jason, for his part, seems to have exhausted his store of seemly arguments. If nothing else, Medea's brutality has laid bare Jason's emotions as well. His own raw hatred and grief come to the fore, and he becomes an authentically tragic character.

Euripides makes it hard not to map the conflict between Jason and Medea onto the divide between men and women generally. Women and men seem to inhabit different worlds, a fractured universe. The Chorus of Corinthian women in the *Medea* participates in the battle of the sexes and, up to a point, takes Medea's side. In one famous instance, the Chorus observes that women have been unfairly represented in poetry, because poetry has been dominated by the perspective of men. Euripides seems to announce a new emphasis on the female viewpoint in poetry. This viewpoint confers, in turn, power and energy on his tragedy. Medea is not simply a caricature of wickedness, a predictable example of what goes wrong when a woman refuses to remain docile and subordinate. Despite the immense horror of Medea's actions, the play does not allow us simply to decide in favor of male rationality over female passion. Medea's plan is appalling, but there is inescapable logic to it, and she commands awe to the very end.

Medusa   See GORGONS.

Megara   See HERACLES.

Meleager (Meleagros) The hero of the Calydonian Boar hunt. Son of Althaea and either ARES or Oeneus, king of Calydon (Aetolia) and brother to DEIANIRA. Classical sources

are Apollodorus's LIBRARY (1.8.2–3), Diodorus Siculus's LIBRARY OF HISTORY (4.34, 4.48), Homer's ILIAD (2.642), Ovid's METAMORPHOSES (8.266–546), and Pausanias's *Description of Greece* (10.31.3–4). Oeneus neglected to perform a sacrifice to ARTEMIS following the harvest, and as punishment for his lack of piety, the goddess sent a wild boar to ravage the country. Faced with this menace, Meleager gathered together a group of hunters—ATALANTA, the DIOSCURI, JASON, PHOENIX, THESEUS, and TELAMON among them—to hunt the boar. Atalanta, whom Meleager loved, struck the first successful blow at the boar. Meleager managed to finish off the boar and angered his uncles, Althaea's brothers, by offering the prized skin to Atalanta. The sources differ as to whether Meleager killed one or both of his uncles. In another version, he kills them accidentally. At Meleager's birth, the FATES had revealed to Althaea that her son would live only so long as a certain log burning in the fire was intact; Althaea had removed the log and preserved it to keep him safe until she realized that he had murdered her brothers. She then threw the log into the fire, and once it was consumed, Meleager died.

Book 9 of the *Iliad* offers a different version. Phoenix recounts the story of the Calydonian Boar hunt to Achilles, who is still holding aloof from the war. The Aetolians and the neighboring Curetes were warring over the head and skin. Meleager's mother cursed him for killing his uncles, and he withdrew from battle. The Aetolians had been winning until then, but now the tide turned. Meleager refused all pleas that he return to the fight, until at the last moment, just as the Curetes were on the point of victory, his wife Cleopatra prevailed on him. The Aetolians were ultimately victorious, but Meleager died in battle.

The Calydonian Boar hunt is the subject of a painting described by Philostratus the Younger in his IMAGINES (15) and appears on the neck of the François Vase of ca. 570 B.C.E. (Museo Archeologico Nazionale, Florence). Here, the enormous boar is trampling hunters and is surrounded by the heroes, whose names appear next to their images. From the same period, a black-figure kylix (J. Paul Getty Museum, Malibu) shows the boar surmounted by hunting dogs and being given chase by the heroes of the hunt. A second-century B.C.E. Roman copy of a Greek original statue of Meleager (Galleria Borghese, Rome) shows the hunter holding a spear and accompanied by a hunting dog.

Memnon   Son of Eos and Tithonus; king of Ethiopia. Classical sources are Apollodorus's *LIBRARY* (3.13.3, Epitome 5.3), Homer's *ODYSSEY* (4.187–188), and Ovid's *METAMORPHOSES* (13.576–622). Memnon went to the Trojan War, in its post-Iliadic phase, to help his uncle PRIAM against the Greeks. There he killed Antilochus, who died in the act of saving the life of his father, NESTOR. ACHILLES, to avenge Antilochus's death, challenged him, and as they fought, Eos and THETIS each appealed to ZEUS, who weighed their respective souls in the balance. Achilles killed Memnon. In one version, Memnon was granted immortality. Ovid's *Metamorphoses* 13 offers a more elaborate variant.

Menelaus   King of Sparta. Son of ATREUS and Aerope. Husband of HELEN. Menelaus and his brother AGAMEMNON are known as the Atreidae. Menelaus is a character in Euripides' *ANDROMACHE*, *HELEN*, *IPHIGENIA AT AULIS*, *ORESTES*, and *TROJAN WOMEN*, and in Sophocles' *AJAX*. Additional classical sources are Apollodorus's *LIBRARY* (3.10.8–3.11.2, Epitome 2.15–6.1, 6.29), Homer's *ODYSSEY* (3.276–302, 15.56–181), and Pausanias's *Description of Greece* (2.18.6, 3.14.6, 3.18.16, 3.19.9, 8.23.4). The many suitors of Helen, the most beautiful woman in the world, swore to her father, TYNDAREUS, to uphold the rights of whichever one of them married Helen. Helen or Tyndareus chose Menelaus as her husband. The daughter of Menelaus and Helen was HERMIONE. While Menelaus was away

from Sparta to attend his grandfather's funeral, his Trojan guest PARIS abducted Helen. Menelaus and Agamemnon accordingly organized the expedition against Troy, calling on the other suitors and Greek heroes to join them. In Homer's *Iliad*, Menelaus is a warrior of respectable powers, but not as ferocious and indomitable as other Greek heroes such as AJAX, ACHILLES, and DIOMEDES. His brother Agamemnon also appears to be a superior warrior and is the leader of the expedition. Menelaus has the better of Paris in a duel in *Iliad* 3, but APHRODITE saves Paris by carrying him off the battlefield. According to Homer's *Odyssey*, Menelaus, like many other Greek heroes, had difficulty making his way home after the war. He ended up stranded in Egypt and had to consult the god PROTEUS to find out how to get home; in the course of his conversation with Proteus, he also learned information about ODYSSEUS, which he was able to relay to TELEMACHUS. Menelaus appears as a genial host of Telemachus in the *Odyssey*, although the differences between his own and his wife Helen's reminiscences about the war underline some lingering tensions in their marriage. In a variant version of the Helen story in Euripides' *Helen*, Helen never goes to Troy with Paris but remains in Egypt for the course of the war, while a phantom image of her, created by the gods, goes to Troy. While Menelaus is taking the phantom image back with him, it suddenly vanishes. When he arrives in Egypt, he encounters the real Helen and must escape with her from the barbarian king Theoclymenus. While the character of Menelaus is largely positive in this play, in other tragedies Menelaus is more negatively depicted. In Euripides' *Trojan Women*, Menelaus is too weak to punish his wife for her destructive actions. In Euripides' *Andromache*, Menelaus and Hermione persecute the guiltless ANDROMACHE, while in Euripides's *Orestes*, he is irritatingly noncommittal, unwilling either to help ORESTES or to admit that he will not help him. In the *Iphigenia at Aulis*, Menelaus wavers between pressuring

Agamemnon to sacrifice his daughter and giving up the whole plan in the name of fraternal friendship. In Sophocles' *Ajax*, Menelaus is a tyrannical figure who forbids Ajax's burial.

Mercury See Hermes.

Merope (1) One of the Pleiades, the seven daughters of Atlas and Pleione (an Oceanid). Wife of Sisyphus, king of Corinth. Classical sources are Apollodorus's *Library* (1.9.3, 3.10.1), Hesiod's *Theogony*, and Ovid's *Fasti* (4.175–176). Merope and her sisters were set in the sky as a constellation. In the *Fasti*, the Pleiades appear in the night sky just before dawn, and although there are seven of them, only six shine brightly. Ovid designates the dim star as Merope, who hides in shame for having married Sisyphus, a mere mortal, or Electra, who hides her eyes in grief at the fall of Troy. In Hesiod's *Works and Days*, the seven sisters are visible to the eye from May to November; their rise determines the schedule for sowing and harvesting.

Merope (2) A queen of Messene. Daughter of King Cypselus of Arcadia. Classical sources are Apollodorus's *Library* (2.8.5), Hyginus's *Fabulae* (137), and Pausanias's *Description of Greece* (4.3.3). Merope was married to the king of Messene, Cresphontes (a descendant of Heracles). Polyphontes, another Heraclid, murdered Cresphontes and two of his sons by Merope, and forced Merope to become his wife. According to Pausanias, it was not Polyphontes but the aristocracy of Messene that conspired against Cresphontes. Unbeknown to Polyphontes, Merope had sent her third son, Aepytus (or Telephon), to be brought up by her father. When he reached maturity, Aepytus returned to avenge the death of his father. He killed Polyphontes and assumed the throne of Messene.

Metamorphoses Ovid (8 c.e.) According to the traditional dating, Ovid completed the

Metamorphoses in the years preceding his exile in 8 c.e. Some scholars believe, however, that he continued to revise the work while in exile, and that an exilic perspective informs the narrative. The *Metamorphoses* is Ovid's longest and most ambitious work. Fifteen books in length, Ovid's epic tells the history of the world, with a special focus on metamorphoses, or changes in form, from the beginning of creation down to his own times. While the poem's vast scope and formal features support its epic identity, the *Metamorphoses* remains notoriously difficult to categorize in generic terms. The poem's frequently erotic subject matter, the absence of a central hero figure, and the complex, episodic structure of interwoven stories mark it as distinct within the epic tradition. Ovid includes epic subject matter—the Trojan War, the wanderings of Odysseus and Aeneas, the voyage of the *Argo*—and yet he also draws on other sources of mythological material and other genres, including pastoral and tragedy. It might be argued that Ovid's true subject matter is mythology itself, in all its complicated interconnections. The main organizing theme is change, yet this theme is inherently fluid and elusive. Change, moreover, works on many levels: Mythological figures undergo changes or transformations, the world and human society change, and the poet transforms his material and models in the very act of writing his own version of inherited stories.

In representing a world in endless flux, Ovid engages with the teleological vision encoded in Virgil's recently completed *Aeneid* (19 c.e.): Virgil's epic represents the long march of historical destiny starting with Aeneas and culminating in the reign of Augustus. By contrast, the Ovidian conception of change, as represented by the long speech of Pythagoras in Book 15, is nonlinear and nonprogressive. The confrontation between Ovid's world of perpetual flux and the Augustan reading of history intensifies in the closing books of the *Metamorphoses*, where Ovid explores developments in his own time, including the apotheosis of Julius Caesar and the Augustan principate.

SYNOPSIS

Book 1

The poet introduces his topic of metamorphosis and tells the story of the creation of the world out of chaos, the ages of humankind, Lycaon, the flood, DEUCALION and PYRRHA, APOLLO and DAPHNE, Io, and PHAETHON. The book ends as Phaethon reaches the palace of the Sun.

Book 2

The poet completes the story of Phaethon, then goes on to tell the story of CALLISTO, the raven and the crow, Ocyrhoe, Mercury (see HERMES) and Battus, and EUROPA.

Book 3

The poet then tells of CADMUS, ACTAEON, SEMELE and BACCHUS's birth (see DIONYSUS), TIRESIAS, NARCISSUS and ECHO, and PENTHEUS.

Book 4

After Pentheus's death at the end of Book 3, the Thebans recognized the divinity of Bacchus and agreed to perform his rites. The daughters of Minyas, however, refuse to celebrate his rites and deny that he is indeed Jupiter's son (see ZEUS). Instead of participating in a festival in the god's honor, they remain at home spinning and telling stories. One of them tells the story of Pyramus and Thisbe; then Leuconoe tells the story of the Sun and LEUCOTHEA. Next, Alcithoe tells of Salmacis and HERMAPHRODITUS. At the end of the story, the power of the god transforms their weaving into grapevines and the women into bats. Then the poet tells of INO and ATHAMAS, Cadmus's transformation into a serpent, and PERSEUS and ANDROMEDA.

Book 5

The poet completes the tale of Perseus's adventures, then recounts the meeting of Minerva (see ATHENA) and the MUSES. A Muse tells Minerva how the daughters of Piereus challenged them to a singing contest. The PIERIDES sang a song belittling the gods and praising the giants. In response, Calliope sang a song that the Muse now repeats: It is the story of the rape of Proserpine (see PERSEPHONE), and it incorporates another story. After her reunion with her daughter, Ceres (see DEMETER) asks the spring Arethusa, who had revealed her daughter's whereabouts in the underworld to her, why she fled and how she became a sacred spring. Arethusa relates her story. Then the Muse tells the story of TRIPTOLEMUS and ends by reporting how they transformed the unrepentant Pierides into magpies.

Book 6

Athena understands the Muses' indignation, since she faced a similar challenge from Arachne. The poet goes on to tell the story of Arachne and Niobe. A Theban, impressed by the power of Latona, recounts the story of the Lycian peasants; another citizen tells of Marsyas. The poet then briefly mentions Pelops and tells at length the story of Procne, Tereus, and Philomela, followed by the story of Boreas and Orithyia.

Book 7

The poet tells the story of MEDEA, JASON, and the Golden Fleece, the restoration of Aeson's youth through Medea's magic, the murder of Pelias, the murder of Jason's children and new wife in Corinth, and Medea's marriage to AEGEUS in Athens. The story of Theseus, whom Medea almost succeeds in poisoning, follows. Next comes the story of MINOS's conflict with Athens over the death of Androgeos, and Aeacus follows with a description of the plague at Aegina. CEPHALUS, an Athenian prince on a diplomatic mission to obtain Aegina's support against Crete, tells the story of his marriage and how he came to kill his wife, PROCRIS, accidentally.

Book 8

The poet tells the story of SCYLLA and Minos, the MINOTAUR, DAEDALUS and Icarus, Perdix, MELEAGER and the Calydonian Boar, and Althaea and Meleager. In the meanwhile, Theseus, who had joined the hunt for the Calydonian Boar, encounters the river ACHELOUS, who tells him how he punished five nymphs by turning them into islands, and how another nymph, Perimele, whom he loved, was also transformed into an island. Theseus's friend PIRITHOUS is scornful and refuses to believe the story. In response, another guest at the gathering, Lelex, tells the story of BAUCIS AND PHILEMON. Finally, Achelous tells the story of Erysichthon and his daughter.

Book 9

Achelous relates his encounter with HERACLES. The poet then tells of Hercules, NESSUS, and DEIANIRA, and of the death and apotheosis of Hercules. Heracles' son HYLLUS marries Iole, to whom Heracles' mother, ALCMENA, recounts the story of Heracles' birth and how Galanthis tricked Lucina, the goddess of childbirth. In response, Iole tells the story of her half sister Dryope. The poet then tells of Iolaus and the sons of Callirhoe, of Miletus, Byblis, and Caunus, and finally, of IPHIS and Ianthe.

Book 10

Then the poet tells the story of ORPHEUS and EURYDICE, and of Cyparissus, and of how Orpheus sang of GANYMEDE, HYACINTH, PYGMALION, Myrrha, Venus (see APHRODITE), and ADONIS. He then recounts the story of ATALANTA as told by Venus to Adonis.

Book 11

When Orpheus ends his song, a crowd of Maenads, mistaking him for an enemy, attack him and tear him apart. To punish them, Bacchus transforms them into trees. The poet then tells of MIDAS, the foundation of Troy by Neptune (see POSEIDON) and Apollo and its subsequent destruction, and PELEUS and THETIS. Peleus, guilty of his half-brother Phocus's murder, takes refuge at the court of King Ceyx, who tells him the story of Daedalion. A herdsman bursts in at the end of the story and informs Peleus that a wolf has killed his cattle. Peleus realizes that this has been caused by his murder

of Phocus, and he tells the story of Ceyx and ALCYONE, and then the story of Aesacus, told by an old man who had seen and admired Ceyx and Alcyone in their bird forms.

Book 12

The poet tells the story of the Trojan War and of the encounter between Achilles and Cycnus. Nestor then tells the story of Caenis and the battle of the Lapiths and centaurs. Then, spurred on by Tlepolemus, he continues with the story of Heracles and his own brothers, the sons of Neleus. Finally, the poet tells the story of Achilles' death and how afterward a dispute arose among the Greeks over the disposition of his arms.

Book 13

There follows the story of Ajax's and Ulysses' (see ODYSSEUS) dispute over the arms of Achilles; the sack of Troy; the story of HECUBA, Polyxena, and Polydorus; and the wanderings of Aeneas, which includes the story of the daughters of Anius, related by Anius himself. As Aeneas reaches Sicily near the twin perils of Scylla and CHARYBDIS, the poet then recalls how the nymph GALATEA once told Scylla the story of Acis and Galatea. There follows the story of Scylla and GLAUCUS.

Book 14

The story of Scylla and Glaucus is concluded. Then the story of Aeneas's wanderings is resumed. At length Aeneas and his companions arrive in Cumae, where Achaemenides, a Greek who had been one of Ulysses's crewmen and whom Aeneas had rescued, meets his former crewmate Macareus. Achaemenides tells the story of the Cyclopes, his abandonment, and eventual rescue; Macareus for his part reports the story of CIRCE and Picus and Canens, as told by one of Circe's acolytes. Then the poet tells of the unsuccessful embassy to Diomede, the transformation of the Trojan fleet into sea nymphs, Aeneas's victory over Turnus, Aeneas's apotheosis, and the story of POMONA and VERTUMNUS, who in turn tell the story of Iphis and Anaxarete. The poet ends the book with the foundation of Rome, the conflict with the Sabines, and the apotheosis of Romulus/Quirinus and Hersilia/Hora.

Book 15

The poet tells how Numa visits Croton and hears the story of its foundation. Pythagoras, who lives in Croton, delivers a long speech on his doctrine of vegetarianism, perpetual change, and the soul's immortality. Instructed in these precepts, Numa returns to rule. After his death, his wife, the nymph Egeria, goes in her grief to the sanctuary of Diana Nemorensis at Aricia, and is consoled by HIPPOLYTUS/Virbius, who tells his story. There follows the story of Cipus, Aesculapius, and the apotheosis of Julius Caesar. The poem ends with the praise of Augustus as son of a god and future god himself, and with the poet's closing claim of immortality.

COMMENTARY

Ovid's *Metamorphoses* is epic in length and meter: He employs the dactylic hexameter meter common to all ancient epics, and his poem comprises 15 books. Like other epic poets, he represents both the actions of mortals and the interventions, designs, observations, and prophetic signs of the gods. The action swivels between events in the human world and discussion among the gods as to the ways in which the outcome of those events may, or may not, be influenced. The subject matter treated by Ovid, moreover, includes substantial portions that correspond to the heroic material traditional for epic poetry: Jason and the voyage of the Argonauts; Odysseus; Achilles and the Trojan War; Aeneas's wanderings; the early history of Rome. Nonetheless, here as in his other works, Ovid displays a subtle awareness of genres and a willingness to manipulate genre in innovative ways. It is not enough to state that the *Metamorphoses* is an epic poem in hexameter verse; we must understand how Ovid's poem is different from other surviving epics, and how he creates a novel epic mode.

One key question concerns subject matter. Many of the most memorable stories that make up the poem, and that, in sheer frequency, predominate, are love stories—the loves of mortals, love among gods, and the love of gods for mortals. There is nothing inherently unepic about love and women. We can easily think of examples in which love is crucial to an epic poem (PENELOPE, Circe, DIDO, ANDROMACHE, Medea). Typically, however, warfare is a key focus, and even if it is not the sole focus—as in the case of the *Odyssey* and the *Voyage of the Argonauts*—female figures still tend to function as either helping or obstructing the efforts of a central *male* protagonist (Aeneas, Jason, Odysseus), who is motivated by goals other than simple erotic fulfillment (Italy, the Golden Fleece, return to Ithaca and reassertion of control over the household).

In Ovid, there is no central male protagonist, nor even a long line of heroes, as in Ennius's *Annales* and other historical epics. Instead, there is a proliferation of intricately interlocking stories—stories, moreover, that do not end with the fulfillment of a male, heroic quest. Rather, Ovid's stories end as frequently in frustration, defeat, and aporia as in fulfillment and success; most important, they end with a transformation. Apollo chases Daphne, but he cannot possess her sexually. She is transformed into a laurel tree, which, however, he now claims as one of his key attributes as a god. This paradoxical ending, which combines possession and loss, fulfillment and frustration, is very different from the ending of a typical heroic quest; it is an ending, moreover, that is repeated, inflected, and, indeed, transformed in the multiple narrative units that compose the poem.

Ovid represents diverse trajectories of desire and their often surprising outcomes in ways that recall his highly successful work in love elegy. We are reminded that Ovid spent a great deal of his poetic career viewing epic as the generic "other," against which he defined his position as love poet and teacher of love. Now that he writes epic, he does so with a lively sense of the possibilities and perspectives of other genres. A perceptible feature of Homer is the tendency to exclude from or play down in his narrative myths that which does not cohere with his idealizing vision of heroic behavior—Ajax's suicide (tacitly assumed but not described in the *Odyssey*), Achilles' early transvestitism. Ovid tends to give much fuller narrative attention to episodes of this kind, and much else besides. Ovid's POLYPHEMUS is not the epic Polyphemus of Homer but the lover of Theocritean bucolic poetry; his Scylla is not simply a monster feared by seafaring heroes but also a beautiful young woman pursued by a multitude of suitors. Ovid takes the mythic episodes that frequently adorn love poetry as illustrative examples, and in his epic narrative treats each as worthy of a story in its own right.

Yet what, exactly, does Ovid's narrative comprise besides a diverse collection of mythological stories? In the opening lines, he makes the startling claim that he will trace a path in "continuous song" (*carmen perpetuum*) from the beginning of the world until his own times. The claim is at once ambitious and provocative. Even though he writes refined, esoteric poetry in the Alexandrian style, he still manages to exceed other epic poets in temporal scope. The paradox is built into the phrasing: He will "lead down" (*deducere*) his poem from creation to the present age, a term that refers at the same time to the "fine-spun poetry" of contemporary taste (*deductum carmen*). Virgil managed to write an epic that encompasses both the legendary times of Aeneas and, through anticipatory devices such as the shield and the visit to the underworld, later Roman history up to the Augustan age. Ovid surpasses this feat in raw terms and, at the same time, makes greater claims of inclusiveness: His work will encompass the subject matter of Virgil's *Aeneid*, early Roman history, the *Odyssey*, the ILIAD, the *Voyage of the Argonauts*, and many other mythological and legendary episodes. A truly comprehensive

narrative of world history would be impossible, but Ovid goes out of his way to show how narrow, comparatively speaking, are the temporal segments carved out by his competitors. Ovid's mega-history is part of a broader Augustan phenomenon; we might compare it not only with Virgil's *Aeneid* but also with Livy's *From the Foundation of the City*. Even amid these competitors, Ovid maximizes narrative scope to an impressive degree. He writes a poem that is vaster, in terms of world-historical scope, than Virgil's, yet no less refined in the composition of its individual episodes.

A major influence is the Alexandrian Greek poet Callimachus, whose fragmentary *Aetia* ("Causes," "Origins") similarly interweaves different myths in a complex, erudite manner. Ovid's *Metamorphoses* betrays a persistent fascination with origins stories: His myths explain the origins of animals, place-names, trees, and flowers. The theme of transformation, however, introduces a distinctive emphasis to the etiological matrix and points as well to the destabilizing possibility of future change. In Ovid's world, the stability afforded by origins is balanced, if not undermined, by the broader pattern of constant transformation and destruction of previous forms, bodies, and certainties. It is not simply a matter of tracing a current, stable entity to its point of origin, thereby satisfying curiosity and anchoring the present state of things in the past. For Ovid, radical, identity-transforming change is possible at any time, and we have very little control over final outcomes. Human beings are at the mercy of larger forces, and we cannot necessarily assume that an orderly sequence of changes is leading progressively toward some meaningful purpose. Change is at once continual, cyclical, a part of the very air we breathe, and, at the same time, irruptive, transgressive. The pattern—if there is one—is not obvious.

On this point, Ovid comes into conflict with an aspect of the epic tradition, and with Virgil in particular. Virgil's epic project is at once etiological (focusing on origins) and teleological (focusing on final purpose and end). The *Aeneid* tells the story of the origins of the Roman race. The intent is etiological in the large picture (the origination of the Romans through the fusion of Trojans and Latins) and in the finer details (rights, customs, language, place-names, the Julian family line). This interest in origins is not simply academic curiosity, the foundation of Rome is an ongoing struggle—it continues into the present day. Aeneas *must* succeed in establishing himself in Italy; otherwise, there will be no Rome, no "empire without end," no Augustus—all outcomes that have been promised by destiny. There is a teleological force driving forward the narrative of the *Aeneid* and of Roman history itself, demanding sacrifices and victories and further sacrifices. Virgil has some precedent for this mode of epic narrative in the *Iliad*, where the "destiny of Zeus" imposes an end/purpose (telos). Homeric destiny, however, does not incorporate a comparable concept of progress and moral necessity. Virgil establishes a new degree of congruity between the teleological drive of history and the mechanism of epic plot.

Ovidian change does not easily accommodate the teleological linearity driving Virgilian epic. The opening of the epic does indeed represent the emergence of distinct realms of the world out of the undistinguished mass of chaos. The stories that follow, however, present little in the way of progress or of a pervasive sense of an ultimate aim underlying the action. Gods pursue, and sometimes rape, nymphs and mortal women. Gods and goddesses, when neglected or hubristically challenged, punish the transgressors with appropriate penalties. Lovers tragically misunderstand each other and proclaim their devotion in their dying words. Ovid's favored story lines focus on the ironies of misunderstanding, the capricious cruelty of eros, love triangles, the capacity of envy and pride to motivate violent retribution—in other words, the recurrent flaws of human and divine character that recombine to create piquant and infinitely varied situations. The basic principle

of change pervading the universe, as described by Pythagoras in Book 15, is radically directionless. Change itself is mandatory, but pattern and progress are not—the very fact of continual change would naturally work against the emergence of a persistent design.

Certain features of Ovidian narrative cohere with the poet's vision of continual, directionless change. First, and conspicuously, Ovid does not begin his epic in medias res in the manner of Homer or Virgil. He begins his epic at the utter beginning of everything, the creation of the world, and proceeds from there to the present day. Ovid could not have taken a further position from the limited slice of time carefully chosen by Homer for his *Iliad*. Ovid does not give the impression that he wishes to proceed from a significant beginning point to a specified end point, i.e., to enact a defined narrative trajectory. He is writing about the history of the transformation of bodies in the broadest possible sense. There is no determinate path or end point to such a history. A second important, formal/structural feature of Ovid's poem relating to the theme of change might be accurately termed narrative "flow." Consciously, and for the most part successfully, Ovid avoids creating the impression of clear narrative boundaries. He makes it difficult to mark definitively where one structurally integral segment ends and the next begins. Ovid prefers, instead, to nest one story segment within another, so that neither has full autonomy within the broader narrative. Often a narrative episode constitutes a detour within a larger story that continues afterward. Frequently, moreover, Ovid does not allow the end of the story to coincide with the end of the book; instead, he deliberately spreads it from the end of one book into the beginning of the next.

Ovid also avoids giving the impression of a deliberately structured, purposeful narrative trajectory through a strategy that might be called the dispersal of voice. Embedded narrative is a traditional feature of epic. We might think of Nestor's stories in the *Iliad*, the massive section of internal narrative in the *Odyssey*, or *Aeneid* Books 2–3. In the *Metamorphoses*, however, the internal speakers are multiplied and layered one on top of the other. In some cases, the layering of narrative is so thick that it is difficult to recall how the different frames relate to one another. Many of these speakers are significant mythological characters in their own right: Arethusa, Hippolytus, the daughters of Minyas. A significant number, however, are identified with what appears to be a deliberately casual vagueness ("a neighbor," "someone who happened to be watching nearby," "a citizen," and so on).

The rhetorical effect of such embedded narration varies, depending on the speech context, the identity of the speaker, and his or her relation to the story told. Knowledge of the punishment of the daughters of Minyas at the end of their storytelling session affects how we may read the stories they tell before their transformation. We would argue, however, that another outcome of the dispersal of voice throughout Ovid's poem is to promote a broader sense of storytelling and human voice through history. We are given the impression of countless stories interwoven with and embedded in further stories, storytelling as an ongoing, age-old process, extending from one generation to the next, throughout the various regions of the world. The stories are in one sense repetitive, circular, part of a shared system of archetypes and recurrent patterns, yet from another perspective, each story presents its own distinctive insight and vision. The indefatigable human voice and *its* changes and transformations through innumerable variations on the traditional themes is arguably the central theme of the epic.

This vision of human and divine storytelling undermines in yet another way Virgilian teleological drive. It is as if Ovid were saying: "These are the stories that have been told for centuries, and will continue to be told in their myriad, ever-changing forms." There is no determinate structure or end-driven design to this metamorphic, continual *(perpetuum)* flow

of voice. Again, we might compare the *Aeneid*, a poem that exerts considerable influence on Ovid, even as he resists its founding assumptions. In Virgil's poem, a series of authoritative voices accompanies the forward progress of the narrative: Anchises, Jupiter via Hermes, Apollo via the Sibyl, Jupiter himself on Olympus in conversation with Venus and Juno. Prophecies and omens announce the will of the gods, constantly demonstrating to Aeneas that he is doing the right (occasionally the wrong) thing, that his struggle and sacrifice are worth it. It does not seem likely that one could elicit similarly directional and didactic messages from the diverse instances of voice in the *Metamorphoses*. For one thing, many of these voices tell their own stories in the first person and thus do not notionally participate in a larger story plan. Ovid weaves subtle thematic interconnections among his various stories and internal narrators, but he does so in such a way as to create an enlivening tension between the autonomy of the story and its place in a broader fabric of stories. The singularities of individual tales and voices constitute yet another obstruction to an overarching narrative teleology.

Far from establishing a dominant teleological strand, Ovid displays a meta-discursive awareness of the stakes involved in different modes of representation and mythological narrative; i.e., some of his stories reflect on the nature of storytelling itself as an interested and inevitably biased endeavor. The story of the contest between the Muses and the daughters of Piereus in Book 5 is a good case in point. The nine daughters of Piereus insultingly challenge the Muses to a singing contest. One of their number sings of the GIGANTOMACHY and the various animal forms taken by the Olympian gods to escape the terrifying TYPHOEUS. The Muse who reports this song suggests that this version of the Gigantomachy was spurious and distorting, although many of the same details are supported by other sources. The Muse then goes on to report the winning song of Calliope. She sings of the rape of Proserpine, but within this narrative, Arethusa, questioned by Ceres, tells her own story; then Calliope goes on to tell of Triptolemus, and finally, the unnamed Muse narrates the outcome of the contest: Calliope is hailed as winner, yet the Pierides continue to be abusive; they are accordingly punished by being transformed into magpies. The story of Proserpine can be read at least in part as a response to the Pierides' account of the Gigantomachy. In Calliope's tale, the gods manage to settle their differences; Jupiter succeeds in negotiating an agreement and achieving an acceptable balance. Rather than showing the gods challenged and routed, Calliope depicts a stable system of power relations effectively maintained by an authoritative ruler.

The entire performance is a tour de force on the part of the Muse and of Ovid: It represents the most complex layering of narrative within narrative in the entire poem. The Pierides do not appear to be exceptionally talented singers, yet the ending of the story, in which they are transformed into chattering magpies, also serves to remind us that the Pierides are no longer in a position to present their side of the story. Their song is dismissively rendered in the Muse's brief paraphrase, while the song of Calliope is lovingly reproduced, complete with elegant detours and inset narrative. The punishment is cruelly appropriate. The continual chattering to which they are forever consigned mocks their love of speech, yet the unintelligible, repetitive, and—the most pointed insult of all—unoriginal twittering of the magpie deflates the Pierides' poetic pretensions. The magpie was known as a mimic. There is a further point concealed here: The term "Pierides" ("daughters of Piereus") sometimes serves as a variant term for "Muses." The Pierides, both in their number (nine sisters) and their ambitions, mimic the Muses and are their natural competitors. The Muses in Ovid's text succeed both in establishing their predominance and in controlling the reputation of their challengers.

Not accidentally, Minerva's story about ARACHNE in Book 6 follows immediately on the story of the Pierides that ends Book 5. In this famous myth, Arachne challenges Minerva to a weaving contest, and the two weave magnificent tapestries: Minerva's work represents the dispute between herself and Neptune over the naming of Athens and patronage of the city; Arachne's represents the various acts of rape and deceitful seduction of mortal women perpetrated by the gods. Minerva's tapestry appropriately shows gods in the act of competing to bestow their gifts on mortals; the gods, according to Minerva's tapestry, have mortals' best interests at heart and contribute to human civilization. She also represents the 12 Olympian gods, including a regal Jupiter, in all their grandeur. It is no accident that the specific story in question favors Minerva and celebrates the city that came to be named after her. In addition, the goddess, intimating Arachne's future fate, adds smaller scenes in the corners representing the gods' punishment of transgressive mortals.

It has not escaped scholars' attention that Arachne's tapestry in particular echoes the subject matter of Ovid's *Metamorphoses*, which is full of stories of the rape and deception of mortal woman by unscrupulous gods. On one reading, Ovid's poem could be seen as such a tapestry—an analogy strengthened by the metaphor of weaving traditionally employed to signify poetic composition. Athena's depiction of the gods' contributions to human civilization, however, also has parallels in Ovid's epic (e.g., the story of Ceres and Triptolemus), and her stories of divine punishment inflicted on presumptuous mortals correspond thematically to the sequence of myths in Books 5 and 6 (the Pierides, Arachne, NIOBE, MARSYAS, the Lycian peasants). The episode has been interpreted as programmatic for the poem itself, and it is easy to understand why. It encompasses many of Ovid's key themes, including the relation between mortals and gods, just and unjust punishment, and the risks undergone by an ambitious and transgressive artist. A certain amount of caution is required, especially in regard to the last-mentioned theme, since modern readers are naturally inclined to sympathize with the punished mortals rather than with the punishing gods, and to consider artistic pride if not admirable at least understandable. There is the danger of assimilating Ovid to the familiar modern paradigm of the heroically rebellious artist oppressed by an authoritarian regime.

On the other hand, Ovid did continue to revise the *Metamorphoses* after Augustus relegated him to the shores of the Black Sea, and it may reflect aspects of his exilic perspective. Jupiter in the *Metamorphoses* is often the threatening thunder-wielding figure to whom Ovid assimilates the emperor Augustus in the *Tristia*, the work he wrote during and about his exile. Several stories in the *Metamorphoses*—Arachne, Marsyas, Daedalus—concern a human artist harshly treated by a tyrant or angry god. Book 6, picking up on the themes of the Pierides story of Book 5, includes a series of stories examining harsh punishments imposed by gods on presumptuous mortals: Arachne, Niobe, Marsyas. Again, we cannot presume that ancient readers would have necessarily sided with the mortals. The temple of Apollo built by Augustus on the Palatine Hill included a representation of the punishment of Niobe on its intricately carved ivory doors. Ovid's representation of Niobe gives a prominent role to her excessive pride, and there is no doubt she acted hubristically. Still, Niobe displays a magnificent defiance, even in the midst of her suffering, and Ovid describes the children's murder in horrific detail. Marsyas's narrative is more compressed. Ovid depicts only the moment of his punishment, as Apollo removes his skin. Ovid intensifies the pathos by employing a pastoral motif: Nymphs, woodland deities, and his fellow shepherds all lament the flayed Marsyas. Ovid does not overtly tip his hand, but he certainly leaves open to his readers the option of judging the god's cruelty excessive.

In the Arachne story, Ovid does appear to tip his hand in favor of the human victim. He specifies that neither Minerva nor Envy could find any fault in Arachne's tapestry—it was a masterpiece. This very flawlessness seems to have angered Minerva more than anything else and to have catalyzed her decision to make an enduring example of Arachne. The punishment, as in the case of the Pierides, sadistically suits the "crime." Arachne, as a spider, must now perpetually create weaving devoid of artistic value and human expression. Her punishment resembles the transformation of the Pierides into magpies and the transformation of the daughters of Minyas into bats. Motifs of weaving, speech, artistry, and defiance of gods are common features of these stories and together suggest Ovid's preoccupations as imperial and exilic writer: He, too, suffered a change in being sent to the Black Sea, as he states in poetry written during this period. A writer eminently suited to the city of Rome, he received a punishment that was all too carefully and cruelly designed to deprive him of his creative dignity.

Ovid's myths understandably reflect the concerns of a love poet. Many of his myths are about love. Poetry, however, is also a major focus. In the foreground of several of his most elaborately developed mythological episodes are voice (Canens, Orpheus, the Pierides, the daughters of Minyas, Narcissus), music (Orpheus, Marsyas), and artifice (Daedalus, Pygmalion). The culmination of the epic's 15 books is the poet's own metamorphosis described in the closing lines. Ovid predicts that he, too, will undergo a change, from living person to immortal work. In the last word of the poem, he proclaims, at once triumphantly and enigmatically, "I shall live." Ovid himself will die, like all mortals, but his work will live on: The "I" that lives in the epic's final line both is and is not the poet Ovid. It is "his" voice that speaks, yet this voice, in becoming entombed in the work, the poet's living monument, is already only partially his. We might compare the way in which, for example, the weeping Niobe, as she is transformed into stone, becomes her own monument.

So many of Ovid's transformed bodies attain an identity and a meaning they themselves never imagined or expected: Their new form and meaning transcend their former selves. Now, Ovid anticipates that he himself will be subject to a similar process. Weaving oneself into a poem entails an exciting, but also disturbing, transformation, the loss of self in a work that is ultimately independent of the writer's physical existence and limited temporal span. The closing self-reference only makes explicit what has been only hinted at throughout: This cosmic history of transformations is at some level a portrait of the literary artist. A universe saturated with the principle of transformation is a universe saturated with the dynamic principles of literary creation, reception, and posthumous survival. Ovid transforms stories by retelling them and resituating them within a new narrative framework; when his text comes into the hands and minds of others, perhaps it will, in its turn, become something other than what he had intended. Transformation is the theme of Ovid's stories, yet transformation is also constantly at work as an internal process in the poem itself. Instead of adapting his art to the cosmos, Ovid paints a cosmos that conveniently and richly reflects his artistic concerns.

The sense of exhaustive completeness of the mythic repertoire is another interesting and ambitious feature of the poem. True exhaustiveness is, of course, impossible. Ovid concedes as much, when, for example, he has one of the daughters of Minyas hesitate among a number of different options in choosing the next story to tell. A close reader of the *Metamorphoses*, moreover, will come to appreciate Ovid's exclusions, truncations, and silences as much as his inclusiveness. As a general (but not strict) rule, he tends to move quickly through narrative episodes that contemporaries such as Virgil have treated extensively and to develop at greater length figures and stories that have been previously neglected or marginalized. Writing

any myth involves suppressing other and/or fuller versions of the same myth. It is also possible, however, to allude to those other versions even while suppressing them. In general, Ovid errs on the side of inclusiveness: His versions of the myths of Niobe, Orpheus, Ceres and Proserpine, and Perseus are amply developed and filled with colorful narrative detail. Where other authors are allusive and selective, so as to flatter their elite audience's self-conscious erudition, Ovid is generous in providing basic background and a satisfyingly complete tale. It is no accident that most modern handbooks of mythology base not only their individual stories but their broader construction of the mythic repertoire on Ovid. Ovid infuses such modern accounts as *Bulfinch's Mythology*, and his versions, because of their very completeness and accessibility as narratives, have become standard. A reader of Ovid's older contemporary Propertius will find typical Alexandrian compression and obliquity in his treatment of myth. Ovid, by contrast, tells the story in the manner of a lively raconteur conscious of the demands of entertaining a broad audience of readers: "There once was a woman/man, who lived in x . . ." Many of Ovid's most memorable tales, such as the myth of Midas or of Pygmalion, are largely his invention. Mythological figures with these names existed, but their stories had not yet acquired the vivid, distilled, and unforgettable form of the Ovidian version. Part of Ovid's intervention consists in making *stories* out of material that is incoherent or otherwise lacking in narrative sparkle.

Ovid is perfectly capable of the difficult density of the Alexandrian style and occasionally demonstrates this capacity (e.g., the sequence dealing with Iolaus and the sons of Callirhoe in Book 9). His expansive and colorful narratives, moreover, can be read on more than one level, depending on the attentiveness and erudition of the reader. A fully enjoyable and fluidly narrated tale still contains many small comments, allusions, and "footnotes" for the connoisseur of poetic mythography. It is possible that

Ovid's seeming transparency, which explains much of his popularity among modern readers, is misleading, or at least only part of a more complicated story. Ovid seems so accessible to us insofar as the totalizing ambitions of his mythological compilation contribute to and are part of the prehistory of our modern concept of mythology. Yet, what to us appears natural and familiar was in many respects a provocative experiment in mythological narration in the epic genre.

Ovid manages to include most of the major mythological figures and sequences, yet he does so under the inclusive rubric of change or transformation. The topic is announced in the opening lines: The poet tells of bodies changed into other forms. The emphasis remains constant to the very end. In Book 15, Ovid reports the long discourse of Pythagoras in which the philosopher presents change as the central principle at work in the universe. Individual myths either themselves constitute transformations (e.g., the formation of the world out of chaos) or culminate in a transformation (Apollo and Daphne, etc.). The closer we examine the *Metamorphoses*, the more it becomes apparent how devotedly Ovid has made change his poem's central theme and accorded special privilege to stories of transformation and figures endowed with special powers of transformation. Midas, for example, coheres perfectly with Ovid's program of metamorphosis, since he both acquires the ability to transform whatever he touches into gold, and himself later undergoes a transformation when Apollo gives him ass's ears. Ovid neatly imposes a unifying theme on the Midas story. For Midas, transformation is negative, whether as an active ability (golden touch) or a passive experience (ass's ears). In the final phase of the story, Midas's barber can barely keep the secret of his master's ears, so he digs a hole, whispers the secret into the hole, then fills it up with earth again. Reeds grow there and speak the story of Midas's ass's ears as they sway in the wind. This final transformation might be termed a meta-transformation, i.e., a metamorphosis that comments on its own conversion into Ovidian poetry: A secret became a story, and the story now forms part of Ovid's widely disseminated text.

A sequence in Book 8 is especially explicit in its articulation of Ovid's thematic focus on metamorphosis. Theseus and his company meet the river Achelous, who tells first how he transformed five nymphs into islands as a punishment for neglecting him, and then how another nymph whom the river god loved fled him and was transformed into an island. Theseus's companion Pirithous laughs at this "fable" and mocks the idea that the gods can change the shape of things at will. All the rest of the company are horrified at this outburst; significantly, Ovid does not here mention Pirithous's name, but refers to him as the son of IXION, the famous sinner and outlaw. It is not accidental that Ovid thus stigmatizes an opponent of his poem's organizing idea. Ixion's very name, moreover, would appear to disprove Pirithous's position, since, among other disreputable deeds, Ixion (as references elsewhere in the *Metamorphoses* confirm) fathered the race of CENTAURS when he coupled with a cloud image of HERA created by Zeus to entrap him. Zeus's deception provides an instance of a god changing the shape of things, and the final product, the centaur, which combines human and equine features, is itself suggestive of metamorphosis.

Another member of the party, Lelex, then offers the story of Philemon and Baucis as a response to Pirithous's impious comment. This story explicitly confirms the power of the gods to effect transformations: Jupiter and Mercury visit a humble household, where an old man and old woman host graciously. When the couple reach the end of their natural lives, the gods reward them by transforming them into two trees rising from a single trunk. This story of piety and reward presents metamorphosis in an especially good light, and further supports the implied equation between belief in transformation and a respectful attitude toward the power of the gods. Ovid's narration derives its broader scenario and many of its motifs from Callimachus's *Hecale* and thus also suggests transformation on the literary plane. The book's final story of Erysichthon (another tale previously told by Callimachus) is stranger and darker, but it still puts metamorphosis itself in the foreground. Erysichthon violated a grove sacred to Ceres, and as punishment is afflicted with unending, inexhaustible hunger. His daughter, who is compared in the story's opening lines to the shape-changing god Proteus, acquires food for her desperate father by undergoing a series of transformations. Yet, she cannot save him, and in the end, he devours himself. Finally, the narrator, Achelous, reveals that he himself has the power of changing his own shape. This capacity is further illustrated in the story of the river god's encounter with Hercules at the opening of the next book. This sequence of myths centered in Book 8 overtly examines the theme of transformation and affords special attention to figures capable of changing their own shape and/or the shape of others.

Other stories bear traces of the metamorphic focus. Proteus's words open Ovid's version of the story of Peleus and Thetis in Book 11. Peleus, to have intercourse with the goddess, must follow Proteus's advice and tie her up to prevent her from changing, Proteus-like, into a multitude of different shapes. In yet another witty variation on his theme, the culmination of Ovid's story is the opposite of metamorphosis, a return to original form: Peleus finally possesses his bride when she returns to being simply Thetis. An even more elaborate story following a similar narrative arc concerns the Roman god of change and transformation, Vertumnus. Romans derived the name of this god from the word denoting transformation (*verto*, "to turn," "change," "transform"). The god Vertumnus loves the Latin nymph Pomona, who has so far resisted all her suitors. He tries various guises and at length gains access to her in the form of an old woman. He/she delivers a long speech in support of Pomona's suitor Vertumnus, including an exemplary tale that includes yet another metamorphosis. She is not persuaded by the old woman's words. Vertumnus then assumes his own handsome shape as youthful god, and she immediately accepts him. Ovid ingeniously fashions a story about the change-god par excellence that ends, like Thetis's story, in a nonchange, a return to original form, which turns out to be much more effective than all the god's previous disguises.

Figures who combine powers of metamorphosis and artistic powers are for obvious reasons of special interest to Ovid. Ovid's version of the story of Pygmalion endows him with skill as a sculptor, whose sculpture of a beautiful woman ultimately comes to life and becomes his lover. Here the key themes of metamorphosis, aesthetics, mimesis, and the transforming power of eros come together in a single figure. Daedalus combines a similar set of themes. As artisan, he succeeds in transforming himself and his son into birds—an artificial bird-metamorphosis to complement and echo the numerous miraculous bird-metamorphoses throughout the poem. Daedalus's artifice also played a key role in creating, then containing, the metamorphic bull-man, or Minotaur. Finally, Orpheus plays an important role in Ovid's poem. The story of Orpheus and Eurydice comes at the opening of Book 10. Here, Orpheus reveals aspects of his transformative power as poet: Not only can he inspire rocks and trees to move; he is able to create life out of death. Yet when he turns back and gazes on Eurydice, she suffers a second death. For the rest of the book, Ovid accords Orpheus the role of extended internal narrator; he tells the stories of Ganymede, Hyacinth, Pygmalion, Myrrha, Venus and Adonis, and Atalanta. Some of these stories reflect themes of evident concern to the bereaved Orpheus: love, the death of a loved one, the artist's power to create life. At the beginning of Book 11, Ovid relates the singer's death at the hands of Maenads.

Orpheus's story and the songs he himself sings articulate an important set of themes concerning the transformative power of song and the limits of that power.

While Ovid clearly chooses topics consonant with his major preoccupations, he also assimilates and adapts subject matter not obviously suited to his epic of transformation. Books 12–14 together offer a "metamorphic" version of the three major epics of the ancient world: the *Iliad*, the *Odyssey*, and the *Aeneid*. Ovid's treatment of epic subject matter in these books systematically exploits the tension between his own and traditional epic narrative modes. The most obvious strategy he pursues is to compress and flatten the main lines of development, while expanding narrative detours, eccentric episodes, and the role of marginal characters. In roughly a hundred lines at the beginning of Book 12, Ovid runs through the main events leading to the Trojan War, including the sacrifice of IPHIGENIA, yet he exuberantly squanders some 30 of those lines on an elaborate imitation/travesty of the Virgilian description of Rumor *(Fama)* in the *Aeneid*. There follows an epic duel—not the duel between Hector and Achilles, but that between Cycnus and Achilles. Achilles cannot even fight a conventional fight against the invulnerable Cycnus and so must resort to battering and then throttling his adversary, who earns his place in Ovid's metamorphic narrative by turning into a swan at the moment of his death. Ovid deliberately plays on this non-Iliadic substitution by observing that Achilles was seeking either HECTOR or Cycnus in battle and engaged Cycnus, since, after all, he will not fight Hector until the war's 10th year. Yet the end of the book, fewer than 500 lines later, narrates Achilles' death. In both cases, Ovid conspicuously avoids Iliadic content by singling out episodes either long before or shortly after the events of Homer's *Iliad*.

The intervening episodes of the book include Nestor's tale about Caeneus, the grotesque battle of the Lapiths and centaurs, and Heracles' slaughter of Nestor's brothers. There is a subheroic tinge to all these stories. Caeneus was previously a woman named Caenis, who, after being raped by Neptune, persuaded the god to transform her into a man. Caeneus then became a renowned warrior. The battle of the Lapiths and centaurs is the longest episode in the book and tells how a marriage party degenerated into a drunken bloodbath. This gory narrative about largely undistinguished warriors and half-animal adversaries gets weighed down (deliberately, one assumes) in a series of ghastly mutilations and subheroic taunts. This substitution for Iliadic battle has the appearance of well-calculated travesty. Finally, Nestor's tale reveals his personal grief at the loss of his brothers and deeply held anger at Heracles—a very different Nestor from the Nestor of the *Iliad*, whose tales of past battles typically recalled the great men of old in order to stir the present generation to deeds of valor.

Book 13 begins with another post-Iliadic episode, the dispute of Ajax and Ulysses over the arms of Achilles. This story is a prime example of the kind of material that Homer largely avoids and that sets heroes in an unflattering light. Particularly notable in Ovid's version is the extent to which heroic deeds have been utterly displaced by words. Even Ajax, who stresses the value of his deeds by contrast with his opponent's clever eloquence, delivers a full-fledged oration. The remainder of the post-Iliadic narrative includes one of the most unpleasant episodes in mythology, Hecuba's vicious blinding of Polymestor for the death of her son Polydorus.

The end of the story of Troy allows for a smooth transition to the beginning of Aeneas's wanderings. In this case, too, Ovid runs rapidly and irreverently through events that, in Virgil's account, were of great moment and consequence, while developing at greater length figures and episodes that, in a more conventional epic frame, would be deemed minor. In general, Ovid favors relatively self-contained episodes within epic, or episodes marginally connected with the epic hero's story, rather than the core series of events that constitute the linear narrative drive. In this case, Ovid begins his metamorphic "Aeneid" in a fluid, almost casual style, relating the beginnings of Aeneas's wanderings with great geographical erudition but with little or nothing of the momentousness and ominous weight of the Virgilian narration. Even before he builds up any narrative momentum, the story veers off into the tale of Acis and Galatea, narrated by Galatea herself, followed by the tale of Scylla and Glaucus. We return to Aeneas's wanderings only about a hundred lines into Book 14. The impression of casual unconcern and levity with which Ovid drops Aeneas only to pick him up in the middle of the next book is masterful and calculated. The story of Dido and Aeneas, which attains the stature of a major tragedy within Virgil's epic, Ovid rapidly dispatches in a handful of deflating lines. Aeneas's trip to the underworld takes place with comparable rapidity and absence of ceremony. Greater attention is lavished on the figure of the Sibyl, condemned to live an immensely long life, growing older and older, more and more insubstantial, until she exists only as a voice. This desiccated Sibyl responds to Virgil's formidable figure and overpowering voice. Ovid deliberately attenuates her, but arguably, he also makes of her a more compelling and less pretentious figure. The reasons behind Ovid's interest in the Sibyl relate at least in part to the poetological concerns that pervade the poem: Her slow metamorphosis into disembodied voice anticipates the poet's own metamorphosis at the end of Book 15.

The continuation of Aeneas's story involves a sophisticated assimilation of Odyssean material that reflects and competes with Virgil's own incorporation of Odyssean figures and episodes. In Virgil's epic, Aeneas and his crew rescue Achaemenides, a member of Ulysses' crew who had been unscrupulously abandoned on the island of the CYCLOPES. The episode implicitly replays aspects of the Philoctetes story, while continuing to build up a negative image of Ulysses' duplicity by contrast with the "dutiful" and humane Aeneas. Ovid, in Book 14 of the *Metamorphoses*, intensifies the intertextual game by having Achaemenides meet yet another former member of Ulysses' crew, Macareus, at Cumae, where the two exchange stories that rework portions of the *Odyssey*. Achaemenides tells the story of his terrifying sojourn on the island of the Cyclopes and eventual rescue. Macareus then relates what happened to Ulysses and his crew after they departed from the island and in particular, their visit to the island of Circe. The entire sequence brilliantly explores the effects of internal narration in the epic tradition, kaleidoscopically shifting among different models, speakers, and viewpoints. The Polyphemus and Circe episodes in the *Odyssey* were themselves narrated by Odysseus in Phaeacia, while Achaemenides tells his story in Virgil's *Aeneid*. In Ovid's version, however, it is the lowly crew member, and not the hero Odysseus, who narrates the Circe episode. We thus see the episode from the perspective of one of the unlucky men turned into swine rather than of the leader who slept in Circe's bed. Comparably, Achaemenides recalls how Ulysses' loud taunting caused Polyphemus to hurl a boulder that nearly sank the departing ship. The shift in narrative focalization shows, among other things, how the same story undergoes a metamorphosis, depending on who is telling it. Ovid removes as speaker the self-confident and self-interested hero Ulysses, thereby transforming the episode's meaning and impact.

Ovid, furthermore, adds the story of Picus and Canens, which is told in neither the *Odyssey* nor the *Aeneid*. Significantly, however, the figure of Picus is mentioned in Virgil's description of the statues of ancestors in the palace of Latinus in *Aeneid* Book 7. Ovid thus carefully navigates between the two predecessor epics: Homer's *Odyssey* affords Circe a major role but makes no mention of Picus; Virgil's *Aeneid* consciously skirts Circe's shore without succumbing to the temptation of longer narrative yet does (merely) mention Picus. The poet of the *Metamorphoses* pointedly places the statue of Picus in Circe's palace, and appropriately exchanges the rustic, Italian cedarwood for white marble. Ovid demonstrates once again that he can make magnificent poetry out of other poets' leavings: He deftly puts two different epic poems in dialogue and at the same time makes his own poem, the meta-epic, that masterfully encompasses both.

The reasons for the extended focus on Circe are not hard to divine. Circe, with her divine status, powers of magical transformation, and erotically motivated vindictiveness is a perfect *Metamorphoses*-figure. We have already seen her use her powers of transformation in a previous story of frustrated desire and revenge (Scylla and Glaucus). While the *Aeneid* consciously avoids a Circe episode, Ovid makes Circe (naturally enough) the heroine of his metamorphic "Aeneid." In the story of Picus and Canens, Circe desires king Picus of Latium, who, however, already loves Canens, whose name means "singing" and who has a lovely singing voice. Picus refuses to yield to Circe, so she transforms him into a woodpecker (the literal meaning of his name). Canens slowly wastes away in grief in a place that came to be called by her name and was particularly honored by the Italian Muses, the Camenae. This story has among its themes transformation, voice, and song. Specifically, the story pits the aesthetically pleasing songs (*carmina*) of Canens against the vindictive spells (the same word in Latin, *carmina*) of Circe. Ovid thus accords a prominent place to a myth that foregrounds both his abiding theme of metamorphosis and his interest in the metamorphic aspects of voice and poetry.

The completion of Aeneas's story follows the same pattern of detour and compression. Ovid devotes a great deal of space to the Latin embassy to Diomedes, who refuses to help and, in the process, tells another story of metamorphosis. In similar fashion, Ovid goes on to describe the transformation of Aeneas's ships into sea nymphs—one of the stranger episodes in the *Aeneid*, but one that fits in perfectly with the tone and themes of the *Metamorphoses*. The actual conflict between the Trojans and the Rutulians receives only a brief description, the outcome an even briefer description: "and Turnus fell." Ovid, moreover, characterizes the conflict in a notably un-Virgilian way: He states that

as the war went on, they no longer fought for the realm nor for Lavinia, but for victory itself and pride. Turnus and Aeneas in this description appear quite starkly as late republican civil warriors—e.g., Caesar and Pompey, or Octavian and Antony—who cannot admit a rival or an insult to their dignity. Civil war is a constant subtext of the latter half of the *Aeneid*, but Aeneas's divinely justified motives remain largely untarnished. Finally, following the pattern established in his treatment of the Trojan War and Achilles, Ovid pursues Aeneas's story to the very end, narrating his death at the river Numicius and subsequent deification as Jupiter Indiges. Virgil imitates the more selective technique of Homer, who, in both epics, begins in medias res and does not end the poem with the end of the hero's life (although prophecy furnishes foreshadowing). The ending of Apollonius of Rhodes's *Voyage of the Argonauts* leaves Jason's life only partially told: The worst is yet to come. Ovid flouts the epic tradition by completing each hero's biography. Death and apotheosis, after all, are important phases in the history of transformation.

A pattern of heroic death followed by apotheosis begins to emerge near the end of the poem, and to import a hint of the narrative teleology that Ovidian epic otherwise largely avoids. After the story of Vertumnus and Pomona, Ovid returns again to heroic founder figures and tells the story of Romulus's foundation of Rome, the conflict with the Sabines, and the apotheosis of Romulus and his wife, Hersilia. Once again, the historical narrative is notably compressed. A brief sentence relates Romulus's founding of Rome, while the murder of his brother Remus goes unmentioned altogether. Book 14 ends, then, with the deification of Romulus and Hersilia; we are reminded that Book 12 ends with Achilles' death, while Book 15 culminates (but does not quite end) with the apotheosis of Julius Caesar. In the middle of Book 14, Aeneas dies and becomes a god. In the case of both Aeneas and Romulus, the divine parent—Venus and Mars, respectively—seeks deification for his or her child from Jupiter. Ovid now engages directly with key facets of Augustan ideology. Julius Caesar built the Temple of Venus Genetrix (Venus the Begetter) in his forum; Augustus built the Temple of Mars Ultor (Mars the Avenger) in his own forum adjacent to Caesar's. Romulus and Aeneas, sons of these gods and founders of Rome, are honored by statues in Augustus's forum and in the relief sculpture on the Altar of Augustan Peace. These two figures are significant in ideological terms because both Julius Caesar and, in a more circumspect way, Augustus associated themselves with Romulus as founder and monarch, while Aeneas is considered the originator of the Julian clan, and thus the ancestor of both Julius Caesar and Augustus.

Ovid's narrative closely follows the blueprint provided by this ideologically freighted genealogy. When the time for Caesar's death comes in Book 15, Venus complains bitterly to Jupiter. He responds that she cannot alter destiny, and he consoles her with a prophecy of Augustus's future career and with the opportunity to deify Julius Caesar's soul in the form of the famous star or comet that supposedly appeared after his death. With this series of deifications, Ovid is encouraging us to appreciate the metamorphosis of the epic tradition itself. Achilles, at the end of Book 12, simply died. The irreversibility of the Homeric hero's mortality is the basis of the tragic power and poignancy of the *Iliad*. Rome's heroes remain subject to death, as Jupiter insists, but they now receive a new compensation in the form of apotheosis. In observing this development, Ovid is also tracing a shift in the composition of the gods and in the very concept of divinity.

The *Metamorphoses* up to this point has explored the relations between gods and humans, and the difference in human and divine perspectives and experiences. Gods have not always been kind and merciful to mortals, as stories such as the punishment of Arachne demonstrate. The inclusion of Aeneas, Romulus, Julius Caesar, and, prospectively, Augustus among the gods brings us into new, specifically Roman and imperial territory. There are examples of apotheosis in Greek mythology (e.g., Heracles), and the idea of the leader as god in imperial Rome

appears to have been modeled on the concept of the divine ruler in the Hellenistic monarchies. For Ovid, however, the politics of deification comes to the fore explicitly in the Roman context near the end of the epic. He famously observes that Julius Caesar had to be made divine, lest Augustus be born of mortal seed. The comment reveals, by nakedly expressing, the teleological devices at work in the phenomenon of ruler deification in Rome and in literary texts such as the *Aeneid*.

It is not clear, however, that Ovid is willing to afford more than window dressing to such teleological schemes. Book 15, which tells of Caesar's apotheosis, is dominated by the long speech of Pythagoras on change as the underlying principle of the cosmos. Pythagoras's speech revisits the speech of Anchises in *Aeneid* Book 6 and its Platonic doctrine of metempsychosis. But the outcome of the Virgilian speech is to show Aeneas the long procession of the souls of the prospective great men of Rome waiting to assume their future bodies. Ovid's Pythagoras, by contrast, frequently alludes to the way that human souls will, in some future form, belong to an animal, and vice versa—hence his strong recommendation of vegetarianism. Change is continual, cyclical, and not obviously linear or progressive: There is no grand vision of Rome's future destiny at the culmination of Pythagoras's speech. The Hericlitean motto of *cuncta fluunt* ("all is flux . . .") cited by Pythagoras offers little traction to a teleological conception of historical progress, and some of Pythagoras's examples explicitly point to the evanescence of cities and civilizations. Ovid, moreover, juxtaposes the more ideologically charged transformations of Aeneas, Romulus, and Caesar with metamorphic love stories (e.g., Pomona and Vertumnus), which often occupy greater space. Teleology remains submerged within the fabric of continual, directionless change.

When Ovid does incorporate aspects of the teleological vision of the *Aeneid*, he does so in such a way as to lay bare deliberately the devices of historical narrative. Jupiter's consoling speech to Venus regarding the death of Julius Caesar not accidentally replays, in its basic outline, Jupiter's consoling speech to Venus in *Aeneid* Book 1 regarding the struggles of Aeneas. In Ovid's condensed and deliberately transparent version, Aeneas and Romulus participate in a patent ideological device. They are being mapped onto Augustus. History is telescopically shortened, and Aeneas prefigures Augustus with a directness Virgil might have abhorred. In the closing prayer, Ovid mixes the still-living Augustus in among the rest of Rome's major gods, some of them made into gods rather than born as gods—Aeneas, Romulus, Mars, Apollo, Jupiter, and Vesta (whose shrine has been incorporated into Augustus's house). Augustus, Ovid declares, will be a greater god than his father, as Agamemnon surpassed Atreus; Theseus, Aegeus; Achilles, Peleus; or, to choose the most appropriate comparison, as Jupiter surpassed Saturn. This series of mythological comparisons, with its mixture of overt panegyric and disturbing undertones, is an appropriate culmination of Ovid's exploration of continual change in the human and divine worlds. And yet this closing prayer is not quite the poem's end. There remains the coda, in which Ovid proclaims his own immortality and that of his work. Ovid, in the form of his monumental work, will live for all eternity—the poem's final instance of metamorphosis and final conversion of mortal achievement into immortal glory.

Metis A TITAN or OCEANID. Wife of ZEUS. Classical sources are Apollodorus's LIBRARY (1.2.1, 1.3.6) and Hesiod's THEOGONY (358, 886–900, 924–929). The parentage of Metis, whose name means "cunning intelligence," varies according to the source: She was either a Titan (in Apollodorus) or an Oceanid (in Hesiod). Metis helped Zeus defeat his father, CRONUS, by giving him the potion that Zeus used to induce Cronus to disgorge the other children he had swallowed. In some sources Metis is the mother of ATHENA. Zeus learned from GAIA and URANUS that Metis would bear Athena and that Metis's second child would be a son who would overthrow him. In order to forestall the prophecy, Zeus swallowed her. He afterward developed an agonizingly painful headache, and when HEPHAESTUS struck his head with an ax, Athena emerged, fully grown, wearing a helmet and carrying her armor.

Midas A king of Phrygia. Classical sources are Herodotus's *Histories* (8.138), Hyginus's *Fabulae* (191), and Ovid's *METAMORPHOSES* (11.85–193). Midas has two main myths, one involving SILENUS and DIONYSUS, and another featuring APOLLO and PAN. In the *Metamorphoses*, Midas rescued the inebriated Silenus, a follower of Dionysus, from peasants who were maltreating him. (Herodotus's *Histories* places Silenus's captivity in Midas's garden, where fragrant, abundant roses grew magically.) Midas liberated Silenus and gave him hospitality. In gratitude, Dionysus granted Midas a wish. Midas asked for the ability to turn objects to gold with his touch, but he soon regretted his wish when he found he could neither eat nor drink. He turned to Dionysus for help, and the god recommended that Midas wash himself in the river Pactolus to rid himself of his gift. The cure was successful, and the river afterward ran with gold. In the another legend, Midas observed the musical contest between Apollo and Pan but disagreed with the judgment of Tmolus in favor of Apollo. For uttering this judgment, Apollo punished Midas by giving him asses' ears. Ashamed, Midas attempted to hide his ears under a headdress and swore his hairdresser to secrecy, but his hairdresser could not resist speaking about what he saw. He dug a hole into which he whispered Midas's secret, and reeds that grew up there reported Midas's disgrace.

In classical art, Midas is bearded and sometimes crowned. In the context of his troubles with Apollo, he has asses' ears and wears either a headdress or a turban. Midas is depicted on an Attic red-figure amphora from ca. 480 B.C.E. (Johns Hopkins University Museum, Baltimore). The other side of the vase shows a captive Sile-

Apollo, Marsyas, and the Judgment of Midas. *Engraving, Melchior Meier, 1582 (Metropolitan Museum of Art, New York)*

nus accompanied by a hunter. An engraving by Melchior Meier from 1582, *Apollo, Marsyas, and the Judgment of Midas* (Metropolitan Museum of Art, New York), shows Apollo holding the flayed skin of Marsyas in the presence of Midas. It is evident that the bearded Midas has already pronounced his unfortunate preference for the music of Pan, because long asses' ears rise from his crown. A less common aspect of the myth is treated in Nicholas Poussin's *Midas Washing at the Source of the Pactolus* of 1624 (Metropolitan Museum of Art, New York).

Minerva   See ATHENA.

Minos   King of Crete. Son of ZEUS and EUROPA, brother of SARPEDON and Rhadaman-

thys. Classical sources include Apollodorus's LIBRARY (1.9.1, 1.9.26, 2.4.7, 2.5.7, 3.1.1–4, 3.15.1, 31.15.7–8, Epitome 1.7–15), Diodorus Siculus's LIBRARY OF HISTORY (4.60.2–62.1, 4.77, 4.79.1–4, 5.78), Herodotus's *Histories* (1.171, 3.122, 7.170), Homer's ILIAD (13.450–451, 14.322) and ODYSSEY (11.568–571, 19.178–180), Ovid's ARS AMATORIA (1.289–327) and METAMORPHOSES (7.456–458, 8.1–176), and Virgil's AENEID. Zeus, in the form of a bull, abducted Europa, took her to Crete, and had three children by her: Rhadamanthys, Sarpedon, and Minos. Minos was brought up by King Asterius of Crete and married PASIPHAE: His children by her include Deucalion, Glaucus, Androgeus, ARIADNE, and PHAEDRA. When Asterius died, there was a dispute over kingship, and Minos, to prove that the gods supported him, asked POSEIDON to send

Minos. *William Blake, illustration for* The Divine Comedy, *1824–27 (National Gallery of Victoria, Melbourne, Australia)*

him a bull from the depths, promising to sacrifice it to the god. Poseidon sent a magnificent bull, but Minos, instead of sacrificing it, kept the bull among his herds. Poseidon therefore punished Minos by making his wife, Pasiphae, fall in love with the bull. The Athenian artisan Daedalus contrived a wooden cow, in which Pasiphae was able to mate with the bull. The offspring of their union was Asterius, better known as the MINOTAUR, a creature that was half man and half bull. Daedalus was asked to build the Labyrinth to contain it.

When Minos's son Androgeus was killed in Athens after an athletic competition, Minos went to war against Athens. At one point, he was laying siege to Megara, and the daughter of King Nisus of Megara, Scylla, fell in love with him. She betrayed her father by stealing from his head the purple lock of hair that

guaranteed the preservation of his kingdom. In Ovid's *Metamorphoses*, Minos recoils from her act and departs in his ship. Scylla pursues him desperately, and both she and her father are transformed into birds: She is a bird called ciris, and he is an osprey pursuing her. In Apollodorus, Minos binds Scylla to the prow of his ship and drowns her. As the war with Athens dragged on, Minos prayed to Zeus for vengeance. The Athenians were afflicted with famine and plague, and an oracle informed them that they had to submit to Minos's conditions. He demanded an annual tribute of seven girls and seven boys to be handed over to the Minotaur. One year, THESEUS managed to be selected as one of the victims, and he slew the Minotaur with the help of Minos's daughter Ariadne, who had fallen in love with him. She helped Theseus escape the Labyrinth by giving him a thread, on Daedalus's advice, so that he could retrace his path. Ariadne was later abandoned by Theseus on the island of Naxos.

Minos, angered by the help Daedalus gave to Theseus, imprisoned him and his son ICARUS in the Labyrinth. Daedalus constructed wings for himself and his son, and they escaped by flight, but Icarus died when he flew too close to the Sun, which melted the wax holding together his wings. Minos pursued Daedalus to Sicily, where the artisan had taken refuge with King Cocalus. Herodotus reports that Minos died a violent death there while pursuing Daedalus, and Apollodorus states that Cocalus's daughters killed him, possibly by scalding him with boiling water. Minos had a reputation as a wise king and lawgiver, and after his death, he became one of the judges of souls in Hades, in addition to Rhadamanthys and AEACUS. Yet he also had a reputation as a philanderer and a cruel tyrant. This bifurcation of Minos's tradition is further complicated by references to a second Minos, son of Minos's son Lycastus and thus grandson of the Zeus-born Minos. Possibly the second Minos was invented to account for apparent contradictions in his mythic reputation.

Minotaur (Minotauros)   A hybrid creature, half human and half bull. Classical sources are Apollodorus's *LIBRARY* (3.1.4, 3.15.8, Epitome 1.7–9), Diodorus Siculus's *LIBRARY OF HISTORY* (1.61, 4.61, 4.77), Ovid's *HEROIDES* (10.101–102) and *METAMORPHOSES* (8.155–173), and Virgil's *AENEID* (5.588–591). During a battle for kingship, King MINOS of Crete asked that a sacrificial bull be sent to him by POSEIDON. Poseidon obliged, expecting that the bull would be sacrificed to him, but Minos was taken with the bull's beauty and decided not to sacrifice it. In revenge, Poseidon inflamed King Minos's wife, PASIPHAE, with a passion for the bull, which, with DAEDALUS's connivance, she was able to satisfy and the Minotaur was the result of this union. Upon its birth, it was kept in a labyrinth built by Daedalus. Sacrifices of seven young women and seven young men were regularly made to the

Theseus Dragging the Minotaur from the Labyrinth. *Detail from Attic cup, ca. 440 B.C.E. (British Museum, London; photograph © Marie-Lan Nguyen)*

Minotaur until the hero THESEUS killed it with the help of Minos's daughter, ARIADNE.

The Minotaur was frequently represented in classical art, usually with the head of a bull and the lower body of a man. The Minotaur is often shown with Theseus, as in an Attic black-figure hydria from ca. 550 B.C.E. (Harvard University Art Museums, Cambridge, Mass.). Here, Theseus holds the creature while stabbing it with a sword. A similar scene is shown on an Attic red-figure clay cup from ca. 440 B.C.E. (British Museum, London).

Minthe (Menthe)   See PERSEPHONE.

Mnemosyne   A TITAN, the personification of Memory. Daughter of GAIA (Earth) and URANUS (Heaven). Sister of IAPETUS, HYPERION, COEUS, Crius, Cronus, OCEANUS, PHOEBE, RHEA, TETHYS, THEIA, and THEMIS. The classical source is Hesiod's *THEOGONY* (53–62, 132–136, 915–917). Mnemosyne lay nine nights with ZEUS, and the nine MUSES were born from their union. Mnemosyne appears in genealogies from the time of Hesiod, but she does not otherwise appear in mythology or cult practice.

Muses   Greek goddesses of poetic inspiration. Daughters of MNEMOSYNE (Memory) or HARMONIA and ZEUS, or of GAIA and URANUS. Classical sources are Apollodorus's *LIBRARY* (1.3.1–4, 3.5.8, Epitome 7.18), Hesiod's *THEOGONY* (1–115, 915–917), Homer's *ILIAD* (2.594–600) and *ODYSSEY* (8.63–64), Pausanias's *Description of Greece* (5.18.4, 9.34.3), and Pindar's *Pythian Odes* (3.86–92). The Muses were said to live on Mount Olympus and inspire the arts, literature, and philosophy; in this, they are similar to the GRACES, and like the Graces, they are attributed different origins, number, and associations. Mount Helicon was sacred to them, but they were worshipped in other regions. According to Hesiod, there were nine Muses: Calliope, Clio, Euterpe, Terpischore, Erato, Melpomene,

The Allegory of Painting. *Johannes Vermeer ca. 1666 (Kunsthistorisches Museum, Vienna)*

Thalia, Polyhymnia, and Urania. Later the Muses became associated with specific literary genres—epic, history, lyric, etc.—but these associations were not fixed. The Muses were closely associated with APOLLO in his role as god of music and poetry, and they were the judges in the musical competition between him and the satyr MARSYAS. The Muses themselves engaged in a musical competition with Thamyris, whom they defeated and afterward blinded. The skilled musician ORPHEUS was the son of Calliope and was buried by the Muses after his death.

Muses are frequently addressed in literary works, their most famous invocation being the opening verses of Homer's *Iliad* and *Odyssey*, but they were also invoked by Virgil, Dante, Milton, and Shakespeare. Postclassical aesthetic writings, particularly during the Renaissance, placed great importance on the Muses and their role in the arts, and solidified their respective associations with history, music, and poetry.

Like the Graces, the Muses were represented in classical sculpture and painting, though, unlike the Graces, who tended to appear as a group, the Muses were represented both individually and as a group of nine. The Muses were depicted as long-robed figures, sometimes carrying attributes: a lyre, pipes, scrolls, or tablets. All nine Muses appear on a Roman sarcophagus from ca. 225 C.E. (Galleria Borghese, Rome). They also appear on the main image of the Attic black-figure François Vase from ca. 570 B.C.E. (Museo Archeologico Nazionale, Florence). A single Muse appears, holding a lyre, on an Attic red-figure kylix from ca. 440 B.C.E. (Museum of Fine Arts, Boston) in the company of Apollo.

A 17th-century painting by Vermeer, *The Allegory of Painting*, shows an artist painting the portrait of a young woman in contemporary dress as Clio, Muse of History. As in the classical images, Clio is crowned with laurel and carries a musical instrument and book.

Myrrha (Smyrna)   See ADONIS.

N

Naiads See NYMPHS.

Narcissus Son of the river god Cephisus and the nymph Liriope. Classical sources are Ovid's *METAMORPHOSES* (3.339–510) and Pausanias's *Description of Greece* (9.31.7–9). Narcissus was a handsome youth who fell in love with his own reflection. He persisted in gazing at his reflection in a river until he was transformed into the flower that bears his name. Ovid links Narcissus's fate to his rejection of many suitors, among them the nymph ECHO. Echo fell in love with him but, with her limited speech, was unable to make him understand her, and in her grief, the nymph withered away to nothing but a voice. Pausanias claims Narcissus loved his own image because it brought to mind the image of a beloved twin sister who had died.

In classical art, Narcissus is depicted perched on the edge of a stream or together with the disappointed Echo, for example, in a third-style wall painting from the House of Marcus Lucretius Fronto of ca. 20 B.C.E. in Pompeii. In a similar Pompeian fresco (Museo Archeologico Nazionale, Naples), Narcissus's reflection appears in the stream, a cupid points at Narcissus, and Echo gazes longingly at Narcissus. Postclassical images include Benjamin West's *Narcissus* of 1805 (Alexander Gallery, New York) and J. W. Waterhouse's *Echo and Narcissus* of 1903 (Walker Art Gallery, Liverpool).

Narcissus and Echo. *Pompeian fresco, first century C.E. (Museo Archeologico Nazionale, Naples)*

Nemean Lion An enormous Lion, impervious to weapons, offspring of Orthus and CHIMAERA. Classical sources are Apollodorus's *LIBRARY* (2.5.1), Diodorus Siculus's *LIBRARY OF HISTORY* (4.11.3–4), and Hesiod's *THEOGONY* (326–332). HERACLES defeated the Nemean

Lion in the first of his Twelve Labors. He cornered the lion in a rocky impasse, strangled it, then skinned it. The skin, which became one of his principal attributes, protected him during his further adventures. A black-figure (white-ground) oinochoe from ca. 520 B.C.E. (British Museum, London) shows Heracles grasping the standing lion during their struggle.

Neoptolemus   Son of ACHILLES and Deidamia. Neoptolemus is also called Pyrrhus. Neoptolemus appears in Euripides' ANDROMACHE and ORESTES and in Sophocles' PHILOCTETES. Additional classical sources are Apollodorus's LIBRARY (3.13.8, Epitome 5.10–11, 6.56.12–14), Homer's ILIAD (19.326–333) and ODYSSEY (3.188–189, 4.5–9, 11.505–540), Pindar's *Nemean Odes* (7.34–48), Strabo's *Geography* (9.3.9), and Virgil's AENEID (2.469–558). Achilles sired Neoptolemus during an episode on the island of Scyros, when he disguised himself as a woman (see Statius's ACHILLEID). In Homer's *Odyssey*, Odysseus tells Achilles' shade in the underworld how he brought Neoptolemus to Troy, where he displayed valor in battle; he was among the warriors in the wooden horse and was crucial to the success of the Trojan War after Achilles' death. According to PINDAR and Virgil's *Aeneid*, Neoptolemus killed PRIAM, who had sought refuge at the altar of *Zeus Herkeios*. In some versions, he is said to have killed ASTYANAX and to have led the sacrifice of POLYXENA. In Sophocles' *Philoctetes*, Neoptolemus accompanies the unscrupulous ODYSSEUS on his expedition to obtain PHILOCTETES, whose bow, according to prophecy, was required to win the Trojan War. In Sophocles' play, Neoptolemus is an honorable young man who sympathizes with the ruthlessly manipulated Philoctetes. On his return home, Neoptolemus marries HERMIONE, daughter of MENELAUS and HELEN, since Menelaus offered her to Neoptolemus to firm up his support of the war. According to Euripides' *Orestes*, however, Tyndareus had previously offered her in marriage to ORESTES. In Euripides' *Andro-*

mache, Orestes persuades Hermione to depart with him despite her marriage to Neoptolemus. According to the same play, Neoptolemus loved his captive ANDROMACHE, with whom he had a son, Molossus, but had no feelings for Hermione. Orestes arranges to have Neoptolemus ambushed and killed at Delphi. The stories of his death vary greatly, however. In other versions, Orestes himself killed him, or according to Pindar, Neoptolemus was killed in a dispute over sacrificial meat at Delphi. Neoptolemus had a tomb and received cult at Delphi.

Nephele   See ATHAMAS; PHRIXUS.

Neptune   See POSEIDON.

Nereids   Nymphs of the sea. Daughters of Nereus and Doris (an OCEANID). Classical sources are Apollodorus's LIBRARY (1.2.7, 1.9.25, 2.4.3, 3.13.6), Apollonius of Rhodes's VOYAGE OF THE ARGONAUTS (4.922–964), Hesiod's THEOGONY (240–264), and Homer's ILIAD (18.35–69) and ODYSSEY (24.47–64). Like the other nymphs, the Nereids were targets for the amorous proclivities of gods, satyrs, and other sylvan creatures. The Nereid AMPHITRITE was the wife of POSEIDON, god of the sea. In Hesiod's *Theogony*, Amphitrite is fair-ankled and can calm the waves of the sea, but in Homer's *Odyssey*, she represents the sea in a darker capacity: She breeds sea monsters, and her great waves crash against the rocks. Another Nereid, GALATEA, was loved by the cyclopes POLYPHEMUS. Nereids appear in the company of POSEIDON, APHRODITE, who was born from the sea, or TRITONS, male sea divinities. Their attributes are dolphins and other sea creatures. A postclassical image of a Nereid is Raphael's *Triumph of Galatea* from 1511 in the Villa Farnesina (Rome).

Nessus   A CENTAUR. Classical sources are Apollodorus's LIBRARY (2.7.6), Ovid's METAMORPHOSES (9.101–133), and Sophocles'

TRACHINIAE (555–581). When Nessus attempted to abduct HERACLES's bride, DEIANIRA, Heracles killed him with an arrow. The dying Nessus tricked Deianira, however, into preserving some of his blood as a "love potion," and years later she unwittingly poisoned Heracles with it, causing his death.

Visual representations of Nessus center on his abduction of Deianira, as on an Attic black-figure hydria from ca. 560 B.C.E. (Louvre, Paris), where Nessus, with Deianira astride his back, flees from a pursuing Heracles.

Nestor   King of Pylos. The youngest son of Neleus and Chloris (Meliboea). Classical sources .are Apollodorus's LIBRARY (1.9.9, 2.7.3), Homer's ILIAD (passim) and ODYSSEY (3.4–485, 24.43–57), Ovid's METAMORPHOSES (8.365–368), Pausanias's Description of Greece (3.26.8–10, 4.36.1–2), and Pindar's Pythian Odes (6.28–42). Nestor was the sole survivor of Heracles' massacre of the sons of Neleus (see Metamorphoses Book 12). Nestor helped MENELAUS assemble the Greek heroes for the Trojan expedition and went to the war himself with his sons Antilochus and Thrasymedes. He is an important figure in Homer's Iliad. Nestor is especially valued for his wise counsel and skill in speaking; he is often a voice of diplomacy. He attempts to arbitrate between ACHILLES and AGAMEMNON during their quarrel, and suggests the embassy to Achilles. On other occasions, he tries to rouse the spirits of his fellow warriors and recalls the great battles of his youth, e.g., his conflicts with the neighboring Epeians and the battle of the Lapiths and CENTAURS. Nestor's long speeches about the superior valor of the old days and his tendency to offer wordy advice have made him seem in the eyes of some modern readers like a Greek Polonius, prolix and tedious, yet in an ancient Greek context, his great capacity for fluid, persuasive speech appears to have been valued. Later in the Trojan War, MEMNON attacked Nestor, and his son Antilochus died in the act of saving him. Exceptionally among the major Greek heroes, Nestor arrived safely back in Pylos without notable difficulty. TELEMACHUS visits him there in search of news about his father in Homer's Odyssey. Nestor, who lived three generations, became a byword for long life in antiquity. There is no known account of his death.

Niobe   Daughter of TANTALUS and wife of Amphion of Thebes. Classical sources are Diodorus Siculus's LIBRARY OF HISTORY (4.74), Euripides' PHOENICIAN WOMEN (159–160), Homer's ILIAD (24.599–620), Ovid's METAMORPHOSES (6.146–312), Sophocles' ANTIGONE (823–835), and Statius's THEBAID (6.124–125). Amphion and Niobe had a large number of children, between five and 10 of each sex (depending on the source), called Niobids. Niobe was very proud of her children and boasted that she was a superior mother to LETO, who had only two children. Leto's children, APOLLO and ARTEMIS, sought revenge for the insult to Leto: Apollo's arrows killed her sons and Artemis's her daughters. In the Iliad, Niobe's dead children remained unburied for 10 days until the gods themselves buried them on the 11th day. In her grief, Niobe turned to stone from which tears continued to stream. In another version of the story, the sole survivor of the Niobids was Meliboea, later called Chloris. Meliboea became the wife of Neleus and the mother of NESTOR.

Two aspects of this myth have been represented in the arts. The massacre of the Niobids by Apollo and Artemis is usually shown as the Niobids run to escape the shower of arrows rained down upon them; and Niobe is shown grieving for her lost children. These images have appeared on antique vases, on sarcophagi, and in painting.

Notus   The offspring of Eos (Dawn) and Astraeus. The classical source is Hesiod's THEOGONY (378–380, 869–871). Notus is one of the ANEMOI (the Venti, for the Romans), the storm winds associated with the four cardinal points: BOREAS, the North Wind; Notus, the

South Wind; ZEPHYRUS, the West Wind; and EURUS, the East Wind. In some accounts, they are descended from TYPHOEUS, and according to Homer, Ovid, and Virgil, they were under the control of AEOLUS. "Swift-pathed" Notus, although associated with the south, brings severe storms in late summer and autumn. In visual representation, the winds were depicted as men, sometimes winged.

Nymphs Young female nature spirits. Classical sources are the *Homeric Hymn to Pan* (19–23), the *Homeric Hymn to Dionysus* (3–10), and the *Homeric Hymn to Aphrodite* (5.259ff), Callimachus's *Hymns* (4.79–85), Hesiod's THEOGONY (129–130, 184–187), Homer's ILIAD (20.7–9) and ODYSSEY (6.105–108, 122–124; 13.103–104, 347–350, 355–360; 17.210–211, 240–246), and Ovid's FASTI (4.231–232) and METAMORPHOSES (6.453f, 8.738–810, 11.47f). Nymphs were associated with either water (springs, fountains, rivers), trees, or mountains. Freshwater nymphs were Naiads, while sea nymphs, daughters of NEREUS and OCEANUS, were NEREIDS and OCEANIDS, respectively. Oreads were mountain nymphs. Hamadryads were tree nymphs, and Dryads were specifically connected with oak trees. Nymphs appear in myths that take place in a sylvan setting, in the company of ARTEMIS, PAN, and DIONYSUS. In the myth of HYLAS, the nymphs of a spring fall in love with and abduct the youth. ECHIDNA and SCYLLA were two nymphs transformed into monsters by angered Olympian gods.

Nyx (Night) A primordial being representing night. Classical sources are Hesiod's THEOGONY (123–125, 211–225) and Homer's ILIAD (14.256–261). In Greek genealogies, Nyx is a primordial spirit from which various personifications are born. In the *Theogony*, Nyx emerges from Chaos and is sister to Erebus. With Erebus, Nyx conceives and gives birth to Aether (Brightness) and Hemera (Day). Next, Nyx parthenogenetically brought forth Blame, Death, Deceit, Destinies, Distress, Doom, Dreams, Fate, Nemesis, Old Age, Sleep, and Strife. From Nyx also emerge the HESPERIDES and the FATES. In general, the children of "black" Nyx are dark aspects of life. In Homer's *Iliad*, Nyx has power over mortals and immortals, and even ZEUS is wary of her. Zeus did not punish HYPNUS for lulling him to sleep at HERA's request, because he did not want to displease Nyx.

Oceanids Nymphs of the sea. Daughters of Oceanus and Tethys. The Oceanids form the chorus in PROMETHEUS BOUND. Additional classical sources are the *Homeric Hymn to Demeter* (5, 415), the *Orphic Hymn to the Nymphs*, Apollodorus's *LIBRARY* (1.8.1), Catullus's *Carmina* (3.12, 40), and Hesiod's *THEOGONY* (346). The Oceanids were said by Hesiod to number 3,000. As with other nymphs, Oceanids attracted the amorous attentions of gods, satyrs and other sylvan creatures. Oceanids appear in the company of Poseidon and Aphrodite or with Tritons, male sea divinities. Their attributes are dolphins and other sea creatures.

Oceanus (Okeanos) A Titan, the Greek personification of the Sea. Son of Gaia (Earth) and Uranus (Heaven). Brother of Iapetus, Hyperion, Coeus, Crius, Cronus, Mnemosyne, Phoebe, Rhea, Tethys, Theia, and Themis. Classical sources are the *Homeric Hymn to Demeter* (418ff), Apollodorus's *LIBRARY* (1.1.3, 1.2.2ff, 1.5.2), Hesiod's *THEOGONY* (133ff, 337–370, 787–791), Homer's *ILIAD* (14.200–210, 246, 301–308; 21.193–199; 23.205) and *ODYSSEY* (4.567f, 11.13, 639, 12.1), and Ovid's *METAMORPHOSES* (13.949–955). Oceanus married his sister Tethys, and their offspring were the 25 Rivers (among them the Nile) and the 3,000 Oceanids. The most important of the rivers descended from Oceanus

and Tethys is the river Styx, which marks the boundary between earth and Hades. Oceanus appears with some frequency in the *Theogony*, as he personifies the most important freshwater river that encircled the earth and also provided a physical location for the "ends of the earth." Though Oceanus appears in genealogies beginning with Hesiod, he does not otherwise appear in mythology or cult practice.

Odysseus (Ulysses) King of Ithaca. Son of Laertes and Anticlea. Husband of Penelope and father of Telemachus. Odysseus appears in Euripides' *IPHIGENIA AT AULIS*, *HECUBA*, and *TROJAN WOMEN*; Homer's *ILIAD* (passim); and Sophocles' *PHILOCTETES*. Homer's *ODYSSEY* treats Odysseus's return journey from Troy. Additional classical sources are Apollodorus's *LIBRARY* (Epitome 7), Hyginus's *Fabulae* (14, 125–127, 141), and Ovid's *METAMORPHOSES* (13, passim). According to a more hostile tradition, Sisyphus seduced Anticlea before her marriage to Laertes and was the father of Odysseus. Odysseus was one of the suitors of Helen, hence obliged to join the Trojan expedition. According to a story in the *Cypria*, a poem in the Epic Cycle, he feigned madness to avoid going to war, but Palamedes revealed the deception. Odysseus later concocted a plan to have Palamedes killed (see Palamedes).

Odysseus is credited with retrieving ACHILLES from Scyros and exposing his feminine disguise (see Statius's ACHILLEID). In Homer's *Iliad*, Odysseus consistently displays excellence in battle and is a shrewd tactician and counselor. His quick thinking prevents the exodus of the Greek army after AGAMEMNON's badly miscalculated speech following his dream in Book 2. In Book 9, Odysseus leads the embassy to Achilles. His eloquence is impressive, if ineffectual in this instance. He participates successfully in the night raid of Book 10. Throughout, Odysseus is shrewd, tactically alert, courageous, and ruthless in pursuit of martial advantage.

Odysseus's post-Iliadic career at Troy is no less remarkable. In one instance, he had himself flogged and dressed in rags to infiltrate

Odysseus Consulting the Shade of Tiresias. *Detail from a calyx krater, Fourth century B.C.E. (Louvre, Paris)*

the city of Troy as a beggar. In the wooden horse, Odysseus restrained the other Greeks who were tempted to cry out in response to Helen's simulation of their wives' voices (both stories are told to Telemachus at Sparta in the *Odyssey*). Odysseus and DIOMEDES are credited with stealing the Palladium, the cult statue of Athena, from Troy. After the death of Achilles, AJAX and Odysseus each claimed the honor of being the Greek hero most worthy of inheriting his armor. Odysseus won the dispute, and Ajax committed suicide. *Odyssey* Book 11 alludes to the affair, which is also the subject of Sophocles' *AJAX* (see also Ovid's *Metamorphoses* 13). ASTYANAX's killer is sometimes identified as Diomedes, sometimes as Odysseus.

Others Greek warriors had difficulty on their return journeys *(nostoi)* from Troy, but Odysseus's return was exceptionally difficult and long (10 years). His return became even more difficult after he destroyed the single eye of POSEIDON's son POLYPHEMUS, thereby attracting the god's anger. The canonical account of Odysseus's voyage home is Homer's *Odyssey*. At the epic's beginning, Odysseus is detained by the nymph CALYPSO, while his son and wife, besieged by suitors for Penelope's hand, wonder whether he is still alive. Penelope holds out desperately against the suitors, who pressure her to choose a new husband from among them, all the while consuming Odysseus's household resources. Odysseus departs from Calypso's island, then is shipwrecked on Scheria, where King Alcinous hosts him, and Odysseus tells the long story of his adventures (the lotus-eaters, Polyphemus's cave, AEOLUS and the bag of the winds, the Laestrygonians, the voyage to the underworld, the SIRENS, SCYLLA and CHARYBDIS, the cattle of the Sun). Alcinous and the Phaeacians send the hero home to Ithaca laden with great treasures. He stays with the loyal swineherd Eumaeus, meets his son, then disguises himself as a beggar to infiltrate his own household in preparation for the final battle with the suitors. After the slaughter, and Odysseus and Penelope's long-awaited reunion,

Odysseus, Telemachus, and Laertes face the parents of the murdered suitors in battle, and Athena imposes peace after a brief encounter. The post-Homeric *Telegony*, a poem in the Epic Cycle, tells how Telegonus, son of Odysseus by Circe, kills Odysseus by accident. According to the Homeric Tiresias, a mysterious, peaceful death "from the sea" will come to Odysseus in his old age. Odysseus is also credited with the foundation of various Italian cities and is identified as the father of Italian founder figures such as Ardeas and Latinus.

In Athenian tragedy, Odysseus is usually a heartless practitioner of realpolitik (see Euripides' *Iphigenia at Aulis*, *Trojan Women*, and *Hecuba*). The Odysseus of Sophocles' *Ajax* is magnanimous enough to recognize the greatness of his dead adversary; in the *Philoctetes*, he is unscrupulous. In Roman texts, the negative image takes root even more fixedly, both because of the influence of the Euripidean characterization and because of the Romans' lower estimate of the qualities of cunning and guile. Odysseus is magnificent in Homer above all as a trickster, the versatile man of "many turns." Odysseus is, not coincidentally, nephew of the trickster Autolycus, who gave him his name and identity, in addition to providing a significant etymology for Odysseus's name ("man of hatred"). The story of Sisyphean paternity stresses the same traits of outrageously controversial character and cunning trickery. Particularly notable are Odysseus's nearly compulsive lying tales, the suppression of his identity and name, and his seemingly infinite capacity for self-restraint and self-degradation in the name of ultimate tactical advantage. Odysseus is the complementary opposite of the frank and emotionally unrestrained Achilles. Between his two epics, Homer manages to describe the full range of heroic virtues.

Odysseus's adventures were well represented in classical art. In a fourth-century red-figure calyx krater by the Dolon Painter, Odysseus is shown consulting Tiresias's ghost in Hades (Louvre, Paris). Odysseus's adventures were less frequently represented in the postclassical period; an interesting example is J. W. Waterhouse's *Ulysses and the Sirens* of 1891 (National Gallery of Victoria, Melbourne). The crew of Odysseus's ship have stopped their ears, and Odysseus is bound against the mast, so that they may not be affected by the Sirens' song.

Odyssey Homer (eighth/seventh century B.C.E.) While we know little to nothing about the poet called Homer, the epic poems ascribed to him were probably composed in the eighth or seventh centuries B.C.E. Sometimes scholars have argued that the *Iliad* was composed earlier, but there is no secure basis for this argument. The style of the poems strongly suggests that they come out of an oral tradition of improvisatory song, but their transmission as texts demands the intervention of writing at some stage. To what extent writing is integral to the composition of Homeric epic is debated. In short, a great deal of uncertainty surrounds the identity of the author(s) of the Homeric epics, the date of their composition, and the circumstances in which they came to be written (see Homer).

While the *Iliad* narrates a series of events in the Trojan War, the *Odyssey* concerns the postwar phase of *nostos* ("return journey"). Many of the returning Greek heroes paid for their destructive acts at Troy with failed *nostoi*, whether they were lost at sea or, as in Agamemnon's case, encountered violence at home. While Odysseus (Ulysses) was among the preeminent warriors at Troy, he truly excels in his return to Ithaca. His return is long, difficult, and painful. He loses all his companions by the end, faces the constant opposition of Poseidon, and makes it home only after 10 years of wandering. That he does finally return, however, and drive out the suitors who have occupied his palace attests to his extraordinary qualities. A ferocious temperament and unmatched excellence in battle characterized Achilles. Odysseus, by comparison, displays the qualities of patience, diplomatic tact, strategic cunning, and

Ulysses and the Sirens. *John William Waterhouse, 1891 (National Gallery of Victoria, Melbourne)*

an unusual capacity for self-concealment and self-restraint. The *nostos* hero must often check his impulses, withhold information about himself, and consider how most tactfully and skillfully to manage the many hosts with whom he is obliged to stay on his long journey. Through these qualities, Odysseus not only survives the war but manages to return home successfully and to enjoy the remainder of his life.

SYNOPSIS

Book 1

The poet calls on the MUSES to tell the story of Odysseus, who returns home after long wanderings and having lost all his companions. Now the nymph CALYPSO holds him prisoner in her cave; the enmity of Poseidon obstructs his return, but ATHENA pities him, and, in conversation with ZEUS, decides to visit Odysseus's son, TELEMACHUS, in the guise of the mortal, Mentes, while sending HERMES to Calypso to demand Odysseus's release. Suitors for PENELOPE's hand in marriage now occupy Odysseus's palace on Ithaca and are eating away his property. The young Telemachus cannot turn them out, but Athena, in the form of Mentes, encourages him to address the suitors, bid them return to their homes, then go on his own to seek news of his father from NESTOR in Pylos and MENELAUS in Sparta.

Book 2

Telemachus calls together a public assembly and addresses the issue of the suitors' ruinous occupation of Odysseus's palace. They claim, in response, that Penelope has been leading them on with delays, and that they will leave if she will only choose a husband from among them. Telemachus responds that he will go to Pylos and Sparta to seek news of his father, and if he hears that Odysseus is alive, he will wait for him for another year, and if not, he will conduct burial rites and give away his mother in marriage. Athena, in the form of Mentes, discusses plans with Telemachus for his voyage. The suitors offer further insults, but Telemachus obtains aid from the faithful nurse Eurycleia in preparing provisions for his voyage. Athena prepares the ship and crew, and they depart.

Book 3

They arrive in Pylos and are hospitably received by Nestor. Telemachus eventually asks for news of his father. Nestor recalls the events at Troy, and how, on their return, the Greek fleet was separated into different groups; he does not know what happened to Odysseus and his companions. At Telemachus's urging, he also tells the story of Aegisthus, Clytaemnestra, Agamemnon, and Orestes. Athena, as she departs, turns into an eagle to everyone's amazement. Nestor bids them sacrifice to the goddess and congratulates Telemachus on the divine favor shown to him. The next day, Telemachus, accompanied by Nestor's son Peisistratus, departs for Sparta.

Book 4

Telemachus arrives in Sparta amid wedding festivities and is hospitably welcomed by Menelaus. He does not reveal his identity immediately, but Helen and Menelaus soon guess that he is Odysseus's son. As the guests recall with sorrow their personal losses because of the Trojan War, Helen puts a drug into their wine that will induce forgetfulness. Helen and Menelaus tell stories of Odysseus's exploits at Troy, and they go to bed. The next day, Telemachus asks Menelaus whether he has heard any news of his father, and Menelaus replies at length: While in Egypt, he learned of Agamemnon's and Ajax's deaths from the shape shifter Proteus, but also that Odysseus was still alive, imprisoned by Calypso. In the meanwhile, in Ithaca, the suitors learn of Telemachus's trip and plot to kill him on his return. Medon the herald conveys the plan to Penelope, who is deeply distressed. Athena sends a phantom image of a mortal woman, Iphthime, to comfort Penelope. The suitors prepare their ambush.

Book 5

At Athena's behest, Zeus sends Hermes to Calypso's island to command her to release Odysseus. She consents reluctantly and helps Odysseus build and fit out a boat. After he departs, Poseidon sends a violent storm against him, but with the help of Athena and Cadmus's daughter Ino (now the goddess Leucothea), he manages to swim naked to the shores of Phaeacia. He takes shelter under bushes and falls asleep exhausted.

Book 6

Athena appears in the dreams of Nausicaa, princess of Phaeacia, and inspires her to go with her companions to the seaside to wash clothing in preparation for her marriage. Odysseus awakes at the sound of the girls at play, covers his nakedness with a leafy branch, and speaks with Nausicaa. She gives him clothing, food, and directions to the palace of her father, Alcinous.

Book 7

Athena surrounds Odysseus with a mist so that the Phaeacians, who are not noted for being friendly to strangers, cannot see him, and, in the form of a young girl, directs him to the palace. Odysseus enters the richly adorned palace with its elegant gardens. He supplicates Queen Arete directly, seeking conveyance back to his homeland. Alcinous and Arete graciously offer hospitality and help; they ask him who he is, but Odysseus reveals only that he has suffered misfortune, has come from the island of Calypso, and seeks to return home. After renewing offers of help, they withdraw for the night.

Book 8

Alcinous commences preparations for a ship to convey Odysseus home, and, in the meantime, holds festivities in his honor. The bard Demodocus sings of the Trojan War and of a quarrel between Odysseus and Achilles. Odysseus must cover his face with a cloak to hide his tears. In the discus throwing that follows, Odysseus, challenged by an insolent young man, wins the contest. The subsequent entertainment includes Demodocus's telling of the story of Ares, Aphrodite, and Hephaestus. The Phaeacians continue to honor Odysseus, and Odysseus asks Demodocus to sing of the Trojan horse. He weeps uncontrollably as he listens. Demodocus then asks Odysseus to reveal his identity; otherwise, the Phaeacians' magically self-guided ships will not know where to take him.

Book 9

Odysseus reveals his name and the land of his origins. He then relates his adventures since he left Troy. He and his men stop first at the land of Cicones, where they enter into a pitched battle with the local inhabitants, in which some of Odysseus's companions die. They next go to the land of the lotus-eaters: Some of the men eat the lotus plant and do not wish to leave; Odysseus must drag them back to the ships. Finally, they arrive at the land of the CYCLOPES, an uncivilized race of herdsman. Odysseus and his men explore the island, and come upon the cave of a giant. Odysseus's men wish to take provisions from the cave and leave, but Odysseus insists on waiting for a proper exchange of hospitality. The one-eyed Cyclopes POLYPHEMUS arrives, refuses hospitality, and devours some of Odysseus's men. They are trapped inside because of the massive stone set in the cave's doorway. Odysseus entices Polyphemus to drink an unusually potent wine and tells him his name his "Nobody." When the giant falls into a drunken sleep, Odysseus and his men put out Polyphemus's single eye with a fire-hardened stake. Polyphemus calls on his fellow Cyclopes, who, however, see no point in coming to help, since Polyphemus states that "Nobody" has assaulted him. Odysseus and his men escape by concealing themselves beneath the bellies of the rams in Polyphemus's flocks. As they are sailing away on the ships, Odysseus taunts Polyphemus and reveals his name. Polyphemus calls on his father, Poseidon, to avenge his injury, and the god hears him.

Book 10

Next they arrive at the floating island of Aeolia. AEOLUS, guardian of the winds, receives Odysseus, shows him hospitality, and sends him

Head of Odysseus. *Detail from a Greek second-century B.C.E. marble group at the Villa of Tiberius at Sperlonga (Museo Archeologico Nazionale, Sperlonga)*

off with a bag containing the winds tightly bound inside. They are in sight of Ithaca, when Odysseus's crew begin to suspect that Odysseus is concealing some treasure inside the bag; they open it, the winds escape, and they are driven back to Aeolia. Aeolus now sees him as a man hated by the gods and refuses to give further help. They sail on to the land of the Laestrygonians, who turn out to be violent cannibals. They lose some of their comrades in the attack and sail next to the island of Aeaea, where CIRCE lives. Odysseus sees the smoke from her dwelling, divides the crew into two groups, one headed by Eurylochus and one by himself, and draws lots: Eurylochus and his group must go and explore the island. Circe invites them in and turns all the men into swine—except Eurylochus, who sensed a trap and now returns to Odysseus. Odysseus himself goes to investigate and meets Hermes on the way, who gives him an antidote to Circe's magic and detailed instructions on how to conduct himself. Circe's magic has no effect on him; he threatens the amazed goddess with a sword, demands that the enchantment be lifted from his comrades, and becomes her lover. The entire crew enjoys her hospitality for a year. Reminded by a comrade of his homeland, Odysseus tells Circe he wishes to leave; she assents, but informs him he must first seek out the prophet TIRESIAS in the land of the dead. One of Odysseus's crew, Elpenor, dies by falling off a ladder on the day of departure, unbeknown to his comrades.

Book 11

Odysseus and his crew sail to the edges of the world and the land of the dead. They make offerings and sacrifices, and Odysseus is able to speak with souls of the dead who drink sacrificial blood from a pit. He first meets Elpenor, who explains his fate, then speaks with Tiresias, who offers predictions and instructions regarding Odysseus's return to Ithaca. Odysseus then speaks with his mother, Anticleia, who confirms his wife Penelope's loyalty and describes the decrepitude of his heartbroken father, Laertes. He then sees famous women—Tyro, ANTIOPE, ALCMENE, Epicaste (see JOCASTA), LEDA, ARIADNE, and others. At this point, Odysseus ceases speaking and proclaims to the gathered Phaeacians that it is time for sleep, but Alcinous encourages him to continue his story. Odysseus reports his conversation with Agamemnon and Achilles; AJAX refuses to speak with him out of resentment over the armor of Achilles. Then he describes famous figures from the underworld (MINOS, ORION, TITYUS, TANTALUS, SISYPHUS) and his conversation with HERACLES, who sympathizes with Odysseus's misfortunes. At last, sudden fear that PERSEPHONE may send up a monster of some kind drives him to prepare the ship and depart.

Book 12

Odysseus and his crew return to Aeaea and bury Elpenor. Circe gives them supplies and offers advice to Odysseus. She tells him how to survive his coming experiences with the SIRENS and SCYLLA and CHARYBDIS, and on the island of Thrinacie, where the cattle of the Sun are kept. They depart. To resist the song of the Sirens, which entices sailors to shipwreck, Odysseus stops the ears of all his crew with wax, but has them tie him to the mast, so that he may hear their song. As they pass the monster Scylla in her cliff-top cave, she devours six of Odysseus's men; they avoid the whirlpool Charybdis. Finally, against Odysseus's wishes, they land on the island of HELIOS, and Odysseus, forewarned by Circe, commands his men not to eat the god's cattle. At length, trapped on the island by unfavorable winds, and facing starvation, Odysseus's men slaughter and eat the cattle, while their leader is asleep. When they depart, ZEUS sends a terrible storm, and all perish except Odysseus, who manages to survive. He makes it to Ogygia, Calypso's island.

Book 13

Odysseus finishes his story. The next day, the Phaeacians send off Odysseus in a ship laden with gifts and treasure. He falls asleep on the voyage. The Phaeacians leave the sleeping Odysseus on the beach with his pile of treasure. Poseidon, to punish the Phaeacians for helping Odysseus, turns the ship into stone. Odysseus awakes and, not recognizing Ithaca, laments that he has been abandoned in an unknown land. Athena appears in the guise of a shepherd and informs him that he is in Ithaca. Odysseus tells a lying tale about his identity. Athena is amused and reveals her true identity. They begin to plot the overthrow of the suitors, and Athena changes his appearance to that of an old beggar. Announcing that she will now go to bring Telemachus back from Sparta, Athena directs Odysseus to seek the loyal swineherd Eumaeus.

Book 14

Eumaeus receives Odysseus, in the guise of a beggar, hospitably in his hut. In conversation over dinner, Eumaeus reveals his deep loyalty to and longing for his absent master, Odysseus, and complains of the depredations of the suitors. Odysseus tells a long, lying tale about his identity and adventures and claims that he has heard news of Odysseus's imminent return. The swineherd is reluctant to believe it. He generously offers Odysseus a warm cloak for the night.

Book 15

Athena goes to Sparta and urges Telemachus to return to Ithaca. She warns him of the ambush the suitors are planning, and instructs him to go to Eumaeus's hut on arrival. Helen and Menelaus send Telemachus off with gifts. As he is preparing to depart, he encounters Theoclymenus, a descendant of the prophet Melampus, who has been exiled from Argos for kin slaying. Telemachus offers him passage on his ship. In the meanwhile, Odysseus continues to enjoy Eumaeus's hospitality, and Eumaeus tells him the story of his life—how he was kidnapped and sold as a slave to Laertes. Telemachus now reaches Ithaca. He recommends that Theoclymenus go to the house of Eurymachus, while he goes to the hut of Eumaeus.

Book 16

Telemachus arrives at the hut and is greeted by Eumaeus. Telemachus sends him to inform his mother of his safe return. Athena appears outside, summons Odysseus, and restores him to his former appearance. Odysseus goes back inside and reveals his identity to the astonished Telemachus. Together they begin to plan the downfall of the suitors. The suitors, in the meanwhile, learn of Telemachus's return from his voyage; they hold a meeting, and some suggest the murder of Telemachus. Penelope learns of the suitors' plans and rebukes them. Eumaeus returns to his hut, but Athena has again made Odysseus take on a beggar's appearance.

Book 17

The next day, Telemachus announces his plan to go to the palace to see his mother; he instructs Eumaeus to take the visitor into town. Telemachus goes to the palace and reports to

his mother what he learned from Menelaus of Odysseus's whereabouts. In addition, the prophet Theoclymenus claims to know that Odysseus is actually present in Ithaca. In the meanwhile, Odysseus and Eumaeus are making their way into town when they meet the disloyal goatherd Melanthius, who insults and kicks Odysseus. On the palace steps, Odysseus's hound Argus, in a sad state of neglect, sees his master, raises his head, and pricks his ears, then dies. Odysseus begs in the palace; the suitor Antinous insults him and strikes him with a stool. Penelope asks to speak with the stranger to see if he has any news of Odysseus. He agrees to speak with her in the evening. Eumaeus departs for his hut.

Book 18

A beggar named Irus insults and threatens Odysseus. Antinous suggests a boxing match between the two of them. Odysseus easily defeats him and throws him outside the palace. Penelope appears before the suitors, enflames their desire, and rebukes Telemachus for allowing a stranger to be treated so disgracefully. She further rebukes the suitors and, leading them on with hopes of marriage, elicits gifts from them. The maid Melantho and the suitor Eurymachus insult Odysseus.

Book 19

Odysseus and Telemachus put away the weapons in the storeroom to make sure that the suitors will not have weapons at hand. Penelope speaks with the stranger (i.e., Odysseus). She tells him how she deceived the suitors by promising them that she would marry one of them when she had finished weaving a shroud for Laertes, when all the while she unraveled every night what she had woven during the day. But now they have discovered the ruse, and she cannot think of how to escape them. The stranger tells how Odysseus had once been his guest; he includes persuasive details about his clothing and appearance, and he adds that Odysseus is on the verge of returning. Afterward, he agrees to let the old servant Eurycleia wash his feet. As she is doing so, she recognizes him by the scar on his leg; he got the scar when hunting with his grandfather Autolycus, who gave Odysseus his name. The nurse is about to cry out, but Odysseus covers her mouth and enjoins secrecy. Penelope tells the stranger of a dream in which in an eagle slaughters her geese, and Odysseus interprets it as a sign of the coming slaughter of the suitors at his own hands. Penelope also announces her intention to hold an archery contest among the suitors. They retire for the night.

Book 20

Penelope and Odysseus each spend a restless night of anxiety, and Odysseus receives a sign from the gods portending the success of his plans for revenge. Odysseus and Telemachus trade sharp words with the suitors and Melanthius, while the herdsman Philoetius expresses his sympathy for the beggar and his longing for the return of Odysseus. Sinister omens disturb the suitors' feasting, and Theoclymenus departs after making dire predictions; but the suitors continue with their present behavior.

Book 21

Penelope prepares the archery contest and brings out Odysseus's bow from storage. She offers herself in marriage to whichever one of them is able to use Odysseus's bow to shoot an arrow through 12 ax heads lined up in a row. Telemachus tries first and almost succeeds in stringing the bow—but Odysseus discourages him with a shake of his head. The suitors struggle unsuccessfully to string the bow. In the meanwhile, outside, Odysseus, having assured himself of the loyalty of Eumaeus and Philoetius, reveals his scar to them and enlists their aid in the plan. He reenters the hall and, over the suitors' objections, is allowed to try the bow. Eurycleia, at Odysseus's bidding, locks the doors of the hall. Odysseus easily strings the bow and shoots an arrow through the ax heads.

Book 22

Odysseus begins the slaughter by shooting Antinous with an arrow; then he reveals his identity to the suitors. Eurymachus blames Antinous and begs him to spare them. Odysseus shows no pity, and the suitors resolve to fight. Melanthius manages to obtain some arms for the suitors. The two herdsmen tie up Melanthius in the storeroom. Athena joins the fight in the guise of Mentor. Leodes the priest begs for his life but is slain; Medon the herald and Phemius the bard are spared—for they were forced to take part by the suitors. After all the suitors have been killed, the 12 serving maids who behaved disloyally are summoned to clean up the carnage and then hanged in the courtyard. Melanthius is mutilated. Odysseus has the palace disinfected and asks Eurycleia to summon Penelope.

Book 23

Eurycleia reports the news of Odysseus's return and the slaughter of the suitors to Penelope, who is slow to believe her. She descends to where Odysseus is sitting but, to Telemachus's dismay, holds back from embracing him. Her husband and son consider how to prevent news of the slaughter from circulating. Odysseus now bathes and is endowed with beauty by Athena. Penelope still doubts and tests him by asking Eurycleia to move the bed out of the bedroom for him; he protests that the bed is immovable, since he made it himself out of a great olive tree rooted in the ground. Penelope is finally convinced: Her husband has confirmed his identity, and she embraces him. They go to bed and make love and tell each other the stories of what they did in each other's absence. The next morning Odysseus prepares to visit his father, Laertes.

Book 24

Hermes, in the meanwhile, gathers the souls of the suitors and conveys them to the underworld. Achilles and Agamemnon are in conversation. Achilles regrets that Agamemnon did not die and receive a glorious tomb on the fields of Troy; Agamemnon describes Achilles' lavish funeral. Hermes and the shades of the suitors arrive. Amphimedon, one of the suitors, tells the whole story of their pursuit of Penelope and Odysseus's revenge. Agamemnon praises Odysseus and compares Penelope favorably with his own wife, CLYTAEMNESTRA. Odysseus, in the meanwhile, arrives at Laertes's estate and at first conceals his identity with a lying story, but then takes pity and embraces his father. The story of the suitors' slaughter now spreads abroad, and the Ithacans prepare for battle. Odysseus, Telemachus, Laertes, and their followers likewise prepare for battle against the families of the suitors. Battle commences and, although Odysseus seems to be prevailing, Athena establishes a peace treaty between the two sides.

COMMENTARY

The *Odyssey* is one of two great epic poems ascribed to the poet Homer, about whom little is known. Scholars have debated the existence of a historical person named Homer and, if such a person existed, whether or not he wrote both poems (see *HOMER* for more detailed discussion of the "Homeric Question"). Putting aside the question of the historical author(s), it remains striking how the two epics complement each other and avoid replicating each other. The *Iliad* is an epic focused on warfare in a single setting, the fields of Troy. The *Odyssey* concerns the aftermath of the Trojan War and, in particular, the return journey *(nostos)* of the hero; the settings are multiple, since it is an epic of wide-ranging travel and adventure. The *Iliad* depicts largely the conflict and interactions among heroes on the battlefield, yet also includes some domestic scenes within the walls of Troy. The action of the *Odyssey* occurs largely within houses and palaces. Questions of hospitality, manners, decorum, and family dynamics, therefore, occupy a great deal of space in the epic, by contrast with the martial focus of the *Iliad*. Women, moreover, enjoy more significant roles in the *Odyssey*, since the household as a sustained setting affords more scope for their actions than the battlefield or the besieged city.

The *Iliad* is about destroying a city, a civilization, and the royal house of PRIAM. In the course of this terrible process, individuals gain glory *(kleos)* through their deeds. The *Odyssey* shows the crucial counterpart to the hero's acquisition of martial glory. To make it all worthwhile, the hero must return home with his material treasures and his immaterial glory in tow and reestablish himself in his ancestral home. Dying on the battlefield is undoubtedly a fine thing in the Homeric view, but best of all, perhaps, is to return home and enjoy the prestige conferred by successful warfare. If the *Iliad* is about the desperate struggle to win glory and to win a war, the *Odyssey* is about the struggle to regain enjoyment of one's life afterward. The two epics between them manage to address what contemporary Greeks would have seen as the most important aspects of life: the pursuit of glory in battle and the cultivation of prestige, happiness, and security at home.

The *Iliad* and *Odyssey*, then, manage to share out portions of the archaic Greek worldview between them with impressive economy. This principle of nonreplication and complementarity extends even to individual episodes. The *Odyssey* includes narration of certain key post-Iliadic episodes, for example, that are not contained within the tight narrative focus of the *Iliad*. Prime among these are the story of the Trojan Horse (related by the bard Demodocus) and the funeral of Achilles (described by Agamemnon in the underworld). We also hear stories of the return journeys *(nostoi)* of the Greek heroes and are even able to satisfy our curiosity as to the restored domestic life of Menelaus and Helen. The *Odyssey*, in short, does not provide a continuous, full account of everything that happened between the death of HECTOR and the return of the Greeks, but does offer, through ingeniously embedded narratives, significant glimpses and résumés of some of the key developments.

The fundamental values of the epic match the character of the epic hero. Underlying all of Achilles' decisions and an integral part of his greatness is the awareness of his early death: He is not fated to return home from Troy. Achilles is violent, impulsive, unrestrained, and ferociously honest. He must maximize his *kleos* for the short time he is alive, and so the virtues of the survivor—patience, restraint, diplomacy, tactical deception—are irrelevant and even despicable to him. In his withdrawal from battle, or in his abuse of Hector's corpse, Achilles is unreasonable and impolitic, since, ultimately, he does not have a great investment in the banal maintenance of polite social relations with those around him: He is locked in a struggle with the limits of his own mortality. Odysseus's situation and goals are profoundly different. He has survived the war and now needs to survive the journey home. He must constantly restrain himself and check his impulses. He needs to keep his hosts (even his violent, lawless ones) reasonably happy to gain his own way in the end. Odysseus is a master of concealing his identity, testing his interlocutors, withholding strategically valuable information, and enduring outrageous insults. Odysseus possesses character traits that are nearly the diametric opposite of Achilles', and although, in the end, he shares with him the basic substratum of the warrior ethos—which includes the primacy of honor and revenge—the means of attaining his goals are markedly distinct. Odysseus possesses the virtues necessary for survival, continuing on after the war, and enjoying the remainder of his life.

The *Odyssey* is a return or *nostos* epic, and thus the qualities of the hero are suited to the challenges of long voyages, unexpected situations, and extended sojourns as a guest in others' houses. Few other Greek heroes were as successful in their return home as Odysseus. We learn from Menelaus that Athena was angry at the Greeks for sacrilegious acts during the sacking of Troy, and punished them with a terrible storm. Many perished in the storm itself; others, such as Menelaus and Odysseus himself, were forced to endure long wandering before arriving back home. Agamemnon managed to arrive home, but his wife Clytaemnestra's lover, Aegisthus, killed him. This story of a failed *nostos* is particularly relevant to Odysseus's situation and recurs throughout the epic as a foil. His wife is also tested by men who wish to replace her husband and usurp his role, and his son, like Orestes, is in danger of losing his inherited estates, if not his life. Odysseus's extreme caution and circumspection on arriving home in Ithaca effectively counter the negative example of the heedless Agamemnon, who fell instantly into the trap laid in his absence. Likewise, we may contrast Penelope's steadfast loyalty with Clytaemnestra's betrayal.

Both Agamemnon and Achilles, as represented in the voyage to the underworld in Book 11, are dead but find solace in the knowledge of their sons' deeds. Odysseus, we are to understand, is more fortunate than both. He will return to his loyal wife, enjoy the company of his son, and console his aging father in person. Achilles' shade emphatically states that he would rather be the lowliest serf among the living than the king of all the dead. We see here clearly marked the difference in underlying values between the *Iliad* and the *Odyssey* as represented concretely in the aims and character of the central heroes. Achilles, in the *Odyssey*, is made to renounce, in effect, the Iliadic primacy of maximum glory within a short lifespan. Now that he is dead, he appears to admit the value of life itself independent of status or honor. Odysseus is only a sojourner in the land of the dead; he still has his life to return to. Odysseus, as it happens, will manage to win both life and glory. His fate is superior to Agamemnon's in that he will retain possession of his house and wife, and superior to Achilles' in that he wins glory without losing his life. His fate is also arguably superior to that of Menelaus in that he happily possesses a wife of proven virtue and loyalty, whereas Menelaus's domestic peace in Sparta is marred by barely suppressed tensions and the difficult legacy of the past.

We will not see the full span of Odysseus's life within the epic, but the dead Tiresias offers a prophetic vision of it: Odysseus will live to a ripe old age, surrounded by his prosperous people, and a gentle death will come, as he mysteriously declares, from the sea. The sea, controlled by the angry god Poseidon, is Odysseus's chief antagonist, and thus it makes sense that, on returning home, he must ritually remove himself from the sea's power. According to Tiresias, Odysseus must go so far inland that the local inhabitants will mistake the oar on his shoulder for a winnowing fan. Then he must plant his oar in the ground and offer a sacrifice to Poseidon. The sea will still claim Odysseus's life in the end, but gently and painlessly, and only after he has been allowed to live out all the years allotted to him. This emphasis on Odysseus's life span as peacefully completed is very different from the Iliadic focus on Achilles' tragically brief flash of brilliance.

Both epic poems, despite their significant differences, have one striking trait in common: They intensify suspense and anticipation by withholding the appearance of the hero. Achilles astonishingly withdraws from battle for the majority of the epic devoted to his *kleos*. The withdrawal magnifies his *kleos* by demonstrating his crucial importance to the Greeks and building up the importance of his return to battle. The *Iliad*, up to the point of Achilles' return, represents the courage and diverse aptitudes of warriors in battle. When Achilles finally does return, we can appreciate both the framework of Homeric warfare and his extraordinary status within that framework. The anticipation of Achilles becomes particularly intense as we near the point of his return, since PATROCLUS takes on his appearance and (to a limited degree) his excellence in donning his armor. He represents a weaker version of Achilles—an inferiority we can appreciate all the more when Achilles subsequently takes the field.

The *Odyssey*, similarly, withholds the appearance of its hero: Odysseus is kept from the view of both his family and the audience of his epic. At the opening of the poem, we learn that Calypso holds Odysseus prisoner in her cave. Commentators have noted that Calypso's name is related to the Greek word meaning "hide, conceal." Odysseus remains hidden in the straightforward sense that his family does not know where he is or even whether he is alive; but he also risks being hidden in the sense of losing his distinctive *kleos* by simply disappearing from the face of the earth. In short, he risks losing his identity. If he returns to Ithaca, he has property, a wife, a son, and a story of accomplishments with a clear beginning and end. If he vanishes mysteriously, there is no tomb to maintain his memory, no completed life story to cement his reputation. Odysseus will remain in this difficult condition of concealment for the first four books of the epic.

In the meantime, the narrative focus falls on his son, Telemachus. Telemachus does not know whether his father is alive or dead and, if alive, where he is. At Athena's urging, he goes on a voyage to learn news of his father from Nestor in Pylos and Menelaus in Sparta. Telemachus, who was an infant when Odysseus departed for Troy, is now on the verge of manhood. His travels allow him to begin to build his own network of *xenia* (guest-host relations, guest friendship) to introduce himself to his father's friends and comrades, and to build up his own reputation in the world at large. These four books of the *Odyssey*, sometimes called the *Telemacheia*, may well be one of the earliest examples of the bildungsroman in Western literature.

Growing into manhood means various things for Telemachus. First, it means occupying a more commanding role as Odysseus's heir and ruler of his own household. Unfortunately, he cannot assume this role forcefully, because, as he observes, the suitors are more numerous and powerful than he is, and his ability to control them is tenuous. All the same, under Athena's tutelage, he begins to assert himself more aggressively—very much to the surprise of the suitors. He also surprises his mother by occasionally rebuking her and reminding her of her proper role within the household. Penelope, in Odysseus's absence, has had to take on more of a masculine role as head of the household, but Telemachus now begins to assert his rights and to claim authority over his mother.

Growing into manhood also means assuming some aspects of his father's character, albeit on a smaller scale and in less masterful ways. Friends and hosts comment on his amazing resemblance to Odysseus, but the similarity goes beyond appearances. The opening books, which tell of Telemachus's travels in search of news about his father, are focused on the fine points of social behavior in the aristocratic households of heroic Greece. Telemachus must learn to be sensitive to etiquette; at the same time—and this is more difficult—he must also understand how to exert a modest degree of independence and to insist on his own priorities. Telemachus is at first diffident and overawed by Nestor. Nonetheless, encouraged by Athena, he learns to act decisively on his own behalf, controlling, rather than being controlled by, the rules of hospitality. The ability to refuse politely an inappropriate gift (Menelaus's offer of horses), or to avoid an occasion of extended hospitality when the moment calls for swift departure, is crucial for a man who wants to be, and to *appear* to be, in control of his own affairs. In small matters, Telemachus shows the beginnings of his father's shrewd practical judgment and tough-minded self-determination.

It is impossible to overrate the importance of *xenia* in the Homeric worldview. Zeus, as Homer frequently reminds us, is the guardian of hospitality. The Iliadic expedition against Troy is premised on a violation of *xenia*: PARIS stole his host Menelaus's wife. The *Odyssey* presents a more fine-grained, varied, and quotidian picture of guest-host relations. Odysseus, in his travels, must seek hospitality in the different lands he visits, and his hosts represent different standards and styles of hospitality. Odysseus, for his part, is a master of *xenia*: No one understands the rules as thoroughly as he does, and consequently, no one is as masterful in stretching, breaking, or manipulating them when necessary. In a relatively short time, and without even revealing who he is, he impresses king Alcinous in Phaeacia to the extent that the king effectively offers him his daughter Nausicaa in marriage. Circe is a host who turns her guests into swine, but Odysseus, with Hermes' help, controls the situation, rescues his men, and becomes Circe's lover. Odysseus's true tour de force is saved for last: He makes himself a guest in his own palace in the guise of beggar. In this humble condition, he manages to gain the trust and admiration of the mistress of the household, and even to inspire fear in the arrogant suitors. At the same time, he secretly makes preparations for their slaughter.

A major component of Odyssean heroic character is his ability to conceal his identity and exert control over his emotions and impulses. When Odysseus stays as a guest among the Phaeacians, he conceals his identity from them for a surprising extent of time; only after Antinous observes Odysseus hiding his tears behind his cloak during Demodocus's songs about the Trojan War does he finally insist on knowing who he is. He similarly conceals his identity from Polyphemus, calling himself "Nobody," and from the suitors, before whom he assumes the guise of a beggar. Again, Telemachus offers a prelude to Odysseus's astonishing feats in this arena. When he goes to visit Menelaus, he does not immediately announce who he is. This suppression of identity is perhaps a sign that, after his experience at the palace of Nestor, he is gaining confidence, self-awareness, and restraint. There is no obvious tactical reason for Telemachus to conceal who he is, and Menelaus and Helen are not fooled for long, but the ability to withhold information about himself is nonetheless potentially useful in other contexts. Telemachus is coming into his inheritance of Odysseus's distinctive character.

The *Telemacheia* thus performs a precise narrative function. Not only does it introduce the character of Telemachus, provide an opportunity for him to garner *kleos*, and keep us in suspense regarding the appearance of Odysseus; these first four books also enable us to appreciate better the amazing feats of *xenia*, concealment, and self-control of the seasoned hero himself when he finally takes the stage. Telemachus performs a function comparable in some ways to that of Patroclus in the *Iliad*: He lays the narrative groundwork for the main player, whose exceptional abilities will be all the more conspicuous in comparison with the actions of his admirable, but still inferior, predecessor on the epic stage. Telemachus enacts his own miniature odyssey. He goes on a trip to Pylos and Sparta and is entertained by genial hosts without serious incident or challenge. Odysseus's assignment is more difficult: He is the prisoner of a man-eating giant, sojourns with a witch who turns men into swine, and goes on a trip to the underworld.

The episodic adventures narrated by Odysseus to the Phaeacians present exotic extremes of hospitality behavior. The Cyclops Polyphemus undoubtedly represents the most reprehensible version of the bad host. Homer's framing of the episode in terms of the *xenia* theme is explicit. On arriving in the empty cave, Odysseus's men wish simply to steal some provisions and flee, while Odysseus (with ruinous consequences for some of his men) insists on carrying out the proper rituals of hospitality. He will wait for the Cyclops and exchange hospitality-gifts. The Cyclopes, however, are stereotypical barbarians. They do not practice civilized arts such as farming and sailing; nor do they have laws. Polyphemus, rather than offering his guests food and lodging, eats them. It is hard to imagine a more total subversion of *xenia* principles. To Odysseus, he tauntingly offers the "*xenia* gift" of eating him last. Odysseus offers a *xenia* gift that is more appropriate, yet conceals a hidden sting. The powerful wine, which the Cyclops in barbaric manner drinks

unmixed with water, causes him to fall into a deep sleep, thereby rendering him vulnerable to attack. The entire episode is an allegory of *xenia* in its confrontation between the barbaric Cyclops and civilized Greekness.

It is hardly coincidental that the Phaeacians are the audience of these stories. As hosts, they could hardly be more civilized, but it would not be beyond Odysseus's cunning to offer self-serving paradigms of hostly behavior. Indeed, they end up sending Odysseus home laden with immense treasure. The culmination of this sequence is Odysseus's assumption of the guise of beggar in his own house. We have been schooled in the distinctions between good and bad hospitality throughout the course of the epic, and have had occasion to appreciate Homer's fundamental equation between *xenia* behavior and moral worth. The suitors are unruly and unwanted guests, who are eating their way through their host's stores without permission, sexually exploiting the serving maids, threatening Odysseus's son and heir, and attempting to steal his wife. They represent a shocking perversion of *xenia* on a mass scale. Conversely, when Odysseus arrives on the scene, they turn out to be terrible hosts. They effectively (if illegitimately) control the household and its resources, yet they do not even share out another man's resources generously and hospitably. In numerous scenes, Penelope and Telemachus must protest the suitors' discourteous treatment of the stranger, appealing to Zeus's guardianship of strangers and beggars.

Homer is preparing in advance the justification for the suitors' slaughter. The carefully recorded insults—e.g., throwing a stool or cow's hoof at the stranger—are implicit acts of war, which will be avenged later in earnest. It is hardly accidental that an especially sinister omen, which occurs shortly before the killing of the suitors, takes the explicit form of a grotesque perversion of banqueting: Athena makes the suitors laugh uncontrollably, and it seems to them that they are spattering blood on their food. The seer Theoclymenus suddenly sees a palace filled with ghosts. When the time for killing comes, Homer is attentive to the convivial nature of the suitors' transgression. In his first kill, Odysseus targets Antinous, who is reaching for a goblet of wine. Before he can swallow, Odysseus's arrow pierces his neck, and blood sprays onto his food. The *Odyssey* culminates with this strikingly original battle scene in a banqueting hall, where blood flows instead of wine, and groans are heard instead of laughter. The location of the slaughter is not merely novel, however, but thematically appropriate, for the punishment is meted out in the very setting of the crime. The suitors deserve punishment precisely for their behavior as guests and perpetual banqueters in the absent Odysseus's hall. Now they die amid their cups and half-eaten food.

The final episode of the epic thus represents an intensification and expansion, as in the *Iliad*, of the themes and narrative patterns enacted throughout the entire poem. Just as Achilles' terrible display of excellence in battle near the epic's close wildly exceeds the battle fury of lesser warriors exhibited previously, so Odysseus's mastery of *xenia* and punishment of *xenia* transgression rises to a new level in the closing books. Other patterns are expanded and intensified as well; in particular, we might note the recurrent scenario of being trapped in a hostile environment, humiliated, threatened, and deprived of status and identity. In Polyphemus's cave, Odysseus assumes the identity of "Nobody," miserably watches his comrades being eaten, and endures the Cyclops's grotesque taunts. He is trapped in a hostile environment and must rely on his wits to overcome his adversary. When he finally escapes the cave and is sailing away, he taunts the Cyclops, revealing his name. Odysseus goes from "Nobody" to a hero with a name, a father, and a place of origin. Commentators have observed that the alias "Nobody" conceals a further play on words. One form of "no one" in Greek resembles the word for cunning (*metis*).

The use of such an alias was itself an act of cunning, and gave Odysseus his victory over the Cyclops.

We might compare a similar narrative pattern in Helen's story about Odysseus. He flogged himself and dressed in rags to look like a beggar, infiltrated Troy in this disguise, gathered information, killed a number of Trojans, and returned to the Greek camp triumphant. The pattern is distinctive to Odysseus: self-abasement and negation/concealment of identity followed by a victorious revelation of identity at the moment the *kleos* (fame) of his deed has been established. Odysseus's story follows a recurrent arc from concealment to revelation, from absence and namelessness to triumphant, glory-conferring return. Again, at the heart of Odysseus's victory is his self-control, powers of concealment, and *metis*.

This pattern characterizes both the microcosm of individual episodes and the larger narrative drive of the epic itself. We should not be surprised if the same pattern characterizes the final portion of the epic in intensified and expanded form. Here, Odysseus conceals himself in rags once again, suffers humiliating insults, hides his identity, and survives by his wits and resilience in a dangerous environment, surrounded by numerous enemies. Then, in a surprise reversal, he takes possession of his bow, announces his identity as Odysseus, and inflicts terrible vengeance on the suitors. What provides this episode with its culminating power is, first, that Odysseus's enemies are so numerous and, second, the fact that his period of self-concealment has been expanded remarkably. He must live under his assumed identity for a significant amount of time, deceiving not only all the suitors but even his own wife. Finally, the reclamation of his identity is now total and concretely grounded in a place and role. Odysseus reinstalls himself as the master of his bow, his household, his wife, his immoveable bed, his property, and his kingship of Ithaca. In a single battle, he reassumes his full identity as Odysseus.

Recovering one's identity after so many years demands not only cunning but also memory. Eurycleia remembers Odysseus's scar instantaneously. The loyal herdsmen cherish the memory of Odysseus, and the final reunion of Odysseus and Penelope is premised on their shared memory of how he constructed their bed. Returning home requires memory on the part of both the hero and those to whom he returns. The opposing impulse is forgetfulness, which recurrently threatens to destroy the hero's *nostos* (return journey). While Calypso conceals Odysseus in her cave, he is threatened with the fate of oblivion. In an especially explicit version of this theme, the lotus-eaters nearly cut off the possibility of *nostos* for some of Odysseus's men by giving them the memory-destroying lotus plant to eat: They immediately lose all desire to return. At Circe's luxurious palace the days go by so smoothly that Odysseus spends a year there before one of his men finally reminds him of their *nostos*. The alluringly beautiful voices of the Sirens cause sailors to abandon their destination and wreck their ships on the rocks. Homer aligns oblivion and abandonment of *nostos* with pleasure and feminine allure. A particularly intriguing instance arises during Telemachus's visit to Sparta. Helen mixes into the drinks a drug that causes oblivion and forgetting of sorrows. Her feminine guile includes an ability to make others forget about the Trojan War and, presumably, her role in causing it.

If a numbing, pleasurable oblivion obstructs *nostos*, remembering one's true identity and homeland usually involves pain. When, at the court of Alcinous, Demodocus sings of the Trojan War and Odysseus's role in it, the hero covers his face with his cloak to hide his tears. The episodes recounted are not particularly sad ones; the Trojan Horse, for example, constitutes a signal victory for the Greeks in general and Odysseus in particular. The reason Odysseus cries is because he is being reminded of who he is, what he has done and suffered, and how he continues to be doomed to wandering.

It is painful for Odysseus to hear his name and be reminded of his heroic status in the world, because he has been exiled from his own identity. This painful awareness of exile, however, is a necessary, catalyzing pain, because without it, Odysseus would have no motivation to continue struggling to achieve his *nostos*. The Sirens, Calypso, Circe, and the lotus-eaters all offer forgetfulness and the absence of pain. Odysseus, although repeatedly subjected to the temptations of pleasurable oblivion, steadfastly weeps for his homeland and yearns to return to his imperfect, mortal wife.

Homer is capable of manipulating the themes of *nostos* and forgetfulness in surprising and subtle ways. When Odysseus finally sails in to the coast of Ithaca in a magical Phaeacian boat laden with treasures, he is blissfully asleep. The poet makes a point of noting the poignant irony. A man who has suffered so much on land and sea is now, as he approaches his goal, shrouded in deep sleep, oblivious of everything he has endured. More vigilance and endurance will soon be required, but for the moment, Odysseus is at last allowed to rest. Perhaps now that his return to Ithaca is assured, he can finally relax his watch and cease to subject himself to the constant, painful struggle to remember who he is and where he comes from.

Identity is at the center of the epic. Odysseus's deeds are important and justly famous, but the simple fact that he *is* Odysseus is of fundamental importance. Homer marks key moments in his epic through reference to concrete tokens of Odysseus's identity. At one such moment, the nurse Eurycleia recognizes Odysseus from the distinctive scar on his leg while washing his feet. This moment of recognition leads into an inset narrative of how Odysseus got the scar. The embedded narration in turn establishes crucial aspects of Odysseus's identity. His mother's father, Autolycus, gave Odysseus his name. Drawing on the similarity between the name "Odysseus" and the Greek word for "hate," Autolycus declares that he names the child for the many enemies he has made for himself in the world. Homer describes Autolycus, whose name means "the very wolf," as the most notable thief and liar of his times. We can already see how aspects of Autolycus correspond to elements in Odysseus's distinctive character. Later, when Odysseus is older, he visits Autolycus and his sons and is wounded in a boar hunt, in which he also wins glory by slaying the boar. This visit represents Odysseus's coming-of-age, the beginnings of his *kleos* and public identity. The scar that confirms the hero's identity is inflicted, significantly, during this initiatory episode that occurs in the company of the man who gave him his name.

The scar is at the center of Odysseus's identity. Other concrete tokens establish specific aspects of his character. The bow represents Odysseus's heroic status and his position as master of his household. As significant object, the bow has a multilayered story: Odysseus received it from Iphitus, who inherited it from his father, Eurytus. We also hear that Heracles subsequently hosted Iphitus in his own house, then killed him. The bow thus interestingly carries associations with slaughter in a specifically domestic setting: Its previous owner was killed in this way. Odysseus chose not to bring the bow with him to Troy but kept it in his house for use on his own estate. The bow—thus defined as a domestic weapon—is appropriately used in Odysseus's banqueting hall to kill the suitors. In Odysseus's case, however, the killing is not an outrageous violation of *xenia*, as Iphitus's murder was, but a merited punishment of *xenia* violators on the part of the lord of the household. Finally, the story of the bow confirms Odysseus's identity by his flawless mastery of it: He strings it effortlessly, and his arrow flies straight through the 12 ax heads. The arrow's perfect trajectory represents the irreducible specificity of Odysseus, the "perfect fit" between object and owner. Odysseus's reclamation of his household from the suitors naturally follows.

Odysseus's bed serves a function similar to that of the bow in grounding and authenticating his identity, but this time specifically as Penelope's husband. Penelope cunningly tests Odysseus by affecting to request that the bed be moved from the bedroom. She know that the bed cannot be moved, since Odysseus made it out of a deeply rooted olive tree, and the hero is accordingly outraged at the suggestion that it might be moved. The symbolism here is overpoweringly clear: The bed has not been moved, and cannot be moved. Odysseus has wandered the world and even sojourned with other women, but his true bed and loyal wife have remained steadfastly in place. These three tokens of Odysseus's identity—the scar, the bow, the bed—thus concretely establish his name and *kleos* as hero, his mastery of his household, and his marriage to Penelope.

Penelope is not simply loyal in the passive sense of not welcoming the advances of a lover or new husband. Resisting the constant pressure of the suitors occupying her home requires a more active and cunning resistance. In putting up such resistance, Penelope assumes a quasi-heroic feminine role unparalleled by anything in the *Iliad*. The most famous instance of Penelope's active defense of her fidelity is the ruse of Laertes' shroud. She claims that she will choose one of the suitors to marry only when she has completed the shroud, yet every night she unravels what she wove during the day. Penelope thus maintains the suitors' goodwill by leading them on, yet continually defers the day of decision that would force her to marry. Later, she induces the suitors to give her gifts, counteracting, to some extent, the damage they have done to the house's resources. Odysseus, in beggar's guise, secretly rejoices in her act. Penelope's accomplishments in many ways recall and even match Odysseus's own. Like Odysseus, she is a master of deception and succeeds in eliciting valuable gifts from others. Odysseus typically tests his interlocutors with leading remarks and suggestions; Penelope brilliantly succeeds in testing Odysseus himself with the pretense of the movable bed. It is significant that Odysseus, as beggar, opens his speech to Penelope with praise of her fame, which he compares to that of the king of a prosperous people. In ruling her household, Penelope has indeed taken on an almost masculine role, and like her husband, she has won *kleos* through her cunning deeds.

There is no question but that Odysseus is allowed relations with other women that Penelope could not have entertained with other men without damage to her reputation; and there is no question but that in broader terms, she occupies a subordinate role and that her *kleos* is of a lesser kind in accordance with her status as woman. It is still striking that she occupies so substantial and positive a role in an epic poem. The *Iliad*, by contrast, is firmly centered on masculine action and prestige. Also remarkable is Homer's highly nuanced picture of married, companionable, middle-aged love—a rare occurrence even in later literature. Odysseus and Penelope are well matched in many ways, and one of the highlights of their reunion is the long-anticipated opportunity to talk with each other and to share stories with each other.

The telling of stories supplies a fitting closure for the sequence of reclamation and reunion. The reunion can be complete only when Penelope and Odysseus possess not only each other but the stories of what happened to each other during their long separation. Odysseus as a hero, moreover, is endowed with a special meta-narrative significance: He himself is a masterful teller of tales and is, in fact, the narrator of a key portion of the epic. The traveler's tales that Odysseus tells to the Phaeacians in Books 9–12 constitute, not by accident, the most exotic, colorful, and supernatural episodes in the poem. Given Odysseus's immense propensity for lying and misrepresentation of his life story even in relatively benign circumstances, it is not overly ingenious or perverse to ask (and many have asked) to what extent these stories are strictly true.

Yet, since there can be no answer to this question, it is perhaps more helpful to consider how the traveler's tales recapitulate in more insistent form the broader question of poetic fiction and truth that informs the epic as a whole. Odysseus displays a seemingly endless capacity to produce stories about himself and invent identities for himself. Like a Hesiodic Muse, he knows how to make false things seem true, and sometimes also tells the truth. His lying tales include a multitude of singular, authenticating details and are just near enough to the truth to deceive. The broader motifs of exile, wandering, adventure, suffering, and misfortune help the teller shape his tales convincingly. Odysseus hides his true identity behind the stories, and yet the stories could only have been produced by Odysseus: Like the alias "Nobody," the deceiving fiction contains an inalienable kernel of truth about the hero. Athena laughs when Odysseus attempts to lead even her astray with an improvised narrative on the shores of Ithaca. What trait is more inveterate and singular to Odysseus than the nearly compulsive invention of fictional identities?

All this staging of metafictional scenarios must reflect at some level the activity and position of the epic poet himself. The *Odyssey* situates us in a post–Trojan War world in which song traditions based on stories of the war are beginning to emerge: Demodocus and Phemius sing about the war and its heroes; aristocratic lords in their palaces are trading stories and reminiscences. Everyone has heard of the fame *(kleos)* of the main heroes such as Odysseus, Achilles, and Agamemnon. Deeds continue to be done, by Odysseus in particular, but the *nostos* phase has as its special concern the establishment of reputations and story traditions when the heroes return laden with the prestige of what they have done. In this *nostos* phase, the talents of a master narrator become extremely valuable, and it is no accident that the hero of Homer's return journey epic is unique for his capacity to do great deeds and simultaneously to recount/create/invent them with words. Not by accident does

Eumaeus the swineherd advertise the stranger's merits to Penelope by praising his ability to tell spellbinding tales and by comparing him explicitly to a bard. Once again, the nature of the epic accords with the character of the epic hero. The sublimity and extremity of the *Iliad* match Achilles' own ferocious and exhilaratingly transgressive character. The *Odyssey*, with its intricately inset narratives and subtle interweaving of truth, fiction, and deception, matches Odysseus's own mastery and cunning as teller of tales.

Oedipus   King of Thebes. Son of Laius and Jocasta. Husband of Jocasta. Oedipus appears in Euripides' Phoenician Women and Sophocles' Oedipus the King and Oedipus at Colonus. Additional classical sources are Aeschylus's Seven against Thebes (742–1,084), Apollodorus's Library (3.5.7–9), Hyginus's *Fabulae* (66, 67), Pindar's *Olympian Odes* (38–42), and Sophocles' Antigone. The account of Oedipus's life that has become canonical is contained in Sophocles' *Oedipus the King*. According to this play, Oedipus's father, Laius, received a prophecy that his son would kill him. He therefore had the infant Oedipus exposed on Mount Cithaeron; the shepherd charged with the task, however, did not leave him to die, but instead Oedipus was brought up by Polybus, king of Corinth, and his wife, Merope. Because Oedipus learned of an oracle

Antigone Leads Oedipus out of Thebes. *C. F. Jalabert, 1843 (Musée des Beaux-Arts, Marseilles)*

stating that he would kill his father and marry his mother, he left Corinth. While traveling, he unwittingly killed Laius in a dispute at the meeting point of three roads. He then saved the Thebans from the SPHINX by answering the riddle, became king of Thebes, and married Jocasta. At the opening of the play, a plague afflicts the city, and Oedipus resolves to find out the cause. Eventually, through persistent investigation, he discovers that he is the cause of pollution, since he killed Laius and married his mother, Jocasta. She hangs herself, and Oedipus blinds himself with the brooch pins of her robe.

The impressive elegance of Sophocles' concentrated plot structure lends a special authority to his version of events, but other versions existed. These include a poem in the Epic Cycle, the *Oedipodia*, an epic called the *Thebais*, an Aeschylean tragic tetralogy comprising *Laius, Oedipus, Seven against Thebes* (extant), and the satyr play *Sphinx*, and Euripides' lost *Oedipus*. Roman versions include Statius's *THEBAID* and Seneca's *Oedipus*. There are significant variations in the tradition. Oedipus does not have children by Jocasta (sometimes Epicaste) in all versions; he does not always go into exile or blind himself; it is not clear that in all versions he defeats the Sphinx by solving a riddle. According to Homer's *Odyssey*, Oedipus killed his father and married his mother, and Epicaste hanged herself, but Oedipus continued to rule at Thebes, afflicted by his mother's FURIES.

After the revelation of his father's murder and his incestuous marriage, Oedipus cursed his sons by Jocasta, POLYNICES and ETEOCLES, condemning them to divide their inheritance by the sword. Various reasons are given for the curse. In some versions, Oedipus's sons behaved in an insulting manner toward him, e.g., by serving him the wrong joint of meat. The result of this curse is the conflict between Eteocles and Polynices over rule of Thebes and the expedition of the Seven against Thebes (see also ADRASTUS, CREON, Aeschylus' *SEVEN AGAINST THEBES*, and Statius's *THEBAID*).

Another divergence in the tradition arises in the question of Oedipus's location in this phase of the story. In Euripides' *Phoenician Women* and Statius's *Thebaid*, the blinded Oedipus remains in the palace, albeit no longer ruling over Thebes. In Sophocles' *Oedipus at Colonus*, the hero goes into exile, accompanied by his daughter ANTIGONE, and ends up finding refuge in the grove of the Eumenides at Colonus, near Athens. THESEUS protects him, as Creon and Polynices attempt to take Oedipus back to Thebes. A prophecy has stated that possession of Oedipus will be a guarantee of power. In this play, Oedipus dies in a place revealed only to Theseus: His tomb will protect Athens from future Theban attack. Sophocles' career betrays a lasting preoccupation with Oedipus and his family. His powerful plays have accordingly had a decisive impact on the image of the hero. The myth of Oedipus does not seem to have been well represented in classical art. In postclassical art, several images of Antigone and a blind Oedipus exist. One example is C. F. Jalabert's mid-19th century *Antigone Leads Oedipus out of Thebes* (Musée des Beaux-Arts, Marseilles).

Oedipus at Colonus SOPHOCLES (ca. 401 B.C.E.) *Oedipus at Colonus*, produced posthumously in 401 B.C.E., was Sophocles' final play. OEDIPUS, blinded, near death, and accompanied only by his daughter ANTIGONE, is wandering in exile, seeking a place to die and be buried. On the basis of a prophecy of APOLLO, he determines that the grove of the Eumenides at Colonus, an Athenian village, is the destined site of his life's end. Sophocles, in his final play, consciously brings his own famous hero's story to a close and, at the same time, weaves together the major themes and preoccupations of his life's work as a tragedian. *Oedipus at Colonus* at once recalls the playwright's previous work and alludes more broadly to the tragic tradition. Sophocles engages especially closely with his other Theban plays, *OEDIPUS THE KING* and *ANTIGONE*, but also returns to some of the central themes of Aeschylus's *EUMENIDES*. As in Aeschylus's play, the role of Athens is central. Oedipus will be buried in Athenian territory and will serve as a protection against future Theban invasion. Sophocles thus situates Oedipus's heroization within the context of the contemporary conflict between Athens and Thebes during the Peloponnesian War.

SYNOPSIS

The scene is set in front of the grove of the Eumenides at Colonus, an Athenian village. The blind Oedipus enters, led by his daughter Antigone. They seek a place of refuge. They know they are near Athens, but are not certain exactly where. A stranger enters; he tells them they must leave the spot where they are resting, since the grove is sacred to the Eumenides. Oedipus announces that he will never leave the place. The stranger replies that the issue lies in the hands of the city. In response to Oedipus's questions, he says that they are at Colonus, and that the ruler of the land is THESEUS. Oedipus asks him to summon Theseus, and the stranger leaves after having promised to do so. Oedipus addresses the Eumenides and recalls that Apollo's prophecies spoke of a land of refuge that he would reach after his wanderings; he also calls upon Athens and asks for pity. Antigone and Oedipus withdraw as they observe the Chorus of citizens of Colonus entering.

The Chorus is searching for the old foreigner it heard was in the grove of the Eumenides; it is affronted by the violation of the sacred grove. Oedipus, revealing himself, proclaims that he is no outlaw. It encourages him to come forth from the sacred spot first, and then present his case. Oedipus consents and is led forth by Antigone. Reluctantly, he reveals that he is Oedipus. The Chorus insists that he depart. Antigone argues that Oedipus, while not innocent, did not intend harm and was destroyed by the gods. Oedipus likewise defends himself and entreats it to give him refuge. The Chorus decides to allow Oedipus to appeal to the ruler

of Athens, who will come himself to see him. Antigone and Oedipus then observe Ismene approaching; she enters. Ismene reveals that Oedipus's sons ETEOCLES and POLYNICES are locked in a struggle over the kingship of Thebes, and that CREON, because he has heard from an oracle that the power of Thebes depends on the presence of Oedipus's tomb, has come to capture Oedipus and hold him within Theban territory. Oedipus is not to be granted a tomb within the city of Thebes itself, because of the taint of kin killing, but at the margins of the land. It is prophesied that the anger of Oedipus's ghost will one day cause a Theban defeat near his tomb. Oedipus sharply criticizes his sons, who, unlike his daughters, did not help him in his time of need and did not prevent his exile, when, after time, he no longer wished for exile or death. Nor will Oedipus give in to Creon. Addressing the Chorus, he states that he will be a great savior for its city and a source of troubles for his enemies.

The Chorus then instructs him to make atonement with libations to the Eumenides, and to offer prayers to them. Ismene agrees to carry out the rites on her aged father's behalf, while Antigone remains with him. Ismene exits. The Chorus asks Oedipus to tell his story. He relates, first, how he came to marry his mother and produce offspring by her; he claims that he was obliged to do so for the sake of the city. Then he tells how he killed his father though without murderous intent, in self-defense, and was thus legally innocent. Theseus enters. He recognizes the blinded Oedipus and declares that he has suffered adversity and exile himself, so is inclined to be sympathetic. Oedipus asks permission to be buried in Athenian territory; he relates that an oracle had predicted doom for Thebes in Athenian territory. Theseus is puzzled, since Athens is not at war with Thebes, but Oedipus declares that in the full extent of time, friendship and enmity alternate, and one day the two cities will be at war. Theseus is persuaded; he offers Oedipus the rights of a citizen and the right to remain where he is, or to follow him. Oedipus chooses to stay in Colonus. Theseus assures Oedipus that he will not allow the Thebans to force him to leave. He exits.

The Chorus sings the praises of Colonus and Athens. Antigone and Oedipus observe Creon approaching. Creon and his attendants enter. Creon expresses pity for the suffering of Oedipus and Antigone and entreats them to return to Thebes. Oedipus rebukes Creon for his subtle, deceptive speech and refuses his false favor; he proclaims that he will inhabit Thebes only as an avenging spirit, and that as an inheritance, he leaves his sons only enough land to die in. As they exchange bitter remarks, Creon announces that he captured Ismene and will also take Antigone. The Chorus protests and threatens to fight him. Creon's men manage to seize Antigone. Creon threatens to seize Oedipus. The Chorus calls for help, and Theseus enters. Oedipus tells him what happened, and Theseus sends men to prevent the removal of Antigone and Ismene. He chastises Creon for lawlessly seizing people in his land and demands that the two girls be returned. Creon blames Oedipus for the action and accuses him of incest and parricide. Oedipus defends himself on both counts at some length, and then accuses Creon of false speech and flattery. Theseus calls an end to words and commands Creon to lead him to the abducted daughters. Creon, overpowered, assents but threatens retaliation once he has returned to Thebes. Theseus and Creon exit.

The Chorus sings an ode in excited anticipation of victory and the recovery of the two sisters. Antigone and Ismene enter with Theseus. They are happily reunited with their father. Oedipus thanks Theseus profusely, praising him and Athens. Theseus reports that he met a man from Argus who had taken sanctuary beside the altar of POSEIDON, and he wishes to speak with Oedipus. Oedipus realizes that it is probably his son Polynices and is reluctant to hear him. Antigone pleads with him to allow

his anger to relent and at least to hear out his son. Oedipus yields. Theseus exits.

The Chorus sings of the unpleasantness of old age. Polynices enters. He expresses dismay and guilt on seeing his father's condition. Then he tells how Eteocles deprived him of the rule that was his right as elder son; he has formed an alliance with Adrastus against Thebes, and now, according to the prophecy, he will prevail if Oedipus is on his side. He wishes Oedipus to join him. Oedipus bitterly recalls how Polynices sent him into exile and did not pity him, and now renews his curses against him: He will not win Thebes or return to Argos but die by a kinsman's hand. Antigone attempts to dissuade Polynices from going to battle against his brother, but he holds fatalistically to his purpose. He exits.

Thunder begins to rumble. Oedipus sees it as a sign of his coming end and calls for Theseus. Theseus enters. Oedipus says that he will lead Theseus to the secret location of his death, a location that will be revealed only to his heir, and thenceforth from heir to heir. Oedipus, Theseus, Antigone, and Ismene exit. A messenger enters. He reports that Oedipus is gone and tells how it happened. Despite his blindness, Oedipus had taken the lead and the others followed him. He sent his daughters to fetch him water for washing and for libations. Then it thundered. Oedipus tenderly took leave of his daughters, telling them that they were about to lose their father. As he wept, he told them his great love for them. A voice was heard summoning him. His daughters were led away, and Oedipus went on with Theseus. Theseus alone saw Oedipus's departure; he shaded his eyes as though it had been terrible to look upon. It was not known what had taken Oedipus away or how it was done. Antigone and Ismene enter. The two sisters lament their loss and their fate. Theseus enters. They wish to see Oedipus's tomb. He replies that it is not permitted: Oedipus made him swear an oath to keep it secret. Antigone and Ismene resolve to go back to Thebes to attempt to head off the conflict. All exit.

COMMENTARY

In terms of mythological chronology, *Oedipus at Colonus* comes after *Oedipus the King* and before *Antigone*. Within the chronology of Sophocles' career, however, *Oedipus at Colonus* comes last. Although written around 406, shortly before Sophocles' death, it was finally produced posthumously by his grandson in 401 B.C.E. The entire play is about endings and how to make an ending. The key question is the location of Oedipus's tomb, which will provide powerful help to whichever city-state possesses it. Oedipus, then, is in the process of settling on a place to die. Sophocles himself, at the same time, is bringing his career as tragedian, and his own life, to a close; thus there is a conscious parallelism between his famous hero's end and his own. The ending place of Oedipus, the Athenian village of Colonus, is known to have been Sophocles' birthplace. The playwright therefore brings his hero to a remarkable end in his own hometown. *Antigone*, moreover, appears to have been one of Sophocles' earliest plays. Hence, by dramatizing events immediately preceding the actions represented in *Antigone*, Sophocles, in a certain sense, completes the circle. At this stage the grand old man of tragedy, Sophocles contemplates the ending and beginning of his life and career, and brings his hero's life to an end in a place of both patriotic and personal significance.

It is not surprising, then, that the passage of time and change over time are central preoccupations of the play. Sophocles has, once again, taken his hero and challenged his audience to note the differences. From the moment the blinded Oedipus first comes onstage, Sophocles' audience is asked to compare him with the Oedipus they know from his earlier play, *Oedipus the King*. The changes are striking. Oedipus's opening speech is especially designed to bring out the differences. At the beginning both of *Oedipus the King* and the present play, Oedipus has the first speech, consisting of 13 lines, in which he first addresses someone, then launches into a series of questions. The syntactic parallelism is notable, and seems deliberate. In the earlier play, however, Oedipus was at the height of his power and prestige, and in the play's very first words, he addressed the Thebans as "children" (*o tekna*), the "recent offspring of Cadmus of old." In the present play, he addresses his own "child" (*teknon*), Antigone, the offspring of "a blind old man." He has gone from the position of leader, paternalistically adopting the entire populace as his "children," to a blind old man being led by his one daughter. If we push the parallelism further, we might note that Cadmus, founder figure of Thebes and famous exile in serpentine form, is now replaced by Oedipus himself, wandering in exile and also transformed physically. Oedipus's status is at once reduced and, in being compared with that of Cadmus, newly exalted.

Other changes are equally striking. In the opening scene of *Oedipus the King*, Oedipus was being petitioned by a group of suppliants. At the opening of *Oedipus at Colonus*, Oedipus and his daughter are the suppliants, seeking refuge in a foreign land. They are now truly foreigners/guests (*xenoi*), dependent on the hospitality of others. Not only is the hero's situation changed; his mood is changed as well. Learning, teaching, suffering, and the passage of time are recurrent themes: Oedipus has learned through his suffering, and time has transformed him. Now, he often expresses willingness to yield and subordinate himself to others' wishes and commands. He is humbly thankful to Theseus, when, later in the play, the Athenian hero recovers his daughters; in the play's opening speech, he observes that strangers must do as they are asked. There are flashes of his old self; when the stranger tells him he must leave the grove of the Eumenides, he replies that he will never leave it. Later, however, at the Chorus's insistence, Oedipus withdraws from the sacred space to make his request respectfully in proper fashion.

Toward Creon and Polynices, Oedipus remains harsh and stubborn, unmovable and insistent on self-determination. The major difference in the present play is that, whereas previously, in *Oedipus the King*, he exerted his domineering will to resist, and at times deny, the destiny prophesied by the gods, now he stubbornly refuses to deviate from the gods' designs as prophesied by Apollo's oracle, even when subjected to tremendous pressure from Creon and his own son. Oedipus now seems possessed of an inner sight, not accidentally recalling Tiresias of the earlier play. Now he is led onstage by a "child," as Tiresias was, and now, guided by his divine knowledge, he will stand up to the threats of an angry Theban king, who wishes to control, rather than accept, Apollo's prophecies. Oedipus has effectively turned into his old adversary, while Creon has taken on Oedipus's previous role as violent, self-deluding ruler.

Oedipus at Colonus answers the pressing question left significantly open at the ending of his previous play: What happens to Oedipus after he blinds himself? At the same time, the play surveys and comments on Sophocles' own previous work, both *Oedipus the King* and *Antigone* and other, non-Theban plays as well; for example, we might well recall PHILOCTETES (produced 409 B.C.E.), in which a physically mutilated, long-suffering hero, banished from his community, violates, as Oedipus does, a sacred grove and stubbornly resists being exploited as a tool of political and military power. In both plays, there is a strong connection between the hero and a specific place. AJAX and TRACHINIAE, moreover, afford a comparable focus on death as the occasion of heroization. *Oedipus at Colonus* thus provides a supremely self-conscious ending to the playwright's career, the resumption and culmination of his dominant themes.

Sophocles' play not only responds to his own previous work, it also engages more broadly with the tragic tradition. The play's setting, in front of the grove of the Eumenides, notably recalls the final play of Aeschylus's *Oresteia*, the *Eumenides*. Oedipus, like ORESTES, is a kin killer who, wandering in exile from his own city-state, is afforded refuge in Athens. Creon even refers to the court of the Areopagus and its etymology, although in precisely the wrong spirit. On presenting a proper defense, Oedipus should, in analogy with Orestes, be absolved of his crimes, for he, too, was driven to fulfill the pronouncements of APOLLO and was not fully culpable. Creon, however, views the refuge afforded Oedipus as contrary to justice. Creon, among other things, is shown to be insufficiently attentive to the tragic tradition and the Aeschylean background to Oedipus's current reception in Athens.

What is especially striking about *Oedipus at Colonus*, by contrast to *Oedipus the King*, is the new emphasis on the defense of Oedipus's crimes and his exculpation. He is not innocent of wrongdoing any more than Orestes is. Yet, as he explains at some length on more than one occasion, he did not kill his father or commit incest on purpose, and he killed his father only in self-defense; in both cases, the gods and destiny doomed him to doing what he did. This new emphasis is appropriate for a play that is more about establishing Oedipus as a hero with beneficent powers for Athens than it is about dramatizing his spectacular downfall. Oedipus, moreover, like the Aeschylean Orestes, is a foreigner who defends himself and his actions before a group of Athenians. Finally, he presents this defense at the grove of the Eumenides, just as Orestes had to defend himself in the presence of the Furies/Eumenides. Having both murdered his father and violated his mother's bed, Oedipus would notionally be subject to the hounding of the Furies, and so it is no accident that he ends up in their grove as he moves toward his final transformation into a beneficent hero figure.

Establishing Oedipus as a hero in Athenian territory is a major outcome of the play. Hero worship in ancient Greece was closely linked with the site of the hero's tomb. A hero, when duly propitiated, could be a powerful protective influence on the land. For this reason, it is very important where Oedipus chooses to end his life and establish his tomb. The entire play is centered around this struggle. Whereas Creon aims to hold him in the outlying areas of Theban territory to take advantage of his power as hero while limiting his damage as polluting presence, the Athenians accept Oedipus's self-defense and receive him into their community. The long description of his death suggests that he has been singled out by the gods, and by Zeus in particular: The rumble of thunder heralds his mysterious end, and rather than dying in a conventional way, he is simply taken by the gods. Oedipus, who even in *Oedipus the King* appeared to have a special connection with the gods, is now transformed into a semidivine figure himself.

The location of Oedipus's tomb in Athenian territory has contemporary political implications. The Thebans chose the Spartan side in the Peloponnesian War. They were a formidable enemy of Athens and were seen as such especially in the aftermath of the Athenian defeat at Delium (424 B.C.E.). It is no accident that tragedies in this period incorporate an anti-Theban dimension. In Euripides' *HERACLES* (ca. 416 B.C.E.), the hero, after going mad and slaughtering his family in Thebes, is received by Theseus in Athens, and in the same playwright's *SUPPLIANT WOMEN*, Theseus recovers the Argive war dead, whom the Thebans refused to bury, and grants them burial in Attic territory. In these two plays and in Sophocles' *Oedipus at Colonus*, the Athenians, represented by the legendary hero Theseus, succeed in situating the burial sites of prestigious heroes from other city-states within their territory, and specifically offer a refuge and final resting place for heroes from Thebes. Athens effectively appropriates the prestige and beneficent power of foreign heroes for itself. In *Oedipus at Colonus*, it is prophesied that this beneficent power will serve the specific purpose of stopping a Theban assault and granting victory to the Athenians over their enemies. Diverse elements of the play—choral odes in praise of Athens and Colonus, the characterization of Theseus as an idealized warrior king who values deeds over mere words, the propagandistic references to Athens as a "city of men," by contrast with the unmanliness of some Thebans—are resonant of contemporary patriotism and conflict. Athens comes off as a city-state of sound principles, justice, and hospitality, while the Thebans are false rhetoricians and self-interested political players, who do not honor Oedipus as a hero but view him simply as an instrument with which to dominate others.

In the end, Oedipus refuses to be controlled by the Theban agenda but chooses his own place of death. Though blind, he does not need to be led; he is guided by some inner sense. Although an outcast and a beggar, Oedipus has become an honored figure whom major city-states compete to possess. In raising Oedipus's status, Sophocles is exalting his own character, the Oedipus he created out of the existing fabric of myths.

Oedipus the King SOPHOCLES (ca. fifth century B.C.E.) It is not known in what year Sophocles' *Oedipus the King* was produced. Sophocles wrote three plays on Theban mythology and the house of OEDIPUS—*Oedipus the King*, *OEDIPUS AT COLONUS*, and *ANTIGONE*—but, unlike Aeschylus's *Oresteia*, they did not form part of a continuous trilogy of plays performed on the same occasion. The three plays, however, do respond to one another in their underlying themes and preoccupations, and attest to Sophocles' enduring interest in Thebes and the figure of Oedipus. In the present play, Oedipus goes from being a savior-hero and king to whom the distressed citizens of Thebes turn in the beginning for help to a destroyed, pitiable figure at the end, self-blinded and destined for exile. A key theme is knowledge and especially self-knowledge. The clear-eyed, commanding, intellectually impressive Oedipus of the beginning of the play does not know who he truly is and how he has acted toward his closest kin. The physically blinded Oedipus at the end, however, does know the truth about himself, and this truth paradoxically makes him a figure of awe and terrible grandeur.

SYNOPSIS

The scene is set in Thebes before the palace of Oedipus. Theban suppliants are seated before the altar, a priest of Zeus at the front. The priest tells Oedipus how the city is suffering from blight and plague; they now look to Oedipus, who previously saved them from the SPHINX. They see him as god-inspired and ask him now to raise up their city from its present catastrophe. He replies that he has racked his brain to find a cure and sent CREON to consult the Delphic Oracle. Creon arrives almost immediately. APOLLO's oracle has stated that the Thebans must extirpate the pollution (*miasma*) from their land. Whoever killed the previous king, LAIUS, was identified by Apollo as the source of pollution; the guilty party, moreover, still lives in Thebes. Creon recalls that Laius was killed when he was traveling to Delphi, that a witness stated that not one person, but a group of bandits, attacked him, and that no investigation was made because of the troubles brought by the Sphinx. Oedipus commits to pursuing the investigation himself, bids the suppliants to summon the Theban people, and exits along with Creon. The priest prays for success, then exits with the suppliants.

The Chorus of Theban elders expresses anxiety regarding the unknown cause of the pollution. It calls on the gods—Apollo, ATHENA, ARTEMIS, ARES, ZEUS, DIONYSUS—for aid and support. Oedipus enters. He announces to the citizens that Laius's killer should come forward and he will receive only banishment as punishment, not death; he calls down a curse on whoever committed the deed, if he keeps silent. The Chorus concurs and recalls

that travelers were said to have killed Laius. TIRESIAS, summoned previously by Creon at Oedipus's behest, enters, led by a boy. Oedipus asks him to reveal the meaning of Phoebus's words. Tiresias speaks darkly, but refuses to reveal the truth; Oedipus becomes furious and insults Tiresias. At length, Tiresias declares that Oedipus himself is the source of the pollution, and that he is living in a shameful manner with those closest to him. Oedipus denounces him as truly blind in all senses and accuses him of participating in a plot with Creon to seize the throne. Tiresias predicts that Oedipus will be banished and be blinded. They exchange angry words, and Tiresias makes further predictions about the man who killed Laius. Tiresias and Oedipus exit.

The Chorus wonders whether to believe Tiresias. Creon enters, indignant at being charged with treachery. Oedipus enters. He rebukes Creon harshly for trying to take his crown and does not let him reply. He interrogates him and learns that Tiresias never made such charges before. Finally, Creon has a chance to defend himself and repudiates the accusation that he wants to be king. Oedipus is not persuaded, and they exchange further angry remarks. JOCASTA enters. She counsels peace and reminds them of the public distress. The Chorus prevails on Oedipus not to banish or execute Creon, but he remains stubbornly angry with him. Creon exits. Oedipus tells Jocasta of Tiresias's charge that he killed Laius. Jocasta, to demonstrate the fallibility of prophecies, tells the story of the prophecy that Laius, who was slain where three roads meet, would be killed by his own son; yet their child was abandoned on the mountainside, his ankles pinned together. Oedipus is startled to hear that Laius was killed where three roads meet; he asks Jocasta for further details about the event. She tells him that a single servant, a herdsman, survived; Oedipus orders that he be summoned. At Jocasta's request, he explains his concerns, starting from the beginning. His father was Polybus of Corinth, his mother

Merope; but one day he heard a rumor that he was not the true son of his parents; so he sent to Delphi. Apollo replied that Oedipus would mate with his mother and kill his father. He fled Corinth, until he came to the place where three roads meet. There he encountered a chariot, in it an old man who attempted to drive him from the path; jostling turned to violence, and Oedipus ended up killing the entire group. He is horrified that he may have killed Laius, then taken his wife, and is now doomed by his own curse to be banished; he even fears that, in his banishment, he might end up slaying his father and marrying his mother. He awaits the witness who previously claimed a group, not a single man, did the deed. Jocasta insists that prophecies are not to be trusted, since Apollo had prophesied that Laius would die by his own child's hand. Jocasta and Oedipus exit.

The Chorus sings of the dangers of hubris and the importance of showing proper honor to the gods; then it laments that, if the prophecies regarding Laius are not shown to be true, Apollo will be abandoned and faith will dwindle. Jocasta enters. She reports that Oedipus is prey to anxieties and seeks help from Apollo. A Corinthian messenger enters with the news that King Polybus is dead, and that the Corinthians wish to make Oedipus King. Oedipus is summoned and enters; he confirms that Polybus died a natural death in old age. Oedipus proclaims the uselessness of the oracles. Yet, he still fears he may wed his mother. The messenger, thinking he will dispel Oedipus's fears, reveals he himself years ago brought the baby Oedipus to Polybus as a foundling who had been discovered on Mount Cithaeron; he recalls the pinned ankles that still cause Oedipus pain and that gave him his name. He cannot reveal who the child's father was, because he received him from someone else, the very herdsman who has already been summoned. Oedipus is keen to discover the secret of his birth, but Jocasta is suddenly reluctant to continue investigating, and as she leaves the scene calls him unfortu-

nate, and ominously proclaims that these are her last words.

Oedipus is determined to press on, believing that Jocasta is afraid merely that her husband comes from a low lineage. The Chorus joyfully hails Cithaeron as Oedipus's birthplace and then wonders if he was the son of a god. The herdsman enters. Oedipus and the messenger question him, but he is unwilling at first to speak. When threatened with force, however, he admits that he gave the child to the messenger, and that the child came from Laius and Jocasta, who had abandoned him because of a prophecy that Laius's child would slay him. Oedipus exits, cursing himself as he goes. The Chorus sings of the fragility of mortal glory; it cites Oedipus as an example of a mortal who ascended the heights, then fell to ruin. He shared his father's bed, and this sin has now been punished. A second messenger enters. He tells how Jocasta rushed, distraught, to her bridal chamber, shut the doors behind her, and called on Laius. Then Oedipus had come, frantically shouting for a sword and for Jocasta. He broke down her door and discovered her hanging dead from a noose. He took her body down, then removed the brooch pins from her robes, and pierced his eyeballs with them, proclaiming that his eyes would no longer look on what he had done and suffered. He now invites all of Thebes to look upon him and is resolved to go into banishment, though he lacks a guide.

Oedipus enters, blinded. He laments his wretched life. The Chorus wonders whether he might have been better off dead than blinded. Oedipus replies that he might have had to look on his father or mother among the shades; nor does he wish to look on his monstrous offspring. It would have been better if he had perished on Mount Cithaeron rather than leading the life he has led. Creon enters. Oedipus begs to be sent away. Creon agrees, but he has consulted the gods and is waiting for his answer before exiling Oedipus. Oedipus wants to go to Mount Cithaeron and die where he ought to have died long ago. He asks for his daughters to be brought before him. ANTIGONE and Ismene are led in, and he mourns tenderly over them. He predicts that they will lead sad lives and find no husbands because of their father's infamy. He commends them to Creon. Creon bids him go inside. Oedipus pleads once more to be exiled, but Creon still awaits the gods' response. He still wishes to hold his children, but Creon reminds him not to try to be master of everything. The Chorus observes that one must wait and see the outcome of a life before counting a person blessed. All exit.

COMMENTARY

At some level, Sophocles' *Oedipus the King* simply enacts a well-established pattern in Greek tragedy and Greek thought generally, the reversal of fortune to which mortals are prone. Sophocles' masterful dramatization of this pattern shows the destruction within the span of a single day of a powerful and successful man's entire conception of self and reality. Sophocles himself stresses this time span more than once to emphasize the swift overturning of Oedipus's existence: If a man can go from being an honored king to a wretched exile in a single day, this speaks to the fragility of mortal lives and the weakness of human self-knowledge.

It is worth reviewing the stages of Oedipus's fall. At the beginning of the play, he is besieged by citizens hoping he will save them from the plague afflicting Thebes. He had saved them previously from the Sphinx and still enjoys the status of a savior-hero. The cause of the plague is pollution (*miasma*), a Greek term that signifies the baneful influence of the presence of a person whose impure acts work a kind of contagion on those who touch him or are near him. The effect of pollution is not local, in this case, but total: The crops are blighted, people die of disease, infertility afflicts the fields and women. The land itself has become tainted, along with everything that lives on it, and the polluting presence needs to be driven out for it to recover. A good king was thought to have the opposite effect. The king's beneficent presence

as representative of Zeus's kingly power was thought to bring fertility and prosperity to the land. Oedipus, though he does not know it yet, has become the very opposite, a polluting king who brings blight and death. Oedipus's first illusion, then, is that he, as king, is working to help his people and will, he believes, save them once again, whereas, in fact, it is his continuing presence that is destroying the city.

Another gap in Oedipus's self-knowledge relates to his place in the city and his relation to the city. In the opening scenes, he is both of the city and separate. It is revealing that the priest specifies that the people are not praying to him as a god but as the first among men. Oedipus has a special, quasi-divine status and enjoys the glamour of an outsider who was able to save the city when no Theban was able to do so. The opening sequence of the play is very much concerned with the relation between Oedipus and his city. He at times takes up a paternal role, calling the citizens "children" and stating that he is more concerned for them than for himself. The citizens have a problem, and he comes as an outside savior-figure to solve *their* dilemma: He truly cares about their misery. Oedipus explains that he comes as a stranger (*xenos*) to the report of Laius's death and the deed itself, and thus needs the citizens' help in finding the killer. Dramatic irony is particularly intense at this point, since Oedipus was not only present during the deed, he perpetrated it; no one could be less a "stranger" to it than he.

The irony goes even deeper, however. Oedipus, as a man from Corinth, is both the king of Thebes and an outsider (*xenos*), a glamorous savior-hero. Yet, in reality, as we will learn, he is a native Theban, born of the king and queen of Thebes, and abandoned on Mount Cithaeron. Oedipus, then, takes the role of outsider/stranger/savior-god, who displays a beneficent willingness to save the Thebans whom he has taken under his wing, and yet, as the play goes on, he will realize that he himself *is* the problem, the pollution. He is not a savior coming from outside, but a Theban polluting his own city. Tiresias pointedly remarks that the man who killed Laius is reputed to be an alien resident (*xenos . . . metoikos*) but is actually Theban-born. When Oedipus finally understands his true Theban origins, however, he is destroyed and, as the polluting presence, must banish himself from the land, according to the terms of his own curse. At the beginning of the play, then, Oedipus is an alien resident who strives to save the city as paternalistic ruler; by the end, he is a native-born Theban acknowledged to be destroying the city and must leave it. He is revealed to be not a Corinthian by origin but a Theban, yet he is to be banished from Thebes: He has no true place. The entire play negotiates the hero's place in the community, first as beneficent outsider, then as baneful presence to be expelled.

Sophocles pays close attention, both at the beginning and throughout the play, to first-person pronouns and adjectives, and reflexives ("myself"). In Greek, the use of the personal pronoun (e.g., "I," Greek *ego*) is not grammatically necessary, and thus conveys emphasis. In *Oedipus the King*, the central protagonist's use of "I" is often pointed and ominous, as when he states, regarding the lapsed investigation into Laius's death, "*I* will start from the beginning and make things clear . . ." He will indeed "clarify" the issue by the end of the day, but not with the outcome he imagines. Oedipus, moreover, will undertake the investigation "himself" *(autos)*; for finding the murderer not only serves the murdered Laius but "himself" as well—since he, too, is vulnerable to assassination. As things turn out, Oedipus will conduct the investigation himself, but discovering the murderer of Laius is hardly useful to him, given that he himself turns out to be the murderer. "Casting light on" or "clarifying" the issue, moreover, takes on a somewhat different sense: Oedipus will receive the terrible illuminating realization of who he truly is, and at the same time, he will serve as a lucid example, making plain to Thebes and all mortals the ineluctabil-

ity of destiny and the fearsome power of the gods' designs.

It is true that Oedipus's use of first-person pronouns and reflexives are an instance of dramatic irony, which pervades the play, but such irony is not merely a clever effect; it is integral to the play's meaning. The central puzzle of the play concerns the nature and identity of Oedipus's "I," who he is and where he came from. Thus we begin the play with the insistent, at times overbearing "I" of a ruler-hero confident in his own powers: "I will take this in hand"; "I will endeavor to bring aid to my suffering people"; "I solved the riddle of the Sphinx." As the play goes on, however, the Oedipal "I" becomes more and more ominous and fraught with the anxious beginnings of a terrible realization: Oedipus was, indeed, always central, but not in the way he thought. His powerlessness before destiny and the gods matters the most in the end, not his capacity to take matters in hand as a controlling agent. By the end of the play, he will realize what it means to be Oedipus, whose name is etymologized in the play itself as referring to his swollen foot deriving from the pinning of his ankles as a newborn baby. Oedipus's "I" goes from being the dogged investigator to the solution of the mystery. By the end of this play, his first-person statements take more or less the following form: "I am Oedipus; I am wretched, born to fulfill a horrifying destiny." The emphasis shifts from actions denoted by transitive verbs and verbs of intention to first-person statements of identity: Oedipus now rehearses to himself and others what he is, has always been, and is now openly shown to be.

One approach to reading the play is to view it as the unfolding of a grim riddle. The Sphinx's famous riddle, to which the answer was "man," was imbued with a taunting circularity: The man attempting to solve the riddle ends up being killed by the Sphinx for not realizing that the answer to the riddle is, in effect, himself. It is not accidental that Sophocles' play constantly refers to Oedipus's victory over the Sphinx, setting up a parallel between this past act of heroism and the present situation. In the past, there was a deadly threat to Thebes, and the solution involved an act of intellectual discovery. In the present of the play's action, there is again a deadly threat to Thebes, and the solution must be discovered by investigation. Oedipus assures the citizens that he has been "traveling many roads of thought" in his attempt to identify the problem. No doubt, we would be at least partially right in viewing the play's outcome as a chastisement of Oedipus's intellectual hubris, his assumption that he can resolve any dilemma through his mental powers. From another perspective, however, it would be equally valid to point out that he *succeeds* in identifying the source of pollution, solving the riddle once again, and thus opening up the path to purification. The riddle, moreover, repeats the form of the original deadly riddle of the Sphinx: The answer to the question posed to Oedipus—"who is the source of pollution?"—is, quite specifically, himself.

The play moves Oedipus from one aspect of Greek heroism (ridding the world of monsters) to another (being banished from the community as a harmful presence). The answer to the first riddle, "man," is general and unproblematic; the answer to the second riddle, "Oedipus," involves the specific fate of an individual and the tangled paths of his conception, birth, and upbringing. A central problem in all this is how to *see* the truth about oneself and the world around one. As many have noticed, Sophocles' *Oedipus the King* is crowded with references to seeing, vision, and eyes. The references to seeing begin to intensify with the entrance of Tiresias, the blind seer. Throughout the passage, Sophocles plays on the paradox that Tiresias, though blind, sees the truth clearly, while Oedipus, increasingly enraged by the prophet's answers, calls him truly blind in every sense, though it is he himself who is blind to his own situation and true origins. Oedipus does not see with whom he shares his bed, what sort of offspring he has produced, who he truly is, and in that sense, he is blind to the meaning of his

entire existence. Tiresias, for his part, predicts Oedipus's act of self-blinding: "[T]he eyes that now see will see darkness." Creon later complains that Oedipus is not seeing straight when he charges him with treason.

Finally, when Oedipus discovers his true identity, he calls upon the light and wishes that he may look on it now for the last time. We subsequently learn that he blinds himself with the brooch pins from his dead wife's robes, proclaiming that he will never have to look on what he has suffered and done. Self-blinding, he states, is preferable to suicide, because otherwise he might have to look upon Laius's or Jocasta's shade in the underworld. He has no desire to look on his own "monstrous" children or the buildings of Thebes. Then Oedipus himself becomes a spectacle, a thing "terrible to look upon"; the Chorus wishes both to gaze on him and to avert its gaze. Oedipus himself, though now blinded, sees the truth about his life in a new way, and thus has uncannily become the mirror image of Tiresias, his hated adversary earlier in the play. His ocular blindness betokens a new, inner vision. The sight of him is fearsome, yet he now displays a certain majesty and suffering in the full realization of his sublimely terrible destiny.

By the end of the play, when the dark design of destiny has become clear, Oedipus is an example to behold and contemplate, a lesson for humankind. But what kind of lesson does his life teach the audience? There is no single answer to this question, but the authority and power of the gods are surely part of the answer. Apollo's oracle predicted that Laius would die at the hands of his offspring, and also predicted that Oedipus would kill his father and marry his mother. One simple lesson to be learned is that the god's truth, while sometimes difficult to interpret or apply to one's life, is unerring. Oedipus and the herdsman, as they unravel the secret of his life in a dialogue of mounting, nearly unbearable tension, declare at a crucial point that they are on the razor's edge, the turning point of realization, which will either mean salvation or disaster. A disastrous realization for Oedipus is the result: Apollo's and Tiresias's words are confirmed.

Yet, from another perspective, the outcome is positive, since it confirms the authority of the gods. Previously, Jocasta dismissed prophecy and oracular truth, since, as far as she knew, the oracles were disproven by the manner of her husband's death. Oedipus similarly triumphs in the revelation that King Polybus has died a natural death. Apparently thinking that he is not subject to the grim destiny (*moira*) assigned him, he proclaims himself the "child of chance/fortune" (*tukhe*). The Chorus responds joyfully to the new wealth of possibilities that opened up regarding Oedipus's birth, including divine parentage. Earlier, the Chorus had sung that the authority of the oracles and faith in Apollo would diminish if it turned out that the prophecies regarding Laius and Oedipus were not confirmed by events. In one sense, the play sets up a wager, a test of the authority of the gods, and, with rising suspense, weighs Oedipus' fate against the word of the gods. In the end, the gods' truth is overwhelmingly confirmed. The manner in which it is confirmed must have inspired feelings of Aristotelian "pity and fear" in the audience, but also relief: The gods still exist, and their truth orders human life.

Oedipus himself is, in one sense, blameless, and in another, utterly guilty. (In this regard, he is a classic scapegoat figure.) He is blameless insofar as he did not know he was killing his father and wedding his mother. The killing of his father was certainly a violent act, but then again, the most admired Greek heroes rarely put up with insolent treatment at the hands of others. The description of the killing suggests a sudden brawl in which neither party was strictly guilty; indeed, it would appear that Laius's party arrogantly pushed Oedipus to the side and began the conflict. Certainly, Oedipus is not a pacifistic character, and the play repeatedly suggests that he needs to be in command of any given situation. In itself a desire

to be in control is not ethically damnable, yet Oedipus risks hubris in moments when he seems confident in being able to evade the pronouncements of Apollo, and when he violently denounces Creon and Tiresias. It is no accident that the Chorus devotes one of their odes to the importance of showing respect for the gods and shunning hubris. The characterization of Oedipus as a man who values control and self-determination, doing things "himself" (*autos*), and taking his destiny into his own hands only underlines more emphatically the power of the gods and fate. Even Oedipus, king of Thebes, slayer of the Sphinx, is shown to be, in the end, pitifully subject to his destiny. Oedipus, who presents himself as being supremely self-confident, thus furnishes the ideal object lesson in the fragility of mortal understanding and self-determination. The lesson goes beyond mere personal culpability—and that is essential to the point.

Oedipus, who, so far as he knows, is living a very successful and morally acceptable life, has nonetheless violated fundamental moral laws. These laws go deeper than mere mortal comprehension and vision, and operate independently of them, i.e., even if a man is socially acceptable and lives a conventionally laudable life, if he violates these laws, the punishment of the gods is still inevitable. While he is carrying on with his transgressions, the land is blighted and the people of Thebes suffer and die. Even if the Thebans are happy with Oedipus as their king, the gods, as keepers of fundamental moral rules, are not. Oedipus's two major transgressions relate to the acts of creation and destruction: He extinguished the life of the man who created him and himself created monstrous offspring by "sowing the same field" as his own begetter. Begetting and killing have become horribly intertwined in Oedipus; the revelation of the incestuous marriage effectively kills Jocasta, while their male offspring, Polynices and Eteocles, will end up killing each other in battle. Sophocles' language throughout the play is replete with words signifying "creation," "coming into being," and "begetting" from the very first line. Employing language that, in retrospect, seems ominous, Oedipus hails his fellow Thebans as "children," the latest "offspring" of old CADMUS. With an inevitable logic, Oedipus's presence as polluting begetter/destroyer brings death, blight, and infertility on the land. In a certain sense, *Oedipus the King* displays the same set of concerns as Antigone, in which the social order of the city-state is opposed to deeper moral laws overseen by the gods. However great Creon's authority as ruler of the city, he cannot violate the rules of burial; when he attempts to do so, he is punished. Oedipus, though king of Thebes, is subject to the fundamental laws prohibiting incest and parricide. When he is revealed to have broken them, he becomes as vulnerable and wretched as any beggar.

It is not quite adequate, however, to state simply that punishment was meted out to Oedipus for his sins. His only punishment is the knowledge of what he has done. As he states emphatically, he blinded himself; no god did this to him. The broader outlook is not wholly negative; now, at least, Oedipus comprehends who he is and what he has done; he is now in a position to save the citizens once again by going into exile. Nor is Oedipus utterly destroyed at the end of the play. His fate is left, suggestively, up in the air. Oedipus himself desires to return to the place that should have been the scene of his death long ago, Mount Cithaeron. Creon is hesitant and wants first to consult the oracle. Oedipus, though brought low by his fate, has hardly been utterly crushed. He is still very demanding and even controlling. He insists that his daughters come to see him; he argues with Creon over his fate; he insists on his autonomy as self-punisher. In his last words, Creon must remind Oedipus not to continue to try to lord it over others and to exert mastery. Oedipus is thus still a fairly awe-inspiring figure, even with his eye socket dripping gore. He retains an astonishing resilience and insistent desire to control his fate—an insistence that will be on display again in Sophocles' last, posthumously produced play, *Oedipus at Colonus.*

Oedipus the King, like other plays of Sophocles, is a showcase for the playwright's mastery of plot, staging, and buildup of suspense as the culminating scene of self-recognition and revelation approaches. The workings of the plot, while not utterly seamless, are impressively designed and, as Aristotle appreciated, impressively self-contained. No outside intervention or deus ex machina is needed; there is no episodic extension of the plot. Oedipus's tragedy, from the beginning, is implicit in his very identity, and thus needs only to be unfolded on the stage. What at first appears to be an external problem to be solved—a murderer polluting the citizens—neatly collapses onto Oedipus himself by the end: The hero himself is at once cause and solution of the problem. Many scholars have viewed Aristotle's prescriptions about tragedy in the *Poetics* as based on Sophocles' *Oedipus the King* as idealizing paradigm. Aristotle's criteria of coherence and self-containedness of plot, of a "single action" not divisible into separate episodes, for example, are largely satisfied by Sophocles' play, but not by most other Athenian tragedies. Perhaps paradoxically, Aristotle's brilliant interpretation of *Oedipus the King* has sometimes derailed understanding of it, insofar as he presents it as the essential tragedy, or tragedy in its perfect form. The interesting particularities of Sophocles' play are thus in danger of being overlooked as its status as classic paradigm is accepted. Another even more famous interpretation—that of Sigmund Freud—has presented a broadly comparable danger: Oedipus's murder of his father and marriage with the mother are interpreted as an emblematic expression of underlying psychological tendencies of the human mind. In the end, it is a testament to Sophocles' compelling character that readers have persistently sought universal human significance in Oedipus's particular fate.

Oenomaus   King of Pisa. See PELOPS.

Oenone   A nymph of Mount Ida. Daughter of the river god Cebren. Classical sources are Apollodorus's *LIBRARY* (3.12.6), Ovid's *HEROIDES* (5), and Quintus Smyrnaeus's *Posthomerica* (10.262ff, 484). The sources give slightly differing accounts of Oenone. She fell in love with PARIS (also called Alexander), who had been abandoned on Mount Ida as an infant and had been brought up there. They had a son, Corythus. In the Judgment of Paris, the young mortal was called on to choose the most beautiful of the trio of goddesses, APHRODITE, ATHENA, and HERA. Paris chose Aphrodite. He then abandoned Oenone for HELEN, the bribe that Aphrodite promised him in return for choosing her. Oenone foresaw the tragic consequences of Paris's abduction of Helen and tried to persuade him to remain in Troy. Having accepted his resolution to leave, she promised to heal him should he be injured. Oenone knew that she alone could do so.

When Paris was wounded during the Trojan War by the poison-tipped arrows of PHILOCTETES, he appealed to Oenone, but the nymph, nursing the sorrows of his betrayal, refused. Oenone repented, but too late—by then Paris had died from his wounds. In grief, Oenone took her own life by either hanging herself or flinging herself on Paris's funeral pyre.

In classical art, Oenone was represented less often than the Judgment of Paris. In postclassical art, the Judgment of Paris continued to inspire artists. An early 20th-century Impressionist example of this theme by Pierre-August Renoir, *The Judgment of Paris* (Phillips Collection, Washington, D.C.), shows Paris offering the golden apple to Aphrodite, while Athena, Hera, and Hermes look on. Less commonly, artists have represented the relationship between Helen and Paris. An example of the latter is J. L. David's painting *The Love of Helen and Paris* from 1788 (Louvre, Paris).

In 1892, Alfred Lord Tennyson wrote a poem entitled "The Death of Oenone." A relief from a Hadrianic-period sarcophagus (Palazzo Altemps, Rome) depicts Oenone holding pan pipes, accompanied by Paris and EROS, and a scene showing the Judgment of Paris. In the postclassical period, the 19th-century American sculptor Harriet Hosmer lends the figure a tragic grandeur in her *Oenone* of 1854–55 (Mildred Lane Kemper Art Museum, Washington University, St. Louis).

Omphale   A queen of Lydia. Classical sources are Apollodorus's *LIBRARY* (2.6.3), Diodorus Siculus's *LIBRARY OF HISTORY* (4.31.5–8), and Ovid's *"ARS AMATORIA"* (2.11), *FASTI* (2.303–358), and *HEROIDES* (9). To purify himself for the murder of Iphitus, HERACLES undertook to become the slave of Queen Omphale of Lydia. In some sources she became his mistress and bore him a son, Agelaus. As Omphale's slave, Heracles was made to play the woman's role. According to Ovid, he had to wear feminine clothes while Omphale wore his lion's skin; in other sources, he had to do women's work, such as spinning. Ovid also relates another episode in which Heracles surprised Faunus (see PAN) in Omphale's bed.

In visual representations, Omphale is shown either in the act of taking possession of Heracles' attributes—the club and lion skin—as in Lucas Cranach's *Heracles and Omphale* from 1531–37 (Minnesota Museum of Art, St. Paul), or as his amorous interest, as in François Lemoyne's *Heracles and Omphale* from 1724 (Louvre, Paris).

Oresteia   See *AGAMEMNON; LIBATION BEARERS; EUMENIDES*.

Orestes   Son of AGAMEMNON and CLYTAEMNESTRA. Brother of ELECTRA and IPHIGENIA. Orestes appears in Aeschylus's *AGAMEMNON, LIBATION BEARERS,* and *EUMENIDES,* Euripides' *ELECTRA* and *ORESTES,* and Sophocles' *ELECTRA.* Additional classical sources are Apollodorus's

LIBRARY (Epitome 6.14, 6.23–28), Hyginus's *Fabulae* (101, 117, 119–123), and Ovid's HEROIDES (8) and METAMORPHOSES (15.489). The earliest known episode in Orestes' mythology takes place during the Trojan War. ACHILLES wounded the hero Telephus in Mysia, and an oracle told Telephus that only the same weapon of Achilles could cure it. Telephus went to Aulis and kidnapped the infant Orestes, threatened to kill him, and forced Achilles to heal him. The main episode in Orestes' life was his murder of AEGISTHUS and his mother, Clytaemnestra, to avenge the murder of his father, Agamemnon. Orestes had been removed from Argos to be brought up by his uncle Strophius, king of Phocis, alongside Strophius's own son Pylades, who was to become Orestes' steadfast companion. Orestes' sister Electra sent Orestes to Strophius to protect him at the time of Agamemnon's murder by Clytaemnestra, or in the version supplied by Aeschylus's *Agamemnon*, Clytaemnestra herself removed him earlier. In either case, Orestes returned, accompanied by Pylades, instructed by APOLLO to avenge his father. Homer's ODYSSEY describes Orestes' act as a glorious deed that conferred fame on the hero. Homer explicitly mentions only Aegisthus's death, although it may be that Clytaemnestra's is implied. Homer either does not acknowledge or does not know of any negative outcomes of Orestes' deed. In the Homeric view, Orestes has shown his manly courage in defending his father's honor and household, just as TELEMACHUS ought to do for the household of his father, ODYSSEUS.

The tragic tradition places greater stress on Orestes' killing his mother, his sister Electra's role in the plot, and his subsequent persecution at the hands of the FURIES. Aeschylus's trilogy of tragedies provides a crucial version of the story. In the *Oresteia*, Orestes and Pylades arrive in Argos, and in a recognition scene that will be repeated in novel forms in the later tragic tradition, he encounters and is reunited with his sister Electra. Together they plan the murder of Aegisthus and Clytaemnestra, which is carried out by Orestes and Pylades. Orestes needs to be encouraged by his friend to go through with the disturbing murder of his mother. Immediately after killing his mother, the Furies appear and begin to hound him. In the final play of the trilogy, *Eumenides*, Orestes has been purified by Apollo at his shrine at Delphi and proceeds to Athens, where he is put on trial at the Areopagus. ATHENA casts the tie-breaking vote in his favor, and the Erinyes are reinvented as the Eumenides ("The Kindly Ones"); they receive a shrine and cult in Athens.

Euripides' *Electra* and Sophocles' *Electra* cover the same ground with different emphases. Orestes' sister Electra plays an even more significant role in these plays. Sophocles' play is more self-contained, almost Homeric in its focus on the act of just vengeance: The play ends with Aegisthus's demise. Euripides gives Electra an even more active role, but at the same time renders the siblings' actions more problematic. Their victims appear sympathetic, and the play ends with a sense of moral chaos rather than justification and resolution. In Euripides' *Orestes*, Aegisthus and Clytaemnestra have been killed, but Orestes and Electra remain at the palace of Agamemnon. The people of Argos plan to execute them for their crimes, and Orestes, Electra, and Pylades conceive of a plan to kidnap HERMIONE, daughter of MENELAUS, to force him to defend them. Apollo resolves the crisis by commanding Menelaus and Orestes to make peace, and Orestes to marry Menelaus's daughter Hermione. In Euripides' ANDROMACHE, Menelaus broke his word and promised Hermione to NEOPTOLEMUS, but Orestes makes off with her in Neoptolemus's absence. He also arranges to have Neoptolemus killed at Apollo's sanctuary at Delphi. Orestes is a less noble and more morally compromised figure in Euripides' plays than in Homer and Aeschylus.

In another story line in Orestes' mythology, the hero learns from Apollo that he will be rid of his affliction only if he brings back the statue of Artemis from Tauris. This story forms the basis of Euripides' IPHIGENIA AMONG

THE TAURIANS. Now Orestes meets his other sister, IPHIGENIA, in another recognition scene. Orestes and Pylades are in danger of falling victim to the local practice of stranger sacrifice at the shrine of ARTEMIS, where Iphigenia is a priestess. Through an elaborate deceit, they manage to escape with the statue of Artemis. According to the Romans, Orestes transferred the rite of stranger sacrifice to Aricia in Italy, where a well-known sanctuary of Diana featured the rite of human sacrifice described in Frazier's *Golden Bough*. In this version of his legend, Orestes died in Aricia, but his bones were later transferred to Rome and buried beneath the temple of Saturn.

Orestes EURIPIDES (ca. 408 B.C.E.) Euripides' *Orestes* was produced in 408 B.C.E. The topic of the play coheres with Euripides' broader areas of interest in his later plays: the Trojan War and its aftermath, the house of Atreus, the terrible sacrifices made in the name of the war, and the figure of HELEN. At the same time, Euripides returns to subject matter he previously treated in his *ELECTRA*: the dilemma faced by ORESTES and ELECTRA after their father's murder. The present play, written near the end of the playwright's life, and in the wake of a long string of disasters suffered by Athens in the Peloponnesian War, presents a highly pessimistic view of war and of human society generally. Orestes and Electra, victims of their mother's treachery, are now faced with further danger: The citizens of Argos are on the verge of condemning them to death for CLYTAEMNESTRA's murder. In their desperation, they plan to kill Helen, who is sojourning in the palace at Mycenae with her husband, MENELAUS, and to kidnap their daughter HERMIONE. The victims are in danger of becoming unscrupulous victimizers, as the family now reaches a new degree of disintegration. Orestes and Menelaus effectively divide the house into two opposing factions. TYNDAREUS condemns all of them, including his own daughters, Clytaemnestra

and Helen, his son-in-law Menelaus, who went to war in pursuit of Helen, and his grandson Orestes, who killed Clytaemnestra. APOLLO appears above the palace just as the situation is on the verge of utter chaos, forces a reconciliation between Orestes and Menelaus, arranges for the main characters' marriages, and instructs Orestes to go into exile and thence to Athens. Apollo's epiphany, while it stems the disorder of the immediate conflict, does little to resolve the play's troubling moral and theological questions.

SYNOPSIS

The scene is set in front of AGAMEMNON's palace at Mycenae. It is six days after the murder of Clytaemnestra, and Orestes lies asleep. Electra laments the grim history of the house of TANTALUS, then summarizes the situation. After killing their mother, Electra and Orestes are treated as outcasts, and the Argives are holding a vote to determine whether they will live or die. In the meanwhile, Menelaus has arrived with Helen, who here rejoins her daughter Hermione, previously entrusted to Clytaemnestra's care. Helen enters; she and Electra converse with barely concealed dislike, and Helen sends Hermione to place a lock of hair on Clytaemnestra's grave and offer libations. The Chorus of noble Argive women enters, and Electra bids it sing softly so as not to wake Orestes. At length, Orestes awakes; he is tormented by the FURIES and begins to rave. When he returns to his senses, he blames Apollo for his predicament. Electra comforts him, and the Chorus prays to the Furies to free Orestes.

Menelaus enters. He has heard the news of both murders. Orestes beseeches him to save them from disaster, explaining that the Argives are voting on his fate. Tyndareus, Clytaemnestra's father, enters. He greets Menelaus but is filled with horror. While roundly condemning the behavior of Clytaemenstra, Helen, and Menelaus, he maintains that instead of killing Clytaemnestra, Orestes should have had her exiled. Orestes responds by painting a vivid picture of his moral dilemma, and then blaming both Apollo and Tyndareus himself for producing an evil daughter. Tyndareus exits in a rage, warning Menelaus not to help Orestes. Orestes then tries to persuade Menelaus to take his side, reminding him of his debts to his brother Agamemnon—both for Agamemnon's help in conducting the war and for the sacrifice of Iphigenia. Menelaus responds tepidly that he will try to help Orestes with diplomacy, and exits. Orestes denounces him as a traitor.

Pylades enters, and Orestes explains the situation to him. Pylades, for his part, has been banished by his father for taking part in Clytaemnestra's murder. With Pylades' help, Orestes resolves to appear before the Argives and argue his case. They exit. The Chorus sings of the curse of the house of Atreus and Clytaemnestra's murder. Electra now enters in search of Orestes. An old man arrives with the report that the Argives have voted in favor of putting them to death. He was present at the trial and describes at length how a hireling of Tyndareus won the day with his speech, securing a death sentence, despite Orestes' appeals and the speeches of others who supported him. Orestes only managed to persuade the Argives to allow them to commit suicide instead of being stoned to death. The Chorus mourns the extinction of the royal house. Electra recalls the horrors that have afflicted the house, beginning with Tantalus.

Orestes and Pylades enter. Orestes and Electra prepare for death; Pylades insists that he, too, will die with them and will bring about Helen's and Menelaus' deaths as well. Electra suggests that they take Hermione hostage and, after killing Helen, threaten to kill her, if Menelaus tries to take revenge. At length, Orestes and Pylades enter the palace to carry out the plan. Helen's cries are heard from within by Electra and the Chorus. Hermione enters. Electra deceives the naive but well-intentioned Hermione into accompanying her into the palace. Hermione is seized as they are entering

the palace. The Chorus sings that divine justice has come to Helen. A Phrygian slave comes out from the palace, lamenting the destruction of Troy for Helen's sake. He then sings how Orestes and Pylades locked up the slaves and attacked Helen. They defeated the Phrygian slaves in battle, snatched Hermione, and were on the verge of finishing off Helen, when they realized she had disappeared. Orestes enters and spares the slave; they leave together. The Chorus laments, then notices smoke coming from the roof of the palace. Menelaus enters. Electra, Orestes, and Pylades appear on the roof, holding torches, with Hermione held hostage. Orestes threatens to kill Hermione and set the palace on fire if Menelaus does not persuade the Argives to spare them. Menelaus is calling on the Argives for help, when Apollo appears above the roof.

Apollo announces that he saved Helen at Zeus's orders: She is going to be immortal, enthroned alongside her brothers Castor and Polydeuces (see DIOSCURI). He commands Orestes to go into exile for a year, then proceed to Athens to be tried for matricide, where he will be acquitted. He is to marry Hermione, while her suitor NEOPTOLEMUS will die at Delphi. Electra is to marry Pylades. Menelaus is to allow Orestes to rule in Argos and must return to Sparta and marry again. Apollo reveals that Helen was employed as a tool of the gods to create war and relieve the earth of its glut of men. Orestes hails the god, removes the sword from Hermione's throat, and seeks her father's permission to marry her. Menelaus offers his best wishes for the marriage. Orestes and Apollo agree to end their quarrels. Apollo leads Helen to Olympus, and all exit.

COMMENTARY

Euripides succeeds in finding an unexploited interval in the story of the house of Atreus and the career of Orestes. Orestes has killed Clytaemnestra but has not yet undergone his trial and received his acquittal in Athens. He and Electra remain as yet in Argos, where the local citizens have turned against them and are on the verge of condemning them to death. At the same time, Euripides engineers the situation so as to bring Menelaus, Helen, and Hermione to the palace of Agamemnon at the same moment. As elsewhere, Euripides lays claim to fresh mythic territory and makes it his own, exploiting an oblique moment in the mythological trajectory to rewrite the story from his own perspective and imbue it with his interests and themes.

A key element of originality here lies in expanding the family conflict to include Menelaus, Helen, Hermione, and even Tyndareus. The web of connections now becomes especially dense. The story, which, in Aeschylus's version, is tightly situated within Agamemnon's immediate family (Clytaemnestra, Orestes, Electra), now also includes Helen and Menelaus, both of whom play key roles in instigating the war and its consequences, and Tyndareus, whose daughter Clytaemnestra has been slain. He, too, was a prime mover of the war. Euripides thus brings into view a complex family story inextricably bound up with the war and its aftermath. The oath of the suitors, the abduction of Helen, the sacrifice of Iphigenia, the war itself, the return and murder of Agamemnon, and the slaying of Clytaemnestra are now all viewed as part of the same densely woven fabric of events.

It is inevitable that, in choosing so familiar a topic as Orestes, Euripides should refer to previous tragedies on the house of Atreus. Evocation of the *Oresteia—Libation Bearers* in particular—is prominent. In the opening scenes of the present play, Orestes, hounded by the Furies, lies asleep. We might compare the opening of *Libation Bearers*, where the Furies lie asleep, rendered dormant by Apollo. Euripides wants the audience to try to figure out where in the story line of Orestes' career the action of the play lies. How long has Clytaemnestra been dead? Will he go to Athens? Euripides plays with our expectations as he fleshes out his topic, ingeniously fitting his play between the two plays of Aeschylus's trilogy.

Part of Euripides' strategy is to banalize the story line of Aeschylus's *Oresteia*, converting a story of revenge killing and the emergence of civilized institutions into a sordid family quarrel. In the early dialogue between Electra and Helen, the latter is smugly self-satisfied with her good fortune, the former angry, self-pitying, and rebarbative. There is an undercurrent of insult traded back and forth in their conversation. The moment Helen leaves, Electra cannot restrain herself from remarking on Helen's characteristic vanity. Self-interest, not familial loyalty, drives the actions of the main characters. Menelaus is happy to express sympathy for Orestes' plight, but when it becomes clear that saving Orestes will require more than polite words, he hurriedly bows out. Orestes sharply reminds Menelaus of the profound debt of gratitude he owes to the dead Agamemnon and, by extension, to his son. Menelaus, however, simply wants to avoid trouble for himself.

We might expect greater wisdom from the aged Tyndareus, and he does offer some bracing arguments. In particular, he castigates Orestes for choosing the path of murder instead of seeking Clytaemnestra's banishment. He analyzes the fruitless cycle of revenge with notable lucidity, offering an effective critique of both Orestes' actions and their justification in Aeschylus's *Oresteia*. Did he really need to *kill* Clytaemnestra? Was no other path of justice available? On the other hand, Tyndareus's overall attitude seems pointlessly negative and meddlesome. He condemns Helen, Clytaemnestra, Orestes, and Menelaus. Tyndareus condemns Menelaus for going to war in pursuit of his unchaste wife, yet without considering his own culpability in demanding the oath that catalyzed the war. Later, he displays the full extent of his vindictiveness by having his agent ensure that the death penalty is decreed for Orestes and Electra. What has happened to his previous recommendation of banishment and lucid critique of the logic of revenge killing? Anger undermines Tyndareus's logic, making him as violent and culpable as anyone else.

Euripides rejects the austerity of traditional tragic plotlines to include an almost chaotic variety of characters driven by a diversity of motives. Orestes is nominally and loosely the focus, yet the play at times resembles a family melodrama. The pessimistic, complaining, but devoted sibling Electra often dominates the stage, while Menelaus's family fills up the stage with their own knotty story lines. Who will marry Hermione? Will Helen be punished for having been the cause of Trojan War? Will Menelaus show loyalty to the dead brother who sacrificed his daughter's, and ultimately his own, life for the sake of retrieving his morally questionable sister-in-law? Even the normally mute, token companion Pylades has a story of his own. He has been exiled by his father, Strophius, and is now in danger of having his promised wife, Electra, forced to commit suicide. Euripides does not display the Sophoclean trait of focusing a steady, isolated light on the doomed, recalcitrant hero figure. Instead, he revels in the multifariously branching plotlines of the different tragic families. Their marriages, the ups and downs of their material fortune, and their relations with their cities and relatives become the topic of a decentered, but no less acute and intense, tragic mode.

Orestes' madness is a case in point. The opening scene, in which Orestes sleeps while Electra laments his condition, makes much of Orestes' raving and the terrible persecution of the Furies. The prominence of this feature of Orestes' situation soon fades, however, as more urgent priorities take over the plot. Verbal fencing with Tyndareus and Menelaus, touching scenes of friendship with Pylades, and heated plan making in the latter portion of the play trump the importance of Orestes' guilt-driven sufferings. At one point, when Orestes and Pylades proceed to the town to plead their case, Orestes' haunted condition returns. In this instance, however, the pollution caused by his mother's murder emphasizes Pylades' utter devotion to his friend, whom he does not shrink from accompanying and supporting. The hero's

evident suffering, moreover, makes him seem pitiable instead of calculating when he unsuccessfully pleads his case before the Argives. His piteous state is forgotten, however, in the play's closing sequence, when he engages in pitched battle with the Phrygian slaves. Orestes' madness and persecution at the hands of the Furies represents one aspect of the hero. It is to be activated at convenient moments, but it is not his overriding feature. The play's plot is simply too various and wide-ranging to accommodate a single, brooding obsession.

Euripides' complicated plotting here is comparable to the intricately plotted *ANDRO-MACHE* (ca. 426 B.C.E.)—not accidentally, since the *Orestes* functions as prequel for some crucial aspects of the earlier play. At the end of *Orestes*, Apollo declares that Orestes is to marry Hermione, at whose throat Orestes melodramatically holds his sword. Neoptolemus, Orestes' main competitor for her hand, will die at Delphi. Hermione, who is an insignificant if largely benign character in the present play, vindictively persecutes Andromache in the earlier play and questionably allows herself to be abducted by Orestes, while her husband, Neoptolemus, perishes in a subheroic ambush at the god's shrine. As in other cases, Euripides shows an interest in exploring the prehistory of, and to a certain extent in rewriting, the plots of his earlier plays.

The earlier play, written, it may be argued, in a period when the playwright's and his audience's enthusiasm for the war with Sparta was still fresh and their outrage at Spartan actions not yet complicated by profound doubts regarding the merits of Athens's involvement, presented the Spartan characters—Menelaus, Hermione—in a relentlessly bad light. The Phthians—Neoptolemus, Peleus—were generally good. Now, Euripides appears to retract some of his criticism of the Spartans. Hermione, in the present play, naively but good-naturedly agrees to enter the palace to help Electra and Orestes, who are actually plotting to kidnap her. Helen comes off as vain and self-satisfied, but not quite the monster Electra makes her out to be, and in the end, Apollo accompanies her to the dwelling of the gods, where she will live as an immortal. Menelaus's character has less to recommend it, but his sins are venial, and he displays no more than the uxorious mediocrity usually ascribed to him by Homer and the tragedians. The final revelation, that Orestes is to marry the very Spartan whom he threatens with death, evokes hopes of an alliance between two previously hostile parties. In the play's closing speeches, Orestes and Menelaus resolve to mend their differences. The mood of the play is one of reconciliation at the end of a long series of regrettably and dispiritingly violent acts.

Hope for the future begins to emerge only at the play's end. Up to that point, the prospect seems fairly grim. Electra opens the play with the recollection of the long, troubling history of the house of Atreus, beginning with Tantalus. Electra recalls Tantalus again when she receives news of the death sentence. Like other plays of this period, however, Euripides does not end with the classic tragic closure of death and lamentation; instead, an exciting action sequence culminates in an escape from death and a god's intervention. The house will survive; its last male scion, Orestes, will live on to marry Hermione. Euripides arguably focuses even more on the household and its survival than Aeschylus. Aeschylus is interested in the emergence of polis institutions and the new position of the cult of the Eumenides (Furies) in Athens. At the same time, Aeschylus explores the cosmic significance of the male/female conflict that emerges in the house of Atreus. Euripides more concretely makes arrangements for the future marriages of Orestes, Electra, and the now wifeless Menelaus.

The other danger that the brother and sister escape, besides a death sentence, is imprisonment within an endless cycle of revenge killing. Orestes has already killed Clytaemnestra in revenge for her slaying of Agamemnon. Now, without any real hesitation, he seeks to revenge himself on Helen for causing the Trojan War. The parallel with the plot of *Libation Bearers* is striking. Once again, Orestes, Pylades, and Electra plan the murder of a woman; and once again, Orestes and Pylades proceed inside the palace of Agamemnon, while Electra waits to hear the news. Naturally, they call on the shade of Agamemnon to support them in this venture as well. Finally, in targeting both Helen and Menelaus, they aim to carry out another double murder of a ruling couple (cf. Clytaemnestra and AEGISTHUS). The siblings are trapped in a cycle of obsessive repetition. In Euripides' *Electra*, Electra resents her mother's luxurious lifestyle, while she herself lives in a cottage. Now, she resentfully envies Helen's and Hermione's resplendent good fortunes. When they kidnap Hermione, she is said, in language reproducing the recurrent metaphor of the *Oresteia*, to be caught in a "net."

Violence, however, has become disconnected from the sense of moral obligation it carried in the *Oresteia*. Orestes casually countenances slaughtering the innocent Hermione without offering any moral justification whatsoever. When Electra first introduces the idea of kidnapping Hermione and threatening her life, she takes an almost perverse relish in it. She was previously despairing and emotional; Orestes complained that she was undermining his virile stoicism. Electra's rapidly conceived plan to hold a sword to Hermione's throat seems to revive her spirits. Brother and sister are already revenge killers. Now, by extension, they are in danger of simply becoming killers. Euripides, as also in *Hecuba*, demonstrates an interest in the degradation of moral scruples through suffering, victimization, and violent precedent. The innocent victim, seeking to bring his or her victimizer to justice, becomes a killer in turn, thereby attaining the same moral status as the victimizer. Not only have Orestes' and Electra's sufferings exhausted their pity and caused them to lose their moral compass; they have become desensitized to violence and now consider violent acts without the kind of inner torment and hesitation that characterizes Orestes' decision to kill Clytaemnestra in *Libation Bearers.*

Euripides' *Orestes* presents a scenario of degradation and moral chaos comparable to that of his *Electra.* Orestes himself possesses a worrisome capacity to adapt to different roles for reasons of expediency. At first, when he still hopes to gain Menelaus's help, he fawns on him and speaks reverently of Helen, overcoming his own repulsion and sense of self-degradation. Later, when it becomes clear he will receive no effective help from Menelaus and Helen, he coolly plans their slaughter and blames Helen as the cause of the war.

The battle that follows does not redound unambiguously to his credit. Orestes and Pylades easily best the effeminate Phrygian slaves who attempt to protect Helen. They are, after all, true, virile Greeks. The description of their prowess includes comparison with Iliadic heroes like AJAX, Agamemnon, and ODYSSEUS. Employing a familiar Homeric simile, the slave who describes the battle compares them to two lions. This domestic battle against effeminate Phrygians, however, is arguably more a travesty of the Trojan War than a true imitation of it. Now, rather than fighting to retrieve Helen from Troy, two young men, who did not fight in the war themselves, attempt to slaughter Helen as a last-resort plan when faced with extinction themselves. They do not succeed in their mission and are in the act of threatening to kill a hostage and torch the palace when Apollo intervenes to sort out the now nearly irretrievable mess.

Does he succeed? Apollo certainly averts the imminent crisis, and he neatly resolves the remaining questions in the plot by revealing Helen's new status and arranging the main characters' futures and marriages. In moral terms, however, and in terms of making sense of the series of catastrophic events leading to the present moment, he does not. Aeschylus, in the final play of his trilogy, continues to build up arguments supporting Orestes' decision to kill his mother. The present play shows Orestes petulantly irritated with the god for leading him down the wrong path. He appears resentful that the god gave him a command that has led to some inconvenient circumstances. Driven to extremity in his argument with Tyndareus, Orestes even goes so far as to suggest that Apollo is the guilty one for having authorized his murderous course of action, and that the god should be killed as punishment for his sins. Orestes is arguably raving, demented by the persecution of the Furies, but it is still a shocking line of argument. For Orestes, moreover, the Trojan War was simply wrong: Agamemnon waged it for generous reasons, but it was still basically wrong. On the whole, the tone is one of bitterness and futility rather than the difficult, painful progress toward expiation and dawning comprehension of the designs of the gods that characterize the *Oresteia.*

All that Apollo achieves, through his direct, authoritative intervention, is a practical resolution of the crisis, which appears to suffice for Orestes. He immediately hails Apollo as a great god and source of truth. Orestes' bitterness fades now that the god arrives to save him at a worrisome moment. But perhaps we should not expect true moral clarity at this point. The moral problem of Orestes' act of murder doubtless remains to be resolved in the next phase, when he goes to Athens for trial. It does not seem accidental, however, that Euripides chose to write his play about a phase in Orestes' story when no credible moral, religious, or legal resolution has yet presented itself. The characters remain in a chaotic world without stable values.

The deus ex machina ending, while superficially reassuring, attests to the *need* for divine intervention. Family members who ought to behave honorably and sympathetically toward one another are at one another's throats; citizens are voting to put to death their rightful king; victims become victimizers. Apollo saves them from their own heedless impulse toward violence, but his message is not deeply reassuring. He shockingly states that Helen was an instrument wielded by the gods for killing mortals. Now she is to become a goddess. Comparable to Euripides' conception of Helen in his play *Helen* as a cruel illusion created by the gods with disastrous consequences, the present formulation drains the great struggle of the heroic age of its motivation and moral premise. No one was truly in the right. There was no larger aim. It was all simply a device of the gods to thin out the number of human beings. Such is the Euripidean conception of war in the waning years of Athenian power.

Orion A giant and hunter of great renown. Son of either GAIA or of POSEIDON and Euryale. Classical sources are Apollodorus's *LIBRARY* (1.4.2–5), Homer's *ODYSSEY* (5.121–124, 11.572–575), Hyginus's *Fabulae* (195), Ovid's *FASTI* (5.495), and Virgil's *AENEID* (10.763ff). Several myths, some contradictory, exist concerning Orion. According to the *Odyssey*, Eos (goddess of the dawn) fell in love with him and carried him off to be her consort. Orion was also the lover of one of the PLEIADES, MEROPE (wife of SISYPHUS) or, in Apollodorus, of another Merope, daughter of King Oenopion of Chios. Oenopion blinded Orion as punishment for his seduction of Merope. He regained his sight by walking toward the rising sun on the eastern horizon, with a young boy astride his shoulders to guide him. ARTEMIS sent a scorpion to sting him to death for having tried to force himself either on her or on one of her followers. After death, he was favored by the gods; he was transformed into a constellation with his dog, Sirius, who became the "dog star." Orion's loss of sight is the subject of Nicholas Poussin's *Landscape with Orion (Blind Orion Searching for the Rising Sun)* from 1658 (Metropolitan Museum of Art, New York).

Orithyia (Oreithyia) Daughter of ERECTHEUS, king of Athens, and Praxithea. Wife of BOREAS. Classical sources are Apollonius of Rhodes's *VOYAGE OF THE ARGONAUTS* (1.213ff) and Ovid's *METAMORPHOSES* (6.679ff). While playing by the river Ilissus, Orithyia was abducted by Boreas, the North Wind. They had two sons, the BOREADAE, Calais and Zetes, who, on attaining manhood, grew wings. They also had two daughters, Cleopatra and Chione. Cleopatra became the wife of PHINEUS, king of Thrace, who was tormented by the HARPIES until he was delivered by Zetes and Calais.

Boreas's abduction of Orithyia appears on an Attic red-figure pelike attributed to the Niobid Painter from ca. 460 B.C.E. (Wagner Museum, University of Würzburg), which depicts Boreas pursuing Orithyia. A more modern representation is a lunette fresco from the Galatea stanza of the Villa Farnesina (Rome) painted by Sebastiano del Piombo in ca. 1511 showing Boreas abducting Orithyia.

Orpheus and Eurydice Orpheus was a legendary musician from Thrace. A son of APOLLO (or Oeagrus) and Calliope (one of the MUSES). Husband of Eurydice (a DRYAD). Father of Musaeus. Classical sources are Apollodorus's *LIBRARY* (1.3.2, 1.9.25), Apollonius of Rhodes's *VOYAGE OF THE ARGONAUTS* (passim), Diodorus Siculus's *LIBRARY OF HISTORY* (4.25), Euripides' *BACCHAE*, (560–564), Hyginus's *Fabulae* (14.27), Ovid's *METAMORPHOSES* (10.1–85, 11.1–84), and Virgil's *GEORGICS* (4.315–558). Orpheus was famed for his musical skills and his association with DIONYSUS, whose rites he is said to have established in Greece. Orpheus's skills as a musician and poet were held in such high esteem that he was said to be able to wield power over stones, beasts, trees, and humans with his music. He joined the expedition of JASON and the Argonauts and with his music secured a safe passage for the *Argo* past the SIRENS, who were trying to lure the crew to destruction by their song.

Orpheus's music entranced even the underworld. On the day of Orpheus's wedding to Eurydice, she was pursued by ARISTAEUS, who

Orpheus and Eurydice. *Engraving,*
Marcantonio Raimondi, ca. 1505 (Metropolitan
Museum of Art, New York)

was infatuated with her, and bitten by a poisonous snake that caused her death. The grieving
Orpheus descended to HADES to bring his
much-loved wife back. The *Metamorphoses* and
the *Georgics* describe the cessation of all activity
and all punishments in Hades as dead souls and
tormentors alike paused to listen to Orpheus's
song. Moved by Orpheus's lament for his lost
wife, Hades, god of the underworld (in some
sources, his queen, PERSEPHONE), gave Orpheus
permission to lead Eurydice out of Hades on
the condition that he not turn around to look
at her as he did so. Just as the couple had gained
the upper world, Orpheus, too eager to have his
wife returned to him, cast a glance at Eurydice
and lost her to Hades a second time. In the
Metamorphoses, the distraught Orpheus sat on
the banks of the river STYX for seven days, but
he was not permitted to reenter.

Orpheus was killed by a group of women
(according to some, MAENADS, followers of
Dionysus), either because he had offended
their god or because his devotion to his wife
made him insensible to their charms. Ovid
describes his death as a grisly affair: The Maenads attacked him with stones, branches, and
farming tools and tore him limb from limb.
Even in death, Orpheus's voice could still be
heard calling Eurydice's name.

Orpheus's attribute is his lyre. In classical art,
he is commonly shown charming animals and
rocks with his music or in his descent to Hades
to rescue Eurydice. In a 16th-century engraving by Marcantonio Raimondi, *Orpheus and
Eurydice* (Metropolitan Museum of Art, New
York), Orpheus carries a musical instrument and
Eurydice sadly raises her arm to him. Another
postclassical example is Jean-Baptiste Corot's
Orpheus Leading Eurydice out of Hades from 1861
(Museum of Fine Arts, Houston). Operas on the
theme include Monteverdi's *Orfeo* (ca. 1609) and
Gluck's *Orpheus and Eurydice* (1910).

Orphic Hymns (second century C.E.) The
Orphic Hymns are 87 short poems of uncertain
date (ca. second century C.E.) based on a loosely
connected set of religious tendencies called
"Orphism." The *Orphic Hymns* belong to the
broader category of Orphic literature—texts
ascribed to the mythic figure ORPHEUS and
used in connection with religious cult. These
texts include an Orphic theogony in which a
succession myth differing markedly from that
of Hesiod's *THEOGONY* is offered. In Orphic
mythology, DIONYSUS and PERSEPHONE are especially important, as they are associated with
death and the afterlife—a major preoccupation
of mystery cult. In 1962, the discovery of the
Derveni papyrus—a commentary on an Orphic
theogony—dramatically expanded scholars'
understanding of Orphic beliefs.

Ovid (45 B.C.E.–17 C.E.)   Publius Ovidius Naso
was a Roman poet from Sulmo, author of

the *METAMORPHOSES*, *AMORES* ("Love Poems/ Loves"), *ARS AMATORIA* ("Art of Love"), *FASTI* ("Calendar"), *HEROIDES* ("Heroines"), the *Remedia Amoris* ("Cure for Love"), *Medicamina Faciei Femineae* ("Cosmetics"), the *Tristia* ("Sad Poems/Sorrows"), *Epistulae ex Ponto* ("Epistles from Pontus"), *Ibis*, as well as a lost tragedy, the *Medea*. Ovid was born in 43 B.C.E. and died in 17 C.E. He came from a good family of equestrian status and might have pursued a political and/or forensic career, but instead devoted his life to writing poetry. Ovid was the major literary figure of his generation and, in addition to writing poetry, performed as a declaimer (a practitioner of rhetorical display speeches). Among Ovid's earlier works are the *Amores* and *Heroides*: Both are on erotic topics and written in the meter of Roman love poetry, the elegiac couplet. The genre of love elegy is a theme running throughout Ovid's career. His *Ars Amatoria* and *Remedia Amoris* deftly pick apart the conventions of the genre, while the *Fasti*, a poem on the Roman calendar, is written in elegiac couplets and engages in a complex way with the generic conventions of elegy. The *Ars Amatoria* was published around 1 B.C.E., while the *Fasti* and *Metamorphoses* were being written up until, and possibly after, Ovid's relegation to Tomis in 8 B.C.E. The real reason for Ovid's exile by decree of the emperor Augustus to the shores of the Black Sea remains a mystery. Ovid, in his poetry written in exile (the *Tristia* and *Epistulae ex Ponto*), alludes to "a poem and a mistake" as the reason, and hints that he may have seen or been privy to some compromising scandal regarding the imperial family. The poem was Ovid's morally subversive *Ars Amatoria*, which no doubt displeased Augustus by contravening the spirit of his legislation on marriage and adultery. Yet most scholars find it difficult to sustain a causal link between Ovid's relegation and a poem published several years earlier. Ovid continued to petition Augustus, and then Tiberius, but was never recalled and died in exile in 17 C.E. Ovid's poetry has been accused in the past of a witty artificiality, but more recent scholarship has explored the depths of his erudition, his genius as a storyteller, and his conscious manipulation of literary traditions. As a poet exiled by Rome's first emperor, Ovid remains a key figure for understanding the relations between poetry and power in imperial Rome, and his poems have been mined by interpreters for subversive nuance. Ovid's greatest poem is his *Metamorphoses*, which, in 15 books of intricately interwoven stories, recounts the world history of "transformation" and has profoundly determined our modern canon of classical myths.

P

Palamedes Son of Nauplius and Clymene. Classical sources are Apollodorus's LIBRARY (2.1.5, 3.2.2, Epitome 3.7–8, 6.8–11), Hyginus's *Fabulae* (95, 105, 116, 277), and Ovid's METAMORPHOSES (13.34–62, 308–312). Palamedes is known as a clever hero who participated in the Greek expedition against Troy. When ODYSSEUS was feigning madness and ploughing his fields with salt to avoid going to Troy, Palamedes either threw Odysseus's son TELEMACHUS in front of Odysseus's plough or threatened Telemachus with a sword. In either case, Odysseus acted to save Telemachus, thereby revealing his sanity. Odysseus took his revenge at Troy: He planted a forged letter from PRIAM offering a bribe of gold to Palamedes for betraying the Greeks, then hid the same amount of gold in Palamedes' tent. AGAMEMNON was persuaded of Palamedes' guilt and had him stoned by the army. His father, Nauplius, avenged his son's death by setting up false beacon lights at Cape Caphareus and causing the wreck of the Greek fleet. Nauplius is also said to have persuaded the wives of Greek heroes to be unfaithful. Palamedes is credited with creating certain letters of the alphabet, the game of dice, and various other inventions. Lost tragedies on the subject of Palamedes are attested for Euripides, Aeschylus, and Sophocles.

Pan (Faunus) A bucolic god, or SATYR, from Arcadia. Classical sources are the *Homeric Hymn to Pan*, the *Orphic Hymn to Pan*, Apollodorus's LIBRARY (1.4.1), Ovid's METAMORPHOSES (1.689–713, 11.146–171), Pausanias's *Description of Greece* (1.28.4, 8.36.8, 8.42.2–3, 8.54.6–7, 10.23.7), Philostratus's IMAGINES (2.11), Theocritus's *Idylls* (1.15–18), and Virgil's ECLOGUES (2.31–33, 10.26) and GEORGICS (3.391–393). Pan was half man, half goat. He was goat-footed, hirsute, and wore a crown of pine needles. Pan, whose name is related to the Greek word for "herdsman," was primarily a protector of herds (sheep, cattle, and horses) but also a hunter of small game. Pausanias also links him to warfare. The word *panic* was derived from the emotion induced by Pan during battle. In addition, Apollodorus credited Pan with having taught the art of prophecy to APOLLO. Romans conflated the figure of Pan with that of Faunus, like him, a bucolic satyr.

In the *Homeric Hymn to Pan*, Pan is the son of HERMES and the nymph Dryope; his father brought him before the Olympian gods, to the delight of all. Ancient authors often associate the name Pan with the Greek word for "all." This association with the universal gave Pan authority over the wide realm attributed to him in this poem.

Pan is closely associated with DIONYSUS, in whose company he frequently appears in classical literature and art. Perhaps he is best known for his association with music and for his amorous pursuit of nymphs. In Book 11 of the *Metamorphoses*, Pan entered into a musical competition with APOLLO and his lyre. King MIDAS expressed a preference for Pan's double flute, and for this judgment, Apollo gave Midas asses' ears.

True to his satyr nature, Pan was lascivious. In the *Orphic Hymn to Pan*, Pan spends his time among the mountain nymphs of Arcadia, playing the panpipe, or syrinx, the instrument he invented after the failure of one of his amorous initiatives. In Book 1 of the *Metamorphoses*, Ovid describes Pan's attempted seduction of the nymph SYRINX, who chastely rejected his advances and fled to the river Ladon. She called on the water nymphs to change her form, and Pan was left clutching the marsh reeds into which she had been transformed. From these reeds, Pan fashioned the panpipe. Pan's pursuit of the nymph Pitys ended in similar rejection; she metamorphosed into a pine tree. His other loves included the nymph ECHO and the shepherd Daphnis. According to Virgil's *Georgics*, Pan succeeded in attracting the amorous attention of SELENE, goddess of the moon. In several sources, the reader is warned not to disturb the sleeping Pan in his domain because his behavior can be erratic.

Visual representations of Pan commonly show him with Dionysus in both the classical and the postclassical periods. In an early third century sarcophagus (Museum of Fine Arts, Boston), Pan participates in a Dionysian procession, along with EROS, SILENI, MEANADS, and other satyrs. He can be identified by his attribute, the syrinx, and is often bearded as in a Lucanian red-figure volute krater from ca. 380 B.C.E. (Toledo Museum of Art, Ohio). Here, Dionysus and ARIADNE appear in a section of the scene while a satyr picks grapes and hands them to Pan.

Pandora   The first mortal woman. Classical sources are Apollodorus's *LIBRARY* (1.7.2),

Hesiod's *THEOGONY* (570–612) and *WORKS AND DAYS* (47–105), Hyginus's *Fabulae* (142), and Pausanias's *Description of Greece* (1.24.7). Pandora's name means "all-gifted," because she was presented with virtues (and vices) by all the Olympian gods. ZEUS commanded HEPHAESTUS to create Pandora—he fashioned her out of earth and water—to punish PROMETHEUS for stealing fire from the gods to give to men. Pandora was designed to be beautiful, skilled, and charming. She was gifted with grace by APHRODITE and clothed and ornamented by ATHENA, who also taught her crafts. Hephaestus created a finely wrought golden headband etched with figures of all the monsters that roam the earth and sea and placed it on Pandora's head. But she was intended to be the bane of mankind. Zeus commanded HERMES to provide her with a thieving, conniving disposition. Pandora was sent as a gift to EPIMETHEUS, brother of Prometheus, and despite having been warned by Prometheus against accepting gifts from Zeus, Epimetheus was tempted by Zeus's offer of Pandora for a wife. Pandora had been given by the gods a storage jar containing daimones or spirits, which, once in the company of Epimetheus, she unintentionally loosed on the world of man: Out of the jar flew all the miseries that would assail mankind. Only one daimon—hope—was left in the jar. In later periods, the storage jar was conceived of as a box giving rise to the expression "Pandora's box."

The daughter of Epimetheus and Pandora was PYRRHA. She married DEUCALION, and they alone of humanity survived the deluge sent by Zeus to destroy human civilization and repopulate the earth. In her questionable nature and her responsibility for the introduction of miseries and hardship into the world, Pandora is comparable to the biblical Eve. Her daughter, like Eve's descendants, survived a great flood to repopulate the earth.

The *Description of Greece* refers to Hephaestus's creation of Pandora in relief around the base of the pedestal of the statue of Athena on the Acropolis. In a red-figure white-background kylix from ca. 470 B.C.E., Pandora is shown flanked by Hephaestus and a smiling Athena as the gods perfect their creation (British Museum, London). In the postclassical period, it was not until the 19th century that a renewed interest in the myth gave rise to new images of Pandora. An example is Dante Gabriel Rossetti's *Pandora* from 1878 (Liverpool National Museum, Liverpool), which depicts Pandora as a beguiling feminine creature with perhaps some intimation of knowledge of the role she will play in human affairs.

Paris (Alexander)   Son of HECUBA and PRIAM, king of Troy. Paris is also called Alexander, especially in Homer. Classical sources are Apollodorus's LIBRARY (3.12.5–6, Epitome 3.1–5, 5.3, 5.8), Homer's *ILIAD* (passim), Hyginus's *Fabulae* (91, 92), and Ovid's *HEROIDES* (5, 16, 17), and *METAMORPHOSES* (12.597–611). Euripides and Sophocles wrote tragedies entitled *Alexander*, now lost. Paris was abandoned as an infant on Mount Ida because of a prophecy revealed to his parents that he would one day bring about the destruction of Troy. In one version, Paris was suckled by a bear and rescued by Priam's servant Agelus, who had come back to check days after he had been ordered to leave the infant on the slopes of Mount Ida. In another version, Paris was found and raised by shepherds.

The story of the return to his family is as follows. Funeral games had been established in memory of Priam's son who had died in infancy—none other than Paris himself—and Paris took part, winning several competitions. He was either recognized by his sister CASSANDRA or he proved his own identity by the token of the clothes he had worn when he had been abandoned.

Paris's abduction of HELEN sparked the Trojan War. The story begins with the famous Judgment of Paris. At the wedding of PELEUS and THETIS, Eris (Discord or Strife) threw a golden apple into the midst of the revelers, which was to be given to the most beautiful of ATHENA, APHRODITE, or HERA. Since none wished to be the arbiter of the competition, ZEUS asked HERMES to bring the three goddesses to Mount Ida and there be judged by Paris. The goddesses attempted to sway Paris's judgment: Athena offered Paris wisdom and unparalleled military victory; Aphrodite offered him the love of the most beautiful mortal woman—Helen of Sparta; and Hera promised him the rule of Asia. Paris accepted Aphrodite's proposal and presented her with the golden apple. Paris abandoned his lover, the nymph OENONE. Oenone had foreseen the tragic consequences of Paris's pursuit of Helen and attempted to persuade him to remain in Troy. Having accepted his resolution to leave, Oenone promised to heal Paris of his injuries. She foresaw that she alone could do so.

Paris sought Helen in Sparta and returned with her to Troy, setting off the Trojan War. At the beginning of the war, the Greeks and Trojans agreed that a one-to-one combat between Paris and Helen's husband, MENELAUS, would resolve the conflict. Paris was on the point of being killed by Menelaus when Aphrodite interceded on his behalf and saved him. During the Trojan War, Paris wounded DIOMEDES but had to be drawn into the fighting by HECTOR. Later, as Hector lay dying, he prophesied that ACHILLES would be killed by Paris, with the help of APOLLO. This came to pass when Paris, guided by Apollo, shot Achilles with an arrow.

Later, Paris was wounded during the war by the poison-tipped arrows of PHILOCTETES. He appealed to Oenone, but the nymph, nursing the sorrows of his betrayal, refused. Oenone repented, but too late; by then, Paris had died from his wounds. In grief, Oenone took her own life, by either hanging herself or flinging herself on Paris's funeral pyre.

Parthenopaeus   See *SEVEN AGAINST THEBES*; *THEBAID*.

Pasiphae   Daughter of HELIOS and Perseis. Wife of king MINOS of Crete. Mother of ARIADNE and the MINOTAUR. Classical sources include Apollodorus' *LIBRARY* (3.1.3, 3.15.1), Hyginus's *Fabulae* (40), Ovid's *ARS AMATORIA* (1.289–322), and Virgil's *ECLOGUES* (6.45–60). According to Apollodorus, Minos asked POSEIDON to send a bull from the depths and promised that if Poseidon did so, he would sacrifice the bull to the god. Poseidon sent a magnificent bull, but Minos sacrificed another bull instead and kept Poseidon's bull among his herds. To punish Minos, Poseidon made Minos's wife Pasiphae fall in love with the bull. DAEDALUS, the famous artisan in exile from Athens, helped her by constructing a wooden cow on wheels covered with a real cow's skin: Pasiphae went inside the artificial cow, and the bull mated with her. Their offspring was Asterios, better known as the Minotaur, a creature with the head of a bull and the body of a man. Daedalus then constructed the labyrinth to contain the Minotaur. After the murder of Minos's son Androgeus in Athens, the Athenians were required to send seven boys and seven girls each year as a sacrifice to the Minotaur, until the Athenian hero THESEUS slew it. Apollodorus also states that Pasiphae gave Minos a drug to prevent him from sleeping with many other women according to his usual inclination: The drug made him ejaculate poisonous creatures into his partners in adultery, thereby killing them. Procris (see CEPHALUS) succeeded in sleeping with Minos by giving him an antidote to Pasiphae's drug. Hyginus tells a slightly different version in which Pasiphae was punished with lust for the bull by APHRODITE, since she failed to perform sacrifices for the goddess. King Minos, in Hyginus's version, imprisoned Daedalus for constructing the wooden cow, but Pasiphae unshackled him, allowing him to escape with his son ICARUS. Roman poets made much of the strangeness of Pasiphae's passion. Virgil's sixth eclogue includes a pathetic scene in which Pasiphae yearns with passionate, unrequited love for the bull. In Ovid's *Ars Amatoria*, a jealous, vindictive Pasiphae condemns bovine "rivals" to be sacrificed, and then mockingly refers to their attractive appearance as she holds their entrails in her hands.

Patroclus   (Patroklos)   A hero of the Trojan War. Son of Menoetius and Sthenele. Close friend of the great hero of the Trojan War, ACHILLES. Classical sources are Apollodorus's *LIBRARY* (3.13.8, Epitome 4.6–7), Homer's *ILIAD* (1.337–347, 9.189–221, 11.599–848, 15.390–404, 16–19, and 23 passim), and Pausanias's *Description of Greece* (3.19.13). Patroclus fought alongside Achilles on the side of the Greeks in the Trojan War.

As a boy, Patroclus was exiled from Opus for killing a boy, Clitonymous, over a game of dice. He came to Thessaly and was raised by PELEUS with Achilles. The two were close friends: They went to the Trojan War together, and when Patroclus was injured, Achilles nursed him to health. When Achilles refused to enter combat because of his quarrel with AGAMEMNON, Patroclus, with Achilles' permission, wore Achilles' armor into battle. The Trojans believed that Achilles had reentered the fray and became frightened. Patroclus, in his borrowed armor, killed many, but during battle he was killed by HECTOR, who afterward stripped his armor. A struggle over possession of Patroclus's corpse ensued. On learning of Patroclus's death, Achilles rushed into battle without armor. His shriek put the Trojans to flight, and Patroclus's body was left for Achilles to claim. Achilles built a tomb for Patroclus near his funeral pyre. The death of Patroclus is a crucial turning point in the *Iliad*: Hector's slaying of Achilles' comrade effectively dooms him to be slain by Achilles.

The death of Patroclus was represented in vase painting and relief in the classical period. The relief on an Etruscan urn from the second

Menelaus and Meriones Place Patroclus's Corpse in a Cart. *Alabaster Etruscan urn, second century* C.E. *(Museo Archeologico Nazionale, Naples)*

century C.E. shows Menelaus and Meriones placing Patroclus's corpse in a cart (Museo Archeologico Nazionale, Naples).

Pausanias (fl. second century c.e.) Pausanias was a Greek writer from Magnesia who flourished around the middle of the second century C.E. He wrote the *Description of Greece* in 10 books. He describes the monuments, sanctuaries, cults, rituals, and topography of cities in Greece and especially Achaia. Pausanias refers to myths and mythological figures in the course of his discussions. Mythology was inextricably connected with the local cults and traditions of ancient Greece.

Pegasus A winged horse. Offspring of MEDUSA and POSEIDON. Classical sources are Apollodorus's *LIBRARY* (2.3.2, 2.4.2), Hesiod's *THEOGONY* (270–286), Ovid's *METAMORPHOSES* (4.785–786), Pindar's *Olympian Odes* (13.60–92), and Strabo's *Geography* (8.6.2, 5.254–268). Pegasus sprang from Medusa's body at the moment she was being beheaded by the hero PERSEUS. The warrior CHRYSAOR also emerged from the wound. In Pindar's *Olympian Odes* 13, ATHENA gave BELLEROPHON a charmed bridle to capture Pegasus as he drank from a spring. Astride Pegasus, Bellerophon fought and defeated the AMAZONS and slew the CHIMAERA, a fire-breathing creature. According to Pindar, Pegasus threw Bellerophon from his back when, in his temerity, Bellerophon attempted to rise to Mount Olympus. When not accompanying Bellerophon on his adventures, Pegasus was stabled on Mount Olympus. By striking the ground with his hoof, Pegasus created the Hippocrene spring near Parnassus.

In visual representations, Pegasus appears at the moment of his birth and also in myths associated with Bellerophon. A white-ground lekythos attributed to the Diosphos Painter from ca. 500–450 B.C.E. (Metropolitan Museum of Art, New York) shows Perseus fleeing from the decapitated body of Medusa while the fully formed Pegasus springs from her neck. Similarly, a black-figure (white-ground) pyxis from ca. 525 B.C.E. (Louvre, Paris) depicts the death of Medusa and birth of Chrysaor and Pegasus. In a postclassical work by Andrea Mantegna, *Parnassus*, dating to 1497 (Louvre, Paris), Pegasus is shown

Pegasus and a Muse. *Odilon Redon, ca. 1900 (private collection)*

among the pantheon of gods, standing beside HERMES. *Pegasus and a Muse* by Odilon Redon is an early 20th century symbolist representation of the mythical flying horse.

Peleus　King of Phthia in Thessaly. Son of AEACUS. Father of ACHILLES. Peleus is a character in Euripides' *ANDROMACHE*. Additional classical sources are Apollodorus's *LIBRARY* (3.12.10–3.13.8), Catullus's poem 64, EURIPIDES' *IPHIGENIA AT AULIS* (1,036–1,079), Homer's *ILIAD* (passim), Hyginus's *Fabulae* (54), and Ovid's *METAMORPHOSES* (11.229–409). Peleus and his brother TELAMON were banished for killing their half-brother Phocus. Peleus went to Phthia and married Antigone, daughter of Eurytion, but he killed Eurytion by accident in the Calydonian Boar hunt. Exiled again, he went to Iolcus, where Astydamia, wife of Acastus, fell in love with him. When he refused her advances, she accused him of rape. Astydamia also sent a letter to Antigone, Peleus's wife, that Peleus intended to marry Sterope, Acastus's daughter. Antigone hanged herself. Acastus attempted to have Peleus killed by abandoning him on a hunting expedition amid CENTAURS and hiding his sword. He escaped, in one version with the help of CHIRON, in another with the help of the gods. He took vengeance on Astydamia by cutting her into pieces. ZEUS and POSEIDON arranged to have the mortal Peleus marry the goddess THETIS, because it was prophesied that her son would be more powerful than his father. Her union with a major male god was thus out of the question. Peleus, in order to win Thetis, had to hold on to her as she assumed many different shapes. This story is told in OVID's *Metamorphoses*. The gods attended their wedding and brought gifts. The goddess Strife (Eris) is said to have attended. By throwing an apple to be awarded to the most beautiful goddess, she inspired the strife among APHRODITE, HERA, and ATHENA, which led to the Judgment of PARIS and the Trojan War. The first meeting and wedding of Peleus and Thetis are recounted in CATULLUS's poem 64. In Catullus's version, the FATES predict the violent later career of their son Achilles. When Peleus interfered with Thetis's attempt to make Achilles immortal by dipping him into fire, she left him. In Homer's *Iliad*, Achilles feels pity for his father Peleus's lonely old age. In Euripides' *Andromache*, Peleus supports ANDROMACHE when HERMIONE schemes against her and persecutes her. At the end of the play, it is revealed that Peleus will be reunited with Thetis and made immortal.

Pelops Son of TANTALUS. Father of ATREUS and THYESTES. Classical sources include Apollodorus *LIBRARY* (Epitome 2.3–10), Apollonius of Rhodes's *VOYAGE OF THE ARGONAUTS* (1.752–758), Diodorus Siculus's *LIBRARY OF HISTORY* (4.75), Ovid's *METAMORPHOSES* (6.401–411), and Pindar's *Olympian Odes* (1.25–96). Pelops's father, Tantalus, killed him when he was a child and served him in a stew to the gods in order to test them. DEMETER, distracted by the loss of her daughter Persephone, ate his shoulder. The gods brought Pelops back to life and replaced his shoulder with an ivory one. PINDAR is appalled by the story of a greedy Demeter consuming human flesh and insists that the episode never occurred. According to Pindar, Tantalus was punished in the underworld because he stole nectar and ambrosia from the gods. Pelops was abducted by Poseidon, who made Pelops his lover. Later, Pelops wished to marry Hippodamia, daughter of Oenomaus. Oenomaus would give his daughter only to the man who could take her in a chariot and escape the father's pursuit. Pelops is said to have bribed Oenomaus's charioteer Myrtilus to loosen the linchpins of his chariot, causing Oenomaus's death. Oenomaus cursed Pelops in his dying words. In some versions, Pelops killed Myrtilus as well. Pindar does not mention the bribe of Myrtilus but states that Pelops won due to Poseidon's gift of horses. In Greek tragedies on the subject of the house of

AGAMEMNON, the name of Pelops or Tantalus is often mentioned to evoke the ancestral curse of the family, passed down from generation to generation. See also ORESTES.

Penelope Daughter of Icarius. Wife of ODYSSEUS and mother of TELEMACHUS. The principal classical source is Homer's *ODYSSEY* (passim). Additional classical sources include Apollodorus's *LIBRARY* (3.10.6–8, Epitome 3.7, 7.2.6–39), Hyginus's *Fabulae* (125–127), Ovid's *HEROIDES* (1), and Pausanias's *Description of Greece* (3.20.10–11, 8.12.5–6). Penelope was the paradigm of marital fidelity in the ancient world: She waited 20 years for her husband to return from the Trojan War, while the suitors occupying her house continually pressured her to choose a new husband from among them. She deceived the suitors by claiming that she had first to weave a shroud for LAERTES before choosing one of them. Each night, however, she would undo her weaving. At length, the ruse was discovered. She then announced an archery contest: She would marry whichever suitor could string Odysseus's bow and shoot an arrow through 12 ax heads. Odysseus, disguised as a beggar, was the only one to perform the feat successfully. He then commenced slaughtering the suitors with the same bow. In Homer's *Odyssey*, Penelope makes a good match for Odysseus; she, like Odysseus, is capable of cunning and deception. After Odysseus kills the suitors, she still does not trust him and tests him to see whether he knows the secret of their unmovable marriage bed. Odysseus similarly tests his interlocutors. The first letter in Ovid's collection of *Heroides* is from Penelope to the absent Odysseus. See also TELEGONUS.

Penthesilea A queen of the *AMAZONS*. Daughter of ARES and Otrere. Classical sources are Apollodorus's *LIBRARY* (Epitome 5.1–2), Diodorus Siculus's *LIBRARY OF HISTORY* (2.46), Quintus Smyrnaeus's *Posthomerica* (Book 1), and Virgil's *AENEID* (1.491–493). Penthesilea, the daughter of an Amazon queen and the

The Battle of Achilles and Penthesilea. *Detail from bell-krater, late fifth century* B.C.E. *(Museo Arqueológico Nacional, Madrid)*

Olympian god of war, accidentally killed her sister Hippolyte (or Glauce or Melanippe) and promised to fight on the side of King PRIAM in the Trojan War in return for being purified of blood guilt by him. In the *Aeneid*, her army carried shields imprinted with crescents, and she herself wore a golden belt. During the battle, she performed bravely but was eventually killed by ACHILLES. Her father, Ares, grieved and in his rage was almost drawn into the conflict to exact revenge, but ZEUS prevented him. In the episode recounted in Quintus Smyrnaeus, after her death, Achilles saw her beauty and fell in love with her. Achilles killed his comrade Thersites when the latter mocked him for his infatuation. According to Diodorus Siculus, Penthesilea was among the last of the great Amazon warriors. Achilles' killing of Penthesilea was represented in antique vase painting, for example, on an Attic black-figure amphora by Exekias from ca. 530 B.C.E. (British Museum, London) and a red-figure bell-krater from the late fifth century B.C.E. (Museo Arqueológico Nacional, Madrid).

Persephone (Proserpina, Kore) Goddess of the underworld. Daughter of DEMETER and ZEUS. The classical sources are the *Homeric Hymn to Demeter*, the ORPHIC HYMN TO PERSEPHONE, Apollodorus's LIBRARY (1.3.1, 1.5.1–3), Hesiod's THEOGONY (767–774, 912–914), Hyginus's *Fabulae* (146), and Ovid's METAMORPHOSES (5.346–571), and FASTI (4.417–620). Persephone is the wife of HADES, god of the underworld. They have no offspring. The *Orphic Hymns*, however, name three children born to Persephone from Zeus, who seduced her in the form of a snake: Melinoe (a goddess of the underworld), the FURIES (whose parentage is normally attributed to the TITANS), and DIONYSUS (also not the usual parentage). Hades, in some version with Zeus's consent, abducted Persephone from a field in Sicily (or Athens, Crete, or Boeotia, depending on the source), where she was gathering flowers with her companions, and took her with him down to the underworld. Her distraught mother searched in vain for her and, in her grief, caused a famine. Zeus finally persuaded Hades to free Persephone, but since she had eaten a seed (or several seeds) of a pomegranate in the underworld, she was obliged to spend a part of each year there.

Persephone occupies a dual role. As daughter of Demeter, she is connected with youthful vitality and is closely associated with her mother as goddess of the fertility of the fields and the abundance of the crops. Her time in the underworld coincides with winter, and her reappearance above with spring and summer, seasons in which vegetation is most productive; she is, thus, representative of springtime fertility. But as queen of the underworld, she is connected with death. Persephone, also called Kore ("girl"), and Demeter are the central cult figures of the Eleusinian Mysteries.

In minor myths, Persephone is said to have loved ADONIS. In another myth she transformed a rival, Minthe, into the plant that bears her name. On the rare occasion that a hero travels to Hades (ODYSSEUS, AENEAS), he visits and pays his respects to Persephone. Persephone was moved by ORPHEUS's lament for his bride, EURYDICE, and she consented to allow him to remove her from Hades. According to Apollodorus, Persephone granted a similar favor to King Admetus, by releasing the soul of his wife, ALCESTIS, who had agreed to die in his stead (Euripides' play *ALCESTIS* is based on this myth).

Persephone makes an appearance in the THESEUS legends as the intended bride of his best friend, PIRITHOUS. They make an abortive attempt to kidnap her from Hades and end up in captivity there themselves.

HERACLES' visit to the underworld had more favorable results; Persephone welcomed him warmly and allowed him to take CERBERUS from Hades to fulfill the requirements of his Twelfth Labor. He was also permitted to rescue Theseus and, in some versions, Pirithous from their underworld captivity.

In antiquity, visual representations of Persephone show her varied aspects: as an object of worship, usually in conjunction with her mother, in the myth of her abduction by Hades, and in her role as a chthonic deity. Her images are found on vases, reliefs, sarcophagi, and mosaics. Persephone and Demeter are often depicted together. Both are clothed in long gowns and carrying their attributes: Demeter with a scepter, sheaf of wheat, ears of corn, and, occasionally, a crown of flowers; Persephone with a four-tipped Eleusian torch or a scepter. Among her other attributes are the pomegranate, or the seed of a pomegranate, and a cornucopia (horn of plenty) to represent fertility. At times the cornucopia is held by Hades, as in an Attic red-figure kylix from ca. 450 B.C.E. (British Museum, London). In her role of chthonic deity, Persephone is shown crowned and holding a scepter, for example, on an Apulian red-figure krater from ca. 330 B.C.E. (Antikensammlungen, Munich), where she is standing in front of an enthroned Hades. A frequent visual theme was the abduction of Persephone by Hades. A wall painting dating to the fourth century B.C.E. from a royal tomb at Vergina shows the main iconographic elements of this theme: the bearded Hades bearing the half-clothed and struggling Persephone away

in his chariot. Representations of her abduction are also to be found on sarcophagi and pottery, for example in a red-figure hydria from the fourth century B.C.E. (Metropolitan Museum of Art, New York), which shows Hades fleeing with Persephone. In later periods, her abduction was the most popular theme for artists; see, for example, Luca Giordano's *The Rape of Persephone* of ca. 1684 and Gianlorenzo Bernini's sculpture *The Abduction of Persephone* from 1622 (Borghese Museum, Rome), which forms a thematic pair with *Apollo and Daphne* from ca. 1625 (Borghese Museum, Rome). A 19th-century painting by Dante Gabriel Rossetti, *Persephone* from 1873 (Tate Gallery, London), shows Persephone in portrait holding her attribute, the pomegranate.

Perseus A Greek hero. Son of DANAE and ZEUS. Classical sources are Apollodorus's *LIBRARY* (2.4.1–5), Hesiod's *THEOGONY* (280–283), Homer's *ILIAD* (14.319), Hyginus's *Fabulae* (63, 64), Ovid's *METAMORPHOSES* (4.605–5.249), and Pausanias's *Description of Greece* (2.21.5–7). Acrisius was the father of Danae. An oracle foretold that Acrisius would be killed by Danae's future son, so he imprisoned her in an underground chamber constructed of bronze. Zeus was, nonetheless, able to visit her in the form of a shower of gold, and in due time, Danae gave birth to PERSEUS. In a second attempt to forestall his fate, Acrisius cast Danae and the infant Perseus adrift in a wooden chest. The two survived the ordeal and, according to Apollodorus, washed up on the shores of Seriphos. They were rescued by Dictys, a fisherman, the brother of Polydectes, king of Seriphos, and given shelter. Perseus was raised to young adulthood by the fisherman. Polydectes fell in love with Danae, and to rid himself of Perseus, he sent the young man on a quest to capture the head of MEDUSA, one of the GORGONS, whose face was so terrible that one glance turned the beholder to stone. Perseus was helped in this task by ATHENA and HERMES, who suggested that he begin his adventure by finding the GRAEAE, winged and gray-haired hags, sisters who shared a single tooth and a single eye among them. The Graeae knew where the Gorgons were to be found, and Perseus forced them to reveal Medusa's location by stealing their one eye and tooth and returning them in exchange for the information. Hermes gave Perseus an adamantine sickle and winged shoes; nymphs provided him with a *kibisis* (shoulder bag) and the Helmet of Hades, a cap that gives its wearer invisibility. Accompanied by Athena, Perseus found Medusa asleep. Athena held her shield as a mirror to guide Perseus so that he would not have to gaze upon Medusa directly. Aloft on winged sandals, Perseus cut off her head with the sickle. He then placed Medusa's head in the *kibisis*, and by putting on the Helmet of Hades, which made him invisible, he escaped from the pursuit of Medusa's sisters.

On his way home with the head of Medusa, Perseus became involved in another adventure. He saw ANDROMEDA, daughter of Cepheus, bound to a rock and awaiting death; she was to be sacrificed to a sea serpent sent by POSEIDON. Perseus fell in love with her, and having gained the consent of her father to marry her, Perseus rescued her, slaying the sea monster either with his sword or by using the Gorgon's head. Cepheus's brother Phineus, who had been promised Andromeda in marriage, attacked Perseus, but Perseus defeated Phineus and his allies by turning them to stone with Medusa's severed head.

When Perseus returned to Seriphos with Andromeda, he turned Polydectes to stone with Medusa's head for having mistreated Danae during his absence. Perseus returned the magical objects that Hermes and Athena had lent him. Athena placed Medusa's head on her shield. Perseus returned with Andromeda and Danae to Argos in search of his grandfather, but Acrisius, still fearing Perseus, fled to Pelasgiotis. Perseus followed and, while competing in the funeral games for the king of Larissa, accidentally killed Acrisius with a discus, thus

Perseus and Andromeda. *Fresco from the House of Dioscuri, Pompeii, first century* C.E.

fulfilling the oracle's prediction. Perseus and Andromeda traveled from Argos to Tiryns, were they remained and where Perseus became king. The offspring of Perseus and Andromeda are Alcaeus, Electryon, Heleius, Mestor, Sthenelus, Gorgophone, and Perses, an ancestor of the Persian kings. Andromeda and Perseus are great-grandparents of HERACLES.

Visual representations of the adventures of Perseus were frequent in classical art and appeared in a variety of media: architectural reliefs, vase and wall painting, as well as ivories and coins. The childhood of Perseus is a common visual theme. An Attic red-figure lekythos from ca. 480 B.C.E. (Toledo Museum of Art, Ohio) depicts Acrisius urging Danae to enter the chest that will soon be set adrift; the infant Perseus, already within the chest, gestures to his mother to enter. Perseus's adventures among the Graeae are represented in a red-figure krater from the classical period, which shows Perseus in winged sandals and the Helmet of Hades, furtively stealing the eye from the Graeae. An Attic red-figure amphora from ca. 490 B.C.E. (Antikensammlungen, Munich) shows Perseus pursuing the running Medusa, here shown as winged and snake-haired, with her tongue hanging between her teeth. Another example of the same theme is an Attic red-figure hydria from ca. 500 B.C.E. (British Museum, London), where the Gorgon's winged and headless body falls to the ground as Perseus strides away with the head peeking out of his bag. Perseus's rescue of Andromeda was also frequently depicted, as in an Apulian red-figure krater from ca. 430 B.C.E. (J. Paul Getty Museum, Malibu), which shows the hero gaining the consent of Cepheus while a chained Andromeda awaits. A similar scene is represented in a first-century C.E. fresco from Pompeii. In such representations, Perseus is shown as a powerfully built young man, wearing winged sandals while carrying a sickle and the head of Medusa. A Roman fresco from Pompeii from the first century C.E. shows the nude hero with a cloak slung around his shoulders and his customary attributes. Andromeda is sometimes shown bound with chains to the rock or at the moment in which Perseus takes her arm to deliver her from her fate. A sea creature representing the monster is also often present. In Piero di Cosimo's *Perseus and Andromeda* of ca. 1513 (Galleria degli Uffizi, Florence), the story is set within a multifigured landscape that shows Perseus floating in the sky, seeing Andromeda's plight, and, within the same painting, killing the sea monster.

Persians AESCHYLUS (472 B.C.E.) Aeschylus's *Persians* was produced in 472 B.C.E., eight years after the battle of Salamis, at which the fleet of King Xerxes, the play's central figure, was defeated by the Athenians. The historical background of the play is the conflict that arose between the Persian Empire and Greek city-states, notably Athens and Sparta, in the early fifth century B.C.E., as Persia sought to maintain control over, and suppress rebellion among, its Greek possessions, such as Miletus.

The defeat of the Persian army of Darius at Marathon in 490, then the subsequent defeats of Xerxes' forces at Salamis (480) and Plataea (479), were surprising, given the immensity and prestige of the Persian army, and contributed signally to the Athenian sense of pride and importance as a rising power in the Aegean. Aeschylus's play encapsulates, and transforms for the tragic stage, key themes in the process of Athenian identity formation, while at the same time commenting on certain core themes in the Greek meditation on the human condition: the dangers of hubris, the unpredictability of fortune. *Persians* was performed in a group of four plays—including the nonextant *Phineus*, *Glaukos*, and *Prometheus the Fire-Bringer*—with which it did not share direct mythical connections or narrative continuity. The evident separateness of content of the four plays contrasts with Aeschylus's usual preference for a connected tetralogy, although more oblique, thematic connections are not ruled out. The tragedy skillfully focuses on, and manages to narrate, the main episodes in the conflict through the viewpoint of the Chorus of elders and the Persian queen at Sousa. Only at the end does the magnificently debased figure of Xerxes return, clothed in rags and crushed by the immensity of his defeat. Xerxes comes to exemplify the gods' power to bring low human arrogance and to punish hubris.

SYNOPSIS

The scene is set at Sousa before the palace of the Persian king Xerxes. The tomb of Darius is visible on the stage. The Chorus of elders, who oversee the land and palace in Xerxes' absence, has dark premonitions about the expedition to Greece. It recounts all the warriors from various regions of the realm who have gone to Greece. They are the flower of Asia and are desperately wanted home by their families. Xerxes has built a bridge of boats across the Hellespont and led his army to Greece. His army is like a mighty, irresistible ocean, yet the fate decreed by the gods wins in the end. The Chorus expresses its fear and closes with a description of the Persian wives alone in their beds. It begins to discuss matters of state, but then turns toward the queen as she enters. It addresses the queen as the mother of Xerxes and widow of King Darius. The queen reveals her anxiety. All the prosperity brought by Darius will not help the Persians if the master of the house is gone; they may come to ruin despite their great wealth. She then relates a dream: Two women, one in Persian, the other in Greek clothing, but of common stock, lived in Asia and Greece, respectively; her son Xerxes tamed and yoked them, and one stood proud but submissive, whereas the other ripped off the yoke; Xerxes fell, Darius looked on him with pity, and Xerxes tore his clothes. Then, after making an offering to the gods, she saw an eagle flee to Apollo's altar and a hawk fly at the eagle and rip it apart. The Chorus tries to reassure her, offering a positive interpretation of the dream. She asks about Athens, and the Chorus supplies answers.

The messenger enters, running at high speed. He reports immediately that the prosperity and entire army of Persia have been destroyed. The messenger can provide an eyewitness report—he was there. The worst damage was done at Salamis. The Chorus laments. The messenger then gives a more detailed account, relating how Xerxes lives, but many of the Persian commanders (and, in particular, many of those previously mentioned) were killed. The Athenian ships were by far fewer, but the gods supported them against the Persians. He saves his most vivid account for the battle of Salamis: A Greek went over to the Persian camp and persuaded Xerxes that the Greeks were fragmented and about to flee separately; Xerxes decided to attack at dawn; but instead, the Greeks attacked in fearsome unison; the Persian forces were hemmed in and then scattered; it was the greatest massacre of human beings ever on a single day. There was further humiliation and suffering, however. The Persians stationed on an island to kill any fleeing Greeks were themselves sur-

rounded by the Greeks and hacked to death. Xerxes, watching from a throne on a high mound by the shore, tore his clothes and gave orders for retreat. The queen, on hearing this, laments that a daimon (spirit) has deceived the Persians and lured them, by the hope of vengeance for their previous defeat at Marathon, to further destruction. Finally, the messenger tells how many were lost on the return journey, some dying of thirst and hunger, while others tried to cross the frozen Strymon and perished when the ice partially melted; a very few managed to return to Persia. The messenger exits. The queen laments the fulfillment of her dream, and directs the Chorus to pray to the gods and make offerings. She expresses concern for her son, and exits.

The Chorus mourns the destruction of the Persian army and the widowhood of Persian wives. It sets the blame on Xerxes and recalls Darius with nostalgia. The king himself barely escaped by going through Thrace; most of the others were left behind, and now the power and reputation of Persia have been undermined.

The queen returns, but now, in her current misfortune, she is in a constant state of fear and is attired without her usual adornments. She makes offerings to the spirit of Darius and the gods below.

The Chorus sings to the gods below in support of the queen's libations. They ask the gods, Earth, HERMES, and Pluto (see HADES) to send up the spirit of Darius, so that he can help them in their current predicament. It praises Darius as beloved king and god, who, it claims, never brought his people to harm in war.

The shade of Darius enters. He asks the Chorus what misfortune the city is undergoing. He has heard the earth groan and saw the queen in her fear, and has come to the world above despite the difficulty involved. The Chorus is afraid to answer, and so he asks the queen. She praises his reign of old, then announces that Persia is now utterly destroyed. She informs him in dialogue of the defeat of the expeditionary force, and he acknowledges that the oracles and prophecies of Zeus have come true. He observes that it was madness and hubris for Xerxes to suppose that, by bridging the Hellespont, he could bind the sea and make it his slave, in defiance of the mighty POSEIDON. The vast wealth accumulated by Darius is now vulnerable. He recalls the history of the rulers of Asia, beginning with the Medes, then going through Cyrus, Mardos, Maraphis, and himself; in his youthful folly, Xerxes has done more damage than any previous ruler. He recommends never sending a force to Greece again; he predicts that even the soldiers still remaining in Greece will not return, but as punishment for the defilement of Greek temples, they will suffer and perish there; he further predicts the battle of Plataea. Darius interprets the present harvest of misfortune as the natural outcome of the crop sowed by violence and of excessive pride. He advises the queen to meet Xerxes and console him; he exhorts the Chorus to enjoy its wealth even amid its sufferings. Darius exits. The queen resolves to obtain fine clothes for her son to help him in his present crisis and humiliation.

The Chorus recalls the better days of Darius's reign. He came back from war without excessive losses and conquered many cities. Now, the gods have changed the Persians' fate, and they suffer losses in war.

Xerxes enters, in rags, with an empty quiver. He laments his fate, and the cruelty of the daimon, and wishes that he were himself among the dead. He acknowledges that he is the cause of the disaster, while the Chorus greets his homecoming with dirges and cries of grief. It asks after the other commanders one by one, and Xerxes reports them all dead. Persia has no more means of defending itself. Xerxes leads the Chorus of Elders in a song of lament as they exit.

COMMENTARY

This early play by Aeschylus crystallizes the essence of human hubris in a powerful and lucid example and, at the same time, condenses important developments in Athenian history and civic identity. Aeschylus had some important predecessors in this effort. Phrynicus's tragedy *Sack of Miletus* was produced in 493 B.C.E. and told the story of the Persian suppression of the rebellion of Miletus, a revolt that the Athenians had supported with their own troops. (Phrynicus was fined by the Athenians for staging a play that incited too much emotion.) The same playwright later successfully produced the *Phoenician Women* on the subject of Xerxes' defeat in 476 B.C.E. Herodotus's *Histories* tells a comparable story of the hubris of the Persian kings, the hard lessons they had to learn about the unpredictable rise and fall of fortune, and the importance of showing proper respect for the gods' irresistible power.

Telling stories can be one important way of constructing a civic identity, and both Aeschylus and Herodotus (as presumably would Phyrnicus, had his plays survived) provide insight into the kinds of stories Athenians might have been telling themselves as they emerged as a formidable city-state in the late sixth and early fifth century B.C.E. The Athenian polis, on this emerging model, is characterized by modesty in wealth, respectful cultivation of its protector gods, determination, cunning, loyalty and cohesion among citizens, resourcefulness, flexibility, and an abhorrence of servitude. But as can be observed in many different instances, the most effective mechanism for self-definition is often categorization and description of the "other," a social group or people who help to define one's own group through their systematically opposed set of traits. The Persians, in the broadest terms, are non-Greeks, and hence categorized as barbarians: Their names and place-names sound different; their clothes and everyday material culture are different; in works such as Aeschylus's *Persians*, these serve as clear markers of barbarian status. More specifically, however, Persia functions as an anti-Athens. As other accounts also confirm, Athenians especially liked to emphasize the vast yet servile Persian army in contrast to the

Athenians fighting as free men, the immensity of Persian wealth and empire in contrast to Athens's lean self-determination and democratic citizenry; and finally, the hubristic arrogance of the Persian kings in contrast to the Athenians' humility and sensible concern to keep the gods on their side.

The question of what attitude is proper to show to the gods is especially conspicuous throughout the *Persians*. The Persians consider their own kings gods—a mistake that, in the Greek view of things, will need to be corrected by a signal punishment. The gods save and protect Athens, whereas, as the Persian characters and Chorus themselves come to recognize, a daimon has been opposing them and bringing about the destruction of their might and empire. Later, we hear that Persian soldiers, who previously thought that the gods were not important, come to respect their great power and begin praying to them. Too late, perhaps, the queen becomes attentive to the goodwill of the gods and offers libations and prayers. The ghost of Darius comments on the punishment reserved for Persian soldiers who have destroyed and defiled the gods' statues and shrines in their invasion of Greece. Finally, there is the worst instance of disrespect for the gods' power: Xerxes, in a legendary act of hubris, "yoked" the sea in building a bridge of boats across the Hellespont. For Xerxes, no doubt, this act of bridge building would have been seen as a fine engineering solution to a difficult problem in the transportation of men and supplies, but the Greeks interpreted it as the case of a tyrannical ruler who had the arrogance to think he could enslave the sea itself and make the god Poseidon submit to his will.

It is not surprising that Aeschylus makes the Persians subject to Greek gods and religious scruples. There are clear limits to Aeschylean, and ancient Greek, ethnography. The marks of "Persianness"—use of the bow versus the spear, magnificence of Asian dress, luxury, an emphasis on wealth, courtly attitudes, divine treatment of rulers, and so on—are everywhere present in the play, yet, in some fundamental ways, Aeschylus still Hellenizes the Persians, putting in their mouths modes of self-descriptions that only Greeks would employ, and even making them describe themselves within the fabric of Greek mythology. The Persians are thus made to derive themselves from the "son of DANAE"—i.e., PERSEUS—and Greeks are considered to derive from the same stock, much as Egyptians and Danaans are seen as having common ancestors in the vast ethnographic vision of Aeschylus's *SUPPLIANTS*. Even more tellingly, the Persians identify the site of their downfall as Ajax's island. Ajax came from Salamis, the location of the sea battle that was so catastrophic for the Persians. Perhaps this reference merely marks an obvious mythic association of the place, but we might also suppose that the Greek hero is seen as defending the place against the invaders or, even more intriguingly, that his act of self-destruction has been repeated by the Persian invaders. Ajax, like Xerxes, is a tragic hero who ends up isolated from the rest of humanity and goes from a position of great honor in society to humiliation and abasement.

Tragedy, when viewed from the perspective of this play, is a distinctively Athenian invention that tends to represent the downfall of tyrants and arrogant rulers, both barbarian and Greek. It is a genre developed in the context of the democratic polis and its institutions, which thematically isolates the aristocratic or regal ruler figure and makes him subject to the omnipresent tragic daimon: All wealth is viewed as potentially ephemeral, power as unreliable, and high position as inherently dangerous. The more humble person will certainly have less to lose than a Xerxes, OEDIPUS, or Ajax and may have compensating qualities of versatility and flexibility in the face of changing circumstances. Are the content and themes of Athenian tragedy, then, attuned to the task of justifying the political ideology of the Athenian polis? In general, it is unwise to oversimplify our picture of Athenian tragedy to merge it with an unproblematic democratic ideology, but in the case of the

Persians, the contrasts articulated in the course of the tragedy tend to oppose the traits of the tragic ruler figure to the emerging identity of the Athenian city-state. Particularly salient is the contrast between slavery and freedom, and Greek identity as distinct from the barbarian.

Alongside the political and military celebration of Athenian victory, however, is the familiar tragic motif of the destroyed household viewed in its generational span. One key measure of a household was its wealth and the preservation of that wealth through its transmission from father to son. The queen, in voicing, first, her anxieties and, later, her grief, lays emphasis on the squandering of the wealth of their house. As wife of the previous ruler, and mother of the present one, she is in a good position to appreciate both how that wealth was built up and how it is now in danger of being lost in a dangerous venture. This point is also made in a physically visible way. When the queen first comes onstage, she will be decked in fine clothes and surrounded by the magnificent trappings appropriate to her station as a member of the Persian royal house, whereas, when she comes out later, after the changed circumstances of that house have been made clear, she is no longer richly adorned and has only a few attendants. All that wealth seems to invite further punishment, now that it has been revealed how the gods punish those with the most grandiose designs and greatest display of arrogance. Darius, however, has a more practical viewpoint; he sensibly urges the Elders to enjoy the use of their wealth amid their coming worries and discomfort. He is represented as a great conqueror and ruler, but without the added hubris characteristic of Xerxes. He added to Persia's territory and wealth, and while he did lose the battle of Marathon, it seems to be implied that he did not stake too much on his ambitions in Greece, nor tempt the punishment of the gods.

It might have been possible to represent Darius in other ways. He might have been shown as a hubristic tyrant keen on enslaving others. He, too, crossed over to Greece from Asia with imperialistic ambitions. In Aeschylus's version of this historical legend, however, Darius displays all the more moderate traits, while all the marks of excess and transgression are accumulated in Xerxes. Darius gives a speech in which he recalls the previous kings of Persia and announces that none caused such damage as Xerxes. In general, Aeschylus has chosen to intensify and isolate the present dereliction of Xerxes, to make it appear that he alone has destroyed a great empire. Naturally, this claim also tends to magnify the importance of Salamis and to frame the liberation of Greece as a particularly Athenian victory. Aeschylus is not simply writing Athens-centered propaganda, however: Plataea, where the Spartans played a greater role, merits a conspicuous passage.

It is interesting, in any case, that Aeschylus chooses to focus the tragedy on Xerxes, for this focus differentiates the *Persians* from the Theban trilogy and the *Oresteia*, in which successive generations are haunted by a primeval curse or act of wrongdoing and an associated daimon relentless in bringing about their doom. The trilogy is an ideal vehicle for tracing a transgenerational curse, since the successive plays correspond to different phases of tragic action. The *Persians*, however, does not seem to have been part of a tragic trilogy and, in terms of its mythic/historical content, stood alone. In terms of dramatic structure, then, Aeschylus heightens the focus on a single hubristic figure who has brought about a catastrophic fall through his pride, rather than emphasizing a transgenerational taint in which later-born figures find themselves enmeshed, sometimes against their will. In historical terms, Aeschylus heightens the effect of a powerful, world-changing event—the battle of Salamis—with its consequent liberating effect on Greece and powerful chastening of Persian ambitions.

The ending of the play shifts the focus onto Xerxes in a particularly dramatic fashion. The subject of anxiety throughout the play, he finally appears on stage in rags, his quiver emblematically spent, to form part of the exodos, in which the abased king and the Chorus weave together a dirge. The king's rags represent an even sharper contrast between past riches and present degradation than the previous transformation in the queen's appearance. He admits that he is the cause of Persia's destruction and wishes that he himself were dead along with all the others. The long lists of Persian commanders, both at the beginning, when their safety was an object of anxiety, and at the end, when their horrific doom has been ascertained, stress the harm that has come to the king's own host through his ambitions and flawed leadership. Unlike the cohesive Greek army, which did not—contrary to the false report designedly sown by the Greeks themselves—splinter into individual self-interested groups, Xerxes is represented as having left his commanders to their diverse fates. He is now almost fully isolated in the manner of other well-known tragic characters. The reiterated emphasis on Xerxes' slain commanders sets up the king's shameful survival as the play's grim culmination. The pathos of this humiliating homecoming is the fitting conclusion of the king's hubristic expedition. On the way to Greece from Asia, he arrogantly made the sea accommodate itself to his needs; now, defeated and largely stripped of his magnificent fleet, he straggles home in ignominious flight.

Given the key role played by a sea battle, water imagery and water metaphors understandably play an important role throughout the play. Earlier on, the massive expeditionary force mustered by Xerxes against Greece is described as a mighty ocean, vast, irresistible, and violent. In more anxious moments, however, the Chorus views the ocean that Xerxes' men are traversing as vast and the men and their boats themselves as slender and fragile. After the revelations of the messenger's speech, we hear that a "sea" of suffering has burst upon the Persians and Asia. Xerxes makes himself infamous by attempting to yoke, tame, and enslave the sea. At the heart of the play is a struggle over whether or not the Persians and the king will control the sea—taking the form of an ungovernable, oceanlike force themselves—or whether the sea will control and subdue them. In the grim outcome of the battle of Salamis, it becomes clear that Xerxes' hubristic desire to tame the ocean has been singled out for significant punishment. He must sit on a slope near the beach and watch his mighty fleet being sunk, the bodies of his men clogging the waters in a gruesome visual echo of the bridging of the Hellespont. Just as he arrogantly affected to make traversable dry "land" out of ocean, so now, at his nadir, Xerxes must look upon water that has been rendered paradoxically "solid" with the corpses of his Persians. The sea—source and symbol of Persian power—now destroys Xerxes and his empire. Conversely, the sea has become a symbol of the power and liberation of Greece and the Athenians. No longer associated with Xerxes' hubristic ambitions, it now calls to mind the resourcefulness and determination of the Athenians, their impressive mastery of seafaring as a medium of travel and warfare. Poseidon, with whom the Athenians have a close, mythic association, has come out on their side against the king who insulted him.

There was no clearly discernible line between history and myth in fifth-century Athens, and we can see in Aeschylus's *Persians* aspects of the formation of an Athenian mythology. This more recent set of myths, however, is built out of older, existing mythic paradigms, and, in particular, the mythology of the Trojan expedition is often an implicit subtext. For Herodotus, the Trojan War and the Persian expeditions against Greece are part of the same, long historical conflict between East and West, a series of transgressions and reprisals stretching back to the earliest phase of mythic/historical memory. In Aeschylus's *Persians*, Greeks have once again defeated enemies from the East, but now they have done so, not as the seafaring aggressors, but as the defenders of their own land and city. The opening list of commanders and their contingents recalls the Homeric catalog of ships and concretely sets up the expectation of a quasi-Iliadic expedition—this time launched by an Eastern power. Aeschylus, however, avoids infusing Xerxes' invasion with the positive, heroic connotations of the *Iliad*, while effectively applying all the negative paradigms of the Trojan mythology. The long-suffering anxiety and expectation of the family members of the absent warriors, departed on a long, dangerous expedition across the sea, recall comparable evocations in both the *Iliad* and the *Odyssey*. Even more strikingly, Aeschylus applies the mythic paradigm of the punitive *nostos* (return journey) familiar from post-Iliadic stories of the return (or failed return attempt) of heroes. In these stories, the hero, who has offended a god, returns after a long trial (Odysseus, MENELAUS), is denied return because of a signal act of transgressive impiety (the lesser Ajax), or is murdered on his return (AGAMEMNON). The Persian commanders, likewise, suffer terrible trials as they attempt to find their way back, and in some cases are punished for acts of transgression against the gods committed during the war.

The Chorus of elders, as it hears of these dismaying events, expresses, by turns, horror, anxiety, sadness, and concern for the future security of Persia. As in *Suppliants*, *Seven against Thebes*, and *Agamemnon*, the Chorus provides a vehicle for the expression of the communal experience of war and aggression, either anticipated (*Suppliants*, *Seven against Thebes*) or completed (*Seven against Thebes*, *Agamemnon*). As in other instances, tragedy develops a counter-heroic viewpoint on heroic mythology, stressing, variously, the destructive nature of the warrior hero, the damage done to the community, and the overpowering fear of imminent suffering. Here, the destruction appears to be total, even though the war was not carried out on Persian soil, and the principal figures (Xerxes, queen, elders) remain alive and well. Aeschylus, in order to stress the totality of Xerxes' reversal of fortune and status as tragic

hero, emphasizes the weakness and vulnerability of his kingdom: He suggests that its collapse is all but imminent. Here, as in many aspects of the play, Aeschylus creates a suitable tragic myth rather than hewing closely to historical reality. Modern scholarship emphasizes the extent to which central aspects of our picture of the "Persian Wars" were created by the Greeks. The notion of the free Greeks' keener fighting spirit vs. the Persians' dispirited conscripts, the claim of the Greeks' consistently superior tactical cunning, the Persians' arrogance and revenge-based motivation, and the supposedly devastating effect of Salamis and Plataea on Xerxes' reign overall have all been challenged in recent works. While the Greeks won impressive and surprising victories, it is clearly false that Persian power was fundamentally undermined by the losses in Greece. The Great King of Persia continued to be a major figure in struggles for Aegean hegemony and played at times a key role in the conflict between Athens and Sparta.

Despite his emphasis on Athenian triumph and the totality of the Persian defeat, Aeschylus avoids undermining the tragic dignity of his characters, and in his depiction especially of the stately queen and Elders, he creates the basis for considerable sympathy on the part of the Athenian audience. Even Xerxes has the good grace to acknowledge his own error and grieve for the damage he has caused. This line of observation has led some to stress the universal dimension of Aeschylus's play: *Persians* is not a boastful story of Athenian triumph but a play about human hubris and the unreliability of fortune. Yet, one could equally argue that, to preserve the power and gravity of the tragic mode, Aeschylus necessarily avoided blatantly denigrating characterization of Persian figures, such as would render them risible and despicable. It no doubt pleased the Athenians to contemplate their own victory while indulging in sympathy for their defeated foe. The victory is all the more admirable if the foe is dignified, rather than negligible. A potentially enlightening comparison can be made with other, specifically Greek tragic heroes. The aristocratic warrior heroes who people tragedy hardly represent the values of a democratic city-state, yet the Athenians liked to experience "pity and fear" in viewing their magnificent downfall. In the case of the *Persians*, however, there is one crucial difference: The Persian king Xerxes is not a Greek hero, and his cult will not be absorbed into the religious fabric of the city-state. As a man whose pride outstrips his abilities, Xerxes embodies a fundamental flaw in human character, and yet, as Persian king and enemy of Athens, his example must always remain to a significant extent alien and distant. The Persians, in their magnificent hubris, have not yet learned the basic lesson that the more humble and pious of the Greeks have internalized.

Phaedra   Wife of the Athenian hero THESEUS. Daughter of King MINOS of Crete and PASIPHAE. Phaedra is a major character in Euripides' *HIPPOLYTUS* and Seneca's *PHAEDRA*. Additional classical sources are Apollodorus's *LIBRARY* (Epitome 1.17–19), Diodorus Siculus's *LIBRARY OF HISTORY* (4.62), Hyginus's *Fabulae* (47), Ovid's *METAMORPHOSES* (15.497ff) and *HEROIDES* (4), Pausanias's *Description of Greece* (1.22.1–2, 2.32.1–4), Plutarch's *Life of Theseus*, and Virgil's *AENEID* (7.765–766). A lost tragedy by Sophocles, *Phaedra*, also contributed to the myth. After the death of the Amazon ANTIOPE, the mother of Theseus's son HIPPOLYTUS, Theseus married Phaedra, the sister of ARIADNE, whom Theseus had abandoned on Naxos. Phaedra and Theseus had two sons, Acamas and Demophon. When Hippolytus was a young man, Phaedra fell in love with him. Hippolytus was a follower of ARTEMIS and chastely refused Phaedra's advances. Sources differ on what followed. In some, a scorned Phaedra told Theseus that Hippolytus had attempted to seduce or rape her. Theseus was not sure whom to believe and sent for Hippolytus, who succumbed to an accident while driving his chariot. In

another account, Theseus was convinced of his son's guilt and called on POSEIDON to kill him. Whether from shame or fear, Phaedra hanged herself.

In Euripides' *Hippolytus*, Phaedra's passion for Hippolytus was incited by APHRODITE, angered by Hippolytus's lack of piety toward her. The goddess planned to use Phaedra's love for her stepson to bring about his death. Euripides' Phaedra is a victim of Aphrodite's ploy. She is a chaste, faithful wife who sees her passion as an affliction and, as long as she can, struggles to keep it a secret. When her nurse, who pried it out of her, betrays it to Hippolytus, she hangs herself in shame. To protect her reputation, however, she leaves a suicide note for Theseus in which she accuses Hippolytus of having tried to seduce her. The enraged Theseus banishes his son and invokes against him one of three curses that his father, Poseidon, had given him. Accordingly, a bull from the sea charges Hippolytus's chariot as he is on the way to exile, and Hippolytus dies. Afterward, Artemis reveals to a devastated Theseus that his wife has lied to him.

The theme of the hero as the target of unwelcome advances from a married woman and then as the victim of false accusations is found also in the myth of BELLEROPHON and Stheneboea and in the biblical story of Joseph and Potiphar's wife.

Phaedra is a descendant of EUROPA (a paternal grandmother), and a bull figures in her story, as in the stories of the other women of her family. Europa is abducted by ZEUS in the form of a bull and taken from Argos to Crete. Minos is one of the sons of this union, and his wife, Pasiphae, develops a passion for a bull sent by Poseidon and, from her union with it, gives birth to the monstrous MINOTAUR. Ariadne, daughter of Minos and Pasiphae, falls in love with Theseus and helps him defeat the Minotaur. And Phaedra's passion for Hippolytus results in his death in an accident caused by a bull sent by Poseidon.

The death of Hippolytus in his chariot was represented on an Apulian calyx krater from ca. 350 B.C. (British Museum, London). Here, Phaedra is shown with her nurse and EROS, the cause of her affliction. This theme is the subject of a wall painting from Herculaneum dating from 75 B.C.E.

Phaethon   Son of Clymene and the sun god HELIOS (Sol). Classical sources are Apollonius of Rhodes's *VOYAGE OF THE ARGONAUTS* (5.595–611), Diodorus Siculus's *LIBRARY OF HISTORY* (5.23), Hyginus's *Fabulae* (152a), Ovid's *METAMORPHOSES* (1.750–2.380), Pausanias's *Description of Greece* (1.4.1), and Philostratus's *IMAGINES* (1.11). Two lost tragedies, Aeschylus's *Heliades* and Euripides' *Phaethon*, dealt with his myth. Phaethon traveled to the realm of the sun to seek confirmation from Helios that he was indeed his father. Helios acknowledged Phaethon as his son and offered him a gift to prove it. Phaethon asked to drive his father's chariot, which bore the sun across the sky, for one day. Helios, aware of the numerous dangers of such a voyage, tried in vain to dissuade his son. Phaethon lacked the experience and skill to drive the chariot and lost control of the horses. As the chariot plunged downward, the sun began to scorch the earth, and Zeus was obliged to strike Phaethon with a thunderbolt. Phaethon crashed into the river Eridanos (the modern river Po). In their grief, Phaethon's sisters, the HELIADES, were transformed into trees with amber sap.

Philemon   See BAUCIS AND PHILEMON.

Philoctetes   Son of Poeas. Hero of the Trojan War. Philoctetes is the central character in Sophocles' *PHILOCTETES*. Additional classical sources include Apollodorus's *LIBRARY* (3.10.8, Epitome 3.14, 3.27, 5.8, 6.15b), Homer's *ILIAD* (2.716–728) and *ODYSSEY* (8.219–220), Hyginus's *Fabulae* (102), Ovid's *METAMORPHOSES* (9.229–234), Pausanias's *Description of Greece* (8.33.4), Quintus Smyrnaeus's *Fall of Troy* (10.179ff.), and Virgil's *AENEID* (3.401–402). Philoctetes obtained the bow of HERACLES either from his father or from Heracles himself as a reward for lighting his pyre on Mount Oeta. Philoctetes joined the Trojan expedition with seven ships but was bitten by a snake on Chryse, Tenedos, or Lemnos (Sophocles' version) and abandoned there by the Greeks because of the excessive stench of the wound and his loud cries of pain. He lived there for 10 years during the war and survived by hunting for animals with his bow. Later, the Trojan seer Helenus, captured by the Greeks, revealed that Troy could be captured only with the presence of Philoctetes' bow. In Sophocles' play *Philoctetes*, ODYSSEUS, and NEOPTOLEMUS go to Chryse to bring back Philoctetes. Neoptolemus, more honest and more averse to deception than Odysseus, hesitates to carry out the plan; in the end, Heracles appears as deus ex machina and commands Philoctetes to go to Troy. At Troy, Philoctetes killed PARIS. Aeschylus and Euripides also wrote plays on the subject, which do not survive. In some versions, Philoctetes went to southern Italy after the war and founded cities there.

Philoctetes   SOPHOCLES (ca. 409 B.C.E.) Sophocles' *Philoctetes* was produced near the end of his career, probably around 409 B.C.E. PHILOCTETES, a Greek hero abandoned by the Greeks on Lemnos on the advice of ODYSSEUS because he was afflicted by a reeking wound that made him howl with pain, turns out to be necessary for the capture of Troy: It is prophesied by the captured Trojan Helenus that both NEOPTOLEMUS, ACHILLES' son, and Philoctetes with his bow are equally needed for success. At the opening of the play, Odysseus and the young, naive Neoptolemus have arrived on Lemnos, and Odysseus is instructing Neoptolemus on how to gain Philoctetes' confidence and thereby trick him into being taken back to Troy. Neoptolemus, however, will have to decide for himself what forms of action are consistent with his sense of his own identity. Philoctetes will also ultimately have to make a choice—to go or to stay. Sophocles has produced yet again an example of the radically isolated hero, who is faced with the choice of supporting his community or pushing himself further away from it on the basis of his own unbending principles and convictions. One key difference in this play is that the hero—albeit by means of the irresistible persuasion of the deus ex machina—*will* bend and rejoin his community, i.e., the Greek army. The element of playacting and deceit is also unusually prominent in this play. Sophocles has produced a different kind of tragedy—in some ways reminiscent of late Euripides—that, nonetheless, wields a deep tragic power. In the three central characters—Neoptolemus, Odysseus, and Philoctetes—we see the tense, complicated interaction of expediency and honor, trickery and honesty, youth and experience. Neoptolemus's choice lies at the crux of the central moral dilemmas of the Trojan War.

SYNOPSIS

Odysseus and Neoptolemus enter. They are on the island of Lemnos. Odysseus introduces the place to Neoptolemus: It was here that the Greeks abandoned Philoctetes years earlier. His screaming was unbearable, and he profaned their festivities. He describes the cave where Philoctetes dwells and informs Neoptolemus that he will require his help with Philoctetes, because Philoctetes will not trust Odysseus. They see some signs of Philoctetes' habitation—a simple hutlike structure, rags for his wound—but not his cave yet. Odysseus then stresses to Neoptolemus that he must be loyal to the expedition with more than his body; he must trick Philoctetes with words, winning his confidence. He should proclaim who he is and feign to be alienated because the Greeks would not give him his father Achilles' armor. Neoptolemus is reluctant, because deception is not suited to his character. Odysseus at length persuades him by pointing out that there is no

other way to capture Philoctetes when he is armed with his bow, and that he is needed for Neoptolemus to defeat Troy: They are both needed. Odysseus indicates that he will send a sailor disguised as a trader to help things along if necessary. He exits.

Neoptolemus proceeds with the Chorus of sailors under his command. The Chorus agrees to follow Neoptolemus and expresses pity for the fate of Philoctetes—a savage existence of hunger and pain. Neoptolemus rationalizes his suffering as being part of divine design. The Chorus hears Philoctetes approaching; Philoctetes enters and asks the strangers who they are. Neoptolemus answers that they are Greeks, introduces himself, and explains that he is sailing from Troy. Philoctetes tells his own story, explaining how he contracted a cursed wound by walking unawares into a sacred grove and being bitten by a viper. He then blames Odysseus and the Atreidae above all for abandoning him on Lemnos. He describes at length the miseries of his nine years alone on the island as he struggled to stay alive. He has begged the occasional sailors to take him home, but none has agreed.

Neoptolemus then claims that he, too, has reasons for anger against Odysseus and the Atreidae. After his father's death, he agreed to join the expedition, as it was prophesied that Troy would not fall without him. When he asked for his father's armor, however, the Atreidae refused, informing him that Odysseus had it. Alienated, he departed for his home island of Scyros. Philoctetes and Neoptolemus discuss how all the best of the Greek warriors have died or suffered a catastrophe, whereas the morally inferior ones have survived without serious trouble. Neoptolemus then announces that he is going, but Philoctetes begs him at some length to take him home. The Chorus urges pity, and Neoptolemus agrees to the plan. Philoctetes blesses his luck, and the sailor disguised as a trader enters. The sailor affects to have arrived by chance with news regarding the plans of the Greeks. Phoenix and the two sons of Theseus are pursuing Neoptolemus, while Odysseus himself is pursuing Philoctetes, and plans to take him to Troy by force if necessary. He explains that the captured Trojan seer Helenus prophesied that Philoctetes and his bow would be necessary for the capture of Troy. An angry and indignant Philoctetes urges them to withdraw quickly to avoid meeting Odysseus's party.

Neoptolemus asks to hold Philoctetes' famous bow; Philoctetes allows him to hold it as a special favor. The Chorus expresses amazement at the degree of suffering to which Philoctetes is exposed, second only to that of Ixion. Following this, Philoctetes begins to succumb to a fit of pain from his wound, which, he explains, will end in sleep. He screams as the pain intensifies and entrusts his bow to Neoptolemus for safe keeping as the fit comes over him. Before falling unconscious, he extracts an oath from Neoptolemus, making Neoptolemus swear that he will not leave the island without him. They cannot leave without him in any case, as Neoptolemus observes, because he is needed in Troy along with his bow. Philoctetes wakes up, expresses his gratitude to Neoptolemus, and suggests that they leave promptly. Neoptolemus then experiences a crisis: He cannot decide whether or not to carry out Odysseus's dishonest scheme. It does not fit his character. Philoctetes is confused by Neoptolemus's remarks. At length, Neoptolemus explains that he intends to take Philoctetes to Troy. Philoctetes laments this betrayal and the breaking of his oath; he pictures his dire existence and probable death without his bow, and expresses hope that Neoptolemus may change his mind in accordance with his true self.

Neoptolemus begins to observe a feeling of compassion in himself. Odysseus enters and demands the bow. Odysseus and Philoctetes have a heated exchange, in which Odysseus insists that Philoctetes will be taken by force and Philoctetes refuses to comply. In a long speech, Philoctetes curses Odysseus and demands vengeance. Odysseus then shifts strategies, proclaims that they do not need

Philoctetes, and affects to be on the point of departure. Neoptolemus tells his crew to wait for now. Neoptolemus and Odysseus exit.

Philoctetes has an exchange with the Chorus. He laments that he will be doomed in the cave without his bow; the Chorus suggests that he has a better choice, and that the gods have made his fate. Philoctetes complains of Odysseus and Neoptolemus, and predicts his own death, while the Chorus attempts to counsel calm and restraint. He is desperate and considers suicide, but refuses to go to Troy no matter what the Chorus says.

Odysseus and Neoptolemus enter in mid-conversation. Odysseus wants to know why Neoptolemus has turned back; Neoptolemus announces that he is going to right the wrong he has done to Philoctetes by returning his bow. Odysseus threatens to prevent him by force and to lead the Greeks against him; but Neoptolemus remains confident that he is acting according to principle and will not be intimated. Odysseus exits. Philoctetes asks what new treachery is afoot; Neoptolemus returns the bow. Odysseus enters just as he is doing so and attempts to forbid it. Philoctetes wishes to kill Odysseus with the bow, but Neoptolemus prevents him. Odysseus exits.

Philoctetes regrets that he could not kill Odysseus, but praises Neoptolemus's good character and genealogy—a true son of Achilles, not of Sisyphus. Neoptolemus then argues at length that Philoctetes clings too tightly to his sufferings and has become savage, incapable of forgiveness or good sense; he also points out that when he goes to Troy, he will be cured of his sickness and will conquer alongside Neoptolemus; and finally, he beseeches him to come to Troy and end the misery of the war. Philoctetes responds that he feels that Odysseus and the Atreidae are wicked men and that he will suffer new wrongs and villainy if he goes to Troy. Considering how he has been treated so far, Neoptolemus himself should not be so eager to go to Troy. Neoptolemus concedes the point but reminds him of the will of the gods.

They argue back and forth, but Philoctetes remains firm: He will not go to Troy and wishes to be taken home. Neoptolemus realizes he cannot convince him, and so they begin their departure. At this point, Heracles appears as a deus ex machina from above and speaks. He addresses Philoctetes, reminds him of the suffering he himself endured to attain glory, then reveals that at Troy he will be cured of his sickness, will slay Paris, and capture Troy. He then addresses Neoptolemus, declares that both he and Philoctetes are required for the capture of Troy; that he himself will send Asclepius to heal Philoctetes; and that, when he sacks Troy, Neoptolemus must remember to remain pious and respect the gods. First Philoctetes and then Neoptolemus agree to obey Heracles. Philoctetes bids Lemnos farewell. All exit.

COMMENTARY

The *Philoctetes* presents one of several examples of the radically isolated Sophoclean hero and is especially comparable with the *Ajax* and *Oedipus at Colonus*. Like the demented Ajax amid the carcasses of slaughtered livestock, Philoctetes' appearance and condition evoke repulsion and disgust. He lives like a desperate animal. His foot, oozing infection and smelling horribly, causes Philoctetes to writhe along the ground, groan in agony, and eke out an uncivilized existence of subsistence hunting. He is different from these other heroes, however, in that he has done little if anything to deserve his condition. Oedipus and Ajax are represented as having, in varying degree, merited their undoing. At a higher level, though, the question of merit recedes in importance: Everyone must accept the fate that the gods give him and learn to live with it as best he can. Learning this lesson is all the more difficult for a hero who has a hard time understanding what he could have done to earn his fate.

As in the case of the *Ajax*, the action of the play is set among the events in the post-Iliadic Trojan War, Achilles is dead, and the other heroes fight over his legacy. No single Greek now enjoys an obvious preeminence in the way that Achilles did, and the struggle over his armor is suggestive of this ambiguous and contentious situation. In this play, as in the *Ajax*, a central character (Neoptolemus) has a right to resent that Odysseus ended up with Achilles' armor rather than he himself, and in this play, too, Odysseus and the Atreidae are allied as representatives of the political/military authority of the Panhellenic expedition. This trio is again represented as ignoring or dismissing the concerns of individual heroes and chieftains in favor of the broader Trojan War endgame. The two sons of Atreus tend to stand for raw, blustering authority, Odysseus for tactical ingenuity and coldly effective privileging of ends over means. Our sympathy, however, is directed to a disgraced warrior at odds with these three figures and to the paradoxes of his singular fate.

Sophocles has gone out of his way to find a highly sympathetic hero, precisely to set up the fierce struggle for the soul of Neoptolemus that ensues. If he were less sympathetic, the terrible conflict between sympathy for a wronged, suffering man and the destiny meted out by the gods would not be so total and overwhelming for the young, inexperienced warrior. Neoptolemus has a conception of what his natural character ought to be: He is, after all, the son of Achilles. Achilles, we recall, stated in response to Odysseus's speech in the famous "embassy" episode in the *Iliad* that he hated more than anything a man who says one thing and thinks another. He is presented by Homer as the diametric opposite of Odysseus, and the two Homeric epics can be interpreted as celebrating complementary opposites in heroic temperament: They represent very different and even conflicting types of excellence, both of which are nonetheless simultaneously valued and operative in Greek society. Here, Neoptolemus and Odysseus thus represent a suggestive pair. They have two profoundly different approaches to the same problem. Their opposition, however, is asymmetrical. Odysseus is much older, more self-assured, and fixed in his opinions than the labile and sometimes self-contradictory Neoptolemus. Neoptolemus is only just coming into the inheritance of the Achillean temperament and, most difficult of all, must learn how to resemble a father he has never met. This play represents an important phase in the struggle to acquire his true character: He learns from Philoctetes some aspects of what his father was like, and how he would have acted in comparable situations.

One fairly prominent strand of the play's meaning derives from Neoptolemus's youth and the initiatory experience he undergoes on Lemnos. At various moments, he comments on the exceedingly difficult dilemma in which he finds himself. No doubt, as a young man, he thought that war would be all about bravery and glory. Sophocles' play shows us that the most testing challenges of the war are ethical: Hard decisions must be made regarding one's position vis-à-vis authority, the validity of trickery as a tactic, and so on. Some initiatory rites require adolescents to engage in trickery, thieving, cunning, and disguise; they must explore the boundaries of ethical behavior and even transgress the rules before assuming an ethically normative adult male identity. This possibility of an initiatory dimension in the *Philoctetes* is further enriched if we accept one scholar's hypothesis that the members of the Athenian tragic Chorus were young men of military age, and that service as a chorus member was a kind of initiatory rite involving disguise and impersonation (John J. Winkler in Winkler and Zeitlin, eds., *Nothing to Do with Dionysus?*). Certainly the *Philoctetes* incorporates a conspicuous metatheatrical dimension, i.e., the play shows awareness of its own status as theater. Neoptolemus is coached by the master impresario Odysseus for the role he must play. Philoctetes will be the unwitting audience. Odysseus further instructs Neoptolemus that a sailor disguised as a trader will make an entrance at a certain point, and that Neoptolemus must "play along" with whatever role and story line the sailor/trader devises for him, i.e.,

like a trained actor, he must be able to fall in with an improvisatory scenario in dialogue with another actor.

The consequences of such role-playing for Neoptolemus, however, are all too real. This dimension of role-playing is brought out brilliantly by Sophocles as Neoptolemus struggles through his challenging script and attempts to bring the story line to a satisfactory conclusion. He discovers primarily that it is not so easy to play a role while remaining detached from the statements, promises, and self-defining utterances that one makes in the course of acting one's part. Odysseus is masterful at simultaneously playing a role and remaining detached from it. He keeps his strategic role and his true self and interests separate. Neoptolemus, in part because he is young, and in part because it is not in his character to play a role in the Odyssean manner, finds it much more difficult to remain detached from the commitments that his "Neoptolemus" persona makes. The subtle yet powerful mechanism of Sophocles' play relies on Neoptolemus's gradual absorption into the role he is playing. Some of this role is quite natural and straightforward. He claims his own identity as Neoptolemus, son of Achilles, as suggested by Odysseus. Odysseus has cannily realized that Neoptolemus's natural candor will serve him well in this setting. He is a natural actor, and the lies that he is asked to tell are effective insofar as they are not far from the truth. He *is* Neoptolemus, and *did* join the Trojan expedition; he was indeed deprived of his father's armor. While he clearly did not abandon the expedition out of indignation, it seems probable that Odysseus has shrewdly divined a real kernel of resentment in Neoptolemus that can be exploited for its underlying plausibility, even while being exaggerated. Odysseus as tragic playwright has thus masterminded a minidrama, in which Neoptolemus's own emotions and experiences are brought into play to create a sense of complicity between him and Philoctetes.

What Odysseus did not adequately calculate, perhaps, was the degree to which Neoptolemus would begin to identify and merge with his role as "Neoptolemus." When he becomes aware that he empathizes with Philoctetes, and that he is deeply reluctant to deprive him of his bow, he admits that he had been sympathetic toward him from the beginning. In other words, even at the start, when he was ostensibly more committed to his role-playing and deceit, the seeds of empathy were already present and were gradually cultivated over the course of their interaction. It is difficult to point to the moment when Neoptolemus ceases to feign resentment toward Odysseus and the Atreidae and begins actually to feel some justified indignation. In taking this position, he is, after all, inheriting a central aspect of the attitude of his father, Achilles, toward the Greek expedition and its leaders. He comes over to the view that Philoctetes has been badly treated and that it is wrong to deceive him. He also makes emotional and verbal commitments to Philoctetes. In particular, he makes an oath that he will not abandon him but will take him home. Finally, Neoptolemus, as a young man deprived of his father and seeking to establish his identity and reputation as a warrior, wants to maintain the esteem he enjoys in the eyes of the older, legendary hero Philoctetes. Philoctetes, before learning of the plot, constantly refers to the young man's good character and upbringing, the excellence he has inherited from his father. He will lose this image of himself, which has been validated through Philoctetes' esteem, if he goes fully over to the side of Odysseus. He discovers that he likes aspects of the role he is playing, and begins to incorporate them into his adult identity. In other words, he begins to change the script Odysseus wrote for him and to invent his own.

Odysseus and Philoctetes, on this reading, are competing father figures for the young orphaned Neoptolemus, or, at least, competing heroic mentors. Neoptolemus largely appears to accept the Achillean character of honesty and candor attributed to him by Philoctetes, but he remains independent. It is a measure of his maturation in the course of the play that he stands up to Odysseus with Achilles-like ferocity and scorn for Odysseus's famous cleverness, yet remains committed to the Trojan expedition and rebukes Philoctetes for clinging to his misery and resentment. He is beginning to define his own role and character as hero as distinct from the roles foisted on him by his mentors and elders.

Commentators have worried over the ending of the play. Heracles, as deus ex machina, resolves the problem of Philoctetes' resistance by bidding him go to Troy. Aristotle famously criticized this type of ending. The deus ex machina violates the Aristotelian principle of whole and integral action that resolves itself through its own internal structure, as opposed to a miraculous outside intervention. Modern critics, however, have noted that Aristotle's theory of tragedy was produced some time after the flourishing of Athenian tragedy and seems to deduce its core principles from Sophocles' OEDIPUS REX. The dramatic intervention of the gods in human affairs to bring about the required course of action is hardly exceptional or disturbing in Greek tragedy or epic. One purpose it serves here is to allow Philoctetes, as a hero of the Sophoclean type, to remain unbending on the human plane. It is not unnatural, however, that he should bend to the thundering words of the divine Heracles. Some conflicts, in the Greek estimation, are truly irresolvable on a human plane. The *Oresteia*, for example, required the conspicuous intervention of ATHENA to reach its resolution. Here, Heracles, as the prime example of Greek heroism, and as a hero who suffered isolation, madness, and seemingly endless suffering and labor to achieve eventual glory, is an effective choice as intervening god. Philoctetes has seemed to many a strikingly "modern" play, yet there are clear limits to applying a modern conception of naturalistic psychology and plot resolution to Athenian tragedy of the fifth century B.C.E.

Heracles' closural intervention, moreover, is not simple or happy in its implications. He initiates a new phase in Philoctetes' fate as a warrior. His old phase of suffering caused by the violation of the sacred grove is coming to an end, and a new phase of undoubtedly difficult cooperation with his sworn enemies, and warfare on the plains of Troy, is beginning. Neoptolemus himself, who, we might be in danger of forgetting, is equally the object of Heracles' admonitions, faces a long path ahead of him. His very name—Neoptolemus ("New War")—represents the future of the Trojan expedition, and to a certain extent, this play is concerned with the question of what ethical form the new phase of the war will take. Will it be Achillean or Odyssean? Will the end justify the means? Will the warriors' honor and reputations be tarnished in the process of capturing Troy? The answer is not simple, but surely not wholly optimistic. Heracles specifies that Neoptolemus must take care to be pious and respectful of the gods, but not all the mythological traditions about Neoptolemus suggest such pious behavior. (Compare, for example, the grim representation of Neoptolemus in *Aeneid* 2: He slays the wretched, defenseless Priam as he takes refuge at an altar.) The Greek heroes, in sacking Troy, will violate fundamental laws of religion and civilized behavior and will be punished for it in the years to come. The drama in which Philoctetes and Neoptolemus play such poignant roles is revealed at the end to have been a mere interlude in a much greater history of violence and destruction.

Philomela   See TEREUS.

Phineus   King of Thrace. Son of Agenor. Classical sources are Apollodorus's *LIBRARY* (1.9.21, 3.15.3), Apollonius of Rhodes's *VOYAGE OF THE ARGONAUTS* (2.176–499), Diodorus Siculus's *LIBRARY OF HISTORY* (4.43.3–44.7), Hyginus's *Fabulae* (14.18, 19–20), Ovid's *METAMORPHOSES* (7.3), and Virgil's *AENEID*

(3.212). Phineus's first wife was Cleopatra (daughter of BOREAS, the North Wind, and ORITHYIA). He had two sons by her, Plexippus and Pandion. His second wife, Idaea, convinced Phineus that his sons had attempted to seduce her. Phineus punished them by blinding them, or according to the *Library of History*, he imprisoned instead of blinding them. They were eventually liberated by the crew of the *Argo*, among whom were their uncles the BOREADAE, Calais and Zetes. In this version, Phineus was killed by HERACLES, and his two sons, now freed from their unjust imprisonment, succeeded to his throne. However, other texts tell a completely different story. Phineus's blinding of his sons incurred the wrath of the HARPIES, who snatched food away from his mouth but allowed him a reeking morsel of food, just enough to allow him to linger in a weakened, aged, and blind state. When the crew of the *Argo* came upon him in this condition, the Boreadae chased the Harpies until their sister IRIS defended them, promising that they would torment Phineus no longer. In still another version, that of Apollonius of Rhodes, APOLLO had endowed Phineus with prophetic powers. He was punished not because of crimes against his family but because he had offended ZEUS by his prophecies. In either case, Phineus, in gratitude for his deliverance, guided the crew of the *Argo* through the dangers in their voyage, advising them, in particular, how to avoid the Clashing Rocks. The winged Boreadae are shown rescuing Phineus in an Attic red-figure column-amphora attributed to the Leningrad Painter from ca. 460 B.C.E. (Louvre, Paris).

Phobus   See ARES.

Phoebe   A TITAN, the daughter of GAIA (Earth) and URANUS (Heaven). Sister of IAPETUS, HYPERION, Coeus, Crius, Cronus, MNEMOSYNE, OCEANUS, RHEA, TETHYS, THEIA, and THEMIS. Classical sources are Apollodorus's *LIBRARY* (1.1.3, 1.2.2), Hesiod's *THEOGONY* (132–136,

404–410), and Hyginus's *Fabulae* (Theogony 10). Phoebe married her brother Coeus, and their children were Asteria (mother of Hecate) and Leto (mother of Apollo and Artemis). Although she appears in the genealogies beginning with Hesiod, there are no myths or cult practice associated with Phoebe.

Phoebus   See Helios and Apollo.

Phoenician Women   Euripides (409 b.c.e.) Euripides' *Phoenician Women* was produced at some point in the years 411–409 b.c.e. Scholars have doubted the authenticity of large parts of the text and hypothesized that it was altered by the play's fourth-century producers. There is no unanimous agreement as to the extent and precise location of the later interpolations. Even if individual sections have come under scrutiny, however, the play can be considered in large part the work of Euripides.

SYNOPSIS

The action takes place in front of the royal palace of Thebes. Jocasta, wife of Oedipus and mother of Antigone, Eteocles, and Polynices, emerges from the grand central doors of the palace. Jocasta begins by outlining her lineage and recounting the suffering that her family has had to endure. An oracle prophesied that the son of Laius, her first husband, would grow up to murder his father and marry his mother, but Laius disregarded the oracle and fathered Oedipus upon Jocasta, thus setting in motion a chain of events that brought the prophecy to fruition and cast the family into unimaginable suffering. The misery continues still. Eteocles and Polynices, sons of an unlawful marriage, have locked Oedipus away, blinded and mad as he is. He cursed his sons to war on one another. Eteocles became king in his father's stead, with the intention that the throne would alternate between him and Polynices every other year. But he has decided to retain the throne and has exiled his brother. While in exile, Polynices

has married an Argive princess, and now with an Argive army at his command, he is besieging Thebes. Jocasta, anxious for her sons, has persuaded Eteocles and Polynices to accept a truce and hopes that a meeting between the two will end in peace for all. Following her speech, Jocasta enters the palace followed by the pedagogue and Antigone. She wants to go up to the roof to survey Polynices's force gathered around the walls of Thebes, and the pedagogue precedes her up the stairs to ensure her safety. Antigone is alarmed at the number of the host. The pedagogue, who negotiated the truce between the two camps, points out the heroes in the Argive force: Hippomedon, Tydeus, Parthenopaeus (son of Atalanta), and Capaneus. Polynices stands with Adrastus, his father-in-law. The pedagogue suggests that they reenter the palace to avoid the crowd of women now coming toward it, and the two disappear inside.

The crowd of women approaches; they are the Chorus of Phoenician women, anxious about the siege of Thebes.

Polynices enters with sword drawn and, in his speech, expresses his doubts about the truce that he has accepted—he fears that he has walked into a trap. Seeing the women, Polynices asks them whence they come, and they reply that they come from Phoenicia; they have been sent to serve at Apollo's shrine at Delphi, but now the war detains them in Thebes. When they realize that they are talking with Polynices, they call to Jocasta to come out and greet her son. Jocasta is joyful to see her son. She tells him that Thebes has longed to see him and that Oedipus has regretted the curse he called down upon his sons. She is dismayed at his marriage to a foreign bride, however, and the exclusion of his family from the marriage rites. Polynices asks after his father and his sisters, and Jocasta replies that they are all suffering from the consequences of their parents' unnatural marriage.

In the ensuing dialogue, it emerges that Polynices has suffered many hardships as an exile. Adrastus interpreted an oracle of Apollo to mean that Polynices and Tydeus, fellow wanderers in exile, would marry his two daughters; that is how Polynices came to have the force of the Argive army with him.

Eteocles enters, and the Phoenician women voice their hope that Jocasta will be able to reconcile her sons. Polynices begins the dialogue by laying out his cause simply: In good faith, he left Eteocles to rule until such time as he might take the throne, but instead Eteocles has denied him his rightful place on the throne and in Thebes. He is prepared to regain what he considers properly his, by force if necessary. Eteocles responds that he finds no sense in giving up his rule. Why should he retreat before his brother? For his brother comes not to negotiate but to lay siege. He is also prepared to go to war to defend his rights and his city. The Chorus finds justice in the words of Polynices and are less convinced by Eteocles' argument.

Turning to Eteocles, Jocasta advises her son to pursue equality and common sense rather than ambition. She counsels restraint to Polynices, to compensate for the folly of coming to make war on his own city.

Eteocles' patience has worn thin, however. He repeats his refusal to lay down his scepter, asks Jocasta to leave off her counsels, and orders Polynices beyond the city walls. In the ensuing exchange, the brothers' tempers rise, and they exchange accusations, which end in threats against the other's person. Eteocles refuses to allow Polynices access to his father or sisters, and Polynices responds with the hope that he will kill his brother during the battle to come. Neither brother can see beyond his argument to realize that he is bringing about the realization of Oedipus's curse. A dismayed Jocasta enters the palace as Polynices abruptly leaves.

The Phoenician women sing of the founding of Thebes and call on the protection of DEMETER to save the city.

CREON, brother of Jocasta, enters and, on finding Eteocles, reports that an Argive prisoner has given them information about the strength of the army encircling the city. They discuss military strategy, and Eteocles takes Creon's counsel to fortify the seven gates of Thebes with troops. Eteocles himself will captain one such defense. Before he takes his leave, Eteocles consents, in the event of a Theban defeat, to the marriage of Antigone and Creon's son, Haemon. Eteocles reminds Creon that should he die, Creon must care for Jocasta. And if Polynices should die, too, Eteocles charges Creon to deny Polynices a proper burial in Thebes. He then leaves for battle.

Acting on Eteocles' advice, Creon sends for the blind seer TIRESIAS. The seer is led in by his daughter and accompanied by Creon's son Menoeceus. Tiresias foretells the doom of Thebes and the death of Eteocles and Polynices by each other's hand. This fate is the consequence of Oedipus's birth. Tiresias intimates there may be a way to forestall the destruction of Thebes, but he is reluctant to speak, especially in the presence of Menoeceus. Pressed by Creon, Tiresias reveals that only the sacrifice of this youth, Creon's own son, will absolve the crimes of the royal house of Thebes. Menoeceus's blood, Tiresias continues, will appease ARES, whose dragon was slain and its teeth sown to create the first families of Thebes. Creon's family is one such descendant of the dragon's sown teeth, and the blood sacrifice of Menoeceus will expatiate the injury done to Ares. Tiresias exits, leaving Creon with the choice of saving his city or his son. Creon does not hesitate; he decides immediately to send Menoeceus out of Thebes for his safety, and exits himself with the intention of procuring gold with which to make good his son's escape. Alone with the Chorus, Menoeceus reveals that he agreed to escape only to calm his father's fears. He intends to take his life and allow his death to be the salvation of Thebes. He exits.

The Phoenician women bemoan Thebes's bloody fate and praise Menoeceus's courage.

An armed messenger enters and calls for Jocasta, who quickly answers his summons. The messenger reports that Thebes has been successfully defended, that both her sons are still alive, and that Menoeceus has given his life for Thebes. He goes on to describe the seven heroes who have come against Thebes, the emblems on their shields, and the successful defense of the Theban gates. He reluctantly reveals that Eteocles and Polynices have agreed to single combat, the outcome of which will decide the war. The messenger exits and Antigone enters. She is apprised of the battle between her brothers and, with her mother, rushes off to plead with them for peace.

Creon enters with attendants bearing the body of Menoeceus, and the Phoenician women tell him where Antigone and Jocasta have gone. A messenger enters, sorrowfully announcing the deaths of Eteocles and Polynices, and that of Jocasta as well. The messenger describes the terrible combat between the brothers, how each slew the other; then Jocasta in grief plunged a sword into herself and collapsed on her sons. Such was the outcome of the combat. Then the Argives took the Theban army by surprise and defeated it. The messenger exits, and Antigone enters. Attendants bring in the bodies of her brothers and mother. Antigone, grief-stricken, calls out for her father, who emerges from the palace. Antigone relates the manner of their deaths to Oedipus, who is beside himself with grief.

Creon accepts the rule of the city, as had been ordained by Eteocles. His first decree is to banish Oedipus, whose cursed existence brings suffering on Thebes. Furthermore, Creon proposes to bury Eteocles and cast the body of Polynices outside the city limits. Antigone is to marry Haemon the following day.

Antigone attempts to persuade Creon not to banish Oedipus and to bury Polynices, but to no avail. Creon exits, leaving Antigone with her father, whom she wishes to accompany in exile. Her father persuades her not to come with him, and they bid each other a tearful farewell. She promises that she will defy Creon and bury Polynices's body. She leads Oedipus as he begins to make his way toward exile.

COMMENTARY

Thebes was always the tragic setting par excellence in Athenian tragedy, a place where, from generation to generation, things always go wrong in tragic ways. It may be argued that the curse that dooms successive generations of the Theban royal household even exceeds the curse afflicting the house of Atreus. The source of doom goes back to the founder figure, CADMUS, who killed the serpent of Ares and thus brought down on Thebes the anger of the war god. The Chorus of the present play does not fail to drive this point home. It refers both to Cadmus's ancient deed and to the predominance of Ares in Thebes's present plight and the lack of Dionysus's more positive presence.

In choosing Thebes as setting, Euripides necessarily engages with the works of the other major tragedians. The play's notional dramatic frame corresponds roughly with Aeschylus's SEVEN AGAINST THEBES, but Euripides focuses more closely on the dynamics of the Theban royal family and the ways in which the present tragedy of Eteocles and Polynices ripples outward into past and present. Euripides uses the moment of the attack on Thebes to create a truly panoramic tragedy that explores the diverse ramifications of the conflict and its connections with other tragic episodes. Euripides' dialogue with Sophocles' Theban plays is especially insistent. Antigone emerges as an important character in the play, even though she does not really affect the central action. Euripides quite explicitly foreshadows her fate as narrated in Sophocles' ANTIGONE. At the close of the play, Creon threatens to make her marry his son Haemon immediately, while she threatens to perform burial rites for Polynices. The choice between fidelity to her brother's corpse, on the one hand, and a normal life of married womanhood, on the other, are precisely the options that define Antigone's tragedy in Sophocles.

Euripides' foreshadowing of later events is sometimes suffused with grim irony. In a notable instance, Creon values his son Menoeceus's life over the welfare of the polis, and makes much of the importance of burial. He will reverse this stance in Sophocles' *Antigone*, insisting on the priority of polis over kinship obligations. He will end up losing his other son, Haemon, through his rigidity. In a classic instance of the double bind, he loses a son through suicide whether he prioritizes his kin or the polis.

The ending of the play looks forward to the events depicted by Sophocles' *Oedipus at Colonus*: The blind Oedipus, forbidden by Creon to remain in Thebes, totters off toward exile with the support of his daughter Antigone. Other passages inevitably recall OEDIPUS THE KING. We hear the story of Oedipus's life in detail from different sources, and Oedipus himself is a presence constantly alluded to even before he appears on stage at Antigone's bidding. The moment of Polynices's attack on Thebes becomes the perfect vantage point from which to view the cross-generational horror. We are able to look back on Oedipus's fate and consider how the curses he inflicted on his sons led to the present situation, and at the same time observe how the foundations are being laid—by Eteocles and Creon in particular—for the next tragic phase involving Antigone and Haemon. Euripides even seems to go out of his way to concentrate as many sources of grief as possible in one place. He places Jocasta's suicide in the present sequence of events, following her sons' deaths—not, as in Sophocles, after the revelation of Oedipus's birth. Finally, and perhaps most intriguingly, Euripides provides insight into the genesis of Antigone's unforgettable character. At the opening of the play, she is under the guardianship of a pedagogue, subject to the dictates of female modesty, limited in her capacity to appear in public. By the end, she throws aside the scruples of modesty and the decorum of female humility; she is fiercely devoted to her principles and willing to stand up for them publicly; in other words, she is Antigone.

If *Oedipus the King* comes closest of any Greek tragedy to satisfying the Aristotelian criteria of complete action, Euripides goes to the other extreme of a purposely decentered and structurally diffuse tragic panorama. As in other Euripidean plays, grief is piled on grief in long succession, and we are left to contemplate the cruelty of fate and the apparent indifference of the gods. More than one messenger scene is required to narrate this string of deaths. Euripides does not make an effort to set up an all-important moment of decision for the tragic hero; there is no true, central tragic hero in this play, but only a long string of victims of fate. The outcomes seem predestined. Polynices's and Eteocles' mutual slaughter is amply prepared for in the preceding scenes, and as tragic spectators, we have the feeling of going through the motions of a fait accompli. Menoeceus decides instantaneously on suicide. The only work he must do (which he does easily) is deceive his father as to his intentions.

This sense of weariness and exhausted expectation of the next inevitable mishap extends to the point of mild humor. Creon summons Tiresias as a sort of afterthought, as if summoning him is routine, the sort of thing one always does in a Theban tragedy. Tiresias hobbles onstage with a certain self-consciousness regarding his own character as physically debilitated but prophetically accurate seer. When he leaves the scene, he grumbles and grouches about the mistreatment of prophets such as himself. No one ever listens to Tiresias, and the consequences are always grim—no matter how many tragedies he appears in, and no matter how often he is proven right.

The Chorus of Phoenician women who views and comments on this tragedy as it unfolds is exiled from its homeland and thus in a position to appreciate some of the play's key themes (both Polynices and Oedipus are exiles). It identifies with the Theban community, with whom it has shared ancestors, but at times, it also enunciates its difference: It is at once foreign and yet somehow part of the community.

This dual status creates a strange effect of sympathetic distance throughout the play: It does not wish for the horrors of warfare and rejoices at the victory of Thebes. Its joy, however, is at times jarringly juxtaposed with the unfolding of the royal family's personal tragedy. In the end, it is difficult to elicit a synthetic viewpoint from the play's contradictory perspectives: We are encouraged to view the action sympathetically and yet with detachment, as insiders and outsiders, as members of the common people and as voyeurs of the imploding royal household. It seems likely that Euripides intended such disjunctions, and that they are at the core of his tragedy's conception.

Pholus   See CENTAURS.

Phrixus   Son of ATHAMAS and INO. Brother of Helle. Classical sources are Apollodorus's *LIBRARY* (1.9.1, 1.9.16, 1.9.21), Hyginus's *Fabulae* (1–3), and Pausanias's *Description of Greece* (9.34.5).

Before his marriage to Ino, Athamas had two children, Phrixus and Helle, by Nephele, a cloud goddess. Ino bore her stepchildren malice and planned to do them harm. First, she caused the crops to fail. Athamas sent a messenger to consult the Delphic Oracle, and Ino then persuaded the messenger to say, on behalf of the Oracle, that the sacrifice of Phrixus would be necessary to bring fertility to the fields. Athamas prepared to sacrifice his son, but before the child was killed, Nephele placed Phrixus and Helle on the Golden Ram that HERMES had given her. The flying ram carried them off through the sky. Helle fell into the sea and drowned; these waters came to be known as the Hellespont in her honor. Phrixus survived and was received into the household of AEETES, ruler of Colchis. Phrixus sacrificed the Golden Ram to ZEUS, and its fleece was placed in a grove sacred to ARES. The same fleece would later be sought by JASON and the Argonauts. Phrixus married Chalciope, one of the royal daughters; their children were Argus, Cytisorus, Melas, and Phrontis.

Pierides   Daughters of Pierus. Classical sources include Ovid's *METAMORPHOSES* (5.294–345, 662–678) and Pausanias's *Description of Greece* (9.29.3–4). The nine daughters of Pierus insultingly challenged the MUSES to a singing contest. One of their number sang of the GIGANTOMACHY and the various animal forms taken by the Olympian gods to escape the terrifying TYPHOEUS. In Ovid's *Metamorphoses*, the Muse who reports this song suggests that this version of the Gigantomachy is spurious and distorting. The Muse then reports the winning song of the Muse Calliope. She sang of the rape of PERSEPHONE. Calliope was hailed the winner, yet the Pierides continued to be abusive. They were accordingly punished by being transformed into magpies.

Pindar   (518 B.C.E–ca. 445 B.C.E.)   Pindar, a lyric poet from a town near Thebes in Boeotia, was born in 518 B.C.E. and died ca. 446–444 B.C.E. He appears to have come from an aristocratic family. He is known mainly for his epinician poetry, i.e., his choral odes written for athletic victories. Starting at the age of 20, Pindar accepted commissions from athletic victors from various Greek cities and became a famous, well-paid, much sought-after poet. In addition to *epinicia*, he wrote hymns, paeans, dithyrambs, processional songs (*prosodia*), maiden songs (*partheneia*), dance songs (*hyporchemata*), encomia, and dirges (*threnoi*). Pindar's works comprised 17 books in the Alexandrian edition, but his only fully extant works are the victory odes. Pindar's epinician poetry was organized into four books corresponding to the four great Panhellenic athletic competitions: Olympian, Nemean, Isthmian, and Pythian. Pindar's patrons, who commissioned the victory odes, were aristocratic victors from all over the Greek world, including Sicilian tyrants such as Hieron of Syracuse. The victory ode was performed by a chorus either at the festival following the victory or at the victor's city on his return. Pindar's style is dense, difficult, at times dazzling; in metrical terms, his victory odes are complex and highly demanding, and no ode follows exactly the same pattern as any other. Pindar conceives his poetic work simultaneously as a reward, memorial, and compensation for the efforts of the successful athlete. The poem, like the athlete's feat, is an intense, agonistic endeavor; it partakes of the same spirit of struggle and competition (agon). In Pindar's view, the life of mortals is dark and difficult, but in rare moments, bright flashes of greatness and fame are granted by the gods to extraordinary individuals such as athletic victors, heroes, and, presumably, poets.

The typical epinician ode praises the victor and his home city, while the central section contains a myth that relates in some way to the victor, his family, his city, and/or his accomplishment. The relation between myth and victor may not be obvious or direct. Heroes such as PERSEUS, HERACLES, PELEUS, ACHILLES, AJAX and his father, TELAMON, are treated in the mythic section of Pindar's odes. To take one example, AEACUS, father of Peleus and grandfather of Achilles, was the son of ZEUS and the nymph Aegina, after whom the city Aegina is named. Pindar received many commissions from victors from Aegina; thus, he often stresses the nobility of their heroic, and ultimately divine, ancestry by including myths involving Aeacus and his descendants.

In some cases, Pindar asserts his independence in relation to the mythological tradition. In a famous instance in *Olympians* 1, written for the victory of Hieron of Syracuse in the horse race, Pindar vehemently rejects the more familiar story: TANTALUS, in an attempt to deceive the gods, chopped up his own son PELOPS, cooked him in a stew, and served him to the gods; DEMETER ate Pelops's shoulder, distracted as she was by the loss of her daughter. The other gods were not fooled, according to this version of the myth, and Zeus brought Pelops back to life and replaced his shoulder with an ivory one. Pindar expresses moral indignation at the idea that Demeter would have gluttonously devoured Pelops's shoulder. He admits that Tantalus was punished by the gods, but for stealing the gods' nectar and ambrosia, not for serving them his murdered son. Pelops, moreover, was shown divine favor in a different way: POSEIDON became enamored of him and swept him off to the home of the gods, just as Zeus abducted GANYMEDE. Pindar goes on to tell how Pelops fell in love with Hippodamia and defeated her father, Oenomaus, in a chariot race, thereby winning her hand. Pindar makes no mention of the usual story, in which Pelops bribes and later murders Oenomaus's charioteer. Instead, Pelops wins the race through Poseidon's gift of horses. The myth of Pelops, then, is refashioned to stress his status as a hero favored by the gods and to remove the taint of moral turpitude. In general, although not always, Pindar stresses the glories and triumphs of heroes in keeping with his glorification of athletic victory.

Pirithous (Peirithous)   A Lapith. Son of ZEUS and Dia (IXION's wife), or son of Ixion and Dia. Classical sources are Apollodorus's *LIBRARY* (1.8.2, 2.5.12), Diodorus Siculus's *LIBRARY OF HISTORY* (4.63), Homer's *ILIAD* (2.740–744, 14.317–318) and *ODYSSEY* (11.630–631), Hyginus's *Fabulae* (33, 79), Ovid's *METAMORPHOSES* (12.210–535), and Pausanias's *Description of Greece* (1.2.1, 1.17.4, 2.22.6). Pirithous generally enters mythological stories as the companion of THESEUS. Their friendship was proverbial, like the friendship of Pylades and ORESTES. Thus he participated in Theseus's abduction of HELEN, the Calydonian Boar hunt, and the war with the AMAZONS. When Pirithous married Hippodamia, the CENTAURS were invited, presumably because of their descent from Ixion; they became drunk and attempted to rape Hippodamia. A battle between the Lapiths and centaurs broke out, narrated with comic relish by Ovid (*Metamorphoses* 12), and the Lapiths won. Theseus accompanied Pirithous to the underworld to abduct PERSEPHONE for Pirithous. They were captured and held in the underworld. In some sources HERACLES managed to rescue Theseus, but not Pirithous who remained imprisoned in HADES.

Pleiades   Seven sisters, daughters of ATLAS and Pleione. Classical sources are Apollodorus's *LIBRARY* (3.10.1–3), Hesiod's *WORKS AND DAYS* (383–384, 619), Hyginus's *Fabulae* (192), and Ovid's *METAMORPHOSES* (13.293) and *FASTI* (4.165–199). The seven sisters are Alcyone, Asterope, Celaeno, ELECTRA, Taygete, MAIA, and MEROPE. The Pleiades and their mother were pursued by the huntsman ORION, who had fallen in love with them. To escape him, the sisters were transformed into doves and, rousing the pity of Zeus, were then transformed into constellations. An alternate explanation for their transformation is that it was compensation for the misery endured by their father, Atlas, who carried the weight of the heavens on his shoulders. In the *Fasti*, the Pleiades appear in the night sky just before dawn, and though they number seven, only six shine brightly. Ovid designates the dim star as Merope, hiding in shame for having married SISYPHUS, a mere mortal, or Electra, who hides her eyes in grief at the fall of Troy, since the house of Troy descended from her. In the *Works and Days*, Hesiod reports that the seven sisters are visible to the naked eye from May to November, and their appearance sets the schedule for sowing and harvesting.

Pluto   See HADES.

Polynices   Younger son of OEDIPUS; brother of ETEOCLES. Classical sources are Aeschylus's *SEVEN AGAINST THEBES*, Euripides' *PHOENICIAN WOMEN*, Sophocles' *ANTIGONE* and *OEDIPUS AT COLONUS*, and Statius's *THEBAID*. Additional classical sources are Apollodorus's *LIBRARY* (3.6.1–3.7.1) and Homer's *ILIAD* (4.376ff). After Oedipus discovered the truth about his life and blinded himself, Polynices and Eteocles insulted him. Oedipus pronounced a terrible curse against them (see, for example, the opening of Statius's *Thebaid*). The two brothers agreed to rule Thebes in alternate years. Eteocles ruled first, and Polynices left Thebes. Eteocles refused to give up the throne at the end of the year, however, and Polynices, with his new father-in-law ADRASTUS, mounted the expedition of the Seven against Thebes. The two brothers met in battle and killed each other simultaneously, fulfilling Oedipus's curse. According to Sophocles' *Antigone*, Creon, ruler of Thebes, afterward refused burial to Polynices, since he attacked the city. ANTIGONE defied his decree and gave her brother burial rites—an act that led to her death by entombment in a cave. In Sophocles' *Oedipus at Colonus*, Oedipus departs for Athens with Antigone, and Polynices seeks him out because of a prophecy that predicts victory for the side in possession of Oedipus. Oedipus refuses and renews his curses against Polynices and his brother. Antigone makes an unsuccessful attempt to persuade Polynices to desist from the conflict. Note also his role in Euripides' *Phoenician Women*.

Polyphemus   A CYCLOPS. Offspring of POSEIDON and the nymph Thoosa. Classical sources are Apollodorus's *LIBRARY* (Epitome 7.3–9), Homer's *ODYSSEY* (Book 9), Lucian's *Dialogues of the Sea-Gods* (2), Ovid's *METAMORPHOSES* (14.160–220), and Theocritus's *Idylls* (11). Polyphemus belongs to a race of lawless, primitive, one-eyed giants living in Sicily called Cyclopes. They live in caves among their animals, eat humans, and ignore the Olympian gods. The most famous of these is Polyphemus, best known for his encounter with Odysseus in the *Odyssey* and his failed romance with the nymph GALATEA in Theocritus's *Idylls*.

According to Theocritus, while still a youth, Polyphemus fell in love with the nymph Galatea; he sang her love songs but she ignored his overtures. Philostratus's *IMAGINES* describes

Polyphemus. *Marble head, Roman copy of Greek original from the second century* B.C.E. *(Museum of Fine Arts, Boston)*

a painting on the subject of Polyphemus's unrequited love. Within a landscape of harvesting Cyclopes, a lovelorn Polyphemus, panpipe under his arm, a single bushy eyebrow crowning a single eye atop a broad nose, gazes at Galatea astride a team of four dolphins. According to the *Idylls*, Polyphemus offered the nymph the wealth of his flocks of sheep and his orchards. But Galatea loved Acis, son of PAN, and would not be tempted. Surprising Galatea and Acis one day, Polyphemus became enraged and crushed the fleeing Acis with a boulder. In another, less frequent, version of the myth, Galatea later became the wife of Polyphemus, and from them are descended the Galates or Gauls.

In Book 9 of the *Odyssey*, Odysseus and his men were imprisoned in a cave with Polyphemus's flock of sheep. Every morning and evening, Polyphemus ate two of his men. In return for Odysseus's gift of a flask of wine, Polyphemus "rewarded" him by telling Odysseus he could eat him last. While the Cyclops lay in a drunken stupor, Odysseus and his men drove a sharpened stake into his eye, blinding him. Odysseus had told him that his name was "Nobody," so when Polyphemus cried out for help, the other Cyclopes asked who was doing him harm. Polyphemus replied "Nobody," and so the Cyclopes went away. At dawn, Odysseus and the rest of his men escaped from Polyphemus by hiding among the sheep and clinging to their bellies when they were being let out to pasture. Having reached the safety of their ship, Odysseus revealed to Polyphemus his true name, and Polyphemus realized that his blinding by Odysseus had been foretold in a prophecy. Angered by Odysseus's treatment of his son, Poseidon endeavored to prevent Odysseus from reaching home safely.

In visual representations, Polyphemus can be distinguished by his size and his single eye, though in some images he is given three eyes, as in the fourth-century C.E. mosaic from the Villa Romana del Casale in Piazza Armerina, Sicily. In a more familiar representation, a marble head of Polyphemus, possibly a Roman copy of the second-century B.C.E. Greek original (Museum of Fine Arts, Boston), shows Polyphemus with one large eye above a broad nose. Images of Polyphemus usually represent either the Odyssean adventure or Polyphemus and Galatea. Examples of the former include an Archaic proto-Attic black-figure amphora from ca. 650 B.C.E. (Archaeological Museum of Eleusis, Eleusis) and an Attic black-figure oinochoe attributed to Theseus Painter from ca. 510–490 B.C.E. (Louvre, Paris). The latter shows a scene in which Odysseus and his men heat a wooden stake and another in which they are shown plunging it into the Cyclops's eye.

Visual representations of the myth of Galatea and Polyphemus were popular in the classical period. Polyphemus is often shown in a pastoral setting playing or carrying a panpipe. A first-century B.C.E. fresco from the Imperial Villa at Boscotrecase, Italy (Metropolitan Museum of Art, New York), depicts Galatea in a rocky landscape with Polyphemus holding a pipe and surrounded by a flock of goats. Galatea is shown with her attributes—dolphins and sea animals—and she holds a windblown cloth above her head. Two well-known Renaissance images of Polyphemus and Galatea exist: Raphael's *Triumph of Galatea* from 1511 in the Villa Farnesina (Rome) beside its thematic pair, Sebastiano del Piombo's *Polyphemus*. Annibale Carracci's paired frescoes, *Polyphemus Wooing Galatea* and *Polyphemus Slaying Acis* in the Palazzo Farnese from ca. 1597 (Rome) are also examples of the theme. A fine 19th-century example is Gustav Moreau's *The Cyclops (Observing a Sleeping Nymph)* of ca. 1898 (Rijksmuseum, Amsterdam).

Polyxena   Daughter of Priam and Hecuba. Classical sources include Euripides' HECUBA and *TROJAN WOMEN* and SENECA's *Trojan Women*.

Additional classical sources include Apollodorus's *LIBRARY* (Epitome 5.23), Hyginus's *Fabulae* (110), and Ovid's *METAMORPHOSES* (13.439–532). In the *Iliu Persis* ("Destruction of Troy"), a poem of the Epic Cycle, NEOPTOLEMUS sacrifices Polyxena on ACHILLES' tomb to appease his spirit and thus allow the Greek ships to return after the war. Her sacrifice thus balances the initial sacrifice of IPHIGENIA needed to begin the expedition. Her sacrifice contributes to Hecuba's sufferings in Euripides' *Hecuba* and *Trojan Women*. CATULLUS includes her death in the grim career of Achilles predicted by the FATES at the wedding of PELEUS and THETIS.

Pomona   A Roman nymph or goddess of fruit trees. Textual sources are Ovid's *METAMORPHOSES* (14.623–771) and Pliny's *Natural History* (23.2). Pomona carefully tended a grove sacred to her outside of Rome. According to the *Natural History*, Pomona imbued her fruits with natural healing properties. In the *Metamorphoses*, Pomona carried a pruning hook, a symbol of her

Vertumnus and Pomona. *Hendrick Goltzius, 1613 (Rijksmuseum, Amsterdam)*

skill in horticulture. The god VERTUMNUS fell in love with her, and knowing her chaste reputation, he took on different forms, including that of an old woman, to plead his case. In this guise, he told Pomona the story of IPHIS and Anaxarete, a hard-hearted young woman who refused her suitor and was consequently turned to stone. When he removed his disguise, Pomona was enthralled by his beauty and reciprocated his love. Her attributes are the apple, grape, or pruning knife. Postclassical artists treated this theme, closely following Ovid's *Metamorphoses*, in painting and sculpture. Representations of the myth include Hendrick Goltzius's *Vertumnus and Pomona* from 1613 (Rijksmuseum, Amsterdam). Here, as is common in postclassical treatments, Vertumnus is disguised as the old crone and Pomona carries a pruning knife. Jean-Baptiste Lemoyne's *Vertumnus and Pomona* from 1760 (Louvre, Paris) shows the god removing the mask of an old woman, while Pomona looks on. Edward Burne-Jones executed a tapestry on this theme in 1885.

Poseidon (Neptune) Son of Cronus and RHEA; Olympian god of the sea. Classical sources are the *Homeric Hymn to Poseidon*, Apollodorus's *LIBRARY* (1.4.3–5, 2.1.4–5, 2.4.2–3, 2.4.5, 3.1.3–4, 3.14.1–2, 3.15.4–7), Hesiod's *THEOGONY* (278–283, 453–506, 732–733), Homer's *ILIAD* (passim) and *ODYSSEY* (passim), Lucian's *Dialogue of the Sea-Gods* (2, 3, 5, 6, 8, 9, 13) and *Dialogues of the Gods* (1, 12), Ovid's *METAMORPHOSES*, and Virgil's *AENEID* (1.124–156, 5.779–826). In the division of realms among Zeus and his brothers, Zeus won the sky, Hades the underworld, and Poseidon the sea. Poseidon's chief role is to cause storms or calm the waters. His wife is AMPHITRITE. There are often tensions between Poseidon and his brother Zeus: Poseidon joined HERA and ATHENA's conspiracy to put Zeus in chains and, in the *Iliad*, often insists on asserting his independent authority. According to Homer, Poseidon supported the Greeks in the Trojan War and continued to do so actively,

even after Zeus forbid the other Olympians from interfering with the war. In one instance, however, Poseidon saved AENEAS from ACHILLES and prophesied that Aeneas's line would one day rule over the Trojans. In the *Odyssey*, Poseidon constantly opposed ODYSSEUS on his voyage home because Odysseus blinded his son POLYPHEMUS. Unlike Zeus, Poseidon is not associated with human society and institutions but with violent natural phenomena such as the sea and earthquakes. He wields the trident and rides a chariot through the waves. Poseidon is also associated with horses.

Poseidon had a dispute with ATHENA over patronage of the city of Athens. Each god offered his or her own gift. Poseidon used his trident to cause seawater to well up on the Acropolis, whereas Athena planted an olive tree. Athena was chosen as the city's patron goddess by Cecrops, the first king of Athens.

Poseidon and Apollo are said to have built the walls of Troy for Laomedon, king of Troy who refused to pay their promised wage. Poseidon accordingly summoned a sea monster to terrorize the Trojans. Poseidon complains in the *Iliad* when the Greeks build their own fortifications: He resents any other walls beside the ones he built, and he will later destroy the Greeks' walls.

Poseidon had many loves, as Ovid's ARACHNE elaborates on her tapestry. By Thoosa, Poseidon sired Polyphemus; by MEDUSA, CHRYSAOR and PEGASUS; and by Amymone, Nauplius (the father of PALAMEDES).

Visual representations of Poseidon in antiquity commonly depict a mature, bearded, regal figure. He sometimes carries a trident (and can thus be confused with TRITON), occupies a seascape, and is accompanied by Amphitrite, Triton, and other mythological marine figures and sea creatures. Poseidon uses his trident to kill the GIANT Polybotes on the tondo of an Attic red-figure kylix of ca. 475 B.C.E. (Bibliothèque Nationale de France, Paris). He is also sometimes depicted driving a chariot. A first-century fresco from Pompeii shows

The Triumph of Neptune. *Nicholas Poussin, 1634–37 (Museum of Art, Philadelphia)*

Poseidon and Amphitrite accompanied by a sea creature. Poseidon, driving four horses out of the sea, and Amphitrite are pictured in the postclassical *The Triumph of Neptune* by Nicholas Poussin from 1634–37 (Museum of Art, Philadelphia).

Priam Son of Laomedon, and king of Troy. Classical sources are Apollodorus's *Library* (2.6.4, 3.12.3–5), Homer's *Iliad* (passim), Hyginus's *Fabulae* (89, 91, 105–106, 108–111), and Virgil's *Aeneid* (2.506–558). Priam was the youngest son of Laomedon and the only one to survive Heracles' sack of Troy. Priam had many children, including 50 sons, by his concubines and his wife, Hecuba. His children include Hector, Paris, and Cassandra. Priam was king at the time of the Trojan War, when the Greeks besieged Troy to retrieve the abducted Helen. In Homer's *Iliad*, Priam is represented as wise, gentle, and respected. Zeus himself has great esteem for Priam, although he knows that Priam's city must fall. He is even kind to Helen, when, in *Iliad* 3, she points out to him the Greek warriors from the walls of Troy. Priam grieves wretchedly when Achilles kills his son Hector and abuses Hector's body. At length, the gods decide to intervene, and Hermes accompanies Priam to Achilles' tent at night. In a striking scene, Priam and Achilles arrive at sympathy in their mutual grief, and

Achilles accepts a ransom for Hector's body. During the sack of Troy, NEOPTOLEMUS kills Priam as he takes refuge at the altar of Zeus. Virgil depicts this slaying with great pathos in the second book of the *Aeneid*.

Procne   See TEREUS.

Procris   Daughter of ERECHTHEUS. Sister of ORITHYIA. Wife of the hunter CEPHALUS. Classical sources are Apollodorus's *LIBRARY* (1.9.4, 3.15.1), Hyginus's *Fabulae* (48, 160, 189), Ovid's *ARS AMATORIA* (3.687–746) and *METAMORPHOSES* (7.672–862), and Pausanias's *Description of Greece* (1.3.1). Ovid tells the story of the tragic death of Procris by the hand of her unwitting husband. One morning, Eos, goddess of Dawn, fell in love with Cephalus when she saw him hunting and carried him off. Cephalus protested his love for his wife, and a scorned Eos sent him back to Procris, although, according to some sources, not before he fathered on her a son named Phaethon. In one version of the myth, Eos caused Cephalus to be suspicious of Procris's fidelity or tricked him into believing that she had been unfaithful. Cephalus therefore set about testing Procris to set his mind at ease. He changed his appearance (with the help of Eos) and attempted to seduce his wife. The faithful Procris for a long time resisted his advances, but at length she appeared to be on the verge of yielding to him. At this moment, Cephalus revealed his true identity to her. A distraught and ashamed Procris sought refuge in the woods of ARTEMIS (in some sources, on the island of Crete), but Artemis refused to accept her into her company because she was married. She was moved by Procris's story, however, and did not send her away empty-handed, but presented her with a javelin that never missed its mark and a dog that always tracked its prey. Cephalus eventually won Procris back by begging forgiveness. The couple lived together happily for some time, and Procris presented her husband with the javelin and hound. But later Procris heard

rumors that he was unfaithful to her. Following him one day into the woods, she surprised him and he, thinking that she was a wild animal, killed her with his javelin. Apollodorus presents a less virtuous Procris, who sleeps with MINOS and, in return, receives the javelin and hound from him.

In visual representations, Cephalus is depicted as a hunter, sometimes carrying the javelin given to him by Procris. In postclassical periods, the predominant theme for artists became the devotion of Cephalus and Procris. Examples here include Nicholas Poussin's *Cephalus and Eos* from 1624 (National Gallery, London), where the hunter spurns the amorous attention of Eos, and Claude Lorraine's *Landscape with Cephalus and Procris Reunited by Diana* from ca. 1630 (National Gallery, London), which shows the reconciliation of Cephalus and Procris orchestrated by Artemis, as well as the goddess's gifts of the javelin and hound.

Prometheus   Son of IAPETUS and the sea nymph Clymene (or Asia). Brother of ATLAS and EPIMETHEUS and a cousin of ZEUS. Classical sources are Aeschylus's *PROMETHEUS BOUND*, Apollodorus's *LIBRARY* (1.2.3, 1.3.6, 1.7.1–2, 2.5.4, 2.5.11, 3.13.5), Hesiod's *THEOGONY* (507–616) and *WORKS AND DAYS* (47–105), Hyginus's *Fabulae* (54, 142, 144), Pausanias's *Description of Greece* (1.30.2, 2.19.5, 2.19.8), and Plato's *Protagoras*. Prometheus, whose name Hesiod interprets as meaning "forethought," is the inverse of Epimetheus, whose name means "afterthought." Prometheus is clever and wily, while Epimetheus is muddleheaded. Prometheus aroused Zeus's anger because of his continued protection of humanity. Some sources claim that Prometheus created humanity, fashioning the original humans out of clay. According to Plato, Epimetheus and Prometheus were charged by the Olympian gods with distributing positive qualities between humans and other animals. Epimetheus began by giving out a number of virtues to the other animals and too late realized that he had left very little for humanity. To help mankind survive, Prometheus tried to steal and give to man some of ATHENA's skill or craft and fire from HEPHAESTUS. In Hesiod's version, Prometheus, having been denied fire by the gods, contrived to steal it from them by hiding it away in a fennel stalk and brought it to man. Prometheus is also said to have attempted to deceive the gods into eating bones and fat rather than the better sacrificial meat. PANDORA, meaning "many-gifted"—because she was made by Hephaestus and provided with virtues by all the gods—was the Olympians' retribution for Prometheus's crimes. Despite having been warned by Prometheus against accepting gifts from Zeus, Epimetheus was tempted by Zeus's offer of Pandora for a wife. Pandora brought with her a storage jar (or box) containing evil daimones—spirits—which she unwittingly loosed on the world of man.

Prometheus's punishment for his continued protection of humanity was severe. Zeus commanded Hephaestus to chain Prometheus to a pillar (or boulder) in the Caucasus and set an eagle to tear at his liver. Since Prometheus was a Titan, his liver regenerated itself, to be torn again by the eagle. Prometheus was finally rescued by HERACLES, who killed the eagle and released him from his chains.

In *Prometheus Bound*, Prometheus refuses to reveal a prophecy concerning THETIS, whom Zeus desires—the prophecy was that her son would supersede his father. In anger, Zeus throws a thunderbolt at Prometheus and casts him into an abyss. In some versions, Prometheus later regains Zeus's favor by revealing the contents of the prophecy. Aescyhlus's Prometheus is a courageous defender of humanity. The need to help mankind is his justification for his crimes against Zeus. He maintains that this was why he stole fire for man and gave him the gift of hope, the sole daimon remaining in Pandora's jar. Aeschylus's Prometheus also gifted humanity with arts (agriculture, prophecy) and sciences (mathematics, medicine). Prometheus married Clymene, and their children are Chimaereus, DEUCALION, and Lycus. Deucalion married Epimetheus and Pandora's daughter, PYRRHA. Pyrrha and Deucalion were the sole humans to survive the deluge sent by Zeus. Advised by Prometheus, they constructed a chest in which they survived the flood and later repopulated the earth.

In classical art, Prometheus is shown stealing fire from the gods or in his punishment. In a Laconian black-figure kylix from ca. 560 B.C.E. (Louvre, Paris), a stylized eagle swoops down before a seated and bound Prometheus. A postclassical example of the myth is Gustave Moreau's 19th-century painting *Prometheus* (Musée Gustave Moreau, Paris). Here, a stoic Prometheus is seated, bound, in a dark landscape, an eagle at his side.

Prometheus Bound AESCHYLUS? (ca. 440 B.C.E.) *Prometheus Bound* is a tragedy of uncertain date and debated authorship. The most recent scholarship has rejected Aeschylean authorship on grounds of style, dramatic technique, and overall quality. The play's techniques and concerns fit better the period of 440–430 B.C.E., by which time Aeschylus was dead. The play was transmitted among his works but is not independently attested as his. It is possible that it was written by his son Euphorion in imitation of the father's style. The play possibly formed part of a trilogy on the fate of PROMETHEUS, of which the later plays are lost except for fragments of *Prometheus's Release*. In this play, the suffering protagonist is a god who cannot die yet, because of his prophetic mind, is aware of all the future events of his existence and the immense duration of his future sufferings. He also knows that there will be a threat to ZEUS's rule: Zeus will be drawn to a marriage that could prove his undoing if he sires a son greater than himself. *Prometheus Bound* represents the suffering of a god and dramatizes the encounter between divine authority supported

Prometheus. *Gustave Moreau, 1868 (Musée Gustave Moreau, Paris)*

task and announces Prometheus's punishment to him. In the following dialogue, Might presses Hephaestus to complete his task of binding Prometheus, while Hephaestus complies reluctantly. Might taunts Prometheus, the "fore-thinker," for not thinking ahead sufficiently in the present instance. Might and Hephaestus exit.

Prometheus laments his suffering, calls the winds, rivers, seas, earth, and sun to witness, and resolves to bear the fate that he foresaw. He recounts how he is punished for stealing fire for humankind. The Chorus of daughters of OCEANUS enters. It expresses sympathy for Prometheus's fate. Prometheus predicts that one day Zeus will have need of him to foil a plot against his throne. The Chorus asks him to tell the story behind his punishment. Prometheus tells how his mother, THEMIS (called Earth), prophesied that the contest between the TITANS and Zeus would be won by guile, but the Titans trusted only to force. Therefore, he and his mother switched over to the side of Zeus, who defeated Cronus and his allies. Zeus distributed different parts of his empire among the gods but consigned mankind to destruction. Prometheus alone took their side and now suffers for it. He goes on to reveal that he gave men fire and hope.

The daughters of Oceanus declare that he made a mistake in opposing Zeus. Oceanus enters. He offers his support and asks Prometheus how he can help him. Prometheus at first believes that Oceanus has come to mock him, as he had first believed of his daughters. Oceanus advises Prometheus to change his tune and to cease speaking angrily of Zeus. He, for his part, will intercede for Prometheus to have him freed. Prometheus replies that Zeus cannot be swayed but thanks Oceanus and advises him to stay away and preserve himself. He recalls others with whom Zeus has dealt ruthlessly—ATLAS, who was condemned to support forever the weight of the heavens on his shoulders, and Typho (see TYPHOEUS), who was blasted by Zeus's lightning and now lies, defeated, beneath Mount Aetna and yet will one day send forth rivers of fire. In dialogue with Oceanus, Prometheus

by absolute strength and the rebellious spirit of an advocate of humankind.

SYNOPSIS

The scene is a stark mountainside in the Caucasus. Might, Violence, and HEPHAESTUS enter. Might instructs Hephaestus to construct adamantine fetters for Prometheus and nail him to the rock, so that he may learn to accept Zeus's sovereignty instead of standing up for men. Hephaestus observes that Might is likely to fulfill the command of Zeus, whereas he himself hesitates to bind a god who is his own kin. Nonetheless, he knows he must carry out his argues that Oceanus is foolish for meddling and risking his own safety, and soon persuades him to leave. Oceanus exits.

The Chorus laments Prometheus's fate, calling Zeus a haughty tyrant, and claims that all the peoples of the world, the waters, and HADES lament for him. The only god previously treated this way was Atlas. Prometheus thereupon expresses his indignation and anger at this treatment. He gave the gods their present honors and, furthermore, gave humans all the various trappings of civilized life. He taught them about building, the seasons, the constellations, numbers, writing, domestication of animals, and shipbuilding. Yet he cannot devise anything to save himself. He goes on to point out that he invented medicine, prophesy, the interpretation of omens, sacrifice, the mining of metals, and, in general, all the arts of humankind. He then states that necessity is greater than craft and that fate is more powerful than Zeus, but only alludes darkly to Zeus's future destiny—for it is to his advantage to keep this knowledge to himself.

The Chorus then stresses the importance of honoring Zeus and of not protecting one's own life. The example of Prometheus inspires fear, for he defied Zeus by his excessive regard for humanity. Men are inferior to gods and are too weak to repay Prometheus for what he gave them. Io enters. She asks who is being tortured, then speaks of her own torture: The gadfly, as the incarnate spirit of the dead ARGUS, who previously guarded her, hounds her relentlessly and gives her no rest. She wishes for death in preference to her current fate and asks Zeus, son of Cronus, why he continues to torment her. Prometheus recognizes Io, but she does not recognize him. Once again she asks who he is and if he knows how her suffering may be ended. Prometheus now reveals his identity and explains that Zeus has had him nailed to the cliff for stealing fire for humankind. He is reluctant to discourage Io by telling her the true extent of her future suffering, but consents. The Chorus, in the meantime, expresses its wish to hear her story.

Io tells how, when she was a virgin, night after night dreams came to her, bidding her to go forth from her father's house to have intercourse with Zeus, who desired her. She told the dream to her father, Inachus, who sent to oracles and was told that if she were not sent forth from his house, Zeus would destroy his people. Her father, therefore, sent her out into the world, her form was changed into that of a cow, and she was put under the guard of Argus. After his death, she was tormented by the gadfly and now wanders from land to land seeking to escape her torment. The Chorus laments her fate. Prometheus then predicts her future destiny, telling her she will travel through the dangerous lands of the Scythians and Chalybes, cross the peaks of the Caucasus Mountains, go southward to the AMAZONS, travel thence to Cimmeria, cross the channel of Maeotis, henceforth to be called the Bosphorus ("cow's ford"), and then, leaving Europe, go to Asia. Prometheus pauses to comment on the cruelty of Zeus and reveals that these travels are only a prelude. He further comments, however, that in his case suffering truly has no end, since he is immortal. Prometheus then tells the sympathetic Io that Zeus will bring danger to his throne by marrying a wife who will bear him a son mightier than his father. Only by releasing Prometheus will he be able to save himself. He reveals, moreover, that it is one of Io's descendants who will release him from his chains.

Prometheus then continues his story. Io must continue to the land of the GORGONS and Arimapsians, and finally to the Nile. There she will establish a colony for herself and her descendants. He then gives proof of his special powers of mind by telling, in detail, portions of Io's journey that she has already made. Finally, he predicts that Io will come to Canopus, near the mouth of the Nile, and will be healed by the touch of Zeus, a touch that will also make her pregnant with EPAPHUS (whose name resembles the Greek word "touch"). From him will come the DANAIDS and the sons of Aegyptus. The latter will pursue the former to force marriage on them, but the Danaids will slay the sons of Aegyptus on their wedding night; one only (Hypermnestra) will not kill her groom, and from her will descend a race of kings in Argos, from which Prometheus's liberator, HERACLES, will eventually arise. The gadfly's sting begins again to drive Io into a frenzy. The Chorus expresses horror at her fate, the fate of those who marry too far above their station. Prometheus, however, remarks on the irony of the situation: Zeus one day will seek a marriage that will threaten to dethrone him.

The Chorus counsels milder words, but Prometheus remains unrepentant. HERMES enters and demands that Prometheus tell him the secret of the threat to the throne. Prometheus despises Hermes as Zeus's servant. Their rule is young, and Zeus will be overthrown like his predecessors. Prometheus opposes himself to the gods. Hermes promises further tortures: Zeus will strike him with his thunderbolt, he will be buried for a long time in the depths of the rock, an eagle will come each day to feast on his liver. Prometheus remains magnificently defiant. Hermes insists that Prometheus is bringing his fate on himself, and the Chorus recoils from Prometheus in horror, calling him a traitor. In this closing speech, Prometheus realizes that it is no longer merely a matter of threats. Zeus's storm is being sent against him in all its fury. Prometheus and the daughters of Oceanus are buried under rock (how this was represented on stage is unclear).

COMMENTARY

The author of *Prometheus Bound* is unknown, its exact date of production uncertain (see above), and its place in relation to other plays of a possible trilogy is also doubtful. *Prometheus's Release*, of which fragments survive, followed the present play, but it is not known whether *Prometheus the Fire-Bearer* preceded or followed these two in sequence or whether there were only two linked plays and no trilogy at all.

A traditional theme in the debate about Aeschylean authorship of the *Prometheus Bound* concerns the representation of Zeus. Aeschylean cosmology is traditionally seen as supportive of a divine order in which Zeus is the ultimate power and brings the ultimate end (telos) of things to pass. The Zeus of the present play, however, is viewed in a much more critical light. Prometheus himself is fiercely critical throughout the play, representing Zeus as a tyrant newly come to power who makes his own whim into "law," is ungrateful to those who put him into his present position, and acts with ruthlessness and cruelty when anyone contradicts his will. He is presented as essentially a hubristic tyrant. The Chorus, at the beginning at least, is sympathetic to Prometheus and cannot believe that anyone would make a god suffer what Prometheus is suffering. Hephaestus is hesitant to be an accomplice in binding Prometheus, while Might—participating to the point of sadistic enthusiasm—is not a particularly sympathetic character. Oceanus offers to try to help Prometheus, and Io largely shares Prometheus's view of Zeus's ruthlessness and indifference to the suffering of others. Perhaps most strikingly, Prometheus states that Zeus himself is subject to the Fates and at their mercy—a view with precedents elsewhere in Greek thought, but remarkable if expressed by Aeschylus, who tends to present Zeus as the embodiment and driving force of destiny.

Modern readers, however, are conditioned to respond to rebels against absolute authority with sympathy—a tendency evident in the romantic reception of the Prometheus myth, most notably in Shelley's *Prometheus Unbound*. Sophocles' *Antigone* represents a similar challenge to modern sensibility and entails a similar risk of anachronism. Modern readers and audiences almost always sympathize with Antigone's rebellion against the dictates of Creon without fully considering the extent to which she may also be culpable, tragically obstinate, and self-willed like her father. The Chorus, of course, is not always right in Greek tragedy, any more than conventional opinion is right in everyday life, but it is notable in the case of the present play that the Chorus, at the beginning sympathetic, by the end recoils in horror when it perceives the full extent of Prometheus's hubristic defiance of Zeus. Oceanus himself, while presented as "loyal" to Prometheus and willing to be his advocate, exits hastily after hearing Prometheus's warning not to become involved in his own downfall. Prometheus's only true "friend" in the play is Io. He can trust her because she has suffered similarly at Zeus's hands, and only she can truly understand his bitter perspective.

Prometheus is not "right" nor Zeus "wrong," even though the sympathetic Hephaestus and Io are much more attractive characters than Might and Hermes, and even though the audience, presented with the spectacle of Prometheus's suffering throughout the play, no doubt experienced Aristotelian "pity and fear" on his behalf. We never see Zeus, and thus can only imagine his motives and attitude through the reports and comments of the characters. Even on the appearance of things, however, he has right on his side on at least some counts: Mortals really are inferior to gods in the Greek worldview and should not be given preference over gods or championed against gods. Any reader of Homer knows that, ultimately, the gods are detached from the spectacle of human suffering, however willing they are to take sides and to support one human or another for a time. Mortals, however interesting and sympathetic, are in the end simply that—mortal, of limited existence and importance. Moreover, the criticism that various characters, and especially Prometheus, make of Zeus and the Olympians throughout the play—namely, that his is a young regime—can actually be read as a possible justification of Zeus's actions. He must establish his authority and, having seen his predecessors felled in succession, is in no position to put up magnanimously with defiance and insubordination from the crafty and powerful Prometheus. There is a risk, if we take Prometheus's side, of wishing for a weaker and more vulnerable Zeus. Finally, there is

space for questioning Prometheus's motives. His indignation at his treatment results in no small amount from pride in his own status and a sense of worth, and when he lists the benefits he conferred on mankind, a note of vanity creeps into his account. He seems inordinately proud of all the things he has done for humanity and appears to value his own status as inventor, discoverer, and benefactor above the needs of the mortals whom he benefited.

We should not imagine that we are seeing an alternative anti-Olympian theology in action. Whether the play is the work of Aeschylus (currently viewed as unlikely) or, more likely, of an imitator, it can be interpreted as fitting the broader paradigm of the Aeschylean play that sets a household conflict within the broader context of cosmic concerns. The *Prometheus Bound* offers a clear example of an *oikos* conflict viewed in relation to the cosmos: Here, the tragic *oikos* (household) is the family of the gods themselves. We are reminded of their kinship on more than one occasion, e.g., Hephaestus shrinks from binding Prometheus because they are kin; Io is the niece of the daughters of Oceanus. Nor can we forget the violent succession myth that has only recently played out for this "young" regime: Zeus violently overthrew Cronus, who in turn had castrated and dethroned Uranus, while Gaia played the part of helper in this series of palace coups. The gods, as the playwright reminds us, are the original tragic family—violent destroyers of their own kin and hubristic enablers of their own destruction.

In other ways, however, Prometheus is hardly a typical tragic hero, and this play, in presenting him as its main protagonist, is unusual. First, he does almost nothing onstage except be nailed to a rock and suffer. All that he deploys during the action of the play are words, since all he has now, and has had for a very long time, is speech and thought. It is significant that, at the end, Prometheus observes that the time for words is over: The play has been almost entirely composed of words and properly ends when Zeus's punishment begins to be put into action. Second, Prometheus is a god, and thus his suffering is both disturbing and different from mortal suffering in its implications. Unlike most tragic protagonists, he cannot die—a point he explicitly makes in his dialogue with Io. The cosmic scale of the action becomes clear when we consider the ramifications of this fact. Perhaps *Prometheus's Release* saw his liberation from the torment of the eagle through the intervention of Heracles. The action of this later play, as *Prometheus Bound* makes clear, must be set more than 13 generations into the future, in the distant heroic age of Heracles, followed by that of ACHILLES. The suffering of the immortal hero of the play, then, surpasses the scope of individual human lifetimes and spans the emergence of civilizations.

The fact that Prometheus has foreknowledge of the future, and of his own fate in particular, completes this picture. He is able to comprehend the centuries of his pain in advance. Many tragic protagonists do not live long beyond their comprehension of their destiny. For Prometheus the "fore-thinker," however, depth of comprehension and chronological scale are altogether different. The drama of Prometheus's suffering is truly cosmic.

One of the old saws of tragic experience is the idea of "learning through suffering"; this idea applies in interesting ways to the present trilogy. Hermes, in the closing dialogue, describes Prometheus as a newly broken colt, still obstinate and defiant. From the extant fragments of *Prometheus's Release*, preserved in a translation by Cicero, Prometheus appears to have become exhausted eventually with his suffering and to be "in love with death." Zeus, in the meanwhile, is described as being still "young" in his rule. It is not clear what occurs to bring about Prometheus's release, and what is the basis of any latter rapprochement between Zeus and Prometheus, but it seems possible that their perspectives will change as time goes on.

Prometheus's most important interlocutor, for his own understanding of his future, is Io. She is the only human figure to come onstage during the tragedy, and thus the only example of those on whose behalf Prometheus exerted his fatal advocacy. The scope of Io's suffering, while it can never quite reach Promethean dimensions, expands as he makes her party to his own farsighted knowledge. There is an end to her wanderings, but it is painfully far off. She, like him, must steel herself for nearly infinite misery, caused by Zeus. Yet, whereas Prometheus experiences Zeus's punitive force, Io experiences Zeus as the object of his desire and will eventually be impregnated by him. This Zeus is ultimately the same one who is invoked as the protector of the Danaids in the SUPPLIANTS and whose "touch" created Epaphus, the originator of their line and thus of the Danaans. The suffering caused by Zeus, then, is not always and necessarily simple cruelty and ruthlessness: A further end (telos) may eventually come into view, however hard it is to imagine or appreciate amid the unpleasantness of the present. This particular result, moreover, has important implications for Prometheus, as he himself is at least partly aware. It is from Io's line that Prometheus's liberator, Heracles, will ultimately arise, and thus Prometheus's liberation is one important outcome (telos) of Zeus's "touching" of Io.

For all that Prometheus is a novel tragic protagonist, he is also less psychologically convincing and interesting than the protagonists of the dramas that belong among Aeschylus's known works. As a god, unable to die, he lacks some of the urgencies of the mortal condition that create the complexity and poignancy of truly tragic characters. The play, while impressive in scope and cosmic vision, falls flat in other respects. The Chorus of Oceanids is not well integrated into the action; Prometheus's role is necessarily static throughout the play; Oceanus's character is not particularly rich or absorbing, almost risible at times; even the more arresting Io fades at the close. Many passages are made up of long enumerations, e.g., the geographical locations that Io will visit or the human arts and practices invented by Prometheus. The play begins and ends with scenes of horrific violence not fully earned by complexity and power of dramatic treatment. Yet, the play remains important as a treatment of the myth of Prometheus, a figure who came to represent the emancipation of humankind in the romantic period.

Propertius (ca. 54 B.C.E.–2 B.C.E.)   Roman love poet. Propertius was born between 54 and 47 B.C.E. at Assisium; he was dead by 2 B.C.E. Propertius's property appears to have been diminished in the confiscations of 41–40, and at the end of his first book of love elegies, he recalls Octavian's brutal siege of neighboring Perugia in 41 B.C.E. Despite this gesture of independence, Propertius addresses the great literary patron Maecenas, Octavian's close associate, at the opening of his second book. Propertius wrote four books of love elegies, or possibly five, if, as some scholars argue, Book 2 is really two books merged together. Propertius's literary mistress was named Cynthia, and he claimed to be "enslaved" by Love. As Love's slave, Propertius declared himself unfit for public life. Propertius's third book of elegies, however, is less narrowly focused on love and his "one and only girlfriend." Book 4 moves away even further from erotic obsession to explore Roman monuments and rites from an etiological perspective. Propertius, especially compared with his contemporary TIBULLUS, enthusiastically incorporates references to mythology. He constantly compares his beloved Cynthia with mythological heroines and draws upon mythological exempla ("examples," "paradigmatic comparisons"). Propertius is also obsessed with death, and these two great themes combined—myth and death—have a tendency to project his love affair onto the plane of posthumous exemplarity, to make it resemble a canonical story already inscribed in the literary tradition.

Proserpina   See PERSEPHONE

Protesilaus   The first Greek to die during the Trojan War. Son of Iphiclus. Classical sources are Apollodorus's LIBRARY (3.10.8, Epitome 3.14, 3.29–30), Catullus's *Carmina* (68.73–130), Homer's *ILIAD* (2.695–710), Ovid's *HEROIDES* (13), Pausanias's *Description of Greece* (1.34.2, 3.4.6), and Virgil's *AENEID* (6.447–448). Protesilaus and his brother Podarces were suitors of HELEN and were thus drawn into the Trojan War. Protesilaus left behind a new bride, LAODAMIA, and sailed to Troy with his brother. An oracle had predicted that the first to touch land in Troy would be the first to die. None was willing to be the first to disembark at Troy until Protesilaus forged ahead. He fought bravely until he was killed by HECTOR. Laodamia begged that Protesilaus be allowed to return to her—a favor the gods granted for a brief time—and then Protesilaus returned to HADES. In her grief, Laodamia committed suicide.

Proteus   A sea god. Classical sources are Euripides' *HELEN*, Herodotus's *Histories* (2.113–119), Homer's *ODYSSEY* (4.349–570), Hyginus's *Fabulae* (118), Ovid's *METAMORPHOSES* (8.728–737), and Virgil's *GEORGICS* (4.386–529). In Homer, MENELAUS inquires of Proteus how he is to get home from Egypt. Proteus changes into many different shapes, and Menelaus must hold on to him to receive answers. Virgil offers a similar story regarding Aristaeus, who wishes to know the cause of the illness killing his bees (*Georgics* Book 4). According to Euripides' *Helen*, HERMES entrusted HELEN to Proteus. The English term "protean" refers to the god's capacity for transformation.

Psyche   A mortal whom EROS married. The principal classical source is Apuleius's *Metamorphoses* (Books 4–6). Psyche's beauty was universally admired. This drew the envious attention of Aphrodite, who asked Eros (Cupid) to make Psyche fall in love with an unworthy object. On seeing her, however, Eros pricked himself accidentally with his arrow and so become enamored of Psyche, in effect succumbing to his own weapon. Zephyrus, the West Wind, carried Psyche to an isolated place where Eros visited her by night but warned her that she must not see him. One night, needled by the envy and curiosity of her sisters, Psyche examined the sleeping Eros by the light of a candle. He awoke and fled in anger. Psyche, however, loved Eros and went in search of him. She finally won him back after performing a variety of tasks imposed on her by Aphrodite. The myth inspired several later retellings, of which the best known is *The Beauty and the Beast*.

Pygmalion   King of Cyprus. The classical sources are Apollodorus's *Library* (3.14.3) and Ovid's *Metamorphoses* (10.243–297). In Ovid's version of the story, Pygmalion creates a sculpture of a beautiful woman that comes to life with the help of Aphrodite, and she becomes his wife. They have a daughter named Paphos. In previous versions, Pygmalion is not a sculptor but falls in love with the cult statue of Aphrodite.

Pyrrha   See Deucalion.

Rhea A TITAN, the offspring of GAIA (Earth) and URANUS (Heaven). Sister of IAPETUS, HYPERION, COEUS, Crius, Cronus, MNEMOSYNE, OCEANUS, PHOEBE, TETHYS, THEIA, and THEMIS. Classical sources are Apollodorus's *LIBRARY* (1.1.3–7), Hesiod's *THEOGONY* (132–136, 493–506), and Homer's *ILIAD* (14.200–204, 15.187–188). Cronus wed his sister Rhea, with whom he produced the generation of Olympian gods: DEMETER, HADES, HERA, HESTIA, POSEIDON, and ZEUS. Wishing to prevent the succession of his own children, Cronus swallowed each child whole shortly after its birth. After the birth of their sixth child, Zeus, Rhea wrapped a stone in swaddling clothes and gave it to Cronus in place of the infant. Zeus was thus spared the fate of his brothers and sisters and grew to maturity on the island of Crete. The Curetes sheltered the infant Zeus by creating a racket to drown out his cries. With Gaia's help, Zeus made his father disgorge his siblings and eventually fulfilled the prophesy of unseating his father.

Pausanias describes a relief on the Temple of Hera at Plataea in Boeotia, depicting Rhea offering Cronus a swaddled stone to swallow in place of her last-born child, Zeus. A similar representation appears on an Attic red-figure pelike from ca. 475 B.C.E. (Metropolitan Museum of Art, New York).

Romulus Founder of Rome. Son of Mars (see ARES) and Rhea Silvia. Brother of Remus. The principal classical sources are Dionysius of Halicarnassus's *Roman Antiquities* (1.76–2.56), Livy's *From the Foundation of the City* (1.3.10–1.17), and Ovid's *FASTI* (2.381–421; 3.11–76, 179–228). Numitor, king of Alba Longa, was driven from the throne by his brother Amulius. Amulius then made Numitor's daughter, Rhea Silvia, a Vestal virgin, since this priesthood required the maintenance of chastity, which, in Rhea's Silvia's case, would prevent the birth of an avenger of Numitor. The god Mars, however, raped her, and she gave birth to twin sons, Romulus and Remus. Amulius ordered the twins to be thrown into the river Tiber. The Tiber was in flood, and the twins were washed ashore near a fig tree called the Ficus Ruminalis. A she wolf came upon them, suckled them, and brought them up. Eventually, Faustulus, the royal herdsman, came upon them, and he and his wife brought them up as their own children. As the boys grew up and became involved in various bold deeds, including robbery, Remus was taken prisoner by Amulius, while Faustulus revealed to Romulus the secret of his parentage. Romulus rescued his brother, defeated Amulius, and reinstalled Numitor as king. The twins then decided to found a city, according to Roman tradition in the year 754 B.C.E. According to

Livy, Romulus set himself up on the Palatine hill, Remus on the Aventine. When they took augury, six vultures first appeared to Remus, but 12 vultures afterward appeared for Romulus. In the subsequent dispute over priority, Romulus killed Remus for daring to jump over his walls. Romulus became Rome's first king.

Romulus's main problem was a lack of population in his newly founded community. He addressed this problem first by setting up an asylum for fugitives of all sorts, who wished to join the Roman citizenry, next by tricking the nearby Sabines into coming to a festival in honor of Neptune and then stealing their wives. A war ensued, which eventually was brought to an end through the intervention of the women themselves, who had begun to feel part of the Roman state. After a reign of about 40 years, Romulus vanished mysteriously amid a storm at a place called the "Goat's Marsh." He was thought to have been abducted by the gods and was worshipped under the name Quirinus. (Ovid tells the story of Romulus's deification in the METAMORPHOSES.) A cynical rumor also existed to the effect that the senators had ripped Romulus to pieces, then spread the more benign story to conceal their deed. Romans in later years could see the Lupercal, or wolf cave, in which Romulus and Remus were supposedly suckled, on the side of the Palatine hill. Likewise, a "hut of Romulus" was preserved as a shrine on both the Palatine and the Capitoline hills. Comparably, another site on the Palatine was designated as Romulus's original settlement, called Roma Quadrata. The emperor Augustus, who saw himself as a second founder of Rome, aligned himself with both Aeneas, son of Venus, and Romulus, son of Mars. While Augustus wished to avoid too close a connection with the monarchical and fratricidal Romulus, and thus chose to assume the honorific title "Augustus" rather than "Romulus," Romulus appears in his key ideological monuments, the Ara Pacis and the Forum of Augustus. Romulus often served to focus Roman awareness of the relation between violence and the foundation of their civilization, between political power and the constant danger of civil war.

Sappho (fl. seventh–sixth century B.C.E.) Sappho of Lesbos was a lyric poet who flourished in the seventh–sixth century B.C.E. Her poetry was collected into nine books in the Alexandrian edition and arranged by meter. She became known as the "the tenth Muse." Mostly fragments of her work survive. She wrote hymns, wedding songs, and poems about love among women and girls. Little is known about Sappho's life, and what does survive is a species of biographical myth (see, for example, the letter of Sappho to Phaon in Ovid's *HEROIDES*). Sappho, who wrote about the beauty and desirability of young women in her social group, became an icon of modern homosexuality. Scholars in recent years, however, have tended to point to patterns of premarital, institutionalized homoeroticism in ancient Greece. In one enigmatic and incomplete poem (fr. 31), she apparently speaks of her physically overpowering experience of jealousy as she watches a female member of her group sitting next to and speaking with an unnamed man. In fragment 1 (complete), Sappho addresses the goddess APHRODITE, asking her to help her in her current state of love, although she recognizes, with graceful humor, that Aphrodite has received this request from the poet frequently in the past.

Like other lyric poets, Sappho sometimes makes use of mythology, which she adapts to the situations and occasions of her poetry. In one

fragment (fr. 44), we find a description of the arrival of HECTOR and his bride, ANDROMACHE. The fragment forms part of an epithalamium (marriage poem): The mythological episode enriches and confers prestige on the marriage celebrated in poem. In another fragment (fr. 16), Sappho declares that while some people value war, she values love above all else; she recalls HELEN's desertion of her husband, MENELAUS, and then thinks of Anactoria, whose lovely manner of walking and radiant face she prefers to any number of chariots and infantry. The mythological reference to Helen plays into Sappho's opposition of love and war, lyric poetry, and epic. In a fragment discovered in 2004, Sappho compares herself, growing older, to Tithonus in his old age, the husband of "an immortal wife," the goddess Eos (Dawn). The Roman poet CATULLUS produced Roman versions of the Sapphic strophe and wrote a free imitation of fragment 31. HORACE also admired Sappho, but professed a preference for Alcaeus.

Sarpedon A Lycian hero of the Trojan War. Son of LAODAMIA and ZEUS. Cousin of GLAUCUS. The classical sources are Apollodorus's *LIBRARY* (3.1.1.–2), Diodorus Siculus's *LIBRARY OF HISTORY* (5.79.3), and Homer's *ILIAD* (12.290–414, 16.419–683). Sarpedon fought on the side of Troy during the Trojan War. He was a formidable warrior in the battle against the Achaeans. When Sarpedon was badly injured by PATROCLUS during battle, his cousin Glaucus attempted to rescue him but was prevented because he sustained a wound himself. Glaucus prayed to APOLLO to be quickly cured, a prayer that the god granted. Glaucus could not save Sarpedon, but brought back Sarpedon's body. Sarpedon's armor, in the meantime, had been stripped by the Greeks. Zeus, Sarpedon's father, wished to save his son from death but was reminded by HERA that he could not oppose destiny. In tribute to his dead son, Zeus sent down a rain of blood. In some post-Homeric authors, Sarpedon is the son of EUROPA and Zeus.

Saturn   See CRONUS.

satyrs   Human male and animal hybrids. Satyrs have in common with FAUNS and SILENI their sylvan domain and their association with revelry and music. Classical sources are AESOP's *Fables*, Euripides' *CYCLOPS* (passim), Ovid's *METAMORPHOSES* (passim), Pausanias's *Description of Greece* (1.20.1–2, 1.23.5–6), and Virgil's *ECLOGUES* (passim). Satyrs have human torsos and a goat's (or horse's) legs and are known for their lascivious behavior. Ovid classifies them with other sylvans and bucolic divinities to whom Zeus granted the right to live in peace in the woods and forests. CENTAURS and fauns resemble satyrs in some of their physical features, but the former are more violent, and the latter more playful. Satyrs, fauns, and Sileni as well as their female associates—nymphs and maenads—participate in the Bacchic processions of DIONYSUS. A satyr play was a type of comic play that was performed last in a tragic tetralogy. Euripides' *Cyclops* is the sole fully extant example.

Satyrs were frequently depicted by classical vase painters in one of two themes: a Bacchanalia or the satyrs' amorous pursuit of a woodland nymph. They appear with Dionysus on an Attic black-figure amphora from ca. 560

Satyr and Maenad. *Kylix detail, ca. 460 B.C.E. (Louvre, Paris)*

B.C.E. (Louvre, Paris), and they appear disturbing the sleep of a nymph in an Attic red-figure kylix from ca. 490 B.C.E. (Museum of Fine Arts, Boston). A satyr and maenad are depicted on the tondo of an Attic red-figure kylix by the Penthesilea Painter from ca. 460 B.C.E. (Louvre, Paris).

Scylla (1)   Daughter of King Nisus of Megara. Classical sources are Aeschylus's *LIBATION BEARERS* (612–622), Apollodorus's *LIBRARY* (3.15.5–8), Hyginus's *Fabulae* (198), and Ovid's *METAMORPHOSES* (8.6–151). King MINOS of Crete laid siege to Megara, but Nisus was invulnerable, thanks to his lock of purple hair. For six months, the siege continued without success, until Scylla, who had fallen in love with Minos while observing him from the citadel of Megara, betrayed her father and cut or pulled out his protective lock of hair as he slept. According to the *Libation Bearers*, however, Scylla betrayed her father for a bribe, a Cretan golden necklace, not for love. In the *Metamorphoses*, Minos was horrified and repelled by her act. Shamed and scorned, Scylla taunted Minos with the passion that his wife, Pasiphae, had conceived for a bull. As Minos sailed away, Scylla leapt into the sea after him and was transformed into a sea bird, the ciris that is continually chased by the osprey, the bird into which her father had been metamorphosed. An alternate version in Hyginus's *Fabulae* makes Minos an accomplice in Scylla's treachery, and his refusal to bring her back with him to Crete is a betrayal of a promise he had made to her. In this version, Scylla is turned into a fish preyed upon by the osprey. In Apollodorus's *Library*, after Minos captured Megara, he tied Scylla to the stern of a ship for her treachery toward her father and she drowned. This myth is represented in a lunette of Sebastiano del Piombo's fresco decorations, from ca. 1511, of the Villa Farnesina in Rome. Here, Scylla prepares to cut off the lock of hair of a sleeping Nisus while a ciris and osprey fly overhead.

Scylla (2) A monstrous canine creature. Scylla's lair was a cave above a narrow sea passage across from an equally terrible CHARYBDIS. Classical sources are Apollodorus's *LIBRARY* (Epitome 7.20–23), Apollonius of Rhodes's *VOYAGE OF THE ARGONAUTS* (4.825–831), Homer's *ODYSSEY* (Book 12), Hyginus's *Fabulae* (151, 199), and Ovid's *METAMORPHOSES* (13.730–14.74). Scylla's parentage is not certain. In Apollodorus's *Library*, Scylla is either the daughter of HECATE and Phorcys or Trienus and Phorcus. Scylla has a variety of representations in classical literature, but the canine element is common to most. Homer describes her as having 12 legs and six heads sitting on six long necks from which issues the barking of a dog; she uses her three rows of teeth to devour passing sea creatures and sailors. In Apollodorus's *Library*, she has six dog heads and 12 paws. According to Ovid, Scylla had once been a mortal, a nymph loved by the sea divinity GLAUCUS and who thus incurred the jealousy of CIRCE. Circe poisoned a bathing place that

Scylla. *Engraving, John Flaxman, illustration for Homer's* Odyssey, *1795 (University College, London)*

Scylla frequented so that Scylla emerged from bathing one day transformed into a monster with dogs growing from her torso. Scylla and Charybdis (a whirlpool) were a threat to all who sailed past their rocks on the opposite sides of what was believed to have been the Strait of Messina. Scylla devours six of ODYSSEUS's crewmates in Homer's *Odyssey*, but in Apollonius of Rhodes's *Voyage of the Argonauts*, Jason and his companions safely pass by Scylla under Hera's protection.

Scylla. was depicted on vases, coins, and other media as having a serpent's tail topped by a nude female torso, flowing hair, and dogs emerging from her midsection. Scylla is thus depicted on a Boeotian red-figure bell-crater from ca. 450 B.C.E. (Louvre, Paris) and in a neoclassical engraving by John Flaxman in his illustrations for Homer's *Odyssey*. Scylla-figure adorned helmets appear on some antique coins.

Selene An early Greek personification of the moon. Daughter of the Titans HYPERION (a sun god) and THEIA. Sister of Eos (Dawn) and HELIOS (Sun). Classical sources are the *Homeric Hymn to Selene*, Apollodorus's LIBRARY (1.2.2, 1.7.5), Apollonius of Rhodes's VOYAGE OF THE ARGONAUTS (4.57), Hesiod's THEOGONY (371–374), Pausanias's *Description of Greece* (5.1.3–5, 5.11.8), and Virgil's GEORGICS (3.391–393). Selene is sometimes merged with the Roman personification of the moon, Luna. In the *Homeric Hymn to Selene* and the *Orphic Hymn to the Moon*, the goddess has a radiance that waxes and wanes with the lunar cycles as she drives her chariot (drawn by horses or oxen, depending on the source) across the sky. Diodorus of Siculus's *Library of History* relates that the Titans murdered Hyperion and Helios, whereupon Selene, who dearly loved her brother, killed herself in grief. Selene and Helios were afterward made into immortal celestial beings representing the moon and the sun. During the GIGANTOMACHY, Zeus prevented Selene, Eos,

and Helios from shining, a tactic that helped defeat the GIANTS.

In her most popular myth, Selene fell in love with the mortal youth ENDYMION. Zeus granted Endymion perpetual sleep during which he would neither die nor grow old. Selene visited Endymion in a cave on Mount Latmus at the dark phase of the moon. In Virgil's *Georgics* (3.391), Selene succumbed to the amorous advances of the bucolic god PAN.

In visual representations, Selene appears with her attribute, the moon, or in the company of Eos and Helios. In the *Homeric Hymn*, Selene is given wings, while in the *Orphic Hymn*, she has horns; in art she is usually depicted with a crescent moon crowning her head but without wings. In antiquity, she appears on various media: reliefs, vase paintings, gems, and coins. Selene also appears on the Pergamon Altar in a scene representing the Gigantomachy. In an Attic red-figure kylix krater from ca. 430 B.C.E. (British Museum, London), Selene is shown in company with her siblings. Here, Helios drives a four-horse chariot, and Eos pursues the hunter CEPHALUS on foot, while Selene rides on horseback.

Semele Daughter of CADMUS and HARMONIA. Consort of ZEUS and by him, mother of DIONYSUS. Also called Thyone. Classical sources are Apollodorus's LIBRARY (3.4.2–3, 3.5.3), Diodorus Siculus's LIBRARY OF HISTORY (4.2.1–3, 4.25.4, 5.52.2), Euripides' BACCHAE (1–12, 23–31, 242–245, 286–297), Hesiod's THEOGONY (940–942), and Ovid's METAMORPHOSES (3.259–312). According to Apollodorus's *Library* and Ovid's *Metamorphoses*, HERA became aware of Zeus's love for Semele. Disguised as Semele's nurse, she persuaded Semele to ask him to show himself to her in his full divinity as proof that he was, indeed, Zeus. Zeus repented that he had already promised to grant her a request, but he was obliged to fulfill his promise. Zeus appeared in the form of the lightning bolt, and Semele was consumed in the blaze. Zeus plucked the unborn Dionysus from her womb and sewed him into his thigh until the child was ready to be born. Later Dionysus would descend into HADES by way of the bottomless Alcyonian Lake and return with Semele, whom he made immortal.

Seneca the Younger (ca. 4 B.C.E.–65 C.E.) Lucius Annaeus Seneca was a Roman philosopher, poet, and statesman born at Córdoba in Spain between 4 B.C.E. and 1 C.E. He was the son of Seneca the Elder, the writer on declamation. Seneca was exiled under Claudius. He was subsequently recalled by Agrippina after Claudius's death. He became, first, Nero's tutor, then, along with the praetorian prefect Burrus, his chief adviser. As time went on, however, Nero appears to have come to resent his former tutor's moral stringency, while Seneca found it difficult to tolerate Nero's actions, including his murder of his mother in C.E. 59. In 62, Seneca retired from the court, and in 65, he was forced to commit suicide for alleged involvement in a conspiracy. Seneca was a committed Stoic philosopher and wrote a number of philosophical tracts and philosophical epistles. He also wrote tragedies: *Hercules, Troades, Phoenissae* (unfinished), *Medea, Phaedra, Oedipus, Agamemnon,* and *Thyestes.* The *Octavia* and the *Hercules Oetaeus* have been ascribed to Seneca. The former is certainly and the latter probably not Senecan. Scholars have debated whether or not the plays were meant for performance or merely recitation; the latter view has largely prevailed. While Seneca shows knowledge of Greek tragedy and models his plays on Greek predecessors, in many ways Seneca writes within the Roman poetic traditions of the early empire centered around Augustan classics such as Virgil's *AENEID* and Ovid's *METAMORPHOSES.* As a Neronian writer, he shares in the broader tendencies of the age: He both betrays his deep preoccupation with the Augustan classics and pursues a counterclassical poetics in his focus on the dark, gruesome, and perverse aspects of human nature and the futility of action in a hopeless environment. The best example is provided by the *Thyestes,* which dwells with increasing horror on the apparently limitless sadism of ATREUS and Thyestes' realization that he has consumed his murdered children.

Seven against Thebes AESCHYLUS (467 B.C.E.) Aeschylus's *Seven against Thebes* is the last play in his Theban trilogy. The plays were produced in 467 B.C.E. and included a fourth satyr play. The background is the cursed history of the Theban royal house: LAIUS was warned not to have children but begot OEDIPUS, who, although abandoned, survived to kill his father and marry his mother. In rage and horror, Oedipus cursed his two sons, ETEOCLES and POLYNICES, predicting that they would divide their inheritance with iron, i.e., the sword. After Oedipus was banished from Thebes, the two brothers were to reign alternately, but Eteocles refused to hand over power at the end of the year. Polynices, exiled from his homeland, found refuge and help in Argos. Both he and the exiled Tydeus happened to come to the palace of Adrastus one night, and each ended up marrying one of Adrastus's daughters. This alliance was the origin of the expedition of the Seven against Thebes. The action of the present play begins at the moment when the assault on Thebes is imminent. We see the action from the perspective of the Theban people, afraid for their lives and freedom, and their king Eteocles, who is concerned that he will be blamed for any misfortune that befalls the city. Aeschylus's play dramatizes the terror of war in the tense moments before the Argive attack and, at the same time, examines the complicated fate of the aristocratic ruling house and the polis over which it rules. The terrible denouement—the simultaneous killing of brother by brother—is both fitting emblem and grim culmination of the cursed destiny of the house of Laius.

SYNOPSIS

The scene is the Theban acropolis. Images of ZEUS, HERA, POSEIDON, APOLLO, ATHENA, ARES, APHRODITE, and ARTEMIS are on the stage. Men, old men, and boys of Thebes enter. Eteocles enters. He comments on the blame that falls on rulers for the misfortunes of a city, but encourages the Theban males to take matters in their own hands by defending their city against the onslaught of the attackers. He has heard from a prophet that their enemies are planning a major assault and awaits confirmation from spies. The group of Theban men exit. A scout enters. He confirms that seven captains have sworn an oath together that they will each lead their troops against a gate of the city and suggests that Eteocles counter their forces at each gate. Eteocles calls on the gods to save Thebes from slavery and submission, then exits.

The Chorus of unmarried Theban women enters. It laments and expresses its fear as it hears the sounds of oncoming soldiers and sees the seven captains take their place at each gate. It calls on the eight Olympian gods whose images are onstage for help.

Eteocles reenters. He chastises the Chorus for merely calling on the gods and lamenting: It is breeding panic rather than helping. He suggests harshly that it stays indoors and not meddle in matters of war. The Chorus and Eteocles debate the extent to which one should rely on the gods' help in a time of crisis. The women, as they hear the sounds of war, are increasingly terrified, while Eteocles brusquely insists that this is the nature of war; they should go inside and keep quiet. Eteocles prevails on them: They will be silent and endure. He further exhorts them to offer a prayer for victory. He announces his plan to place seven heroes along with himself at the gates to the meet the Argive attack. Eteocles exits.

The Chorus declares that it will make an effort, but it is still terrified of the enemy attack. It exhorts the gods to throw panic and madness on its enemies and save the city. Then, in vivid detail, it enumerates the horrors of a successful siege—the destruction wrought on people's homes and the fate of the captured, especially women and girls.

The scout enters followed by Eteocles. The scout informs Eteocles of the movements of the enemy, the situation of each enemy captain, their character, and the emblems on their shields. Tydeus is at the Proitid gate, but he can go no farther because the sacrifice was ill omened; he is angry and arrogant, as the emblem of the moon blazing amid smaller stars suggests. Against Tydeus, Eteocles sets Melanippus. The scout then describes Capaneus at the Elektran gate. He boasts that even Zeus's lightning will not stop him, and his shield shows a man holding a lamp with the words "I will sack this town" on it. Against Capaneus, Eteocles sets Polyphontes. The scout then relates that Eteoclus is set to attack at the Neis gate. His shield shows a besieging hoplite next to words stating that not even Ares could throw him down. Magareus is slated to stand up against him. The scout next describes the gigantic and monstrous Hippomedon, whose shield depicts Typhon and coils of snakes. He is hailed as Terror itself. Eteocles opposes Hyperbius to Hippomedon and states that the Zeus on his shield will defeat Hippomedon's Typhon. The scout then describes Parthenopaeus at the Northern Gate. On his shield—as a taunt to Thebes—is depicted the SPHINX carrying a Theban man in her claws, so that Theban spears will have to be aimed at the image of a Theban. To Parthenopaeus, Eteocles opposes Actor. The scout indicates that the prophet Amphiaraus is at the Homolian gates. He is formidable for his very piety and wisdom; he opposes Tydeus's bloodthirstiness and criticizes Polynices, questioning his attack on his own home city. He predicts that he himself will be buried under Theban soil and has no emblem on his shield. Eteocles laments that Amphiaraus must join an expedition of bad men and that he must share their fate; against him, he sets Lasthenes. The scout reports that the last invader is Eteocles' own brother, Polynices. He will end up facing his own brother in combat, who bears the emblem of Justice represented as a woman modestly leading a warrior. The image represents his claim of his right to return to his own city. The scout exits.

Eteocles mourns the fate of the race of Oedipus and the enmity of the gods: His father's curse has been fulfilled. He denies the association of Polynices, "man of much strife," with the figure of Justice. He resolves to face his brother in combat. The Chorus encourages him not to stain himself with the blood of kin, but Eteocles insists that this evil fate inflicted by the gods cannot be resisted. Eteocles exits.

The Chorus cries out that a Fury is fulfilling Oedipus's curses, bringing new violence and pollution on the house. It explains that the story of crime and the gods' enmity goes back to Laius, who, despite the warnings of Apollo's oracle at Delphi, lay with his wife and begot a child—Oedipus, who killed his father and married his mother. It is was in a rage at his cursed union that Oedipus cursed his own children, saying that one day they would divide their property with iron.

The scout enters. He reports that the city has been saved: The defense at six of the gates was successful, but Apollo brought to bear Oedipus's curse at the seventh. The two brothers have slain each other, as the Chorus learns in a dialogue with the scout. The scout exits. The Chorus is uncertain whether to rejoice at the city's salvation or lament the brothers' demise. It observes that Oedipus's curse has been fulfilled and the consequences of Laius's act have now all come to pass, not merely in word, but in deed. Attendants enter with the corpses of Eteocles and Polynices. The Chorus views their bodies and comments on these double deaths. The household itself was pierced by the death blow they dealt each other. It expresses sympathy for the profound misfortune of JOCASTA, the mother of the two dead men, and observes that the Curses have sung a victory song, Destruction has set up a victory monument, and the hostile daimon of the

house is the true victor. In the closing section, the Chorus, exchanging verses rapidly among its various members in succession, laments the fate of the dead brothers and the disaster for the house and the land. In the play's final lines, the Chorus contemplates their burial and the grim irony of the two brothers being laid to rest beside their father.

COMMENTARY

As the culminating play of Aeschylus's trilogy on the tragic destruction of the royal house of Thebes, the *Seven against Thebes* must be seen as a cataclysmic finale of a mythological trajectory beginning with Laius and ending with the burial of the two enemy brothers. Laius was warned not to have children, but did anyway: Oedipus was born, abandoned, and survived to kill his father and marry his mother, Jocasta. The horror of his realization caused him to curse his own children, that they would "divide their inheritance with iron." Aeschylus's trilogy *Laius*, *Oedipus*, and *Seven against Thebes* dramatizes each stage of this grim series of family disasters. The last play in the trilogy, and the only one to survive, supplies a fitting climax by broadening and intensifying the scope of the previous plays. Now the division within a family has brought about the massing of two armies, an attack on a great city, and the terror of its people. Oedipus was, at first, the savior of his city, defeating the murderous Sphinx; now, his sons and his curse are on the brink of destroying the polis over which his family rules.

At the opening of the play, Eteocles is isolated in the unenviable role of leader of a besieged city. He addresses the old men and boys, who represent the warriors of the past and of the future, while the warriors of the present moment take the field. The city is thus conceived as an entity that extends over time—an idea that is all the more appreciated by an audience that has viewed the family of Laius and its involvement with Thebes over successive generations. The Thebans are associated with legends of autochthony (e.g., some of the city's heroes derive from the Sown Men, who sprang from the ground itself), and Earth (GAIA) is mentioned more than once as a protective deity. Finally, the images of the gods are arranged across the scene; throughout the play, as in this opening scene, the city will be closely associated with the protective power of the gods, above all, Zeus. It is clear to Eteocles, however, that while the gods will receive credit for victory, the leader will take the blame for any failure. He is trying to encourage proper respect and reverence for the gods in this moment of crisis—Earth, Thebes's native daimones, Zeus, the other Olympians—and at the same time, he exhorts the citizens to do their part for the war effort rather than give in to panic or blame casting.

While the old men and boys apparently hear Eteocles' speech without complaint, the city's unmarried women, who make up the Chorus are less docile, perhaps for good reason. The emotional tenor of their address to the city's acropolis deities is of a very different sort from that of Eteocles and derives from the immediacy of their terror: They can hear the approaching din of warfare. The evocation of the panic-inspiring sights and cacophonous sounds of imminent warfare is a powerful one in the opening choral passage (the parodos), and effectively sets the tone for the play. By setting the emotive pitch high, Aeschylus's Chorus infuses with dynamism, tension, and even suspense a plot that otherwise is in danger of being static and one-dimensional. For the Greeks, moreover, and for the Athenians especially, warfare was a continual aspect of life. Of its various outcomes, the fate of a city that has fallen to a siege would have been among the most pathetic and terrible: families destroyed, populations enslaved, women raped, children and babies violently mistreated or killed. The young, unmarried women of Thebes not unnaturally feel the approach of the Argive force as a physical threat to their bodies and freedom: They will be made into

servants and bedmates of the conquerors, and their only "hope," as they put it with grim sarcasm, will be to suffer forced intercourse with their new masters. Their plight is all the more poignant because they are maidens and have not therefore reached the culmination of normal womanhood in marriage; instead, they are in danger of suffering this violent travesty of marriage before they enjoy the proper rite. The polis, in this case, becomes like one violently overturned household: Its resources are plundered and wasted by looters, its structures destroyed by fire, and its fundamental cohesion dissolved.

The first choral sequence is especially tense and fragmented, as it moves rapidly from exclamation to rhetorical question to piecemeal observation or description. Aeschylus brilliantly simulates a moment of mass panic in its diverse articulation. While the Chorus later calms down somewhat, its more overtly emotional and pessimistic viewpoint enriches the texture of the play by presenting a constant counterpoint to the plans and militaristic declarations of Eteocles. War is viewed simultaneously as a moment of valor and civic cohesion and as an occasion of terror, foreboding, and suffering. Eteocles appears to be (or presents himself as) levelheaded and self-controlled by contrast with the women of the Chorus. He objects not to the mere fact that they turn toward the gods in time of crisis but the manner in which they do. He claims they do so in a spirit of fear and panic and thus fail to uphold the fighting spirit of others. He suggests that instead they pray that the gods will be their allies in victory. In the case of victory, the Thebans will offer thanks by animal sacrifice and by setting up trophies and dedicating spoils of war.

It is noteworthy that here, as elsewhere, Aeschylus sets up a sharp division between male and female principles as an organizing tension of the play. The women represent the perspective of those who suffer and cannot fight on their own behalf, the most helpless and pitiable victims of war. Their position of relative vulnerability also seems to bestow on them an insight into the potential for suffering that men ignore. Men suffer in war as well as women, they point out. The broad lines of this conflict can be compared with the male-female divide that pervades and drives the *Oresteia;* at an even more detailed level, the panicked, vulnerable female Chorus in conversation with a more self-possessed—but ultimately violent and vengeful—male leader figure resembles the Chorus of Danaids panicked at the imminent arrival of the sons of Aegyptus in Aeschylus's *Suppliants.* Here, too, an invading mob of insolent, hubristic men threatens to take a group of women by force, and the women, in turn, look to the gods and their leader to protect them. (In Suppliants, however, the Argives ultimately offer a place of refuge to the fleeing women, whereas in *Seven against Thebes,* the Argives are the invaders.) This complex dynamic of adversarial tension and common cause defines the interaction of Eteocles and Chorus throughout the play. As he departs for the fatal encounter with Polynices, the Chorus continues to express foreboding and to attempt to dissuade him, whereas the Theban leader continues to insist on the perverse necessity and even nobility of the fate demanded by the gods and his father's curse.

The Chorus focuses on the sufferings caused by war and the ancient curse of the royal house; Eteocles focuses on the present crisis, war, and strategy. The battle itself, in accordance with the conventions of ancient drama, is not shown onstage, and thus the composition of the opposing forces and their disposition are represented through an elaborate, prospective strategy discussion between Eteocles and the scout that occupies the central portion of the play. The scout gives information on the seven main enemy warriors, one stationed at each of Thebes's seven gates, reports the warrior's attitude and words, and describes the emblem (or lack of emblem) on each warrior's shield. For each warrior thus described, Eteocles offers an opposing Theban warrior, as well as an adversarial interpretation of the enemy's attitude, character, and emblem. The invaders' emblems typically associate them with hubris, arrogance, and unbridled violence; they are described, moreover, as massive, monstrous, and lacking self-control. Eteocles in each instance elicits a meaning from the symbols different from their ostensible import; e.g., the night scene on Tydeus's shield, that shows him great like the moon amid lesser stars, is reinterpreted to refer to the night that will come over his eyes in death. Against the arrogant, foreign invader, moreover, Eteocles sets Melanippus, descended from the Sown Men, an appropriately autochthonous defender of his native soil and fitting answer to Tydeus's boastful celestial imagery.

Other notable instances include the intensely hubristic attitude of Capaneus, who boasts that Zeus's thunderbolts will not stop him (in fact, they will), and whose shield depicts a man carrying a blazing lamp that itself emblazons the words "I will sack this town." On Hippomedon's shield is the figure of Typhon (see Typhoeus) flanked by coiling snakes. In both cases, the invaders are emblematically allied with the rebellious, monstrous, hubristic enemies of Zeus and the Olympians; as elsewhere, Gigantomachy symbolizes the defeat of unprincipled might and transgressive violence. Typhon and snakes represent the *wrong* kind of earthborn creatures—the monstrous as opposed to the autochthonous. The cosmic symbolism of their shields is itself an omen of their failure. Topographical details support this symbolism; e.g., Hippomedon stands near the temple of Athena—one of the central warriors of the Gigantomachy and mainstay of Zeus—and Parthenopaeus stands by the tomb of Amphion, son of Zeus. The gods themselves, prominent in the play's dialogue and staging from the outset, will act as defenders of the city's gates in highly concrete and visible ways.

In a certain sense, then, although the battle is not shown taking place directly, Aeschylus has created a scene in which the battle is fought, not with swords, but with symbols and interpretations. The tragedian's script wages its own tense, violent war of words that parallels and gives literary form to the battle it represents. Writing and even "texts" are emphasized to an unusual degree. The lamp on Capaneus's shield bears an aggressive written message, and Eteoclus (an Argive invader, to be distinguished from Eteocles) bears a shield decorated with the image of a soldier climbing a ladder accompanied by words representing his speech: Not even Ares himself can cast him down. All these words, scripts, and symbols, however, are ultimately inscribed with the marks of their own failure. Besides their sometimes patently self-incriminating gestures of hubris, the bearers of the emblems commit the more fundamental hubris of claiming more than they have actually achieved.

The only positively represented enemy captain is the prophet Amphiaraus, described as a good, prudent man. He was forced into joining the expedition by a trick. His wife, Eriphyle, married him on the condition that she would be the arbiter of any dispute between him and her brother Adrastus, the leader of the Argive force. Polynices bribed her with the necklace of HARMONIA (a significant, mythologically laden emblem of Thebes) to support Adrastus in their dispute over the proposed attack on Thebes. Amphiaraus, although he disapproved on the basis of his prophetic knowledge of the expedition's doom, was forced to join as a condition of his marriage. None of this story is told here except that he is contemptuous of Tydeus's violent attitude and Adrastus's course of action. It is significant, however, that his shield has no emblem whatsoever, since, as Aeschylus's scout observes, he was a deep thinker and did not wish merely to seem, but to be, the best. Amphiaraus's own words are quoted: He will "enrich" the land and be buried under hostile soil. This may refer darkly to a story told explicitly only much later in Statius's *Thebaid*—namely, that Amphiaraus did not die in battle but was swallowed up alive by the earth at Zeus's behest and became an immortal prophet-hero. Certainly, the Athenians will recognize a foreshadowing of Amphiaraus's cult and status as oracular hero, as embodied in his shrine located near the border of Attica and Boeotia.

Arguably the most important and complex emblem of the sequence is the last, the emblem that Eteocles' brother and adversary, Polynices, bears on his shield: A warrior represented in gold is led by a woman representing Justice, accompanied by a written text of Justice's words. She declares that she will bring Polynices back home, where he will inhabit the city of his fathers and his own house. Polynices's claim is not a nakedly violent boast of might and conquest but a more subtle combination of claims, both a prediction of victory and a justification of his deeds. Polynices mixes together a pose of deference and modesty—he does not attack brazenly but is led modestly by a woman—with an implication of superiority and victory over his enemies. Eteocles is enraged by these claims and pointedly contrasts Polynices's name—"much strife"—with his supposed alliance with Justice. His claims, however, are not quite so easy to dismiss, and it is noteworthy that, in the succession of warriors, Polynices comes last, immediately following Amphiaraus. The two culminating figures are the most ambiguous morally and least obviously condemnable, since Amphiaraus was unwilling and Polynices had at least some arguable basis for wishing to return to his homeland.

The danger, as the Chorus observes, is that Eteocles ("true fame") will become all too similar, through his actions, to his brother ("much strife"). The apparently clear and distinct division of moral roles implied by the two names is profoundly muddled by the actual turn of events, the merging of their different paths of action into a single, horrifically symmetrical act of mutual slaughter. No matter how intense and, at times, effective is Eteocles' effort to distinguish himself morally from his ostensibly hubristic adversary, in the end their rivalry fuses them into a single, undifferentiated image of a destroyed household. They were fated by Oedipus to "divide" their inheritance with iron, and yet, in a terrible irony, by this same iron they are merged into a unified doublet in death.

A great deal of the irony here is generated by the previous focus on the close reading of signs and Eteocles' adversarial explication of his enemies' emblems, his careful labor of exegesis distinguishing self and enemy, hubristic invader and morally worthy, autochthonous defender, good brother, and bad brother. The limit of his capacity to define his fate through such an act of heroic exegesis arises when he himself becomes, as a corpse, part of the tragedy's culminating sign or emblem. Following the announcement of the Thebans' victory, the Chorus learns that Apollo brought to a grim fulfillment Oedipus's curse on his two sons: They killed each other with their own hands in battle. As the Chorus laments, the two corpses are brought onto the stage to be viewed. The Chorus, which was just singing of Laius's deed and Oedipus's curse, declares that the proof now can be seen before it: "his words are visible." The "double death" of the two brothers has made visible the dark workings of the destiny decreed by the gods, and its ineluctable fulfillment over generations. It is significant that in the Chorus's closing lament, the two brothers' names are no longer used to distinguish them; they have been merged into a single fate, a single image of double destruction. Together, the corpses represent a household extinguished. Instead of naming the one or the other, the Chorus laments how "brother" fell upon "brother," how the killer was killed, and vice versa. The staccato division of words and phrases in the closing sequence at once intensifies the emotional pitch and renders distinction of one individual from the other meaningless: "you struck and were struck / You killed and died / killed with a spear / died with a spear . . ."

The opposing emblems and interpretations that dominated the central section of the *Seven against Thebes* have now faded in importance. It is not the confident, militaristic, strategizing voice of Eteocles, but the Chorus in its raw grief, that pronounces the final words of the play. Eteocles demanded a prayer for victory with the gods as allies and promised trophies and the dedication of spoils. The Chorus, whose pessimism and foreboding now appear justified, describes the actual outcome with savage, sorrowful accuracy: Curses now sing a perverted victory song for their triumph over a family; Destruction has erected a victory monument before the gates of the city; and the true victor is the daimon (spirit). It is important to note the other, less obvious winner in this conflict, if only implicitly: While the aristocratic ruling family has perished dreadfully, the polis has survived and won out over its enemies. Here as elsewhere, Athenian spectators at the tragic competition lamented the deaths of great heroes and kings, even while tacitly acknowledging the survival of the polis itself through the power of its gods and cults.

Sileni Followers of Silenus. Human male and animal hybrids. Sileni have in common with FAUNS and SATYRS their sylvan domain and their association with revelry and music. Classical sources are Ovid's *Metamorphoses* (11.88–105), Pausanias's *Description of Greece* (1.4.5, 3.25.2–3), and Virgil's *Eclogues* (6). In the *Metamorphoses*, Sileni are classed with other sylvan creatures and bucolic divinities and granted by Zeus the right to live in peace in the woods and forests. Satyrs, fauns, and Sileni, as well as their female associates, nymphs and maenads, participate in the Bacchic processions of DIONYSUS. According to the *Description of Greece*, the name "Sileni" was given to the oldest satyrs.

Classical vase painters favored two themes in their depiction of Sileni: their amorous pursuit of woodland nymphs and their participation in Bacchanalia.

Silenus A human and animal hybrid with the legs of a goat or horse. The tutor, or foster father, of DIONYSUS. Classical sources are Apollodorus's LIBRARY (2.5.4), Ovid's *METAMORPHOSES* (11.89–105), Pausanias's *Description of Greece* (1.4.5, 3.25.2–3), and Virgil's *ECLOGUES* (6). The parentage of Silenus varies according to the source; he is the son of either PAN or HERMES, both of whom have bucolic associations. In some texts, Silenus or Sileni are not carefully distinguished from satyrs, while in others, they are seen as older figures. The followers of Silenus are Sileni, who, with SATYRS, FAUNS, and their female associates, nymphs and maenads, participate in the Bacchic processions of Dionysus. In the *Orphic Hymn to Silenus*, Silenus leads the Bacchanalia, followed by the satyrs, Naiads, and Bacchantes. In the *Eclogues*, Silenus is a pastoral bard to be found in his cave, sleeping off effects of the previous evening's wine in the company of fauns. In the *Metamorphoses*, Silenus, as a member of Dionysus's entourage, is described as being old, leaning on his staff, and drunken or riding a donkey. Elsewhere in the *Metamorphoses*, a disoriented Silenus is captured by Phrygians, who take him to the court of King MIDAS. Midas recognizes and frees him. Dionysus then rewards Midas with the gift of the golden touch. In Apollodorus's *Library*, Silenus is the father of Pholus, a peaceable CENTAUR whose feast with HERACLES unwittingly brings about his own death.

Silenus appears on an Attic red-figure neck amphora of ca. 480 B.C.E. (Johns Hopkins

Bacchanal with Silenus. *Engraving by Andrea Mantegna, by 1494 (Metropolitan Museum of Art, New York)*

University Museum, Baltimore). In this image, Silenus is the captive of a hunter; Midas appears as well. Images of Silenus were carved in reliefs, including images on sarcophagi of Dionysiac triumphal processions. Other visual themes relating to Silenus were scenes of the drunken Silenus and bacchanals. A postclassical example of the bacchanal is the 15th-century engraving by Andrea Mantegna, *Bacchanal with Silenus* (Metropolitan Museum of Art, New York).

Sirens Sea nymphs who lure sailors to their death with their song. Classical sources are Apollodorus's LIBRARY (1.34, 1.7.10, 1.9.25), Apollonius of Rhodes's *VOYAGE OF THE ARGONAUTS* (4.891–921), Homer's *ODYSSEY* (12.39–54, 158–200), Hyginus's *Fabulae* (141), Ovid's *METAMORPHOSES* (5.552–563), and Pausanias's *Description of Greece* (9.34.3, 10.5.12, 10.6.5). In the *Voyage of the Argonauts*, the Sirens stand poised on the dangerous rocks off the island Anthemoessa, onto which they tempt passing seamen to their doom. In the *Odyssey*, the Sirens sit in a meadow surrounded by the moldering bones of those whom they lured to their deaths. There is some disagreement among the sources as to the parentage, names, and number of the Sirens. In Apollodorus's *Library*, the Sirens are the daughters of the river god ACHELOUS and the Muse Melpomene (or Sterope), and their names are Aglaope, Pisinoe, and Thelxiope, while according to the *Voyage of the Argonauts*, their mother is the Muse Terpischore. Hyginus's *Fabulae* agrees with Apollodorus as to the Sirens' parentage, but here the Sirens are named Molpe, Raidne, Teles, and Thelxiope. Sophocles and Homer recognize only two Sirens, and in the *Odyssey* they are not named. The Sirens were skilled in playing the flute and lyre and in singing. Ovid speculates that the Sirens were originally the mortal companions of PERSEPHONE, who searched for her after she had been abducted and were transformed partially into birds. Their

thighs (or feet) were bird-shaped. Pausanias describes an episode in which HERA persuaded the Sirens to compete against the MUSES in song. The victorious Muses plucked the Sirens' feathers and wore them as crowns. In the *Odyssey*, at the suggestion of CIRCE, Odysseus had his shipmates plug their ears with wax to prevent them from being tempted by the Sirens' song. Meanwhile, Odysseus had himself bound to the mast so that he could hear their song without endangering his ship; though he begged his crew to stop and let him listen longer, they could not hear him, and the ship sailed on past the danger. In Hyginus's *Fabulae*, the Sirens lived only as long as none escaped their song; accordingly, after Odysseus's safe passage, they threw themselves into the sea and died. In Apollonius of Rhodes's *Voyage of the Argonauts*, it was the skilled musician ORPHEUS who enabled the *Argo* to sail safely past the Sirens by filling his comrades' ears with his song, so that they could not hear that of the Sirens.

In visual representations, the Sirens are shown with birds' bodies and female heads. An example from the classical period is an Attic red-figure stamnos from ca. 480 B.C.E. (British Museum, London). Here, Odysseus is bound to the mast as his crew row past the Sirens, bird-like creatures who sing and fly around the ship. A similarly presented scene of the postclassical period is J. W. Waterhouse's *Ulysses and the Sirens* of 1891 (National Gallery of Victoria, Melbourne).

Sisyphus King of Corinth. Son of AEOLUS and Enarete. Brother of ATHAMAS, husband of MEROPE, father of GLAUCUS, and grandfather of BELLEROPHON. Founder of Corinth and of the Isthmian Games in honor of Melicertes. Classical sources are Apollodorus's LIBRARY (1.7.3, 1.9.3, 3.4.3, 3.10.1, 3.12.6), Homer's *ODYSSEY* (11.593–600), Hyginus's *Fabulae* (60, 201), Ovid's *METAMORPHOSES* (4.460ff), Pausanias's *Description of Greece* (2.1.3, 2.3.11, 2.5.1), and Virgil's *AENEID* (6.616). Sisyphus is one of a group—which includes Ixion, Tantalus, and Tityus—of primordial violators of the social order and of divine authority. Ixion committed parricide, Tantalus was accused of cannibalism, Tityus tried to rape Zeus's consort Leto, and the wily Sisyphus attempted to steal fire from the gods and defeat death. Their crimes varied, but all deeply offended morality and/or challenged the authority of the Olympian gods, especially that of Zeus, and their punishments were ingeniously devised to provide gruesome spectacle and admonition. In his descent to Hades in the *Odyssey*, Odysseus witnessed the torments of Sisyphus, Tantalus, and Tityus, and in the *Aeneid*, Aeneas encountered Tityus and Ixion. In Ovid's *Metamorphoses*, their punishments were momentarily stilled when Orpheus sang his lament for Eurydice, his dead bride.

Sisyphus was known for his craft and cunning. According to Diodorus Siculus, Sisyphus caught the thief who had been stealing his prize cattle by cleverly marking the hooves of his cattle. He discovered that the culprit was Autolycus, who had been given the talent to thieve by Hermes, and in revenge Sisyphus seduced Autolycus's wife, Anticlea. Anticlea was later married to Laertes and gave birth to Odysseus, but some sources claim that Sisyphus was in fact the child's father, not Laertes.

According to Apollodorus and Pausanias, Sisyphus revealed to Asopus, the river god, that Zeus had carried off and seduced his daughter Aegina. For this crime, Zeus consigned him to Tartarus and imposed an arduous punishment on him: Sisyphus must to roll a heavy boulder up a hill, but once the summit is achieved, the boulder propels itself back down the hill to its starting point, and Sisyphus must begin the task anew. In other accounts, Sisyphus earned that punishment for cheating death; he managed to convince Hades to let him go back to the world of the living, then refused to return. In another version, Sisyphus captured Thanatos (Death), and while he held Thana-tos imprisoned, no one could die. Thanatos was finally rescued by Ares. In modern usage, a Sisyphean task is one that is exhausting, unceasing, and, ultimately, aimless.

In classical art Sisyphus is shown as a bearded male carrying or pushing against a boulder as, for example, in an Attic black-figure nekyia amphora from ca. 530 b.c.e. (Antikensammlungen, Munich). His task is here overseen by Persephone, who, in some accounts, shows some favor to Sisyphus. Sisyphus is an easily recognizable inhabitant of Hades and appears in images that represent the underworld, such as an Apulian red-figure volute krater from ca. 330 b.c.e. (Antikensammlungen, Munich). Here, Hades and Persephone are shown with other figures associated with the world of the dead, including Orpheus and Hermes, and Sisyphus straining against the boulder. Titian's cycle of paintings *The Four Condemned* included paintings of Ixion, Sisyphus, Tantalus, and Tityus: *The Punishment of Sisyphus* of 1548–49 (Prado, Madrid) shows Sisyphus pushing his boulder up an incline.

Sol   See Helios.

Sophocles (ca. 496 b.c.e.–ca. 401 b.c.e.)   A major Athenian playwright of the fifth century b.c.e. His contemporaries included Aeschylus, Euripides, and Aristophanes. Sophocles' tragedies won many prizes, and his long, distinguished career was marked by the admiration of his contemporaries and great popularity with audiences. He was involved in public life, serving in public office in several instances, and he was active in the promotion of the cult of Asclepius at Athens. Only seven plays remain by Sophocles, though he was said to have completed more than 100. The extant tragedies are *Ajax*, *Antigone*, *Electra*, *Oedipus the King*, *Oedipus at Colonus*, *Philoctetes*, and *Trachiniae*, of which only two, *Oedipus at Colonus* (ca. 401 b.c.e.) and *Philoctetes* (ca. 409 b.c.e.), may be securely dated.

According to Aristotle, specific innovations of Sophoclean tragedy include the expansion of the number of actors (from two to three), scene painting, and expansion of the chorus from 12 to 15. In his *Poetics*, Aristotle notes Sophocles' self-professed tendency to depict people as they might be, in comparison with Euripides' tendency to depict people as they are. For Aristotle, Sophocles' tragedies are, in terms of their development, unity of theme and characterization, the best possible examples of drama; he cites *Oedipus the King* in particular. Other sources note that Sophocles broke from tradition in presenting at festivals a number of plays that did not share a common story, breaking with the idea of the trilogy and producing self-sufficient single dramas.

Sphinx A hybrid creature. Offspring of ECHIDNA (or CHIMAERA) and Orthus. Classical sources are Aeschylus's *SEVEN AGAINST THEBES* (773ff), Apollodorus's *LIBRARY* (3.5.8), Diodorus Siculus's *LIBRARY OF HISTORY* (4.64.3–4), Hesiod's *THEOGONY* (326–329), Pausanias's *Description of Greece* (9.26.2–4), and Sophocles' *OEDIPUS THE KING* (130–131, 391–398). The Sphinx is a creature with Mesopotamian variants and Egyptian origins. In the Greek genealogies, she is descended from TYPHOEUS, who mated with Echidna (part nymph and part snake) to produce Orthus (a huge dog), as well as CERBERUS, the HYDRA OF LERNA, and CHIMAERA. Echidna then produced the Sphinx by mating with Orthus. Like the Chimaera and the Griffon, the Sphinx is composed of different animal and human parts; she is most often depicted as having a lion's torso topped by a human head, male or female according to the source, and she is also sometimes given wings. Like her siblings, the Hydra of Lerna and Cerberus, the Sphinx protects a specific terrain or location. In Sophocles, the Sphinx was a guardian of Theban territory. In Hesiod's *Theogony*, the Sphinx is called destroyer of the Cadmeians, because she would devour all who passed and failed to

Oedipus and the Sphinx. *Jean-Auguste-Dominique Ingres, ca. 1808–27 (Louvre, Paris)*

answer a riddle correctly. The riddle (which, according to Apollodorus, had been given to her by the MUSES) was the following: "What has one voice yet is four-footed, then two-footed, then three-footed?" In a later addition to the story, Oedipus encountered her and correctly solved the riddle—the answer was "man." He either killed the Sphinx or she jumped to her death following Oedipus's success.

In a red-figure amphora attributed to the Achilles Painter from ca. 450 B.C.E. (Museum of Fine Arts, Boston), the Sphinx sits on a pedestal before Oedipus. Her upper torso is distinctly feminine. Grave steles not uncommonly used images of the Sphinx. An archaic example from ca. 540 B.C.E. exists in marble (Metropolitan Museum of Art, New York). A famous postclassical image of the Sphinx's encounter with Oedipus is Jean-Auguste Dominique Ingres's *Oedipus and the Sphinx* of 1808–27 (Louvre, Paris).

Statius (ca. 45 C.E.–ca. 96 C.E.)   Publius Papinius Statius was a Roman poet from Naples, author of the *THEBAID*, the *ACHILLEID*, and the *Silvae*. He was born between 45 and 50 C.E.; the exact date of his death is unknown, but he is believed to have died ca. 96 C.E. Statius's father was a professional poet who wrote and performed in Greek at festival competitions. For Statius, then, poetry was a family métier, and both his father's vocation and Statius's connection with the culturally Greek city of Naples explain his deep immersion and erudition in Greek literature. Statius praises the emperor Domitian in his poetry, who was notorious among Roman emperors for his encouragement of flattery. Statius was a victor in the poetry competition at Domitian's Alban Games but was defeated at the Capitoline Games—a humiliating outcome that appears to have contributed to the poet's decision to leave Rome and retire to Naples with his wife. Statius's major work is the *Thebaid*, an epic poem in 12 books on the expedition of the Seven against Thebes published in 91–92 C.E. He also commenced an epic poem on the life of Achilles, the *Achilleid*, which remained unfinished at his death. Finally, Statius wrote five books of *Silvae*, occasional poems in hexameters that treat a wide diversity of topics and are addressed to Statius's friends and patrons. These poems were published starting in 93 C.E., while Book 5 was published posthumously.

Stheneboea   See BELLEROPHON.

Styx   The river that encircles the underworld (HADES) nine times, forming the boundary between it and the world of the living. Styx is the eldest daughter of OCEANUS and TETHYS. Classical sources are the *Homeric Hymn to Demeter* (424), Apollodorus's *LIBRARY* (1.2.2–5, 1.3.1), Callimachus's *Hymns* (1.36), Hesiod's *THEOGONY* (361, 383–403, 775–806), Hyginus's *Fabulae* (97), Pausanias's *Description of Greece* (8.17.6), and Virgil's *AENEID* (6.439). By the Titan Pallas, Styx is the mother of Bia (Strength), Cratus (Power), Nike (Victory), and Zelus (Zeal). The Styx was a river with magical properties, some of which were harmful. In the *Theogony*, the gods swear solemn oaths by its waters, which IRIS fetches in a golden jug. The gods were punished severely for breaking such an oath: They were deprived of breath, food, and water for a year, then forced to endure nine years of exile. It was into the Styx that THETIS dipped ACHILLES to provide him with almost complete invulnerability.

Suppliants   AESCHYLUS (463 B.C.E.)   Recent evidence has shown that the *Suppliants*, previously considered one of Aeschylus's early plays on grounds of style and dramatic structure, was produced around 463 B.C.E. and was thus among his mature works. The *Suppliants* was the first in a trilogy of plays on the subject of the Danaid myth. The daughters of DANAUS are pursued by their cousins, the sons of Aegyptus, who wish to force them into marriage, and whom they eventually murder on their wedding night. The other plays, which do not survive, are known to be the *Egyptians*, *Danaids*, and a satyr drama, *Amymone*. The *Suppliants* presents the arrival of the Danaids in Argos, where they seek refuge from their pursuers. There they attempt to persuade King Pelasgus to protect them and to allow them to settle among the Argives. He consents eventually, thereby incurring war with the sons of Aegyptus and sealing his own fate. While we do not know the precise series of events that occur in the later plays of the trilogy, it seems likely that a gender-based conflict, as in Aeschylus's *Oresteia*, will be played out with murderous consequences, and presumably divine intervention will bring about a final resolution. Aeschylus's powerful play dramatizes the violent origins of peoples.

SYNOPSIS

The Chorus of Danaids enters carrying suppliants' wands. The women relate that in accordance with the plans of their father, Danaus, they have come from Egypt to Argos as suppliants, in the hope that they will receive protection there. They are fleeing their cousins, the sons of Aegyptus, who wish to marry them by force. They call on the gods of the land, on the gods of vengeance, and on ZEUS, their ancestor, for aid. They derive their ancestry from Zeus through Io. Her son, EPAPHUS (whose name refers to the word "touch"), evokes Zeus's sexual contact with Io. In their lament, the Chorus compares itself to Metis (elsewhere called Procne), the wife of Tereus, who was transformed into a nightingale. It observes the inscrutability of Zeus and calls on him, and on ATHENA, to help it in its current plight. After the harsh treatment of Io by HERA, he owes something to her descendants. The Chorus's women threaten to kill themselves if they are not saved.

Danaus enters. He reports that an armed force is coming their way and advises the Chorus to take shelter at the altars of the 12 gods, adopting the attitude and manner appropriate to suppliants. It does so and calls on the various Greek gods represented by the altars to protect it. King Pelasgus enters with soldiers, observes their foreign appearance and suppliant stance, and expresses wonder that the women have come so far. On being asked, Pelasgus gives his ancestry and declares that he rules the land of Argos, which is called Apian after the healer Apis, who once cured a plague and cleared the land of monsters brought forth by Earth. The Chorus claims Argive ancestry through Io. In dialogue, Pelasgus and the Chorus work out the details of the story of Io, who was a priestess of Hera in Argos, and, thus, their common ancestor. On this basis, the Danaids ask Pelasgus to protect them from the sons of Aegyptus, who seek to marry them against their will. Pelasgus faces a dilemma; if he yields to their plea, he will become involved in a war; if he rejects it, he incurs the anger of the gods, at whose altar the suppliants have taken refuge, and Zeus's anger in particular. The suppliants continue to press their claims and insist on the power of Zeus in his capacity of protector of suppliants and of kinship. Pelasgus is uncertain and states that he must ponder the matter deeply.

The Danaids continue in their supplication, and Pelasgus considers his impossible choice. Then the Danaids press him yet harder: They will hang themselves by their waistbands if he denies them protection. Pelasgus is still conflicted but recognizes the horror of the ensuing pollution, should they hang themselves, and also the ultimate authority of Zeus as god of suppliants. He agrees to harbor them and instructs them to place their suppliants' wands on all the gods' altars to make their status and the justness of their cause clear to the people. Danaus consents, then departs with an escort of soldiers that he had requested. Pelasgus calls the Danaids forth from the altars into a sacred grove and prepares to summon his people and persuade them of the justice of his actions. Pelasgus and the remaining soldiers exit.

The Chorus sings: It addresses Zeus as king of the gods, recalls its ancestry from him, and beseeches him to ward off its pursuers. It relates the myth of Io: how she was chased by the gadfly from Argos to Egypt, where she conceived Epaphus. It praises Zeus's power and greatness.

Danaus enters with the news that the Argives voted in their favor. Pelasgus had persuaded them of the force of Zeus's protection of suppliants and of the Danaids' Argive ancestry. They will be allowed to remain as settlers, and all Argives will be obliged to protect them from seizure on pain of losing their civic rights. Danaus exits.

The Danaid Chorus then prays that the polis of the Argives will not suffer for their just and reverent decision: They have respected the power of Zeus and should not have to suffer the horrors of war. The Chorus further asks the gods to look after the Argives' childbirths, harvest, and flocks.

Danaus enters. He reports some alarming news: A ship approaches, sailed by men with black skin and white clothes. He encourages the Chorus not to panic; he will begin to seek support and protection for them. The Chorus expresses its fear: The sons of Aegyptus are ruthless warriors without concern for the gods or their altars. Danaus encourages them again. They will not be able to attack immediately, the Argives will defend them, and the gods are not on the aggressors' side. Danaus exits.

The Chorus, terrified, asks where it can go to escape the sons of Aegyptus; it expresses its horror of being forced to accept husbands it does not want, and again beseeches Zeus to protect it from the violence and lust of its pursuers.

The herald of the sons of Aegyptus enters with soldiers. In abrupt, harsh language, he orders the Danaids to go to the ships, threatening them with violence if they do not. The Danaids stand firm, however, and refuse, defiantly wishing the herald and his companions ill. As the herald advances, the Chorus compares him to a black spider advancing and calls on Zeus and Earth (GAIA) for aid. The herald and the soldiers begin to seize the suppliants as they cry out in dismay. Pelasgus enters and rebukes them for their behavior. Do they think they have to deal with a land where there are only women? Do they not know how to behave as strangers in the land of Greeks? In the following exchange, Pelasgus and the herald bandy comments about each other's gods and dispute the question of the suppliants. According to the herald, they are the possessions of the sons of Aegyptus; Pelasgus, however, insists that they will not give them up to the sons of Aegyptus on threat of violence. The herald threatens war, and exits. Pelasgus promises the Danaids continuing protection and bids them find places to live in the city. They will seek advice from their father, Danaus. Pelasgus exits.

Danaus enters with an escort of Argive soldiers. He expresses gratitude for their good fortune. The Argive citizens support them against their cousins, and he has been given a bodyguard. He also remarks on the good fortune of being offered lodging in the city free of rent; but he reminds the Danaids of the power of desire and APHRODITE, of their own "ripeness," and the dangers of incurring a bad reputation. The Danaids assure him that he need not worry. They will keep to their present course. In the final choral sequence, the Danaids find themselves in dialogue with a competing chorus, perhaps of Argive soldiers. The Danaids express their thanks and loyalty to Argos, their rejection of the Nile, and their determination to avoid marriage. The soldiers respond by proclaiming the paramount importance and sacred power of Aphrodite; no one can resist the power of Zeus, and, perhaps, the Danaids may, in fact, marry. The Danaids continue to ask Zeus to protect them from their cousins, while the soldiers suggest that they moderate their prayers. The Chorus turns once again to Zeus for help, reminding him how he saved Io. All exit.

COMMENTARY

Aeschylus's *Suppliants* dramatizes a grim episode in Greek mythology that involves the suffering of not merely one or two main characters, but conflict and violence on a mass scale. Danaus and Aegyptus, according to the usual version of the myth, are the two sons of Belus, who was a son of Libya, who, in turn, was descended from Io and Zeus through Epaphus. The sons of Aegyptus seek to marry the daughters of Danaus. Each set of sons and daughters are conventionally considered 50 in number. Danaus and his daughters, in the Aeschylean version, flee from Egypt to Argos, where they seek protection from the local population ruled by King Pelasgus. In requesting protection and invoking the right to hospitality, the Danaids are able to point to ancient kinship ties with the Argives, since Io herself was a priestess of Hera before being driven to Egypt by the gadfly. By harboring the suppliant Danaids, the Argives bring war with the sons of Aegyptus down on themselves. Danaus ends up as the ruler of the

Argives—presumably because Pelasgus dies in the fighting—but eventually is driven to make peace with the sons of Aegyptus, agreeing to his daughters' marriage to his brother's sons. He instructs his daughters, however, to kill their bridegrooms with concealed knives on the wedding night. All do so except one, Hypermnestra, who spares her bridegroom, Lynceus, for reasons that are represented differently by different sources. In some accounts, it is because he spares her virginity; in others, because she loved him or wanted children.

The final outcome of the story also depends on the source. It may be that, in Aeschylus's version, Hypermnestra and Lynceus end up ruling the Argives after some kind of intervention from one or more of the gods, including Aphrodite. In other versions, however, Lynceus avenges his brothers by killing the Danaids and their father. We do not know the exact sequence of Aeschylus's version, since *Suppliants* is the only surviving play of his trilogy on the subject. In all likelihood, *Suppliants* was the first in the sequence of three plays performed together, followed by *Egyptians*, then *Danaids*. The whole trilogy was then followed by a satyr play entitled *Amymone*, which tells the story of one of the Danaids, who, searching for water, is first saved from the assault of SATYRS by POSEIDON, then seduced by him. The problem of how the rest of the trilogy proceeded has much exercised scholars but cannot be resolved with certainty or in detail. It seems likely, however, that, as in the *Oresteia*, some kind of reconciliation between the opposing forces—male and female—is brought about, after great suffering and horrific violence, with the help of the gods and perhaps the polis. The attempt to reconstruct the remainder of the trilogy has been aided only slightly by the survival of a fragment from a later play, in which the goddess Aphrodite speaks, vaunting her powers and the core principle of EROS that pervades the cosmos. The question of love and marriage is already shaping up as a central theme in *Suppliants* and

presumably plays some part in a divinely aided resolution later on.

In formal terms, the play is strongly focused on the shifting emotions and actions of the Chorus of suppliant Danaids. The title in Greek simply means "those who have come" *(hiketides)*, but in coming from Egypt to Argos, where they have no home, the Danaids have inevitably put themselves in the role of supplicating the local population, and the dynamics of the play are centered around their role as suppliants of the Argive king Pelasgus. The play is not so much concerned with individual character and psychology as many other Greek tragedies, and for that reason has sometimes been considered to be early or "primitive," but that view of the play is not now so much in favor. It is anachronistic to suppose that Greek tragedy was evolving toward a less chorus-centered and more psychological form along modern lines. The most recent evidence points toward a production date of 463 B.C.E., which would make it a work of Aeschylus's mature period, and its themes and structures are reminiscent on many levels of his last work, the *Oresteia*.

The effect of the focus on the Chorus of Danaids is very powerful, and it is helpful when reading the play to try to imagine the dancing and singing of the Chorus and the staging of different scenes. Essentially, the sons of Aegyptus are intent on mass rape. As the male kin of unmarried women, they view the Danaids as their property and intend to claim them as their own and subjugate them in physical, dynastic, and sexual terms. When the herald comes on stage near the end of the play, we can sense the raw, mass panic of the Danaids as their pursuers land in a fleet of ships and attempt to capture them. The words exchanged between the Chorus and herald are few and brutal, and the herald's comments in particular are the brutal, misogynistic remarks of a man intent on carrying out an act of rape. He is like a "black spider" advancing on its prey.

The male/female dynamic of the *Suppliants* recalls the gendered opposition that underlies the plot of the *Oresteia*. In the latter play, the sacrificial killing by AGAMEMNON of IPHIGENIA is in part the cause of CLYTAEMNESTRA's rage and alienation. She kills her husband and is, in turn, slain by ORESTES, who is consequently hounded by his mother's FURIES. The whole trilogy is resolved by the intervention of Athena, who is female yet "takes the part of the male," as a warrior goddess with masculine traits, and is especially allied with her male parent, Zeus, who produced her without the involvement of Hera. This violent opposition of family member against family member is multiplied many times over in the *Suppliants* to include one entire set of male cousins set against an entire set of female cousins. Here, too, an act of male violence (the pursuit of the Danaids and the attempt to take their bodies by force) will be balanced by another act of female violence. The violence is specifically sexual in this case, and the Danaids' response corresponds nicely to the threat of male penetration: Instead of penetrating their newly won brides on their wedding night, the sons of Aegyptus will themselves be penetrated by the knives that the Danaids have concealed. Their own attractiveness as erotic objects will become weapons of war, and the men will, in turn, be disarmed and destroyed by the very lust that made them aggressive in the first place.

It is impossible to say how, or to what extent, this male/female conflict came to be resolved in the later plays of the trilogy. We must suspect that, as in the case of the *Oresteia*, Aeschylus has manipulated and shaped the myth to fit his own ends and interests. Other versions do not emphasize a resolution of the conflict through divine intervention, but the surviving play of the trilogy shows some signs that this will be so in Aeschylus's version. The Danaids, however just and sympathetic their cause is made out to be, are clearly represented as underrating the value of marriage and the importance of Aphrodite as incarnation of sex/reproduction. Their own overemphasis on integrity and control over their own bodies will be corrected, in the Aeschylean dialectic of reconciliation through violence and expiation, by some later insight or divine pronouncement. Certainly, the case of Hypermnestra represents an important dissenting view that could prove crucial to the plot's final formulation.

Hypermnestra, like Amomyne in the satyr play, is an exception, an individual singled out of the mass of Danaids. Mythographers like to list the names of the Danaids and the sons of Aegyptus they killed, but this is essentially an exercise in filling in blanks. The exceptional Danaid who chooses marriage over murder in the mythological tradition is an important figure in the context of the play, because she represents the potential for dissent within the otherwise unified choral group. One could argue that Aeschylus, rather than producing an old-fashioned or primitive tragedy with its emphasis on choral song, has done something highly innovative. His Chorus at times resembles not so much a traditional chorus as a tragic protagonist. In the exodos, or exit procession of the Chorus, members of the Chorus engage in debate with another apparently male speaker or group of speakers—interpreted variously by scholars, but most likely representing a group of Argive soldiers—who recommend a more moderate attitude toward marriage and love. Other characters in Greek tragedy who fail to appreciate a major god or goddess—however destructive some of their attributes appear to be (e.g., desire, inebriation)—are corrected, if not harshly punished (PENTHEUS, HIPPOLYTUS).

The Chorus of Danaids, in this case, becomes themselves like a tragic character, who, in dialogue with the mild, conventional *communis opinio* of the Chorus, is revealed in his or her extremism. It is for this very reason that the choral role must split at this stage, because the choral unit has begun to resemble a tragic agent. The Danaids will, like many tragic protagonists, find themselves in the unbearable

position of having to choose between two terrible options—either killing their own cousins
or suffering rape at their hands. They will end
up murdering their own kin in a typically tragic
perversion of the marriage rite, and will be persuaded to do so by their own father. By making
the Chorus into a tragic character, Aeschylus
approaches the limits of tragic form and, in
the process, creates a highly original tragedy.
It is unfortunate that we cannot know how he
completed this striking sequence of action, but
it is not difficult to imagine further innovations
in the use of the Chorus and the interaction of
choral groups. Certainly, the sons of Aegytp-
tians will themselves form a Chorus (as the title
of the trilogy's second play indicates), but it also
seems possible that the Danaids as opposing
Chorus might interact on the same stage with
their pursuers.

A key aspect of Aeschylus's representation
of a plurality of protagonists on the tragic
stage derives from the focus of the play on the
dynamics of race and ethnic origination. The
daughters of Danaus as a plurality are suggestive not just of a group of sisters but (prospectively) of a racial or ethnic group, the Danaans.
Similarly, the sons of Aegyptus inevitably suggest, by metonymy, the Egyptian people or
Egypt. Even the local king, Pelasgus, has an etiological toponym as name, i.e., his name makes
him the originator of the Pelasgians. There is
a complicated dynamic of similarity and differentiation at work here. Both Danaids and sons
of Aegyptus are Egyptians and even belong to
the same family; yet the latter, when they arrive
by boat, are described in strong terms as having black skin, whereas the Danaids have been
described more as "dusky" or "sunburned." For
the Greeks, it is a naturally masculine trait to
have darker skin: Women spend more time in
the household, whereas men spend time outside
in the sun, laboring in agriculture or engaging
in warfare. Greek vases regularly employ this
distinction in representing men and women.
Still, Aeschylus includes many comments on
physical appearance as marker of ethnic dif-

ference, and the sons of Aegyptus are singled
out for their foreign appearance. When they
arrive in ships, they are presented as invaders
from Egypt, foreign enemies attempting to
abduct local women—a typical cause of war in
Greek myth. In the taunts offered by Pelasgus,
the sons of Aegyptus are represented as typical
beer-drinking barbarians—not proper, civilized
men, by contrast with the Argives.

The sons of Aegyptus might have made
equally valid claims to descent from Io, and
thus to being of Argive origin, yet it is the
Danaids who successfully make this claim
and win a place within the Argive community.
The myth, viewed from this perspective, is a
myth of origination through division. Once
part of a single family, the Danaids broke
off to form the Danaans as distinct from the
Egyptians. The Danaids' lack of desire to have
the sons of Aegyptus as husbands explains the
ethnic differentiation, and their unwillingness
is partly justified in hindsight: To members
of Aeschylus's audience, the "black" Egyptians may not have seemed appropriate mates
for the lighter-skinned Danaids, whom the
Greeks viewed in some sense as belonging to
their own ethnic group.

The tragedy of an *oikos* ("household")
expands to the level of community and even
civilization as a whole in Aeschylus's immense
tragic vision. This may explain one aspect of his
interest in the myth: The *Oresteia* comparably,
but not identically, expands the focus from the
implosion of the aristocratic *oikos* to the emergence of polis institutions. The polis is clearly
part of the picture in the present play as well.
As often in tragedy, the polis is represented by a
more or less monarchical leader concerned with
the city as a cohesive unit, yet the exact nature
of the government and laws are left somewhat
vague. Pelasgus displays a notable concern for
his people's view of the affair and wishes to
absolve himself of the charge that he harmed
his own people by gaining their enthusiastic
consent for the harboring of the Danaids in the
first place. He is eager not to be seen as acting

on his own. There is also mention of voting and of specific provisions for the accommodation of the Danaids within the community. Danaus will later become the leader of the Argives when Pelasgus dies, a further degree of integration of the Danaids within the polis. The play thus explores questions of endogamy and exogamy (marriage within or outside the kinship group) in connection with the issue of citizenship and community—a strong concern for the Athenians. Like the Athenians, the Argives have authochthonous origins (i.e., indigenous, born from the earth, rather than coming from abroad). Pelasgus's father is called Palaichthon, which means something like "earth of old." Earth, however, also produces monsters, as in the origins story that Pelasgus himself tells: The land had to be cleared and the plague cured by the local hero/healer figure, Apias. Pelasgus's own words, then, concern a complicated relation between autochthony and the intervention of outsiders, the value of indigenous origins and the scourge of earth-born monsters that must be cleared away to make space for true civilization.

The Danaids, then, are dangerous as outsiders because, among other things, they bring war and conflict. But they are also important as originators of civilization. At its broadest level, the trilogy concerns the origins of peoples and civilizations, and the institution of marriage as an instrument of such processes. The fragment in which Aphrodite speaks of the cosmic dimension of eros is one illustration of this concern; another is the frequently iterated story of Zeus and Io. The erotic drive of the king of gods, and his impregnation of Io, constitute the origins story of the present play, but also of its different ethnic outcomes. Zeus is the ultimate progenitor of human races, since he, by impregnating Io, was the father of Epaphus, from whom both Danaan and Egyptians will be derived. Even the satyr play takes a part in working out these themes on a less serious level: Amymone, like the Danaids, is in danger of being raped by male aggressors (satyrs) but,

like Io, ends up being impregnated with the offspring of a god.

The role of Zeus is salient throughout the play. He is the Danaids' divine ancestor, and just as he protected the wandering, vulnerable Io, so they, as suppliants, hope to receive Zeus's protection. The pervasiveness of Zeus is similarly a feature of *Prometheus Bound*—also, debatably, of Aeschylean authorship. Zeus upholds relations of hospitality *(xenia)*—the hosting of strangers, beggars, and, especially relevant in this instance, suppliants. Furthermore, Zeus, as in the *ILIAD*, is the god who "brings things to their end/purpose/resolution *(telos)*." Zeus the resolution-bringer—the god who oversees the fulfillment of a sometimes complex, difficult, and violent destiny—will presumably be crucial to the outcome of the trilogy.

Suppliant Women EURIPIDES (ca. 420 B.C.E.) Euripides' *Suppliant Women*, produced in the late 420s B.C.E., is set in the Attic town of Eleusis after the defeat of the Seven against Thebes. ADRASTUS and the mothers and sons of the Seven have come to ask Athens for aid in recovering the bodies, which CREON, king of Thebes, refuses to give back for burial. *Suppliant Women* is a tragedy imbued with relevance to contemporary politics and the Athenian city-state. It refers to alliances among city-states, Athenian democratic government, the origin of cults and festivals, the legendary history of Attica, and the human cost of war. Euripides' play recalls the basic structure and concerns of Aeschylus's *SUPPLIANTS* and Sophocles' *ANTIGONE*, while establishing its own highly political, Athens-centered perspective. Euripides appears to offer praise of Athenian equality and democracy, but the example afforded by Argos and Thebes may also contain a warning about the dangers of hubristic ambitions.

SYNOPSIS

The scene is set in front of the temple of DEMETER and Kore at Eleusis in Attica. The

Chorus of the mothers of the Seven against Thebes, Adrastus, and the sons of the Seven are supplicating Aethra, mother of THESEUS, king of Athens. Aethra, praying to Demeter, identifies herself and relates how the Seven have been refused burial, and how Adrastus and the mothers have appealed to her for aid. She in turn has sent for her son Theseus. The Chorus further entreats her to pity it; for she also has a son, and can sympathize with its suffering.

Theseus enters. He questions Aethra, and she tells him who the suppliants are. Adrastus asks Theseus to help him recover Argos's fallen sons, for his own city is in ruins and cannot do so on its own. Theseus then interrogates Adrastus about his motives for going to war. Adrastus admits that he went to war against the gods' will and despite the warnings of the seer AMPHIARAUS. Theseus disapproves. Adrastus makes a final plea for Theseus's sympathy, pointing out that those with good fortune should look with pity on those in misfortune; he has come to Athens because, unlike savage Sparta, Athens is capable of pity and strong leadership. Theseus replies that mortals have been given more good than bad in life, and that they ought to be grateful for what they have, rather than, like Adrastus, foolishly seeking more against the will of the gods. Theseus see no reason why Athens should have to become involved in the consequences of Adrastus's rash actions. Adrastus is affronted by Theseus's judgment and begins to depart. The Chorus renews its pleas, reminding Theseus of their common ancestry through PELOPS. Aethra begins to weep in pity; she encourages Theseus to win glory by helping those who have been wronged, and by upholding the universal laws governing burial of the dead, rather than incur a reputation for inaction and cowardice. Theseus does not retract any of his previous criticism but begins to see the advantages of pursuing a course of heroic action. He will put the case before the Athenians to ratify his decision. Theseus, Aethra, and Adrastus exit.

The Chorus anticipates the happy outcome of the alliance and praises Athens. Theseus reenters with Adrastus and an Athenian herald. He sends a message to Thebes asking as a favor that they bury the dead; but he goes on to warn that if they refuse, they should expect a "group of shield-bearing revelers" at their door. Unexpectedly, a Theban herald arrives. Theseus and the herald argue over which form of government is superior, a democratic one (Athens) or monarchical rule (Thebes). The herald then delivers his message: Athens should expel Adrastus, and mind its own business, rather than attempt to give the Argive dead a proper burial; intervention will cause war, and peace is far preferable; moreover, the will of the gods destroyed the impious Seven. Adrastus is enraged, but Theseus insists on responding himself. He is right in maintaining the Greek custom of burial, regardless of the justice or injustice of the acts of the Seven; Thebes and Creon are foolish to disregard these customs, and Theseus will maintain them by force if necessary. The herald accuses Theseus and his city of being busybodies. The exchange ends in mutual threats. The herald departs. Theseus commands that preparations for war begin, and he and the Athenian herald also leave.

The Chorus debates the danger of the coming war and the possibility that the gods will bring about a favorable outcome. The messenger enters. He introduces himself as Capaneus's servant, captured by the Thebans, now returning with news of Theseus's victory. Theseus himself turned the tide of battle and put the Thebans to flight, but he restrained himself from entering the city. Adrastus reflects on how the Thebans (like the Argives once) acted insolently in their prosperity and are now being punished for it. In dialogue with Adrastus, the messenger reveals that the bodies of the Seven have been recovered, and the rest are buried near the glens of Cithaeron, in the Attic village of Eleutherae. Theseus and other free Athenians recovered the bodies, carried them to the burial sites, and washed the wounds. Adrastus laments his losses and that he himself has survived. Adrastus and the messenger exit.

The Chorus dreads having to look on its sons' corpses. Adrastus and Theseus enter with five draped corpses. Adrastus and the Chorus lament bitterly, the Chorus bemoaning the outcome of Phoebus's prophecy on the marriage of Adrastus's daughters and declaring that the FURIES have left Thebes and come to Argos. Theseus asks Adrastus for an account of the bravery of the fallen Argive heroes. Adrastus then praises the simplicity and forthright character of Capaneus; Eteoclus's incorruptibility; Hippomedon's robust virility; the handsome Parthenopaeus's modesty, restraint, and support for the Argive cause; and Tydeus's pride in glorious deeds. In his turn, Theseus praises Amphiaraus, who was swallowed up alive by the earth, and POLYNICES. He specifies that Capaneus's body is to be buried apart from the others; it is sacred to the gods, since he was struck down by Zeus's lightning; his tomb will be built beside the temple. The others will be cremated on a single pyre. The Chorus continues its lamentation.

Evadne, wife of Capaneus, appears on the cliffs behind the temple of Demeter and Kore, above her husband's tomb; she is splendidly garbed. The Chorus leader observes her there and asks what she is doing. She proclaims her intention to leap from the cliff, then join her husband's pyre: Their "marriage" will take place in the underworld. Iphis, father of Eteoclus and Evadne, enters. He wishes to take home his son's body and find Evadne, who escaped the close watch of the house. In dialogue with his daughter, he learns what she intends to do. She throws herself from the cliff. Iphis, horrified and embittered, declares that he wishes he could live his life over again, and avoid having children. He no longer cares to retrieve his son's body and leaves, determined to starve himself in order not to prolong his life any further.

Theseus and the sons of the Seven enter, carrying urns of ash. The mothers and sons lament in alternation. The sons vow future vengeance on Thebes. Theseus reminds them of what Athens has done for Argos. Adrastus promises enduring gratitude on the part of Argos. ATHENA appears from above. She commands Theseus to exact an oath from Adrastus that Argos will never attack Athens and will oppose any who do so. Sacrifices are to be made, the sacrificial knife buried, and the oath to be inscribed on the tripod that HERACLES had Theseus dedicate at Delphi after sacking Troy. Athena prophesies that the sons of the Seven will avenge their fathers' deaths and will be called the Epigoni. After Theseus agrees to carry out her commands, Athena exits. The Chorus leader bids Adrastus join in taking the oath before Theseus. All exit.

COMMENTARY

Euripides' *Suppliant Women* occupies a somewhat unfamiliar place within the broader terrain of tragic mythology: The action occurs after the story of OEDIPUS, after the expedition of the Seven against Thebes, and after the mutual slaying of ETEOCLES and Polynices. Euripides does not choose to represent the figure of the Theban ANTIGONE and her struggle to bury her brother Polynices—a subject definitively treated by Sophocles—but moves the action away from Thebes altogether and sets his scene in Attic Eleusis, where Adrastus and the mothers and sons of the slain Argives supplicate Theseus for help in recovering the bodies. Yet while Euripides chooses a novel mythic setting, he constructs his drama out of well-established scenarios in the tragic tradition.

The first and most important of these is the scenario of supplication. The title (literally, "women who have come . . .") is the same as Aeschylus's *Suppliants* and is foregrounded by the supplicant role of the Chorus. This play, unusually, has two choruses: one, the Chorus of suppliant women, is the main Chorus throughout the play; the other, the Chorus of sons of the Seven, is also present throughout and contributes to the choral song near the play's end. The basic structure of the play closely resembles Aeschylus's play of the same title: a group of women constituting the Chorus, represented and led by a male figure (Adrastus, compare Danaus), arrives in a foreign polis and seeks aid against an impious act of hubris (Thebes's refusal to allow burial of the dead; compare the sons of Aegyptus's attempt to force marriage on the Danaids). Furthermore, specific correspondences between the two plays include the sacred setting (compare the altars of the gods in Aeschylus's play) and the ratification of the choice to help the suppliants by a vote of the polis. At the same time, Euripides refers to Aeschylus's *Seven against Thebes.* He specifically alludes to Aeschylus's description of the Seven in the exchange between the herald and Eteocles. Euripides, however, implicitly "corrects" the Aeschylean characterization of the Argive captains as hubristic and insolent. In his description, they are restrained, diplomatic, humble, virtuous.

Euripides also distinguishes himself from Aeschylus in his arrangement of the identities of suppliant and supplicated. Whereas Aeschylus has the Danaids and their father supplicate Argos, in Euripides' play, the Argives supplicate Athens. The Argives thus received suppliants—with all the difficult consequences that entailed—in an earlier phase of their mythic history. Indeed, the choice to receive the suppliants was a formative one for their genealogy and identity as a people. Euripides consciously plays on this earlier tragic/legendary episode of supplication, when, for example, the Argives refer to themselves as the "offspring of Danaus" and derive themselves, just as the Danaids did in Aeschylus's play, from Zeus via Io and Inachus. Like the Danaids, moreover, the Argive suppliants remind their hosts of their common genealogical link, in this case, Pelops. Now, however, it is the Argives who are supplicating, and the Athenians who are being supplicated—a shift that both establishes the distinct

perspective of Euripides' play and traces a shift in the dynamic of hegemony.

The central dramatic tension derives from the same basic set of forces in the two plays. Supplication has a binding force and, if wrongly rejected, can bring plague and misery on the land. The supplicated leader is thus put in a difficult position: He risks, on the one hand, the danger of pollution and divine displeasure if he refuses, and on the other hand, if he accepts, the danger of implicating his polis in the contentious affairs of another city-state. The suppliants themselves are at once vulnerable and menacing. They are weak and in need in support, yet as they encircle the one whom they are supplicating and chant their pleas, holding suppliant boughs, they resemble a kind of invading force that aims to bend the local ruler to their will. The supplicated ruler is naturally cautious when confronted with a request for help, especially if he feels that the supplicating party has acted unethically or against the wishes of the gods. Theseus, for this reason, interrogates Adrastus at length as to the ethics of his expedition against Thebes. Adrastus admits his folly but still insists on demanding Theseus's aid. In the end, the importance of the Greek custom of allowing burial of war dead overrules any scruples that Theseus may have had. He must tread a narrow path between taking the side of a morally questionable warrior, on the one hand, and displeasing the gods by not supporting the burial of the dead, on the other. The Argives were wrong to attack Thebes, but Thebes is now wrong in refusing burial.

The moral crux of the play thus recalls that of Sophocles' *Antigone.* The laws of burial governed by the gods of the underworld are opposed to the decrees of the polis forbidding burial of its enemies. Yet even as Euripides' plot occupies the well-established tragic scenarios of supplication and burial, he expands the scope of political resonance. Tragedy most frequently concerns events within a single royal house—Thebes, Argos, Troy—whereas here three city-states and kings (Thebes-Creon, Argus-Adrastus, Athens-Theseus) are all involved at once. The dramatization of intricate inter-polis relations, diplomacy, and rhetorical posturing is evocative of the tense political situation in Euripides' day during the Peloponnesian War. *Supplicant Women* was produced in the late 420s, when Athens was involved in the Archidamian War phase of the Peloponnesian War. During this period, Thebes was a major adversary and member of the Spartan confederacy. In 424, after the battle of Delium, the Boeotians refused to allow the Athenians to bury their dead; Euripides' play apparently alludes to this contemporary event. The Argives, in the meanwhile, were consistently allied with Athens. *Supplicant Women* positions Athens simultaneously in relation to an enemy (Thebes), portrayed as impiously refusing burial and subsequently punished by the victorious Athenians, and in relation to the Argives, portrayed as loyal allies, since they are perpetually indebted to Athens for receiving them as suppliants.

Euripides' play about inter-polis relations is thus rich in contemporary political resonance. The themes of war and peace, the complex logic of alliance and enmity, hegemony and hubris belong equally to the mythic situation represented in the play and the actual conditions of the Peloponnesian War. On a first reading, Argos and Thebes are, in different ways, morally inferior to Athens, and represent instances of a polis becoming excessively ambitious in prosperity. Adrastus, with his new allies, dared to attack Thebes and was punished by the outcome; the victorious Thebans, in turn, attract the anger of the gods by refusing burial to the Argives. The Athenian Theseus, by contrast, is able to claim that he is upholding the moral standard of all Greeks in attacking the impious Thebans. Like many great empires, the Athenians back up their hegemony and aggression with claims of moral right. The enemies of Athens accused them of polypragmosyne ("being a busybody"), and here the Thebans accuse Theseus of the same;

yet the Athenians might claim, as in the present instance, that when moral standards are at stake, inaction is cowardly and unworthy. Finally, the Athenians displayed pride in their own democratic government. When Theseus trades sharp words with the Theban herald, he champions a democratic state, where citizens hold yearly offices, and there is an "equal vote" for all, both rich and poor. Argos, by contrast, is a monarchy.

It is hard not to conclude that Euripides' play carries a strongly pro-Athenian message, as we might expect, given that the play was performed (and judged) before an Athenian audience in wartime conditions. This sensible conclusion does not rule out the possibility that the play's positive picture of Athens also contains warnings and even potential criticism. Argos and Thebes demonstrate how an overweening pride can come before a fall, and moral aphorisms throughout stress the importance of tempering one's ambitions. The Thebans' victory over the impious invaders quickly yielded to an impious act of their own. The support of the gods is not guaranteed, and continuing successes depend on the exercise of restraint as well as bravery, and the consultation of the gods' will in all matters.

The Euripidean representation of the cost of war is acute and may reflect the harsh conditions and heavy losses incurred by the conflict with Sparta. The devastation on the Theban side is almost total, and as elsewhere, Euripides focuses on the pathos of parents grieving for lost children. More than once, a character or the Chorus wishes they had never had children or wishes that they had not lived to see them die. Women, who must grieve for dead husbands and sons, thus have a certain prominence in the play. The suppliant Argive women of the Chorus constitute the play's central focus, and their emotions of grief drive the action. Aethra is a mother herself, and thus can sympathize with the sufferings of the mothers of the Seven. Her intervention persuades Theseus and is accordingly the main pivot of the plot.

The theme of grieving women culminates in the terrible scene of Evadne's death: She commits suicide by leaping from a cliff before her father Iphis's eyes. In his despair, Iphis departs to end his own life by starvation without even obtaining his son's body—his main purpose in coming in the first place. Iphis, whose household is utterly destroyed, comes off as the play's most tragic character. His desolation and disgust with his life are total. It is telling, however, that Euripides includes this story of domestic horror almost as a subplot, even as he frames the larger structure of his plot in terms of the Aeschylean themes of civilization, history, and the emergence of polis cults and institutions. Euripides' play depicts grieving and suffering on a mass scale, not simply the implosion of a single household, and thus resonates with the contemporary conditions of war among the Greek city-states.

Euripides, as in other plays, displays an interest in mythography, etiology, and topography. He makes specific reference to Theban topography—Amphion's tomb, Ares' Spring, and the like—and throughout the play is attentive to the etiological history of Athens and Attica, e.g., the reference to the different regionary contingents, led by Paralus and Theseus, that are to make up Attica. Even more strikingly, we learn that the main portion of the Argive dead have been buried at Eleutherae, an Attic village on the border of Boeotia. According to Pausanias, Eleutherae joined Attica to gain Athenian citizenship and because they hated Thebes. Eleutherae thus symbolizes, in a certain sense, the opposition between Thebes and Athens. There is also a story that Eleutherae, when it sought to join Attica, presented Athens with a statue of the god DIONYSUS. Athens at first rejected the offer but then, after suffering a plague, instituted a procession to placate the god. This procession was the origin of the festival of the City Dionysia, held in honor of *Dionysos Eleuthereus.* Even in Euripides' day, the festival procession symbolically reenacted the path of the statue: It was carried on the road in the direction of Eleutherae and then brought back into the city by the same road. Euripides' reference to Eleutherae as a site of burial of the Argive dead thus combines the theme of Theban-Athenian enmity and the origins of the festival at which Athenian tragedy was performed.

Syrinx A chaste Arcadian nymph. The principal classical source is Ovid's *METAMORPHOSES* (1.689–712). Syrinx caught the eye of the lascivious satyr PAN. She rejected his advances and fled. Coming to the river Ladon, she called on the water nymphs to save her by changing her form, and Pan was left clutching the marsh reeds into which she had been transformed. From these reeds, Pan fashioned the panpipe, also called the "syrinx." This myth echoes the attempted seduction of DAPHNE by APOLLO: both myths involve the transformation of the object of desire into the pursuer's attribute, the syrinx for Pan and the laurel for Apollo.

Talos See Daedalus; Hephaestus; *Voyage of the Argonauts*.

Tantalus King of Sipylus in Lydia. Son of Zeus and the nymph Pluto. Tantalus married Dione (a Pleiad, daughter of Atlas). Their children were Niobe and Pelops. Classical sources are Homer's *Odyssey* (11.583ff), Hyginus's *Fabulae* (82), Lucian's *Dialogues of the Dead*, Ovid's *Metamorphoses* (4.458–459; 6.172–176, 403–411), and Pindar's *Olympian Odes* (1.54–64). Tantalus is one of a group—which also includes Ixion, Sisyphus, and Tityus—of primordial violators of the social order and of divine authority. Ixion committed parricide, Tantalus was accused of cannibalism, Tityus tried to rape Zeus's consort Leto, and the wily Sisyphus attempted to steal fire from the gods and defeat death. Their crimes varied, but all deeply offended morality and/or challenged the authority of the Olympian gods, especially that of Zeus, and their punishments were ingeniously devised to provide gruesome spectacle and admonition. In his descent to Hades in the *Odyssey*, Odysseus witnessed the torments of Sisyphus, Tantalus, and Tityus, and in the *Aeneid*, Aeneas encountered Tityus and Ixion. In Ovid's *Metamorphoses*, their punishments

were momentarily stilled when Orpheus sang his lament for Eurydice, his dead bride.

There are several versions of Tantalus's crime. In Pindar, he is accused of stealing ambrosia and nectar of the gods after having dined with them and of having revealed secrets of the gods to mortals. In another version, he is accused of serving his own son, Pelops, to the gods to see whether they could perceive his trick. Only Demeter, distracted by the loss of Persephone, ate some of Pelops's shoulder before Tantalus's treachery was discovered. (But note an alternate version in Pindar.) In punishment for his crime, Tantalus was consigned to Tartarus, where he could never quench his thirst or sate his hunger: The water and fruit tree for which he reached shrank continually away from his grasp. The word "tantalize" derives from the name of Tantalus.

Tartarus The extremity of Hades. Classical sources are Hesiod's *Theogony* (119, 713–735, 820–822), Homer's *Iliad* (8.10–17, 478–481), and Virgil's *Aeneid* (6.548–627). In the *Theogony*, Tartarus lies as far beneath Earth (Gaia) as Heaven (Uranus) lies above Earth. It would take an anvil nine days and nights to fall from the heavens to the earth and nine days and nights again for the anvil to reach

Tartarus. "Misty" Tartarus is in a pit encircled by a bronze fence itself encircled three times by night. Uranus consigned the Hundred-Handed Ones, and the Cyclopes, Uranus's offspring by Gaia, to Tartarus. They were released by ZEUS during the TITANOMACHY and played a critical role in the defeat of the TITANS by the Olympian gods. Zeus then imprisoned Cronus and the other defeated Titans in Tartarus, where they were surrounded by a bronze fence with a bronze gate and were guarded by the Hundred-Handed Ones.

Telamon   Son of Aeacus and Endeis. Brother of PELEUS, and father of AJAX and TEUCER. Classical sources are Apollodorus's *LIBRARY* (1.8.2, 1.9.16, 3.12.6–7), Apollonius of Rhodes's *VOYAGE OF THE ARGONAUTS* (1.93–94), Ovid's *METAMORPHOSES* (13.21–28), and Sophocles' *AJAX* (202, 433ff). Telamon and Peleus killed their half-brother Phocus and were banished. Telamon departed for Salamis, where he became king. He married Periboea (or Eriboea), by whom he had his son Ajax. Telamon participated in the voyage of the *Argo*, the Calydonian Boar hunt, and HERACLES' sack of Troy. Heracles gave him HESIONE, daughter of LAOMEDON, as a prize, and she gave birth to Teucer. When Teucer returned from the Trojan War without his half-brother Ajax, Telamon exiled Teucer, who subsequently founded a second Salamis on the island of Cyprus (a story told by HORACE in *Odes* 1.7).

Telegonus   Son of ODYSSEUS and CIRCE. Classical sources are Apollodorus's *LIBRARY* (Epitome 7.16, 7.36–37), Hesiod's *THEOGONY* (1,014), and Hyginus's *Fabulae* (125, 127). Telegonus is not mentioned in Homer's *ODYSSEY*. His story arises in the *Telegony*, a lost poem of the Epic Cycle summarized by Proclus, where he is said to have returned to Ithaca in search of his father and to have unwittingly killed him in a chance encounter. Telegonus then returned with PENELOPE to Circe's island to bury Odysseus.

Circe then immortalized Odysseus, Penelope, and their son, TELEMACHUS. Telemachus married Circe; and Telegonus married Penelope. According to Hyginus, the son of Circe and Telemachus was the Latin king Latinus and the son of Penelope and Telegonus was the similarly eponymous Italus.

Telemachus   Son of ODYSSEUS and PENELOPE. Classical sources are Homer's *ODYSSEY* (Books 1–4 and passim), Hyginus' *Fabulae* (127), and the lost *Telegony* as summarized by Proclus. Odysseus, bound by his oath to go to Troy, pretended madness and began plowing his fields with salt. PALAMEDES either threw Telemachus in front of the ploughshare or threatened him with a sword, and so caused Odysseus to reveal that he was not insane. Odysseus thus went to Troy when Telemachus was an infant. In Homer's *Odyssey*, the early books of the epic focus on Telemachus, who is coming of age as a young man in his father's absence in a household filled with suitors of his mother, Penelope. This early portion of the epic, in which Telemachus begins to establish his social identity, is sometimes called the *Telemacheia*. Telemachus is only just starting to stand up to the suitors and to assume authority over his household; on a few occasions, he surprises Penelope by admonishing her. Encouraged by ATHENA, Telemachus goes in search of news of his father, first to NESTOR at Pylos, then to the palace of MENELAUS and HELEN at Sparta. He evades the suitors' attempt to ambush him on his return and is reunited with his father at the hut of the loyal swineherd, Eumaeus. He then participates in his father's plot to kill the suitors and joins him in the final battles. In the *Telegony*, a poem in the Epic Cycle, Telemachus marries CIRCE, who makes him immortal. In general, Telemachus's mythology is closely tied and subordinate to that of Odysseus. Within the narrative economy of Homer's epic, he functions as a prelude to his father. He is only starting to learn the subtleties of foreign travel, hospitality, concealment, and public speaking—all areas in which his father is a world-renowned master.

Tereus King of Thrace. Classical sources include Aeschylus's SUPPLIANTS (58–67), Apollodorus's LIBRARY (3.14.8), Homer's ODYSSEY (19.518–523), Hyginus's *Fabulae* (45), Ovid's METAMORPHOSES (6.424–674), Pausanias's *Description of Greece* (1.41.8–9), and Virgil's ECLOGUES (6.78–81). Sophocles wrote a lost play entitled *Tereus*. According to Apollodorus, Procne and Philomela were daughters of King Pandion of Athens. King Tereus of Thrace was summoned by Pandion to help him in a war with Thebes over a boundary dispute. Pandion subsequently gave in marriage to Tereus his daughter Procne by whom Tereus had a son, Itys. However, Tereus also came to desire Procne's sister Philomela, raped her, and then hid her away and cut out her tongue. She wove the story of Tereus's act into a robe and thereby revealed the truth to Procne. Procne, in revenge, killed her son, Itys; boiled him; and served him as a meal to her husband and then fled with Philomela. Tereus pursued them with an ax, but the gods transformed Procne into a nightingale, Philomela into a swallow, and Tereus into a hoopoe. Hyginus presents a slightly different version: Tereus lied to King Pandion, telling him that his wife, Procne, died, in order to persuade him to hand over Philomela as his new wife. He subsequently raped her. In this version, Philomela became a nightingale, Procne a swallow, and Tereus a hawk. According to Pausanias, however, Tereus committed suicide. He also notes that the story of the transformation of the sisters into a swallow and nightingale was probably due to the plaintive sound of these birds' songs. In Homer's *Odyssey*, PENELOPE refers to a very different version of Philomela's story in which the nightingale, daughter of Pandareus, laments that she unwittingly killed Itylus, son of King Zethus.

Ovid follows the basic outlines of the version in Apollodorus but elaborates the story with rich, often horrifying detail and heightened pathos: Ovid's Tereus, for example, continued to rape the captive Philomela repeatedly even after cutting out her tongue. Later, both Procne and Philomela stabbed the innocent Itys in their rage for revenge, and Philomela hurled his severed head at Tereus after he had eaten the boy's flesh. In Greek and Roman poetry, the plaintive lament of the nightingale and Philomela's suffering are associated with songs of lamentation.

Tethys A TITAN, the offspring of GAIA (Earth) and URANUS (Heaven). Sister to IAPETUS, HYPERION, Coeus, Crius, Cronus, MNEMOSYNE, OCEANUS, PHOEBE, RHEA, THEIA, and THEMIS. Classical sources are Apollodorus's LIBRARY (1.1.3, 2.1.1), Diodorus Siculus's LIBRARY OF HISTORY (4.69, 4.72), Hesiod's THEOGONY (132–136, 337–370), Homer's ILIAD (14.200–210), and Hyginus's *Fabulae* (177). Oceanus married his sister Tethys, and their offspring are the 25 Rivers (among them the Nile) and the 3,000 OCEANIDS (Ocean nymphs). The most important of these rivers is the STYX, which marks the boundary between Earth and HADES. Though Tethys appears in the genealogies beginning with Hesiod, she does not otherwise appear in mythology or cult practice.

Teucer Son of TELAMON and Hesione. Half-brother of AJAX. See *AJAX*.

Thebaid STATIUS (91–92 C.E.) Statius's *Thebaid*, published in 91–92 C.E. under the emperor Domitian, is the epic masterpiece of an early imperial Roman poet who is only now beginning to receive the critical attention and admiration he merits. Statius is an intensely self-aware poet who weaves into his poem a rich fabric of allusions to his predecessors. His epic poem on the Seven against Thebes responds both to the tradition of Greek and Roman epic

(Homer, Apollonius, Virgil, Lucan, and Ovid, to name only a few) and Greek and Roman tragedy (Aeschylus, Sophocles, Seneca). Statius's tragic epic enacts a striking dialogue of genres, while exploring the darker aspects of the epic tradition: violence, extreme hatred, madness, moral and religious defilement, mourning, and bereavement. Statian characters are exhausted by the violence they enact and are at times filled with a sense of the futility of their own actions, even as they carry them out. This sense of saturation and exhaustion reflects Statius's self-consciousness as a poet who occupies a belated position in the literary tradition, coming after Virgil and other canonical writers. Yet Statius deploys his poetics of exhaustion to dazzling effect and creates great poetry out of a sense of weariness and satiety. Statian epic is thus densely packed on many levels—packed with literary allusions, accumulating violence and bodies, and ornate rhetorical figures and descriptions. He also inserts into his poem complicated reflections on political power and, implicitly, the early imperial political culture of his times.

SYNOPSIS

Book 1

The poet reviews potential subject matter, rejects early Theban mythology, and chooses to focus on the house of OEDIPUS. He then praises Domitian as a god, who, he hopes, will nonetheless remain content with ruling mortals. He predicts that he will sing of Domitian's deeds in the future. The poet, deliberating where to begin, chooses the already self-blinded Oedipus. He addresses Tisiphone and the infernal deities. After he blinded himself, his sons despised him; he now curses them and bids Tisiphone destroy his line. The ghastly Tisiphone hears, and eagerly makes her way to Thebes. She fills the two sons of Oedipus, who now share the rule of Thebes in alternate years, with rivalry for dominance. The people of Thebes become restless under ETEOCLES, the first to hold rule. The gods hold a council. Jupiter (see ZEUS) complains of the wearisome transgressions of mortals. He

is fatigued in particular by the house of Oedipus and the royal house of Argos, and vows to punish both. Juno (see HERA) complains that he singles out Argos, a land particularly dear to her. Jupiter calmly refuses to be persuaded and sends Mercury (see HERMES) to send for the spirit of LAIUS in the underworld. In the meanwhile, POLYNICES, wandering in exile, is overtaken by a sudden storm. He takes shelter at the palace of ADRASTUS at Argos. Tydeus, in exile for killing his brother, happens to take shelter there on the same night. The two heroes quarrel and come to blows; Adrastus arrives to break up their fight; Tydeus and Polynices become close friends. Adrastus notices that Polynices wears the emblem of a lion and Tydeus the emblem of a boar, suggesting the fulfillment of a prophecy regarding his daughters' marriage. Adrastus holds a feast in honor of the guests and tells the story of Phoebus APOLLO and Coroebus. Phoebus raped the Argive king's daughter. The child of their union was abandoned and devoured by dogs; when the mother found out, she lamented inconsolably, thus revealing her secret. Her father put her to death. Apollo, angry at his paramour's treatment, sent a monster to devour Argive children; Coroebus killed it; Phoebus sent a plague against the Argives as punishment for the slaying; Coroebus offered himself as expiatory victim, and Phoebus spared him. After the story, on being asked by Adrastus, Polynices reveals his ancestry. Adrastus offers prayer to Phoebus.

Book 2

Mercury, sent by Zeus to retrieve Laius, travels to the underworld and takes him back to Thebes. The Thebans are enjoying a festival in honor of Bacchus (see DIONYSUS). Eteocles is asleep after feasting. Laius, as bidden by Mercury, disguises himself to look like the Theban seer TIRESIAS and speaks to Eteocles. He warns him of his brother's marriage and intentions and bids him make preparations for war. Then he pulls off his disguise, revealing himself to Eteocles as his murdered grandfather. Eteocles is now stirred to rage against his brother. In the meanwhile, Adrastus offers his daughters, Argia and Deipyle, in marriage to Polynices and Tydeus, respectively. They accept, and Adrastus vows that he will help them regain their rightful realms. News of the alliance reaches Thebes. The wedding day arrives in Argos, but as they approach the temple of Pallas the unwedded, a shield falls from above, and a trumpet blare is heard from within. The omen is ascribed to the fact that Argia was wearing the necklace of HARMONIA. Vulcan (see HEPHAESTUS) originally made the necklace as bridal gift for Harmonia, Venus's (see APHRODITE) daughter by Mars (see ARES), and in revenge for his wife's continued adultery, he imbued it with violence, grief, and discord. Harmonia, wife of CADMUS, founder of Thebes, ended up being transformed along with her husband into a serpent; next the doomed SEMELE owned it; after her, Jocasta had it. Now, Argia owns the necklace, but Adrastus's sister Eriphyle, married to the prophet AMPHIARAUS, covets it intensely. Bribed by it, Eriphyle persuades her husband to go on a doomed expedition, and her son, in vengeance, will slay her. Polynices, in the meantime, begins to turn his eye on Thebes. His wife is reluctant to see him go. It is decided that Tydeus will go to Thebes to request humbly Polynices's return. Eteocles is committed to holding his throne by force, however, and Tydeus's speech to him is excessively candid and harsh. Eteocles flatly refuses, and Tydeus leaves in anger. Eteocles sends a band of soldiers after Tydeus, despite his role as ambassador. They attempt to ambush him at the foot of the cliff from which the SPHINX fell to her death. He crushes four immediately with a boulder, and begins to slay the rest. Exhausted, he is persuaded by Athena to return to Argos. He spares one Theban to convey the outcome to Eteocles. Then he fastens the enemy's armor to a tree and dedicates it to Pallas ATHENA. He prays to Pallas and vows to build her a temple in Argos.

Book 3

Eteocles cannot sleep, feeling shame and anxiety over his act of perfidy. The spared Theban, Maeon, a prophet, returns in deep lamentation.

He brings the news of Tydeus's success to Eteocles, condemns the king and his evil war, and commits suicide before the king can have him killed. Eteocles forbids his burial. The Thebans rush to the place of the slaughter, and family members mourn and collect the remains of their slain kin. A Theban mother, Ide, finds the remains of her slain twin sons. The aged Aletes compares the present slaughter with Theban catastrophes of old, and condemns Eteocles. Jupiter on Olympus summons Mars and bids him stir up the Argives to a frenzy of bellicose rage. Jupiter insists that the war is destined and cannot be prevented: The peoples must pay for their sins. The other gods are cowed and agree. As Mars descends to carry out Jupiter's commands, Venus meets him and begs him not to destroy their race, the Thebans, descended from their daughter, Harmonia. Mars is moved by her plea, and while he must foment war as commanded by Jupiter, he declares that he will strive to protect Thebes and oppose the Argives in battle. In the meantime, Tydeus returns to Argos and proclaims to the king and his council that the war has begun: The Thebans ambushed him and were slain. Polynices expresses outrage and offers to send himself alone to Thebes to die, instead of bringing war and grief on Argos. His words succeed in manipulating the Argives into desiring war. Adrastus is more restrained. Tydeus tells the full story and inflames Polynices further. Mars fills the land with eagerness for war. The seers Melampus and Amphiaraus are dispatched to observe omens. The entrails are discouraging, but they go on to read the sky. The birds and their actions are even more disturbing, and in one instance, a group of eagles attacking a "city" of swans presages with some precision the defeat of the Seven. The seers are disheartened. Melampus retires to his country dwelling, while Amphiaraus retreats to his chamber and refuses to speak. At length, as the tide of war rises, Capaneus expresses impatience and demands that the prophet speak. Amphiaraus, coming forth at last, predicts doom as the outcome of the war. Capaneus is scornful and hubristically casts doubt on the gods. The crowd roars approval. Just before dawn, Argia goes to see her father with her child Thessander and, anguished by her husband's unhappiness, pleads with Adrastus to go to war against Thebes, though she knows she may regret it. He cautiously agrees.

Book 4

Three years pass. The Argive forces are now on the verge of departing for war. Adrastus is weary and reluctant, Polynices and Tydeus fierce and eager for war. The poet then rehearses the catalog of forces from various places that contribute to the Argive expedition, including the seven famous heroes. The giant Capaneus leads one troop. Hippomedon leads the Peloponnesians. Amphiaraus has finally relented and comes to war. Argia has agreed to give up the necklace of Harmonia so that Eriphyle may be bribed to persuade her husband, the seer Amphiaraus, to join the expedition he knows is doomed. Parthenopaeus, son of ATALANTA, is young and inexperienced in war, but very handsome. He leads the Arcadians—a rough, hardy, and ancient people—into war. Atalanta, when she hears of Parthenopaeus's desire for battle, leaves the woods and confronts him, vainly attempting to persuade him to stay clear of war until he is older. In the meantime, the Thebans reluctantly and without eagerness or pleasure prepare for war. They resent their leader's bidding and do not wish to leave their families. Sinister rumors run through the city of Thebes; dire omens are observed; the leader of the Bacchantes cries out to Bacchus that she can no longer keep up his rites properly and complains of Eteocles' rule and war. Bacchus himself withdraws. Eteocles, alarmed, consults Tiresias. Tiresias offers rites to HADES and the other gods of the underworld and bids them release the spirits of the dead to the upper world. Tisiphone is to lead them up. The underworld is opened, and Theban and Argive ghosts come forth. The priestess who is helping Tiresias, Manto, describes to him the well-known figures of Theban mythology as they approach. Then, surprisingly, Tiresias himself is able to see and describes the Argive dead that appear, including the 50 slain warriors who tried to ambush Tydeus. In order to speak, the ghosts must drink the blood of the sacrifice. Tiresias seeks out Laius in particular and persuades him to speak, although he is initially reluctant. He predicts terrible war and Theban victory, but also that the FURIES will possess the city, and there will be a "double crime" in which the father will triumph. Meanwhile, the advancing Argives reach Nemea. But Bacchus, leading his train from Haemus, land of the Getae, sees the Argive army and complains that Juno, in anger at Semele, is contriving to do further damage to his city. He decides to delay them. He persuades the water nymphs to close up their springs, so that Nemea parches, and the soldiers become desperate. Only one spring, Langia, still flows. In their search for water, they come upon Hysipyle, daughter of Thoas, king of Lemnos, who, however, has been captured by pirates and sold as a slave to Lycurgus, the Spartan king, whose son, Opheltes, she looks after. Adrastus mistakes her for the goddess Diana (see ARTEMIS) and begs her to help them find water. She responds that she is not a goddess, although of royal lineage, and informs them of the spring Langia. She puts Opheltes down on the ground to guide them more rapidly. They find the spring and drink deeply. An Argive leader praises the stream.

Book 5

Adrastus asks Hysipyle her lineage and origins. She names her place of origin, Lemnos, alluding to the killing of the Lemnian women's husbands, and gives her name. Adrastus asks to hear her story. She tells how the Lemnian women neglected the rites of Venus, and she came with a Tartarean entourage to banish conjugal love from the island. The men of Lemnos preferred to wage war in Thrace than to remain with their families. An old Lemnian woman named Polyxo went into a frenzy and summoned the women together. She suggested violence against their husbands and children. The women made an oath sealed by the slaughter of a male child. The husbands returned, and their wives celebrated with them; Venus even breathed love into the husbands for one last night. During the night, the Lemnian women slaughtered the males of the island, including those of Hypsipyle's family, although she did not join in the slaughter. Instead, she chose to save her father, Thoas, leading him out of the city. Bacchus appeared to them and urged Hypsipyle to send her father away by ship. She did so, then returned to the city. She held a sham burial of her father to escape notice. She was made queen. The Lemnians began to regret their deeds and to remember the dead. The Argonauts arrived. The Lemnians mistook them for their enemies. A great storm fell upon the ship. The Lemnians attacked them while they were reeling from the storm. In a lightning flash, the heroes were revealed to them, and they ceased their attack. The two sides established a truce. The Lemnian women welcomed the men and accepted them in their beds; Hypsipyle herself was taken by Jason against her will and gave birth to twin sons. Eventually, the Argonauts departed. A rumor circulated that Hypsipyle did not kill her father, the Lemnians became angry and resentful of her innocence, and she departed for the shore, where she was captured by pirates; she was brought to her present location as a slave. While Hypsipyle tells her story, Opheltes falls asleep in the grass unmonitored. In the meantime, a giant serpent sacred to Jupiter is searching for water in the area and, without knowing it, strikes and kills the infant with its tail. Hypsipyle hears the death cry and goes on a frantic search. She comes on the serpent, shouts, and Capaneus slays it with his spear, declaring his indifference to any protector god the creature may have. The serpent dies in Jupiter's temple, and Jupiter decides not to kill Capaneus yet. Hypsipyle grieves for Opheltes, also called Archemorus ("beginning of doom/destiny"), whose death fulfills a prophecy

that Lycurgus would offer the first death in the war. Maddened by grief, Lycurgus calls for Hypsipyle's death. The Argive heroes interpose themselves, and Tydeus exchanges harsh words with Lycurgus. There is a report that Hypsipyle is being dragged to death. Panic, confusion, and armed conflict ensue. Adrastus, displaying Hypsipyle in his chariot, calms the crowd of soldiers. Unexpectedly, Hypsipyle's sons, Thoas and Euneus, from whom she had been long separated, appear and, after she recognizes them, enjoy a reunion with their mother. Amphiaraus addresses the Nemeans, declaring that the entire sequence of events was the inevitable outcome of destiny and that Archemorus should be honored as a hero.

Book 6

Rumor spreads through Greece that the Argives are establishing the Nemean games as part of Opheltes' funeral rites. The royal household mourns. The mother and father of Opheltes are inconsolable, and an elaborate funeral ceremony is carried out. The Argive army, at Amphiaraus's bidding, at the same time makes offerings to expiate the slaying of the sacred serpent. The cutting of wood required to build the altars is a scene of extravagant destruction. Eurydice, the mother, delivers a speech expressing her rage, sorrow, and resentment toward Hypsipyle—who enjoyed her child's company before causing his doom—and calls for her death. Lycurgus expresses his grief, and the body is burned on the sumptuous pyre. Afterward, they build a temple on which relief sculptures represent the story of Opheltes' death. They choose a wood-fringed vale as the site for the games and gather there. Statues of heroes are brought to the place. Polynices (driving Adrastus's horse Arion); Amphiaraus; Admetus; the two sons of Hypsipyle, Thoas and Euneos; Chromis; and Hippodamus line up to compete in chariot racing. Apollo, singing of the gods and cosmology on Olympus, observes the competition at Nemea and sees that two mortals favored by him, Admetus and Amphiaraus, are involved. He pities the short, unhappy life remaining for Amphiaraus and speeds down to Nemea. Polynices has difficulty controlling Arion, who senses an alien rider. Apollo, moreover, makes a ghastly phantom appear, and a terrified Arion causes Polynices to fall onto the ground. Polynices (unfortunately for Thebes and the Argives) survives; Amphiaraus wins as rider, but Arion, continuing riderless, crosses the finish line first; Admetus comes second. All three, including Polynices, are rewarded. Then the foot race is held. Parthenopaeus, son of the swift Atalanta, competes. Near the finish line, Parthenopaeus leads Idas, but Idas pulls him back by his long blond hair. In the following dispute, Adrastus rules that they must run again on separate tracks. Parthenopaeus wins. Next comes the ring toss. Hippomedon wins. After that comes the boxing match. Capaneus challenges the crowd, and at length, the Spartan Alcidamas comes forth. Capaneus despises his opponent. The skillful Alcidamas, trained by Pollux, consistently gets the better of the powerful, raging Capaneus and knocks him down, but Adrastus, seeing Capaneus's rage redoubled and fearing fatal violence, calls off the match. Alcidamas is hailed as winner, while Capaneus seethes and vaunts that he will send the boy's corpse back to Pollux. The vast, but somewhat unwieldy Agylleus, claiming descent from Hercules (see HERACLES), then challenges the sinewy Tydeus in wrestling. Tydeus raises him aloft and pins him to the ground, winning the match. Agreus and Polynices wish to fight with swords, but Adrastus forbids them, exhorting them to save their strength and lives for the war to come. Adrastus gives prizes to both, and has Polynices garlanded and proclaimed victor of Thebes. The others bid Adrastus perform a feat with bow and arrow. He is to strike a tree across the plain. The arrow hits its target but then, amazingly, turns around and falls before Adrastus. They debate the cause, but the poet reveals the meaning of the omen: Unbeknown to them all, the arrow is singling out Adrastus as the only one who will survive the war.

Book 7

Jupiter, watching from on high, is angered at the Argives' lack of progress and sends Mercury to chide Mars, currently among his favored Thracians, for ignoring his task; he threatens to supplant him with Athena as leader in the war. Mercury goes to the north and arrives at Mars's temple, grim, made of iron, and decorated with representations of the deities and trappings of warfare. Mercury approaches Mars and reports Jupiter's commands; Mars assents. At Nemea, the funeral games have ended, and Adrastus, praying to Opheltes, vows a temple to him in return for victory at Thebes. Mars, approaching, sends Panic *(Pavor)* ahead. Panic confuses the Argives with phantom images and sounds and makes them believe they are under attack from the Thebans. They snatch up arms. Bacchus, dismayed to see them making their way toward Thebes, goes before Jupiter. He complains that Jupiter, in allowing unwarlike Thebes to be attacked, singles him out for dishonor, whereas the birthplaces of other gods are peaceful and protected. A smiling Jupiter declares that destiny, not his personal will, is bringing about the present war. Thebes will not be destroyed until a later age. In the meantime, a report of the approaching Argive army comes to Eteocles, who calls on his allies. On a lonely tower, ANTIGONE questions Phorbas, who was once an attendant of Laius, about the war. He provides information on the various contingents joining their side in the war. He lingers on the story of Lapithaon and his son Alatreus, who appear very close in age because the nymph Dercetis seduced Lapithaon when still a boy. He also singles out Hypseus, who was the son of the river god Asopus, who raged against Zeus for abducting his daughter Aegina. Near the close of his catalog, he is reminded of Laius's death and breaks off in sobs. He remarks that he has put off his death only to look after Antigone and deliver her safely to her marriage. Eteocles then delivers a speech from a high mound and disposes the troops. The Argives march toward Thebes relentlessly, indifferent to the many dire omens. They cross the swelling Asopus and settle on a ridge overlooking Thebes. The city is wracked with fear and anticipation of war. Oedipus wanders abroad and prays to have his eyes back. Jocasta, supported by her daughters, goes forth from the city to meet the enemy. She calls for her son; he embraces her, and she berates him bitterly. She pleads that he go to the city with her and enter into negotiation with his brother. He is disposed to go, but Tydeus intercedes, recalls Eteocles' treachery, and stirs up warlike feelings in the army. As it happens, two tigers, brought by Bacchus from the East and treated as beloved manifestations of the god by the Thebans, are stung by the Fury and fall on some Argives, including Amphiaraus's charioteer, until they are driven, wounded, to the gates by Aconteus. The Thebans are outraged, and Aconteus is killed. The camp is thrown into tumult, Jocasta flees, and, with Tydeus's encouragement, battle begins in earnest. The poet calls on the Pierian Muses to sing of wars waged in their own country. Capaneus kills a priest of Bacchus; Eteocles fights fiercely, Polynices fights reluctantly against his own countrymen. Amphiaraus shines in battle with Apollo's support and, doomed to die by no mortal hand, slays many. When Hypseus kills his charioteer, Apollo, in mortal guise, takes his place. At length, Apollo reveals himself and proclaims the irreversibility of the prophet's fate. Amphiaraus, in his last words, commends to Apollo the punishment of his wife. The earth begins to shudder and rip apart; all cease their activity; an abyss opens and engulfs the horses and Amphiaraus, who rides on into the underworld as the earth closes above him.

Book 8

Amphiaraus enters the underworld, and all the shades are amazed and frightened. Pluto complains at length about the invasion of his realm. He sees it as an act of war and expresses his defiance of Olympus. He further wishes the two brothers to slay each other, that one war-

rior will feed on his enemy's head, that another will prevent the burial of corpses, and that one will make war on the gods. Then he turns to Amphiaraus and questions him. Amphiaraus swears that he does not come to the underworld as an aggressor, nor as a guilty soul; he was betrayed by his wife for gold and thus tricked into joining the Argive expedition. He expresses respect for Pluto and begs to become a shade. Pluto yields to his prayers. On Earth above, no one can find traces of his chariot, and they fear the place of its disappearance. The news is brought to a horrified Adrastus. Soldiers begin to retreat, and night falls. The Argives mourn the loss of Amphiaraus; they now have no prophet and have lost a brave warrior; the oracles will fall silent; and he will be worshipped at his own shrine. In Thebes, there is revelry and singing; the inhabitants rejoice in the enemy prophet's death, and they sing the legendary history of Thebes. Even Oedipus, pleased with the commencement of war, joins the feasts. Adrastus sits in gloomy anxiety. At dawn, the Argives choose Thiodamas, son of Melampus, as their seer. In his first act as seer, Thiodamas sets up altars and prepares offerings to appease Earth. He prays to Earth and to Amphiaraus. Thebes then sends forth warriors from all its seven gates. The Argives proceed less eagerly, still feeling the loss of their prophet. The poet calls on Calliope and Apollo to commence his battle narrative. The two sides meet in battle. A series of killings are described: Theban Hypseus and Haemon, supported by the divine Hercules (see HERACLES), distinguish themselves, as does Argive Tydeus, supported by Pallas Athena. Hercules and Pallas meet, and Hercules, expressing gratitude and reverence before Minerva yields; she is satisfied. Haemon senses the loss of his divine support and retreats; he is wounded by Tydeus but spared by Minerva. Tydeus goes on to kill others. Atys, betrothed to Ismene, enters the fray in splendid clothes and, at first successful, challenges Tydeus, who disdainfully and briefly spears him. In the meanwhile, Antigone and Ismene, in their bedroom, converse. They lament the misfortunes of Thebes and doubt whom to support in the war, but silently support Polynices. Ismene confesses she dreamed that she was a bride and recalls an omen of fire that appeared when once she saw Atys by accident. Atys, mortally wounded, is brought in. He has called for Ismene, and when she is alone with him, she closes his eyes in death. Tydeus is still preeminent on the battlefield. He even encounters Eteocles, but Enyo, the goddess of war, prevents Eteocles from being killed. Tydeus begins to falter eventually amid the immense slaughter. He is wounded in the groin by Melanippus. After hurling a spear back at Melanippus, he is dragged to the side of the field, where, dying, he demands Melanippus's head. Capaneus finds the dying Melanippus and carries him to Tydeus. Driven by Tisiphone, Tydeus eats Melanippus's brains. Minerva, looking on, was about to request immortality for the dying Tydeus, whom she favored, but now, seeing him defile himself in this way, averts her eyes and withdraws.

Book 9

All are disgusted by Tydeus's act, and the Thebans attempt to seize his corpse. Polynices, learning the news of his friend's death, grieves. He is restrained from committing suicide by his comrades. A group of Thebans led by Eteocles advance toward the corpse. The two sides fight over Tydeus. Tisiphone, taking human form, occupies the battlefield. Hippomedon—the mainstay of the corpse's defense—is misled by Tisiphone into thinking that Adrastus is in peril and follows her until she reveals her true form, and he sees Adrastus unharmed. The Thebans obtain the corpse and mutilate it. Hippomedon mounts the horse of Tydeus and continues his onslaught. Hippomedon comes to the river Ismenos and terrorizes the enemy there. The river is choked with bodies. Crenaeus, grandson of the river Ismenos, fights with a great sense of security in the water. He challenges Hippomedon. Hippomedon kills

him, and he calls on his mother in his dying breath. His mother, Ismenis, searches for him in the crowded waters, at length finds him, mourns him, and calls on her father, Ismenos, to exact vengeance. He hears her from far off and comes. He complains to Jupiter that, despite his support of Jupiter's amours, his river is choked with gore. The stream swells, and Hippomedon is battered by its force, yet still fights against, and taunts, the god. Hippomedon, beginning to be overwhelmed, grabs a tree trunk, which, however, falls onto him, and he begins to drown; he calls on the gods to save him from an ignominious death by drowning, and Juno hears. Jupiter, at his wife's request, causes the waters to subside. Hippomedon crawls onto the bank, where he is killed by the Thebans. Hypseus displays Hippomedon's helmet and vaunts over the corpse; Capaneus kills him and offers Hypseus's spoils to the dead Hippomedon. Atalanta, in the meantime, has been having ominous dreams about her son and Thebes. She prays to Diana for his safety. Diana makes her way through the heavens to Thebes and on the way meets her brother Apollo, saddened by the death of Amphiaraus. Apollo knows why she goes to Thebes and points out that he had to endure the death of his prophet: Fate is immutable. She replies brusquely that she can still ensure that Parthenopaeus will win glory by his death, and that his death is avenged. Parthenopaeus, gloriously arrayed, is much admired on the battlefield. Diana laments to see him there and enters into the field herself. With Diana's aid, he kills many in a fierce onslaught. At one point, Diana attempts to dissuade him from battle, but he insists on remaining. From on high, Venus observes Diana's actions at Thebes and chides Mars for standing aloof from battle while the normally unwarlike Diana does harm to their race. Mars descends and commands Diana to depart; she has no choice but to comply. Mars summons Dryas, descendant of ORION and thus enemy of Diana's follower. Parthenopaeus, struck by Dryas's weapon, falls. Dryas himself mysteriously falls, apparently untouched by any weapon. Parthenopaeus's comrades bear him from the field, and as he dies, he sends a carefully worded message to his mother.

Book 10

Night falls, hastened by Jupiter. The Thebans, emboldened by the killing of four Argive captains and encouraged by Eteocles, keep watch on their enemies' retreat rather than their own camp. In Argos, women and children pray for the men's return. They make offerings and pray to Juno for the defeat of Thebes. Juno knows she cannot change Argos's destiny but is determined to do what she can. She observes the Theban sentinels and sends Iris to the palace of Sleep, which is described in exquisite detail. Iris manages to rouse him with her brilliance and bids him put the Theban guards to sleep. Sleep descends on the battlefield and lulls the Thebans, but not the Argives, into slumber. Thiodamas is seized by a prophetic frenzy and goes to Adrastus's tent, where the chieftains (some newly appointed) are gathered, and tells them that he has received a prophetic message from Amphiaraus, who rose up from the underworld to speak to him: The Thebans are asleep and vulnerable to attack. Thiodamas chooses 30 to accompany him, though many more wish to go. They slaughter many Thebans in their sleep, aided by Juno herself. Thiodamas becomes weary with so much slaughter. At length, Actor suggests they set a limit to their havoc. Thiodamas agrees and prays to Apollo that he may one day return to his homeland. Two warriors on the expedition, however, Hopleus and Dymas, companions of Tydeus and Parthenopaeus, respectively, decide to search for the bodies of their slain captains. They obtain bright moonlight by praying to Diana. They find the bodies of Tydeus and Parthenopaeus and begin carrying them back. A troop led by Amphion calls on them to halt, and Hopleus is shot down. They capture Dymas, and he begs them not to mistreat his captain's corpse. Amphion commands him to

reveal the Argives' war strategy, and Dymas commits suicide. In the meanwhile, there is rejoicing at the Argive camp when Thiodamas returns, and Amphion's band, discovering the slaughter, turns back in horror. The Argives pour forth in eagerness for war, while the Thebans shut the gates. The Argives besiege the town and attempt to break its defenses; the Thebans defend the city from the walls. Inside, the inhabitants express a variety of sentiments and call on Tiresias, who, taking the omens, declares that the latest-born of the serpent race must die as the price of victory. Creon immediately understands that his son Menoeceus is meant. The goddess Virtue, who rarely visits Earth, on this occasion comes down from heaven in the form of the mortal prophetess Manto. Menoeceus is fighting alongside his brother Haemon, but Virtue approaches and bids him embrace his noble destiny. He agrees to do so and returns to the city. His father, realizing his son's intent, desperately attempts to dissuade him. The son affects to have no such intention and departs, leaving his father in confusion, although he ends by believing his son. Capaneus rages on the battlefield. Menoeceus stands on the wall. He prays to Apollo for victory, stabs himself with his sword, sprinkling the walls with his protective blood, and falls lightly to the ground. They bury him, and his mother laments inconsolably. The poet now works up to the more daring act of representing the wild audacity of Capaneus. Weary of slaughter, Capaneus looks upward, takes a ladder, and climbs the battlements. The Thebans hurl missiles at him. Not at all deterred, Capaneus continues climbing, reaches the summit, and taunts the Thebans. He begins destroying the walls and hurling down pieces onto the city below. Around Jupiter the various deities are arguing, each presenting the case of their favored side. Jupiter remains calm. Capaneus cries out, taunting the gods—Bacchus, Heracles, and, finally, Jupiter himself—asking them if any will come to Thebes's defense. Jupiter laughs and strikes him with a thunderbolt.

Capaneus is set on fire but manages to die still standing defiantly on the battlements.

Book 11

Capaneus lies immense on the ground, with a grim look on his face, having performed famous deeds that are even praiseworthy in the eyes of Jupiter. The Argives are scattered on the field in their fear of an angry Jupiter. Tisiphone, weary of the war, decides to bring it to a conclusion by the brothers' duel, and summons Megaera to help her. Tisiphone informs Megaera that while she has inspired the war's frenzy quite effectively thus far, she is wearying and needs her help for the final chapter—the duel of the brothers. Megaera will incite Polynices, Tisiphone will handle Eteocles and Thebes. Jupiter, anticipating the coming events, bids the gods, himself included, turn their eyes away from the earth. Polynices, who has seen an ominous vision of his wife, Argia, is lashed by the Fury into violent rage. He approaches Adrastus and announces his intention to meet Eteocles in a duel. He has caused the shedding of enough Argive blood. Megaera, in human guise, hastens him to the field of battle. Eteocles, in gratitude for the lightning bolt that struck down Capaneus, makes sacrifice and prayer to Jupiter. News of Polynices's approach reaches the king, and Creon fiercely demands that Eteocles, hesitating among various councils, face Polynices: Thebans, his son Menoeceus in particular, have suffered enough for their king's perjuries. Eteocles prepares for battle, threatening that he will punish Creon afterward. His mother passionately attempts to dissuade him. At the same time, Antigone, from the walls, attempts to dissuade Polynices. Polynices begins to waver, when Tisiphone abruptly smashes the gate and sends forth Eteocles. After exchanging harsh words, the two brothers meet in battle, each supported by his own Fury. Adrastus attempts to intervene and, failing, drives away from Thebes. The goddess Piety (*Pietas*), who long has dwelled in a remote region of the sky, alienated from gods and men, complains of the present strife and comes down to prevent it in mortal guise. For a moment, the two brothers repent of their actions and weep. Tisiphone harshly rebukes and intimidates Piety, who flees to Jupiter. They exchange blows, and neither is wounded, but Eteocles' horse is wounded. They rush at each other in a torrent of uncontrolled rage, and the Furies, no longer needed, stand aside in admiration and envy. Polynices drives his sword into Eteocles' groin and taunts his brother. Eteocles purposely falls to the ground, and as Polynices leans over him to strip him of his arms, Eteocles stabs him in the heart. Polynices, predicting Eteocles' punishment in the underworld for his treachery, falls dead on his brother. Oedipus, on hearing the news, comes out from his chamber and, supported by Antigone, is led to the bodies and flings himself on top of them. He feels a belated sense of duty and affection toward his sons and regrets his curse. Antigone foils his suicide attempt. Jocasta also attempts suicide. Creon holds power, becomes tyrannical, denies burial to the Argive dead, and sends Oedipus into exile. Oedipus responds with harsh, sarcastic words. Antigone pleads on his behalf. Creon responds that Oedipus may inhabit Theban territory in the wilds of Cithaeron. The remainder of the Argives flee under cover of darkness.

Book 12

The Thebans emerge cautiously from their city and attempt to sort out their kinsmen's bodies from the jumbled heap. They burn their dead, while leaving the Argives' bodies, Polynices's included, unburied. Menoeceus receives an elaborate burial, and Creon reiterates his decree against burial of the Argives. A group of women from Argos approaches Thebes in mourning: Argia, Deipyle, Atalanta, Evadne, Eriphyle, and others. They are aided by sympathetic gods, but meet along the way a lone, wounded, fleeing Argive soldier, Ornytus, who warns them that Creon will not allow them to bury their loved ones and that they are in danger of their own lives. The women entertain various options, but Argia, driven by love for her slain husband, decides to entreat the king personally, while the rest of the group appeals to THESEUS of Athens for aid. Accompanied by her old tutor Menoetes, Argia embarks on a long, relentless quest for the Theban battlefield. Once there, she searches through the bodies for her husband's by torchlight. Juno aids her by bidding the moon to shine more brightly and Sleep to put the watchmen to sleep. Argia recognizes first her husband's cloak, and then his body. She speaks to his corpse in grief. In the meanwhile, Antigone manages to slip past the guards out of the city. The two women meet over the corpse and join as partners in mourning. They tell each other the stories of Argos and Thebes, respectively. They prepare the body and, in their search for fire, come on the still burning pyre of Eteocles, although they do not know it is his. They place Polynices on the same pyre. The very flames and timbers strive against each other and push away from each other. The women realize their error, and Antigone calls on their ghosts to be appeased and cease their discord. The pyre's discord only increases with a great tremor, and the watchmen wake up. The two women fiercely contend with each other to take credit and demand punishment. The rest of the Argive women, meanwhile, approach Athens as suppliants, supported by Juno and Athena. They come to the shrine of Clemency, a specially designated place of refuge. Theseus returns from his Scythian wars in triumph. Spoils of his victory over the AMAZONS are led in procession. Capaneus's wife presents their case to him: Creon wrongly forbids burial of their kin. Theseus, deeply offended by Creon's conduct, commits to immediate war. The Athenians march against Thebes in eager spirits led by Theseus. Creon, however, is sending Antigone and Argia to their deaths. When they are about to be executed, a message from Theseus arrives, threatening war. Creon hesitates, then sends back a taunting response. The exhausted Thebans drag themselves listlessly out to war

yet again. The two sides meet in battle. After barely missing Haemon with his spear, Theseus seeks out Creon. Creon taunts him, but Theseus merely laughs and, offering Creon up as a victim to the Argive dead, throws his spear, which strikes the death blow. Theseus, stripping Creon of his armor, assures him of burial. A treaty is made, and Theseus is welcomed as a guest in Thebes. The Argive women come down to find and bury their dead. The poet then affects inability to tell of the funeral that followed and its diverse episodes and declares the end of his poem's journey. He further prays for the survival of his poem into future ages, a poem that, he remarks, has already achieved a measure of fame and is known to the emperor (Domitian). He exhorts his poem to avoid direct rivalry with the *AENEID*, but instead to follow reverently in its footsteps.

COMMENTARY

Statius came from the Bay of Naples, a very Greek part of Italy, and his father was a professional poet who composed in Greek. Given Statius's deeply Greek cultural background, it make sense that the subject matter of his epic poem draws on Greek mythology and displays his impressive erudition in Greek literature, myth, geography, and ethnography. At the same time, Statius writes in Latin, and the literary conventions of his poem are formed within the context of the tradition of imperial Roman epic. These two major dimensions of Statius's work—Greek subject matter and Roman literary matrix—create an enlivening tension throughout his epic poetry. Statian epic is informed by the set of concerns specific to the sociopolitical conditions of the emerging and early Roman Empire: Foundation, empire, city and world, conflicts over land and hegemony, the relation between the cosmic and the mundane, race, and destiny. Those concerns are submerged within and, yet at the same time, infuse a distinctly Greek mythological setting.

To understand Statius's position within the Roman epic tradition and its ideological framework, it is necessary to recall its development over the previous century and the figures of Virgil and Lucan especially. Virgil, who founded the tradition of imperial Roman epic, appropriately wrote an epic of foundation, the story of how the Trojan fugitive AENEAS comes to Italy and establishes the basis for Roman civilization. Aeneas must first fight a long war with the native Latins, with whom eventually his own Trojans will join to form the Roman race. The sacrifices Aeneas and his comrades make, and the deaths they both suffer and cause in war, are thus notionally justified within the broader scheme of the destiny of the Roman people. Virgil provides plenty of space for the dissenting reader to ponder the sacrifices of Roman destiny and to wonder whether the violence involved in founding civilization is truly worth it—whether that means the early Roman civilization Aeneas and later Romulus founded or the imperial civilization Augustus founded at the cost of civil war. Yet the driving engine of Virgilian narrative is teleological, i.e., devised so as to suggest that great labors and suffering are directed toward some end or goal. The teleological framework remains available and always at least *potentially* operative.

Lucan, an epic poet writing under Nero, inherits the same set of concerns with empire, destiny, foundation, and violence, yet he in many ways inverts the ideological emphasis of Virgil's foundation epic. His *Civil War* treats the relatively recent conflict between Caesar and Pompey that formed part of the disintegration of the Roman Republic. This story, too, presents a teleological dimension, yet perversely so. As Lucan notes, without the civil war that destroyed republican government, there would be no principate, and no Nero. Caesar and Pompey, in their relentless discord, are arguably founders of the imperial system no less than Augustus. Yet they accomplish their "foundation" through civil violence and *nefas* ("not-right"). Although we know that the Julio-Claudian emperors (and

their putative glories) are yet to come, there is no strong impression of worthwhile destiny pervading the narrative, which is filled instead with mangled bodies and a sense of purposeless brutality. Civil war is about discord rather than fusion and thus presents a darker, more divisive view both of foundation and of the civilization that is founded.

Statius, like Lucan, at once inherits the ideological matrix of Virgilian epic, while developing its subversive tendencies to the point of undermining the central link between narrative drive and teleological justification. As in Lucan, there is a profound sense of purposeless violence in Statius, a relentless war drive that pushes along the narrative toward its destined outcomes without providing any positive justification for the massive suffering caused along the way. Statius situates his narrative even further from the chain of Roman historical causation, however, in choosing to write about the Seven against Thebes. There is arguably even less teleological motivation, from a Roman point of view, than in Lucan, since, in the latter case, we can at least fill in the succeeding periods of Roman history in our minds. Later mythological events are in store for the future, but there is no sense of a particular, worthwhile goal toward which the current sequence tends. Theban mythology is thus, in a certain sense, cut off from Virgilian epic destiny, trapped in a bubble of nonteleological violence. Violence that is cyclical, inescapable, and purposeless, that ends in lamentation and emotional exhaustion, is more reminiscent of tragedy than epic, and Thebes is the tragic city par excellence. The central problem of Thebes is tragic repetition, the recurrence of patterns of violence and defilement across generations. Thebes wins the war, but the victory is Pyrrhic, to say the least, and Statius's Jupiter, far from guaranteeing some future "empire without end," as in the *Aeneid*, guarantees only that one day Thebes, in a future age, will be defeated and fall. The Argives have no greater hopes: The only "hopeful" prophecy of their future is that Adrastus, alone of the Seven, will survive the war.

In developing this antiteleological vision, Statius is not so much rejecting Virgil as developing and intensifying some aspects of Virgil at the expense of others. Or, to put it another way, he develops a reading of Virgil that privileges elements congruent with his own project. One of those elements is the presence of tragedy within epic. Thebes as a place, as mentioned above, has strong tragic associations. The assault of the Seven was the subject of an Aeschylean tragedy, which was itself the culminating play in a Theban trilogy; Sophocles' oeuvre includes a famous group of Theban plays (*Oedipus Rex, Antigone, Oedipus at Colonus*). Euripides' PHOENICIAN WOMEN affords yet another tragic version of Theban mythology, and his meta-tragic tragedy, the *Bacchae*, is set in Thebes. For Roman writers and readers, Thebes and Mycenae were common metonyms for the tragic.

The place itself, however, does not establish the presence of the tragic genre within epic, for Statius might have developed his theme in a more straightforwardly epic manner. He chooses, rather, to emphasize and maximize the tragic and—a closely related theme—the Dionysiac in his representation of Thebes. The association of Bacchus and Thebes is a constant theme, reinforced by references to Pentheus, AGAVE, and Semele. Pentheus and Agave, are tragic characters, and Dionysus/Bacchus, who brings about Pentheus's downfall for his resistance to Dionysiac rites, is the presiding deity of Athenian theater. Bacchus himself appears on the scene in the epic's narrative and plays a key role in bringing about the delay of the Argives at Nemea. It is Bacchus in this play, not Juno as in the *Aeneid*, who complains to Jupiter of his dishonor and the fate of a favored city. Other figures are equally distinctive in their tragic resonance. Tiresias, for example, is close to being a stock character in Theban tragedies; Hypsipyle is likewise the subject of tragedy. Oedipus was, at least since Aristotle, the prototypical tragic character.

Argos, for its part, presents almost equally impeccable tragic credentials. While Mycenae is the usual setting for the house of Atreus, Aeschylus places it in Argos. The abominable act of Atreus, who served up Thyestes' own children to him as a meal, is alluded to several times throughout the epic. When, near the beginning of the epic, Jupiter complains that two cities in particular have committed transgressions that demand punishment, he singles out Thebes and Argos. Argos, like Thebes, can call on a longer history of dark myths. Just as Thebes can claim Cadmus and Harmonia, Semele, ACTAEON, Pentheus, and NIOBE, so Argos can claim the Danaids' murder of their husbands and other grim stories of ancient legend. The expedition of the Seven appeals to Statius because both sides are almost equally tainted with criminality; neither has right on its side, and both are associated with cycles of recurrent violence and ancestral curses that undermine the hopes of the living.

The most vivid embodiment of tragic rage and violence is to be found in Statius's omnipresent Furies, sometimes designated, in an Aeschylean reminiscence, as Eumenides. The epic tradition provides precedents for this dialogue with the tragic genre: Apollonius's *VOYAGE OF THE ARGONAUTS* is hardly unaware of the tragic MEDEA's later career. Even more strikingly, Virgil stages his DIDO episode, as some commentators have observed, and as Virgil himself encourages us to observe, as a tragedy within the epic. Dido, trapped in the circuit of incurable desire, resists the epic's teleological drive and, ultimately, is destroyed in its wake. She lives out the plot of a tragedy, while Aeneas goes on to complete his epic destiny. Aeneas's forward momentum defeats the self-imploding tendency of the tragic character, while Virgil's narrative overcomes the nonprogressive tendency of tragic closure. Statius vastly expands the presence of the tragic within epic, and even allows tragic cyclicality to eclipse epic progress. The forward drive of the Argive expedition in the end only serves to confirm the recurrent cycle of doom within the house of Oedipus. Apparent progression collapses into repetition, the fulfillment of the blind old man's curse, while the Fury becomes the poem's presiding deity.

Related to the Statian concern with cyclicality and lack of progression is his version of the epic motif of delay *(mora)*. Delay can be a powerful narrative device for building up expectation and tension and is used with great effectiveness by Homer in both his epics: Achilles' awe-inspiring return to battle is delayed for most of the poem, and ODYSSEUS's return to the role of master in his household is tantalizingly and spellbindingly delayed, even after he has arrived home in Ithaca. Virgil ensures that Aeneas wanders for most of the first half of the epic before arriving in Italy and commencing his war with the Latins. Statius, however, manages to push the poetics of delay to the breaking point. Statius has, first of all, chosen a subject that, in mythological terms, does not obviously present a large number of major narrative units into which to break up his epic. The assault of the Seven was compactly treated by Aeschylus in a single play. It took a tour de force of expansion to fill the Virgilian number of 12 books with these events. Statius manages to make the beginning of his war fall in the seventh book, as in Virgil's *Aeneid*, even though relatively little, in raw terms, actually happens in the interval between Oedipus's curse and the start of the conflict.

The episode of Opheltes and Hypsipyle is notable for its richly learned expansiveness and its incorporation of multiple layers of narrative. Statius seems almost to have gone out of his way to include a highly complicated episode with only a glancing relation to the epic's central plotline. The principle of *mora* is maximized. But the Hypsipyle detour is only the most obvious instance: Adrastus, even after agreeing in principle to the war, still waits three years before commencing the expedition. Amphiaraus, the other morally admirable Argive hero, is equally slow and reluctant. Both would prefer to delay indefinitely the attack on

Thebes and its fated outcomes. Aeneas was a reluctant warrior in some respects and claimed, when justifying himself to Dido, that he was going to Italy against his will. Yet Aeneas ultimately accepted his destiny as the founder of a civilization. Amphiaraus and Adrastus present the case of heroes who would do anything to put off or evade their destiny.

The destiny that the *Thebaid* enacts is ultimately a negative one. Statius's Jupiter announces from the outset that he will employ infernal power to punish two cities that have sinned against morality and the gods. In thus framing his epic, Statius distinguishes himself from his Virgilian model. He foregrounds the destruction, rather than the foundation, of cities, and at the same time, he confounds the Virgilian opposition between infernal and Olympian powers and deities. In Virgil, Jupiter, the sky god, supports the hero Aeneas in his quest for Italy and, along with other Olympians such as Neptune (see POSEIDON), restores order after Juno and her hellish lieutenants have wreaked havoc and created obstruction. This scheme may be too simple in the end, but as a basic blueprint, it provides insight into an important aspect of the *Aeneid*'s narrative dynamic. No such dichotomy can be applied to the *Thebaid*. From the very beginning, Jupiter turns to the underworld in handling the matter of Thebes and Argos. Tisiphone, the epic's first deity to make an appearance, continues directing the action through to the final act, when the two brothers kill each other.

The idea of complicity between an Olympian god and infernal forces derives from the *Aeneid* itself: Juno employs the terrifying figure of Allecto, the direct literary ancestor of the Statian Tisiphone. Even Jupiter, at the epic's close, summons the hell-demons called Dirae to help bring Turnus's story to a close. The pervasive presence of the infernal in the *Thebaid*, however, presents yet another case where Statius develops a Virgilian feature to the point where sheer quantity transforms literary quality. Statius's gods routinely employ

Furies and hellish forces, and as Statius is keen to emphasize, there is often no clear dividing line between the devices of the gods and the devices of Thessalian witches. Many instances illustrate Statius's Fury-saturated world and the inextricable link between Olympian and infernal powers. Venus employs the infernal powers to make Lemnos a hell on earth. Phoebus afflicts the Argives with a hellish child-eating monster. The fearsome serpent that emerges to kill the infant Opheltes is sacred to Jupiter. Minerva, when Tydeus feasts on the brains of Melanippus, averts her gaze, and as she turns away, the image of the Gorgon on her shield seems to grow in stature and overshadow the goddess's face. Furies dominate the scene and sometimes make disturbing, unexpected appearances. Polynices, as he turns toward the city to face his brother in battle, glances back to see the sinister omen of the Fury's looming shadow.

Just as it is hard to distinguish between infernal and Olympian powers and projects, given Statius's insistent and informed mixing of the two, so also does he go out of his way to make the boundary between the world of the living and the world of the dead unusually permeable. The journey to visit the dead is an epic motif that goes back to the *Odyssey* and was notably revived in significant form by Virgil in the sixth book of the *Aeneid*, where Aeneas visits the underworld to learn of Rome's future greatness. We might compare with Aeneas's journey the ghastly retrieval of the ghost of Laius by Mercury at Jupiter's behest. Statius's Pluto justly complains that the boundaries of his realm are all too permeable, and that people seem to be able to go back and forth with impunity. Laius himself is a prime example. On his first exit from Hades, he appears to Eteocles and, in his dream, covers him in blood from the fatal wound on his neck, thereby stirring up feelings of violence and war in his descendant. Before revealing himself, however, he grotesquely dresses up as Tiresias—at once a highly self-conscious reference to tragic the-

ater and an allusion to Tiresias's role as ghostly prophet in the *Odyssey*.

Later, in an even more explicit travesty of Odysseus's consultation of the shades, Eteocles has Tiresias release the shades from the underworld, and this time Laius is consulted as prophet of the coming war. The contrast with the *Aeneid* is pointed: Laius predicts Theban victory, but also the "twin death" and the horrific triumph of the father's curse. Laius's and Tiresias's roles, with cruel irony, are doubled. Laius caused the misfortunes of the household by not heeding prophecy, and now he becomes, on two occasions, a posthumous Tiresian prophet. Tiresias himself becomes a somewhat absurd figure, closer to a witch practicing necromancy than the revered prophet of Greek tragedy. Finally, rather than sending a hero down to visit the dead, Statius brings up legions of the dead from the underworld, effectively undermining the barrier between the two realms. In doing so, he at once recalls and expands Lucan's ghastly scene of necromancy.

In one instance, Statius does send a hero, still living like Aeneas, down to the underworld. The prophet Amphiaraus is swallowed up by a chasm in the earth. Amphiaraus, however, will not return; the finality of his doom is forcefully impressed on the hero, when, descending to the land of the dead, he has the unpleasant experience of observing the earth closing up again above him. Pluto, when he observes this trespass on his realm, becomes infuriated and complains that the Olympians are attempting to undermine his sovereignty. The point is well taken. The boundaries of hell in Statius's epic are not hard; they are softer even than in the *Aeneid*, to the point that their constant permeability becomes almost comic. Pluto himself is surprisingly loquacious in the epic and comes off as a much more lively and important character than elsewhere in epic. The pervasive infernal coloring of the narrative extends to the characters as well. Argia's epic quest to find her husband's body is compared by the poet to Demeter's relentless search for her abducted child Persephone. Adrastus, departing from Thebes, is compared to Pluto, his spirits dashed at the sudden realization that, in drawing the underworld as his lot, he has lost the sky. This haunting vision of eternal loss would make Adrastus the king of a dead world. The only one of the seven heroes to survive the war, Adrastus now inhabits a desolated ghost realm. Everyone who mattered is dead.

Ghosts fill the air at various moments in the narrative and whistle about the heads of the living. Near the end, Argia must walk through fields filled with corpses to find Polynices's. To avoid contaminating the epic's least tainted and most unproblematically heroic character (Theseus), Statius must find a bit of ground unoccupied by bodies for the epic's final battle. The scarcity of undefiled space signifies in literary terms as well. Statius, in writing about Thebes, is traversing a literary terrain that is both thick with previous practitioners and thick with corpses. The site of Tydeus's slaughter of 50 Thebans is emphatically identified by Statius with the site of the Sphinx's murderous perch and suicidal fall. Statius effectively imitates and expands the scene in *Aeneid* 3, where the very soil is tainted by Polydorus's murder, but *not* the sequence in Book 8, where Aeneas is shown the as yet humble sites of Rome's future greatness. Statius focuses on the violence of the past and its defilement of the present. The many mythologically famous ghosts of Thebes—the Sown Men, Semele, Actaeon, Pentheus—remind us of the city's legions of violently killed dead who continue to haunt its soil.

The soil's saturation with gore is only one among many Statian figures for exhaustion, both in martial and in poetic terms. The cluster of terms that belong to the semantic domains of fatigue and satiety—filling, exhausting, drinking to the dregs, wearying, wearing down—occurs with striking frequency throughout the epic, and in their overuse, the words themselves afford an example of the theme they express. The horror of Thebes is overdetermined and all too predictable. A plethora of signs and omens accompanies the Argives as they march toward Thebes. Their plurality makes the effort to ignore them all the more incredible. Every death is presaged by disturbing dreams and omens; every phase in the narrative is preceded by multiple emblems of future woe. This sense of hypersaturation extends to the temporal register as well: Generation after generation at Thebes has replicated the pattern of violence and pollution. Statius consciously points up the effect of crowding; his narrative is dense with dark mythic exempla, just as it is almost cloyingly enriched by its multiple layers of allusion to previous epic. Statius succeeds, in other words, in making poetic exhaustion an absorbing poetic theme.

To take only one of many possible examples, the night raid scene in Book 10 knowingly plays on the idea of exhaustion on multiple levels. On the level of the narrated events, the raid intensifies the ordinary glut of violence that constitutes epic warfare: Uncounted Thebans are murdered in their sleep without effort or struggle, to the point that the killers become disoriented by the possibilities for slaughter. Eventually, they must set an arbitrary limit, even though it seems like the waste of an opportunity to do so. The prophet Thiodamas, who urged the expedition in the first place and is its prime hero, himself becomes weary and even disgusted with the mechanical killing. It is no accident that the night raid scene is one of the most venerable in ancient epic and goes back to Homer's *Iliad*. Apollonius included a confusing night battle in his epic, and more important for Statius, the night raid passage in the *Aeneid* was singled out by its author as important and worthy of enduring the passage of time. Statius, imitating Virgil's gesture, expresses the hope that his Hopleus and Dymas will be famous and immortal like Virgil's Nisus and Euryalus. Statius is unusually explicit about his act of emulation in this passage. It may not be accidental that Statius foregrounds here his Virgilian inheritance, given that the entire episode is about exhaustion, repetition, and weariness.

Another example is afforded by the cutting of trees in Book 6 to build altars. Tree cutting is yet another epic type scene that goes back to Homer, is featured in Virgil, and can even now be found near the beginning of Derek Walcott's *Omeros*. Statius, not surprisingly, surpasses his predecessors' violation of nature, multiplying the devastation to new extremes. Yet there is added irony in this instance, since, by ruthlessly hewing down an ancient grove, the Argives aim to appease an angry god and thus display their piety. "Wood," in Latin, is one way of referring to material or poetic subject matter. Thus, a scene featuring the violent hacking of a wood is at the same time a violent metaphor for literary creation and the extravagant, exploitative use of the age-old materials provided by one's revered predecessors in the epic tradition. Statian imitation has an edge of violence and carries suggestions of conscious exploitation and defilement that are in tension with the reverent tones of his poem's closing envoi.

Another area where literary imitation is at once inevitable and problematic is the description of the violence of warfare. Death and wounding have been exhaustively described by epic poets. Already in Homer, various modes of extinguishing life were employed to add variety to battle narration. What can a new poet add, except greater accumulation and novel provocations, to disgust and horror? Statius has the dubious honor of writing in the wake of Lucan, who seemingly maximized epic's potential for the fragmentation and destruction of bodies. Extreme violence of warrior heroes, then, is itself paradoxically the site of fatigue. This paradox creates a continual narrative tension between weariness and the dynamism required for fresh acts of destruction. Statius's achievement mirrors that of some of his heroes. Aware of the immense power of the past over his present venture, of the wearisome nature of repetition, and even of a certain futility, he

nonetheless forges on and holds our interest as he does so.

Statius goes beyond recording the exhaustion of the better-established areas of epic narrative, however; he also injects new energy into areas of the epic tradition that, while certainly important, had not been developed to their full potential. One of these areas is the representation of grief, and especially mourning for the loss of children. The interest in dead children on Statius's part seems consistent and even programmatic. Recurrent mythic reference is made to the killing of Thyestes' children, the slaughter of the children of Niobe, and, perhaps more distinctively, the story of Ino/Leucothea and Palaemon/Melicertes. In that story, Athamas, driven mad at Juno's behest, killed one of his wife Ino's children, and she dove with the other into the sea, where they were transformed into sea creatures and renamed. The two latter stories are carefully chosen: They are both Theban and concern grief for dead children.

The theme of dead children comes up throughout the epic. In the story told by Adrastus in Book 1, the Argive king's daughter abandoned her child by Apollo, then learned to her immense grief that the child was devoured by dogs. After her execution, Apollo's punishment came in the form of a child-eating monster. The Lemnian women killed both male adults and male children of the island—murders they later come to regret. The most elaborate development of the theme is the Hypsipyle episode, in which Opheltes/Archemorus dies due to Hypsipyle's neglect. Her own grief and the grief of the child's mother and father are represented in painful detail, and his funeral rites and subsequent funeral games take up a significant portion of the epic. Statius has a sharp eye for the pathos of the heartrending detail, which he uses to powerful effect. Creon's fatherly concern for Menoeceus, and later his heartless political exploitation of his son's memory, contribute to a memorable psychological portrait. Statius's comparison of Argia's search for Polynices's body to Demeter's search for Persephone assimilates her grief to the loss of a child. Many of these parents and caretakers are at least in some way responsible for their children's death—a detail that may help to explain the pattern and its larger significance for Statius. Oedipus, who furnishes the beginning point of the narrative, reemerges near the end: He regrets cursing his sons and throws himself on top of their corpses. The culmination of the epic's central myth is the slaying of two children through the dreadful agency of their father.

Epic poets since Homer made the cost of war and thus the glory of the hero's death manifest by embedding miniature biographies into the battle narrative. Before he dies, we learn the warrior's city of origin and information about the father, mother, or wife who will mourn his death. These small but often vividly evocative details of the hero's life story intensify the emotional power of the battle narrative and give war its emotional and moral complexity. Virgil made a decisive intervention in the epic tradition by introducing his distinctive mode of pathos. There is a much-noted mournful quality to some of Virgil's poetry that some critics have seen as a counterpoint to the martial drive of his epic and its patriotic themes. Virgilian mournfulness, his sense of the "tears of things" *(lacrimae rerum)*, builds on and transforms the Homeric awareness of the cost of war. Virgil goes beyond the Homeric paradigm of the hero as object of mourning for his kin and community and ponders broader aspects of sadness and tragedy in human existence. There is even some precedent for Statius's interest in grief for the death of children. In a key passage in Book 6, Virgil describes the Temple of Apollo built by the master artisan Daedalus, who represented in relief sculpture various stories from Cretan mythology, but not the death of his own son, Icarus.

Roman epic, starting with Virgil, extends the space of grief within epic, so that it gradually begins to take on a weight and importance of its own and no longer merely functions as a measure of war's cost, the warrior's heroism, and the community's loss when its defenders are slain. The Homeric Achilles' grief for the dead Patroclus does play a major role in the *Iliad* and continues to drive Achilles' actions even after he has avenged his friend's death by killing Hector. At the same time, however, Achilles' grief for Patroclus must be understood as a means of justifying his return to battle and magnifying his battle fury to magnificent proportions. Grief fuels Achilles' rage, and his rage makes him a splendid and memorable warrior. Virgilian and post-Virgilian epic, with its assimilation of tragic paradigms of action and emotion, gives new scope to the expression of grief and, as in the case of Dido, explores the destructive power of emotion outside the battlefield. Grief, especially in Statius, begins to come into its own as a feature of mortal life and is the more vividly and intensely evoked in certain cases where the object of mourning is not an adult warrior.

There are many cases where grief is expressed for a warrior, but even in these cases, the theme of grief itself begins to overshadow the exposition of war, and the proportion subtly shifts in favor of emotive response over action and deed. The Theban Atys, who is engaged to be married to Ismene, calls out her name when he is brought into the city mortally wounded, and it is his bride-to-be, alone with him for the first and only time, who closes his eyes in death, then mourns her dead fiancé. This small, private scene has great power. The culmination of the whole narrative sequence concerning Atys takes place outside the battlefield, in an unmarried girl's wordless expression of grief. We might compare the death of Parthenopaeus. Like a Homeric hero, he enjoys a display of martial splendor, supported by a patron god, before he dies, and the pathos of his death is heightened by descriptive attention to his youth and beauty. Yet, intertwined with the sequence of his glory in battle and subsequent demise is a long, richly detailed narrative of Atalanta's premonitions, anxieties, and actions on her son's behalf. In a certain sense, the central meaning of the episode is the mother's grief, and yet, in this instance, Statius brilliantly subverts our expectation of an elaborately described mourning scene. He ends the sequence instead with Parthenopaeus's dying directions for the messenger who will, eventually, inform his mother of his death. In this case, the sense of Atalanta's terrified concern for her son has been so profoundly built up that the choice *not* to represent her actual grief is much more powerful than a more conventional grieving scene would have been.

The overt emotionalism of Statian epic is only one facet of a hypercharged literary style that constantly intensifies the impact of the events and surrounds events with a rich fabric of associations. The epic simile is a traditional feature of epic and goes back to Homer; Apollonius and Virgil inherited and reworked it in turn. In Statius, similes come with striking frequency. They are so densely packed, at times, that they seem to equal the narration to which they are notionally subordinate. Statius, moreover, often uses simile not simply as a comparison that adds vividness to the narrated event but as a juxtaposed field of meaning that is often with tension with, or even supplants, the narration. The simile can bring out darker implications and a more disturbing emotional tenor than the events themselves directly suggest, and thus functions as a complex counterpoint to the narrative, interweaving it with double entendres and imbuing it with a rich tonal dissonance. Another feature of Statius's densely ornate style is the sometimes whimsical detail of his physical description. The magnificently described Tisiphone descends holding a funeral torch in one hand and a live water snake in the other. Mercury, on his voyage to the northern lands, finds that his broad Arcadian hat is ill designed to ward off the hail rattling about his head. Statius presses at the boundaries of epic decorum, and his descriptions are the richer for it. One final feature worth remarking is his use

of learned periphrasis and a hypererudite style of naming. Rarely will Statius simply employ a hero's name, but uses instead a topographical adjective that itself only obliquely indicates his place of origin; in other cases, he uses a patronymic. Both features are traditional in epic, and yet Statius is so consistently oblique in his manner of reference as to create an overt effect of opacity.

Statian allusion is perhaps the most conspicuous dimension of his epic poetry and has been the object of much study in recent years. Not surprisingly, Statius retreads his predecessors' ground in a manner that is at once exhaustive and eccentric, reverent and laced with aggression, self-denigrating and ambitious. He is constantly allusive and, above all, alludes to Virgil. To take only a few examples: The funeral games for Opheltes replay the funeral games both for Hector in the *Iliad* and, yet more closely, the funeral games for Anchises in the *Aeneid;* the terrible storm in Book 1 of the *Thebaid* reworks the storm of *Aeneid* 1; in both Virgil's and Statius's epic, a wounded animal or animals especially favored by the local population are the cause of the beginning of hostilities. The poet's closing remarks, in which he claims to follow Virgil at a reverent distance, has been traditionally taken at face value but is more recently viewed as at once concealing and expressing proud poetic ambitions. Certainly, Statius is not hesitant about inviting direct comparison with Virgilian epic as, for example, in his explicitly declared emulation of Virgil's Nisus and Euryalus episode. Statian allusion typically works at several levels and alludes to more than one predecessor text at once, and thus reflects, on the level of literary inheritance, the rich exuberance of his style. One example among a vast multitude will have to suffice. Hypsipyle, when she tells the story of the events on Lemnos, is likened to Aeneas telling the story of the fall of Troy in *Aeneid* 2: The Lemnos episode, like *Aeneid* 2, is a first-person narration, and as in Virgil, the narrator tells how she dutifully saved her aged father from the ruin of her own city. Equally, however, we might think of the Lemnos episode in Apollonius, which, likewise, fulfills the function of narrative delay within the broader frame of the epic journey. The list could be expanded. Statius combines multiple, intertwining allusive strands in fashioning his narrative, and invites multiples lines of comparison and interpretation.

The epic genre has a long tradition of incorporating elements that are, at least ostensibly, opposed to the "classic" version of its identity as the narration of heroic deeds. From the time of Homer, delay, narrative detour, representation of women, the expression of emotions such as grief and erotic desire, the display of erudition apparently for its own sake, and a concern with the subheroic and ignoble have formed an important part of epic poetry, constituting its identity at least in part through tension and contrast and paradox. Statius, in this perspective, is no different from his predecessors going back to Homer. And yet, in another sense, he is distinctive precisely in his determination to maximize the presence of the anti-epic within epic, creating a paradoxical epic of the sinister, the defiled, the pointless, the baroque, and the absurd. Stylistic and allusive ornateness play into the same project. The medium, with its allusive density, stylistically baroque texture, hypererudite manner, and simile-burdened narration, is in constant tension with the narrated message, baffling and obstructing the unrolling of the plot. It thus makes sense that there are multiple instances in the *Thebaid* of blocked, fragmentary, and elliptical speech. Statius, a poet capable of tremendous fluidity when he wishes, combines verbal profusion and blockage, speech and a sense of the futility of speech.

Related to the theme of speech and silence is that of seeing and not seeing. The entire epic begins with the gory spectacle of the blinded visage of Oedipus. Statius, moreover, has developed a distinctive version of the myth, which resembles Euripides' *Phoenician Women*, and in which Jocasta, rather than committing suicide, is still alive, and Oedipus, rather than going into exile, remains at Thebes during the war. His blind presence is crucial to Statius's thematic emphases. The verb Statius uses to describe Oedipus's act of self-blinding (*scrutor*) means "to search, explore, probe." This unusual usage suggests that the poet is consciously playing on the irony of Oedipus's character, a figure who, in Sophocles' play, was a great scrutinizer and investigator of his own life and fate. Now, he has probed and delved into his own eye sockets so as to look no longer on the horror of what he has discovered—his wife/mother, his misbegotten children, his life, and himself. Moreover, in a dark travesty of the motif of the blind seer endowed with inner sight, Oedipus is afflicted with a "cruel daylight" that shines with harsh brightness in his mind. Later, Tiresias, although blind, will be unexpectedly capable of seeing the ghosts of dead Thebans as they come up from the underworld, as if, by a logical inversion, blindness in the world of light and life conversely conveys sight in the realm of death. Jocasta, in turn, when Eteocles is on the verge of dueling with his brother, will call to mind the blinded Oedipus and suggest the same treatment for her own eyes and ask why the present day must be gazed upon. Finally, when Oedipus comes to regret the curse he earlier inflicted in the wake of his self-blinding, he will wish, on feeling the dead bodies of his sons, that he had his eyes back so that he could tear them out again.

Mortals are not the only ones who wish they could not look upon the horror of their fate. The gods also sometimes choose not to see. Minerva, when Tydeus feeds on the skull of Melanippus, averts her gaze so as not to watch the polluting act. Even more strikingly, when the two brothers are about to enter battle against each other, Jupiter calls on the other gods to join him in turning their gaze away from the coming events. This injunction is a fairly disturbing idea. The culminating action of Statius's epic is unworthy even to be seen by the gods and, uniquely in the epic tradition, goes ahead *without* the spectating Olympians. We, the readers/audience, do view/read the final act of the two brothers' story and, presumably, defile ourselves in being privy to their grotesque end. Statius plays with his readers' simultaneous sense of disgust and continuing desire to see it all played out nonetheless. This concern with violence and the desire to see/not see is not unrelated to broader cultural developments. The emergence of spectacle and spectatorship as defining paradigms for literature and reading in the early empire has often been observed in recent scholarship. The spectacles of violence in Lucan's *Civil War* can be interpreted as responding to the violent spectacles that become increasingly popular in the early imperial period: beast hunting, public executions, and gladiatorial combat. Statius, writing under the Flavian dynasty, lived in a period when ampitheatrical spectacle was given enduring and conspicuous public form. The Colosseum, a massive monument to the Roman taste for spectacle, was built by the Flavians. Statius effectively integrates the contemporary cultural paradigm of spectacle into the mythological framework of the *Thebaid*, where blindness and sight have thematic prominence.

Another reflection of contemporary culture in the *Thebaid* can be found in the epic's many artistic and architectural ecphrases, i.e., extended descriptions of artworks and buildings. The most famous example of artistic ecphrasis is the Homeric "Shield of Achilles" in the *Iliad*, to which Virgil responded with his shield of Aeneas. Yet Virgil also goes beyond his Homeric model by including further ecphrastic passages describing temples, palaces, relief sculptures, and the early topography of Rome. Virgil is responding to the increasing monumentalization of the city under Augustus, the transformation of Rome's visual culture to create an imperial capital city. Statius inherits the Virgilian vocabulary and interest in visual culture, not least because the Flavian emperors under whom he wrote manifested a renewed interest in urban monumentalization

and infrastructure. The Temple of Mars, the Palace of Sleep, and the Shrine of Clemency are all described in extended ecphrastic passages that illustrate how a building, its location, and artistic adornment belong to a broader program congruent with the qualities of the particular deity. Statian ecphrasis reflects the way in which Roman emperors since Augustus used public architecture, including temples and forums, to articulate the ideology of their regimes.

Statius's description of the necklace of Harmonia, insofar as it responds both to Homer's shield of Achilles and to the Virgilian shield of Aeneas, is a good example of how he uses ecphrastic description of a work of artisanship to define his poetic project. Ecphrasis of an art object, insofar as it describes the process of making and artistic representation, has been interpreted as a metapoetic device, i.e., a device that comments on the poet's own creation of the literary work. Homer, for example, describes Hephaestus, the divine artificer, in the act of making the shield. The shield of Aeneas appropriately represents the political history of Rome and its great men—a subject that is central to the poem's identity as epic of civilization. Apollonius, by focusing ecphrastic attention on the cloak of JASON given him by Hypsipyle, emphasizes his hero's status as lover and attractive young man, as opposed to indomitable warrior. Statius interestingly follows Apollonius in choosing an object associated with the world of women and adornment rather than the battlefield, yet his ecphrastic object is imbued with sinister signs, black magic, and destructive forces: gorgons' eyes, embers from the thunderbolt, serpents' crests. Hephaestus resembles a witch in his use of certain ingredients, and he is driven by malicious intent: Harmonia, daughter of Venus and Mars, receives the present as a bridal gift, and Hephaestus is taking revenge on their continuing adultery. He is driven not by love for his wife or positive eros, as in other cases, but by "Grief and Rage and Pain and Discord"—a fair sample of the emotions driving Statian epic. The object is also inherited, a curse passed from woman to woman, and its making goes back to the very origins of Thebes. Now in the hands of an Argive woman, once among the Thebans, it is a perfect physical embodiment of the two doomed cities. In the end, it will destroy Amphiaraus's family, sending him to war, bringing about the death of his wife, and the pollution of his son. Statius thus announces the dark principles of his poetics through an emblematic object.

A key question informing the epic narrative is the degree to which the politics of Thebes and Argos relate to Roman politics in the early empire. The *Aeneid*, while focusing on early legendary history, did not disguise its interest in the broader span of Roman history and especially recent history in the late republican and Augustan periods. The hero of Virgil's epic was the ancestor of Julius Caesar and thus of Augustus himself, and its subject was the creation of the Roman community in Italy. In writing such a poem, Virgil participates in the Roman tradition of political/martial epic about Roman history, a tradition that goes back to Ennius and Naevius. Lucan, who chose to write not only about history, but relatively recent history, and who removed the Olympian gods from his narrative, brought about an even more striking convergence of epic poetry and Roman history.

Statius, by contrast, does not write about a subject overtly connected with Roman history: His epic is both mythological and Greek. For the ancients, however, there was no hard and clear line between history and myth, and thus the world of the *Thebaid*, for all its apparent remoteness, is not totally dissociated from Roman historical themes. In Thebes, as well as Rome, there is contention over political supremacy, inheritance, and the problem of tyrannical rule. The political categories and terms that Statius uses—e.g., *patres* ("senators"/"elders")—are often anachronistic and distinctly Roman as opposed to Greek.

For the Romans, moreover, "war between brothers" was a common way of referring to civil war, and their myth of foundation—the slaying of Remus by Romulus—represents the first of many civil conflicts as an instance of discord between brothers. Statius also knowingly invites comparison in minor but telling details. The Argive exile Polynices at times recalls the exiled Trojan prince Aeneas, who similarly is destined to marry into a royal family, and who likewise ends his siege on a city by a one-to-one duel. The Thebans, for their part, are seen as descended from both Mars and Venus, since their child was Harmonia, wife of the Theban founder, Cadmus. In this respect, the Thebans are being made to resemble the Romans, descended from Venus through Aeneas and from Mars through Romulus. The Romans, who were apt to view violent episodes of discord in their own history as a manifestation of the gods' anger at their race, might have sympathized with the Thebans, and may have seen themselves reflected in them.

Readers of Statius may also be struck by the initial resemblance between Statius's and Lucan's central theme: civil war and the discord it embodies. Statius's significant literary inheritance from Lucan would thus only work to further underscore the *Roman* dimension of his Theban civil war narrative. Lucan wrote about the civil discord that preceded the establishment of the Augustan principate, and thus also the Julio-Claudian dynasty under which he lived. Statius wrote under the Flavians, whose regime had been preceded by a particularly unpleasant bout of civil war: In the year 69 C.E., after Nero's death, there was a succession of three short-lived emperors, who fought bloody and ultimately ineffectual battles for supremacy, sometimes in the very center of Rome. Vespasian managed to hold on to power in the wake of these violent skirmishes and, as an experienced general, made his way slowly to Rome before establishing a dynasty that would last nearly three decades. His two sons, first

Titus, then Domitian (under whom Statius wrote), succeeded him.

When we consider these political circumstances, Statius's choice of mythological subject—two brothers who enter into rivalry for power after their father's abdication and end up killing each other—is striking, if not provocative. There are even hints in the historical record of rivalry between Titus and his brother Domitian. While Statius is probably not intending to criticize the Flavian dynasty through some kind of implicit, coded narrative, he does bring to the fore tensions and ambiguities endemic to the system of imperial government, conditions that contributed to the crisis in 69 C.E. It is no doubt significant that the Flavian trio of father and two sons largely succeed where the Theban royal family failed, and thus may be seen to represent everything the house of Oedipus is *not*. Still, the possibility of renewed civil war must have remained in the back of many Romans' minds, even under the relatively stable regime of the Flavians. Such fears would not have been entirely ungrounded. Domitian, who became one of the most hated emperors in Roman history, was increasingly terrified of conspiracies, and he ended his reign by being assassinated.

The themes of tyrannical rule and the repression of free speech provide similar fodder for speculation without offering any explicit criticism of Domitian. The tyrant was a cliché of Roman philosophical writing and rhetorical exercises, and so we should not be surprised to see Eteocles accommodated to this role by Statius. He does not brook dissent and displays a savage anger when provoked. He has a tyrant's capacity for cruelty and openly threatens his critics. Yet despite the conventional nature of the tyrant's role, the resemblance between Eteocles' character and negative traits in Roman emperors as viewed by the Roman upper classes cannot be entirely accidental. We note, for example, a minor but significant theme of feigned sentiments and flattering speech that matches well with Tacitus's repre-

sentation of the relation between the emperor and the senate in the historical works he wrote under the Antonine emperors in the following generation.

Statius's Eteocles is a far more dominant and lonely figure than the Eteocles in Aeschylus's *Seven against Thebes*. In that play, he engages in a spirited debate with the Chorus and works out his strategy in open discussion with the messenger. Statius's representation of Eteocles' role as ruler can be read as responding to the shift toward a more authoritarian style of imperial role in this period. There is a further potential parallel with the figure of Jupiter. In court poetry under Domitian—primarily Statius's and Martial's—the emperor is straightforwardly put on the same plane as, or even made out to be superior to, Jove himself. Domitian was treated as a god during his own life, and not only that, as the supreme god. The Statian Jupiter perhaps not accidentally wields a degree of authority that seems to rule out any serious dissent from the outset. By comparison with the fierce struggle between Juno and Jupiter in the *Aeneid*, dissenting acts of other gods in the *Thebaid* are few, minor, and limited. Statius's Jupiter may be read, on this line of thought, as an idealized version of Flavian imperial authority.

An even more strikingly Roman and imperial scenario arises in the narrative of Creon's rule near the end of the epic. Creon, who spoke out as a voice of *libertas* ("freedom of speech") against the tyrannical Eteocles, appears in retrospect to have been calculatingly ambitious in his comments, as Eteocles himself suspected. He may well have wanted power for himself from the start, and in the event, he turns out to be a tyrant just as deplorable as his predecessor. Statius displays here a shrewd insight regarding the capacity of power, and the "imperial" system itself, to corrupt those who hold and aspire to power. Even more subtly, Statius demonstrates how a justifying ideology is fashioned to reinforce the ruler's position. In this instance, Menoeceus, Creon's son, is made into a kind of martyr figure symbolizing the piety and sacrifice of the ruler's family. While the Argives are allowed to lie unburied, Menoeceus is awarded a spectacular hero's funeral—an episode whose resemblance to the various public rituals and pageants involving members of the imperial family would not have gone unnoticed by Statius's readers. Creon cynically manipulates his son's memory and sacrifice to fortify his rule against criticism.

In the latter portion of Book 10, in which Statius represents Menoeceus's act of sacrifice, he intriguingly juxtaposes it with the hubristic assault of Capaneus. The parallels are conspicuous: Menoeceus kills himself and falls from the city walls as an act of piety, obedience to the gods, and self-sacrifice, to save the city of Thebes; Capaneus, in an attempt to destroy Thebes, ends up suicidally and impiously challenging Jupiter himself and, struck by his thunderbolt, falls from the walls to the ground. Statius does not allow us to remain content with this apparently lucid juxtaposition of piety and impiety, self-sacrifice and bloodthirsty aggression, however. Menoeceus's self-sacrifice ends up serving politically dubious ends, while Capaneus unexpectedly emerges as a hero. Even Jupiter seems to harbor a bemused admiration for his immensely spirited rage, and he is described by Statius, like Theseus, as "greatspirited" *(magnanimus)*. Statius's treatment of questions of authority, rebellion, and the ideology of imperial rule offers no easy dichotomies or moral lessons, and in that sense, he follows in the tradition of Virgilian ambiguity and complexity of political vision. He offers a depiction of authoritarian rule that could be read as implicitly critical of the Roman imperial system, although we do not know to what extent it can be applied to any particular emperor. Statius's Jupiter is, on the one hand, supremely powerful and authoritative and, at the same time, the author of destruction and mayhem.

The ending of the epic should logically come with the mutual slaying of the two brothers. Virgil's *Aeneid* ended in Book 12 with the duel between Aeneas and Turnus. Statius provocatively offers his own closural duel, but instead of depicting a slaying motivated by a sense of justice and duty toward a slain comrade by the founder of the future Roman race, he depicts two brothers killing each other in a grim, impious duel that the gods themselves refuse to watch, and that ends only in a tragic sense of defilement and loss. Aeneas, defeating his political rival and thus paving the way for the fusion of the two peoples, has truly come into his own as Achillean warrior and civilization founder. Statius's closural duel, by contrast, is not *for* anything. Yet neither does it coincide with the actual close of the epic. The penultimate, as opposed to final, position of the duel is signified by its placement in Book 11, not Book 12, as in the *Aeneid*. The duel is the logical culmination of the plot, yet that plot continues with what might be called a supplemental phase. Here, Statius draws special attention to his mythography and his choices in ordering his Theban narrative. In Sophocles' *Antigone*, Creon, who rules Thebes after the death of the two brothers, condemns Antigone to death, and her death is followed by that of his own son Haemon. Here, however, Statius follows a version in which Theseus slays Creon while Antigone and Haemon remain alive at the end of the poem (compare Theseus's role as guarantor of burial rites in Euripides' Suppliants.) Statius thus brings in Theseus as a kind of deus ex machina, who effectively saves Antigone and Argia, while restoring proper rites for the dead.

The ending is unusually positive after an epic that had few bright spots. Theseus comes off as a heroic figure in a way that none of the epic's other main characters does. The "good" ending of the poem may point gently toward a positive Flavian ending to the civil conflict of 69 C.E. Theseus, a relatively untainted hero, is welcomed as a guest in a city defiled and wracked by civil war. Even as he conquers, he installs a restored set of moral values. We might compare Vespasian, a figure who similarly comes from abroad, as an experienced general, to a city tainted by civil conflict, and restores order and piety: The end of civil war, in both Theban and Roman terms, may be the beginning of a positive new phase in history. Still, the Theban story, in any case, is not unequivocally positive, and the epic's close is tantalizingly open-ended. Just as Statius begins his poem with deliberation as to where to start (since there are many possible beginning points for the story of Thebes), so also at the end he engages in a highly conspicuous *praeteritio* ("passing over"): He will not tell of the funerals that followed and their diverse episodes. Nor do we hear the fate of the city and the surviving characters. Following in Virgil's footsteps, Statius ends his epic with a new beginning and many still unanswered questions.

Theia   A Titan, the offspring of Gaia (Earth) and Uranus (Heaven). Sister of Iapetus, Hyperion, Coeus, Crius, Cronus, Mnemosyne, Oceanus, Phoebe, Rhea, Tethys, and Themis. Classical sources are Apollodorus's Library (1.1.3, 1.2.2) and Hesiod's Theogony (233–239, 265–269). Neither Diodorus Siculus's Library of History nor Hyginus's Fabulae lists Theia as one of the Titans: the total number of Titans in their genealogies is six male and five female. Theia does appear, however, in the genealogies of Apollodorus and Hesiod. Theia married her brother Hyperion, and their offspring are Eos (Dawn), Helios (Sun), and Selene (Moon). Though Theia appears in the genealogies of Hesiod, she does not otherwise appear in mythology or cult practice.

Themis   A Titan personifying concepts of Justice and Law. Daughter of Gaia (Earth) and Uranus (Heaven). Sister of Coeus, Crius, Cronus, Iapetus, Hyperion, Mnemosyne, Oceanus, Phoebe, Rhea, Tethys, and Theia. Classical sources are the *Homeric Hymn to Apollo* (12.3–5), Apollodorus's Library (1.1.3, 1.3.1, 1.4.1, 3.13.5), Diodorus Siculus's Library of History (5.66), Hesiod's Theogony (132–136, 901–906), Homer's Odyssey (2.68–69), Hyginus's Fabulae (Theogony 3.25), and Ovid's Metamorphoses (1.321, 379; 4.643; 9.403, 418). Themis was the second Titan wife of Zeus (after Metis) and with him she produced the Horae (Seasons), the Fates (Atropos, Clotho, and Lachesis), as well as Order, Peace, and Justice. The *Homeric Hymn to Apollo* links her particularly to Apollo as an oracular deity.

Theocritus (fl. third century b.c.e.)   A poet of the third century b.c.e. Very little is known of his life. He almost certainly came from Sicily but also seems to have spent some time writing in the Ptolemaic court at Alexandria. Theocritus is the inventor of the pastoral genre. His *Idylls* are poems written in the meter of epic, the dactylic hexameter, yet are much shorter than any epic and profoundly different in subject matter and style. His typical form is the mimetic dialogue. We see the pastoral figures in dialogue with each other, and from these dialogues, gain glimpses of their rural existence. Theocritus was a highly sophisticated poet who subscribed to the Alexandrian aesthetic of intricately learned, highly crafted poetry for educated readers. Yet, he often chooses to represent very humble figures in the midst of ordinary circumstances, expressing naive sentiments with little sophistication. This contrast between aesthetic sophistication and "primitive" subject matter is central to Theocritus's poetic project: Theocritean pastoral's "rustic chic" only serves to highlight further the elegant, learned dimension of the poetry.

Theocritus is a poet extremely sensitive to place, and many of his poems are set in specific locations throughout the Mediterranean. While he favors Sicily to some extent, Theocritus does not use any one location exclusively but evokes a broader, more varied concept of Greekness. In this regard, he is an eminently Hellenistic poet: Greek culture, for Theocritus, is not rooted in a particular place and its traditions. Rather, with the aid of a deep reservoir of erudition, he evokes different Greek locations, traditions, rites, and dialects throughout the Hellenic world. Nor are all his locations rural. Some of the surviving idylls occur in urban settings, including Ptolemaic Alexandria. Here, too, the characters are humble, the observations homely and naive, and the literary form dialogue. Theocritus was later associated with an exclusively rural milieu, but his own topographical orientation was more complex.

The Theocritean poems that have played a central role in creating the Western concept of pastoral are dialogues among humble herdsmen/singers who, in their spare time, exchange observations, casual conversation, anecdotes, and songs on various subjects. Music, including song, is an essential feature of the pastoral world, and thus pastoral is a richly self-reflexive poetic genre, which includes within its own mimetic fiction the representation of the contexts and mechanisms of poetic production, circulation, and criticism. Unlike epic, the "heroes" of pastoral are not major mythic figures but generic herdsmen who inhabit an idealized countryside. Pastoral is in many ways a counter-epic genre: Its very premise—the tranquil life of simple herdsmen in the countryside—lies at the opposite extreme from epic warfare and the pursuit of martial glory.

Theocritean pastoral elaborates certain myths central to its conception as a poetic genre. In Theocritus 1, one of the herdsmen/singers tells the story of Daphnis, who takes on the role of an archetypal pastoral herdsman. Daphnis is a shadowy mythological figure, but the stories about him concern love and his status as pastoral singer and/or subject of pastoral song. He is sometimes the son of HERMES, and his name associates him with the laurel (*daphne*). In one version, he is loved by a nymph (variously named), but a princess gets him drunk and has sex with him. The nymph then blinds or even kills him. In Theocritus's version, however, the less idealizing elements in the myth have been edited and transformed. Daphnis now resembles Hippolytus: Although loved passionately by a nymph, he resists APHRODITE and chooses to perish rather than give in to the antagonizing goddess. Daphnis thus becomes an originating hero of the pastoral myth, a semidivine herdsman who establishes the pastoral landscape as a space of tranquility and refuge from desire. Daphnis, not accidentally, refers to the myth of Adonis—another mythic figure with pastoral associations, a connection with Aphrodite, and a tragic demise. Daphnis is hardly an epic hero. His central act is to die by mysteriously melting into a river.

Theocritus does not relate a multitude of myths, but the mythological stories that he does tell are chosen with exquisite care. Like Apollonius of Rhodes, he relates the story of HYLAS, the beautiful youth stolen away from HERACLES by water nymphs. The sylvan setting of this story and Hylas's elegant idyll of desire and disappearance integrate well with Theocritus's pastoral, counter-heroic aesthetic. The brutish strength of Heracles will not be the main focus here. Perhaps the most explicitly anti-epic mythological narrative in Theocritus is his versions of the love songs of the CYCLOPS POLYPHEMUS. In Theocritus (7, 11), it is not the Odyssean Polyphemus who makes an appearance—the repulsively violent and brutish eater of Odysseus's men—but Polyphemus in his earlier, lesser known guise as Sicilian herdsman/singer desperately in love with the sea nymph GALATEA. Theocritus thus lays claim to a mythological figure who sustains associations with his place of origin (Sicily), his genre (pastoral), and its central themes: the naive pastoral idyll and the intrusion of desire. Like Apollonius, Theocritus cunningly achieves chronological priority over Homer, reaching back into the pre-Homeric mythological past. To put pastoral on the literary map, Theocritus transforms elements of the mythic tradition and makes them his own.

Theogony HESIOD (ca. eighth–seventh century B.C.E.) Hesiod wrote in the eighth or possibly seventh century B.C.E., around the time of Homer. He was a native of the town of Askra. Unlike Homer, Hesiod reveals aspects of his life and personality in the first person. He has a brother, Perses, with whom he had a dispute over inheritance, and he won a prize at a poetry contest at a festival. Hesiod's two major works extant are *Theogony* and WORKS AND DAYS. In the *Theogony*, Hesiod writes about the birth of the gods and, in a broader sense, about the origination of the divine order prevailing in his time, in which the Olympians were preeminent and ZEUS was king of the gods.

Poetry itself, and Hesiod's role as singer, enjoy an important place in this order of things. Hesiod, like Homer, begins his poem by invoking and stressing his own connection with the divine, namely, the MUSES who inspire him. The Muses' origins are of some significance, since they are the daughters of Zeus through MNEMOSYNE (Memory). They sing for Zeus on Olympus, and the content of their song mirrors with some precision the content of Hesiod's *Theogony*: the origins of the gods, giants, and men, and of Zeus's ascendancy. They also infuse earthly rulers with the power of persuasion and can dispel sorrows. By a marked irony, the daughters of "Memory," Hesiod observes, are able to bring "forgetfulness" of cares to humankind.

In a passage that would inspire imitation and emulation in later poets, Hesiod recalls how the Muses filled him with inspiration and gave him song. While he was tending sheep on Mount Helicon, the Muses addressed him, breathed inspiration into him, and gave him a staff. They are the divine patrons of his song, and while he is to sing of the gods in general, he is to offer the Muses special honor, singing of them first and last. It is surely significant that both Hesiod and Homer, writing roughly in the same period, place great emphasis on their indebtedness to the Muses for their special knowledge as poets and for their poetic gift.

The characterization of the Muses in Hesiod, however, is richer and more nuanced than in Homer. The Hesiodic Muses are at once delightful, generous, and harshly intimidating (they refer to shepherds such as Hesiod as "mere bellies"); they make false things seem true, yet they also, sometimes, tell the truth. Hesiod thus begins his poem with an intriguingly ambiguous vision of his inspiring deities.

At this point, the account of the gods' origins itself commences: first Chaos (more literally "Chasm" or "yawning gap"), then Earth (GAIA), EROS, and Night (NYX). Earth brought forth URANUS (sky/heaven). Hesiod is presenting the formation of the basic constituents of reality and the universe. Earth and Uranus then go on to bring forth further deities through sexual intercourse. Throughout the poem, Hesiod continues to unravel the tangled story of a multitude of genealogical connections among a vast multitude of gods, goddesses, giants, monsters, water deities, divine personifications, heroes, and so on. Some sections are close to being a pure catalog of names and acts of conception. It is easy to become overwhelmed by the intricate texture of genealogical knowledge that Hesiod's poem weaves, but it is also important to remember the crucial importance of the information contained in the poem for his audience. Through his privileged access to the Muses, the singer Hesiod is able to reveal the emergence of the divine order and the vast family of the gods in their myriad interconnections. Just as Homer, through the power of the Muse, is able to tell the stories of heroes who lived in the distant past, Hesiod is able to narrate the beginnings of the universe. The breadth of vision is impressive: We move, by degrees, from the primeval "gaping" of Chaos to the family relations of gods and, finally, to mortal heroes.

Nor is Hesiod's account of genealogy unstructured in thematic and narrative terms. The broader trajectory of the poem represents the violent succession of sky gods and ultimate ascendancy of Zeus. Uranus, to check the threat of a son stronger than him, buries his children within the earth, i.e., keeps them imprisoned within Gaia's womb so they cannot emerge. Gaia, in great pain, enlists the help of her son Cronus, who castrates his father when he comes to have intercourse with Gaia. One striking consequence of this act is the birth of APHRODITE from the foam that rises up in the sea around the discarded genitals of Uranus. Cronus, in turn, attempts to profit from his father's example. He does not entrust his children to Gaia (the consequences were unpleasant for Uranus) but swallows them himself. Gaia once again comes up with a counter-scheme: Zeus is spirited away to Crete, where he is allowed to grow into strength, while a stone is deposited in Cronus's stomach instead.

The female principle in Hesiodic myth is often destructive and subversive in its effects. Gaia is constantly bringing forth from her womb new threats with the potential to destabilize the current power structure. She is the mother of monsters and giants. Her capacity for reproduction and "feminine" cunning are a constant source of danger for the sky gods whom she also produces. Hesiod thus thematizes the tension between male and female, sky and earth, in his account of the origins of the divine order and of our world.

In the earlier stages of this succession, Gaia remains effective and dangerous as a political player. Zeus, however, ultimately establishes his reign as one in which the male sky god is permanently in control. A key question that Hesiod must answer is how Zeus stabilized his regime—what made him successful where Cronus and Uranus were not. One challenge comes from PROMETHEUS, the son of IAPETUS, who acts as patron of humankind in his attempts to deceive Zeus. Prometheus hides good flesh in unattractive tripe and bones and misleads Zeus into choosing the wrong portion at Mekone. This story offers an origins myth of Greek sacrifice, explaining why the gods get the less valuable parts of the animal, while humans receive the edible portion. Even in this case, Hesiod

is unwilling to admit that Zeus was truly deceived. To avoid imputing such a weakness to Zeus, he resorts to the problematic idea that Zeus saw through Prometheus's deception and also foresaw the punishment he would inflict on mortals as a result (the removal of fire). He knew that he was choosing the inferior portion, justifying in advance the punishment he would later inflict.

For Hesiod, Zeus is both physically powerful and cunning, and Prometheus's story demonstrates how Zeus gets the best of a challenger. When Prometheus subsequently steals fire in a fennel stalk, Zeus has an answer: He inflicts another punishment on mankind in the form of woman. This first woman, not named here but called Pandora ("all-gifted") in *Works and Days*, presents a further example of the Hesiodic mistrust of the female: Except in rare cases, a woman will wear down a man's resources while contributing nothing herself, yet men need women, without whom they cannot generate an heir. The themes of male and female, sex and reproduction, have now been transposed to the human sphere, yet it is by no means clear that mortal men can maintain mastery over the feminine element in the way that the god Zeus has succeeded in doing.

Even HERACLES' rescue of Prometheus, narrated proleptically at the beginning of the entire passage, is purposely brought about by Zeus. Though angry at Prometheus, he wishes his son Heracles to obtain glory. Zeus's will is behind everything. The entire passage ends with an explicit declaration of the moral of the story: It is impossible to evade Zeus, whose will has the force of necessity. Subsequent sections in the poem contribute to confirm this idea: The defeat of the TITANS—a battle on a truly cosmic scale—removes Zeus's main remaining rivals from the field and shows how he deploys the brute force of the HUNDRED-HANDED ONES when he needs them—a diplomatic coup. Finally, Gaia brings forth one more monstrous threat, TYPHOEUS, who is almost a caricature of an earthborn monster. He has a multitude of serpents' heads that make the sounds of a bull, a lion, and a dog in alternation. Zeus overwhelms him with the power of his thunderbolt, and Typhoeus is reduced to living on as the source of occasionally destructive storm winds. Zeus's rivals in general are relegated to the edges of the world in the isolated prison compound of TARTARUS.

At length even Gaia admits Zeus's supremacy, and at her suggestion, he is made king of the gods. His first act as king is to wed, and subsequently ingest, METIS, whose name means "cunning" or "practical intelligence." Zeus thus absorbs into himself the subversive power of the feminine and of cunning—ideas that are here closely associated—and the outcome is that their offspring ATHENA is born from his own head. Gaia and Uranus had predicted that the second child of Zeus and Metis after Athena would be a son who would challenge Zeus's rule. Zeus thus heads off this threat and at the same time produces a female child loyal to himself. In Aeschylus's *EUMENIDES*, Athena supports her father and the male side in general. Zeus's solution to the problem of succession thus involves a neutralization of the subversive effects of women and of cunning (Metis). The episode, moreover, is linked thematically with the Prometheus episode: Prometheus, whose name is interpreted as meaning "fore-thinker," from the same root as *metis* ("cunning"), is dangerous chiefly because of his intelligence. Zeus, however, outmaneuvers him, just as he absorbs the potential threat of Metis.

The remainder of the poem recounts Zeus's other marriages and liaisons (THEMIS, DEMETER, HERA, LETO, MAIA, SEMELE) and the gods born from these unions (PERSEPHONE, APOLLO, ARTEMIS, ARES, and HERMES, among others). To these, Hesiod adds Athena born from Zeus's own head, and HEPHAESTUS, produced by Hera on her own without Zeus's help. Significantly, he does not fail to mention Mnemosyne, and Zeus's children by her, the Muses, with whom the poem began. Hesiod then moves on to heroes born from gods, paying special atten-

tion to Heracles, who marries HEBE. After he bids the Olympian gods farewell, he calls upon the Muses to sing of the unions of goddesses with mortal men and the children of those unions: Ploutos, Geryon, Memnon. Finally, he summarizes the story of JASON and the births of ACHILLES, AENEAS, and Nausithous (the child of CALYPSO and ODYSSEUS). Hesiod does not develop longer narratives from any of these figures, and thus the closing portion of his poem is largely a catalog of heroes and the circumstances of their begetting. The lines with which our text ends evidently serve as a transition to Hesiod's *Catalog of Women*, which is not extant. (The poem that does survive under this title is not considered to be Hesiod's.) Hesiod has taken us from the origins of the universe and the gods to the birth of heroes and the human world. The *Theogony* is at times baffling for modern readers, who might expect more narrative sweep and structure, yet we must attempt to appreciate its great power within an ancient context. Hesiod's divinely inspired poetry affords access to the realm of the divine and the sequence of begettings that form the basis of the world that we inhabit and know.

Theseus A famous Athenian hero. Son of either POSEIDON or AEGEUS (king of Athens) and Aethra. Theseus is a descendant of Erectheus and PELOPS. Classical sources are Apollodorus's *LIBRARY* (1.8.2, 2.6.3, 3.10.7, 3.15.6, Epitome 1.24), Diodorus Siculus's *LIBRARY OF HISTORY* (4.16, 4.28, 4.59–63), Euripides' *HIPPOLYTUS*, Homer's *ODYSSEY* (11.321–325, 631) and *ILIAD* (1.262–265), Hyginus's *Fabulae* (37–38, 42–43, 47, 79), Ovid's *HEROIDES* (4, 10) and *METAMORPHOSES* (7.404–452, 8.155–182), Pausanias's *Description of Greece* (1.17.2–6, 1.22.5, 1.27.7–10, 2.33.1, 10.28.9), Plutarch's *Life of Theseus*, and Virgil's *AENEID* (6.617–618). Theseus first loved ARIADNE and later married PHAEDRA, both daughters of King MINOS of Crete and PASIPHAE. Two sons, Acamas and Demaphon, were born to Theseus and

Phaedra. Theseus's relationship with the Amazon ANTIOPE (or Hippolyta) produced a son, HIPPOLYTUS. Theseus was known as clearheaded, astute, strong, brave, and a fierce warrior. He is credited with the unification of Attic territory, the establishment of Athens as its capital, and the introduction of key Athenian political institutions.

In some sources, Poseidon is said to be Theseus's father, which lends the hero semi-divine status, but his paternity is more commonly ascribed to Aegeus. Aegeus had traveled to Delphi to consult the Oracle on the subject of his future heirs. The prophecy warned him not to beget a child before his return home to Athens. He misunderstood the prophecy and fathered Theseus on Aethra, the daughter of Pittheus, king of Troezen. Before he returned home, and suspecting that Aethra was pregnant with his child, Aegeus hid a sword and shoes under a rock for the child to recover. He asked Aethra to send his son to him once he was capable of lifting the stone concealing the sword and shoes. When Theseus reached young manhood, he took the tokens left by Aegeus and set off for Athens to claim his birthright.

While he was making his way to Athens, Theseus sought to emulate Heracles in exploits similar to those he had performed in the course of the Twelve Labors. Theseus subdued a series of villains. These included Corynetes, who killed with a club; Sinis, who tore his victims apart by tying their arms to two pine boughs bent together then loosened; Sceiron, who forced his victims to wash his feet in a precarious spot overlooking the sea, then kicked them down the cliff to their death; Cercyon, who killed whomever he defeated in a wrestling contest. The most infamous of these villains was Procrustes. Procrustes' gruesome technique of killing his victims—forcing them to lie on a bed and cutting off those parts that did not fit within its confines or, alternately, stretching them to fit the bed—was applied to Procrustes himself by Theseus. (From this villain originates the concept of a Procrustean principle,

Theseus Fighting the Minotaur. *Detail from Kylix, ca. 430 B.C.E. (Museo Arqueológico Nacional de España, Madrid)*

one in which conformity is achieved by violent and indiscriminate methods.) In addition, Theseus slew the Crommyonian sow, an enormous wild sow that had killed many people. Before arriving at Athens, Theseus was purified of the blood he had shed in the course of these early adventures, and he had also become a father (by rape) of a son, Melanippus, by Perigune, daughter of Sinis.

In the intervening years, Aegeus had married MEDEA. She saw Theseus as a threat to her own children's position in the household. She first persuaded Aegeus to send Theseus to confront the Marathonian bull. This was the bull that Poseidon had given to King Minos of Crete and that sired the MINOTAUR on Minos's queen, Pasiphae. Heracles had brought it from Crete and set it free, but it was now wreaking havoc in Marathon. Theseus killed the bull, sacrificed it to APOLLO, and returned triumphant to Athens. Medea then attempted to poison Theseus, but when Aegeus discovered Medea's plot, he drove her out of Athens. Aegeus did not recognize his son until he saw Theseus's sword, the token that proved his ancestry. Aegeus officially recognized Theseus and appointed him his successor, thereby angering the sons of Pallas, who had hoped to succeed him. The Pallantidae laid an ambush for Theseus, but he survived the attack.

Theseus is perhaps most famous for his adventure with the Minotaur, the half-man, half-bull monster whose sire he had killed in Marathon. Every year, Athens had to send seven young men and seven young women as tribute to Crete, to be sacrificed to the Minotaur in its lair, the tortuous labyrinth that DAEDALUS had constructed for it. Theseus volunteered to be one of the sacrificial victims so that he could kill the monster. MINOS's daughter Ariadne fell in love with Theseus and gave him a ball of string. Theseus used the string to lay a trail he followed out of the daunting labyrinth, once he had located and killed the Minotaur. Theseus brought Ariadne with him when he left Crete, but he later abandoned her on the island of Naxos (accounts vary as to the reasons for his abandonment). In some versions of the story, Theseus and Ariadne were together long enough to have had children. Ovid's *Heroides* features a lament by Ariadne, who, awakening, finds herself abandoned on Naxos and watches in anguish as the sails of his ship disappear from sight. She was later rescued by DIONYSUS, who carried her away from Naxos to be his companion.

Aegeus had asked Theseus to hang a white sail as a sign that Theseus had survived his adventures in Crete. Theseus neglected to hang the correct sail because he had forgotten the prearranged signal. When Theseus's ships were sighted without the white sail, Aegeus assumed the worst and, in grief, threw himself into the sea, which was afterward known as the Aegean Sea in his honor.

Theseus assumed the throne of Athens and married Phaedra, Minos's daughter and Ariadne's sister. In Apollodorus's account, the Amazonian Antiope, with whom Theseus had fathered Hippolytus, threatened the wedding celebration but was killed before she could make good her threat. We learn from another version of his life that Theseus had captured Antiope, thus provoking an Amazonomachy (battle with the Amazons).

Theseus took part in other adventures as well. He joined in the Calydonian Boar hunt led by MELEAGER. King Oeneus of Calydon neglected to perform a sacrifice to ARTEMIS following the harvest, and as a consequence, the goddess sent a wild boar to ravage the country. Meleager gathered a group of hunters who included ATALANTA, the DIOSCURI, Jason, Phoenix, TELAMON, and Theseus, with his best friend PIRITHOUS.

Theseus also took part in the Centauromachy (battle with the CENTAURS). Pirithous, king of Lapiths in Thessaly, had graciously invited the centaurs to his wedding with Hippodame. During the wedding feast, the centaurs drank wine and became unruly. The centaur Eurytus attempted to carry off the bride and was killed by Theseus. This sparked the battle between the Lapiths and the centaurs, which Ovid depicted in the *Metamorphoses* as a gruesome, violent struggle that ended in the defeat of the centaurs.

During a period of exile from Athens, Theseus came to live in Troezen, near Athens, with his family. It was during this time, when Hippolytus was a young man, that Phaedra became enamored of him. As a follower of Artemis, Hippolytus rebuffed her chastely. Sources differ as to what followed. In some, a scorned Phaedra told Theseus that Hippolytus had attempted to seduce her. Theseus was unsure whom to believe and sent for Hippolytus, who succumbed to an accident while driving his chariot to meet his father. An alternate account sees Theseus convinced of his son's guilt and asking Poseidon to kill Hippolytus; Poseidon sent a bull that caused the chariot accident in which Hippolytus died. Out of guilt Phaedra hanged herself.

After Phaedra's death, Pirithous and Theseus agreed to help each other abduct brides worthy of their lineage. Together they kidnapped HELEN, who was at the time very young, as a bride for Theseus, and then descended to HADES to kidnap Pirithous's desired bride, PERSEPHONE. The plot was foiled, and the two remained trapped in Hades until Heracles rescued them. In some accounts, it was only Theseus who returned to his life above ground. In the meantime, Helen's brothers, Castor and Polydeuces (the Dioscuri) rescued Helen from Theseus and, in retaliation, abducted his mother, Aethra.

Theseus returned to Athens after his rescue from Hades, but he found that he had become the object of hostility for various political groups. He left Athens in despair, sent his children away from the city, found refuge on the island of Scyros, and there died, either accidentally, as a result of a fall down the steep cliffs of Sycros, or because he was murdered by Lycomedes, the local king. His remains were eventually brought back to Athens for burial.

In literature, the myth of Theseus provided the inspiration for Giovanni Boccaccio's *Teseida* of ca. 1340. In visual representation, the adventures of Theseus, either as a cycle or in isolated incidents, were frequently depicted in Attic art, especially in vase painting. An example is an Attic red-figure cup from ca. 480 B.C.E. (Louvre, Paris) showing Theseus's adventures with Procrustes, Sinis, and the Crommyonian sow. His defeat of the Minotaur, perhaps the most popular visual theme, is depicted on the François Vase of 570 B.C.E. (Archaeological Museum, Florence), where he appears as a youthful and powerful nude figure. Athena is present in an image showing Theseus defeating the Minotaur, on the tondo of an Attic red-figure kylix, ca. 430 B.C.E. (Museo Arqueológico Nacional de España, Madrid). A postclassical treatment of the myths is by Paolo Uccello, *Episodes from the Myth of Theseus* from ca. 1460 (Seattle Art Museum, Seattle).

Thetis A sea nymph brought up by HERA. Daughter of Nereus. Wife of PELEUS, and mother of ACHILLES. Classical sources are Aeschylus's *PROMETHEUS BOUND* (767), Apollodorus's *LIBRARY* (1.2.7, 1.3.5, 1.9.25, 3.5.1, 3.13.5–8, Epitome 3.29, 6.5, 6.12), Catullus's poem 64, Euripides' *ANDROMACHE* (12.31ff), Hesiod's *THEOGONY* (1,003–1,007), Homer's *ILIAD* (1.348–430, 493–533; 9.410–416; 18.35–147; 18.369–19.39; 24.74–142), Hyginus's *Fabulae* (54, 96, 106), Pindar's *Isthmian Odes* (8.26–47) and *Nemean Odes* (4.62–68), Ovid's *METAMORPHOSES* (11.217–269), and Statius's *ACHILLEID*. According to Pindar *Isthmian* 8 and the *Prometheus Bound*, Thetis was destined to bear a child greater than his father, and since ZEUS and POSEIDON were courting her, it was deemed prudent to marry her to the mortal Peleus. The great warrior Achilles was their son. She is said to have left Peleus after he interfered with her attempt to make Achilles immortal, although at the end of Euripides' *Andromache*, she returns to Peleus and makes him immortal. In HOMER'S *Iliad*, Thetis pleads on the angry Achilles' behalf to Zeus, persuading Zeus to turn against the Greeks to intensify the Greeks' need for Achilles and magnify his prestige. She also persuades HEPHAESTUS to make new armor for Achilles' after PATROCLUS's death and conveys to Achilles the gods' command to give back HECTOR's body.

Thucydides (second half of the fifth century B.C.E.) The Greek historian Thucydides was born between 460 and 455 B.C.E. and died ca. 400 B.C.E.. Thucydides was a member of the Athenian upper class and was a general during the Peloponnesian War in 424 B.C.E. He was not able to arrive early enough to defend Amphipolis against the Spartan general Brasidas and was exiled. Thucydides fits the pattern of the statesman sidelined from active participation in public life, who then turns to history. In Rome, the historian Sallust is an example of a similar pattern. Thucydides wrote the *History of the Peloponnesian War* between Athens and Sparta, which, however, remained incomplete at his death. Thucydides stresses the seriousness of his concern for fact, detail, chronology, and the accuracy of his research: He strives to base his account on autopsy, documents, and interviews. Thucydides has often been compared favorably with HERODOTUS, who relies a great deal on oral tradition and legend. The contrast between the two, however, may be overstated, and now Herodotus is less often criticized. Thucydides himself, in the opening portion of his history, examines Homer's account of the Trojan War in order to prove his point that the Peloponnesian War was greater than previous conflicts.

Thyestes Son of PELOPS and Hippodamia. Twin brother of ATREUS. Father of AEGISTHUS and Pelopia.

Tibullus (ca. 50 B.C.E.–19 B.C.E.) The Roman poet Tibullus was born between 55 and 48 B.C.E.; he died in 19 B.C.E. Among the poets of his generation, Tibullus is distinctive in having the Roman aristocrat M. Valerius Messalla Corvinus, and not Maecenas, the close associate of the emperor Augustus, as his patron. He makes no direct mention of Augustus in his poetry, nor, however, is there any sign that he belongs to a dissident or anti-Augustan set. The works of Tibullus came down to us in a collection of three books of poetry called the Tibullan corpus. Only the first two books are by Tibullus; the third book is composed of poems written by various members of Messalla's circle. Tibullus, like Propertius, Cornelius Gallus, and OVID, was an elegiac love poet. His poetic mistress in the first book of elegies is called Delia, in accordance with a tradition that names mistresses after cult titles of APOLLO; in the second book, his mistress has become the more all-absorbing and destructive Nemesis. Tibullus, unlike his fellow Augustan elegists Propertius and Ovid, also wrote love poems to boys, specifically, a boy named Marathus. Tibullus is also unusual in combining love as the main occupation and focus of his life with military service under Messalla and the role of country gentleman and farmer.

Love poets generally occupy an urban milieu; Tibullus provocatively combines the tranquility of the countryside with Love's perpetual worries and emotional turbulence. By comparison with Ovid and Propertius, Tibullus makes very few references to mythology. In one notable exception, however, he refers to the myth of Apollo and Admetus: The myth refers to Apollo's labors as guardian of Admetus's flocks. Tibullus, who accommodates poetry and the countryside, love and farming, in his own poetry, makes much of the contrast between the refined lover poet Apollo and his rustic surroundings.

Tiresias The famous seer of Thebes. Classical sources are Apollodorus's *LIBRARY* (2.4.8, 3.6.7, 3.7.3–4), Euripides' *BACCHAE* and *PHOENICIAN WOMEN*, Homer's *ODYSSEY* (10.490–495, 11.84–151), Ovid's *METAMORPHOSES* (3.316–338), and Sophocles' *ANTIGONE* and *OEDIPUS THE KING*. The stories about how Tiresias became blind and received his gift of prophecy vary. In one version, he was blinded because he saw Athena nude while she was bathing, but at the request of his mother, Chariclo, a nymph favored by Athena, he received the gift of prophecy in compensation for his loss of sight. In another version, Tiresias saw two snakes copulating, and when he wounded them, or separated them, or killed the female snake, he was turned into a woman. Later, when he saw two snakes copulating again, he was turned back into a man. Zeus and Hera, when they were disputing whether men or women had greater pleasure from intercourse, referred the question to Tiresias, since he had experience of both roles. He replied that women's pleasure was much greater, thereby angering Hera, who deprived him of his sight. Zeus, in compensation, gave him the gift of prophecy and an exceptionally long life. (He is supposed to have lived seven generations, starting from the time of Cadmus.) Tiresias appears frequently in Greek tragedy, especially in the plays of Sophocles. His role in Sophocles' *Oedipus the King* is crucial. In general, Tiresias is the morally stringent purveyor of a truth those in power may not wish to accept, although his very frequent appearances in tragedy begin to become a cliché, which Euripides exploits. (For example, note his somewhat less than respectable appearance in the *Bacchae*, or his nearly comic weariness and irritation in *Phoenician Women*.) When Odysseus, in Book 11 of Homer's *Odyssey*, travels to the underworld, he seeks, above all, to speak with the spirit of Tiresias, who offers prophecies and instructions regarding the remainder of his journey home and the outcome of his life.

Tisiphone   See Furies.

Titanomachy   See Titans.

Titans   A generation of deities preceding the Olympian gods. The classical sources are Apollodorus's Library (1.1.2–1.2.5), Hesiod's Theogony (132–138, 207–210, 389–396, 617–735, 807–814), and Homer's Iliad (14.277–279, 15.224–225). The Titans were the offspring of Gaia (Earth) and Uranus (Heaven) and, according to the genealogy given in the *Theogony*, numbered 12: six male and six female: Coeus, Crius, Cronus, Iapetus, Hyperion, Mnemosyne, Oceanos, Phoebe, Rhea, Tethys, Theia, and Themis. Some sources include Metis in the list of Titans, while others classify her as Oceanid. Uranus and Gaia also produced the Hundred-Handed Ones and the Cyclopes. Uranus prevented the birth of his children, keeping them inside Gaia. Cronus, encouraged by Gaia, castrated his father with a flint (or adamant) sickle, liberated his brothers and sisters, and succeeded Uranus. Cronus swallowed his children by Rhea, but Zeus, with Rhea's help, escaped his fate and dethroned Cronus (see Theogony). Following the Titanomachy, a 10-year battle for supremacy between Titans and the Olympian gods, the Titans were defeated and consigned to Tartarus, which lies at the extremity of Hades

and is surrounded by a bronze fence with bronze gate, where they were guarded by the Hundred-Handed Ones. Some of the Titans were personifications of elements such as the sun (Hyperion) and the sea (Oceanus) or abstract concepts such as memory (Mnemosyne) and law (Themis); these functions were later identified with various Olympian gods. Titans such as Coeus, Crius, Phoebe, Theia, and Tethys appear in the genealogies of Hesiod but are not associated with other myths or cult practice. In Hesiod, Helios rode through the sky in a horse-drawn chariot, bringing the light of day with him—an image later applied to Apollo. Hyperion married his sister Theia, and their children were Eos, Helios, and Selene. Tethys married her brother Oceanus, and their offspring were the 3,000 Oceanids (sea nymphs) and the major rivers. Iapetus married Klymene (an Oceanid); their offspring were Atlas, Epimetheus, Menoetius, and Prometheus. Cronus wed his sister Rhea, with whom he produced the generation of Olympian gods: Demeter, Hades, Hera, Hestia, Poseidon, and Zeus. Phoebe married her brother Coeus, and their daughters were Asteria (mother of Hecate) and Leto (mother of Apollo and Artemis by Zeus). Mnemosyne bore Zeus the Muses, and Themis bore him the Horae (Seasons) and the Fates (Atropos, Clotho, and Lachesis), as well as Order, Peace, and Justice.

Tithonus   See Eos (Aurora); Sappho.

Tityus   (Tityos)   Son of either Gaia or Elara and Zeus. Tityus is the father of Europa (a consort of Zeus). Classical sources are Apollonius of Rhodes's Voyage of the Argonauts (1.761), Homer's Odyssey (11.576–581), Hyginus's *Fabulae* (55), Ovid's Metamorphoses (4.457–458), Pausanias's *Description of Greece* (10.4.5–6, 10.29.3), and Virgil's Aeneid (6.595–600). Tityus is one of a group—which includes Ixion, Sisyphus, and Tantalus—of primordial violators of the social order and of divine authority.

Ixion committed parricide, Tantalus was accused of cannibalism, Tityus tried to rape Zeus's consort Leto, and the wily Sisyphus attempted to steal fire from the gods and defeat death. Their crimes varied, but all deeply offended morality and/or challenged the authority of the Olympian gods, especially that of Zeus, and their punishments were ingeniously devised to provide gruesome spectacle and admonition. In his descent to Hades in the *Odyssey*, Odysseus witnessed the torments of Sisyphus, Tantalus, and Tityus, and in the *Aeneid*, Aeneas encountered Tityus and Ixion. Ovid relates that their punishments were momentarily stilled while Orpheus sang his lament for Eurydice, his dead bride.

There are several versions of Tityus's origins. In one, Zeus hid the pregnant nymph Elara within the earth until Tityus, a giant, emerged. According to Homer and Virgil, Tityus was simply the son of Gaia. In Apollonius of Rhodes's *Voyage of the Argonauts*, Tityus was born of Elara but nursed by Gaia. Tityus was killed for his attempt to rape Leto either by the arrows of Apollo and Artemis or by Zeus's thunderbolt. Zeus consigned him to Tartarus as punishment. He is bound across nine acres while two vultures or serpents (depending on the source) tear at his liver in perpetuity.

Because of the similarity in their punishments, Tityus can be confused with Prometheus in visual representations. Pausanias mentions that the defeat of Tityus by Apollo and Artemis was carved in relief on the base of the throne of Apollo at Amyclae. An Attic red-figure pelike from ca. 450 b.c.e. by Polygnotes (Louvre, Paris) shows the giant Tityus shot through with Apollo's arrows in the presence of a modest Leto. In postclassical art, Titian included Tityus in his cycle of paintings *The Four Condemned*.

Trachiniae Sophocles (latter half of the fifth century b.c.e.) Scholars have offered various hypotheses as to the date of production of Sophocles' *Trachiniae*, or *Trachinian Women*, but there is no reliable evidence for a date.

Trachiniae takes place in Trachis, a Spartan settlement located close to Thermopylae and Mount Oeta. Heracles and Deianira have come there from Tiryns, after Heracles killed Iphitus, son of Eurytus, king of Oechalia. *Trachiniae* tells the story of the death of Heracles through the agency of his wife, Deianira. Many years before, Heracles had shot an arrow dipped in the blood of the Hydra and killed the centaur Nessus as he attempted to abduct Deianira. Before his death, Nessus encouraged Deianira to collect the blood around his wound and keep it as a love potion for Heracles. Deianira later sent Heracles a robe that she anointed with Nessus's "love potion." Realizing too late that she has unwittingly poisoned her husband, Deianira commits suicide. Heracles suffers great physical anguish until he ends his life on a funeral pyre on Mount Oeta.

The *Trachiniae* presents both a familiar and an unfamiliar Heracles. He is physically powerful, courageous, and nearly indomitable. Yet, he is no longer the endlessly resilient hero who accomplishes one seemingly impossible task after another but a figure coming to his end—an end both mysterious and terrible. He is also a hero more in danger from the impulses and vulnerabilities of his own character and body than from the threats of external enemies. The present crisis is motivated by eros ("love"/"desire"), both his own and Deianira's. Zeus and Aphrodite, in their different ways, are the presiding gods of the tragedy, and the hero is at once singled out as the son of a god and brought down to the level of everyone else by being humbled by an infatuation. His final choice will be determined not by his mighty hands and their power to vanquish foes but by the magnitude of his helpless suffering.

Sophocles, in telling the story of Heracles, draws on an immensely rich and intricately varied mythic tradition embodied both in poetry and in works of visual art. He has many Heraclean heroes to choose from, and in a sense, they are all present, although Sophocles consciously constructs his own particular story line. The messenger Lichas first tells one version of Heracles' motives for sacking Oechalia, and then, when pressed, tells another—the true one, given the demands of Sophocles' tragic plot. Yet, in the broader picture, both are valid mythic variants and known as such. Deianira and the Chorus are constantly asking about Heracles—his whereabouts, condition, and destiny—and, in a very real sense, so is Sophocles' audience. Even the hero's death brings no certainty or final clarity.

SYNOPSIS

The scene is set in front of Deianira and Heracles' house in Trachis. Deianira pours out her anxieties about Heracles' absence to the nurse, who suggests that Deianira send HYLLUS in search of news of his father. Hyllus enters and tells his mother that he has heard that Heracles is waging war on Eurytus. Deianira reveals to him that she is particularly concerned for Heracles' safety, because it was prophesied that he would either have died by now or, having completed his task, would live happily the rest of his life. A concerned Hyllus agrees to find Heracles and sets off to do so.

A Chorus of Trachinian women enter; the substance of its speech is ever-changing fortune, sometimes good, sometimes bad, and its unknowability; it attempts to console Deianira with the observation that Heracles is typically buoyed up by good fortune in the end. Deianira reveals to the Chorus the nature of the prophesies concerning Heracles' fate. One year and three months previously, Heracles had left behind tablets indicating that either he will have survived one year and three months on his current adventure or he will perish at the end of that time. A messenger arrives reporting that Heracles is alive and well, and victorious. He has heard as much from Heracles' herald, Lichas, who is on his way to Heracles' home. Deianira is relieved and gives thanks to Zeus. In its joy at the news, the Chorus sings the praises of APOLLO and ARTEMIS.

Lichas comes before Deianira; he is leading a group of captive women who stand silently by during his exchange with Deianira. Lichas tells Deianira that Heracles is indeed well; he is at the moment in Euboea consecrating an altar to Zeus and will shortly return home. Lichas recounts Heracles' adventures. Eurytus, king of Oechalia, had insulted Heracles, and as vengeance, Heracles killed Eurtyus's son Iphitus by guile. For this act of deceit, Zeus sold Heracles into slavery to OMPHALE for a year. Therefore, Heracles killed Eurytus, whom he blamed for his humiliation, and sacked Oechalia, so that its population, too, would know the humiliation of bondage. The captive women are, Lichas tells Deianira, the result of Heracles' sack of the city. Noticing Iole, one of the women, Deianira approaches her and asks whether she is of royal blood and whether she is a maiden or a mother. Iole remains silent, but Lichas replies to the questions: Iole may be of royal blood, but he does not know who she is, not even her name. Lichas enters the house with the captured women in preparation for returning to Heracles.

In the meantime, the messenger approaches Deianira indicating that the truth has not been fully revealed to her by Lichas. According to the messenger, Heracles did not capture the city of Oechalia for the sake of wounded pride but for love of Iole. In fact, Heracles had wished to take Iole as a concubine, but her father, Eurytus, had refused, and so for her sake, Heracles had waged war against Eurytus and enslaved Iole. Emerging from the house, Lichas is confronted by Deianira and the messenger. Deianira appeals to Lichas to be truthful, insisting that she fears a lie more than a painful truth, and that if the messenger's version of events is true, she does not harbor any anger toward the girl or Lichas. Lichas finally reveals the truth, confirming the messenger's story. Furthermore, Lichas says, the dissimulation was his alone: Heracles did not ask him to lie and has no wish to conceal the fact that Iole was brought home to be his concubine.

Deianira goes into the house with the messenger and Lichas to prepare a gift for Heracles that she will send back with Lichas, leaving the Chorus to recount the history of the battle fought between ACHELOUS and Heracles over Deianira. Deianira emerges from the house with a copper urn, and she recounts another episode from her history—her abduction by Nessus and Heracles' slaying of him with arrows dipped in the Hydra's venom. Before his death, however, Nessus told Deianira that if she gathered the blood around the wound in his side made by Heracles' arrows, she could obtain a love potion that would keep Heracles from desiring another woman. Deianira has kept this salve and has just now rubbed it onto a robe that she will send to Heracles via Lichas. She refuses to act in anger or wickedly toward Heracles and Iole, but this charm, she believes, is a benign action with which she hopes to keep Heracles' love. The Chorus responds cautiously but does not dissuade her. Lichas enters, and Deianira bids him bring the robe to Heracles; he assents and departs. Deianira goes back into the house. The Chorus sings hopefully of its longing that Heracles may return, having succumbed to Deianira's love potion.

Deianira returns in a state of nervous agitation, regretting her use of the love potion. The piece of wool she had used to rub the salve onto the robe has all but dissolved in the sunlight in which it lay. She fears that Nessus has tricked her into harming Heracles. She resolves that if Heracles is destroyed, she will also die. The Chorus objects that it is yet too early to know the result of her actions. Hyllus enters; he has just seen his father, and he confirms Deianira's fears. He is convinced that his mother has acted with deliberate malice and in his rage recounts bitterly what he has seen: Lichas presented Heracles with Deianira's gift, but when he put it on, the robe caused excruciating physical agony. Heracles, enraged, threw Lichas from the cliff, killing him. Heracles denounced his marriage to Deianira and his association with her father, Oeneus, and asked Hyllus to bring him home. When he finishes, Deianira turns and silently enters the house.

The Chorus sings a lament. Too late, it perceives the extent of Nessus's manipulation of Deianira. The Chorus hears wails of lament, and inquiring of the nurse, who has emerged grief-stricken, it finds out that Deianira has stabbed herself with a sword on Heracles' bed. The nurse had tried to warn Hyllus, but they were too late. Hyllus, when he found out, groaned at the consequences of his accusation and lamented his orphanhood.

Hyllus enters with an old man and attendants bringing Heracles. Heracles wakes to terrible pain and decries his fate and denounces his wife. Hyllus prevails on him to listen to an explanation of what had happened: It was Nessus's trick that killed him. Heracles does not comment on Deianira's role; he laments his doom and recognizes that the revenge wreaked on him by Nessus fulfills the prophecy he received from his father Zeus's grove at Dodona: His death would be caused by one already dead. Heracles then extracts two promises of Hyllus—that he will build a funeral pyre on Mount Oeta, on which Heracles means to throw himself, and that Hyllus will marry the captive Iole. Hyllus reluctantly assents, unwilling to help his father to his death or to marry the woman who was the cause of his mother's death and his father's suffering. In the closing words of the tragedy, Hyllus expresses dismay at the gods' lack of compassion, above all at Zeus's apparent indifference to the suffering of his own son and grandson.

COMMENTARY

Central to Sophocles' *Trachiniae* is the relationship between Deianira and Heracles. Even though the two do not appear in any scene together, their relations as husband and wife and their domestic drama are fundamental to the logic of Heracles' destruction. Especially notable is the contrast between Deianira's focus on the domestic realm and Heracles' conspicuous neglect. Deianira, patiently (if anxiously) awaiting the return of her long-departed husband to the household, calls to mind that paragon of female domestic virtue, PENELOPE. Yet unlike Heracles, ODYSSEUS comes home from his adventures to his wife and home, leaving his affairs with other women discreetly behind. By contrast, Heracles is out in the world, waging war and imperiling himself, not only neglecting his wife and falling in love, but bringing his current mistress, Iole, into his home. This last sign of carelessness with his domestic life decides his fate. When Heracles has transferred his affection to another, his wife does not respond with anger, but in a last attempt at keeping her husband's interest, she turns to Nessus's "love potion."

The pathos of Deianira's actions emerges when contrasted with MEDEA, another female character whose husband joins himself to a younger woman. In Euripides' version of the play, Medea uses magic to revenge herself on the adulterous Jason—sending his new bride a poisoned robe—and murdering their children. Deianira knowingly dabbles in magic, also sending a tainted robe, but her naïveté in such matters—why would the blood of a centaur dying from a poisoned arrow be a love potion?—results in unanticipated and tragic consequences. Deianira's unwitting actions earn her the enmity of her husband, the realization of her worst fears. Even after Hyllus defends his mother's innocence, Heracles does not regret or recant his savage anger; he simply ceases to speak of her altogether.

Deianira's lack of control over her fate is several times referred to over the course of the play. Her marriage to Heracles was the result of his fight with another suitor, the river god Achelous, in the form of a bull, while Deianira waited, too frightened to watch the battle. The Chorus thus describes her as a prize of battle, a spear-won bride. The second part of her story, her abduction by Nessus, is an equally frightening ordeal in which Deianira again plays a passive role. For the second time, Heracles comes to her rescue, delivering her from the threat of yet another union with a beast, this time a centaur. Her life as Heracles' wife has not been easy. Heracles is present only occasionally—for the conception and birth of his children—then goes off on his adventures. Deianira's anxiety regarding his safety was already at a high pitch at the opening of the play, because before he left, Heracles revealed a written oracle, stating that he was destined either to die on his present task or return home to safety. She is relieved to hear that Heracles is alive and well and on his way home, but her happiness turns out to be short-lived: She learns that Heracles has fallen in love with another woman. Her desperation at this revelation leads her to take the only real action of her life—with tragic consequences.

Is Deianira culpable? Sophocles certainly makes her out to be a good woman in most respects; even when sending the love potion, she is hardly malevolent or ill intentioned. She becomes stingingly eloquent at the moment she realizes that she has been betrayed, evoking the image of two women under a single bedsheet awaiting with erotic longing the return of the same man. She is not tranquil, and not fully passive, but hardly a Medea, and not even deeply angry. Deianira does admit to feeling ashamed, however, and in general, the "love potion" is associated with secrecy and darkness. The potion, in accordance with the centaur's instructions, had to be stored in the dark depths of the household—a lurking source of destruction over the years. The potion resembles the sword Hector gave to Ajax, ostensibly a gift, but one that turned out to be a fatal one. A gift from an enemy in Sophocles is generally a bad thing, and this particular gift—composed of blood from the centaur and venom from the Hydra—is doubly inimical. The centaur's true intention, however, remained hidden for a long time, as did the poison itself. It becomes fully destructive only at the moment when it comes into the light and touches Heracles' skin. Deianira has a premonition of what this destructive force is like when she leaves a piece of wool soaked with the poison out in the sun for a few minutes, then watches it burn away and dissolve into shreds. The Chorus, in its first entrance (or *parodos*), apostrophizes the Sun that sees all things, and a theme of seeing and light is sustained throughout the play. Heracles, when the agony of the robe possesses him, wishes to be taken from the sight of men. Hyllus emphasizes that he had to look on his father's horrible ordeal. At the end, Heracles no longer keeps his eyes open to see.

Much hinges on what is visible and known as opposed to what is dark and hidden. The playwright lays significant stress on Lichas's deception. Deianira delivers a speech on how unworthy it is of him to be dishonest. At length, she prevails on him to tell the truth. Then, driven by her own passions, she concocts a deception of her own, and sends Lichas back with the cloak. Lichas, who was condemned for deceitfulness, is now being sent on a new mission of deceit, of which he is unaware. He is all too faithful to his mistress in this instance and, for his reward, is smashed against a rock by his master. If Heracles is untrue to his marriage with Deianira, and yet forthright and honest about it, Deianira is deeply faithful to Heracles in affection, yet for that very reason deceives him. The two worlds, of masculine and feminine, husband and wife, are tragically out of joint. The dual status of the poison/potion is an effective emblem of the disjointedness: What the female Deianira intends as a love cure becomes, when it passes into Heracles' masculine domain, an enemy's weapon. The tragedy occurs, in a certain sense, due to a profound misalignment of understanding.

While both main characters occupy different mental worlds, they are equally, if differently, affected by the power of eros. Next to Zeus, Aphrodite is the most powerful god in the play. In its opening lines, Deianira recalls her fear of marriage because of the unwanted attentions of the multiform river god Achelous. Her own beauty, she notes, was baneful to her on more than one occasion. She later has occasion to observe that the captive Iole's beauty was the cause of destruction of her city and the suffering of her people. Beauty incites desire, and desire causes irrational and violent behavior. Heracles sacks an entire city out of

lust for Iole. Lust, in turn, is associated with the part-wild element in human nature. Achelous took the form of a snake and a bull, while the centaur Nessus represents a classic instance of the mixture of human/civilized and animal/uncivilized. It is his animal side in particular that is meant to suggest lack of sexual restraint, although human beings are the species notoriously driven to self-destructive action by eros. The venom/love potion bestowed by the lustful then dying Nessus affords a rich emblem of the conjunction of eros with violence, darkness, and the monstrous. Heracles, who slew the Hydra, could not control the many-headed monster of eros that ultimately brought him to his destruction.

Sophocles' emphasis is not moralizing in the Victorian sense. Desire is not the sign of a moral flaw but a compulsion to which, unfortunately, all human beings are sometimes subject. As Deianira herself concedes on learning of Heracles' infatuation with Iole, eros is not in a person's control and cannot be blamed on him. In its most destructive form, eros can have a violent, identity-eroding force. The venom/potion of Nessus, though not truly a love potion, is nonetheless suggestive of eros's violence, insofar as it is motivated both in its creation and in its deployment by a context of desire. Its effect, as it is described, is the dissolution of form. It melts away whatever it touches, taking away its shape and internal structure. In its identity-destroying aspect, eros resembles a kind of madness, and Deianira's action in sending the love potion no longer seems fully rational. (We might compare other scenarios in tragedy, e.g., Sophocles' *AJAX*, in which a character acts in a state of frenzied emotion or madness then recovers mental clarity, only to realize the tragic consequences of his or her action.) When Heracles insists on forcing his son Hyllus to marry Iole after his death, his son believes his father to be mad. In a sense, he is.

Heracles is excellent at killing monsters and completing seemingly impossible tasks. He runs into serious trouble, however, when it comes to domestic matters—women and children in particular. In a famous fit of madness (the subject of Euripides' HERACLES) he slew his entire family (this was before his marriage to Deianird). Here, it is a domestic matter—a wife's neglected love—that brings an end to the labors and to the hero himself. In general, Heracles has more trouble with women than with male adversaries. Omphale, to whom Heracles was sold as a slave, provides another example of humiliation at the hands of a woman. Or was he humiliated? It is perhaps significant in the present context of Heracles' womanizing that some versions of the Omphale story make Omphale into Heracles' mistress during the duration of his servitude. According to another story, however, he ended up wearing women's clothing at Omphale's behest—a humiliation for this most masculine of heroes. In a more serious vein, Heracles proclaims that the atrocious physical pain inflicted on him by the poison of Nessus has made him like a woman, and that after defeating so many monsters, he is being defeated by feminine wiles.

In cultic terms, the rites of Heracles are known for their focus on male initiates—ephebes (young men on the verge of manhood and military service)—and for explicitly excluding women. The structure of the present play, in a certain sense, replicates the ritual exclusion of women in Heraclean cult. The first portion of the action consists largely of the dialogue between Deianira and the Chorus of Trachinian women; the latter part, after Deianira is dead, consists of the exchange between two men, Heracles and his son Hyllus. The play's dramatic structure, in other words, itself embodies the radical division between husband and wife, Heracles and the world of women. Heracles and Deianira never speak to each other and effectively inhabit different worlds.

At the play's end, Heracles is even more profoundly divided from his wife. She is dead and apparently no longer much of a concern to him. His own life is ending, and at the same time, a major mythological sequence is coming to an end. Zeus, who brings things to their completion, oversees the terrible process. The Heraclean mythology is eminently serial in nature—a long series of labors, one after another, and he succeeds at each one only to commence another. In Euripides' ALCESTIS, we meet him between labors—one of the few moments that Heracles might be inserted into a narrative that does not form part of his canonical labors. He is constantly defined by the ongoing sequence of tasks. Thus, bringing that sequence to an end requires a special situation, a culminating labor or task distinct from the rest. Zeus, who in the ILIAD is the one who brings things to the final end/completion/purpose (telos), is thus somehow behind everything that happens to his suffering son, yet he is also strangely and disturbingly absent. The relation of Zeus and Heracles' final end are metonymically signaled on more than one occasion when a character, without apparent awareness of the fatal significance, refers to Mount Oeta as being sacred to Zeus.

The last, uncanonical labor of Heracles that culminates there, however, does not feature a positive task to be accomplished or a foe to be overcome. Mount Oeta will witness only the horrors of the hero's own self-consuming body. Reduced to suffering, Heracles experiences the purest labor he has had—relentless, unimaginable pain—and, rather than having an outlet for his aggressive, masculine valor, the hero is turned in upon his own nature and resources. Heracles does the best he can, given the circumstances, and assumes control of his own death. By having himself burned alive, he forces himself to endure the ultimate in pain to escape his present humiliation. We might compare Ajax, who escapes the grotesquery of his deeds and subsequent mental anguish by suicide, or PHILOCTETES, whose unbearable wound makes him wish for death. In being thus turned onto himself and his own suffering, grotesque body as the object and goal of his final labor, Heracles becomes a truly Sophoclean hero.

The big question that surrounds this end is the question of Heracles' apotheosis.

In *Philoctetes*, Heracles appears as a deus ex machina: He is linked with the play's central figure, Philoctetes, not only because Philoctetes inherits Heracles' bow, but also because both heroes are associated with Mount Oeta. Furthermore, Heracles presents himself as an example of heroic labor and suffering rewarded in the end with greater things. Are we also to understand in the present play, then, that after his sufferings, Heracles will be rewarded with Olympus and immortality? If so, Sophocles gives us no indications of such an afterlife. The end of suffering, as far as we know from the *Trachiniae*, is simply the end for Heracles. There is no further purpose.

A hero is not quite a god, and Sophocles likes to focus his plays on the magnificent self-destruction of heroes. When they are worshipped, it is as chthonic figures, in close connection with their tomb. Possibly Sophocles chooses not to comment, or is strategically agnostic on the question of immortality, since this would needlessly dilute the purity of Heracles' suffering and heroic end. The intimation of a divine Heracles would dissolve the tragic tensions and contradictions that define the suffering hero Heracles—godlike, yet a man; son of Zeus, yet cruelly humiliated; the master of his fortunes, yet pathetically at the mercy of destiny. The tragedians in general focus on episodes in Heraclean mythology that have tragic potential. The exception of *Philoctetes* is thus perfectly conformant with the broader rule: Heracles can appear as a god in a play where he is *not* the tragic hero. We are not allowed to forget his divine blood at any time, however. Mount Oeta, alluded to ominously and powerfully throughout the play as the site of Heracles' final conflagration, is also associated with Zeus. Zeus is bringing about a strange and horrible end for Heracles, but we, as mortals, cannot fully comprehend what that end is or what it means. Human beings can never fully comprehend the ways of gods—an admission that, while it does not predict apotheosis, does not quite rule it out.

Deianira's suicide provides another perspective on Heracles' end, coming before it and even prefiguring it. We might compare it with Jocasta's suicide by hanging followed by Oedipus's own separate yet complementary self-blinding in *Oedipus the King*. Deianira's death is located indoors, in her bedroom, on their very marriage bed—a clear emblem of her focus in life and the motive of her death. Before she dies, she looks sadly on the household items she will not use again and her household servants. Yet, in other ways, she dies like a man: Notably, she employs a sword. The irony of the fact that Heracles himself dies by feminine deceit and poison, groaning and defeated by pain like a woman, would not be lost on the Athenian audience. Yet, in the end, he heroically embraces his end, and rather than being surrounded by the trappings of domestic life, he is isolated on a mountain, engulfed by his own funeral pyre, perishing under the gaze of Zeus.

The character who will ensure this ending for Heracles is his son, Hyllus. Just as Zeus makes his son Heracles suffer in carrying out his destiny, so Heracles enforces a hard series of tasks on his son. Not only in the case of his wife, but here, too, Heracles appears monumentally egotistical. He does not care about his son's pain but only that he himself achieves the death he wishes, and that Iole's body will not be possessed by a man outside his family. Still obsessed with her, he passes her on as a kind of sexual inheritance. Hyllus agrees and, in agreeing, comes into his own proper tragic legacy—killer of his father and husband of the woman who was the cause of his father's and mother's deaths. Hyllus is an intriguing figure, as he is the one person who can truly appreciate both halves of the tragedy. He shuttles back and forth between father and mother and, for a moment at least, sees truly the perspective and motives of each. In that sense, he is the play's linchpin, the only thing that keeps this disturbingly fractured tragedy together.

Triptolemus Inventor of agriculture, follower of Demeter. Classical sources are the *Homeric Hymn to Demeter* (153, 474); Apollodorus's LIBRARY (1.5.1–2); Hyginus's *Fabulae* (147, 259, 277); Ovid's FASTI (4.507–560), METAMORPHOSES (5.642–616), and *Tristia* (3.8.1–2); and Pausanias's *Description of Greece* (1.4.1–3, 1.38.6, 7.18.1). Son of Celeus and Metaneira, or of Eleusis (or Eleusinus) and Cothonea, or of OCEANUS and GAIA. In the *Homeric Hymn to Demeter*, Triptolemus is only one of several local notables of Eleusis to whom Demeter teaches her rites. In later versions, however, he plays a more important role. In Apollodorus, Triptolemus is the son of King Celeus of Eleusis and Metaneira. (Apollodorus also reports that Pherecydes, in a variant tradition, identifies Oceanus and Gaia as the parents of Triptolemus.) Demeter, wandering after the abduction of her daughter PERSEPHONE, arrives at Eleusis, where, disguised as an old woman, she becomes the nurse of Demophon, son of king Celeus and Metaneira. She attempts to immortalize the child by placing him in the fire at night, burning away his mortality. Metaneira interrupts the goddess in the midst of this rite, causing the child to be destroyed in the fire. The goddess reveals herself and then gives Demophon's brother Triptolemus a chariot with dragon wings and seeds of wheat. He spreads the practices of agriculture around the world. In one of several similar stories, Triptolemus's host, King Lyncus of Scythia, becomes jealous of his glory and benefaction to humankind and tries to kill him. Demeter transforms Lyncus into a lynx before he can strike with his sword (Ovid's *Metamorphoses*, Hyginus).

In other versions, as in Ovid's *Fasti*, Triptolemus, not Demophon, is the child whom Demeter attempts to immortalize. But whereas in Ovid, Celeus and Metaneira are Triptolemus's parents, Hyginus identifies his parents as Eleusinus and Cothonea. Demeter attempts to immortalize Triptolemus and is interrupted by Eleusinus, whom she kills. She gives Trip-tolemus the chariot and grain, and he spreads the practice of agriculture, but when he returns home, King Celeus, who succeeded the dead Eleusinus, tries to kill Triptolemus. Demeter, however, prevents the murder and orders Celeus to give his kingdom to Triptolemus, who names it Eleusis after his father and establishes the Thesmophoria (a festival in honor of Demeter and Persephone).

In visual representations, Demeter and Persephone are sometimes joined by Triptolemus in a wheeled or winged chariot given to him by Demeter. An example is a bas-relief from Eleusis dating to ca. 440 B.C.E.

Triton A sea god. Son of AMPHITRITE and POSEIDON. Classical sources are Apollodorus's LIBRARY (1.4.6, 3.12.3), Apollonius of Rhodes's *VOYAGE OF THE ARGONAUTS* (4.1,588–1,622), Hesiod's THEOGONY (930–933), Lucian's *Dialogues of the Sea-Gods* (8, 14), Ovid's METAMORPHOSES, Pausanias's *Description of Greece* (7.22.8, 9.20.4), Pindar's *Pythian Odes* (4.19ff), and Virgil's AENEID (1.44–145). Sea deities with no specific mythology are called tritons and are not to be confused with Triton, the offspring of Poseidon. In the *Theogony*, Triton's domain is the seafloor, where he lives in a golden palace close to Amphitrite and Poseidon. In some sources, Triton's home is located either in Boeotia or near Libya. In Apollodorus's *Library* and Pausanias's *Description of Greece*, Triton was associated with a specific river. Triton is similar in appearance to another sea creature, GLAUCUS, who also has a human upper body and a lower body in the form of a fish's tail. Triton's attributes are a trident and a conch shell, into which he blows to control the seas. According to Ovid, the flood witnessed by DEUCALION ceased in obedience to Triton's command.

Triton appeared in human form to the crew of the *Argo*, which had been blown off course. The Argonauts gave him the tripod of APOLLO; in exchange, he offered them the gift of a bit of earth and guided them out of the Tritonian Lake. In the *Aeneid*, Misenus challenged the gods to surpass his skill in blowing a conch shell and was drowned by Triton for his hubris. There are few myths specifically related to Triton, but he appears regularly in the retinue of his parents, Poseidon and Amphitrite, as well as with nymphs and goddesses associated with the sea, such as GALATEA and APHRODITE.

In visual representation, Triton, like Glaucus, is represented as mature and bearded. In postclassical art, Triton often appears with Poseidon in the decoration of fountains or on his own as in Gianlorenzo Bernini's Triton fountain in Piazza Barberini (Rome) dating from 1642.

Trojan Women EURIPIDES (415 B.C.E.) Euripides' *Trojan Women* was produced in 415 B.C.E. as part of a tetralogy that included *Alexander*, *Palamedes*, *Trojan Women*, and *Sisyphus*. The first play concerns the life and destructive destiny of PARIS; the second an episode in which ODYSSEUS treacherously brings about the death of a fellow Greek, Palamedes, at Troy; and the final satyr play deals with the famous trickster and liar SISYPHUS. The first three plays are united by the theme of Troy and its destruction. Some commentators have suggested that the last play, *Sisyphus*, is connected to the others by the figure of Odysseus, whose true father, in some stories, is said to be Sisyphus. The *Trojan Women* represents the series of misfortunes that afflicts the women of Troy after its defeat: ANDROMACHE, CASSANDRA, HECUBA, and many others are enslaved; POLYXENA is sacrificed to ACHILLES' ghost; and Odysseus persuades the Greeks to kill HECTOR's son, ASTYANAX, by throwing him from the walls of Troy. The play's main themes include human cruelty, slavery, degradation, and the apparent absence or indifference of the gods. There is little plot development and no hope for salvation, although Cassandra's frenzied words, and the dialogue between ATHENA

and POSEIDON at the play's opening, look forward to the compensatory suffering and deaths of the Greeks on their journeys home. It does not seem accidental that what is arguably Euripides' bleakest tragedy was produced in the wake of some of the more disturbing events of the Peloponnesian War, including the killing and enslavement of the population of Melos in 416–415 B.C.E.

SYNOPSIS

The scene is set on the plains of Troy, with the city in the background, before the tents of the captive Trojan women. Troy has been taken, and the Greeks are preparing to depart with their captives and plunder. The god Poseidon surveys the destruction of the city he helped build and summarizes the situation: Polyxena has been sacrificed to Achilles' ghost, Hecuba mourns endlessly, PRIAM is dead, and Cassandra has been allotted to AGAMEMNON as concubine. Athena enters. Although she destroyed Troy, she is appalled by the victorious Greeks' religious offences; Poseidon agrees to help her punish them with terrible storms at sea. The gods depart, and Hecuba, who has been lying down on stage, oblivious to the presence of the gods, arises and together with the Chorus of captive Trojan women, laments the fate of Troy and her own and other Trojan women's enslavement. The Greek herald Talthybius enters and reports the fate of well-known Trojan women: Cassandra is allotted to Agamemnon, Andromache to NEOPTOLEMUS, Hecuba to the hated Odysseus; Polyxena's fate is darkly alluded to but not stated outright. Cassandra enters and, in what appears to be a demented frenzy, sings of her "marriage" to Agamemnon. She rejoices in the destructive effect it will have on their enemies. She is dragged offstage, and Hecuba mourns her degraded status. As the Chorus sings, Andromache is led onstage on a wagon, along with her son, Astyanax. Together, she and Hecuba bewail Troy's fate, and Andromache reveals to Hecuba that Polyxena has been slain as a sacrifice. She declares that it is preferable to die like Polyxena than to live on as a slave and be forced to go to another man's bed. Hecuba is urging Andromache to forget Hector and be obedient to her new master, and to place hope in Astyanax as future rebuilder of Troy, when suddenly Talthybius enters and reports that Odysseus has persuaded the Greeks to kill Astyanax by throwing him from the walls of the city. Andromache must relinquish her child to the herald, who takes the boy away. After the choral ode, in which the Chorus laments that the gods have abandoned Troy, MENELAUS enters with his soldiers: He rejoices that he has killed Paris, destroyed his kingdom, and reclaimed his wife as captive slave; he intends to execute her in Sparta. Hecuba encourages him to kill her but to beware of her enchanting looks. Helen is brought forth and asks to be allowed to defend herself. Hecuba agrees to speak for the prosecution in a kind of "trial." Helen blames Hecuba for giving birth to Paris; she claims that the Trojan War was to the Greeks' advantage and observes that it was impossible to resist the power of APHRODITE. She finally claims that she was held in Troy against her will. Hecuba refutes these arguments, declaring that Helen was motivated by lust and the luxury of Paris's household. Menelaus agrees with Hecuba, but sends Helen to the ships rather than executing her immediately. As the Chorus sings of Helen's vileness, Talthybius enters with the body of Astyanax: Andromache was sent off on one of Neoptolemus's ships before she could bury her son, and so she has asked Hecuba to prepare his burial. Talthybius exits, and Hecuba prepares Astyanax to be buried with Hector's shield. As the rites are carried out, and the Chorus laments, the city of Troy begins to burn and to fall into ruin. Hecuba and the Chorus sing a dirge for the city's destruction as they are led offstage.

COMMENTARY

Euripides' *Trojan Women* represents the ruin of a city. The atmosphere of hopelessness and loss is total, and there is almost no plot in the ordinary sense of the word. Critics of the play have noted its lack of articulated structure and development, but this seems to be the point: There is no more story to be told. The story of Troy is finished, and all that remains is lamentation and exploration of the effects of the defeat of the city on those who survive.

Such exploration is indeed the substance of Euripides' play. One significant action takes place, but the decision that brings about the action is made offstage, and we see only its lamentable outcome. Otherwise, the play consists of a series of dialogues and long speeches that elaborate the main characters' sense of despair and loss. The figure who endows this series of lamenting voices with a certain unity is the enslaved queen of Troy, Hecuba. Exceptionally, she remains on stage throughout the entire tragedy and absorbs each new shock of misfortune in its turn. When Poseidon begins the play with his speech, Hecuba is lying down, weeping continuously. As queen, and mother of so many children—now mostly dead—she stands as an emblem of Troy's endless suffering. She is widowed, deprived of her children, reduced in status, and enslaved all at once. She encapsulates Troy's suffering. Like other Euripidean characters, she is a figure who, once grand, has been brought low, a slave in rags rather than Priam's royal consort.

Not surprisingly in a play that focuses on the sufferings of newly enslaved women, and that features a chorus of captive Trojan women, slavery is a major theme. The main characters now have the opportunity to meditate on what it means to lose all control over one's fate, what it means to become another person's property. At the end of the play, the herald Talthybius gives an order to prevent Hecuba from killing herself. She is not allowed even this freedom, since she is now the property of Odysseus. Andromache cannot stay in Troy long enough to bury her own son, Astyanax, since Neoptolemus is in a hurry to return to Phthia to help his grandfather PELEUS. She is simply cargo, and so has no choice about her departure. The destructive effect of subjugation on human relations is a theme Euripides explores in his other post–Trojan War plays as well: *HECUBA* and *ANDROMACHE*, which take their titles from two of the main characters of this play, are deeply concerned with the condition of slavery.

Andromache, in particular, considers the question of whether or not a life of servitude is worth living. She compares her own condition unfavorably with that of Polyxena, who was fortunate enough to die. A dead person, she points out, cannot experience pain and cannot compare previous happiness with a present state of grief. Andromache further reflects on the unexpected result of her own virtue and modesty. She restrained herself from going outside her house, practiced modest behavior, and subordinated herself to her husband. Now, by a cruel irony, her reward for this voluntary obedience is to be specially singled out for slavery as another man's bedmate. Because of her excellent reputation for virtue, Neoptolemus chose her as his slave. Andromache's thinking on this point is both subtle and pointed. She knows that her life as a woman was hardly "free" in the fullest sense of the term, yet crucially, she *chose* to be obedient, silent, modest. Now, as her reward, she can no longer even choose her habitual self-restraint: Subservience is forced on her. Worst of all, from her perspective, she must accept another man as lover. Andromache is a paragon of loyalty, and she is being forced to betray Hector after his death. Euripides has already explored these themes to a certain extent in *Andromache*, where we see the outcome of her life as slave and reluctant bedmate of Neoptolemus.

Cassandra's case is at once typical and exceptional. Like other Trojan women, she must accept a master and lover she despises: Agamemnon. She no longer has control over her own life and fate. Cassandra's manner of perceiving and describing her situation, however, is very different and points toward events well beyond the ending of the play.

As priestess of APOLLO, who receives prophecies from the god, yet is doomed never to be believed by others, Cassandra speaks an ominous idiom, full of hints and suggestions that we, the audience, can understand from our broader knowledge of the myths, but that the other characters within the frame of the play cannot fully comprehend. In particular, she bids Hecuba rejoice at her servitude to Agamemnon, since it will do harm to their enemy. She understands, in other words, that her status as Agamemnon's bedmate will function as catalyst of his murder at the hands of CLYTAEMNESTRA and thus will contribute to the implosion of the house of Atreus. In a significant allusion to Aeschylus's *Oresteia*, Cassandra declares that the house of Atreus will be destroyed in compensation for the destruction of Priam's house.

Cassandra further offers a condensed account of the wanderings of Odysseus. His homecoming, in the Homeric view, was ultimately successful, by comparison with the negative example of Agamemnon: He wandered for 10 years but came home laden with treasures and *kleos* (fame), and successfully drove out the suitors with the help of his son. Yet, Cassandra here emphasizes the misfortunes and sufferings of Odysseus, which, in the present context, seem merited. He does not appear on stage in the present play, but in the *Palamedes*, a lost play that preceded the *Trojan Women* in Euripides' sequence of four plays, Odysseus would have certainly played the part of villain. The present play singles out Odysseus as author of Astyanax's death. Moreover, in what might appear to be a sophistic performance, Cassandra argues that the Trojans enjoy a happier fate than the Greeks. They died defending their city and were buried in the earth of the homeland; the Greeks have died far from home, and their families have suffered terribly in their absence. The argument, while apparently counterintuitive, has some justification. At the opening of the play, the dialogue of Poseidon and Athena shows the gods turning against the victorious

Greeks, plaguing their return voyage with a catastrophic storm. The punishment of the Greeks is only just beginning.

Cassandra, whose words seem barely comprehensible to her immediate auditors within the play, speaks over their heads to the audience, just as Poseidon and Athena spoke (literally) over the head of the weeping Hecuba. Beyond the immediacy of suffering, there is the deeper question of justice, and yet, to all but a very few, the gods' justice is incomprehensible and inaccessible. Cassandra is one of the few who has access to it, yet she cannot communicate her knowledge to others. Helen presents a difficult case in point. Her punishment would appear to be especially merited, yet it does seem likely that she will be punished in any way. Helen also presents an exceptional case within the sequence of captive speakers. On the one hand, she is explicitly presented as a captive woman, Menelaus's slave, and yet, in other ways, it becomes clear that she is not truly and irrevocably a slave in the same way as the Trojans. As an (apparently willing) abductee of Paris, she caused the sufferings of both the Greeks and the Trojans, and thus, if there is any justice, she should be a prime candidate for punishment. Menelaus, in fact, declares that he is bringing her back to Sparta to be executed. Hecuba, however, warns Menelaus not to look at her or bring her back in the same boat with him; her immense, and immensely destructive, power of attraction will surely master him. Menelaus's inability to put Helen to death immediately implies that she is already beginning to bring him under her sway. Hecuba's refutation of Helen's defense is fairly devastating and convinces Menelaus at least on a rational level, but the deeper power of persuasion clearly resides in Helen's person. Her terrible beauty destroyed Troy and decimated the Greek warrior class. Words, set against the divine power of her beauty, are of minor import.

Helen appears as an exception to both the rules of slavery and of justice. She ought to be punished, yet will not be, whereas Andromache ought to be rewarded for her virtue, yet ends up a slave instead. The play's structure encourages and intensifies the juxtaposition. The episode of Helen's "trial" falls between the removal of Astyanax and the scene of the preparations for Astyanax's burial. Andromache is the mirror opposite Helen: She is loyal, steadfast, virtuous, yet she must lose her husband and her child and live out her life as a slave. Helen, whose disloyalty caused the war, will return to Sparta to live with her husband. In the very moment she relinquishes Astyanax, Andromache fiercely denounces the Greeks, and Helen in particular. She denies that Tyndareus or Zeus was Helen's father, but Vengefulness, Hate, Blood, and Death. The playwright thus draws a direct link between Helen's actions and the death of Andromache's child. Even more pointedly, the body of Astyanax is brought in at the very moment that the Chorus of captive Trojan women is expressing the wish that Menelaus be denied a successful return to Sparta after forgiving Helen's shameful betrayal. The enslaved members of the Chorus are cut off from the homeland and their dead husbands, while Menelaus and Helen return to their homeland together to live out their lives comfortably.

Despite these sharp condemnations, however, the case of Helen is not simple, and Euridipes' present play takes part in a long debate over her culpability in the Trojan War, to which Herodotus, Stesichorus, Homer, and others variously contribute. Homer made a good case for the bullying power of Aphrodite over Helen, and so Helen's present argument regarding the goddess's irresistible force is less implausible than it seems. Moreover, *Alexander*, the first play in Euripides' tetralogy, may well have provided some support for the arguments that Helen makes: Paris was fated, from his birth, to destroy Troy, and if that is the case, Helen's personal culpability becomes even more debatable. Helen is the offspring of Zeus, and from that perspective, her destructive effect on humankind ultimately has its divine origin in Zeus's rape of LEDA. The problem of Helen, therefore, is not simply one of personal culpability but also has a theological dimension. One could truly say that Zeus's act of lust in swan form caused the central, catastrophic event in Greek mythology, the Trojan War.

Hecuba and the Chorus are clearly disturbed by the theological implications of the fall of Troy. The gods are abandoning the city that honored and worshipped them; they are abandoning their own temples to destruction. Troy was a city traditionally favored by the gods, and as the Chorus points out, the gods are known to have very close relations with Trojans. The Trojan GANYMEDE serves as Zeus's cupbearer and sexual object; the goddess Dawn (Eos) chose the Trojan Tithonus as spouse; Apollo and Poseidon built the walls of Troy, which they now allow to fall into ruin. Hecuba, in two brief speeches near the end of the play, comes close to nihilistic despair: The gods have done nothing except cause suffering for Hecuba and Troy, which they now annihilate and consign to oblivion.

The play's darkest moment, which deprives Hecuba of her last vestiges of hope, is the appearance on stage of Astyanax's corpse. The killing of Astyanax is the play's one true action. Polyxena is already dead at the opening of the play, Priam has been killed, and the fates of the Trojan captives have been decided. Hecuba earlier consoled Andromache with the survival of her son and the possibility that he might one day renew the greatness of Troy. This hope is cruelly extinguished by his murder. Hecuba's long, poignant speech over his corpse, which she prepares for burial, maximizes the emotional impact of his death. Both symbolically and concretely, Hecuba is burying what is left of Troy. She buries him, significantly, with Hector's shield, the same shield that defended the city against the Greek invaders. The symbolism here functions in parallel to the manner of Astyanax's death—being thrown from the walls of Troy. The walls stand metonymically for the city, and, specifically, for the defense of the city. Thus the fact that Astyanax, whose name means "lord of the city" in Greek, falls from those walls to his death produces a doubly cruel irony: The boy born to inherit Hector's role as city defender dies by falling from the city's defensive walls. The scene of his burial is followed immediately and significantly by the destruction of the city itself by fire.

By contrast with several other late Euripidean plays, no deus ex machina intervenes to save the day and vindicate the justice of the gods. To console us, we have only the opening dialogue between Poseidon and Athena, which promises that the Greeks will be punished for their crimes. The destruction of Greek lives and households, however, is not the same thing as any kind of salvation for Troy. The prospect remains bleak for Trojans and Greeks alike. The political background of the period, as commentators have observed, may have something do with the dark mood of the play and its exposure of human cruelty in war. By the time Euripides produced *Trojan Women* in 415 B.C.E., he had had the opportunity to observe some of the grimmer moments in the Peloponnesian War and, in particular, the recent events on the island of Melos in 416–415. The Melians, who sought to maintain neutrality, were besieged by Athens and surrendered. The men were killed, and the women and children enslaved. The focus of the play on the pointless sufferings inflicted on women and children, and on the cold realpolitik that motivates characters such as Odysseus, resonates strikingly with the punishment of the Melians. In certain passages, Euripides refers to Athens, albeit in broadly positive terms. The Chorus of captive Trojan women wishes to be sent to Athens and later recalls how Telamon, from Salamis near Athens, participated in an earlier sack of Troy. While the references are not openly critical, Athens is implicated in the Greek war effort and its subsequent inhumanity. Euripides reminds us that the Athenians, both in the play and in contemporary history, have done their share of killing and enslaving innocents civilians.

Turnus King of the Rutulians and Italian hero. Son of Daunus and the nymph Venilia. Brother of the nymph Juturna. Classical sources are Dionysius of Halicarnassus's *Roman Antiquities* (1.64), Livy's *From the Foundation of the City* (1.2.1–6), and Virgil's *AENEID* (Books 7–12). In Virgil, Turnus is the favored suitor of Lavinia, daughter of King Latinus. When AENEAS arrives in Italy, Latinus recalls a prophecy that he should give his daughter in marriage to a stranger and offers Lavinia to Aeneas. Turnus, at first inclined to diplomacy, is maddened by the hell demon Allecto at Juno's instigation and raises his Rutulians and other Italian allies against Aeneas. Latinus withdraws into his palace and refuses to participate in the war. Aeneas slays Turnus in a duel at the close of the epic. Other versions existed as well, in which Turnus and Latinus fought against Aeneas, or Aeneas and Latinus joined forces against Turnus.

Tyndareus Husband of LEDA. See HELEN; MENELAUS; *ORESTES*.

Typhoeus (Typhon) A monstrous offspring of GAIA and TARTARUS. Classical sources are Apollodorus's *LIBRARY* (1.6.3), Hesiod's *THEOGONY* (820–880), Ovid's *METAMORPHOSES* (5.321–358), and Pindar's *Pythian Odes* (1.15–28). Typhoeus is described as an enormous creature with fiery eyes glittering in 100 snake heads rising from his neck. Apollodorus claims that he was larger than a mountain and that his head brushed the stars. The sounds issuing from the multiple heads varied from the animalistic to the human and were horrible to hear. APHRODITE incited the union of Gaia and Tartarus, and Typhoeus was born during the period when the TITANS were being defeated by ZEUS and the other Olympian gods. Gaia encouraged Typhoeus to battle against Zeus and the Olympians in revenge for their imprisonment of the Titans. Zeus perceived the danger that Typhoeus represented and quickly tried to destroy him by setting his many heads on fire with his thunderbolts. In the *Theogony*, Zeus succeeds without serious difficulty and confines Typhoeus in Tartarus. According to Apollodorus, Typhoeus initially had the upper hand. Many of the gods fled to Egypt and transformed into various animals. Typhoeus captured Zeus, cut Zeus's sinews out with the god's own adamantine scythe, and imprisoned him in his cave is Cilicia. Zeus was rescued by HERMES and finally defeated Typhoeus. As he crashed to earth, Typhoeus created a volcanic eruption (Mount Etna, with which Typhoeus is identified). Zeus then consigned him to TARTARUS among the Titans.

Before his defeat, Typhoeus mated with ECHIDNA, partly a beautiful nymph and partly a serpent, and she gave birth to the dog Orthus; CERBERUS, the dog that guards the gates of HADES; the HYDRA OF LERNA; the CHIMAERA; and the SPHINX. In other sources, his descendants include the NEMEAN LION, the Crommyonian sow, the eagle that ate at PROMETHEUS's liver, and the dragon of the HESPERIDES. In some accounts, Typhoeus also fathered the great and terrifying winds that destroy sailors on the open sea and cause chaos on land. A Chaldician black-figure hydria from ca. 540 B.C.E. (Antikensammlungen, Munich) shows Zeus in battle with Typhoeus. Here, Zeus draws back a hand holding thunderbolts and faces Typhoeus, who is depicted as having wings, a serpentine lower body, long hair, and beard. In the postclassical period, Gustav Klimt's *Beethoven Frieze* in Vienna from 1902 shows Typhoeus with a more simian aspect.

Ulysses See ODYSSEUS.

Uranus (Ouranos) The Greek personification of the sky or heaven. A primordial divinity. Offspring and consort of GAIA (Earth). Classical sources are Apollodorus's *LIBRARY* (1.1–5) and Hesiod's *THEOGONY* (126–182, 363–473, 886–893). Uranus was conceived of as the sky, a dome-shaped entity surrounded by stars. Uranus's offspring with Gaia were the TITANS: IAPETUS, HYPERION, Coeus, Crius, Cronus, MNEMOSYNE, OCEANUS, PHOEBE, RHEA, TETHYS, THEIA, and THEMIS. They also produced the HUNDRED-HANDED ONES and the CYCLOPS, whom Uranus consigned to TARTARUS. Uranus, to prevent his many children from being born, kept them inside Gaia, in the Earth. Cronus, encouraged by Gaia, castrated his father with a flint (or adamant) sickle, liberated his brothers and sisters, and succeeded Uranus. Cronus cast Uranus's genitals away, and when they touched Earth, they produced the FURIES and the GIANTS. Cast into the sea, the genitals produced APHRODITE. Following his defeat, Uranus foretold the downfall of the Titans at the hands of the Olympian gods.

Uranus was not a frequent subject in ancient art, nor is there evidence of cult practice surrounding the god in the classical period. In visual representation of later periods, he appears in the company of Gaia, and his attributes are stars. A 16th-century fresco by Giorgio Vasari and Cristofano Gherardi, *The Castration of Uranus*, from ca. 1560 (Palazzo Vecchio, Florence) shows Cronus attacking a prone Uranus with a sickle made of flint.

Venus   See Aphrodite.

Vertumnus   A Roman god of the orchard and other vegetation. Classical sources are Ovid's *Fasti* (6.409–410) and *Metamorphoses* (14.623–771), Propertius's *Elegies* (4.2), and Varro's *On the Latin Language* (5.46). The Romans derived the name of this god from the word denoting transformation (*verto*, to turn, change, transform). Some texts cite his skill in taking on various human shapes; others identify him as the god who receives the harvest, the fruit of the turning year; while another mentions that he was able to turn back (or reverse the flow of) a river. Propertius's *Elegies* establishes the god's origins in Etruria. In Ovid's *Metamorphoses*, Vertumnus fell in love with Pomona. Knowing her chaste reputation, he took on various forms, including that of an old woman, to plead his case. In this guise, he told Pomona the story of Iphis and Anaxarete, a hard-hearted young woman who refused her suitor and was consequently turned to stone. When he removed his disguise, Pomona was enthralled by his beauty and reciprocated his love.

Postclassical artists treated this theme in painting and sculpture, closely following Ovid's *Metamorphoses*. Such images include Hendrick Goltzius's *Vertumnus and Pomona* from 1613 (Rijksmuseum, Amsterdam). Here, as is common in postclassical treatments, Vertumnus is disguised as the old crone, and Pomona carries a pruning knife. Jean-Baptiste Lemoyne's sculpture *Vertumnus and Pomona* from 1760 (Louvre, Paris) shows Vertumnus removing his crone's mask before the seated Pomona.

Vesta   See Hestia.

Virgil (70 B.C.E.–19 B.C.E.)   Publius Vergilius Maro was a Roman poet, author of the *Eclogues*, *Georgics*, and *Aeneid*. Virgil came from Mantua; he was born in 70 B.C.E. and died in 19 B.C.E. In the closing lines of the *Georgics*, Virgil claims that, while Octavian was at war, he himself spent time in literary leisure at Naples; he is also known to have studied Epicureanism in the same area. Virgil's literary career began in the wake of Julius Caesar's death, the rise of Octavian (the future emperor Augustus) and his rival Mark Antony, and Octavian's unpopular land confiscations in Italy. Virgil's *Eclogues* suggest that his own family may have suffered from the confiscations in Mantua, but also that Virgil's patrons and connections—Pollio, Varus, and possibly Octavian himself—interceded to help him. In the *Georgics*, Virgil addresses Maecenas, the close associate of Octavian/Augustus, as patron. He also came to enjoy a friendship with the emperor Augustus, to whom he is said to have recited portions of his work. Scholars debate, however, the extent to which the *Aeneid* in particular can be seen as the official voice of the Augustan regime, given its sometimes pessimistic reflections on history, violence, and the project of civilization. An enduring preoccupation of Virgilian poetry is the land of Italy, first in the *Eclogues* as threatened refuge, then in the *Georgics* as the site of agricultural labor, and finally, in the *Aeneid*, as the final goal of Aeneas's wanderings, the prize of war, and the future location of Rome. Virgil's epic treated the ideologically crucial myth of Aeneas's voyage from Troy to Italy and foundation of the Roman race—an origins story both for Roman civilization and for the Julian clan. Virgil's poetry almost immediately achieved the status of a classic, and his work became the quintessential school text throughout the Roman Empire.

Voyage of the Argonauts APOLLONIUS OF RHODES (third century B.C.E.) Apollonius of Rhodes's *Voyage of the Argonauts*, or *Argonautica* (the Greek title), is the work of an extremely erudite scholar-poet working under the patronage of the Ptolemies in Hellenistic Alexandria. Apollonius's poem tells the story of the hero JASON's voyage to Colchis, the land ruled by king Aeetes, at the edges of the known world. Jason and his companions—a group comprising the most eminent Greek heroes of the time—sought to retrieve the Golden Fleece, which, according to Greek mythology, had previously made its way to Colchis from Greece, when PHRIXUS and HELLE, fleeing their stepmother's violent designs, fled through the sky on a magical golden ram. While this epic poem about a heroic voyage across the seas recalls the similarly episodic tales of islands, monsters, and dangers at sea in Homer's ODYSSEY, Apollonius engages knowingly with, and at times subverts, epic conventions in presenting a new kind of hero and a different perspective on heroism. Jason's story intersects with the formidable MEDEA, daughter of King Aeetes, and while

the tragic outcome of their union lies outside the scope of Apollonius's epic, his readers are frequently reminded of Medea's violent tendencies. Jason himself is in many ways a problematic hero: He is notable chiefly for his good looks; he requires the witch Medea's help to perform his main heroic tasks; and he is often represented as helpless in the face of the many challenges he faces on his journey.

SYNOPSIS

In the first book, King Pelias of Iolcus sends Jason on a quest for the golden fleece. With the aid of Athena, Jason's ship, the *Argo*, is built, and a crew of 50 heroes is assembled in Thessaly. Among their number are HERACLES, HYLAS, ORPHEUS, MELEAGER, ZETES, CALAIS, PELEUS, LAERTES, TELAMON, CASTOR, and POLLUX. They choose Jason as their leader. The Argonauts sail from Thessaly to Lemnos, where they discover a population composed only of women. Their Queen Hypsipyle conceals the fact that the women have murdered their husbands, and she convinces the Argonauts to help repopulate the island. The Argonauts continue on their voyage, sailing through the Hellespont and arriving among the Doliones. There, Jason accidentally kills King Cyzicus, and his wife, Cleite, commits suicide. He makes sacrifices to the gods in atonement for his action. Then Heracles abandons the expedition to say behind in Propontis to look for his companion, Hylas, who was taken away by nymphs.

In the second book, the *Argo* arrives among the Bebryces, where Pollux accepts the challenge of a boxing match with King Amycus, killing him in the process. The Argonauts then rescue the blind seer Phineus from the Harpies, and in return, Phineus helps them navigate through the Clashing Rocks (Symplegades) with little damage to the *Argo*. The successful crossing of the *Argo* puts an end to this maritime hazard—henceforth, the Rocks clash no more. The crew continues its voyage, passing through the land of the Amazons, the land of the Mossynoikoi, and an island sacred to Ares before arriving in Colchis.

In the third book, King Aeetes challenges Jason to perform two impossible tasks before he will give him the Golden Fleece: to harness and plough with fire-breathing bulls and to sow the field with dragon's teeth. But Eros, in response to Hera and Athena's request, intervenes. He makes Medea, Aeetes's daughter, fall in love with Jason, so that she would help him succeed. She gives him a protective potion to help him harness the bulls and plough the field. But even after having accomplished the challenges set him, Aeetes refuses to allow Jason the golden fleece.

In the fourth and final book, Medea offers to help Jason steal the fleece if he promises to take her back with him on the *Argo*. He accepts her offer, and she uses a magic potion to put to sleep the dragon guarding the fleece, while Jason makes away with the prize. As the Argonauts are fleeing from Colchis, Aeetes and Medeas's brother give pursuit. Jason kills the boy to delay the pursuit, and the *Argo* makes good its escape. Following some minor adventures (one in which the Argonauts meet Talos, the giant of Crete), the *Argo* returns home to Thessaly.

COMMENTARY

Apollonius of Rhodes, a major poet of the third century B.C.E., may have come from Rhodes, or merely lived there for a certain period. His literary career, however, was centered in Alexandria, where Ptolemy I Soter (367–282 B.C.E.) and Ptolemy II Philadelphus (308–246) provided substantial support to literary culture. Two institutions in particular, the Museum ("temple of the Muses")—an institution that housed scholars and writers—and the great Library of Alexandria, were the products of royal patronage. The institutionalization of literature in Egypt had important consequences for poetry. The poets who received patronage from the Ptolemies were also scholars—there was no distinction between the two, as there often is in the modern world. This applies above all

to Apollonius of Rhodes: He was appointed chief librarian at the Alexandrian library. In this period, texts of classic works of Greek literature were being collected, edited, and catalogued in the Library. The scholar/writers who carried out and enjoyed the benefits of this work were no longer rooted in the cultural traditions of traditional Greek city-states but belonged to the Greek ruling class of Hellenistic Alexandria. Greekness for them was vitally tied to literature and literary culture; but their sense of Greekness was also notably eclectic, a synthesis of a multitude of local cultural traditions now being sifted and collected in the form of texts. At the same time, by the very act of defining a canon of classic works, they excluded themselves from that canon and, accordingly, developed a sense of "coming after" the major period of Greek poetry. The Alexandrian scholar/writers thus write as connoisseurs and scholars of the literary tradition: Their poetry is intricately erudite, richly allusive, and pervaded by a sense of their own distance from the great writers and cultural traditions of the past, even as they engage obsessively with those writers and traditions.

These broader features of Alexandrian poetry are strongly in evidence in the case of Apollonius of Rhodes's *Voyage of the Argonauts*. By virtue of choosing to write in the epic genre, Apollonius necessarily engages with *the* canonical poet of Greek culture, Homer, and especially (although not exclusively) with Homer's *Odyssey*. Like the *Odyssey*, the *Voyage of the Argonauts* is a travel epic that involves seafaring, diverse adventures and perils throughout the world, and a return home to Greece at the end. Like the *Iliad*, it features an expedition of Greek heroes to a foreign land to retrieve an invaluable object/person that came originally from Greece: in the case of the *Iliad*, a person, Helen of Troy; in the case of the *Voyage of the Argonauts*, a unique object, the golden fleece. The fleece, like Helen, originally left Greece under unusual mythological circumstances. Athamas, king of Orchomenus, and his first wife, Nephele, had two children, Phrixus and

Helle. Ino, his second wife, became jealous of her stepchildren and attempted to persuade Athamas to sacrifice Prixus to avert a pestilence. Phrixus and Helle escaped on the back of a magical winged, golden-fleeced ram sent to them by Zeus. Helle fell off and drowned, giving her name to the "Hellespont." Phrixus made it to the far-off land of Colchis, where the ram was sacrificed to Zeus and the golden fleece given to Aeetes, king of Colchis. In return, the king gave Phrixus his daughter Chalciope in marriage, and they had four sons. Thus, as in the *Iliad*, the core mythological material concerns the relation between Greeks and barbarians (including intermarriage) and a Panhellenic expedition mounted to bring a prestigious object back to Greece. In both cases, the king of the gods, Zeus, plays a central role in the story: In Homer, *Zeus xenios* (Zeus as guardian of guest/host relations) drives the plot and guarantees the outcome of the Greek expedition to Troy (Paris wronged his host, Menelaus, when he stole Menelaus's wife). In Apollonius, it is Zeus who gave the ram and who drives and authorizes the expedition to bring it back to Greece. Apollonius, then, manages to engage with both Homeric epics, combining the "expedition of heroes" scenario with the "adventures at sea" scenario, and exploring above all the relations between Greeks and foreign peoples—whether in warfare, marriage, or hospitality.

A great advantage of Apollonius's chosen subject is that it offers a large cast of heroes and a major cache of myths not treated, or not fully treated, by Homeric epic. The ship *Argo* is manned by the generation of heroes *preceding* the heroes of Homer's *Iliad*. In *The Voyage of the Argonauts* Book 1, Apollonius, like Homer, produces a catalog of heroes, which includes, significantly, Telamon and Peleus, fathers of Diomedes and Achilles, respectively. The centaur CHIRON comes down with Peleus's wife to watch the *Argo* depart, and she holds up the baby Achilles for his father to see. Apollonius here subtly signals his own and his

readers' awareness of the later Iliadic expedition. Even though, as a writer, Apollonius is intensely aware of coming after Homer, he positions himself, through his epic subject matter, *before* Homer. "Coming before" is one way of maintaining continual, allusive contact with Homer, while avoiding redundancy and direct competition: He stays within the frame of the pre-Homeric expedition yet continually looks forward to the *Iliad* by allusive foreshadowing. By this careful strategy of self-positioning, Apollonius manages to confer on his own epic expedition a paradoxical priority over that of his revered predecessor. Apollonius's approximate contemporary Theocritus achieves something similar in his 11th *Idyll*, where he presents a pre-Homeric POLYPHEMUS—not yet the man-devouring monster depicted by Homer but a gentle shepherd in love with the sea nymph Galatea. The very nature of Apollonius's mythological material, then, positions him in relation to Homer and creates the conditions for literary allusions that combine elements of both homage and competition.

Even as Apollonius sends the Argonauts on a pre-Iliadic expedition, he sends Jason on a pre-Odyssean voyage to the limits of the known world and back. The basic pattern is highly comparable: The hero departs to encounter perils and win *kleos* ("renown") and treasure, both of which he then brings back with him to Greece. Odysseus went to Troy, won glory as both a warrior and a traveler, and, unlike other major Iliadic heroes who were denied a *nostos* ("return journey"), returned to his home island of Ithaca laden with treasures. Similarly, Apollonius's Jason travels to a faraway kingdom where he defeats his enemy in battle, then returns to Greece, having won both glory and the golden fleece.

As we look more closely at Apollonius's narrative, however, striking differences begin to appear. Consider, for example, the traveling hero's marriage. Homer's Odysseus refuses to stay with goddesses such as Calypso and Circe and does not take up Alcinous's offer of his daughter Nausicaa's hand in marriage, but instead remains fixed in his purpose of returning to Ithaca and his wife, Penelope. Odysseus, by the end of the epic, will be reunited with his wife and will regain control over his household. Exotic alternatives such as the witch goddess Circe have been rejected, and Odysseus's own sensible Greek wife, Penelope, has proved herself loyal and is rewarded. Jason's marriage takes on an entirely different aspect: Instead of returning to a Greek bride, he brings a markedly exotic foreign bride back to Greece. Not only is Medea a foreigner, she is also a witch. The dangerous, irrational forces of black magic are opposed, in Homer's *Odyssey*, to more acceptable traits of Greek womanhood, even when, in Penelope's case, those traits include (necessary) cunning and deception. Odysseus's house will remain integral and free of such taint, however much the *Odyssey's* governing pretext of enforced seafaring is designed precisely to allow him contact and even intimacy with the thrillingly dangerous Circe. As with the Sirens, Odysseus is allowed both to enjoy and to experience feminine allurements and to remain safe from any permanent harm. Jason, by contrast, will bring the dangerous, violently passionate Medea home with him. Readers of Euripides' *Medea* know that this choice will eventually destroy his house, his marriage, his children, and his entire life. The dangers of feminine magic and passion that Odysseus was careful to control, confine, and finally curtail are allowed almost unlimited scope in the mythology of Jason and Medea.

Concepts of Greekness are at stake, yet Apollonius, while clearly interested in mapping the boundaries of Hellenic culture, creates a hero whose actions lead to a transgressive importation of a powerful barbarian witch into Greece. Homer's epic ends with the reintegration of Odysseus within his own community, the resolution of his journeying in a satisfying return that brings the Greek hero back to his own Greek soil. Apollonius scrupulously brings his hero back to the Greek mainland in the poem's closing lines, but he hardly brings the dialectic of Greek and foreign to a neat, reassuring resolution: We know that the pairing of Jason and Medea will only escalate to further violence and destruction. The carefully designed contrast between barbarian and civilized values that organizes Homer's epic narrative can be seen at work in the *Voyage of the Argonauts*, but the relatively stable oppositions of the *Odyssey* are not allowed to remain fully intact. Because Odysseus is a traveler for much of the epic, the poem is, not surprisingly, composed of a series of connected scenes of hospitality, good and bad. At one extreme lies Polyphemus, who eats his own guests (*xenoi*) and, as a guest-friendship gift (*xenion*), awards Odysseus the privilege of being eaten last. The Cyclopes, as Homer relates, lack laws, assemblies, agriculture, the art of seafaring, and other practices of a civilized society. Polyphemus represents the archetypal barbarian, and his grotesque parody of hospitality concretely represents his barbarity. The Greek Odysseus, by contrast, proves himself the consummately perfect guest again and again; he brilliantly manages to defeat Polyphemus even while presenting him with a model hospitality gift (a sack of strong wine that puts him to sleep). Jason and his fellow Greek heroes similarly travel to diverse lands and are treated differently by their various hosts. Naturally enough, they expect to encounter what they would consider to be appropriate hospitality and to obey their culture's traditions of good behavior. Apollonius's darkly inventive narrative, however, often frustrates this intention, leading to scenes of violated or otherwise bizarre guest-host relations unforeseen by the heroes. In Book 1, Jason and his comrades are hospitably entertained by the Doliones and their king, Cyzicus, but the following evening, strong winds drive them back to the Doliones's shores. In the darkness, the Doliones do not recognize the Argonauts and attempt to repel the invaders: They fight, many are killed, and Jason himself kills Cyzicus. The next day, they realize with horror that they have killed their own hosts. Such a scene of random moral catastrophe would have been unthinkable in Homer's *Odyssey*.

Even the core events of the quest are tainted by concerns with the violation of guest-host relations. Jason and the Argonauts are the guests of King Aeetes—a role that carries moral obligations, however rude and unpleasant a host he may be—and yet they end up making off with the golden fleece and his own daughter. They may have some moral justification on their side, given King Aeetes' own hostile and uncooperative behavior, but the opposition is hardly a simple or unworrisome one. The treacherous slaying of Medea's brother Apsyrtus carries yet further Apollonius's destabilization of heroic civility, and draws Jason and his comrades further from any kind of moral high ground. The Greek/barbarian divide and its corresponding panoply of moral distinctions are progressively and at times violently undermined as the epic goes on.

Just as the paradigms of heroic morality are destabilized by Apollonius, so also is his central hero, Jason, represented in an untraditional and certainly un-Homeric light. First and most important, Jason's quest is achieved not by traditional feats of martial prowess or Odyssean tactical cunning but by his good looks and attractiveness to women. We are given a foreshadowing of his ability to gain the support of a woman in the Lemnos episode, where he becomes the lover of his host, Queen Hypsipyle. Apollonius describes the images on the cloak she gives him in an extended passage carefully designed to parallel and answer Homer's description of the shield of Achilles, yet the contrast could not be greater: on the one hand, a hard, divinely forged weapon that will accompany the great warrior into battle; on the other, a lover's gift, a richly woven textile to complement Jason's remarkable good looks. Later, Medea falls in love with him, and as Apollonius makes utterly clear, it is solely through her magical devices and knowledge that Jason is able to yoke the fire-breathing bulls, defeat the earth-sown men, and, finally,

obtain the fleece. His display of excellence in battle—called his *aristeia* in the terminology of Homeric scholarship—is a pharmaceutically enhanced *aristeia*, the product of a barbarian woman's drugs. Again, Apollonius deliberately tampers with core paradigms of heroic achievement: Jason is patently and wholly dependent on the barbarian, the irrational, and the feminine for his defining feat as Greek hero. In other episodes, Jason displays no greater valor or capability. Repeatedly, Apollonius describes him as being at a loss or "resourceless" when faced with a difficult problem—the exact opposite of the irrepressibly resourceful Odysseus. What ought to have been his scenes of heroic valor—battle scenes, scenes in which he slays an adversary—turn out to be grotesque or morally dubious: He kills his own host Cyzicus and slays Apsyrtus by treachery and deception. Even the battle of the earth-born men, with which the third book significantly ends, is marked by a pervasive note of grotesquery. Jason kills them as they sprout from the ground, some of them only half "grown," and the entire scene is described by Apollonius as a dark travesty of agriculture and harvest: Their blood flows in the furrows, and they lie scattered in various position on the ground, "looking like monsters from the sea."

Jason's unconventional heroism is not necessarily and exclusively negative. Heroic feats and virtues in the expedition of the *Voyage of the Argonauts* are more equitably dispersed among the various heroes than in Homer's *Odyssey*—and Apollonius is quite careful to demonstrate throughout the epic how different capabilities are required to overcome different obstacles: in some cases speed, in some cases agility, in some cases intelligence or prophecy. The contrast with a Homeric hero such as Odysseus is stark: Odysseus is a highly isolated, even lonely hero who knows that he can ultimately rely only on himself. At the end of the epic, he is assisted by his son Telemachus and some loyal servants, but even then, Odysseus is the prime strategist and architect of the suitors' slaughter. Homer emphatically makes it clear that Odysseus cannot rely on his crew, who fail to listen to him and betray him in various instances, until at last they are utterly destroyed for eating the cattle of Helios. Apollonius, however, pointedly devises heroic tasks not likely to be completed successfully by any single person or set of competences. Indeed, none of the heroes could have been capable of circumventing Aeetes and obtaining the fleece were it not for the highly specialized skill of Medea with magic and drugs. Above all, the use of raw force is subtly denigrated and sidelined by Apollonius. When Heracles, in a comic manner, breaks an oar by the sheer force of his rowing, then, later, disappears from the epic when he goes off in angry pursuit of the stolen Hylas, Apollonius is giving strong indication of the kind of epic he is writing and the kind of heroes he is interested in representing: The hypermasculine model of the hero is literally displaced from the pages of his poem. Comparable, the quarrelsome Idas appears repeatedly in confrontation with Jason, a confrontation that usually follows the same outlines: Idas complains whenever the old-fashioned masculine approach to a problem is not employed, and he is shown to be wrong by the outcome. In the boxing episode at the opening of Book 2, the agile, light-footed Polydeuces defeats the massive brute Amycus.

In his restless confrontation with the epic tradition, Apollonius not only adapts and redefines the concept of heroic virtue; he also blurs the boundaries of the genre itself and invites an element of tragedy into his epic quest-narrative. The character of Medea, for third-century B.C.E. readers of Apollonius, would have been inextricably linked with Euripides' tragedy of the same name. At least at first, Apollonius's Medea, like Theocritus's pre-Homeric Polyphemus, appears more naive and incapable of the horrific violence that marks her later mythological career. This pre-Euripidean Medea, however, already bears traces of her later self and is made to allude simultaneously to her future actions and her past literary representations. Like Medea in Euripides' tragedy, she is a profoundly divided figure who plays out her contradictory plans and impulses in extended, self-punishing soliloquies; like her tragic version, Apollonius's Medea is driven by extreme passion, is capable of betraying her own family, and already shows signs of disturbing possessiveness and dark depths of passion. Medea's brother Apsyrtus becomes implicitly a prototragic victim, an innocent slain with the collusion of a member of his own family, in a grim travesty of sacrificial killing. Like his contemporaries, Apollonius did not hew strictly and single-mindedly to his chosen genre but engaged in a sophisticated dialogue of genres—a dialogue newly made possible by the array of canonical works in different genres catalogued and gathered in the Alexandrian Library. Apollonius, at once scholar, poet, and librarian, created a work of poetry that embodies the intellectual energies and innovations of a great age of literary erudition.

Vulcan   See HEPHAESTUS.

W

Works and Days HESIOD (ca. eighth–seventh century B.C.E.) Hesiod's *Works and Days*, like his *THEOGONY*, opens with reference to ZEUS and the MUSES—the two keystones of his poetry. Zeus is the king of the gods, who, in the *Theogony*, proves himself to be both strong and cunning, an unbeatable combination; the Muses are his daughters and the source of Hesiod's song. Hesiod's poetry is thus connected with the divine figure (Zeus) who oversees human life. A major difference in the present poem is that Hesiod also addresses a mortal man, his brother Perses. The vague hints the poem affords suggest that Hesiod was involved in a dispute with Perses over an inheritance from their father, and that Perses bribed rulers in their capacity as arbitrators of lawsuits. If we take the poem's injunctions literally, we will also conclude that Perses was in debt and unwilling to work hard to increase his property. It is difficult to say, however, how accurate a portrait of Perses the poem represents, insofar as his presence as addressee is intrinsically related to the poem's didactic mode. Hesiod's *Works and Days* is the earliest example we have of didactic, or instructional, poetry, and it provides the model for later didactic poems (Lucretius's *De Rerum Natura*, Virgil's *Georgics*). The didactic speaker typically treats his addressee as a slow or witless pupil, offering constant admonition and castigation.

For Hesiod to highlight his central themes of justice, toil, maintenance of property, and proper social behavior effectively, logically the didactic addressee Perses ought to require instruction in all these areas, i.e., as someone who perverts justice, avoids hard work, and fails to maintain his property.

Hesiod opens with a distinction between two types of Strife: bad Strife, which puts people at odds with each other and causes war, and good Strife, which motivates people to work hard and increase their possessions. Perses is influenced too much by the former and not enough by the latter. This opening distinction is in keeping with the dominant perspective and themes of the poem. Hesiod's world is a harsh one, in which constant hard work is required for survival. The myth of the Ages of Man provides an illuminating background to this emphasis. Hesiod develops the first version of a motif that will recur in various forms throughout ancient poetry: There were five ages of man—gold, silver, bronze, the age of heroes, and the iron age, in which the poet himself lives. Each generation of men was completely demolished before being replaced by the next, and there is a general (although not wholly unvarying) pattern of decline. The golden age is perfect and arguably the most unlike the human world we know: No toil or labor was required; people lived without effort.

We might contrast this age with the present iron age, in which humans are full of toil and sorrow. The golden age, it seems, was designed to be the inverse of the human reality that we all inhabit, in which hard work and suffering are an inherent part of life—indeed, are requisite for even moderate success. The people of the golden age lived in the time when Cronus was still king of the gods, just as, in Roman versions of the myth, Saturn reigned instead of Jupiter. Hesiod, however, lives under the regime of Zeus, and it is to Zeus that he constantly refers as a moral compass and authority throughout the poem. Living under Zeus, in the iron age, means constant hard work.

The poem's subject matter, in contrast to the divine and cosmic perspective of the *Theogony*, is the human world: social relations, maintenance of the household, agriculture, marriage, friendship, justice, work, money, and time as measured out in days of human toil and activity. Hesiod has moved away from the cosmic time span of the *Theogony*, which takes us back to the origins of the universe and then moves forward to the age of heroes. In the *Works and Days*, the time scales are smaller and more minutely graded. The ending of the poem is a detailed catalog of days: Hesiod offers advice as to which days are appropriate for specific activities. This passage offers the clearest and starkest version of the "work and days" referred to in the poem's title.

The perspective of the *Theogony* might be termed Olympian, and the mode is revelatory. Hesiod shows his audience the history of the gods' coming into being. The *Works and Days* offers an emphatically earthbound perspective, albeit with constant reference to the gods and especially Zeus. The two poems represent, in a certain sense, two sides of the same coin. The Zeus of the *Works and Days* is not shown as a narrative figure in action; rather, the poet gestures upward to Zeus on Olympus as an all-powerful, yet largely absent, reference point for human conduct. We do not see Zeus interacting with and dominating the other gods, as in the *Theogony;* instead, Hesiod refers to Zeus as the upholder of human morality, the guarantor of "straight" justice by contrast with the "crooked" ways of those who accept bribes. The *Theogony* narrates the establishment of Zeus's regime among the gods; the *Works and Days* focuses on what it means to live under his regime as a human being.

The main mythic element of the poem, besides the Ages of Man, is a version of the myth of PROMETHEUS, this time with special focus on PANDORA. The central importance of the Prometheus myth for Hesiod is now manifest: He represents a key link between divine and human realms and also brings to the fore the problem of human toil and suffering. In the *Theogony*, which focuses on the world of the gods, Prometheus appears as a patron and protector of human beings, for which role he is savagely punished by an all-powerful and seemingly omniscient Zeus. Now, in the *Works and Days*, which focuses on human life, Hesiod presents the story of Prometheus as a proof, not primarily of the omnipotence of Zeus, but of the ineluctability of toil and struggle. Cronus's golden age has passed, and now nothing comes without effort. Hesiod is grappling with a central theological problem: If the gods are great and worthy of human worship, why do they make life so difficult, and why must we toil to live? Nothing comes without a price; gaining one resource (fire) triggers a counterbalancing difficulty and pain (Pandora, or, in general terms, the problem of Woman). Hesiod, in fact, explicitly describes Pandora as a source of sorrow that counterbalances the theft of fire. In Hesiod's vision of the world, nothing is perfect or easy. Accepting this state of things allows one to understand, as he famously states, that half is better than the whole. Accepting what is incomplete or imperfect is the best we can do.

The story of Pandora as related in *Works and Days* is distinct from the version in the *Theogony* and represents the version better known in the modern period. The focus now falls on a detailed list of Pandora's various attributes as conferred by the different gods (whereby she comes to be "all-gifted"), and especially her physical attractiveness. Hermes, in addition, confers on her a cunning and thieving character. The combination, of course, is fatal. Prometheus was enough of a "fore-thinker" to understand that gifts from the gods are dangerous, but his more thick-witted brother EPIMETHEUS ("after-thinker") accepts the gift of Pandora without anticipating the consequences.

Hesiodic misogyny can be seen here in full force. Pandora herself, as Woman, and threat to the integrity of Man's property and household, is already a source of pain. In this instance, however, she also brings with her the famous "jar" (called a "box" in modern versions) that contains the various forms of suffering and disease that, when she opens it, plague the world. Pandora is thus an Eve figure, the source of human suffering. The only potentially positive aspect of the story concerns hope. Hope is the one thing that Pandora manages to keep within the jar after all the ills spill out. The interpretation of this passage, however, is difficult, since we might logically expect hope to escape into the world in order to have a benign effect rather than remaining trapped within the jar. The outlook, in any case, is largely bleak, and the passage on Pandora is significantly followed by the passage on the Ages of Man, which effectively explains the same aspects of the human condition from a different viewpoint.

The content of Hesiod's didactic advice for getting on in such a world is both general and highly specific. In general, he advocates hard work, justice, and common sense. His ethical recommendations refer insistently to the authority of Zeus and a link between morality and prosperity. Those who are just and ethical will flourish in material terms; those who are not will suffer famine and misfortune. Hesiod's world is harsh, but it is not morally arbitrary. Animals, he states, do not have to live by the

rules of human morality. In one animal fable, he describes how the hawk ruthlessly rejects the nightingale's request for pity as it is being carried away in the hawk's talons. Such behavior is expected from a bird of prey but not from a human being, and it is perhaps significant that the victim is the nightingale, a bird singled out here and elsewhere as a bird of song symbolically linked with poetry. Hesiod appears to be offering implicit critique of his brother's unscrupulous behavior.

Hesiod's more specific pieces of advice are too many to discuss fully here, but a brief summary will give a general idea of the scope of his comments: how to dress in the winter, how to fend off the summer heat, how to make wine, how to take care of boats, when to sail, how to get married, how to treat friends, and so forth. If there is a theme or locus that unifies these diverse instances, it is the household and its property. Hesiod speaks to the head of the household, who must manage his crops, merchandise, wife, animals, neighbors, friends, and kinsmen. Some of Hesiod's advice is surprising and eccentric, as, for example, when he advises farmers to plough and sow their fields in the nude, or when he compares a delicate maiden, bathed and anointed, retiring to the inner recesses of the house on a cold winter's day to an octopus, the "boneless one," gnawing its foot in the depths of the ocean. The passage of which this is part concerns the winter and sharp winter winds. Hesiod's poetic imagination at times takes utterly surprising turns that have no obvious relation to his poem's stated didactic purpose. In this regard, he anticipates future didactic poetry (Aratus, Virgil) and the constant tension between the stated aim of utility and the broader aesthetic aims of the poem.

Like the *Theogony*, Hesiod's *Works and Days* contains a few, tantalizing autobiographical references. We learn that Hesiod's father came from Cumae to the town of Ascra, and that Hesiod does not like Ascra in the least. Furthermore, Hesiod won the prize of a tripod at a poetry contest given in honor of Amphida-mus at Chalcis, and that, although generally averse to sailing, he went there by boat. The *Theogony* concerns the gods, and so, logically, the self-representational material in that poem focuses on Hesiod's relation to the divinities most relevant to him, the Muses. The *Works and Days* concerns the human world, and so the autobiographical references in this poem offer revealing glimpses into Hesiod's activities as a member of human society—as son, brother, and, above all, singer.

Z

Zephyrus (Zephyros, Zephyr) One of the Anemoi. A personification of the West Wind. Progeny of Eos (Dawn) and Astraeus. Classical sources are Hesiod's *THEOGONY* (378–380, 869–871), Ovid's *FASTI* (9.201–12,319), and Philostratus's *IMAGINES* (1.24). Hesiod considers "clear and fresh-blowing" Zephyrus to be the son of Astraeus, but another account makes him the son of Typhoeus. The Anemoi were storms winds associated with the four cardinal points

Primavera. *Sandro Botticelli, ca. 1478 (Galleria degli Uffizi, Florence)*

and included BOREAS, the North Wind; NOTUS, the South Wind; EURUS, the East Wind; and Zephyrus. In the *Fasti*, Zephyrus carried off the nymph FLORA, following the courtship example of his brother wind Boreas, who abducted his own bride. After their marriage, Zephyrus granted Flora the privilege of reigning over flowers.

Another myth blames Zephyrus for the death of HYACINTHUS, the youth whom Apollo loved. Zephyrus was said to have deliberately blown off course a discus that Apollo had thrown; it struck Hyacinthus and killed him. The reasons given are either anger at Apollo or jealousy because Zephyrus was also in love with Hyacinthus. Philostratus relates in the *Imagines* that as PHAETHON fell to his death, Zephyrus joined the swans in lament for the pitiful death of the son of the sun god.

In visual representations of the classical period, Zephyrus is depicted, like Boreas, as a winged man. The most famous postclassical image of Zephyrus is Sandro Botticelli's *Primavera* of ca. 1478 (Galleria degli Uffizi, Florence). Here, Zephyrus is depicted as a forceful youth blowing wind through his mouth arriving on the right-hand side of the image, preceded by his bride, Flora, under whose feet flowers spring and out of whose mouth tumble more blooms (see GRACES).

Zetes   See BOREADAE.

Zeus (Jupiter, Jove) Olympian god of the sky. King of the Gods. Son of the TITANS CRONUS and RHEA. Classical sources include the *Homeric Hymns*, the *Orphic Hymns*, Aeschylus's *AGAMEMNON*, *LIBATION BEARERS*, *EUMENIDES*, *SUPPLIANTS*, and *PROMETHEUS BOUND*; Apollodorus's *LIBRARY*; Diodorus Siculus's *LIBRARY OF HISTORY*; Hesiod's *THEOGONY* and *WORKS AND DAYS*; Homer's *ILIAD* and *ODYSSEY*; Hyginus's *Fabulae*; Ovid's *FASTI* and *METAMORPHOSES*; Pausanias's *Description of Greece*; and Virgil's *AENEID* and *GEORGICS*. (This list of sources is necessarily selective; it is not

practical to list precise passages, since Zeus is pervasive in ancient literature.) Zeus was the dominant god of the Olympian pantheon, both a paternalistic figure and a symbol of ultimate authority. Zeus was associated with the heavens, the sky, clouds, and weather formations, especially of thunder and lightning. His epithets relate to his various functions and domains: for example, *horkios* (protector of sanctity of oaths), *xenios* (protector of hospitality relations), *hikesios* (protector of suppliants). Zeus oversees human life and action, sees all things, and controls outcomes and the lot of mortals. He is especially concerned with the relations among human beings, on which civilization is premised and which require good faith and justice: property, commerce, hospitality, relations between strangers, the sanctity of oaths, friendship. Zeus was syncretized with the Roman god Jupiter.

Cronus wed his sister Rhea, with whom he produced the generation of Olympian gods that included DEMETER, HADES, HERA, HESTIA, POSEIDON, and Zeus. Not wishing to be superseded by his own children, Cronus swallowed each child shortly after its birth. Following the birth of their sixth child, Zeus, Rhea wrapped a stone in swaddling clothes and gave it to Cronus in place of the infant. Zeus was thus spared the fate of his brothers and sisters and grew to maturity on the island of Crete. The Curetes sheltered the infant Zeus by creating a racket to hide the infant's cries. With his mother's help, Zeus later succeeded in having his father disgorge his other children. In some versions of the myth, Zeus received the aid of METIS, who provided him with a potion that induced vomiting in Cronus and thus made it possible for the children to be born.

Zeus engaged in the TITANOMACHY, a protracted war between the Olympian gods and Cronus and the other Titans, and eventually fulfilled a prophecy that he would succeed his father. To achieve this victory, he released from TARTARUS the HUNDRED-HANDED ONES, the GIANTS and the CYCLOPES (who fashioned

Zeus's thunderbolts) and persuaded them to fight on the side of the Olympian gods. After their defeat, Zeus and the Olympian gods consigned the Titans to Tartarus, where they were guarded by the Hundred-Handed Ones.

Having achieved supremacy, Zeus and the Olympians established their respective domains of authority. Zeus, Poseidon, and Hades divided up the realm by drawing lots; Zeus ruled the heavens, Poseidon the oceans, and Hades the underworld. Even after defeating their rivals the Titans, however, the Olympians still encountered challenges from other enemies. Gaia, angered by the imprisonment of the Titans, incited the giants to rebel. The GIGANTOMACHY ensued, in which Heracles, a mortal, aided the gods. Zeus and the Olympians defeated the giants. Finally, Zeus had to contend with the monstrous giant TYPHOEUS, the son of GAIA. He used his thunderbolts to set Typhoeus's many heads on fire, but according to Apollodorus, Typhoeus cut Zeus's sinews with the god's own adamantine scythe and imprisoned him in his cave in Cilicia. Zeus was rescued by HERMES, who helped reattach his sinews, and finally defeated the monster with his thunderbolts. Zeus's ascendancy was complete.

Yet even so, Zeus had to contend with other possible threats to his power. He was especially concerned with the pattern of succession, begun with Cronus and URANUS, whereby each son violently usurped his father's throne and was then deposed in turn. In Hesiod's *Theogony*, Zeus learned from Gaia and Uranus that Zeus's first wife, Metis, would bear a daughter and then a second child, a son, who would overthrow him. Zeus solved the potential threat by swallowing Metis. Zeus afterwards developed a painful headache. When HEPHAESTUS struck his head with an axe, Athena emerged, fully formed, wearing a helmet and carrying her armor. Zeus thus succeeded in heading off the threat of succession to which Cronus and Uranus had succumbed. Specifically, he ingested Metis, whose name means "clever-

ness" or "intelligence"—the very means by which his predecessors were defeated. The threat to Cronus and Uranus, moreover, came from the clever devices of a female figure, Gaia. Zeus ingeniously swallows the female Metis and then gives birth to the female, yet loyal, Athena. In a comparable story, Zeus learned from PROMETHEUS that the son of THETIS would be greater than his father. He refrained from having a child by her and arranged to have her married to the mortal Peleus instead.

Zeus was married to two Titans (Metis and THEMIS) and two Olympians (Hera and Demeter). He also had love affairs with a number of nymphs and mortal women; he had numerous progeny, both mortal and immortal. After Zeus's marriage to Metis, Themis, his aunt, was his second wife, and with her Zeus produced the HORAE (Seasons) and the FATES (Moirai). Zeus then married his third wife, Eurynome (an Oceanid), on whom he fathered the Charites (see GRACES). His fourth wife was his sister Demeter, with whom he had a daughter, PERSEPHONE. MNEMOSYNE, a Titan, who was his aunt, became his fifth wife; together they produced the nine MUSES.

The Titans COEUS and PHOEBE had a daughter, LETO, who became Zeus's sixth wife and the mother of the Olympians APOLLO and ARMETIS. Finally, Zeus married his sister Hera, and their children were ARES, HEBE, and EILEITHYIA. Hephaestus is considered to be either Zeus's child by Hera or Hera's parthenogenetic child. Two extramarital affairs produced two more gods: Zeus fathered Hermes by the Pleiad MAIA, and SEMELE bore him DIONYSUS. With his first series of wives and loves, Zeus completed the Olympian pantheon and, in addition, sired goddesses personifying key concepts related to law, justice, and time (Themis, Horae) and culture and society (Eurynome and Mnemosyne).

Zeus's loves, particularly during his marriage to Hera, were numerous. A recurrent theme is the length to which he would go to seduce a beautiful mortal or nymph. He inevitably provoked the rage of Hera, whose jealousy was sometimes directed at the woman with whom he betrayed her and, at other times, focused on the offspring of the affair. The most famous example of the latter is the story of HERACLES, whom Hera persecuted throughout his life. Zeus's affairs with mortals and nymphs produced several important heroes, among them the DIOSCURI and PERSEUS. Other children include (depending on the version): Arcas (by CALLISTO), Aeacus (by the nymph AEGINA), AMPHION and Zethus (by ANTIOPE), Epaphus (by IO), MINOS, Rhadamanthys, and SARPEDON (by EUROPA). An aspect of Zeus's love affairs emphasized in Ovid's *Metamorphoses* is his tendency to undergo transformation for the purpose of seduction. To Antiope he appeared as a satyr, to Danae as a shower of gold, to Europa as a bull, to Leda as a swan. When he fell in love with the boy GANYMEDE, Zeus transformed himself into his own attribute, the eagle, and carried him off to become his cupbearer. Sometimes Zeus took on human shape: He appeared to Callisto in the form of Artemis, and to ALCMENE as her husband, AMPHITRYON.

Zeus often assumes the role of enforcer of justice and punisher of transgressions in his relations with human sinners and with benefactors of humankind. Prometheus, in representing the interests of mortals, provoked the enmity of Zeus repeatedly: He tricked, or attempted to trick, Zeus into accepting the inferior portion of the sacrificed animal, and he stole fire from Mount Olympus and gave it to mortals. Zeus, in turn, commanded Hephaestus to make the first mortal woman, PANDORA, who brought with her all the miseries and ills that afflict society. Zeus also visited retribution upon violators of social and moral codes and divine authority, of which the prime examples are IXION, TANTALUS, TITYUS, and SISYPHUS. Their punishments, witnessed by ODYSSEUS and AENEAS in their descent to HADES, were ingeniously devised to provide gruesome, perpetual spectacle as a warning to others. Hubris was, similarly, ruthlessly punished, notably in

Jupiter and Thetis. *Jean-Auguste-Dominique Ingres, 1811 (Musée Granet, Aix-en-Provence)*

the case of CAPANEUS, who challenged Zeus himself and was struck down by the god's thunderbolt (see Statius's *THEBAID*).

Jupiter, the Roman counterpart of Zeus, was the most important god of the Romans, and his temple on the Capitoline Hill was the religious center of the city and a symbol of Rome itself. Jupiter was worshipped alongside Juno (see HERA) and Minerva (see ATHENA) in a tripartite temple cella. Jupiter was especially associated with military power and victory: The Roman triumphal procession ended with sacrifice at the Capitoline temple.

In visual representations, Zeus is depicted as an older, regal, bearded figure holding a scepter. His attributes, the eagle and bolts of lightning, often accompany him, as in the sculpture from the Pergamon Altar (Pergamonmuseum, Berlin). His images are found on a variety of media in classical period: vases, coins, gems, reliefs, and painting. Pausanias's describes a relief on the Temple of Hera at Plataea, Boeotia, showing Rhea offering Cronus a stone to swallow in the place of her last-born child, Zeus. A similar representation appears on an Attic red figure pelike from ca. 475 B.C.E. (Metropolitan Museum of Art, New York). The major themes concerning Zeus reflect either his status and functions or his many loves. Zeus was also a frequent subject of Renaissance and baroque artists' works. In later periods, the loves of Zeus were particularly well represented. Excellent examples include Antonio Correggio's *Danae* from ca. 1531 (Galleria Borghese, Rome) and *Ganymede* from ca. 1530 (Kunsthistoriches Museum, Vienna). A 19th-century example of Zeus enthroned was painted by Jean-Auguste-Dominique Ingres, *Jupiter and Thetis*, from 1811 (Musée Granet, Aix-en-Provence).

SELECTED BIBLIOGRAPHY

This bibliography is by no means intended as an exhaustive list of works on classical mythology. Under various headings, we have suggested some basic works for further reading. In addition to these general works, useful collections of essays on specific topics can be found in the Cambridge Companions to the Ancient World series and the Blackwell Companions to the Ancient World series.

THE CLASSICAL WORLD: HISTORY, CIVILIZATION, AND GENERAL REFERENCE

Boardman, John, Jasper Griffin, and Oswyn Murray. *The Oxford History of Greece and the Hellenistic World.* Oxford: Oxford University Press, 2002.

Cartledge, Paul. *The Cambridge Illustrated History of Ancient Greece.* Cambridge: Cambridge University Press, 2002.

Edwards, I. E. S. *The Cambridge Ancient History.* Cambridge: Cambridge University Press, 1970.

Hornblower, Simon, and Antony Spawforth. *The Oxford Classical Dictionary.* Oxford: Oxford University Press, 1996.

———. *Who's Who in the Classical World.* New York: Oxford University Press, 2000.

Howatson, M. C., and Sir Paul Harvey. *Oxford Companion to Classical Literature.* Oxford: Oxford University Press, 1989.

Pomeroy, Sarah B. *Ancient Greece: A Political, Social, and Cultural History.* 2d ed. New York: Oxford University Press, 2007.

CLASSICAL MYTHOLOGY: HANDBOOKS, DICTIONARIES, AND INTERPRETATIONS

Bremmer, Jan. *Interpretations of Greek Mythology.* London: Routledge, 1988.

Buxton, Richard. *Complete World of Greek Mythology.* London: Thames and Hudson, 2004.

———. *Imaginary Greece: The Contexts of Mythology.* Cambridge: Cambridge University Press, 1994.

Caldwell, Richard. *The Origin of the Gods: A Psychoanalytic Study of Greek Theogonic Myth.* Oxford: Oxford University Press, 1989.

Detienne, Marcel. *The Creation of Mythology.* Translated by Margaret Cook. Chicago: University of Chicago Press, 1986.

———. *The Gardens of Adonis: Spices in Greek Mythology.* Translated by Janet Lloyd. Princeton, N.J.: Princeton University Press, 1994.

———. *The Writing of Orpheus: Greek Myth in Cultural Context.* Translated by Janet Lloyd. Baltimore, Md.: Johns Hopkins University Press, 2003.

Detienne, Marcel, and Jean Pierre Vernant. *The Cuisine of Sacrifice among the Greeks.* Translated by Paula Wissing. Chicago: University of Chicago Press, 1989.

Doherty, Lillian E. *Gender and the Interpretation of Classical Myth.* London: Duckworth, 2001.

Dowden, Ken. *Death and the Maiden: Girls' Initiation Rites in Greek Mythology.* New York: Routledge, 1989.

———. *The Uses of Greek Mythology.* London: Routledge, 1992.

Edmunds, Lowell. *Approaches to Greek Myth.* Baltimore, Md.: Johns Hopkins University Press, 1990.

Fontenrose, Joseph Eddy. *The Ritual Theory of Myth.* University of California Publications, 18. Berkeley: University of California Press, 1966.

Forbes Irving, P. M. C. *Metamorphosis in Greek Myths.* Oxford: Clarendon Press, 1990.

Gantz, Timothy. *Early Greek Myth: A Guide to Literary and Artistic Sources.* Baltimore, Md.: Johns Hopkins University Press, 1993.

Graf, Fritz. *Greek Mythology: An Introduction.* Translated by Thomas Marier. Baltimore, Md.: Johns Hopkins University Press, 1993.

Grant, Michael, and John Hazel. *Who's Who in Classical Mythology.* London: Weidenfeld and Nicolson, 1973.

Grimal, Pierre. *The Dictionary of Classical Mythology.* Translated by A. R. Maxwell-Hislop. Oxford: Blackwell, 1996.

Hansen, William F. *Handbook of Classical Mythology.* Oxford: Oxford University Press, 2004.

———. *Ariadne's Thread: A Guide to International Tales Found in Classical Literature.* Ithaca, N.Y.: Cornell University Press, 2002.

Harris, Stephen L., and Gloria Platzner. *Classical Mythology: Images and Insights.* Mountain View, Calif.: Mayfield, 1995.

Kirk, G. S. *The Nature of Greek Myths.* Woodstock, N.Y.: Overlook Press, 1974.

Lefkowitz, Mary. *Women in Greek Myth.* London: Duckworth, 1986.

Morales, Helen. *Classical Mythology: A Very Short Introduction.* New York: Oxford University Press, 2007.

Nagy, Gregory. *Greek Mythology and Poetics.* Ithaca, N.Y.: Cornell University Press, 1990.

Nilsson, Martin P. *The Mycenaean Origin of Greek Mythology.* New York: Norton, 1965.

Penglase, Charles. *Greek Myths and Mesopotamia: Parallels and Influence in the Homeric Hymns and Hesiod.* London: Routledge, 1994.

Peradotto, John. *Classical Mythology: An Annotated Bibliographical Survey.* Urbana, Ill.: American Philological Association, 1973.

Powell, Barry B. *Classical Myth.* Upper Saddle River, N.J.: Prentice Hall, 1998.

———. *A Short Introduction to Classical Myth.* Upper Saddle River, N.J.: Prentice Hall, 2002.

Sergent, Bernard. *Homosexuality in Greek Myth.* Translated by Arthur Goldhammer. London: Athlone, 1987.

Slater, P. E. *The Glory of Hera: Greek Mythology and the Greek Family.* Princeton, N.J.: Princeton University Press, 1992.

Tyrrell, W. B. *Amazons: A Study in Athenian Mythmaking.* Baltimore, Md.: Johns Hopkins University Press, 1984.

Vernant, Jean Pierre. *Myth and Society in Ancient Greece.* Translated by Janet Lloyd. New York: Zone Books, 1988.

———. *Myth and Thought among the Greeks.* Translated by Janet Loyd. London: Routledge and Kegan Paul, 1983.

Veyne, Paul. *Did the Greeks Believe in Their Myths? An Essay on the Constitutive Imagination.* Translated by Paula Wissing. Chicago: University of Chicago Press, 1988.

Vidal-Naquet, Pierre. *The Black Hunter: Forms of Thought and Forms of Society in the Greek World.* Translated by Andrew Szegedy-Maszak. Baltimore, Md.: Johns Hopkins University Press, 1986.

West, M. L. *The Hesiodic Catalogue of Women: Its Nature, Structure and Origins.* Oxford: Oxford University Press, 1985.

Woodard, Roger D. *The Cambridge Companion to Greek Mythology.* New York: Cambridge University Press, 2008.

GREEK LITERATURE

This list is highly selective and is meant merely as a starting point for further study. More specialized studies have not been included but can be found by consulting the bibliographies of the general studies included below.

Dihle, Albrecht, and Clare Krojzl. *A History of Greek Literature: From Homer to the Hellenistic Period.* London: Routledge, 1994.

Dougherty, Carol, and Leslie Kurke. *Cultural Poetics in Archaic Greece: Cult, Performance, Politics.* New York: Oxford University Press, 1998.

Easterling, P. E., and Bernard M. W. Knox. *Greek Literature.* Vol. 1 of *The Cambridge History of Classical Literature.* Cambridge: Cambridge University Press, 1985.

Goldhill, Simon. *The Poet's Voice: Essays on Poetics and Greek Literature.* Cambridge: Cambridge University Press, 1991.

Lesky, Albin. *History of Greek Literature.* New York: Crowell, 1996.

Nagy, Gregory. *Best of the Achaeans: Concepts of the Hero in Archaic Greek Poetry.* Baltimore, Md.: Johns Hopkins University Press, 1998.

Taplin, Oliver. *Literature in the Greek World.* Oxford: Oxford University Press, 2001.

Whitmarsh, Tim. *Ancient Greek Literature.* Cambridge: Polity, 2004.

Greek Religion

Burkert, Walter. *Greek Religion: Archaic and Classical.* Oxford: Blackwell Publishing, 1985.

———. *Structure and History in Greek Mythology and Ritual.* Berkeley: University of California Press, 1979.

Buxton, Richard. *Oxford Readings in Greek Religion.* Oxford: Oxford University Press, 2000.

Harrison, J. E. *Themis: A Study of the Social Origins of Greek Religion.* Cambridge: Cambridge University Press, 1912.

Nilsson, Martin P. *A History of Greek Religion.* Translated by F. J. Fielden. Westport, Conn.: Greenwood Press, 1980.

Ogden, Daniel. *A Companion to Greek Religion.* Malden, Mass.: Blackwell Publishing, 2007.

Parker, Robert. *Athenian Religion: A History.* Oxford: Oxford University Press, 1997.

———. *Miasma: Pollution and Purification in Early Greek Religion.* Oxford: Oxford University Press, 1999.

Price, Simon. *Religions of the Ancient Greeks.* Cambridge: Cambridge University Press, 1999.

Greek Literature Relevant to Mythology: Translations and Editions

Good translations of a range of ancient writers can be found in the Oxford World's Classics series and the Penguin Classics series. The Loeb Classical Library (Harvard University Press) offers facing Greek-English texts of major works and also lesser-known works that are otherwise difficult to find in English.

Apollodorus

Apollodorus' Library *and Hyginus'* Fabulae: *Two Handbooks of Greek Mythology.* Translated by R. Scott Smith and Stephen M. Trzaskoma. Indianapolis, Ind.: Hackett, 2007.

Apollonius of Rhodes

Jason and the Golden Fleece: The Argonautica. Translated by R. L. Hunter. Oxford: Oxford University Press, 1998.

Callimachus

The Poems of Callimachus. Translated by Frank J. Nisetich. Oxford: Oxford University Press, 2001.

Diodorus Siculus

Diodorus of Sicily. Translated by Charles Henry Oldfather. Loeb Classical Library. London: W. Heinemann, 1961.

Greek tragedy

There are innumerable translations of the plays of Aeschylus, Sophocles, and Euripides. The *Complete Greek Tragedies,* edited by David Grene and Richard Lattimore, University of Chicago Press, is standard.

Herodotus

Herodotus: The Histories. Translated by Carolyn Dewald and Robin Waterfield. Oxford: Oxford University Press, 1998.

The Histories. Translated by Aubrey De Sélincourt and John Marincola. Penguin Classics. London: Penguin Books, 2003.

Hesiod

The Shield, Catalogue of Women, Other Fragments. Translated by Glenn W. Most. Cambridge, Mass.: Harvard University Press, 2007.

Theogony, Works and Days. Translated by M. L. West. Oxford: Oxford University Press, 1999.

Homer's *Iliad*

Homer's Iliad. Translated by Robert Fagles. Penguin Classics. New York: Penguin, 1998.

The Iliad of Homer. Translated by Richard Lattimore. Chicago: University of Chicago Press, 1961.

Homer's *Odyssey*

The Odyssey. Translated by Robert Fitzgerald. New York: Farrar, Straus and Giroux, 1998.

Homeric Hymns

Foley, Helene. *The Homeric Hymn to Demeter: Translation, Commentary, and Interpretive Essays.* Princeton, N.J.: Princeton University Press, 1994.

Shelmerdine, Susan C. *The Homeric Hymns.* Newburyport, Mass.: Focus Publishing, 1995.

Pausanias

Guide to Greece. Translated by Peter Levi. Penguin Classics. New York: Penguin, 1984.

Pindar

Pindar's Victory Songs. Translated by Frank Nisetich. Baltimore, Md.: Johns Hopkins University Press, 1980.

Pindar: The Complete Odes. Translated by Anthony Verity. Oxford: Oxford University Press, 2008.

ROMAN MYTH

Braund, David, and Christopher Gill. *Myth, History and Culture in Republican Rome: Studies in Honour of T. P. Wiseman.* Exeter, Devon, U.K.: University of Exeter, 2003.

Fox, Matthew. *Roman Historical Myths: The Regal Period in Augustan Literature.* Oxford: Oxford University Press, 1995.

Grant, Michael. *Roman Myths.* New York: Scribner, 1971.

Wiseman, T. P. *The Myths of Rome.* Exeter, Devon, U.K.: University of Exeter, 2008

———. *Remus: A Roman Myth.* Cambridge: Cambridge University Press, 1995.

ROMAN RELIGION

Ando, Clifford. *Matter of the Gods: Religion and the Roman Empire.* Berkeley, Calif.: University of California Press, 2008.

———. *Religions of Ancient Rome.* Toronto: University of Toronto Press, 2008.

Beard, Mary, John North, and Simon Price. *A History.* Vol. 1 of *Religions of Rome.* Cambridge: Cambridge University Press, 1998.

———. *A Sourcebook.* Vol. 1 of *Religions of Rome.* Cambridge: Cambridge University Press, 1998.

Dumezil, Georges. *Archaic Roman Religion.* Translated by Philip Krapp. Baltimore, Md.: Johns Hopkins University Press, 1996.

Feeney, Denis. *Literature and Religion at Rome: Cultures, Contexts, and Beliefs.* Cambridge: Cambridge University Press, 1998.

Rives, James B. *Religion in the Roman Empire.* Malden, Mass.: Blackwell Publishing, 2006.

Rüpke, Jörg. *The Religion of the Romans.* Cambridge: Polity, 2007.

Scheid, John. *An Introduction to Roman Religion.* Translated by Janet Lloyd. Bloomington: Indiana University Press, 2003.

ROMAN LITERATURE

This list is highly selective and is meant merely as a starting point for further study. More specialized studies have not been included but can be found by consulting the bibliographies of the general studies included below.

Braund, Susanna Morton. *Latin Literature.* New York: Routledge, 2002.

Conte, Gian Biagio. *Latin Literature: A History.* Baltimore, Md.: Johns Hopkins University Press, 1994.

Fantham, Elaine. *Roman Literary Culture: From Cicero to Apuleius.* Baltimore, Md.: Johns Hopkins University Press, 1996.

Feeney, D. C. *The Gods in Epic: Poets and Critics of the Classical Tradition.* Oxford: Oxford University Press, 1991.

Hardie, Philip. *The Epic Successors of Virgil: A Study in the Dynamics of a Tradition.* Cambridge: Cambridge University Press, 1993.

Harrison, S. J. *A Companion to Latin Literature.* Blackwell Companions to the Ancient World. Malden, Mass.: Blackwell Publishing, 2005.

Hinds, Stephen. *Allusion and Intertext: Dynamics of Appropriation in Roman Poetry.* Cambridge: Cambridge University Press, 1998.

Kenney, E. J., and W. V. Clausen. *Latin Literature.* Vol. 2 of *The Cambridge History of Classical Literature.* Cambridge: Cambridge University Press, 1982.

Taplin, Oliver. *Literature in the Roman World.* Oxford: Oxford University Press, 2001.

Von Albrecht, Michael. *A History of Roman Literature: From Livius Andronicus to Boethius with Special Regard to Its Influence on World Literature.* Revised by Gareth L. Schmeling and translated with the assistance of Ruth R. Caston and Francis R. Schwartz. Leiden, The Netherlands: E. J. Brill, 1997.

ROMAN LITERATURE RELEVANT TO MYTHOLOGY: TRANSLATIONS AND EDITIONS

Good translations of a range of ancient writers can be found in the Oxford World's Classics series and the Penguin Classics series. The Loeb Classical Library (Harvard University Press) offers facing Latin-English texts of major works and also lesser-known works that are otherwise difficult to find in English.

Catullus

Catullus: The Complete Poems. Translated by Guy Lee. Oxford: Oxford University Press, 1998.

Horace

The Odes of Horace. Translated by David Ferry. New York: Farrar, Straus & Giroux, 1997.

Hyginus

Apollodorus' Library and Hyginus' Fabulae: Two Handbooks of Greek Mythology. Translated by R. Scott Smith and Stephen M. Trzaskoma. Indianapolis, Ind.: Hackett, 2007.

Livy

Luce, T. J. *The Rise of Rome: Books One to Five.* Oxford: Oxford University Press, 1999.

Ovid

Ovid: Fasti. Translated by James George Frazer. Loeb Classical Library, 5. Cambridge, Mass.: Harvard University Press, 1989.

Ovid: The Love Poems. Translated by A. D. Melville. Oxford: Oxford University Press, 2008.

Ovid: Metamorphoses. Translated by Charles Martin. New York: Norton, 2005.

Ovid: Metamorphoses. Translated by A. D. Melville. Oxford: Oxford University Press, 2008.

Ovid: Metamorphoses: A New Verse Translation. Translated by David A. Raeburn. Penguin Classics. London: Penguin, 2004.

Parthenius

Erotika Pathemata: The Love Stories of Parthenius. Translated by Jacob Stern. New York: Garland, 1992.

Propertius

Propertius: Elegies. Translated by G. P. Goold. Loeb Classical Library, 18. Cambridge, Mass.: Harvard University Press, 1990.

Statius

Statius: Thebaid. Translated by A. D. Melville. Oxford: Oxford University Press, 1995.

Valerius Flaccus

The Voyage of the Argo. Translated by David R. Slavitt. Baltimore, Md.: Johns Hopkins University Press, 1999.

VIRGIL

The Aeneid. Translated by Robert Fagles. Penguin Classics. New York: Penguin, 2008.

The Aeneid. Translated by Robert Fitzgerald. New York: Vintage, 1990.

The Eclogues and Georgics. Translated by C. Day Lewis. Oxford: Oxford University Press, 2009.

Virgil: The Eclogues. Translated by Guy Lee. Penguin Classics. New York: Penguin, 1984.

ARTISTIC REPRESENTATIONS OF CLASSICAL MYTH

Ackermann, Hans Christoph, Jean-Robert Gisler, and Lilly Kahil. *Lexicon Iconographicum Mythologiae Classicae (LIMC).* Zurich: Artemis, 1981.

Agard, Walter R. *Classical Myths in Sculpture.* Madison: University of Wisconsin Press, 1951.

Aghion, Irène, Claire Barbillon, and F. Lissarrague. *Gods and Heroes of Classical Antiquity.* Flammarion Iconographic Guides. Paris: Flammarion, 1996.

Carpenter, T. H. *Art and Myth in Ancient Greece: A Handbook.* London: Thames and Hudson, 1991.

Henle, Jane. *Greek Myths: A Vase Painter's Notebook.* Bloomington: Indiana University Press, 1973.

Impelluso, Lucia, Stefano Zuffi, and Thomas Michael Hartmann. *Gods and Heroes in Art.* Los Angeles: J. Paul Getty Museum, 2002.

Keuren, Frances van. *Guide to Research in Classical Art and Mythology.* Chicago: American Library Association, 1991.

Reid, Jane Davidson, and Chris Rohmann. *The Oxford Guide to Classical Mythology in the Arts, 1300–1990s.* Oxford: Oxford University Press, 1993.

Schefold, Karl. *Myth and Legend in Early Greek Art.* New York: Harry N. Abrams, 1966.

Schefold, Karl, and Luca Giuliani. *Gods and Heroes in Late Archaic Greek Art.* Cambridge: Cambridge University Press, 1992.

Seznec, Jean. *The Survival of the Pagan Gods: The Mythological Tradition and Its Place in Renaissance Humanism and Art.* Translated by Barbara Sessions. New York: Harper and Brothers, 1961.

Shapiro, H. A. *Myth into Art: Poet and Painter in Classical Greece.* London: Routledge, 1994.

Woodford, Susan. *Images of Myths in Classical Antiquity.* Cambridge: Cambridge University Press, 2003.

ONLINE RESOURCES

Bonefas, Suzanne, and Barbara F. McManus. VRoma: A Virtual Community for Teaching and Learning Classics. URL: http://www.vroma.org. Accessed March 31, 2009.

Bowman, Laurel. Classical Myth: The Ancient Sources. URL: http://web.uvic.ca/grs/department_files/classical_myth/index.html. Accessed March 31, 2009.

Crane, Gregory, editor in chief. The Perseus Project Digital Library. URL: www.perseus.tufts.edu. Accessed March 31, 2009.

Grout, James. Encyclopaedia Romana. URL: http://penelope.uchicago.edu/~grout/encyclopaedia_romana/romapage.html. Accessed March 31, 2009.

Kurtz, Donna, director. The Beazley Archive. URL: http://www.beazley.ox.ac.uk.index.htm. Accessed March 31, 2009.

Malitz, Jürgen, with the collaboration of Gregor Weber. Gnomon Online: The Eichstätt Information System for Classical Studies. URL: www.gnomon.ku-eichstaett.de/Gnomon/en/Gnomon.html. Accessed March 31, 2009.

Matheson, Philippa M. W., and Jacques Poucet, current Web site managers; original conception by R. Morstein-Marx. TOCS-IN: Tables of Contents of Journals of Interest to Classicists. URL: www.chass.utoronto.ca/amphoras/tocs.html. Accessed March 31, 2009.

Pantelia, Maria. Electronic Resources for Classics: The Second Generation. URL: www.tlg.uci.edu/index/resources.html. Accessed March 31, 2009.

Scaife, Ross. Diotima: Materials for the Study of Women and Gender in the Ancient World. URL: www.stoa.org/diotima. Accessed March 31, 2009.

———. The Stoa Consortium. URL: www.stoa.org. Accessed March 31, 2009.

Stevenson, Daniel C. Internet Classics Archive. URL: http://classics.mit.edu. Accessed March 31, 2009.

Thayer, Bill. Lacus Curtius: Into the Roman World. URL: http://penelope.uchicago.edu/Thayer/E/Roman/home.html. Accessed March 31, 2009.

INDEX

Boldface page numbers indicate main entries. *Italic* page numbers denote illustrations.